Modern Compliance

BEST PRACTICES FOR SECURITIES & FINANCE

Compiled and Edited by
David H. Lui & John H. Walsh
Jason K. Mitchell, Associate Editor

This book is a summary for general information only.
It is not a full analysis of the matters presented and should
not be relied upon as legal advice.

©Modern Compliance 2015

No part of this book may be reproduced, in any form or by any means, without permission in writing from the publisher.

ISBN 978-0-8080-4301-0

All rights reserved.

Printed in the United States of America.

*For Amy,
Debbie and Jill,
whose endless patience and encouragement
made this project a reality.*

© MODERN COMPLIANCE 2015

It is not the critic who counts; not the man who points out how the strong man stumbles, or where the doer of deeds could have done them better. The credit belongs to the man who is actually in the arena, whose face is marred by dust and sweat and blood; who strives valiantly; who errs, who comes short again and again, because there is no effort without error and shortcoming; but who does actually strive to do the deeds; who knows great enthusiasms, the great devotions; who spends himself in a worthy cause; who at the best knows in the end the triumph of high achievement, and who at the worst, if he fails, at least fails while daring greatly, so that his place shall never be with those cold and timid souls who neither know victory nor defeat.

— Theodore Roosevelt
April 23, 1910

Modern Compliance Editorial Board Members

We would like to express our appreciation to the following individuals for their work as members of the Editorial Board of Modern Compliance. Their guidance and feedback assured that Modern Compliance adhered to the highest standards for scholarship, relevance to the Compliance mission and readability. Without their help, this book would not have been possible.

R. Gerald Baker, *SIFMA*

Michael Caccese, *K&L Gates*

Andrew J. Donohue, Jr., *Principal Global Investors, LLC*

James A. Fanto, *Brooklyn Law School*

J. Christopher Jackson, *Calamos Investments*

Keith Loveland, *Loveland Consulting*

Richard D. Marshall, *Katten Muchin Rosenman LLP*

David E. Rosedahl, *Briggs & Morgan*

Brian L. Rubin, *Sutherland Asbill & Brennan LLP*

David Sobel, *Abel/Noser Corporation*

Robert Stirling, *National Regulatory Services*

Eric R. Vercauteren, *Galliard Capital Management, Inc.*

Kurt Wachholtz, *WellSpring Compliance, LLC.*

Craig Watanabe, *Core Compliance & Legal Services, Inc.*

About the Editors

JOHN H. WALSH

Mr. Walsh was a key regulator at the SEC for 23 years, serving as Chief Counsel and Acting Director of the Office of Compliance, Inspections and Examinations. In that capacity he was instrumental in creating OCIE and one of the key figures overseeing the development of the standards governing securities compliance. Mr. Walsh has a Ph.D. in History from Boston College, and a juris doctor degree from Georgetown University. He is currently a Partner at Sutherland Asbill & Brennan and admitted to practice in New York and the District of Columbia.

DAVID H. LUI

Mr. Lui was chair of the industry's trade group, the National Society of Compliance Professionals, and has been a chief compliance officer for some of America's largest investment advisers, including Charles Schwab Investment Management, Franklin Advisers (Franklin Templeton), U.S. Bancorp Asset Management, and Galliard Capital Management, an $85 Billion subsidiary of Wells Fargo. Mr. Lui is currently a Principal with Galliard Capital Management.

Mr. Lui is a graduate of Brown University with a bachelor of arts degree with Honors in History and a juris doctor degree from the University of California, Hastings College of the Law. He is admitted to practice in California and Minnesota.

JASON K. MITCHELL

Jason K. Mitchell serves as the chief compliance officer for Summit Creek Advisors, LLC in Minneapolis, Minnesota. Jason has over 15 years of experience in the financial services industry, with 10 years dedicated to the compliance profession. Prior to joining Summit Creek Advisors, Jason served as a senior compliance associate for Galliard Capital Management, overseeing the Investment Advisory functions of the firm. Jason also previously served as a compliance manager at U.S. Bancorp Asset Management, where he supervised the firm's compliance training program, as well as Code of Ethics administration and SEC examination coordination responsibilities. Jason graduated with a bachelor of arts degree in economics and management from the University of Minnesota, Morris.

Foreword

The role of a compliance professional is one of the most difficult in the modern business world. Compliance professionals are called on to ferret out activities that fail to comport with increasingly complex laws and regulations, and they function under the specter of personal liability if they fail. At the same time, they are called on by their management to keep their firms "out of trouble," but the resources necessary to change internal behaviors are scarce and compliance may not be given the priority it deserves.

The compliance officer can be squeezed between being responsible for everything and being responsible for nothing. On one side of the spectrum, management can perceive compliance as an obstacle, and on the other, government can hold compliance responsible for management's failures. In the face of this challenging backdrop, the compliance profession is faced with an existential question: Can the regulatory model for American business be governed by controls emphasizing ethics from within and strong internal procedures? Compliance professionals believe that it can, and they work every day to deliver these values.

With this as a backdrop, we created this book to give compliance professionals the best chance of success. We have dedicated our professional lives to strengthening the practice of compliance, and we dearly want to see the experiment in ethical and strong compliance succeed.

Generally speaking, compliance professionals have access to the black letter law that governs their work. Very little energy and scholarship, however, have been expended on developing the "best practices" that help a compliance professional achieve success. Recognizing this, *Modern Compliance* delves not only into the black letter law requirements of the compliance professional's job, but also into the attitudes, soft-skills, and finesse required to do it effectively.

In creating this book, we worked to bring together the compliance community's foremost thought leaders: individuals who are intellectually and professionally vested in developing and enhancing the practice of compliance. Contributing authors have spent decades working as chief compliance officers, practicing compliance law, serving as senior regulators, leading professional organizations, or teaching and researching compliance as a field of academic study. Each chapter focuses on an area of expertise that the writer is uniquely positioned to analyze. By bringing together these contributing authors, we hope to provide unique insight into the skills needed for the successful practice of compliance.

Compliance is a relatively small profession. But given the trillions of dollars of the nation's—and even the world's—wealth that compliance professionals work to protect, we firmly believe it is a high and noble calling. We wish each of you the best of luck in fulfilling your compliance responsibilities, and thank you for helping to pioneer *Modern Compliance*.

John H. Walsh
David H. Lui

Contents

CHAPTER 1: Introduction
By Lori A. Richards 1

CHAPTER 2: A History of Compliance
By John H. Walsh

I.	Introduction	5
II.	Foundations	7
III.	Origins	10
IV.	Development	19
V.	Recognition	44
VI.	A Half-Century of History	60

CHAPTER 3: What Is Compliance?
By R. Gerald Baker

I.	Introduction	63
II.	Distinguishing Between the Little c and the Big C	63
III.	Responsibilities Generally Ascribed to Compliance	66
IV.	Authoritative without Owning Supervision Responsibility	71
V.	Regulatory Expectations	75
VI.	Diverse Firm and Business Structures	75
VII.	Availability and Use of Resources: People and Technology	77
VIII.	Working with Senior Management	78
IX.	Conclusion	78

CHAPTER 4: Fiduciary Duty
By Karen Barr and David Tittsworth

I.	Introduction	81
II.	Origins of Fiduciary Principles	82
III.	Aspects of Fiduciary Duty	82
IV.	Regulatory Framework	84
V.	"NonRegulatory" Examples	86
VI.	Key Areas: Disclosure and Conflicts of Interest	88
VII.	Other Fiduciary Standards	89
VIII.	Fiduciary Duty and Broker-Dealers	89
IX.	Conclusion	91

CHAPTER 5: Core Requirements of a Compliance Program
By David H. Lui

I.	Introduction	93
II.	Culture of Compliance	95
III.	Tone at the Top	97
IV.	Written Procedures	100
V.	Testing	107
VI.	Annual Review or Written Report	115
VII.	Requirement to Designate a Chief Compliance Officer	128
VIII.	Reporting Structure	128
IX.	Conclusion	139

CHAPTER 6: Overview of the Regulatory Framework for SEC-Registered Investment Advisers
By Eric R. Vercauteren

I.	Introduction	141
II.	Understanding the Regulatory Objectives of the U.S. Securities and Exchange Commission	142
III.	Understanding the Regulatory Framework of The Financial Industry Regulatory Authority (FINRA)	152
IV.	Understanding the Regulatory Framework of the U.S. Commodity Futures Trading Commission	157
V.	Understanding the Regulatory Framework of the Comptroller of Currency	162
VI.	Conclusion	167

CHAPTER 7: Game Plan for the New CCO
By Robert Stirling

I.	Introduction	169
II.	Acclimating Yourself to the Firm's Culture	170
III.	Triage	171
IV.	Taking the Firm's Temperature	172
V.	Deploying Your Team (If You Have One)	172
VI.	The Listening Tour	173
VII.	The SEC's Document Request List: Who, Not What	174
VIII.	IT, Human Resources, and Accounting: Your New Best Friends	175
IX.	A Roadmap for Your First Year	176

CHAPTER 8: How Compliance Can Teach Ethics
By Lee Augsburger

I.	Introduction	179
II.	Corporate Entities Behave on an Ethical Spectrum, Whether Intentionally or Not	179

III.	Unethical Corporate Attitudes Affect Compliance and Business Results	181
IV.	Other Drivers of Corporate Ethics Programs	183
V.	Implementing an Effective Ethics Program	185
VI.	Similarities and Differences between Compliance and Ethics Programs	190
VII.	Conclusion	191

CHAPTER 9: Ethics Standards Governing Compliance Professionals
By Richard D. Marshall

I.	Introduction	193
II.	Competence and Empowerment	193
III.	Independence	199
IV.	Conflicts of Interest	200
V.	Confidentiality	204

CHAPTER 10: Soft Skills: Presenting Compliance
By Michelle Hawkins

I.	Introduction	207
II.	Your Road Map	208
III.	Self-Evaluation	208
IV.	Hindsight is 20/20	209
V.	Your ToolKit	210
VI.	Building Your Compliance Community	210
VII.	Communication	212
VIII.	Talent Management	215
IX.	Conflict Management	217
X.	Demonstrating your Expertise and Talent	219
XI.	Survival Skills	221
XII.	Additional Thoughts and Resources	222

CHAPTER 11: Compliance Training
By Kurt Wachholz

I.	Introduction	225
II.	Reasons for Conducting Compliance Training	226
III.	Learning Approaches	228
IV.	Learning Model	231
V.	Training Development	235
VI.	Training Evaluation	250
VII.	Ten Training Session Keys	252
VIII.	Conclusion	254

CHAPTER 12: Compliance and Risk Management
By Andrew J. (Buddy) Donohue and Andrew J. (Drew) Donohue, Jr.

I.	Introduction	257
II.	Enterprise Risk Management Framework and Identification of Types of Risk	259

III.	Responsibilities	261
IV.	Regulatory Requirements	263
V.	The Impact of the Dodd-Frank Act	271
VI.	Developing and Implementing Effective Risk Management in Financial Firms	272
VII.	Relationship Between Compliance and Risk Management	274
VIII.	Limitations of Risk Management Systems	277
IX.	Conclusion	277

CHAPTER 13: Navigating Marketing and Distribution
By Michael Caccese and Douglas Charton

I.	Advisers Act Section 206(4) and Rule 206(4)-1	279
II.	Performance Advertising	297
III.	FINRA	311
IV.	GIPS	323
V.	CFTC	345
VI.	Differences Among Regulatory Bodies	351
VII.	Conclusion	357

CHAPTER 14: Corporate Transactions: The Role of the Compliance Department
By A. Brad Busscher

I.	Introduction	361
II.	Corporate and Related Transactions	362
III.	Legal Department Versus Compliance Department	372
IV.	The Role of the Compliance Department in Corporate Transactions	378
V.	Conclusion	404

CHAPTER 15: Affiliated Transactions Under the Advisers Act
By Joseph McDermott

I.	Introduction	407
II.	Identifying Affiliates	409
III.	Legislation and Adopting Rules	410
IV.	Principal and Cross Trades	412
V.	Affiliated Brokerage	417
VI.	Other Considerations	420

CHAPTER 16: Adviser Custody: What You Need to Know
By Elizabeth M. Knoblock

I.	Introduction	423
II.	Why is Custody So Important?	423
III.	What Does "Custody" Mean?	425
IV.	What Does the Custody Rule Require?	425
V.	Procedures for Complying with the Custody Rule	426
VI.	Custody Review Process	431

VII. Monitoring and Testing 432
VIII. Conclusion 433

CHAPTER 17: Protecting the Privacy of Client Information
By David E. Rosedahl, Keith Loveland, and Andrew C. Small

I. Introduction 435
II. Gramm-Leach Bliley Act 435
III. SEC Regulation S-P: Broker-Dealers/Investment Advisers 436
IV. Regulation S-AM: Limitations on Affiliate Marketing 452
V. Identity Theft Prevention Programs: The Red Flags Rule 454
VI. Recent SEC and FINRA Initiatives 460
VII. SEC Enforcement Actions 464
VIII. States' Efforts to Safeguard Customer Information 472
IX. Developing Customer Data Security Processes 474
X. Customer Self-Protection of Data 475
XI. Safeguarding Examinations 476
XII. "Report on Cybersecurity Practices" 477
XIII. Conclusion 478

CHAPTER 18: Cybersecurity
By Krista Zipfel and Craig Watanabe

I. Introduction 493
II. The Growing Cyber Threat 494
III. Regulations, Policies, and Guidance 495
IV. Enforcement Cases 499
V. The NIST Cybersecurity Framework 502
VI. SEC Office of Compliance Inspections and Examinations (OCIE) Cybersecurity Initiative 503
VII. User Awareness: NINE Training Memos 515
VIII. Cyber Insurance 528
IX. Vulnerability Assessments and Penetration Testing 529
X. Risk Analysis Checklist 531
XI. Conclusion 531

CHAPTER 19: Forensic Testing
By Jeffrey Hiller

I. Introduction 533
II. Forensic Testing Defined 533
III. Tests and Analysis 536
IV. Conclusion 567

CHAPTER 20: Regulatory Examinations and Audits
By Michelle Jacko

    I.   The Purpose of SEC Examinations 569
    II.   The Examination Process 571
    III. Customary Regulatory Requests 577
    IV. Preparing for a Regulatory Audit. 580
    V.   Managing a Regulatory Examination 585
    VI. Final Stages of the Examination Process 588
    VII. Conclusion 595

CHAPTER 21: Your Relationship with FINRA
By David Sobel

    I.   Introduction 643
    II.   Developing a Rapport. 644
    III. Getting Involved. 644
    IV. Examinations 646
    V.   Enforcement. 647
    VI. Conclusion 648

CHAPTER 22: Compliance Professionals' Relationships with Endangered Populations
By Theodore J. Sawicki and Melissa J. Gworek

    I.   Introduction 649
    II.   Duties Owed to Senior Investors. 650
    III. Regulatory Concerns About Sales Practices and Investment Products 660
    IV. Suggested Best Practices 668
    V.   Conclusion 676

CHAPTER 23: Seeking to Avoid Chief Compliance Officer Liability
By J. Christopher Jackson

    I.   Introduction 679
    II.   The Role of Compliance and the CCO. 680
    III. The Question of Supervision 684
    IV. Enforcement Actions Against CCOs. 691
    V.   Key Steps to Take to Seek to Avoid Liability 692
    VI. Conclusion 701

CHAPTER 24: Avoiding Supervisory Liability
By Ted Urban

    I.   Introduction 703
    II.   Legal Bases for Supervisory Liability 704
    III. The Evolution of Commission Standards for Supervisory Liability 706
    IV. The *Urban* Matter. 715

V.	Developments After *Urban:* Seeking Clarity in Murky Waters.	721
VI.	Practical Considerations	727
VII.	Conclusions	731

CHAPTER 25: Enforcement Actions Against Chief Compliance Officers
By Brian L. Rubin and Irene A. Firippis

I.	Introduction	733
II.	The Relevant Rules and the Role of the CCO	734
III.	Theories of Liability	735
IV.	Direct Violations	736
V.	Aiding and Abetting and/or Causing a Violation	742
VI.	Failure to Supervise	746
VII.	Conclusion	750

CHAPTER 26: Preparing to Become a Compliance Officer, and the Academy
By James A. Fanto

I.	Introduction	753
II.	Traditional Backgrounds of Compliance Officers	754
III.	Increased Focus on Legal Training for Compliance Officers	756
IV.	Skills Training for Compliance Officers in the Academy	760
V.	Conclusion	763

CHAPTER 27: Is It Time to Go?
By Kathleen Edmond

I.	Introduction	765
II.	Read the Tea Leaves	766
III.	Do You Really *Have* to Go?	768
IV.	Protect Yourself When You Depart	769
V.	Consider Other Precautions	770
VI.	Conclusion	772

CHAPTER 28: Compliance as a Profession
By John H. Walsh

I.	Introduction	773
II.	Is Compliance a Profession?	773
III.	Progress Toward Professionalism	776
IV.	Getting to the Next Level	788
V.	Unfinished Business	794

Index 797

CHAPTER 1

Introduction

By Lori A. Richards

We have all heard the phrase "good compliance is good business." I have used it many times over the years, and its repetition in the industry has made it something of a truism. Why then, do I repeat it here? Because I have come to believe that it reflects a false choice and that it was born in a time before we could see clearly what compliance could become. Let me explain why.

First, you simply cannot operate a business (or for very long) without effective compliance. Rather than just being good business, it is an imperative to operating a business. If you lack effective compliance, eventually your customers will walk, you will suffer negative press stories, generate whistleblower complaints, or be subject to regulatory actions. And, the scrutiny on the financial services industry is such that these consequences will occur much faster than in the past. Think of the changes we've seen in the rigor and expectations of investors, boards, consultants, and the public, even apart from regulators.

Second, the phrase implies that the staff in the business (i.e., the front office) and compliance (i.e., the people in the Compliance Department) somehow have separate interests, and I don't think that is true, or should be the case. I believe that the business owns its compliance obligations, and failures in compliance are most always due to a failure to appreciate that fact.

It was more frequently the case in the past that companies operated in a kind of "catch me if you can" mentality that held that the business was just responsible for generating sales and revenue, and it was compliance's job to see and stop any compliance problems along the way. Ask front office people in a company like that who was responsible for its compliance with [*insert any regulatory requirement here*], and they were likely to name their compliance officer. What a failed model that was! The business didn't see its obligations as its own and perhaps didn't confide in or fully inform compliance personnel of issues or changes in its activities that would be questionable, and compliance officers may have lacked the resources, metrics, or standing to adequately call out the Business on its practices. The phrase "good compliance is good business" was born of that time, in an effort to convince the business that compliance was not just a revenue-reducing part of the firm's overhead.

I think we've come a long way, even if all firms are not on the same growth path. I'm thinking here of a chief compliance officer (CCO) friend at a private fund firm whose owner considers the CCO to be the personal embodiment of all regulators and regulations. So, whenever a regulator adopts a new rule, or the CCO's compliance testing or monitoring reveals an issue, the owner gets annoyed with the CCO! The owner has conflated a compliance responsibility (little c) with the Compliance program (big C). This has serious consequences as, taken to its logical extension, any compliance-related failing would be per se the failure of compliance—an untenable model for compliance professionals certainly because they cannot shoulder the responsibility or liability it suggests but it's also an ineffective model in terms of fostering healthy compliance in the industry.

I suggest that while they have different functions, the business and compliance do not have separate interests. Another friend (in the business at a regulated firm), describes this in the following way: "we are a We," meaning that the business and control functions share a common interest in reaching the right result, together. This supposes that there is mutual interest, but also that the business itself owns its compliance responsibilities. When a new rule is proposed [*insert any regulatory requirement here*], the person or persons responsible for establishing, maintaining, and supervising compliance with the obligation are in the business. Compliance provides assistance and guidance, and performs monitoring, testing, and credible challenge, but responsibility is clearly vested in the business.

Likely, your firm is somewhere on this journey from convincing the business that good compliance is good business to we are a We. How do you help move your firm closer to the latter sentiment, where the business feels more responsible for its own obligations? Do you educate your colleagues on the appropriate activities expected in first, second, and third lines of defense? On the duty to supervise? If not, you should think of these obligations as you would other compliance obligations that must be owned by the business.

Business executives increasingly understand the value of good compliance. Compliance programs are now receiving more resources, larger staffs, much more executive attention, and the proverbial "seat at the table." This has been a positive development in recent years.

When I served as director of the SEC's examination program, I frequently worried that compliance programs were not receiving the attention and support they deserved. When the "Compliance Rule" for advisers and funds was adopted in 2003, it institutionalized and supported a function that had previously been less formally structured and sometimes lightly resourced. Broker-dealers, transfer agents, and insurance companies were similarly at different stages of their compliance program development. In later years, CCOs and their compliance programs grew in stature and professionalism. During the financial crisis of 2008, I was afraid that much of the progress in compliance programs could be swept away in a few weeks of budget-cutting. We made it our purpose to reach out to the regulated community, especially to CEOs of regulated firms, to remind them of the importance of compliance and not to cut back on funding to compliance programs. We had been speaking about the importance of compliance to CCOs, but delivering that message to chief executive officers (CEOs) and business managers was more impactful. There were a few bad weeks and months, but compliance rode out the storm and emerged even stronger.

This history and development of compliance programs—only touched upon here but now many years long—has allowed for some important developments. First, we have developed a significant number of professional practitioners, people who have been working as CCOs or compliance professionals for many years, and who have individual and shared experiences of what has worked and what has not (many of whom are contributors to this book). Second, we know that compliance programs have stood the test of time, and crisis, and are not going away. Third, compliance has absorbed the best learning from other doctrines and toolsets: governance, ethics, technology, risk, audit, legal, and the "soft" skills that surround persuasion. Fourth, we're now seeing compliance programs develop more rigorous and defined core practices functions, i.e., advisory, policies and procedures, risk assessment, surveillance, monitoring, testing, and training. Fifth, there is more commonality in compliance programs globally, leading to a drive toward common global standards to facilitate growing global compliance efforts. Finally, the use of technology is radically reforming testing, monitoring and front-end compliance controls, and helping compliance evolve and expand its reach.

The practice of Compliance today bears scant resemblance to the compliance practiced thirty or forty years ago. In producing this book, the coeditors John Walsh and David Lui have assembled chapters by many of the leaders of modern compliance. Over the years I have had the opportunity to work with both John and David, as well as many of their contributors. In this book, they delve into the history of Compliance, ask about its nature, describe its core functions, and consider how it can be applied in various settings. This book should be of interest both to practitioners and consumers. Practitioners can use it to better appreciate their profession, sharpen their skills, and give themselves a benchmark in assessing their own efforts. Consumers—business executives, regulators, and others—can use it to better understand what compliance is and what it can do. In every case, by deepening our understanding of the field, and how it can be practiced, John, David, and all of the contributors have helped prepare us to realize our opportunities and address our challenges.

ABOUT THE AUTHOR

Lori A. Richards served on the staff of the U.S. Securities and Exchange Commission from 1985 to 2009. Among other positions, she was a senior enforcement attorney, executive assistant to Chairman Arthur Levitt, and director of the SEC's examination program (the Office of Compliance Inspections and Examinations). In these roles Ms. Richards was at the center of many of the important regulatory actions of the last several decades. Following her government service, Ms. Richards provided compliance services as a principal of a major accounting firm. She is currently the CCO of a leading asset management firm. In 2013, Ms. Richards was the recipient of the first Joan Hinchman Award of the National Society of Compliance Professionals, which honors lifetime contributions to compliance.

CHAPTER 2

A History of Compliance

By John H. Walsh
    Sutherland, Asbill & Brennan

I. INTRODUCTION

Modern compliance has a short history. It first appeared in the 1960s, only half a century ago. Indeed, even 50 years seems over-long, because many of compliance's modern features began to emerge only in the 1990s. Given the brevity of its history, it is remarkable how much compliance has developed and changed from its point of origin. The speed of its growth suggests that compliance addresses important contemporary goals.

The historical foundations of compliance suggest several relevant goals. At the deepest level, there is an ancient and worldwide aspiration for voluntary compliance with the public interest. Examples of this type of thinking can be found in both European and Asian traditions. Closer to the surface, when modern financial regulation was first developed, early in the 20th century, two more specific aspirations took shape. The first was a vision of a simple code of ethics that would govern finance. The second was a vision of self-regulation, in which the financial community would regulate itself. Compliance provides a practical solution for achieving all of these goals.

The origins of modern compliance can be dated with precision. It first appeared in the early 1960s, when the securities markets were shaken by a terrible scandal. Regulators and political leadership leapt into action. Investigations, enforcement, a major study, and recommendations quickly followed. Congress enacted legislation imposing liability on broker-dealers when they fail reasonably to supervise persons who commit violations. In this setting, securities firms began to give attention to their own internal enforcement of governing laws and rules. Within a few years these internal processes had become sufficiently widespread among broker-dealers that the United States Securities and Exchange Commission (SEC) undertook to publish its expectations. The SEC organized an advisory committee that issued a *Model Guide for Broker-Dealer Compliance in 1974*. The guide was a seminal work that articulated many of the practical and continuing features of a compliance system. By the 1980s compliance was recognized as an established function within broker-dealers, but at this point, only as a "first line" of law enforcement for the regulators.

In the early 1990s compliance entered a period of intense development and growth. This took several forms:

- Contemporaries settled on certain essential institutional structures, including a designated compliance officer, policies and procedures, access to the highest levels in the organization, and periodic self-evaluations;
- They articulated a mission beyond local law enforcement that included the realization of affirmative values such as creating a preventive control environment and an effective code of ethics; and
- They extended compliance into multiple fields including global financial regulation, criminal law enforcement, bank regulation, corporate governance, health care, public company financial disclosure, and the regulation of asset managers.

Moreover, contemporaries began to debate the nature of compliance: was it inherently supervisory, inherently advisory, or something else? By the middle of the first decade of the twenty-first century compliance had grown into a highly articulated function that had been deployed across multiple sectors.

Recognition of compliance began to follow. This recognition took various forms: regulators stepped forward to protect compliance in the midst of the financial crisis; a global association of regulators recognized its value; and the United States Congress began to incorporate compliance into major legislation as a tool of public policy. Perhaps most importantly, regulators, industry groups, and others began to recognize that compliance is a unique field that must be endowed with certain key characteristics, including senior level governance, objectivity, and independence. There were missed opportunities. Nonetheless, the trend toward recognition has been unmistakable, including, most recently a multinational initiative to publish a global standard for compliance management.

After a half-century of accelerating development, compliance has become a dynamic and highly institutionalized field of endeavor with distinctive structures and characteristics. No longer simply a "first line" of enforcement for a single regulator, compliance provides a unique and independent service across multiple sectors. Compliance practitioners work every day with systems and practices that deliver compliance with the public interest and ethical standards. Through self-control of business, by itself and for itself, compliance is achieving true self-regulation.

Nonetheless, much work remains to be done. Compliance remains divided into multiple discrete areas defined by the rules or standards with which practitioners work. Many compliance practitioners and the firms they work for continue to see themselves as craftsmen, who apply specific tools to specific problems, instead of professionals, who share a common professionalism with other compliance practitioners around the globe. Perhaps the greatest challenge facing compliance today is to recognize that despite its multiple internal specializations, it is one field, one practice, and one profession. Perhaps the next major development in the ongoing history of compliance will be practitioners' recognition of their own shared professionalism across all of these specialized fields.

II. FOUNDATIONS

Modern compliance is built on deep foundations. Some stretch back thousands of years. From ancient times, voluntary compliance with the public interest has been seen as a positive and even inspiring value. These values reside at the roots of many contemporary ideas, including modern compliance.

The ancient Greeks believed the laws of the *polis* should be constructed to foster and enhance voluntary compliance, because it was through such compliance that citizens grew in virtue and reason. A modern commentator has described Aristotle's views:

> Voluntary compliance is essential to the law attaining its fundamental end of making citizens virtuous, or in other words of enabling them to fulfill their *telos* [or purpose] by helping them become rationally self-governing in their dealings with other people. If legislation does not take place in a way that encourages and permits voluntary compliance or consent, then it is inconsistent with the attainment of its citizens' ends, and is thus unjust.[1]

Hence, voluntary compliance is not simply submission to the dictates of the state. Rather, it is an essential element in the creation of a virtuous and rational society. Legislation should contemplate voluntary compliance, so that citizens can respond accordingly. Understood in this light, law creates a potential for reason and virtue, and voluntary compliance realizes and implements that potentiality among the citizens.

Ancient values regarding voluntary compliance were not limited to Europe. They can also be found in Asian thinking. Confucius taught that compliance obtained through the threat of punishment is insincere and unstable; those threatened with punishment will always find ways to circumvent such laws.[2] True social harmony—in Confucius's words, the harmonious oneness of heaven and humanity—comes from voluntary inner compliance with moral principles, known collectively as *li*. These principles are inculcated through training and education, establish moral expectations, and have a self-disciplinary effect on individuals. In ancient China most commercial relationships were regulated by *li*, not punitive law, and disputes were resolved through self-reflection, self-regulation, compromise, and the voluntary acceptance of decisions made by clans, guilds, and business associations. Again, rather than simple submission to the punishing power of the state, voluntary compliance with *li* was the expression of an individual's harmony with society. Modern scholars are reconsidering these Confucian ideals in the hope of creating commercial regulations in China that are suited to its culture and traditions.[3] The aspiration for voluntary compliance is so deeply seated in cultural and

---

[1] Randall R. Curren, 22 *Reason Papers* 144, at 147 (Fall 1999) (emphasis in original) (review of Fred D. Miller, Jr., *Nature, Justice, and Rights in Aristotle's Politics*, Oxford University Press, 1995).

[2] Angus Young, *Conceptualizing a Hybrid Approach in Enforcement and Compliance in China: Adopting Responsive Regulation and Confucian Doctrines to Regulate Commerce* (August 10, 2013), available online.

[3] *Id.*

intellectual norms that any selection of examples seems invidious. Countless other instances could be cited from ethics, philosophy, theology, or political science. This general approbation of voluntariness gives compliance much intuitive appeal. But we need not limit ourselves to theoretical values. Compliance is ultimately a practical hands-on venture, and its inspiration should be found in practical values. With this in mind, perhaps the best example of the foundational goals animating the history of compliance will be found in a conversation between two consummate men of the world.

In the early 1930s, at the birth of national financial regulation in the United States, two senior executives met to discuss the financial crisis then gripping the country. Securities markets were crashing, banks were failing, and unemployment was surging. One of the executives, the newly elected president of the United States, proposed a solution to the other, the president of the New York Stock Exchange. Ethics—and what we would today call compliance—played a central role.

A Simple Code of Ethics

In April 1933, shortly after his inauguration as president of the United States, Franklin D. Roosevelt met with Richard Whitney, president of the New York Stock Exchange. The only record of the meeting is a follow-up letter Whitney sent to President Roosevelt.[4] Hence, our understanding of the conversation is entirely based on Whitney's description. Nonetheless, Roosevelt's policy vision for the financial sector can be heard in Whitney's words.

Roosevelt raised the possibility of the New York Stock Exchange adopting a code of ethics—simple enough, he said, for the public to understand. He also told Whitney that he hoped the code "might become a universal standard." The two presidents spent some time talking about how regulations adopted by the New York Stock Exchange could be made applicable to other exchanges. Whitney expressed some doubt about whether any code for the securities business could be made simple enough for the public to understand. But he assured Roosevelt that the vast majority of the exchange's members were "anxious to put the security business on a higher plane than it has ever been before."[5]

This conversation is remarkable on several levels. First, in the midst of the financial crisis of the early 1930s, the two presidents spoke of an ethical code and placing business on a higher plane. They explicitly considered ethics as a pragmatic policy solution. Second, they spoke of making the code a universal standard. To some extent this was a reflection of the power of the New York Stock Exchange. Given his position, Whitney could influence other market centers and actors. Beyond that, however, their discussion showed that the two presidents were reaching beyond the exchange and seeking to remake business at large into a new image. Third, although they did not use the term compliance, we can see it in their conception of the code as something so simple

---

[4] Letter of Richard Whitney to Hon. Franklin D. Roosevelt (April 14, 1933), unpublished letter available in the archives of the Franklin D. Roosevelt Presidential Library and Museum, Hyde Park, New York.
[5] For a more detailed discussion of the historical context in which this conversation occurred, *see* John H. Walsh, "A Simple Code of Ethics: A History of the Moral Purpose Inspiring Federal Regulation of the Securities Industry," 29 *Hofstra Law Review* 1015, 1039–40 (2001).

even a layperson would understand. Whitney questioned whether this was possible, and experienced compliance professionals may agree. Yet, the conception of the code as something simple suggests both voluntariness (it should be simple to understand and simple to follow) and visibility (onlookers should be able to appreciate that it is being followed). This is a powerful policy vision: ethical, universal, simple: and demonstrable.

Although Roosevelt's vision of a simple code of ethics played a role in the early development of financial regulation in the United States,[6] it did not lead immediately to modern compliance. Several more decades would pass before compliance appeared on the scene. Nonetheless, this vision reflects an aspiration that compliance could eventually fulfill. Could finance be governed by its own internal ethical code?

The conversation between the two presidents revealed another concept that has had a foundational role in modern compliance. Roosevelt asked Whitney whether the New York Stock Exchange could develop the simple code. In other words, at least in its initial expression, the code would be a creation of the private sector. This expressed the contemporary idea that finance should regulate itself.

Self-Regulation

In early 1933, during the same period in which he discussed the simple code of ethics with President Whitney of the New York Stock Exchange, President Roosevelt was embarking on a major initiative to bring self-regulation to the American economy. The National Industrial Recovery Act of 1933[7] established the National Recovery Administration (NRA). The NRA sought to eliminate unfair trade practices through mandatory codes of fair competition prepared by trade associations, subject to NRA approval.[8] The NRA applied to the entire economy, and hundreds of codes were adopted. As part of this adoption effort, an Investment Bankers Code Committee prepared a code of conduct for the securities business. This code contained provisions that continue to play a role in financial regulation, including broker-dealers' obligation to adhere to "just and equitable principles of trade," and their duty to consider the suitability of investments when making recommendations to customers. The NRA, however, did not survive. In 1935 the Supreme Court held that it was unconstitutional.[9] Roosevelt's expansive vision of an entire economy subject to self-regulation had failed.

The failure of the NRA did not end self-regulation in finance. During the heyday of the NRA, Congress had enacted the Securities Exchange Act of 1934, which provided for self-regulation by securities exchanges, such as the New York Stock Exchange.[10] Moreover, when the NRA was disbanded, the Investment Bankers Code Committee voluntarily remained in operation and worked to obtain legislation authorizing self-regulation that passed constitutional muster. In 1938 the Securities Exchange Act was

---

[6] *Id.*
[7] National Industrial Recovery Act, Ch. 90, 48 Stat. 195 (1933).
[8] For a more detailed discussion of these events *see* Walsh, *A Simple Code of Ethics.*
[9] *A.L.A. Schechter Poultry Corp. v. United States,* 295 U.S. 495, 550 (1935).
[10] Securities Exchange Act of 1934, Ch. 404 § 6, 48 Stat. 881, 885–886 (1934).

amended to authorize securities associations, and the committee reorganized itself as the National Association of Securities Dealers (NASD),[11] which has since been reorganized into a successor organization known as the Financial Industry Regulatory Authority (FINRA). Roosevelt's vision lived on in finance.

Self-regulation had much in common with the simple code of ethics. Both sought to elevate business to a new level, higher, in Whitney's words, than it had ever been before. With a code, business people would adhere to a standard of conduct, and with self-regulation other business people would enforce that adherence. The legacy of this effort can be seen in modern standards of conduct, including those first developed by the Bankers Code Committee, and others since. Moreover, it was upon these foundations—ethics and self-regulation—that compliance would eventually be built.

III. ORIGINS

In the early days of national financial regulation in the United States, contemporaries seem to have divided the business community into two groups: people who were honest, and people who were not. The purpose of self-regulation was to muster the support of the former in controlling the latter. A 1938 statement by Senator Alben Barkley, who was later vice president of the United States, captures this understanding:

> While I know that most of the people in the banking business are honest and would need no regulation or supervision, I know as well that there are some who, because of incompetency or a careless regard of fair practices, need the influential guidance of government supervision…the 1938 self-regulatory law described in § 2.02[B] above] is written upon the theory that regulation can best be achieved by the efforts of honest brokers and dealers themselves.[12]

In this environment, attention was focused on how honest business people could regulate others who were less so. The major breakthrough that led to modern compliance took place when honest people began to recognize that they needed to keep an eye on themselves. Self-regulation, they came to understand, should be internalized within each firm.

Special Study of the Securities Markets (1963)

In early 1960, serious violations of the securities laws came to light at the American Stock Exchange, then the second largest stock exchange in the country. A member firm, Re, Re and Sagarese, and the father and son who controlled it, Jerry and Gerard F. Re, were accused of wide-ranging misconduct. They had distributed securities in violation of the registration requirements, delivered prospectuses containing false and misleading

---

[11] Securities Exchange Act Amendments of 1938, Ch. 677, 52 Stat. 1070 (1938).
[12] Senator Barkley, Extension of Remarks, 83 Congressional Record 790 (1938) (capitalization conformed).

information, made purchases on the basis of undisclosed material information, engaged in inappropriate transactions as specialists on the exchange, failed to maintain required books and records, manipulated the prices of securities, and more.[13] The SEC initiated an enforcement action, expelled the two Res from the business, and revoked their firm's registration as a broker-dealer.[14]

As often happens in the aftermath of a scandal, regulatory attention quickly turned from the misconduct to the conditions that had allowed it to occur. In the spring of 1961 the SEC announced that it would conduct an inquiry of the American Exchange "to see why," in the words of a member of the SEC staff, "it was possible for something like this to happen."[15] At the time, the investigation was described as "the most extensive of its kind" since the 1930s.[16]

Congress, however, decided an even more comprehensive review of conditions in the securities industry was in order. On September 5, 1961, Congress enacted an amendment to the Securities Exchange Act authorizing and directing the SEC to make "a study and investigation of the adequacy, for the protection of investors, of the rules of national securities exchanges and national securities associations, including rules for the expulsion, suspension, or disciplining of a member for conduct inconsistent with just and equitable principles of trade."[17] The chairman of the SEC indicated that it would include a "new and comprehensive look" at exchange practices in a number of areas.[18] The study's director, Milton Cohen, later remembered that the scandal at the American Stock Exchange had been the principal thing Congress had in mind when it decided that the SEC should look at the total industry.[19]

A special staff of the SEC conducted the study, which was eventually known as the "Special Study of the Securities Markets." The SEC's chairman later indicated that the intent of the study had been to give special focus to the integrity of broker-dealers and their salesmen. "It is the broker-dealers," he said, "employing these salesmen, who must bear a responsibility of maintaining the necessary standards by adequate supervision. Responsible conduct on the part of broker-dealers and their salesmen can, and should be, our keystone."[20] The study was a priority for the agency. By the fall of 1962, the SEC indicated that it would curtail the expansion of other operations to fund the study's completion.[21]

---

[13] A summary of the case can be found at: *Securities and Exchange Commission News Digest* (Aug. 25, 1960).
[14] See *Securities and Exchange Commission News Digest* (May 5, 1961).
[15] See "SEC to Probe Am. Exchange; Rules, Policies, Practices to Be Scrutinized," *Chicago Daily Tribune*, page B5 (May 15, 1961).
[16] *Id.*
[17] SEC, *Report of the Special Study of the Securities Markets of the Securities and Exchange Commission*, Part 1, page 1 (Apr. 3, 1963) (hereinafter cited as "Special Study Report").
[18] See William L. Carey, Chairman, SEC, *Speech to the Investment Bankers Association of America*, page 12 (Nov. 28, 1961).
[19] Milton Cohen, statement at *The Roundtable of the 1963 SEC Special Study*, SEC Historical Society, transcript at pages 15–16 (Oct. 4, 2001).
[20] SEC, *Special Study Report* at 7.
[21] "SEC May Delay Enforcement Step-Ups to Obtain Funds for Stock Market Study," *Wall Street Journal*, page 8 (Oct. 16, 1962).

© MODERN COMPLIANCE 2015

In the event, the study group issued its report in 1963. Contemporaries noted that the reaction of the securities industry was "amazingly quiet."[22] So quiet, in fact, that as the report was issued it was headline news that members of the investment community declined to comment.[23] They did, however, take it seriously. The New York Stock Exchange, for example, established five special committees to analyze the study's recommendations.[24] Indeed, the most noteworthy controversy was a public spat between the chairman of the SEC and the study's chief counsel. The chairman described the report as "mild," and the chief counsel took issue.[25] The controversy would be nothing more than a footnote, except it revealed the thinking of the study staff. The chief counsel was concerned that the mild characterization would have an adverse effect upon the prospects that the study's recommendations would be carried out, including, "one of the most important recommendations of the study…its suggestions for upgrading standards for securities salesmen."[26]

In fact, the study had paid careful attention to the standards applicable to securities salesmen. The starting point was the ethical standards they currently followed. The report found they used multiple inappropriate practices.[27] These abuses included "come-on" and "bait" advertising, "cold turkey" telephone calls, "boiler room" organizations, the use of special compensation to generate intense selling efforts, self-dealing, and more.

The problems documented by the study, the chairman of the SEC reported to Congress, resulted from "inadequacies in established enforcement machinery, both government and industry."[28] His language was significant. The problems arose because of inadequate "enforcement machinery." Moreover, the machinery was in "government and industry" alike. This revealed the study's fundamental vision of how to address abusive practices. Problems arose because of a lack of enforcement, which should include enforcement by the industry itself. This vision would characterize compliance for years to come.

Beyond the failures of enforcement, the study discussed existing methods of supervision and control within firms over selling practices. Broker-dealers, the study noted, had the ultimate responsibility for the conduct of their agents and employees.[29] The study went on to identify several of the controls used by the better firms to implement this responsibility, including through line managers, centralized oversight, review of transactions, oversight committees, internal audits, firm policies, approved lists, and even, at the largest firms, the use of "electronic data processing equipment (EDP)" to provide a daily "run" of information about transactions. In transmitting the Special

---

[22] David G. Mutch, "SEC Study Lauded," *Christian Science Monitor*, page 13 (Apr. 18, 1963).
[23] Robert E. Nichols, "SEC Study Evokes Icy 'No Comment,' Investment Community Cautious in Reacting to Lengthy Report," *Los Angeles Times*, page B8 (August 4, 1963).
[24] "Five Special Big Board Groups Reviewing Recommendations of SEC's Staff Report," *Wall Street Journal*, page 2 (Oct. 21, 1963).
[25] Arelo Sederberg, "Terming SEC Study 'Mild' Seen Unfair," *Los Angeles Times*, page C7 (Nov. 14, 1963).
[26] *Id.*
[27] *Special Study Report*, at 237 et seq.
[28] Letter of Transmittal of the Report of the Special Study of the Securities Markets, William L. Carey, Chairman SEC, to the President of the Senate and the Speaker of the House of Representatives (Apr. 3, 1963).
[29] *Special Study Report*, at 290 et seq.

Study Report to Congress, the chairman of the SEC said these voluntary efforts by responsible firms should be made generally applicable in regulations.[30]

In the immediate aftermath of the study, the SEC recommended to Congress that it enact new legislation requiring securities firms to internalize regulation through more effective supervision of their agents and employees.[31] Congress did so by authorizing the SEC to bring disciplinary actions against supervisors who failed to supervise reasonably persons who commit violations. These provisions, applicable to broker-dealers and investment advisers, have played a role in securities regulation ever since.[32]

Through the attention it gave to internalized responsibilities and controls, the Special Study of the Securities Markets played a critical role in the development of compliance. It shows an interesting trajectory. It began by investigating a failure by a traditional self-regulator: the American Stock Exchange. Then, as soon as the study staff began to examine the standards and practices of securities salesmen, their attention moved to a new type of self-regulation: the responsibilities and controls internalized within each securities firm. Years later, in a roundtable sponsored by the SEC Historical Society, study Associate Director Ralph S. Saul cited the development of compliance as one of the study's major accomplishments.[33] He said, "Setting up the whole supervisory compliance structure within firms, I think a lot of that is due to the Special Study. We emphasized that." Other observers have agreed that it was in the 1960s and 1970s that a small number of practitioners first began to create the compliance function within broker-dealers.[34]

Model Guide to Broker-Dealer Compliance (1974)

In the years after the Special Study of the Securities Markets, responsible broker-dealers worked to implement its recommendations. They began to draft compliance manuals, including, at one major firm, an "original 1971 manual" that served as the backbone of all that was to come.[35] As this work unfolded, the SEC decided that it had a role to play.

In early 1973, G. Bradford Cook, chairman-designee of the SEC, announced that an initiative to prepare a model compliance program for broker-dealers had begun in October 1972 as a cooperative venture with the regulated community.[36] In the near future, he said, an industry advisory group would submit its recommendations. The

---

[30] *Special Study Report* at pages III–IV.
[31] *See* House Report No. 1418, to accompany H.R. 6793 (May 19, 1964).
[32] The provisions regarding firms are now codified at Securities and Exchange Act § 15(b)(4)(E) and Investment Advisers Act § 203(e)(6). The provisions regarding individual supervisors are now codified at Securities and Exchange Act §15(b)(6) and Investment Advisers Act § 203(f).
[33] Ralph S. Saul, statement at *The Roundtable of the 1963 SEC Special Study*, SEC Historical Society, transcript at pages 55–56 (Oct. 4, 2001).
[34] Edward H. Fleischman, Commissioner, SEC, *Perspectives from the Commission Table: Supervision; Address to the Compliance and Legal Division Seminar of the Securities Industry Association* (Apr. 5, 1989).
[35] *Id.*
[36] G. Bradford Cook, Chairman-Designee, SEC, *Keynote Address to PLI's "The SEC Speaks Again"* (Feb. 23, 1973).

goal was not to change the SEC's rules, but rather to conduct an educational project on existing requirements and day-to-day practices in the brokerage industry.

In early 1974 the advisory committee issued a public draft,[37] and in late 1974, it submitted its report to the SEC.[38] The report indicated that the objective of the advisory committee, as defined by the SEC, had been to provide an awareness of existing requirements and to suggest procedures by which the industry could comply with them. Participants in the effort had included securities firms, such as Merrill Lynch & Co., Inc., Goldman Sachs & Co., Baker, Weeks & Co., Inc., and First Southwest Company, as well as self-regulators, including the New York Stock Exchange, NASD, American Stock Exchange, and Midwest Stock Exchange. The committee had held 50 days of meetings to discuss the drafts and the report was 272 pages long. As the advisory committee noted, the size of the final report demonstrated the length and complexity of its undertaking.

The Guide to Broker-Dealer Compliance, or "Model Guide" that issued from the advisory committee's work bears a striking resemblance to countless compliance manuals since. It contained nineteen topical sections devoted to supervision, registration, financial and operational responsibility, customer accounts, oversight of branch offices, advertising and sales literature, investment advisory services, private placements, proprietary trading, research and recommendations, underwriting, as well as several more devoted to specific types of securities products. Each section had three parts: a statement of applicable laws or regulations, special problems arising in the area, and compliance procedures for addressing the problems.

Many of the procedures in the Model Guide would be familiar to compliance practitioners in the early 21st century. The guide contained checklists, outlines for interviews, specific controls, training, periodic inspection visits, forms to complete, due diligence information to collect and consider, regional compliance personnel, and similar procedures. Perhaps most suggestive of future developments, it contained a chapter on electronic data processing (EDP), with a discussion of compliance controls over manual input of data, review of printouts, consideration of "special computer codes to highlight certain types of accounts," and the possibility of using EDP for regulatory filings.

The SEC's Model Guide initiative demonstrates the energy and creativity of compliance. Within a decade of the Special Study, an array of compliance controls had been developed, deployed, debated by leading representatives of the business community, and included in the Model Guide. When viewed as indicative of what compliance practitioners did, and continue to do, the Model Guide was a landmark development. One could view much of compliance's later history as an elaboration on the controls first set out in the Model Guide.

---

[37] "SEC Panel Issues Draft of Its Compliance Guide," *Wall Street Journal,* page 4 (Jan. 28, 1974).
[38] *Guide to Broker-Dealer Compliance, Report of the Broker-Dealer Model Compliance Program Advisory Committee to the Securities and Exchange Commission*, Securities Exchange Act Release No. 11,098, 5 SEC Docket 472 (Nov. 13, 1974). A copy of the full report is available in the SEC Library.

On another level, though, the Model Guide also demonstrated contemporaries' perception of compliance. The Model Guide's treatment of the "compliance official" is revealing in this regard. The guide said:

> The Compliance Official of a broker-dealer is the person or persons vested by management with the ultimate authority and responsibility for supervisory controls and procedures designed to achieve compliance by the broker-dealer and associated persons with applicable securities laws, rules and regulations. The term "Compliance Official" does not denote a particular management or supervisory person, but rather it is used as a term of description to identify the person to whom authority and responsibility is delegated, regardless of the office he holds in the business entity involved.[39]

In other words, the compliance official was the manager responsible for achieving compliance. As the guide put it, the official must be "vested with sufficient authority and full support [of] senior management so that he is fully empowered to carry out his responsibilities successfully."[40]

The Model Guide appears to have intended the compliance official to be a member of senior management, because it stated that ultimate responsibility for compliance rested with senior management.[41] The guide also compared compliance to supervision, and the contrast is noteworthy. Supervisory responsibility could be delegated, and the term "supervisory person" meant those "subordinates" to whom such responsibilities had been delegated.[42] The perception this conveys identifies the compliance official as among the senior managers of the firm, and the supervisory person as among the subordinate officials, such as office manager, resident manager, sales manager, or administrative manager.[43] In short, in this sense, compliance described a function of senior line management: achieving regulatory compliance. It was not a specialized function within the firm dedicated to compliance. Indeed, the Model Guide expressly contemplated that this function would be assigned to persons holding other offices.

In the 1970s, when the Model Guide was created, compliance was seen primarily as a body of procedures for enforcing substantive rules or standards. One could summarize the overall approach of the guide as identifying rules and enforcing them. It was not a specialized function managed by specialized experts. Quite the contrary, it was assigned to senior managers of the firm who were often expected to hold other offices as well. Nonetheless, when viewed from the perspective of the shop floor, where specific procedures were applied to specific issues, broker-dealer compliance had taken a significant step forward.

---

[39] *Guide to Broker-Dealer Compliance*, at 2–3.
[40] *Guide to Broker-Dealer Compliance*, at 3.
[41] *Guide to Broker-Dealer Compliance* at 2.
[42] *Guide to Broker-Dealer Compliance*, at 2 and 49, note 1.
[43] *Id.*

Compliance in the 1980s

By the 1980s, compliance had acquired several years of practical experience and had grown and flourished in many broker-dealer firms. Indeed, by the end of the 1980s, the work of the prior decades was already taking on something of the air of compliance's heroic period.

In a 1989 speech, Edward Fleischman, a commissioner of the SEC, spoke about the progress of compliance.[44] He noted the small number of practitioners in the 1960s and 1970s who had first begun to mold the compliance and legal functions within their firm and to draft the early compliance manuals. From those earliest days, he said, compliance had been working "to deploy new tools, to perform even more effectively, and to convey to line management (and to regulators) an articulate perspective on the profitability of compliance." The spirit penetrating a compliance conference, he said, should be pride: "pride in all that's been accomplished in the [last] quarter century."

These sentiments demonstrated the progress compliance had made since the publication of the Special Study of the Securities Markets. The original manuals had been developed and expanded until the earlier work served only as a backbone for larger and more sophisticated bodies of practice. Nonetheless, when we examine what contemporaries meant by compliance, we find that their understanding of compliance had hardly advanced beyond the days of the study and Model Guide. Compliance, in the contemporary understanding, remained an enforcement mechanism.

In the mid-1980s Aulana Peters, a commissioner of the SEC, articulated a vision of compliance that expressed the contemporary understanding. She was speaking about the SEC's enforcement program, and in doing so she described it to be like a pyramid. The SEC was at the top, she said, self-regulatory organizations for broker-dealers were in the middle, and finally, at the bottom, were the securities firms.[45] Because the SEC did not have the resources to pursue every violation, the commissioner said, the commission had to rely on brokerage firms as its "first line" of defense "to police their own ranks."

The commissioner's speech provided a powerful simile for the work of compliance. So powerful, in fact, that it would long outlive the 1980s. Even decades later, from time to time some of the images it expressed reemerge into public discourse. One must ask, however, what it means. As a simile for compliance, the pyramid communicates three propositions.

First, compliance is a police activity. The commissioner stated this two ways. Compliance was a substitute for SEC enforcement, and the SEC relied on broker-dealers to police their own ranks. In American terms, the police power has special meaning, because it is a power identified by the U.S. Constitution and conferred on the states to enforce

---

[44] Fleischman, *Perspectives from the Commission Table*.
[45] Aulana L. Peters, *Investor Protection: The First Line of Defense: Address to Brooklyn Law School's Securities Regulation Symposium* (Mar. 15, 1985).

their own laws and regulation.[46] Within any legal regime, however, the police power can readily be understood as a coercive exercise of public or governmental authority. In short, in this view, compliance did within the firm—coercive enforcement—what the government could do to the firm.

Second, compliance is at the bottom of a hierarchy. The image of a pyramid suggests both that compliance practitioners outnumbered regulators and self-regulators, and also that compliance was secondary, and even tertiary to them in regards to status. The commissioner heightened this imagery in her speech by calling compliance the "first line" of defense. Much like a Roman Legion of old, for which the first line was occupied by the youngest and least trained soldiers, with the better and more experienced soldiers in the second and third lines behind, the image of a first line continues to suggest lesser rank and skill.

Third and finally, the commissioner communicated that compliance's highest value was to serve as an agent of the regulators "higher-up" in the hierarchy. If, she suggested, the SEC had the resources to pursue every violation on its own, compliance would be unnecessary. It was only because the regulator lacked sufficient enforcement resources that compliance had a role.

The image of compliance expressed in Commissioner Peters' speech is unmistakable. Compliance was a police activity conducted by low-status personnel who served as local enforcement agents for the regulators. Indeed, one should emphasize, this was the image communicated by someone who was otherwise—at least judging by the remainder of her speech—a friend of compliance who rose to speak on its behalf. In this environment, one can understand why business managers and line personnel might view compliance as an outside imposition on their activities.

Many of the themes of Commissioner Peters' simile can be found in other contemporary statements regarding compliance. Public officials emphasized that firms' internal efforts were necessary to "stretch" the SEC's "thin resources."[47] SEC Chairman John Shad, who challenged the private sector to exercise more responsibility for its own ethics,[48] spoke of how compliance, specifically in regards to insider trading, could "continue to assist" the regulators, through a "joint assault of the securities industry and the Enforcement Division of the SEC."[49] Formal statements of the SEC, such as in an opinion issued by the full commission sitting as an adjudicative body, spoke of compliance as a form of enforcement: that is, as a responsibility of firms in which they must have the internal power and authority to compel compliance with applicable standards and requirements.[50]

---

[46] United States Constitution, 10th Amendment.
[47] Bevis Longstreth, commissioner SEC, *The Duty to Supervise: Self-Discipline Within the Securities Firm: Remarks to the Fifteenth Annual Rocky Mountain State-Federal-Provincial Cooperative Securities Conference* (Oct. 29, 1982).
[48] In addition to serving as chairman of the SEC, John Shad was a leader in advocating business ethics.
[49] John S.R. Shad, chairman SEC, *The SEC and the Securities Industry, Speech to the Securities Industry Association* (Dec. 2, 1981).
[50] *In the Matter of Prudential-Bache Securities, Inc.*, 48 S.E.C. 372 (1986).

In the 1980s regulators also began to see opportunities to extend compliance to other areas. In 1985 the director of the SEC's division responsible for asset managers gave a speech in which she coined a phrase that would resonate for years: "Good compliance is good business."[51] Yet, when one looks behind the phrase, the speech itself mostly deals with the SEC's own regulatory actions such as its compliance inspections, its rulemaking and application processes, and a proposal then under consideration for a self-regulatory organization for investment advisers. The director only briefly mentioned firms' internal compliance. Firms must stress it, she said; they must keep their procedures up to date; and resources spent on new product development and marketing must be matched with more resources spent on compliance. Hence, the speaker suggests, even as good business, compliance remained secondary to regulatory activity.

Finally, in a hint of the development of compliance in following years, in the late 1980s Congress responded to a wave of insider trading scandals by enacting compliance requirements for broker-dealers and investment advisers. In 1988, the House Committee on Energy and Commerce noted that insider trading was a "serious problem in our securities markets."[52] The Committee went on to express concern about "the types of procedures Wall Street firms have in place to prevent insider trading violations given the great numbers of firm employees who have access to potentially invaluable confidential information and the apparent ease with which that information can be disseminated."

The time had come, the House Committee concluded, to require broker-dealers and investment advisers to design effective procedures to restrict and monitor access to highly sensitive materials, and prevent insider trading. The result was the Insider Trading and Securities Fraud Enforcement Act of 1988 (ITSFEA).[53] Codified at Section 15(f) of the Securities Exchange Act (now at Section 15(g)), and Section 204A of the Investment Advisers Act, the act required broker-dealers and investment advisers to "establish, maintain, and enforce written policies and procedures reasonably designed, taking into consideration the nature of such broker's [or adviser's] business, to prevent the misuse…of material, nonpublic information." In 1990, the SEC staff issued a report entitled "Broker-Dealer Policies and Procedures Designed to Segment the Flow and Prevent the Misuse of Material Nonpublic Information."[54] The report described the steps firms were taking to implement ITSFEA, including training, employee trading restrictions, physical barriers to separate departments, and surveillance procedures. The staff concluded that although firm procedures varied widely "in scope and comprehensiveness," certain minimum procedures were needed including: the maintenance of watch lists and restricted lists, review of employee and proprietary trading, documentation of procedures, and an active and responsible role for compliance.

---

[51] Kathryn McGrath, director Division of Investment Management SEC, *Good Compliance Is Good Business: Keynote Address to the 1985 ICI/SEC Procedures Conference* (Oct. 31, 1985).
[52] H.R. Rep. No. 100-910, at 13 (1988).
[53] P.L. No. 100-704, 102 Stat. 4677 (1988).
[54] SEC Division of Market Regulation, *Broker-Dealer Policies and Procedures Designed to Segment the Flow and Prevent the Misuse of Material Nonpublic Information*. (Mar. 1990).

By the late 1980s compliance had established itself in the broker-dealer community. Practitioners could look back with pride on all they had achieved, and ideas were already circulating about how compliance might apply in other areas, such as among asset managers. Moreover, Congress's response to the wave of insider trading cases in the 1980s hints at the future development of compliance. In ITSFEA Congress responded to a concern about a problem in the securities markets with requirements for better compliance. This response would be seen again, repeatedly, after 1990. Yet, at the same time, compliance was the bottom level of a regulatory pyramid. Nonetheless, despite this low starting position, in the coming years compliance would experience remarkable growth and development.

IV. DEVELOPMENT

In the early 1990s, compliance began to develop and grow with remarkable speed. It was an idea whose time had come. Perhaps like other ideas whose time suddenly arrives, compliance began to spring up in multiple locations, with multiple applications, and no apparent sense that individual efforts were part of a larger movement. Time and again, political leaders, task forces, prosecutors, commissions, regulators, courts, and others announced a newfound appreciation for compliance, as if no one had ever noticed it before. Only rarely, and only late in this period of ferment and growth, were efforts made to survey the movement as a comprehensive whole. It all began with a policy initiative directed from the highest level of global political leadership.

FATF Recommendation 20 (1990)

In July 1989, the heads of state or government of the seven leading industrial powers, known as the Group of Seven (G-7), held a summit in Paris. The conference was called the Summit of the Arch because it was held at the top of the newly constructed Grande Arche de la Defense. This was the fifteenth meeting of the G-7. Delegates in attendance included the president of host France, the presidents of the United States and the European Commission, the chancellor of West Germany, and the prime ministers of the United Kingdom, Canada, Italy, and Japan.

The summit addressed a variety of contemporary problems including: managing the debt of the world's poorest countries, the decline in rates of savings, the Uruguay round of trade negotiations, the environment, and drug issues.[55] In regards to the latter, the summit found that the "drug problem has reached devastating proportions." It stressed "the urgent need for decisive action, both on a national and an international basis." Among other initiatives, the summit decided to convene a financial action task force from summit participants and other interested countries to consider "additional preventive efforts" that could be taken "to prevent the utilization of the banking system and financial institutions for the purpose of money laundering."

---

[55] G-7 Paris Summit, *Economic Declaration* (Paris, July 16, 1989).

The task force, known as the Financial Action Task Force (FATF), was established in Paris under French presidency, and immediately began operations.[56] During the following months its membership was expanded to include additional countries. The task force also moved quickly to prepare recommendations for fighting money laundering. In April 1990, less than a year after its formation, the FATF issued a report containing forty recommendations.[57] A month later, in May 1990, the task force's member nations endorsed the report at the ministerial level.

Most importantly, in Recommendation 20, FATF endorsed the idea that financial institutions should develop internal programs to prevent money laundering. Moreover, FATF set out the minimum elements that each financial institution's program should contain. The recommendation stated:

> 20. Financial institutions should develop programs against money laundering. These programs should include, as a minimum:
>   a. The development of internal policies, procedures and controls, including the designation of compliance officers at management level, and adequate screening procedures to ensure high standards when hiring employees;
>   b. An ongoing employee training program; and
>   c. An audit function to test the system.

Although short and to the point, this recommendation was a powerful statement on the essential elements of a compliance program. Moreover, the institutional structure it described for compliance could be universally applied. It was inherently scalable and flexible. Every element could be adjusted depending on the size and nature of the firm. This provided an open-architecture for a compliance program that could be given any number of specific applications within specific firms.

After 1990, FATF has revised its recommendations several times. Nonetheless, each time it has preserved the statements in the original Recommendation 20 in one form or another. In 1996 and 2003 it renumbered the Recommendation, first to number 19 and then to number 15. Then, in 2012, FATF moved its text from the recommendations to the interpretative notes, where it now resides.[58] However, FATF's later treatment of this recommendation is less significant than its role in establishing a global model for compliance in the early 1990s.

FATF Recommendation 20 has played a significant role in the history of compliance. FATF's endorsement of internal programs with certain universal elements gave compliance credibility around the world. As a matter of prestige, FATF stood close to the

---

[56] A history of the origins of FATF can be found in *Financial Action Task Force on Money Laundering, Report 1990–1991* (Paris, May 13, 1991).
[57] *The Forty Recommendations of the Financial Task Force on Money Laundering 1990.*
[58] The current recommendations can be found in: *International Standards on Combatting Money Laundering and the Financing of Terrorism & Proliferation: The FATF Recommendations* (Paris, Feb. 2012). The relevant text appears in the interpretative notes to Recommendation 18.

pinnacle of global political leadership, and was supported by the leading economic nations of the world. As a matter of education, FATF worked actively in the years after 1990 to spread the implementation of its recommendations throughout the world economy. Finally, as a matter of enforcement, states that failed to cooperate were listed as "non-cooperative countries or territories," and every effort was made to treat them as pariahs in the global financial community. By 2014 only a handful of countries remained on the uncooperative list. Thanks to FATF, the desirability of internalized compliance—specifically in regards to antimoney laundering—has become a familiar concept around the world.

United States Sentencing Guidelines (1991)

The next major step in the development of compliance took place in the United States when a domestic commission issued guidelines on the appropriate sentences for business organizations convicted of criminal misconduct. The commission, known as the United States Sentencing Commission ("Sentencing Commission"), had been established by an act of the United States Congress in 1984. Over the next several years it held public hearings and issued public analyses of its goals. In 1987 it began issuing guidelines for sentencing individual defendants. Then, in November 1991, it issued guidelines for sentencing business organizations.

The guidelines for organizations were set out in Chapter 8 of the United States Sentencing Guidelines Manual (USSG Manual).[59] They operate by assigning points to a defendant's misconduct to create a culpability score, and then subtracting points known as mitigating credit to obtain a final score.[60] A source of mitigating credit was the business organization's compliance program. Moreover, the Sentencing Commission explained what a minimally effective program should contain. It did so by setting out seven key elements.

First, the organization must have standards and procedures to prevent and detect criminal conduct. As with FATF Recommendation 20, and indeed, the SEC's Model Guide for broker-dealers, policies and procedures were at the heart of the standards set out in the USSG Manual.

Second, the organization's governing authority must be knowledgeable about the content and operation of the compliance and ethics program, and must exercise reasonable oversight. A specific person within high-level personnel must be assigned overall responsibility for the compliance and ethics program, and day-to-day operational responsibility should be delegated to an individual who will report to higher-level personnel. The compliance program should be given adequate resources, appropriate authority, and direct access to the governing authority of the firm (or an appropriate

---

[59] United States Sentencing Commission, *Federal Sentencing Guidelines Manual*, Chapter 8, "Sentencing of Organizations, Part B, Remedying Harm from Criminal Conduct, and Effective Compliance and Ethics Program" (1991).
[60] A short summary of the guidelines can be found at Paula Desio, Deputy General Counsel, United States Sentencing Commission, *An Overview of the Organization Guidelines* (no date given).

subgroup thereof). This level of detail regarding compliance governance made the USSG Manual unique. Unlike prior guidance, the manual set out a specific chain of command, with a senior official, day-to-day manager, as well as resources, funding, authority, and reporting access.

Third, reasonable efforts should be made to not give substantial authority to an individual who has engaged in illegal activities or other conduct inconsistent with the compliance and ethics program. Of course, the screening of employees had played a role in both prior broker-dealer compliance and the FATF recommendation.

Fourth, the organization should take reasonable steps to communicate its standards and procedures, and conduct effective training programs appropriate to individuals' respective roles and responsibilities. Again, training was deeply engrained in prior compliance.

Fifth, the organization should conduct monitoring and auditing to ensure the compliance and ethics program is followed, and provide mechanisms for confidential or anonymous internal reporting or guidance. The organization will also periodically evaluate the program's effectiveness. Internal monitoring was inherent in compliance from its earliest days, and the idea of periodic evaluations had also been recommended by FATF.

Sixth, the compliance and ethics program should be consistently promoted and enforced through both incentives and discipline. This was an interesting aspect of compliance that had not received much prior attention. It would quickly come to be known as a "culture of compliance." The USSG Manual recognized that compliance includes both internal promotion and dealing with those who fall short.

Seventh, after criminal conduct has been detected, the organization should take appropriate steps to respond and prevent any similar conduct. One could expect this element to be given prominence in the USSG Manual because, as a source of sentencing guidelines, one can assume the manual would only be considered after some serious problem had occurred.

As can be seen, the USSG Manual reflected many previous developments in compliance. Nonetheless, it also presented new features that warrant special note. For example, the manual provided a much more detailed outline for compliance governance than previous sources. It also spoke to both compliance and ethics and included cultural concerns that could be overlooked if compliance is viewed solely as an enforcement mechanism. Finally, the manual focused on how a firm behaves after a problem is discovered, which highlighted compliance's role in crisis management.

The USSG Manual has played a role in many criminal proceedings. The Sentencing Commission reports that since the guidelines were implemented more than 1 million defendants—individual and organizational—have been sentenced under them.[61] The manual has also drawn litigation, including before the United States Supreme Court.

---

[61] *An Overview of the United States Sentencing Commission,* available online.

In 2005 the Court ruled that the detailed guidelines were voluntary for judges, that is, they could consider them but need not strictly follow them.[62] Finally, the manual's influence has spread beyond sentencing. Standards similar to those in the manual can be found in the principles federal prosecutors use to determine whether to bring charges against organizations.[63]

Beyond criminal proceedings, the guidelines have had a significant impact on compliance. The USSG Manual laid out a well-developed institutional structure for compliance, including policies and procedures, governance and management, employee screening, training, monitoring, a culture of compliance, and crisis management. In addition, the guidelines created incentives for adopting a compliance program. In the words of William W. Wilkins, Jr., chairman of the Sentencing Commission, the guidelines helped establish a "carrot and stick" approach.[64] The guidelines, he said, were intended to provide "incentives for organizations to establish meaningful compliance programs."

The USSG Manual played a crucial role in the development of compliance in the United States. It had an immediate impact. Press and commentators followed the progress of the Sentencing Commission and the guidelines, and emphasized how compliance programs could help companies avoid criminal prosecution, even when the programs were unsuccessful.[65] Twenty years after the guidelines were adopted an independent review of their application found that the guidelines had "achieved significant success in reducing workplace misconduct by nurturing a vast compliance and ethics movement and enlisting business organizations in a self-policing effort to deter law-breaking at every level of their business."[66] Much like FATF's promotion of the basic structure of compliance throughout the world, the USSG guidelines served to promote the fundamental structures and goals of compliance throughout the business community in the United States.

Arthur James Huff and the Nature of Compliance (1991)

In the early 1990s, an SEC enforcement case challenged the contemporary understanding of compliance. The legal question presented was whether a broker-dealer compliance official was a supervisor and responsible for the misconduct of an employee. As discussed above,[67] after the Special Study of the Securities Markets of the 1960s, the U.S. securities laws had been amended to make broker-dealers liable for the violations of supervised persons, if they had failed to supervise them reasonably. The enforcement case in the early 1990s addressed what this legal standard meant when applied to a

---

[62] *U.S. v. Booker*, 543 U.S. 2200 (2005).
[63] See Principles of Federal Prosecution of Business Organizations, Title 9, Chapter 9-28.800.
[64] "Plan on Corporate Crime," *The New York Times*, page D2 (Oct. 29, 1990).
[65] Daniel B. Moskowitz, "Compliance Programs Could Help Companies Avoid Criminal Prosecution," *Washington Post*, page 13 (Apr. 23, 1990).
[66] Ethics Resource Center, *The Federal Sentencing Guidelines for Organizations at Twenty Years, A Call to Action for More Effective Promotion and Recognition of Effective Compliance and Ethics Programs: Report of the Ethics Resource Center's Independent Advisory Group on the 20th Anniversary of FSGO* (2012).
[67] See § 2.03[A].

compliance officer. As a matter of law, the case did little to resolve the issue, and the law of supervision remains unsettled to this day when applied to compliance professionals. Regardless, the case marked a turning point in the history of compliance.

Arthur James Huff worked in the Compliance Department of a major broker-dealer.[68] A securities salesman in the firm's Miami branch office engaged in a major fraud. The salesman conducted an investment scheme called either an "arbitrage" or a "short term trading" program and ran up millions of dollars in losses, mostly through trading options. He concealed these results from his customers by intercepting the broker-dealer's accurate account statements and sending customers fake versions of his own. The salesman was eventually caught, convicted of a criminal offense, and sentenced to ten years in federal prison.

Huff had been given certain responsibilities regarding options, including being named senior registered options principal (SROP), a position required by the broker-dealer's self-regulatory organization.[69] In various informal documents, such as an educational handbook, the SRO had suggested that an SROP had supervisory responsibility. When the salesman's misconduct came to light, the SEC staff charged the salesman's branch manager, regional manager, and Huff with a failure to supervise. The branch and regional managers settled the charges, leaving only Huff to contest them.

The SEC action against Huff was carried out in two steps. First, it was tried before an administrative law judge (ALJ); then the case was appealed to the commissioners who sat as a panel of adjudicators. Both the ALJ[70] and the commission[71] issued written decisions on the merits of the case. As the case made its slow progress—the commission ruled more than three years after the ALJ—it posed the question, what is compliance?

Before the ALJ, Huff described his duties as advisory in nature. He said he was responsible for developing and implementing policies, setting up compliance guidelines, reviewing activity in options accounts on a selective basis, preparing policies and procedures, following through on options situations when there were appearances of a concern or problem, investigating options problems and complaints, having in place supervisory procedures for the review of large or active options accounts, and assisting branch managers. This was a different activity, he said, than the "line supervision" provided by the firm's business managers, such as the branch manager in the Miami office. As a contested legal issue, within the enforcement action, Huff concluded from this that he was not a supervisor, and therefore not liable for the rogue salesman's violations.

The ALJ disagreed. The Compliance Department, he said, "As its very name suggests, is an integral part of the supervisory process, particularly in a large geographically dispersed" firm such as Huff's employer. Moreover, the ALJ said, Huff's employer

---

[68] *In the Matter of Arthur James Huff,* Initial Decision of SEC Administrative Law Judge (Dec. 15, 1987) (hereinafter cited as "Huff, ALJ Decision").
[69] In this case the self-regulator was the Chicago Board Options Exchange (CBOE), the primary U.S. market for trading options.
[70] Huff, ALJ Decision.
[71] *In the Matter of Arthur James Huff,* 50 S.E.C. 524 (Mar. 28, 1991)(hereinafter cited as "Huff, SEC Decision").

considered the Compliance Department an integral part "of the 'team' that shared responsibility for ensuring compliance by and supervision over" both the salesman and the branch manager. In short, the ALJ said, line officers and compliance personnel shared supervisory responsibilities. The ALJ also noted Huff's position as SROP, and said it "would be a travesty of the self-regulatory process" to ignore the self-regulatory organization's description of the position as supervisory. The ALJ found Huff liable for failure to supervise and suspended him from the brokerage business.

The sanction against Huff drew considerable attention, particularly because it was rare for the SEC to target compliance officials. In press coverage on the case, even the head of the SEC regional office that had prosecuted Huff admitted that it was "pretty unusual, in that there aren't that many cases against individual officers of compliance departments."[72] The enforcement action may have been rare, but within its historical context, the ALJ's analysis was highly conventional. One could see it as an echo of the SEC's Model Guide of the 1970s, which had described the compliance officer as the senior manager designated by the firm to provide supervision and ensure compliance. With this understanding of compliance, as the ALJ notes, its "very name" signifies supervisory responsibility. Moreover, the ALJ's decision revealed a deep commitment to the self-regulatory context in which compliance had emerged in the 1960s and had been understood through the 1980s. The broker-dealer's self-regulator had apparently intended this particular compliance position to have supervisory responsibility, and, in the ALJ's words, it would be a "travesty" to defeat that self-regulatory purpose.

If the Huff case had ended here, with the ALJ's decision, it would have marked a moment of continuity, even though the case itself had been rare. But Huff appealed the decision to the full commission. This gave all of the parties an opportunity to revisit their arguments. In addition, the Compliance and Legal Division of the Securities Industry Association (SIA), a broker-dealer industry group, submitted a friend-of-the-court brief.[73] The SIA questioned whether compliance officers should ever be deemed supervisors. Compliance practitioners, the SIA said, are advisors, not supervisors. They provide support, guidance, and systems to those charged with line management, but they do not have the power to hire, fire, reward or punish employees. In 1991 the commission issued its decision. The result can best be described as a muddle.

One of the commissioners recused himself from the decision, and the other four split evenly into two groups of two. All four agreed that the case should be dismissed, and it was. But each of the two groups had its own reasons and wrote its own opinion. As a result, as one of the four commissioners later said, "Huff is a difficult case to make much sense out of with these two somewhat disparate opinions."[74] The first opinion declined to decide whether Huff was a supervisor, and instead held that regardless of

---

[72] "Paine Weber Inc. Compliance Aide Suspended by SEC," *Wall Street Journal*, page 29 (Dec. 22, 1987).
[73] A 1988 statement by the head of the SIA's Legal and Compliance Division summarizing the argument was quoted in Fleischman, *Perspectives from the Commission Table*.
[74] Richard Y. Roberts, *Failure to Supervise Liability for Legal and Compliance Personnel: Remarks to the Securities Law Committee of the Federal Bar Association* (Dec. 7, 1992) (hereinafter cited as "Roberts, 1992 Speech").

his responsibilities, under the particular facts of the case, his actions were reasonable.[75] The second opinion, on the other hand, held that he was not a supervisor because he did not control the salesman, and therefore the commission need not consider whether his conduct was reasonable.[76] Despite the muddle, the decision marked a turning point for compliance for two reasons.

First, all four commissioners rejected the ALJ's reasoning that the self-regulatory process was a paramount consideration. With varying levels of analysis both opinions held that the views of the self-regulator did not control their assessment of whether Huff was a supervisor. Anne Flannery, a distinguished attorney who later served as the CCO of a major broker-dealer, helped represent Huff in his appeal to the commission. She indicates that a key part of the strategy on appeal was to focus on the statutory requirements for supervision.[77] In the early 1990s, Flannery indicated, compliance's regulatory and legal structure was relatively undeveloped. By focusing on the statutory requirements for supervision, Huff's legal team could argue that the self-regulator's position was relevant, but not binding in any respect. The commission agreed. The self-regulator's view, all four commissioners agreed, did not control their determination of the compliance position's legal responsibility. From a historical perspective—at least symbolically—one could see this as the moment when compliance began to emerge from the bottom layer of the enforcement pyramid. Compliance, the commissioners suggest, was not inherently below and subordinate to the traditional self-regulators.

Second, all four commissioners, again with varying levels of analysis, addressed the ALJ's reasoning that compliance was inherently supervisory. Three visions of compliance were before them. The ALJ reasoned that compliance's supervisory nature was suggested by its "very name." At the opposite extreme, the SIA argued that compliance was inherently advisory, and therefore necessarily never supervisory. In the middle was Huff's defense team. Flannery remembers that Huff's attorneys had "something of a difference of opinion" with the SIA over this point. Instead of arguing that compliance was inherently advisory, Huff's attorneys argued that although compliance was mostly advisory, there were circumstances under which it could be supervisory, but in the presenting case there was no evidence that the rogue broker had ever been subject to Huff's supervision. This more nuanced approach carried the day. Two of the commissioners opined that Huff was not a supervisor, which rejected the ALJ's view, and all four stated that their decisions were not based on the function Huff performed (i.e., "as a staff compliance officer"), which rejected the SIA's view. Instead, two of the commissioners opined, Huff's ability to control the salesman's behavior was the decisive question, irrespective of the department in which he worked. Again, from a historical perspective—here more than symbolically—one could see this as the moment when compliance began to emerge from its origins in the Special Study and the early compliance programs that had been designed to address the supervisory obligations

---

[75] Huff, SEC Decision (opinion of Chairman Breeden and Commissioner Roberts).
[76] Huff, SEC Decision (opinion of Commissioners Lochner and Schapiro).
[77] Interview with Anne Flannery (Nov. 2014). Interviews will be cited only once. Absent further citation, all following quotations or references to the statements of the same individual are based on the interview.

that had resulted therefrom. Compliance, the commissioners found, was not simply another name for supervision.

The Huff case has an interesting historical legacy. One could say that the most important statements it made about the nature of compliance were purely negative. Unlike the views of the ALJ and the SIA, the SEC's opinion suggests that compliance has no special nature. Indeed, in the opinion of the two commissioners who most thoroughly considered these issues, the nature of compliance was irrelevant: The same supervisory "control" standard would apply to compliance practitioners as would apply to anyone else. Of course, in light of compliance's early history, this negative statement was a powerful message.

In the immediate aftermath of the Huff case, the SEC took up other cases involving legal and compliance personnel. Although those cases had important legal implications, they had less of a role in marking historical changes within compliance. However, the legacy of Huff lingered in public discourse. For example, in 1992, SEC Commissioner Roberts, who had joined the opinion finding that Huff had acted reasonably, gave a speech in which he continued to blast the SIA's view of the nature of compliance.[78] He said: "At a minimum the proposition that a…compliance officer could never be deemed a supervisor should be laid to rest." In 1993 SEC Commissioner Schapiro, who had joined the opinion holding that Huff was not a supervisor, also returned to the topic, and reiterated the view that legal responsibility should follow actual responsibility.[79] She said: "In the 1990s, compliance and legal personnel are part of the life blood of securities firms and have had to adjust to that reality.…Increased actual responsibility in some cases may mean greater legal responsibility." From a historical perspective, her most noteworthy observation may have been that compliance had entered broker-dealers' "lifeblood."

Interagency Standards for Bank Safety and Soundness (1995)

In the mid-1990s compliance came to bank regulation. As with its arrival in broker-dealer regulation three decades before, the rise of compliance was born in an atmosphere of crisis. In this case, the crisis focused on retail banks and savings and loan associations (S&Ls), a type of retail bank in the United States that takes deposits and primarily provides home mortgage loans.

In the 1980s rising interest rates had posed a financial challenge to many retail banks and S&Ls. With most of their assets invested in fixed-rate, long-term mortgages, the S&Ls were unable to respond to customers' demand for higher interest rates for their deposits. This created a maturity mismatch: The banks were raising funds through demand deposits, which were vulnerable to fluctuations in short term interest rates; and they were investing those funds in long-term mortgages with fixed interest rates. Caught by sharply rising interest rates, numerous institutions failed. As they failed,

---

[78] Roberts, 1992 Speech.
[79] Mary Schapiro, commissioner, SEC, *Remarks at the National Association of Securities Dealers, Inc., Sixth Annual Education Seminar* (Oct. 5, 1993).

serious abuses were revealed across the sector, including fraud, accounting irregularities, self-dealing, extravagant compensation, poor lending decisions, and more. This led to multiple enforcement actions, criminal convictions, and widespread public disgust. This environment was quickly labeled the "S&L Crisis."

To respond, the U.S. Congress passed legislation requiring bank regulators to establish operational and managerial standards for a variety of relevant practices, including loan documentation, credit underwriting, asset growth, and compensation for bank and S&L insiders, such as directors, officers, and employees.[80] In the United States, bank regulation is conducted by a number of different agencies: the Board of Governors of the Federal Reserve System, the central bank; the Federal Deposit Insurance Corporation (FDIC), which administers the national deposit insurance program; the Office of the Comptroller of the Currency (OCC), which regulates national banks; and the Office of Thrift Supervision (OTS), which at that time regulated S&Ls. In July 1995, the agencies jointly released the new standards.[81]

The joint Standards for Safety and Soundness focused on the specific controls identified by Congress in the enabling legislation. These were the primary areas in which misconduct had occurred. However, the standards also addressed compliance on a more generalized level. Two aspects of this generalized statement warrant note.

First, the joint Standards addressed compliance with applicable laws and regulations. Initially, each of the substantive standards had recited that it included compliance with applicable laws and regulations. Then, in the final text, the regulators stated that repetition in each substantive standard was unnecessary. As a result, the regulators included a single statement requiring "compliance with applicable laws and regulations." The agencies explained, "The express requirement to ensure compliance with applicable laws and regulations is a necessary standard for internal controls and information systems."

Second, the joint standards addressed the bank regulators' practice of imposing compliance plans. The standards stated that if an institution failed to meet any of the standards, the relevant regulator could require it to submit an acceptable plan to achieve compliance. Such compliance plans would be required, the agencies said, when the failure to meet one of the standards was of such a severity that that it "could threaten the safe and sound operation of the institution." In addition, as the agencies noted, they would likely take additional supervisory actions until the deficiency had been corrected, including possible enforcement action.

The bank regulators' compliance plans illustrate an alternative path in the development of compliance. Unlike the sector-wide developments seen with broker-dealers, compliance plans were imposed on individual banks after an institution had otherwise

---

[80] Federal Deposit Insurance Corporation Improvement Act of 1991 (FDICIA) § 132, 105 Stat. 2236 (Dec. 19, 1991) (adding a new Section 39 to the Federal Deposit Insurance Act).

[81] Office of the Comptroller of the Currency, Board of Governors of the Federal Reserve System, Office of the Comptroller of the Currency, and the Office of Thrift Supervision, *Standards for Safety and Soundness*, 60 *Federal Register* 35674 (July 10, 1995).

failed to meet applicable standards. This individualized remedial approach would play a role in other sectors as well.

Development of the joint Standards for Safety and Soundness mimicked, to a remarkable degree, the historical process in which compliance had initially emerged. A crisis shakes existing institutions: in this case, retail banks and S&Ls. High-level public policy, again led by the U.S. Congress, requires action to prevent a recurrence. Then, specialized regulators take action both to address the specific issues that led to the crisis and to require more generalized compliance with applicable laws and regulations, hopefully to address future and yet unidentified problems. Compliance, at least at the regulatory level, was becoming an attractive policy response to crises.

In re Caremark International (1996)

By the mid-1990s, compliance was spreading far beyond its origins among broker-dealers. In 1996, a state court decision was handed down that introduced it into corporate governance. Specifically, the decision indicated that a board of directors, the most senior internal supervisory body for most large businesses in the United States, could escape private liability for corporate misconduct if it had exercised a good faith judgment that the corporation had a reasonable compliance system.

State courts in the United States play a critical role in corporate governance, because the laws of a corporation's state of domicile govern its practices. In this regard, the State of Delaware is especially important. It claims to be the home of 50 percent of all U.S. public corporations and 64 percent of the largest 500.[82] Caremark International, Inc., was a public company domiciled in the State of Delaware.[83] As a result of its domicile, claims by the company's shareholders against its board of directors were judged in the Delaware courts.

In 1994, a group of Caremark's shareholders claimed that the directors had breached their duty of care when they failed to exercise appropriate attention and had allowed the company to engage in a pattern of violations that eventually drew regulatory and criminal sanctions. Specifically, as a healthcare provider Caremark entered into contracts with doctors that were problematic under the Anti-Referral Payments Law. That law prohibits the payment of referral fees for patients whose medical bills are paid with government funds under the public health insurance programs known as Medicare and Medicaid. Instead of referral fees, Caremark paid referring doctors for other services, such as monitoring patients, consultations, and research. The Delaware court noted that these payments were not illegal in and of themselves, but they did raise the possibility of unlawful "kickbacks." The inspector general of the U.S. Department of Health and Human Services (HHS) conducted an investigation of the payments; federal criminal prosecutors eventually joined in; and Caremark pled guilty on a charge of mail fraud, paid a criminal fine, and made civil reimbursements, all of which totaled approximately $250 million. The shareholders did not claim that the board of directors knew about

---

[82] These statistics are made available by the Delaware Department of State, Division of Corporations.
[83] *In re Caremark, Inc.*, Derivative Litigation, 698 A. 2d 959 (Del. Ch. 1996).

the wrongful conduct. Instead the shareholders alleged that the directors were ignorant of the misconduct, and therefore, the shareholders said, liable for their inattention or negligence. Rather than contesting the claims, the directors entered into a proposed settlement with the shareholders, which under Delaware law had to be approved by the court.

This procedural background has some bearing, because the historical importance of the Caremark decision has dwarfed its legal authority. The judge decided only whether the proposed settlement was fair. But the reasoning by which he arrived at that conclusion had a dramatic impact on compliance.

The judge said that when a claim is made against directors predicated on the directors' ignorance of wrongful conduct, "in my opinion only a sustained or systematic failure of the board to exercise oversight—such as an utter failure to attempt to assure a reasonable information and reporting system exists—will establish the lack of good faith that is necessary to establish liability." In other words, the board will avoid liability if it exercises a good faith judgment that the corporation's "information and reporting system is in concept and design adequate to assure the board that appropriate information will come to its attention in a timely manner as a matter of ordinary operations, so that it may satisfy its obligations."

The judge then considered whether Caremark had such a system. In his decision the judge noted that Caremark had a "Guide to Contractual Relationships" that prohibited the misconduct under investigation; had issued an ethics manual; conducted internal training; had an internal audit plan designed to assure compliance with its business and ethics policies; established new policies requiring local branch managers to secure home office approval for certain transactions; and had appointed a compliance officer. In sum, the judge held, Caremark's information systems appear to have represented a good faith attempt to be informed of relevant facts. "If," he concluded, "the directors did not know the specifics of the activities" that led to liability, "they cannot be faulted." He approved the settlement ending the litigation.

Contemporaries viewed the *Caremark* opinion as creating "an incentive to create compliance systems to detect corporate wrongdoing."[84] One lawyer quoted in the press described the opinion to say: "Look, Mr. Director, you're going to have to take compliance seriously."[85] Moreover, the opinion had added weight because of Delaware's importance as a domicile for United States corporations. Much like the USSG Manual, the *Caremark* decision made compliance relevant to any type of business, especially, in this case, the largest corporations, many of which are incorporated in Delaware.

Open Letter to Health Care Providers (1997)

Caremark's problems with the Anti-Referral Payments Law illustrate the complexity of the legal regimes in which many businesses operate. From time to time particular

---

[84] Dean Starkman, "Compliance Ruling May Shield Directors," *Wall Street Journal,* page B5 (Dec. 24, 1996).
[85] Starkman, "Compliance Ruling," quoting Kirk S. Jordan.

lines of business draw heightened regulatory concern and enforcement. In the early 1990s, health care providers like Caremark found themselves under intense scrutiny. A series of investigations by the inspector general of HHS led to criminal actions against multiple providers. Violations included fraudulent claims on public medical insurance programs, kickbacks, violations of laws governing medical referrals, and others. In 1997 HHS addressed these problems with a compliance initiative.

In early 1997, HHS's inspector general was June Gibbs Brown. She had previously served in the Department of Justice, where she had worked with the Sentencing Guidelines, and with the mandatory compliance programs often required in the settlement of criminal actions against business organizations. In February, she issued *An Open Letter to Health Care Providers* that described a comprehensive regulatory compliance program.[86]

The 1997 letter was brief but to the point. It had three major elements. The first invited health care providers to join her in a national campaign to eliminate fraud and abuse from Medicare, Medicaid, and other health and human development programs. The second warned that her office had been given new resources to combat health care fraud, such as investigative and audit staff, and that it was pursuing "an intensified crackdown." She was committed, she said, to "vigorously pursue civil and criminal action against those who defraud this nation's health care programs." Finally, in the third element, she turned to compliance. Her office, she said, had been meeting with representatives of health care provider groups to draft model compliance programs. The effort had already led to the preparation of general guidelines containing the fundamental elements of any health care compliance program. Soon, she indicated, it would produce sector-specific models for each component of the health care community, such as clinical laboratories.

Although the letter did not recite the fundamental elements to which Inspector General Brown alluded, the first model was made available to the public the following month. In March 1997 HHS published model compliance guidance for clinical laboratories.[87] The model was notable for two reasons.

First, it stated that it was based on the inspector general's fraud investigations and the requirements imposed on clinical laboratories in corporate integrity agreements. These agreements were compliance obligations imposed on individual health care organizations following the inspector general's determination that they had violated the health care laws, such as, for example, by submitting false invoices for medical services, paying medical referral fees, and so on. The practice of entering into these agreements has continued, and in recent years more than 30 companies remain subject to them.[88] In practical terms, these agreements have created an ad hoc compliance structure for affected firms much like the Compliance Plans administered by bank regulators.

---

[86] June Gibbs Brown, *An Open Letter to Health Care Providers*, HHS Inspector General, Open Letter 02-1997 (Feb. 1997).
[87] Office of Inspector General HHS, *Publication of the OIG Model Compliance Plan for Clinical Laboratories*, 62 *Federal Register* 9435 (Mar. 3, 1997).
[88] Office of Inspector General HHS, *Focus on Compliance: The Next Generation of Corporate Integrity Agreements* (Aug. 27, 2012).

Second, the model described a compliance program with many familiar elements. They included written policies and procedures, in this setting including standards of conduct for lab employees and for limiting tests to those that are medically necessary; oversight of relations with physicians, including ongoing monitoring of those who direct both publically insured and other business to the same lab; controls over billing and marketing; record retention; naming a chief compliance officer; audits; corrective action; training; and more. The following year, HHS issued another model guide, this time for hospitals.[89] Since that time, several more have followed.

Beyond its specific messages, the Open Letter's tone and tenor were noteworthy. Inspector General Brown indicated that she and her staff were "committed to creating an atmosphere that encourages voluntary compliance and self-disclosure by health care providers." She admitted that "compliance programs are not a novel idea." Nonetheless, she indicated, "They are becoming increasingly popular as affirmative steps toward promoting a high level of ethical and lawful corporate conduct." Numerous providers had expressed an interest in them to protect their operations, and, she said, when her office or the Department of Justice investigate health care fraud, they would consider the entity's compliance efforts when considering the level of sanctions and the penalties that should be imposed.

Three years later, Inspector General Brown issued another open letter describing the progress of her compliance initiative. Her Open Letter of 2000[90] reported that the number of guidelines had risen to seven. In addition to clinical laboratories and the hospital industry; new guidelines had been issued for home health agencies; third-party billers; the durable medical equipment, prosthetics, orthotics, and supply industry; hospice providers; and Medicare+Choice organizations. Others were in store, such as one for the nursing home industry. Her successors in the position have continued the practice of issuing open letters, and they continue to discuss health care compliance and regulatory issues of interest to the health care community.

Inspector General Brown's Open Letter of 1997 and the following model guidance set out a complete regulatory program for health care compliance. It stated the regulator's policy of fostering compliance; described the regulator's specific expectations, in this case, through model compliance guidelines published in cooperation with the affected business segment; and revealed how the standards would be enforced, in this case through HHS's Corporate Integrity Program.

The introduction of compliance to the health care sector was a major development for compliance. At one level, it showed how compliance was reaching into new areas of human activity. A field initially developed to control the sales practices of securities salesmen had reached medical practitioners. At another level, the entry of

---

[89] Office of Inspector General HHS, *Publication of the OIG Model Compliance Program Guidance for Hospitals*, 63 *Federal Register* 8987 (Feb. 23, 1998).
[90] June Gibbs Brown, *An Open Letter to Health Care Providers*, HHS Inspector General, Open Letter 03-02-2000 (Mar. 9, 2000).

compliance into medicine showed how pervasive compliance was becoming in the modern economy. Health spending has been estimated to constitute approximately 17 percent of the gross domestic product of the United States, and significant percentages of other countries as well.[91] Entering this field was a major extension of compliance's reach.

The Sarbanes-Oxley Act (2002)

In the early years of the twenty-first century, financial markets were rocked by the failure of several leading businesses. Enron, a giant energy company, went bankrupt amid allegations of accounting and securities fraud. Leading executives would later be indicted, and some spent time in prison. At the time, it was the largest bankruptcy in history. Enron's collapse led to calls for regulatory reform. However, as Senator Paul Sarbanes, at the time chairman of the Senate Banking Committee later recalled, the pressure for reform quickly began to dissipate.[92] Then, WorldCom, an even larger communications company, went bankrupt and assumed the title of largest bankruptcy in history. Its CEO would eventually find himself in prison. After WorldCom failed, Senator Sarbanes recalled, everything changed in Washington, and everyone was in "full roar." Even the president demanded immediate action. The result was the Sarbanes-Oxley Act of 2002,[93] named for Senator Sarbanes and his colleague in the House of Representatives, Congressman Michael Oxley.

The act, often called "SOX," focused on financial accounting and internal controls. It contained a number of provisions, including a new self-regulatory organization for auditors, new grounds to sanction individuals who interfere with an audit, and many more. Most relevant to the history of compliance, it required senior executives to certify to the accuracy of their company's financial statements[94] and required companies to prepare an annual report on their internal controls, which would be audited by the company's outside auditors.[95]

As a result of the certification and internal control requirements, many companies established internal processes in which lower level employees certified the accuracy of information up to the executives, who were required to prepare the statutorily mandated certification. Special units, sometimes in the Compliance Department, were often created to manage the certification process and address any exceptions or problems that were uncovered. Many companies also undertook major initiatives to review their internal controls and prepare the reports that would be subject to audit. Risk control frameworks were highlighted. For example, the Committee of Sponsoring Organizations of the Treadway Commission (COSO) had promulgated risk control guidance

---

[91] The World Bank, *Health Expenditure, Total (% of GDP)* (2015).
[92] Joseph Nocerra, "For All Its Cost, Sarbanes Law Is Working," *The New York Times*, page C1 (Dec. 3, 2005).
[93] Sarbanes-Oxley Act of 2002, 116 Stat. 745 (July 30, 2002).
[94] Sarbanes-Oxley, § 302.
[95] Sarbanes-Oxley, § 404.

in the 1990s that drew renewed attention after SOX. COSO had described internal controls as having five interrelated components.[96] They were:

- The control environment, which set the tone for the organization and the foundation for other controls, including how employees are assigned and controlled, firm culture, and the attentiveness of the board of directors;
- A risk assessment, which was a mechanism for identifying the firm's objectives and associated risks;
- Control activities, which are policies and procedures to ensure that management directives are carried out;
- Information and communication, which includes both the flow of clear messages down from leadership and providing employees with a means to provide important information upward; and
- Monitoring, which includes both ongoing monitoring and separate evaluations, or audits.

In many firms, implementing SOX resulted in a chain of certifications and newly enhanced internal controls reaching from deep in the organization up to the senior executives and auditors.

SOX focused primarily on financial reporting, but it had a dramatic impact on compliance. Indeed, in its aftermath surveys reported 80 percent of participating companies planned to update their compliance initiatives because of SOX.[97] One observer, whose firm conducted annual compliance surveys, was *quoted* in the press saying: "It's like a newfound religion has formed around SOX compliance."[98] Many large public companies hired their first CCO.[99] SOX also had an impact on the tools used by compliance professionals. A variety of providers stepped forward with enhanced electronic monitoring tools, such as tools designed to detect expense account fraud.[100] Certification programs were developed to train company employees.[101] Boot camp ethics programs taught how to spot fraud.[102] In the aggregate, billions of dollars were spent, with one survey estimating the total at $3.5 billion[103] and another estimating that approximately $1 million was spent on compliance for every $1 billion in revenue.[104] As a professor at Stanford University Law School noted, "Compliance is becoming an industry unto itself."[105]

---

[96] COSO, *Internal Control—Integrated Framework* (1992 and 1994).
[97] Eve Tahmincioglu, "Profiting from Cures for the Sarbanes-Oxley Blues," *The New York Times*, page C5 (Dec. 29, 2005).
[98] Tahmincioglu, "Profiting from Cures" (quoting John Hagerty).
[99] Harry Hurt III, "Drop That Ledger! This Is the Compliance Officer," *The New York Times*, page B5 (May 15, 2005).
[100] Paul Burnham Finney, "Gotcha! Software, Tools Can Catch Expense-Account Padders (and Make Filing Easier)," *The New York Times*, page C8 (June 27, 2006).
[101] Tahmincioglu, "Profiting from Cures."
[102] Melinda Ligos, "Boot Camps on Ethics Ask the 'What Ifs'," *The New York Times*, page BU12 (Jan. 5, 2003).
[103] Tahmincioglu, "Profiting from Cures."
[104] Hurt, "Drop That Ledger!"
[105] Hurt "Drop That Ledger," quoting Joseph A. Grundfest.

SOX contained another requirement that warrants note: codes of ethics. Section 406 of the act directed the SEC to issue rules requiring public companies to disclose whether they had adopted a code of ethics that applies to its senior financial officers, and if the company had not adopted such a code, to explain why not. When the SEC adopted rules, it extended the code to cover the Chief Executive Officer (CEO) as well as the financial officers.[106] The SEC indicated that it seemed reasonable to do so, because the CEO is a superior official to the financial officers. It also defined a code of ethics and established standards for company to follow when disclosing it to the public.

The SEC defined a *code of ethics* as an assembly of written standards that are reasonably designed to deter wrongdoing and promote five goals. Those goals were:

- Honest and ethical conduct, including the ethical handling of actual or apparent conflicts of interest between personal and professional relationships;
- Full, fair, accurate, timely, and understandable disclosure in reports filed with the SEC as well as in other public statements;
- Compliance with applicable governmental laws, rules, and regulations;
- Prompt internal reporting of violations of the code; and
- Accountability for adherence to the code.

The SEC noted that it was not specifying every detail that a code of ethics must contain nor prescribing any specific language. Instead, it noted, it wished to "strongly encourage" companies to "adopt codes that are broader and more comprehensive than necessary to meet the new disclosure requirements."

The SEC also established disclosure requirements for the codes of ethics. The specific venues for disclosure chosen by the SEC are of less importance than its decision that codes must be disclosed. As a result, the specific ethical codes formulated by each issuer company would be revealed to the public. Moreover, Congress required, and the SEC implemented, rules requiring companies to disclose changes to or waivers from the code. Waivers of the code of ethics drew a great deal of attention at that time because it was believed that the problems at Enron had resulted, at least in part, from waivers to its code of ethics.[107] Going forward, early disclosure of such waivers could be a warning sign about potential trouble at a company.

SOX created a new focus on compliance in American business. The substance of SOX compliance was limited to financial reporting, with attendant internal controls and codes of ethics. But it introduced the concept, practice, and tools of compliance to large numbers of senior corporate executives. It was also a high-profile development. As one analyst said at the time, SOX became "the gold standard for governance, transparency and controls."[108] Moreover, because it involved major legislation and impacted the

---

[106] SEC, *Disclosure Required By Sections 406 and 407 of the Sarbanes-Oxley Act of 2002*, Release Nos. 33-8177, 34-47235 (Jan. 24, 2003).
[107] Frank Navran and Edward Pittman, "Corporate Ethics and Sarbanes Oxley," originally published in *Wall Street Lawyer* (July 2003), available from the Ethics Resource Center.
[108] David S. Joachim, "A New Law and Lots of Headaches," *The New York Times*, page G2 (Feb. 21, 2006).

highest levels of the business community, it drew extensive press attention, during both enactment and implementation. As one CCO said, SOX "helped create a new sense of urgency."[109] There were also complaints. Many business executives indicated that they supported the new law, although they were concerned about its cost.[110] Smaller firms in particular were challenged by the cost.[111] These issues would create considerable controversy. Nonetheless, as the debates and controversy continued, so did the enhanced attention to compliance. Perhaps more than any other single development in compliance's history, the Sarbanes-Oxley Act helped make compliance a household word, or at least, a word well known throughout the business community.

Compliance Rules for Asset Managers and Broker-Dealers (2003–2004)

In 2003 the SEC embarked on rulemaking to mandate compliance functions among asset managers—funds and investment advisers. The value of compliance for asset managers had been recognized as early as the 1980s, as discussed above.[112] Now, the SEC's rulemaking would establish a mandatory institutional structure for compliance including codes of ethics. Moreover, by the time the process had run its course, it had surveyed contemporary examples of compliance, restated compliance's goals, identified best practices, and added codes of ethics to the core compliance structure. While the SEC was engaged in this process, the NASD conducted its own rulemaking for broker-dealers. In many respects, this process could be viewed as a capstone to the development of compliance.

Before turning to the specifics of the rules, it would be helpful to briefly review the SEC's rulemaking process. When the SEC issues rules, it conducts a two-step process. First, it issues a document called a *proposing release* that sets out the rules it expects to issue, with the agency's commentary upon them, as well as a request for public comments. Within the administrative process of the United States government this is known as "notice and an opportunity for comment." After the public has had an opportunity to review the rules and provide comments, the SEC will make changes in the rules it believes appropriate to respond to the comments, and then issue a document called an *adopting release*. The adopting release finalizes the rules, that is, makes them binding and official, with updated commentary by the agency based on the public comments it had received. In addition, there is a third type of release, known as a *concept release*. A concept release does not propose specific rules. Instead it states ideas for possible future proposals and asks for public comments. Finally, when a self-regulatory organization wishes to issue new rules, it must submit them to the SEC for approval, which publishes the proposed rules for notice an opportunity for comment. All four of these types of releases—proposing, adopting, concept, and self-regulatory—played a role in the SEC's compliance rules.

---

[109] *Id.*
[110] Jonathan D. Glater, "Here It Comes: The Sarbanes-Oxley Backlash," *The New York Times,* page B5 (Apr. 17, 2005).
[111] Joachim, "A New Law and Lots of Headaches."
[112] *See* the discussion of compliance during the 1980s; "*Compliance in the 1980s*

Unlike many other compliance initiatives, the proposed rules for asset managers were not issued in the midst of a crisis. Robert Plaze, associate director and later deputy director of the SEC's Division of Investment Management, played a leading role in drafting the compliance rules. He remembers that although no crisis had shaken asset managers, the SEC's chairman, Harvey Pitt, called together his senior staff and highlighted the recent crisis in financial disclosure that had led to the Sarbanes-Oxley Act.[113] He instructed the staff to consider measures to avoid crises in other areas. In Plaze's words, the chairman said, "The next scandal may be yours, so you need to begin doing something to deal with it." As Plaze notes, in light of subsequent events: "He was prescient!"

In February 2003 the SEC issued a proposing release describing potential new compliance rules for asset managers.[114] Separate rules were proposed for investment advisers (Rule 206(4)-7) and investment companies (Rule 38a-1), but the two rules had many similarities. The release explained the SEC's views on why the rules were appropriate and should be considered. Four elements should be noted.

First, the release explained the role of compliance. In this regard, the SEC's proposing release took a traditional approach. SEC examiners, it said, "cannot be everywhere at all times." Moreover, the SEC said, it had learned to regard weak compliance controls as an indicator that undetected and uncorrected violations may have occurred. Accordingly, the SEC said, it could leverage its limited examination resources by focusing on firms with weaker compliance controls. The release continued, "Our ability to protect fund and advisory clients has in many respects come to rely upon the effectiveness of these compliance programs. They provide the first line of investor protection."

One could read this rationale for compliance as a throwback to the 1980s, when compliance was seen as nothing more than a "first-line" extension of the regulators. Certainly, the proposing release had much of that flavor. However, at the same time it also demonstrated a much more sophisticated appreciation of compliance. It said, "Funds and advisers with effective internal compliance programs administered by competent compliance personnel are much less likely to violate the federal securities laws." Also, when violations do occur, "they are much less likely to result in harm to investors." Finally, it added, "Many funds and advisers have established effective programs staffed with competent and trained professionals." In short, when discussing the role of compliance, the proposing release showed an interesting juxtaposition of thinking from the 1980s—compliance is a first line substituting for regulators who cannot be everywhere—with a more sophisticated appreciation for the field, including its practitioners' competence, training and professionalism.

---

[113] Interview with Robert Plaze (Dec. 2014). As noted above, interviews will be cited only once. Absent further citation, all following quotations or references to the statements of the same individual are based on the interview.

[114] SEC, *Compliance Programs of Investment Companies and Investment Advisers*, Proposed Rules, Release No. IC-25925, IA-2107 (Feb. 5, 2003) (hereinafter cited as "Compliance Rules Proposing Release").

Second, the proposing release surveyed contemporary examples of compliance systems. This survey of existing compliance systems, both domestic and foreign, was fairly unique. In prior cases, compliance initiatives were simply announced with no effort to trace the legacies that had informed them. Multiple parties, in multiple sectors, it appeared, had independently discovered the benefits of compliance, including a responsible compliance official, policies and procedures, and so on. There were a few exceptions. For example, in deciding the *Caremark* case, the Delaware court cited to the United States Sentencing Guidelines.[115] Then, some months later, when HHS issued its *Model Compliance Program Guidance for Hospitals*, it cited to the *Caremark* case when describing the duties of hospital directors.[116] However, this type of explicit line of descent was rare. Thus, the effort by the SEC to survey the field stands out. Plaze remembers that the staff conducted the survey because they "were looking to borrow good ideas."

The SEC's survey highlighted the chaotic state of contemporary compliance.[117] It cited to the Sarbanes-Oxley Act as an example of a system of internal controls used to ensure the integrity of financial reporting. Coming shortly after the highly publicized compliance initiatives triggered by SOX, this element of the survey is understandable, particularly in light of how Chairman Pitt had initiated the SEC's rulemaking process. The survey also pointed to bank regulators' safety and soundness standards, including compliance. As discussed above, bank regulators had adopted these standards after massive problems among S&Ls. The survey also pointed to a self-regulatory rule, specifically NASD Rule 3010(b) that required broker-dealers to adopt compliance procedures. The cited rule is interesting because it provided for the supervisory requirements of broker-dealers. Plaze has indicated that he recognized the NASD rule was narrower than the asset manager initiative, but many advisers are also registered as broker-dealers, and the SEC staff sought to anticipate objections that they should have taken account of existing requirements for broker-dealers.

The SEC's survey also identified several foreign compliance systems.[118] Plaze indicated that while travelling abroad on SEC business, he became aware that foreign regulators would cite to U.S. law as support for a regulatory change, "but we never did." The survey was intended to remedy this oversight. It cited to the Financial Services Authority of the United Kingdom, whose handbook said firms should take reasonable care to establish and maintain effective systems and controls for compliance with applicable requirements as well as to counter the risk that the firm may be used to further financial crime. The Fund Manager Code of Conduct of the Securities and Futures Commission of Hong Kong included provisions on appointing a designated compliance officer with a line of report directly to the firm's senior management; and sufficiently detailed compliance procedures to give senior management reasonable assurance that the firm complies with all applicable requirements at all times. In a harbinger of future

---

[115] *In re Caremark, Inc.*
[116] HHS, *Model Compliance Program Guidance for Hospitals*.
[117] SEC, Compliance Rules Proposing Release.
[118] The survey of foreign compliance systems, including citations to the relevant sources, can be found in note 25 of the Compliance Rules Proposing Release.

developments, the Hong Kong Code of Conduct also stated that compliance functions should be separated from operational functions. Finally, the SEC also pointed to the business governance standards promulgated by the French securities regulator, the Commission des Operations de Bourse. Although the governance standards, as such, do not appear directly relevant to compliance, governance and compliance had previously been linked in several settings.

Third, the SEC's proposing release set out the goals for a compliance system. Much of its discussion would be of interest only to compliance practitioners who work with asset managers; that was, after all, the point of the rulemaking. But in this context the SEC also made more general statements that had a bearing beyond any one particular sector. Most memorably, the SEC said that it would not enumerate specific elements that must be included in a firm's policies and procedures. Firms are too varied, the SEC said, to impose a single set of requirements. Rather, policies and procedures:

> ...should be designed to *prevent* violations (by, for example, separating operational functions such as trading and reporting), *detect* violations of securities laws (by, for example, requiring a supervisor to review employees' personal securities transactions), and *correct* promptly any material violations [emphasis in original].

Plaze recalls that these goals were drafted in consultation with the SEC's examination program, particularly with the help of Gene Gohlke, a long time examination manager. In formulating these goals—prevent, detect, and correct—the SEC gave compliance a mission statement.

Fourth and finally, the SEC's proposing release contained a discussion of the specific rules it was considering, Rule 206(4)-7 for advisers and 38a-1 for investment companies. In keeping with the development of compliance over the prior several years, the rules established certain key institutional structures: policies and procedures; a CCO; access for compliance to the senior levels of the organization, specifically funds' boards of directors; and an annual review. Perhaps most noteworthy in the proposed rules was the SEC's decision to require not just a designated compliance official but a specific position with a specific title: the CCO. The release stated that many funds and advisers had already designated a person to serve in this role, but it was not required, and some had not. Plaze indicated that "the most successful SEC rules are ones that obligate regulated entities to follow best practices," and that was the goal with the compliance rules. No matter how well-crafted policies and procedures might be, the SEC's proposing release said, they will be ineffective unless "well-trained, competent personnel administer them."

The SEC's proposing release provided a major statement on the purpose, status, and goals of compliance, as well as serving as an example of its development. It also contained some hints of the field's future. In a separate section of the release it indicated that it was exploring ways in which the SEC could make the best use of its own resources. One promising way, the release said, would be to rely more heavily on the private sector. It suggested four concepts for comment. Two of the concepts, a self-regulatory organization for asset managers and fidelity bonding, need not detain us. But the other two were more directly applicable to compliance. The first was to require firms to undergo a third-party compliance review. The release pointed to the use of independent reviews in fighting money laundering, which, as noted above, had been identified in FATF Recommendation 20. It also indicated that compliance consultants and others already performed "mock audits." The second was to require auditors reviewing the financial statements of investment companies to include a compliance review similar to their review of internal controls. The agency asked for comments on both.

Following publication of the SEC's proposing release and receipt of public comments, the SEC held an open meeting and adopted the final rules in December 2003.[119] On one level, the Compliance Rules Adopting Release was something of an anticlimax. The rules were adopted largely as proposed: policies and procedures, a CCO, access to fund boards of directors, and an annual review. More notable was the change in tone. Whereas the proposing release spoke of the need for a "first line" for the SEC, the adopting release focused instead on asset managers' own fiduciary duties and conflicts of interest. This change reflected the new conditions in which the adopting release was issued. In the months following the proposal events had taken a new and sudden turn.

In late 2003, Chairman Pitt's prescience about the danger of other crises bore fruit. A number of enforcement actions were developed against asset managers, by both state attorney-generals and the SEC, alleging that they had abused their fiduciary duties by allowing unfair special trading privileges to certain favored clients in return for various quid pro quo arrangements (a practice known as *market timing*). The adopting release highlighted these cases. Plaze remembers, "This was the first significant scandal in the mutual fund industry." There were anger and indignation about the scandals and the involvement of many fund advisers. For the staff drafting the compliance rules, in Plaze's words, "It was a challenge to find language that was forceful yet dignified and that the commissioners could all support." However, most remarkable about the SEC's response to the crisis was the speed of its response. Regulatory proposals often languish for years. In this case, the SEC adopted the compliance rules only ten months after they had been proposed.

The adopting release also reconsidered the concept items. The SEC announced that none would move forward at that time, except, it said, it may in the future reconsider requiring asset managers to obtain compliance reviews from third-party compliance experts. Plaze recalls that requiring third-party audits was viewed as a form of privatizing the SEC's examination function and could be considered analogous to the work of independent auditors. However, in his words, "The analogy was difficult." Compliance firms are not regulated and have no standards of review similar to those applied by financial auditors. Plaze also consulted with SEC enforcement attorneys who had been involved in administering enforcement settlements that required third party

---

[119] SEC, *Final Rule, Compliance Programs of Investment Companies and Investment Advisers*, Rel. Nos. IA-2204, IC-26299 (Dec. 17, 2003) (hereinafter cited as "Compliance Rules Adopting Release").

audits. They informed him that the settlements often worked only because the SEC staff could impose quality assurance, such as by requiring the firm to retain a highly qualified consultant instead of the least expensive and least competent available. This type of quality assurance, Plaze said, would be impossible across the entire industry. As a result, the concept item did not move forward at that time.

A few months after the SEC proposed Rules 206(4)-7 and 38a-1 for asset managers, the NASD proposed compliance rules for broker-dealers.[120] Although the NASD had long standing supervisory rules that included compliance policies and procedures—the SEC cited to these existing supervisory rules in its own proposing release—the NASD rules considered in 2003 focused on developing compliance's institutional structure. Much like the SEC's rules, the NASD required broker-dealers to designate one or more CCOs. They also gave the CCO access to the highest levels of the firm, in this case to the broker-dealer's CEO. Finally, they included an annual review and report, with the addition of a certification by the CEO that the firm has in place processes to establish, maintain, review, test, and modify policies and procedures that are reasonably designed to achieve compliance. The NASD had initially proposed a dual certification by both the CEO and the CCO, but eventually decided on the CEO alone, perhaps in the same spirit as the SEC's SOX code of ethics rulemaking, which had also focused on the CEO.

When the NASD proposed these rules, senior officials emphasized that their purpose was to support and enhance compliance. Robert R. Glauber, chairman of NASD, was quoted in the press saying:

> The purpose of this is to empower the brokerage firm compliance officer…We think it is absolutely crucial as part of the process of creating an environment in the firms that puts high standards of behavior first. We think this is a very important step to rebuilding investor confidence.[121]

This support was reiterated in the SEC's release publishing the NASD's rules for comment prior to SEC approval. The SEC recited the NASD's purpose for the rules as ensuring that compliance is given "the highest priority" by the firm's senior executive officers.[122]

The SEC's release also contained an interesting change in tone. Still describing the NASD's purpose, it said, "Comprehensive compliance and supervisory systems

---

[120] The NASD proposed the rules in June 2003, NASD, *NASD Requests Comment on Proposal to Amend Rule 3010 and Adopt Interpretative Material 3010-1*, Special Notice to Members 03-29 (June 2003); and issued them in final form, after SEC approval, in November 2004. NASD, *SEC Approves New Chief Executive Officer Compliance Certification and Chief Compliance Officer Designation Requirements*, Notice to Members 04-79 (Nov. 2004).

[121] Gretchen Morgenson, et al., "Accountability Is Focus of Rule Aimed at Chiefs of Wall Street," *The New York Times*, page C1 (June 4, 2003).

[122] SEC, *Self-Regulatory Organizations; Notice of Filing of Amendment No. 2 to a Proposed Rule Change by the National Association of Securities Dealers, Inc. Relating to Chief Executive Officer Certification and Designation of Chief Compliance Officer*, Release No. 34-50105 (July 28, 2004).

constitute the bedrock of effective securities industry self-regulation." This passage was notable because it recognized that compliance is a form of self-regulation. The release went on to describe compliance as "the primary strata of investor protection." This passage was notable because of its dramatic change in rhetoric. Indeed, it reversed the language in the SEC's proposing release for the asset manager rules. Now, instead of serving merely as a front line for the regulators, compliance was itself the "primary strata" of investor protection. In this new rhetorical environment, regulators and traditional self-regulators now occupied the secondary and tertiary strata. The compliance pyramid of the 1980s had been turned upside down.

In July 2004, a few months after adopting Rules 206(4)-7 and 38a-1 for asset managers, the SEC followed in the footsteps of SOX and required investment advisers to adopt codes of ethics. The regulatory vision sustaining this effort can be seen in a contemporary statement by William Donaldson, the SEC's chairman. Firms, he said, need a "company-wide environment that fosters ethical behavior and decision-making."[123] This environment, he continued, should be a "moral compass" guiding hiring decisions, operating practices, and internal policies and procedures. Moreover, when adopting the rule requiring advisers to adopt a code of ethics, the SEC said, "A good code of ethics should effectively convey to employees the value the advisory firm places on ethical conduct, and should challenge employees to live up to not only the letter of the law, but also the ideals of the organization."[124]

The rule adopted by the SEC was similar to an existing rule for funds that required them to establish codes of ethics to monitor employees' personal trading.[125] Plaze notes that extending similar requirement to advisers was another example of the SEC adopting a best practice in the industry.

The new code of ethics rule required advisers to include in their codes:

- A standard or standards of business conduct that the adviser requires of all of its supervised persons that must reflect the adviser's fiduciary duties;
- Provisions requiring the adviser's supervised persons to comply with applicable law;
- Provisions requiring certain advisory personnel to report their personal securities transactions and the adviser to review them;
- Provisions requiring supervised persons to promptly report any violations of the code of ethics; and
- Provisions requiring advisers to provide each of their supervised persons with a copy of the adviser's code of ethics and obtain from them a written acknowledgement of receipt.

As a result, codes of ethics under the new rule were far more extensive than reporting and monitoring personal securities trading.

---

[123] William Donaldson, *Remarks Before the Caux Roundtable* (Nov. 30, 2004).
[124] Investment Adviser Codes of Ethics, Release No's IA-2256 & ICA-26492 (July 9, 2004).
[125] SEC Rule 17(j)-1 under the Investment Company Act.

The SEC's Compliance Rules Adopting Release reflected the broad sweep of its goals for rule. A code of ethics, it said, should be more than a compliance manual. Rather, it said, a code of ethics should set out "ideals for ethical conduct," premised on fundamental principles of "openness, integrity, honesty, and trust." Indeed, after the SEC's rulemaking, the Investment Adviser Association issued guidance for a model code that covers a wide variety of topics, including gifts, entertainment, service on outside boards of directors, confidentiality, and numerous other issues that could implicate an adviser's ethics and fiduciary duty.[126]

One final aspect of the SEC's compliance rules drew considerable interest at the time. In the course of discussing a requirement that a fund's board of directors must approve the hiring or dismissal of the fund's chief compliance officer, the SEC said:

> The board, and the board alone can discharge the officer if she fails to live up to her position. Thus a chief compliance officer who fails to fully inform the board of a material compliance failure or who fails to aggressively pursue noncompliance within the service provider, would risk her position. She would also risk her career, because it would be unlikely for another board of directors to approve such a person as chief compliance officer.[127]

The SEC then stated in footnote 90, "If such a person were approved by another fund, our staff would enhance its scrutiny of the fund accordingly." This immediately triggered an outpouring of concern that the SEC would track CCOs of whom it disapproved from fund to fund. Plaze reports that he has "taken a lot of heat" for footnote 90. He also states, in light of later events, that he continues to stand by it. The goal of the 2003 rulemaking, he says, was to help upgrade compliance to a profession, and that includes professional obligations beyond those to a particular employer or client. The SEC does not have licensing authority over compliance practitioners, so footnote 90 was "what we came up with." He adds: it has worked. In his words, "Compliance professionals have really picked up their game and are playing a much more significant role in many asset management firms. There are really some impressive people who have been attracted to the profession."

Moreover, a few years later, the SEC clarified how it would deal with CCOs of whom it disapproved by beginning to issue compliance bars. In compliance bars the SEC resolves enforcement proceedings against compliance practitioners by barring them "from association in a compliance capacity with any broker, dealer, or investment adviser."[128]

---

[126] IAA, *Best Practices for Investment Adviser Codes of Ethics* (July 20, 2004).
[127] SEC, Compliance Rules Adopting Release.
[128] *See, e.g., In the Matter of Consulting Services Group L.L.C., et al.,* Release Nos. 34-56612 and IA-2669 (Oct. 4, 2007).

One could view the SEC's and NASD's compliance rules as a capstone to the institutional development of compliance. Over the preceding decade and a half compliance had become increasingly institutionalized, with certain components consistently appearing in different setting: policies and procedures, compliance officers, access to the senior levels of the organization, and periodic assessments. All of these were codified in the SEC's and NASD's rules. Moreover, when considering the rules the SEC surveyed the field and adopted best practices. The concepts published by the SEC suggested possible routes forward in the field's future development, particularly third-party compliance audits, if the implementation issues identified by Plaze could be resolved. Finally, the SEC's decision to include codes of ethics in its compliance rulemaking demonstrates the continuing linkage between compliance and ethics. Compliance was more than a tool for building a control environment. Compliance carried in its "DNA"—to use a phrase made popular by then SEC Chairman William Donaldson[129]—an aspiration for creating ethical as well as law-abiding behavior. Through these rules compliance and ethics had become operational realities, with a defined institutional structure and a defined mission statement: to prevent, detect, and correct violations.

V. RECOGNITION

By the middle years of the first decade of the 21st century, compliance had reached an important moment in its history. From broker-dealers, sector of its origin, it had spread to global financial regulation, criminal law enforcement, bank regulation, corporate governance, health care, financial disclosure, asset managers, and ultimately back to broker-dealers in a new form. From a manual of control procedures it had grown into an institutional structure that embodied widely accepted forms: dedicated officials, policies and procedures, access to senior levels of the firm, and periodic assessments. From local law enforcement it had acquired the affirmative mission of creating a preventive control environment and codifying ethics. Nonetheless, despite this rich diversity of growth, recognition of compliance remained uneven.

In the years after 2004, the most noteworthy trend in the ongoing history of compliance was whether and how the development of the field would be recognized. This recognition took various forms, including: acknowledging compliance's new role, protecting it when threatened, and using it as an affirmative tool at the highest levels of public policy. However, a recurring theme came to dominate this period: compliance's role as a distinct control function that must be endowed with certain characteristics to fulfill its mission. Objectivity, in particular, would draw considerable attention, usually under the rubric of making compliance independent.

---

[129] *See,* e.g., William H. Donaldson, chairman, SEC, *Remarks Before the Economic Club of New York* (May 8, 2003) ("moral DNA" must be embedded within a company).

Board of Governors of the Federal Reserve System and Compliance Risk Management (2008)

In October 2008 the Board of Governors of the United States Federal Reserve System issued Supervisory Letter SR 08-8 that gave recognition to compliance.[130] This letter was a significant development in the history of compliance for several reasons:

- It identified compliance as a tool for public policy; it implemented global best practices;
- It recognized the unique characteristics of compliance risk;
- It articulated and elaborated a sophisticated vision of compliance; and
- It identified certain core features of a successful compliance regime.

In late 2008 the world financial system had entered a period of extreme crisis. On September 15, 2008, Lehman Brothers, a major financial services firm, filed for bankruptcy. Almost immediately, the Reserve Primary Fund, a major money market fund holding Lehman debt, experienced a run. That is, investors experienced a crisis of confidence in the entity and immediately sought to withdraw all of their funds. The run quickly spread to other money market funds. A few days later, on September 25, regulators shut down Washington Mutual, the largest S&L in the United States, after a massive run by its depositors. Central banks in the United States and Europe took extraordinary measures to address the crisis, including extending public insurance to nondepository money market accounts, buying newly issued stock to give banks more capital, and otherwise providing emergency liquidity to markets and institutions. This was in the environment in which the Federal Reserve issued SR 08-8.

SR 08-8 began with considerable understatement, given the crisis environment in which it was issued:

> In recent years, banking organizations have greatly expanded the scope, complexity, and global nature of their business activities. At the same time, compliance requirements associated with these activities have become more complex. As a result, organizations have confronted significant risk management and corporate governance challenges, particularly with respect to compliance risks that transcend business lines, legal entities, and jurisdictions of operation.[131]

The letter continued, "To address these challenges, many banking organizations have implemented or enhanced firm wide compliance risk management programs and program oversight."

---

[130] Board of Governors of the Federal Reserve System, *Compliance Risk Management Programs and Oversight at Large Banking Organizations with Complex Compliance Profiles*, SR 08-8 (Oct. 16, 2008) (hereinafter cited as "SR 08-8").
[131] SR 08-8.

The Federal Reserve indicated that it had previously emphasized the need for such firmwide compliance risk management through its examination program. The letter, however, was intended to clarify the Federal Reserve's views. For example, it said: "Organizations supervised by the Federal Reserve, regardless of size and complexity, should have effective compliance risk management programs that are appropriately tailored to the organization's risk profiles." Among banks, such a statement from the Federal Reserve could be expected to have the same effect as a rule issued by a nonbanking regulator.

The Federal Reserve also indicated that it believed its expectations, as set out in SR 08-8, were consistent with "global sound practices."[132] Specifically, it said, they were consistent with the global principles enunciated by the Basel Committee on Banking Supervision. The Basel Committee is a forum of bank regulators from around the world that has met since the 1970s in Basel, Switzerland. In April 2005 a task force of the committee had issued a high-level paper on compliance risk and the compliance function in banks.[133] Many of the propositions in SR 08-8 had been set out in the task force's paper. Several elements of the supervisory letter are worthy of note.

First, the letter recognized the unique nature of compliance risk. It said that although the guiding principles for sound risk management are the same for compliance and other types of risk, the former presents several unique challenges. Specifically, the letter noted that the quantitative analyses used for other risks, such as risk limits or aggregation and trend analysis, are less meaningful for compliance. These distinguishing characteristics, the letter said, underscored the need for large and complex organizations to establish firmwide compliance risk management programs and establish strong cultures of compliance.

Second, the SR 08-8 articulated a sophisticated vision of compliance governance. The board of directors, senior management, and the corporate compliance function are responsible for working together "to establish and implement a comprehensive and effective compliance risk management program and oversight framework that is reasonably designed to prevent and detect compliance breaches and issues." Boards, it continued, are responsible for setting an appropriate culture of compliance, establishing clear policies regarding the management of key risks, and ensuring that the policies are adhered to in practice. Senior management is responsible for communicating and reinforcing the culture established by the board, and implementing and enforcing the firm's compliance policies and compliance risk management standards. Finally, senior management of the corporate compliance function should report to the board, or a committee thereof, on significant compliance matters and the effectiveness of the compliance risk program.

Third, the letter identified certain core features of a successful compliance regime. Compliance, the Federal Reserve said, must be independent of the business lines for which it has compliance responsibility:

---

[132] *Id.*
[133] Basel Committee on Banking Supervision, *Compliance and the Compliance Function in Banks*, Bank for International Settlements (Apr. 2005).

> Federal Reserve supervisory findings at large, complex banking organizations consistently reinforce the need for compliance staff to be appropriately independent of the business lines for which they have compliance responsibilities. Compliance independence facilitates objectivity and avoids inherent conflicts of interest that may hinder the effective implementation of a compliance program.[134]

The letter went on to provide specific guidance on reporting lines for compliance, particularly in large banks, which the Federal Reserve defined as those with more than $50 billion in assets. For example, if compliance staff report to a business manager, the Federal Reserve said, they should also have a dual reporting line to a compliance official for their compliance functions.

SR 08-8 bears comparison to the prior joint Standards on Safety and Soundness. In 1995 the bank regulators simply issued a single statement—indeed, a single sentence—on compliance. Thirteen years later, based on its supervisory experience, in the midst of a major financial crisis, the Federal Reserve updated this guidance with a highly elaborated statement about its expectations for compliance. The contrast between the statement in 1995 and SR 08-8 highlighted how much compliance had developed and grown over the intervening period. The Federal Reserve recognized that compliance is a unique field that requires sophisticated governance as well as objectivity and independence. This was a mature vision of compliance as a unique control function.

Financial Crisis and Compliance Resources (2008)

The financial crisis of 2008 had a direct impact on compliance practitioners. Major financial firms declared bankruptcy, banks and money market funds suffered depositor or investor runs, and financial activity dramatically slowed around the world. Many financial firms took steps to save money such as reducing their payrolls. News of layoffs and reductions in staff were inescapable during those months. Estimates of financial sector layoffs were in the tens of thousands and growing. In early 2008, one estimate placed the total at 34,000 in New York City alone since the previous July.[135] By November the press was reporting that accelerating financial sector layoffs could reach 200,000 by the end of the year.[136] In this environment, concerns grew that layoffs and other reductions in resources would disproportionately fall on compliance.

On December 2, 2008, Lori A. Richards, director of the SEC's examination program, published the program's *Open Letter to CEOs of SEC-Registered Firms*.[137] The letter reviewed the importance of the compliance function. It was, she said, critical

---

[134] SR 08-8.
[135] "20,000 More Layoffs on Wall Street?" Deal Book, *The New York Times* (Mar. 28, 2008).
[136] Joel Bel Bruno, "Wall Street Layoffs Could Surge Past 200,000," *Huffington Post Business* (Nov. 23, 2008).
[137] Lori A. Richards, SEC Office of Compliance Inspections and Examinations, *Open Letter to CEOs of SEC-Registered Firms* (Dec. 2, 2008).

to ensure firms' operations compliance with the law and rules for industry participation and to ensure that the interests of "customers, clients, and shareholders are protected." She continued, "Compliance is a vital control function that helps to protect the firm from conduct that could negatively impact the firm's business and its reputation."

Having established the importance of compliance, Richards turned to the current circumstances in the financial sector. Many firms, she said were considering reductions and cost cutting measures. She wished to remind them, she continued, of their legal obligation "to maintain an adequate compliance program reasonably designed to achieve compliance with the law." She then quoted the chairman of the SEC, Christopher Cox, who had said:

Compliance programs have made huge strides in recent years in becoming more formalized and more robust…Now more than ever, companies need to take a long-term view on compliance and realize that their fiduciary responsibility requires a constant commitment to investors. That means sustaining their support for compliance during this market turmoil and beyond it as well.[138] The letter stated that firms' interactions with investors should meet high standards, and that by fulfilling their obligations, regulated firms in the financial services industry "can help restore and bolster public confidence in the fairness and integrity of our markets and market participants." It concluded: "Providing adequate resources to compliance programs and functions and ensuring that CCOs and compliance personnel are integrated into the activities of the firm are essential to that process."

A few months later, Richards returned to the topic. In a speech in March 2009, she indicated that firms should ask: Does the compliance program have adequate resources to do the job?[139]

"At the SEC," she said, "many of us have cautioned against making resource reductions to compliance programs that could undercut their effectiveness." CCOs, she continued, should consider whether their programs have sufficient resources, and include information about shortfalls in the annual compliance report. Finally, she said, firms should consider alternative ways to better target their resources, such as by having compliance leverage resources available elsewhere in the firm, or by investing in technology.

The crisis of 2008 impacted compliance practitioners, and Richards responded with support. Her efforts were in the nature of moral suasion—the CEOs who received her letter were under no obligation to respond. Nonetheless, in the midst of a crisis, Richard's letter demonstrated that regulators recognized compliance and that they were ready to protect it when necessary.

---

[138] *Id.*
[139] Lori A. Richards, SEC Office of Compliance Inspections and Examinations, *Compliance in Today's Environment: Step Up to the Challenge: Remarks Before the IA Compliance Best Practices Summit 2009* (Mar. 12, 2009).

IOSCO Principle 31 (2010)

In 2010, the world community returned its attention to compliance. In this instance, it did so through the International Organization of Securities Commissions (IOSCO), a global body composed of regulators from around the world. Currently, IOSCO reports that it has 120 member securities regulators, as well as 80 other participants, such as self-regulators and securities exchanges. The precise format for IOSCO's attention to compliance was its review and revision of existing guidance. This was not headline news. Yet, IOSCO's actions demonstrated the global community's recognition of compliance.

In the late 1990s IOSCO had undertaken to identify the essential elements of securities regulation. As a result of this effort, in 1998 it issued a set of thirty principles intended to guide securities regulators.[140] Most of the principles addressed issues of only indirect interest to compliance, such as information sharing among regulators. One principle, however, was directly relevant to compliance.

Among the principles applicable to the regulation of market intermediaries, that is, those in the business of managing individual portfolios, executing orders, dealing or distributing securities, and providing information relevant to the trading of securities, in 1998 IOSCO stated:

> 21. Market intermediaries should be required to comply with standards for internal organization and operational conduct that aim to protect the interests of clients, ensure proper management of risk, and under which management of the intermediary accepts primary responsibility for these matters [emphasis added].

In commentary, IOSCO articulated a number of potential regulatory actions to implement Principle 21, including: the observation of high standards of integrity, fair dealing, and diligence; terms of engagement with customers; information about customers; protection of customer assets; market practices; operational controls; conflicts of interest; and proprietary trading. Many of these comments are familiar elements of a compliance program. Nonetheless, the 1998 Principle 21 revealed an enforcement-centric world, in which regulators require and intermediaries comply. This would change in 2010.

Following the financial crisis of 2008, IOSCO undertook to bring its principles up-to-date. To do so, it issued new principles and revised several of the old.[141] Of greatest interest, Principle 21 was renumbered as Principle 31 and amended to read as follows:

> 31. Market intermediaries should be *required to establish an internal function that delivers compliance* with standards for internal organization and operational conduct, with the aim of protecting the interests of clients and their assets and ensuring proper management of risk, through which management of the intermediary accepts primary responsibility for these matters [emphasis added].

---

[140] IOSCO, *Objectives and Principles of Securities Regulation* (Sept. 1998).
[141] IOSCO, *Objectives and Principles of Securities Regulation* (June 2010).

One could view this 2010 statement of principle as marking the global triumph of compliance. Now, instead of regulators requiring and firms complying, IOSCO recognizes that intermediaries themselves should "establish an internal function that delivers compliance." Buried deep within the activity of a global association of securities regulators, the ground had moved.

After years of development for compliance, the IOSCO principle does not break new ground. Rather, it codifies in a globally sanctioned principle the development of compliance over the previous decades. The most important aspect of new Principle 31 is the recognition it conveys. Requiring an "internal function that delivers compliance" is now among the guiding principles of global securities regulation.

The 111th Congress of the United States (2010)

In 2010 the Congress of the United States recognized compliance. It was the 111th Congress elected since the beginning of the republic and hence is known by that designation. Within the space of a few months in 2010, the 111th Congress enacted high-profile and headline-grabbing legislation, including the Patient Protection and Affordable Care Act,[142] often called "Obamacare" after President Barack Obama, and the Dodd-Frank Wall Street Reform and Consumer Protection Act,[143] named for its sponsors Senator Christopher Dodd of Connecticut and Congressman Barney Frank of Massachusetts. These laws fundamentally revised how the United States government provides public insurance for health care, and how it regulates new financial products such as derivatives and swaps. The compliance provisions in these laws, on the other hand, were not high profile. Instead of grabbing headlines, they were obscure and deeply buried in legislative text. Nor did they produce any groundbreaking new compliance standards. Nonetheless, provisions in both laws showed that compliance had been recognized at the highest levels of policy making in the United States.

In the Patient Protection and Affordable Care Act, Subtitle E addressed integrity programs for Medicaid and Medicare, the leading programs through which the United States government provides health insurance. The act authorized HHS, in consultation with the HHS Office of the Inspector General, to establish core elements in compliance programs for medical providers and suppliers who wish to serve covered patients.[144] In other words, to be eligible to receive payments under the public insurance programs, a physician or supplier would need to establish a compliance program meeting the core requirements. A few months after enactment, the chief counsel of HHS's Office of the Inspector General indicated that the new provisions were consistent with his office's longstanding view that "well-designed compliance programs can be an effective tool for promoting compliance and preventing fraud and abuse."[145]

---

[142] Patient Protection and Affordable Care Act, 124 Stat. 119 (Mar. 23, 2010).
[143] Dodd-Frank Wall Street Reform and Consumer Protection Act, 124 Stat. 1376 (July 21, 2010).
[144] Patient Protection and Affordable Care Act § 6401.
[145] Lewis Morris, Testimony before the Committee on Ways and Means, Subcommittee on Health, Subcommittee on Oversight, United States House of Representatives (June 15, 2010).

In the Dodd-Frank Act, Title VII established a new regulatory regime for swaps and securities-based swaps (together referred to here as "swaps"), a common type of derivative financial instrument. The law established new requirements for derivative clearing organizations,[146] swap information processors,[147] swap dealers,[148] and major swap participants.[149] In each case, the newly registered entities were required to establish compliance programs in which a CCO would report directly to the entity's board of directors, review the organization's compliance, consult with the board of directors to resolve conflicts, administer policies and procedures, ensure compliance, and establish procedures for the remediation of noncompliance issues. The following year, while proposing rules to implement some of these provisions, the SEC indicated that it was explicitly basing its proposals on compliance rules already in place for self-regulatory organizations.[150]

The compliance legislation of the 111th U.S. Congress did not shake up compliance practices. Rather, it enacted fairly straightforward requirements that would have been familiar in concept to any experienced compliance practitioner. Moreover, the responsible agencies then responded to these enactments by stating that they understood them to be consistent with each agency's own longstanding practices. These were not radical provisions. Rather, the importance of these enactments can be seen in the recognition compliance had achieved in the public policy process. In reforming governmental health insurance and in creating a new regulatory regime for swaps, the United States Congress recognized compliance as a public policy tool.

Theodore W. Urban and the Nature of Compliance (2012)

In October 2009 the SEC instituted an enforcement action that revisited the nature of compliance. The case was brought against Theodore W. Urban, general counsel and head of compliance for a broker-dealer.[151] In many respects, this action resembled the case approximately twenty years earlier against Arthur James Huff. A salesman at the firm engaged in serious misconduct, and the SEC charged Urban with failure to supervise the rogue employee. Again, as with Huff, the case against Urban precipitated an outpouring of views about compliance with third parties filing friend-of-the-court briefs that raised arguments about the nature of compliance. However, as with Huff, the results were inconclusive.

Urban was the general counsel and head of compliance of a well-known regional broker-dealer headquartered in Baltimore, Maryland.[152] A salesman in an office in Beachwood, Ohio, and later in Baltimore, conducted a significant fraud, in which he manipulated

---
[146] Dodd-Frank Wall Street Reform and Consumer Protection Act §§ 725 & 763.
[147] Dodd-Frank Wall Street Reform and Consumer Protection Act § 728.
[148] Dodd-Frank Wall Street Reform and Consumer Protection Act §§ 731 & 764.
[149] *Id.*
[150] *Business Conduct Standards for Security-Based Swap Dealers and Major Security-Based Swap Participants*, SEC Release Number 34-64766, Proposed Rule, page 157, note 281 (June 29, 2011).
[151] Mr. Urban is a contributing author to this book.
[152] *In the Matter of Theodore W. Urban,* Initial Decision, Initial Decision Release No. 402 (Sept. 8, 2010).

the value of a company's stock by placing clients into highly concentrated positions, with significant margin debt, active trading of positions, and little client benefit. The salesman eventually pled guilty to a criminal charge and was sentenced to prison. When the misconduct came to light, the SEC charged Urban, the broker-dealer, and several line supervisors at the firm. The firm and all of the other individuals settled, leaving only Urban to contest the charges.

As with Huff, the SEC's enforcement action against Urban proceeded in two steps: first before an Administrative Law Judge, then before the five commissioners. As with Huff, the litigation focused on whether Urban was a supervisor within the meaning of the relevant legal standard, and if so, whether his supervision was reasonable. The ALJ found that Urban was a supervisor because other employees at the firm usually took his advice, but in the case of this salesman, it was reasonable for Urban to take no further action because his advice would have been futile. This legal formulation poses significant analytical difficulties that need not detain us here.[153] More interesting from an historical perspective is what this case said about the nature of compliance.

Many compliance practitioners believed the Urban case presented significant public policy issues. R. Gerald Baker, executive director of the Compliance and Legal Division of the Securities Industry and Financial Markets Association (SIFMA), a successor organization to the SIA, has indicated that the action against Urban was "the case we always hoped for."[154] SIFMA believed it presented an opportunity to obtain a clearer statement from the SEC about the nature of compliance. SIFMA filed a friend-of-the-court brief.[155] In addition, in a press release issued by the National Society of Compliance Professionals (NSCP), a professional organization for compliance officers, Charles Senatore, former chairman of the organization, said: "This matter raises public policy issues critical to the effectiveness of the role of a robust compliance program in a securities firm."[156] NSCP also filed a friend-of-the-court brief.[157]

SIFMA's brief was prepared jointly with the Association of Corporate Counsel, a group representing in-house attorneys. Regulators and the securities industry, they argued, have recognized the distinct role of legal and compliance professionals. These professionals advise and assist in developing policies and procedures, monitor business activity, investigate and report instances of misconduct, and offer recommendations

---

[153] For a discussion of the analytical difficulties raised by this approach as a matter of law, see John H. Walsh, "The Time Has Come to Reconsider the Gutfreund Standard," 45 *Review of Securities & Commodities Regulation* 177 (Sept. 2012).

[154] Interview with R. Gerald Baker (Dec. 2014). Mr. Baker is a contributing author to this book. As noted above, interviews will be cited only once. Absent further citation, all following quotations or references to the statements of the same individual are based on the interview.

[155] *In the Matter of Theodore W. Urban*, Brief of Amici Curiae: The Securities Industry and Financial Markets Association, Including Its Compliance and Legal Society, and the Association of Corporate Counsel in Support of Appellee-Cross Appellant Theodore W. Urban, Admin. Proceeding 3-13655 (Nov. 22, 2010).

[156] NSCP, *NSCP Files Amicus Brief in the Matter of Theodore W. Urban* (Nov. 23, 2010).

[157] *In the Matter of Theodore W. Urban*, Amicus Brief of National Society of Compliance Professionals on Review of Initial Decision, Admin. Proceeding 3-13655 (Nov. 22, 2010).

for remediation efforts. In short, these professionals play important advisory and monitoring roles. Moreover, the friends-of-the-court argued, the independence and objectivity of the legal and compliance departments is crucial when they assess and advise on legal and compliance matters. "Management," they said, "benefits greatly in its supervisory decisions by obtaining balanced, impartial, and informed advice from professionals who do not individually stand to gain or lose depending on the decision's outcome."

Baker believes this position reflected a significant change from the SIA's arguments in the Huff case. Instead of arguing that compliance is inherently advisory and therefore cannot supervise, SIFMA argued that as a control function compliance should be independent and objective, and therefore should not be supervisory. Anne Flannery who had, in her words, "something of a difference of opinion" with the SIA while litigating the Huff case, agrees that SIFMA is now taking a much more sophisticated position.

NSCP's brief also argued that independence is crucial to an effective compliance program. Compliance programs, the friend-of-the-court brief argued, were intended to supplement supervision "with independent observation and advice." Specifically, the NSCP said:

Vigorous compliance programs are a key aid to management's efforts to combat misconduct and malfeasance. In order to maintain the ability to root out misconduct, compliance personnel must have open communication with business personnel and advise feely on suspect behavior.

Moreover, in its brief, NSCP explicitly compared the work of a compliance official to an attorney's ability to provide "unbiased, independent legal advice." The SEC, the friend-of-the-court argued, should not interfere with the compliance officer's ability to deliver "unvarnished opinions" on problems faced by a firm.

In sum, both friend-of-the-court briefs emphasized that compliance should be independent and free to deliver objective or—in NSCP's words—"unvarnished" opinions. In the context of the pending litigation, the parties intended this analysis to bear on whether Urban was legally liable for the salesman's misconduct. More generally though, regardless of how it might have been applied to Urban's conduct,[158] this analysis reflected changing contemporary views on the nature of compliance. The Federal Reserve, for example, had already recognized that compliance must be independent to preserve its objectivity.

In January 2012 in an odd refrain from the result in Huff, three of the five commissioners recused themselves from the Urban matter, and the remaining two declared themselves

---

[158] The author wishes to note that while a member of the SEC staff, he played a small role in the prosecution of Mr. Urban. He also wishes to note that in commenting on the historical significance of the case, and particularly the policy arguments raised in the friend-of-the-court briefs, he states no view on the merits of the SEC staff's case, Mr. Urban's defense, or how the policies articulated in the friend-of-the-court briefs might have been applied to the specifics of Mr. Urban's conduct.

"evenly divided" as to whether the facts alleged by the staff had been established.[159] As a result, the proceeding was dismissed and, as the commission noted in its order of dismissal, the ALJ's initial decision had no effect. The SEC issued no opinions.

The Urban case was a missed opportunity to recognize the changes that were taking place in compliance. Flannery has reflected on the odd similarity between the commission's resolution of the Urban case and the earlier Huff case. In her words, the disposition of the Urban case "was either an elegant solution or very heavy handed." In either event, Flannery says, the SEC has failed to clarify its expectations for compliance and has created a "real muddle."

After compliance has spread to vast new fields and taken on new roles and new missions within firms, the SEC appears to remain deeply ambivalent about its own progeny. Did it create a mere first line of defense for itself, or did it set in motion a developmental process that has created a new and independent field of endeavor, with roles and values far beyond anything envisioned in the 1960s and 1970s? In 2010, the SEC missed an opportunity for leadership. As can be seen elsewhere in this chapter, others are stepping forward to fill the vacuum.

ESMA Guidelines on MiFID Compliance (2012)

In July 2012 the European Securities and Markets Authority (ESMA) issued guidelines on the compliance function in certain types of financial institutions.[160] The guidelines concluded a process that had begun in 2011 with a consultation paper[161] and had included public comments. The guidelines themselves are of interest, because they demonstrate the importance of compliance in one of the world's most significant economic areas. They are equally of interest because they reflect the global trend toward recognizing the essential features of a successful compliance regime.

ESMA is an independent authority of the European Union, located in Paris, France. It was created in 2011 to serve as the supervisory authority for securities, within the European System of Financial Supervisors. Michel Barnier, at that time European commissioner for the Internal Market and Services Directorate General, described the role of the supervisory authorities when they started their work.[162] The authorities do not replace national supervisors. Rather, Barnier said, although national regulators remain responsible for "daily surveillance," the European authorities are responsible for "coordination, monitoring, and if need be arbitration between national authorities, and will contribute to the harmonization of technical rules applicable to financial institutions."

---

[159] *In the Matter of Theodore W. Urban,* Order Dismissing Proceeding, Release No. 34-66259 & IA-3366 (Jan. 26, 2012).
[160] ESMA, *Final Report, Guidelines on Certain Aspects of the MiFID Compliance Function Requirements,* ESMA 2012/388 (July 6, 2012).
[161] ESMA, *Consultation Paper, Guidelines on Certain Aspects of the MiFID Compliance Function Requirements,* ESMA 2011/446 (Dec. 2011).
[162] Michel Bernier, "A Turning Point for the European Financial Sector, Declaration of Michel Barnier on the Start of the Three New Authorities for Supervision," European Commission Press Release Database Memo 11/1 (Jan. 1, 2011).

ESMA's guidelines on compliance were prepared to clarify the compliance requirements set out in a directive of the European Union that had harmonized members' regulation of investment services. The Directive on Markets in Financial Instruments (MiFID) regulates firms providing investment services and activities.[163] Among other things, MiFID required firms to establish effective risk management and compliance processes. In the words of ESMA's consultation paper, the compliance initiative was undertaken because the financial crisis had "highlighted the need for better and tighter monitoring and managing of risk (including reputational risk) by investment firms, and for a more comprehensive and proactive compliance strategy, especially in view of the plethora of evolving legislation and increasing levels of scrutiny from both regulators and investors."[164]

ESMA's guidelines were set out in a numbered series. They included several that addressed the compliance function. ESMA stated that the compliance officer must have "sufficiently broad knowledge and experience and a sufficiently high level of expertise so as to be able to assume responsibility for the compliance function as a whole and ensure that it is effective." Firms should ensure that compliance had sufficient resources, authority, and information. Also, much like the Federal Reserve a few years before, ESMA held that the compliance function should be independent. It said:

Investment firms should ensure that the compliance function holds a position in the organizational structure that ensures that the compliance officer and other compliance staff act independently when performing their tasks. The compliance officer should be appointed and replaced by senior management or the supervisory function.[165]

Again like the Federal Reserve, ESMA went on to address the combination of compliance management with other functions. ESMA noted that compliance management could be combined with other control functions, but not with internal audit.

ESMA's guidelines also addressed how a compliance program should operate. The guidance stated that firms should ensure that the compliance function:

- Takes a risk-based approach;
- Establishes a monitoring programme;
- Sends regular written compliance reports to senior management;
- Fulfills its advisory function through training, day-to-day assistance, and establishing new policies and procedures;
- Operates on a permanent basis (that is, by appropriately substituting for the compliance officer when he or she is absent); and
- Ensures that all applicable requirements are fulfilled when outsourcing some or all of the compliance function.

---

[163] European Union, Directive 2004/39/EC (Apr. 21, 2004).
[164] ESMA, *Consultation Paper*.
[165] ESMA, *Final Report*.

Like many of the other sources of recognition for compliance, ESMA's guidance was not headline news. Much of compliance's most important development has taken place in obscure settings, known only to specialized practitioners. In this case, even ESMA appears to have done little to publicize the guidelines. In the words of a consulting firm, published five months after issuance of the final guidance, ESMA had "hardly given any publicity to the guidelines."[166] This silence does not detract from the importance of the initiative. ESMA's guidance harmonized several key elements of a compliance regime across the European Union's financial sector. Just as important, the guidelines reflected several developments seen elsewhere, such as compliance's need for independence. Although the ESMA guidance differed in several details from the Federal Reserve's SR 08-8, a common spirit could be found animating them both.

SIFMA White Paper (2013)

In March 2013, SIFMA's Compliance and Legal Division released a document on the state of compliance, entitled *White Paper: The Evolving Role of Compliance.*[167] From time to time, SIFMA, or its predecessor the SIA, had issued white papers when the moment seemed opportune to review the current state of the field. R. Gerald Baker, executive director of SIFMA's Compliance and Legal Division reports that the paper was triggered by the "turmoil the industry experienced in the late 2000s." The aftermath of the financial crisis seemed opportune for a new white paper because compliance was being challenged by multiple new developments—globalization, new technology, new regulatory priorities, and even new regulators—as organizations entered new jurisdictions or new lines of work. For their part, regulators were enhancing their enforcement programs and establishing self-reporting mechanisms, which placed extra pressure on compliance. Finally, because of budgetary restraints, many firms were asking compliance to assume greater responsibilities with limited resources. As the white paper expressed it, because of these changes, compliance officers had come to inhabit an "increasingly complex world."

From the perspective of contemporary compliance, the white paper is a valuable source regarding many current issues and concerns. Moreover, from a historical perspective, the white paper provides a benchmark that allows for an assessment of the changes in the field. In this regard, the contrast between the white paper and the Model Guide of the 1970s is striking. In particular, three contrasts are worthy of note.

First, the white paper focused on the role of compliance as a risk and control function. To be effective in this role, compliance must have clearly defined duties, which distinguish its activities both from the business and other control functions. Beyond this, the white paper said, firms must protect compliance's independence. The paper set out three means of ensuring appropriate independence for compliance: its advice should not be subject to the approval of senior management; its personnel should be

---

[166] Charco & Dique, Risk Management & Compliance, *ESMA on Organization Compliance Function* (Jan. 13, 2013), available online.
[167] Securities Industry and Financial Markets Association, *White Paper: The Evolving Role of Compliance* (Mar. 2013).

solely responsible for performing compliance functions; and it should have sufficient tools and expertise to fulfill its responsibilities. Forty years before, in the Model Guide, there was no discussion of compliance's independence. Instead, the Model Guide had focused on the authority of the manager charged with the organization's compliance. The difference between these two documents marks the rise of compliance as a unique field of endeavor, distinct from day-to-day management.

Second, the paper discussed the complex responsibilities of compliance in its dealings with the firm's management, including the control group, firm committees, legal staff, internal audit, and risk management. The image of compliance that emerges from this discussion, particularly in regards to what the paper calls "front-office centered" activities, is a senior-level function that participates at the highest levels of firm governance. The Model Guide, on the other hand, focused on the operational controls that compliance could exercise. In other words, where the white paper discussed high-level strategic participation in firm leadership, the Model Guide had discussed specific operational control procedures. The difference between these two documents marks the rise of compliance out of an operational function on the shop floor—where, to this day, compliance operations remain in place—to an executive function that participates with the highest levels of the firm.

Third, the white paper discussed the importance of technology. Technology has facilitated and enhanced many compliance operations. At the same time, the paper notes, rapid changes in technology have posed significant challenges to compliance. New technology platforms allow employees to engage in both business and personal communications; business functions can use multiple data sets in real time to make decisions; accelerated business practices generate vast quantities of data; and algorithmic trading strategies challenge surveillance and monitoring. New technology has also given compliance new responsibilities, in areas such as data protection and privacy. The white paper notes that compliance is struggling to obtain the resources and expertise it needs to keep up. Forty years ago, at the time of the Model Guide, computer technology was just beginning to have an impact on business. The challenges discussed in the Model Guide were related to issues like controls over the manual entry of data, review of printouts, and consideration of special coding. The contrast between the white paper and the Model Guide marks the transformation of modern society as computational power has become cheap and widely distributed. It also marks how technology has changed from a tool that can assist compliance to a dynamic and fluid area that carries as many compliance challenges as opportunities. From a simple consumer of computer technology, compliance has become a player in addressing the challenges it raises.

The *White Paper: The Evolving Role of Compliance* discussed concerns and challenges facing compliance. The concerns are real and the challenges serious. Nonetheless, as a historical document, the document can help us understand the changes in compliance over its brief life. In it we can see how compliance had changed from its origins, only a few decades before. Compliance has become an independent field of endeavor, an executive function participating in the highest levels of firm governance, and a player in meeting the challenge of technological change.

ISO Standard 19600 (2014)

The most recent recognition of compliance was finalized in late 2014. An international group stepped forward to exercise global leadership for compliance, through the preparation of a global standard for compliance management. Just as the institutional development of modern compliance was first seen at the global level, with a recommendation from a task force established by the G-7, today another important development regarding compliance has taken place on the global stage. As the new standard is disseminated around the world, it can be expected to have an impact on every compliance practitioner.

The standard was developed under the auspices of the ISO. The ISO's name is an acronym translated variously, depending on one's language. In English it is taken to mean the "International Standards Organization." ISO is a global organization headquartered in Geneva, Switzerland, which claims to work with more than 160 countries. The ISO has issued standards in a wide variety of settings, including quality management, the ISO 9000 series; information security, the ISO 27000 series; and many others. The compliance management standard was issued as ISO Standard 19600.

Martin Tolar, chair of the International Committee developing ISO Standard 19600, has described its purpose and the process followed in its development.[168] The initiative began in 2012, he said, to provide "overarching guidelines" on what companies could and should do to respect their compliance obligations, irrespective of the source of the obligations. With such a standard, he continued, companies will be able to "benchmark their framework against international best practice." Australians stepped forward to lead the effort, and held the first meeting in Sydney in April 2013. A second meeting was held in Paris in October of the same year, and the standard was further discussed in a meeting in Vienna, Austria, in July 2014. The focus of participating nations, Tolar said, was to achieve a standard "that will serve the compliance profession in a practical way." Participating nations included Australia, Austria, Canada, China, France, Germany, Malaysia, Netherlands, Portugal, Singapore, Spain, and Switzerland. Several others, including Japan and the United Kingdom, had observer status.

The new standard was issued in its final firm on December 15, 2014.[169] The Standard begins by saying:

> Organizations that aim to be successful in the long term need to maintain a culture of integrity and compliance, and to consider the needs and expectations of stakeholders. Integrity and compliance are therefore not only the basis, but also an opportunity for a successful and sustainable organization.

---

[168] "What Are the Origins of the New ISO Standard on a Compliance Management System?" *Ethic Intelligence* (Nov. 2013).
[169] ISO, *Compliance Management Systems—Guidelines*, ISO 19600, First Edition (Dec. 15, 2014).

The standard states say that compliance is made sustainable by "embedding it in the culture of an organization and in the behavior and attitude of the people working for it." Policies and procedures must be integrated into all aspects of how the organization operates. In a refrain from the guidance provided by the Federal Reserve, ESMA, and the friend-of-the-court briefs in the Urban case, the standard also highlights compliance's independence, even as it is integrated into the organization's financial, risk, quality, environmental, and health and safety management processes, as well as its operational requirements and procedures.

The standard's discussion of integrity and the values provided by compliance is worth noting. Compliance has a role to play in safeguarding integrity, avoiding noncompliance, and enhancing socially responsible behavior. Specifically, the draft states:

> Organizations are increasingly convinced that by applying binding values and appropriate compliance management they can safeguard their integrity and avoid or minimize noncompliance with the law. Integrity and effective compliance are therefore key elements of good, diligent management. Compliance also contributes to the socially responsible behavior of organizations.

To implement these goals, the standard contains several elements, including: scope, context of the organization, leadership, policy, planning, support, operations, performance evaluation, and improvement. In regards to "scope," the standard is intended to apply to all types of organizations. In regards to the "context of the organization," the standard identifies the needs and expectations of interested parties, principles of good governance (including independence of the compliance function, its direct access to the governing body, and its authority and resources), as well as the identification, analysis, and evaluation of compliance risks. "Leadership" focuses on the organization's governing body and top management, and includes specifics on how they can demonstrate their commitment to compliance. "Policy" addresses the development of compliance policies for the organization, including the different roles of the governing body, the compliance function, and other managers and employees. "Planning" includes aligning compliance risks and objectives, and considering the steps that will be taken to achieve the objectives. "Support" includes the resources available to compliance, the competence of those responsible for compliance, internal awareness, communication, and documentation, as well as steps toward developing a supportive culture of compliance. "Operations" delves into operational planning and control of the compliance function, including in an outsourced environment. "Performance evaluation" includes monitoring, measurement analysis and evaluation of the compliance function. Finally, "Improvement" addresses how the organization should respond to nonconformity and noncompliance, including escalation of issues, with the goal of achieving continual improvement.

The development of a global standard for compliance management, with the active participation of several leading economies and observer status for several more, promises to be a major turning point in the recognition of compliance. Through an ISO standard, compliance management has achieved global recognition and a global benchmark. In addition, by writing a standard that is applicable to any regulatory regime, and any regulator, as well as any type of business—finance, manufacturing, or service—compliance is slipping free of its early constraints. One could view the ISO standard as final recognition for compliance. Compliance is ready to function in any organization, in any regulatory regime, in any country, and in any business sector. In sum, in the ISO standard integrity and effective compliance are being recognized on a global scale as key elements of, in the words of the ISO Standard: good, diligent business management.

VI. A HALF-CENTURY OF HISTORY

Over the last fifty years compliance has been transformed from an enforcement mechanism in one sector of one economy under the direction of one regulator, into a global phenomenon that is being applied in a wide variety of critical economic activities. To expand upon the words of SEC Commissioner Schapiro, spoken in the early 1990s about broker-dealers, by the early 21st century compliance was entering the lifeblood of the global economy.

Domestically, in the United States, compliance continues to spread and grow. Private entities are increasingly adopting compliance for their own purposes. Any number of examples could be highlighted. Two distinctively American activities are college athletics—particularly football—and charitable giving—with U.S. foundations leading the fight against diseases and other social ills. Many college athletic programs in the United States have established compliance systems to enhance their ethics and compliance with the rules of the National Collegiate Athletic Association (NCAA). In keeping with developments elsewhere in compliance, an electronic tool known as Compliance Assistant is now available to help college administrators, athletic departments, and student-athletes.[170] Also, the Council on Foundations, a private nonprofit group serving endowed grant-making organizations, offers compliance assistance to its members, and has published compliance guidance for their assistance.[171] Many other examples could be given. Public entities are also adopting compliance as a regulatory tool. A short list in the United States would include: the United States Equal Opportunity Commission (EEOC), a federal agency charged with enforcing laws against discrimination, which has been issuing a Compliance Manual, a section at a time, over several years;[172] the United States Department of Labor, which issued a Federal Contract Compliance Manual in July 2013;[173] the United States Federal Maritime Commission (FMC), which is promoting voluntary compliance with regulations governing international shipping;[174] and the Environmental Protection Agency (EPA), the agency responsible for enforcing the environmental protection laws which has, in its own words, "established programs to promote environmental compliance and correction of violations by offering incentives

---

[170] NCAA, *Compliance Assistant,* available on the NCAA website.
[171] Council on Foundations, *Check This: A Compliance Check List for Private Foundations* (2010).
[172] EEOC, *Compliance Manual*, available on the EEOC website.
[173] United States Department of Labor, *Federal Contract Compliance Manual*, available on the DOL website.
[174] FMC, *Regulating the Nation's International Ocean Transportation for the Benefit of Exporters, Importers, and the American Consumer*, available on the FMC website.

to the regulated community in exchange for agreements to self-assess, disclose, correct and prevent future violations."[175] The list could go on.

As compliance has grown and spread, both continuity and change can be seen in its practice. In regards to continuity, on an operational level, a modern compliance practitioner would recognize the control procedures identified in the SEC's Model Guide of the 1970s. At the same time, over the last fifty years, compliance has been transformed by new developments. These have come in two waves. First, beginning in the early 1990s compliance was transformed into a distinctly institutionalized practice. Time and again, the core institutional structures essential for compliance management have been articulated: a designated compliance officer, policies and procedures, periodic assessments, and a special relationship with the highest levels of the organization. Repeatedly, these elements have been rediscovered, recognized, and applied in diverse settings, until now, pursuant to the draft ISO standard, they could be applied in any type of business anywhere in the world. Second, more recently, compliance has been transformed again, this time by the growing recognition that it is unique. It is not regulation or supervision, or a front line of defense for someone else. Compliance is a unique control function with its own goals and ethos. To achieve those goals, it must be independent and objective. Attention to establishing and protecting these characteristics, in an operational environment, has risen to the top of the agenda of many compliance practitioners. In many cases, the issue has been framed as a practical question: which institutional association—legal, risk, senior governance, or something else—best achieves both independence and effective integration into the firm?

Compliance is a new function, only fifty years old, yet it fulfills aspirations as old as civilization. Ancient philosophers, European and Asian, described voluntary compliance with the public interest as a path to reason and virtue. More recently, in the early 20th century, ethics and self-regulation were advanced as practical policy goals. Modern compliance practitioners continuously demonstrate how organizations can achieve these goals, even in the absence of compulsory or punitive state power. Compliance has transformed business ethics and self-regulation from aspirations into operational realities. Each firm, each business, each entity, organizes itself for its own self-control. The visionaries who first articulated these goals, early in the twentieth century or before, would likely be surprised by the operational forms their ideas have taken. Certainly, they would be amazed by the global nature of the current effort. But assuredly, they would have recognized and applauded modern compliance.

Although compliance has made great strides, a unique feature of its history has been its constant rediscovery. Viewing each development in isolation, it would appear that the benefits, structures, and implementing procedures of compliance have been rediscovered anew in each arena in which it has been applied. Much compliance literature continues to frame compliance solely in relation to the discrete requirements of a particular field of practice. Because of this, compliance remains highly balkanized, with compliance

---

[175] EPA, *Compliance Incentives Programs*, available in the EPA website.

practitioners in different areas working separately, with little communication and often less understanding of each other's work. Today, many compliance practitioners believe they are craftsmen who know how to apply specific compliance tools to specific local problems. Yet, when we look back on the last fifty years, we can imagine compliance as a building wave—rolling slowly at first, and then with more and more power—until it has swept through countless businesses, sectors, and countries. In the next half-century of compliance's history, perhaps compliance practitioners will come to recognize their participation in a common movement. When they do, they will see that despite their specializations, compliance is one field, one practice, and one profession.

ABOUT THE AUTHOR

John H. Walsh has a law degree from Georgetown University and a doctorate in History from Boston College. He has published widely on the law and practice of compliance, including coauthoring the *Investment Adviser's Legal and Compliance Guide, Second Edition*, published by Wolters Kluwer Law & Business, as well as articles in multiple journals. Mr. Walsh served for many years with the SEC in the Division of Enforcement, as special counsel to Chairman Arthur Levitt, and as associate director, chief counsel and acting director of the examination program. He is now a partner of the law firm Sutherland Asbill & Brennan. From his vantage point, Mr. Walsh has had the opportunity to observe and participate in many of the more recent events he describes.

CHAPTER 3

What Is Compliance?

By R. Gerald Baker
  Former Executive Director, SIFMA Compliance & Legal Society

I. INTRODUCTION

This chapter will discuss the role of the Compliance Department in a securities firm and the ways in which the department works with the firm's senior and line management in developing, implementing, and maintaining compliance programs throughout the organization. The chapter will look at what is, and is not, included in the mission of a Compliance Department. Market, regulatory, and enforcement events in recent years have spotlighted the Compliance function and the roles of Compliance professionals. Although the traditional responsibilities of the department have remained intact, there are increasing demands and expectations within firms and by regulators on what Compliance should be. The long-held view of Compliance as primarily an advisory function is being challenged by some regulators and the complex structures of many firms.

Firms have expanded the role of Compliance and consequently the risk that Compliance officers may be held to higher standards and potential supervisory liability by regulators. This chapter will discuss this and ways to mitigate that risk. It will also cover the diversity of firms, their expansion into new services and product lines, and the global growth of many firms. The importance of resources—people and technology—is covered as well. Finally, the chapter will review the many ways in which a firm can integrate Compliance responsibilities across the organization and its senior management.

II. DISTINGUISHING BETWEEN THE LITTLE c AND THE BIG C

How many times have you heard or read the expression "Where was Compliance?" If you are an industry Compliance professional, you have probably heard this more times than you care to remember, especially if the question was directed at you. Having been a Compliance professional for many years in the securities and financial services industry, I cannot begin to count the number of times I heard or read it, but I usually remember who said it. And the speakers of that oft-used comment are in many instances persons who can make your life as a Compliance professional frustrating, if not miserable: business managers at your firm, litigators, media, and (worst of all) regulators. More often than not, the question "Where was Compliance?"

unfortunately reflects a total misunderstanding or disregard of the role and functions of a Compliance professional.

To better understand the role of the compliance professional we need to distinguish what many others and I call "big C" compliance, the Compliance Department and compliance professionals, from "little c" compliance, the organization's obligation and commitment to establish and maintain compliance and supervisory programs for all of its businesses and activities. Both are required by rule and regulation. The Securities and Exchange Commission (SEC), self-regulatory organizations (SROs), states and other regulators all require a member organization to designate a chief compliance officer or (CCO) and also to establish a compliance program reasonably designed and maintained to meet regulatory obligations for its broker-dealer business.[1] Although the CCO and program are not mutually exclusive, there are distinctions between the Compliance Department and compliance program.

First consider "little c" compliance. In recent years regulators and others recognizing the distinction of "big C "and "little c" have often used the term *culture of compliance* to reference a firm's compliance program.[2] The SEC did not invent this term. It has been around for many years and used to describe how an organization, not only in the financial services industry but in many others as well, establishes and maintains a culture of compliance that addresses its ethical standards, legal and regulatory obligations, rights and interests of the end-users of its services or products, and conduct and character of its employees, most importantly those charged with managing the firm's businesses.

Obviously, the intent of the phrase is to endorse and recommend an enterprise-wide culture that requires, not just endorses, a strict adherence to the highest standards of professional and personal conduct by all employees, both management and staff personnel. This means more than giving lip service to the culture of compliance or just having a written code of conduct for supporting ethical behavior and compliance. I do not think anyone has yet seen a firm that openly supports misbehavior or lack of compliance. However, as everyone knows, there has been a seemingly endless stream of corporate misbehavior, some of which violates even criminal law and is not just a subject of administrative or civil proceedings. This misconduct has not been confined to a small number of obviously deviant organizations, but includes a widespread, global list of some of the most prominent and highly regarded institutions. In virtually every case, each firm had a code of conduct in place, compliance and other internal control programs and volumes of written policies, procedures and supervisory controls.

---

[1] See Securities and Exchange Commission Form BD, *Uniform Application for Broker-Dealer Registration*, Schedule A. Direct Owners and Executive Officers, Question 2 (a)...Chief Compliance Officer; Securities and Exchange Act of 1934, Rule 15(b)(4)(E); FINRA Rule 3130 *Annual Certification of Compliance and Supervisory Processes*, (a) Designation of Chief Compliance Officer(s); FINRA Rule 3110, *Supervision*, (a) Supervisory System; and FINRA Rule 3120 (a) *Supervisory Control System*.

[2] See former Securities and Exchange Commission, Office of Compliance Inspections and Examinations (OCIE) Director, Lori A. Richards' address, *The Culture of Compliance* at the spring conference of National Regulatory Services, Tucson, Arizona (Apr. 23, 2003).

I am not suggesting all misconduct suggests or implies a deliberate intent to commit wrongdoing or illegal activities, but it does mean that the organization's culture of compliance message has been lost within the organization. Where does an organization's culture of compliance begin? Obviously, at the top! The chief executive officer (CEO), president, senior management, the board of directors, or, simply put, those responsible for running the show. This "tone at the top" concept is not exactly groundbreaking or brilliant. It has however, been discussed on more than one occasion by senior officials at the SEC and other legal and regulatory professionals frequently for more than a decade.[3] Yet the number of enforcement cases and regulatory investigations involving financial services firms, large and small, has not diminished, and the magnitude of the illegal activities, the failures of internal controls, and ill-gotten profits or losses to investors are jaw dropping, as are the penalties to the firms.

Certainly in many instances, the perpetrators of the illegal activities were rogue or over-zealous employees benefitting themselves personally through enhanced compensation and recognition, or concealing activities prohibited by the firm or law or resulting in significant losses for customers and/or the firm. This misconduct occasionally occurs even in an organization that has a very strong compliance culture and has devoted significant personnel and technological resources to supervise and monitor its business activities. Sadly though, there are too many examples in which firms profess to have strong compliance and other internal control programs in place and can point to volumes of policies and procedures and internal reports as evidence, whereas the facts of their actual compliance refute their argument. During a recent meeting, Preet Bharara, the U.S. Attorney for the Southern District of New York, discussed the role of Compliance professionals and compliance programs in general. He pointed out that prosecutors hear all the time how great a firm's compliance program is and how seriously the firm takes its compliance responsibilities, yet the prosecutors' investigations and the evidence expose just the opposite. Prosecutors find, for example, that policies and procedures have not been updated in years or, even worse, sit gathering dust on office shelves, while, in many cases, red flags identifying wrongdoing are ignored or missed.[4]

The examples of the prevalence of this misconduct suggest the following: Although board members and senior managers recognize their responsibilities to operate a business with the highest ethical standards, in full compliance with regulatory and legal requirements, and with the rights and best interests of their clients foremost at all times, this recognition fails to reach the next levels of management in the organization. Even if the philosophy of compliance is communicated throughout the organization, as I expect it is, there are the ever present and challenging conflicts with the philosophy that are

---

[3] *See* former Securities and Exchange Commission Director of Enforcement, Steven M. Cutler's address, *Getting It Right* at the Second Annual General Counsels' Roundtable, December 3, 2004, Washington, DC, and SEC Chairman Mary Jo White's remarks at the National Society of Compliance Professionals National Membership Meeting, October 22, 2013, Washington, DC.

[4] *See United States v. S.A.C. Capital Advisors LP, et al.* Prepared Remarks for U.S. Attorney Preet Bharara, July 25, 2013, and U.S. District Court Southern District of New York, *United States of America v. S.A.C. Capital Advisors, L.P., S.A.C. Capital Advisors, LLC, CR Intrinsic Investors, LLC, and Sigma Capital Management, LLC*, Indictment.

ignored or never addressed. In every firm there are performance expectations for every employee. When those expectations include or are exclusively focused upon revenue and profit targets, the business unit, its managers, and employees tasked with meeting or exceeding those goals may be tempted with using creative, and even illegal, methods to reach their targets. It is at this point that decisions about compliance are made. This is where the organization's culture of compliance is tested. Staff members know whether the culture of compliance has been communicated, is ingrained throughout the firm, and is buttressed by operating standards and controls that have zero tolerance for a corner cutting, "profits first at any cost" approach. If that culture, in which the client or end-user is foremost in every decision, is in practice, it is reasonable to expect that the opportunities to make illegal or unethical decisions are mitigated, monitored, and controlled.

Even with the best compliance culture, there will be ethical failures or lapses, rules will be violated, and illegal activities may occur. People make mistakes; some people purposely commit wrongdoings. How that happens, for how long, and how it was discovered reflect on the adequacy of the firm's supervisory and control programs, not so much on its compliance culture. Obviously, if the firm discovers malfeasance through its own internal compliance and control programs, that's a big plus unless the issue went undetected for so long that a question arises as to just how well internal controls actually worked. However, if the problem is discovered by regulators through their routine oversight examinations or through other methods, the efficacy of the firm's compliance and supervisory systems will immediately be suspect.

One of the challenges in designing and implementing a robust compliance and internal control program is having adequate resources, both people and technology, for it. How many Compliance and control officers are needed, how are they allocated, and what are their responsibilities? These are several of the big questions that all firms must answer. And of course, the answers will depend upon the size of the firm as well. These are the main reasons that there is no one-size-fits-all solution, or more importantly a very proscriptive regulatory requirement, about compliance. There are, however, clearly articulated regulatory expectations, which can be simplified as requiring each firm to have reasonably adequate systems of supervision, compliance, and other internal controls.

III. RESPONSIBILITIES GENERALLY ASCRIBED TO COMPLIANCE

Advisory

As discussed earlier, a firm's Compliance Department falls under the big "C" category and serves as a component of the firm's overall compliance program. What are the typical functions of the Compliance Department, and what roles does it have?

The first role that immediately comes to mind is advisory. Many other functions that the Compliance Department performs eventually find their way into the advisory function. As an advisor, the department provides a firm's management and its business units with guidance on how to meet their respective regulatory obligations within the firm's revenue and profit goals. The information and sources used to provide this guidance compose much of the department's functions.

Regulatory compliance guidance provides the firm with information on new rule initiatives and rule interpretations. It also includes assessments of how well a firm is meeting current regulatory requirements. These assessments may be made exclusively by compliance professionals or in concert with other control functions at the firm. New rule or rule interpretation advice may also involve the firm's legal and other control functions. Unless the rule requires the Compliance Department to implement and maintain the rule, compliance ownership also becomes the responsibility of the business unit. Simply put, compliance with sales practice rules becomes the responsibility of the sales function, compliance with trading rules that of the trading departments, compliance with operations and financial reporting that of the financial and operations management. However, assigning ownership to the business functions does not mean Compliance's role is finished. I will discuss compliance's ongoing role later in this chapter.

New products and services constitute a constantly evolving and moving part of the financial services industry. The past decade has evidenced just how extensive, creative, and fast moving the introduction of new products and services can be. The firms engaged and providing them were not just large domestic and global organizations, but included modestly sized and small firms as well. Nor was the sale of often complex and elaborately structured products limited to institutional or sophisticated investors; they were offered and sold to retail investors. Compliance professionals have an important role to play when new services and products are being considered. First and foremost, a compliance representative has to have a seat at the table, which means being able to review and be educated on what the objectives and the risks are for any new product or service. A compliance professional also has to have the opportunity to make his or her own independent review of existing regulatory requirements and the expectations of regulators. In an advisory capacity, a compliance professional can opine on who the intended investor audience is, what training and education of those on the business side, including brokers, is needed, and ultimately who will provide the training, and how supervision will be carried out.

At many firms the development and offering of new services and products is a committee process. Compliance has to participate on such committees, but whether or not a compliance representative has a vote can be a vexing issue. Using the advisory role as the basis of an argument, the answer would be that a compliance representative should not be a voting participant. If, however, the representative is a voting member, that voting participation should not in and of itself create any special regulatory liability, especially supervisory liability for the compliance officer. The argument can still be made that the Compliance Department's participation is limited to its advisory role, despite its representative's voting power. Again, the size and structure of the organization is also a major factor, and a compliance representative's participation on any committee—product or management—raises the same issues. Regulators appear to accept that the mere presence on any committee by a compliance officer does not create any unique or special supervisory liability for a compliance officer.[5] This gives some comfort to the concerns about a compliance officer liability.

Monitoring, Testing, and Assessing

The Compliance Department is also responsible for monitoring, testing and assessing the adequacy of the firm's compliance and supervisory programs. The methods used to perform these functions are generally similar among firms. In some cases these responsibilities may be shared with other departments, most frequently, the Internal Audit Department. Obviously, the actual reports or tools used will vary among firms and are designed for specific purposes. Many larger firms perform these functions within specifically designed units or silos to achieve a balanced and efficient use of resources throughout the organization and among its affiliated entities. For example, units responsible for monitoring daily trading activities may be reviewing retail, institutional, and proprietary trading across an entire organization. Onsite examinations may be similarly handled within a unit designated with that function. In other cases large firms may have designated compliance units assigned to specific businesses—retail, institutional, proprietary, etc.

In medium and smaller firms, the compliance structure is not as extensive or elaborate and everything may be assigned to one department. In many firms, that department is one person who sometimes wears more than one hat—one of them being a business hat. Staffing is not the only resource challenge. Technological resources in smaller firms are limited both by internal resources and the costs of obtaining them from third-party service providers, whereas, large organizations typically have extensive internal technology with the ability to develop and maintain internal reporting tailored for specific needs and purposes.

The assessment of a firm's overall compliance and supervisory program is essential to meeting and maintaining regulatory obligations. The Financial Industry Regulatory Authority (FINRA) requires its members to perform an annual review and assessment of its compliance programs and to provide a report of that review to the firm's senior management.[6] FINRA recognizes the extensive diversity among its members in terms of business conducted, size, and organizational structure and resources. This knowledge results in firms being encouraged to use a risk-based approach in making their annual assessments. However, there is no assurance that FINRA, through its examination programs—routine or for-cause—will necessarily agree with any member's risk-based evaluations. FINRA may thus issue deficiency reports that identify business activities that in FINRA's view are not adequately supervised or reviewed.

---

[5] See SEC Division of Trading and Markets, *Frequently Asked Questions About Liability of Compliance and Legal Personnel at Broker-Dealers Under Sections 15(b)(4) and 15(b)(6) of the Exchange Act,* September 30, 2013, Question 5.

[6] See FINRA Rule 3120, *Supervisory Control System* and FINRA Rule 3130 *Annual Certification of Compliance and Supervisory Processes*

Any self-evaluation report card raises the question of just how objective and accurate it can be. It also creates, usually unintentionally, finger pointing. In large, complex organizations, other units necessarily have to participate and be included in the preparation of the annual assessment report. Although the Compliance Department might be the ultimate owner of the report, the data collected has to involve groups such as internal audit, risk, and legal. In more modestly sized firms the source of information for the report likely does not involve as many sources or groups.

Although enforcement cases specifically addressing a firm's overall compliance program and its internal assessment have been relatively few, a recent SEC action against a firm's CCO was based on the inadequacy of its weak compliance program.[7] To date FINRA has not brought enforcement proceedings against a firm or person for violation of Rule 3120 and an alleged failure to properly prepare an annual assessment report.

Education and Training

If the culture of compliance or the tone at the top is the cornerstone of a firm's compliance program, how that is communicated and instilled throughout the organization is critically important. Regardless of the size of the firm, the education and training of its employees are essential. Education and training are not limited to an orientation program for new employees, and the effort is not exclusive for positions in the organization requiring regulatory examination qualifications.

The importance of training and education is evidenced by FINRA's Rule 1250, Continuing Education Requirements,[8] which superseded NASD Rule 1120[9] of the National Association of Securities Dealers (NASD) in October 2011. Initially, NASD Rule 1120 applied only to a limited number of registered persons—registered representatives and certain principals, and required the completion of a regulatory element and a firm element as proscribed in the rule. Other registered persons were exempted from the Rule. However, in 2004 the NASD revised the entire Rule 1120 and eliminated all previous exemptions.[10]

Regulatory Relationships

Compliance plays an important role in the relationship a firm has with regulators. Much of the direct contact between regulators and a firm involves compliance. Even as regulators rely on other means to gather information on a firm—regulatory filings, financial reports, media, and third-parties ultimately they must have direct contact with the firm. In most instances, that contact is first with the firm's Compliance Department,

---

[7] *Securities and Exchange Commission vs. Thomas E. Meade,* Administrative Proceeding, File No. 13-15927, June 11, 2014.
[8] See FINRA Rule 1250, *Continuing Education Requirements,* which requires all registered persons to complete a regulatory element examination on the second anniversary of their initial registration and every three years thereafter, and the firm element designed and administered by the Member annually.
[9] See NASD Rule 1120, *Continuing Education Requirements.*
[10] See NASD Notice to Members, October 2004, *Regulatory Element Exemptions.*

with the possible exception of inquiries regarding the firm's financial reporting. Consequently, regulators may quickly form an opinion about a firm based simply on how that initial interaction is handled.

Establishing and maintaining a strong, respectful, and mutually beneficial relationship with every regulator is therefore a responsibility of compliance. Today, this relationship has become increasingly important because the number of regulators overseeing a firm's businesses has grown to include not only more domestic regulatory authorities but also, for many firms, authorities outside of the United States. This growth has resulted in differing and sometimes conflicting expectations on what Compliance's role and responsibilities are. Although this is obviously a challenge for Compliance, it really serves to underscore the importance of each regulatory relationship. FINRA designates a coordinator for each of its members. This person is typically located in the FINRA district office where the firm's headquarters is located. Other regulators, such as the CFTC, SEC's Office of Compliance Inspections and Examinations (OCIE) and Division of Trading and Markets and banking regulators, have persons specifically designated to provide guidance and rule interpretation for their subject firms. Firms are strongly encouraged to use these resources without the risk of inviting heightened scrutiny about their activities. Another component of a healthy regulatory relationship is self-reporting. Although the rules issued by FINRA and other regulators require self-reporting of certain events and possible rule violations, how and when a firm initiates a report have a direct bearing on the relationship between the firm and the regulator.

The objective, then, is to build relationships that encourage dialogue. The ideal relationship is one in which the firm can use the regulator as a resource for guidance on rule interpretations, business plans and developments, and the resolution of problems and other events that the firm may encounter. Likewise, the firm should build and maintain a profile that is seen by the regulator as responsive and cooperative even in cases defending its position or approach.

Interaction with Other Control Functions

In today's firms, with perhaps the exception of some small firms, multiple groups perform control functions, and compliance is just one of them. In fact, many of the very largest organizations contain specialized units, with some of those functions including compliance. Typically, these other control functions are legal, internal audit, and risk. Each has a core responsibility, but by necessity interacts with compliance professionals as well as with each of the other groups. Some of the functions that each unit performs may also overlap with functions conducted by the others, including compliance. This is not a duplication of the functions; in every instance, the purpose of the control function being performed has a different objective. For example financial risk, operational risk, market risk, and compliance may all be viewing the firm's equity trading activities. Financial and market risk specialists would be looking at inventory valuations, size, and age. Operational risk staff would review for late reporting, trade errors, and internal reporting compliance. And, compliance professionals could be reviewing trades for patterns of customer or desk trading violations—trading ahead, best execution, etc. In some cases they may share functions. For example, on-site inspections of branch offices or business units may be jointly performed by compliance and internal audit personnel, each with their own objectives and targets.

Even though these groups may operate independently, there is a need to coordinate and share information and data among them. Compliance and legal groups often jointly interact with regulators in connection with regulatory examinations, inquiries, or enforcement matters. They may also work together on developing and implementing new policies and procedures as well as training programs for them. Similarly, internal audit through its reviews may identify matters requiring the attention of Compliance, legal or risk. Another example would be risk specialists performing a review or monitoring and then forwarding the results to compliance or internal audit. As I noted previously, these are generally independent control functions with their own proscribed responsibilities, but they cannot nor should not operate in a vacuum. Units interact with one another, whether through regularly scheduled meetings (highly recommended), and/or through well-defined policies and procedures requiring the exchange, forwarding, or sharing of data and information is a necessary component of a firm's compliance and internal control programs.

IV. AUTHORITATIVE WITHOUT OWNING SUPERVISION RESPONSIBILITY

Without any question or doubt, one of the biggest challenges for firms' CCOs and other compliance professionals is establishing a robust compliance program and culture that does not result in compliance or compliance professionals ending up as "supervisors," other than for their own department and responsibilities. In other words, the issue is "how to be authoritative without becoming the boss." This, by no means, is a new issue or concern, but in recent years the number of enforcement cases brought against Compliance professionals has seen a dramatic increase. Although every case is based on "facts and circumstances," as the regulators like to say, there are several underlying and avoidable facts in many of them that caused or contributed to a compliance professional being charged with failing to supervise. Even among regulatory officials there is sometimes a lack of clarity on where the "supervisory" line is for compliance officers, and some have suggested written guidance to address this issue.[11]

First, let me acknowledge that when the conduct involves the failure to properly carry out or supervise activities directly under the control or direct supervision of the compliance person, he or she is going to get charged. However, when the misconduct or violations occur in activities under the direct supervision of a business person, the role of the compliance professional should not be seen as supervisory.

---

[11] *See*, e.g., Securities and Commission Commissioner Daniel M. Gallagher's *Introductory Remarks at the Evolving Role of Compliance in the Securities Industry Presentation*, May 12, 2014 Washington D.C. and Commissioner Kara M. Stein's *Keynote Address Compliance Week 2014*, May 19, 2014, Washington D.C.

However, having an authoritative voice within the organization's overall compliance program is absolutely necessary for a compliance professional. Being authoritative is necessary in any role normally associated with a compliance professional—advisory, monitoring, assessing or testing. The SIFMA March 2013 White Paper, *The Evolving Role of Compliance,* includes an excellent discussion on when, why and how a Compliance professional could be subject to supervisory liability.[12]

Note that, although not evident in any rule changes or rule proposals, regulators seem to have developed a more expansive view of the roles and responsibilities of the Compliance Department and compliance officers, as evidenced in some recent enforcement actions. Like many others, I see this as a dangerous trend because it implies that compliance is expected to be authoritative, and that, when it is authoritative, there are greater supervisory liabilities that result.

This section summarizes recommendations that firms and compliance professionals should consider to avoid or mitigate the risk of becoming the target in a potential enforcement action.

Job Description

Regardless of the size of the organization or the department, every compliance position should have a clear written description of the functions and responsibilities associated with it. The job description should contain information on what the professional is expected to do, the specific procedures and processes to be used, the frequency of specific tasks, resources for them, reporting lines, and the procedures for escalating matters. Positions that involve the supervision of persons or specific Compliance Department functions should be identified and the procedures for performing the supervisory functions clearly articulated.

Written Policies and Procedures and Supervisory Policies and Procedures

FINRA, SEC, and other regulators require that every firm maintain "reasonably" adequate written policies and procedures (WPPs) and written supervisory procedures (WSPs) for the purpose of meeting the firm's regulatory, compliance, and supervisory obligations. These have the potential of becoming a minefield for possible and unintended regulatory and supervisory liability for the Compliance professional.

In many firms, compliance is the outright "owner" of the firm's WPPs/WSPs. This means the Compliance Department is responsible for developing, writing, implementing, updating, and monitoring and testing their compliance. Typically, this "ownership" is found in small or modest sized firms reflecting the type of business, size, structure and available resources in the organization. However, in the larger and more complex organizations you are more likely to find that compliance's role is only part of the process

---

[12] See SIFMA White Paper *The Evolving Role of Compliance*, March 2013, Sec. II. Defining the Role of Compliance, C. Compliance and Supervision: Enforcement of Existing Standards.

of developing, implementing, monitoring and testing effective and adequate policies and procedures. The idea that "one-size-fits-all" simply cannot work in an industry as complex and diverse as ours.

In large organizations, designing and implementing policies and procedures are a collaborative effort involving not only compliance staff but also the affected business unit(s), the supervisors and management of the affected businesses, intellectual technology, legal representatives, other control functions (financial risk, operational risk), internal audit, and often, operations. Care is given to drafting policies and procedures that satisfy the applicable regulatory requirements and/or the internal firm objectives without imposing unreasonable or unnecessary burdens on the firm. Often, new policies and procedures, particularly those any requiring new or enhanced technology or reports, are subjected to testing before they are permanently implemented. Introducing new policies and procedures almost always includes, or should include, training of all personnel who will have some role or responsibility related to those introduced.

The idea that "one-size-does-not-fit-all" is most evident in smaller firms. These firms, subject to the same regulatory standards and expectations as their bigger siblings, often do not have the same access to the resources available in the larger firms. To meet their obligations to develop, implement, and maintain adequate policies and procedures suited to their businesses, these firms frequently rely on third parties as the source of their written policies and procedures. There is nothing inherently wrong with this, but using third parties sometimes comes with additional risks, exposures, and liabilities not just for the firm and supervisors, but also for the CCO and other compliance professionals. My comments on the use of "off-the-shelf" manuals are in no way intended to criticize the firms that provide these services or the manuals and services they provide. When all is said and done, it's the subscriber or end user who owns its regulatory compliance responsibilities.

Whether the policies and procedures manuals are developed in-house or purchased from a third party, there are "must have" components for every policy and procedure in the manuals. The following list identifies the most important:

- A clear description of the policy and procedure;
- A generic reference, when necessary, to the regulatory requirement for such policy or procedure;
- The person(s) or positions(s) responsible for performing the required functions (I strongly recommend using the position(s) rather than the name(s) of individuals for this, and it must also name the person with the ultimate supervisory authority for compliance);
- The tools, reports, etc. used for the task;
- The frequency for performing the task;
- The methods used for documentation; and
- The process or procedure followed for resolving exceptions, which should include the escalation process for unresolved exceptions.

Although there are other important steps that might have to be included, these features at least serve as a starting point.

Why are the written guidelines important? Because, the manuals assign specific responsibilities to specific individuals, and most importantly the policies and procedures identify who owns the supervisory responsibilities, as well as what responsibilities are ascribed to others. During my career I have seen and even helped to write a number of policies and procedures manuals for firms both enormous and small in size. These manuals included those prepared in-house and those purchased from service providers. Usually, manuals prepared in-house are designed as described above, thus limiting or confining supervisory responsibilities and the attendant liabilities to the right person or parties. Because off-the-shelf manuals are designed for a wider and more diverse group of users, designing and tailoring them to a specific firm is a challenge. The end user or subscriber should carefully review every policy and procedure contained in the manuals and relevant to its businesses. Because some documents may be generic, the subscriber should either amend, enhance, or use attachments to match the firm's resources and structure. A CCO or Compliance professional should make sure that he or she is not unintentionally identified as the person ultimately responsible for compliance with any policy or procedure other than those specifically assigned to the Compliance Department. Even then, it's just as important to not have the ultimate authority to deal with violations—internal discipline, firing, etc.

A final comment on policies and procedures is this: They are not written just to impress a regulator. They need to be adequate to meet requirements so they can be followed or performed with the resources available in the firm.

Committee Participation

In virtually any firm you will find or expect to find a Compliance Department representative presence on almost any committee established by the firm for evaluating products and services, risk management, internal controls, regulatory changes, business lines and management, internal or regulatory investigations, and internal disciplinary matters. As noted before, this generally is a traditional advisory role for Compliance and not one where ownership of any supervision is ascribed to Compliance. The SEC has also provided some clarity on this issue.[13] However, as some recent enforcement cases have disclosed, there is no clear definition by a regulator as to when a Compliance professional moves from being in an advisory role to one taking on supervisory liability for committee decisions. Among firms there is no common answer on whether Compliance participants have a "vote" in any committee decision, or simply provide advice. Obviously, a voting role could create potential, even unintended, supervisory liability for the Compliance member. My strong belief, is that committee participation

---

[13] *See* Securities and Exchange Commission, Division of Trading and Markets, *Frequently Asked Questions About Liability of Compliance and Legal Personnel at Broker-Dealers under Sections 15(b)(4) and 15(b)(6) of the Exchange Act,* Question 5.

is absolutely essential in any compliance program, and compliance participation can still be justified to regulators as being solely advisory.

V. REGULATORY EXPECTATIONS

Clearly, every regulator expects that the firms subject to its authority develop and maintain robust compliance and supervisory programs to reasonably comply with their respective rules and regulations. There are no standard models to meet these expectations, which not surprisingly might differ among the different regulators. In fact, there are examples where there appears to be no coordination or consistency among regulators in their respective expectations on how firms should meet compliance requirements for the same services or products regulated by different regulators.

The other evident challenge posed by regulators, and one that they usually deny, is competition among them. This means that firms subject to SEC, FINRA, varying state regulators, banking regulators, and their domestic and foreign counterparts have to carefully sort out how they can meet each regulator's compliance expectations. There is no easy answer to this dilemma. And regulators do not generally agree among themselves whose rules are more important for a firm to follow. As firms develop, implement, and maintain controls designed to meet the expectations of one regulator, they have to be mindful that complying with other regulators' requirements cannot be overlooked.

Where this conundrum is very evident is in the challenges posed by complying with the requirements of securities regulators and at the same time meeting the demands of banking regulators. Add to that challenge the requirements posed by foreign regulators.

The role of compliance in all of this is equally complex. Foreign regulators, both securities and banking, and U.S. banking regulators see the role of compliance not only as authoritative but also as a control position. Even among only U.S. banking, securities, investment advisory, and commodities futures regulators, there are varying definitions and consequent expectations for firms and their compliance professionals.

VI. DIVERSE FIRM AND BUSINESS STRUCTURES

The composition of organizations in today's financial services industry reflects an ever-changing pattern of growth, businesses, and structure. Almost every firm is unique in some way from its competitors. The products and services offered by firms are similarly varied. As a result, the organizational structures of firms are often designed along their client, business, and product lines. It is not unusual to see firms that have separate business units, or in some cases affiliated companies, dedicated to a specific client base such as individual investors, institutional clients, trust services, advisory services, or counterparties. Add to that diverse model similar activities in foreign jurisdictions and it is easy to see the challenges these organizations confront in developing compliance programs and a compliance structure that are both effective but also efficient. In many of these firms compliance resources are shared. For example, branch office inspections may be conducted across affiliated company lines by teams dedicated solely to doing these reviews. Other shared functions might include antimoney laundering (AML) compliance, trading surveillance, regulatory interaction, etc. The sharing of resources is a very efficient way of managing the costs of these programs, and at the same time benefiting from the information gathered from multiple sources. The sharing of resources is not confined to compliance and will often include other risk or control functions—internal audit, legal, risk, etc.

The reporting lines for compliance are also experiencing changes. Again, in larger organizations the CCO often now reports to the head of risk for the firm, whereas in the past the compliance manager generally reported to the head of legal or the general counsel and was considered part of the firm's legal department. There are reasons for these changes. Because many firms today are themselves or part of an organization subject to U.S. and/or foreign banking regulations, there is an expectation by banking regulators that all risk and control functions be independent within the organization and focused on monitoring, testing, and assessing. Obviously, this differs somewhat from how compliance has traditionally functioned in the securities industry.

Another change that has occurred within the larger organizations is the designation of multiple CCOs. Firms that have affiliated broker-dealers will have a CCO named for each. Similarly, if the firm has separately registered investment adviser or commodities futures affiliates, they too will often have their own CCO. In some firms there are even separate CCOs for specific business activities.

In smaller firms the Compliance Department structure is far less complicated. Generally, there is one CCO, even if the firm might be dually registered as a broker-dealer and investment adviser or have affiliated entities registered as broker-dealers and investment adviser. Compliance staffing in these firms usually entails assigning multiple responsibilities to personnel or designating each compliance professional with a specific function. It is quite common for many of these firms to use third parties for some of their compliance functions. Firms that operate on the independent contractor platform often have a large number of branch office locations widely dispersed geographically and rely on third-party service providers to conduct on-site examinations of these offices. Service providers are often used to monitor trading activity, communications with clients, movements and transfers of client assets-funds and securities, or other functions requiring technology resources.

Reporting lines in these firms are much simpler and streamlined. Usually the CCO reports to the firm's CEO or president. If the firm has an on-site general counsel, the CCO would likely report to that person as well. In most of these firms, although there may be an organizational structure along its business lines, the CEO often ultimately makes most of the key decisions. As I noted earlier, this is an example of a structure for which it is imperative that the duties and responsibilities of the CCO and other compliance professionals are clearly described in a written job description.

VII. AVAILABILITY AND USE OF RESOURCES: PEOPLE AND TECHNOLOGY

The short comment on this subject is that there is never enough of either! That said, this issue is always a major consideration in any organization. First, people. As noted previously, in large, complex organizations sharing personnel resources is commonly employed. Redundant or duplicate functions are costly, often inefficient, and lacking in coordination. Most certainly costs are often the driving force to consolidate and share resources. However, another big benefit from consolidation is consistency across the organization. As a result, the collection and coordination of information become more meaningful and useful in making business and management decisions. Analysis of gathered information can identify trends or patterns of activity, more efficiently enabling the firm to respond to potential problems more quickly. Committees composed of personnel, including compliance, from different, affiliates, business units, or control functions can share information and data benefiting each and the firm.

Smaller firms can gain the same benefits by having regular meetings to share and discuss information for the same purpose of spotting trends or patterns that require greater attention. Again, these firms also use third parties to provide support to their compliance programs, and in such cases it is important to include those providers in the discussions when necessary.

Technological support and development will always be featured in every organization's compliance programs. One of the challenges compliance faces is the competition within the firm for these resources. This limitation on technological resources is exacerbated because of new and evolving regulatory demands, which can easily add to the strain on technology. Many of the larger organizations have addressed this by providing the Compliance Department with its own dedicated technology support. The benefits of this are significant. Compliance can develop programs tailored for specific purposes, even one-time needs and respond promptly to new regulatory rules and demands. In firms where technology remains an independent support unit, access usually depends on compliance professionals and other control functions getting in a queue. Often in these situations, unless there are clear regulatory or significant risk needs, business and revenue sources may get priority.

Almost all smaller firms rely on third-party service providers for their technology needs. Often these services are included in the execution, clearing, and operational support provided by another broker-dealer as part of an introducing arrangement. The introducing broker-dealer can usually select from a menu of services and reports those it wishes to include in the arrangement, although certain reports and information are required under regulatory rules. Some firms using these arrangements may also have in-house technology resources, which sometimes can be coordinated with reports and information from the service provider or, in other cases, used separately by the firm. These third-party arrangements have obvious limitations, and access to specialized reports and information can be difficult. Larger firms will also use third parties for certain types of information rather than design their own programs to access the same information. In many instances the data and information obtained from the third party is downloaded and merged with the firm's data for the firm's reports.

VIII. WORKING WITH SENIOR MANAGEMENT

It is generally agreed that compliance needs to function independently. That said, the department also cannot operate in a vacuum. Consequently, the working relationship between compliance professionals and senior management and business units is the ultimate measure of a firm's culture of compliance. Senior management must clearly articulate and demonstrate support for the role of compliance. The Compliance Department must demonstrate that it is a resource that management can call and rely on for advice and information on the adequacy of the firm's compliance needs or for specific guidance as issues develop. Business managers should feel comfortable and encouraged to use the Compliance Department as a partner for providing guidance as they perform their respective supervisory duties. Management must also accept and acknowledge that its members carry the ultimate responsibility for the supervision of business activities and personnel engaged in those activities.

While there is no one preferred method of interaction between compliance and senior management, FINRA rules proscribe at a minimum certain annual reports and meetings.[14] In most organizations meetings between compliance and senior management occur more frequently than annually. Similarly, various compliance reports are prepared and circulated to senior management on a regular basis.

IX. CONCLUSION

As I have been writing this chapter, the world of compliance and CCOs continues to be a focus of regulators. One change that is most apparent concerns the traditionally held view that compliance serves an advisory role in its organization.[15]

However, some regulators—banking and foreign ones in particular—believe that compliance is not an advisory function but rather an oversight function serving as the firm's watchdog and policeman. They believe that the advisory role is better provided by a firm's legal professionals. Consequently, many large, global firms here in the United States have restructured their Compliance Departments to no longer report to the firm's legal director, but instead to the firm's risk specialists. This reporting preference is privately expressed by some U.S. regulatory officials.

So far, the firms affected by this view have not made major changes in the functions or roles played by their compliance professionals, who continue to serve as advisers

---

[14] *See* FINRA Rule 3120, Supervisory Control System, (a)(1), (2) and FINRA Rule 3130(b) Annual Certification Requirement, (c) Certification (1)(A), (B), (C), (2), (3), (4).

[15] *See* Securities Industry and Financial Markets Association (SIFMA)'s White Paper, *The Evolving Role of Compliance*, March 11, 2013, at II. C.

and to provide guidance on supervisory and compliance issues. Continuing that role is critically important. Successful compliance programs rely heavily on the interaction and cooperation between a business function and a compliance professional. Making the compliance professional's role nothing more than the cop-on-the-beat would severely undermine, if not eliminate, the business-compliance relationship.

One thing is certain. Compliance and the compliance professional remain necessary in financial firms, but their role is also challenging, not without risk and constantly evolving.

ABOUT THE AUTHOR

R. Gerald Baker is the former executive director of the Compliance and Legal Society of the Securities Industry and Financial Markets Association (SIFMA) and served as a member and special adviser of its Executive Committee for more than 20 years.

Mr. Baker has more than 50 years of experience in the securities and investment advisory field, and held the position of CCO with some of the industry's major firms. His expertise includes compliance, supervision, sales, trading, financial reporting, and training. He currently provides compliance and supervisory consulting services and works with regulators on rule initiatives and other regulatory issues. He was the recipient of the Alfred J. Rauschman Award in 2009 in recognition of his contributions to the compliance and regulatory community.

CHAPTER 4

Fiduciary Duty

By Karen Barr, *Investment Adviser Association*
David Tittsworth, *Ropes & Gray, LLP*

I. INTRODUCTION

Fiduciary duty is a key distinguishing characteristic of the U.S. investment advisory profession. The duty emanates from the sensitive nature of the relationship between an investment adviser and its clients—a relationship based on trust that requires a higher legal standard of care. The fiduciary duty under the Investment Advisers Act is an overarching duty that requires investment advisers to place the interests of their client ahead of their own interests at all times. Although the word *fiduciary* does not appear in the Advisers Act, the U.S. Supreme Court concluded decades ago that the law imposes a strict fiduciary duty on investment advisers, confirming previous pronouncements of the Securities and Exchange Commission (SEC).

The Advisers Act fiduciary duty derives from a combination of the nature of the advisory relationship and the broad antifraud provisions of the law that prohibit an investment adviser from engaging "in any act, practice, or course of business which is fraudulent, deceptive, or manipulative."[1]

Fiduciary duty is an integral part of the largely principles-based regulatory framework of the Advisers Act. As SEC Chairman Arthur Levitt stated in 2000, "Unlike some of the other securities laws, the Advisers Act does not contain detailed rules governing the way advisers conduct their businesses. Rather, the act broadly prohibits fraud and holds advisers to rigorous fiduciary standards when dealing with clients."[2]

Although some regulations under the Advisers Act explicitly reference an investment adviser's fiduciary duty, many aspects of fiduciary duty are not readily susceptible to command-and-control specifications and requirements. Instead, the Advisers Act fiduciary duty requires an investment adviser to consider the particular facts and circumstances of its relationship with its clients and then to conform its activities according to fiduciary principles. These principles include a duty of loyalty and a duty of care.

---

[1] Investment Advisers Act of 1940, Sec. 204(d).
[2] Amendments to Form ADV: Opening Statement, Hon. Arthur Levitt, Jr. (Apr. 5, 2000).

II. ORIGINS OF FIDUCIARY PRINCIPLES

The origins of American fiduciary duty find their roots in British law that developed several centuries ago.[3] Without belaboring the details of how the law has emerged over time, the basic concept is straightforward: A person who is entrusted with another's property should be held to higher legal standards than the standards that apply to mere commercial transactions.[4] In fact, fiduciary duty is consistently described as the highest legal duty. The heart of the duty is the relationship of *trust* between two parties.

In a typical investment advisory relationship, the context for fiduciary duty is also straightforward: the client entrusts the investment adviser with valuable property—the client's money!—for the purpose of receiving advice about how to invest the client's assets. The vast majority of SEC-registered investment advisory clients' assets are managed on a discretionary basis—that is, the client has authorized the investment adviser to make investment decisions without the client's preapproval. Many other investment advisers provide recommendations to their clients on how to invest or allocate their assets or provide more comprehensive financial planning services. Because advisers are entrusted with managing or giving advice about their clients' savings and investments, the fiduciary duty that governs the advisory relationship is critically important.

III. ASPECTS OF FIDUCIARY DUTY

There are two basic components of the Advisers Act fiduciary duty: the duty of loyalty and the duty of care. The duty of loyalty requires an adviser to:

- Serve the best interests of its clients;
- Subrogate its own interests to that of its clients; and
- Fully disclose and eliminate or mitigate conflicts of interest.

The duty of care requires, among other things, an adviser to provide only suitable advice and to "make a reasonable investigation to determine that it is not basing its recommendations on materially inaccurate or incomplete information."[5]

However, the Advisers Act fiduciary duty encompasses additional duties and obligations. Among the specific obligations that flow from an adviser's fiduciary duty, in addition

---

[3] For a discussion of how fiduciary law evolved, see http://www.bu.edu/law/central/jd/organizations/journals/bulr/documents/SEIPP.pdf

[4] Thomas P. Lemke and Gerald T. Lins, *Regulation of Investment Advisers*, Thompson Reuters (2010), at 2:33; see also *SEC v. Capital Gains Research Bureau*, 375 U.S. 180 (1963) ("Capital Gains").

[5] SEC, "Study on Investment Advisors and Broker-Dealers, as Required by Section 913 of the Dodd-Frank Wall Street Reform and Consumer Protection Act," page 22.

to the duty to act in the client's best interest and to make full and fair disclosure to clients of all material facts, are:[6]

- The duty to place the clients' interests first;
- The duty to have an adequate, reasonable basis for its investment advice;
- The duty to inform itself about clients' situations and circumstances;
- The duty to use only those strategies for which the adviser is reasonably competent;
- The duty to follow client instructions, guidelines and governing documents;
- The duty to perform due diligence on subadvisers and other third parties;
- The duty to seek best execution for clients' securities transactions where the adviser directs such transactions;
- The duty to render advice that is suitable to clients' needs, objectives, and financial circumstances;
- The duty to vote proxies in the best interests of clients;
- The duty to allocate investment opportunities fairly among clients;
- The duty not to subrogate clients' interests to its own;
- The duty not to use client assets for itself; and
- The duty to maintain client confidentiality.

Similarly, the Standards of Practice of the Investment Adviser Association set forth the following aspects of fiduciary duty and professional responsibility:

> An investment adviser stands in a special relationship of trust and confidence with, and therefore is a fiduciary to, its clients. As a fiduciary, an investment adviser has an affirmative duty of care, loyalty, honesty, and good faith to act in the best interests of its clients. The parameters of an investment adviser's duty depend on the scope of the advisory relationship and generally include:
>
> 1) The duty at all times to place the interests of clients first;
> 2) The duty to have a reasonable basis for its investment advice;
> 3) The duty to seek best execution for client securities transactions where the adviser directs such transactions;
> 4) The duty to make investment decisions consistent with any mutually agreed upon client objectives, strategies, policies, guidelines, and restrictions;
> 5) The duty to treat clients fairly;

---

[6] See *Amendments to Form ADV*, Investment Advisers Act, Rel. No. IA-2106 (July 28, 2010); *Suitability of Investment Advice Provided by Investment Advisers; Custodial Account Statements for Certain Advisory Clients*, Investment Advisers Act, Rel. No. IA-1406, n. 3 (Mar. 16, 1994) (noting duty of full disclosure of conflicts of interest, duty of loyalty, duty of best execution, and duty of care, citing various sources); *Applicability of Investment Advisers Act to Financial Planners, Pension Consultants, and Other Persons Who Provide Investment Advisory Services as a Component of Other Financial Services*, Investment Advisers Act, Rel. No. IA-1092 (Oct. 8, 1987) (1092 Release) (discussing fiduciary duties). See also IAA Standards of Practice, https://www.investmentadviser.org/eweb/dynamicpage.aspx?webcode=StandardsPractice

6) The duty to make full and fair disclosure to clients of all material facts about the advisory relationship, particularly regarding conflicts of interest; and
7) The duty to respect the confidentiality of client information.

The Standards of Practice also address professional qualifications, responsible and ethical business practices, fair and reasonable compensation, and appropriate communications with clients and the public. However, the fiduciary duty standard is overarching, and, because it is principles-based, cannot be completely captured in or reduced to a checklist.

In practical terms, fiduciary duty means that, in the course of providing advice to clients, advisers must disclose all material information and conflicts of interest to their clients, including the fees that they charge, how they plan to recommend securities to clients, and any material disciplinary information involving the firms or their investment personnel. Moreover, as fiduciaries, advisers must treat their clients fairly and not favor one client over another, especially if they would somehow benefit from favoring one particular client or type of client. Most important, whenever the interests of investment advisers differ from those of their clients, advisers must explain the conflict to the clients and act to mitigate or eliminate it, ensuring they act in the interests of the client and not for their own benefit.

IV. REGULATORY FRAMEWORK

The Advisers Act regulatory framework that has developed over the years includes numerous rules that are based on fiduciary principles as well as statutory provisions of the Advisers Act. At the same time, the regulatory framework recognizes that the fiduciary duty permeates all of the adviser's activities, which can vary among advisers. The regulations require that advisers adopt and follow policies and procedures in certain areas, but do not prescribe the content of the policies and procedures.

For example, the so-called Compliance Program Rule (which is likely the single most important regulation promulgated by the SEC under the Advisers Act) requires all SEC-registered investment advisers to:

- Adopt and implement written policies and procedures reasonably designed to prevent violation of the federal securities laws;
- Review those policies and procedures annually for their adequacy and the effectiveness of their implementation; and
- Designate a chief compliance officer to be responsible for administering the policies and procedures.[7]

The release approving the final Compliance Program Rule notes that the rule "requires advisers to consider their fiduciary and regulatory obligations under the Advisers Act and to formalize policies and procedures to address them."[8]

---

[7] *Compliance Programs of Investment Companies and Investment Advisers,* Rel. Nos. IA-2204; IC-26299; File No. S7-03-03 (Dec. 17, 2003).
[8] *Id.*

A few months after the Compliance Program Rule was adopted, the SEC approved the Investment Adviser Codes of Ethics rule. The rule requires all SEC-registered investment advisers to adopt codes of ethics that set forth standards of conduct expected of advisory personnel and address conflicts that arise from personal trading by advisory personnel. The proposing release for the rule states that:

> We propose that each code of ethics set forth a standard of business conduct that the adviser requires of all its supervised persons. *This standard must reflect the adviser's fiduciary obligations and those of its supervised persons, and must require compliance with the federal securities laws. These obligations are imposed by law and thus would establish a minimum requirement for a code of ethics complying with the rule.* Advisers would be free, however, to require higher standards such as those we described above [emphasis added].[9]

Thus, SEC-registered investment advisers are required to undertake specific actions relating to policies and procedures and, in doing so, to consider their fiduciary obligations. In addition, investment advisers must adopt codes of ethics that specifically reference the adviser's fiduciary duty. All advisers are required to provide clients with a description of the firm's code and to state that the firm will provide a copy of the code to any client or prospective client upon request.

An example of instances when the fiduciary duty influences a firm's policies and procedures in developing a code of ethics is personal trading by the firm's employees. For example, although not required by SEC rules, firms may impose "blackout periods" during which firm personnel cannot buy or sell securities in their personal accounts. Policies on blackout periods, the length of such periods, and the persons or categories of persons to whom they apply will vary to meet the particular nature and practices of individual firms. However, each firm's goal is typically to avoid even the appearance that firm employees may be benefiting from the firm's recommendations to clients. These policies are enforced in various ways, including preclearance, employee reporting and certifications, ongoing monitoring, and periodic testing.

The Advisers Act proxy voting rule is yet another example of how SEC rules reflect the fiduciary duty of an investment adviser. The proposing release for the rule clearly states how an investment adviser's duty to vote proxies is shaped and controlled by the adviser's fiduciary duty:

> The federal securities laws do not specifically address how advisers must exercise their voting authority. Under the Advisers Act, an investment adviser is, however, a fiduciary that owes its clients a duty of "utmost good faith, and full and fair disclosure of all material facts," as well as an affirmative obligation "to employ reasonable care to avoid misleading"

---

[9] *Investment Adviser Codes of Ethics*, Rel. Nos. IA-2209, IC-26337; 69 Fed. Reg. 4039, 4041 (Jan. 27, 2004) (footnote omitted).

its clients. An adviser owes its client a fiduciary duty with respect to all services undertaken on the client's behalf, including the voting of proxies. An adviser's fiduciary duty includes the duty of care and the duty of loyalty to clients. The duty of care requires an adviser given authority to vote proxies to monitor corporate events and to vote the proxies. The duty of loyalty requires an adviser to vote proxies in a manner consistent with the best interest of its client and precludes the adviser from subrogating the client's interest to its own.[10]

These examples serve to demonstrate the connection between the overarching fiduciary duty under the Investment Advisers Act and its connection with specific regulations governing the advisory profession. In addition, these provisions recognize that advisers do not satisfy their fiduciary duty through compliance with detailed, command-and-control requirements, but rather by establishing and following policies and procedures that are tailored to the adviser's own clients.

V. "NONREGULATORY" EXAMPLES

In other instances, the Advisers Act fiduciary duty operates to create practices that reflect the general principle of putting the client's interest first when no specific regulatory obligations govern particular situations.

As a general matter, investment advisers recognize the importance of "tone at the top" in establishing a fiduciary culture, which informs all firm personnel in the conduct of their duties. The message conveyed by senior management to firm personnel in written policies and procedures, codes of ethics and conduct, and regular training, is that the clients' best interests are the main concern of the firm. Tone at the top guides each firm's decision making in addressing all aspects of its business, including the establishment of policies in areas that are not addressed specifically in SEC rules. These policies are monitored and reviewed to ensure that the adviser is serving the best interests of its clients.

For example, trade errors may occur when an investment adviser conducts a certain activity for a client account that was unintended or mistaken, and that negligence results in a financial gain or loss for the client.[11] There is no specific provision in the Advisers Act (or any regulation) that deals with trade errors. However, the SEC staff has interpreted investment advisers' fiduciary duty to include an obligation to "make their clients whole when they have made a trade error."[12] Thus, it is a common practice among investment advisory firms to absorb any losses resulting from a trading error.

---

[10] *Proxy Voting by Investment Advisers*, Rel. No. IA-2059; File No. S7-38-02 (Sept. 20, 2002) (footnotes omitted).
[11] Robert Helm and Megan Johnson, "Dealing with Investment Errors," *Investment Lawyer*, Vol. 20, No 3.
[12] Investment Adviser Association Comment Letter, *Response to Request for Data and Other Information*, Rel. No. 34-69013; IA-3558; File No. 4-606, at 5 (July 3, 2013) ("IAA Comment Letter July 2013"), https://www.sec.gov/comments/4-606/4606-3108.pdf

The rationale behind this is that a fiduciary has a responsibility to take due care in performing its duties, and this means that the adviser must institute and follow policies and procedures that minimize the risk of trade errors.[13]

A similar example is best execution. There are no specific provisions of the Advisers Act that define best execution or detailed regulations that require written policies or specific practices. However, numerous pronouncements of the SEC and its staff clearly state that an investment adviser has the duty to seek best execution on behalf of its clients. In seeking best execution, an investment adviser should consider relevant situations that may present potential conflicts of interests, such as soft dollar arrangements and allocations of limited investment opportunities (such as IPOs). The investment adviser should have a process in place that allows it to weigh appropriate considerations, such as the price of the trading commission, the client's need for confidentiality, the complexity of the trade, the broker's past experience and financial strength, speed of execution, and value of any research provided. Thus, although there are no written regulations requiring an investment adviser to seek and achieve best execution, the Advisers Act fiduciary duty dictates that an investment adviser consider potential conflicts of interest and put in place a process to evaluate relevant factors in order to fulfill its duties of loyalty and care.[14]

In addition, investment advisers under the fiduciary standard typically establish policies and procedures concerning allocation of investment opportunities, which apply when a particular investment may be appropriate for multiple clients, especially when the investment opportunity is limited. The SEC does not require such procedures by rule; however, these procedures are prevalent in the industry. In order to ensure that the adviser is serving the best interests of clients, it may establish a pro rata rule to allow all applicable clients to invest in equal amounts or may establish a rotation system to ensure that clients are treated equally over time. Firms will review trades regularly to confirm that these procedures are being followed and that they treat all clients fairly. As part of these policies, firms may require that any proprietary trades by the firm and personal trades by firm personnel be made only after all client orders have been filled.[15]

It is important to recognize that the fiduciary standard applies beyond the context of specific policies and procedures and should guide investment advisers in their day-to-day interactions with clients. For example, investment advisers working with individual clients routinely advise their clients to use their assets for purposes other than investing, even though this advice would reduce the amount of funds under the firm's management and accordingly reduce the adviser's fee. Such instances arise when

---

[13] Helm and Johnson, "Dealing with Investment Errors."
[14] *See*, e.g., Thomas P. Lemke and Gerald T. Lins, *Soft Dollars and Other Trading Activities*, 2014–2015 ed., Thomas Reuters, at 7:18.
[15] Allocation is a good example of the flexibility and scalability of principles-based duties where firms may need different policies and procedures depending on their investment strategies. Thus, firms investing in only liquid large cap securities or open-end mutual funds for their clients would need different policies and procedures from those investing in small- or micro-cap or other less liquid securities. In addition, the allocation policies for fixed income investments often differ from those with respect to equities.

the firm advises a client to pay off his or her mortgage, make gifts for tax reasons, or engage in other estate planning measures.

VI. KEY AREAS: DISCLOSURE AND CONFLICTS OF INTEREST

Investment advisers are required to provide extensive disclosures about their businesses, services, practices, and material conflicts of interest. SEC Form ADV Part 2A, which is available publicly, specifically requires disclosures regarding a firm's advisory business, fees and other compensation, management of conflicts arising from "side-by-side management," types of clients, methods of analysis, investment strategies, risk of loss, conflicts of interest, disciplinary information, other financial industry activities and affiliations, code of ethics, participation or interest in client transactions and personal trading, brokerage practices, review of accounts, client referrals and other compensation for business, custody, investment discretion, proxy voting, and any material concerns about the adviser's financial condition. In addition, Form ADV Part 2B requires specific disclosures regarding an adviser's supervised persons, including information regarding educational and business background, disciplinary history, other business activities, additional compensation, and supervision.

Responding to the specific items and questions in Form ADV, however, is just a starting point. The instructions to the form emphasize that:

> Under federal and state law, you are a fiduciary and must make full disclosure to your *clients* of all material facts relating to the advisory relationship. As a fiduciary, you also must seek to avoid conflicts of interest with your clients, and, at a minimum, make full disclosure of all material conflicts of interest between you and your *clients* that could affect the advisory relationship. This obligation requires that you provide the client with sufficiently specific facts so that the client is able to understand the conflicts of interest you have and the business practices in which you engage, and can give informed consent to such conflicts or practices or reject them. To satisfy this obligation, you therefore may have to disclose to *clients* information not specifically required by Part 2 of Form ADV or in more detail than the brochure items might otherwise require. You may disclose this additional information to *clients* in your *brochure* or by some other means.

As fiduciaries, investment advisers must assess what conflicts they have, in effect compiling an inventory of such conflicts. They then must determine how to address conflicts by avoiding or mitigating them through instituting policies and procedures to ensure that the firm places the best interests of its clients first. The adviser must also provide full and fair disclosure of the nature of its practices and the conflicts they present and how the adviser addresses them. Advisers must provide a detailed, narrative explanation of conflicts identified by the SEC in Form ADV Part 2. In addition, as fiduciaries, investment advisers must disclose any other conflicts in Part 2 or by other means. Part 1 of Form ADV also requires advisers to provide additional information about potential conflicts.

A good example of how the fiduciary duty works with respect to conflicts and disclosure in practice arises in the area of compensation. If investment advisers receive payment from others for recommending certain types of products, the advisers must tell clients about the compensation and how the compensation may potentially affect or influence the investment advice that is given. For example, advisers paid by commission are required to disclose that commission-based compensation may motivate them to trade more frequently or to recommend trades because the advisers would receive more compensation. In addition to disclosing this information to clients, investment advisers must act to recommend securities that are in the best interests of the clients regardless of the additional compensation they may receive. They must also periodically monitor the application and the continued effectiveness of their policies to ensure that conflicts do not result in actions contrary to the best interests of clients.

VII. OTHER FIDUCIARY STANDARDS

As noted above, the Advisers Act fiduciary duty is well-established. Although aspects of the duty are not susceptible to precise definition, the duty has been confirmed by the U.S. Supreme Court and in numerous pronouncements of the SEC for many decades.

Investment advisers should be aware that other laws or circumstances may impose fiduciary duties that differ in some respects from the Advisers Act fiduciary duty.

For example, the Employee Retirement and Income Security Act of 1974 (ERISA) imposes a strict fiduciary duty on those who provide investment advice to private pension plans. Although the basic concepts of fiduciary duty are the same as the Advisers Act fiduciary duty (a relationship of trust and the duty to place the interests of the client ahead of one's own interests), certain aspects of ERISA are different.[16] Advisers therefore may need to consult resources in addition to the Advisers Act and SEC regulations and guidance in order to comply fully with their duties to clients.

VIII. FIDUCIARY DUTY AND BROKER-DEALERS

The fiduciary standard currently applies to certain activities of broker-dealers as well. If a broker-dealer provides discretionary asset management to a client for a fee, then the Advisers Act and its accompanying fiduciary duty apply with respect to that account.[17] Broker-dealers also may be subject to state law fiduciary duty under certain circumstances, depending on state law and the relationship between the broker-dealers

---

[16] Similarly, the fiduciary duties of a trustee or a board member may differ from those of an investment adviser.
[17] These firms generally are dually registered as both broker-dealers and investment advisers.

and their client.[18] Further, the SEC staff has taken the position that brokers providing discretionary asset management based on commissions and brokers that charge a separate fee for advice also are subject to the Advisers Act and its fiduciary standard.[19] On the other hand, broker-dealers whose performance of advisory services is "solely incidental" to the conduct of its business as a broker-dealers and who receives no "special compensation" for such services are excluded from coverage under the Advisers Act and its overarching fiduciary duty.

Thus, the services for which broker-dealers and investment advisers currently are subject to different standards of care are primarily nondiscretionary investment advisory services, such as making recommendations about securities to brokerage customers.[20] The existing standard of care for broker-dealers that engage in such activities is that specified in FINRA Rule 2111, which requires that a broker-dealer ensure that the advice is "suitable" to the client.[21] In addition, FINRA Rule 2010 requires broker-dealers when dealing with customers to "observe high standards of commercial honor and just and equitable principles of trade."[22]

The suitability standard is not as broad as fiduciary duty. Indeed, as noted above, the duty to provide suitable investment advice is merely one aspect of the fiduciary duty. For example, brokers under a suitability duty may make recommendations or make

---

[18] In some states, courts have found a broker-dealer to owe a fiduciary duty to a customer in limited circumstances in which the broker-dealer has discretion over an account or, because of a special relationship of trust and confidence, has *de facto* discretion. See, e.g., *Hecht v. Harris*, 430 F.2d 1202 (9th Cir. 1970) (holding that despite a nondiscretionary account, a broker-dealer owed fiduciary duties to a 77-year-old customer who was unable to understand confirmation slips); *Kravitz v. Pressman, Frohlich & Frost*, 447 F. Supp. 203 (D. Mass. 1978) (holding that a broker-dealer owed fiduciary duties in a nondiscretionary account when the customer was clearly unable to understand confirmation slips and completely relied on decisions of the broker, who the customer was dating at the time). Unlike investment advisers under the Advisers Act, however, broker-dealers are not considered fiduciaries by operation of law.

[19] *Interpretive Rule under the Advisers Act Affecting Broker-Dealers, Investment Advisers Act,* Rel. No. IA-2652 (Sept. 24, 2007). Although the proposed interpretations have not been finalized, they are the most recently expressed views of the commission on this subject, and it is understood that they continue to represent the commission's interpretation.

[20] See Letter from Christopher Gilkerson, senior vice president, deputy general counsel, Charles Schwab & Co., Inc. to Elizabeth M. Murphy, secretary, SEC, re: Release No. IA-3058 Study Regarding Obligations of Brokers, Dealers, and Investment Advisers, at 7–8 (Aug. 30, 2010).

[21] FINRA Rule 2111 provides, with respect to noninstitutional customers: "(a) A member or an associated person must have a reasonable basis to believe that a recommended transaction or investment strategy involving a security or securities is suitable for the customer, based on the information obtained through the reasonable diligence of the member or associated person to ascertain the customer's investment profile. A customer's investment profile includes, but is not limited to, the customer's age, other investments, financial situation and needs, tax status, investment objectives, investment experience, investment time horizon, liquidity needs, risk tolerance, and any other information the customer may disclose to the member or associated person in connection with such recommendation."

[22] FINRA Rule 2010 prohibits broker-dealers from: (1) filing misleading information about membership or registration; (2) trading ahead of a customer limit order; (3) failing to abide by FINRA's front-running policy; (4) engaging in certain purchases or sales in initial public offerings; and (5) failing to register its employees. See FINRA Rule 1122, Filing of Misleading Information as to Membership or Registration; IM-1000-3 Failure to Register Personnel; IM-2110-2 Trading Ahead of Customer Limit Order; IM-2110-3 Front Running Policy; FINRA Rule 5130, Restrictions on the Purchase and Sale of Initial Equity Public Offerings.

investment decisions as long as they are "suitable" for that client under his or her particular circumstances even if they are not in the best interests of the client. Moreover, even if the brokers are motivated to provide particular advice because significant benefits accrue to them (such as receipt of a financial benefit for recommending a particular security), suitability does not require disclosure of such conflicts.

IX. CONCLUSION

Investment advisers—of all sizes and business models—all owe each of their clients a fiduciary duty. They must act in the best interests of their clients and place their clients' interests above their own. Although the Advisers Act fiduciary duty is embedded in many SEC regulations, it is an overarching responsibility. The fiduciary duty informs and guides all actions and decisions by investment advisers and their personnel, not only compliance officers. Investment advisers need to establish a fiduciary culture within their firms, starting with the tone at the top.

All professionals need to have a firm grasp of the Advisers Act fiduciary standard in order to carry out their responsibilities (as well as an appreciation for other fiduciary standards that may be applicable, such as the strict fiduciary standard under ERISA). The Investment Advisers Act principles-based approach stands in stark contrast to the rules-based regulatory regime governing broker-dealers. The Advisers Act fiduciary standard is not readily susceptible to a "check the box" mentality. Instead it requires an examination and assessment of a firm's practices and activities—on an ongoing basis—to determine whether these activities are in the best interest of clients.

ABOUT THE AUTHORS

Karen L. Barr is president and CEO of the Investment Adviser Association (IAA), the nonprofit organization dedicated to serving and representing the interests of SEC-registered investment adviser firms. The IAA serves as the voice of the adviser community on key policy issues before the U.S. Congress, SEC, CFTC, DOL, and other regulators, and connects advisers with the latest information, resources, and opportunities to share best practices. Before assuming the role of president and CEO in 2014, Ms. Barr served as the IAA's general counsel for 17 years, with responsibility for the wide range of legal and regulatory matters affecting the Association and its members.

Prior to joining the Investment Adviser Association in March 1997, Ms. Barr was in private practice at Wilmer, Cutler & Pickering (now Wilmer Hale). Ms. Barr received her bachelor's of arts from the University of Pennsylvania and her juris prudence degree from the University of Michigan Law School.

 **David Tittsworth** serves as counsel with Ropes & Gray, LLP. Prior to joining the law firm in 2015, he served as president and CEO of the Investment Adviser Association from 1996 until 2014. The IAA is the nonprofit organization dedicated to serving and representing the interests of SEC-registered investment advisory firms. Before joining the IAA, Mr. Tittsworth served in senior positions in federal and state government, including counsel/minority counsel to the U.S. House Committee on Energy and Commerce from 1992–1996, where he handled a variety of legislative and oversight matters, from transportation (railroad) to consumer protection (FTC) issues.

The authors would like to thank IAA Associate General Counsel Kathy Ireland and former IAA interns Brian Farnkoff and Sanjana Nafday for their contributions to this chapter.

CHAPTER 5

Core Requirements of a Compliance Program

By David H. Lui
Galliard Capital Management, Inc.

I. INTRODUCTION

This chapter will describe the basic framework presented by the Securities and Exchange Commission (SEC) compliance rules and give compliance professionals and others a sense of the common compliance requirements applicable to broker-dealers, investment advisers, and mutual funds.

Reliance in the securities compliance arena on the Federal Sentencing Guidelines, yielded in 2004 to the passage of the "compliance rules." The Federal Sentencing Guidelines set out a uniform sentencing policy for individuals and organizations convicted of felonies and serious misdemeanors in the United States federal court system, and set forth certain "mitigating factors" that would be considered in reducing the severity of sentencing, such as: training programs, well-developed control procedures and self-reporting.

The thought was that corporations that had implemented these safeguards voluntarily, even if those control structures had not prevented a violation, had proven their willingness to comply with legal requirements and therefore, they were deserving of a lessened sentence by virtue of their efforts to voluntarily implement control structures.

These general guidelines yielded in 2004 to the creation of three sets of rules, each set governing compliance in one of the separate areas of the securities industry: broker-dealers, investment advisers, and mutual funds. The enactment of this model created a formalized requirement for an internal control structure, transitioning "compliance" from the realm of sentencing mitigation to a legal requirement in the securities industry.

The compliance rule that governs the compliance activities of Investment Advisers is Rule 206(4)-7 under the Investment Advisers Act of 1940 ("Advisers Act").[1] It is a deceptively simple rule. It is less than a third of a page long and lays out the broad framework of the requirements of the compliance rule paradigm: (a) an annual review by (b) a chief compliance officer (CCO), who is (c) responsible for administering procedures of the Adviser that are adequate and effective in satisfying the requirements of the Advisers Act.

---

[1] 17 CFR 275.206(4)-7 (Rule 206(4)-7).

The Advisers Act model is elaborated upon and more detail is added for its application to registered investment companies (mutual funds) in Rule 38a-1 under the Investment Company Act of 1940.[2] Under Rule 38a-1, the model provided under Rule 206(4)-7 is extended from procedures reasonably designed to prevent, detect, and correct violations of the Advisers Act to procedures reasonably designed to prevent, detect, and correct violations of seven separate enumerated "federal securities laws." Although the coverage of the rule is limited to the activities of an investment adviser in the Advisers Act Rule, in Rule 38a-1, the CCO must report on the activities of many "service providers," including investment advisers and subadvisers, transfer agents, fund administrators and principal underwriters, in addition to the mutual fund itself.[3] Finally, the requirement of a "review" under Rule 206(4)-7 becomes the requirement to create a "written report" on material compliance matters and other compliance concerns. Although few advisers actually conduct a review that is unwritten, the Advisers Act standard, unlike Rule 38a-1, would allow for a review that remains undocumented.

The compliance rule that governs the activities of broker-dealers is Rule 3130 under the Securities Exchange Act of 1934. These rules are governed by the Financial Services Regulatory Agency (FINRA, the self-regulatory organization for broker-dealers) and essentially accomplish much the same objective of Rule 38a-1, but translates the Broker-dealer rule into the vernacular of the Broker-dealer world, referencing the role of registered principals and written supervisory procedures. Rule 3130(c) calls for the creation of a written compliance report (certification) mirroring the documentation requirements of Rule 38a-1.

The compliance rules represent a creative and innovative approach to the problem of how to address conflicts of interest within the securities industry. The compliance rules seek to create highly tailored processes, reflected by procedures that are individually crafted by each firm to cover the requirements of the federal securities laws in the innumerable situations where conflicts may arise between the need of the firm's client needs and firm structures. In that sense, the rules address a highly complex topic in a very simple framework.

It leaves the answer to the question of how to achieve compliance with the requirements of the federal securities laws within each firm's purview, as long as compliance is critically assessed and found to be both adequate and effective by an individual who is designated to make the review: the CCO. The rules might even be viewed as being fundamentally deregulatory in their effect, relying not on volumes and volumes of federal requirements, but leaving the design of ethical processes essentially in the hands of the industry that it seeks to regulate.

What could have otherwise required thousands and thousands of pages of regulation is elegantly disposed of with the requirement that a firm maintain procedures that are "reasonably designed to prevent, detect, and correct violations of federal securities laws"

---

[2] 17 CFR 270.38a-1, Compliance Procedures and Practices of Certain Investment Companies (Rule 38a-1).
[3] See Rule 38a-1(a)(1).

and that those procedures be "effective in their implementation"—as determined by a CCO who is made to care as a result of the imposition of his or her personal liability. This is the heart of securities law compliance, and once this fundamental principal is understood, the paradigm adopted by the SEC for compliance becomes perfectly clear.

II. CULTURE OF COMPLIANCE

In implementing the compliance rules, the SEC staff has often emphasized the key importance it assigns to establishing and maintaining a "culture of compliance." But what are the attributes of a culture of compliance?

Most compliance professionals would probably agree that the primary distinguishing element of firms that have a strong culture of compliance is that the rules that govern their activities are not read with an eye toward limiting these rules to their minimal applicability but are looked at in light of the purpose they are trying to achieve.

In this vein, many of the biggest compliance failures of our generation—including the failure of Enron—were executed by individuals who claimed to believe that they were operating within the letter of the law. However, judging by the collapse of the firm and the misconduct that later came to light, one could fairly suspect that these individuals had totally lost sight of the spirit of what the law intended to achieve. The requirements that had been lost in translation were often encapsulated by innocuous phrases like "disclosures that fairly represent," or references to "other material exposures" that allow certain discretion in interpretation but are very unforgiving if abused. A firm with a strong culture of compliance demands a response not just to the question asking, "What rule does this break?" but "Is this action fair to our clients and properly reflect our fiduciary obligation to put their interests before our own?"

Relationship of Ethics and a Culture of Compliance

A compliance function that elevates its mission from working to ensure that the staff is "following the rules" to working to build a culture that emphasizes its ethical duties to clients, shareholders and each other, is a firm that is more likely to have a strong culture of compliance.

An analogy in this regard may help make the point. On a ship, the role of compliance (in its narrowest sense), could be viewed as the role of the night watchman, who periodically checks whether the watertight doors are shut, the running lights are on, and the sound of the engine seems right as he makes his rounds, testing that everything is working as it should. Risk management mans the crow's nest, dutifully scanning the horizon for icebergs, ensuring the course is free of imminent danger, and ethics is the role of the captain, steering the ship to a point on the horizon. The engines could run just so, the lights all be blazing, no icebergs in sight—but if the captain lacks an ethical compass, the purpose of the business could be money laundering, facilitating the work of a drug cartel or identity theft—and no person attracted to the role of compliance could countenance his energies turned to that result.

Elevating the compliance function to have impact on the direction that the ship is steered is very important to each of us, and the challenge becomes how we gain the influence in the firm in which we work so that the role of compliance is not just that of the night watchman, but is that of the navigator, advising the captain how to steer the ship. In a firm with a strong culture of compliance, the CCO is not just the night watchman, but a "trusted adviser" to the captain. It is the single most important component of a successful compliance program.

Supervisory Buy-in

Another attribute of a firm with a strong culture of compliance is how deeply the supervisors within an organization, from the chief executive officer (CEO) downward, view the compliance mission as their own mission, as opposed to a series of requirements to be fulfilled by a Compliance Department or a CCO.

As will be discussed below, a strong supervisory structure is the first line of defense with respect to the implementation of compliance requirements. If the firm's supervisors don't grasp this duty and communicate the importance of compliance clearly, their direct reports will never value compliance because they will not be rewarded for the energy they take toward maintaining good compliance practices or punished if they fail in their efforts to achieve it. Supervisory "buy-in" to the mission of compliance is critical because the compliance professional, who has no direct supervisory responsibilities outside of a very limited sphere, must lead by influence. Without the buy-in of a firm's supervisory structure, he or she will not have the seniority and authority to fulfill the compliance function.

Attitudes Toward Controls

One of the most telling attributes of a culture of compliance is a firm's attitude toward controls.

When probed, very few people will hold themselves out as being unethical. The compliance professional who tries to distinguish him- or herself as having the "moral high ground" ethically will probably be disliked reasonably quickly. In a world where the people feel themselves to be acting ethically, a real question exists as to whether they will be accepting of the need for control structures that they might not view as being entirely necessary. That's to say that if "our people" would never cheat the system—frontrunning, acceptance of significant personal gifts from vendors, improper allocations—why implement "cumbersome" control practices? By and large, in that context, the controls can be viewed as just a "waste of time."

If, on the other hand, the firm accepts the notion that even if no one on its staff would ever knowingly abuse the process, the industry as a whole does need the controls, it is an important acknowledgment that supports a culture of compliance. Because it is impossible to call out where a problem may exist in the industry at any point in time, the controls must represent a communal standard that should exist across the board.

Thus, an attribute of a strong culture of compliance is the knowledge that the controls are necessary, not for any perceived problem within the firm, but as a reflection of the fact that the industry as a whole is subject to very real conflicts of interest, and even if employees know that they would not "cave in" to the pressures of a conflict of interest, that the industry needs these controls as a whole and that they exist for a larger good. Thus, the attitude toward controls itself is an important indicator of the firm's culture of compliance.

III. TONE AT THE TOP

Because achieving a culture of compliance depends on achieving buy-in from the various levels of management within a firm to maximize the compliance influence, that level of supervisory support is most effectively achieved when the message comes from the top of the firm. Thus, a strong message regarding the importance of compliance, when it comes from the highest level of the firm, is highly prized by all compliance professionals. But what is it that the CEO, chairman of the board or president of a company must do to set the right "tone at the top?"

Public Support of Compliance Goals

First and foremost, explicit public support of the goals and objectives of compliance by the highest level of management of the firm is essential. There must be no doubt in the minds of the leaders (or rank-and-file) of the firm that compliance is important to each level of management of the firm and that forwarding the firm's compliance program is equivalent to forwarding the CEO's own personal agenda for the firm.

There must be no doubt that as the ultimate manager of the firm, the CEO views the compliance program as the *firm's* compliance program. That is to say, that the program is not viewed as being the goal solely of the Compliance Department or, worse still, the goal solely of the CCO. Achieving the goal of the compliance program, as laid out by CCO, should be viewed as a goal of the firm—a goal that the success or failure of the firm might be measured by.

This type of support can take a fair amount of coordination to achieve. As will be discussed below, the compliance professional must create a clear vision and proposal for what the firm's compliance program should be. The compliance professional must present it to the leadership of the firm (not just the head of the firm) to assure all stakeholders that the plan is viable and deserves the support of management. They must create the opportunity for the firm's CEO to know that the plan has the support of the management team, and with that, give the CEO the comfort to support it whole-heartedly.

This type of management buy-in may take one or many rounds of back-and-forth negotiation to achieve, but it is well worth the effort, as it creates the environment necessary for the CEO to cautiously (at first) claim the compliance program as their own and go forward and endorse the importance of the compliance effort.

Public Support of Compliance Professionals

Like any of the people who directly or indirectly report to the CEO, he or she will not always agree with decisions of the firm's compliance professionals. However, a public disagreement with compliance can model a behavior that suggests that the CEO does not necessarily share the compliance goals being put forward.

Where a public rebuke is warranted, a strong tone at the top delivers a message that although a particular decision might have been executed poorly, the goal of promoting compliance should not suffer, and thus the compliance professional should redouble their efforts to achieve the plan and not allow a "poorly executed" decision to impact the need to continue to move forward. When a message delivered by the CEO impacts the firm's communal view of compliance, a strong compliance professional uses that as a teaching opportunity to help management understand how to reinforce the compliance mission.

Incorporating Compliance Goals Into the Firm's Mission Statement

One way for management to impact the way that a firm views compliance is the incorporation of compliance goals into the mission statement of the firm.

Reinforcement of the values of the firm relating to "strong ethical standards" and "integrity" or dealing with clients "fairly and honestly" can seem noncontroversial and innocent when added to the statement, but can be useful points of reference when passions become inflamed over particular issues that arise from time to time. It keeps in easy view those values that the compliance professional can leverage at important junctures.

If the opportunity presents itself to incorporate compliance goals into the mission statement of the firm, it should not be missed.

Compliance Goals and Compensation Incentives

One of the strongest statements of the importance of compliance within an organization is the inclusion among the goals and objectives of each person in his or her annual performance review process of a deliverable reflecting the employee's attitude toward fulfillment of compliance requirements.

Nothing speaks to working people as strongly as hitting them in the "pocketbook." Having an explicit goal that relates to procedures that employees must comply with, procedures that they must fulfill as supervisors, the attitude that they communicate to others regarding the importance of compliance and their ability to identify and properly respond to compliance exceptions, is a powerful statement of the firm's emphasis on having a strong culture of compliance.

Compliance goals cause supervisors to have conversations regarding compliance with their direct reports on an annual basis, and perhaps more importantly, it gives a compliance professional a reason to provide supervisors with useful input and feedback regarding their direct reports. Goal setting is a process vehicle that emphasizes the importance of compliance and where it can be had. It is a mark of an organization with a superior "tone at the top."

When you take a job as a CCO, probing management about the firm's attitude toward incorporating these compliance goals into the annual performance review process is desirable. It sends a strong message about how you feel compliance should be integrated into the management process of the firm, and is a moment when you may have significant leverage to make changes to a firm's processes.

Repetition

Repetition of the compliance message itself is a strong indicator of the strength of the firm's tone at the top.

Any propagandist knows that the more you say something, the more apt people are to believe that the opinion expressed is true. Compliance goals are not exempt from this truism. The more that management says that compliance with firm procedures is a priority for the firm, the more likely it is that the staff will "drink the Kool-Aid."

Repetition of the compliance message is also a useful tool when firm representatives answer SEC examination questions regarding the tone at the top. A file collecting the CEO's presentations, comments, emails, and other communications espousing the importance of compliance goals is strong evidence that the compliance message at a firm is heartfelt and real, not window dressing created for the needs of a moment.

Repeated messaging is also a form of protection that the compliance professional can offer the firm's CEO. It is his or her "insurance policy" that when executives were called to support compliance, they were right there and gave their Compliance Department the tools they needed to be successful. This repetition of the compliance message is not only for the firm's benefit, but for the personal benefit of the CEO. It protects executives from the charge that they were ambivalent toward the importance of the firm's control processes or that they did not understand the example they needed to portray. The compliance professional can use this self-interest to help the firm's leadership understand how this compliance goal can be important to them personally.

Tone at the top and culture of compliance are two of the basic underpinnings that help to create the right environment for the compliance message at a firm to be well-received and grow strong. It serves as fertile soil for the compliance message. With this ground prepared with the help of management, the compliance professional works to set the foundation of the framework of the three basic requirements of the compliance rules.

Basic Requirements of the Compliance Rules

Compliance rules are distinguished by certain core requirements that are fundamental to the creation of a compliance program whether you operate a broker-dealer, an investment adviser or a mutual fund. These fundamental elements are (a) written procedures that are adequate and effective; (b) a review or report on the firm's compliance program; and (c) a CCO who is personally liable for known but undisclosed issues.[4] Each of these fundamental elements will be discussed in turn will be discussed in turn.

IV. WRITTEN PROCEDURES

The most fundamental element of the compliance rules revolves around a requirement that a firm adopt procedures that are (1) adequate, or "reasonably designed to prevent, detect, and correct violations of the applicable federal securities laws;" and (2) are effective in their implementation.[5]

But what's the practical difference between "adequacy" and "effectiveness" from the standpoint of the work that a CCO needs to accomplish? Understanding the answer to this simple question is fundamental to fulfilling the compliance role, and may be most quickly and effectively answered by using a simple analogy.

Procedures are adequate if they are the right "tool for the job." Adequacy looks to whether the control process that you have put in place—scaled up or down to take into account the complexity of your firm—is up to the challenge presented to mitigate potential conflicts of interest, meet regulatory concerns and requirements, and provide supervisors with appropriate guidance regarding how to exercise their discretion. It reflects the needs of the task at hand: if you need a hammer, you can't do the job with a screwdriver.

The question of whether that tool is "effective," is a question that strikes a different chord. Issues of effectiveness emphasize the analysis of whether the tool (even assuming that it was the right tool for the job) is working as expected. Thus, an adequate and effective procedure is the right tool, and the knowledge that that tool is operating as it should makes you know it is adequate and effective.

How does developing effective procedures work? It really depends on the nature of the job you are trying to do. If, for example, you wanted to mow a lawn and that lawn really amounted to nothing more than a small patch of grass, an old-fashioned rotating blade push lawnmower might be all that was called for. If you had acres and acres of grass to

---

[4] *See* Rule 206(4)-7 under the Investment Advisers Act of 1940 for investment advisers (17 CFR 275.206(4)-7), Rule 38a-1 under the Investment Company Act of 1940 for mutual funds (17 CFR 270.38a-1), and FINRA Rule 3130 under the Securities Exchange Act of 1934 for broker-dealers.

[5] In Rule 38a-1(a)(1), the fund must adopt procedures that are "reasonably designed to prevent violations of enumerated federal securities Laws." These procedures are approved by the mutual fund's board in Rule 38a-1(a)(2), and in Rule 38a-1(a)(3), the annual report is designated as a review of the "effectiveness of implementation."

mow, a large tractor, with a seat, gas engine, and rotating blades might be the order of the day, and choosing the right tool is only the first step. That tool has to work. If the bearings have fallen out of the push mower, the blades won't turn. If you turn the key of the tractor, and nothing happens, you're sunk. It has to be the right tool, *and* it has to work. Adequacy and effectiveness: Those are what a CCO should seek in a firm's compliance procedures. Let's take each one of these concepts in turn.

Adequacy

In the parlance of the SEC, "adequate" procedures are procedures that are "reasonably designed to prevent, detect, and correct violations of applicable federal securities laws."[6] The procedure must work to accomplish this goal. But how does this work in operation?

Reasonably Designed. According to the compliance rules, a firm's procedures must be "reasonably designed to prevent, detect, and correct violations of the applicable federal securities laws." But why is the standard set to "reasonably designed" as opposed to "absolutely designed" or just "designed," and what significance does the standard of "reasonableness" in this context have?

These are very important questions, because they acknowledge that if a procedure is designed reasonably, even in the face of a violation, the compliance responsibility may have been adequately executed. Reasonableness is a key concept because compliance can't ever guarantee that people with free will who are employed by a securities firm won't intentionally or unintentionally cause violations of rules, no matter how well written those rules might be. So, the question of when, in light of a problem, a firm's compliance procedure still serves to protect the firm is a question of fundamental importance to a CCO.

SEC administrators will also generally acknowledge that there is no way for a CCO to stop business line managers and employees from breaking the rules applicable to their areas of concern. However, they would be quick to add that processes to prevent such violations can be put in place—even if you can't be sure that those processes will be 100 percent effective. Likewise, a CCO can design systems and various testing methodologies to test for and detect violations of law, and if found, correct them. But there is never a guarantee in life that all problems will be detected. But the SEC standard —reasonableness—is that our role requires that we should work hard to try.

Thus, the yardstick is not the absolute success of the procedures in preventing a violation (although this may be a piece of the puzzle), but whether they were thoughtfully designed. Part of an assessment of that design will be whether there were multiple

---

[6] Although Rule 38a-1 specifically references only the "prevention" of violations of federal securities laws, the Adopting Release of the rule broadens this mandate and calls for procedures that "prevent, detect, or correct" violations of those laws. *See* Release Nos. IA-2204; IC-26299; File No. S7-03-03 (the "Adopting Release"). Because the standard is that the procedures must be "reasonably designed," the lack of precision inherent to a standard based on "reasonableness" has preempted any discussion of whether the standard should be limited to "prevention."

checkpoints, safeguards, and other creative redundancies used within each procedure to prevent a violation, and, if a problem was still not prevented, whether it was detected quickly through thoughtfully created supervisory touch points or other separations of duties, and—after it was detected—whether there was a process employed by the firm that provoked a wholehearted effort to correct any damage that was caused. Thus, the issue is whether the prevention mechanism is robust and, if it does not prevent an issue, whether it can catch the issue quickly and resolve it. Reasonable design equals sound process.

This is a point of key importance and perhaps the greatest value a compliance person can bring to his or her firm. Even if a "bad actor" at a firm violates the federal securities laws, the procedures themselves should protect the firm from liability.

The impact of this construction of the compliance rules—seeking only that the procedures of a firm be "reasonably designed"—becomes clearest when a compliance officer assesses who may be liable for a violation. The natural progression of possible liability will be first to assess the liability of the individuals directly involved; secondly, look for failures to supervise those individuals and failures to supervise the levels of management above them; and then, to look for failures of the compliance program.

Even in the case of an intentional violation by an employee, if the procedures can be held out to be reasonably and effectively implemented, a claim of a failure of the firm's compliance program can be avoided, and as will be discussed below, so can the claims of failures to supervise. The creation of reasonably designed and effectively implemented procedures is the most effective way to prevent limited violations caused by individuals at a firm from growing into failures of the firm itself. It limits the scope of the violation to the "bad actor" and does not allow the liability to flow across the firm.

The challenge of the CCO in fulfilling this function is to effectively balance this emphasis on process on one hand while also having an eye to creativity on the other, so that the CCO is not simply a bureaucrat. The notion of how these "reasonable" redundancies, supervisory touch points, and separations of duties are put forward and incorporated in the procedures is all a matter of experience, insight, and intuition: It is a creative exercise, working with line management to understand the "art of the possible."

The successful CCO can point to the procedures in the face of a problem and fairly say, "Look, we thought about this risk—worked to avoid it—and even if someone stepped over the line, we found the damage quickly and made the injured party whole. Yes, someone may have gone 'off the ranch,' but as CCO, I can't prevent that. I can only work to see that processes that I believe to be reasonable are in place and that they have been effectively implemented."

If a CCO can say that, he or she should be able to avoid the firm's liability for the bad acts of an errant employee. This is when compliance adds the most value to the controls of a firm. It is compliance at its best.

Designating Desktop and Compliance Procedures. Although a firm has to satisfy the requirements of the compliance rules to be "adequate," are there processes in a firm that, although they need to be documented, are not necessary for compliance purposes, that is, their purpose is not to prevent, detect or correct violations of federal securities law. The question is which documents are actually "procedures" for the purposes of the compliance rules?

Clearly, there are many types of documents at a firm that are necessary to help employees understand how to do various tasks. There are manuals on how to operate systems, how to file expense reports, and even a sign over most coffee makers saying, "Turn off after 5 p.m." Which of these are the procedures that the compliance rules call on firms to maintain?

Many firms distinguish between "desktop procedures" and "compliance procedures." When designating whether a certain document is a compliance procedure, the CCO should ask whether the purpose of the procedure is to facilitate compliance with the applicable federal securities laws. In the broadest sense, all procedural documents support the goals of the federal securities laws. Even the sign over the coffee maker helps prevent fires and can be thought of (in the broadest sense) as supporting the firm's record retention requirements. Likewise, a document giving instructions on how to use the code of ethics system helps detect frontrunning, but does it help the employees running the system understand how to use their discretion or supervisory authority?

The most important practical distinction between compliance and desktop procedures is that compliance procedures:

- Will have to be tested and the results of that testing reported upward; and
- Will have to be monitored on an ongoing basis for the impact of changes in law, changes in business model, and other learnings that can be gleaned from patterns of compliance exceptions.

An incorrect designation of a procedure suggests that the Compliance Department did not think it worthy of testing, and if a problem emanates from that process, it will be a per se violation of the compliance rules.

Procedures that merely give instructions on how to use a system may have some value in maintaining smooth execution of operations, but they tend not to give much insight into whether the system (even if it is being competently used) is accomplishing its associated compliance objective. For example, the procedure regarding how to use a code of ethics system doesn't tell you much about what standards you should choose for monitoring the securities transactions of the access persons in your firm.

A key distinction between desktop procedures and compliance procedures is that any procedure that can be said to be used to mitigate conflicts of interest within a firm should be viewed as a compliance procedure that requires testing. To use any strategy that would relieve compliance from testing procedures that are used to address conflicts of interests should be fastidiously avoided because that strategy strikes at the heart of the SEC's vision in the creation of the compliance rules. Plus that strategy will almost certainly be flagged by regulators as a compliance failure if things go wrong.

Federal Securities Laws. In Rule 38a-1, procedures must be created to prevent, detect, and correct violations of the "federal securities laws," and the coverage of this term is clear because *federal securities laws* is defined in the rule. Because Rule 38a-1 is designed for mutual funds, the federal securities laws cover the various regulatory areas that may be applicable to a fund, including (1) the Investment Advisers Act of 1940; (2) the Investment Company Act of 1940; (3) the Securities Act of 1933; (4) the Securities Exchange Act of 1934; (5) the Bank Secrecy Act; (6) the Employee Retirement Income Act; (7) Title V of the Gramm-Leach-Bliley Act (regarding privacy of consumer information); and (8) the Sarbanes-Oxley Act of 2002.[7]

For investment advisers outside of the realm of managing mutual funds, the standard is a bit less clear. Although Rule 206(4)-7, on its face, relates only to the Investment Advisers Act of 1940 and not the six other acts that constitute the federal securities laws, the Advisers Act contains a code of ethics requirement under Rule 204A-1 that requires the reporting of violations of federal securities laws generally. Thus, a question may exist as to whether the broader code of ethics requirement subsumes the narrower compliance rule requirement. In other words, when an adviser's CCO tests for violations of the code of ethics requirement, must his or her review touch the broader array of federal securities laws?

Although the SEC has never availed itself of this "bootstrap" theory, a compliance officer should be mindful of the possible conflict between the two requirements, which could result in their extending their reviews beyond the confines of the Advisers Act to the other acts constituting the federal securities laws.

The Broker-dealer version of the rule seeks only that the CCO test and verify that the supervisory procedures are reasonably designed with respect to the activities of the FINRA member and its registered representatives and associated persons to achieve compliance with "applicable securities laws, regulations, and FINRA Rules." Arguably, this is the broadest provision of the three because it would touch any applicable securities law, which might be thought to go beyond the seven acts enumerated in the mutual fund version of the compliance rules. However, as a practical matter, the coverage is generally taken as being equivalent.

Use of Risk Inventories to Assess Adequacy. Developing adequate procedures as a matter of internal control processes presents unique challenges. How do you create a process to programmatically identify the procedures needed for your firm? How do you confirm that a certain set of procedures are the "right tools" to prevent, detect, and correct violations of the applicable laws? Generally speaking, the device that the industry has focused on to do this is a *gap analysis* or *risk inventory*.[8]

---

[7] See Rule 38a-1(e)(1).
[8] See Lori A. Richards, Working Towards a Culture of Compliance: Some Obstacles in the Path, National Society of Compliance Professionals 2007 Annual Meeting, Washington, DC (Oct. 18, 2007), www.sec.gov/news/speech/2007/spch101807lar.htm

A risk inventory addresses the issue of adequacy by assessing the risks and conflicts of interest confronting a particular firm, looking to which rule governs the issue and assessing whether a procedure of the firm actually exists to govern the issue. If there is no procedure to address the issue, a gap has been detected and the procedure needs to be created or enhanced.

Because the types of risks and conflicts affecting the firm can be wide ranging and difficult to identify, another best practice has developed among CCOs to take the processes of the firm and attempt to trace them through diagrams or checklists to see whether each portion of the process is covered by one of the firm's procedures. A diagram of this sort can be constructed as a type of flow chart, detailing the control points of each process of the firm: trading, custody, code of ethics reviews, reconciliations, marketing reviews, new product development, etc. Each such review seeks to identify conflicts of interest and as these conflicts are identified, the question becomes what controls exist to mitigate those conflicts? Once the risks of the firm are matched to governing procedures that are "reasonably designed to prevent, detect, and correct violations of federal securities laws," you have properly defined the scope of the firm's procedure base.

Conflicts of Interest: Follow the Money. Understanding the risks of loss and the conflicts of interest that may exist in your firm generally boils down into a familiar mantra that was made famous during the Watergate scandals of the Nixon Administration in the 1970s: "Follow the money."

The Watergate scandal, for anyone who was politically aware in the 1970s, will forever represent the granddaddy of all failure to supervise events. A scandal that ultimately caused a president to resign was broken wide open when a whistleblower from within the government approached two journalists at *The Washington Post* and told them some of the details surrounding the Republican-sponsored break in of the Democratic National Committee headquarters at the Watergate Apartments in Washington. The informer also gave details of the Nixon Administration's attempts to conceal the truth, leading to another famous mantra for compliance professionals: "The cover-up is worse than the crime."

The Nixon whistleblower (forever after known as "Deep Throat") wouldn't give *The Washington Post* journalists the complete story, but only told them to "follow the money," and eventually, the trail of money led back to President Nixon and his senior staff. Follow the money has since then stood for the notion that knowledge of financial incentives is a key element of understanding why things are structured the way they are. For a control person, such as a compliance professional, understanding when those incentives cause conflicts of interest or are otherwise at odds with a firm's stated values or ethical standards is a vital piece of the puzzle.

In the compliance context, following the money might mean fully understanding each team's bonus, salary, and other elements composing their compensation structure. It might mean understanding how vendors (and broker-dealers) are selected and what benefits might flow back to the firm by selecting one vendor over another. Soft dollar relationships can trigger this concern. It might mean understanding how the firm is compensated in various contexts and what elements of the relationship might represent a disclosable conflict between the interests of various clients.

Following the money is a time-tested prerequisite to understanding the conflicts that might exist in your firm. Without that knowledge, a compliance profession is ill-equipped to identify the issues that will govern whether the firm's procedures are adequate.

Another key learning from the Watergate scandal, "the cover-up is worse than crime," is worth a quick nod here as well. When a problem occurs, oftentimes it is an inadvertent issue or a bad choice made by a limited number of people. When a determination is made to hide something "under the carpet," invariably more people are involved; then it becomes a clearly intentional action and almost always represents a supervisory breakdown. For this reason, the Watergate cover-up, which ultimately included actions by the president of the United States, caused the downfall of the Nixon Administration and has since that time stood as a reminder of the dangers of a supervisory cover-up.

The Process of Creating a Procedure Draft. Once the process of identifying gaps is complete, there must be some form of programmatic involvement of business line managers, attorneys and compliance professionals to assess the nature of the reasonable controls required.

Generally speaking, it will be the role of the compliance professional to set out a strawman about what a reasonable control would be. The compliance officer will create the draft procedure. At times, this may instead be done by a proactive attorney or business line manager, but in the absence of such a draft, the creativity for the genesis of the document generally comes from compliance. In many ways, this is the best part of the job, because it lends itself to the greatest creativity: Should a committee be formed, or is a supervisory sign off enough? Does the task require a separation of duties among people or can it be done by a single person? Do multiple stakeholders need to formally sign off, and how and often should that sign-off be required and by whom should the output be reviewed? Addressing these needs in a creative way is what elevates the practice of compliance out of the realm of creating bureaucracy and into the creative realm necessary to truly add value to the firm.

Then these creative ideas must receive the buy-in of the other stakeholders. If the compliance person thinks a particular control is the right tool, but the attorney thinks it is more than what's necessary, and the business person thinks it's too cumbersome to implement, it's time to go back to the drawing board. It is the interplay of these three groups, working together under a management portraying a strong tone at the top that emphasizes the importance of compliance and creates the greatest likelihood that a firm's procedures will be deemed to be "adequate."

V. TESTING

The compliance rules call for a firm's procedures to be not only adequate (that is, as discussed above, reasonably designed to prevent, detect, and correct violations of federal securities laws) but also "effective in their implementation."[9] This requirement is the basis for the testing done by compliance that should be memorialized in an annual written compliance report.

There is no set requirement for how procedures should be tested, exactly what aspects of the procedures should be tested, or how often they should be tested. The fact that the written compliance report under Rule 38a-1 is required to be issued annually suggests that an ongoing recurring annual review is desirable, but even this is not required.

Types of Testing

Commonly, compliance officers recognize three types of testing: (1) transactional testing, (2) periodic testing, and (3) forensic testing.[10] Each of these will be discussed in turn.

Transactional Testing. Transactional testing (or monitoring) is testing that is done on a real-time, ongoing basis. The monitoring of trading on a daily basis would be an example of this testing type. With portfolio trading there is no tolerance for compliance violations because any purchase of securities outside of client guidelines is impermissible, and the damage caused made right generally by refunding the purchase price if the price of the security has decreased since the time of purchase. It essentially creates the potential for the creation of a put by the adviser in favor of the client. Code of ethics approvals are another example of providing ongoing, real-time approvals of permissible trading. This form of transactional testing is an effective mechanism for ensuring that individuals remain in compliance with applicable procedures and do not place their own interests in front of the interests of their clients.

Periodic Testing. For the items that don't require ongoing monitoring, some level of periodic review is still required to be able to assert—as the compliance rules require—that the firm's procedures are "effective in their implementation." The issue is what should be tested and how often those controls should be put through the discipline of testing.

Forensic Testing. Senior officials of the SEC staff have time and time again emphasized the need for firms to engage in a regimen of forensic testing to complement the monitoring and other forms of transactional and periodic testing that a firm might do. So what is forensic testing? How does it differ from other forms of testing?

Forensic testing is a form of testing that uses inferences and other indirect information to understand when a compliance program's controls are not acting as they should. For example, testing that identifies disparities in investment returns between clients

---

[9] Rule 38a-1(a)(3) and Rule 206(4)-7(b).
[10] *See* US Compliance Consultants, http://uscomplianceconsultants.com/3-types-of-compliance-testing/

may suggest improper allocation issues, and disparities between the personal accounts of portfolio traders and their clients allow a reviewer to infer that the trader may be misappropriating investment opportunities or front running. In either case, this type of forensic testing would point the compliance professional toward potential issues and allow him or her to make further inquiries to follow up on potential issues. Endless varieties of forensic testing can be designed, but they all share the attribute of testing indirectly for elements that the testers are seeking to assess.

What to Test

After going through the process of constructing a risk inventory that identifies the conflicts of interest in your firm, assesses the supervisory needs that call for documentation, and reviews other applicable regulatory requirements, a CCO should have a reasonably good idea about what procedures would be necessary to fulfill the requirement of adequacy. The next question is how to test them for effectiveness.

More than anything else, the question of whether a procedure is effective is one of whether the essential control points within that procedure are operating as anticipated. So how do you identify those essential control points that should be tested for effectiveness?

You first need a clear idea of what the procedure is attempting to accomplish. In this vein, many procedures are drafted to begin with a summary "purpose" section. As a preliminary matter, finding the controls that support this purpose can be as simple as going through each procedure document with a yellow highlighter to find the "testable" items. If after doing this, you find that some elements of the purpose have no controls, the exercise was a good one because it has helped you understand whether more is necessary to meet the standard of adequacy: prevention, detection, and correction of violations.

For example, a single procedure document might have three controls—or ten— that you deem to be "essential." A firm that has several dozen procedure documents constituting its "compliance manual" might be confronted with the need to test several hundred essential controls, or more, depending on the size and complexity of the firm. Once those controls are identified, the issue then turns to how often each control requires testing.

How Often to Test

The adopting release to the compliance rules calls upon the CCO to construct a compliance program that is nimble and responsive to events around him or her. Specifically, it emphasizes a program that reports annually regarding (1) changes in law, (2) changes in business model, and (3) patterns of compliance exceptions.[11] Let's take each one of these in turn, because understanding this requirement is key to knowing how often to subject your procedures to review.

---

[11] *See* the Adopting Release to Rule 38a-1 and Rule 206(4)-7, Rel. Nos. IA-2204; IC-26299; File No. S7-03-03, at Section II(B)(1).

Changes in Law. Changes in law, in this context, should be considered very broadly. It would include not only actual changes to the rules underlying the federal securities laws, but the guidance given in the proposing and adopting releases supporting those changes. It would include enforcement actions (hopefully always against other firms), whether successful or not, as they give insight into what types of activities the SEC might pursue and how regulators might view related, but slightly different, fact patterns. The notion of a change in law should take into consideration relevant SEC no action letters and exemption requests that might be applicable to a firm and the indications of how the staff might respond to related fact patterns. It should also respond to available reconnaissance regarding SEC examination requests and follow ups.

But perhaps most importantly, the notion of changes in law would apply to the changes that relate to your own firm: SEC deficiency letters and your responses, enforcement proceedings against your firm (if any), responses to whistleblower complaints, and any other communications in which your firm has made a factual undertaking to the commission staff suggesting how your policies and procedures are being implemented. Each of these items forms an important trigger in assessing how often to review the essential control contained in your firm's procedures.

Changes in Business Model. Changes in business models can arise from many different sources. They can result from the pressures that arise out of the growth of a firm or a firm's reduction in force. They can surface in the introduction of new products or the termination of product lines. They can develop even when a product line never changes but is marketed to new audiences. Changes can sprout with the employment of new mechanisms of marketing. In other words, a change in business model can emerge from any modification of product line, marketing techniques, or client base. They changes are a broad reading of the factors that may precipitate a requirement to modify the procedure's governing your firm's activities.

Changes in Patterns of Compliance Activity. The third element that the SEC recognizes as a spur to the need to revise compliance procedures arises out of results of the compliance program itself: the recognition of patterns of compliance exceptions that suggest that the monitoring regimen must be revised to tighten up the controls to change behaviors internally. Examples of this element might arise from testing that suggests that a certain supervisor needs to have more formalized guidance or information to be considered in his or her decision making, trading patterns that suggest that blackout windows on person trading need to be extended, or patterns of violations that need greater internal emphasis and sanctions to communicate the importance of avoiding such violations in the future. Even minor compliance violations should spur the question of whether a procedure needs to be changed.

The adopting release to the compliance rules suggested that the firm's response to these types of changes should be reported on annually in the CCO's compliance report.[12] Thus, the testing that looks at the firm's essential control points should at least mirror

---

[12] *Id.*

this annual review requirement. However, as discussed above, although some forms of testing are transactional and should be done on an ongoing basis, others may warrant weekly, monthly, quarterly, or annual testing. The issue of how often to test for the changes referenced above and other violations ultimately is a reflection of the degree of risk each such matter presents to the firm. Thus the risk inventory, which is a key element of assessing the adequacy of the firm's procedures, can also be the touch point for assessing whether the risk profile of a particular process or essential control warrants testing more frequently than annually.

Updating Procedures

Understanding when the impact of these testing results reaches a critical mass requiring revisions to procedures is more of an art than a science. This understanding requires the input and integration of three different disciplines within a firm to accomplish: the legal staff, compliance, and the applicable business lines. The creation of a formalized (or, if you work in a small firm environment, informal) Procedure Review Committee or a Compliance Committee should periodically gather together to assess whether changes in the environment have created a need to revise individual procedures to respond to the changes.

Meetings for these constituencies to review each of the firm's procedures can be done on a rotating basis according to a procedure review calendar. All procedures should be scheduled for a periodic update, and industry best practices suggest that that update cycle should not extend beyond a year for any required procedure. The bottom line is as long as there is a process and methodology for how you have decided to address this issue, as long as you have reasonably designed a program that functions to respond to change and your program reviews each procedure's effectiveness of implementation, you have met professional standards. The selection of a reasonable methodology is left to the discretion of each firm: it is a form of self-regulation that is a fundamental premise of a compliance regimen.

However, that having been said, the closer a procedure gets to not having been reviewed for a full year, most compliance professionals would probably agree that the less likely it is that the procedure is still up-to-date. The passage of time itself at a certain point becomes a factor regarding whether it is reasonable to consider a procedure as being current. Even if no change is made, the procedure should still be reviewed and the review date recorded. If no such review is made, such a procedure is generally referred to within the industry is being "stale."

Leveraging the Testing of Other Control Groups

One of the issues faced by any compliance organization in a larger firm, and even some smaller firms, is that they are not the only entity in the organization that is responsible for "testing." For example, operations units will routinely engage in some degree of exception testing, audit functions will engage in "deep dive" reviews of particular issues, and the risk management area will often conduct stress testing of various types on portfolio holdings to ascertain how the portfolio might respond under certain scenarios.

The key factor here for compliance is to work carefully to see that none of the testing that they are doing is duplicative with the testing being done by other control groups. When the compliance rules were first issued, one of the most biting comments regarding the new testing regimen of the rules was that they duplicated the work that other internal organizations were doing. However, this perspective was quickly discredited. The compliance rules do not necessarily call on the Compliance Department to do all the testing required to assess the adequacy and effectiveness of a firm's procedures, only to conduct an annual review or create an annual report that includes an assessment of adequacy and effectiveness of implementation.

Thus, coordination is essential in determining who will test what and how the findings of that testing will be funneled into compliance to be reflected as part of the annual report (or review). For example, the Internal Audit Department may make an assessment of which areas that department will review at the beginning of the year. To the extent that the compliance group has no reason to believe that the audit team will execute their reviews in anything but a professional manner, compliance may rely on that review and turn its attention elsewhere rather than conducting a redundant review of the same areas.

Thus, it is important to ascertain early in the compliance review process which other control functions are "claiming" functional areas to review, and to steer clear of "doubling up" on the review of a single area in a single year. Not only would such a review yield little additional value, it would likely be destructive. The group targeted for multiple reviews would likely to balk at the added burden imposed by two uncoordinated reviews that might offer little marginal improvement to their internal processes. The broad-based compliance review of processes should therefore be molded around the "deeper dives" that may be conducted by other controls groups who may occupy the same regulatory space.

Three Lines of Defense

In the context of leveraging the other control functions that exist within a firm, it is often commonly said that securities firms have "three lines of defense." In the broadest sense, these are:

- The supervisory structure;
- The compliance structure; and
- The more specialized control functions, which tend to grow more and more robust as a firm grows larger.[13]

---

[13] Carlo V. di Florio, Director, Office of Compliance Inspections and Examinations, Address at the Private Equity International Private Fund Compliance Forum, New York, NY (May 2, 2012).

These more specialized control functions include internal audit, accounting, operations, legal staff, and "trade support." Understanding this model can be useful in helping the business lines understand the role of compliance and each of their own roles in a firm's control structure.

Supervision: The First Line of Defense. The first line of defense at any firm is the firm's supervisory structure. This is because, as a matter of Human Resource Department requirements, this supervisory structure is empowered with the responsibility to set goals and objectives for the employees reporting to them and to assess the quality of the work accomplished toward completing those goals. A necessary outgrowth of this authority is the "carrot and stick" of the power to hire, fire, and award or withhold compensation.

A strong supervisory structure, reinforced by compliance as a second line of defense (discussed below), offers other benefits as well. Supervisors who understand their obligations to maintain regulatory requirements can be the most important exponents of a strong compliance program within a firm. It is far more important that a supervisor be an advocate of measuring up to compliance standards than of merely looking to a Compliance Department to apply the procedures. This broader view of supervisory duties, one including a compliance call-to-action, diffuses compliance responsibilities throughout a firm and underlines the axiom of all firms that have a strong culture of compliance: "Compliance is everyone's responsibility." This disbursement of compliance duties within a firm is a far more effective way of communicating the compliance message than having the single voice of a Compliance Department stand behind the firm's compliance procedures.

This disbursed structure can be more intuitive to supervisors in the broker-dealer world, because the supervisory requirements in the world of Series 7 Registered Representatives and Series 24 Principals have a very explicit compliance component associated within the professionals' roles. Under the licensing regimen of FINRA, supervisors are trained to understand the compliance components of their role, and the maintenance of their license depends on it.

Failures to follow compliance practices by a supervisor will often trigger questions of "failures to supervise," and a regulatory examiner will quickly attempt to take a compliance failure at one level of a firm and move up the supervisory food chain. As discussed below, the only defense that the SEC recognizes in this vein also emphasizes the importance of the using of reasonably designed procedures under the supervisor's oversight to avoid the claim of a failure to supervise. Thus, the first stop for implementing compliance at any firm resides with this first line of defense: supervisory oversight.

The Compliance Department: The Second Line of Defense. The compliance emphasis on the administration of procedures is designed, as a regulatory matter, to support the supervisory function of a firm. By facilitating the creation of reasonably designed procedures, the compliance role works to protect line managers from claims that they have failed to supervise their staff.

The SEC in its panoply of rules has never defined "good" supervision. In fact, there is no rule even saying when a failure to supervise exists. The Investment Advisers Act does, however, in Section 203(e)(6), outline a defense to regulatory claims of a failure to supervise.[14]

Rule 203(e)(6) creates a safe harbor of sorts if: (a) a supervisor is acting pursuant to reasonable procedures, (b) has a system for applying them, and (c) knows of no red flags that exist that would otherwise spur the supervisor to action.

This standard is fully consistent with (and served as a model for) the requirements of the compliance rules. As such, it presents an important opportunity to show how the businessperson's supervisory needs mesh with compliance objectives. From a compliance standpoint, the development of procedures that are reasonably designed to prevent, detect and correct violations of federal securities law, are from a businessperson's standpoint, the same tools that he or she needs to avoid supervisory liability.

Using this common objective, the creation of these procedures can be presented as the fulfillment of a business need, and the businessperson can look at the support being provided by the compliance professional as being absolutely necessary for his or her own personal protection, as well as the protection of the firm. In this, compliance and the business are "sitting on the same side of the table," and share a common need.

The commonality of objectives between the supervisory line and compliance reinforces compliance as the firm's "second line of defense" (as discussed below) behind the firm's supervisors, and positions compliance as the best ally that the business line will ever have against a determination that they have failed in supervising the functions entrusted to them. With this assertion, most businesspeople will see the wisdom of supporting the compliance function, if only out of recognition of their own enlightened self-interest, to create a "shield" against claims of their failure to supervise a function.

A well-placed reminder that working to create reasonably designed procedures to personally protect the supervisor is a key element of the compliance mission can be just the argument needed to sway the business line toward working to keep the firm's procedures current. This is because the converse of this argument is also true. When a procedure doesn't track the supervisor's actions or isn't reasonably constructed, it stands as a dangling "sword," waiting at any moment to fall and injure the line manager it is supposed to support. A regulatory examiner could use the failure to follow or update a procedure (even if it somehow did not meet the business need) prior to claiming a failure to supervise by the line manager. The regulator will attempt to follow flawed procedures and supervisory practices "up the food chain" supervisor to supervisor as high in the supervisory structure of the firm as possible. In this sense, the procedures act much like the dividers that divide the oil tanks in an oil tank farm—preventing a fire in one from spilling out to the others and engulfing the whole facility in a conflagration.

---

[14] *See* 15 USC Section 80b-3(e)(6).

In one context, the procedure is the line managers' shield against claims that they failed to properly supervise their functions and in the other, a sword to be used against the managers to show that they have not properly fulfilled their role. This paradigm can be used to show the business professional that the help of the compliance professional is essential to the success of line management and compliance is operating at its best when the supervisors using a procedure understand that compliance does them a great service by facilitating the creation of procedures that can help the supervisors avoid a failure to supervise.

Internal Audit and Other Control Functions: The Third Line of Defense. If business line supervisors within a firm are the firm's first line of defense, and Compliance Department activities the second, are there other lines of defense? The answer is yes. Legal groups, accounting control groups, operations reconciliation groups and external counsel, auditors, trade control groups, and consultants can all fill specialized control functions. But at larger firms, the control group that stands out with a mission that is strikingly similar to the mission of compliance is the Internal Audit Department.

Like compliance, an internal audit team is tasked with testing the effectiveness of certain controls. Unlike compliance, there is generally no regulatory requirement that this review be undertaken. So the question becomes, with two groups occupying a similar space, how do they effectively coordinate and coexist?

The key here is a close reading of the regulatory requirement governing compliance. While the CCO is held to a standard of reviewing the adequacy of the firm's entire compliance control structure annually and testing the effectiveness of implementation, most audit groups annually determine the scope of their reach reasonably narrowly and schedule the particular reviews that they believe are necessary for them to conduct. Thus while compliance is charged with reviewing the entire control structure across a broad front, the auditors characteristically take deep dives into particular topics of concern. One is more shallow but far broader; the other is far more concentrated and deep.

The key element for compliance to successfully coexist with the Internal Audit Departments is close coordination. Best practices here would suggest periodic coordination meetings between the chief audit officer and CCO to share thinking on where control lapses might be. Whereas the Audit Department wishes to review certain topics that could also be reviewed by compliance, it is perfectly reasonable for the compliance person to use these meetings as due diligence to build comfort that the audit team will do a thorough job of testing that area and their tests prove reliable. There is nothing in the compliance rules that says that compliance must do all the testing itself. Only that the CCO must be satisfied that the procedures are effective, which can be determined on the basis of an audit report.

Likewise, the meetings with compliance can form an important feedback loop for internal auditors. A heads up from compliance about where issues seem to be developing can focus the auditor toward much more productive work in the coming cycle.

Similarly, calling on the resources of the audit team in this way is a way of leveraging existing control resources available to assist in the compliance mission.

This positive outcome, like many other facets of the business arena, depends on building trust. The Audit Department generally reports up through a separate supervisory line. To the extent that audit and compliance representatives become competitors in the same space, little coordination will be possible, and the win-win of leveraging resources will yield to a zero-sum game. Ongoing meetings and open conversations in periodic meetings help to avoid this result. With so many processes to test, there's little real need to fight over what to test; the goal should be to make space for all and leverage off of each other's successes.

Viewing the SEC as a Fourth Line of Defense. Avoiding preventable client/investor losses is the goal of all control structures. From time-to-time, it's important to remind ourselves that all internal control structures are aligned with the SEC in this result.

At times, however, the industry is less than graceful in achieving that result, and "bad apples" in our community can deceive their SEC examiners. At other times, the SEC is too strident in fulfilling its mission at the expense of an overwhelmingly honest industry. At the end of the day, most compliance professionals hope they never lose sight of the fact that they would far rather have an SEC examiner find an issue than endanger the investments of those who rely on us for the safety of their hard-won savings and investments. Occasionally, though, we have to be reminded of that just as the SEC may have to be reminded to tone down its rhetoric.

Each of the compliance rules has three common elements: adequate and effective procedures, an annual review, and a CCO. Now that we have reviewed the best practices surrounding the creation and maintenance of procedures, we'll turn our attention to the second requirement: an annual review or written report.

VI. ANNUAL REVIEW OR WRITTEN REPORT

The second of the three basic requirements of the compliance rules calls for an annual review or report that must be provided by the CCO and, at a minimum (in the mutual fund version of the rule) that must address the operation of the policies and procedures of each service provider and each material compliance matter that has occurred since the issuance of the previous annual report.[15] But although the mutual fund version of the rule calls for a written report, the investment adviser formulation of the rule calls only for an annual "review," without requiring that the review be actually written.[16] The broker-dealer standard is similar to the mutual fund formulation, seeking that the designated principal (the CCO) must submit to member's senior management no less than annually a report detailing the member's system of supervisory controls, the summary of the test results and significant identified exceptions, and any additional

---

[15] Rule 38a-1(a)(4)(iii).
[16] Rule 206(4)-7(b).

or amended supervisory procedures created in response to the test results.[17] Let's take each of these three different standards in turn.

Investment Company Act Standard

The Investment Company Act version of the compliance rules, Rule 38a-1, offers the clearest guidance regarding how the annual report should be documented and to whom it should be made. Rule 38a-1 calls for a written report to be delivered at least annually to the fund's Board of Directors.[18] The key elements are the fact that the report must be written and then distributed to the board, which then includes the board's counsel.

Service Providers and Other Similar Entities. The Investment Company Act standard demands that the activities of not only the mutual fund be reported to the fund's Board of Directors, but also certain enumerated "service providers" including the fund's: (a) investment advisers (including any subadvisers); (b) principal underwriters; (c) fund administrators; and (d) transfer agents.[19] In the Adopting Release to Rule 28a-1, the SEC took pains to note that although the term *service provider* refers only to a fund's advisers, principal underwriters, administrators, and transfer agents, the commission did not consider itself to be lessening a fund's obligation to consider compliance as part of its decision to employ other entities, such as pricing services, auditors, and custodians.[20] Thus, although inclusion of the activities of these other entities in the compliance report is discretionary, it is not beyond the scope of what an examiner, or a fund board, might find desirable.

This question often leads, especially in a post-Madoff regulatory environment, to whether the annual compliance report should include a review of the policies, procedures, and activities of the fund's custodian. Although an inclusion about the custodian is discretionary on the part of the fund's CCO, given the importance of the soundness of the controls offered by the custodian, going an extra distance to include an assessment of the custodian's controls carries certain logic. In most cases, this question will be settled by counsel for the independent trustees of the fund, who will make their own feeling known regarding whether they consider a Compliance review of the Custodian to be important. The board will almost universally follow their counsel's logic, and the CCO will find his or her hand all but forced to include it.

But regardless of which service providers are included, there is a bigger issue that exists with respect to the fund's service providers. The question is, especially when these service providers are unaffiliated to the advisers, how a compliance professional can have access to adequate information to give the same robust review to a service provider that the compliance person gives his or her own internal control structures? The answer to this question can be found in guidance known as the ICI Report issued by

---

[17] FINRA Rule 3130(b) and Rule 3130(c).
[18] Rule 38a-1(a)(3).
[19] *Id.*
[20] Adopting Release of Rule 38a-1(2)(3), at note 7.

the SEC in response to an inquiry by the Investment Company Institute shortly after the compliance rules were adopted.[21]

The ICI Report gives important guidance regarding the level of review necessary for a service provider under Rule 38a-1. Specifically, it addresses the question of the degree of review required by a CCO of a service provider in the fund's annual compliance report by stating that a compliance professional looking at service providers may rely on "summaries" they provide in making the CCO's assessment of the service providers' policies and procedures.

Although the degree of detail provided to the recipient of the summary is generally in large part under the control of the service provider, these summaries must be robust enough to provide basic insights into:

- The adequacy and effectiveness of the service provider's procedures;
- Any material compliance matters that might have occurred at the service provider; and
- The resolution of any discovered issues.

Without these basic elements, additional information must be requested.

In addition to summaries provided by the service provider, most CCOs value the opportunity to actually visit a service provider and get a "feel" for its operations. It bears saying that if a firm relies on a summary, but could have easily seen that that elements of the summary were untrue by taking the time to visit the service provider's principal place of business, the CCO's review will likely have been considered to be inadequate.

Reasonable people will differ as to how often a service provider should be visited. Although some firms may hold out for periods of up to two years between visits (longer periods are unusual), others may seek to visit their service providers more frequently than annually, although this is unusual as well. Most CCOs attempt to maintain an annual schedule of visits to compliment the annual need to issue a revised compliance report.

It should also be recognized that not all service providers need be visited on the same schedule. For example, a mutual fund may wish to visit its transfer agent on a biennial basis, but visit subadvisers annually. A subadviser that has issues that, in the reviewer's opinion, need to be addressed may be visited more frequently for progress reports. Although there is no rule governing these activities, it is fair to say that any distinctions between service providers in the review process should be susceptible to a clear and cogent explanation to a regulatory examiner, mutual fund board member, or management.

Due Diligence Process. It is important that the service provider's reviewer develop an effective process when conducting due diligence. Commonly, the due diligence process should commence with a letter to the provider setting expectations for the coming review. A coordination call to kick off the review process is also much appreciated by the

---

[21] Investment Company Institute Report, Assessing the Adequacy and Effectiveness of a Fund's Compliance Policies and Procedures ("ICI Report") (Dec. 2005), at page 12.

target provider, and if this step is missed for any reason, the service provider should not be reluctant to initiate contact and work with the reviewer to outline a timetable and deliverables that will be sought in the review. Proactivity in this regard by the service provider will often be appreciated.

Prior to an on-site visit, the reviewer will often submit a written questionnaire to the service provider. A proactive reviewer will not only use a previous year's questionnaire (if available) as a starting point, but will solicit questions from other internal groups outside of the Compliance Department to seek input regarding service issues and conflicts that compliance professionals may not know.

Characteristically, the questionnaire will drill down on the service provider's compliance processes, key procedures, conflicts of interest, relationships to other firms, supervisory structures, and personnel issues. It will seek insight as to "how things work" at the service provider and who is responsible for what. It will also seek information as to how changes in law, changes in business model, and compliance concerns have been addressed since the last visit. In addition, a written questionnaire to a service provider will also generally ask that certain written materials be provided. These documents can include:

- *Annual compliance reports.* With the exception of the requirement that a broker-dealer, investment adviser, or mutual fund share its own annual report with management, a mutual fund's Board of Directors, and SEC examiners, there is no regulatory requirement that a service provider share its annual report with anyone else. However, such an obligation can be imposed by contract. For example, a mutual fund may incorporate terms into a contract with a subadviser that make the continued use of that entity conditional on an agreement to provide a copy of a subadviser's annual report. Thus,
    - When a service provider is unwilling to give a copy of its annual report (as is often the case), there are several common fallbacks that may serve as proxies to satisfy this request. Often, the service provider will be willing to give the due diligence reviewer a written summary of the annual report with a focus on any material compliance matters that are contained in the report and include a summary of the outcome of any deficiencies noted by the SEC in its most recent examination,
    - At times, if the service provider is not willing to provide this summary in writing, it can be presented orally, giving the reviewing CCO an opportunity to confirm the oral statements with their own written summary, which can be sent back to the service provider, and
    - Another work around can be had if a service provider is comfortable allowing the due diligence reviewer to review its annual report "on site" in a way that it cannot be reproduced. The idea in this context is that it is not objectionable that the report be read by the due diligence reviewer, as long as controls are in place to prevent its distribution to any third party;
- *Communications with regulatory examiners.* Generally speaking, on a periodic basis, every investment adviser, mutual fund, and broker-dealer is subject to regulatory examinations. These regulatory examinations may be conducted by any one of a

number of governmental agencies or self-regulatory organizations. A request for materials related to these regulatory contacts should be broad enough to take in examinations as well as other communications, and communications that go beyond discussions with the entity's primary regulator, to include any discussions with the SEC, FINRA, the Department of Labor (DOL), Office of the Comptroller of the Currency (OCC), Federal Reserve, Municipal Securities Rulemaking Board (MSRB), state regulators, and non-U.S. jurisdictions, just to name a few. An examination can be "for cause" or "routine." An examination generally concludes in one of three ways:

- No further action taken (often, this outcome is not documented), a deficiency letter, or a referral to the Enforcement Division of the SEC to assess whether legal action by the SEC is warranted as a follow-up to examination findings,
- The overwhelming percentage of examinations conclude with an exit interview that orally communicates the noted deficiencies, and then a more formal written "deficiency letter" is sent to the registrant. A SEC deficiency letter notes the examiner's observations and gives the registrant a certain amount of time to draft a deficiency response letter. A due diligence reviewer of a service provider will generally want to see any deficiency letter and any responses or follow-ups to ensure that no material issues were discovered and that all issues were resolved. Many registrants treat the confidentiality of their communications with examiners and other regulators with the same eye to confidentiality that they treat their annual compliance review, refusing to provide copies of these communications for due diligence purposes. As with access to annual reports, a reviewer can pursue some of the same strategies to gain insight into the existence of any findings, seeking to use summaries or viewing the deficiency response letter in a way that it cannot be reproduced, and
- If the service provider refuses to provide a copies of the actual regulatory correspondence, a report on the regulatory relationship to the due diligence reviewer is an essential part of the due diligence process. Were any material issues identified? Were all the issues that were discovered—material or not—addressed to the satisfaction of the examiners or other regulators? Were there any issues that touch the services that the service provider provides to the company doing the due diligence? Any questions that the target company is willing to answer regarding their regulatory relationships is of value to a due diligence reviewer, and should be memorialized in a memorandum back to the service provider from the person responsible for conducting the due diligence;

- *Key procedures.* A question often arises in the context of a due diligence review as to whether is a benefit to request all of the service provider's written procedures. The majority view on this question is that you should request only those documents that you intend to review and assess. Generally speaking, only "key" procedures should be requested. To have a cabinet full of documents that were never reviewed by the recipient is probably less desirable than never having requested them in the first place. But knowing what you need to see, asking to see those documents, reviewing them, assessing them and providing feedback is clearly the progression that represents the most proactive response. There will be many documents in the file of the service

provider that you won't request, to request many and never crack the cover probably starts to set out the facts of a review that is less than perfect. Which procedures you request and review depends totally dependent on the scope of the due diligence that you are conducting, but a good starting point might include:
- Portfolio management processes, including allocation of investment opportunities among clients and consistency of portfolios with clients' investment objectives, disclosures by the adviser, and applicable regulatory restrictions,
- Trading practices, including procedures by which the adviser satisfies its best execution obligation, uses client brokerage to obtain research and other services (e.g., soft dollar arrangements), and allocates aggregated trades among clients,
- Proprietary trading of the adviser and personal trading activities of supervised persons,
- The accuracy of disclosures made to investors, clients, and regulators, including account statements and advertisements,
- Safeguarding of client assets from conversion or inappropriate use by advisory personnel,
- The accurate creation of required records and their maintenance in a manner that secures them from unauthorized alteration or use and protects them from untimely destruction,
- Marketing advisory services, including the use of solicitors,
- Processes to value client holdings and assess fees based on those valuations,
- Safeguards for the privacy protection of client records and information, and
- Business continuity plans;

- *Disclosure documents.* Access to current disclosure documents is also an important part of any due diligence review. Ideally, these documents should be requested and reviewed prior to a due diligence visit because they should provide a preview for your understanding of how things work in the shop that you are visiting. If you read the documents before you arrive and still don't have a clear idea of the business model, operations, and potential risks or conflicts that may exist at the shop you are visiting, it is an indication that the disclosure is not fulfilling its function. Reviewing these documents should set the baseline for understanding the questions that you should ask in your questionnaire prior to your arrival. The types of disclosure documents that may be among your targets would include:
  - The Form ADV,
  - Any mutual fund prospectuses,
  - Any 408(b)(2) disclosure documents,
  - Representations and warranties contained in investment management or other contracts, and
  - Client advertising materials.

After analyzing the answers to their questionnaire, most due diligence reviewers will prepare an agenda for the meeting and a list of individuals who should be made available for interview. These people should represent the senior leadership of each area of the service provider as well as specific subject matter experts who are most familiar with the systems and processes that are the subject of the review. Prior to arrival, it is essential that the interview schedule be set, or the due diligence reviewer might find him- or herself with a wasted trip. In addition, the reviewer should prepare a list of questions to be asked on-site as a result of the review of disclosure documents, requested procedures, and the questionnaire. These questions may, or may not, be shared with the service provider prior to the visit.

The visit generally will take a single day or less; seldom does a due diligence reviewer stay for two days, unless there are particular issues requiring additional focus.

After the visit, it is imperative that the reviewer document the visit to preserve the information accumulated and the effort expended in the due diligence effort. A memorandum to management (or file) setting out the review process, dates of telephone contacts and visits, and the conclusions reached will be an essential backup to the conclusions contained in the annual report regarding the service provider. A memorandum to the service provider is a useful memorialization of the information provided, because if the information the memo contains is not contradicted, it can be assumed to be accurate.

Reviewers may also go through the exercise of preparing a "scorecard." A service provider scorecard, pioneered by Katie Kloster of Varde Partners in Minneapolis, takes a number of important issues, such as code of ethics violations, trading processes, and supervisory structures, and creates a heat map of red, yellow, orange, and green scores to summarize the adequacy of the service provider's controls in a format that can be quickly assessed by management.[22] It is a useful reference tool, as each of the reviewer's service providers can be assessed on a single sheet across a standardized group of important topics. Often, these heat maps (as they relate to the adequacy and effectiveness of service provider controls) can be incorporated into the due diligence reviewer's annual report as well as an important summary of the reviewer's due diligence program.

How Much Detail Is Appropriate for the Annual Report?

The question of how much detail to put forth in the annual report represents an important concern. On the one hand, creation of a thorough inventory of the issues that exist at an investment adviser, broker-dealer or mutual fund is a road map for a regulator or litigant who wishes to find fault with the adviser. On the other hand, a compliance professional's annual report is a legally required document that stands as proof of the CCO's reasonable diligence and satisfaction of his or her obligations because the CCO might otherwise be assessed with personal liability for a failure to appropriately execute due diligence.

In this sense, it is often thought (especially by attorneys) that the compliance obligation to report on violations of federal securities laws diverges from legal needs. This is especially true because the annual compliance report is required to include all material

---

[22] Katie Kloster, Service Provider Risk Evaluation Scorecard: A CCO's Tool, Mutual Fund Governance Consulting (Jan. 2007).

compliance matters and cannot be made subject to any legal privilege as a document legally required to be produced to SEC examiners (see below).

However, although the inclination of the legal staff may be to minimize the creation of a written record of compliance concerns, thereby creating less of a roadmap of the adviser's issues, its creation is exactly the mission of the compliance professional. But even having said this, an issue, even when discovered, cannot and should not be presented in anything but the best light possible, so long as information presented is completely truthful and not misleading. In this regard, the report should highlight (a) the process that uncovered the issue; (b) the issue itself; and (c) what has been done to resolve the issue. The documentation represented by the annual report offers an opportunity for the compliance officer to underscore the reasonableness of the process that they have created. As stated above, this underscores a fundamental goal of compliance.

The true role of the compliance professional is a person who can never "ensure" compliance with the federal securities laws. Instead, the call to action for compliance professionals is "to call it as they see it." The compliance formula runs as follows:

- I am the CCO;
- I am responsible for the administration of the firm's policies and procedures;
- As such, I have created a testing program to assess the adequacy of those procedures (that is, whether they are reasonably designed to prevent, detect, and correct violations of federal securities law) and whether
    - Those procedures are effective in their implementation,
    - This testing program has discovered the issues contained in the report (or "no material compliance matters," if that was the conclusion of the report), and
    - If any such issues have been uncovered, they have been resolved to the satisfaction of Compliance Department and management.

Whenever the CCO is called on to make an affirmation that speaks to their "assurances" that the firm is in compliance with federal securities laws—he or she should quickly recognize that this type of certification is a fact that, at any given moment, is unknowable to a moral certainty. The CCO is well served to use the formula referenced above to more precisely lay out his or her duties and the information possessed about the firm's compliance profile.

Although there is no set profile regarding how the report must be structured: to lay out (1) the CCO's responsibilities, (2) details of the testing program, (3) the findings, and (4) remedial actions taken. This formulation, in response to questions regarding compliance with the requirements of the firm's procedures, probably represents a best practice in the industry.

An annual compliance report should consist of the following elements described here.

Description of the Testing Process in the Report. The annual report should contain not only a discussion of the testing findings, but a reasonably thorough description of the testing process itself. It is an important statement of the due diligence that the CCO has conducted to be able to fairly assert, as most annual reports do, that "there were no material compliance violations" during the year.

There is no single formula that covers the endless permutations of how testing programs or their descriptions in an annual report can be structured. In fact, the allowance for this type of variety is a central theme of the compliance rules, which allows for any control structure to be reflected in a firm's policies and procedures so long as those policies and procedures are adequate and effective. However, when trying to look at the wide array of possible testing programs, it is fair to say that SEC guidance that a CCO work to make the success of the program "measurable" has special applicability here. Best practices in compliance testing require an expectation that a certain number of tests will be done in an annual review period and the results of each test retained, aggregated and reported annually.

For the methodology used to assess the adequacy of the firm's procedures, the report should discuss the process used to support the conclusion that a firm's procedures used are the right "tools," that is, whether they are reasonably designed to prevent, detect, and correct violations of law. This description of the process helps memorialize and support the "reasonableness" of the process and is thus an important element of the compliance program.

This work can take many forms. Most commonly, a discussion of a gap analysis or risk inventory will be created to discuss how the compliance reviewer looked for practices within the firm that should be covered by a procedure. Other times, discussion of the work that resulted in diagramming processes to look for lapses in the coverage offered by a firm's procedures will be used. No matter how the CCO achieved the outcome, it is a best practice for the annual report to describe the measures taken to assess the adequacy of the procedures and to recount any changes made in response to that assessment.

With respect to effectiveness, management and regulators will often respond to the notion that the annual report describes measurable "compliance deliverables"; that each procedure has a certain number of "essential control points" that serve to prevent, detect, or correct violations of law; and that each of these control points has been subjected to a recurring testing regimen over a period of time. In doing this, for example, a CCO might be able to say that a firm with 43 procedure documents in its "compliance manual" may have in each procedure an average of 8 essential control points, yielding an aggregate of 344 "essential control points."

A proactive compliance program may then feature creation of a testing calendar showing how often these items were scheduled to be tested. Other items may be added to the testing calendar on an ad hoc basis as new tests are developed or any other work that might be considered, for this purpose, a "test" is completed, and with this accomplished, a measurable and well-defined testing program can be described in this annual report.

However, although the structure just outlined is one way to approach this testing issue, it is not the only way. There are many. As long as a testing program is well defined and measurable, it is one of the areas where a CCO's creativity can shine through. The trick is, once this path has been discovered and paved, it should be clearly recounted in the annual report, so that the SEC and others who will assess "reasonableness" of the CCO's work have knowledge of why the compliance officer can feel comfortable in making affirmations regarding compliance to management, the government, or third parties regarding the adequacy and effectiveness of a firm's compliance program.

Discussion of Testing Findings. Once the process surrounding the assertion of the adequacy and effectiveness of the firm's procedures has been drafted, a separate section of the annual report should discuss the results of testing.

The mutual fund version of the Rule, Rule 38a-1, calls for the annual report to address (1) material changes to fund policies; and, more importantly, (2) material compliance matters. A great degree of judgment is required of the CCO in determining what constitutes a *material compliance matter,* basically distilling that definition to any matter about which the fund's Board of Directors would reasonably need to know to oversee fund compliance. The definition also goes on to specifically call out material compliance matters to be material weaknesses to process designs.

Assessing "Materiality." As a practical matter, only a small minority of annual reports will ever call out the existence of a material compliance matter. Most compliance professionals view this term, in practice, to be synonymous the type of matter that one would self-report to the SEC. This was almost certainly not the original vision for Rule 38a-1, but that is result as certainly reported by external counsel and others who have access to numerous reports.

However, many compliance professionals have developed a best practice that, if they have no issues that they would call out as material, still uses the annual report to disclose "high-priority, medium-priority, and even low-priority" nonmaterial issues to the board. This way, even if the SEC or a litigant were to disagree with the person who drafted the report about the characterization of an item as "material" or "nonmaterial," the fact that that item had been appropriately disclosed as part of the report would mitigate any damage that was incurred by the mischaracterization; the disclosure would have essentially fulfilled the necessary purpose of reporting the item.

In addition, this reporting strategy has the effect of implicitly securing the buy-in of the board to the imputed dividing line between material and nonmaterial issues. Presumably, if the board considered an item that the CCO had characterized as "nonmaterial" to be "material," board members would be under an obligation to suggest the change. How else, the compliance professional would rightly argue, could a compliance person know "what a board member would reasonably need to know to oversee fund compliance"? It is a useful mechanism to functionally share this burden of designating compliance issues as material with the board itself, and has thus become a best practice.

Following Up on Previously Reported Compliance Issues. In addition to functioning as the vehicle to recount the testing methodology and report on material compliance matters and other high priority nonmaterial items, the annual report is often used as a vehicle to report on the current disposition of items that were reported in the prior year.

Using the annual report in this manner makes sense because it closes the loop on the items previously reported and creates an official record of the resolution of those items. This is true even if quarterly "compliance reports" have been provided to a mutual fund board to show progress in the resolution of these items. If there are a large enough number of nonmaterial reportable items, using a heat map can quickly show which items have been resolved, are nearing resolution, have been started, or are not started.

Include Compliance Strategic Plan. A strategic plan for compliance, as the final section of the annual report, is not a required part of the annual report, but the moment of the issuance of the annual report is an opportune moment to set forth the resources that the Compliance Department needs to be successful and to build a consensus regarding the measures by which compliance should be judged in the coming year.

Having a strategic plan for compliance makes sense for several reasons. First, like any business unit, success is generally measured by the completion of agreed upon "deliverables." For the CCO to propose and achieve alignment on what these deliverables should be is an important milestone in determining an agreed-upon definition of the successful administration of a compliance function. Otherwise, the success of compliance is merely subject to the question of whether any issues were uncovered (easily viewed as an unsuccessful year for compliance) or the discovery of no issues (no news is good news, but still difficult to get excited about).

The execution of an agreed upon set of goals as set forth in a compliance strategic plan avoids the trap that exists if the best that compliance can achieve is "nothing to report." Instead, the use of the annual report to create a strategic plan takes the moment when the compliance reviewer has the greatest visibility in the organization, and uses it to assess personnel and system needs. The strategic plan, therefore, helps to successfully produce deliverables related to the creation of the tools required to assess adequacy and effectiveness.

Using the annual report to define the objectives of the Compliance Department also gives these objectives the communal visibility necessary in the organization to be able to hold them out universally as the firm's compliance program. Thus, the plan is enterprise wide rather than "the Compliance Department's plan," which other groups may or may not buy into, or, worse still, "the CCO's goals and objectives, "which may not be shared by anyone else. Progress on these goals and objectives can become a major focus of the activities of the firm's Compliance Committee, the vehicle created by most investment advisers (as discussed below) to be the recipient of the annual report.

The importance of creating a strategic plan for compliance is that it can be used to turn the perception of compliance into a group that, like other business line organizations, is essentially delivering a product—deliverables such as a defined number of different types of compliance tests through the year, or revising a certain number of procedures or emphasizing a particular type of gap analysis review. The underlying premise is that a strategic plan has made the completion of compliance goals measurable, and you can be proactive in completing a plan. No longer is success in compliance merely about the "luck of the draw" of finding a problem or not; it is about defining your success and being rewarded for creating a measurable and proactive compliance program. This goes to the heart of what the SEC called for in its creation of the compliance rules, and puts the compliance officer more squarely into the heart of controlling his or her own destiny.

The Advisers Act Standard

On its face, the Advisers Act standard for the annual review is very different from the Investment Company Act standard for the annual report. The Advisers Act standard allows for the possibility that the annual review not be memorialized in a written document, but that instead it merely be an unwritten "review." Presumably, the minimum requirement would be that a review of the adequacy and effectiveness of the procedures be done and "reported" orally. But even an oral report is not required. Because no report is required, it is not surprising that the Advisers Act also does not specify to whom any report would be made.

In a mutual fund context, the Advisers Act standard and the Investment Company Act standard work in tandem. For investment advisers to mutual funds who have no other clients, the overlap is complete, as the federal securities laws that the investment adviser must report on include the Investment Advisers Act, and there are no clients or regulatory needs that present issues that run beyond the requirements of what is anticipated in Rule 38a-1 for the firm's mutual fund clients.

However, most firms that serve as investment advisers to mutual funds also service nonmutual fund clients. In these cases, the side-by-side conflicts that may exist between these two types of clients demand a separate treatment of the Advisers Act issues that may exist for non-mutual fund clients. Likewise, These "Advisers Act only" clients may have distinct issues that do not arise in the context of the firm's management of mutual fund clients.

Thus, some advisers who service mutual fund and nonfund clients "side by side" will tend to write a report that separately analyzes the two groups or even write two separate annual reports—one under Rule 38a-1 with respect to mutual fund clients and the other with respect to Rule 206(4)-7 nonmutual fund clients.

Who Writes the Report? While Rule 38a-1 does say that a CCO must "provide" the annual report to the board, there is no requirement that a CCO must actually draft the annual report. However, given the fact that a CCO can have personal liability if he or she knows of material compliance matters that are not contained in the report, it is of central importance to the CCO to be given the authority to draft (or at least freely revise) the report. The ability of the CCO to do this, and the willingness of management to allow him or her to draft the report, can be fairly viewed as something of a litmus test of management's trust in compliance in one direction, and the ability and sensitivity of the CCO running in the other direction.

That's not to say, however, that other constituencies should not have the opportunity to comment on what the CCO has drafted before the report is issued, but it is clearly considered a best practice in the industry to have the CCO control the production of the annual report. This also serves to protect the firm from a claim that it has exercised "undue influence" on the CCO to avoid reporting on a particular item. The "undue influence" provision of the mutual fund version of the rule has been little used, but if the annual report is crafted in the CCO's own words, it is surely harder to make the case that the CCO was compelled not to disclose an item.

A Report to Whom? In the mutual fund context, Rule 38a-1 calls for the annual report to be delivered to the mutual fund's Board of Directors. But, in the adviser context, the question of who should receive the report is left unanswered. The reason for this is easy to understand because the Advisers Act does not even require that a report be written—it only calls for an "annual review."[23]

However, most investment advisory CCOs (as described above) take the review requirement to be best served when it is properly documented by an actual written report. Without a strict legal requirement to write a report, the question of to whom the report should be delivered is left to the discretion of the compliance professional.

As a supervisory matter, there would be little question that the report should be delivered to whoever supervises the compliance function. If the supervisor of the compliance function is not the CEO of the firm, as a matter of fulfilling the SEC emphasis on the importance of the firm's tone at the top, the CEO and other selected members of the management (if one exists) should also receive the annual report.

But most compliance professionals go a step further and use the standard in Rule 38a-1, which calls for the delivery of the report to "a board," as a guidepost. For advisers that have an Executive Committee, this standard is easy to fulfill because the report can be distributed to the members of that committee. If there is no such committee, the report can be distributed to the senior executive officer and his or her direct reports or group leaders.

But perhaps the best practice in this regard is to create a structure that mirrors the board delivery requirement called for by Rule 38a-1. This mirror structure is best accomplished through the creation of a Compliance Committee. A Compliance Committee, composed of members of the firm's management team, can serve many important compliance functions. Meeting on a periodic basis, it forms a body that can monitor the progress of the firm's compliance program or the implementation of a strategic plan, provide the compliance officer with an environment to receive feedback, discuss

---

[23] *See* Rule 206(4)-7(b).

resource needs, and generally heighten the profile of compliance concerns within the firm and emphasize the firm's culture of compliance. With the CCO as the chair of the committee, it also provides a forum in which the CCO can exert the influence necessary to administer a successful compliance function.

Broker-Dealer Annual Report Standard

Rule 3130 states that a designated principal (the CCO) must submit a report to member's senior management no less than annually detailing the member's system of supervisory controls, the summary of the test results and significant identified exceptions, and any additional or amended supervisory procedures created in response to the test results.

This standard for the production of an annual report is, of course, very similar to the standards set forth under the mutual fund and investment adviser versions of the rule. Here, as in the mutual fund version of the compliance rules, an actual report (rather than a review) is required. Like the mutual fund rule, the recipient of the report has been designated. Instead of the "material compliance matters" that are earmarked for reporting in the mutual fund rule, the notion of "significant identified exceptions" seems to suggest reporting that might theoretically be a little broader, but in practice, generally covers the same ground.

VII. REQUIREMENT TO DESIGNATE A CHIEF COMPLIANCE OFFICER

The third foundational requirement of the compliance rules is the requirement that the firm designate a CCO.[24] This compliments the other two requirements (the requirements of written procedures and an annual report) because it is the CCO who must administer the firm's procedures and provide the report to the board (in the case of a mutual fund) or senior management (in the case of a broker-dealer).

VIII. REPORTING STRUCTURE

Framing the reporting lines of the CCO can be difficult. On the one hand, the CCO is designed to serve as the leading control function to a firm, and that suggests that a separation of duties might be desirable, making the CCO independent of the firm's management to the extent possible. Outside of the mutual fund context, however, there is only one entity, and all functions generally flow up to a single CCO. An actual separation of that function from the advisory or brokerage firm itself would have been difficult (if not impossible) to orchestrate. In the mutual fund context, however, a mutual fund CCO could have reported to the fund board alone, without a connection to the investment adviser firm's management.

---

[24] Rule 38a-1(a)(4) for mutual funds, Rule 206(4)-7(c) for SEC-registered investment advisers, and Rule 3130(a) for broker-dealers.

The SEC rejected this approach however, and the rationale is instructive. The commission's thinking was that the CCO would ultimately have more access to information and greater influence in the organization if he or she were an "insider"—that is, if the CCO was a member of the investment adviser firm's senior management team.[25] This fundamental underpinning of the compliance rules, while taken for granted today, was for many, a reasonably close call. The issue was, at its base, whether a separation of duties in the compliance context was necessary to fulfill the control function. Was the CCO a "spy," the eyes and ears of the board—or even the eyes and ears of a regulator—or should the CCO be a "trusted adviser" of management sitting on the "same side of the table" as the executive team? The compliance rules opted for the approach that attempted to focus on the CCO as trusted adviser.

In the adopting release to the compliance rules, the SEC noted that a fund's CCO will often be employed by the fund's investment adviser or administrator.[26] The commission did not adopt a requirement that the CCO be employed by only the mutual fund (and not the adviser) because the SEC believed that such a provision would actually have weakened the CCO's effectiveness. Funds typically have no employees and delegate management and administrative functions, including the compliance function, to one or more service providers. If the SEC, in the rationale set forth in its adopting release, had precluded the CCO from being an employee of an adviser or any other service provider, the compliance officer would have to be divorced from all fund operations."[27]

If a separation of the fund CCO had been required by the SEC, the adviser's CCO would have continued to administer the adviser's compliance programs, and the role of the fund's CCO would have been limited to the oversight of service providers' compliance policies and providing advice to the board on their operation. As a result, the fund's CCO would have been almost entirely dependent on information filtered through the senior management of the fund's adviser rather than, for example, information received directly from a trading desk. Moreover, fund management would be unlikely to consult with an "outside" compliance officer on a prospective business decision to ascertain the compliance implications.

The SEC recognized, however, that a CCO who was an employee of the fund's investment adviser might be conflicted in his or her duties, and that the investment adviser's business interests might discourage the adviser from making forthright disclosure to fund directors of its compliance failures. The rule, as it was adopted, was designed to address these concerns by requiring a fund's CCO to report directly to the board. For many CCOs, this creates a dual reporting line.

The board, and the board alone, was then empowered to discharge the officer as fund CCO if he or she failed to live up to the position. Thus, the Adopting Release continued, "a Chief Compliance Officer who failed to fully inform the board of a material

---

[25] Adopting Release, Rule 38a-1, at note 89.
[26] *Id.*
[27] *Id.*

compliance failure, or who failed to aggressively pursue noncompliance within a service provider, would risk their position. The SEC noted that they would also risk their career, because it would be unlikely for another board of directors to approve such a person as Chief Compliance Officer."[28]

Although these provisions do not directly impact investment adviser or broker-dealer-only registrants, most mutual fund registrants are dual registrants, and the mutual fund standard has direct bearing on them. But the notions set forth in Rule 38a-1 also have "moral" applicability to the other versions of the compliance rules too. This is a relationship that many of the more detailed Rule 38a-1 standards have to the more abbreviated standards in the other rules, especially for investment advisers in Rule 206(4)-7. When SEC examiners and others look for how to interpret the skeletal version of the compliance rules offered to investment advisers, the joint adviser and fund guidance in the adopting release and the "buffed out" requirements for funds, although not directly applicable, cast a long shadow over the world of investment adviser compliance.

Seniority and Authority

The Adopting Release to Rule 38a-1 and 206(4)-7 makes a special point to affirm that a CCO should be competent and knowledgeable regarding the Advisers Act and should be empowered with full responsibility and authority to develop and enforce appropriate policies and procedures for the firm.[29] Thus, the CCO should have a position of "sufficient seniority and authority" within the organization to compel others to adhere to the compliance policies and procedures.[30]

The adopting release goes on to say in the fund context, that a fund's CCO should be "competent and knowledgeable" regarding the federal securities laws and should be empowered with full responsibility and authority to develop and enforce appropriate policies and procedures for the fund. The CCO of a fund, like the CCO of an investment adviser, should have sufficient seniority and authority to compel others to adhere to the compliance policies and procedures. Although this is the standard set forth in the adopting release, most CCOs know that it is not desirable to actually go so far in the power to "enforce" procedures and to actually usurp the position of business line management as the supervisor of the various functions of a firm. Doing that has significant implications for the CCOs personal liability if and when things go wrong.

But beyond this, there is no requirement for any particular educational background, certification, or license applicable to compliance as a discipline or compliance professionals as individuals. As a practical matter, however, many CCOs come to the position with a legal background. Either they are attorneys or have worked in a law firm in some capacity. Many others come to the profession from accounting and operations, and still others have worked strictly in compliance.

---

[28] Adopting Release, Rule 38a-1, at note 90.
[29] Adopting Release, Rule 38a-1, at note 73.
[30] Adopting Release, Rule 38a-1, at note 88.

At one time the New York Stock Exchange maintained a Series 14 certification for compliance professionals within a NYSE-Registered firm. That certification did not long survive the merger with the NASD into FINRA. Various other organizations offer a proprietary credential, such as the National Society of Compliance Professionals, which offers a credential known as the Certified Securities Compliance Professional (CSCP). National Regulatory Services, a prominent compliance consultant offers individuals a credential known as the Investment Adviser Certified Compliance Professional (IACCP). None of these credentials, while offering good insights into compliance duties and an individual's proficiency, is required to maintain any role in compliance.

Finally, many institutions of higher learning, such as the Wharton School of Business at the University of Pennsylvania, offer certificates focusing on compliance training, and these are generally very well regarded, but again, not required. The reality in this area is most of the background people have in compliance comes from doing the work rather than any form of formal training. Many other organizations and compliance consultants offer robust compliance training programs, both in person and online. It is generally considered desirable for each compliance professional within a group to attend at least one such training session in person annually, both for networking and training purposes.

However, in a more basic sense, the requirement that a CCO have the "seniority and authority" necessary for the role speaks to the CCO's stature and gravitas within the organization. It is a question of whether, without directly supervising the individuals within a firm, the CCO has the ability to affect conduct. Is the advice that they provide listened to or are they ignored? Is the person included in meetings or is compliance excluded? Are they given access to the information necessary to do the job? Are they viewed, not because of their role or title, but because of their bearing, as a trusted adviser and as being a necessary part of the decision-making process? In this vein, the stature of the CCO within the organization speaks to whether they have the seniority and authority necessary to do the job.

Competence Regarding Activities of Service Providers

This sense of gravitas extends to the CCO's relationships with service providers. The CCO, in exercising his or her responsibilities under Rule 38a-1, will also oversee the fund's service providers, which will have their own compliance officials. A CCO should diligently administer this oversight responsibility by taking steps to assure him- or herself that each service provider has implemented effective compliance policies and procedures administered by competent personnel.

The CCO should be familiar with each service provider's operations and understand those aspects of the operations that expose the fund to compliance risks. The CCO should maintain an active working relationship with each service provider's compliance personnel. Arrangements with the service provider should provide the fund's CCO with direct access to these personnel and should provide the CCO with periodic reports and special reports in the event of compliance problems. In addition, the fund's contracts with its service providers might also require service providers to certify periodically that they are in compliance with applicable federal securities laws, or could provide for third-party audits arranged by the fund to evaluate the effectiveness of the service provider's compliance controls. The CCO could conduct (or hire third parties to conduct) statistical analyses of a service provider's performance of its duties to detect potential compliance failures.

The CCO with Dual Roles

In many organizations, especially those investment advisers with a smaller number of employees, a single individual will tend to wear more than one hat. The chief financial officer (CFO) may be the head of marketing; the CEO may also be a portfolio manager and trader. The lead attorney may be the CCO (a special case discussed below); the CCO may be the head of operations. As the firm grows and becomes more complex, the roles tend to differentiate themselves so that individual roles coalesce around particular people. This is only natural. In a one-person firm, the owner is CEO—and everything else.

However, special issues arise when the compliance officer fills more than one role. For each "hat" that the compliance officer wears, a potential conflict arises. The supervisory duties of the noncompliance-related role (whether operations, trading, marketing, or legal) cannot be easily complemented by the control function that compliance would generally fulfill, which is to help ensure that the procedures under which that area operates are "reasonably designed to prevent, detect, and correct violations of federal securities law and are effective in their implementation." Simply put, when the CCO executes a supervisory, or "first line of defense" function, the role of compliance as a "second line of defense" is compromised, because the CCO is attempting to control his or her own activities.

This is a circumstance that calls for a significant degree of creativity, because the answer to the conflict lay in creating mitigating and compensating controls: finding creative ways where other mechanisms will backstop the conflict that the CCO has in controlling his or her own activities. This is more art than science, and thus the need for creativity.

For example, where the head of operations is also the CCO, a second level of business line sign-off may be required to approve "nonstandard" transactions to compensate for the fact that a review of those transactions by the same person (first as operations officer and then as compliance officer) may not produce an effective safeguard. The reason to introduce the additional level of control has nothing to do with any implication that the operations/compliance person is honest or dishonest, but just that if that particular person has missed an issue as the business line supervisor, there's no reason to believe he or she will spot it in the compliance role. The real purpose behind the need for a compliance review might be just to get a second set of eyes, with a different perspective, on the transactions.

If the CCO is in charge of marketing, similar "workarounds" should be sought. Perhaps the firm's attorney may be designated to review marketing materials for appropriate disclosures. The general theme is that when the CCO holds another role, the separation of control duties that the presence of a compliance function is designed to facilitate is compromised, and creativity must be used to design another way to achieve. It is in these types of contexts when a compliance person bringing creativity to bear on an issue is most valued.

The Attorney as CCO

A special issue exists with respect to the assertion of legal privilege when the firm's CCO is also working in a capacity as an attorney.

Courts have long recognized a common law privilege for attorneys to maintain certain information with a privilege against disclosing that information to the court. This is an outgrowth of an attorney's ethical obligation to maintain client confidences.[31] The attorney-client privilege exists because, an attorney must be able to possess full access to information about the client's circumstances in order to mount the most effective defense. The client has to be comfortable that he or she can tell this information to another person without fear of compelled disclosure. Not everyone can go to law school, but everyone in our system is due a zealous defense. This is only possible if the information given the attorney in anticipation of litigation, or the output of their work product, is shielded from discovery that could itself disadvantage the client.

Whereas others would have to answer a question in court, information given pursuant to an attorney/client privilege gives the attorney the right to respectfully decline to answer. From the attorney's perspective, this "right" is actually an ethical obligation, because the obligation to keep client confidences confidential is perhaps the highest ethical obligation of the legal profession.

However, where an attorney takes on a compliance role, compliance is not afforded a similar legal privilege. In fact, the essence of the compliance role is the reporting of all known material issues to management in a report that is designed to be reviewed by regulatory authorities as well. Thus, although the essence of the legal role emphasizes confidentiality and nondisclosure of work product, the essence of the Compliance role emphasizes reporting of any known material issues and disclosure of those issues in a required report.

As a result, it is very hard for an attorney working in a compliance role, such as a person who has accepted a role as "general counsel and CCO" to parse out when he or she is functioning as an attorney and when as a compliance professional. Clearly, the SEC will not recognize the annual compliance report as being subject to a legal privilege, but other communications, if impacting the compliance role, could be hard to shield as well.

---

[31] Geoffrey C. Hazard, Jr., "An Historical Perspective on the Lawyer-Client Privilege," Yale Law School Legal Scholarship Repository, Faculty Scholarship Series, http://digitalcommons.law.yale.edu/cgi/viewcontent.cgi?article=3288&context=fss_papers

If a privilege is claimed by an attorney who also works in a compliance role, regulators have made clear that the claim cannot be made as an afterthought. The regulators will look for a well-planned assertion of the privilege, including documents that are clearly marked "confidential-attorney client privilege" and a reference to the document entered into a "compliance log."

In this context, a privilege log is a list of documents for which the attorney is claiming privilege containing a description of the document (in a general sense), the date created and the distribution list. Documents that are distributed to a group that include others beyond those client representatives who have an absolute need-to-know can cause the document to lose its privilege, and thus narrow distribution lists are preferable to broad distributions. Documents produced in this way may also be marked "do not distribute," as the privilege may also be lost if the document is given to nonattorneys by any recipient.

Needless to say, working simultaneously as both an attorney and compliance officer can conflict—providing the key protections and ethical needs by the attorney can be compromised. Attorneys are well advised to carefully consider the legal requirements of the ethical obligation of confidentiality prior to accepting a compliance role.

This conflict, however, does not apply if an attorney is working strictly in a compliance role and not in a legal capacity. The fact that a person happens to be an attorney does not present an issue by itself so long as the attorney fulfilling the compliance role does not claim the role as the organization's legal adviser.

Serving as CCO of Multiple Entities

Other conflicts may arise where one individual serves as CCO for multiple related entities, especially if those entities are doing business together. Most commonly, these conflicts arise in two circumstances, serving as CCO for (1) a mutual fund and its investment adviser, or (2) an investment adviser and an affiliated broker dealer.

Serving as CCO of a Fund and Investment Adviser. Often, if an investment advisory firm is the sponsor of a mutual fund, a single CCO will serve both as the CCO for the fund under Rule 38a-1 and the adviser's CCO under Rule 206(4)-7. This type of structure is especially common if the fund is the adviser's sole client.

The issue here is that the adviser and the fund may have different interests and that given the adviser's almost complete control over the activities of the fund, a conflict between the two may be resolved in favor of the adviser. If the CCO of the fund is the same person as the CCO of the adviser, an important safeguard may have been lost.

The situation may became even more acute if the adviser services other separate account clients in addition to the mutual fund, as the interests of one group of clients may be favored over the interests of the other. Without separate CCOs, there would be no "independent watchdog" at each level exclusively tasked with looking out for the interests of their clients.

So what are the equities of resolving this potential conflict? In addressing this issue, one needs to turn back to the adopting release of the Rule 38a-1, which sought to make the CCO an "insider" rather than a type of independent examiner. As a result, the SEC chose to have the CCO report to management, to make the CCO be "part of the team" rather than an "outsider." It was thought that this would give the CCO better access to information, and in the long run, more influence to create compliant structures. And that decision was made with the full knowledge that a potential conflict existed.

When the fund is the adviser's sole client, if the CCO role for fund and adviser were separated and the fund CCO reported to the fund's board only, that would create the greatest possible separation of duties but would run counter to the "part of the team" approach that the SEC staff put forward in the adopting release. If the two were separate CCOs (one for the adviser, and one for the fund) with both reporting to the adviser's supervisory structure, although there might be a benefit to having a second person focus on the same issues from a distinct perspective, it's more an issue of having a second set of eyes. The second CCO would not have achieved a meaningful independence through a separate reporting chain.

The key element in the effectiveness of a fund CCO who is in the investment adviser's reporting chain is probably not the separation of duties, but the nature and quality of the confidentiality that the CCO shares with the board—specifically the board member who is the chair of the Compliance Committee or the chair of the board. Even if one person serves in both roles, to the extent the CCO can use the confidential relationship with the board to sound the validity of issues and the board can confidentially get comfort about the nature of the adviser's operations, in the long run, this will be far more effective than having a separate individual fill the fund CCO role. When the board doesn't have sufficient confidence in the adviser's culture of compliance, or lacks confidence in the individual designated as adviser's CCO, the board may demand the addition of a fund-only CCO.

When the adviser has other clients besides the mutual fund, side-by-side advisory issues may form another rationale for separating the role of adviser compliance from fund compliance. Side-by-side issues emerge when one class of advisory client is favored over another. This may occur as a result of differences in compensation structure to the adviser when, for example, separately managed accounts pay higher management fees than a fund client. The question that can arise in that context is whether the clients paying higher fees are being given the better investment opportunities to "keep them happy." Differences in the perceived importance of the client cause certain clients to be favored, causing side-by-side issues—the implication being that bigger, "more important" clients are receiving the best information and opportunities. In a third context, side-by-side issues can exist when one client funds the payment of expenses that benefit another client, such as when investment research is shared.

These situations call for additional sensitivity and care as the addition of the side-by-side issue adds complexity to the CCO's duties. It is a context in which the additional burden of focusing on controls to safeguard a separate population of clients might benefit from having a second professional involved who focuses on the adviser's issues from the point of view of a second group of clients. Although having a second CCO in this context might be more desirable to mitigate the perception of any potential conflicts, the adviser may also field a larger staff of compliance professionals, some of whom are tasked with reviewing procedures from the independent perspective of the different groups of clients within a firm. The question is the same one that the SEC originally grappled with. How can the fund CCO have an independent reporting line and still be an "insider?"

Like most compliance issues, where to deploy limited compliance resources most effectively becomes the heart of the issue.

Serving as CCO of an investment adviser and affiliated broker-dealer, dual broker-dealer and investment advisory registrants also often share a single CCO, and of course, with the differing interests of these two entities, each having a distinct purpose, may find their interests in conflict.

Potential conflicts in their regard may express themselves, from the adviser's perspective, in whether the use of the "captive" broker-dealer is in the best interest of the advisory client (especially if the broker-dealer is the exclusive broker executing the trades). This often distils itself into a discussion of "best execution."

To the extent that the brokerage services provided include fees for security selection, what is the benefit to the client of paying for that service again by selecting a separate investment adviser? To the extent that the fees are coordinated in a wrap arrangement of some type, why is selection of that particular adviser or broker in the best interest of the client as advisory client or brokerage client, respectively?

This question is made somewhat more complex by the fact that broker-dealers and investment advisers are legally subject to different standards of care with respect to their interactions with clients. Advisers must provide their advisory clients with a standard of care as a "fiduciary," but broker-dealers need only buy "suitable securities" for their clients. The fiduciary standard, which is often characterized as the "highest standard of care known to law," is generally not applicable to brokers.

It is generally conceded that these different standards arose out of unique historical reasons related to the passage of the Securities Exchange Act in 1934 for broker-dealers and the Investment Advisers Act in 1940 for advisers. The result has precipitated calls for "normalization" of the two standards of care in recent years, the existence of a different yardstick for the two types of financial intermediary does add a layer of complexity to the recognition of conflicts in dual registrants.

Clearly, given the nature of the relationships described above, serving as both a BD and IA CCO to a dual registrant or affiliated entities, the potential arises for conflicts that must be addressed in a way that is specific to the facts and circumstances of the entities.

Whether the result of this analysis is a desire to split the role or to create compensating controls is a determination that the CCO who holds the two roles that may conflict must continually validate throughout their tenure and they must stand ready to either defend or restructure.

CCOs Reporting to CCOs

In the largest securities conglomerates in the nation, CCOs for one entity may report to other CCOs. This may be true in the case of a large mutual fund complex in which a single family of mutual funds may be led by a worldwide fund CCO who then has the individual CCOs of the various investment advisers owned by that complex reporting to him or her.

On the one hand, a structure such as this complex may ameliorate the conflicts that might exist between the adviser and the fund. Having a separate adviser CCO reporting into the compliance chain would be desirable, just in the context of having a second set of eyes to look at an issue. On the other hand, when, for example, the mutual fund CCO is the investment adviser CCO's supervisor, one may well ask whether a true independence has been achieved.

Instead of truly creating an independent safeguard, one reason to create a structure such as this is to make a firebreak between the two CCOs, so that any material compliance issues that might be found to exist in the adviser can be said to be the responsibility of the lower-level CCO rather than actually flowing through to the global CCO. This structure has never been tested; however, whether a liability for failures can be avoided by the designation of two levels of CCOs probably depends on whether the superior CCO knew, or should have known, that the issue existed at the lower level—a standard that arises as a matter of the liability of a supervisor and probably exists for the supervisory CCO whether or not they designate their subordinate as a CCO.

Compensation Models

A lively discussion has surrounded the best way to compensate a CCO without creating a conflict of interest. As discussed above in the adopting release of the compliance rules, the SEC made the point that the commission had considered having the CCO reside outside of the organization that he or she serves. However, in seeking that a CCO be an insider to management, the question arises about whether it is appropriate for the CCO to participate in other types of incentive programs that the firm may allow its senior executives, such as stock option plans and incentive bonus plans.

The question is whether a CCO, if incentivized with a special bonus or in possession of a large number of stock options, will have a reason not to report or address important issues to enhance his or her own personal compensation package. The majority view on this issue is that when these forms of compensation are available to other key executives, they should be available to the CCO. Otherwise, the firm runs the alternative risk that the CCO will not be viewed as being in the "same league" as other key executives. He or she will not be viewed with the requisite seniority and authority afforded the other key executives.

Bonuses. The risk of the use of bonuses (single, lump-sum compensation payments that rely on the discretion of a supervisor for disbursement) as part of the compensation structure for a compliance professional is that they can be used to incentivize bad as well as good behaviors. Issuance of a bonus is often given broad discretion by a supervisor, and for a senior compliance professional reporting into the business line, the behavior rewarded may be minimizing the firm's regulatory risk exposure or approving otherwise "marginal" transactions.

A lump-sum payment can be an easy way to reward compliance people who avoided confronting issues that might be damaging to their supervisor. Even fair and honest businesspeople can fall prey to the notion that a compliance person is expressing opinions that "do not reflect the culture of the firm" and they should "loosen up." Whether this type of discussion is the primary feedback received by compliance after the first of the year, when bonuses are usually paid out, is often a concern in a room filled with senior compliance people.

Like most conflicts in the compliance arena, there are ways to mitigate this concern. A detailed annual strategic plan outlining deliverables to be provided by year end, or even goals and objectives outlined with an eye to measurable success factors, can serve to normalize expectations as to what constitutes a "successful" year, and thus what types of behaviors warrant the payment of a bonus. The key is to temper the otherwise absolute discretion of the supervisor to instead reflect the fulfillment of goals set at the beginning of the year.

The most important point here is that in the long run, denying a compliance person a bonus because of the risk that the bonus might be abused is generally viewed as having a long-term effect of separating the CCOs from the other executive-suite members of the firm. And it doesn't really solve the issue of abuse of compensation discretion either because merit increases in pay might be "held hostage" to the same type of concerns and are harder to regulate. Most firms have come to the conclusion that it is better to keep the CCO in the compensation structure shared by the other executives of the firm, and keep him or her as a "member of the team," as the SEC envisaged in the Adopting Release of Rule 38a-1. That way, when the CCO is successful in creating a strong compliance structure for the firm, the tools will exist to properly reward them for innovative and creative work.

Restricted Stock and Stock Options. The award of stock options raises concerns that seem, on their face, to be more difficult to address.

The concern in this regard is that by being given compensation that essentially represents the ownership of a piece of the company for which the compliance professional is structuring controls, the compliance professional is subject to an irreconcilable conflict of interest. If the CCO calls out a material compliance matter in a public way, if that issue is of significance, it may impair the value of the company and work against the economic interest of the compliance professional.

This is a concern, but it could also be just as forcefully argued that the compliance officer who has an ownership stake in the company would be more anxious to use his or her skills to protect the company and thus preserve or enhance personal ownership interest.

Another consideration in the mix is that these forms of compensation generally vest over four or five years and thus tend to facilitate the creation of an environment that involves less staff turnover and greater stability. Low turnover tends to create a stronger compliance environment. A more attractive compensation package also tends to attract better compliance talent, and participation in option programs generally attracts a more entrepreneurially minded compliance person. Both these attributes may be fairly looked upon by a firm as desirable from the standpoint of building a culture that is viewed as being more conducive to growth.

Use of options as also a "promise" of good things to come gives a small firm a shot at finding the best talent available and goes a distance toward equalizing the "playing field" between small and big firms in the search for talent.

Finally, if the use of options could prevent a compliance person from reporting issues, would this same rationale extend to the payment of normal salary? If an issue identified by compliance were of such great import as to affect the firm's viability, wouldn't that suggest that even the potential to disrupt normal payment of normal salary could weight the scale toward nonreporting, thereby making the mechanisms of the payment, be they stock, bonus or salary, inconsequential?

On balance, the majority view supports the notion that an award of stock does not represent a conflict so great as to guide the hand of the compliance professional to ignore their legal and ethical duty to report on issues discovered and to create the strongest control environment possible for the firm. In fact, many would argue that it enhances need to fulfill that role fully.

IX. CONCLUSION

The regulatory paradigm that governs the securities world places a strong emphasis on the development of internal controls through a discipline that has come to be known as compliance. A series of rules adopted in 2004 recognizes three pedestals on which the compliance structure in the securities arena stands:

- Designation of a CCO with the seniority and authority to execute the control functions assigned to him or her;

- Procedures adopted by the firm that are reasonably designed to prevent, detect and correct violations of applicable federal securities laws and are effective in their implementation; and
- An annual review, generally distilled into an a written report, that identifies all material compliance matters and discusses the firm's responses to changes in law, changes in business model and compliance matters during the past year.

Although the model is deceptively simple on its face, it conceals the underlying complexity of the firms it is designed to govern. Because no two securities firms share exactly the same business model, the SEC was confronted with the question of how to create standards to govern the innumerable potential conflicts of interest among the various elements of those business models are sliced together and torn apart by the dynamic processes of the American financial system. It is the compliance professional who is on the front line of finding the appropriate balance of creativity and process, control, and innovation that allows their firm to thrive while at the same time reducing regulatory risk to an acceptable minimum.

ABOUT THE AUTHOR

David H. Lui was chair of the industry's trade group, the National Society of Compliance Professionals, and has been a chief compliance officer for some of America's largest investment advisers, including Charles Schwab Investment Management, Franklin Advisers (Franklin Templeton), U.S. Bancorp Asset Management, and Galliard Capital Management, an $85 Billion subsidiary of Wells Fargo. He is a graduate of Brown University with a bachelor of arts degree with Honors in History and a juris doctor degree from the University of California, Hastings College of the Law. He is admitted to practice in California and Minnesota.

CHAPTER 6

Overview of the Regulatory Framework for SEC-Registered Investment Advisers

By Eric R. Vercauteren
   Galliard Capital Management, Inc.

I. INTRODUCTION

The regulatory framework for investment advisers registered with the Securities and Exchange Commission (SEC) consists of a complex web of federal and state statutes and a broad range of far-reaching rules and regulations. It is safe to say that a compliance professional could spend a career becoming an expert in just one area of this expansive regulatory regime. The goal of this chapter is to provide the reader with a foundational understanding of the fragmented regulatory framework that applies to SEC-registered investment advisers. Each of the four sections of this chapter discusses a different regulatory agency, providing a history along with a summary of the current regulatory objectives of the agency. This chapter is not intended to be a comprehensive review of everything a compliance professional of an SEC-registered investment adviser needs to know; rather it is intended to offer you a broader perspective of the applicable regulatory framework and highlight some of the more important statutes, rules, and regulations.

The quest for effective regulation of securities markets has historically been a function of the United Sates Congress and the legislative bodies of the states. Government has typically been the leader when it comes to regulatory reform, and the vast majority of the regulatory framework in place today is a function of governmental agencies. But government is not the only regulator responsible for spearheading the development of rules and regulations with an effort to create a marketplace where investors are willing to allocate capital. Self-regulatory organizations and the SEC-registered investment advisers themselves play a critical role in carrying out the regulatory objectives of the various regulatory agencies.

This chapter will explain how the existing regulatory framework puts a significant amount of responsibility on compliance professionals of SEC-registered investment advisers. The array of rules and regulations of which compliance professionals need to have command of in order to be effective in their roles is continuously evolving and becoming increasingly complex. Many variables can determine the extent to which a compliance professional will have to engage with various regulators. Some of those variables include the investment strategy of the advisory firm, the products it sells or provides advice about, and the firm's ownership structure. In order to be effective, compliance professionals are expected to have a baseline understanding of not only what the regulatory agencies are and what they do but, perhaps more importantly, the professionals must possess the ability to anticipate the regulatory expectations of the agencies and be able to interact with them successfully.

The four key regulatory agencies covered in this chapter are:

- The U.S. Securities and Exchange Commission (SEC);
- The Financial Industry Regulatory Authority (FINRA);
- The U.S. Commodities Futures Trading Commission (CFTC); and
- The Office of the Comptroller of the Currency (OCC).

The size of the investment advisory profession today makes it clear how important the role of these regulatory agencies and compliance professionals is to the protection of investors. The investment advisory industry alone employs more than 700,000 professionals employed in a total of 10,533 firms with assets under management of nearly $55 trillion.[1] By comparison, investment companies subject to registration with the SEC managed approximately $17 trillion in assets as of the end of 2013.[2] The assets under management by investment advisers is equivalent to more than three times the annual gross domestic product (GDP) of the United States and approximately than six times the total savings deposits at all U.S. depository institutions.

II. UNDERSTANDING THE REGULATORY OBJECTIVES OF THE U.S. SECURITIES AND EXCHANGE COMMISSION

Historical Perspective of the SEC

The SEC is the federal agency primarily responsible for, among other things, administering and enforcing federal securities laws and regulating the securities industry. The events that led to the creation of the SEC are well known, but a brief history is helpful to an understanding of the SEC as it exists today. The stock market crash in October 1929 was the impetus that led to the enactment of federal legislation to regulate capital markets. The first federal statute, the Securities Act of 1933 ("Securities Act"), focused on regulating the offer and sale of securities and making sure that the persons buying such securities were receiving sufficient and accurate information regarding the risk of the securities. The second federal statute, the Securities Exchange Act of 1934 ("Exchange Act"), focused

---

[1] Investment Advisor Association and National Regulatory Services, *Evolution Revolution 2013: A Profile of the Investment Adviser Profession* (2013), https://www.investmentadviser.org/eweb/docs/Publications_News/Reports_and_Brochures/IAA-NRS_Evolution_Revolution_Reports/evolution_revolution_2013.pdf
[2] Investment Company Institute, *2015 Investment Company Fact Book* (2015), http://www.icifactbook.org/fb_ch1.html#investment

on regulating the market participants—brokers, dealers, and exchanges—that facilitate the buying and selling of securities and setting up a framework under which investors are treated fairly and honestly. The SEC was created by Section 4 of the Exchange Act.

These two statutes were entirely necessary because prior to the adoption of the Securities Act, regulation of securities was chiefly governed by state laws, commonly referred to as "blue sky" laws. The primary difference between the Securities Act and state blue sky laws was that the philosophy of the Securities Act was, and continues to be, focused on disclosure of material information whereas the philosophy of state blue sky laws was to impose a "merit review" procedure by which state securities administrators would review the terms and aspects of securities against qualitative fairness standards, or guidelines, to determine their soundness, and to make a determination whether the securities should be permitted to be offered in the state. Over time, most states abandoned merit review for a disclosure based review process similar to the Securities Act.

The big change to the interaction between the SEC and state securities regulators came in 1996. After more than 60 years of a two-tier review system for securities offerings, Congress enacted the National Securities Markets Improvement Act (NSMIA) of 1996. NSMIA preempted states from applying registration and qualification requirements of blue sky laws to securities offerings and transactions that are national in character, or which have characteristics as to bring them within the scope of federal preemption by falling within any of several categories of "covered securities." Following NSMIA, the SEC became the exclusive regulator for the vast majority of securities offerings in the United States and substantially all of the capital-raising transactions. The SEC is responsible for administering and enforcing Exchange Act, the Securities Act, the Trust Indenture Act of 1939, the Investment Company Act of 1940 ("Investment Company Act"), the Investment Advisers Act of 1940 ("Advisers Act"), the Sarbanes-Oxley Act of 2002, portions of the Dodd-Frank Wall Street Reform and Consumer Protection Act of 2010, other statutes, and a broad swath of regulations.

The history of the Securities Act and Exchange Act is interesting in its own right, but the Advisers Act is where a compliance professional of an SEC-registered investment adviser is most likely to encounter the regulatory objectives of the SEC. The Advisers Act and its companion statute, the Investment Company Act, were enacted over a decade after the stock market crash of 1929. Although different in scope, the Advisers Act and the Investment Company Act have similar regulatory objectives to the Securities Act and Exchange Act, but the emphasis is on different market participants.

The Advisers Act was created primarily as a disclosure and recordkeeping statute. Similar to the framework of the Securities Act, for many decades investment advisers were subject to regulation by the SEC and state securities authorities. The Investment Advisers Supervision Coordination Act, which was adopted in 1996 as a part of NSMIA, amended the Advisers Act to divide the responsibility for regulating investment advisers between the SEC and state securities authorities. The allocation of responsibility was updated again in 2010 through amendments to the Advisers Act made by the Dodd-Frank Act.

From 1996 until 2010, the SEC generally had regulatory responsibility for registered advisers with at least $25 million in assets under management (AUM). The Dodd-Frank Act updated the Advisers Act such that now generally only investment advisers with at least $100 million in regulatory AUM are allowed to register with the SEC.

The emphasis of the Advisers Act is a "principles-based" regulatory regime rather than a rules-based regime. This point has been reiterated time and again by the courts and top ranking members of the staff of the SEC.[3] The main purpose of the Investment Company Act is to protect the investing public by regulating conflicts of interest in investment companies and securities exchanges, so it is generally considered more of a rules-based regulatory regime when compared to the Advisers Act. Over time through rule making and enforcement actions by the SEC, the Advisers Act and the Investment Company Act have been broadened such that today there are a substantial number of standards of conduct imposed on investment advisers registered under the Advisers Act as well as registered investment companies subject to the Investment Company Act.[4]

The Organizational Structure of the SEC

The SEC consists of five presidentially appointed commissioners, one of whom is appointed by the president of the United States as chairman of the commission. The work of the SEC is carried out by approximately 3,500 staff in five divisions and 23 offices, which are summarized in Table 1.

TABLE 1.

SEC Divisions	SEC Offices	
■ Corporation Finance ■ Enforcement ■ Economic and Risk Analysis ■ Investment Management ■ Trading and Markets	■ Administrative Law Judges ■ Chief Accountant ■ Chief Operating Officer ■ Acquisitions ■ Financial Management ■ Human Resources ■ Information Technology ■ Support Operations ■ Compliance Inspections and Examinations ■ Credit Ratings ■ Equal Employment Opportunity ■ Ethics Counsel	■ General Counsel ■ Inspector General ■ International Affairs ■ Investor Advocate ■ Investor Education and Advocacy ■ Legislative and Intergovernmental Affairs ■ Minority and Women Inclusion ■ Municipal Securities ■ Public Affairs ■ Secretary

---

[3] See e.g., Andrew J. Donohue, Keynote Address at the 9th Annual International Conference on Private Investment Funds (Mar. 10, 2008), http://www.sec.gov/news/speech/2008/spch031008adj.htm (quoting "When enacting the Investment Advisers Act of 1940, Congress recognized the diversity of advisory relationships and through a principles-based statute provided them great flexibility, with the overriding obligation of fiduciary responsibility").

[4] For a good description of the SEC's development of a conduct-based regulatory scheme, see Barry Barbash, and Jai Massari, "The Investment Advisers Act of 1940: Regulation by Accretion," *Rutgers Law Journal*, Volume 39, pp. 627–656.

The SEC's primary office is located in Washington, DC. The work of the Office of Compliance and Inspections (OCIE) and the Division of Enforcement, two areas of the SEC a compliance professional is most likely to come into contact with, is carried out through regional offices across the country. The SEC's regional offices are located in the following cities:

- New York Regional Office
- Boston Regional Office
- Philadelphia Regional Office
- Atlanta Regional Office
- Miami Regional Office
- Chicago Regional Office
- Fort Worth Regional Office
- Denver Regional Office
- Salt Lake City Regional Office
- Los Angeles Regional Office
- San Francisco Regional Office

The SEC's Division of Investment Management regulates investment companies, variable insurance products, and federally registered investment advisers. OCIE is responsible for administering the SEC's National Exam Program, which serves as the mechanism by which the SEC staff promotes registered investment advisers' compliance with federal securities laws.[5]

When the circumstances warrant, OCIE will make referrals to the SEC's Enforcement Division, whose primary function is investigating and enforcing securities law violations and bringing civil actions on behalf of the SEC. Beginning in 2012, following some well-publicized acts of fraud (most notoriously the Bernie Madoff Ponzi scheme), both OCIE and the Enforcement Division underwent significant reforms with a focus on improving the regulatory outcomes of both divisions. Through these efforts, OCIE and the Enforcement Division have become much more coordinated in their efforts to protect investors through the examination process and enforcement actions.

The SEC's Regulatory Framework and the Impact on the Compliance Professional

The mission of the SEC is to protect investors; maintain fair, orderly, and efficient markets; and facilitate capital formation.[6] The SEC's mission is broad and, given the nature of the securities market, highly complex. The SEC is charged with direct oversight of over more than 10,000 investment advisers with more than $48 trillion of assets under management.[7] It is expected to perform that oversight with a budget that is surpassed thousands of times over by staffing budgets of the firms it seeks to regulate. That is likely one of the reasons why the role of the compliance professional and, in particular, the chief compliance officer (CCO) of each SEC-registered investment adviser firm, has become so important in the eyes of the SEC. In February 2003 the SEC proposed rules that mandated the involvement of the firms they are charged with regulating. Those

---

[5] SEC, National Exam Program: Offices and Program Areas, http://www.sec.gov/ocie/Article/about.html
[6] SEC, The Investor's Advocate: How the SEC Protects Investors, Maintains Market Integrity, and Facilitates Capital Formation, http://www.sec.gov/about/whatwedo.shtml
[7] SEC, National Exam Program.

rules were unanimously adopted by the SEC and became effective in February 2004 (Rule 38a-1 for investment companies, Rule 206(4)-7 for investment advisers, plus amendments to Rule 204-2, collectively known as the "Compliance Program Rule"); thus, an industry of securities compliance professionals was created with the effect of assisting the SEC in overseeing the industry the SEC is charged with regulating.[8]

Summary of the Compliance Program Rule. The Compliance Program Rule significantly expanded the role of the compliance function within SEC-registered investment advisers.[9] As adopted, the Compliance Program Rule established a framework of regulation from inside the firms the SEC is charged with regulating. The Compliance Program Rule requires each investment adviser registered with the SEC to:

- Adopt and implement written policies and procedures reasonably designed to prevent violations of the federal securities laws;
- Review those policies and procedures annually for their adequacy and the effectiveness of their implementation; and
- Designate a CCO to be responsible for administering the compliance program.[10]

For compliance professionals working in SEC-registered advisers, understanding the Compliance Program Rule—both in its intent and application—are critical components of the job. This chapter offers a general outline of the Compliance Program Rule's intended purpose.

The SEC document creating the Compliance Program Rule begins with a few prescriptions of the types of activities the SEC expected from an adviser's compliance program. Specifically, the SEC identified the "critical areas" that an investment adviser should review:

- Portfolio management, including the allocation of investment opportunities among clients and the consistency of portfolios with clients' investment objectives, disclosures, and regulatory restrictions;
- Trading practices, including satisfying the duty of best execution and the use of client commissions to obtain execution, research or other services;
- Proprietary trading of the adviser and personal trading by employees;
- The accuracy of disclosures made to investors, clients, and regulators, including account statements and advertisements;
- Safeguarding of client assets from conversion or misuse;
- Accuracy of books and records;

---

[8] SEC, Final Rule: Compliance Programs of Investment Companies and Investment Advisers, SEC Release Nos. IA-2204; IC 26299 (Original Compliance Date Oct. 5, 2004), www.sec.gov/rules/final/ia-2204.htm

[9] *See* SIFMA White Paper on the Role of Compliance (Oct. 2005), http://www.sifma.org/uploadedfiles/societies/sifma_compliance_and_legal_society/role_of_compliance_white_paper%20(2).pdf?n=25175 (last accessed Apr. 14, 2015) (quoting Lori Richards, then director of OCIE in 2003 "In the past, [SEC-registered investment advisory] firms were only required to have written policies and procedures governing a fairly narrow scope of activities—insider trading, privacy issues, proxy voting, codes of ethics, and antimoney laundering. Now, the coverage of compliance is comprehensive, as the fund must have written policies and procedures to prevent the fund from violating the federal securities laws. These procedures will be critical tools for your compliance personnel to be able to perform their jobs effectively.").

[10] SEC, Final Rule: Compliance Programs.

- Marketing advisory services, including the use of solicitors;
- Valuing client holdings and assessing fees;
- Protecting the privacy of client records and information; and
- Business continuity plans.[11]

Subsequent guidance from the SEC staff indicates that the SEC's expectations go much further then what was set forth in the initial rule. The staff has emphasized that the firms "annual review" of its compliance policies should really be a continuing process throughout the year. It has also said that an effective compliance program should be an "activist" program that continues to evolve.[12] The staff believes that the annual review process will help compliance professionals identify needed changes to the compliance program to ensure that there is an effective "activist" compliance program on a go-forward basis. For example, in the adopting release, the SEC staff noted that the annual review should consider: (1) any compliance matters that arose during the previous year, (2) any changes in the business activities of the adviser or its affiliates, and (3) any changes in the Advisers Act or applicable regulations that might suggest a need to revise the policies or procedures.[13] The SEC's guide, "Questions Advisers Should Ask While Establishing or Reviewing Their Compliance Programs," is a good resource for compliance professionals to consult when preparing a compliance program or performing an annual review of an existing program.[14]

Summary of the Code of Ethics Requirement. Although the Compliance Program Rule is a significant component of the SEC's regulatory framework for registered investment advisers, it represents only one of the many areas compliance professionals need to be cognizant of when seeking to satisfy the regulatory expectations of the SEC. Another area of SEC regulation that is closely related to the Compliance Program Rule is the requirement that SEC-registered investment advisers establish, maintain, and enforce a written code of ethics as set forth in SEC Rule 204A-1.[15] SEC Rule 204A-1 requires an SEC-registered investment adviser's code of ethics to set forth the standards of business conduct expected of the investment adviser's "supervised persons" and to address personal securities trading by such individuals.

An SEC-registered investment adviser is not required to adopt a particular standard of business ethics. Rather, the standard that an investment adviser selects should reflect the investment adviser's fiduciary obligations to its investment advisory clients, the fiduciary obligations of the individuals it supervises, and compliance requirements of the federal securities laws. A code of ethics should set out ideals for ethical conduct premised on fundamental principles of openness, integrity, honesty, and trust.[16] According to the

---

[11] *Id.*
[12] See Lori Richards, "*Speech by SEC Staff: Remarks before the Investment Adviser Compliance Best Practices Summit: Compliance Programs: Our Shared Mission,*" U.S. Securities and Exchange Commission https://www.sec.gov/news/speech/spch022805lar.htm (last accessed June 20, 2015).
[13] SEC, Final Rule: Compliance Programs.
[14] See *Questions Advisers Should Ask While Establishing or Reviewing Their Compliance Programs* (May 2006), http://www.sec.gov/info/cco/adviser_compliance_questions.htm (last accessed June 20, 2015).
[15] SEC Release No. IA-2256 (Aug. 31, 2004).
[16] *Id.*

SEC, "A good code of ethics should effectively convey the value that the investment adviser places on ethical conduct and the code of ethics should challenge the employees to meet not only the letter of the law, but also the ideals of the organization."[17] Investment advisers may set higher ethical standards than the requirements set forth in Rule 204A-1, such as those established by other professional or trade groups.[18]

In order to prevent unlawful trading and promote ethical conduct, an investment adviser's code of ethics should include certain provisions relating to personal securities trading by investment advisory personnel. At a minimum, an investment advisor's code of ethics must include the following requirements[19]:

- A standard (or standards) of business conduct that the investment adviser requires of its supervised persons reflecting the investment adviser's fiduciary obligations;
- Provisions requiring the investment adviser's supervised persons to comply with applicable federal securities laws;
- Provisions that require all of the investment adviser's "access persons"[20] to report their personal securities transactions and holdings periodically, and the review of such personal securities transactions by the investment adviser;
- Provisions requiring supervised persons to report any violations of the investment adviser's code of ethics promptly to the CCO; and
- Provisions requiring the investment adviser to provide each of its supervised persons with a copy of the investment adviser's code of ethics and any amendments, and requiring its supervised persons to provide the investment adviser with a written acknowledgment of their receipt of the code of ethics and any amendments.

SEC-registered investment advisers must describe its code of ethics in response to Form ADV Part 2A, Item 11, and must offer to provide, upon request, a complete copy of its code of ethics to an investment advisory client.[21]

SEC-registered investment advisers are also required to establish, maintain, and enforce written policies and procedures that are reasonably designed to prevent the misuse of material nonpublic information. The prohibition on insider trading is often included in the SEC-registered investment adviser's code of ethics.

Summary of the Antifraud Rules. Section 206 of the Advisers Act addresses "prohibited transactions by registered investment advisers." Section 206, among other things, makes it unlawful for an investment adviser to engage in any fraudulent, manipulative, or deceptive act with respect to an advisory client or prospective client. It also prohibits an adviser from engaging in "principal transactions" (i.e., transactions between the

---

[17] Id.
[18] Id.
[19] Id.
[20] Id. (defining *access person* as "a supervised person who has access to nonpublic information regarding clients' purchase or sale of securities, is involved in making securities recommendations to clients or who has access to such recommendations that are nonpublic").
[21] See SEC Release IA-3060 (effective date Oct. 12, 2010).

client and the adviser acting on its own behalf) unless the client has been informed of all relevant facts and provides written consent in advance of each transaction. Over time, the SEC has adopted a number of rules designed to add clarity to the types of conduct that could be deemed to be prohibited by the antifraud language in Section 206. The vast majority of the rules governing investment adviser conduct, including the Compliance Program Rule, have been adopted pursuant to the SEC's rulemaking power in Rule 206(4).[22] The following rules apply to SEC-registered investment advisers:

- *The Advertisement Rule.*[23] Rule 206(4)-1 prohibits an SEC-registered adviser from distributing any advertisement that is false, is misleading, or that contains
  - An untrue statement of material fact,
  - Testimonials,
  - References to past investment recommendations without reference to all recommendations in a period,
  - Charts, graphs or other information that would lead an investor to determine specific securities to buy or sell, or
  - A statement that purports to offer a report, analysis or other service without charge if it commits the recipient to any obligation;
- *The Custody Rule.*[24] Rule 206(4)-2 prohibits an SEC-registered adviser from maintaining custody of client funds or securities unless certain steps to safeguard client assets are taken, such as the use of a qualified custodian;
- *The Cash Solicitation Rule.*[25] Rule 206(4)-3 prohibits an SEC-registered adviser from making cash payments, directly or indirectly, to unaffiliated third parties that have solicited client accounts for the adviser unless certain conditions are met, including that the solicitor not be subject to a court order or administrative sanction, that the payment is made pursuant to a written agreement, and that written disclosure is provided to the client;
- *Pay-to-Play.*[26] Rule 206(4)-5 was adopted to address the "pay-to-play" issues relating to relationships between investment advisory firms and political officials who have control over, or the ability to appoint someone to control, the investment decision making for public pension plans. The rule limits the political contributions (federal, state, and local) that investment advisers and certain current and prospective employees can make;
- *Proxy Voting.*[27] Rule 206(4)-6 prohibits an SEC-registered adviser from exercising proxy voting authority over client securities unless it has adopted, implemented, and described to its clients written policies and procedures to ensure that the adviser

---

[22] (15 USCS § 80b-6), Section 206 provides "It shall be unlawful for any investment adviser, by use of the mails or any means or instrumentality of interstate commerce, directly or indirectly—...
(4) to engage in any act, practice, or course of business which is fraudulent, deceptive, or manipulative. The Commission shall, for the purposes of this paragraph (4) by rules and regulations define, and prescribe means reasonably designed to prevent, such acts, practices, and courses of business as are fraudulent, deceptive, or manipulative."
[23] See 17 CFR 275.206(4)-1.
[24] See 17 CFR 275.206(4)-2.
[25] See 17 CFR 275.206(4)-3.
[26] See 17 CFR 275.206(4)-5.
[27] See 17 CFR 275.206(4)-6.

votes such securities in the best interest of clients and to disclose to clients how they can learn information on how such securities were voted. The authority to vote proxies is often provided for under an investment advisory agreement. The "Compliance Program Rule,"[28] Rule 206(4)-7 requires an SEC-registered adviser to adopt a compliance program. The Compliance Program Rule is discussed in more detail above.

- *"Pooled Vehicle Antifraud."*[29] Rule 206(4)-8 prohibits fraudulent and deceptive practices by investment advisers (whether registered or not) for many types of pooled investment vehicles, including private funds. A *private fund* is an issuer that would be an investment company under Section 3 of the Investment Company Act but for the exclusions from the definition of *investment company* under Sections 3(c)(1) or 3(c)(7) (15 USCS § 80a-3) of the Investment Company Act. The SEC passed Rule 206(4)-8 to clarify that action can be against advisers to pooled investment vehicles regardless of their registration status because many "private funds" are sold without a public offering to a restricted pool of investors satisfying certain criteria for sophistication and/or wealth. Prior to the adoption of Rule 206(4)-8, the *Goldstein v. SEC*[30] decision created uncertainty about whether the SEC could proceed in cases where investors in the "private fund" were defrauded by the adviser to that pool, because only the pool was treated as a client in *Goldstein*.

Fiduciary Duty. Section 206 of the Advisers Act has been interpreted as imposing a duty on investment advisers to act as fiduciaries in dealings with their clients, meaning that the adviser must hold the interests of its clients above its own in all matters.[31] Through the promulgation of various regulations and formal guidance, the SEC has articulated an investment adviser's fiduciary duty as including five major duties: (1) duty of care, (2) duty of loyalty, (3) duty of obedience, (4) duty to act in good faith, and (5) duty of disclosure.[32] The biggest challenges for an SEC-registered investment adviser often relate to actual or perceived conflicts of interest of the adviser. In these instances, the adviser must clearly and accurately describe those conflicts and how the adviser will not violate its fiduciary obligations to its clients. Since the passage of the Dodd-Frank Act, the SEC and other securities industry regulators have been pushing for a uniform fiduciary standard that would apply to all investment professionals overseen by the SEC, but that standard does not yet exist.

Books and Records Rule. Rule 204-2 of the Advisers Act requires investment advisers registered with the SEC to make and keep true, accurate, and current certain books and records relating to its investment advisory activities. Generally, SEC-registered investment advisers will be required to maintain and preserve most books and records in an easily

---

[28] *See* 17 CFR 275.206(4)-7.
[29] *See* 17 CFR 275.206(4)-8.
[30] *Goldstein v. SEC*, 451 F.3d 873 (D.C. Cir. 2006) (*"Goldstein"*).
[31] *See SEC v. Capital Gains Research Bureau*, 375 U.S. 180 (1963) (citing the "delicate fiduciary nature of an investment advisory relationship").
[32] *See* Lorna A. Schnase, "An Investment Adviser's Fiduciary Duty" (Aug. 1 2010), http://www.thefiduciaryinstitute.org/wp-content/uploads/2013/02/lornaschnaseFiduciary-Duty-Paper.pdf

accessible location for five years from the end of the fiscal year during which the last entry was made on the record or, in the case or marketing pieces or other forms of communications, from the end of the fiscal year during which the adviser last published or otherwise disseminated the document. The most recent two years of the required books and records must be maintained in an appropriate office location of the adviser. Information must be provided on Form ADV Part 1A if any of the investment adviser's books and records is kept in a location other than the investment adviser's principal office location.

Books and records are subject to review during an SEC examination. An investment adviser's written policies and procedures should at a minimum address what documents should be maintained, how the documents will be maintained, where the documents will be maintained, how long the documents will be maintained, and the persons responsible for ensuring the proper maintenance of required books and records.

Examination Power. Section 204 of the Advisers Act grants the SEC the right to conduct periodic, special, or other examinations of investment advisers. An SEC examination may cover or focus on any area of regulatory requirements or the adviser's operations that the SEC examiner deems appropriate. Each year, OCIE identifies certain selected examination priorities that reflect the focus areas for that year.[33] In addition to periodic inspections, the SEC may conduct "for cause" examinations of an adviser's activities if the commission has reason to believe, on the basis of a complaint, rumor, or otherwise, that an adviser or person associated with the adviser has violated the securities laws. For a thorough discussion of this subject see this book's chapter entitled "Regulatory Examinations and Audits," by Michelle Jacko.

Failure to Supervise Liability. Compliance professionals need to be aware of the risk of liability that can come with the violation of certain regulations by other professionals within their own firm. Most compliance professionals, notably CCOs, are well aware of the SEC enforcement actions when CCOs are alleged to be personally accountable for failing to maintain an adequate compliance program.[34] These cases are typically brought under a theory of liability available to the SEC known as "failure to supervise."[35]

The current statement of the SEC's failure to supervise theory of liability was first announced in the administrative proceeding known as *In the Matter of John H. Gutfreund et al.*[36] In *Gutfreund*, the commission stated that, under certain circumstances, legal or compliance officers of broker-dealers could be found to be supervisors. In order to have liability for the conduct of another employee, a compliance professional generally must have "the requisite degree of responsibility, ability, or authority to affect the conduct of the employee whose behavior is at issue."[37] When evaluating

---

[33] OCIE's examination priorities are located on its website, http://www.sec.gov/ocie
[34] See e.g., *In the matter of Consulting Services Group, LLC, and Joe D. Meals*, Rel. IA-2669 (Oct. 4, 2007); Thomas Meade, Private Capital Management case (July 31, 2012).
[35] SIFMA White Paper Note 9, FN 56 (quoting "for a Compliance Department officer to be liable for deficient supervision, the employee who violates a securities law must be 'subject to the supervision' of the individual"; see 1934 Act § 15(b)(4)(E).)
[36] *John H. Gutfreund*, Exchange Act Release No. 31554 (Dec. 3, 1992).
[37] *Id.*

what it means to have the "requisite degree of responsibility, ability, or authority to affect the conduct of another employee," the standard from *Gutfreund* that "a person's actual responsibilities and authority, rather than, for example, his or her 'line' or 'nonline' status, determine whether he or she is a 'supervisor.' "[38] Compliance professionals must be mindful that to the extent they make, or are viewed to be responsible for, business or managerial decisions, they may assume business or supervisory liability.[39]

III. UNDERSTANDING THE REGULATORY FRAMEWORK OF THE FINANCIAL INDUSTRY REGULATORY AUTHORITY (FINRA)

Historical Perspective of Self-Regulatory Organizations and FINRA

The existing regulatory framework of the securities markets in the United States relies heavily on self-regulatory organizations (SROs). A self-regulatory organization is an organization that exercises some degree of regulatory authority over an industry or profession. The ability of an SRO to exercise regulatory authority may derive from a grant of authority from the government.

The role of self-regulation of the securities markets in the United States has its roots in the member-owned stock exchanges of the 19th century and goes back more than two hundred years.[40] The earliest forms of SROs in the securities markets were the member-owned exchanges such as the New York Stock and Exchange Board, which later became the New York Stock Exchange, and the Boston and Philadelphia Stock Exchanges. These early membership-based forms of SROs generally adopted constitutions that prescribed rules on trading, the admission and discipline of members, and fixed commissions.[41] The form of self-regulation by members of the exchanges continued to evolve through the 19th century and had a number of challenges during that time. The challenges to the early forms of SROs generally centered on the fairness and effectiveness of such forms of regulation. Despite knowing of issues with the existing form of SRO regulation, lawmakers believed that this early model of SROs had great promise, and so it continued until the market crash of 1929 caused such a level of distrust in the SRO model that Congress was forced to act.

The question of exactly what to do to change the existing SRO model was a challenging one for Congress. The members of Congress involved in creating the Securities Act and Exchange Act also had to decide between direct governmental intervention and day-to-day supervision of all activities, or a less invasive approach. Ultimately, Congress at the time had to make a compromise and opted to allow the SROs to

---

[38] *Gutfreund*, at note 24.
[39] SIFMA White Paper, pp. 6–7, http://www.sifma.org/issues/item.aspx?id=8589942363 (last accessed Apr. 14, 2015).
[40] The Institution of Experience: Self-Regulatory Organizations in the Securities Industry, 1792–2010, http://www.sechistorical.org/museum/galleries/sro/ (last visited Apr. 14, 2015).
[41] *Id.* (citing the February 25, 1817, Transcript of Constitution of the New York Stock & Exchange Board).

continue in their current form and have them register with the SEC as "national securities exchanges." This public-private partnership model of regulation, which began with the creation of the SEC, launched the partnership between the private member-owned stock exchanges and federal regulators that exists today.[42] Under this model, the SROs were expected to enforce compliance with their own rules and federal securities laws. In 1938 the Exchange Act was amended by the Maloney Act, which authorized the formation and registration of national securities associations, which would supervise the conduct of their members subject to the oversight of the SEC. In 1939 the National Association of Securities Dealers (NASD, which later became FINRA) was designed to regulate and license member brokerage firms, broker-dealers, their sales staffs, and the exchange markets.

The relationship between the SROs and the SEC continued for decades, with the SROs operating relatively autonomously until the Securities Act Amendments of 1975 ("1975 Amendments"). The changes brought about by those amendments were generally seen as the most comprehensive revisions to the Securities Act and Exchange Act passed by Congress since the passage of the original securities laws in the 1930s. As it pertained to the public-private partnership between SROs and the SEC, the primary objective of the 1975 Amendments was to "make uniform the SEC's authority over self-regulatory organizations."[43]

A few of the changes in the 1975 Amendments covering this point were very specific:

- Any new rule or change in the rules of an SRO had to be filed with the SEC, and with minor exceptions, approved by SEC;
- The SEC was given the power to deny the adoption of, or to amend, any rule of an SRO;
- The SEC was given the authority to review all disciplinary actions by the stock exchanges; and
- Stock exchanges were only able to deny membership in accordance with provisions specified in the 1975 Amendments.

These changes began to tip the scale from what had been for 40 years a private-public partnership to one where the SEC had much greater responsibility for ensuring that the SROs were regulating themselves in ways that the commission found to be acceptable. An interesting historical fact comes from the 1975 Amendments, when the phrase "self-regulation" was almost abandoned for what the House Committee concluded was better phrased as "cooperative regulation."[44] The Senate Committee thought that phrase might be misleading about the "relative functions and authority of industry and government," and the phrase "self-regulatory organization" made its way into Section 3(a)(26) of the Exchange Act, where it remains defined today.[45]

---

[42] *Id.*
[43] P.L. 94-29, June 4, 1975.
[44] Address by Phillip A. Loomis, Jr., Joint Securities Conference 1975 (Nov. 18, 1975).
[45] *Id.*

The presence and importance of SROs in the United States regulatory framework has significantly increased from its roots in the early 1900s. There are currently a large number of SROs participating in the regulation of the securities industry. A current list of them is available on the SEC's website and consists of the national securities exchanges (e.g., the New York Stock Exchange, NYSE Arca, NASDAQ stock market, and BATS Exchange); registered securities associations (FINRA); securities futures associations (National Futures Association); and registered clearing agencies (e.g., Chicago Mercantile Exchange, Depository Trust Company, and Fixed Income Clearing Corporation), among others.[46] One SRO in particular, the NASD (now known as FINRA), has become arguably the most prominent SRO in the United States securities industry, and as such it is the focus of the remainder of this section on SROs.

The Organizational Structure of FINRA

Like the SEC, FINRA has a big job to do when it comes to enforcing compliance with the rules and regulations applicable to the securities industry and its members. To carry out its regulatory agenda, FINRA has approximately 3,500 employees in more than 20 offices across the United States. FINRA was established in 2007 through the combination of the NASD and the member regulation, enforcement, and arbitration operations of the New York Stock Exchange. Although sometimes mistakenly viewed as a part of the U.S. federal government, FINRA is not a government agency. FINRA is the largest SRO in the securities industry in the United States.

FINRA functions under the umbrella and jurisdiction of the SEC as the SRO for the securities industry in the United States. FINRA's supervisory responsibility includes more than 4,000 firms and more than 600,000 brokers.[47] It monitors and regulates all securities trading (monitoring approximately 6 billion share trades each day[48]), operations and records, exchange platforms, and personnel in the industry. It also acts as a buffer organization between the securities markets and the SEC. FINRA supervises only broker-dealers; it does not currently have direct responsibility for the regulation of registered investment advisers. Nevertheless, registered investment advisers will in all cases have contact with FINRA because the Investment Adviser Registration Depository (IARD), the platform by which all investment adviser firms register and file their annual updates to Form ADV, is operated by FINRA.

FINRA's stature as a market regulator has grown and its regulatory scope continues to evolve as the securities industry changes and the public's perception of the ability of securities regulators to effectively protect investors grows more circumspect. The financial crises and the massive fraud committed by Bernard Madoff made 2008 a very difficult year for the SEC and FINRA. After the onset of the financial crisis and the revelation of the Bernard Madoff Ponzi scheme, FINRA worked with the SEC to further expand

---

[46] *See* SEC, Self-Regulatory Organization Rulemaking, http://www.sec.gov/rules/sro.shtml (last accessed June 20, 2015).
[47] FINRA, About FINRA, http://www.finra.org/AboutFINRA/
[48] *Id.*

the ways it could assist in the effective regulation of the securities markets. In March 2009, FINRA created the Office of the Whistleblower Protection, and later that year it introduced a number of internal initiatives to help prevent another Madoff scenario.[49] In its 2008 Year in Review and Annual Financial Report, FINRA started laying the groundwork to expand its supervisory responsibilities beyond broker dealers to include investment advisers. After more than four years of effort, FINRA stepped back from this initiative in 2013, but it is possible that FINRA might seek regulatory oversight of investment advisers again in the future.

FINRA's Regulatory Framework and the Impact on the Compliance Professional

FINRA has five main regulatory objectives, which can be categorized as follows:

- Deter misconduct by enforcing the rules;
- Discipline those who break the rules;
- Detect and prevent wrongdoing in the U.S. markets;
- Educate and inform investors; and
- Resolve securities disputes.[50]

FINRA performs many important functions, including being tasked with the responsibility of maintaining an orderly marketplace. FINRA's mission is to safeguard the investing public against fraud and bad practices. FINRA pursues that mission by writing and enforcing rules and regulations for every single brokerage firm and broker in the U.S. and by examining broker-dealers for compliance with its own rules, federal securities laws, and rules of the Municipal Securities Rulemaking Board (MSRB), another SRO.[51]

FINRA also licenses individuals and admits firms to the industry; writes rules to govern their behavior; examines them for regulatory compliance; and disciplines registered representatives and member firms that fail to comply with federal securities laws and FINRA's rules and regulations. FINRA maintains the Central Registration Depository, a database of all registered individuals and firms. In addition, FINRA provides education and qualification examinations for securities industry professionals. FINRA members include all securities firms that do business with the public. Through agreements with the various markets and exchanges, FINRA also provides oversight and enforcement to the New York Stock Exchange, NASDAQ, MSRB, American Stock Exchange, International Securities Exchange, industry utilities, and other over-the-counter operations.[52]

FINRA works with the SEC in the detection and prosecution of issuers when regulatory infractions occur. Although FINRA in and of itself does not possess the legal authority to prosecute issuers, it actively engages in investigations related to market fraud and

---

[49] *See* 2009 Year in Review, Enhancements to FINRA's Regulatory Program, https://www.finra.org/sites/default/files/Corporate/p121646.pdf) (last accessed Apr. 16, 2015).
[50] FINRA, What We Do, http://www.finra.org/AboutFINRA/WhatWeDo/ (2015).
[51] *Id.*
[52] *Id.*

shares its findings with prosecutorial authorities (i.e., the SEC for civil actions and either Department of Justice or State Attorney for criminal violations). FINRA maintains a vital role in the enforcement of securities laws by providing prosecutorial bodies with crucial data that substantiates when a violation has occurred.

Although FINRA and the SEC are distinct in their emphases of market regulation, many similarities exist in the rules and agendas they have in place. One area in which FINRA and the SEC have adopted similar approaches to their regulatory objectives is through the requirements of FINRA Rule 3100, Supervisory Responsibilities. FINRA's supervisory requirements are in many ways similar to the requirements of the SEC's Compliance Program Rule. The next section will explore the implementation of FINRA Rule 3100 in more detail.

Adoption and Implementation of the Supervisory Responsibilities Rule

On the heels of the SEC's adoption of the Compliance Program Rule, FINRA submitted a similar rule to the SEC, which was approved by the SEC in December 2004.[53] Originally implemented as NASD Rule 3013, Annual Certification of Compliance and Supervisory Processes, and IM-3013-1, Annual Compliance and Supervision Certification, FINRA's Compliance Program Rules were consolidated as FINRA Rule 3130 in the Consolidated FINRA Rulebook following FINRA's formation in 2007. FINRA Rule 3130, as enacted, had many parallelisms with Rule 206(4)-7. The general requirements of FINRA Rule 3130 are:

- Designate one or more CCOs and report these individuals on the firm's Form BD and on the FINRA Firm Contact System;
- A firm may designate a co-CEO;
- Have the CEO(s) complete an annual certification that the member has in place *processes* to establish, maintain, review, test, and modify written compliance and supervisory policies and procedures that are reasonably designed to achieve compliance and that the CEO has conducted one or more meetings with the CCO in the preceding 12 months to discuss the processes;
- Prepare a report evidencing the member's processes and have it reviewed by the CEO(s), CCO(s), and any other officers the member deems necessary; and
- Provide the report to the member's board of directors and Audit Committee (or equivalent bodies), either prior to execution of the certification or at the earlier of the next scheduled meetings or within 45 days of execution of the certification.

In early 2014, FINRA issued Regulatory Notice 14-10 ("FINRA Notice 14-10"), announcing that Rules 3110 and 3120 (together, the "Consolidated Supervision Rules") would become effective on December 1, 2014, thereby superseding NASD Conduct Rules 3010 and 3012 and various NASD interpretive material and related New York Stock Exchange rules (NYSE rules).[54] FINRA Notice 14-10 discusses the Consolidated

---

[53] NASD Notice to Members 04-79 (Nov. 2004).
[54] FINRA, SEC Approves New Supervision Rules, Regulatory Notice 14-10, https://www.finra.org/industry/notices/14-10

Supervision Rules that require member firms to "have a supervisory system for the activities of its associated persons that is reasonably designed to achieve compliance with the applicable securities laws and regulations and FINRA rules, and sets forth the minimum requirements for a firm's supervisory system."[55]

The Consolidated Supervision Rules have minimum requirements for supervisory systems that are similar to those required by current rules, including the adoption of written supervisory procedures, designation of registered principals to carry out supervisory responsibilities, and conducting an annual compliance meeting or interview.[56] Some of the requirements in the Consolidated Supervision Rules update existing FINRA compliance rule requirements by specifying:

- Which personnel are permitted to act as supervisors of other personnel;
- Which personnel may perform office inspections;
- Requirements for review of certain internal communications;
- Obligations to monitor for insider trading, including a requirement to conduct internal investigations and report certain related information to FINRA; and
- Obligations related to the supervision of firms' Offices of Supervisory Jurisdiction (OSJs).

In addition, the Consolidated Supervision Rules impose a new requirement that, for a member that reports more than $200 million in gross annual revenues on its FOCUS report, the annual report to senior management must include: "a tabulation of reports made to FINRA during the year regarding customer complaints and internal investigations; and a discussion of the prior year's compliance efforts, including procedures and educational programs relating to trading and market activities, investment banking, antifraud and sales practices, finance and operations, supervision, and anti-money laundering."[57]

The adoption of the Consolidated Supervision Rules is a good reminder of the need for firms to review their existing supervisory policies and procedures periodically and revise them as necessary to meet changing regulatory requirements.

IV. UNDERSTANDING THE REGULATORY FRAMEWORK OF THE U.S. COMMODITY FUTURES TRADING COMMISSION

Historical Perspective of the CFTC

The purchase and sale of futures contracts for agricultural commodities has a long history in the United States, with many of the commodity exchanges in operation

---

[55] Id.; *see also* Note 4 (quoting Notice to Members 99-45 (June 1999) ("NASD Rule 3010's 'reasonably designed' standard 'recognizes that a supervisory system cannot guarantee firm-wide compliance with all laws and regulations' but that the 'reasonably designed' standard requires that the system 'be a product of sound thinking and within the bounds of common sense, taking into consideration the factors that are unique to a member's business.'")
[56] *See* Id.
[57] Id.

tracing their origins back to the 1800s.[58] These exchanges functioned as self-regulatory organizations free from federal regulation until the 1920s.

The Future Trading Act (FTA) was enacted on August 24, 1921. Under the FTA, the regulation of "contract markets" fell under the authority of the Secretary of Agriculture. The FTA was the first comprehensive effort to regulate these markets with the goals of preventing manipulation of prices and the dissemination of misleading information.[59] The FTA did not last long, and the Supreme Court declared the entire act unconstitutional less than 12 months after its enactment. Later in 1922, however, Congress passed the Grain Futures Act (GFA), which created the Grain Futures Administration within the Department of Agriculture and created the independent Grain Futures Commission.[60]

The Grain Futures Act remained in effect until June 15, 1936, when Congress passed the Commodity Exchange Act (CEA).[61] The CEA, 7 U.S.C. § 1 *et seq.*, prohibits fraudulent conduct in the trading of futures contracts. The CEA amended the GFA and added several new sections and regulatory requirements. With the passage of the CEA, the Grain Futures Commission became the Commodity Exchange Commission and the Commodity Exchange Authority was created. The CEA extended the regulatory authority of the Secretary of Agriculture to include futures on exchange-traded commodities, other than grain futures. However, the CEA did not prove to be effective in the prevention of market manipulation and abuse.[62]

With the exception of the Onion Futures Act of 1958,[63] which imposed a ban on the trading of futures contracts on onions, the commodities markets continued to operate without much change for close to forty years. However, by the 1970s, the trading of futures contracts had expanded beyond traditional and agricultural commodities into a vast array of financial instruments, including foreign currencies, U.S. and foreign government securities, and U.S. and foreign stock indices. With the evolution of the futures markets, the need for additional regulation became apparent, and the Commodities Futures Trading Commission Act of 1974 (CFTCA) was passed on October 23, 1974.[64]

The passing of the CFTCA resulted in the creation of the U.S. Commodity Futures Trading Commission (CFTC), which replaced the Commodity Exchange Commission and the Commodity Exchange Authority as the independent federal agency responsible for regulating the futures trading industry. Under the CEA, the CFTC is the federal agency responsible for the regulation of trading in instruments such as commodity futures, commodity options, security futures products, retail forex transactions, and

---

[58] U.S. Commodity Futures Trading Commission, History of the CFTC, http://www.cftc.gov/about/historyofthecftc/index.htm
[59] Futures Trading Act § 5, 42 Stat. at 188.
[60] Grain Futures Act of 1922, ch. 369, 42 Stat 998(1922).
[61] Community Exchange Act of 1936, ch. 545, 49 Stat. 1491 (1936).
[62] *See* Shifting Risk to the Dumbest Guy in the Room: Derivatives Regulation After the Wall Street Reform and Consumer Protection Act (citing Jerry W. Markham, "Manipulation of Commodity Futures Prices: The Unprosecutable Crime," 8 *Yale J. on Reg.*(1991), 281, 313–31).
[63] 7 U.S.C. § 13-1(b).
[64] Commodity Futures Trading Act of 1974 §201, P. L. No. 93-463, 88 Stat 1389 (1974).

other commodity interest transactions in the U.S. markets. Although the CFTCA made significant strides to enhance the regulation of futures and commodities trading, there were many areas of the market that were left unregulated. The lack of regulation, most notably the failure to regulate certain financial products known as over-the-counter derivatives,[65] would, in substantial part, give rise to the financial crisis that began in 2008.

In 2010, the Dodd-Frank Act[66] further amended the CEA to expand the CFTC's jurisdiction to include trading in certain swaps. The SEC was given jurisdiction over security-based swaps, and the SEC and CFTC share jurisdiction over the limited category of securities referred to as "mixed swaps." The Dodd-Frank Act tightened the regulations on participants in the futures and swaps markets, predominantly futures commissions merchants, swap dealers, and major swap participants. Among the provisions arising out of the Dodd-Frank Act, the CFTC and SEC established rules and guidelines regarding business conduct standards for swap dealers and major swap participants, futures commission merchants, and introducing brokers.

The Organizational Structure of the CFTC

The CFTC organization[67] is made up of five commissioners, the offices of the chairman, and the agency's operating units.[68] The five commissioners are appointed by the president of the United States, with the advice and consent of the Senate, to serve staggered five-year terms. The president designates one of the commissioners to serve as chairman. No more than three commissioners at any one time may be from the same political party. The CFTC operates similarly to the SEC in many ways. For example, the CFTC also has rulemaking authority and is also authorized to establish regulations in accordance with the authority granted to it by the CEA.

The CFTC has four divisions: (1) Division of Clearing and Risk; (2) Division of Enforcement; (3) Division of Market Oversight; and (4) Division of Swap Dealer and Intermediary Oversight.

The CFTC has eight offices that assist the CFTC with carrying out its mission: (1) Office of the Chief Economist; (2) Office of Data and Technology; (3) Office of the Executive Director; (4) the Office of General Counsel; (5) the Office of the Inspector General; (6) the Office of International Affairs; (7) the Office of Legislative Affairs; and

---

[65] The Commodity Futures Modernization Act of 2000 (CFMA) clarified the CEA so that most over-the-counter (OTC) derivatives transactions between "sophisticated parties" would not be regulated as "futures" under the Commodity Exchange Act of 1936 (CEA) or as "securities" under the federal securities laws. Instead, the major dealers of those products (banks and securities firms) had their dealings in OTC derivatives supervised by their federal banking regulators under general "safety and soundness" standards.

[66] Dodd–Frank Wall Street Reform and Consumer Protection Act (Enrolled Final Version—HR 4173) (Dodd-Frank Act).

[67] The CFTC Organization, http://www.cftc.gov/ucm/groups/public/@aboutcftc/documents/file/cftcorgchart.pdf

[68] U.S. Commodity Futures Trading Commission, CFTC Organization, http://www.cftc.gov/About/CFTCOrganization/index.htm

(8) the Office of Public Affairs. In addition to its headquarters in Washington, DC, the CFTC has three regional offices in Chicago, Kansas City, and New York.

CFTC's Regulatory Framework and the Impact on the Compliance Professional

The stated mission of the CFTC is "to foster open, transparent, competitive, and financially sound markets, to avoid systemic risk, and to protect the market users and their funds, consumers, and the public from fraud, manipulation, and abusive practices related to derivatives and other products that are subject to the Commodity Exchange Act."[69]

Compliance professionals at SEC-registered investment advisers are most likely to encounter the complex rules and regulations of the CFTC when evaluating whether the firm itself meets the definition of a commodity trading advisor (CTA). A CTA is any person who, for compensation or profit, whether directly or indirectly, engages in the business of advising others, or as part of a regular business issues reports or analysis, about the value of or the advisability of trading in, among other things, any futures contract or swap.[70] For SEC-registered investment advisers, there are two exemptions from registration with the CFTC that are generally available. Both of the exemptions summarized below are self-executing (that is, there is no filing requirement).

- *CEA Section 4m(1) and CFTC Rule 4.14(a)(10)—15 or Fewer Clients.* Section 4m(1) of the CEA provides that a person need not register as a CTA if, during the course of the preceding 12 months, the person has not furnished commodity trading advice to more than 15 persons. In addition, the person must not hold itself out generally to the public as a CTA; and
- *CEA Section 4m(3)—Certain SEC-Registered Investment Advisers.* Section 4m(3) of the CEA provides that a person need not register as a CTA if that person is registered with the SEC as an investment adviser under the Investment Advisers Act, provided that the person's business does not consist "primarily" of acting as a CTA and does not act as a CTA to any commodity pool that is engaged primarily in trading commodity interests. For this purpose, the CTA provides that a CTA or a commodity pool shall be considered to be "engaged primarily" in the business of being a CTA or commodity pool if it is or holds itself out to the public as being engaged primarily, or proposes to engage primarily, in the business of advising on commodity interests or investing, reinvesting, owning, holding, or trading in commodity interests, respectively.

Even though the above exemptions are self-executing, in some cases, an SEC-registered investment adviser may desire to make a notice filing so that the counterparties it deals with can independently verify that the adviser has properly filed an exemption from registration with the CFTC.

---

[69] CFTC, Mission & Responsibilities, http://www.cftc.gov/about/missionresponsibilities/index.htm
[70] *See* CEA Section 1a(12) and Commission Regulation 1.3(bb). The CEA and the Commission's regulations may be accessed through the commission's Web site, www.cftc.gov

Not all exemptions from CFTC registration are self-executing. The Rule 4.14(a)(8) exemption requires a notice filing.[71] The details regarding this notice filing are described here.

CFTC Rule 4.14(a)(8): Certain SEC-Registered Investment Advisers; Exempt and Excluded Investment Advisers. CFTC Rule 4.14(a)(8) provides that an SEC-registered investment adviser does not need register as a CTA, provided that:

1. The firm's commodity trading advice is directed solely to, and for the sole use of, one or more:
    - "Qualifying entities" for which a notice of eligibility for the Rule 4.5[72] exclusion has been filed with the NFA;
    - Collective investment vehicles excluded from the definition of "commodity pool";
    - Certain non-U.S. commodity pools;
    - A CPO claiming the exemption from CPO registration under Rule 4.13(a)(3);
    - A registered CPO that may treat each pool it operates that meets the criteria of Rule 4.13(a)(3) as if it were not so registered; or
    - A registered CPO that may treat each pool it operates that meets the criteria of Rule 4.13(a)(3) as if it were not so registered;
2. The firm provides commodity trading advice "solely incidental" to its business of providing securities or other investment advice to the aforementioned clients;
3. The firm does not otherwise hold itself out as a CTA;
4. The firm files an exemption with the NFA and affirms at the end of each calendar year that it is conducting its activities in accordance with the terms of the exemption (if it cannot do so, the firm must withdraw its claim of exemption); and
5. The firm must make and keep certain books and records prepared in connection with its commodity trading advice.

An entity that makes a notice filing under CFTC Rule 4.14(a)(8) is still relying on an exemption from the CTA registration requirements. Any entities that are exempt from CTA registration may nonetheless be subject to certain regulatory requirements. For example, a CTA (whether registered or unregistered) may not refer to any testimonial or to any simulated or hypothetical performance of the CTA or any of its principals, unless certain disclosures are made in accordance with CFTC regulations.

Although many SEC-registered investment advisers are able to avail themselves of an exemption from CFTC registration, any entity that is required to register as a CTA and who manages or exercises discretion over customer accounts must be a member of the National Futures Association (NFA) in order to conduct futures business with the

---

[71] See CFTC, http://www.cftc.gov/IndustryOversight/Intermediaries/CPOs/cpoctaexemptionsexclusions
[72] Under Rule 4.5(b) "qualifying entities" generally include SEC-registered investment companies, insurance company separate accounts, bank custodial accounts and trust accounts, and ERISA pension plans.

public. As mentioned earlier in this chapter, the NFA is an SRO. Accordingly, CTA registration is an example of a regulatory regime in which the public-private partnership of government (CFTC) and self-regulatory organizations (SRO) overlap.

Implementing the CFTC and NFA CTA Compliance Program Rules

A CTA that is registered with the NFA is required to design and implement a program for complying with the rules and regulations of the CFTC and the NFA. For SEC-registered investment advisers, the CFTC and NFA requirements such as the disclosure booklet, reporting, and recordkeeping requirements can be incorporated into their existing policies and procedures.[73]

V. UNDERSTANDING THE REGULATORY FRAMEWORK OF THE COMPTROLLER OF CURRENCY

Historical Perspective of the OCC

The Office of the Comptroller of the Currency (OCC) is the oldest regulatory agency of the U.S. government, tracing its roots back to the National Currency Act, which was adopted in February 1863. The OCC continues to operate as a bureau of the U.S. Department of the Treasury and it serves to charter, regulate, and supervise all national banks and thrift institutions, as well as the federal branches and agencies of foreign banks in the United States.

The OCC's original purpose was focused on creating a national banking system, establishing a national currency, and creating a uniform set of rules enforced by bank examiners who were compensated by the banks they examined.[74] With its origins in the Civil War, it is also no surprise that the OCC has undergone more change in its regulatory duties than any other U.S. government agency.

The first major overhaul of the OCC came with the Federal Reserve Act of 1913, which created and established the Federal Reserve System. The Federal Reserve System became the central banking system of the U.S. and it assumed the legal authority to issue Federal Reserve notes, now known as U.S. dollars. The Federal Reserve Act required that all nationally chartered banks become members of the Federal Reserve System and to set aside stipulated amounts of noninterest-bearing reserves with their respective reserve banks. Importantly, the OCC retained its role of maintaining supervision over national banks, including examinations by the OCC's Division of Examinations.

The stock market crash of 1929 and the bank failures that followed necessitated another overhaul that came with the passage of the Glass-Steagall Act of 1933.[75] The

---

[73] *See* the NFA's website at http://www.nfa.futures.org/nfa-compliance/index.HTML for additional information on CFTC and NFA compliance requirements.
[74] *See* Office of the Comptroller of the Currency, *A Short History,* http://www.occ.gov/about/what-we-do/history/OCC%20history%20final.pdf
[75] The term *Glass-Steagall Act of 1933* generally refers to four provisions of the U.S. Banking Act of 1933 that limited commercial bank securities activities and affiliations within commercial banks and securities firms.

Glass-Steagall Act had, at its core, the notion that the riskier activities of investment banking should be separated from the traditional activities of commercial banks. On the one hand, it prevented investment banks from taking deposits. On the other hand, it prohibited commercial Federal Reserve member banks from:

- Dealing in nongovernmental securities for customers;
- Investing in non-investment grade securities for themselves;
- Underwriting or distributing nongovernmental securities; and
- Affiliating (or sharing employees) with companies involved in such activities.

The Glass-Steagall Act also created a system of federal deposit insurance that helped shore up the public's confidence in putting money back into banks, which helped the nation recover from the Great Depression. State banks were also eligible for federal deposit insurance protection, and those who accepted it became subject to supervision by the newly created Federal Deposit Insurance Corporation (FDIC) and state banking regulators. With the creation of the FDIC, it became clear that with three main federal regulatory bodies—the OCC, the Federal Reserve, and the FDIC—the start of new era of heightened bank supervision and regulation was set to begin.[76]

The United States banking system experienced tremendous growth and change from the mid-1930s through the 1960s. The 1960s saw a general relaxation of certain restrictions imposed by the Glass-Steagall Act, and by the 1980s, many of the restrictions had been phased out or interpreted in such a way that the original intent of the Glass-Steagall Act was nonexistent. The Office of Thrift Supervision (OTS), the successor to the Federal Home Loan Bank Board, was established by Congress on August 9, 1989, as the primary federal regulator of all federal and state-chartered savings institutions across the nation that belong to the Savings Association Insurance Fund.[77] Another significant development came in November 1999, when Congress passed the Gramm-Leech-Bliley Act[78] and effectively removed the separation of investment banking and commercial banking activities that was the hallmark of the Glass-Steagall Act.

The financial crises of the late 2000s spawned another new era in regulation with the passage of the Dodd-Frank Act. The main emphasis of the Dodd-Frank Act was principally focused on national banks, with the stated goal of the Dodd-Frank Act being:

> To promote the financial stability of the United States by improving accountability and transparency in the financial system, to end "too big to fail," to protect the American taxpayer by ending bailouts, to protect consumers from abusive financial services practices, and for other purposes.[79]

---

[76] Office of the Comptroller of the Currency, *A Short History*.
[77] U.S. Department of the Treasury, Office of Thrift Supervision, http://www.treasury.gov/about/history/Pages/ots.aspx
[78] Also known as the Financial Services Modernization Act of 1999, (P.L. 106–102, 113 Stat. 1338, enacted Nov. 12, 1999).
[79] *See* preamble to Dodd-Frank Act.

Another significant change brought about by the Dodd-Frank Act was the establishment of the Financial Stability Oversight Council (FSOC). The FSOC was established in 2010 with the goal of bringing together federal and state financial regulators to look across the financial system to identify risks to financial stability, promote market discipline, and respond to emerging threats to the stability of the U.S. financial system. The FSOC is composed of 10 voting members and 5 nonvoting members.

TABLE 2.	
FSOC Voting Members	**FSOC Nonvoting Members**
■ Secretary of the Treasury (also serves as the Chairperson of the FSOC) ■ Chair of the Board of Governors of the Federal Reserve System (Federal Reserve) ■ Comptroller of the Currency ■ Director of the Consumer Financial Protection Bureau ■ Chairman of the Federal Deposit Insurance Corporation ■ Chair of the Securities and Exchange Commission ■ Chairman of the Commodity Futures Trading Commission ■ Federal Housing Finance Agency ■ Chairman of the National Credit Union Administration ■ Independent member with insurance expertise who is appointed by the president	■ Director of the Office of Financial Research ■ Director of the Federal Insurance Office ■ A state insurance commissioner ■ A state banking supervisor ■ A state securities commissioner

After much anticipation and debate about whether the FSOC would and should designate individual asset managers (a nonbank financial firm) as systemically important financial institutions (SIFIs), which would subject them to greater oversight, the FSOC announced in August 2014 that rather than designating individual asset managers as SIFIs, it would focus on examining systemic risk posed by asset managers' products, and activities. As a result of FSOC's announcement, the SEC is expected to take a prudential supervisory role of individual asset managers, in addition to exercising its traditional mandate of investor protection.[80]

The Organizational Structure of the OCC

The OCC is a bureau of the U.S. Department of the Treasury and is headed by the comptroller of the currency.[81] The president appoints the Comptroller to head the agency for a five-year term. The comptroller serves a five-year term and is also a director of the FDIC and the Neighborhood Reinvestment Corporation.[82] The OCC is one of a number

---

[80] Additional information regarding the regulatory purview of the FSOC is available at http://www.treasury.gov/initiatives/fsoc/Pages/home.aspx
[81] Office of the Comptroller of the Currency, About the OCC, http://www.occ.gov/about/what-we-do/mission/index-about.html
[82] *Id.*

of bureaus of the U.S. Department of the Treasury that includes the Internal Revenue Service, the Financial Crimes Enforcement Network, and the U.S. Mint.[83] The OCC also enforces MSRB rules that apply to national banks that deal in municipal securities.

The comptroller works with an Executive Committee composed of the heads of the OCC's major business units. The executive committee advises the comptroller on policy and other issues. Smaller committees also report to the comptroller and the Executive Committee. These committees are the audit, bank supervision, budget and finance, human capital, regulatory policy, legal and external affairs and technology and systems committees.

The OCC is not funded by Congress. Its operating budget continues to come from assessments on national banks, which pay for their examinations and for processing certain applications. The OCC also supplements its budget with income on the investment of this revenue.

Washington, DC, is home to the OCC headquarters, but a nationwide staff of bank examiners in more than 50 field offices performs the onsite reviews of national banks. The OCC is divided into four geographic regions: Western (headquartered in Denver), Central (headquartered in Chicago), Southern (headquartered in Dallas), and Northeastern (headquartered in New York). The OCC is the only regulatory agency that has resident examiners inside the offices of the entities it regulates. Presently, the OCC has resident examiners at the largest banking companies in the United States.

OCC Regulatory Framework and the Impact on the Compliance Professional

The OCC exists to ensure the safety of the banking system, foster banking competition, provide efficient supervision, and ensure fair and equal access to financial services for all Americans. It polices the lending and investment activities of national banks, and it issues operating rules, legal interpretations, and important decisions regarding national bank activities. The OCC also has the power to approve or deny charters for new national banks or bank branches.

The primary task of the OCC is to regularly examine national banks. These examinations include analyses of a bank's loans and investments, how it manages its funds, the risk profile of the bank (that is, the liquidity and profitability of the bank), and the bank's compliance with consumer banking laws. The OCC examiners also review the bank's internal controls and management ability.[84]

Each regulatory agency of a bank has the right to examine the bank, but the regulators usually cooperate with each other and accept the examinations of other authorities. So, although the FDIC wants to conduct an examination at least annually, it will often

---

[83] U.S. Department of the Treasury, Bureaus, http://www.treasury.gov/about/organizational-structure/bureaus/Pages/default.aspx
[84] Investing Answers, Office of the Comptroller of the Currency (OCC), http://www.investinganswers.com/financial-dictionary/laws-regulations/office-comptroller-currency-occ-934

accept a recent examination by the Federal Reserve or the OCC. States will often accept the reviews of federal regulators rather than performing their own.

To assess the safety and soundness of a bank, banking examiners use a scoring system called CAMELS, which stands for Capital adequacy, Asset quality, Management, Earnings, Liquidity, and Sensitivity to risk. A score of 1 (highest) to 5 is assigned to each category, which is then used to select banks for greater scrutiny.[85] CAMELS scores are not publicly disclosed because they are only the opinions of bank examiners. Bank examiners also consult with bank managers on how to do a better job of managing risk, since most of them examine multiple banks and learn the best practices of the different banks. An additional rating category noted as "Other" is also considered in the safety and soundness assessment.[86]

The OCC also has responsibility for examining the operating subsidiaries of banks, which may include SEC-registered investment advisers. This is the point at which a compliance professional of an SEC-registered adviser owned by a national bank is likely to encounter the OCC. The OCC has certain procedures that are to be used when examiners conduct a risk assessment of a national bank's SEC-registered investment adviser subsidiary in the case where the subsidiary provides investment management services to the bank.[87] A compliance professional for an SEC-registered investment adviser within a national bank ownership structure should be familiar with the examination procedures that apply to the entity's national bank parent. This will allow the compliance professional to anticipate the types of requests that will likely come from the bank or the OCC when the bank's investment management activities are under examination and will help the compliance professional in responding to requests from the bank's internal audit functions.

Implementing the Compliance Program Rules for Bank-Owned Investment Advisers

The regulatory framework applicable to the investment management activities of a national bank has its foundation in the maintenance of policies and procedures designed to manage the risk of those activities and to ensure the safety and soundness of the bank. The procedures should address the monitoring and controlling of all significant risks associated with the advisory activity, including legal, operating, reputational, fiduciary, and financial risks. A significant component of the policies and procedures of the investment adviser will be on the adviser's compliance with SEC requirements, which requires an effective Rule 206(4)-7 program.

Investment advisers owned by national banks generally have to maintain specific policies that a nonbank-owned adviser would not necessarily have to maintain. The nature and extent of those policies will depend on the types of funds the investment adviser advises

---

[85] Office of the Comptroller of the Currency, Comptroller's Handbook, http://www.occ.gov/publications/publications-by-type/comptrollers-handbook/index-comptrollers-handbook.html

[86] *Id.*

[87] *See* Comptroller's Handbook, Investment Management Services, http://www.occ.gov/publications/publications-by-type/comptrollers-handbook/invmgt.pdf (Aug. 2001), pp. 77–78.

for the bank, the services the investment adviser performs for the bank, and the types of clients the adviser maintains. A bank-owned investment adviser is expected to fully understand how the risks involved in any investment product it recommends could impact a fund that is sponsored by the bank. Investment advisers should have policies and procedures that subject funds sponsored by the national bank to appropriate "stress testing" or contingency planning on a periodic basis in an effort to determine whether the investments will continue to conform to the bank-sponsored funds' objectives in periods of market uncertainty and volatility.

The Federal Reserve's guidance on compliance programs should be considered by compliance professionals of SEC-registered investment advisors that are part of a bank-owned holding company structure.[88] From the perspective of the Federal Reserve, a strong compliance function is focused on implementing a firmwide, global approach to risk management and oversight that goes much further than the role of compliance in an SEC-registered investment adviser.[89]

VI. CONCLUSION

Compliance professionals at SEC-registered investment advisers need to have an awareness of a broad range of highly technical and complex rules and regulations in order to be positioned to meet the demands of the current regulatory environment. The regulatory framework that applies to SEC-registered investment advisers today is made up of an evolution of regulation that has been in response to one or more highly publicized market events that drove the perceived need for enhanced regulations.

One of the most significant evolutions in the regulation of securities markets was the enactment of the SEC's Compliance Program Rule in 2004. The Compliance Program Rule created a paradigm that was put forward first by the SEC and, later, by other regulators, as an effective means to enlist the parties responsible for following the rules to develop compliance programs to test whether those rules are actually being adhered to on an ongoing basis. As described in this chapter, this model has gone beyond compliance with the Advisers Act and is now serves as a basis for regulation by agencies other than the SEC.

---

[88] See Federal Reserve Board, *Compliance Risk Management Programs and Oversight at Large Banking Organizations with Complex Compliance Profiles*, SR 08-8/CA 08-11 (Oct. 16, 2011).

[89] *Id.*

ABOUT THE AUTHOR

Eric R. Vercauteren currently serves as director, Contract Strategy & Negotiation, at Galliard Capital Management, Inc., a wholly owned, independently operated subsidiary of Wells Fargo Bank, N.A. Galliard is a registered investment adviser that manages investment portfolios for more than 230 institutional clients, including corporate retirement/benefit plans, operating funds, insurance reserves, foundations and endowments, healthcare funds, Taft Hartley plans, and public entities. Prior to joining Galliard, Mr. Vercauteren spent several years as an attorney in the corporate finance and transactions practice group of Oppenheimer Wolff & Donnelly LLP where he advised registered and unregistered investment advisers, underwriters, and issuers on various securities law and regulatory compliance matters.

Mr. Vercauteren is licensed to practice law in Minnesota. He holds a juris doctor degree from the University of Minnesota and a bachelor of science in Finance from Winona State University.

CHAPTER 7

Game Plan for the New CCO

By Robert Stirling
National Regulatory Services

I. INTRODUCTION

Certainly any person who is about to take on the role of chief compliance officer (CCO) should do research about the firm he or she is considering joining. Google searches and reviews of Securities and Exchange Commission (SEC) documents are a must. However, the research should not stop there. Key to determining whether you will have a productive career in the new firm is getting a clear understanding of whether the new firm truly sees the CCO as a true C-level officer.

During the interview process, ask whether there are any boundaries to what the CCO can do. For example, ask whether the CCO will have access to all meetings, discussions, and business plans. Apart from discussions of the CCO's own employment, every CCO needs unfettered access to the decisions being made within the firm. Be alert to any signs of reluctance on the part of senior management to include you in meetings that may have nothing to do with your specific role.

If the firm is closely held by the firm's officers, ask whether excellent performance on your part could result in an opportunity for ownership. Even if the answer is no, this will put your prospective employers on notice that you see yourself as a peer and expect to be treated as such.

Ask why the position is open. Ask how many CCOs the firm has had in the previous five years. If there has been high turnover in the position, find out why.

Get some basic data from the firm. What were the firm's regulatory assets under management (RAUM) for the past three years? Is the firm growing, contracting, or staying at the same size?

Be sure to insist on being included in any directors and officers (D&O) policies as a condition of employment.

II. ACCLIMATING YOURSELF TO THE FIRM'S CULTURE

In your first few weeks, it is important to learn about your new firm on its own terms. Even if you have been brought in to address a specific problem, you will need to learn how to work with your new colleagues to solve that problem. Successful compliance people can achieve this by learning and living the firm's culture. Moreover, by including yourself in that culture (even without being invited), you can demonstrate that you belong. Some of the elements of a firm's culture include ones covered here.

Language

Every advisory firm has developed its own jargon. At times a firm may use certain words in ways that to you seem incorrect or confusing. For example, at one firm I have worked with, the term *directed brokerage* means that the adviser can direct a client's trades to any broker the adviser chooses – something I had always referred to as *discretionary brokerage* I have seen the term *soft dollars* used to mean everything from research purchased with client commissions to paying solicitor's fees to directing brokerage in exchange for client referrals. Many firms refer to investment adviser (IA) representatives as *investment advisers*. Some firms distinguish between *investment advice* and *wealth management*—a distinction that would certainly surprise the SEC.

It is important in your early days on the job to refrain from trying to change a firm's jargon. Although such a change is a laudable goal over time, in your initial months on the job it is vital to create clear lines of communication, which will not happen if people are afraid they're going to be corrected when they ask a question or raise a concern.

Of course, if incorrect language is leading to problems—say, for example, a firm refers to both its own representatives and unaffiliated subadvisers as "investment advisers," and the firm's manual places requirements on investment advisers that clearly shouldn't apply to the subadvisers—you need to take action to correct this language. As a general rule, however, be sure you're fluent in the existing language before you start trying to change it.

Systems

A vital part of a firm's culture is its electronic systems: what they are, how they are organized, and who has access. Even if your technical background is limited, your ability to share information with and learn from your colleagues will depend heavily on being able to understand where they go for information and the various systems they use each day. For example, if someone says "I sent the client an Axys report," take the time to learn what Axys is, what it is used for, and who uses it.

Lunch

Never underestimate the importance of lunch! If you can get the budget to take your new colleagues out to lunch in small groups, great! If not, invite yourself to lunch with everyone in the firm. Eat what they eat—brown-bag it with the admins, hit a fancy restaurant with sales, share a pizza with the information technology (IT) crowd. Make sure that you take the opportunity to spend time with your colleagues so that you can see them (and they can see you) as human beings rather than simply as functions.

Meetings

From your first day on the job, you should invite yourself to every meeting you can. Don't ask permission; simply show up and take a seat at the table. Let all the attendees know that you take your role as a C-level officer seriously and that they should do so as well. In addition, this puts you in a position to learn what plans are being put in motion that could have compliance implications. Finally, even if you sit silently at the table, your presence will be registered (like Banquo's ghost in *Macbeth*), and others will be prompted to ask compliance-related questions.

Attitude Toward Your Role

However warmly you may have been welcomed, you may face resistance and even open hostility from some quarters. At a minimum, review all code of ethics and compliance violations for the two years preceding your hire date. If violations were noted, ask what (if any) sanctions were assessed. Use this information to get a handle on where resistance may be encountered.

As CCO, you will have access to the firm's e-mail system. Take the time to review e-mail to and from your predecessor to see what problems he or she experienced. If you see ongoing clashes with certain persons or departments, make a special effort to reach out to them.

On the subject of e-mail, some CCOs I know have searched all e-mail regarding their own hiring. Some might find this ethically dubious—a use of one's authority to review messages that are not needed to do one's job. On the other hand, I know of one CCO who discovered an e-mail in which the firm's president stated that the CCO was being hired to be "a sacrificial lamb for the SEC." I think knowing that this is the firm's attitude toward the CCO overcomes any moral qualms. (Incidentally, that CCO went on to have a successful career at that firm and developed a strong mutual respect with the president.)

III. TRIAGE

Although it would be nice to gently ease one's way into the CCO role, there are often issues that need to be addressed immediately—particularly if the position has been vacant for some time prior to your hire date. To discover what matters you must promptly resolve, consider the following in this order:

1. *Deadlines.* The first thing to do is to ensure that all SEC and state filings are current and required mailings have been sent to clients. As a reminder, here are some relevant deadlines:

a. Form ADV—must be updated w/in 90 days of the firm's fiscal year end.
b. Disclosures— material amendments to Form ADV Part 2A, or the complete Part 2A, must be delivered to clients within 120 days of the firm's fiscal year end.
c. Form 13F—Firms filing 13F must do so within 45 days after the end of each calendar quarter.
d. Privacy statement—must be delivered annually.
e. IARD renewals—renewal statement is available in mid-November, with the filing date in mid-December (the exact dates change from year to year).
f. Other filings—based on the nature of the firm's business, Forms 13D, 13G, 13H and/or PF must be filed at intervals to be found on the instructions for each form.
2. *Previous SEC deficiencies.* The next order of business is to make certain that any issues identified in previous SEC examinations have been resolved. Recent history indicates that the SEC is far more likely to initiate enforcement actions against advisers who have failed to correct past problems.
3. *Annual review.* If the annual review has not been completed, this should be done using the existing risk assessment and supervisory procedures (if any), even if you feel they are inadequate.
4. *Specific concerns of senior management.* Speak to corporate management and the heads of the various departments to learn what their concerns are. You may not necessarily agree that their concerns should be priorities, but by promptly addressing their concerns you can build up a reservoir of good will and a reputation for getting things done. If their concerns are, in fact, serious problems, you will have an ally in getting the needed resources to solve the problem.

IV. TAKING THE FIRM'S TEMPERATURE

Here are some quick ways to identify the firm's general approach to compliance:

- *Personal securities trading.* Have annual and quarterly reports been provided in a timely manner? If not, this may indicate a lax attitude toward compliance.
- *Trade errors.* Have trade errors been identified quickly and have clients promptly been made whole?
- *Marketing materials and website.* Do these materials contain testimonials, past specific recommendations, poorly disclosed performance data, or promissory or hyperbolic language?
- *Comparing Form ADV, advisory agreements, and marketing materials.* Do these documents conflict?

V. DEPLOYING YOUR TEAM (IF YOU HAVE ONE)

If you are fortunate enough to have compliance staff, I strongly recommend seeing their most important role as being a resource for the rest of the firm rather than for you. The greatest challenge a compliance officer faces is getting the rest of the firm to ask whether their activities may have implications for compliance. Most compliance departments sit together and perform their duties in relative isolation from the rest of the firm. This has the unfortunate effect of forcing people outside the department to seek out a compliance person if they have a compliance-related question. I often wonder how many questions go unanswered because someone simply forgets that he or she wanted to see a compliance person, or decides the question isn't important enough to make the effort.

I suggest scattering the compliance staff throughout the firm. I have found that most questions come from trading, client service, and marketing, and so I recommend stationing a compliance person as close as possible to each department. This not only puts a compliance person in a situation in which compliance questions can be asked frequently and informally but also puts the compliance person within earshot of current developments well before they may be presented to the CCO.

Regardless of where your team members sit, you should instruct them to always be available for questions, comments, and suggestions. Encourage them to linger in the various departments they may be called to visit, to inquire as to what is going on, and, at least initially, to listen and report back to you before offering opinions that have not been requested.

VI. THE LISTENING TOUR

Once triage is complete, the next step is to learn how the firm actually works and how closely the procedures are followed.

When starting at a new firm, you shouldn't expect the decision-making processes to follow the steps described in the firm's written supervisory procedures. Instead, follow the decision-making process from start to finish in several key areas:

- Investment decision making;
- Trading;
- Sales;
- Client onboarding; and
- Development of marketing materials.

Learn how decisions are actually made and who has the authority to make them. If this turns out to agree with your procedures, terrific! If not, you'll not only learn which procedures need to be corrected but have a better sense of who actually holds the levers of power in your firm.

Pay special attention to those times when duties pass from one person or department to another. These hand-offs are often when problems occur.

Immediately correct violations of applicable rules or the adviser's fiduciary duty. Work with the various departments to help them draft procedures that are both effective and practical.

© MODERN COMPLIANCE 2015

Once immediate problems have been addressed, the next step is to take a more granular look at the remaining policies and procedures to identify which are being followed, which are being ignored, and which really work. To do this, visit each employee in the firm and review his or her daily activities together. (In a large firm, you may have to deputize other compliance staff to assist with this function.) Again, your initial role is to listen; find out what employees think works well, what may not work so well, what they don't understand, and what improvements they think should be made.

After you have a reasonable understanding of a person's role, compare what the employee does with the written procedures. Review the applicable procedures with the employee and identify areas that are incorrect and areas that can be improved. Work with the employee to develop draft procedures that the employee would agree are reasonable and practical, and that you have determined are consistent with applicable regulations and the adviser's fiduciary duty.

Work your way up the food chain, starting with the clerical and administrative employees and working your way up to the chief officers. Along the way, share suggestions for improvement made by the lower-level employees with their superiors, and see what changes the supervisors feel are useful and practical.

By the time you have reviewed the procedures with your fellow chief officers, you should have buy-in from everyone in the firm. Assemble suggestions for new procedures, share them with the managers and chief officers, and work with them to draft new procedures. Once the revised procedures have been approved, introduce them to the firm.

Once the procedures have been completed, reverse-engineer the procedures to develop a risk assessment that is mapped to the procedures. (For example, if you have a procedure that says all marketing materials must be reviewed for compliance with the advertising rules, that procedure presupposes a risk that marketing materials may violate the advertising rules.) Compare procedures to any existing risk assessment and identify any gaps. Circulate the revised risk assessment to all personnel to see if additional risks can be identified; for any new risks, work with the various departments to create appropriate procedures.

VII. THE SEC'S DOCUMENT REQUEST LIST: WHO, NOT WHAT

Obtain a recent copy of the document request list the SEC sends advisers prior to an examination. (If possible, use one from the regional office responsible for your geographic area.) Review this with the department heads. In reviewing the list, identify:

- Which requested items do not apply to your firm;
- Which requested items are readily available;
- Which requested items are available but not in the format requested by the SEC; and
- Which requested items are unavailable.

For each applicable item, identify which persons will be responsible for producing the item in the event of an SEC examination. Be specific; get the name and title of the individual who will be charged with producing each item. Do not be satisfied with a general statement that the department or a particular group will produce it.

Do not yet be concerned about the content of the requested documents. You can consider content when you request the documents later in the year. Initially, focus on the documents and the persons charged with providing them. For unavailable documents, work closely with the responsible persons to make sure that the documents can be created upon request. For documents that are available but not in SEC-requested format, find out whether they can readily be put into the requested format. If not, determine whether the required format is something that your firm would need to effectively supervise the activity involved. (For example, if you have trade blotters but they do not contain all the information the SEC requests, determine whether you need the additional information to supervise the portfolio management and trading functions.) Many of the documents requested by the SEC do not appear in the books and records rules. If you believe that the SEC is asking for something that (a) is not a required record, (b) you don't have, and (c) your firm doesn't need for effective supervision, be prepared to explain to the SEC why you believe you do not need it.

VIII. IT, HUMAN RESOURCES, AND ACCOUNTING: YOUR NEW BEST FRIENDS

Compliance touches every aspect of the advisory firm; it is part of the firm's connective tissue. As such, it has common interests with other firm-wide services such as accounting, information technology, and human resources. Forming alliances with these departments can provide a mutually beneficial support structure.

Information Technology

Cybersecurity has risen to the top of the SEC's priority list and is likely to remain there for the foreseeable future. Thus, you will need to become intimately familiar with your firm's data security procedures. Make a point of meeting the head of IT as soon as possible, explaining the level of your knowledge (or ignorance) of the tech world and asking for her help in bringing you up to speed on how your firm is addressing cybersecurity issues. You do not have to be a computer expert yourself; be sure the head of IT understands in the event of an SEC examination he or she will have to explain the system to the examiners. Work with IT to find ways to describe the security function in terms an intelligent layperson can understand.

Apart from security issues, compliance and IT are both deeply invested in maintaining readily accessible books and records. You can be a tremendous ally in helping IT obtain adequate resources for data storage and document retrieval. By the same token, IT can help you by making sure that your concerns are heard and addressed in all issues concerning data storage and destruction. This is a natural alliance that you should cultivate.

Finally, IT serves as the gatekeeper to your firm's website. It is important to make sure that those in charge of the website work with you to ensure that only information approved by compliance can be uploaded to the website.

Human Resources

One good way to introduce yourself to the human resources (HR) department is to ask the manager's opinion of the process by which new hires learn what their compliance responsibilities are and receive compliance training. Although HR is often not directly involved with this, the HR staff can become involved in the fallout if the process is poorly handled; for example, if a new hire complains that he was never told that he would have to report his spouse's securities holdings and transactions in addition to his own. Anything you can do to reduce these types of complaints will be greatly appreciated.

HR can provide important information about other employees that you may need to know. For example, if a trader has been admitted to drug rehab, this will clearly indicate a need for heightened supervision upon his or her return. Also, HR may have early information about changes in the firm (if, for example, the firm is looking to hire employees for a new branch office).

HR folks must be very careful about what types of information they can share, the persons with whom they can share it, and the circumstances under which it can be shared. They are bound by federal and state regulations and company policies. Do not demand information from them! Instead, open a dialogue about the types of information that would be important to you and the circumstances under which the staff could potentially share it.

Accounting

In addition to maintaining required books and records and handling client billing, accounting can provide valuable support to compliance personnel. Introduce yourself to the accounting folks and regularly drop by to say hello. Periodically ask to review records of consulting charges, political or charitable contributions, and expense reports, because these can be used to disguise improper solicitation fees or kickbacks. Let the accounting folks know what you are looking for and why. Even if (as in most firms) you will find nothing, you will have made them aware of your concerns, and they may alert you to any signs of questionable payments that they encounter.

IX. A ROADMAP FOR YOUR FIRST YEAR

Much of what you do in your early months on the job will be driven by the calendar and the immediate needs of your firm. Taking that into consideration, here is a (very) rough guide to scheduling your first year on the job.

- Days 1–30
  - Begin acclimating yourself to firm;
  - Take firm temperature; and
  - Begin triage.
- Days 31–90
  - Complete triage;
  - Begin listening tour; and
  - Conduct SEC document request list review.
- Days 91–180
  - Complete listening tour;
  - Based on listening tour, provide new risk assessment and procedures manual to firm; and
  - Develop tests for new procedures.
- Days 180–365
  - Initiate program for testing new procedures; and
  - Obtain all applicable items on SEC document request list.

Of course, you will have to accomplish all this while making required filings, conducting an annual review, and putting out at least one fire a day. Please remember that these are suggestions and can be moved around to accommodate all the unexpected events that you will encounter. That said, however, by following this guide you will not only make a start at having a well-organized compliance program but will have taken steps toward becoming a respected and vital part of your new firm.

ABOUT THE AUTHOR

Robert Stirling has worked with National Regulatory Services (NRS) as a senior consultant for much of the past twenty five years: from October 1991 to June 2000, from May 2002 to June 2004, on a part-time basis staring in December 2007, and returning full-time in August 2008. He has prepared and/or reviewed hundreds of ADVs representing firms of all sizes and engaged in every aspect of investment advisory services. He regularly reviews advertising and marketing materials, including websites, for compliance with SEC guidelines. Mr. Stirling has also audited dozens of advisory firms and has spoken at numerous compliance conferences and seminars.

During his times away from NRS, Mr. Stirling was himself a compliance officer. He was chief compliance officer of Private Accounts, Inc., from July 2000 to October 2000, when Private Accounts, Inc., was purchased by E*TRADE Financial, where he worked as a compliance manager from November 2000 to May 2002. He was chief compliance officer and general counsel of Eubel Brady & Suttman Asset Management, Inc., of Dayton, Ohio, from June 2004 through July 2008. Mr.

Stirling graduated from the American University in 1975 with a bachelor of arts in religion and received a juris doctor degree from the University of Connecticut School of Law in 1997. He has also been admitted to the Connecticut bar.

CHAPTER 8

How Compliance Can Teach Ethics

By Lee Augsburger
Prudential Financial, Inc.

I. INTRODUCTION

You may wonder why there is a chapter in this book on "ethics." After all, isn't this a discussion about compliance programs? Sure, you might be saying, I know that there is a rule that investment advisers and mutual funds have to follow about a code of ethics, but that's really just about personal securities trading restrictions. What does ethics have to do with the SEC's rules and regulations that I need to prove are being followed in my business? What do "ethics" have to do with my system of policies and procedures, monitoring and testing, training, and reporting that make up my compliance program? It turns out that there is nothing more important to your compliance program. Ethics is the one indicator that dictates whether your program is successful or likely to catastrophically fail.

Over the years, there have been countless enforcement cases that have nothing to do with the sufficiency of the registrant's compliance program. Indeed, as enforcement cases are handed down, only a very few actually address deficiencies in compliance programs. We all know the litany of Enron, Madoff, Stanford Partners, and so on. So where did all these cases come from? At the heart of all these cases is a simple lapse of integrity in one or more persons within the registrant that ultimately culminated in a violation of the general antifraud provisions of one or more the various substantive securities regulations.

Failing to address the issue of integrity places you, your career, and your firm at risk. Integrity is the most important element of a complete compliance program. Focusing only on the specific rules and regulations will ultimately lead to a failure of your compliance program and that failure can be career altering.

II. CORPORATE ENTITIES BEHAVE ON AN ETHICAL SPECTRUM, WHETHER INTENTIONALLY OR NOT

Background on Corporate Behavior

Let's lay out some background perspective. First, just like individuals, corporate entities behave on an ethical spectrum. Sometimes a corporation or firm will do this intentionally, usually for good. An example of this might be the sponsorship of a local little league baseball team or a contribution to a local shelter. Other times a firm may act without any clear intention through actions that simply grow out of its "culture." Whether intentional or not, actions of a company are seen by the general public as being good and bad.

A great deal of public dialogue has addressed the ethics of environmental decisions by corporations. We would all agree that the company that pollutes is seen as bad. The company that behaves with clear focus on sustainability is viewed as good. In the case of the polluter, did the company make a conscious decision to dispose of waste in a detrimental way? Perhaps a high level decision was made to save expenses with a hope of not getting caught. Yet, it is just as likely that the decision started with a middle manager who believed that pollution was no big deal, simply reflecting the company's culture. That manager believed the harmful result really did not matter. Either way the manager and business viewed it, the company is seen as a wrongdoer, violating society's greater interests.

This behavior is important because companies and organizations of human enterprise have the effect of leveraging behavior. Organizations have proven over and over again that joining 200 people together will generate a greater output and greater results than if the 200 people simply work as 200 individuals. The whole truly is greater than the sum of its parts. In business settings, companies accomplish this by allowing individuals to develop specializations and expertise in a given area and then routing all appropriate activity through that specialist.

This funneling means that when a company does something bad, it is has a greater effect than if each of the company's employees had done the same wrong thing as individuals. Companies concentrate the effect of ethical decisions. Great good can be accomplished on a magnificent scale, and so too can great harm be perpetuated on society. Bernie Madoff's fraud was magnified by many other employees and was even assisted by third-party agents that identified potential investors. The simple fact is that if Bernie Madoff had worked as an individual to accomplish his fraud, it would never have reached the size that it did. Company concentration magnifies the consequences of ethical decisions.

Part of the problem is the definitional nature of corporate efficiency. Just as efficiencies are gained by routing specific processes to those with the appropriate expertise, so too are decisions. To gain the efficiency in decision making, choices are intentionally reduced the lowest possible level of the company. It makes no sense to have the CEO deciding on office supply purchases; his or her time must be spent on more critical decisions with respect to the strategy and future of company in light of current competitive pressures.

Most companies find that a hierarchical pyramid of accountability is the most efficient. Few companies operate as democracies. Consequently, as decisions are pushed to the most junior levels possible and spread broadly across the organization for the sake of efficiency, it is impossible for one person to be aware and individually accountable for generally monitoring all decision making and its relative ethicality. Ultimately, questionable decisions sometimes only become obvious when their negative impact is felt or their unfortunate outcome discovered.

Firms of broker-dealers and investment advisers are no different. The actions of such organizations may not be obviously good or bad. And given the size of many smaller registrants, it is unlikely that they might attract the attention of a newspaper reporter. However, the actions of such smaller organizations are just as laden with ethical implications. The question is whether anyone is thinking about this and trying to do something about it.

III. UNETHICAL CORPORATE ATTITUDES AFFECT COMPLIANCE AND BUSINESS RESULTS

What Does Ethics Matter, Anyway?

The truism is that good ethics is good business. But just because it's a truism, it is really true? Assume for the moment that I run a window manufacturing company with exceptionally high-quality products. Does it matter that the shop steward is stealing tools off the assembly line? Does a customer care whether there is employment discrimination taking place in the factory? How many customers will be concerned if my senior sales personnel are cheating on their expense reports? The costs of this misbehavior may, in some small way, be passed on to the customer, but hey, if the product is the best in the industry, do I really care?

It turns out that I should care because although the effect may not manifest itself today, permitting an environment where these kinds of actions are tolerated will absolutely compromise business activity. The effect may not be immediate, but it will inevitably impact the company at some future point. This outcome is all the more critical in a business based on customer trust like banking, securities brokerage, asset management or insurance. In essence, each of these businesses promises to work on behalf of their customer. The firm asks the customer to trust it with a most precious possession: their money. Anything that compromises that trust strikes at the very basis of their customer relationship and potentially drives a customer away to a more trustworthy firm.

A Sampling of the Empirical Evidence Proving That Ethics Matters in Business

Interestingly, strong empirical data support the generalized conclusions discussed above. The Ethics Resource Center (ERC), established in 1922, has been surveying and analyzing the ethical climate of American business since 1994. The ERC now conducts its National Business Ethics Survey (NBES) every two years specifically focusing, among other things, on the effect ethics and formal business ethics programs have on the behavior of employees in following company policies, as well as other applicable rules. Figure 1 from the survey conducted in 2013 reflects the positive impact that ethics programs have.

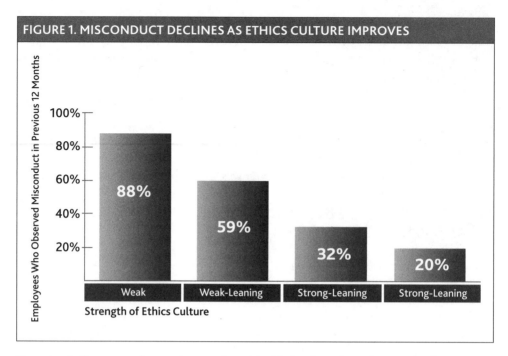

Focusing influence and attention on the ethical behavior of employees clearly connects to the adherence to company policies and procedures.

The Corporate Executive Board serves as forum for senior leaders of Fortune 500 companies and maintains a specific group focused on compliance and ethics called the Compliance and Ethics Leadership Council (CELC). The staff supporting the CELC has developed a similar integrity survey that has been administered to over a million employees worldwide. The results of the CELC data confirm the conclusions drawn from the NBES and add an important element. Not only do the CELC results confirm the connection between a focus on ethics and adherence to policy, they also indicate that employees in strong integrity environments are approximately 2/3s more willing to raise concerns when they observe violations.

When taken together, isn't this connection exactly what every compliance officer wants? Don't we all want to have employees who are less likely to violate policies in the first instance and employees who, if they see a violation, are more likely to raise the violation to someone's attention?

The Corporate Executive Board also facilitates a forum for human resource professionals that discovered another fascinating facet of corporate ethics activities. The CEB's human resources group attempted to identify the primary drivers that caused employees to exert discretionary work effort—in other words, what makes people want to work harder when they don't have to? As it turns out, paying people more does *not* elevate an employee's discretionary work effort. (I know this from painful personal experience because in 2010 the Chicago Cubs had the third highest payroll in major league baseball behind the New York Yankees and the Boston Red Sox, and the Cubbies not only missed the playoffs but finished in fifth place in their division.)

In fact, the research shows that aligning corporate values with ethical behavior of managers is the most important driver of discretionary employee effort. To elicit greater effort from employees, companies should have managers of highest integrity that exude the corporate values and mission.

Finally, although the causal connection is not clear, more and more studies suggest that the truism "good ethics is good business" is, in fact, true. Ethisphere Institute has been identifying the 100 World's Most Ethical Companies (WME's in the chart below) since 2007. These companies have consistently outperformed their peer groups based on their market price.

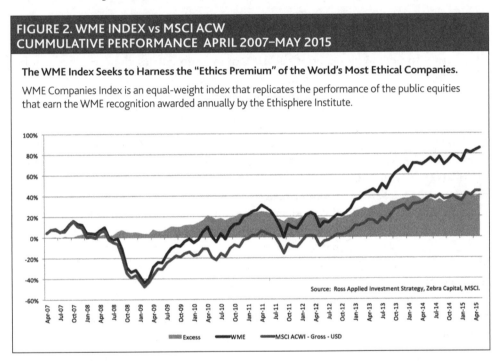

Obviously market factors add a great deal of complexity and variability to this analysis, however, the overall trend is compelling.

IV. OTHER DRIVERS OF CORPORATE ETHICS PROGRAMS

Other Reasons for Corporate Ethics Programs

Apart from anecdotal and common sense support for organizations to focus on integrity and ethics, studies from other parts of society suggestion that because corporations involve humans and because humans bring their own limitations into their corporate activities, corporations should implement structures to counteract these human tendencies.

All of Us Lie, at Least a Little Bit. Dan Ariely argues in *The (Honest) Truth About Dishonesty* that all of us cheat, at least a little bit. His brilliantly conceived testing asked a roomful of people to complete a relatively simple addition task. A page was handed out with 25 4 × 4 grids of numbers, within each grid were four numbers when added together totaled 100. Within a limited timeframe, participants were asked to identify the four numbers in each grid and complete as many grids as possible. They were paid $1 for each correctly solved grid. Initially, all participants turned in their worksheets, thus establishing a performance baseline.

In the next iteration, he changed the submission process by directing the participants to shred their worksheets and turn in only a slip of paper with the number of grids the participants correctly analyzed. Remarkably, all the participants became much smarter! *Everyone* inflated the number in order to get paid more, not a lot, but just a little bit.

Wondering how to change the outcome in subsequent groups, the tester added proctors, asked participants to sign undertakings of honesty, and even asked one group of people to write down as many of the 10 Commandments as they could remember before doing the test. Ariely's book describing his conclusions is fascinating and well conveys the notion that all of us cheat (at least all college students; where else could he find all these participants?).

We Don't Trust Each Other. Well-known author and speaker Stephan Covey estimates in his book *Speed of Trust* that the lack of trust in our economy costs America trillions of dollars every year. He notes that one study estimated the expense to implement just one section of the Sarbanes-Oxley Act at over $35 billion. (Ironically, these regulations were designed to strengthen confidence in financial statements.) This lack of trust in our economy results in untold hours of attorneys' time just to document our agreements and to negotiate penalties that encourage each party to keep the agreements. To underscore Covey's conclusions, Edelman, the world's largest public relations firm, has been measuring trust since 2001 among consumers. Edelman found in its 2014 Trust Barometer that only one in four general public respondents trust business leaders to correct issues and even fewer—one in five—to tell the truth and make ethical and moral decisions.

Trust is premised, argues Covey, on two dimensions: the competence of the counterparty, i.e., *can* that party deliver on the agreement, and the character of the counterparty, i.e., will that party *choose* to deliver on the agreement? Most companies have the capability of delivering on their agreements, so competence is not the question. The real question is the "character" of companies and for that, integrity and ethics are essential ingredients. If a customer is to trust companies, they must exude a character of integrity.

Our Regulators Require Ethics Programs. The Federal Sentencing Commission laid out a set of principles for compliance programs in 1991, which, if followed by a company facing criminal sentencing, would have the effect of reducing the sentence by up to 60 percent of the penalty otherwise imposed. The commission intended to create a "carrot" for companies to incentivize them to create effective compliance programs. In 2004, following the Enron debacle, the commission amended the Federal Sentencing Guidelines such that any sentencing credit was contingent upon the company having *both* effective compliance *and* ethics programs. Interestingly, the same components that supported an effective compliance program were also seen by the Sentencing Commission to support an effective ethics program (although clearly the subject matter is different).

At about the same time the Federal Sentencing Commission amended its guidelines to add ethics; the Securities and Exchange Commission (SEC) adopted one and amended another very important provision under the Investment Advisers Act of 1940 and the Investment Company Act of 1940. Under both acts, registrants are obligated to maintain a code of ethics. This code is admittedly focused on the personal securities trading of employees as contrasted securities trading for customers, but the adopting release suggests that the portion of the rule focused on the overall standard of care for employee behavior should be grounded in overarching principles of integrity and ethics. Specifically, the adopting release states:

> …A code of ethics should set out ideals for ethical conduct premised on fundamental principles of openness, integrity, honesty, and trust. A good code of ethics should effectively convey to employees the value the advisory firm places on ethical conduct, and should challenge employees to live up not only to the letter of the law but also to the ideals of the organization.

Although the balance of the release addressed many questions about personal securities trading, the primary principle stands that all advisory and investment company codes of ethics should address so much more than simply the details of securities trading policy and in fact ought to clearly lay out a company's principles of integrity and ethics.

V. IMPLEMENTING AN EFFECTIVE ETHICS PROGRAM

By now you may be saying, "Enough already. I get it. I need to think about this and figure out how to make it part of my organization, but how do I do that?" I am glad you asked that question. There are a number of aspects to weaving ethics into the fabric of your business culture and your business environment. As this field has matured, there are certain nonnegotiable elements that any business organization should pursue in effecting attitudes to reflect high integrity. The good news is it can be done as a small or as a very large company.

As you read this discussion and consider the elements that are described, note that certain aspects are more important than others. For example, the first program element is a written code of conduct. A written code of conduct alone does not significantly influence employee behavior. Enron's code of conduct was a beautifully written document that clearly was not worth the paper it was written on (although ironically, today on eBay you can often find this document auctioned off for hundreds of dollars). Taken together, all of the elements described here can have a profound effect on how your employees behave. However, remember it is about the total picture, not just a single element.

Written Code of Conduct

Surprisingly, many organizations have never thought about the standards that apply to their employees' behavior, and in many organizations that have thought about their standards, the yardsticks have not been consolidated and written down. A written code of conduct is the place to start. The code should identify the overarching values of the company and the foundational expectations that management has for the way all employees should act. There are excellent examples of codes of conduct easily available today simply by exploring the home pages of companies on the internet. One particularly good example is GE's *The Spirit and the Letter*. In the GE case, you will find a well-written and easily understandable document that clearly articulates the expectations of the board and senior management with respect to employees' behavior.

The code of conduct should be a document that management supports from the top down. It will not succeed for the code to be written and owned only by the compliance or ethics officer. It needs to have the full support of senior leadership. Once the document is crafted, it is helpful to have employees initially attest to the code, with an annual attestation thereafter.

Anonymous Reporting Process

A second element for an effective ethics program is a means for reporting issues and concerns anonymously. This idea gained particularly currency following the adoption of the Sarbanes-Oxley Act in 2002, when an anonymous "helpline" or hotline was made mandatory for all companies whose stock is listed on an American exchange. Research analyzing helpline calls in 2014 across multiple industries and business conducted by NAVEXGlobal shows that approximately 5 percent of all significant complaints are raised through such a reporting mechanism. Accordingly, no one should view such a process as the primary method of identifying and addressing violations of policy or regulation. In fact, the anonymous reporting process should be seen as a relief valve or as a last resort for employees to voice concerns. Still, the presence of such a reporting process communicates clearly to employees that senior management is intentional and open to the concerns of the company. Sometimes this message is the most important aspect of establishing and maintaining such a reporting process.

Training

As a parent and a compliance officer, I find it hard to think about training without drawing the parallel between employees and children. Parents know intuitively that expecting children to do what parents want them to do without explanation is unlikely to garner the behavior that parents desire. Instead, parents provide careful direction and explanations. For younger children without the capacity to understand reasons for the preferable behavior, parents often simply direct it; later, as children mature, that direction will be supplemented with the underlying logic for the direction, and indeed, as that maturation process concludes, parents often simply provide the reason for behavior preferences without even giving direction.

For employees, much the same process is used. Some rules will simply be provided to staff as must follows because the company or regulator or CEO requires them. Other rules will be communicated with full explanation regarding the underlying reasoning. And still other situations will have a degree of flexibility that permits an employee to exercise a degree of discretion based upon overarching principles.

Secondly, as known from children, training requires constant reiteration. The need for constant reiteration is actually amplified in the corporate setting because unlike children, employees tend to change periodically. With adults, however, mere reiteration can result in people tuning out. Constant messaging creates a degree of inoculation. Accordingly, when trainers train repetitively, variation is critical. The periodic use of humor is helpful as well. Some of the most compelling business ethics training videos in the marketplace have been produced by Second City, the improvisational comedy team that has given us such comedians as John Candy, Martin Short and many others.

Another critical aspect of training also harkens from parenting. When training, trainers and our business leaders must "walk the talk." Well known is the anecdote of a two-year-old swearing a blue streak because he or she heard bad language from his or her parent. This experience has embarrassed many moms and dads (and led to long-told family stories). The quickest way to communicate to employees that it is acceptable to break with company policy is to have extensive training that senior management does not support or, worse, does not follow.

Finally, the preceding discussion has focused on the general means of training, whether administered through computer based programs, large in-person events, or even media campaigns within an office. There is another very important training mechanism that often is not included in these more generalized training activities: one-to-one conversations between a manager or ethics leader and the employee. Within this relationship, CELC research shows that there are certain points within an employee's career when he or she is more open to integrity messages. Not surprisingly, these moments are at critical career junctures, such as taking a new position or getting a significant promotion. At these critical moments, employees are more teachable and willing to absorb integrity training. Taking advantage of these windows of opportunity enhances a good ethics training program.

Investigations

When violations occur, and they will, an effective ethics program must have a good protocol for investigations. In the world of business ethics, this requires a high degree of sensitivity and skill. Allegations, if proven true have long-term impact on a person's reputation and potentially on his or her overall career. Even if proven untrue, the visibility and publicity of an investigation may still have a meaningfully negative impact, so the investigator must take care in analyzing these types of allegations.

Many well-considered and thoughtful articles and treatises have been written on conducting investigations. Those focusing on allegations of discrimination and harassment are particularly helpful when one considers an investigation into ethics allegations. Suffice it to say, that this is an area where unskilled investigators can do a great deal of harm. When faced with a serious business ethics allegation, it may well pay to seek out and retain a highly skilled investigator to ascertain the facts of the case. Many large corporations maintain experienced investigatory teams for just such situations. However, irrespective of determining the best way to develop and maintain investigatory experience, having a clear plan for addressing investigations is an essential element of an effective ethics program.

Discipline

"Tone at the top" is the phrase commonly describing the degree to which senior executives support a compliance program. The same concept applies to ethics programs, and the area that most conveys the attitude of senior executives is that of discipline. In other words, how do senior executives determine discipline for employees who violate company policy? This is the most critical factor in creating an effective ethics program. Again, disciplining employees is analogous to raising children. If parents do not discipline effectively, children quickly learn that the applicable rules are not necessarily those that they hear from parents. They learn that the true rules are those that are enforced with meaningful discipline.

Apart from anecdotal perspectives on how discipline was meted out in childhood or as a parent, empirical evidence shows that discipline and the way a company handles discipline are the most important factors in whether employees believe themselves to be working in a high-integrity environment.

Confidence in organizational justice results from transparency and fairness in the process of discipline. That confidence stands in stark contrast to what might be called "water cooler" justice. This occurs when employees are left to speculate around the water cooler about what happened to an employee who is suddenly terminated. Too often, in a misguided effort to protect the guilty, management chooses not to talk about an employee who is terminated; instead, the rest of the staff is left to speculate about what happened until a memorandum is issued that reinforces or restates the company policy that was violated by the terminated employee (although nowhere in the memorandum is that employee's name mentioned).

First, for discipline to be trusted, it needs to be open and transparent. This is challenging, admittedly, because a company wants to insulate itself from potential libel or slander actions. However, there are many ways to communicate about these instances. One way is to publish fact-based scenarios that describe the violation without using names, often changing key details to disguise the location, business unit, and the actual employee involved. Usually these scenarios are published long after the activity occurred to further distance the story from the individual.

Second, the *process* of determining the discipline itself must be transparent. A secret "star chamber" process does nothing to enhance employee confidence and does much to cause higher levels of suspicion. Publishing a document describing the process by which discipline is reached and precisely who is accountable for the discipline decisions greatly helps in providing a sense of fairness to employees.

Finally, overall discipline statistics should be transparent. Another way to demonstrate fairness and thereby achieve employee belief in the system is to periodically publish the results of disciplinary decisions, indicating the number of cases, the levels of the employees involved, and the types of discipline administered. Many companies publish these types of statistics annually to demonstrate the evenhandedness of disciplinary outcomes (obviously, without using specific employee names).

Make no mistake, getting to a point of true transparency on employee disciplinary matters is not easy without senior management support. Achieving this ideal, however, is worth all the effort because this activity is most important in reinforcing the idea that the company employees work for maintains the highest ethical standards.

Measurement

Years ago the management maven Peter Drucker famously stated that "What gets measured, gets managed." Mr. Drucker's quote was aimed at general business practices, but it is absolutely true of ethics programs and is in fact a most challenging consideration given the "softness" of business ethics. However, without some mechanism for quantitatively considering your ethics program, it will be impossible to determine improvement from year to year.

One of the most popular methods of measurement is employee surveys. The advantage of the survey is its ease of administration. The greatest challenge of the survey is the reliability of the data. To develop meaningful data, questions need to be carefully designed to elicit information that is truly predictive and useful rather than being merely interesting. In this regard, organizations like the Ethics Resource Center or the Compliance and Ethics Leadership Counsel can be very helpful. They each have invested years in developing reliable data that accurately reflects employee behavior.

Notwithstanding the ease of obtaining survey data, other measurement mechanisms can be applied, such as direct interviews, monitoring of helpline calls, or other observations of employee behavior. These other types of measurement activities however, tend to introduce an element of subjectivity that the administrator must guard against. Without measurement, no reliable sense of direction can be determined, and it will be unclear whether the program's efforts are effective in influencing higher ethical behavior.

VI. SIMILARITIES AND DIFFERENCES BETWEEN COMPLIANCE AND ETHICS PROGRAMS

Are the basic elements of an effective ethics program any different than what one uses for the purposes of regulatory compliance? In fact, the work efforts are virtually identical. A good compliance program starts with documented policies just as a good ethics program begins with a documented code of conduct. Training for compliance obligations is not at all different than training for ethical obligations. Having mechanisms to report regulatory concerns is as important to a compliance program as it is for an ethics program. Investigating regulatory breaches is a critical as investigating ethical breaches. Enforcing compliance standards is as important as disciplining for ethical violations. Tracking and measuring compliance breaches allows for the management of compliance issues just as measurement of ethical perspectives facilitates the management of ethical matters. The processes for maintaining a compliance program is virtually identical to the processes needed to administer an ethics program. As a result, at least with respect to the mechanical aspects of an ethics program, a competent compliance professional should have no difficulty in establishing and managing an ethics program.

There are, however, some critical distinctions between the two programs. First, compliance programs are imposed by external regulatory pressures whereas ethics programs only exist on the strength of internal commitment. This leads to one of the most important challenges for compliance and ethics programs: the commitment of senior management. A company cannot argue that laws and regulations do not apply to its business. Although a business leader may not be particularly focused on compliance matters, he or she cannot ultimately ignore them. Sooner or later, the SEC, Financial Industry Regulatory Authority (FINRA), or some other regulator has the authority to enforce compliance regulations. Ethics is completely different. No regulator is going to assess an organization for its lack of an ethics program and then bring an enforcement action. As a result, much more so than compliance, establishing an ethics program genuinely requires the true commitment of senior leadership. Without it, creating an effective ethics program is almost impossible.

Another important distinction is that compliance programs are based on clearly articulated laws and regulation. Identifying applicable regulation is relatively straightforward as compared to identifying the ethical standards to which a company intends to adhere (although there excellent models to follow, inevitably these are modified to reflect the personality of each individual company). Determining the specifics of a new code of conduct is the creation of art rather than the discovery of science. Regulation is hard; ethics is soft. In a corporate environment, this can be a challenge.

Given these differences, it is *absolutely essential* to have senior business leaders engaged in support of creating and maintaining an ethics program. Particularly given the fact that it will only be supported by internal commitment rather than having the pressure of external regulators, it is crucial that senior business leaders believe and, indeed, lead an ethics program.

VII. CONCLUSION

Our industry has been focused on rules and regulations since the adoption of the Securities Act of 1933, the Securities Exchange Act of 1934, and the Investment Company and Investment Advisers Acts of 1940. Through the years the SEC, FINRA, and state securities administrators have provided us with volumes of rules and regulations that we have all worked to address within our firms as compliance officers. These rules and regulations, however, have not stopped the most significant and substantial frauds on our customers and the public. The root challenge is the ethical behavior of our firms. The culture of a firm trumps the compliance program of a firm every time.

As compliance officers, we must absolutely focus the attention of our senior management on the creation of a healthy ethical environment within each of our firms. Without a focus on ethics, we will continue as an industry to defraud our customers and bring evermore substantial regulation on our businesses. Only with the development of a higher degree of trust between Wall Street and Main Street will we be able to reinvigorate our industry and our larger economy. Only with trust in the financial services sector can our regulators look to other parts of the industry in order to develop fixes for longstanding operational challenges and be more responsive to industry issues as a partner rather than an adversary. Good ethics is good business—for us, for our industry, and for all of society.

ABOUT THE AUTHOR

Lee Augsburger is senior vice president and chief ethics and compliance officer in the Law, Compliance, Business Ethics & External Affairs unit of Prudential Financial, Inc., responsible for overseeing the company's global compliance organization of more than 500 staff worldwide and the company's global business ethics efforts.

Mr. Augsburger joined Prudential's law department in 1997, later becoming the chief legal officer for the annuities business. In 2000 he moved to the Compliance Department, was appointed global chief compliance officer in 2007, and became global chief ethics officer in 2009. He also has served as vice president, compliance, for the company's Investment Division, where he was responsible for managing compliance programs for the retirement services, institutional brokerage, asset management businesses, and mutual funds.

CHAPTER 9

Ethics Standards Governing Compliance Professionals

By Richard D. Marshall
    Katten Muchin Rosenman LLP

I. INTRODUCTION

No mandated ethical standards apply to compliance professionals, although NSCP has adopted a code of ethics that Certified Securities Compliance Professionals (CSCPs) must obey. However, compliance professionals frequently confront ethical issues and should be guided, in addressing these issues, by high ethical standards. Even if ethical conduct is not mandated by law, reputational and business issues should encourage compliance professionals to adhere to high ethical standards.

II. COMPETENCE AND EMPOWERMENT

Competence

The NSCP Code of Ethics sets forth the following requirements for compliance professionals:

> Compliance professionals should be knowledgeable regarding relevant laws and regulations, relevant policies and procedures within their firms, and their firms' businesses, products, and processes.

* * *

> Compliance professionals should remain familiar with new rules and laws, changes in their firms' businesses and products, and developments in the industry and marketplace. Compliance Professionals must maintain and should strive to continually improve their technical knowledge, as well as the effectiveness and quality of their services.

General standards of due care require a professional to possess "the skill and knowledge normally possessed by members of that profession or trade in good standing."[1] This does

---

[1] Restatement (Second) of Torts §299A.

not mean that a professional is a guarantor of good results.[2] However, it does not mean that conforming with the "average" standards of competence in the industry is sufficient if these "average" standards of competence are too low.[3] It is also not sufficient to conform with the standard of competence in a given locality since modern communication and transportation services should permit a professional to adhere to nationally recognized standards.[4]

Where resource limitations may make it difficult for a professional to adhere to competency standards, these should be disclosed to the employer. It may be necessary for the compliance professional to refuse to perform services if resources are insufficient to perform a minimally acceptable job.[5] Where noncompliance professionals are used to assist the compliance professional, these persons must be properly supervised to ensure that acceptable professional standards of competence are met in their work.[6]

As practical guidance, compliance professionals should understand the businesses in which their firm operates, the products it offers, and the laws and regulations that govern these activities. This requires both formal training and experience, as well as continuing education to keep up to date on new developments.

A former senior official of OCIE has offered the following statement of the competency requirement for compliance professionals:

> In my view, to be competent a CCO should be well qualified in regard to understanding compliance requirements of advisers and how attributes of effective compliance activities relate to those requirements and prevent violations of the [Investment] Advisers Act [of 1940[.]This understanding includes the means or process by which compliance programs are created and maintained as well as the issues they are designed to address. To me, competence requires familiarity with steps needed to create compliance programs such as:
>
> Risk identification and assessment how to identify conflicts and other compliance factors creating risk exposure for the firm and its clients in light of the firm's particular operations. This is the important starting point for establishing effective compliance programs but is also a step many advisers, especially smaller ones overlook.
>
> Creating policies and procedures to address the risks identified—the rule identifies certain issues that should be covered by such policies and procedures to the extent the risks are relevant to an adviser. To be effective, such policies and procedures should address all conflicts of interest

---

[2] Restatement of the Law Governing Lawyers §52, comment b.
[3] *Id.*
[4] Restatement (Section) of Torts §299A, comment g.
[5] Restatement of the Law Governing Lawyers, comment c.
[6] Restatement (Second) of Torts §213. *See also* NSCP Code of Ethics: "A compliance professional can rely upon experts, including attorneys, certified public accountants, and internal auditors, to assist the compliance professional in performing his or her responsibilities."

and other risks the firm is exposed to and not a set of risks that advisers in general may have.

Implementation of the policies and procedures while recognizing principles of good management and controls.

I think competence would also include familiarity with functions required to administer compliance programs, such as:

- Requesting resources to carry out compliance activities;
- Monitoring implementation by managers throughout the firm which requires good interpersonal skills;
- Knowing the business of an adviser; and
- Being proactive, inquisitive, and being able to exercise professional skepticism.[7]

Empowerment

As set forth in the NSCP Code of Ethics:

A compliance professional should not accept employment as a compliance professional unless he or she is given adequate authority and resources to perform his or her responsibilities. These include the following:

- Access to and the ability to gather and test appropriate information; and
- The ability to communicate with appropriate senior management about compliance issues and concerns."

A former senior OCIE official has offered the following guidance on the powers that a CCO should be able to exercise:

In the Adopting Release, the commission said that an adviser's CCO should be empowered with full responsibility and authority to develop and enforce appropriate policies and procedures for the firm. It seems logical, then, to conclude that the compliance officer should have a position of sufficient seniority and authority within the organization to be able to compel others to adhere to the firm's compliance policies and procedures. To achieve this result, CCOs will usually be a member of the senior management of a firm.

---

[7] Gene Gohlke, Practical Guidance for Hedge Fund CCOs (May 5, 2005), http://www.sec.gov/news/speech/spch050505gg.htm. *See also* Lori Richards, The New Compliance Rule (June 28, 2004), http://www.sec.gov/news/speech/spch063004lar.htm:

> The chief compliance officer will need to not only understand the regulations but how the industry works, the products and services offered by the firm, the nature of the services provided by service providers, and the firm's operational and compliance structure. Certainly it will be important for her to be able to "think outside of the box" and to question and reassess past practices. She should look at product, market and regulatory trends to identify existing and emerging compliance risk areas.

The Compliance Rule does not require that a CCO report to a firm's CEO or an equivalent position. However, if other "C" level executives (e.g., CFO, CIO) report directly to the CEO and the CCO does not, the firm should be aware that its staff may interpret this difference in reporting structure to mean that compliance is not as important as those other functions and the ability of the CCO to compel compliance may be weakened. In addition, if legal and CCO roles are combined into a single position or if a CCO reports to the firm's chief legal officer, a number of difficult conflicts may arise.[8]

The Federal Sentencing Guidelines also provide guidance on the empowerment that is expected of compliance professionals:

> Specific individual(s) within the organization shall be delegated day-to-day operational responsibility for the compliance and ethics program. Individual(s) with operational responsibility shall report periodically to high-level personnel and, as appropriate, to the governing authority, or an appropriate subgroup of the governing authority, on the effectiveness of the compliance and ethics program. To carry out such operational responsibility, such individual(s) shall be given adequate resources, appropriate authority, and direct access to the governing authority or an appropriate subgroup of the governing authority.[9]

Two key elements thus emerge from these elements of a compliance professional's empowerment. First, a compliance professional must be given sufficient access to information about firm activities to monitor and test those activities.[10] Second, the compliance professional should have access to the most senior management of the firm to report on the results of that monitoring and testing.

---

[8] Gohlke, Practical Guidance for Hedge Fund. Lori Richards, The New Compliance Rule, stated:

> I know that fund firms are now considering where the chief compliance officer position should fit within the firm's structure. I would not automatically assume that it should be placed within Legal or report through the general counsel (remember that the chief compliance officer also reports directly to the fund's Board of Directors). Intertwining the corporate legal duties and the duties of the compliance officer may create conflicts not only in the implementation of the compliance program but also in the examination of the program. If you decide that the chief compliance officer will report to Legal, counsel will have to clearly articulate instances of client privilege and show great effort to segregate any dual responsibilities. Routine compliance monitoring is not subject to attorney-client privilege, and in particular, take note that the commission recently reminded firms that all reports required under the federal securities laws are meant to be made available to the commission's staff for examination, and thus are not subject to the attorney-client privilege, work product doctrine or other similar protections.

[9] United States Sentencing Commission, *Guidelines Manual*, §8B2.1(b)(2)(C) (Nov. 2012).

[10] With respect to the adequacy of resources devoted to compliance, the NSCP Code of Ethics provides the following:

> 10.2 While the compliance professional should request adequate resources to perform his or her responsibilities, compliance professionals usually do not control the allocation of firm resources to compliance functions. A compliance professional should devote reasonable efforts to the diligent discharge of his or her responsibilities within the staffing, systems, and other resource constraints to which they are subject.

Particularly difficult issues arise when the compliance professional is put on notice of possible misconduct. On October 19, 2009, the SEC instituted an administrative proceeding against Theodore Urban, the former general counsel of a broker-dealer, alleging that he had "failed to supervise" a registered representative of the firm.[11] Urban was alleged to have been alerted to possible wrongdoing by a registered representative of the firm, to have tried to investigate and to stop any misconduct, but to have done too little to stop this misconduct. On first glance, it is difficult to identify a theory of liability under which Urban could be charged. He did not commit illegal acts, did not aid and abet or cause others to commit illegal acts, and was not the line supervisor of any wrongdoer. Nonetheless, the SEC asserted a theory of liability first articulated two decades ago under which a legal or compliance officer holding a senior position within the firm can be held liable for a failure to take affirmative action to investigate and to prevent misconduct that such officer had reason to suspect was taking place. Application of this failure to supervise theory is of particular concern to those within the legal and compliance community because, under such a theory of secondary liability, once a person is found to be a supervisor of a wrongdoer, the supervisor is subject to liability, with the burden shifting to the supervisor to prove the defense that supervision had in fact been adequate.

The *Urban* case has a somewhat unusual procedural history. The SEC's claims were initially tried before an administrative law judge, who accepted the theory of supervisory liability but found that Urban met his burden of proving he had adequately supervised the wrongdoer.[12] The SEC commissioners then denied summary affirmance of this decision.[13] The SEC commissioners then scheduled, then canceled, oral argument on the appeal of this decision. On January 26, 2012, the case was finally resolved, but without in any way clarifying the theory under which legal and compliance officers can be held liable. Instead, the SEC dismissed the case because all but two of the commissioners had recused themselves from the case, and the two remaining commissioners were split in their views of the case.[14] Urban has now been vindicated, but with legal and compliance officers left with no clear guidance as to the standard of liability that applies to their conduct in carrying out their duties and responsibilities.

The theory of liability under which Urban was charged was first asserted in in *In re John H. Gutfreund*,[15] when the SEC stated in dictum that a firm's chief legal counsel, who directly supervised the firm's CCO, could be disciplined for a failure to supervise based on the misconduct of employees for whom he was not the direct supervisor but where the chief legal officer/CCO had knowledge of possible misconduct and the authority to intervene to prevent it. *Gutfreund* represents an expansion of traditional failure to supervise claims to nonline supervisors. This theory was most clearly and forcefully advocated in a 1993 speech by then SEC Commissioner Mary Schapiro, who said, "The facts and circumstances which may make you 'become' a supervisor

---

[11] *In re Urban*, SEC Admin. Proc. File No. 3-13655 (Oct. 19, 2009).
[12] *In re Urban* (Sept. 8, 2010).
[13] *In re Urban* (Dec. 7, 2010).
[14] *In re Urban* (Jan. 26, 2012).
[15] *In re John H. Gutfreund*, 51 S.E.C. 93, Release No. 34-31554, 1992 WL 362753, *15-16 (1992).

vis-a-vis a particular employee, when formerly you were not, are (1) your knowledge and awareness of allegedly improper conduct, and (2), being so situated within a firm that you have some ability to affect the conduct at issue."[16]

According to the SEC, under this theory of supervisory liability, two obligations are imposed on legal and compliance professionals when they learn of possible wrongdoing: a duty to investigate and a duty to prevent misconduct:

> The *"supervisory obligations* imposed by the federal securities laws *require a vigorous response even to indications of wrongdoing."* In re John H. Gutfreund, Exchange Act Release No. 31554, 1992 SEC LEXIS 2939, at *34 (Dec. 3, 1992). Thus, supervisors must respond not only when they are "explicitly informed of an illegal act," but also when they are "aware only of 'red flags' or 'suggestions' of irregularity." *See id.* at *34-35. In addition, "[e]ven *where the knowledge of supervisors is limited to 'red flags' or 'suggestions' of irregularity, they cannot discharge their supervisory obligations simply by relying on the unverified representations of employees."* Id. at *35. *"Red flags and suggestions of irregularities demand inquiry as well as adequate follow-up and review."* In re Edwin Kantor, Exchange Act Release No. 32341, 1993 SEC LEXIS 1240, at *16 (May 20, 1993)." *In the Matter of George M. Lintz,* Exchange Act Rel. 43961 (Feb. 14, 2001).

> Once a person in [the general counsel's] position becomes involved in formulating management's response to the problem, he or she is obligated to take affirmative steps to ensure that appropriate action is taken to address the misconduct. For example, such a person could direct or monitor an investigation of the conduct at issue, make appropriate recommendations for limiting the activities of the employee or for the institution of appropriate procedures, reasonably designed to prevent and detect future misconduct, and verify that his or her recommendations, or acceptable alternatives, are implemented. If such a person takes appropriate steps but management fails to act and that person knows or has reason to know of that failure, he or she should consider what additional steps are appropriate to address the matter. These steps may include disclosure of the matter to the entity's board of directors, resignation from the firm, or disclosure to regulatory authorities.[17]

The NSCP Code of Ethics directly addresses this situation:

> If a compliance professional takes appropriate steps to address a compliance violation but management fails to act effectively and the compliance professional knows or has reason to know of that failure, he or she should

---

[16] Mary L. Schapiro, Broker-Dealer Failure to Supervise: Determining Who Is a "Supervisor?" SIA Compliance and Legal Seminar, at 15 (Mar. 24, 1993).

[17] *In re John Gutfreund* (emphasis added).

consider what additional steps are appropriate to address the matter. These steps may include disclosure of the matter to the entity's most senior management or board of directors, resignation from the firm, or disclosure to regulatory authorities. In the case of an attorney, the applicable Code of Professional Responsibility and the Canons of Ethics may bear upon what course of conduct that individual may properly pursue. Other professionals and members of other professional organizations that adhere to a professional code of ethics may have additional ethical responsibilities.

III. INDEPENDENCE

The NSCP Code of Ethics provides the following guidance on a compliance professional's independence:

> Compliance professionals should seek to avoid coercion, deception, or undue influence by any persons, both inside or outside their firm, in connection with the compliance professional's performance of his or her duties and must report any instances of such conduct to appropriate senior management.

For the CCO to a registered investment company, there is guidance in the SEC's adopting release for Rule 38a-1 about how to preserve the independence of the compliance professional:

> The rule contains several provisions, some of which were not included in our proposal, designed to promote the independence of the chief compliance officer from the management of the fund. First, the chief compliance officer will serve in her position at the pleasure of the fund's board of directors, which can remove her if it loses confidence in her effectiveness. The fund board (including a majority of independent directors) must approve the designation of the chief compliance officer, and must approve her compensation (or any changes in her compensation). The board (including a majority of the independent directors) can remove the chief compliance officer from her responsibilities at any time, and can prevent the adviser or another service provider from doing so.
>
> Second, the chief compliance officer will report directly to the board of directors. She must annually furnish the board with a written report on the operation of the fund's policies and procedures and those of its service providers. The report must address, at a minimum: (i) the operation of the policies and procedures of the fund and each service provider since the last report, (ii) any material changes to the policies and procedures since the last report, (iii) any recommendations for material changes to the policies and procedures as a result of the annual review and (iv) any

material compliance matters since the date of the last report. We have added a definition of the term "material compliance matter" to the rule, to clarify that the report should inform the board of those compliance matters about which the fund's board reasonably needs to know in order to oversee fund compliance.

Third, we are requiring that the chief compliance officer meet in executive session with the independent directors at least once each year, without anyone else (such as fund management or interested directors) present. The executive session creates an opportunity for the chief compliance officer and the independent directors to speak freely about any sensitive compliance issues of concern to any of them, including any reservations about the cooperativeness or compliance practices of fund management.

Fourth, we have added a provision to protect the chief compliance officer from undue influence by fund service providers seeking to conceal their or others' non-compliance with the federal securities laws. Rule 38a-1 prohibits the fund's officers, directors, employees or its adviser, principal underwriter, or any person acting under the direction of these persons, from directly or indirectly taking any action to coerce, manipulate, mislead or fraudulently influence the fund's chief compliance officer in the performance of her responsibilities under the rule.[18]

It is important to note, however, that compliance professionals are not subject to the standard of independence that applies to independent auditors. These professionals must adhere to a very high standard of independence which serves both to maintain the quality of their audit work and also to enhance the public's confidence in the quality of that work. For these reasons, auditors cannot invest in an audit client's securities or provide certain non-audit services to the audit client. These onerous restrictions do not apply to the compliance professional.

IV. CONFLICTS OF INTEREST

The identification and management of conflicts of interest is central to any ethical issues for any professional. Five rationale have been offered for regulating conflicts of interest by professionals:

1. A professional should serve the interests of his or her "client" with undivided loyalty. A conflicted professional may be unable or unwilling to serve the interest of his or her "client" effectively;
2. A conflict of interest can impair a professional's judgment and vigor in performing his or her responsibilities;
3. A conflict of interest may compromise the professional's protection of his or her "client's" confidences;

---

[18] Advisers Act Rel. 2204 (Dec. 17, 2003).

4. A conflicted professional may be tempted to advance his or her own interests at the expense of the "client"; and
5. A conflict of interest rules protect the integrity of the compliance process.[19]

In general, a conflict of interest exists when the compliance professional has an interest that is potentially adverse to the interests the professional is supposed to protect.[20] This is not the same as an "appearance of impropriety," a vague standard that focuses on how an uninformed third party might react to the motivations in question.[21] Rather, a conflict of interest is deemed to exist when the compliance professional might be tempted to act in a manner that is inconsistent with his or her responsibilities.

In general, when a conflict of interest is present, it should be mitigated, monitored, and disclosed. If the conflict of interest is severe, it must be avoided entirely.

The NSCP Code of Ethics identifies five particular conflicts of interest that compliance professionals should address: personal trading, gifts, compensation, self-investigation, and self-monitoring.

Personal Trading

The NSCP Code of Ethics offers the following guidance on this issue:

4.1 Personal Trading

- Compliance professionals must maintain strict adherence to their firms' codes of ethics and any other codes regulating their personal trading; and
- With or without specific employer policies, a compliance professional should avoid any actual or appearance of conflicts of interest in personal transactions in products offered by the employer.

Broker-dealers,[22] investment advisers,[23] and investment companies[24] are required to collect and monitor the personal trading by their employees, including compliance professionals. This does not require a complete ban on personal trading, which was considered and rejected for many reasons:

- The Advisory Group believes that the potential conflicts arising from personal investing activities can be addressed decisively—and the public's trust fully vindicated—through effective restrictions and procedures that do not constitute a total ban. The former commission members and senior officials with whom the Advisory Group met in the course of its work concurred unanimously in this judgment;

---

[19] Restatement of the Law Governing Lawyers, §121, comment b.
[20] Restatement of the Law Governing Lawyers, comment c.
[21] *Id.*
[22] FINRA Rule 3050.
[23] Advisers Act Rule 204A-1.
[24] Investment Company Act Rule 17j-1.

- The Advisory Group is convinced that a total ban on personal investing would arbitrarily and unfairly foreclose, potentially to many thousands of individual employees, wholly legitimate and appropriate investment opportunities. Based on the Advisory Group's review, such a ban would be unprecedented and would far exceed accepted notions of fiduciary conduct or any reasonable expectations of ethical accountability; and
- As senior executives in the industry, the Advisory Group notes the widespread expressions of concern—which are legitimate—that foreclosing portfolio managers from opportunities to invest directly in the markets not only would detract from the very portfolio management abilities on which shareholders rely, but would establish significant and needless disincentives to the continued service of these talented individuals in the industry. This is especially true in the absence of comparable restrictions on other types of asset managers. In the end, the Advisory Group believes that a ban would operate to the detriment of millions of individual fund shareholders and of the industry at large.[25]

The SEC has offered the following guidance of how the mandated review of personal transactions should be conducted:

> Review of personal securities holding and transaction reports should include not only an assessment of whether the access person followed any required internal procedures, such as preclearance, but should also compare the personal trading to any restricted lists; assess whether the access person is trading for his own account in the same securities he is trading for clients, and if so whether the clients are receiving terms as favorable as the access person takes for himself; periodically analyze the access person's trading for patterns that may indicate abuse, including market timing; investigate any substantial disparities between the quality of performance the access person achieves for his own account and that he achieves for clients; and investigate any substantial disparities between the percentage of trades that are profitable when the access person trades for his own account and the percentage that are profitable when he places trades for clients.[26]

Gifts

The NSCP Code of Ethics addresses this issue directly:

> 4.2 Gifts
> - A compliance professional may not solicit the receipt of a gift for the execution of his or her legitimate job duties.
> - A compliance professional may give or receive an unsolicited gift from an individual with whom his or her firm does business only if

---

[25] Report of the Advisory Group on Personal Investing (May 9, 1994), http://www.ici.org/pdf/rpt_personal_investing.pdf
[26] Advisers Act Rel. 2256 (July 2, 2004).

consistent with the firm's policies and procedures and the ability of the compliance professional to exercise independent judgment. This would include gifts from employees of the same firm that the compliance person works for (e.g., holiday baskets).

Although the SEC has not adopted rules governing gifts and entertainment, FINRA Rule 3220 directly addresses this issue:

a. No member or person associated with a member shall, directly or indirectly, give or permit to be given anything of value, including gratuities, in excess of one hundred dollars per individual per year to any person, principal, proprietor, employee, agent or representative of another person where such payment or gratuity is in relation to the business of the employer of the recipient of the payment or gratuity. A gift of any kind is considered a gratuity.

b. This Rule shall not apply to contracts of employment with or to compensation for services rendered by persons enumerated in paragraph (a) provided that there is in existence prior to the time of employment or before the services are rendered, a written agreement between the member and the person who is to be employed to perform such services. Such agreement shall include the nature of the proposed employment, the amount of the proposed compensation, and the written consent of such person's employer or principal.

c. A separate record of all payments or gratuities in any amount known to the member, the employment agreement referred to in paragraph (b) and any employment compensation paid as a result thereof shall be retained by the member for the period specified by SEA Rule 17a-4.

Compensation

The NSCP Code of Ethics addresses the issue of compliance professional compensation as follows:

4.3 Compensation

- A compliance professional should review his/her compensation package and other remuneration and reduce or eliminate, wherever possible, actual conflicts of interest presented by the manner in which the compensation is calculated or paid.

The SEC has also addressed the issues of compliance professional compensation in the Final Rule: Compliance Programs of Investment Companies and Investment Advisers applicable to investment companies, which requires that the fund's independent directors set the chief compliance officer's compensation:

> [C]ompensation should be designed to reinforce or incentivize the objectivity of the chief compliance officer, and to motivate her to perform her responsibilities. In thinking through how to compensate the chief compliance officer, I suggest that the spirit of the new rule should drive compensation and incentives. Some key factors might be: Is the chief compliance officer administering a compliance environment that not only addresses and supports the goals of all the federal securities laws but the intent of those laws? Is the program structured to and does it in fact prevent, detect and correct violations? Does it support open communication between the fund's service providers and those with compliance oversight? Is the program proactive, seeking to identify potential risk rather than reactive, merely plugging holes as they arise?[27]

Self-Investigation

The NSCP Code of Ethics offers the following guidance on a compliance professional's investigation of his or her own conduct:

> 4.4 Allegations against the compliance professional
>
> - When the compliance professional's conduct is directly and explicitly questioned, the compliance professional can continue to perform appropriate responsibilities, unless either appropriate senior management requests that the compliance professional cease to act in matters involving the professional's own alleged misconduct or the compliance professional concludes that he or she can no longer act effectively.

Self-Monitoring

Related to self-investigation is the problem of self-monitoring. The NSCP Code of Ethics offers the following guidance on self-monitoring:

> 4.5 Monitoring the Compliance Professional's Own Conduct
>
> - A compliance professional should avoid testing, monitoring, or supervising his or her own conduct, unless the size of the firm makes any other arrangement impractical.

V. CONFIDENTIALITY

The NSCP Code of Ethics provides the following guidance on a compliance professional's confidentiality obligations:

---

[27] *See* Lori Richards, The New Compliance Rule.

6.1 Compliance professionals should only disclose information conveyed in confidence within their firms to persons outside their firms when permitted by appropriate senior management to do so or when compelled to do so by legal requirements.

6.2 Compliance professionals should warn appropriate persons within their firms, as necessary, that it may be impossible for the compliance professional to preserve the confidentiality of information learned within the firm.

The status of this guidance has been challenged, however, by two developments. First, the self-evaluative privilege, which protects from disclosure certain information reflecting a critical self-evaluation of problems within a firm, is probably unavailable to a compliance professional.[28] Second, the SEC's whistleblower reporting rules expressly prevent a firm from preventing a whistleblower from reporting information directly to the SEC, even if firm procedures prohibit such communications:

> One commenter expressed concern that many employees are required to sign confidentiality agreements that may prevent them from providing information to the commission without a subpoena. *See* letter from David Sanford. We caution employers that, as adopted, Rule 21F-17(a) provides that no person may take any action to impede a whistleblower from communicating directly with the commission about a possible securities law violation, including by enforcing or threatening to enforce a confidentiality agreement. Further, Section 21F(h)(1)(A) of the Exchange Act prohibits any form of retaliation by an employer against a whistleblower because of any lawful act done by the whistleblower in providing information to the commission in accordance with Section 21F. 15 U.S.C. 78u-6(h)(1)(A)(i).[29]

---

[28] *See University of Pennsylvania v. E.E.O.C.*, 493 U.S. 182 (1990); But *see, FTC v. TRW, Inc.*, 628 F.2d 207, 210-11 (D.C. Cir. 1980); *United States v. Noall*, 587 F.2d 123 (2d Cir. 1978), *cert. denied*, 441 U.S. 923 (1979); *United States v. Westinghouse Elec. Corp.*, 788 F.2d 164 (3d Cir. 1986).

[29] Rel. 34. 64545 (May 25, 2011), n. 76.

ABOUT THE AUTHOR

Richard D. Marshall focuses his practice on the representation of financial institutions and their employees who are the subject of investigations by the SEC, U.S. attorneys, FINRA, and state securities regulators. He also counsels broker-dealers, investment companies, and investment advisers on regulatory issues, particularly relating to SEC and FINRA regulation. Rick also frequently counsels clients on compliance and risk management issues and handling of SEC inspections. Prior to entering private practice, Mr. Marshall worked for several years for the SEC as both a branch chief in the Division of Enforcement in Washington, DC, and as senior associate regional administrator in the SEC's New York office, where he supervised a staff of 70 that conducted inspections of investment companies and investment advisers and instituted enforcement actions against those entities.

CHAPTER 10

Soft Skills: Presenting Compliance

By Michelle Hawkins
    Fort Washington Investment Advisors, Inc.

I. INTRODUCTION

Our employers, clients, and regulators expect compliance professionals to be adequately trained and have the requisite technical skills to effectively manage their responsibilities. This includes staying up-to date on new regulations, laws, industry best practices, and proactively managing the ever increasing complexities associated with compliance. Technical skills can, and are, achieved in a variety of ways, including pre- and post-graduate studies, on the job training, attending conferences and seminars, and completing various compliance or financial related certifications and designations.

Having been part of the financial services industry for the past 30+ years, I have diligently worked at honing my technical skills. However, as a compliance professional I have also found that one needs more than technical skills to drive change, build and demonstrate capabilities, obtain a seat at the table, assemble a compliance team, and add value to the compliance community. I have also found that having the right people, in the right seats, doing the right job will help in building and developing a compliance community and compliance team while one is effecting change. In addition to having the right people on the team, a continuous evaluation and ongoing gap analysis is needed to understand the various opportunities available in taking a compliance program and team to the next level while one improves capabilities and skills.

> **Soft skills: desirable qualities for certain forms of employment that do not depend on acquired knowledge; they include common sense, the ability to deal with people, and a positive flexible attitude.**
>
> — World English Dictionary

The majority of this book focuses on the technical skills required for the job and will provide information needed to help the reader in becoming a subject matter expert in compliance, legal, and regulatory requirements. This chapter, however, will focus on the soft skills needed to manage oneself, a team, and the expectations within a firm and its clients, and among peers, all while promoting the role of compliance.

The *World English Dictionary* defines *soft skills* as "desirable qualities needed for certain forms of employment....They include common sense, the ability to deal with people, and a positive flexible attitude." The primary goal of this chapter is to analyze, identify, and address ways to improve soft skills and other skills and tools needed to assist one in adding value within an organization, its clients, and the compliance community.

II. YOUR ROAD MAP

Most self-help and business development books will address what you need to do to help you get where you want to be. This chapter will provide you with an opportunity to think outside of the norm and will help you to develop a road map that will assist you in improving your soft skills. When you develop a road map, it's important to reverse engineer your thought process by asking *what,* before you decide *where,* and then you can decide *how.* In other words, decide what you want to be, and then you can decide how to get there. This becomes your personal road map that provides you with the directions and route(s) needed to be successful. Start with asking do you have a road map or are you driving or working without a preplanned destination or goal? Next, do you know where you want to go? In other words, does your road map include driving instructions, a map, or mission statement that will help you in reaching your desired personal or professional destination? What are the key concepts within your mission statement? For example, will you always do the right things for the right reasons, within the regulatory framework, and in compliance with legal requirements? Or are you directed toward your stakeholders to counsel, protect, and always place their interest first? It is essential for you to first determine your personal mission and goals. This must be done prior to establishing or providing input on the mission statement of the firm or even for your department. A mission statement should contain the goals and desired outcome of your actions. So in developing your road map, you need to determine what your goals are and how you will define success based on the goals established.

> **Successful people do what unsuccessful people are not willing to do. Don't wish it were easier, wish you were better.**
>
> — Jim Rohn

III. SELF-EVALUATION

Determining your goals, both professionally and personally, should first start with a self-evaluation. Using our road map analogy, your self-evaluation can be viewed as making sure that your vehicle is prepared for your journey. Is your vehicle equipped to handle the wear and tear of the road? Will it respond to the instructions necessary to reach your destination?

A yearly self-evaluation is recommended to help identify potential areas and opportunities for improvements. You should also use this process to highlight your success during the prior year. Focus on both the positive and the negative. Focusing strictly on the negative may be defeating before having the opportunity to make necessary changes. Self-evaluation is about understanding what works, what doesn't work, and weaknesses and gaps, both personally and professionally. Motivational speaker Jim Rohn stated, "Successful people do what unsuccessful people are not willing to do. Don't wish it were easier, wish you were better."

The key point is that success begins with you! What are the qualities, skills and habits that you need to work on to become successful? Self-evaluations also provide you with an opportunity for self-reflection.

Following are some examples of self-evaluation questions:

- Who am I?
- What are my strengths?
- What are my weaknesses?
- What are my best qualities?
- How do people perceive me?
- What do I need to work on?
- What can I change?
- Do I demonstrate confidence, knowledge, and expertise?
- How do I add value to the organization?

During your self-evaluation look at areas or skills that proved to be successful during the prior year. Ask yourself what worked and how you can repurpose or build upon your prior success. What can you do to help drive change and improvements? Everyone has different skills and strengths, and the effects of team dynamics will be discussed later in the chapter. However, as an individual contributor, manager, or executive, you need to determine your strengths and weaknesses and focus on improving in each area. You want to focus on the things that you're good at, but you should also review your weaknesses and areas of opportunities rather than allow them to deter you or keep you from being successful.

IV. HINDSIGHT IS 20/20

This portion of the chapter will focus on change from having the benefit of hindsight. Revisiting our road map, you can take the opportunity to look back and determine how where we are now relates to the path we have chosen to take. By reviewing our path, it gives us the opportunity to identify any wrong turns we've taken on our journey, and correct our course for the trip ahead.

© MODERN COMPLIANCE 2015

Reflection on prior activities was illustrated very well in the movie *Groundhog Day*, where the lead character relived the events of a day over and over. When the main character, played by Bill Murray, woke up each day he relived the prior day. Benefiting from reliving his actions each day, he was able to make improvements on his mistakes that resulted in changing the outcomes. Eventually, the Bill Murray character was able to make the necessary changes to reach his desired goal: to win the girl! Unfortunately, you do not have the ability to go back in time and relive prior days; however, you do have the ability of hindsight and to know the things that have worked in the past. You have the ability to change future actions/outcomes by improving what you do on a daily basis. Part of this change arises from having self-awareness, passion, and confidence that you can make improvements to almost anything that you do or touch.

> For me, motivation is a person who has the capability to recruit the resources he needs to achieve a goal.
>
> — Arsene Wenger

Ask yourself the following questions:

- What could I do to add or increase value?
- What have I done today to improve myself?
- What have I done today to improve others?
- What was my biggest contribution today, this week, this month, this year?

V. YOUR TOOLKIT

You should have a personal and professional toolkit. Your professional toolkit will include skills required to help you in becoming a more successful, empowered, and enlightened compliance professional. The sections ahead will focus on the soft skills needed for your compliance toolkit, primarily the following areas:

- Building your compliance community;
- Communication;
- Talent management;
- Conflict management;
- Demonstrating your expertise; and
- Survival skills.

VI. BUILDING YOUR COMPLIANCE COMMUNITY

A main component in your toolkit is your compliance community. Your community consists of the professionals that comprise the talent around you, as well as professionals outside of your organization. In building your community, it is essential that you get the basics right. The basics include managing your talent and the talent of your team. This includes hiring the right person for the team and the organization, and not hiring for expertise alone. For example, in my hiring process each candidate must go through a series of interviews with my team and certain members of our firm. They must also produce a work product of my choosing. Candidates are evaluated on how they approach the assignment and their presentation skills. In general, candidates are well prepared for interviews; however, challenging them with a task involving minimal instruction helps determine what type and level of ongoing direction or guidance they would need. Candidates can be trained. The focus of the assigned task is to see whether the person has the right attitude, confidence, and qualities that could lead to a successful career within our organization. In the compliance community, these qualities include integrity, passion, commitment, and dedication.

During the interview process, you should always look for key qualities that address your goals and desires for the organization and your team. Following is a list of certain qualities that are important to me and compliment my management style. They may be for you as well.

- Passion;
- Integrity;
- Commitment;
- Communication skills;
- Time management;
- Confidence;
- Persuasiveness; and
- Innovation.

It is important to take advantage of opportunities that highlight an individual's unique and diverse capabilities during meetings or even throughout the workday within your organization. Individuals quite often succeed when they are maximizing their strengths.

When it comes to your compliance team, it is important to capitalize on each person's strengths. My team members have diverse backgrounds, and their individual qualities and expertise complement each other and help build a foundation for our compliance program. Identifying these qualities in each person early on has helped our compliance program be very successful. I am very blessed to have a wonderful team.

In addition to your compliance team, it is important to expand your compliance community beyond your firm. Consider the following questions when building your personal community. Do you belong to any professional groups? Do you attend conferences? Do you network? How do you approach your peers? Do you have an elevator speech that you use when introducing yourself? Are you active or passive in your efforts, in other words, do you seek people out or are you more comfortable in the background? Do you take advantage of conference social events or do you prefer to retire to your room at the end of the day?

© MODERN COMPLIANCE 2015

If you exhibit qualities that are not leading to professional connections, it is time to break out of your conundrum and your comfort zone. Networking is part of building those soft skills necessary to make you the best compliance professional possible. You should try to meet at least one new person per day throughout the year. This sounds simplistic, but there are additional steps you need to take. It is not only important to meet new people and exchange contact information. It is also important to proactively reach out to people within your network. Exchanging business cards is the first step, but having a business card is not building your community unless you reconnect with people in your network and interact with some frequency. You should try communicating with at least one person in your network on a weekly basis. This could take the form of an email or telephone call, just to say hello, to discuss new regulations, or summarize the latest strategy or business initiative within your firms. Keep your community and the interaction with your network fluid. You never know when someone in your community can use your help or advice. You do not want to reach out only when you have an issue at hand or need help yourself. Join a compliance roundtable within your region, if you don't have an existing roundtable to join, start one. In general, here is how: Identify the individuals in your region, introduce yourself to them, and bring them together for an informal get together. During your meeting discuss challenges that you are facing. Quite often, your peers are facing similar challenges and are looking for solutions and advice. The great thing about a compliance community is that everyone shares the same focus and is generally willing to share experiences, expertise, and best practices.

VII. COMMUNICATION

If you are old enough to remember growing up during the '60s, '70s or '80s, recall how you were often asked, "What is your zodiac sign?" today the question is "What is your communication style?" Communication styles, like zodiac signs, cover a broad spectrum and can influence how people react and interact with each other. This is not to say you should ask your CEO or your employees their zodiac signs. However, it's important to understand how people communicate (i.e., their communication style) and how your communication style can help you in managing interactions with others and potentially in achieving your personal and professional goals.

> **It is the province of knowledge to speak and it is the privilege of wisdom to listen.**
>
> — Oliver Wendell Holmes

Effective communication skills are one of the most important, if not the most important, skill that a compliance professional should have. The ability to influence others by understanding their goals, aspirations, and values, and how an individual or a group of individuals communicate and process information is instrumental. This will help you in determining how information should be presented, whether you should potentially reframe your message, or communicate your thoughts in a way that will bring about your desired results. The worst thing a compliance professional can do is to immediately communicate from a platform of the enforcer (e.g., "you have to do it because of regulatory requirements") without providing context for the reasons why, and describing an understanding of the impact to the firm, as well as the risk of not doing what is required. Your communication technique should include a discussion of the perception of others, an understanding of the requirements and/or issue(s) at hand, and potential recommendations to reach an amicable resolution. Now I would be remiss, and for those who have not been in the compliance profession for any length of time, to indicate that if you follow my advice that you will not have conflicts during your career. Conflicts are inevitable, and actually if you think about it, one of the "Cs" in compliance could or should stand for "conflict."

In addition to understanding your communication style and the communication styles of others, active listening is also essential and will help you in becoming an effective communicator. Communication is a two-way activity, and you not only need to communicate your desires and thoughts, but you also need to listen to you audience. In his book, *Communicating Clearly*, Robert Heller describes three types of listening skills:

- Empathizing—Drawing out the speaker and getting information in a supportive, helpful way;
- Analyzing—Seeking concrete information and trying to disentangle fact from emotion; and
- Synthesizing—Proactively guiding the exchange toward an objective.

The key takeaway is that you should understand your communication style and how to leverage your style with the communication styles of others. Ask yourself, who do I generally communicate with, and how do I communicate? When communicating, do I have a complete communication loop? Are people able to understand and interpret my message? There are several resources that can help you in improving your communication skills; the following is one of the many resources and tools that you can use to help understand various communication styles that are borne from our social interactions, upbringing or education. The styles are attributable to the work of Dr. Tony Alessandra.

Based on prior studies, Stephanie Reyes devised this list of four main communication styles:

- Interpersonal, also called the Relator;
- Affective, also called the Socializer;
- Cognitive, also called the Thinker; and
- Behavioral, also called the Director.

Relator (Interpersonal)

The Relator is relationship orientated and readily expresses their thoughts and feelings. However, Relator's are generally slower paced and security conscious, so they prefer less intrusive interactions.

Socializer (Affective)

The Socializer prefers to interact with others rather than work alone. Socializers have a fast paced, aggressive communication style and generally work well with others.

Thinker (Cognitive)

The Thinker has a closed, personal style and is analytical in their approach. Thinkers take a while to feel comfortable with others, and tend to take longer to reveal information about themselves.

Director: (Behavioral)

The Director has an aggressive, competitive nature and is very independent. Directors are results orientated and focus less on the people impacts.[1]

Other Tools

Reyes' is just one of the many communication style predictors. Additional resources include:

- Myers-Briggs;
- DISC; and
- Kolbe Index.

After determining your communication style and developing concrete ways to effectively communicate, you should also consider preplanned approaches to spontaneity and uncertainty. This is especially helpful when delivering tough messages to your firm or interacting with senior officers, such as the president, directors, or regulatory authorities. Being prepared for this type of interaction allows you to communicate with skill, confidence, and competence. Being prepared for the unexpected, uncomfortable conversations, hidden agendas, and the occasional outburst or rampages that you may encounter can only help you in your career. Showing your ability to think on your feet is a desired trait for any professional especially for someone who is looking for career growth and advancement.

---

[1] Stephanie Reyes, "Understanding Communication Styles in the Workplace," Workplace Tribes, http://tribehr.com/blog/understanding-communication-styles-in-the-workplace

VIII. TALENT MANAGEMENT

There are four key factors in talent management:

- Effective teams;
- Coaching with heart;
- Strategic planning; and
- Self-awareness.

An effective leader quickly realizes that he or she does not know everything. As an effective leader, you must trust others, but you must do so carefully. You may also need to earn the trust of your team. Leaders should help others as well as themselves do the right things for the right reasons. As a leader one of your primary goals is to set the direction of your team, create and convey your vision and the vision of the team, all the while outlining your future and the future plans of the team and your organization as a whole. This should also be done while you are creating an atmosphere that motivates and inspires, which in turn will help your team become a dynamic, collaborative, and highly functional unit. Coaching from the heart is about taking the desires of your team members and their best interests into consideration when evaluating their career paths and development plans.

Creating highly effective teams is more of an art than science. Effective teams allow you to do more with less, and the world of compliance is often expected to do more with limited resources. It is rare to build your compliance team from the ground up. Generally, you inherit people from other departments or if you are new to your position or firm, you have people who are already in their roles and have developed both good and bad habits. One of the most important tenets when you evaluating your team is that effective teams are built and maintained based on mutual collaboration, cooperation, and respect for the talent that each individual brings to the team. As a manager or leader of your organization or department, you must convey the mission of the team and define the roles of each team member. Developing employees by understanding their desires, strengths, weaknesses, and career aspirations will assist you in determining the functions of each team member, and his or her ultimate role and responsibilities within the team and within the firm. To find the right fit for each individual takes collaboration and a plan to build on the strengths of the individual. No one is good at everything, and one person alone cannot do everything.

> **Leadership is the art of getting someone else to do something you want done because he wants to do it.**
>
> — Dwight D. Eisenhower

Capitalize on the strengths of each team member; you can always support areas of weaknesses or opportunities. You should start with your strongest asset/capability and build up, versus working from a deficit (i.e., weakness); in both cases you are working toward a goal. It is best to start from a strong foundation and build from there. When managing people, you want to make sure that you balance the role of manger/boss with humility and compassion. Remember that your team and coworkers have feelings and want to be treated with respect and reminded that they are important to the overall success of your department and the firm.

I have been very fortunate in my career to have the ability to work with highly motivated, talented, and very capable individuals. I've come to respect the individual talents of each team member and have structured our team to include people who are analytical, inquisitive, data driven, outgoing, and great communicators.

So how did I capitalize on my team's qualities and capabilities from one year to another? Earlier in this chapter, I mentioned conducting an annual personal assessment, and establishing goals for the upcoming year and beyond. Each year my team and I undergo an annual strategic planning exercise. The strategic planning session allows the team and me to revisit our individual accomplishments and goals from the prior year and collectively discuss our individual goals, department goals, and organization goals. During our recent strategy session, the following questions were incorporated to help drive our discussion:

- What is our mission?
- How do you rate our overall compliance program?
- What are the top five things that we need to concentrate on in the upcoming year?
- If you could change one thing about the firm, our department, or other areas or activities conducted within the firm, what would you change?
- What are our top three resource issues?

At the end or our session, the team members reevaluated their answer to the second question. Surprisingly, after reviewing our individual and collective accomplishments, the majority of the members increased their overall ranking of our compliance program. The good news is that we are continuously evaluating and reevaluating our goals, processes, program, and interactions. We recognize we still have work to do.

Talent management also requires that you become a continuous learner. Most people, when starting their career, take time to learn all they can about their area of responsibility. If you are established in your career, have you become complacent? In order to keep abreast of current trends, regulations, and best practices in our field, you must be competent. Competency is based on your ability to continuously learn and develop new skills or improve the skills that you have. How often do you read financial publications? Do you subscribe to or read academic or legal articles and magazines? As a professional you must understand not only the technical aspects of compliance but also your field of practice. Become a sponge or a connoisseur of learning. Take in and absorb as much information as you can. Evaluate whether there are opportunities or skills that will help you in your quest to become a life-long learner. For instance, do you need to increase your reading speed, writing skills, or technical knowledge? If so, take the necessary steps to work on these less honed skills. What got you to this point in your career may not keep you here, so work on self-improvement each day. Establish benchmarks and monitor your accomplishments. Always have a business plan not only for your department but for yourself and for your employees. Learn how to measure the value that you bring to your organization and make sure to find a way to communicate that value.

IX. CONFLICT MANAGEMENT

The following are key points to consider when you are thinking about or addressing conflicts:

- Conflict is inevitable;
- Adversity is a speed bump;
- Goal is to advance the ball;
- Show maturity and manage your emotions;
- Provide encouragement and support;
- Be accountable for your actions; and
- Know your goals and the goals of others.

First and foremost, conflicts are inevitable. The goal in any situation is advancement and understanding, especially in the area of conflicts. Conflicts will happen during your career and in your personal life: Embrace those situations. Remember, they are just a speed bump, not personal. Manage your emotions and understand that your primary goal should be to move toward understanding and agreement. To use a sports analogy, advance the ball! Conflict management is a skill, and as a compliance professional, you must expect and plan for conflicts and develop the requisite skills to arm yourself with tools that can assist you during times of conflict or heated discussions.

One such skill is effective listening. Learn to listen to your associates and key stakeholders and provide them with the opportunity to voice their concerns or disagreement with the situation or topic at hand. Effective listening skills are essential when you are managing conflicts. Listen first, and then ask questions! Look for areas of agreement, and remember that not all conflicts are resolved to everyone's absolute satisfaction. It is best to reserve expressing your opinion until you are further into the negotiation or resolution phase of your discussion.

In the heat of any negotiation, discussion, or conflict, remember to always be professional. Professionalism includes being a credible and knowledgeable resource. If you do not know the answer to a question, respond that you have to conduct additional research or contact other resources, never lie or make something up. Lack of knowledge, understanding, or answering a question on the fly without the proper knowledge can ruin your credibility, and your position of authority. Conflict resolution requires you to look for areas that you can agree on and work toward a mutual compromise. There may be times where you will agree to disagree and you will have to reach a point of resolution or compromise. Always work from a foundation of trust and credibility; never compromise yourself for the sake of reaching an agreement or to avoid a situation.

The bottom line is that during conflict management, you should always follow these simple guidelines:

- Listen effectively;
- Be professional;
- Stay credible, assertive, and effective; and
- Articulate your position, but be willing to compromise.

It is important to remember that there is a human element involved when you try to resolve conflicts. Being a good negotiator will quite often help you during situations in which there are disagreements between you, your coworkers, management, and regulators. Regardless of the situation, you should respond from a platform of trust, respect, and appreciation for the differing views that are presented. You are not required to agree with other opposing views. When disagreement occurs, people may feel threatened or take the situation as a personal affront—to their character, intelligence, or capabilities.

The first step in conflict management is to try to remove the human element of the situation, and to deal with the situation using a solution based approach, which requires you to understand the individual or group's ultimate goal and what everyone is trying to accomplish. Put yourself in the antagonists' shoes first, then work from a knowledge base to explain the options that may exist. During the initial phase of any conflict, try to ask questions before telling your opinion or giving advice. For example, you may hear remarks from employees that your code of ethics is unfair. An initial response should be to gain a better understanding of why the individual feels that way. To ask the individual why he or she thinks the code is unfair, delineate whether it is the entire code or a certain part, something in particular, or in its understanding. You should avoid starting from a platform of the teacher or enforcer; start from a point of understanding and inquiry. Some additional suggestions or questions include the following:

- Let me see: Do I understand what you're saying?
- What exactly are you trying to accomplish?
- Are there any hurdles that you need to overcome?
- What risks are associated with your plan?
- Are you aware of any restrictions, business, regulatory, and/or legal?
- How can I/we help to accomplish your goals?

Remember to hold your opinion until you reach a conclusion on what all parties are trying to accomplish or understand their motivation for wanting an exception.

X. DEMONSTRATING YOUR EXPERTISE AND TALENT

How often do you ask the following questions?

- How do people perceive me?
- Do I convey a confidence when talking with others?
- Do I speak with authority?
- Do I engage people when I'm speaking?
- If I were listening to myself, what flaws could I point out in my communication style?

First impressions are important. It is natural to want to make a good impression when meeting people. However, lasting impressions are just as important, if not more important. How do you want people to remember you? What expertise are you trying to convey? As a compliance professional you should want to demonstrate your command and understanding of regulations, laws, ethics, and the fundamental concept of compliance, as well as how you effectively manage your responsibilities. For example, I was honored and somewhat humbled that the editors of this book invited me to be part of what I consider to be a great and noble undertaking. Initially I thought about declining their offer and walking away from this great opportunity. I considered excuses, such as "I'm too busy, too unsure of my contribution," and so on. However, I questioned my motives or lack of understanding of "why me?" and reached the conclusion that they obviously saw something I had to offer and believed that I could add value to their project. My interactions with John and David over the years have left a lasting impression—an impression that I demonstrated an expertise that they wanted me to share with you. It took courage for me to accept their invitation. Courage can help you increase your personal and professional influence. I believe that I increased my personal and professional influence by accepting this challenge. I encourage you to do the same.

> **Life shrinks or expands according to one's courage.**
>
> — Anaïs Nin

Now ask yourself, where does courage come from? Is courage the lack of fear, the ability to overcome self-doubt, the fear of failure, and/or mistakes? However you define courage, the most important component is that it can help you succeed and do outstanding things. Quite often, professional and personal growth is based on our ability to overcome our fears and self-doubts and to have courage to face the unknown.

Imparting your authority or at the very least how you convey your influence, comes from the way people perceive you. This includes your speaking and writing skills, your ability to convey confidence when talking, how you present yourself, or people's perception of you when you walk into a room or participate in a meeting. How are your speaking skills? Are you a good communicator? Do you enjoy public speaking? Do you strive to continuously improve your presentation and speaking skills, and if so, how? The ability to effectively communicate will help you gain visibility within your firm and in your compliance community. Some people are born with the gift; others have mastered the art of being excellent and engaging communicators. In fact, many contributors to this book have mastered the art. Maybe, like me, you consider yourself to be shy and introverted. You may have to work to overcome different obstacles to master the art of public speaking.

Great communicators inspire or command an audience by words, actions, or their very presence. You can learn from several great speakers/presenter in the compliance community, including the contributors to this book. To be a great speaker, you need to be yourself, letting your personality and persona come through. My best speaking engagements have been those when I was relaxed and presented the materials from my vantage point, just being myself.

Another aspect of being a good speaker is having the requisite knowledge of the topic that you are presenting. Your knowledge and expertise is something you can share with the compliance community. It is important to present information from a position of knowledge, purpose, and consideration of the needs of the audience. Seek opportunities to practice your profession, to share your knowledge and expertise, and to improve your skills. All professionals, like doctors and lawyers, can only get better or become more proficient by practicing their craft. The same is true for you.

What qualities and expertise do you have that should be shared with your organization, with your team, or within our compliance community? Growth requires sharing your assets and knowledge; the more you give, the more you get. Do you volunteer to be a guest speaker at conferences, to mentor, to take on new projects, or to learn new skills? You have unique qualities that provide value—qualities and values that may help others when needing an expert in a particular area or help with a particular topic. When demonstrating your talent, you should find ways to package yourself and your talents and to present those qualities that others may not possess. The key takeaway from this section is to remember that building and demonstrating your expertise requires that you:

- Have and demonstrate courage;
- Master the art of communication;
- Become an expert;
- Build your brand;
- Convey your expertise;
- Share your knowledge; and
- Seek continuous improvement.

XI. SURVIVAL SKILLS

As compliance professionals we need survival skills in our professional toolkit, which includes the following:

- Setting goals;
- Having a good network;
- Developing your team;
- Planning strategically;
- Concentrating on improvements (people and process);
- Reassessing and reevaluating;
- Managing projects;
- Seeking help; and
- Giving yourself a break (nobody's perfect!).

Quite often I ask myself, "How will my team and I survive? How can we be expected to continue at our current pace? How can we work smarter, be more efficient, and leverage other areas?" Do you find yourself asking the same questions and looking for solutions, helpful tools, and ways of maximizing your skills just to survive and make it through the next round of regulatory or business initiatives, or even daily tasks and responsibilities?

A key component of your survival skills that will make your department and your combined efforts sustainable is good planning. As discussed earlier, my team and I conduct an annual strategic planning session. Having the ability to focus on planning for the upcoming one-, three-, or five-year period is very therapeutic. It is not often that you have the ability of hindsight; however, when you evaluate future plans, it is always helpful to look back and discuss what worked and what did not. Conducting a SWOT (strengths, weakness, opportunities, and threats) analysis will help in identifying those areas that are working and those that need your attention.

> **You don't drown by falling in the water; you drown by staying there.**
>
> — Edwin Louis Cole

Based on your SWOT analysis, you can then start your planning phase, and identify the resources that you will need to accomplish your goals. Do not shy away from or be reluctant in asking for help; help can come in a variety of forms or actions. If your resources are limited in the area of actual employees, then evaluate potential technology or vendors who can provide you with cost-effective solutions. Having a good network helps. You may have resources within your network that have gone through similar challenges that can help with solutions. There may be compliance vendors who can help you with your regulatory filings, drafting of policies and procedures, or testing your compliance program. Your compliance networks and compliance roundtables may be able to provide you with potential no-cost solutions.

Another key requirement for survival skills is making sure that you have taken the time and made an investment in developing your team. The transfer of knowledge and proactive coaching and mentoring will assist you and your team, and prepare you for long term success. Your team will gain additional knowledge, which in turn will make the members more self-sufficient, building their individual capabilities. The result of the time and effort that you allocate to their learning will pay dividends in the long run. You will eventually find that you have more time to be strategic, to coach, and to look for improvements.

Being strategic requires that you conduct an assessment and evaluate your processes, people, practices, and goals. Having a strategy is defining how you want something to work out and how you can best achieve your goals. The ultimate goal is to concentrate on improvements that need to take place and execute those plans to achieve your desired goals. You may find yourself in a situation where you have to deliver difficult messages or admit that you need help. Nobody's perfect and compliance professionals need to give themselves a break every now and then; it is okay to say "uncle." This may require you to have that frank discussion with leaders in your organization or to seek other opportunities. In the end, success should be defined and guided by *your* desired outcome.

XII. ADDITIONAL THOUGHTS AND RESOURCES

Hopefully, you found something within this chapter that can help you reach your goals and demonstrate your expertise and talent. As a compliance professional, you must always take time to reflect and concentrate on improvements. Improvements include not only writing new policies and procedures, or developing new monitoring tools and conducting new audits. You need to take time out for yourself and set goals, develop and enhance your communication style, expand your opportunities, and share your knowledge. Reach out to your community and interact on a regular basis. Get out of your comfort zone and volunteer to participate on compliance committees or be a panelist at a compliance conference. Take time to mentor your team or someone else in the compliance community, or get a mentor and become a continuous learner. If you are a manager or supervisor, remember that your team is only as strong as the weakest link; therefore, you have the primary responsibility for building capabilities and developing their expertise. Teams are interdependent and in order for your team to survive and flourish, members must use their combined skills and efforts for a common good: the good of the team and your organization. Find someone in your community or your firm that you can confide in, and give yourself an ally. You are not perfect; you are responsible for your own growth. I encourage you to expand your knowledge; learn, grow, and take advantage of opportunities.

Additional Resources

The following are websites and publications to peruse as you strengthen your soft skills:

- DISC: www.thediscpersonalitytest.com/
- MYERS-BRIGGS: www.myersbriggs.org/my-mbti-personality-type/mbti-basics/
- *Kolbe Index*: www.kolbe.com/assessments/kolbe-a-index
- *Harvard Business Review:* www.hbr.org/Harvard-Business-Review
- Toastmasters: www.toastmasters.org
- "The Art of Public Speaking: Lessons from the Greatest Speeches in History," *The Great Courses*
- New Line Ideas, "Communication Style Self-Assessment": www.newlineideas.com/communication-style-quiz.html
- Leigh L. Thompson, *Making the Team: A Guide for Managers,* Prentice Hall Inc., 2000
- Larry Bosidy and Ram Charan, *Execution,* Crown Business, 2001
- Don Maruska and Jay Perry; *Take Charge of Your Talent,* Berret-Koehler, 2013

ABOUT THE AUTHOR

Michele Hawkins is managing director and chief compliance officer for Fort Washington Investment Advisors, Inc., which she joined in 2000, and its subsidiary, Peppertree Partners, LLC. Fort Washington is headquartered in Cincinnati, Ohio, with $46.4 billion in assets under management (as of December 31, 2013). Ms. Hawkins is responsible for all aspects of the firm's compliance program: training, compliance monitoring, establishment of policies and procedures, auditing, risk management activities, due diligence, and all regulatory related initiatives.

Ms. Hawkins has more than 30 years of experience in the securities and financial services industry, including duties ranged from investment advising; with mutual funds; serving as a broker-dealer; and working with transfer agent compliance, trading, operations, and management. Prior to joining Fort Washington, she worked for Countrywide Financial Services, Inc., Leshner Financial Services, Inc., EF Hutton, and Paine Webber. She earned a bachelor of science degree in Business Management and has received the designation of Certified Regulatory Compliance Professional (CRCP) from FINRA/Wharton School of Business, as well as the NRS Investment Adviser Certified Compliance Professional (IACCP) designation. Ms. Hawkins also serves on the Advisory Board for Xavier University Cintas Institute for Business Ethics and Social Responsibility, serves as chairperson of the Herbert R. Brown Society, and is a member of the National Society of Compliance Professionals (NSCP).

CHAPTER 11

Compliance Training

By Kurt Wachholz
WellSpring Compliance, LLC

I. INTRODUCTION

In my early years as a chief compliance officer (CCO), I struggled with the task of training associated persons on compliance. My struggle was not with its importance, but with its delivery and effectiveness. How do I "train" compliance to associated persons? Many of these associated persons were already established professionals in the industry with vast experience who knew their respective jobs, in some cases, better than I did. How could I, a newly appointed compliance officer, train them on the regulatory aspects of their job and influence their behaviors to ensure compliance with them?

I experimented with training approaches and methods. Some of these approaches succeeded; others failed. Through these trials and tribulations, I learned two important aspects of training on compliance. First, *training* is the wrong word and hence the wrong perspective. Helping associated persons *learn* compliance is what led to more sustainable success in my efforts. The idea that I was *teaching* associated persons an aspect of their job that in some cases stood just outside of their day-to-day focus but was an integral part of their performance was refreshing. Could I help my coworkers understand concepts and requirements that support their activities and then work together on their integration? Yes, I could do that.

To gain perspective on how compliance fits in the workplace, I turned to athletics. With sports, there are a set of rules that define the field of play and the manner in which athletes will compete. When athletes are at the starting line, or at the ready, or about to start a play, they are not thinking about field dimensions, boundaries, or many other defined aspects of the field of play. They are thinking about executing as efficiently and effectively as possible. Before they can do that, they must understand the rules of play for the results to matter. They need to *learn* how to play before they can *train* on how to perform. Athletes train not only to improve performance but also to perform within the framework of the sport's rules and requirements. The top-performing athletes are not successful solely because of sheer talent. They practice, study, compete, and comply with the rules to perform at the highest level. This is not to say that there are not those who bend the rules or shortcut the activities required to succeed, but in the long run their success and place in history is short-lived. If an athlete has limited knowledge of the rules of play, sustainable success is limited.

The check-the-box approach I initially used for compliance training was marginally successful and very dependent on oversight. In my search for a better, more sustainable method, I found a new perspective. Instead of training on compliance, I began *teaching* the application of compliance. By teaching, my focus was on how I could help associated persons understand compliance well enough to apply it to their jobs. Moving my compliance training goals beyond the collection of attestations to the demonstration of compliance procedures being followed consistently in the workplace meant I needed to help associated persons *learn* compliance.

As I explored ways to help associated persons learn compliance, I considered various frameworks. I wanted to find an approach or process that addressed my new learning perspective—something that would keep me centered on my goal of educating and influencing compliant behavior. The elements of this framework were easy to find. They already existed. In the end, I reconstructed existing frameworks to fit the needs of a compliance program. These frameworks helped shape the pages that follow.

II. REASONS FOR CONDUCTING COMPLIANCE TRAINING

Before the discussion proceeds to that of compliance training, it will be helpful to consider the reasons why it matters. For compliance professionals administering a compliance program, training is a way to educate others on their respective compliance responsibilities. The objective of training is to disseminate compliance responsibilities related to policies, procedures, processes, and functions. Documentation of this dissemination is typically captured through sign-in sheets, attestations, and/or certifications. Although these sign-on-the-line or check-the-box approaches may satisfy regulatory requests and provide support for legal defenses, they may not lead to lasting comprehension or sustainable behavior. Helping associated persons of a firm understand compliance enough to result in consistently compliant behavior is one of the reasons why effective training is so critical. As the expectations and interests of the regulators move beyond the requirements codified by law and considerations such as risk management and adequate internal controls stretch compliance departments into new areas, effective training provides compliance programs with an ability to reduce the administrative strain on resources.

Why Compliance Training?

A recent survey of ethics and compliance professionals found that the top three objectives for compliance training are to create a culture of ethics and respect, to comply with laws and regulations, and to prevent future issues or misconduct.[1] With the growing

---

[1] NAVEX Global, *2014 Ethics and Compliance Training Benchmark Report*.

regulatory interest in the understanding and treatment of risk within a firm's operations, it is no surprise that training objectives are changing.

Because a firm's culture influences behavior and decision making, it is an important subject for compliance training. Culture is a soft subject for training in that it may be defined by words but is demonstrated by actions. The significance of workplace perceptions is one of the reasons why addressing culture in training is critical. Effective compliance training programs can clarify perceptions and align actions.

Another objective of compliance training is compliance with laws and regulations. There are many regulated areas in the securities industry. Depending on a particular firm's registration, compliance training may be mandatory. For example, firms that are members of Financial Industry Regulatory Authority (FINRA) are required under FINRA Rule 1250 to have both regulatory and firm element training for certain registered persons of a firm.[2] For investment advisers, training is mentioned under Rule 204A-1 as it relates to the code of ethics.[3] Other regulators also address training—for example, the Municipal Securities Rulemaking Board (MSRB) under Rule G-3 addresses its members' continuing education requirements and has recently proposed to expand the requirements to include additional individuals at a firm.[4]

Training is a consideration when individuals and firms have violations, even when training is not specifically required in laws and regulations.[5] Court proceedings will consider training when determining liability and fault for individuals and their firms.[6] The U.S. Sentencing Commission provides detailed guidance on what it means to have an effective compliance program through the Federal Sentencing Guidelines.[7] One aspect of these guidelines is compliance training. Compliance programs often meet this objective by having associated persons of a firm acknowledge that they understand the policies and procedures that address specific laws and regulations that pertain to their area(s) of responsibility. The challenge of training is whether this acknowledgment leads to the individual's ability to recognize and avoid noncompliant behavior.

Another primary objective of compliance training is the prevention of future issues or misconduct. This objective focuses on addressing noncompliant behavior before it happens. Compliance training addressing this objective focuses on both understanding and skills in the workplace.

Beyond the objectives above, effective compliance training improves productivity, reduces legal and regulatory liabilities, enhances incident response and recovery, manages risk, informs decisions, and empowers employees. It can help integrate compliance policies and procedures into the workplace, which can reduce administrative activities,

---

[2] FINRA Rule 1250, Continuing Education Requirements.
[3] FINRA Final Rule 204A-1, II, F, Investment Adviser Code of Ethics.
[4] Exchange Act Release No. 73368 (Oct. 15, 2014), File No. SR-MSRB-2014-05 (Jul. 22, 2014).
[5] See In the Matter of Du Pasquier & Co., Inc., Adm. Proc. File No. 3-16750 (Jan. 21, 2015).
[6] See SEC v. Peterson, No. 12-2033 (JBW)(E.D.N.Y. Apr. 25, 2012).
[7] See U.S Federal Sentencing 2014 Guidelines Manual, Chapter 8 § 8B.2.1(b)(4).

free up resources, and improve performance. Because effective training can do so much, it is the most precious resource of a compliance program. The pages that follow will provide guidance on developing an effective compliance training program.

III. LEARNING APPROACHES

Effective compliance training programs recognize that individuals learn in different ways. This section reviews the different approaches that relate to how individuals respond and process information. The most effective learning approach for an individual is dependent upon three factors: their learning style, level of education, and prior experience. It is just as important to address the differences in learning styles as it is to select applicable training topics. Because each style approaches material in a different way, recognizing the variety of approaches is important in connecting with a training audience.

Learning Styles

There are three basic learning styles.[8] They may be called by different names, but the following reviews their general characteristics.

Auditory. Auditory learners are the "tell me" participants. They receive information best when they hear it. They respond to training that includes speakers, audio conferences, discussion groups, question and answer sessions, audio recordings, reading aloud and other oral communication.

Visual. Visual learners are the "show me" participants. They receive information best when they see or read it. They respond to training that includes written instructions, workflows, checklists, diagrams, handouts, presentations, videos, making lists, taking notes, and other visual information.

Kinesthetic or Tactile. Kinesthetic or tactile learners are the "let me" participants. They receive information best when they touch or feel it. They respond to training that allows them to experience it through demonstrations, simulations, role playing, group discussions, practice, or actual performance.

An audience for compliance training will most likely include all three kinds of learners. It is important that a compliance training program incorporate a combination of learning styles into its methods and material. In training on regulatory information or compliance concepts, some participants will comprehend better through listening to a presentation (auditory learning); others may prefer reading (visual learning); and others may need to participate in a discussion or exercise (kinesthetic or tactile learning). In training on practical application of policies or actual procedures, some participants will prefer to hear verbal instructions (auditory learning); others will prefer how-to illustrations or diagrams (visual learning); and others will prefer to figure things out as

---

[8] Walter Burke Barbe; Raymond H. Swassing; Michael N. Milone, Jr., *Teaching Through Modality Strengths: Concepts and Practices.* Columbus, Ohio: Zaner-Blosner (1979).

they work (kinesthetic or tactile learning). Using a variety of training methods helps the trainer to address each learning style.

Now that we have discussed styles, it is important to touch on one other aspect of learning as it relates to compliance training: motivations of adult learners.

Adult Learning

The audience for compliance training is not like the audience in an academic setting. It is not made up of students with a quest for knowledge and grades, but rather adults whose motivations and experiences are quite different. Adults have well-established values, beliefs, and opinions. They will relate new information to these established values and experiences. As a result, misperceptions and misunderstandings can occur. In addition, training participants will have varying education and work experience. A training session may consist of individuals with professional designations and advanced degrees as well as those with limited education and extensive work experience. Participants may also be from various levels and functions within the firm. These are all considerations that compliance professionals must take into account when developing training programs and materials. A good place to start is to examine what is consistent among adult learners.

Adults tend to be more self-directed in their learning. They desire to learn what they want, when they want, and how they want. To overcome this challenge, compliance training programs must recognize the need for flexibility in how they address adult learning. There are four elements to adult learning: motivation, retention, application, and reinforcement. For compliance training programs to achieve optimal learning, these four elements must be present.

Motivation. Adults respond to training that is interesting to them or that can benefit them. Because it is rather unlikely to find adults interested in compliance, training should focus on the benefits compliance provides to them. Trainers should avoid using regulatory terminology or quoting rule numbers, instead, using terminology that is more familiar in their workplace. Adults are motivated when learning is open, friendly, and at the proper knowledge level. This is important because adults need to integrate new information with their past experiences and opinions.

To help adults integrate compliance concepts, make sure the training balances the presentation of new material with the sharing of relevant experiences. When a new compliance concept or procedure is introduced, the effective trainer does not just *tell* participants; instead, he or she *discusses* with participants how the new concept changes what they are currently doing and thus encourages participation in training sessions. Adults learn best when there is encouragement. In addition, involving participants can help overcome differences because of the varying degrees of education and experience in the audience through the sharing of knowledge and perspectives. The trainer can recognize and reward helpful participation, and not necessarily monetarily. He or she should make the material difficult enough to challenge participants and specific enough to make the learning points evident. Adults do not learn well when there is too much material; it can lead to information overload. Adults are motivated by specific feedback and measured results from training. Feedback and results help show the benefit of training and their participation.

Retention. As mentioned above, in order for adults to retain material, they must see the benefit and understand the purpose of the training, which includes knowing the level of importance to place on the material. They must be able to understand, interpret, and apply the training material in order to properly retain it. Because how well an adult learns is directly related to how well they will retain the material, compliance training sessions must emphasize the practical application of the material. This stresses the importance of confirming understanding during the sessions through feedback and knowledge tests.

Application. For training to be successful, adults must be able to apply what they learn directly to their workplace. Adults learn best when they connect the information or knowledge to their current job or career path. For compliance training, this means that material must be relevant to the individual's job function. Emphasizing the practical application of compliance, as opposed to abstract or theoretical learning, improves retention and understanding. If training participants are not able to connect the material to their job, they will tune it out. To be successful, training material must provide tailored compliance information that can be used by the participants and applied to their activities. Compliance training that is off the shelf, outdated, unrelated, or abstract will hamper the ability for adults to connect the material to the workplace.

Reinforcement. Reinforcing the training material is also critical to learning. Compliance training objectives need to be communicated with senior management as well as managers and supervisors. This allows the "tone at the top" and "melody in the middle" to support and reinforce training objectives in the workplace.

Adults respond well to both positive and negative reinforcement. The trainer should give positive reinforcement frequently and recognize learning progress and compliant behaviors in order to sustain retention as well as allow for ongoing feedback related to training objectives. Negative reinforcement may also help to end noncompliant behavior in the form of some type of consequence. In order to be effective, the consequence should be at a strong enough level to impact the individual's actions. For example, a $100 fine for the failure of a portfolio manager to respond to a required code of ethics report may not have the same impact as it would to an administrative assistant. The portfolio manager would need an appropriate fine at a level that would have more of a financial consequence.

Effective compliance training programs incorporate training methods and material that address the various learning styles and adult audiences. Participants' background, demographics, education, experience, training expectations, and overall attitude are important elements in creating and providing successful training sessions.

IV. LEARNING MODEL

Knowing your audience is only a small part of developing an effective compliance training program. A learning model helps incorporate other aspects of learning into the training program and provides a way in which to support sustainable results. An effective learning model for compliance, adapted from a successful information technology (IT) training model, consists of three levels: awareness, training and education.[9]

Training on compliance has several challenges. There are compliance policies and requirements that everyone in a firm needs to know and some that are specific to certain roles and duties. There are varying degrees of understanding and application of compliance by individuals and different levels of supervision and oversight. Using a model helps address those challenges. In general, all members of a firm need some form of compliance training. However, portions of the material should be differentiated depending upon the various roles and responsibilities of the audience.

For example, all members of a firm need training on the code of ethics, but not everyone needs training on trading best execution. Board members, senior management, and supervisors need a different type of compliance training than those on the front lines. In order to meet the adult learning need of relevance, training content should be tailored to the roles and responsibilities of the individual. This can be achieved, in part, by using a compliance learning model that starts with promoting an awareness of compliance, followed by training on compliance, and reinforced with education in compliance.

Compliance Awareness

As discussed earlier, adults learn best when they are familiar with the material and understand its relevance to their function. This is difficult to do if the first time participants are exposed to compliance material is in a compliance training session. Compliance awareness sets the stage for training. It is not training. The purpose of compliance awareness is to focus attention on certain compliance initiatives. Initiatives may include upcoming training topics, reporting deadlines, areas of concern and how to recognize them, or how to respond to noncompliant situations. Whereas training is more active in directing specific action and performance, awareness is a passive activity designed to reach an audience with compliance information. Awareness is designed to reach a broader audience through various marketing techniques.

In other words, compliance awareness is a marketing campaign for compliance training. A single awareness activity should be designed for short-term, immediate, and specific learning objectives—for example, a reminder to associated persons that they must report their personal securities transactions. To be effective, awareness campaigns need to recognize that individuals will tune them out over time. If the same materials

---

[9] National Institute of Standards and Technology Special Publication 800-16, *Information Technology Security Training Requirements: A Role- and Performance-Base Model* (Apr. 1998).

are used over and over again, individuals will eventually ignore them. In order to foster attention for learning, awareness materials need to be interesting and dynamic.

Awareness is passive learning that can increase familiarity with compliance policies and procedures and reinforce training information and requirements. Compliance awareness can come from the use of various materials, most commonly printed materials such as posters, flyers, or table tents that are placed in common areas. Giving out trinkets such as coffee mugs or mouse pads with compliance slogans on them can support awareness activities. More elaborate awareness campaigns may involve running compliance reminders on message boards or using distributed video or audio messages.

One of the goals of awareness activities is to help raise an individual's sensitivity to compliance risks and requirements. It can also set the stage for compliance training by introducing information ahead of sessions. And it can help reinforce the culture of compliance by keeping certain compliance topics active.

Levels of Compliance Training

Where awareness sets the stage for training and reinforces compliance in general, training is the mechanism for instilling compliance within the individuals of the firm. We discussed the objectives of compliance training earlier. It is important to remember that training should produce relevant and needed competency and compliance by individuals within their various functions, such as marketing, trading, portfolio management, and client service. Just as there are levels in a learning model, there are also levels in training. These training levels relate to content and can be translated into basic, specific, and advanced.

Basic Training. The basic level of compliance training is the foundation that supports higher-level, specific training. It is an introduction to compliance. At this level, a compliance training program introduces compliance concepts to the workplace, including the core set of regulations that all individuals of the firm need to know and follow. Basic training also translates the regulatory terminology of compliance into a language that is recognizable to all individuals of the firm and integrates it into the firm's vocabulary. As described earlier, adults need to recognize the connection of new information with their current environment in order to achieve understanding. Translating compliance concepts into a vocabulary more common in the firm helps accomplish this.

There are four primary objectives of compliance training at the basic level. First, this level of training should ensure that participants know the terminology, concepts, and general requirements that compose essential regulatory compliance. Basic training should promote personal responsibility and compliant behavior. It should help establish the firm's culture of compliance and risk assessment process. And it should establish consistent compliance training across the organization. By addressing these objectives, the compliance training program will establish a consistent, firmwide approach that ensures that associated persons of a firm have the same understanding of regulatory compliance. This shared foundation will support the area-specific and individual compliance training to follow.

Although the regulatory laws applicable to the operation of a firm may be vast and the underlying rules and requirements continue to change and expand under today's regulatory climate, there are certain common compliance requirements that are a part of all compliance programs, such as regulatory oversight and registration, code of ethics and culture of compliance, administration of the compliance program, whistleblowing or reporting, recordkeeping obligations, and disaster recovery plans. These areas are routinely addressed in existing compliance orientation of new hires or annual compliance meetings and apply to all individuals in a firm.

Specific Training. This level moves beyond the basics, focusing on improving individuals' understanding of compliance policies and procedures specific to the participants' roles and responsibilities. For example, an individual working in the trading department is trained on policies and procedures related to trading activities. Unless the responsibilities include other regulated activities, the individual is not trained on policies and procedures unrelated to his or her current duties. As discussed in the examination of how adults learn, the training must be relevant to an individual for learning to occur. If training is not relevant, the individual will tune it out and see the training as a waste of time. Beyond understanding the applicable policies and procedures, the focus of specific training is also to help individuals understand how to apply the required elements in their day-to-day activities.

With specific training of policies and procedures, it is also important to consider the varying degrees of skill in training participants. For example, some participants may be new to their role; others may have been performing it for years. Especially when it comes to training on specific policies, it is important for training to be open and allow participants to share their experiences. Using participants who may already be familiar with policies and procedures to explain them to those who are not is a good way to foster learning. It also helps with two other compliance program objectives: leveraging of resources and developing compliance supervisors.

Because an individual's need for compliance training changes as their role changes, compliance training must accommodate the changing relationship that individuals have with policies and procedures. For example, as an individual's career develops, he or she may go from being a follower of compliance policies and procedures to a supervisor of policies and procedures. As relationships with compliance policies and procedures change, it adds to the specific training needs of an individual.

Advanced Training. The advanced level of compliance training addresses the administration of compliance within a firm. Various individuals at a firm, both inside the Compliance Department and outside, have additional responsibilities related to the compliance program. Board members, senior management, managers, and supervisors have a unique relationship to compliance policies and procedures. Their compliance responsibilities may include oversight and supervision. Advanced training addresses these responsibilities. It also helps individuals to better understand responsibilities, evaluate regulatory reports, and make informed regulatory decisions related to business initiatives.

Those who manage or supervise individuals subject to compliance policies and procedures have a responsibility to ensure they are in compliance. This level of compliance training helps address the monitoring, reporting, and responding obligations related to compliance policies and procedures. For example, it helps a manager know what to look for to identify noncompliant activities and how to respond, whether directly or through escalation. Advanced training also assists managers and supervisors in the support and reinforcement of compliance training objectives. Because front-line employees are more likely to follow the direction of their direct managers, it is critical for managers to have sufficient understanding of compliance policies, procedures, and initiatives. Advanced training empowers this level of management to take action as necessary should circumstances arise where violations occur or performance falls below established tolerances. In general, this is training on the supervisory aspects related to the administration of a compliance program.

For board members and senior managers, advanced training helps with their responsibilities related to the administration of a compliance program. These responsibilities may include such things as the adoption and implementation of policies and procedures, incident escalation, program reports, and assessments, and setting tone and culture. To accomplish these administrative elements, board members and senior managers need training that helps with evaluation, support, and decision making. In other words, advanced training helps these decision makers to set the *tone at the top,* and helps managers and supervisors recognize and reinforce the *melody in the middle* so that compliance has a consistent *beat at the bottom.*

Compliance Education

To complete the training model, compliance education addresses the need for knowledge and understanding of the laws, rules, regulations, principles, concepts, and skills necessary to effectively administer a compliance program. Primarily, this education is for compliance professionals who require the needed expertise to perform their role in administering compliance within a firm. It also involves board members, members of senior management, legal, internal audit, or other areas depending on the size and structure of a firm as well as the role each plays in the administration of the compliance program. Unlike training, this level of the learning model focuses on the acquisition of knowledge and understanding as it relates to compliance programs, the industry's regulatory framework of laws, industry rules, or membership requirements. Compliance education provides a regulatory competence that can be translated to the business and applied to its operation.

For boards, senior managers, and others outside the Compliance Department, compliance education helps in addressing such topics as the role of the CCO, incidents, deficiencies, violations, risk assessments, regulatory requirements, and laws. For example, a board of directors may need education on antimoney laundering so they can properly evaluate the annual antimoney laundering report; senior managers may need education on changes to the custody rule so they can properly assess the custody risks of the firm and the changes being made to policies and procedures. As part of the compliance learning model, education is necessary in order to appropriately assess a program's effectiveness.

Individuals working in Compliance Departments, including CCOs, have varying degrees of administrative skill and regulatory competence. This can limit the effectiveness of training efforts. Compliance education helps train the trainer. The function of compliance has become too complex to be successfully accomplished by individuals who lack a comprehensive set of competencies. Regulators, stakeholders, boards, managers, and clients continue to create pressures and demands for compliance programs to provide solutions to the growing range of regulatory risks—solutions that can only be achieved by individuals knowledgeable in governance, risk, and compliance.

To summarize the compliance learning model's levels:

- *Awareness* answers the "what" in compliance training; its purpose is to support short-term recognition and retention of compliance requirements;
- *Training* in the learning model answers the "how"; its purpose is to support comprehension and application over the long-term; and
- *Education* in the learning model answers the "why"; its purpose is to provide long-term insight into compliance objectives and administration.

V. TRAINING DEVELOPMENT

Having recognized the ways adults learn and having identified a model for learning compliance, we can now move on to developing a training plan. In this section we will detail the major steps in preparing a program.

Depending on a firm's registration, compliance programs may or may not be required to provide compliance training. As mentioned earlier, firms registered under the Investment Adviser Act of 1940 and regulated by the Securities and Exchange Commission (SEC) are not required to have a written training plan. However, firms registered under FINRA are required to perform a needs analysis and document their training plans annually.[10] The part of the required compliance training conducted by the firm is referred to as the *firm element*. The Securities Industry/Regulatory Council on Continuing Education offers resources that can assist in formalizing annual training plans.[11]

---

[10] *See* FINRA Rule 1250(b)(2)(A).
[11] *See* the Securities Industry/Regulatory Council on Continuing Education Firm Element resources at www.cecouncil.com/firm-element

Whether required or not, a compliance program will benefit from an annual assessment of compliance training needs for the year ahead. Once the training needs are identified, the other levels of the learning model can be determined, such as creating awareness campaigns and planning education activities.

Assessing Training Needs

From year to year, compliance programs should evaluate a number of areas in order to determine training needs. The particular areas and level of assessment may vary depending on the size and activities of a firm. Smaller firms that provide a limited range of services may be able to identify needed training much easier than large organizations that offer a variety of services in various markets. There are six main areas of consideration for determining training needs: audience, services, experience, regulation, performance, and feedback.

Audience. The first area to consider is the worker makeup of the firm. As discussed earlier, knowing the audience is an important part of effective training sessions. Early on the trainer should gather and analyze information related to experience, roles, responsibilities, and workforce to help tailor training to participants. If new hires are expected in the coming year, the trainer creates or updates orientation materials to address roles and current compliance policies and procedures.

The makeup of the current workforce can also influence training needs. For example, if 80 percent of a firm's workforce has 15 or more years of experience and has been with the firm for more than five years, the overall training need will be much different than if the firm had a workforce that is 70 percent younger than age 30 with less than a few years with the firm. The latter group may require more training emphasis on basic compliance learning, whereas the more experienced group requires more specific and advanced training. A larger organization with a diverse workforce may need to factor in cultural considerations required for effective learning.

Within the workforce, the trainer also examines roles and responsibilities to help determine which individuals need certain specific and advanced training. For example, identifying those individuals involved in the process of trading will help determine who needs training on trading-related regulations, policies, and procedures. Identifying the audience accurately also helps determine which managers and supervisors need advanced training on supervising their applicable compliance policies and procedures.

Services. Next, the trainer reviews services and products offered by the firm as part of determining training needs. As discussed with learning approaches geared to adults, the relevancy of information is important to effective learning. It would seem obvious that compliance training should address the regulatory requirements related to the products and services offered by a firm. However, business offerings change, new regulations are enacted, and the services or products themselves or even the processes for delivering them may change. Subtle changes can be overlooked in the day-to-day administration of a compliance program. Training needs may include introducing compliance requirements related to new offerings, or changes to existing policies and procedures as a result of the introduction of new technology. There may also be a need to review existing compliance procedures in order to address performance issues or introduce updates to processes. This type of training is often specific to individual roles and may include some advanced training for supervisors of individuals affected by service changes. Training related to changes in products and services should be timely. In addition, compliance refresher training may be needed for products and services where compliance with initial training has not met expectations.

Experience. Then the trainer considers the experience of the firm and its individuals related to complaints, legal matters, and regulatory actions to help determine training needs. If the firm has experienced a complaint related to individuals or services, training may be needed on the activity, policy, or procedures related to the complaint. Legal or regulatory actions are also sources of training needs in order to help prevent, detect, or correct future occurrences.

Regulation. Changes in regulatory laws and rules that impact compliance policies and procedures will require training for those impacted. For example, changes in the Investment Advisers Act Custody Rule may require firms to update their procedures to meet new requirements that will lead to new training needs. In addition, regulatory emphasis on certain industry practices may warrant refresher training in those areas. As an example, if regulators indicate that current examination priorities are focused on the use of certain products such as variable annuities or exchange traded funds and the firm uses those products, individuals may need refresher training to make sure regulatory concerns are being met.

Performance. Manager and supervisor feedback on performance of subordinates can help the trainer to determine whether additional training is needed to meet compliance objectives. Results from compliance program tests, audits, and monitoring activities can also help determine training needs. For example, if a review of emails indicates an increase in transmitting unsecured nonpublic information, training may help to correct the issue. Examining risk assessment findings and firm risk priorities can also aid in establishing training needs. For example, if the firm wants to reduce the risk level of social media use, compliance training can help to accomplish that objective. Finally, areas of weakness or recommendations for improvement made in annual compliance reports to management may also become training needs.

Feedback. Compliance programs can obtain feedback from a number of sources. Compliance hotlines, employee surveys or questionnaires, training evaluations, manager and supervisor comments, and employee questions received in the Compliance Department are all sources of training needs. Feedback is one of the best resources for determining training needs as it provides an indication of those topics that individuals already have a desire to understand. Remember that adults learn best when the subject interests them.

Reviewing audience, services, experience, regulation, performance, and feedback to determine training needs will help the compliance trainer in developing a training plan. Some training, however, will take place out of necessity and may not be part of the formal plan, such as when unexpected changes occur in the business or performance indicates a need to realign compliance objectives.

Formalizing a Plan

Once information is gathered and analyzed to determine the compliance training needs of the firm, the next step is to create a plan. Most plans consider just the training aspect of compliance. However, this approach falls short of considering the learning process. To improve training results, the plan should recognize the other compliance learning model levels of awareness and education in order to achieve sustained learning. The plan should address the what, who, when, where, and how.

What. The result of a needs analysis will identify areas, policies, and procedures that will benefit from training. As discussed earlier for compliance training, content considerations lend themselves to basic, specific, or advanced training levels.

Basic training covers the common compliance policies and procedures applicable to the majority of the individuals in the workplace. Investment adviser topics, for example, may include regulatory disclosures and registration, fiduciary standard, conflicts of interest, insider trading, gifts and entertainment, outside business activities, personal security transactions and holdings, privacy, social media, cybersecurity, whistleblowing, business continuity, and recordkeeping.

Specific training covers compliance policies and procedures applicable to specific areas or individuals of the firm. For example, depending on the service offering of an investment adviser, roles within the firm may need training on topics such as portfolio management, trading, money movement, new accounts, marketing, custody, vendor due diligence, and solicitation. Specific training plans may involve changes to existing policies and procedures, concerns from performance or testing results, or current regulatory priorities related to roles within the firm.

Advanced training covers compliance program administration that is geared toward supervisors, managers, senior management, and governing boards. This training type covers such topics as supervision, risk assessment, escalation, and examinations. It also involves training on policy implementation, oversight responsibilities, compliance program priorities, compliance culture, and setting the tone at the top. Some of the topics covered in advanced training may require additional compliance education.

Once the training topics are determined, the next step is to identify an associated goal for each topic. For example, the goal may be to raise awareness of a compliance policy, to introduce new policies and procedures, to address new requirements for existing procedures, to improve compliance with procedures, to reduce or remove a specific compliance risk, or to improve overall compliance initiatives. Compliance training goals should be specific for two reasons: so they can be effectively communicated and so they can be measured.

Measuring how closely the training comes to reaching its goal is important to training. There is an old saying, "What gets measured gets done."[12] Without measurement it is hard to assess the effectiveness of training efforts. For example, if the outcome of a training session is to obtain sign-in signatures and collect attestations, it does little to demonstrate that the information from the learning space will translate into application in the workplace. Training measurement quantifies the accomplishment that training provides to its participants by showing improvement in application.

As discussed for overall adult learning, for training to become learning it must be applied in the workplace. Adults want to be challenged and successful, so training metrics should be realistic and achievable targets. For example, the results of compliance tests or audits prior to training are shared with participants along with the desired training objective so that when training ends, participants know that the application of training is expected of them to provide certain performance results. If the measurement of a newly introduced compliance procedure is to have 100 percent of procedure integration within two weeks of training, then participants know the goal and have the expectation when the application will be tested. If the objective is to raise awareness, then a possible measurement is to test the understanding of the material before and after training efforts. Measurement of the achievements of training activities also helps demonstrate the value of time spent training. Using graphical representations, for example, to show management the specific value of training through performance improvements or levels of compliance or improving trends can help improve management's conviction and support. Performance history, benchmarks and other quantitative information will help determine what to measure as well as areas to address in training.

Who. Compliance training can involve many individuals, from participants to trainers. As the plan is developed, it is important to review these two groups. For smaller firms, this may be a very quick assessment.

Participants

Compliance training participants can vary by training topic and objective. Whether training is for new hires, interns, contractors, all employees, certain roles or functions, supervisors, managers, executives, or board members may necessitate different training content. Adults bring past experience, opinions, and beliefs to new information, and adults' experience must be recognized for learning to occur. Knowing the participants helps determine how advanced the material can be and what perspectives they may bring to training sessions. For example, a firmwide audience may require content to be balanced between simple compliance concepts and more involved procedures so as to not overwhelm one segment of participants and bore another.

---

[12] This maxim has been attributed to Peter Drucker, Tom Peters, Edwards Deming, Lord Kelvin, and others.

Trainers

Selection of trainers can vary according to the topic and objective. They can be individuals in the Compliance Department, business area supervisors or managers, senior managers, third parties, or even front-line workers. The more compliance training can involve individuals outside of the compliance staff, the more connected training will be to a participant's workplace—an important part of adult learning. For example, using front-line employees to cover prepared material, discuss examples of applying procedures, or share real world experiences can be very helpful in recognizing and rewarding the right behaviors. If trainers use participants in training sessions, it is important to set the participants up for success in covering material or sharing their experiences.

Management can also help to convey the importance of compliance training. The lack of senior management support and commitment is one of the main reasons why some training does not meet expectations. Involving senior management by having executives start training meetings, introduce topics, attend meetings, or send meeting invitations will help to show support and commitment and set the appropriate tone at the top. When senior management shows interest in the learning process, participants are more likely to apply the policies and procedures to their work.

Likewise, managers and supervisors also influence how individuals react to training. Having managers or supervisors promote, attend, or lead segments of training meetings can have a significant impact on participants' perceptions of compliance responsibilities. For compliance training to resonate among all levels, there needs to be involvement from those that directly influence the activity of participants. Compliance cannot be presented as separate and distinct from the other workday activities. Involving leadership in the training program is vital to achieving compliance and retention.

Identifying training topics and deciding on objectives may reveal the need for further compliance education. Knowledge gaps may require additional education or alternative delivery considerations—for example, if internal training resources do not have the expertise regarding cybersecurity to meet the training need of reducing security risks, or if senior managers or board members do not have a sufficient level of understanding to adequately support training initiatives and assess results. Using outside expertise in training activities can address weaknesses in internal knowledge or experience and may also add credibility to the training material.

When. Most training activities will be scheduled. There will be instances where informal or impromptu training takes place, such as when an individual asks compliance professionals for help with a procedure or process. These spontaneous instructional moments are excellent opportunities for learning because they generally occur in the workplace instead of the training space. Note the topics of these instances so that the topics can be considered for broader training purposes. Also inform supervisors or managers when individuals receive informal training so they can coordinate recognition and follow-up.

Should there be a formal training schedule? Calendaring training activities is a good way to organize what will occur over the course of a year. The trainer should keep training dates tentative until training methods are determined (such as in-person, online, self-directed, or live). If training is self-directed, include specific dates for completion that can be communicated and enforced.

Other scheduling considerations should include makeup provisions for nonparticipants, such as additional dates or timeframes to complete material. Recording live sessions can also add flexibility in scheduling by providing those unable to attend the ability to view the training session at a later time. For more involved compliance information, training may be spread out over more than one session to maximize retention. Likewise, if participants for particular training have varying levels of knowledge or experience, it may be more beneficial to break up the material into such levels as introductory, intermediate, and advanced. Scheduling training sessions that present a logical progression of compliance concepts and information can help participants absorb the information more effectively. Shorter and more frequent training sessions are often preferable to one long session because adults retain information better in small doses. A growing concept in compliance training is *burst learning,* which is training that is short, specific, and on demand.

Where. After identifying the topics, objectives, participants, and dates, the next step is to consider where training will occur. If the training is self-directed, will it be based on distributed materials or accessed online? Do all participants have the necessary tools and supplies to access and use the training technology? Also, the trainer should determine whether compliance resources will be needed to administer technology used in training, such as setting up user accounts and resetting passwords.

If training is location-based, it is important to consider the environment. Whether onsite or offsite, single location or multiple, review the venue to ensure adequate space, equipment, environment, and location. A poor training environment can easily dilute the most effective training presentation and hinder learning.

How. The meatier part of the training plan is determining how it will be executed. This involves considering the budget, available resources, and methods to be used.

Not all firms establish a formal budget for compliance training. Even so, firms should have an expectation of reasonable costs related to compliance training activities. For annual compliance training, a NAVEX Global report indicates that firms provide six hours on average per employee.[13] Another training report indicates that $1,028 is the average annual direct learning expenditure per employee.[14]

The primary consideration for determining where and how to spend training funds should be the ability to achieve training objectives. Decisions about whether to create,

---

[13] NAVEX Global, *2014 Ethics and Compliance Training Benchmark Report* (July 2014).
[14] ATD Research, *2014 State of the Industry* report.

buy, conduct, or outsource training, or whether objectives can be met with one long compliance meeting or several short meetings, are among the cost considerations involved in budgeting. If the Compliance Department does not have the resources or expertise necessary to carry out training objectives, there may be a need to use third-party materials or trainers. Using outside expertise to help in presenting well-structured, customized and impactful training may be necessary in order to accomplish training objectives and ensure that the firm stays in compliance.

Senior management buy-in is critical to the success of training program activities. Compliance professionals should be prepared to present numbers and facts in support of training methods that have been determined best for keeping the firm in compliance. Understanding costs as well as benefits, including potential penalties for inadequate compliance training, is a way to gain senior management buy-in to training efforts and to support a training commitment throughout the firm.

Training methods are the final consideration on how training will be provided. Although it is important to know the training audience, it may be difficult to know the learning style of each training participant. As a result, it is important to use training methods that address all three major learning styles. Methods can include providing publications, holding meetings, or sponsoring online courses. Using more than one method or blending methods in training sessions increases the likelihood that learning objectives will be met.

Learning Methods

There are many methods and materials available to help train participants on compliance. Using several methods in combination may be the most effective way to reach an adult learner and foster retention. In this section we will review the various methods and how they may fit with a learning model and training plan.

Awareness Methods. Some materials lend themselves better to awareness than actual training. As discussed for the learning model, part of effective training is setting the stage for success through familiarity and reinforcement. Examples of common awareness methods that can support compliance training are posters, message boards, emails, marketing trinkets, and social media or corporate intranet postings. Raising awareness pre- and post-training can help support longer-term retention. Posters or other messaging should be attention-getting and brief. The goal is to create interest.

There are also ways to create interest through awareness activities. For example, a firm experiencing inconsistency in employee code of ethics reporting used an awareness campaign in conjunction with training. The Compliance Department created a catchy phrase that was displayed on training posters, coffee mugs, and mouse pads. Individuals seeing the chief executive officer (CEO) using a coffee mug with the catch phrase was a subtle reinforcement of the training objective. The campaign reinforced the compliance training objective and resulted in improved code of ethics reporting.

Another example relates to privacy policy and record safekeeping practices. A firm needed to change the behavior of individuals in their handling of nonpublic information in the workplace. To raise awareness prior to a training session on privacy, the Compliance Department circulated a notice that it would be conducting a surprise audit of work areas within the period prior to training. After work hours one night, the Compliance Department's members used sticky notes stamped with the word *confidential* in red to mark any sensitive information left out in offices and work areas. As employees arrived to work the next day, they encountered a visual display of privacy weaknesses in various workspaces. In some areas the sticky notes were so prevalent that employees began to refer to them as "snow." This visual left a direct workplace impression on the issue and fostered several discussions as well as setting the stage for the training that was to follow. A few weeks after the training concluded, a similar workspace audit showed dramatic improvement in meeting the training objective. Awareness methods are short-term and not meant to train. They are designed to introduce, reinforce, or support actual training objectives.

Training Methods. Compliance training provides information that, when applied in the workplace, will lead to compliant results. Recall that under the learning model there are three levels of training: basic, specific, and advanced. In general, the same training methods can be used for each level of training. However, complex compliance requirements will require smaller audiences with more interaction than the basic level for learning to occur.

Live Training

Live training can incorporate a number of training methods in one session. The most traditional is instructor-led training in which compliance policies, procedures, processes, or requirements are explained. Live training can take place in-person or via audio or video conferencing. The challenge with instruction is avoiding the mistake that telling is training. Although telling may reach some auditory learners, by itself that approach risks being boring, condescending, or overwhelming to other participants. As a result, instruction should be blended with other learning methods.

The use of PowerPoint presentations is a popular method for adding visual elements to compliance training that can address visual learners, whereas handouts of the presentation can provide something for tactile learners. PowerPoint presentations are relatively cost effective and can be archived for reuse, used for self-directed learning, or made available for those who miss a training session. However, their effectiveness relies heavily on the skill of the presenter and design of the slides and overall presentation.

Adults tend to bring a problem-oriented way of thinking to workplace training. Presenting case studies involving regulatory proceedings is a good method to capitalize on this type of adult learning. Most industry regulators post their regulatory proceedings, including the background information related to the violations. These can be great resources for case study training material. By analyzing real and relevant compliance violations, participants can learn how important certain compliance policies and procedures are to their workplace situations. Case study use is also a good way to discuss how to identify and respond to compliance problems. This form of training stimulates discussion and participation, allowing participants to share knowledge and experiences with others so as to capitalize on another adult learning need.

Similar to case studies are scenario analyses. A scenario analysis usually follows a compliance issue. Analyzing a compliance situation in the workplace can be a good way to review decision making and consequences. Reviewing something that has happened can also make sessions more personal or "real" to the participants. "I want to discuss something that's happened with you" can be an attention-getting opener for a training topic. Training sessions that review a compliance event provide an opportunity to train participants on what to look for and how to respond. Scenario analysis is good for issues such as business disruption, cybersecurity, information handling and safekeeping, and marketing. When discussing events that happened in the workplace, the trainer should exercise caution about to how actual scenarios are used, and legal consideration should be made part of the preparation.

A further enhancement to case study or scenario discussion is actual role playing. Although it can be challenging to have adults play roles, these activities are an excellent learning tool because both the role players and nonrole players are able to consider motivations, decisions, and perspectives that provide an involved assessment of compliance's application. By assuming roles and acting out compliance situations that might occur in the workplace, participants can learn how to handle these situations before they may occur on the job.

Demonstration of compliance processes or technologies related to the compliance program are helpful in addressing new steps or information related to compliance procedures or reporting. Demonstrations engage the tactile learners, who want to learn by doing. When demonstrating steps to a process, the trainer may find it helpful to distribute policies, forms, checklists, or other records related to the training topic to help with recognition and application. Similarly, using the actual technology and allowing participants to try it during training sessions can promote more sustainable learning back on the job. For example, showing participants how to enter personal security transactions into a reporting application and then having them try the data entry as well can help them perform the activity more easily when they are on their own. The same type of demonstration can be used for marketing review submissions. Walking through entries on the form that accompanies the marketing piece and having participants fill in the information are good ways to engage tactile learners.

Like demonstrations, drills are another active way to enhance learning. Compliance drills are typically incorporated into disaster recovery training. Drills can be written scenarios, tabletop exercises, dry runs, or actual simulations. Drills are hands-on tools that can also help participants connect the material to their workplace. As an example, a firm was experiencing limited success with receiving completed plans for disaster recovery from various departments. The training objective was to review disaster recovery planning for those areas and have the departments' representatives finish all outstanding items. The participants were separated into two groups and sent to two different rooms. In one meeting room, the participants had a wooden geometric puzzle assembled on the table and a picture of it on an overhead screen. After the group members took their seats, the overhead projector was turned off and the puzzle in the middle of the table was flipped, leaving pieces all over the tabletop. The trainer told the participants that they had three minutes to assemble the puzzle and started counting down the time. No instructions, directions, or answers to questions were provided to the participants. The three minutes were filled with confusion, arguments, and some effort at organizing the wooden pieces. When the three minutes ended, the group was told its members were in a competition with the other group to complete the puzzle in the least amount of time.

The other group in the other room had the same setup. The only difference was when the puzzle was flipped, each participant received an envelope containing a picture of a piece of the puzzle and instructions on where it went in the puzzle. As the time was counted down, the participants quickly reassembled the puzzle. The two groups then joined each other for a discussion on what they learned. The meeting lasted a total of 15 minutes. Within two weeks of the meeting, all of the departments had completed their disaster recovery plans.

Other interactive training methods that can help validate learning are question and answer (Q&A) sessions, active summaries, and quizzing.

Whether formal or informal, Q&A segments of training sessions can provide participants with the ability to confirm understanding. Generally, the larger the audience, the more formal the method for collecting questions should be. For example, using notecards for individuals to write down questions that can then be answered at a predetermined time, such as at the end of the session, works well for larger groups. This method can also help with insecurities if participants can submit questions anonymously. Q&A sessions provide important feedback on how participants are receiving the training information and can indicate the need to adjust content accordingly.

Active summaries involve participants summarizing a training segment. For example, participants are placed into small groups to work through a compliance scenario. Once the group has finished the scenario, members are asked to summarize the issue and their response to it. This learning method uses application and feedback to confirm understanding. Trainers can also provide summaries at the end of training segments to reinforce learning objectives and prompt feedback from participants. Active summaries give members of the training session the opportunity to compare their impressions with others. This form of active feedback can assist the trainer in determining whether training objectives are being met. In the disaster recovery example mentioned above, when the two groups were brought together, they provided an active summary of their challenges and experiences with the puzzle.

Quizzing is a quantifiable way to determine whether training objectives are being met while also incentivizing participants. To avoid academic impressions or adult test anxieties, refer to quizzes as knowledge checks, fact checks, training points, or some other neutral learning term. For long or complex training sessions, administer brief quizzes periodically on information presented up to that point. Another option is to give participants a session prequiz and inform them that they will take a post-training quiz to see whether their understanding has improved. This can encourage participants to stay engaged in order to improve their quiz scores or understand prequiz mistakes. Offer additional motivation by rewarding high or improved scores.

Some of the more successful formats of quizzes are games. Variations of TV game shows such as "Jeopardy," "Who Wants to Be a Millionaire," "$10,000 Pyramid," or "Are You Smarter Than a 5th Grader" can be modified and used to test compliance understanding by having individuals or groups compete against each other. For example, at the end of a cybersecurity training session, the leader can divide participants into three groups that compete against each other in a version of "Jeopardy," with the categories and answers from the cybersecurity policies and procedures covered in the session material and prizes for the team with the most points.

One of the simplest and most cost effective ways to improve learning in training sessions is to include notetaking or written activities. Even with the growth of electronic media, the act of writing something down helps with retention. Using handouts in compliance training sessions that have predetermined questions or blank spaces and directing participants to write down information is a good way to support objectives in training and retention.[15]

Indirect Training

Other activities that can lead to indirect compliance training can be just as important to the success of a compliance training program as formal training sessions. Examples of indirect forms of compliance training are policy and procedure development, cross-training, and mentoring.

The collaboration that takes place when supervisors, managers and front-line employees are involved in discussions related to compliance policy and procedure drafting can lead to training opportunities and workplace learning. Discussions that help integrate the regulatory requirements with workplace activities in joint initiatives are excellent indirect training opportunities.

Firms that use cross-training provide those involved with the ability to experience another person's job and the compliance policies and procedures that go with that job. Beyond enhancing skills and adding bench depth to various roles, cross-training provides the opportunity for individuals to experience a broader application of compliance

---

[15] Kevin Clark, "The Cleveland Browns' Strategy: Write This Down: Why Cleveland Prefers Pen and Paper to Technology; 'To Write Is to Learn' " *The Wall Street Journal* online (Aug. 11, 2014).

procedures. It can allow participants to see how their own compliance responsibilities fit with the work of others, giving them a workplace perspective that fosters adult learning.

Mentoring programs provide training opportunities that extend formal compliance training objectives. Communicating objectives to mentors helps foster support and reinforcement in mentoring activities. This help ensures that part of the mentoring goal is to improve an employee's compliance performance. Knowing compliance training objectives allows mentors to know immediately whether the trainee has learned compliance responsibilities. Because employees are more likely to follow the instruction of their mentor, mentoring is an effective avenue for compliance training.

Self-Directed Training

Distributing compliance policies, procedures, manuals, codes or other guidance with a specific learning response, such as a quiz or certification, is the simplest form of self-paced training. This can be a good approach for visual learners who need to read to understand. However, training is not the act of distributing and confirming receipt of compliance materials. Distributing compliance materials assists more with the awareness and education stages of the learning model. In general, a key component to compliance training is human interaction. The ability for participants to ask questions is often viewed as necessary for an activity to count as training. Training efforts should result in the demonstration of what is taught. Self-directed training requires the individual to translate material into workplace application.

Self-directed compliance training is growing in use as technology advances and user experience improves. Online compliance training is becoming more popular compared to use of live training and print resources.[16] The ability to deliver compliance training on any type of device using various forms of media can be very effective. This also accommodates a more technologically savvy workforce. Online training can be easy to use, cost effective, flexible, and convenient. The material is standardized and measurable. Compliance training materials can be delivered via company intranets or vendor websites. The material can be branded to a firm and include access credentials for tracking participation. A catalog of courses can be available on a variety of compliance topics, which allows for flexibility in training plans and provides users some flexibility in following their interests.

In addition to delivering content, training can be interactive by requiring participants to answer questions, make choices and even experience consequences of decision-making. Participant experience can be recorded to aid in training evaluations. Recent developments in online compliance training have added virtual reality scenarios like video games that guide participants through interactive simulations—for example, a virtual scenario on insider trading in which a participant investigates whether illegal

---

[16] According to NAVEX Global's *2014 Ethics and Compliance Training Benchmark Report*, 71 percent of compliance training programs use online tools.

trading has taken place.[17] These games provide hands-on experience without the risk of actual performance.

The challenge with these methods is that they can be generic in nature and not customized to specific firms or participant needs. Beyond the technological challenges of ease of use, device compatibility, and system requirements, device training programs have little or no interaction with a live person. Live interaction with participants on training is often critical to ensuring that information is understood well enough to be consistently applied in the workplace. Interaction with trainers is also important in identifying poorly designed material that may require modification in order to meet learning needs.

Education Methods. As mentioned earlier, the goal of education in the learning model is to improve knowledge and understanding, not necessarily application. As an individual's competence improves, the ability to apply it in decision making also improves. Following are several methods that can aid in education.

Newsletters can be an inexpensive and self-directed way to improve understanding. Whether distributed in print or by email, newsletters allow individuals to learn at their own pace. Because effectiveness depends on the recipient's level of interest, newsletters should be short, specific, and related to the workplace. Compliance newsletters should be no more than two pages long, easy to read, and attractively packaged.

Written materials for managers is another education tool for compliance programs. Discussion materials can both educate managers and supervisors on compliance objectives as well as provide guidance on compliance program initiatives, training objectives, and performance goals. Having this information will help managers support and reinforce compliance in the workplace. As with newsletters, these communications should be short and provide specific, actionable material for the manager or supervisor to use. For example, a handout might provide supervisors working in customer service positions with a one-page reminder about wire fraud that highlights the signs to look for in communications and important procedures to review in their next staff meeting.

Other methods for improving internal knowledge of compliance involve the use of third-party services. When firms lack the internal expertise necessary for certain compliance training or application, use of outside consultants is often a good solution. Constantly changing compliance regulations and expanding responsibilities can present challenges to individuals trying to keep up.

Many third parties can provide topical materials in print or online that can help alleviate the challenge of staying current. Third parties can provide specific support addressing knowledge gaps and can tailor the support to the specific needs of the firm and its individuals. Whether providing interpretation of new custody requirements

---

[17] Tom Groenfeldt, "Insider Trading—The Training Game—Sounds a Little Like SAC," Forbes.com (June 31, 2013).

to compliance officers, assisting with cybersecurity assessments with compliance and IT departments, or helping a board member understand antimoney laundering and oversight responsibilities, third-party subject matter experts can enhance compliance training by improving compliance knowledge. Sources of this knowledge can include regulators, associations, organizations, law firms, consultants, and vendors.

Another form of education is the use of third-party compliance webinars, seminars, and industry conferences. The value of this education method depends on the quality of the provider and most often is good for improving general compliance knowledge. Sending individuals to conferences and seminars can be an excellent way for them to gain knowledge and network with peers. Both types of events provide an opportunity to improve training efforts. The obvious drawbacks are the cost and time away from work. However, in many cases, especially when there are only a few employees involved and there is a lack of in-house expertise, education derived from conferences and seminars may be well worth the expense.

There are very few colleges or universities that provide formal undergraduate programs on industry compliance. As a result, those professionals currently wanting to gain expertise are limited to a few organizations and their designation programs.[18] Courses related to these designations can provide participants with a broader understanding and application of industry laws and regulations. These programs can help improve individuals' expertise, which will support their involvement in training program objectives.

There are advantages and limitations to each of these education methods. Depending on the facts and circumstances of a firm, some methods may be more appropriate than others because of the participant group size, costs, or other reasons. Using awareness and education methods in conjunction with training can improve results by adding perspective and knowledge in support of training goals. Blending training methods will also help reach the various learning styles of participants and create an optimal learning experience.

Training Materials

Often when training objectives or results are not met, it can be attributed to poorly prepared materials. Preparation for compliance training sessions is critical to success. Just as participant time is a critical element of training cost, time spent on preparation is a critical element in training success. Developing one hour of training can require 40 hours or more of research and development time.[19] Although the in-house preparation of materials may take longer than prepackaged materials, if done properly the firm-specific materials will be more tailored to the needs of the training session. Retaining

---

[18] Examples include the Investment Adviser Certified Compliance Professional (IACCP) sponsored by the Investment Adviser Association and NRS Education, the Certified Securities Compliance Professional (CSCP) developed by the National Society of Compliance Professionals, and the Certified Regulatory and Compliance Professional (CRCP) program developed by FINRA.

[19] Karl M. Kapp and Robyn A. Defelice, Time to Develop One Hour of Training, Association for Talent Development (Aug. 31, 2009).

training materials also helps develop a library of training content that can be reused or updated as needed. This system helps to reduce development time.

In-house compliance training material provides more control over what is trained. However, there are instances where purchasing prepackaged training courses or using outside training vendors can be advantageous. In formalizing the compliance training plan, it may become evident that qualified trainers or resources are not available in-house to accomplish training objectives. Because regulatory compliance can be complex and keeping track of requirements can be overwhelming, third parties may be able to provide quality training programs that can adequately address training needs. Outside compliance content should be customized to the training needs of the firm to be most effective. Off-the-shelf or boilerplate materials often require the removal of inapplicable content or the addition of relevant content to meet tailored training objectives and avoid confusing the participants. Whether in-house or third party, the content should be up-to-date and reflect the latest regulatory changes or hot topics.

VI. TRAINING EVALUATION

Compliance training resistance typically comes from a perception that it is a waste of time. This can be the result of compliance being seen as separate from an individual's day-to-day activities. As mentioned earlier, the time involved in compliance training is an expense. The value of that expense is the results achieved from training. Demonstrating that value is why training evaluation is important. A successful training program is not static; it is a dynamic work in progress. Objectives, methods and materials are constantly changing in a training cycle—a cycle that is not complete without evaluation.

There are many ways to evaluate and measure the effectiveness of compliance training. Tracking training completion rates may help demonstrate who has finished course material but it does not necessarily signify learning. Monitoring feedback from participants and managers, observing behavior or changes in attitude, reviewing reports, hotline calls, incidents or violations are all ways to gauge how well training objectives are being applied. Participant evaluation methods may involve retention quizzes, surveys and performance metrics.

Of the many methods and tools available to assist in evaluation, one of the most popular frameworks is the four-level evaluation system created by Donald Kirkpatrick over 40 years ago that continues to be used today.[20] The four levels are reaction, learning, behavior, and results.

Reaction

The first level of Kirkpatrick's evaluation system is about evaluating how well the participants liked the training session. It provides an opportunity for participants to give

---

[20] Donald L. Kirkpatrick and James D. Kirkpatrick *Evaluating Training Programs: The Four Levels*, Berrett-Koehler Publishers (2006).

feedback on the environment, the trainer, and session material. Reactions of participants are collected through observations during the session and recorded afterward or through written feedback following the session. An effective way of collecting this information is through satisfaction surveys that provide a uniform measure or grade that can be quantified. For overall impressions, a simple rating system is used, such as a 1 through 5 value scale. For participant impressions, closed-ended questions are used, and for feedback, more open-ended questions can be added. It is helpful to include a space for participants to include follow-up questions or future topics to address.

Learning

This level of evaluation deals with the participants' benefits from training—how much participants learned about the compliance policies and procedures, concepts, and responsibilities in the training session compared to what they knew before the training was provided. This can be determined by reviewing compliance audit and test results, communicating with managers and supervisors, and conducting pretraining tests. During the training, quizzes can help to determine whether learning is occurring. Following training, knowledge or performance tests can also assess how much learning occurred.

Behavior

This level of evaluation deals with participant retention of training objectives. Compliance training may help confirm knowledge, but in order to determine that knowledge is being applied, the knowledge must result in compliant behavior. The behavior level measures how a participant's behavior changes as a result of training. For example, the measurement determines whether participants have incorporated the trained policies and procedures and applied them to their activities and decisions. Supervisors, managers, and others who work closely with training participants can observe behavior and provide feedback regarding how well the training objectives are being applied and sustained. To determine whether participants have made sustainable performance changes or have integrated compliance training knowledge, observations should continue for a period of time (three to six months) after the training session. Behavior changes can also be determined by comparing compliance of employees who did not receive training with those who did to gauge how well the learning objective was achieved.

Results

The final level of evaluation is results. This level looks at the impact training has had on the firm rather than on the individual. Instead of focusing on the effectiveness of training on a participant's performance, this evaluation considers the results the training has provided in terms of an increase in compliant activity, decrease in violations, reduction in noncompliant incidents or events, improvement in morale, or changes in the measurement of identified risks. For each of those areas, measurements, tests, or audits can be conducted pre- and post-training to compare changes in results. Post-training measurements should continue for several months to see whether changes are sustained.

As an example, a firm was experiencing limited success in receiving private placement paperwork in good order. Prior to the training, 42 percent of the paperwork was in good order. After the training, 98 percent of the paperwork processed was in good order. The high percentage of good order paperwork continued over the remainder of the year.

The evaluation framework is just one way a compliance training program can be evaluated. The importance of post-training evaluation is that it helps track training benefits. These evaluation measurements can help demonstrate the value of training to participants, managers, and senior management. If evaluations fail to demonstrate the value of training, it is an indication that the training plan needs to change. If evaluations support the training objectives, results will reinforce the value of the activity and strengthen the support of the training efforts.

VII. TEN TRAINING SESSION KEYS

The following steps highlight some of the key points in the sections of this chapter that will help compliance training session be more effective.

1. Prior to sessions, determine the current level of compliance or knowledge and the desired performance objective from training.
2. Set the stage for training sessions by using awareness campaigns. Providing information prior to training to create interest in the material helps foster a more open and friendly training environment.
3. Be a good facilitator by creating a safe environment for participation, keeping topics focused and on-time, neutralizing negative behavior, and promoting a positive image.
4. At the beginning of training sessions, tell participants what will be covered and the training objective. Focus participants by covering the main topics of the session and related goals.
5. During the session, tell and show participants what they need to know. Provide materials that reach all three learning styles. The body of a compliance session should explain key policy and procedure points, demonstrate compliant activities, and relate information to the participants' workplace.
    a. Present subject matter in a logical order. Explain the basics of the topic—and make sure participants understand them—before going on to more detailed and technical information.
    b. Emphasize the points that are most important. Cover the facts or practices that participants absolutely need to understand or know how to do. Plan to spend most of your training time on these items. Allocate less time to less important but still pertinent training points.
    c. Customize training materials to your firm's situation. Training information needs to reflect your business, policies, procedures, and technology.
    d. Introduce new compliance policies or procedures by explaining why something is changing, how it has changed and how it applies. This will help participants know what to look for and what to remember.

e. Use as much interaction as possible. To reach the learning styles of all participants, provide some form of hands-on training so that application can be practiced. When possible, demonstrating and then applying compliance procedures will help with transference to the workplace.
f. Quiz often. Informing participants that they will be tested on material encourages them to pay closer attention to key training points. It also provides feedback on whether training objectives are being met. This can also be done less formally by soliciting feedback throughout the training session.
g. Encourage participation, which is important for adult learning. Interaction provides variety to training material and allows participants to share experiences.
h. When a participant asks a question, repeat it before answering. This helps confirm that the question is understood, ensures that all participants know the context, and provides time to form the answer.
i. Be flexible in the delivery of material. Each session and its participants will vary. Adapting to what works best in reaching the audience is important. If a training method is not working, consider trying another approach and make note of it for future training sessions.
j. Manage training session time. Start and finish as scheduled. Poorly managed time will detract from even the best training materials. If a training discussion leads to some pertinent related material, don't let the issue take over from the planned training objective. Instead, if there is enough interest, schedule a separate session for it.
k. Use games or challenges for the participants to add some entertainment value to the material, which will help to sustain their interest in the training. To avoid stale sessions, alternate training methods so participants have a variety in the delivery of information.
l. Humor can help with participant enthusiasm, if a point can be made with humor rather than theory or statistics. Remember that participants have varying senses of humor, so when humor is used it is better to be personal and self-deprecating.
m. Make compliance materials look attractive. Policies and procedures should appear organized and worth reading. Spend time on making handouts interesting because packaging alone can add interest and create a favorable impression of the subject.
n. Remember that adults like to participate in order to learn. Encourage participation by using discussions, small groups, or exercises when possible.
o. Adults want to know what's in it for them. Compliance is necessary and required, but they need to know why it is important to them. When participants can relate compliance training to their own self-esteem or self-worth, they are more likely to apply that learning to their workplace activities.

6. At the end of the session, tell participants what you just told them. Reinforce the training objectives by concluding the session with a summary of the opening overview. Repetition helps participants grasp and retain information. Include handouts such as checklists and refresher sheets that participants can refer to

back in their workplace. This can very helpful for new procedures or changes to existing procedures.
7. Conclude training sessions with an evaluation. Gather feedback and comments to help measure the effectiveness of the session and to help improve future sessions.
8. Give support and feedback to participants after the training. Contact participants and ask how the application of what they learned is going, if there are any problems or concerns, or if there are suggestions for training improvements. Let participants know there is an open door policy in compliance where they can talk about issues that may come up from training. This can be helpful not only for compliance training but also for the compliance program itself because seeking out input is one way to improve rapport within a firm.
9. At the end of training sessions, establish manager and supervisor support. Provide supervisors and managers with training follow-up that will help collect problems or concerns from participants. Working with managers and supervisors to monitor, support, and reinforce training in the workplace is very important to sustain learning.
10. Report to managers and senior management on the results of training activities. Share information measuring results with participants and supervisors so that value can be recognized from training efforts.

VIII. CONCLUSION

Investing in compliance training is a wise decision for every firm. Training creates more compliant employees, and compliant employees make compliant firms. Keep in mind that training is much more than a one-time event as long as methods and technologies keep changing the way we work. For firms to stay compliant, they must expand their training model and turn their employees into compliance learners.

The steps outlined in this chapter can serve as a guideline to design and run an effective compliance training program. Educating your participants on the importance of compliance and motivating them to incorporate compliance concepts into their roles and responsibilities on an ongoing basis will have significant value to your compliance program as well as to your firm.

ABOUT THE AUTHOR

Kurt Wachholz is the managing director of WellSpring Compliance LLC, an Atlanta-based consulting firm. His firm is dedicated to providing financial service firms and their management practical and strategic guidance, including clarity for compliance programs.

Mr. Wachholz has over two decades of professional experience in the financial services industry. He has worked on the retail side of the banking, insurance, brokerage, advisory, and financial planning organizations. He has also worked in various back office positions including accounting, human resources, technology, and compliance. He has had first-hand experience with SEC and FINRA examinations. Mr. Wachholz has served in several industry organizations, including the National Society of Compliance Professionals, in various capacities. He has supported the efforts of various CCO roundtables, including the CCO Study Group of Atlanta and the Compliance Professionals Network of Atlanta. He has developed and taught "Ethics in Leadership," a MBA program module for the Goizueta Business School at Emory University. He has been a guest instructor for the Investment Adviser Certified Compliance Professional (IACCP) designation. He has presented at national conferences and participated in online webinars. He has been a volunteer judge for the InvestWrite youth program sponsored by the Foundation of Investor Education. Mr. Wachholz earned his bachelor of arts degree from the University of Wisconsin–Eau Claire and his Investment Adviser Certified Compliance Professional designation from the Center for Compliance Professionals. He has also earned various securities and insurance licenses.

I would like to thank the various industry members, from colleagues to clients to coworkers, who have shared their valuable insight with me over the years—whether directly or indirectly in conversations, projects, seminars, and conferences. In addition, special thanks to those who assisted in reviewing and editing the content, especially Tamra Brown and Tracy Wachholz.

CHAPTER 12

Compliance and Risk Management

By Andrew J. (Buddy) Donohue
    Andrew J. (Drew) Donohue, Jr., *Principal Global Investors*

I. INTRODUCTION

Understanding risk and how to manage it is critical for participants in the financial securities markets in order to best serve their clients and protect themselves. Often, these participants seek to avoid, minimize, or at least manage risk. Risk can also be viewed as a valuable tool used to optimize returns for your firm and for your clients. To effectively use this tool, you must correctly identify potential risks, determine how to best measure and monitor them, and ascertain which risks you should enhance, eliminate, or modify. At first blush, this concept might seem counterintuitive. But, we must remember that business and investing are all about the appropriate balancing of risk and reward.

Risk is an essential part of everyday life that is often addressed through any number of risk transfer mechanisms. For example, you can address the risk that your home might burn down or be damaged by weather by purchasing property insurance. You can address the risk of the potential expense of a medical emergency by obtaining medical insurance. Similarly, you can buy life insurance to mitigate the risk that you will not be able to adequately provide for your family's needs due to your premature death. Other risks, such as the risk that you will not be able to provide for your retirement, for the college education of family members, or for emergencies, are often addressed through various types of savings and investment. In order to optimize risk, it is important to have a broad understanding of risk and not fixate on any one particular risk or type of risk. Frequently, in seeking to minimize or eliminate a particular risk or type of risk we unwittingly have accepted a different, often unrecognized, risk. Put differently, we frequently move risk around or unknowingly trade one risk for another.

The debate during 2009 around target date funds is instructive in this regard. Target date funds were developed as a proposed solution to the challenge that retail investors face when planning and investing for retirement. Target date funds are typically identified by the year in which an investor is expected to retire. By design, these funds have changing asset allocations that are usually more aggressive in early years and gradually become more conservative as an investor approaches or enters retirement. During the dramatic decline in the equity markets in 2008, many of the target date funds held by investors close to anticipated retirement dates suffered severe declines in their value and investors watched their nest egg disappear. For example, investors in funds with a target date of 2010 incurred investment losses as high as 41 percent, with an average loss of almost 25 percent.[1] This investment risk (highlighted by the significant losses sustained by investors) became the focus of investors, the press, securities regulators, the U.S. Department of Labor, and Congress. What many did not recognize or appreciate is that the target date funds were seeking to address and balance at least three different types of risk that those planning for retirement face:

- Inflation risk—the risk that inflation will erode the value of a person's assets over time;
- Market risk—the risk that the value of a person's assets will be adversely impacted by the movement of the markets or securities in which those assets are invested; and
- Longevity risk—the risk that a person will outlive the assets that have been accumulated for retirement.

This difference in perception shows how firms and their clients can have quite different views of the relative importance of each of those risks and the appropriate way to balance and address them. The varying losses sustained by the 2010 target date funds in 2008 demonstrate the real world impact that those differing views can have.

There is no shortage of examples of risk or risk management failures that have dramatically affected financial firms and investors. Some that come quickly to mind are:

- The back office failures of brokerage firms in the late 1960s and early 1970s;
- The failure of Long Term Capital Management in 1998;
- The "rogue trader" or other losses suffered by Barings Bank in 1995, Sumitomo Corporation in 1996, Allied Irish Bank in 2002, Societe Generale in 2008, and UBS in 2011;
- The demise of Bear Stearns and Lehman in 2008;
- The demise of MF Global in 2011;
- The huge trading losses incurred by Knight Capital Group as a result of an automated trading error in 2012; and
- The multibillion dollar "London Whale" losses at JPMorgan Chase.

Although the issues and the risks that caused these events may differ, they each demonstrate the importance of properly identifying and assessing risks and then managing those risks effectively while highlighting the possible negative effects of not doing so.

The remainder of this chapter will consider the different types of risk from the perspective of investment advisers, investment companies, and broker-dealers. We will explore the legal and regulatory responsibilities of the firms, their directors, officers, supervisors, and employees as well as those of chief risk officers and chief compliance officers for identifying, managing and disclosing risks to the firms and to their clients. We will also

---

[1] Testimony Concerning Target Date Funds by Andrew J. Donohue, Division of Investment Management, U.S. Securities and Exchange Commission, Before the United States Senate Special Committee on Aging (Oct. 28, 2009), http://www.sec.gov/news/testimony/2009/ts102809ajd.htm

discuss the interrelationship between risk and compliance and the often complementary roles of the chief risk officer (CRO) and the chief compliance officer (CCO).

Risk is a complex area and one that is increasingly the focus of investors and the regulators, especially after the recent financial crisis. We hope this chapter helps to identify the basic framework for installing an effective risk management program and is of some assistance to those who have responsibility for addressing this important financial concern.

II. ENTERPRISE RISK MANAGEMENT FRAMEWORK AND IDENTIFICATION OF TYPES OF RISK

There are many different ways of looking at risk and how risk applies to a particular firm, its products, and its clients. Some define *risk* as "uncertainty" and then categorize risks into those you can measure and those that you can't. For those risks that can be quantified, firms seek to develop appropriate measures of the risks' levels. In the investment arena a few of those quantified measures, often referred to as *risk metrics* are severe loss scenario, Sharpe ratio, standard deviation, value-at-risk, and duration to name but a few.

The risk process within a firm often starts with an identification of the various types of risk that a firm, its products, or its clients are subject to based on a collaborative effort within the firm. It begins with the development of an inventory of the risks faced, an assessment of those risks taking into account the likelihood of the occurrence of that risk, the severity of that risk (*inherent risk*) if it does occur, and then the risk remaining after any moderation or amplification of it (*residual risk*).

Identifying the various types of enterprise risk that may affect a firm or its clients can be a difficult and time-consuming task, especially if the firm does not take into account its strategic vision. In order to help in setting the framework for identifying the appropriate risks that may affect a firm, it is important to identify and categorize the various objectives of the firm.

In 2001, well before risk management became a hot topic within the financial services industry, the Committee of Sponsoring Organizations of the Treadway Commission (COSO) undertook a project to develop a framework to assist firms in their oversight of risk management.[2] COSO defined *enterprise risk management* as follows:

> Enterprise risk management is a process, effected by an entity's board of directors, management and other personnel, applied in strategy setting and across the enterprise, designed to identify potential events that may affect the entity, and manage risk to be within its risk appetite, to provide reasonable assurance regarding the achievement of entity objectives.[3]

---

[2] Enterprise Risk Management-Integrated Framework: Executive Summary (Sept. 2004), http://www.coso.org/documents/coso_erm_executivesummary.pdf
[3] Enterprise Risk Management-Integrated Framework: Executive Summary, page 4.

As a result of this review, COSO has put forth an approach that separates enterprise risk management into four distinct categories in an effort to afford companies the opportunity to adequately identify and assess its risk in a structured manner.

This framework envisions that an organization has an established mission or vision, and that against this backdrop, the organization has established strategic objectives, selected strategies and aligned objectives. The objectives can be categorized as four basic pillars:

- Strategic—high-level organizational goals aligned with the overall vision and strategic outlook of the firm;
- Operations—identifying and monitoring the firm's use of resources to ensure that it is both effective and efficient;
- Reporting—the reliability of the various levels of reporting that is produced by the firm; and
- Compliance—the level and manner in which a firm is complying with the applicable laws and regulations that govern its activities.

The acceptance, avoidance, or management of risk is a large part of day to day business of a financial firm. Firms often identify enterprise risks on the basis of a number of interrelated components. As a firm identifies and reviews the risks of its business, it is not uncommon for a number of items to fall into more than one category. In order for an approach to identifying and managing enterprise risk management to be effective, it is important that both the risk management function and the compliance function work in concert toward a goal that is in line with the firm's overall strategic outlook or mission statement.

This approach includes identifying key risks relative to the various business activities of the firm and ensuring that management has a clear understanding of the risks, a plan to review and assess the risks, and a plan to monitor, mitigate and review those risks. The firm must also ensure that while it is reviewing and assessing these risks, it views them relative to the other risks that are discussed in this chapter.

COSO also identified eight components of enterprise risk management as a tool to use to assess the potential effectiveness of a firm's enterprise risk management program. Those components as defined by COSO are:

- Internal environment—The tone of an organization (also referred to as the "tone at the top") and includes items such as a firm's risk appetite and its core values;
- Objective setting—Enterprise risk management ensures that management has in place a process to set objectives and that the chosen objectives are appropriate and consistent with the firm's risk appetite;
- Event identification—Internal and/or external events that may impact a firm and affect its ability to achieve its objectives;
- Risk assessment—Firm analysis of risks, considerations of the likelihood of occurrence, and notation potential impact. This may be conducted at minimum on an annual basis but is typically reviewed by investment related firms on a more frequent

or ongoing basis. The assessment will also take into account the inherent risk and residual risk;
- Risk response—The identification of a set of actions in line with its risk tolerance and risk appetite (avoidance, acceptance, reduction or sharing of risk);
- Control activities—Establishment and implementation of policies and procedures in order to ensure that the risk responses are effectively carried out;
- Information and communication—The identification and sharing of relevant information across an enterprise; and
- Monitoring—The ongoing review of management activities relative to the above items. This can also be referred to or included in a firm's forensic testing plan.

As you use the four pillars of the risk management framework along with the additional eight components in assessing your firm's current risk program, those responsible for identifying and managing risk at the enterprise level are able to view it in a somewhat structured and replicable manner. These tools will assist those responsible for carrying out the duties and responsibilities discussed throughout this chapter.

Finance and investment professionals must identify, calculate, and assess exposure to many different types of risks that are often cited as important such as market risk, credit risk, interest rate risk, inflation risk, funding risk, liquidity risk, counterparty risk, political risk, foreign exchange risk, model risk, and operational risk. Individuals and firms also discuss risk in terms of absolute risk (the risk that you may lose money) and relative risk (the risk that a particular investment or strategy may not perform as well relative to a benchmark, regardless of whether or not there is an absolute loss or gain). So when a company executive or client asks whether a particular activity is "risky," compliance professionals, risk officers, and others should ask about what particular risk(s) the question relates.

Now that we have identified a number of different ways for a firm to identify, assess and manage the risks that affect its business, let's discuss some of the responsibilities related to risk that fall on the directors and officers, supervisors, and senior managers of a firm.

III. RESPONSIBILITIES

Board of Directors

Directors don't generally have day-to-day management responsibilities but rather have oversight responsibilities and certain decision-making responsibilities.[4] In that regard, a director's responsibility for risk management is generally considered an oversight responsibility, absent a specific legal or regulatory requirement to the contrary.

A Board of Directors generally is responsible for ensuring that the company has established appropriate risk management programs and for overseeing management's

---

[4] See Federal Regulation of Securities Committee, ABA Section of Business Law, *Fund Director's Guidebook*, 3rd ed., 2006.

implementation of such programs. This responsibility is principally derived from state law, which imposes a duty of care that directors and officers owe to their firm and the evolving duty of oversight or duty to monitor. A director's duty of care generally means that the director must exercise the care of an ordinarily prudent person in a like position would exercise under similar circumstances and in a manner the director reasonably believes to be in the best interests of the corporation.[5] The duty of oversight or the duty to monitor refers to the director's responsibility to actively monitor the activities of officers and employees to prevent harm to the firm arising from wrongdoing.[6]

The Delaware Chancery Court[7] has held that the board of directors has a duty to ensure that appropriate "information and reporting systems" are in place to provide the board and top management with "timely and accurate information." The 1996 *Caremont* case and the subsequent cases[8] have set an extremely high bar for finding directors personally liable for breaching their fiduciary duty to monitor. Essentially a sustained and systemic failure to exercise oversight is needed and in the absence of "red flags" or warning signs that the manner in which a company evaluates the risks involved with any given business decision is protected by the business judgment rule.

So it would appear that if the firm has appropriate information and reporting systems in place to provide timely and accurate information and there are no red flags, the directors will have satisfied their fiduciary duties. But is that the correct perspective through which this issue should be viewed? Should directors view their responsibilities to the firm and its shareholders for risk management based on the minimum that they must do to avoid personal liability for their actions (or inactions)? We think not and believe that this will be an area that will continue to evolve where there will be increasing expectations regarding the directors' role. Let's now explore certain specific recommendations or requirements regarding the directors' risk management responsibilities.

In the wake of the global financial crisis, there have been a host of reviews and recommendations regarding the role of risk management and internal controls in the financial firms' distress during the crisis. These will be noted later and you will see that the role of the board regarding risk management, especially in financial firms, is only increasing.

The Securities and Exchange Commission (SEC) in 2009[9] adopted new disclosure requirements for issuers regarding board leadership structure and the board's role in risk oversight. In particular, investment companies must disclose the extent of the board's role in the risk oversight of the company, such as how the board administers its risk oversight function and the effect this has on the board's leadership structure. In

---

[5] *Id.*
[6] *See* Fairfax, Lisa M., "Managing Expectations: Does the Directors' Duty to Monitor Promise More Than It Can Deliver?" *University of St. Thomas Law Journal,* Vol. 10; No. 2, Article 2, http://ir.stthomas.edu/ustlj/vol10/iss2/2
[7] *Caremark International Inc. Derivative Litigation* (698 A. 2d 959 (Del. Ch. 1996)).
[8] *In re Citigroup Inc. Shareholder Derivative Litigation,* 964 A.2d 106 (Del. Ch. 2009) and Goldman Sachs Group, Inc. Shareholder Litigation , 2011 WL 4826104 (Del. Ch. 2011).
[9] *See* Proxy Disclosure Enhancement: SEC Release No(s). 33-9089, 34-61175, IC-29092 (Dec. 2009), http://www.sec.gov/rules/final/2009/33-9089.pdf

addition the NYSE has listing standards that require that the audit committee must meet and discuss policies with respect to risk assessment and risk management.[10] The commentary to that provision is instructive of the role that the Audit Committee is expected to play with respect to risk assessment and risk management.

Officers, Supervisors, and Senior Managers

The role of officers, supervisors, and senior managers regarding risk management is quite different from that of directors, although they are all subject to a duty of care. Unlike directors, the role of officers, supervisors, and senior managers is an active role and is not just one of oversight. Their role also takes into account the extent to which the firm may have an obligation to identify and manage the risks to which the firm is subject. It is the collective obligation of the officers, supervisors, and managers to discharge that obligation.

In the next section, we will discuss a general overview of the regulatory requirements as well as specific requirements set forth for investments advisers, broker-dealers and investment companies.

IV. REGULATORY REQUIREMENTS

Regulatory requirements for broker-dealers, investment advisers, investment companies, and other regulated entities with respect to risk and risk management are not generally explicitly established in the various securities laws[11] or the regulations thereunder. Those statutes and the resulting regulatory structures were largely enacted more than 70 years ago, well before the current understanding of the importance of risk evolved. This absence of explicit requirements is especially true with regard to the proprietary risks assumed by those firms and the management of those risks. The regulators have been more aggressive with regard to the risks to clients and the management of proprietary issues, particularly through disclosure requirements and the application of various antifraud provisions of those laws.

Notwithstanding the absence of explicit requirements, however, regulators expect financial firms to have effective risk management practices in place. This expectation has only heightened following the financial crisis that began in 2007. This expectation was also enhanced when the major broker-dealers became subject to the supervision of the banking regulators and the greater traditional focus of prudential regulators on the risk management practices of firms.

There are many examples of how the SEC, the Financial Industry Regulatory Authority (FINRA), and other regulators have addressed the need for effective risk management

---

[10] See NYSE Rule 303A.07(b)(iii)(D), http://nysemanual.nyse.com/LCMTools/PlatformViewer.asp?selectednode=chp%5F1%5F4%5F3%5F6&manual=%2Flcm%2Fsections%2Flcm%2Dsections%2F

[11] Securities Act of 1933, Securities Exchange Act of 1934, Investment Company Act of 1940, and Investment Advisers Act of 1940.

by the firms they regulate. In 1999, regulators were concerned about the potential impact of the year 2000 ("Y2K") on computer systems used by everyone, including financial firms. In response to that concern the SEC responded in an aggressive manner regarding the preparedness of financial firms for that event.[12] More recently with the potential vulnerability of firms to cyberattacks various regulators have also responded. For example, in March 2014 the SEC held a roundtable to discuss cybersecurity[13] and thereafter the SEC's Office of Inspections and Examinations (OCIE) issued a National Exam Program Risk Alert[14] directed to broker-dealers and investment advisers. That risk alert indicated that OCIE would be focusing on, among other things, the entity's cybersecurity governance, the identification and assessment of cybersecurity risk, risks associated with remote access and funds transfer, and the risks associated with vendors.

On December 11, 2014, SEC Chair Mary Jo White gave a speech titled "Enhancing Risk Monitoring and Regulatory Safeguards for the Asset Management Industry"[15] wherein she discussed the regulatory safeguards and incentives in the regulatory framework governing the investment advisory and investment company industries and the controls on portfolio composition risks and operational risks. Shortly thereafter the Financial Stability Oversight Council (FSOC) issued a notice seeking comment on asset management products and activities.[16] In that notice the FSOC was seeking comment on whether asset management products and activities may pose potential risks to the U.S. financial system in the areas of liquidity and redemptions, leverage, operational functions, and resolution. Risk is clearly of interest to the financial regulators and an area that is and will be subject to increased regulatory oversight and regulation.

Investment Advisers

The Investment Advisers Act of 1940 ("Advisers Act") is a very brief statute that regulates the activities of investment advisers. It is a principles-based statute that embodies the concept that investment advisers are "fiduciaries,"[17] and the SEC enforces that concept through disclosure requirements and the application of the Advisers Act's antifraud provisions.[18] Even though there are no specific statutory requirements in the Advisers Act for risk management, there is increasing expectation among financial regulators that effective enterprise risk management is in place at investment advisory firms for the benefit of both the firm and its clients.

---

[12] SEC, Final Rule: Year 2000 Operational Capability Requirements for Registered Broker-dealers and Transfer Agents Release No. 34-41661, http://www.sec.gov/rules/final/34-41661.htm
[13] SEC Cybersecurity Roundtable (2014), http://www.sec.gov/spotlight/cybersecurity-roundtable.shtml
[14] "OCIE Cybersecurity Initiative," National Exam Program Risk Alert by Office of Compliance Inspections and Examinations , Volume IV, Issue 2 (Apr. 15, 2014), http://www.sec.gov/ocie/announcement/Cybersecurity+Risk+Alert++%2526+Appendix+-+4.15.14.pdf
[15] Mary Jo White, "Enhancing Risk Monitoring and Regulatory Safeguards for the Asset Management Industry," The New York Times DealBook Opportunities for Tomorrow Conference (Dec. 11, 2014), http://www.sec.gov/News/Speech/Detail/Speech/1370543677722
[16] Financial Stability Oversight Council, "Notice Seeking Comment on Asset Management Products and Activities" (Docket No. FSOC-2014-0001), http://www.fsoc.gov
[17] See SEC v. Capital Gains Research Bureau, Inc., 375 U.S. 180 (1963) and Transamerica Mortgage Advisors, Inc. 444 U.S. 11 (1979).
[18] See Investment Advisers Act, Section 206.

With regard to the investment advisory firm itself, the SEC has addressed the need for effective risk management in a number of ways. When the SEC adopted Rule 206(4)-7 under the Advisers Act ("compliance rule")[19] that addressed compliance risk, the commission indicated that the policies and procedures that advisory firms needed to adopt and implement should incorporate a reasonable process for responding to emergencies, contingencies, and disasters and that the advisers' contingency planning process should be appropriately scaled and reasonable in light of the facts and circumstances surrounding the advisers' business operations and the commitment made to clients.

In 2011, the director of the OCIE, Carlo V. di Florio, gave a speech regarding compliance and ethics in risk management[20] in which he discussed a number of areas relating to risk management and the obligations advisers owe to their clients.

This compliance responsibility was more recently highlighted by OCIE in a National Exam Program Risk Alert titled "SEC Examinations of Business Continuity Plans of Certain Advisers Following Operational Disruptions Caused by Weather-Related Events Last Year."[21] In that risk alert, OCIE noted that because of an adviser's fiduciary duty to its clients it needed to take steps to protect the clients' interest from risks resulting from the adviser's inability to provide advisory services after, for example, a natural disaster. Here OCIE has pointed to certain operational risk areas and emphasized the need to identify and manage risks lest client's interests be compromised.

With respect to investment related risks, the SEC's Division of Investment Management (IM) has also recently been raising issues associated with risk management. For example, IM Guidance Update No. 2013-03 was issued in July 2013 and was titled "Counterparty Risk Management Practices with Respect to Tri-Party Repurchase Agreements."[22] More recently, IM Guidance Update No. 2014-1 was issued in January 2014 and was titled "Risk Management in Changing Fixed Income Market Conditions."[23] The IM Division has also established its own Risk and Examinations Office, which enhances its own risk monitoring efforts.[24] Accordingly, we should expect that such focus on risk and risk management will only increase especially as the SEC further develops its own capabilities to identify risks.

---

[19] SEC Release No(s) IA-2204; IC-26299 "Compliance Programs of Investment Companies and Investment Advisers" (December 2003), http://sec.gov/rules/final/ia-2204.htm

[20] Carlo V. di Florio, director, Office of Compliance Inspections and Examinations, "The Role of Compliance and Ethics in Risk Management," NSCP National Meeting (Oct. 17, 2011), http://www.sec.gov/news/speech/2011/spch101711cvd.htm

[21] National Exam Program Risk Alert: Volume II, Issue 3: "SEC Examinations of Business Continuity Plans of Certain Advisers following Operational Disruptions Caused by Weather-Related Events Last Year," http://www.sec.gov/about/offices/ocie/business-continuity-plans-risk-alert.pdf

[22] IM Guidance Update No. 2013-03, Counterparty Risk Management Practices with Respect to Tri-Party Repurchase Agreements (July 2013), http://www.sec.gov/divisions/investment/guidance/im-guidance-2013-03.pdf

[23] IM Guidance Update No. 2014-1, Risk Management in Changing Fixed Income Market Conditions (Jan. 2014), http://www.sec.gov/divisions/investment/guidance/im-guidance-2014-1.pdf

[24] *See* Norm Champ, director, Division of Investment Management, Remarks to the 2014 Mutual Funds and Investment Management Conference (Mar. 17, 2014), http://www.sec.gov/News/Speech/Detail/Speech/1370541168327#.VDAQxlJ0zq4

In considering risk, the primary disclosure documents available for clients of investment advisers is the "brochure" governed by Form ADV, Part 2. Item 8 requires disclosure regarding "Methods of Analysis, Investment Strategies, and Risk of Loss."[25] This is a primary means for advisers to disclose to clients the risks they are taking on and if that disclosure is inadequate, inaccurate, or misleading, then the antifraud provisions of the Advisers Act, particularly Sections 206(1) and 206(2), can be used by the SEC.

So although there may be no explicit requirements regarding risk or risk management in the Advisers Act, it is clear that the SEC expects that advisers have a fiduciary obligation to identify, manage, and disclose risks. Because the expectations of those obligations are not well defined, those parameters will likely be shaped by speeches, alerts, and guidance from IM and OCIE, deficiency letters resulting from OCIE exams, and enforcement actions using the antifraud provisions of the Advisers Act.

As mentioned previously, SEC Chair White in a speech on December 11, 2014, indicated that the SEC's regulatory program needed to fully address the increasing complex portfolio composition and operations of the asset management industry. For investment advisers that likely will include providing additional data to the SEC and the requirement that firms have a plan for transitioning client assets when circumstances warrant. Chair White also stated that the SEC staff was considering ways to implement new requirements for annual stress testing by large investment advisers as required by the Dodd-Frank Act.[26] With this speech, the SEC staff work underway, and the previously mentioned FSOC notice, clearly risk requirements for advisers are a priority item for the SEC and FSOC.

Broker-Dealers

Broker-dealers are subject to a regulatory regime quite different from that applicable to investment advisers. Broker-dealers are subject to the rules of their self-regulatory body, FINRA, as well as those of the SEC. Like investment advisers, there are few specific regulatory requirements of the SEC or FINRA that specifically address risk and risk management obligations of firms. There is, however, clearly an expectation by those regulators that broker-dealers do have effective risk management in place.

In 1999 the Office of Compliance Inspections and Examinations of the SEC, the New York Stock Exchange, and NASD Regulation, Inc. (predecessor to FINRA), issued a joint statement titled "Broker-Dealer Risk Management Practices Joint Statement."[27] These regulators had formed a task force in response to changes in the industry and several instances in which poor systems of internal controls resulted in substantial losses at certain firms. Among the goals of the task force was to assess the industry's awareness

---

[25] Form ADV, Part 2 Item 8:Item 8, Methods of Analysis, Investment Strategies, and Risk of Loss, http://www.sec.gov/about/forms/formadv-part2.pdf

[26] Dodd-Frank Wall Street Reform and Consumer Protection Act, P.L. No.111-203 (July 21, 2010), http://www.sec.gov/about/laws/wallstreetreform-cpa.pdf

[27] NASD Notice to Members 99-92 (Nov. 1999), http://www.finra.org/web/groups/industry/@ip/@reg/@notice/documents/notices/p004054.pdf

of the need for stringent risk management supervisory systems and to compile a compendium of sound practices and weaknesses noted during its review. The statement described a risk management system:

> Risk management is the identification, management, measurement and oversight of various business risks and is part of a firm's internal control structure. These risks typically arise in such areas a proprietary trading, credit, liquidity and new products. The elements of a comprehensive risk management system are highly dependent on the nature of the broker-dealer's business and its structure.

The task force also stated: "As regulators we want to emphasize to management throughout the broker-dealer community the importance of maintaining an appropriate risk management system geared to a firm's business activities."

The staff at the SEC has also been vocal about the need for effective risk management at broker-dealers. In a speech by an associate director of OCIE in 2005,[28] several thoughtful observations were made regarding the risk management framework of broker-dealers and the different roles played by compliance and internal audit. In another speech by the associate director in 2007,[29] it was acknowledged that there were currently no specific rules requiring risk management controls for broker-dealers except those applicable to over-the-counter (OTC) derivatives dealers and consolidated supervised entities. She noted however, that having a well-documented system of internal controls designed to manage risks is a proactive, sound practice to protect against significant financial losses, violations of law, and investor harm. She also provided a list of practices observed during exams that may mitigate certain risks (such as operational risk, market risk, and credit risk) including senior management involvement, effective internal audit, legal, and compliance functions.

FINRA has been active in this area as well. In a FINRA Regulatory Notice in 2010,[30] FINRA discussed its expectation that broker-dealers will develop and maintain robust funding and liquidity risk management practices to prepare for adverse circumstances. In that notice, FINRA discussed certain practices, including those relating to:

- Risk limits and reporting;
- Independent risk oversight;
- Maturity profile and funding sources;
- Red flags of potential funding and liquidity problems;
- Inventory valuation;

---

[28] Mary Ann Gadziala, "Integrating Audit and Compliance Disciplines within the Risk Management Framework," Operational Risk and Risk Magazine Present Compliance '05 USA, New York, NY (Nov. 30, 2005), http://www.sec.gov/news/speech/spch113005mag.htm

[29] Mary Ann Gadziala, "Risk Management for Broker-Dealers" 2007 AICPA/FMD National Conference on the Securities Industry, New York, NY (Nov. 28, 2007), www.sec.gov/news/speech/2007/spch112807mag.htm

[30] FINRA Regulatory Notice 10-57 Risk Management: Funding and Liquidity Risk Management Practices (Nov. 2010), http://www.finra.org/web/groups/industry/@ip/@reg/@notice/documents/notices/p122388.pdf

- Stress testing;
- Contingency funding plan; and
- Use of customer assets.

More recently FINRA announced its regulatory and examination priorities for 2014[31] and under "Financial and Operational Priorities" indicated that it would be asking its larger members to perform stress testing of liquidity positions in four areas of the firm's business and incorporating factors FINRA believes to be relevant. FINRA would also be evaluating the rigor of the firm's counterparty risk management programs.

The SEC has also been incorporating risk management requirements into some of its rulemaking such as a recent amendment to Securities Exchange Act of 1934 Rule 17a-3 which requires certain broker-dealers to document their credit, market and liquidity risk management controls.

So the regulators clearly have an expectation that broker-dealers will have an effective risk management program in place and we should anticipate that, like we discussed with respect to investment advisers, those expectations will only increase.

Investment Companies

The Investment Company Act of 1940 does not directly address the requirement for risk management by the investment company. There are, of course, requirements regarding the disclosure of material risks to investors relating to their investment in shares of the investment company.[32] In order to do this properly, it would seem to require a firm to have a robust program for the identification and assessment of risks. In addition, the SEC has adopted rules requiring disclosure of the board's role in the oversight of risk.[33]

Not surprisingly there have been speeches and other actions undertaken by OCIE and IM that touched on this area. For example, in 2007, IM Director Andrew J. Donohue provided some of his thoughts about risk, operational risk and risk management systems.[34] More recently, as previously discussed, certain guidance provided by the IM had applicability to investment companies.[35] The current Directors of the IM and OCIE, Norm Champ and Andrew Bowden, now regularly visit firms and request extensive presentations on risk management. Clearly this is an area the regulators are focusing on.

This focus was highlighted in a previously mentioned speech provided by SEC Chair White on December 11, 2014. In that speech Chair White indicated that the SEC staff was considering whether broad risk management programs should be required for

---

[31] FINRA 2014 Regulatory and Examination Priorities (Jan. 2, 2014), http://www.finra.org/web/groups/industry/@ip/@reg/@guide/documents/industry/p419710.pdf
[32] See Form N-1A, Form N-2 and Form N-3, http://www.sec.gov/forms#invadv
[33] See Item 17(b)(1) of Form N-1A; Item 18.5(a) of Form N-2 and Item 20(d)(i) of Form N-3, http://www.sec.gov/forms#invadv
[34] Andrew J. Donohue, Remarks Before the Investment Company Institute 2007 Operations and Technology Conference, http://www.sec.gov/news/speech/2007/spch101807ajd.htm
[35] See IM Guidance Update No. 2013-03 and IM Guidance Update No. 2014-1.

mutual funds and ETFs to address the risks related to their liquidity and derivative use. She noted that the SEC staff is also reviewing options for specific requirements such as updated liquidity standards, disclosures of liquidity risks or measures to appropriately limit the leverage created by the use of derivatives. The SEC staff is working on the stress testing requirements for larger funds ($10 billion in assets) mandated by the Dodd-Frank Act as well. The previously noted FSOC notice also is seeking information regarding the potential risks to the U.S. financial system by asset management products and activities in the areas of liquidity and redemptions, leverage, operational functions and resolution, or in other areas. So compliance professionals should expect that the SEC will likely soon be addressing risk in the investment company area.

The investment company industry has produced some useful papers discussing the risk management process for investment companies and the oversight role that fund directors should play. The Mutual Fund Directors Forum[36] and the Investment Company Institute/Independent Directors Council[37] papers are particularly useful in this regard. The Investment Company Institute also produced a survey of investment company organizations regarding chief risk officers and their role within the organization.[38]

The Mutual Fund Directors Forum's paper provides a simplified way for fund directors to think about risk and risk management. It breaks down risk into investment risk and operational risk categories. With respect to investment risk the paper suggests that fund boards should consider whether there are adequate mechanisms in place to address the following issues:

- Monitoring investment performance and investment risk;
- Valuation risk;
- Complex securities; and
- Issuer and counterparty risk.

Operational risk, the paper notes, encompasses issues arising or errors or omissions that will (or might) occur in the ordinary course of business that will adversely affect the business. A few of the risks identified were:

- Compliance risk;
- Fails or reconciliation differences;
- Customer complaints;
- Guideline breaches;
- Systems problems; and
- Disasters.

---

[36] Mutual Fund Directors Forum, *Risk Principles for Fund Directors: Practical Guidance for Fund Directors on Effective Risk management Oversight* (Apr. 2010), http://www.mfdf.org/images/uploads/newsroom/Risk_Principles_for_Fund_Directors_April_2010_Web_Version.pdf

[37] Investment Company Institute and Independent Directors Council *Fund Board Oversight of Risk Management* (Sept. 2011), http://www.idc.org/pdf/pub_11_oversight_risk.pdf

[38] Investment Company Institute, *Chief Risk Officers in the Mutual Fund Industry: Who Are They and What Is Their Role Within the Organization?* (2007), http://www.idc.org/pdf/21437.pdf

The paper suggests that a risk inventory be developed and that red flags may be employed to identify areas where further inquiry or monitoring might be advised. In its Exhibit A, the paper identifies certain components of a risk management framework including:

- Organization and governance;
- Culture;
- Risk management and process:
  - Risk appetite, strategy and asset allocation;
  - Risk identification and assessment;
  - Risk measurement and analysis;
  - Risk mitigation, control and monitoring;
  - Reporting and performance measurement;
  - Periodic review; and
  - Infrastructure.

Other exhibits provide guidance regarding additional areas such as: risk-conscious culture, staffing and organization of the risk function, evaluating risks attributable to new investments, determining mechanisms for controlling operational risks, assessing the adequacy of a fund's investment risk management, assessing the adequacy of a fund's valuation policies and procedures, and issuer and counterparty credit risk management.

In their September 2011 paper, the Investment Company Institute and Independent Directors Council highlighted the following recurring themes for effective risk management:

- Tone at the top is critical to promoting a risk-conscious culture;
- Risk management is a process, not a project;
- Risk management is everyone's responsibility;
- Appropriate independence makes risk management more meaningful;
- Risk management is forward-looking and proactive;
- Clear communication facilitates effective risk management; and
- Organizational structures and policies themselves can serve as risk controls.

Each of these papers provides thoughtful insight and practical guidance regarding effective risk management for investment companies.

Requirements Applicable to All

As examined above, there are not many explicit statutory provisions, rules, or regulations that require investment advisers, broker-dealers and investment companies to have robust risk management practices. What is clear, however, is that regulators expect those entities, in fact, to have robust and effective risk management practices.

In addition, the SEC has indicated that it is considering various risk-related matters and FSOC has expressed its interest in this area, especially regarding investment advisers, investment companies and their activities, and their potential impact on the U.S. financial system.

Regardless of whether the regulators will develop and enforce that expectation through the fiduciary standard for investment advisers, the disclosure obligations applicable to investment advisers, broker-dealers, and investment companies or otherwise may not be that important to the question of whether those firms need to have robust and effective risk management. They do!

The next portion of this chapter will address impact of the Dodd-Frank Act on the risk management function within a firm and what those entities need to do to develop and implement an effective robust risk management system.

V. THE IMPACT OF THE DODD-FRANK ACT

The impact of the Dodd-Frank Wall Street Reform and Consumer Protection Act (the "Dodd-Frank Act") on the role of risk assessment and risk management at financial firms should not be underestimated. Although the provisions affecting risk management obligations may be primarily applicable to large bank holding companies, public midsized holding companies, and certain nonbank financial institutions, those requirements and the risk management framework embodied in the regulations are, at the least, informative about regulators' expectations.

The entities that are covered by these provisions are required to have an enterprise-wide Risk Committee of the Board of Directors that approves and periodically reviews risk management policies, and oversees the operation of its risk management framework. That committee (which must be a separate committee for a large bank holding company) must:

- Include at least one member who has experience identifying, assessing, and managing risk exposures of large, complex firms;
- Be chaired by an independent director;
- Have a formal written charter approved by the board;
- Meet at least quarterly;
- Fully document and maintain records of proceedings, including risk management decisions;
- Establish a risk management framework that is commensurate with its structure, risk profile, complexity, activities, and size, which must include:
  - Policies and procedures establishing risk management governance, risk management procedures and risk control infrastructure for its operations,
  - Processes and systems for:
    - Identifying and reporting risks and risk management deficiencies;
    - Establishing managerial and employee responsibility for risk management;
    - Insuring the independence of the risk management function; and
    - Integrating risk management and associated controls with management goals and compensation structure.

In addition, large US bank holding companies must employ a CRO with specified risk management responsibilities. The CRO must:

- Have risk management experience identifying, assessing and managing risk exposures of large, complex financial firms;
- Report directly to the risk committee and the chief executive officer (CEO) and provide quarterly reports to the Risk Committee;
- Have a compensation and incentive arrangement consistent with providing an objective assessment of risks taken;
- Be responsible for overseeing
  - Establishment of risk limits on an enterprise-wide basis and monitoring of those limits,
  - Implementation of and ongoing compliance with risk management policies and procedures,
  - Development and implementation of the processes and systems to monitor compliance with risk management policies and procedures,
  - Management of risks and risk controls within the parameters of the firm's risk control framework, and
  - Monitoring and testing of firm's risk controls;
- Report risk management deficiencies and emerging risks to the Risk Committee and resolving risk management deficiencies in a timely manner.

At a minimum, one should discern from this list that risk management is considered quite important and that regulators will likely expect that even firms not subject to the explicit requirements of the Dodd-Frank Act will establish a risk management framework tailored to their particular size, activities, and business.

VI. DEVELOPING AND IMPLEMENTING EFFECTIVE RISK MANAGEMENT IN FINANCIAL FIRMS

It is clear that for business, financial, and regulatory reasons, investment advisers, broker-dealers, and investment companies should develop, establish, and implement effective and robust risk management programs in their firms. But how best to do so? One approach is to draw on the guidance provided by the Financial Stability Board (FSB) in 2013. The FSB was established in April 2009 as the successor to the Financial Stability Forum (FSF), which was originally founded in 1999 by the G7 finance ministers and central bank governors to enhance international cooperation and promote stability in the international financial system.[39] The objectives of the FSB as stated in the General Provisions of its Charter are to:

> Coordinate at the international level the work of the national financial authorities and international standard setting bodies (SSBs) in order to develop and promote the implementation of effective regulatory, supervisory, and other financial sector policies. In collaboration with the international financial institutions, the FSB will address vulnerabilities affecting financial systems in the interest of global financial stability.[40]

---

[39] Financial Stability Board, "Our History," http://www.financial stabilityboard.org/about/history.htm
[40] *See* Charter of the Financial Stability Board (June 2012), http://www.financialstabilityboard.org

Here is a synopsis of some aspects of the approach the FSB recommend:

- Develop a Risk Appetite Framework (RAF) that is both actionable and measurable. As pointed out in the FSB's *"Principles for an Effective Risk Appetite Framework,*[41] ("Principles") an effective RAF should:
  - Establish a process for communicating the RAF across and within the financial institution;
  - Be driven by both top-down board leadership and bottom-up involvement of management at all levels;
  - Facilitate embedding the risk appetite into the financial firms risk culture;
  - Evaluate opportunities for appropriate risk-taking and operate as a defense against excessive risk-taking;
  - Allow the risk appetite statement (RAS) to be used as a tool to promote robust discussions on risk and a basis upon which the board, risk management, and internal audit functions can effectively and credibly debate and challenge management recommendations and decisions;
  - Be adaptable to changing business and market conditions;
  - Cover activities, operations, and systems of the financial institution that fall within its risk landscape but are outside its direct control, including subsidiaries and third parties; and
  - Be consistent with principles in that document.
- Develop a risk appetite statement that should articulate the aggregate level and types of risk that the financial institution is willing to accept, or to avoid, in order to achieve its business objectives. It should include both qualitative and quantitative statements. As pointed out by the FSB Principles, an effective risk appetite should:
  - Include key background information and assumptions that inform the financial institution's strategic and business plans;
  - Be linked to the institution's short- and long-term strategic, capital and financial plans, as well as compensation programs;
  - Establish the amount of risk the financial institution is prepared to accept in pursuit of its strategic objectives and business plan;
  - Determine for each material risk and overall the maximum level of risk that the financial institution is willing to operate within, based on its overall risk appetite, risk capacity and risk profile;
  - Include quantitative measures that can be translated into risk limits applicable to business lines and legal entities as relevant, and at a group level which can be aggregated and disaggregated to enable risk measurement;
  - Include qualitative statements that articulate clearly the motivations for taking on or avoiding certain types of risk;
  - Ensure that the strategy and risk limits of each business line and legal align with the institution-wide risk appetite statement; and
  - Be forward looking and, where applicable, subject to scenario and stress testing.

---

[41] *See* Financial Stability Board, *Principles for an Effective Risk Appetite Framework* (Nov. 2013), http://www.financialstabilityboard.org/publications/r_131118.pdf

- Establish risk limits for the financial institution and for business lines and entities. Risk limits should be specific and sensitive to the shape of the actual portfolios, measurable, frequency-based, reportable, and based on forward looking assumptions. As pointed out by FSB Principles, risk limits should:
  — Be set at a level to constrain risk-taking within the risk appetite;
  — Be established for business lines and legal entities;
  — Include material risk concentrations at the institution, business line, and legal entity levels as relevant;
  — Although referenced to market best practices and benchmarks, not be strictly based on comparison to peers or default to regulatory limits;
  — Not be overly complicated, ambiguous or subjective; and
  — Be monitored regularly.
- Establish distinct roles and responsibilities in accordance with the financial firm's organizational structure, but the oversight and control functions should always play a key role. Clear roles and responsibilities should be established for:
  — The Board of Directors;
  — The CEO;
  — The CRO (if there is one);
  — The chief financial officer;
  — Business line leaders and legal entity-level management; and
  — Internal Audit, Compliance, and Legal Departments.

To be sure, these recommendations seem complex and complicated. Let's see if we can simplify them. To develop an effective risk management framework we believe you should engage knowledgeable members of your organization to:

- Identify the various risks that the firm and the firm's clients are exposed to and develop an inventory of those risks;
- Determine the exposures of the firm and the firm's clients to each of those risks and develop acceptable limits or ranges for each of those risks individually and in aggregate;
- Determine a means of managing those risks by eliminating, modifying or, if appropriate, even enhancing them;
- Develop a systematic means to measure and monitor those risks, including appropriate reports;
- Identify responsibilities for each step of the process; and
- Be vigilant and expect the unexpected.

VII. RELATIONSHIP BETWEEN COMPLIANCE AND RISK MANAGEMENT

The compliance function within a financial firm and the role of the CCO require a diverse set of talents and involve a number of critical interdependencies. Thus, to be effective compliance needs to be embedded in the culture of the firm in a manner that allows for ongoing, real-time coordination between the compliance team and vital personnel in areas such as marketing, portfolio management and trading, operations, legal, and internal audit.

An effective risk management program will certainly identify regulatory risks as an important risk category that needs to be managed properly, a responsibility typically assumed by the compliance function and the CCO. So in a way, compliance is clearly a key component of an effective risk management program. To the extent that having an effective risk management program is viewed as a regulatory imperative, then effective risk management is also a key component of the compliance regime.

The reality is that although the two may be viewed as or set up as independent functions within a financial firm, compliance and risk management are important, complementary functions within a financial firm, and they need to have a high degree of effective communication and coordination. This is not unlike the more familiar interplay between compliance and the legal and internal audit areas.

The Compliance and Risk Management Process

When a firm sets out to prepare a comprehensive risk assessment, it would be prudent to begin with the framework that has been provided by COSO and go through each step, beginning with aligning the firm's relative risk appetite with its overall strategy. As discussed earlier in this chapter, enterprise risk management encompasses the following items[42]:

- Aligning risk appetite and strategy;
- Enhancing risk response decisions;
- Reducing operational surprises and losses;
- Identifying and managing multiple and cross-enterprise risks;
- Seizing opportunities; and
- Improving deployment of capital.

These items should be considered as your firm develops its risk management process. Once a potential risk is identified, it is important to further research the risk to better understand the potential impact (negative or positive) that the risk may have on the firm or its clients. Keeping the above factors in mind, it is now possible to move on to reviewing the risk through the relevant components of enterprise risk management and identifying to which portion of the framework it belongs (Strategic, Operations, Reporting, Compliance, or Safeguarding of Resources). The remainder of this discussion will demonstrate how this process can be applied or followed.

Once a risk has been identified, the firm must understand how that risk relates to the underlying components within its *internal environment*. In this step it is important to properly identify where this risk fits based upon the tone and goals of a firm and its overall risk appetite.

---

[42] Enterprise Risk Management-Integrated Framework: Executive Summary.

The next step is to take a look at the overall objective that the firm wishes to seek through the activity noted in or related to this risk. During this phase of *objective setting*, a firm should inquire as to the ultimate objective of using this risk and the intended outcome.

Once this objective is clear, the firm should look to identify potential or predictable events that could affect the firm's ability to manage this risk towards the desired outcome. This process allows for the risk management group to work with the business units to identify potential business opportunities as well as identify the risks associated with them. This step is referred to as *event identification*.

The next area of focus is then on the overall *risk assessment*. During this phase, discussions and analysis take place regarding the identified risk. Multiple factors are taken into account during this analysis, such as probability of occurrence, potential positive (upside) or negative (downside) impact, and proposals or recommendations on how to best manage the risk. Once this has been done, the group can analyze the impact of these items when the group reviews the difference between the inherent risk score and the residual risk score assigned to it.

After this review has been completed, firm managers can then select the appropriate *risk response*. Does the firm wish to simply accept the risk or take appropriate steps to avoid, reduce or share the risk? Compliance and risk professionals can then work toward developing and instituting a program that aligns the firm's response with its agreed upon appetite for risk.

The internal business units can then work with the Compliance Department and Risk Department to put in place adequate *control activities*. These would include the everyday policies and procedures that govern an organization and that are enacted and followed to ensure that the business units have an understanding of the risks along with knowledge of the firm's desired outcome from managing them. Properly aligned policies and procedures help protect the firm's overall plan while assisting it in documenting the framework for and providing guidance to ensure that the desired risk response is followed through at each relevant level within the firm.

These issues, controls, policies, and procedures must then be "rolled out" to the relevant business units. Industry best practice suggests that the *information and communication* portion of this process incorporate an element of training. Training allows for management to explain the process and expectations, along with any anticipated or desired timelines, to the staff. Training can be done in any number of ways, depending on the size, type, or location of staff within your organization. Training may also vary based upon the importance or type of information being communicated to the staff. For example, policies and procedures related to higher risk items or new policies and procedures may be communicated through one-on-one training or group interactive training sessions (in person), whereas lower risk or updates to existing policies and procedures may be addressed through email updates or computer based training modules. In-person training, when conducted properly, provides a direct opportunity for discussion and questions with staff which hopefully help in ensuring that there is a clear understanding of both the risk and the policy.

The final step in this process is the ongoing *monitoring* program, which, from a compliance and risk management perspective, is an ongoing and fluid process that provides oversight while allowing for modifications and changes to policies and procedures in order to ensure their adequacy and appropriateness. This step also allows for a firm to ensure that its policies are being adhered to and that they are having the desired effect or outcome. Typically, the Compliance Department will review and monitor this through ongoing, formal risk-based forensic testing. Some firms may use risk management systems to monitor risk; however, there are some limitations to these systems as described below.

Each of these steps is important in framing out an effective, appropriate compliance and enterprise risk management program. A firm may have an exceptional process in place for seven of the steps listed above but may falter in its communication of the program to its employees, thus having a negative impact on the entire program. Additionally, policies and procedures created through this process must not only accurately reflect its desired outcome but also fit within its business processes and capabilities. Once a firm establishes policies and procedures, it is crucial that they be followed. Regulators will typically hold a firm to its internal policies and procedures (even if not mandated by regulation or law) especially in instances where those internal policies and procedures may be more restrictive than otherwise required.

VIII. LIMITATIONS OF RISK MANAGEMENT SYSTEMS

Risk management systems that seek to identify, quantify, and manage risks can be very valuable tools, but they have their limitations and those need to be recognized upfront. Overreliance on your risk management systems can easily be a significant risk to a financial firm and its clients.

One limitation of risk management systems is the selection of the set of data to be used and how best to weight that data. Another is that by its nature the data is historical, and a basic assumption is that the past is instructive of what the future will likely be. We liken overreliance on risk systems to driving down a steep winding road with cliffs on both sides by looking in your rear view mirror. Sound advice is to drive slowly and frequently get out and look ahead. Focus on what the potential consequences are in the future is much different from the past.

Many of the investment disasters that have occurred were the result of the risk management systems and firms not appreciating the limitations of the systems and the consequences of their being wrong. Keep that in mind and don't abandon common sense. You often hear of "tail risk" or "black swan events" and you should expect that these will occur. The question then is what impact they will have on the financial firm and its clients when they do occur.

IX. CONCLUSION

Risk management is an important concern in any organization, but it is a critical area for financial firms and for their clients. Although the regulatory regimes applicable to investment advisers, broker-dealers, and investment companies may not yet have developed detailed risk management requirements for firms, it would be a serious mistake to conclude that there are none. Especially in light of the financial crisis of 2007 to 2009, regulators and indeed clients will expect that financial firms do have effective risk management in place.

To meet those expectations and to manage your firm to properly serve the interests of your clients, effective risk management is an imperative. We hope this chapter has been of some assistance to you in identifying various types of risk, understanding risk management, and enabling you to develop an effective risk management program within your firm.

ABOUT THE AUTHORS

Andrew J. (Buddy) Donohue has been associated with the investment management industry for more than 35 years. From May 2006 to November 2010 he was the director of the Division of Investment Management at the SEC, where he was responsible for developing regulatory policy and administering the federal securities laws applicable to mutual funds, exchange-traded funds, closed-end funds, variable insurance products, unit investment trusts, BDCs, and investment advisers. Before joining the SEC Mr. Donohue served as global general counsel for Merrill Lynch Investment Managers and as executive vice president and general counsel at OppenheimerFunds, Inc.

Mr. Donohue earned a bachelor of arts cum laude with "high honors" in Economics from Hofstra University in 1972 and a juris doctor degree from New York University School of Law in 1975. He is admitted to practice law in New York and New Jersey.

Andrew J. (Drew) Donohue, Jr., is the director, Global Compliance for Principal Global Investors, LLC (PGI) and has more than 15 years of diversified experience in the financial services industry. In his current role at PGI he manages daily oversight of the firm's global compliance department including professionals located throughout the United States, United Kingdom, Hong Kong, Singapore, Japan, China, and Australia. Oversight responsibilities include a number of registered investment advisers and the creation, implementation, and review of global policies and procedures. Previously Mr. Donohue was responsible for overseeing 206(4)7 and 38a-1 compliance supervision for OppenheimerFunds, Inc., a large mutual fund manager and its related adviser entities, a trust company and related limited purpose broker-dealer entities. In his prior roles he has managed internal audits, routine regulatory examinations, and targeted regulatory examinations.

CHAPTER 13

Navigating Marketing and Distribution

By Michael Caccese, *K&L Gates*
   Douglas Charton, *Grantham, Mayo, van Otterloo, LLC*

I. ADVISERS ACT SECTION 206(4) AND RULE 206(4)-1

As investment firms continually seek to expand their asset-gathering efforts, advertising continues to be a prominent and important tool way to attract additional capital from traditional sources and to tap in to previously untapped investor bases. Meanwhile, deficiencies in investment adviser marketing and performance presentation are among the most common (and most sustained) problem areas identified by the Securities and Exchange Commission (SEC) in its examinations of investment advisers.[1] Further, the SEC, its Office of Compliance Inspections and Examinations (OCIE), and the commission's Asset Management Unit in the Division of Enforcement continue to focus efforts on investment adviser advertising practices.[2]

Although neither the Investment Advisers Act of 1940, as amended ("Advisers Act"), nor the rules thereunder require advisers to submit or file advertisements with the SEC prior to use, advisers should expect a request by the SEC staff during any SEC examination for any and all advertising materials distributed by the adviser during the examination period and all necessary documentation that supports the calculation of the advertised performance. As a matter of policy, the SEC staff will not review advertisements on a preuse basis to determine whether they comport with the advertising rules under the Advisers Act.[3] Therefore, advisers must decipher the regulatory scheme governing adviser advertising themselves by piecing together the SEC and its staff's positions as set

---

[1] The SEC identified marketing/performance as one of the three "core risk" areas—those risk areas that are common to the business model utilized by investment advisers and that have existed for a sustained period and are likely to continue for the foreseeable future—for investment advisers. *See* SEC Office of Compliance, Inspections and Examinations 2014 National Examination Program Examination Priorities for 2014 (Jan. 9, 2014).

[2] In its January 2011 *Study on Enhancing Investment Adviser Examinations*, the SEC's Division of Investment Management identified advertising as one of the six "high-risk areas" on which examinations of registered investment advisers will typically focus (along with conflicts of interest, portfolio management, valuation, performance and asset verification).

[3] *See e.g.*, Trainer, Wortham & Co., Starbuck, Tisdale & Assoc. (Dec. 6, 2004) ("[T]he staff does not review specific advertisements as a matter of policy."); Clover Capital Management, Inc. (Oct. 28, 1986) ("Because of the factual nature of the determination, the staff, as a matter of policy, does not review any specific advertisements."); James B. Peeke & Company, Inc. (Sept. 13, 1982).

forth in sometimes conflicting SEC staff no-action letters, speeches by the SEC's staff, and SEC enforcement actions against investment advisers. Accordingly, investment advisers and their compliance personnel need to be highly cognizant of the applicable rules and regulations governing adviser advertising and marketing before the advisers developing or circulating advertising or marketing materials.

Section 206(4) of the Advisers Act and Rule 206(4)-1 thereunder govern the advertisements of investment advisers. Section 206 applies to all advisers, whether registered or unregistered, whereas Rule 206(4)-1 only applies to those advisers that are registered or required to be registered with the commission.[4] Section 206(4) of the Advisers Act, the general antifraud provision, governs all activities of investment advisers (including marketing and advertising activities), and makes it unlawful for any investment adviser, whether registered or unregistered, to directly or indirectly engage in any act, practice, or course of business that is fraudulent, deceptive, or manipulative.[5] Rule 206(4)-1 promulgated thereunder speaks specifically to four advertising practices, but also contains a "catchall provision" for any additional practices deemed to be false and misleading. Specifically, the rule deems it to be a "fraudulent, deceptive, or manipulative act, practice, or course of business" for any registered adviser to, directly or indirectly, publish, circulate or distribute an advertisement that:

- Makes any direct or indirect references to a testimonial concerning the adviser or its advice, analysis, report or other service it has rendered;[6]
- Makes any direct or indirect references to the adviser's past specific recommendations that were or would have been profitable, unless the advertisement sets out or offers to provide a list of all recommendations made within the immediately preceding period of not less than 1 year, accompanied by certain disclosures;[7]
- Makes any direct or indirect representation that a graph, chart, formula or other device: (a) can in and of itself determine which securities to buy or sell or when to buy or sell securities; or (b) can assist an individual in making such determinations, without prominently disclosing the limitations thereof and the difficulties regarding its use;[8]
- States that any report, analysis or other service is for free, unless such materials or services are entirely free and without any direct or indirect condition;[9] or
- Contains any untrue statement of a material fact, or is otherwise false or misleading.[10]

Rule 206(4)-1 was originally adopted in 1961 under the consideration that "advisers are professionals and should adhere to a stricter standard of conduct than that applicable

---

[4] Section 206 as amended in September 1960 subjects all advisers, whether registered or unregistered, to Section 206 and grants the SEC the power, through rules and regulations, to "define, and prescribe means reasonably designed to prevent, such acts, practices, and courses of business as are fraudulent, deceptive, or manipulative" within the meaning of Section 206(4). Prior to this amendment, the SEC did not have the power to define the specific activities that were deemed to be fraudulent or deceptive within the meaning of Section 206 of the Advisers Act. *See Investment Advisers Notice of Proposed Rule Making*, SEC Rel. No. IA-113 (Apr. 4, 1961).
[5] Section 206 of the Advisers Act.
[6] Rule 206(4)-1(a)(1).
[7] Rule 206(4)-1(a)(2).
[8] Rule 206(4)-1(a)(3).
[9] Rule 206(4)-1(a)(4).
[10] Rule 206(4)-1(a)(5).

to merchants, securities are 'intricate merchandise,' and clients or prospective clients of investment advisers are frequently unskilled and unsophisticated in investment matters."[11] The SEC staff continues to impose a standard of conduct for investment adviser advertisements that is stricter than that for other vendors of products or services. Each investment adviser is accountable for all of the information that is included in an advertising piece that it creates and/or distributes. If information is obtained from external sources, those sources are required to be identified, the information must be truthful and supportable, and if it includes any performance, the investment adviser must have documentation supporting the calculation of that performance, as discussed below.

What Is an Advertisement?

Whether any material, either in written or in oral form, is subject to Rule 206(4)-1 depends upon whether it constitutes as an "advertisement" within the meaning of Rule 206(4)-1(b) under the Advisers Act. As such, before investment advisers and their compliance personnel can understand the intricacies of the SEC's rules governing adviser advertising, they must understand the types of communications that the SEC regards as advertisements. Rule 206(4)-1(b) defines an "advertisement" to include:

- Any notice, circular, letter or other written communication addressed to more than one person; or
- Any notice or announcement in any publication or by radio or television that offers any
  - Analysis, report, or publication concerning securities, or which is to be used in making any determination as to when to buy or sell any security, or which security to buy or sell, or
  - Graph, chart, formula or other device to be used in making any determination as to when to buy or sell any security, or which security to buy or sell, or
  - Other investment advisory service with regard to securities.

In general, "whether any particular communication—or series of communications—constitutes an advertisement under Rule 206(4)-1(b) under the Advisers Act depends upon all of the facts and circumstances."[12]

Although Rule 206(4)-1 does not set forth a specific list of communications that the SEC deems to be "advertisements" under the rule, in a series of no-action letters, the SEC has applied a broad view of what constitutes an advertisement, which generally includes materials designed to maintain existing clients or solicit new clients[13] including form letters; presentation booklets; requests for proposals; a brochure delivered pursuant to Rule 204-3 under the Advisers Act; radio and television broadcasts; magazine or newspaper pieces; and certain electronic communications, such as internet postings.[14]

---

[11] *Advertisements by Investment Advisers,* SEC Rel. No. IA-121 (Nov. 1, 1961) (adopting release to Rule 206(4)-1).
[12] Investment Counsel Association of America, Inc., SEC No-Action Letter (pub. avail. Mar. 1, 2004).
[13] Munder Capital Management, SEC No-Action Letter (pub. avail. May 17, 1996) ("Materials designed to maintain existing clients or solicit new clients for the adviser are considered to be advertisements within Rule 206(4)-1.").
[14] *See also SEC v. Yun Soo Oh Park a/k/a Tokyo Joe and Tokyo Joe's Societe Anonyme Corp.,* N.D. IL, Case No. 00C 0049 (complaint filed Jan. 5, 2000).

Some examples of communications that are generally *not* considered advertisements within the meaning of Rule 206(4)-1 include oral communications other than those in radio or television broadcasts[15] and written communications that do no more than respond to an unsolicited request by a client, prospective client or consultant for specific information about the adviser.[16] In addition, the SEC staff has clarified that documents that relate specifically to investment companies (e.g., prospectuses, advertisements, or sales literature) will not be treated as materials "designed to maintain existing clients or solicit new clients for the adviser unless the documents are directed to such persons or refer to advisory services that are offered to such persons."[17] Written communications to existing advisory clients about the performance of their accounts are also generally not considered advertisements under Rule 206(4)-1.[18] However, if the purpose of the communication is to offer advisory services or maintain the existing client, the communication will likely be deemed to be an advertisement under Rule 206(4)-1.[19]

Although the determination of whether a document constitutes an "advertisement" under the Advisers Act depends on the particular facts and circumstances, Table 1 provides examples of certain types of communications that the SEC is likely/unlikely to deem an "advertisement":

TABLE 1. COMMUNICATIONS CONSIDERED AND NOT CONSIDERED TO BE ADVERTISING

Advertising	NOT Advertising
■ Marketing brochures ■ Paid advertising in periodicals and other publications ■ Television, radio, or other broadcast advertising ■ Internet websites ■ Form letters and mass mailings ■ Email messages sent to multiple recipients ■ Audio/videotapes of marketing presentations ■ Slides used in marketing presentations ■ Press releases and some interviews ■ Reprints of third-party publications ■ Questionnaires from independent rating services ■ Performance presentations used for more than one prospective client ■ Telemarketing scripts ■ Internal material that reaches clients	■ In person, telephone, or other oral conversations ■ Any written communication that does no more than respond to an unsolicited request by a client, prospective client, or consultant for specific information ■ Regular account statements and reports sent only to existing clients (but not to solicit new business from prospective or existing clients) ■ Academic articles that discuss portfolio management methodology but do not offer advisory services

---

[15] Investment Counsel Association of America, Inc., SEC No-Action Letter (pub. avail. Mar. 1, 2004).

[16] *Id.* An adviser that induces an existing or prospective client, or a consultant to request the adviser to provide information on its past specific recommendations or distributes an advertisement indicating that the adviser may provide past specific recommendations upon request is deemed to have solicited such a request. The SEC staff clarified that a response to an unsolicited client request would not be deemed to be an advertisement under Rule 206(4)-1 even if the information was provided to one consultant who submits the request on behalf of several clients, or several consultants, so long as the information was provided "in response to a specific, unsolicited request" for information.

[17] Munder Capital Management, SEC No-Action Letter (pub. avail. May 17, 1996).

[18] Investment Counsel Association of America, Inc., SEC No-Action Letter (pub. avail. Mar. 1, 2004).

[19] *Id.* For instance, if an adviser distributes a communication to an existing client that discusses the profitability of past specific recommendations that were not held or recently held by the existing client, this would suggest that the purpose of the communication was to promote the adviser's services and may therefore constitute an advertisement that contains past specific recommendations in contravention of Rule 206(4)-1(a)(2).

Compliance Notes: Review and Approval of Communications and Advertisements

As further explained above, all communications by an investment adviser are subject to the general antifraud provisions under Section 206(4) of the Advisers Act, but only "advertisements" are subject to the specific prohibitions contained in Rule 206(4) thereunder. Compliance policies and procedures should identify the specific types of communications that the adviser may engage in and differentiate between materials that are (or could be deemed) advertisements and those that are not.

Communications that do not constitute advertisements should comply with content standards designed, at a minimum, to ensure that such communications are not false or misleading. Whether a communication is false or misleading depends on the applicable facts and circumstances; however, when reviewing materials that an adviser intends to use with investors and/or prospective investors, compliance personnel should generally consider the form and content of the advertisement, the implications that may arise out of the advertisement's context, and the level of sophistication of the prospective clients that will view the advertisement. Common problem areas include incorrect and/or missing defined terms and failure to disclose underlying assumptions necessary to understand the information presented in materials such as client reports and materials prepared pursuant to a client's or prospect's request.

Compliance personnel are encouraged to take a broad view regarding what they consider to be an advertisement. For instance, if materials are prepared in response to a client's or prospect's specific request, but the materials go beyond the information requested, the materials could be viewed as an advertisement. Similarly, if materials are prepared for use with existing clients as "client reporting" but the materials include information not specifically related to the client's account and holdings, the materials could be viewed as an advertisement.

Even though communications that do not constitute advertisements are not technically subject to the SEC's rules and interpretations applicable to advertisements, compliance personnel may use such rules, interpretations, and guidance in reviewing and approving advertisements in evaluating what the SEC may consider to be false or misleading under the Advisers Act's general antifraud provisions.

Testimonials

Rule 206(4)-1(a)(1) under the Advisers Act prohibits an adviser from referring, directly or indirectly, to a testimonial of any kind regarding the adviser, its advice or any other services the adviser offers.[20] The prohibition against testimonials is premised on the concern that the testimonial may give the investor the misleading impression that the experience it conveys is representative or typical of the experience of all of the adviser's clients.[21] In adopting the prohibition, the SEC characterized advertisements containing testimonials as innately misleading, citing the temptation for advisers to always present testimonials in an unbalanced manner by publishing only those that are favorable to the adviser and/or its activities.[22] Although Rule 206(4)-1(a)(1) does not define the term *testimonial,* the SEC staff has interpreted the term through a number of no-action letters. In the eyes of the SEC, any statement of a former, current or existing client regarding the client's experience with, or endorsement of, an adviser constitutes a testimonial.[23] Such statements may be deemed testimonials even if unrelated to the adviser's performance, such as statements regarding an adviser's character, diligence, or sensitivity to client needs. For instance, in Gallagher and Associates, Ltd., the SEC staff refused to grant no-action relief with respect to client endorsements that were restricted to the adviser's character.[24]

Partial Client Lists as Testimonials. In Denver Investment Advisors, Inc., the SEC staff's first no-action letter to address client lists as testimonials under Rule 206(4)-1(a)(1), an adviser sought permission to provide consultants with partial client lists assembled using objective criteria (e.g., account size, geographic location, client classification) on an unsolicited basis, except with respect to updates to consultants who originally received the information pursuant to their request.[25] The SEC staff declined to take the position that the client lists were not testimonials under Rule 206(4)-1(a)(1) but stated that it would not recommend enforcement action to the commission if the adviser included a partial client list in its advertisements so long as:

- The adviser did not use performance-based criteria in determining which clients to include in the list;
- Each client list contained a disclaimer that it was not known whether the listed clients approved or disapproved of the adviser or the advisory services provided; and
- Each client list included a statement disclosing the objective criteria used to determine which clients to include in the list.[26]

---

[20] Rule 206(4)-1(a)(1) under the Advisers Act.
[21] See CIGNA Securities, Inc., SEC No-Action Letter (pub. avail. Sept. 10, 1991) (stating that written statements from satisfied financial planning clients are testimonials prohibited by Rule 206(4)-1(A)(1); New York Investors Group, Inc., SEC No-Action Letter (pub. avail. Sept. 7, 1982).
[22] *Advertisements by Investment Advisers.* The SEC added that "[t]his is true even when the testimonials are unsolicited and are printed in full." CIGNA, SEC No-Action Letter.
[23] See DALBAR, Inc., SEC No-Action Letter (pub. avail. Mar. 24, 1998) ("Although the term 'testimonial' is not defined in Rule 206(4)-1, we consistently have interpreted that term to include a statement of a client's experience with, or endorsement of, an investment adviser.").
[24] Gallagher and Associates, Ltd., SEC No-Action Letter (pub. avail. July 10, 1995). The proposed endorsements were restricted to statements about the adviser's religious affiliation or moral character; his community service, trustworthiness and ethical character, diligence and attention to details; ability to listen and be sensitive to client needs; knowledge of investing, insurance and tax strategies (but without referencing performance); and prudence and judgment. *Id.*
[25] Denver Investment Advisors, Inc., SEC No-Action Letter (pub. avail. July 30, 1993).
[26] *Id.*

Approximately four years later, in *Cambiar Investors, Inc.*, the SEC staff pronounced that a partial client list that does no more than identify certain clients of the adviser (i.e., neither emphasizes comments or activities favorable to the adviser nor ignores those that are unfavorable) is not a statement of a client's experience with or endorsement of the adviser and is therefore not a testimonial under Rule 206(4)-1(a)(1).[27] The SEC staff clarified:

> Our position is not conditioned on the adviser's use of nonperformance-related criteria to select clients that appear on the partial list or the presence of any particular disclosure or disclaimer. Our position also is not conditioned on who receives the advertisement (consultant or client) or whether the recipient requested the information. In our view, these factors are not relevant to determining whether the content of an advertisement constitutes a statement of a client's experience with, or endorsement of, a particular investment adviser.[28]

Although an advertisement that does no more than identify select advisory clients is not a testimonial within the meaning of Rule 206(4)-1(a)(1), the SEC staff emphasized that such advertisements are nonetheless subject to the general prohibition against false or misleading advertisements under Rule 206(4)-1(a)(5).[29] For instance, in an action against Reservoir Capital Management, Inc., the SEC admonished the adviser for providing prospective clients with a "representative" client list which contained eight institutional investors.[30] Because institutional clients composed no more than 15 percent of the adviser's assets under management and at least two of the eight investors were not clients of the adviser, the SEC found that the adviser violated Section 206(4) and Rule 206(4)-1(a)(5) thereunder.

The SEC staff has indicated that a partial client list that is *not* distributed in the manner described in Denver Investment Advisors, Inc., is not necessarily false or misleading under Section 206(4) and Rule 206(4)-1(a)(5). However, the SEC staff stated that "an adviser's deviation from one or more of the [Denver Investment Advisors, Inc.] representations could be relevant, but would not necessarily be determinative" in the analysis of whether the advertisement containing a partial client list is false or misleading.[31] In addition, the SEC staff stated that a list that includes only advisory clients who were selected on the basis of performance and the selection bias was not adequately disclosed may be potentially misleading in violation of Rule 206(4)-1(a)(5).[32]

---

[27] Cambiar Investors, Inc., SEC No-Action Letter (pub. avail. Aug. 28, 1997).
[28] *Id. But see* Franklin Management, Inc., SEC No-Action Letter, at n. 14 (pub. avail. Dec. 10, 1998) (stating that the SEC staff agreed not to recommend enforcement action against Cambiar Investors, Inc. so long as the selection criteria for the partial client list were objective and unrelated to the performance of clients' accounts, and the advertisement contained disclosure and the disclaimer set forth in Denver Investment Advisors, Inc.).
[29] Cambiar Investors, Inc. SEC No-Action Letter (pub. avail. Aug. 28, 1997).
[30] *In re Reservoir Capital Management, Inc. and Roann Costin*, SEC Rel. No. IA-1717 (Apr. 24, 1998).
[31] Cambiar Investors, Inc., SEC No-Action Letter (pub. avail. Aug. 28, 1997).
[32] Cambiar Investors, at n. 8.

Compliance Notes: Inclusion of Partial Client Lists in Advertisements

Based on the foregoing, inclusion of partial client lists in advertising materials is not in and of itself misleading, as long as:

- The adviser did not use performance-based criteria in determining which clients to include in the list;
- The criteria for selecting clients for inclusion on the list are disclosed;
- A disclaimer is included stating that it was not known whether the listed clients approve or disapprove of the adviser or its services provided; and
- Client consent is obtained.[33]

Ratings and Rankings Based Solely on Performance. Third-party ratings that are based solely on performance, regardless of whether an adviser compensates the third party to verify and rank its performance, do not constitute testimonials under Rule 206(4)-1, and as such, are permitted provided that their inclusion is not "false or misleading" in violation of the catchall provision under the advertising rule. [34] In order to avoid being deemed false or misleading under Rule 206(4)-1(a)(5), an advertisement that contains any third-party rating should adhere to the following conditions:

- The advertisement should disclose the criteria on which the rating was based;
- The adviser should not be aware of undisclosed facts that would call into question the validity of the rating or appropriateness of advertising the rating (e.g., adviser received numerous client complaints relating to rating category or areas not included in the survey);
- The adviser should disclose unfavorable ratings (if any) when disclosing favorable ratings;
- The advertisement must not state or imply that adviser was a top-rated adviser in a category when it was not rated first in that category;
- The advertisements should disclose clearly and prominently the category for which the rating is calculated or determined, the number of advisers surveyed in that category, and the percentage of advisers that received that rating;
- The advertisement should disclose that the rating may not be representative of any one client's experience because the rating reflects an average of all, or a sample of all, of the experiences of the adviser's clients;
- The advertisement should disclose that the rating is not indicative of the adviser's future performance; and
- The advertisement should disclose prominently who created and conducted the survey, and (if applicable) that the adviser paid a fee to participate in the survey.[35]

---

[33] Although client consent is not explicitly required, many states prohibit disclosure of client identity without client consent and the fact that a particular customer or consumer is an advisory client also constitutes nonpublic personal information under Regulation S-P. Such disclosure without consent could also violate provisions of an adviser's contractual arrangements with a client.

[34] *See* Stalker Advisory Services, SEC No-Action Letter (pub. avail. Feb. 14, 1994). *See also* the later discussion regarding article reprints.

[35] Investment Adviser Association, SEC No-Action Letter (pub. avail. Dec. 2, 2005).

Ratings and Rankings as Testimonials: Ratings Based Primarily on Client Evaluations. The inclusion of third-party rankings and ratings in advertisements can be used to imply a certain level of client satisfaction. Because the SEC has characterized *any* statement of a client's experience with the adviser as a "testimonial," inclusion of third-party ratings or rankings in advertising materials carries the risk of violating the prohibition on testimonials.[36] As such, a third-party rating that contains an implicit statement of a client's experience with an adviser is a testimonial within the meaning of Rule 206(4)-1(a)(1). It is within this context that advisers and their personnel must review advertisements that refer to ratings or rankings published by third parties.[37]

In Investment Advisers Association, the SEC staff clarified that the term *testimonial* includes a third-party rating that "relies primarily" on client evaluations of an adviser, but does not include a third-party rating where client responses about the adviser are considered but deemed to be an insignificant factor in formulating the rating.[38] When determining whether a third-party rating constitutes a testimonial, the adviser should consider the criteria used by the third party in formulating its rating and the significance of client evaluations in the rating's formulation.[39] In making these considerations, the SEC staff indicated that an adviser may need to contact the third party to make this determination.[40]

In a no-action letter issued to DALBAR, Inc., the SEC staff stated that a rating that solicits client views about their experience with an adviser is a testimonial under the rule because the rating "is an implicit statement of clients' experiences with an adviser…and because the rating purports to convey the experience of a hypothetical average, or typical client with an adviser."[41] Nonetheless, the SEC staff believed that the advertising of such ratings would not raise the dangers that Rule 206(4)-1(a)(1) was designed to prevent so long as certain conditions are met. Accordingly, in addition to the factors above that should be considered for all rankings and ratings included in advertising materials, ratings that are based primarily on client evaluations of investment advisers are permitted so long as:

- The rating does not emphasize favorable client responses or ignore unfavorable client responses;
- The rating represents all, or a statistically valid sample, of the responses of the adviser's clients;
- The questionnaire sent to clients was not prepared to produce any predetermined results that could benefit any adviser;
- The questionnaire is structured to make it equally easy for a client to provide a negative or positive response; and
- The research firm did not perform any subjective analysis of the survey results but rather assigned numerical ratings after averaging the client responses for each adviser.

---

[36] *See* DALBAR, Inc., SEC No-Action Letter (pub. avail. Mar. 24, 1998). *See also* the discussion about testimonials.
[37] Investment Adviser Association, SEC No-Action Letter (pub. avail. Dec. 2, 2005).
[38] *Id.*
[39] *Id.*
[40] *Id.*
[41] DALBAR, Inc., SEC No-Action Letter (pub. avail. Mar. 24, 1998).

In taking this position, the SEC staff relied upon the factors above and DALBAR, Inc.'s representations that:

- Participating advisers have met certain eligibility criteria reasonably designed to ensure that a participating adviser has an established and significant history and record free from regulatory sanctions;
- The research firm is not affiliated with any participating adviser;
- The research firm surveys all or a statistically valid sample of a participating adviser's clients;
- All participating advisers are charged a uniform fee, paid in advance;
- The research firm does not issue ratings to an adviser unless the ratings are statistically valid with respect to that adviser; and
- Any survey results published by the research firm contain information that clearly identifies the percentage of survey participants who have received such designation and the total number of survey participants.

Article Reprints. An article drafted by an unbiased third party that discusses an adviser's performance is not a testimonial within the meaning of Rule 206(4)-1(a)(1) unless it includes a statement of a customer's experience or endorsement.[42] However, the advertisements of such reprints will continue to be subject to Rule 206(4)-1(a)(5). The SEC staff has indicated that an advertisement that reprints articles by an independent financial publication may be prohibited pursuant to Rule 206(4)-1(a)(5) if the reprint, together with the advertisement, implied something about or caused a reader to make an inference regarding: the experience of the adviser's clients; the possibility of a prospective client having a similar investment experience to that of prior clients; or the adviser's competence, when there are additional facts that if disclosed would imply different results.[43]

> *Compliance Notes: Misleading Professional Designations*
> *(Advisers Act Section 208)*
>
> Advisers may include professional designations in their advertising materials. Such designations can be seen as symbols of an adviser's professionalism, competence, trustworthiness, and qualifications. The SEC has turned a watchful eye to inclusion of designations in advertising materials. Advisers who include professional designations or qualifications in advertising materials must ensure that such use does not violate the general antifraud provision and/or Section 208 of the Advisers Act, which prohibits investment advisers from representing or implying that any governmental entity or agency has sponsored, recommended, or approved the adviser's business or qualifications.

---

[42] Richard Silverman, SEC No-Action Letter (pub. avail. Mar. 27, 1985); New York Investors Group, Inc., SEC No-Action Letter (pub. avail. Sept. 7, 1982). *See also* Kurtz Capital Management, SEC No-Action Letter (pub. avail. Jan. 18, 1988) (stating that bona-fide unbiased third party reports are generally not subject to the prohibition against testimonials and the distribution of a bona-fide article drafted by an unbiased third party is not subject to the requirements of Rule 206(4)-1(a)(2) where past specific recommendations happen to be referred to within the article).

[43] Stalker Advisory Services, SEC No-Action Letter (pub. avail. Jan. 18, 1994); New York Investors Group, Inc., SEC No-Action Letter (pub. avail. Sept. 7, 1982).

More specifically, Advisers Act Section 208(b) permits advisers to state that they are registered, provided that the adviser is in fact registered, and provided that the adviser does not misrepresent the effect of such registration. In the adopting release replacing Part II of Form ADV with Parts 2A and 2B (the "Form ADV Amendment Adopting Release"), the SEC clarified that, to avoid "misrepresent[ing] the effect of such registration," an adviser who refers to itself as a "registered investment adviser" on the cover page of Part 2A of Form ADV *must* accompany such reference with the disclaimer that such registration does not imply a certain level of skill or training.[44] The SEC is not only concerned with implications accompanying the use of the term *registered* on Form ADV but the commission has also expressed disapproval of the term's use in advertising materials. For example, the Form ADV Amendment Adopting Release states "that the emphasis on SEC registration, in some advisers' marketing materials, appears to suggest that registration either carries some official imprimatur or indicates that the adviser has attained a particular level of skill or ability" in violation of Section 208.[45] Specifically, an adviser's inclusion of the registered designation must not be done in a way that implies any level of professional competence, education or special training. Further, using the term *registered investment adviser* (RIA) in advertising materials is also viewed as inherently misleading because it implies that it is a formally recognized designation—one that requires qualifications to attain—akin to CPA for certified public accountants or CFA for chartered financial analysts.

By the same logic, advisers should avoid including *any* professional designation on advertising materials that tends to indicate a degree of skill/competence where the designation requires no formal qualifications to attain. Inclusion of such a designation might be considered inherently misleading.

Compliance Notes: Third-Party Social Media Communications as Testimonials

In March of 2014, the SEC issued guidance (the "2014 Guidance") on the publication of third-party social media information that was previously considered a grey area of permissible testimonials.[46] Advisers are now permitted to maintain links from their own websites to social media sites containing testimonial commentary from the general public so long as the following guidelines are followed:

- *Independence of the Social Media Website.* The social media website must be independent of the investment adviser and its affiliated parties. The investment adviser could advertise on the social media website if it is apparent that any public commentary is separate from the advertisement, and if the website does not alter the public commentary as a result of receiving advertising revenue from the adviser;

---

[44] *Amendments to Form ADV*, SEC Rel. No. IA-3060 (Oct. 12, 2010) at p.11.
[45] SEC, *Amendments to Form ADV*, at n. 29.
[46] *Guidance on the Testimonial Rule and Social Media*, Guidance Update, Division of Investment Management, SEC, No. 2014-04 (Mar. 2014).

- *Independence of Third-Party Commentary.* Neither the investment adviser nor its personnel may directly or indirectly author any commentary or pay others to author commentary on the linked social media site;
- *Completeness of Content.* All public commentary must be viewable, and any searchable or sortable functions must be in a content-neutral manner; and
- *No Modification of Content.* The social media website must allow for independent commentary on an unrestricted, real-time basis. The adviser may not modify third-party content in any way, including by suppressing or prioritizing any content. However, the social media website may modify or remove content in accordance with its published content guidelines, for example, to remove defamatory statements, profanity, racially offensive statements, or material that infringes on intellectual property rights.[47]

Even with the expanded scope of permissible links, the SEC urged caution regarding client lists and community pages as areas commonly found on social media sites that may continue to be treated as impermissible testimonials. Social media site staples, such as "friends lists," continue to be permissible so long as the list does not indicate that the "friends" have received favorable results and that the list has not been presented or manipulated in a manner that would paint a more favorable picture of the adviser. Community pages from third-party sites should be entirely independent of the adviser and not intended solely to provide information on advisers or investment management in general. For example, third-party content posted to an independent social media site like Facebook or LinkedIn may be viewed differently by the SEC than an adviser linking to a fan page on a site dedicated to offering investment management information.

The 2014 Guidance offers little on how compliance policies should be updated to reflect the clarification of use of third-party social media sites, so it is still advisable to consult OCIE's National Examination Risk Alert addressing investment adviser use of social media (the "OCIE Risk Alert") where it does not conflict with the 2014 Guidance.[48] Otherwise, advisers should consider implementing policies that:

- Expressly identify the social media websites that the investment adviser and its employees may use for business purposes, and require approval by the firm's CCO or another appropriate officer to add websites to this list;
- Prohibit employees from asking clients or the public to post comments about the adviser or any of its personnel, and, in particular, prohibit employees from requesting positive commentary or providing a benefit such as a discount in services in exchange for posting a comment;
- Prohibit employees from posting unauthorized comments on the adviser's social media sites; and
- Prohibit any manipulation of third-party posts on the adviser's social media sites.

The OCIE Risk Alert takes the position that social media communications are *advertisements* and that third-party social media content regarding an adviser *may* constitute prohibited testimonials, whereas the 2014 Guidance addressed independent social media

---

[47] *Id.*
[48] OCIE's National Examination Risk Alert: *Investment Adviser Use of Social Media* (Jan. 4, 2012).

sites. As discussed above, Rule 206(4)-(1)(a) prohibits the use of testimonials in adviser advertisements. The OCIE Risk Alert extends this principle to statements posted by third parties on adviser-sponsored social media pages, saying that such statements, if testimonials, would constitute a violation of federal securities laws. Whether a third-party statement is a testimonial depends on all of the facts and circumstances relating to the statement; however, the SEC generally considers any statement of a former, current, or existing client regarding the client's experience with, or endorsement of, an adviser to be a testimonial, regardless of whether the statements are related to performance.

Past Specific Recommendations

Performance-Based Past Recommendations. In the adopting release to Rule 206(4)-1, the SEC emphasized its belief that advertisements that refer only to profitable recommendations and ignore unprofitable ones are "inherently misleading and deceptive" in absence of a list containing all recommendations made within the immediately preceding period of at least one year.[49] The commission further stated that the underlying concern of the rule was the act of misleading prospective clients regarding the adviser's investment performance by emphasizing profitable recommendations while ignoring unprofitable ones, a practice commonly referred to as "cherry picking."[50] Rule 206(4)-1(a)(2) makes it a fraudulent, deceptive, or manipulative act, practice, or course of business for any registered investment adviser to publish, circulate, or distribute any advertisement that makes a direct or indirect reference to past specific recommendations of the adviser that were or would have been profitable unless the advertisement sets out or offers to furnish *free of charge* a list of all recommendations made within the immediately preceding period of not less than one year;[51] and the advertisement (or list if furnished separately) contains the following pieces of information:

- The name of each security recommended;
- The date and nature of each recommendation (e.g., buy, hold or sell);
- The market price at that time;
- The price at which the recommendation was to be acted upon;
- The market price of each listed security as of the most recent practicable date; and
- The following legend on the first page in print or type as large as the largest print or type used:

> It should not be assumed that recommendations made in the future will be profitable or will equal the performance of the securities in this list.

---

[49] SEC, *Advertisements by Investment Advisers*.

[50] *Id. See also* The TCW Group, Inc., SEC No-Action Letter (pub. Avail. Nov. 7, 2008) (stating that presentation of equal number of best and worst-performing holdings during a measure period under certain conditions would not raise the dangers that Rule 206(4)-1(a)(2) was designed to prevent); Franklin Management, Inc. (pub. avail. Dec. 10, 1998) (stating that use of objective, non-performance based selection criteria of past specific recommendations in reports issued by an adviser will not raise the dangers of cherry picking, which the rule was designed to prevent); National Corporate Sciences, Inc. (pub. avail. July 24, 1976) (rule serves to protect against misleading clients about the adviser's performance by referring only to profitable recommendations while ignoring unprofitable ones); Starr and Kuehl, Inc. (pub. avail. Apr. 17, 1976) (same).

[51] In Scientific Market Analysis, the SEC staff stated that Rule 206(4)-1(a)(2) "could be interpreted to require that such list be furnished free of charge to prospective clients, since an adviser might be able to avoid the rule's requirements by charging a fee for a list of recommendations for which prospective clients might be unwilling to pay." *Scientific Market Analysis*, SEC No-Action Letter (pub. avail. Mar. 24, 1976).

In *Scientific Market Analysis,* the SEC staff clarified that the earliest recommendation referred to in an advertisement would establish the beginning period from which the list of all recommendations must be presented.[52] For instance, if an adviser wanted to refer to profitable securities recommendations made for the period from 2002 to the present, the adviser must include in its list every recommendation made from 2002 to the present.[53]

Partial List of Recommendations. Although contrary to the plain language of the rule, the commission staff interprets Rule 206(4)-1(a)(2) strictly to preclude any references in advertisements to past specific recommendations that were or would have been profitable without setting out all past recommendations during the preceding year, even when accompanied by an offer to provide such information separately.[54] Therefore, an adviser may not refer to select recommendations in its advertisements with an offer to furnish the remainder. Rather, Rule 206(4)-1(a)(2) permits advertisements that either contain a full list of recommendations made during the preceding period of not less than one year with certain disclosures or offer to provide such a list.[55]

Best- and Worst-Performing Holdings Charts. The SEC staff has provided no-action relief to investment advisers to distribute charts to existing and prospective clients showing the best- and worst-performing individual holdings in a representative account for a particular investment strategy during a measurement period.[56] In The TCW Group, Inc., the holdings charts reflected the average weight of the holdings and the contribution of these holdings to the account's return during the period presented.[57] In granting the relief, the SEC staff stated that it relied on the following conditions:

- The best and worst holdings are selected by taking into account consistently the weighting of every holding in a representative account that contributed to the account's performance during a period of time (the "Measurement Period");
- The Measurement Period consists of at least a full calendar month, as computed as of the most recent calendar month's last trading day;
- The presentation of information and number of holdings is consistent from period to period;

---

[52] *Id.* ("[T]he earliest recommendation referred to establishes the pertinent time period.").
[53] *Id.*
[54] *See* Mr. Norman L. Yu & Company, Inc. (pub. avail. Apr. 12, 1971) ("[A]ny advertisement by an investment adviser which contains a partial list of recommendations and an offer to furnish a list of all recommendations made during the previous 12-month period would be viewed by us as an attempt to 'whet the appetite' of the general public and would clearly be in violation of [Rule 206(4)-1] and be deemed to be a misleading and fraudulent advertisement."). *See also* Dow Theory Forecasts, Inc., SEC No-Action Letter (pub. avail. Nov. 7, 1985) ("Rule 206(4)-1(a)(2) under the [Advisers] Act does not permit an advertisement which refers to selected past recommendations of an investment adviser which were or would have been profitable to any person, even if the advertisement offers to provide a list of all recommendations made by the adviser within the past year."); James B. Peeke & Company, Inc., SEC No-Action Letter (pub. avail. Sept. 13, 1982); Scientific Market Analysis (pub. avail. Mar. 24, 1976); J. D. Minnick & Company, SEC No-Action Letter (pub. avail. Apr. 30, 1975); Mr. Charles Swanson, SEC No-Action Letter (pub. avail. Apr. 10, 1972).
[55] *See* Dow Theory Forecasts, Inc., SEC No-Action Letter (pub. avail. Nov. 7, 1985); J. D. Minnick & Company, SEC No-Action Letter (pub. avail. Apr. 30, 1975).
[56] *See* The TCW Group, Inc. SEC No-Action Letter (pub. Avail. Nov. 7, 2008).
[57] *Id.* The calculation used to show the impact on the account's performance during the period was the weight invested in each holding (i.e., percentage of the total account) multiplied by the rate of return for that holding during the period.

- The chart shows no fewer than a total of ten holdings, including an equal number of the best and worst performing holdings during the Measurement Period (i.e., Top 5/Bottom 5, at a minimum);
- The chart includes the following disclosures in close proximity (i.e., on the same page) to the performance information—
  - How to obtain the calculation's methodology,
  - How to obtain a list showing every holding's contribution to the overall account's performance during the measurement period,
  - That the holdings identified do not represent all of the securities purchased, sold or recommended for the adviser's clients, and
  - That past performance does not guarantee future results;
- The chart includes all information necessary to make the chart not misleading, including presenting the best- and worst-performing holdings on the same page with equal prominence, and
- The following records are maintained and made available to the sec staff upon request—
  - Criteria used to select the specific securities listed,
  - A list showing the contribution of each holding in the representative account to the overall account's performance during the measurement period, and
  - All supporting data necessary to demonstrate the calculation of the chart's contribution analysis and to demonstrate the appropriateness of the holdings included in the chart.[58]

Compliance Notes: Best- and Worst-Performing Holdings

Note that in the The TCW Group, Inc. no-action letter the staff did not permit the presentation of actual performance of the best and worst performing securities, but rather only the average weight of the best and worst performing holdings in a representative account during a specified period, and the impact of those holdings on the representative account's return overall. Any presentation of raw actual security performance would be outside the scope of the The TCW Group, Inc. no-action letter and the staff's grant of relief thereunder.

Article Reprints. In New York Investors Group, Inc. and Dow Theory Forecasts, Incorporated, the SEC staff took the position that the inclusion in an advertisement of an article that commends an adviser for its ability to select stocks that perform well in favorable and unfavorable market conditions is an indirect reference to the adviser's past specific recommendations and violates Rule 206(4)-1(a)(2) unless it contains all the recommendations made by the adviser within the preceding year.[59] However, the SEC staff seemingly reversed its position in Kurtz Capital Management when it stated

---

[58] *Id.*
[59] Dow Theory Forecasts, Incorporated, SEC No-Action Letter (pub. avail. Nov. 7, 1985) (advertisement of a *New York Post* article that contains references to past specific recommendations made by an adviser must satisfy the requirements in Rule 206(4)-1(a)(2)); New York Investors Group, Inc., SEC No-Action Letter (pub. avail. Sept. 7, 1982) (finding that quoting an article that lauds the Company or its officer's success in selecting stocks is an indirect reference to past specific recommendations in violation of Rule 206(4)-1(a)(2) without referencing all past recommendations within the preceding year).

that the distribution of an article drafted by an unbiased third party that "happens" to refer to past specific recommendations made by the adviser is not subject to the requirements of Rule 206(4)-1(a)(2), but is still subject to the prohibition against misleading and fraudulent advertisements under Rule 206(4)-1(a)(5).[60]

Nonperformance Based Recommendations. In Franklin Management, Inc., the staff broadened its interpretation of the Rule 206(4)-1(a)(2) to permit discussions of past specific securities bought, sold or held for the adviser's accounts in quarterly reports to existing and prospective clients so long as:

- The securities discussed are selected on objective, nonperformance based criteria;
- The same selection criteria will be consistently applied each quarter;
- The advertisement does not discuss, directly or indirectly, realized or unrealized profits or losses of the named securities;
- The advertisements include cautionary disclosures; and
- The adviser maintains, and makes available to the sec staff upon request, records that evidence:
  – The complete list of all securities recommended by the adviser in the preceding year for the specific investment category covered by the advertisement,
  – The information set forth in Rule 206(4)-1(a)(2) for each recommendation, and
  – The criteria used to select the specific securities listed in each advertisement.[61]

The SEC staff believed that the use of objective, nonperformance selection criteria and the omission of any discussion on the profitability of any security would limit the ability of the adviser to cherry pick profitable recommendations and mislead prospective clients about the adviser's performance.[62] In *Franklin Management, Inc.*, the staff also clarified that advertisements that identify and discuss current or unprofitable recommendations of the adviser are not within the prohibitions of the rule.[63] However, while current or unprofitable recommendations are not prohibited under the rule, it is difficult, if not impossible, to predict whether, at the time such recommendations are written, the listed securities held in the portfolio will subsequently be sold or whether the unprofitable holdings will subsequently become profitable.

> *Compliance Notes: Past Specific Recommendations*
>
> - *Case Studies.* Investment adviser marketing materials commonly include "case studies" intended to illustrate the adviser's application of its investment strategy and the types of investments that the strategy intends to focus on, particularly when advertising self-distributed private funds. These case studies should be considered to be the adviser's past specific recommendations and must comply with staff guidance (i.e., the Franklin

---

[60] Kurtz Capital Management, SEC No-Action Letter (pub. avail. Jan. 18, 1988).
[61] Franklin Management, Inc., SEC No-Action Letter (pub. avail. Dec. 10, 1998).
[62] *Id.*
[63] Franklin Management, Inc., SEC No-Action Letter, at n. 11.

no-action letter) unless the security name and other identifying information are omitted from the advertisement. In the event that such information is omitted, the material must still comply with general antifraud rules and should not overly emphasize successful examples (i.e., cherry picking) in a manner that implies the adviser only picks "winners."

- *Documentation and Disclosure.* The Franklin no-action letter does not explicitly require that the adviser *disclose* the objective, nonperformance based criteria used to select the securities presented; however, as a matter of best practices, compliance personnel should consider requiring disclosure of the selection criteria to give the recipient a better understanding of how the securities were selected for presentation. Such disclosure will help compliance personnel ensure that
    - The criteria are truly objective and not based on performance,
    - The same criteria are applied consistently, and
    - The adviser satisfies the requirement to maintain records of such selection criteria.
- *Press Releases/Current Recommendations.* Many advisers post press releases to their public websites announcing major acquisitions by the firm. Where such acquisitions involve portfolio holdings, such an announcement could be construed to be an advertisement that presents the adviser's "recommendation." The fact that the "recommendation" (if deemed to be a recommendation) would be a recommendation for the adviser (and not advisory clients) does not take it out of the past specific recommendation prohibition because Rule 206(4)-1(a)(2) under the Advisers Act makes it unlawful for an investment adviser to publish, circulate, or distribute an advertisement which refers, directly or indirectly, to past specific recommendations of such investment adviser which were *or would have been* profitable to *any person* (which could be interpreted to include the adviser itself). One could argue that such a press release would constitute a *current* recommendation rather than a past recommendation, but this line becomes blurry as time passes on and the material remains publicly available. An adviser's current recommendations, though not subject to the Rule 206(4)-1(a)(2) prohibition on past specific recommendations, may very well become past recommendations if an advertisement is distributed (or remains publicly available) after the adviser ceases recommending any of the particular securities presented.[64] Accordingly, to avoid violating the prohibition on past specific recommendations, advisers should consider complying with the conditions of the Franklin no-action letter with respect to such press releases (namely, that the adviser publishes such press releases announcing all acquisitions that satisfy specified objective criteria, such as all acquisitions over a certain size).

---

[64] Franklin Management, Inc., SEC No-Action Letter (pub. avail. Dec. 10, 1998), at n. 9.

Charts and Formulas

Rule 206(4)-1(a)(3) under the Advisers Act prohibits an adviser from making any claim in its advertisements that a graph, chart, formula or other device being offered can be used to determine which securities to buy or sell, when to buy or sell the securities, or will assist persons in making such decisions, unless the limitations and difficulties regarding the use of the device are prominently disclosed.[65] The SEC staff has clarified that the former restriction is absolute; that is, an advertisement may never make a claim that a device can be used to make decisions on which securities to buy or sell, or the timing of such decisions, irrespective of what limitations and difficulties are discussed.[66]

> ### *Compliance Notes: Charts and Formulas*
>
> Advertisements that contain charts and formulas (as with all advertisements) are also subject to the catchall provision under the advertising rule. Compliance personnel should be carefully review the disclosures regarding the assumptions underlying charts and formulas included in advertisements and the defined terminology that is used to ensure that all material facts are disclosed (particularly in light of the fact that the omission of a material fact necessary to make the information presented not misleading is a violation of the general antifraud provision).

Free Reports or Services

Rule 206(4)-1(a)(4) prohibits the distribution of an advertisement that states that any report, analysis, or other service will be furnished for free or without charge if there are any conditions or obligations connected with the receipt of such report, analysis, or service.[67]

Antifraud Catchall Provision

Rule 206(4)-1(a)(5) deems it to be a fraudulent, deceptive or manipulative act, practice, or course of business within the meaning of Section 206(4) of the Advisers Act for any adviser to distribute, directly or indirectly, any advertisement that contains an untrue statement of material fact or that is otherwise false or misleading.[68] This is

---

[65] Rule 206(4)-1(a)(3) under the Advisers Act.
[66] Bache & Co. Incorporated, SEC No-Action Letter (pub. avail. Feb. 5, 1976); Mottin Forecast, SEC No-Action Letter (pub. avail. Nov. 29, 1975); S. H. Dike & Company, Inc., SEC No-Action Letter (pub. avail. Apr. 20, 1975); Investor Intelligence, SEC No-Action Letter (pub. avail. Apr. 18, 1975).
[67] Rule 206(4)-1(a)(4) under the Advisers Act. *See,* e.g., Dow Theory Forecasts, Inc., SEC No-Action Letter (pub. avail. May 21, 1986) (stating that an advertisement's offer of a free subscription to an investment newsletter on the condition that the Dow Jones Industrial Average not rise 10 points during the subscription period violates Rule 206(4)-1(a)(5)).
[68] Rule 206(4)-1(a)(5) under the Advisers Act.

a catchall provision that is used by the SEC to sanction investment adviser firms for advertising violations that do not fit within the specific prohibitions listed in subparagraphs (a)(1) through (a)(4) of Rule 206(4)-1. Whether an advertisement is false or misleading under Rule 206(4)-1(a)(5) largely depends upon the particular facts and circumstances.[69] An adviser should consider the following three factors when conducting an analysis under Rule 206(4)-1(a)(5):

- *The form and content of the advertisement:* An adviser should make sure that all relevant information is included in the advertisement so that its audience receives a clear and unbiased picture of the adviser's investment skills;[70]
- *The implications that arise out of the context of the communication:* An adviser should examine its advertisement to determine whether the audience may infer something about the adviser's competence or future investment results that would not be true had the advertisement included all material facts;[71] and
- *The prospective client's sophistication:* An adviser should determine whether the advertisement is being presented to a sophisticated client in a one-on-one presentation, to a retail investor, or distributed broadly through a newspaper, magazine, radio, or on the internet.[72]

An advertisement may be deemed to be misleading even if each individual statement in an advertisement is factually correct. In *In re Spear & Staff, Incorporated*, the SEC found that the advertisements at issue "were deceptive and misleading in their overall effect even though it might be argued that when narrowly and literally read, no single statement of a material fact was false."[73] Generally, an advertisement may be considered false or misleading if it implies something about the adviser or its client's experiences that is not true, or that the client would not have inferred if the adviser had disclosed all material facts.[74]

II. PERFORMANCE ADVERTISING

Definitions

Table 2 defines terms commonly used in performance advertising.

---

[69] Franklin Management, Inc., SEC No-Action Letter (pub. avail. Dec. 10, 1998).
[70] For example, an adviser that directs his or her clients' investments in mutual fund shares has a duty to disclose that in addition to the adviser's fees, additional fees, and expenses associated with an investment in mutual fund shares will be incurred. See James B. Peeke & Company, Incorporated, SEC No-Action Letter (pub. avail. Sept. 13, 1982).
[71] See, e.g., In re Valicenti Advisory Services, Inc., SEC Rel. No. IA-1774 (Nov. 18, 1998) (concluding that an adviser willfully violated Section 206(1) and Rule 206(4)-1(a)(5) thereunder for, among other things, presenting performance of a "composite" that failed to disclose that the performance reflected was achieved only by a small sampling of accounts chosen by the adviser's principal).
[72] See, e.g., In re LBS Capital Management, Inc., SEC Rel. No. IA-1644 (July 18, 1997); Clover Capital Management, Inc., SEC No-Action Letter (pub. avail. Oct. 28, 1986); Anametrics Investment Management, SEC No-Action Letter (pub. avail. May 5, 1977); In re Spear & Staff, Inc., SEC Rel. No. IA-188 (Mar. 25, 1965).
[73] In re Spear & Staff, Incorporated.
[74] Investment Adviser Association, SEC No-Action Letter (pub. avail. Dec. 2, 2005).

TABLE 2. PERFORMANCE ADVERTISING TERMS	
Benchmark	A basis of measurement used to compare investment performance (e.g., Standard & Poor's 500 Composite Index).
Composite	An aggregation into a single performance presentation of individual portfolios or asset classes that are managed pursuant to a similar investment objective or strategy.
Gross-of-Fee Performance	Performance that does not reflect the payment of investment advisory fees and other expenses that would be incurred in the management of an investment account. Gross-of-fee performance under the Global Investment Performance Standards (GIPS) must reflect trading expenses (e.g., brokerage commissions) that were incurred during the periods presented. This performance does not include any fees paid to the adviser.[a]
Hypothetical Back-Tested Performance	Theoretical performance obtained by retroactively applying a particular investment strategy (e.g., quantitative) to historical financial data to show what decisions would have been made and what performance would have been obtained if the strategy had been employed over a select market period.
Model Performance	Performance that is created by adjusting actual performance using hypothetical assumptions.
Net-of-Fee Performance	Performance that reflects the payment of investment advisory fees and all other fees paid to the adviser and other expenses that would be incurred in the management of an investment account, such as transaction costs.[b]
Portability	The ability of one adviser to reference in its own performance presentation the historical performance record of either a predecessor firm or that of the adviser's portfolio managers achieved while at another firm.

[a] In a wrap-fee context, a pure gross number that does not reflect advisory fees or transaction costs may be shown alongside a pure net number.
[b] Although the SEC has not specifically addressed the treatment of performance fees, net-of-fee performance should also reflect the deduction of performance-based fees. This approach is consistent with the SEC position that net performance should reflect the performance actually attained by advisory clients.

General Requirements

Although the SEC does not prescribe the method by which investment advisers must calculate or present their past performance, the SEC does rely upon Rule 206(4)-1(a)(5) to police what it deems to be fraudulent or misleading advertising of performance. In one of the most seminal advertising no-action letters issued by the SEC staff, Clover Capital Management, Inc.,[75] the SEC staff took the opportunity to articulate the advertising practices in connection with the presentation of either model or actual returns that it believed were prohibited under Rule 206(4)-1(a)(5). Advisers should not rely on the Clover Capital no-action letter as a safe harbor when presenting actual and model returns, nor should advisers consider the Clover Capital list to be an exhaustive list of all factors to be considered.[76] However, when advertising an adviser's performance, the adviser must ensure that it at a minimum, it discloses the factors articulated in Clover Capital, including that it disclose:

---

[75] Clover Capital Management, Inc. (Oct. 28, 1986).
[76] Id.

- The effect of material market or economic conditions on the results portrayed;[77]
- Disclose whether and to what extent the results portrayed reflect the reinvestment of dividends and other earnings;[78]
- If the advertisement suggests or makes claims about the potential for profit, disclose the possibility of loss;
- If performance of model or actual results is compared to an index, disclose all material facts relevant to the comparison (for example, disclose, if applicable, that the volatility of an index materially differs from a model portfolio);[79]
- Disclose any material conditions, objectives, or strategies used to obtain the results portrayed (for example, failure to disclose that certain investment practices or instruments contributed overwhelmingly to performance, especially when it is doubtful that the performance could be expected to continue including IPO investments or other material events that may not repeat themselves);[80]
- Disclose, if applicable, that actual results portrayed relate only to a select group of the adviser's clients, the basis on which the selection was made, and any material effect of this practice on the results portrayed; and[81]
- Any other material factors that affected performance.

Moreover, the SEC staff has clearly stated that a disclaimer to the effect of "Past performance is not a guarantee of future returns" may not, in and of itself, be sufficient to cure a misleading presentation.[82] Each communication of the adviser should be reviewed in its totality to determine whether its audience may infer something about the adviser or its competence that would not be true if all material facts were presented.

Model Performance

The term *model performance* generally refers to the actual performance results achieved by applying a particular investment strategy to a model portfolio of securities, but results that do not reflect actual trading or the adviser's decision making for the par-

---

[77] See Edward F. O'Keefe (Apr. 13, 1978) ("Information concerning performance of accounts over a period or periods attended by special market characteristics may imply or cause an inference to be drawn about the competence of the adviser or the possibility of a client enjoying a similar experience that would not arise if such characteristics were also disclosed.").

[78] See e.g., *In re Schield Management Company et al.*, Investment Advisers Act Rel. No. 1872 (May 31, 2000) (finding that an adviser violated Rule 206(4)-1(a)(5) for, among other things, failing to disclose that performance presented reflected the reinvestment of dividends).

[79] See, e.g., *Scientific Market Analysis* (Mar. 24, 1976) (stating that comparison of performance of hypothetical separate advisory accounts with a Lipper Mutual Fund Index may be inappropriate because individual advisory accounts are not likely to be as broadly diversified as a mutual fund portfolio).

[80] See, e.g., *In re The Dreyfus Corporation and Michael L. Schonberg,* Investment Advisers Act Rel. No. 1870 (May 10, 2000) (finding willful violation of section 206(2) for failing to disclose that a large portion of advertised performance was attributable to investments in IPOs); *In re Van Kampen Investment Advisory Corp. and Alan Sachtleben,* Investment Advisers Act Rel. No. 1819 (Sept. 8, 1999) (finding a willful violation of section 206(2) for failing to disclose that IPO securities had a large effect on the fund's return, a disclosure that "would have significantly altered the total mix of information available to investors").

[81] For instance, the SEC staff has indicated that the provision of performance covering select periods or select accounts would be misleading if other periods or other accounts would modify the implication that arises or the inference that is drawn from the information as originally presented. See Edward F. O'Keefe (Apr. 13, 1978).

[82] See Edward F. O'Keefe (Apr. 13, 1978).

ticular strategy presented. Neither Section 206 of the Advisers Act nor Rule 206(4)-1 thereunder speaks to the use of model performance results. The SEC staff, however, has explicitly stated, "The applicable legal standard governing the advertising of model or actual results is that contained in paragraph (5) of the rule, that is, whether the particular advertisement is false or misleading."[83] At least thirty years ago, the SEC staff took the position that the advertisement of model performance was per se misleading and could not be cured by any amount of disclosure.[84] The SEC staff eventually abandoned this position and currently permits model disclosure so long as it is not false or misleading in contravention of Rule 206(4)-1(a)(5). In Clover Capital, the SEC staff clarified that advisers who present model returns must equip prospective investors with additional information in light of the heightened chance that model returns may give rise to an erroneous inference about future investment returns.[85]

In addition to the presentation and disclosure requirements applicable to both model and actual returns, the SEC staff opined that an adviser would be prohibited by Rule 206(4)-1(a)(5) from presenting model performance unless the adviser also discloses:

- The limitations inherent in model results, particularly that model returns do not reflect actual trading and may not reflect the effect that material economic and market factors may have had on the adviser's decision-making had the adviser actually managed client funds;
- Material changes in the conditions, objectives, or investment strategies of the model portfolio during the time period portrayed in the advertisement and the effect of any such change on the results portrayed (if applicable);
- That some or all of the securities or strategies reflected in the model portfolio do not relate, or only partially relate, to the services currently offered by the adviser (for example, the model reflects securities that are no longer recommended for clients) (if applicable);[86] and
- That the adviser's clients had investment results materially different from the results portrayed in the model (if applicable).

Hypothetical Back-Tested Performance

Unlike model performance, back-tested performance presents hypothetical performance based upon the retroactive application of an adviser's investment strategy over a select market period. Great care should be taken when presenting back-tested performance, which is regarded as highly suspect by the SEC. Back-tested returns

---

[83] Clover Capital Management, Inc. (Oct. 28, 1986).
[84] See, e.g., A.R. Schmeidler & Co. Inc. (June 1, 1976) ("In fact, in view of the misleading nature of performance figures of a hypothetical fund it is doubtful whether any form of disclosure would offset the misleading impact of such figures without at the same time making clear that such figures are essentially meaningless."). See also Clover Capital Management, Inc. (Oct. 28, 1986) ("The staff no longer takes the position, as it did a number of years ago, that the use of model or actual results in an advertisement is per se fraudulent under section 206(4) and the rules thereunder, particularly Rule 206(4)-1(a)(5).").
[85] Clover Capital Management, Inc. (Oct. 28, 1986).
[86] The SEC has admonished an investment adviser for advertising hypothetical returns based upon a timing system that was no longer in use by the adviser. See In re Bond Timing Services, Inc. and Vilis Pasts, Investment Advisers Act Rel. No. 920 (July 23, 1984).

should only be presented to sophisticated (that is, nonretail) clients.[87] Through enforcement actions addressing this practice, the SEC has admonished advisers for failing to disclose the following in connection with the presentation of hypothetical back-tested returns:

- Back-tested performance was derived from the retroactive application of a model developed with the benefit of hindsight (for example, disclosure that the adviser began to offer its strategy after the period depicted);[88]
- The inherent limitations of data derived from the retroactive application of a model developed with the benefit of hindsight (e.g., performance results do not represent actual trading) and the reasons why actual results may differ; [89]
- Whether the trading strategies retroactively applied were not available during the periods presented;[90]
- That actual performance with client accounts was materially less than the advertised hypothetical results for the same period (if applicable);[91]
- All material economic and market factors that may have affected the adviser's decision making when using the model to actually manage client funds;[92]
- Whether the advertised performance reflects the deduction of advisory fees, brokerage or other commissions, and any other expenses that a client would have paid;[93]
- All material facts relevant to any comparison between back-tested performance and its benchmark;[94] and
- The potential for loss.[95]

With respect to the requirement that advisers disclose that back-tested performance was derived from the retroactive application of a model developed with the benefit of hindsight, the SEC has indicated that labeling back-tested returns as "pro forma" or "hypothetical," in and of itself, is insufficient to satisfy this requirement.[96] Moreover, the SEC has stated that the inclusion of general disclaimers to the effect of,

---

[87] *In re LBS Capital Management* (stating that in concluding that an advertisement containing back tested performance was misleading, the SEC considered that the advertisement was distributed to existing and prospective retail clients).
[88] *In re Schield Management Company; In re Meridian Investment Management Corp. et al.*, Investment Advisers Act Rel. No. 1779 (Dec. 28, 1998); *In re LBS Capital Management, Inc.*, Investment Advisers Act Rel. No. 1644 (July 18, 1997); *In re Patricia Owen-Michel*, Investment Advisers Act Rel. No. 1584 (Sept. 27, 1996).
[89] *In re Market Timing Systems, Inc. et al.*, Investment Advisers Act Rel. No. 2047 (Aug. 28, 2002); *In re Schield Management Company*. For instance, in *In re Schield Management Company*, the SEC admonished an adviser for failing to disclose that the hypothetical strategy, when actually executed, underperformed its benchmark even though the back-tested performance presented showed that the hypothetical strategy consistently outperformed the benchmark each year.
[90] *See, e.g., In re Leeb Investment Advisors et al.*, Investment Advisers Act Rel. No. 1545 (Jan. 16, 1996) (admonishing an adviser under section 17(a)(2) of the Securities Act and section 34(b) of the Advisers Act for stating that an investor could turn an investment made in 1980 into millions by the 1990s without disclosing that this result would depend on using trading strategies that were not available in 1980).
[91] *In re Market Timing Systems. See also In re Profitek, Inc. and Edward G. Smith*, Investment Advisers Act Rel. No. 1764 (Sept. 29, 1998) (finding a violation of section 206(4) and Rule 206(4)-1(a)(5) thereunder, among other violations, for failing to disclose that performance data of model portfolios were based on hypothetical stock transactions that bore no resemblance to the actual performance of its client accounts).
[92] *In re Patricia Owen-Michel*.
[93] *Id.*
[94] *Id.*
[95] *Id.*
[96] *In re Schield Management Company*.

"Future results based upon past performance, including hypothetical returns, cannot be guaranteed" is also insufficient to remove the erroneous suggestion that the performance was achieved through actual trading.[97] The SEC in *In re LBS Capital Management, Inc.*, noted that disclosure that back-tested returns were "pro-forma" and that "actual results were available upon request" was insufficient to convey that the advertised performance were achieved by retroactive application of a model, or otherwise dispel the misleading suggestion that the advertised performance represented actual trading.[98]

Gross-of-Fee and Net-of-Fee Performance

Net-of-Fee Performance. Generally, investment adviser performance must be advertised after the deduction of advisory fees, brokerage or other commissions, and any expenses that a client paid or would have paid, unless an exception applies.[99] Except under limited circumstances described later, the SEC staff deems the presentation of gross-of-fee performance alone to be misleading under Rule 206(4)-1(a)(5) because an average investor would make an inference about the future returns of the adviser or its competence that would not be true if the adviser had presented returns on a net-of-fee basis.[100] This is largely because gross-of-fee returns fail to reflect the effect that fees have on performance or the compounded effect on performance of not deducting fees.[101]

Custodial Fees. The SEC staff has clarified that custodial fees do not have to be reflected in net-of-fee returns because custodians are ordinarily selected and paid directly by advisory clients.[102]

Multimanager Account Performance. An adviser that manages only a portion of a client's account may advertise performance figures relating only to that portion of the account so long as performance is shown net of all transaction costs and advisory fees or charges paid to the adviser or its affiliates.[103]

Gross-of-Fee Performance. As discussed above, investment adviser performance generally must be advertised after the deduction of advisory fees, brokerage or other commissions, and any expenses that a client paid or would have paid.[104] However, the SEC has permitted the presentation of gross-of-fee performance in three situations, subject to the conditions discussed below.

One-on-One Presentations. In a no-action letter issued to the Investment Company Institute (the "ICI II no-action letter"), the SEC staff permitted the presentation of gross-of-fee performance returns in a one-on-one presentation to certain prospective

---

[97] *In re Patricia Owen-Michel*.
[98] *In re LBS Capital Management*.
[99] *See Clover Capital Management, Inc.* (Oct. 28, 1986).
[100] *See Investment Company Institute* (Sept. 23, 1988). *See also In re Bond Timing Services, Inc. and Vilis Pasts*, Investment Advisers Act Rel. No. 920 (July 23, 1984) (finding an adviser to have fully violated section 206(4) and Rule 206(4)-1(a)(5) thereunder for distributing advertisements of annualized returns that did not reflect advisory fees, sales loads, and transfer fees).
[101] *Id.*
[102] *See Investment Company Institute* (Aug. 24, 1987).
[103] *See Association for Investment Management and Research*, SEC No-Action Letter (Dec. 18, 1996).
[104] *See Clover Capital Management, Inc.* (Oct. 28, 1986).

clients that are in a position to negotiate their advisory fees[105] (for example, wealthy individuals, pension funds, universities and other institutional investors) so long as the adviser provides the following disclosures to the client in writing:

- Performance disclosures do not reflect the deduction of advisory fees;
- The client's return will be reduced by the advisory fees and any other expenses it may incur in the management of its advisory account;
- The adviser's fees are described in part II of its Form ADV; and
- A representative example (for example, table, chart, graph, or narrative) that shows the effect an advisory fee, compounded over a period of years, could have on the total value of a client's portfolio.[106]

To constitute a "one-on-one presentation," the presentation must be private and confidential in nature and the prospective client must have ample opportunity to discuss the type of advisory fees that may be paid.[107] In addition, the presentation must not be publicly available through any print, electronic or other medium.[108]

> ### Compliance Notes: One-on-One Presentations
>
> As discussed in the compliance notes regarding the use of charts and formulas, above, once advertising materials are approved for use by compliance personnel and/or legal in one context, there is some risk that the materials will later be used in another context. Accordingly, compliance personnel should consider labeling the cover of any advertisement that contains standalone gross-of-fees performance (that is, gross-of-fees performance that is not presented side-by-side with net-of-fees performance, as "for use in one-on-one presentations only." In addition, the disclosures accompanying such materials should specify that the materials are only to be used with sophisticated clients in one-on-one settings.

Consultants. An adviser may present performance information to a consultant on a gross-of-fee basis in a one-on-one presentation so long as the adviser instructs the consultant to present such performance data to prospective clients only on a one-on-one basis with the disclosures set forth in the ICI II no-action letter.[109]

Side-by-Side Gross and Net-of-Fee Performance. In a no-action letter issued to the Association for Investment Management and Research, the SEC staff stated that an

---

[105] The SEC staff has acknowledged "a client's ability to negotiate fees with an adviser is directly related to the amount of client assets subject to the adviser's management." Investment Company Institute (Sept. 23, 1988). The SEC staff acknowledged that information on the fees and expenses associated with performance of other advisory clients is not as material to a client that has bargaining power over its advisory fees. *See* Clover Capital Management, Inc. (Oct. 28, 1986).
[106] *See* Investment Company Institute (Sept. 23, 1988).
[107] *Id.*
[108] *Id.*
[109] *See* Investment Company Institute (Sept. 23, 1988); Bypass Wall Street, Inc. (Jan. 7, 1992). In Clover Capital Management, Inc. (July 19, 1991), the SEC staff denied a request to allow the presentation of gross-of-fee performance to plan sponsors and investment consultants without complying with the conditions set forth in ICI II.

adviser may distribute an advertisement that presents composite performance on a gross and net-of-fee basis, so long as:

- The gross and net performance is presented with equal prominence;
- The presentation is in a format designed to facilitate the ease of comparison between the gross and net performance; and
- The advertisement contains sufficient disclosure (for example, that gross-of-fee performance does not reflect the payment of advisory fees and other expenses) that would ensure that the presentation is not otherwise misleading.[110]

Model Fees

An adviser may advertise performance reflecting the deduction of a model fee so long as:

- The resulting performance is no higher than the performance that would have resulted if actual fees were deducted;
- The performance reflects the deduction of the highest fee charged to any account managed in the same investment strategy during the applicable period;
- If the advertisement presents net performance that includes wrap and nonwrap fee accounts, the model fee must be equal to the highest fee charged for each type of account; and
- The advertisement must disclose that
  - For each strategy shown, the performance was reduced by the highest fee charged to any client employing that particular strategy during the period under consideration,
  - Actual fees may vary depending upon, among other things, the applicable fee schedule and portfolio size, and
  - The firm's fees are available on request and also may be found in Part 2A of its Form ADV.

Composites Containing Wrap and Nonwrap Accounts. There are two other situations in which the SEC staff has permitted "model" advisory fees to be used in lieu of the actual fee. These include advertisements that present composites containing both wrap and nonwrap fee accounts may calculate net-of-fee performance using the actual fees from wrap accounts and a model fee from nonwrap accounts, which is equal to the highest fee charged to a wrap fee account, so long as the advertisement contains sufficient disclosure to ensure that the information presented is not misleading.[111] The SEC has also addressed the concept of "pure gross" and "pure net" presentations of performance.[112]

Pure Net. Pure net-of-fees performance is performance shown less the fees charged related to the adviser's management of the account. These include all transaction

---

[110] Association for Investment Management and Research (Dec. 18, 1996).
[111] See Association for Investment Management and Research (Dec. 18, 1996).
[112] See Association for Investment Management and Research, SEC No-action letter (pub. avail. Dec. 18, 1996).

costs and all fees paid to the adviser or an affiliate of the adviser regardless of whether it is a multimanager account or not.[113]

Pure Gross. Pure gross-of-fees performance may be provided alongside the net-of-fees performance so long as both are presented with equal prominence and the presentation contains sufficient disclosure to ensure that the presentation is not misleading.[114]

Multimanager accounts. A composite that includes advisory accounts that consist of a portion of the assets of a multi-manager account[115] can be presented on a net-of-fee basis after deducting only those fees and costs related to the assets managed by the adviser, including transaction costs and all fees and charges paid by the account to the adviser or its affiliate, provided that it is accompanied with a statement that identifies those fees and costs that have been deducted.[116]

Portability

"Portability" of performance refers to the ability of one adviser to reference in its own performance presentation the historical performance record of either a predecessor firm or that of the adviser's portfolio managers achieved while at another firm. A number of SEC staff no-action letters considered whether an adviser's advertisement of performance results of accounts managed by a predecessor would be misleading and therefore deemed fraudulent for purposes of Section 206(4) and Rule 206(4)-1. These no-action letters take the position that an advertisement that includes prior performance of accounts managed by portfolio managers at their prior place of employment will not, in and of itself, be misleading under Section 206(4) and Rule 206(4)-1 thereunder so long as:

- The person(s) managing accounts at the successor adviser are also those primarily responsible for achieving the prior performance results;[117]

---

[113] *Id.*

[114] *Id.* Other than pure gross performance in a wrap fee context, all gross performance should reflect the deduction of transaction costs.

[115] In a multimanager account, different investment firms manage a discrete portion of the account's assets.

[116] *See* Association for Investment Management and Research (Dec. 18, 1996).

[117] Fiduciary Management Associates, Inc. (Mar. 5, 1984) (stating that it is not misleading for a new adviser to use the performance of another adviser when, among other things, the investment personnel are the same). *See also* Bramwell Growth Fund (Aug. 7, 1996) (finding that section 206 does not prohibit the inclusion in a mutual fund's prospectus performance of another registered investment company previously managed by the fund's portfolio manager provided that (1) no other individuals played a significant part in achieving the prior performance, and (2) the performance is not presented in a misleading manner and does not obscure or impede understanding of information required to be in the prospectus); Great Lakes Advisors, Inc. (Apr. 3, 1992) (finding that it may be misleading for an adviser to advertise the performance results of accounts managed at an employee's prior place of employment when the employee was one of several persons responsible for selecting the securities for those accounts). The SEC staff has clarified that whether this requirement is satisfied requires a review of the investment team both at the prior firm and the new firm. That is, the individuals primarily responsible for achieving the prior performance results must also be those individuals primarily responsible for the accounts at the new firm. *See* Horizon Asset Management, LLC (Sept. 13, 1996). In Horizon Asset Management, the SEC staff found that although the sole portfolio manager who was responsible for achieving the prior performance was now a member of an advisory committee at his new firm, this in and of itself would not bar the portability of the prior performance so long as the portfolio manager was actually responsible for making investment decisions without the need for consensus from the other committee members. *See id.*

- The accounts managed at the predecessor adviser are so similar to the accounts currently under management that the performance would provide relevant information to prospective clients of the successor adviser;[118]
- All accounts that were managed in a substantially similar manner are advertised unless the exclusion of any such account would not result in materially higher performance;[119]
- If all accounts that were managed in a substantially similar manner are not advertised, the advertisement discloses the criteria for selecting the accounts presented and/or the reasons why certain accounts are excluded (e.g., sufficient records are not available to substantiate prior firm performance of certain accounts);
- Performance dates back only to the date as of which the current portfolio manager(s) began managing the account at the predecessor firm;
- The advertisement is consistent with SEC staff interpretations with respect to the advertisement of performance results;[120]
- The advertisement includes all relevant disclosures, including that the performance results were from accounts managed at another entity;[121] and
- The successor adviser has records sufficient to comply with Rule 204-2(a)(16) in

---

[118] Horizon Asset Management, LLC (Sept. 13, 1996).

[119] *See* Horizon Asset Management, LLC; Conway Asset Management, Inc. (Jan. 27, 1989) (allowing newly registered adviser solely owned by an employee to use performance data of several accounts managed by employee prior to registration); Fiduciary Management Associates, Inc. (Mar. 5, 1984). Although the advertisement of performance of a prior adviser's select accounts is not per se prohibited so long as such performance is not materially higher than the composite performance, the Global Investment Performance Standards (GIPS) prohibits a firm from linking select accounts of the composite's performance history. *See* Guidance Statement on Performance Record Portability (Revised), Application No. 2 (effective Jan. 1, 2006) (hereinafter "Portability Guidance Statement") ("In addition to meeting all the elements of the Guidance Statement, in order for a firm to be able to link the composite from the old firm to the ongoing performance of the new firm, the entire composite performance history, including all portfolios, must be used.").

[120] *See*, e.g., Clover Capital Management, Inc. (Oct. 28, 1986) (stating that Rule 206(4)-1(a)(5) prohibits an advertisement that
  (i) Fails to disclose the effect of material market or economic conditions on the results portrayed;
  (ii) Includes model or actual results that do not reflect the deduction of advisory fees, brokerage or other commissions, and any other expenses that a client paid or would have paid;
  (iii) Fails to disclose whether and to what extent returns reflect the reinvestment of dividends and other earnings;
  (iv) Suggests the potential for profit without disclosing the possibility of loss;
  (v) Compares model or actual results to an index without disclosing all material facts relevant to the comparison;
  (vi) Fails to disclose any material conditions, objectives or investment strategies used to obtain the results portrayed;
  (vii) Fails to disclose prominently the limitations inherent in model results, if applicable;
  (viii) Fails to disclose, if applicable, that the conditions, objectives, or investment strategies of the model portfolio changed materially during the time period portrayed and, if so, the effect of any such change on the results portrayed;
  (ix) Fails to disclose, if applicable, that any of the securities contained in, or the investment strategies followed with respect to, the model portfolio do not relate, or only partially relate, to the type of advisory services currently offered by the adviser;
  (x) Fails to disclose, if applicable, that the adviser's clients had investment results materially different from the results portrayed in the model; and
  (xi) Fails to disclose prominently, if applicable, that the results portrayed relate only to a select group of the adviser's clients, the basis on which the selection was made, and the effect of this practice on the results portrayed if material).

[121] *See*, e.g., Horizon Asset Management, LLC (Sept. 13, 1996); In re Seaboard Investment Advisers, Inc., Investment Advisers Act Rel. No. 1431 (Aug. 3, 1994) (finding a violation of section 206(4) and Rule 206(4)-1(a)(5) for, among other things, using the prior performance of an adviser's control persons without disclosing the source of the performance).

connection with the performance of accounts managed at the predecessor adviser at which the firm's portfolio managers previously managed accounts.[122]

Recordkeeping

General. Rules 204-2(a)(11) and 204-2(a)(16) under the Advisers Act govern the maintenance of records associated with investment adviser advertising. Rule 204-2(a)(11) requires generally that every registered investment adviser "make and keep true, accurate, and current...a copy of each notice, circular, advertisement, newspaper article, investment letter, bulletin, or other communication that the investment adviser circulates or distributes, directly or indirectly to 10 or more persons."[123] Rule 204-2(a)(16) generally requires that each federally registered investment adviser maintain:

> [A]ll accounts, books, internal working papers, and any other records or documents that are necessary to form the basis for or demonstrate the calculation of the performance or rate of return of any or all managed accounts or securities recommendations in any notice, circular, advertisement, newspaper article, investment letter, bulletin, or other communication that the investment adviser circulates or distributes, directly or indirectly, to 10 or more persons (other than persons connected with the investment adviser).[124]

Rule 204-2(a)(16) applies to any advertised performance, both actual and model.[125] Rule 204-2(a)(16) also provides that an adviser is deemed to satisfy the requirements of the rule if, with respect to the performance of its managed accounts, the adviser retains: all account statements so long as they reflect all debits, credits, and other transactions in the client's account for the period of the statement; and all worksheets that are necessary to demonstrate the calculation of the performance or rate of return of the managed accounts.[126] In the adopting release to Rule 204-2, the SEC emphasized that these account statements must be prepared contemporaneously with the period reported, and that all account statements for the period for which performance is calculated be kept, regardless of whether a particular account is included in the computation of an advertised performance figure.[127] The SEC staff has acknowledged that neither the rule nor the releases proposing or adopting the rule states that this safe harbor for managed accounts is the exclusive method of satisfying the requirements

---

[122] Horizon Asset Management; Taurus Advisory Group, Inc. (July 15, 1993); Great Lakes Advisors, Inc. (Apr. 3, 1992). *See also* In re Seaboard Investment Advisers, Inc., Investment Advisers Act Rel. No. 1431 (Aug. 3, 1994).

[123] Investment Advisers Act Rule 204-2(a)(11).

[124] Rule 204-2(a)(16) under the Investment Advisers Act Rule 204-2(e)(3)(i) generally requires such books and records to be maintained and preserved in an easily accessible place for a period of not less than five years, the first two years in an appropriate office of the adviser, from the end of the fiscal year during which the adviser last published or otherwise directly or indirectly disseminated the advertisement or communication. The Advisers Act performance recordkeeping requirements are applicable to the delivery of performance information to "ten or more persons" in the aggregate. Accordingly, if a specific performance calculation is requested by a potential client, or the client's consultant, that is unique to a particular situation and does not go to more than nine persons, then the performance recordkeeping requirements are not applicable. This exception is relied upon by firms that prepare specific information in response to consultant's questionnaires.

[125] *See, e.g.*, In re Meridian Investment Management Corp. et al., Investment Advisers Act Rel. No. 1779 (Dec. 28, 1998).

[126] Investment Advisers Act Rule 204-2(a)(16).

[127] *Recordkeeping by Investment Advisers*, Investment Advisers Act Rel. No. 1135 (Aug. 17, 1988), at n.3 (adopting release).

of Rule 204-2(a)(16).[128] However, as a matter of policy, the SEC staff will not provide no-action assurances under the rule regarding whether an adviser's particular records are sufficient to form the basis of, or demonstrate the calculation of, the investment performance of an adviser's managed accounts.[129] The SEC's purpose in adopting the rule was to assist SEC examiners in their efforts to substantiate performance claims made by advisers in their advertisements.[130]

Although Rule 204-2(a)(16) may be satisfied through the reliance on internally generated records, the SEC staff has noted that advisers can facilitate the SEC's examination of advertised performance by maintaining records prepared by a third party (for example, custodial and brokerage statements) that confirm the accuracy of client account statements and other performance-related records maintained by the adviser, and reports prepared by an independent auditor that verify performance.[131] On at least one occasion, the SEC staff has indicated a *preference* for independent records to substantiate advertised returns.[132] Lori Richards, the director of the SEC's OCIE, has questioned the reliability of internally generated documents, stating that advisers may easily manipulate their internal statements to support false performance and advisers are therefore encouraged to support their performance claims with third-party records (for example, brokerage or custodial records and statements).[133] The SEC staff has acknowledged the value of third-party records for not only assisting in the verification of performance claims, but also for enabling SEC examiners to confirm client assets and review for the misappropriation of client funds and securities.[134]

---

[128] Salomon Brothers Asset Management, Inc. and Salomon Brothers Asset Management Asia Pacific Limited (July 23, 1999). Rule 204-2(a)(16) may also be satisfied by retaining published materials listing the net asset values of an account together with worksheets demonstrating the performance calculations based on the net asset values, provided the net asset values were accumulated contemporaneously with the management of the account. See Solomon Brothers Asset Management, Inc. (July 23, 1999).

[129] Jennison Associates LLC (July 6, 2000).

[130] *Recordkeeping by Investment Advisers*, at n.3 (adopting release); Recordkeeping by Investment Advisers, Investment Advisers Act Rel. No. 1093 (Nov. 5, 1987) (proposing release). *See also* Jennison Associates LLC (July 6, 2000) ("The purpose of Rule 204-2(a)(16) was to deter the use of false or misleading performance advertisements by advisers by requiring advisers to make and keep for inspection by the commission's examination staff all records necessary to substantiate the performance information in their advertisements.").

[131] Jennison Associates LLC (July 6, 2000). When reviewing auditor reports, the SEC indicated that it will consider all the facts and circumstances relating to the quality of the audit, including whether:
 (i) The auditor is appropriately independent from the adviser;
 (ii) The auditor reports are based on the review of data that were accumulated contemporaneously with the management of the relevant accounts;
 (iii) The auditor reviews sufficient information to afford a reasonable basis for its conclusions (e.g., by reviewing custodian and brokerage statements, and confirming data directly with custodians and brokers) and prepares the auditor reports in accordance with appropriate auditing standards;
 (iv) The adviser or the auditor maintains records underlying the auditor reports (i.e., audit work papers) and the SEC staff has access to such records;
 (v) The performance verified by the auditor is consistent with the performance derived from other records maintained by the adviser; and
 (vi) The auditor reports include a clear and specific description of the standard used by the adviser to calculate performance.

[132] Lori A. Richards, "Compliance Priorities for Investment Advisers," Remarks at the Investment Adviser Compliance Summit (May 1, 2000) ("Because of the possibility of fraud, internal documentation prepared by the adviser may not be adequate alone to substantiate performance claims. In today's technologically sophisticated world, it's relatively easy for an adviser to artificially create internal statements supporting false performance returns. We have seen this scenario too often.").

[133] *Id.*

[134] Jennison Associates LLC (July 6, 2000).

The records required to be made under paragraphs (a)(11) and (a)(16) of Rule 204-2 must be maintained in an easily accessible place for at least five years, the first two years in an appropriate office of the adviser, beginning from the end of the fiscal year during which the adviser last disseminated the advertisement.[135]

Social Media Considerations. The content, not the form, of an adviser's communication triggers the recordkeeping requirement. As such, advisers who communicate using social media must retain records of their communications if the content of the communications triggers the Rule 204-2 recordkeeping requirement, and advisers should adopt policies and procedures for determining what social media communications must be preserved.

Social media's dynamic and interactive nature may make it difficult for a firm to distinguish between the types of communications that are required to be preserved under Rule 204-2 and those that are not. For example, a blog post by an adviser's representative may start out as industry commentary that is unrelated to investment advisory services, but subsequent responses by third parties or by the original poster may transform the communication into a communication relating to investment advice required to be preserved under Rule 204-2(a)(7). Although the 2014 Guidance is silent on its impact on recordkeeping, OCIE recommends that firms take a precautionary approach and preserve *all* records related to social media communications.[136]

OCIE recommends that the social media preservation policies and procedures address, at a minimum:

- Determining, among other things
  - Whether each social media communication used is a required record, and, if so,
  - The applicable retention period, and
  - The accessibility of the records;
- Maintaining social media communications in electronic or paper format (e.g., screen print or .pdf of social media page, if practicable);
- Conducting employee training programs to educate advisory personnel about recordkeeping provisions;
- Arranging and indexing social media communications that are required records and kept in an electronic format to promote easy location, access and retrieval of a particular record;
- Periodic forensic testing (using key word searches or otherwise) to ascertain whether employees are complying with the compliance policies and procedures (e.g., whether employees are improperly destroying required records); and

---

[135] Rule 204-2(e)(3)(i) under the Advisers Act. For instance, if an advertisement contains performance over the last ten years, the documents that form the basis for the adviser's performance for each of the ten years must be kept for five years, the first two years in an appropriate office of the adviser, after the end of the fiscal year in which the advertisement was last published or disseminated. *See* Jennison Associates LLC (July 6, 2000).
[136] OCIE's National Examination Risk Alert: *Investment Adviser Use of Social Media* (Jan. 4, 2012).

- Using third parties to keep records consistent with the recordkeeping requirements.[137]

In addition, compliance personnel should be aware of OCIE's guidance regarding the circumstances under which social media communications may be deemed to be "testimonials," as discussed earlier.

Advertising Policies and Procedures

General. Firms that are registered under the Advisers Act are required to adopt and implement written policies and procedures reasonably designed to prevent violations of the Advisers Act and the rules thereunder, including Rule 206(4)-1.[138] OCIE will likely review policies and procedures of investment advisers in an examination to ensure that advertisements and other marketing materials distributed to existing and prospective clients contain accurate information.[139] In addition, OCIE has identified several features of inadequate policies and procedures governing marketing and performance advertising, including failures to:

- Address the operations or practices of the adviser's businesses;
- Ensure that compliant presentations were being used by third-party consultants;
- Address how cash and cash equivalents are treated when equity and fixed income performance is carved out from balanced accounts;
- Ensure that claims of compliance with the GIPS are accurate;
- Require a consistent comparison of composites to their appropriate benchmarks; and
- Ensure accurate composite descriptions.

Features of advertising policies and procedures that the OCIE commended included:

- Institution of a multilevel process involving an adviser's performance group, investment personnel and marketing group to review advertisements prior to their dissemination;[140]
- Development of monthly reports comparing all composites to their benchmarks and an investigative process to review material discrepancies;
- Review of all managed accounts on at least a quarterly basis to ensure proper composite construction and maintenance; and
- Use of a second independent pricing service to periodically verify prices supplied by the primary pricing service, with investigations of any material discrepancies.

---

[137] *Id.*

[138] Rule 206(4)-7 under the Advisers Act.

[139] Lori A. Richards, "Focus Areas in SEC Examinations of Investment Advisers: the Top 10," Remarks at the IA Compliance Best Practices Summit 2008 (Mar. 20, 2008).

[140] In January 2011, the SEC staff released its Study on Investment Advisers and Broker-Dealers, which recommended that the SEC consider harmonizing the internal pre-use review requirements for adviser and broker-dealer advertisements or requiring advisers to designate employees to review and approve advertisements. *See* Securities and Exchange Commission, Study on Investment Advisers and Broker-Dealers, at 132 (January 2011). The study was required under the Dodd-Frank Wall Street Reform and Consumer Protection Act of 2010 to evaluate the effectiveness of legal or regulatory standards of care for broker-dealers and investment advisers who provide personalized investment advice to retail customers.

III. FINRA

Scope of the FINRA Regime

The mission of the Financial Industry Regulatory Authority, Inc. (FINRA) "is to safeguard the investing public against fraud and bad practices."[141] FINRA enforces its mission by writing and enforcing rules and guidance for brokerage firms, which generally must be members of FINRA.

As used in this section, the term *communications* includes all types of written communications, including electronic communications, seminar handouts and even sales/telemarketing scripts. However, different rules may apply depending on the audience of a communication. In particular, different standards apply depending on whether the communication is deemed to be an "institutional communication," a "retail communication," or "correspondence."

An *institutional communication* is any written (including electronic) communication that is distributed or made available only to "institutional investors," but it does not include the member's internal communications.[142] In addition, compliance personnel should be aware that the term *institutional investors* is defined differently from its common usage definition, and in some cases could include individual investors.[143]

In contrast, retail communication and correspondence are communications with retail, not institutional, investors. The definitions differ only in the number of retail investors to whom the communication is distributed.[144] A *retail communication* means any written (including electronic) communication that is distributed or made available to more than 25 retail investors within any 30-day calendar-day period, whereas *correspondence* means any written communication distributed to 25 or fewer retail investors. For purposes of the applicable FINRA rules, a retail investor is any person other than an Institutional Investor, regardless of whether the person has an account with the FINRA member distributing the communication.[145]

> ### *Compliance Notes: Scope of FINRA Regulation*
>
> - The advertising rules and guidance promulgated by FINRA govern communications by FINRA-member broker-dealers with the public. In addition to FINRA rules, certain products may be governed by additional regimes. For example, communications regarding registered funds, which are distributed by broker-dealers, must comply with FINRA rules and guidance, but also are subject to specific rules under the Securities Act of

---

[141] See FINRA, http://www.finra.org/AboutFINRA/WhatWeDo/
[142] See FINRA Rule 2210(a)(3). Although FINRA does not expressly define *internal communications*, materials used to train and educate internal sales persons would not be considered communications with the public.
[143] Specifically, for purposes of FINRA advertising rules, the term is limited to "banks, savings and loan associations, insurance companies, registered investment companies, registered investment advisers, any person (including natural persons) with assets of at least $50 million, governmental entities, employee benefit plans and qualified plans with at least 100 participants, FINRA members and registered persons, and a person acting solely on behalf of an institutional investor." See FINRA Rule 2210(a)(4).
[144] Compare FINRA Rule 2210(a)(5) with FINRA Rule 2210(a)(2).
[145] See FINRA Rule 2210(a)(6).

1933, as amended (the "1933 Act"), and SEC rules, regulations and guidance.[146] Accordingly, it is crucial for compliance personnel to determine what product is being marketed and to review materials with respect to the rule of each applicable regime; and

- FINRA has issued guidance indicating that a private placement memorandum or other offering document generally will not be considered a communication with the public, unless a broker-dealer assisted in the preparation of that document.[147] Typically, it is the private fund's manager who prepares the memorandum.

General Content Standards

As previously discussed, FINRA's mission is to protect investors from fraud and bad practices. In that regard, all communications are subject to broad antifraud general content standards.[148] The FINRA advertising rules require that each piece of sales literature independently comply with the rules' content standards;[149] thus, it is not sufficient that the risks are described in offering documents to investors. No communication may make false, exaggerated, unwarranted, promissory, or misleading statement or claim. In addition, FINRA members must consider the nature of the audience to which the communication will be directed and must provide information and disclosures appropriate to the audience.

In accordance with the general content standards, and subject to certain limited exceptions described below, communications may not predict or project performance, imply that past performance will recur or make any exaggerated or unwarranted claim, opinion or forecast. There are three exceptions to the prohibition on projected performance:

- A hypothetical illustration of mathematical principles, provided that it does not predict or project the performance of an investment or investment strategy;
- An investment analysis tool, or a written report produced by an investment analysis tool, that meets the requirements of FINRA Rule 2214[150]; and
- A price target contained in a research report on debt or equity securities, provided that the price target has a reasonable basis, the report discloses the valuation methods

---

[146] Rule 156 under the 1933 Act provides guidance with respect to registered fund "sales literature," which generally includes all types of fund sales materials and advertising. In addition, registered fund sales material will fall under, and be subject to, Rule 482 under the 1933 Act. Rule 482 advertisements are the primary manner (outside of a fund's prospectus) for advertising registered funds and for communicating fund performance data to prospective investors. In addition, compliance personnel should be aware that the SEC has proposed, but not yet adopted, rules that would apply Rule 156 to communications concerning private funds. See Release No. 33-9416 (Jul. 10, 2013).

[147] See FINRA Notice 10-22 (Apr. 2010).

[148] See FINRA Rule 2210(d)(1).

[149] See NASD News Release, "NASD Fines Altegris Investments for Hedge Fund Sales Violations" (Apr. 22, 2003).

[150] This limited exemption to the prohibition on hypothetical performance (see Section VIII) permits communications to include statements regarding the results generated by "Investment Analysis Tools." These tools are defined to mean "an interactive technological tool that produces simulations and statistical analyses that present the likelihood of various investment outcomes if certain investments are made or certain investment strategies or styles are undertaken, thereby serving as an additional resource to investors in the evaluation of the potential risks and returns of investment choices." Any communication relating to the results of such Investment Analysis Tools must be accompanied by certain disclosures required pursuant to FINRA Rule 2214. In addition, any member that intends to offer an investment analysis tool under that rule (regardless of whether customers use the member's tool independently or with assistance from the member) must, within 10 business days of first use, provide FINRA's Advertising Regulation Department access to the investment analysis tool, and file with such department any template for written reports produced by, or retail communications concerning, the tool.

used to determine the price target, and the price target is accompanied by disclosure concerning the risks that may impede achievement of the price target.

The most commonly used exemption is the first type using math, which would permit, for example and without limitation, an illustration of the net returns that an investor would earn over an assumed period of time with assumed variables of rates of returns, frequency of compounding, and tax rates.

Compliance Notes: General Content Standards

- Members marketing private funds to investors should be mindful to disclose the risks associated with such private funds in any sales literature[151]—
  - When marketing private funds, a member should disclose that, among other things: (i) the fund is speculative and involves a high degree of risk; (ii) the fund may be leveraged; (iii) the fund's performance can be volatile; (iv) an investor could lose all or a substantial amount of his or her investment; (v) the fund manager has total trading authority over the fund and that the use of a single advisor applying generally similar trading programs could mean lack of diversification and, consequentially, higher risk; (vi) there is no secondary market for the investor's interest in the fund and none is expected to develop; (vii) there may be restrictions on transferring interests in the fund; (viii) the fund's high fees and expenses may offset the fund's trading profits; and (ix) a substantial portion of the trades executed for the fund takes place on foreign exchanges;
- FINRA requires that disclosures are prominently displayed and prefers to see disclosures at the beginning of an advertisement and on each page (as necessary) rather than all placed at the end. Communications may include information placed in a legend or footnote, but only in the event that such placement would not inhibit an investor's understanding of the communication[152]; and
- Retail communications and correspondence in particular should be reviewed to ensure that they can be readily understood by unsophisticated investors. For example, although it is acceptable to include technical terms such as the *Sharpe ratio, beta,* or *efficient frontier* in communications to retail investors, it is important to provide plain English explanations of what these concepts mean so that the recipient can appropriately assess the data and its relevance to the product that is being marketed.

---

[151] *See* NASD News Release, NASD Fines Altegris Investments for Hedge Fund Sales Violations (Apr. 22, 2003). Members should note that "[a]ll member communications must be based on principles of fair dealing and good faith, must be fair and balanced, and must provide a sound basis for evaluating the facts in regard to any particular security or type of security, industry, or service." *See also* FINRA Rule 2210(d)(1)(A). Moreover, "[n]o member may omit any material fact or qualification if the omission, in light of the context of the material presented, would cause the communications to be misleading." *Id.*

[152] *See* FINRA Rule 2210(d)(1)(C).

Testimonials

Testimonials are not prohibited under FINRA rules and guidance. However, prior to marketing a testimonial statement, compliance personnel should first ensure that the communication is not subject to the advertisement rule under the Advisers Act. As described earlier in detail in discussion of the Advisers Act, although FINRA permits broker-dealers to provide testimonials, investment advisers generally are prohibited from doing so.

Under FINRA rules and guidance, if any retail communication or correspondence provides any testimonial concerning the investment advice or investment performance of a member or its products, it must prominently disclose: (i) the fact that the testimonial may not be representative of the experience of other clients; (ii) the fact that the testimonial is no guarantee of future performance or success; and (iii) if more than $100 is paid, the fact that it is a paid testimonial.[153] In addition, if any testimonial (including institutional communications) relates to a technical aspect of investing, the person making the testimonial must have the knowledge and experience to form a valid opinion.[154]

> ### Compliance Notes: Retail vs. Institutional Communication Disclosures
>
> Although the disclosure requirements described above apply only to retail communications and correspondence, institutional communications, as discussed above, remain subject to general antifraud considerations. To that end, as a recommended practice, compliance personnel should consider applying the same disclosure standards to testimonials in their firms' institutional communications.

Comparisons

Any comparison between products, investments, services or indices included in retail communications must be accompanied by disclosure of all material differences between products, investments, services or indices, including (as applicable) investment objectives, costs and expenses, liquidity safety, guarantees or insurance, fluctuation of principal or return, and tax features.[155]

> ### Compliance Notes: Comparisons
>
> - The relevant differences between product types should be clearly stated and should not be described in a footnote or legend; and
> - Although the comparisons rule only applies to retail communications, as described above, compliance personnel are encouraged to make similar disclosures when making comparisons in correspondence and institutional communications.

---

[153] See FINRA Rule 2210(d)(6)(B).
[154] See FINRA Rule 2210(d)(6)(A).
[155] See, e.g., FINRA Rule 2210(d)(2); SEI Investments Distribution Co., Letter of Acceptance, Waiver and Consent No. 2009018186201 (Feb. 2012) ("SEI Investments AWC").

Graphs and Charts

Graphs and charts are not expressly referenced in FINRA Rule 2210, but like narrative text, they are similarly subject to antifraud guidance designed to help investors fully understand the content of what they are reading.[156]

In light of the complexity of the information that can be presented in graphs and charts, they may be subject to unique forms of manipulation. For example, FINRA has found charts to be misleading when they contained unequal distances between plot points on the graph lines, dollar values along the vertical axis that did not correspond to a fund's actual performance over time, and inaccurate labeling of the increments on the axes.[157]

> ### Compliance Notes: Charts and Graphs
>
> When reviewing charts and graphs, compliance personnel should be particularly aware of the following:
>
> - Does the communication identify the indexes, averages, or specific securities on which the performance is based, and disclose that past performance does not guarantee future results?
> - Are all charts and graphs proportionally correct or drawn to scale?
> - Are all axes labeled so that the reader can understand the data presented;
> - Is there sufficient accompanying text that clearly states the purpose and disclosure advertising the relevant assumptions?
> - Do the starting points fairly reflect the performance of the product without exaggeration, and without cherry-picking periods with favorable performance?

Fund Rankings

Independently prepared fund rankings are similarly subject to requirements designed to protect investors from misleading information.[158] In contrast to the Advisers Act regime, which as described earlier provides more flexibility, fund rankings used in communications subject to FINRA rules must be created and published by a "ranking entity" or by a fund or an affiliate of a fund based upon performance measurements of a ranking entity. A *ranking entity* is "any entity that provides general information about investment companies to the public, that is independent of the investment company and its affiliates, and whose services are not procured by the investment company or any of its affiliates to assign the investment company a ranking."[159]

---

[156] *See, e.g.,* NASD RCA (Apr. 1995), Misuse of Charts Comparing Index Returns Concerns NASD; NASD RCA (Summer 2000), Inaccurate Performance Graphs Result in Formal Action.

[157] *See* NASD Press Release, NASD Regulation Fines Kemper Distributors $100,000 for Mutual Fund Advertisement Violations (May 16, 2000).

[158] *See* FINRA Rule 2212. Fund rankings (whether or not based on performance) are not subject to the requirements of Rule 482 with respect to standardized return calculation, presentation and related disclosures.

[159] *See* FINRA Rule 2212(a).

Among other features, the rankings must be of a category choice that provides a sound basis for evaluating the fund's performance and that of the category, and they must be accompanied by disclosure sufficient to allow an investor to assess the relevance and significance of the information presented. For example, a headline or other prominent statement must not state or imply that an investment company or investment company family is the best performer in a category unless it is actually ranked first in the category.[160]

Prominent Disclosure. Fund rankings must be accompanied by prominent disclosure of:

- The name of the category (e.g., large cap equity);
- The number of investment companies or, if applicable, investment company families, in the category;
- The name of the ranking entity and, if applicable, the fact that the investment company or an affiliate created the category or subcategory;
- The length of the period (or the first day of the period) and its ending date; and
- The criteria on which the ranking is based (e.g., total return or risk-adjusted performance).[161]

Certain Additional Disclosure. In addition, fund rankings also must disclose:

- The fact that past performance is no guarantee of future results;
- Whether the ranking takes sales loads into account (if applicable);
- A statement (if applicable) to the effect that:
    - The ranking is based on total return or the current SEC standardized yield,
    - Fees have been waived or expenses advanced during the period on which the ranking is based, and
    - The waiver or advancement had a material effect on the total return or yield for that period, a statement to that effect;[162]
- The publisher of the ranking data and the date on which the ranking appeared (e.g., "ABC Magazine, June 2011"); and
- If the ranking consists of a symbol (e.g., a star system) rather than a number, the meaning of the symbol (e.g., a four-star ranking indicates that the fund is in the top 30 percent of all investment companies).[163]

Relevance of the Ranking. In addition to the disclosure requirements discussed above, it is important that the ranking not be stale. In that regard, the ranking must be current as of the most recent calendar quarter (or more recent if available). If no such

---

[160] See FINRA Rule 2212(c)(1).
[161] See FINRA Rule 2212(c)(2).
[162] In addition, if based on total return, the ranking must be accompanied by rankings based on total return for one, five and ten year periods (if the fund has been in existence for such periods) provided by the same Ranking Entity for the same category. If no such period rankings exist, a FINRA member may use rankings representing short, medium and long term performance for the same required periods.
[163] See FINRA Rule 2212(c)(3).

ranking exists, a FINRA member may use the most current ranking from the ranking entity, unless such ranking would be misleading in which case no ranking may be used. In determining whether a ranking would be misleading, compliance personnel should examine whether there have been any material events subsequent to the date of the ranking that would materially impact the results of the ranking. Furthermore, the ranking may not cover a period of less than one year, unless based upon yield.[164]

Past Specific Recommendations

Pursuant to FINRA Rule 2210(d)(7)(C), retail communications and correspondence[165] may not refer to past specific recommendations made by the FINRA member that were or would be profitable, unless such communications set out or offer to furnish a list of all recommendations as to the same type, kind, grade, or classification of securities made by the FINRA member within the immediately preceding period of not less than one year. Such list must include the following:

- Name of each security recommended;
- Date and nature of each recommendation (e.g., buy/sell/hold);
- Market price of security at the time of the recommendation;
- Price at which recommendation was to be acted upon;
- The most recent market price of each security listed; and
- The following legend prominently on the first page in a size as large as the largest print or type used in the text of the advertisement or list on which it appears: *It should not be assumed that the recommendations made in the future will be profitable or will equal the performance of the securities in this list.*

> *Compliance Notes: Past Specific Recommendations*
>
> Rule 2210(d)(7)(C) was modeled after Advisers Act Rule 206(4)-1(a)(2), which prohibits registered advisers from presenting past specific recommendations. It is worth noting that with respect to a broker-dealer's communications with the public, FINRA Rule 2210(d)(7)(C) applies only to past recommendations by the FINRA member. Accordingly, although not an official FINRA position, compliance personnel should be aware that if a fund is distributed by a broker-dealer, the broker-dealer's presentation of fund investments (i.e., the past-specific recommendations of the adviser) may not be viewed as within the prohibition of FINRA Rule 2210(d)(7)(C). However, communications about those fund portfolio holdings would remain subject to the general antifraud rules. In contrast, for funds that are self-distributed or distributed by their advisers, the communication would be subject to rules and guidance promulgated by

---

[164] *See* FINRA Rule 2212(d).
[165] Similarly to other rules described herein, compliance personnel should keep in mind that past-specific recommendations remain subject to antifraud considerations even when disclosed only in institutional communications. To that end, it is a best practice to comply with the rule in all communications that include recommendations by the FINRA member.

the SEC under the Advisers Act, under which the presentation of past recommendations is limited.[166] For organizations with both registered investment advisers and FINRA member broker-dealers, compliance personnel should adhere to well-defined procedures and use a consistent approach to reviewing fund materials. More specifically, compliance personnel must not apply the less restrictive regime under the circumstances in order to do indirectly what cannot be done directly under the appropriate regulatory regime.

Presentation of Performance in Member Communications

Performance advertising presents a range of issues requiring the particular close attention of compliance personnel. Given the weight that investors place on past performance, it is often the aspect of advertising most heavily scrutinized by FINRA and other regulators during examinations. Accordingly, it is imperative to ensure that such performance is presented in a complete and accurate manner that is not misleading.

The discussion below addresses some of the principal issues with which compliance personnel should be familiar when reviewing performance presentations in communications with the public.

Index or Benchmark Performance. If fund performance is compared to an index or a benchmark, or if an advertisement otherwise refers to an index or a benchmark, the communication should only use a comparative index or benchmark that is appropriate for the product. Typically, this would be (but is not required to be) the index or benchmark identified in the fund's offering document. The communication must also contain clear and prominent disclosures sufficient to provide the reader with a sound basis for evaluating the facts with respect to the product's comparison to the index, noting in particular that investments cannot be made directly in an index.

In addition, it is critical to verify and flag any back-tested index or benchmark performance. Compliance personnel should inquire whether all or a portion of the historical index or benchmark performance presented is calculated retroactively for periods that predate the creation of the index or benchmark (e.g., applying the Russell 2000 index inclusion standard to calculate how the Russell 2000 index would have performed prior to its inception) or if all index performance is actual index performance. FINRA has only permitted the use of back-tested index or benchmark performance in the context of institutional communications regarding passively managed exchange-traded products, subject to various conditions.[167]

---

[166] See Advisers Act Rule 206(4)-1(a)(2).

[167] See FINRA Interpretive Letter to Mr. Bradley J. Swenson (Apr. 22, 2013)("While we do not object to the use of PIP data in institutional communications as discussed herein, this letter does not affect FINRA's long standing position that the presentation of hypothetical back tested performance in communications used with retail investors does not comply with FINRA Rule 2210(d).").

Related Performance. FINRA considers *related performance* to include the performance of other, separate investment companies, funds, portfolios, accounts or composites thereof managed by the same investment adviser, subinvestment adviser, or portfolio manager that manages the fund that the member is promoting. The term also includes the performance of "clone" funds and other similarly managed accounts and funds, the performance of funds or accounts that preceded and were converted into the advertised fund, and composites of other similarly managed funds, accounts, or portfolios.[168]

Related performance may only be presented in sales material for Section 3(c)(7) funds all recipients of which are "qualified purchasers."

> ### Compliance Notes: Related Performance
>
> A Section 3(c)(7) fund that relies on Regulation D may be offered to investors that are not qualified purchasers (as long as those investors are accredited investors). However, if communications contain related performance, FINRA's position effectively imposes a higher restriction requiring recipients to be qualified purchasers. In the absence of related performance, the qualified purchaser requirement is only relevant at the point of sale, rather than during the offering process.

Other than with respect to Section 3(c)(7) funds, no member may publish or distribute sales materials for a hedge fund that presents related performance information, even if the recipient of the communication would be a highly sophisticated investor. For example, this general prohibition extends even to communications that are aimed at qualified institutional buyers (QIBs) that are potential investors in a Section 3(c)(1) fund.[169]

FINRA noted that the distribution of related performance information to QIBs that are potential investors in Section 3(c)(1) funds raises concerns that are not present in the context of Section 3(c)(7) funds. For example, such distribution could create the risk of disparate treatment of potential investors because QIBs would have access to information that is not available to others. Moreover, the FINRA staff was concerned that once communications with the public containing related performance information are created for one class of potential investors, such as QIBs, it could become difficult to ensure that those communications are not subsequently disseminated to other, less sophisticated investors.[170]

FINRA, consistent with the above, also prohibits the use of related performance in registered fund advertisements. However, such information may be included in the statutory prospectus that is filed with the SEC, subject to the SEC staff's requirements.

---

[168] *See* NASD Interpretive Letter to Securities Industry Association (Oct. 2, 2003).
[169] *See* NASD Interpretive Letter to Collins/Bay Island Securities (Sept. 14, 2004).
[170] *Id.*

The staff of the SEC's Division of Investment Management has taken the position that a registered fund may include in its registration statement information concerning the performance of separate accounts and other funds managed by the fund's adviser that have substantially similar investment objectives, policies, and strategies as those of the fund, provided that such information is not presented in a misleading manner and does not obscure or impede the understanding of information that is required to be in the fund's registration statement (including the fund's own performance). Such performance should not exclude the performance of separate accounts or other funds managed by the fund's adviser that have substantially similar investment objectives, policies, and strategies as the fund if the exclusion would cause the performance shown to be materially higher than would be the case if the other funds or accounts were included or if such exclusion would otherwise be misleading.[171]

The term *model performance* generally refers to either a hypothetical combination or a subset of actual performance results achieved by the adviser, but the term does not reflect actual management on a standalone basis of the particular fund or strategy presented. The term *hypothetical back-tested performance* refers to the use of theoretical performance applying a particular investment strategy (e.g., quantitative) to historical financial data to show what decisions would have been made if the strategy were employed.[172]

Communications must not include model or hypothetical back-tested performance data, even when presented in combination with actual historical performance.[173] Nevertheless, as discussed above, communications may show the hypothetical growth of an investment, provided that such performance is calculated using the actual performance of the fund (e.g., how a $10,000 investment would have performed). In addition, although FINRA has not expressly stated its position, it has implied that, under certain conditions, providing hypothetical back-tested performance to institutional investors could be permissible.

Compliance Notes: Pitfalls in Performance Advertising and Due Diligence Requests

- Performance advertising presents multiple traps for the unwary. By way of a simple example, it is important to know that all performance must be shown net of fees. However, the unpublished but current position of FINRA staff is that gross of fee performance may also be presented, provided that net of fee performance is also presented side-by-side and with equal prominence; and

---

[171] See Division of Investment Management IM Guidance Update No. 2013-05 (Aug. 2013); Nicholas-Applegate (pub. avail. Aug. 6, 1996); ITT Hartford Mutual Funds (pub. avail. Feb. 7, 1997).

[172] See, e.g., In re Schield Management Company; In re Market Timing Systems.

[173] See NASD News Release, "NASD Fines Citigroup Global Markets, Inc. $250,000 in Largest Hedge Fund Sales Sanction to Date" (Oct. 25, 2004); NASD Interpretive Letter to Securities Industry Association (Oct. 2, 2003), Bear Stearns Letter of Acceptance, Waiver and Consent No. 2007011145701 (Jul. 30, 2009). In FINRA Interpretive Letter to Mr. Bradley J. Swenson (Apr. 22, 2013), FINRA made reference to its "long standing position that the presentation of hypothetical back tested performance *in communications used with retail investors* does not comply with FINRA Rule 2210(d)" (emphasis added). FINRA's specific reference to "retail investors" may indicate a change in FINRA's position, potentially leading to a new approach where presenting model and/or hypothetical performance to nonretail investors may be permissible under certain circumstances.

- There is no FINRA guidance that expressly allows a member to provide information requested by investors if that information is prohibited by FINRA under Rule 2210. This frequently occurs during a fund's due diligence phase during which investors typically request information such as financial models and projections, back-tested performance, and the performance of other similar funds or strategies managed by the same investment adviser. Although the prohibitions on providing the requested information could unnecessarily restrict the business activities of FINRA members without a corresponding benefit to investors, FINRA has not yet clarified whether providing such information would be permissible under certain conditions.[174]

Administrative Matters

Certain Retail Communications Subject to Approval. All retail communications must be approved by a qualified registered principal of the FINRA member by signature or initial and date before the earlier of its use or filing with FINRA's Advertising Regulation Department.[175]

Retail communications that have previously been approved by the department and have not been materially altered are not required to be approved by a registered principal. However, for such communications, firms must maintain records of the name of the member that filed the retail communication for approval and a copy of the review letter from the department.

Retail Communications Preuse Approval Exemptions. Notwithstanding the above requirements, three categories of retail communications are exempt from the principal pre-use approval requirement; *provided that* all three categories nevertheless must be supervised as correspondence, as described below. Such three categories are as follows:[176]

- Any retail communication that is excepted from the definition of "research report" pursuant to NASD Rule 2711(a)(9)(A), unless the communication makes any financial or investment recommendation. In general, this exemption relates to market letters (i.e., discussions of broad-based indices; commentaries on economic or market conditions; technical analysis concerning the demand and supply for a sector, index, or industry based on trading volume and price; statistical summaries of multiple companies' financial data, including listings of current ratings; recommendations regarding increasing or decreasing holdings in particular; and notices of ratings or price target changes), unless of course the market letter makes any financial or investment recommendation. The exemption also would include white papers and market commentary pieces that meet the foregoing definition;

---

[174] *See* FINRA Interpretive Letter to Mr. Bradley J. Swenson (Apr. 22, 2013).
[175] *See* FINRA Rule 2210(b)(1).
[176] *See* FINRA Rule 2210(b)(1).

- Retail communications posted on an online interactive electronic forum;[177] and
- Retail communications that do not make any recommendation or promote a product or service of the member firm.

Correspondence Subject to Supervision Requirement. Unlike retail communications, correspondence is not required to be approved by a registered principal prior to use. However, correspondence must be subject to written supervisory procedures designed to reasonably supervise the firm's correspondence that complies with NASD Rule 3010(d).[178]

Institutional Communications Subject to Supervision Requirement. Institutional communications are not required to be approved by a registered principal prior to use, but must be subject to written supervisory procedures designed to reasonably supervise the firm's institutional communications.[179] As indicated in FINRA Rule 2210(b)(3), when such procedures do not require review of all institutional communications prior to first use or distribution, they must include provision for the education and training of associated persons as to the firm's procedures governing institutional communications, documentation of such education and training, and surveillance and follow-up to ensure that such procedures are implemented and adhered to. Moreover, evidence that these supervisory procedures have been implemented and carried out must be maintained and made available to FINRA upon request.

Recordkeeping. Recordkeeping policies should be reflected in the FINRA member's procedures, and provide as follows:

- *Retail and Institutional Communications.* Copies of all retail communications and institutional communications must be maintained in a separate file for three years following the date of last use, along with the dates of first and last use, name of the registered principal who approved each item, the date approval was given, and, if registered principal approval is not required, the name of the person who prepared or distributed the communication. In addition, the records must include information concerning the source of any statistical table, chart, graph, or other illustration used by the FINRA member in communications with the public;[180] and
- *Correspondence.* In addition, copies of all correspondence must be maintained in a separate file for three years. The names of the persons who prepared the correspondence and who reviewed the correspondence must be ascertainable from the retained records.[181]

Filing Requirements: Certain Retail Communications. When filing materials with FINRA, the FINRA member must provide with each filing the actual or anticipated date of first use, the name and title of the registered principal who approved the material and the date that the approval was given. Below is a description of the filing requirements applicable to certain retail communications.[182]

---

[177] This could refer, for example, to social media.
[178] *See* FINRA Rule 2210(b)(2). The requirements of NASD Rule 3010(d) are outside the scope of this section.
[179] *See* FINRA Rule 2210(b)(3).
[180] *See* FINRA Rule 2210(b)(4).
[181] *See* FINRA Rule 2210(b)(4); NASD Rule 3010(d)(3) and FINRA Rule 4511.
[182] The requirements described herein do not apply to all communications. *See* FINRA Rule 2210(c)(7) for a list of types of communications that are excluded from FINRA's filing requirements.

Prior to Use Filings. The following types of retail communications must be filed with the Advertising Regulation Department at least 10 business days prior to use:[183]

- Retail communications of new FINRA members for a period of one year beginning on the date that the firm's FINRA membership became effective;
- Retail communications concerning registered funds that include or incorporate performance rankings or comparisons that are not generally published or are the creation (directly or indirectly) of the fund, its underwriter or an affiliate. The filing must include a copy of the ranking or comparison used in the retail communication;
- Retail communications concerning security futures, unless the communication is submitted to another self-regulatory organization with comparable review standards (e.g., the National Futures Association); and
- Retail communications concerning bond mutual funds that include or incorporate bond mutual fund volatility ratings.

After Use Filing. The following types of retail communications must be filed with the department within 10 business days of first use:[184]

- All other retail communications concerning registered funds (including mutual funds, exchange-traded funds, variable insurance products, closed-end funds, and unit investment trusts) not included above;
- Retail communications concerning public direct participation programs;[185]
- Any template for written reports produced by, or retail communications concerning, an investment analysis tool;
- Retail communications concerning collateralized mortgage obligations registered under the 1933 Act; and
- Retail communications concerning any security that is registered under the 1933 Act and that is derived from or based on a single security, a basket of securities, an index, a commodity, a debt issuance or a foreign currency, not otherwise included above.

IV. GIPS

The Global Investment Performance Standards are performance presentation standards that are created, sponsored and interpreted by the CFA Institute (CFAI). The objectives of the standards are to:

- Establish industry best practices for calculating and presenting investment performance that promote investor interests and instill investor confidence;

---

[183] See FINRA Rules 2210(c)(1)(A); 2210(c)(2).

[184] *See* FINRA Rule 2210(c)(3). However, as a practical matter, many mutual fund underwriters require that marketing materials be filed and approved with FINRA prior to their use, in order to avoid the necessity of redistributing materials that require changes to correct deficiencies identified by FINRA.

[185] The term *direct participation program* is defined in FINRA Rule 2310, and it means "a program which provides for flow-through tax consequences regardless of the structure of the legal entity or vehicle for distribution including, but not limited to, oil and gas programs, real estate programs, agricultural programs, cattle programs, condominium securities, Subchapter S corporate offerings, and all other programs of a similar nature, regardless of the industry represented by the program, or any combination thereof."

- Obtain worldwide acceptance of a single standard for the calculation and presentation of investment performance based on the principles of fair representation and full disclosure;
- Promote the use of accurate and consistent investment performance data;
- Encourage fair, global competition among investment firms without creating barriers to entry; and
- Foster the notion of industry "self-regulation" on a global basis.[186]

Compliance with GIPS is voluntary, but once a firm claims compliance, it must comply at all times on a firm-wide basis.[187] The CFAI does not have any authority over a firm that does not claim compliance with the GIPS. However, firms that claim compliance with the standards must comply with all "updates, Guidance Statements, interpretations, Questions & Answers (Q&As), and clarifications published by CFA Institute and the GIPS Executive Committee...."[188] Although the GIPS are not created or maintained by a governmental entity, the SEC's investment adviser monitoring program will review a firm's claim of compliance with the GIPS, including firm definition, discretion definition, composite creation and maintenance, calculation methodology, recordkeeping, and presentations.[189]

Definition of the Firm

Defining the *firm* is both the responsibility of the entity in question and the "foundation for firmwide compliance," creating the boundaries for determining total firm assets and delineating which portfolios must be included in at least one composite of the firm.[190] The definition of the firm must be fairly and appropriately defined and "appropriate, rational, and fair."[191]

Each compliant firm may only be defined as "an investment firm, subsidiary, or division held out to clients or prospective clients as a distinct business entity."[192] Although this approach enables multiple firms to exist within a corporate structure, a GIPS-compliant firm should be "organizationally and functionally segregated" from any other units or divisions within the entity, have discretion over its assets under management and employ an investment strategy without regard to the remainder of the entity's units or divisions.[193] Further, the GIPS encourage a broad definition of the firm, such that it complies with the public's view of the firm.[194] For example, the definition should include all regional offices operating under the same company regardless of the name of the regional management companies.[195]

---

[186] *GIPS Handbook*, 3rd ed. (2012), Introduction.
[187] *GIPS Handbook*, Guidance Statement on the Definition of the Firm.
[188] GIPS Standard 0.A.1.
[189] *See* Lori A. Richards, SEC Roundtable on Investment Adviser Regulatory Issues (May 23, 2000).
[190] *GIPS Handbook*, Guidance Statement on the Definition of the Firm.
[191] *Id.*
[192] *Id.*
[193] *Id.*
[194] *Id.*
[195] *Id.*.

Compliance Notes: Substance over Form in the Definition of the Firm

With regard to specific portfolios, the GIPS endorse a substance over form approach that applies a holistic review, as opposed to a formal structural analysis. Under this approach, advisory-only relationships, such as unified managed account platforms, in which the adviser provides nonbinding investment advice, should be included in the definition of firm. Where a portfolio is subject to oversight by a third party who is theoretically free to follow or ignore the firm's advice, firms must include the portfolio in the firm definition if the firm effectively exercises discretionary investment management and can provide documented evidence to demonstrate that all investment advice has been implemented accordingly.[196]

Definition of Discretion

A GIPS-compliant presentation must contain each portfolio over which the firm has *discretion*, meaning the ability to implement an investment strategy without significant restrictions.[197] Nondiscretionary portfolios, on the other hand, must be excluded from a GIPS-compliant presentation because they do not reflect performance based upon the firm's investment strategy.[198]

Examples of client-imposed restrictions that may render a portfolio nondiscretionary include:

- Restrictions of trading subject to client approval;
- Restrictions on asset allocation;
- Tax considerations;
- Limiting sale of certain securities;
- Restrictions on the purchase of certain securities; cash flow requirements; and
- Legal restrictions.[199]

As a best practice, if a firm classifies a portfolio as nondiscretionary, it should document its reasons for doing so.

---

[196] *See GIPS Handbook*, Guidance Statement on Alternative Strategies and Structures, Question, Q&A 2.
[197] *GIPS Handbook*, Guidance Statement on Composite Definition.
[198] *Id.*
[199] *Id.* The CFAI indicates that a substance over form approach should also be taken with respect to discretion determinations. *See GIPS Handbook*, Guidance Statement on Composite Definition ("May 2012 Guidance"), Q&A 2. *Id.* If the firm provides an investment model or recommendations but has no control over investment decisions of a portfolio, the portfolio is a discretionary portfolio unless the firm's model or recommendation are in fact treated as recommendations. To avoid a misleading advertisement under SEC rules and regulations, a compliant firm including such a portfolio in a composite should disclose that the portfolio is subject to the authority and oversight of a third party.

Compliance Notes: Partial Restrictions and Discretion Determination

If a client-driven investment restriction prevents the firm from fully implementing its strategy to the extent that the portfolio would no longer be representative of the strategy, a firm may either characterize all or a part of the portfolio as nondiscretionary, or create a composite with portfolios carrying similar restrictions.[200] The former option may be appealing to firms with strategies that not only impossible to implement in the restricted portfolio, or portion thereof, but also contain performance information that is not helpful to prospective clients. The latter may be appealing to firms where portfolios are not wholly nondiscretionary (e.g., a client restriction affects a discrete portion of the strategy) and provide useful performance information to prospective clients.

Composite Definition

The standards define a *composite* as an "[a]ggregation of one or more portfolios managed according to a similar investment mandate, objective, or strategy."[201] In order to prevent firms from cherry-picking performance, firms must include all actual, fee-paying, discretionary portfolios in at least one composite, irrespective of whether the firm plans to market the strategy employed.[202]

Composites must be defined according to investment mandates, objectives, and/or strategies and each composite definition must be provided to clients upon request. The CFAI suggests, but does not require, the following hierarchy for defining composites: (i) investment mandate, (ii) asset classes, (iii) style or strategy, (iv) benchmarks, and (v) risk/return characteristics.[203] Composites may be further defined by relevant client constraints or guidelines if such constraints or guidelines result in materially different strategies. This may include the extent of derivatives, hedging and/or leverage use, treatment of taxes, client type, instruments used, portfolio sizes, client characteristics, portfolio types, or base currency.[204]

Compliance Notes: Tailoring Composite Definitions

Note that the GIPS require all portfolios meeting a composite's definition to be included in the same composite.[205] This may present complications for firms seeking to create composites for specific products or underlying assets. An overly broad definition may capture a wider range of portfolios

---

[200] *See GIPS Handbook*, Guidance Statement on Composite Definition.
[201] *GIPS Handbook*, GIPS Glossary, "Composite."
[202] *See GIPS Handbook*, Explanation of Provisions of the GIPS Standards, 3.A.1. Non-fee-paying portfolios may be presented in a composite, if the firm discloses the percentage of assets held in non-fee-paying portfolios as of each annual period end.
[203] *Id.*
[204] *Id.*
[205] GIPS Standard 3.A.4.

than actually intended by the firm, resulting in the inclusion of portfolios that may not truly reflect the intended composite strategy. On the other hand, too narrow of a definition may exclude portfolios that the firm believes to be representative of the strategy, notwithstanding minor restrictions or guidelines from the client.

Prospective Clients

Firms must make every reasonable effort to provide a compliant presentation to all prospective clients, if such prospective client has not received a compliant presentation within the past twelve months.[206] Upon the request of a prospective client, the firm must provide a complete list of composite descriptions and a compliant presentation for any composite listed on the firm's list of composite description.[207]

The GIPS define *prospective client* broadly to include "any person or entity that has expressed interest in one of the firm's composite strategies and qualifies to invest in the composite. Existing clients may also qualify as prospective clients for any strategy that is different from their current investment strategy. Investment consultants and other third parties are included as prospective clients if they represent investors that qualify as prospective clients."[208] Therefore, compliant firms must not only determine who they are advertising to, but in what context, to determine whether a prospective client requiring a compliant presentation exists.

In the context of pooled investment funds, many firms do not deliver compliant presentations to fund investors. These firms interpret a prospective client to refer only to the fund, not the fund's investors. This approach makes practical sense, as the fund or its board/general partner/managing member decides whether to hire the firm and directs the firm to manage the fund in accordance with the composite strategy being marketed. Other firms do not deliver a compliant presentation due to regulatory obstacles.[209]

CFAI has indicated its intent to publish guidance on this topic. Although not yet ready for public comment, an uncirculated early working draft of this guidance (the "Preliminary Draft Guidance Statement") illustrates CFAI's general views on disclosure to prospective clients.[210] The Preliminary Draft Guidance Statement would provide an exception from the compliant presentation delivery requirement if the firm either

---

[206] GIPS Standards, 0.A.9.
[207] GIPS Standards, 0.A.10.
[208] GIPS Handbook, GIPS Glossary, "Prospective Client."
[209] Communications that are distributed by a broker-dealer that is a member of FINRA, such as communications regarding registered funds and many private funds, are subject to FINRA's communications rules and related guidance. Pursuant to FINRA guidance, related performance information may only be presented in communications marketing funds exempt from registration under the 1940 Act pursuant to Section 3(c)(7), in which the member ensures that all recipients of such communications are "qualified purchasers." See NASD Interpretive Letter to Davis Polk & Wardwell (Dec. 30, 2003). Composite performance data included in a compliant presentation constitutes related performance, unless the fund being marketed is the only fund in the composite. Applicable law in other jurisdictions may impose similar or conflicting requirements.
[210] Annie Lo and Ann Putallaz, *Still Swimming in the Deep End: Developing Guidance for Pooled Funds* (Speech delivered at GIPS 2013 Annual Conference (Sept. 19, 2013).

delivers a fully compliant GIPS presentation to all prospective pooled fund investors or follows the GIPS Advertising Guidelines.[211] Currently, a firm may comply with the GIPS Advertising Guidelines without delivering a compliant presentation to each fund investor if the fund's offering materials and related marketing materials do not include a GIPS claim of compliance or reference GIPS.[212] It is uncertain whether such an "opt-in" will survive the future guidance.

> ### Compliance Notes: Investors in Pooled Investment Funds as Prospective Clients
>
> Until more concrete guidance is issued, firms claiming compliance with the standards should continue applying their current approach with respect to pooled fund products (either treating funds or fund boards/general partners/managing members as prospective clients or determining that applicable regulations prohibit firms from delivering compliant presentations to individual fund investors).

Calculation Methodology

A standardized approach to the calculation of returns for each investment firm claiming compliance with the GIPS is crucial to both the goals and utility of the standards. The following conventions must be adhered to when calculating portfolio returns:

- The calculation method must represent returns in a fair manner, applied consistently and not be misleading;
- All returns must be net actual trading expenses incurred;
- Returns must reflect realized and unrealized gains and losses plus income, if any;
- Time-weighted rates of return that adjust for external cash flows must be used and periodic returns must be geometrically linked;
- External cash flows must be calculated consistent with the firm's written composite-specific policy;
- For periods beginning January 1, 2005, the firm must, at a minimum, use approximated rates of return that adjust for daily-weighted external cash flows (i.e., the Modified Dietz Method); and
- For periods beginning January 1, 2010, firms must, at a minimum, value portfolios on the date of all large external cash flows.[213]

---

[211] *Id.* The GIPS Advertising Guidelines require that all advertisements that include a claim of compliance with the GIPS Standards disclose the definition of the firm, how prospective clients can obtain a compliant presentation and/or the firm's list of composite descriptions, and a prescribed GIPS compliance statement for advertisements. In addition, the GIPS Advertising Guidelines require a firm to disclose the composite description, composite total returns calculated in accordance of one of three prescribed methods, whether returns are gross or net-of-fees, benchmark description and total returns for the benchmark, and currency used to express performance, but only if an advertisement includes both a claim of compliance with the GIPS and performance information. *GIPS Handbook*, GIPS Advertising Guidelines.

[212] *See GIPS Handbook*, Explanation of the Provisions of the GIPS Standards, GIPS Advertising Guidelines.

[213] *See GIPS Handbook*, Guidance Statement on Calculation Methodology.

With respect to composite return calculations:

- Individual portfolio returns must be asset weighted to calculate to calculate composite returns using beginning-of-period values or a method reflecting both beginning-of-period values and external cash flows (the aggregate return method is an acceptable asset-weighted approach);
- For periods beginning January 1, 2006, composite returns must be calculated by asset weighting individual portfolio returns at least quarterly and for periods beginning January 1, 2010, monthly; and
- Periodic returns must be geometrically linked. Return calculations may be presented as either gross-of-fees or net-of-fees, as long as the compliant presentation clearly labels the returns one or the other.[214]

Significant Cash Flows

A significant cash flow occurs when a client-directed external cash flow causes the firm to determine that the portfolio cannot implement the composite strategy. A cash flow that merely distorts composite returns is not a significant cash flow. Firms wishing to take action upon the occurrence of a significant cash flow event may either temporarily segregate significant cash flows from the applicable composite or temporarily remove the affected portfolio(s) from the composite.[215]

The firm must act according to an established composite-specific policy regarding significant cash flows, which sets a definition of significant cash flow (expressed as either a specific monetary value or percentage of portfolio assets), provides for the action to be taken upon a significant cash flow event and articulates the appropriate grace period after which the portfolio or cash flows will be reintroduced into the composite for the purposes of calculating returns.[216] The significant cash flow policy cannot be enacted or amended retroactively.[217]

Should a firm choose to temporarily remove portfolios with significant cash flows from a composite, the firm must disclose that the following is available upon request:

- The grace period for the composite;
- If altered, the date and description of change for the significant cash flow definition, policies or grace periods for handling significant cash flows; and
- The number of portfolios removed during the applicable period;
- The number of times portfolios were removed during a given period; and

---

[214] *Id.* Although GIPS provides flexibility in presenting net or gross returns, registered investment advisers and FINRA members must be cognizant of stricter requirements relative to the presentation of gross-of-fee returns. *See e.g.*, Clover Capital Management, Inc., SEC No-Action Letter (Pub. Avail. Oct. 28, 1986).

[215] *See GIPS Handbook*, Guidance Statement on Treatment of Significant Cash Flows.

[216] *Id.* The standards caution that the threshold for "significant cash flow" should be responsive to the portfolio's assets and strategy. For example, the inflows triggering a significant cash flow should be higher, as a percentage of portfolio assets, in the case of portfolio holding highly liquid assets than one holding illiquid assets.

[217] *Id.*

- The amount of composite assets represented by the portfolios affected by the application of these policies.[218]

Compliance Notes: Effect of Temporary Segregation and Removal of Composites

When choosing between temporary segregation of significant cash flows or removal of a portfolio from a composite, compliant firms should weigh the ease of removing a portfolio from the composite against the loss of performance information. Practical considerations, such as which approach is most consistent with the firm's recordkeeping[219] and return calculation infrastructure, should also be considered.

Firms are not required to have a significant cash flow policy for any or all of their composites, and should consider the nature of the composite strategy and number of portfolios, among other factors, in determining whether a significant cash flow policy is appropriate. For example, establishing a significant cash flow policy for a composite with a single account may not be appropriate since the removal of the composite would terminate or create a gap in the composite's performance history.

Materiality

The GIPS incorporate the concept of materiality into certain disclosures (e.g., firms need only disclose relevant details of the treatment of withholding taxes on dividends, income, and capital gains if material, but does not establish a definition for *material* nor, with the exception of the error correction policy, do they require the firm to define it.[220]

Compliance Notes: Materiality Standard

In the absence of guidance from CFAI, firms may consider the SEC's standard of materiality, which investment advisers in the United States are required to use for purposes of the Investment Adviser's Act of 1940's antifraud provision. Under this standard, information is material if there is a substantial likelihood that a reasonable investor would consider it important in making an investment decision.[221] As a best practice, firms should document their analysis for all disclosures deemed unnecessary due to immateriality.

---

[218] *Id.*

[219] Each compliant firm must capture and retain all information necessary to support all items in a compliant presentation, including any supplemental or additional information thereto. *See GIPS Handbook,* Guidance Statement on Performance Record Portability. Many advisers, including those registered with the SEC under the Investment Advisers Act of 1940, are subject to broad recordkeeping requirements. Advisers should not assume, however, that adherence to local law will satisfy their recordkeeping obligations under the standards. Firms should review their existing recordkeeping policies against the information required to be retained under the GIPS and update their retention policies as needed.

[220] *See* GIPS Standards, 4.A.20; *GIPS Handbook,* Guidance Statement on Error Correction.

[221] *See TSC Industries, Inc. v. Northway, Inc.,* 426 U.S. 438, 449 (1976).

Supplemental Information

Firms may include performance-related information as part of a compliant presentation that enhances the required and/or recommended provisions of the standards.[222] Supplemental information must be clearly labeled as supplemental, must be presented separately from the required compliant information, cannot be false or misleading and must accompany, or follow within 12 months of, a compliant presentation.[223]

The GIPS allow for the use of model and hypothetical back-tested performance in a compliant presentation's supplemental information if, in addition to the conditions above, neither is linked to actual performance results and use of the data complies with applicable law.[224]

Compliance Notes: Use of Hypothetical Back-Tested Performance

Note that hypothetical back-tested performance is an important consideration for firms regulated by the SEC because the SEC restricts the use of model and hypothetical back-tested performance.[225] As noted earlier, the SEC requires certain disclosures to accompany this information, as to lessen the chance that model returns create false impressions upon the viewer. All limitations and assumptions underlying the model(s) must be disclosed, as well as any actual client performance results that materially differ from the back-tested or model results presented.[226] With regard to back-tested returns, investment advisers should only present this information to highly sophisticated clients, and only with comprehensive disclosure.[227]

Portability

Under the GIPS portability standards, the performance track records of a past firm or affiliation must be reflected in the compliant firm's GIPS-compliant presentation if, on a composite-specific basis, substantially all investment decision makers are employed by the existing firm, the decision-making process remains substantially intact

---

[222] *See GIPS Handbook*, Guidance Statement on the Use of Supplemental Information.

[223] *Id.* Although there are instances where required and supplemental information may appear on the same page, the Standards recommend that, when in doubt, compliant firms should segregate the two.

[224] *Id.*

[225] *Id.* FINRA prohibits the use of model and back-tested hypothetical performance in broker-dealer advertising materials. However, broker-dealers may include back-tested index performance data if it discloses this fact and must identifies the source of the hypothetical back-tested performance history. *See* SEI Investments Distribution Co. Letter of Acceptance, Waiver and Consent No. 2009018186201 (Feb. 14, 2012). As with all indices, broker-dealers must also provide sufficient information regarding the indices and the differences between the indices and fund to enable the viewer to make a sound evaluation of the facts with respect to the product.

[226] *See* the earlier discussion of the Clover Capital no-action letter and surrounding text (discussing adviser advertising under Section 206 under Advisers Act and Rule 206(4)-1 thereunder).

[227] *See* the discussion of portability and surrounding text (discussing the SEC's regulation of investment adviser performance portability). For more information and additional required disclosures, *see, e.g., In re Market Timing Systems, Inc. et al.*, SEC Rel. No. IA-2047 (Aug. 28, 2002); *In re Schield Management Company*; *In re Leeb Investment Advisers*; and *In re Patricia Owen-Michel*.

and independent within the existing firm, and the existing firm has supporting documents for the performance.[228] In a compliant presentation, the compliant firm must disclose that the performance results from the acquired firm are linked to the ongoing performance records of the compliant firm. If the acquired firm or affiliation is not GIPS-compliant, the compliant firm has one year to bring the acquired firm into compliance with the GIPS.[229]

If an acquired firm or affiliation fails to meet the conditions above and cannot be linked to the ongoing performance records of the firm, the compliant firm may include the acquired firm or affiliation's past performance record as supplemental information to the compliant presentation if the compliant firm possesses all data and information necessary to support the supplemental information.[230]

> ### *Compliance Notes: Portability Recordkeeping Requirements*
>
> Note that the standards do not identify the specific supporting documents required to be retained for performance portability. The recordkeeping requirement likely includes, at a minimum, all underlying data necessary to recreate the performance of its composites for those periods, including beginning and ending fair values of all portfolio holdings and intraperiod cash flows for the composite for each account in the composite, including all custodian statement that include a list of all holdings and inflows and outflows.[231]

Carve-Outs

The GIPS define a *carve-out* as a "portion of a portfolio that is by itself representative of a distinct investment strategy." [232] Carve-outs are "used to create a track record for a narrower mandate from a multistrategy portfolio managed to a broader mandate" and are typically based on characteristics such as asset class, geographic region, or industry sector.[233]

The use of carve-out returns raises two concerns. First, the presentation of carve-out returns may be misleading if it does not represent what would have been achieved in a portfolio that was dedicated to that strategy. Second, if cash is not accounted for separately and not allocated to the carve-out returns, the accuracy of the calculation of the carve-out returns is jeopardized.[234] To address the former concern, the GIPS

---

[228] GIPS Standards, 5.A.8.
[229] *Id.*
[230] *GIPS Handbook,* Guidance Statement on Performance Records Portability.
[231] *See GIPS Handbook,* Explanation of Provisions of the GIPS Standards, 1.A.1. The records requirement for substantiating performance information under Rule 204-2 under the Advisers Act should also satisfy the GIPS requirement.
[232] *GIPS Handbook,* GIPS Glossary, "Carve-Out."
[233] *GIPS Handbook,* Guidance Statement on the Treatment of Carve-Outs.
[234] *Id.*

require that the carved-out segment "be discretionary and structured materially the same as a portfolio dedicated to that strategy and have a risk profile that is substantially similar."[235] A firm may not combine different carve-outs to construct a composite that represents a simulated strategy for purposes of complying with GIPS, but may present such information as supplemental information.[236] The firm is responsible for establishing a policy for creating, using, and calculating carve-out returns and applying this policy on a consistent basis.[237] To manage the latter concern, for periods beginning on or after January 1, 2010, firms may only include a carve-out in a composite if the carve-out is managed separately with its own cash balance.[238]

If the segment is carved-out of a particular strategy, the firm must carve out all similar portfolio segments that are managed to that strategy and include such performance results in the composite.[239] Firms are prohibited from cherry picking specific portfolios to include in the standalone composite, and must include all portfolios that satisfy the criteria for inclusion in the composite.[240] In addition, when presenting net-of-fees performance of composites that contain carve-outs, the carve-out returns must reflect the deduction of fees, which must be representative of the fees charged for a separately managed portfolio for the asset class carved out considering the fee schedule for the composite containing the carve-outs.[241]

GIPS Advertising Guidelines

Firms that include a claim of GIPS compliance in any advertisement,[242] other than a one-on-one presentation that must comply with the full GIPS standards, must adhere to the GIPS Advertising Guidelines, including disclosure of a firm's description, how to obtain a GIPS-compliant presentation and/or a list and description of the firm's composites, and (the GIPS Advertising Guidelines compliance statement ("[Firm name] claims compliance with the Global Investment Performance Standards (GIPS®).").[243]

If performance of the firm is advertised, the GIPS Advertising Guidelines require the following information to be presented:

---

[235] *Id.*
[236] *Id.*
[237] *Id.*
[238] GIPS Standards, 3.A.8. For periods prior to January 1, 2010, if carve-outs were included in a composite, cash must have been allocated to the carve-out in a timely and consistent manner.
[239] *GIPS Handbook*, Guidance Statement on the Treatment of Carve-Outs. However, if a firm decides to carve out a particular segment of a portfolio, it does not have to carve out the remaining portions of the portfolio to form a stand-alone composite.
[240] *GIPS Handbook*, Explanation of the Provisions of the GIPS Standards, 3.A.4.
[241] *GIPS Handbook*, Guidance Statement on the Treatment of Carve-Outs.
[242] The GIPS define *advertisement* as "an advertisement includes any materials that are distributed to or designed for use in newspapers, magazines, firm brochures, letters, media, websites, or any other written or electronic material addressed to more than one prospective client. Any written material, other than one-on-one presentations and individual client reporting, distributed to maintain existing clients or solicit new clients for a firm is considered an advertisement." *GIPS Handbook*, Explanation of the Provisions of the GIPS Standards, GIPS Advertising Guidelines.
[243] *GIPS Handbook*, GIPS Advertising Guidelines.

- The composite description;
- Composite total returns accord to one of the following:
  - One-, three-, and five-year annualized composite returns through the most recent period with the period-end date clearly identified. If the composite has been in existence for less than five years, firms must also present the annualized returns since the composite inception date. (For example, if a composite has been in existence for four years, firms must present one-, three-, and four-year annualized returns through the most recent period.) Returns for periods of less than one year must not be annualized;
  - Period-to-date composite returns in addition to one-, three-, and five-year annualized composite returns through the same period of time as presented in the corresponding compliant presentation with the period end date clearly identified. If the composite has been in existence for less than five years, firms must also present the annualized returns since the composite inception date (For example, if a composite has been in existence for four years, firms must present one-, three-, and four-year annualized returns in addition to the period-to-date composite return.) Returns for periods of less than one year must not be annualized; or
  - Period-to-date composite returns in addition to five years of annual composite returns (or for each annual period since the composite inception date if the composite has been in existence for less than five years) with the period end date clearly identified. The annual returns must be calculated through the same period of time as presented in the corresponding compliant presentation.
- Whether performance is gross or net of advisory fees;
- Total return of the benchmark for the same periods that composite returns are presented and a benchmark description, and if no benchmark is presented, an explanation why no benchmark is presented;
- Currency used to express returns;
- Description of the use and extent of leverage and derivatives if used as an active part of the strategy and has a material effect on returns; and
- For any performance presented in an advertisement for periods prior to January 1, 2000, that does not comply with the GIPS standards, firms must disclose the periods of noncompliance; and
- If the advertisement conforms to laws and/or regulations that conflict with the requirements of the GIPS standards and/or the GIPS Advertising Guidelines, firms must disclose this fact and disclose the manner in which the laws and/or regulations conflict with the GIPS and/or the GIPS Advertising Guidelines.[244]

Compliance Notes: Claims of Compliance and Performance Advertising

A firm choosing to both claim compliance in an advertisement and present performance information must include performance information required by both applicable law and the standards.[245] Certain pooled

---

[244] *Id.*
[245] *See GIPS Handbook*, Explanation of the Provisions of the GIPS Standards, GIPS Advertising Guidelines.

investment vehicles are legally required to present performance information and therefore those that claim GIPS compliance must provide each prospective investor with GIPS compliant performance information.[246] Currently, a firm may avoid this requirement if the firm does not include a claim of compliance or otherwise mention GIPS in its advertisements.[247] However, in light of the Preliminary Draft Guidance Statement, it is uncertain whether this opt-out will survive.[248]

Minimum Asset Levels

Under the GIPS, firms may set minimum asset levels for the inclusion of a portfolio in a composite.[249] If a minimum asset level is adopted with respect to a composite, a firm cannot include portfolios below the minimum asset level in the composite and cannot retroactively amend the minimum asset level.[250] In the composite's GIPS compliant presentation, the minimum asset level and any changes thereto must be disclosed.[251]

If a firm establishes minimum asset levels, the firm must establish and consistently apply both the composite's minimum asset level and policies regarding the valuation of portfolios across the composite.[252] However, the standards grant firms flexibility to utilize different methods of defining the minimum asset values (e.g., plus or minus a certain percentage of a fixed asset level) and valuation calculations (e.g., beginning value, ending value, beginning value plus cash flows). Further, a portfolio's inclusion or removal in a composite may be contingent upon maintenance of the minimum asset value for a given number of valuation periods (e.g., a portfolio may only be included if its assets are greater than [x] for two consecutive years and only removed if its assets are less than [x] for two consecutive years).[253] Although such a hurdle may increase the composite's ramp-up period, firms may find such a buffer from exclusion helpful for portfolios that are highly volatile or when a portfolio is susceptible to significant asset outflows.

In the event a portfolio is removed from the composite due to a low asset level, its performance must remain in the composite. Should all portfolios be removed from the composite, the composite's performance record would cease. Further, if after the removal of all portfolios from the composite, a portfolio reaches the minimum asset value and is added to the composite, the prior performance history of the composite cannot be mathematically linked to the composite's current performance results.[254]

---

[246] See *Advertisements by Investment Advisers*, Rel. No. 1A-121.
[247] *Id.*
[248] See the discussion of the Gallagher and Associates no-action letter in the discussion of testimonials.
[249] GIPS Standards, 3.A.9.
[250] *Id.*
[251] *GIPS Handbook*, Explanation of the Provisions of the GIPS Standards, 3.A.9.
[252] *Id.*
[253] *Id.* Maintenance periods should be symmetrical.
[254] *Id.*

Compliance Notes: Minimum Asset Levels

Firms should consider the implications of empty composites when establishing minimum asset values. An overly aggressive minimum asset level may disrupt a composite's continuity of performance results. Likewise, a minimum asset level that is too conservative may not adequately reflect the asset needs of the strategy marketed. Firms should carefully review historical portfolio asset levels, inflows and outflows, against the strategy's asset needs before establishing a minimum asset level.

Valuation Principles

For periods beginning on or after January 1, 2011, portfolios must be valued pursuant to the definition of *fair value:* "the amount at which an investment could be exchanged in a current arm's length transaction between willing parties in which the parties each acts knowledgeably and prudently" included in the GIPS Valuation Principles; periods prior to January 1, 2011, may continue to use market valuation.[255] In accordance with the GIPS principles of fair representation and full disclosure, a fair value determination must be made using "objective, observable, unadjusted quoted market price for an identical investment in an active market on the measurement date, if available."[256] When such factors are unavailable, the valuation must be made based on the firm's "best estimate of market value."[257]

The standards also require portfolios to be valued at least monthly and on the date of all large cash flows.[258] However, the GIPS recognize that certain assets are not suitable for monthly valuation.[259] In the case of alternative investments, pricing sources often will not provide monthly valuations. When, for example, a fund is not able to obtain a monthly valuation and accepts client cash flows less often than monthly, the standards permit valuations to be performed less frequently than monthly.[260]

Although the GIPS require firms to establish policies and procedures for valuing portfolios, the standards do not require a firm's valuation policies and procedures to use any specific data inputs. However, the following hierarchy is recommended:[261]

1. Investments must be valued using objective, observable, unadjusted quoted market prices for identical investments in active markets on the measurement date, if available. If not available, then investments should be valued using
2. Quoted prices for identical or similar investments in markets that are not active (markets in which there are few transactions for the investment, the prices are

---

[255] GIPS Standards, 1.A.2, 6.A.1, 7.A.1; *GIPS Handbook,* GIPS Valuation Principles, Fair Value Definition.
[256] *Id.*
[257] *Id.*
[258] GIPS Standards, 1.A.3.
[259] For example, real estate investments are required to be valued quarterly and private equity investments annually. GIPS Standards, 6.A.2 and 7.A.2.
[260] *GIPS Handbook,* Guidance Statement on Alternative Strategies and Structures. Additionally, firms must disclose if they are required to conduct monthly valuations but opt out of doing so.
[261] *GIPS Handbook;* GIPS Valuation Principles, Valuation Recommendations.

not current, or price quotations vary substantially over time and/or between market makers). If not available or appropriate, then investments should be valued based on

3. Market-based inputs, other than quoted prices, that are observable for the investment. If not available or appropriate, then investments should be valued based on

4. Subjective unobservable inputs for the investment where markets are not active at the measurement date. Unobservable inputs should only be used to measure fair value to the extent that observable inputs and prices are not available or appropriate. Unobservable inputs reflect the firm's own assumptions about the assumptions that market participants would use in pricing the investment and should be developed based on the best information available under the circumstances.

Although this hierarchy is a recommendation, firms must, for periods on or after January 1, 2011, disclose any material difference between the composite's valuation policy and the recommended hierarchy.[262]

Compliance Notes: Illiquid Asset Valuation

Although the difference between fair value and market value should not affect the valuation of liquid securities in active markets, firms should consider the implication of this distinction during times of illiquidity and for illiquid investments.[263] Should a formerly liquid asset become illiquid, market prices may not be sufficient to satisfy a firm's valuation obligations under the standards. Therefore, firms should regularly consider the efficiency of the market for their portfolios' investments, especially in times of market stress.[264]

Further, if a firm is a registered investment adviser, the firm should have established valuation procedures pursuant to Rule 206(4)-7 under the Advisers Act that addresses the methodology and frequency of alternative investment valuations.[265] In lieu of creating new valuation policies, the firm should consider incorporating these valuation policies into the firm's GIPS policies and procedures.

---

[262] GIPS Standards, 4.A.28.
[263] See *GIPS Handbook,* Explanation of the Provisions of the GIPS Standards, 1.A.2.
[264] For real estate and private equity investments, the standards require enhanced valuation procedures and disclosures due to the illiquidity of the underlying investments. For example, real estate investments must be valued by a third-party in adherence to the practices of "the relevant valuation governing and standard setting body." *GIPS Handbook;* GIPS Valuation Principles, Additional Real Estate Valuation Requirements, Items 9 and 10. Private equity valuation methodologies must be appropriate for a "particular investment based on the nature, facts, and circumstances of the investment." *GIPS Handbook;* GIPS Valuation Principles, Additional Private Equity Valuation Requirements, Item 17.
[265] See *Compliance Programs of Investment Companies and Investment Advisers,* SEC Rel. No. IA-2204 (Dec. 17, 2003) ("We expect that an adviser's policies and procedures, at a minimum, should address the following issues to the extent they are relevant to that adviser:…processes to value client holdings and assess fees based on those valuations.").

Component Parts of a GIPS Presentation

Performance Periods. For each composite presented in a GIPS presentation, the following items must be reported:

- At least five years of performance (or performance of every year since inception of the fund if in existence for less than five years) presented in, as applicable, one, three and five year returns;
- If in existence for more than five years, returns presented for the lesser of the composite's existence and ten years;
- Returns for each full annual period must be clearly labeled as gross-of-fees or net-of-fees; total return of the benchmark(s) that reflects the composite mandate, objective or strategy must be presented for each annual period;
- The number of portfolios in the composite for each full annual period, if greater than five;
- The composite's assets for each annual period end; and
- Either total firm assets as of the end of each annual period or the composite's assets as a percentage of the total firm's assets as of the end of each annual period.[266] When presenting the returns of a portfolio or composite with less than one year of performance history, such performance should not be annualized in the GIPS compliant presentation, it should be presented as year to date.[267]

When stating firm assets in accordance with the last item above, assets cannot be double-counted. For example, if a firm uses a master-feeder structure in managing alternative investment funds or otherwise, the firm must determine which level of the master-feeder structure is relevant for composite inclusion.[268] The basis of this calculation must be documented in the firm's policies and procedures and applied consistently across composites.

Noncompliant Returns. Firms may link non-GIPS-compliant performance to GIPS-compliant performance if all performance information presented for periods beginning on or after January 1, 2000, is GIPS compliant.[269]

Carve-Outs. For periods beginning January 1, 2010, carve-outs may be included if the carve-out is managed with its own cash balance, and its assets are not allocated from another portfolio. For periods prior to January 1, 2010, asset allocation to carve-outs must have been made in a timely and consistent manner.[270]

For periods beginning on or after January 1, 2006, and ending prior to January 1, 2011, if a composite includes carve-outs, the presentation must include the percentage of the composite that is composed of carve-outs as of each annual period end.[271]

---

[266] GIPS Standards, 5.A.1.
[267] GIPS Standards, 5.A.4.
[268] *GIPS Handbook,* Guidance Statement on Alternative Strategies and Structures.
[269] GIPS Standards, 5.A.3.
[270] GIPS Standards, 3.A.8.
[271] GIPS Standards, 5.A.5.

Estimated Values. When the composite includes illiquid assets, asset values may not always be available. Firms may take one of three approaches to deal with this issue:

- Produce a compliant presentation on a timely basis using the estimated value to determine fair value[272] after making a determination that estimated value is a reliable basis for determining fair value;
- Produce a compliant presentation on a timely basis using last available historical final values to determine fair value; or
- Produce compliant presentations with a time lag only after final valuations have been received.

> *Compliance Notes: Estimated Values*
>
> Of the above approaches, the third may be the most preferential from an administrative ease prospective. In the first two approaches, the firm must update the presentations upon receipt of final performance information and evaluate deviations between the estimated figure and final figure under the firm's GIPS error correction procedure. Although the third approach may not create error correction concerns, it would delay the presentation of performance information.[273]

Nonfee-Paying Portfolios. If any composite contains nonfee-paying portfolios, the percentage composition of the composite's assets represented by the nonfee-paying portfolios must be presented as of each annual period end.[274]

Bundled Fees. If a composite contains any portfolios with bundled fees (a combination of, for example, trading, custody, management, and other administrative fees), the compliant presentation must include the percentage of composite assets represented by portfolios with bundled fees as of each annual period end.[275]

Model Fees. When the firm presents returns for a fund with multiple classes of shares or a composite with multiple portfolios, it may not be practicable to reflect all actual fees applicable to all share classes and series. Instead of reporting actual fees, the firm may apply the highest investment management fee and apply it across the composite. If it is not possible to determine the highest fee, either due to performance-based fees

---

[272] *Fair value* is defined as the "amount at which an investment could be exchanged in a current arm's length transaction between willing parties in which the parties each act knowledgeably and prudently. The valuation must be determined using the objective, observable, unadjusted quoted market price for an identical investment in an active market on the measurement date, if available. In the absence of an objective, observable, unadjusted quoted market price for an identical investment in an active market on the measurement date, the valuation must represent the Firm's best estimate of the Market Value. Fair Value must include accrued income." *GIPS Handbook,* GIPS Glossary, "Fair Value." For periods prior to January 1, 2011, firms must value assets based on market value. GIPS Standards, 0.A.13.

[273] *See GIPS Handbook,* Guidance Statement on Alternative Strategies and Structures. Although the guidance statement provides specific examples with reference to funds of funds, we believe the same principles regarding the use of estimated values apply to illiquid investments generally. Private equity and real estate assets are also subject to the GIPS guidance statements specific to such asset classes.

[274] GIPS Standards, 5.A.6.

[275] GIPS Standards, 5.A.7.

or a similarly variable fee arrangement, the net-of-fee returns may reflect the deduction of the highest model fee applicable to the specific prospective client or intended recipient of the GIPS compliant presentation, so long as the model net-of-fee returns are not higher than the returns that would have been presented had actual fees been used.[276]

Fund of Fund Fees. When presenting returns for a fund of funds composite strategy, both gross-of-fees and net-of-fees returns must be net of all the underlying funds' fees and expenses.[277]

Master Feeder Fund Fees. Presentation of net-of-fees returns for master funds must reflect any fees charged at the feeder fund level.[278]

Performance Fees. Presentation of net-of-fees returns must reflect any performance-based fees and/or carried interest.[279]

Stub Periods. When the initial period for a composite with an inception date on or after January 1, 2011, is less than one year, performance must be shown through the initial period end.[280] Where a composite terminates on or after January 1, 2011, performance must be shown from the last annual period end through the composite termination date.[281]

Volatility. The firm must disclose the measure of internal dispersion of individual portfolio returns for each annual period, unless the composite has five portfolios of less in any full year.[282] Further, for all composite performance showing performance ending on or after January 1, 2011, firms must show three-year annualized ex-post standard deviation (using monthly returns) of both the composite and the benchmark as of each annual period end.[283] However, if a firm believes that the three-year annualized ex-post standard deviation is not relevant or appropriate, the firm must show an additional three-year ex-post risk measure for the benchmark (if applicable and appropriate) and the composite, the measure of which must be identical in each case.[284]

Side-Pockets. Disclosure of side-pocket performance varies depending on the discretionary nature of the side-pockets. Although the firm is responsible for distinguishing between discretionary and nondiscretionary side-pockets, the GIPS note that a side-pocket may only be classified as nondiscretionary if all of the following criteria are met:

- It is segregated into a separate subportfolio;
- Its assets are no longer considered in the fund's asset allocation and investment process;

---

[276] *GIPS Handbook*, Guidance Statement on Alternative Strategies and Structures.
[277] GIPS Standards, 7.A.7.
[278] *Id.*
[279] GIPS Standards, 4.A.6.
[280] GIPS Standards, 5.A.1.c.
[281] GIPS Standards, 5.A.1.d. *See GIPS Handbook*, GIPS Glossary, "Composite Termination Date" (defining "Composite Termination Date" as the "date that the last portfolio exits a composite").
[282] GIPS Standards, 5.A.4.
[283] GIPS Standards, 4.A.33.
[284] GIPS Standards, 4.A.34.

- There are no investment decisions for the side-pocket assets (other than monitoring and liquidating); and
- Side-pocket assets are subject to no (or reduced) investment management fees.[285]

If a composite includes discretionary side-pockets and contains only one portfolio, performance must be presented both including and excluding the side-pocket. Where a composite includes multiple portfolios and one or more portfolio includes a discretionary side-pocket, performance must include the performance of the discretionary side-pocket (inclusion of separate performance excluding the side-pocket is not required). Where a side-pocket is nondiscretionary, however, performance of the side-pocket must be excluded from the composite performance.[286]

> *Compliance Notes: Discretionary and Nondiscretionary Side Pockets*
>
> Prior to formulating the enumerated test above, the Standards lent firms more independence to define and apply their own definition of "discretion" with respect to side-pockets. The standards' move to an objective test likely reflects a concern that firms will use side-pockets to remove underperforming investments from a compliant presentation. Although the SEC has not endorsed the factors identified in the GIPS' test, the SEC shares the standards' concern that side-pockets may be used to hide the performance of poorly performing assets.[287] Further, the SEC requires disclosure regarding any material factors that affect performance.[288]

Disclosures

A firm that claims compliance with GIPS must disclose the following information in the GIPS compliant presentation:

- **Firm Definition.** Firm definition used to determine total firm assets and firmwide compliance. When a portfolio is subject to oversight by a third party who is theoretically free to follow the firm's advice or not, firms must include the portfolio in the firm definition if the firm effectively exercises discretionary investment management and can provide documented evidence to demonstrate that all investment advice has been implemented accordingly;
- **Firm Redefinition.** If the firm has been redefined, must disclose the date of, description of, and reason for redefinition;
- **List of Composites.** The availability of a complete list and description of all firm composites;

---

[285] *GIPS Handbook*, Guidance Statement on Alternative Strategies and Structures.
[286] *Id.*
[287] *See* SEC Charges Georgia-Based Hedge Fund Managers with Fraud in Valuing a "Side Pocket" and Theft of Investor Assets, Statement of Robert B. Kaplan, Former Co-Chief of the SEC's Asset Management Unit, *SEC News Digest* (Oct. 19, 2010) ("Side pockets are not supposed to be a dumping ground for hedge fund managers to conceal overvalued assets…deceive[d] investors about the fund's performance and extract[ed] excessive management fees based on the inflated asset values in a side pocket.").
[288] *See* Clover Capital Management, Inc. (Oct. 28, 1986).

- **Composite Description.** Composite description (i.e., general information regarding the composite strategy), including whether illiquid securities are a significant part of the composite strategy or if there is a strategic intent to invest in illiquid investments;
- **Composite Redefinition.** If composite redefined, must disclose data of, description of, and reason for change. Changes to composite cannot be applied retroactively;
- **Composite Name Change.** Any changes to the composite's name;
- **Composite Creation Date.** Composite's creation date;
- **Minimum Asset Levels.** Minimum asset level (if any) below which portfolios are not included in a composite, and any changes to the minimum asset level;
- **Gross-of-Fee Performance.** With respect to gross-of-fee performance, whether any fees are deducted in addition to the trading expense;
- **Net-of-Fee Performance.** With respect to net-of-fee performance, whether any fees are deducted in addition to the investment management fees and trading expenses, if model or actual investment management fees are used and if returns are net of any performance-based fees;
- **Fee Schedule.** The fee schedule appropriate to the presentation;
- **Currency.** The currency used to express performance;
- **Dispersion Measures.** The dispersion measure used;
- **Calculation Policies.** The policies for valuing portfolios, calculating performance and preparing compliant presentations are available upon request;
- **Leverage and Derivatives.** The presence, use, and extent of leverage, derivatives, and short positions, if material, including description of frequency of use and characteristics of the instruments sufficient to identify risks;
- **Significant Events.** All significant events that would help a prospective client interpret the compliant presentation. If a composite contains investment that become illiquid or if an illiquid investment ceases to be managed in a discretionary manner, the firm must disclose this fact to the extent the firm determines the situation rises to the level of a significant event;
- **Noncompliant Periods.** If performance presented prior to January1, 2000, does not comply with GIPS, all periods of non-compliance;
- **Withholding Tax.** Relevant details of treatment of withholding tax on dividends, interest income, and capital gains, if material;
- **Exchange Rates—**
  - Any known material differences in exchange rates or valuation sources used among portfolios within a composite and between composite and benchmark, for periods beginning on or after January 1, 2011, and
  - Any known inconsistencies in exchange rates used among portfolios within a composite and between composite and benchmark, for periods prior to January 1, 2011;
- **Local Law.** If local laws and regulations differ from GIPS, must disclose that presentation adheres to local laws and disclose manner in which law conflicts with GIPS;[289]

---

[289] The standards' requirements are not always consistent with those of the SEC, CFTC or FINRA. *See* later discussion of contrasting positions.

- **Carve-outs.** If, for periods prior to January 1, 2010, carve-outs are included in a composite, disclose the policy used to allocate cash to carve-outs;
- **Side-Pockets.** If any portfolio in the composite contains side-pockets;
- **Bundled Fees.** If composite contains portfolios with bundled fees, the types of fees that are included in the bundled fee;
- **Subadvisers.** For periods beginning on or after January 1, 2006, the use of subadviser and periods a subadviser was used;
- **Month-End Valuations.** *For periods prior to January 1, 2010,* must disclose if any portfolios were not valued at calendar month end or on the last business day of the month;
- **Use of Subjective Inputs.** *For periods beginning on or after January 1, 2011,* must disclose use of subjective unobservable inputs for valuing portfolio investments if the portfolio investments valued using subjective unobservable inputs are material to the composite;[290]
- **Valuation Hierarchy.** *For periods beginning on or after January 1, 2011,* must disclose if the composite's valuation hierarchy materially differs from the recommended valuation hierarchy in the GIPS Valuation Principles;
- **Valuation Frequency.** Firms must disclose if any portfolios in a composite are valued less frequently than monthly and/or are unable to be valued on the date of large cash flows, and must disclose why such valuations are not possible;
- **Estimated Values.** Firms must disclose whether estimated values are used for a composite and any additional information necessary or appropriate in connection with the use of estimated values;
- **Benchmarks—**
  - Firms must disclose the benchmark description and whether benchmark returns are net of withholding taxes (if such information is available),
  - If no benchmark is shown, the firm must disclose why no benchmark is presented;
  - If the firm changes benchmark, must disclose date of, description of, and reason for change.
  - Although GIPS permits custom benchmarks and a combination of multiple benchmarks, the firm must disclose the benchmark components, weights and rebalancing process; and
  - Must disclose if the three-year annualized ex-post standard deviation of the benchmark is not presented because 36 monthly returns are not available;
- **Significant Cash Flows.** If the firm has adopted a significant cash flow policy for the composite, must disclose how the firm defines significant cash flow and for which periods. If a firm temporarily removed portfolios with significant cash flows from a composite, the firm must disclose that the following is available upon request:
  - The grace period for the composite,
  - If altered, the date and description of change for the significant cash flow definition, policies or grace periods for handling significant cash flows,

---

[290] Subjective unobservable inputs should only be used to measure fair value of portfolio investments if observable inputs and prices are not available or appropriate. Unobservable inputs reflect the firm's own assumptions about the assumptions that market participants would use in pricing the investment and should be developed based on the best information available under the circumstances.

- The number of portfolios removed during the applicable period,
- The number of times portfolios were removed during a given period, and
- The amount of composite assets represented by the portfolios affected by the application of the significant cash flow policy;
- **Risk.** Must disclose if the three-year annualized ex-post standard deviation of the composite is not presented because 36 monthly returns are not available. If the three-year annualized ex-post standard deviation is not relevant or appropriate, must describe
  - Why the ex-post standard deviation is not relevant or appropriate, and
  - The additional risk measure presented and why it was selected; and
- **Linked Performance.** Must disclose if performance from a past firm or affiliation is linked to the performance of the firm, pursuant to the GIPS portability requirements.

Annual Notification Requirement

As of January 1, 2015, each firm claiming compliance with GIPS must annually notify the CFA Institute of such claim.[291] The initial compliance date was June 30, 2015, and forms may be submitted electronically through the CFA Institute's website. Firms must decide whether to be listed on the GIPS website as a firm claiming compliance or to opt out of being listed by checking the appropriate box on the form.

Failure to notify the CFA Institute of a claim of GIPS compliance will be deemed a failure to comply with GIPS and may call into question the validity of a firm's claim of compliance, including any claims made in a firm's marketing materials. The SEC has taken a strong position that a firm that advertises its claim of GIPS compliance in marketing materials but that does not comply with all of the GIPS requirements is misleading under Section 206 of the Advisers Act (the general antifraud provision) and Rule 206(4)-1 thereunder (the advertisement rule). Therefore, failing to comply with the GIPS annual notification requirement could result in serious regulatory consequences.

> *Compliance Notes: Regulatory Considerations for Privately Offered Funds*
>
> For firms that manage funds relying on the exemption from registration provided by Rule 506(b) of Regulation D under the Securities Act, listing firm information on the GIPS website may raise questions about whether such listing violates Rule 506(b)'s ban on general advertising and solicitation. Similarly, the posting may jeopardize the safe harbor provided by Regulation S under the Securities Act if the posting would result in a directed selling effort or otherwise condition the United States market for any offered security. If a firm manages funds that are offered under the private placement regime in a foreign jurisdiction, the firm should consider whether posting its information to the GIPS website would affect the continued availability of the applicable foreign private placement

---

[291] CFA Institute, GIPS Executive Committee Approves GIPS Standards Requirement for Firms to Notify CFA Institute of their Claim of Compliance with the GIPS Standards, http://www.gipsstandards.org/news/Pages/detail.aspx?ID=47

exemption. Accordingly, firms should carefully consider the benefits and risks of a public listing on the GIPS website when completing and submitting their notification forms.

V. CFTC

The Commodity Futures Trading Commission (CFTC) has adopted various rules relating to advertising and promotional materials used by commodity pool operators (CPOs) and commodity trading advisors (CTAs).[292] These rules apply to all CPOs and CTAs, regardless of whether they are exempt from registration under the Commodity Exchange Act (CEA).[293] The National Futures Association (NFA) has similarly adopted rules applicable to the advertising and promotional materials used by CPOs and CTAs that are registered with the NFA.[294]

The following section provides an overview of the CFTC and NFA rules applicable to CPO and CTA advertising and promotional materials. The CFTC's general advertising rule applies to any publication, distribution or broadcast of any report, letter, circular, memorandum, publication, writing, advertisement, or other literature or advice whether by electronic media or otherwise, including information provided via internet or email, the texts of standardized oral presentations and of radio, television, and seminar or similar mass media presentations.[295] Similarly, the NFA's general advertising rule applies to promotional materials used by NFA member CPOs and CTAs, or their associated persons,[296] which include:

- Any text of a standardized oral presentation or any communication for publication in any newspaper, magazine, or similar medium, or for broadcast over television, radio, or the electronic medium, that is disseminated or directed to the public concerning a futures account, agreement or transaction;
- Any standardized form of report, letter, circular, memorandum or publication which is disseminated or directed to the public; and
- Any other written material disseminated or directed to the public for the purpose of soliciting a futures account, agreement or transaction.[297]

> ***Compliance Notes: Definition of Promotional Material***
>
> The NFA's broad definition of *promotional materials* is generally understood to include any website content, standardized presentations, and materials sent to prospective clients, standard scripts designed to respond to

---

[292] *See*, generally, CFTC Regulation 4.41.
[293] CFTC Regulation 4.41(c)(2).
[294] *See*, generally, NFA Compliance Rule 2-29. CPOs and CTAs that are registered under the CEA are required to become members of the NFA and are subject to the NFA's compliance rules and guidance.
[295] *See*, generally, CFTC Regulation 4.41.
[296] *Associated persons* are individuals who solicit orders, customers or customer funds (or who supervise persons so engaged) on behalf of a CPO or CTA. Associated persons are required to be individually registered with the NFA.
[297] *See*, generally, NFA Compliance Rule 2-29.

inquiries and content that is provided only to a single prospective investor, even if that prospective investor is characterized as sophisticated or institutional.[298] Some have taken the position that responses to requests for proposals may also be considered promotional materials subject to NFA rules.

General Background and Antifraud Rules

CFTC Regulation 4.41 contains a general antifraud provision, which states that CPOs and CTAs may not advertise in a manner that employs any device, scheme, or artifice to defraud any participant or client or prospective participant or client; or involves any transaction, practice, or course of business which operates as a fraud or deceit upon any participant or client or any prospective participant or client. Similarly, the general antifraud prohibition contained in NFA Compliance Rule 2-29 provides that no registered CPO or CTA may make any communication with the public that operates as a fraud or deceit, employs or is part of a high-pressure approach, or makes any statement that futures trading is appropriate for all persons.[299] Furthermore, no NFA member (including any registered CPO or CTA) may use promotional materials for commodity interest advice or commodity pools that is likely to deceive the public, or contains any material misstatement of fact or that the NFA member knows omits a fact if the omission makes the promotional material misleading.[300]

> #### *Compliance Notes: Antifraud Rules*
>
> "High pressure approaches" are generally understood to include:
>
> - Rushing a customer through account opening forms and glossing over the risk disclosure in haste to open the account;
> - An overnight courier service delivering blank account forms to the customer and waiting while the customer completes the form;
> - Actively attempting to dissuade unsophisticated customers from seeking further advice on their investment decisions;
> - Threatening or intimidating customers; and
> - Phone calls made at unusual hours and with unusual frequency, so as to annoy and harass a customer into opening and account.[301]

Testimonials, Statements of Opinion, and Statements Relating to the Possibility of Profit

Testimonials. CPOs and CTAs may not use testimonials in any promotional materials, advertisements, or sales literature unless the relevant document discloses that the testimonial may not be representative of the experience of other clients, that the testimonial is no guarantee of future performance or success, and, if more than a nominal

---

[298] *See*, generally, NFA Compliance Rule 2-29 and "Guide to NFA Compliance Rules 2-29 and 2-36."
[299] NFA Compliance Rule 2-29(a).
[300] NFA Compliance Rule 2-29(b).
[301] "Guide to NFA Compliance Rules 2-29 and 2-36," at 9–10.

sum is paid, the fact that it is a paid testimonial.[302] Furthermore, any promotional materials of NFA members should include disclosure that a testimonial is not representative of all reasonably comparable accounts, state prominently that the testimonial is not indicative of future performance or success, and state prominently that it is a paid testimonial (if applicable).[303]

Statements of Opinion. Any statements of opinion contained in the promotional materials of NFA members must clearly be identified as opinions and must be supported by a reasonable basis in fact.[304] Generally, the extent of support required for an opinion statement will depend on the nature of the opinion.[305] The NFA has acknowledged that certain opinions by their nature may not be susceptible to ironclad support documentation, but NFA members should be careful to always be able to demonstrate at least a reasonable basis for their claims.[306]

Statements of the Possibility of Profit. Promotional materials that contain a discussion of the possibility of profit must be accompanied by an *equally prominent* statement of the risk of loss.[307] "Equal prominence" is generally understood to require that the possibility of profits and loss must be emphasized proportionally considering font size, the number of times profit is address as compared to the number of times risk of loss is addressed, and whether the risk disclaimer addressing the risk of loss is unique to the futures industry, as opposed to trading activities generally.[308] Furthermore, the discussion addressing risk should stand alone and should not include qualifiers.

> *Compliance Notes: Testimonials and Statements Relating to the Possibility of Profit.*
>
> **Testimonials.** We note to compliance personnel that in light of the vast number of registered investment advisers that have had to register as CPOs and/or CTAs, such dually registered firms must comply with the stricter Advisers Act general prohibition on testimonials, subject to relevant SEC Staff interpretations.[309]
>
> **Statements of the Possibility of Profit.** The NFA provided the following example of qualified risk disclosure that is not acceptable: "Commodity trading involves substantial risk of loss. However, it is less risky than investing in swaps."[310] As a practical matter, the NFA staff typically expects to see the risk of loss disclaimers on the same page as the statements relating to the possibility of profits.

---

[302] CFTC Regulation 4.41(a)(3).
[303] NFA Compliance Rule 2-29(b)(6).
[304] NFA Compliance Rule 2-29(d).
[305] "Guide to NFA Compliance Rules 2-29 and 2-36," at 11.
[306] *Id.*
[307] NFA Compliance Rule 2-29(c).
[308] "Guide to NFA Compliance Rules 2-29 and 2-36," at 10.
[309] *See* Rule 206(4)-1(a)(1) under the Advisers Act ; CIGNA Securities, Inc., SEC No-Action Letter (pub. avail. Sept. 10, 1991) (stating that written statements from satisfied financial planning clients are testimonials prohibited by Rule 206(4)-1(A)(1); New York Investors Group, Inc., SEC No-Action Letter (pub. avail. Sept. 7, 1982).
[310] *Id.*

Performance Information

Past Performance. Any past performance included in the promotional materials used by an NFA member must be accompanied by a statement that past performance is not necessarily indicative of future results.[311] Past performance must be representative of the actual performance of all reasonably comparable accounts for the same time period, and must be calculated in accordance with the relevant CFTC and NFA regulations depending on the type of account. Performance for commodity pools must be calculated in accordance with CFTC Regulation 4.25(a)(7). Performance for separate accounts must be calculated in compliance with CFTC Regulation 4.35(a)(6) and NFA Compliance Rule 2-34. All past performance used in promotional or sales materials of CPOs and CTAs generally must be presented net of fees and must be recent as of a date no more than three months prior to the date of the promotional materials.[312] Senior staff at the NFA, however, have informally indicated that gross of fees information can be presented in one-on-one presentations to wealthy individuals, pension funds, universities and other institutions (clients who have sufficient assets to justify a one-on-one presentation), and consultants as permitted under applicable SEC guidance under the Advisers Act, as described earlier in this chapter provided gross of fees information is presented with net of fees information.

Compliance Notes: Past Performance

Any past performance used in promotional materials by a CPO or CTA:

- Must be balanced with regard to the risk of loss (*See* the earlier discussion about statements of the possibility of profit);
- Must fully disclose the nature of the results (for example, disclose what is meant by and included in "average rate of return");
- Must not be presented as "average" or "cumulative" returns where individual returns for the period have wide fluctuations;
- Must not omit any information that would render the data misleading; and
- Must be accompanied by disclosure of all relevant costs, including commissions, spreads, and fees. [313]

Performance Calculation: Annual Rates of Return. Annual rates of return generally must be based on twelve consecutive months of performance, be computed on a compounded monthly basis, and be calculated by dividing net performance by beginning net asset value for pools, and beginning and end of period portfolio values for separate accounts. CPOs and CTAs may use one of the following three alternative methods for calculating returns discussed in Appendix B of the CFTC's Part 4 regulations; however, CPOs and CTAs must use the method that most accurately depicts client performance:

---

[311] NFA Compliance Rule 2-29(b)(4).
[312] NFA Compliance Rule 2-29(b)(5) and CFTC Regulation 4.25(a)(7).
[313] "Guide to NFA Compliance Rates 2-29 and 2-36," at 11–12.

- Time weighting for additions and withdrawals;
- Only accounts traded; or
- Compounded rate of return.

Once a method of calculating rate of return is selected, it must be used consistently for periods going forward, unless its use would produce misleading results.[314]

With respect to managed accounts, returns may include interest earned on actual funds but may not impute interest on other funds. Furthermore, for partially funded separately managed accounts, rates of return must be calculated using nominal account size (and not actual funds) as the denominator.[315]

The Use of Third-Party Ratings and Rankings. A CPO or a CTA may include third-party ratings or rankings based on performance in their promotional materials only in certain circumstances and with certain disclosures. Third-party rankings may not be accompanied by any implication that the ranking is officially sanctioned by the futures industry and must be supported by all data necessary to support the performance results. Third-party rankings must also be accompanied by disclosure about the basis and limitations of the rankings used. Similarly, the ratings must be based on the rate of return calculations that comply with CFTC rate of return rules (as just discussed). Finally, as with all performance, third-party ratings based on performance must be accompanied by a statement that past performance does not guarantee future results.[316]

Hypothetical Performance. CPOs and CTAs are subject to a variety of restrictions on the use of "hypothetical" performance. The NFA takes a broad understanding of what constitute hypothetical performance, including:

- Any trade or series of trades that was not actually executed for an account;
- Simulated trading;
- Combining the performance of several advisors who have not traded together;
- Applying models or calculations to actual performance; and
- "Extracted performance" (as discussed in more detail below) of one component of a broader trading program.[317]

Regardless of the type of investor that is receiving the promotional materials, hypothetical performance must be clearly so labeled and calculated in the same manner as actual performance. CPOs and CTAs also must be able to demonstrate the validity of the presentation, the underlying theory generating the hypothetical results, and the basis for their calculations.[318]

For promotional materials that are directed solely to nonqualified eligible persons (QEPs) within the meaning of CFTC Regulation 4.7, hypothetical performance may

---

[314] "Guide to NFA Compliance Rates 2-29 and 2-36," at 12.
[315] NFA Compliance Rule 2-34(A).
[316] "Guide to NFA Compliance Rates 2-29 and 2-36," at 21.
[317] "Guide to NFA Compliance Rates 2-29 and 2-36," at 13.
[318] *Id.*

be used, but must be accompanied by a specific disclaimer, displayed as prominently as the results and immediately preceding or following the results (if the hypothetical or simulated results are lengthy, disclosure may need to be made more than once).[319] See Appendix A to this chapter for the full text of the required disclaimer. However, no matter whom promotional materials are directed to, CFTC Regulation 4.41 requires a hypothetical performance disclaimer.

Compliance Notes: Hypothetical Performance

The following restrictions apply to the use of hypothetical performance in CPO and/or CTA promotional materials that are directed to investors that are not QEPs:

- Hypothetical performance may not be used for any program with at least three months of performance; and
- The promotional materials must include disclosure of all material assumptions made in preparing the hypothetical results, including but not limited to
  - The initial investment amount,
  - Whether profits were reinvested or distributed,
  - Commissions and fees that were charged, and
  - The method used for determining the purchase and sales prices for each hypothetical transaction.
- Where both hypothetical and actual results appear, you must show actual results with at least equal prominence;
- The promotional materials must include performance for all discretionary customer accounts for the past five years; and
- The promotional materials must include a prescribed disclosure legend, displayed as prominently as the results and immediately preceding or following the results (again, if the hypothetical or simulated results are lengthy, disclosures may need to be made more than once).[320] See Appendix A to this chapter for the full text of the required disclaimer.

"Extracted performance," meaning the performance of one component of a broader trading program, may only be presented to non-QEPs if the material expressly designates the specific percentage of assets committed to the component being highlighted (i.e., if a pool's disclosure document states that a certain percentage of a fund's assets are dedicated to a particular strategy, the pool may "extract" the results of that strategy). Similarly, it may only be used if the results are adequately labeled as extracted performance, and the trading results of the overall program are disclosed with equal prominence.[321]

---

[319] CFTC Regulation 4.41; NFA Compliance Rule 2.29(c). If you prefer, promotional materials containing hypothetical performance that are directed only to QEPs may also contain the legends provided below that are to be included in non-QEP materials.
[320] NFA Compliance Rule 2-29.
[321] "Guide to NFA Compliance Rates 2-29 and 2-36," at 12.

Procedures for Submitting Advertising/Promotional Materials to the NFA

Certain advertising and promotional materials used by CPOs or CTAs must be submitted to the NFA for preapproval. Advertising materials may be submitted to the NFA in various electronic formats (i.e., Microsoft Word, PDF, rich text, PowerPoint, CD, email, zip file, etc.). The following list of materials is required to be submitted to the NFA for review and approval at least ten days prior to use if such materials include specific trade recommendations or reference past or potential profits:

- Webinars—outline/script of what will be discussed;
- Live feeds—outline/script of what will be discussed;
- Radio advertisements;
- TV advertisements; and
- Any other audio or video advertisement distributed through media accessible by the public.

> ### Compliance Notes: Submission of Promotional Materials to NFA
>
> In order to submit the relevant promotional materials to the NFA, the CPO or CTA must include a cover letter indicating: the purpose for the submission (note that the submission is a required preapproval piece as opposed to a voluntary prereview request), and contact details for the person(s) to whom the NFA should reply. The latter may be someone other than, or in addition to, the person who initially submits the material for preapproval or prereview. To complete the submission, the CPO or CTA must send a hard copy of cover letter and promotional material to:
>
> National Futures Association (NFA)
> Advertising Regulatory Team
> 300 South Riverside Plaza, Suite 1800
> Chicago, IL 60606
>
> or
>
> Send electronic copy of cover letter and promotional material to: art@nfa.futures.org

VI. DIFFERENCES AMONG REGULATORY BODIES

Although the overarching objectives of all advertising regimes are investor protection and full and fair disclosure, there are significant differences in the treatment of marketing and advertising materials. These differences often are a point of confusion for internal compliance personnel when reviewing and approving marketing and advertising materials. This section discusses some of the key differences among the regulatory regimes; also discussed are best practices for compliance monitoring and the review and approval of marketing materials.

When a compliance officer works with divergent marketing rules among the SEC, GIPS, CFTC, and FINRA, it is important to understand both the hierarchy among the regimes and which regimes apply in which contexts. As previously discussed, adherence to GIPS is voluntary. In contrast, compliance with SEC, CFTC, and FINRA (collectively, the "mandatory regimes") rules is always mandatory for any firm falling within the purview of each regulator. To the extent that contradictory positions exist between GIPS and the mandatory regimes, firms must comply with the applicable mandatory regime position.[322] However, where the GIPS are stricter than the mandatory regimes' rules, a GIPS-compliant firm must adhere to the higher standards under GIPS. For firms regulated by more than one of the mandatory regimes, it is important to recognize the jurisdiction of each of the SEC, CFTC, and FINRA and when to apply the rules of each in reviewing materials. An understanding of the scope of jurisdiction of each regime is essential to determining which rules apply to any particular marketing or advertising material.

What Is an "Advertisement"?

The regulatory regimes differ even among the baseline question of which marketing materials are subject to regulatory scrutiny. As previously discussed, the Advisers Act broadly defines the term *advertisement* to include any communication addressed to more than one person or any announcement generally related to investment advice.[323] Although the Advisers Act general antifraud provision governs all activities of an investment adviser, communications deemed to be advertisements are subject to additional regulations.[324] Similarly, the CFTC and NFA broadly define promotional material to include any publication, distribution, or broadcast of any report, publication, literature, or similar item.[325] Recall that FINRA treats communications as retail communications (distributed to over 25 retail investors), correspondence (distributed to 25 or fewer retail investors), or institutional communications (distributed only to institutional investors), with each category subject to varying regulations.[326] Finally, GIPS has created the GIPS Advertising Guidelines to provide firms with options for advertising performance when mentioning the firm's claim of compliance. GIPS generally define an *advertisement* as any material distributed to more than one person designed to maintain existing clients or solicit prospective clients.[327] GIPS advertisements are subject to specific requirements regarding disclosure and performance presentation.[328] However, a firm that does not mention the GIPS standards in a GIPS advertisement is not required to comply with the requirements of the GIPS Advertising Guidelines.

---

[322] Adherence to applicable law or regulation is a requirement under the GIPS themselves. CFA Institute, *Global Investment Performance Standards Handbook*, 39 (3rd ed., 2012) ("GIPS Handbook").
[323] Advisers Act Rule 206(4)-1(b). Refer to the earlier detailed overview of the Advisers Act definition of an advertisement.
[324] Advisers Act Rule 206(4)-1.
[325] NFA Rule 2-29.
[326] FINRA Rules 2210 and 2212-2216. Refer to the earlier examination of FINRA for a more detailed overview of the requirements applicable to each FINRA category of communication.
[327] *GIPS Handbook*, at 291.
[328] *GIPS Handbook*, at 291–301.

Key Substantive Differences

Products Being Marketed. The initial question for compliance professionals to consider for marketing materials is the product being marketed. FINRA rules generally do not apply to the marketing of advisory services (i.e., a strategy) because such marketing is generally done through the adviser performing such services.[329] CFTC/NFA rules apply if the product being marketed (whether a strategy or security) involves trading commodities and/or futures.[330] GIPS may apply to a strategy through the use of composites.[331] If securities are being marketed, FINRA does apply because in most cases funds are sold through brokers registered with FINRA. Where a fund is self-distributed and does not make use of a broker, compliance personnel should review under SEC Advisers Act standards.[332] The Advisers Act and GIPS otherwise generally apply only when marketing separate account advisory services. However, a CFA panel at the 2013 GIPS Conference indicated that the CFA takes the position that the GIPS standards apply to fund marketing materials, a position that is not consistent with GIPS as currently drafted. Should this position be formalized in guidance from the CFA, firms will face even further challenges, including the GIPS requirements to present composite (i.e., related) performance versus SEC and FINRA positions. It is recommended that all GIPS-compliant firms be cognizant of any new guidance or developments on this topic.

A common problematic scenario for determining the applicable regulatory regime comes with dual employee arrangements. Dual employee arrangements, the most common of which involve individual employees acting in the capacity of both a registered representative of a broker-dealer and a supervised person of an investment adviser, are common in the financial services industry, and are recognized by both the SEC and FINRA.[333] Dual employee arrangements can arise when one firm is dually registered as an investment adviser and as a broker-dealer, as well as when an individual employee is employed by both an adviser and a separate but affiliated broker-dealer. Remember that marketing materials are subject to the supervision of the broker-dealer when performing activities in furtherance of the broker's business, and by the investment adviser when relating to the provision of investment advisory (IA) services. The regulatory scheme applicable to marketing materials

---

[329] For example, *see* FINRA Rule 2111 ("A member or an associated person must have a reasonable basis to believe that a recommended *transaction or investment strategy involving a security or securities* is suitable for the customer.") (emphasis added).

[330] NFA Rule 2-29 (" 'Futures account, agreement, or transaction' includes futures accounts and orders, commodity pool participations, agreements to direct or guide trading in futures accounts, and agreements and transactions involving the sale, through publications or otherwise, of non-personalized trading advice concerning futures.").

[331] GIPS themselves define a *composite* as "an aggregation of one or more portfolios managed according to a similar investment mandate, objective, or strategy." *GIPS Handbook*, at 45.

[332] FINRA Rule 0140 ("The [FINRA] rules shall apply to all members and persons associated with a member.").

[333] Dual employment arrangements are not expressly recognized in the federal securities laws, SEC rules, or FINRA rules. However, the SEC's tacit approval of such arrangements is demonstrated by numerous references to dual employee arrangements in SEC staff no-action letters (though such letters all involve discussions of other legal issues), and the SEC staff's express approval for foreign SEC-registered investment advisers to use, in addition to their own employees, persons who were also employees of affiliated banks and advisers not registered with the SEC. ABN AMRO Bank N.V., SEC No-Action Letter (pub. avail. July 1, 1997). Likewise, FINRA has also long recognized that registered representatives of member broker-dealers may also conduct investment advisory or banking business outside the scope of their association with the employing member. *See, e.g.*, FINRA Notice to Members 91-32.

used by dual employees depends on whether the materials relate to promoting the firm's investment advisory services or promoting the firm's securities business. [334]

Pursuant to applicable FINRA guidance, marketing materials are deemed to be promoting the broker-dealer's securities business if they are used to solicit customers for any arrangements in which the broker-dealer or its registered representatives participate in the execution of securities transactions and receive transaction-based compensation in lieu of or in addition to an advisory fee.[335] This distinction follows from the statutory definition of *broker*, which has been regularly interpreted by the SEC to include persons who receive transaction-based compensation with respect to securities transactions.[336] By contrast, materials that promote the firm's fee-based investment advisory services are subject to the Advisers Act.[337]

When a compliance officer determines the appropriate regulatory regime for a dual employee, FINRA advertising rules[338] will apply to marketing materials used by such dual employee if they are deemed to be "related to promoting [the broker-dealer's] securities business." Under FINRA guidance, marketing materials that discuss any securities offered by or through the broker-dealer (e.g., registered or private funds for which the broker-dealer acts as distributor or placement agent) would likely meet the foregoing test. Materials meeting the foregoing test need to comply with FINRA rules and be maintained in the broker-dealer's advertising file. Marketing materials that relate solely to IA services would typically not be subject to FINRA regulation if they were provided to a client or prospective client by the dual employee.[339] Effectively, the dual employee would be acting as an adviser employee in providing adviser materials to the prospective client and the materials themselves would not be under FINRA jurisdiction. Rather, such materials would be subject to the advertising and marketing requirements under Section 206 of the Advisers Act, as well as SEC staff pronouncements on investment adviser advertising.

The question of which regime applies is significant because of the differences in positions taken by each. Recent amendments to CFTC rules have required vastly more advisers to register as CTAs or CPOs (and become NFA members) and become subject

---

[334] *See* FINRA Interpretive Letter to Ms. Dawn Bond, FSC Securities Corporation, Application of Rule 2210 to the Use of Investment Projections and Marketing Material When Registered Persons Are Conducting Advisory Services (Jul. 30, 1998).

[335] *Id.*

[336] *See*, e.g., Brumberg, Mackey & Wall, P.L.C. SEC No-Action Letter (pub. avail. May 17, 2010).

[337] FINRA Interpretive Letter to Ms. Dawn Bond.

[338] *See* FINRA Rule 2210 (Communications with the Public).

[339] *See* FINRA Interpretive Letter to Ms. Dawn Bond. With respect to marketing material used by dual employees, FINRA clarified that the application of then-NASD Rule 2210 depends on whether the materials in question are "related to promoting the member's securities business." Materials are not subject to then-NASD Rule 2210 if they are used exclusively to solicit on behalf of an advisory business, do not contain the member's name, and do not contain references to securities. However, the interpretive letter states that materials would be "soliciting for the member's securities business," and therefore subject to then-NASD Rule 2210, if they are used to solicit customers for any arrangement (such as a wrap-fee program) in which the member or its registered representatives participate in the execution of securities transactions. Therefore, if a broker-dealer is involved in executing transactions for separately managed accounts offered by an investment adviser, it is likely that FINRA would view advertisements related to those programs to be within the scope of its jurisdiction and therefore subject to FINRA Rule 2210 (i.e., FINRA regulation).

to a new set of marketing rules. Because of some of the contrasting SEC and CFTC guidance in the marketing area, the CFTC has informally stated that compliance with certain Advisers Act standards (particularly with regard to performance presentation) will be deemed compliance with CFTC standards until the CFTC issues guidance harmonizing its rules with those of the SEC.

Performance. A major area of substantive difference between the regulatory regimes is regarding the presentation of performance. Table 3 illustrates the applicable standards under each regulator.

TABLE 3. COMPARISON OF PERFORMANCE STANDARDS				
	Advisers Act	**FINRA**	**CFTC/NFA**	**GIPS**[a]
Performance (Fees)	Generally must be net Gross permitted in one-on-one presentations or side-by-side with net	Generally must be net Gross may be presented side-by-side and with equal prominence as net	Generally must be net NFA senior staff has represented that gross is permitted where permitted by the SEC	May be gross or net Must be clearly labeled as gross or net
Related Performance[b]	May be shown if relevant and accompanied by appropriate disclosure	Prohibited unless marketing a 3(c)(7) fund	Permitted with prescribed disclosure Stringent requirements for inclusion in non-QEP-only materials	Permitted as additional information (but, if same strategy, likely included in relevant composite)
Performance Portability	Permitted if including such performance is not misleading.[c] It would not be misleading if: ▪ Persons managing accounts at the successor adviser are also primarily responsible for achieving prior performance ▪ Account at prior firm and current account are so similar that performance provides relevant information ▪ All account managed in a substantially manner are advertised unless exclusion would not result in materially higher performance ▪ Advertisement follows staff interpretations in presenting performance ▪ All relevant disclosures are included, including that performance results were from accounts at another entity ▪ Successor adviser has sufficient records to demonstrate the basis of the performance	FINRA does not expressly address record portability FINRA's treatment of related performance may apply.	The CFTC and NFA do not expressly address record portability The CFTC's and NFA's treatment of related performance may apply.	Permitted subject to GIPS portability standards. Prior firm performance results are *required* to be "linked" to composite performance if: ▪ Substantially all investment decision-makers are employed at the new firm (in contrast to the SEC view, GIPS requires the entire composite history be presented and not solely that achieved by the decision makers employed at the new firm) ▪ Decision-making process remains substantially intact and independent within the new firm ▪ New firm has supporting documents for the performance Under certain circumstances and subject to disclosure, the firm may present performance from a prior firm as supplemental information if the portability standards are not met

TABLE 3. COMPARISON OF PERFORMANCE STANDARDS Cont'd

	Advisers Act	FINRA	CFTC/NFA	GIPS[a]
Model and Hypothetical Back-Test Performance[d]	Only permitted to sophisticated (nonretail) clients with required disclosure May not be linked to actual performance	Prohibited	Permitted with prescribed disclosure Stringent requirements for inclusion in non-QEP-only materials	Permitted as supplemental information May not be linked to actual performance

[a] To the extent that contradictory positions exist between GIPS and a mandatory regime and both apply, firms must comply with the applicable mandatory regime position.
[b] *Related performance* generally refers to the performance of funds or accounts other than the product being marketed (such as similar accounts or predecessor funds) which are managed by the same adviser in a substantially similar manner to the product being advertised.
[c] *See* Horizon Asset Management, LLC, SEC No-Action Letter (pub. Avail. Sep. 13, 1996).
[d] Model performance refers to the inclusion of results for hypothetical or model portfolios that do not reflect the performance of an actual account. Hypothetical back-tested performance is the theoretical performance resulting from the backdated application of an investment strategy to historical financial data.

Testimonials. Another area where the regulatory regimes differ is for testimonials. Testimonials include discussions referring to the investment adviser or any advice, analysis, report, or other service rendered by such investment adviser. Table 4 illustrates the applicable testimonial standards under each regime.

TABLE 4. COMPARISON OF TESTIMONIAL STANDARDS

Advisers Act	FINRA	CFTC/NFA	GIPS
May not include any statements of a former, existing, or prospective client's experience or endorsement Exceptions exist for partial client lists, ratings, and reprints	Must state that it may not be representative Must prominently state that a testimonial is not guarantee of future performance or success Must prominently state if paid (over $100)	Must be representative of all reasonably comparable accounts. Must prominently state that testimonial is not indicative of future performance or success Must prominently state if paid	Not applicable.

Past Specific Recommendations. A final area with notable regulatory regime differences is past specific recommendations. Table 5 illustrates the applicable standards for using past specific recommendations under each regime.

TABLE 5. COMPARISON OF PAST SPECIFIC RECOMMENDATIONS STANDARDS

Advisers Act	FINRA	CFTC/NFA	GIPS[a]
Permitted if specific disclosure requirements are met, fair and balanced, and objective criteria used (no cherry picking) Exceptions exist for nonperformance-based recommendations	Prohibited for FINRA members (but past recommendations of the *adviser* may be shown) FINRA members may include a full list of all recommendations (with appropriate disclosure)	Generally permitted If relating to security futures products, underlying securities of these products, or derivatives thereof, must be accompanied by disclosure of all other similar recommendations	Permitted as supplemental information

[a] As noted, GIPS supplemental information is any performance-related information included as part of a compliant presentation that supplements or enhances the required and/or recommended provisions of GIPS.

Third-Party Rankings. The permitted use of third-party rankings and conditions related to such use is another area in which regulatory regimes differ. Ratings or rankings prepared by a third party may be used under each regime if the conditions in Table 6 are met.

TABLE 6. COMPARISON OF THIRD-PARTY RANKINGS STANDARDS

Advisers Act	FINRA	CFTC/NFA	GIPS
Rankings based solely on performance may be used if not false or misleading. Advisers using such ratings should: ■ Disclose ratings criteria ■ Not know of any facts questioning the rankings' validity ■ Disclose unfavorable rankings ■ Not imply "top-rated" if not rated first ■ Clearly disclose category of ranking, number of advisers ranked, and percentage receiving a ranking ■ Note that ranking may not be representative of any one experience ■ Disclose that rating is not indicative of future performance ■ Disclose who conducted the survey and that the adviser paid to take part in it (if applicable)	Rankings published by a "Ranking Entity"[a] may be used if: ■ Prominent disclosure is included regarding (i) category name, (ii) number of funds, (iii), the name of the Ranking Entity, (iv), length of time and its ending date, and (v) criteria on which ranking is based ■ Additional disclosure notes, as applicable, (i) past performance does not guarantee future results, (ii) whether sales loads are accounted for, (iii) fee waivers are noted, (iv) publisher and date of ranking, and (v) the meaning of any rating system used ■ The rankings are as of the most recent calendar quarter or otherwise most current (if not otherwise misleading) ■ The rankings cover at least one year (unless based upon yield)	Rankings based on performance may be used in certain circumstances. CPOs/CTAs should: ■ Not imply the ranking is sanctioned by the futures industry ■ Ensure all data necessary to support performance results is included ■ Include disclosure about the basis and limitations of the rankings ■ Comply with rate of return calculation rules for ratings based on returns ■ Disclose past performance does not guarantee future results	Not applicable

[a] As noted above, a ranking entity is "any entity that provides general information about investment companies to the public, that is independent of the investment company and its affiliates, and whose services are not procured by the investment company or any of its affiliates to assign the investment company a ranking." FINRA Rule 2212(a).

VII. CONCLUSION

Investment advisers and their compliance personnel must understand that the rules and guidance applicable to marketing and advertising materials can and will differ depending on the product being marketed and the context in which the materials are used. Constant monitoring of the relevant marketing rules, regulations, and guidance from each of the SEC, GIPS, CFTC, and FINRA is crucial to understanding the rules that apply in any particular situation.

APPENDIX A. COMPARISON OF THIRD-PARTY RANKINGS STANDARDS

CFTC and NFA Hypothetical Performance Disclosures

For promotional materials that are directed solely to qualified eligible persons (QEPs) within the meaning of CFTC Regulation 4.7, hypothetical performance may be used, but must be accompanied by the following disclaimer, displayed as prominently as the results and immediately preceding or following the results (if the hypothetical or simulated results are lengthy, disclosure may need to be made more than once). CFTC Rule 4.41(b)(1)(i) says:

> The results are based on simulated or hypothetical performance results that have certain inherent limitations. Unlike the results shown in an actual performance record, these results do not represent actual trading. Also, because these trades have not actually been executed, these results may have under- or over-compensated for the impact, if any, of certain market factors such as lack of liquidity. Simulated or hypothetical trading programs in general are also subject to the fat that they are designed with the benefit of hindsight. No representation is being made that any account will or is likely to achieve profits or losses similar to these being shown.

In promotional materials directed at investors other than QEPs when both hypothetical and actual results appear, the following prescribed disclosure language in the form presented below must be included, as applicable, displayed as prominently as the results and immediately preceding or following the results (again, if the hypothetical or simulated results are lengthy, disclosures may need to be made more than once):

> Hypothetical performance results have many inherent limitations, some of which are described below. No representation is being made that any account will or is likely to achieve profits or losses similar to those shown. In fact, there are frequently sharp differences between hypothetical performance results and the actual results subsequently achieved by any particular trading program one of the limitations of hypothetical performance results is that they are generally prepared with the benefit of hindsight. In addition, hypothetical trading does not involve financial risk, and no hypothetical trading record can completely account for the impact of financial risk in actual trading. For example, the ability to withstand losses or adhere to a particular trading program in spite of trading losses is a material point that can also adversely affect actual trading results. There are numerous other factors related to the markets in general or to the implementation of any specific trading program which cannot be fully accounted for in the preparation of hypothetical performance results and all of which can adversely affect actual trading results.

APPENDIX A. COMPARISON OF THIRD-PARTY RANKINGS STANDARDS *Cont'd*

If the CPO and/or CTA uses the immediately preceding disclosure and has less than one year of experience trading client or proprietary accounts, then the following statement must also be included:

> [The CPO/CTA] has had little or no experience in trading actual accounts for itself of for customers. Because there are (little or) no actual trading results to compare to the hypothetical results, customers should be particularly wary of placing undue reliance on these hypothetical performance results.

If the CPO and/or CTA uses hypothetical performance records that show, through use of a hypothetical composite, what a multi-advisor account or pool could have achieved if assets had been allocated among certain advisors, the CPO and/or CTA should replace the two preceding disclosures with the following:

> This composite performance record is hypothetical and these trading advisors have not traded together in the manner shown in the composite. Hypothetical performance results have many inherent limitations, some of which are described below. No representation is being made that any multiadvisor managed account or pool will or is likely to achieve a composite performance record similar to that shown. In fact, there are frequently sharp differences between a hypothetical composite record and the actual record subsequently achieved.

> One of the limitations of a hypothetical composite performance record is that decisions relating to the selection of trading advisors and the allocation of assets among those trading advisors were made with the benefit of hindsight based upon the historical rates of return of the selected trading advisors. Therefore composite performance records invariably show positive rates of return. Another inherent limitation on these results is that the allocation decisions reflected in the performance record were not made under actual market conditions and therefore, cannot completely account for the impact of financial risk in actual trading. Furthermore, the composite performance record may be distorted because the allocation of assets changes from time to time and these adjustments are not reflected in the composite.

If the CPO and/or CTA uses the immediately preceding disclosure and has less than one year of experience trading client or proprietary accounts, then the following statement must also be included:

> [The CPO/CTA] has had little or no experience allocating assets among particular trading advisors. Because there are [little or] no actual allocations to compare to the performance results from the hypothetical allocations, customers should be particularly wry of placing undue reliance on these results.

ABOUT THE AUTHORS

Michael Caccese is one of three Practice Area Leaders of K&L Gates' Financial Services practice, which includes the firm's Investment Management, Broker Dealer, and Consumer Financial Services practice groups, and sits on the firm's Management Committee. K&L Gates maintains one of the most prominent financial services practices in the United States – with more than 200 lawyers practicing from Australia, Asia, Europe, the Middle East, and the United States, representing diversified financial services institutions and their affiliated service providers.

Mr. Caccese focuses his practice in the areas of investment management, including mutual funds, closed-end funds, registered fund of hedge funds, hedge funds and separately managed accounts, in addition to advising on investment management and broker-dealer regulatory compliance. Mr. Caccese also advises on structuring investment management professional team "lift-outs" and "placement," "soft dollar" compliance, investment performance, the Global Investment Performance Standards ("GIPS"), and the CFA Soft Dollar Standards and the Trade Management (Best Execution) Guidelines, along with other investment management industry standards of practice. His focus is on serving the needs of investment advisory firms of all sizes, including helping them design and comply with the investment industry's "best practices" and policies.

Douglas Charton is legal counsel at Grantham, Mayo, van Otterloo, LLC. Prior to joining GMO in 2015, Mr. Charton spent eight years at K&L Gates, focusing his practice on advising investment advisers, mutual funds, closed-end funds, registered funds of hedge funds, hedge funds, separately managed account programs, and broker-dealers. Mr. Charton has experience drafting and reviewing registration statements, proxy statements, tender offer documents, credit agreements, as well as other legal documentation for the formation, organization, and ongoing operations of registered investment companies and hedge funds. Mr. Charton also deals with legal and regulatory issues, including SEC compliance, advertising and marketing issues under the SEC and FINRA rules, the GIPS, industry best practices and policies, and contract negotiation and drafting.

CHAPTER 14

Corporate Transactions: The Role of the Compliance Department

By A. Brad Busscher
    Incapital Holdings LLC

I. INTRODUCTION

The purpose of this chapter is to explore the integral role played by the Compliance Department with respect to corporate and related transactions. That role has not been well defined and may be overlooked within an organization, either by senior managers or by compliance professionals themselves. Culturally, senior managers may rely on in-house counsel to perform a risk management role in connection with corporate transactions. This delegation to counsel is because the managers perceive the role of the Compliance Department as broadly focused on drafting policies and procedures and performing surveillance activities with respect to arms-length transactions between the registered entity and its clients and counterparties. In that regard, the regulatory expertise of the Compliance Department may be lost in the shuffle as an organization is confronted with time sensitive and material corporate transactions.

Little has been written on the role of the Compliance Department as it relates to corporate and related transactions. The functional responsibilities of the Compliance Department have evolved and have been framed over the years through a combination of securities rules and regulations, interpretive guidance by regulatory bodies and self-regulatory agencies, industry conferences and networking events, industry trade associations such as the Securities Industry and Financial Markets Association (SIFMA) and the National Society of Compliance Professionals, Inc. (NSCP), and scholarly publications written by outside counsel and by in-house compliance and legal professionals. In fact, there is little or no law or guidance available that describes particular duties or responsibilities to guide compliance professionals when they participate in corporate transactions. As an in-house lawyer and general counsel at a variety of regulated entities for the past twenty plus years, I have seen firsthand this crucial risk management role played by compliance professionals with respect to corporate and related transactions.

In this chapter, I will describe a variety of corporate and related transactions wherein the involvement of the Compliance Department will be beneficial to an organization. Likewise, I will discuss the differences in the functional responsibilities between the Legal Department and the Compliance Department. Lastly, I will undertake to describe the functional responsibilities of the Compliance Department as they relate to particular corporate transactions and, where applicable, provide a brief overview of applicable law and best practices. Hopefully, this chapter will assist compliance professionals in identifying and spotting issues so they can be proactive as it relates to their involvement with respect to corporate transactions.

II. CORPORATE AND RELATED TRANSACTIONS

As just described, this chapter is focused on the Compliance Department's involvement in corporate and related transactions. What does that involvement encompass? The focus is on an organization's own transactions with third parties as opposed to an organization's interaction with and services provided to its clients and counterparties, such as providing asset management services, transactional services, and financial advice. Generally speaking, corporate transactions are related to events whereby an organization is making some change with respect to its existing structure or capabilities such as buying another firm, selling a particular division, hiring a group of employees to add an area of expertise, or taking on investors or offering debt to improve the organization's current capital structure.

Accordingly, in this chapter, I will discuss the role of the Compliance Department in mergers and acquisitions (M&A) transactions, private equity transactions, joint ventures, and revenue sharing agreements, lift-outs, and other hiring decisions and corporate restructurings. I will also discuss the Compliance Department's role with respect to the organization's participation in equity or debt offerings, either through an initial public offering (IPO) or a "secondary" offering of equity or debt securities. Curiously, little has been written with respect to the role of the Compliance Department when the broker-dealer is acting as an underwriter or syndicate member in connection with a registered or exempt offering of securities by an unaffiliated issuer of such securities. The same principles outlined herein can be applied to those types of transactions when the organization or an affiliate thereof is involved.

Types of Corporate Transactions

The following is a brief overview of each of the corporate transactions discussed in this chapter.

M&A. M&A encompasses a variety of transactions. Generally speaking, a merger concerns the consolidation of two firms into a newly formed entity. Conversely, an acquisition involves one firm acquiring another firm wherein the acquiring entity remains as the surviving entity. However, in recent years, those terms have become interchangeable and the lines are now blurred.

An acquisition could take the form of an asset purchase where one party, the purchaser, purchases specified assets from another party, the seller. The purchase of assets could involve a purchase of retail or institutional accounts, an investment model, a track record or strategy, particular receivables, a business unit or division in a broader organization, or the entire organization. As part of that acquisition, the buyer might end up hiring registered employees who worked in a particular business unit of the target entity. Normally, in an asset purchase, the buyer is not assuming any liabilities of the seller and is only contractually assuming liabilities relating to the purchased assets following the closing date of the transaction. Asset purchase transactions tend to be a bit less risky for the entity purchasing the assets.

On the other hand, broad-based acquisitions or mergers might involve a stock transaction. In a stock transaction, one entity acquires the equity of another entity. The buyer is generally assuming the liabilities of the selling company and such assumption of liability normally predates the closing date of the transaction. Stock transactions tend to be more risky for the buyer given the assumption of liability on behalf of seller. In that instance, performing a full and thorough review of the target entity and its existing and threatened litigation as well as other areas of potential liability is crucial to ensure that the acquiring entity is obtaining the "benefit of the bargain" and is not subject to unforeseen liabilities.

Public Offerings and Private Equity Transactions. Organizations that seek to grow may avail themselves of the public markets by filing for an IPO. An IPO involves the filing of a registration statement with the Securities and Exchange Commission (SEC) and a listing application with an exchange (e.g., the New York Stock Exchange (the NYSE) or NASDAQ) for the issuer's common shares. The issuer engages underwriters to market the IPO shares, set the price (in consultation with the issuer) at which the shares will be offered to the public, and, in a "firm commitment" underwriting, purchase the shares from the issuer and then resell them to investors. The public offering process is divided into three periods:

- The "prefiling period" is the period between determining to proceed with a public offering and the actual SEC filing of the registration statement when the issuer is in the "quiet period" and subject to potential limits on public disclosure relating to the offering;
- The "waiting or preeffective period" is the period between the SEC filing date and the effective date of the registration statement; during this period, the company may make oral offers, but may not enter into binding agreements to sell the offered security; and
- The "post-effective period" is the period between effectiveness and completion of the offering.

An IPO may consist of the sale of newly issued shares by the company (a "primary offering"), or a sale of already issued shares owned by shareholders (a "secondary offering"), or a combination of these. Underwriters may prefer a primary offering because the company will retain all of the proceeds to advance its business. However, many

IPOs include secondary shares, either in the initial part of the offering or as part of the 15 percent overallotment option granted to underwriters. The company's major shareholders, who may consist of the company's founders, venture capital investors, and private equity investors, generally view a secondary offering as their principal realization event. A company must also consider whether any of its shareholders has registration rights that could require it to register shareholder shares for sale in the IPO. Registration rights are often granted to early stage investors in a company through a registration rights agreement or other shareholders' agreement.

Private equity transactions generally concern a private equity fund making a capital infusion into a company in exchange for an equity stake in the company. The transaction might also entail the private equity fund loaning money to an entity in exchange for a promissory note or debenture, debt securities, or debt securities convertible into equity securities. The equity might take the form of common stock or newly issued preferred stock with a specified dividend. Private equity transactions could involve an investment in a newly formed entity wherein the owners have an idea, strategy, or business plan but no capital to execute on their idea, strategy, or business plan. It could also include an entity that is in a growth mode and needs additional capital to grow the business, as well as a mature organization that lacks adequate capital and management talent to grow the company beyond its current bounds. In that instance or the other instances referenced above, in exchange for providing capital, the private equity firm usually seeks a majority or controlling interest in the company, might replace senior management, or might seek board representation in order to effect a change in leadership, strategy, or firm culture. Private equity firms seek to capitalize on their investment in an organization through a sale of the entity or some form of recapitalization (e.g., the entity takes on debt to repurchase the private equity firm's equity stake).

Private equity funds have a time horizon and seek to monetize their investment within a specified timeframe so they can compensate the investors in the fund. It is prudent for an organization contemplating a private equity investment to conduct "reverse due diligence" on the private equity firm to determine how the private equity firm has dealt with other portfolio companies for purposes of gaining insight into whether the goals of the organization are generally in line with the goals and objectives of the private equity firm. However, one must keep in mind that the primary goal and objective of any private equity firm is to generate realized returns for its investors.

Joint Venture and Revenue Sharing Agreements. Joint venture and revenue sharing agreements are a common form of agreement between registered entities. A common example of a joint venture or revenue share agreement is when one registered entity seeks to monetize a relationship by introducing a client or a transactional opportunity to another registered entity which has particular expertise to represent the client or handle the transaction. Generally speaking, it is appropriate from a regulatory perspective for two broker-dealers to share transactional compensation. However, consideration needs to be given whether the referral arrangement may necessitate disclosure of the arrangement in conjunction with a client transaction.[1] Registered investment advisers may compensate a third-party solicitor in connection with a client referral so long as the referral complies with Rule 206(4)-3 under Investment Advisers Act of 1940, as amended ("Investment Advisers Act"). In that regard, the arrangement may need to be disclosed subject to the type of solicitation arrangement agreed to and the nature of the advisory services being performed. For example, if the adviser offers personalized advisory services through a solicitor unaffiliated with the adviser, at the time of the solicitation, the solicitor must provide the solicited client with a copy of the adviser's brochure and a disclosure document reciting the terms of the solicitation agreement. Consequently, a proposed referral or joint venture agreement may create a conflict of interest, or an appearance thereof. Various regulatory bodies have expressed concern with respect to such conflicts, and disclosure may be necessary to alleviate any concerns about such relationship or transaction.

Joint ventures and revenue sharing agreements could also follow a different path. Accordingly, a form of corporate transaction could seek to exploit specific expertise or capabilities at two independent firms whereby a new legal entity is created to take advantage of resulting synergies. One example might be the formation of a new minority-based firm that is designed to capture minority "set aside business" offered by state, local or municipal government clients or by corporate entities that create minority set asides. Specific federal, state, and local laws need to be followed when a firm seeks to capture such business from governmental entities. Likewise, the representation of governmental clients might create collateral requirements, such as agreeing to maintain an affirmative action employment program, complying with specific reporting requirements, or being subject to particular audit requirements. Therefore, minority set aside business needs to be carefully vetted to ensure that the firm is complying with applicable law as well as any related contractual obligations.

Another example of a joint venture or a revenue sharing agreement might take the form of an "employee lending" relationship. In this case, a broker-dealer might authorize certain registered employees to become affiliated with another broker-dealer. One example of an employee dual registration arrangement might be an insurance company with an affiliated broker-dealer that permits a registered employee to become registered with a nonaffiliated broker-dealer who also distributes variable annuities. Dual registration arrangements in any context require careful supervision because both broker-dealers have responsibility for that registered employee and need to develop an appropriate system to monitor such registered employee's conduct in relation to the services provided to each firm as well as any outside business activities.

Additionally, two entities might enter into an arrangement to create, offer, and/or distribute a new financial product, security, or investment strategy. These types of arrangements might arise between two affiliated subsidiaries within the same organization

---

[1] *See* Carlo V. di Florio, *Conflicts of Interest and Risk Governance*, (Oct. 22, 2012); *FINRA Report on Conflicts of Interest* (Oct. 2013), available at http://www.finra.org/web/groups/industry/@ip/@reg/@guide/documents/industry/p359971.pdf

or between two independent organizations, one of which is located onshore and the other offshore. An example of this arrangement might be the case of an issuer of a publicly offered security and an affiliated broker-dealer firm that has responsibility for underwriting such security.

Revenue sharing and joint venture agreements could also arise between a registered entity and a nonregistered entity. However, the payment of transactional-based compensation by a registered entity to a nonregistered entity may be forbidden by the regulatory provisions applicable to the registered entity. For example, broker-dealers who are members of the Financial Industry Regulatory Authority (FINRA) are generally forbidden from sharing transactional-based compensation with nonregistered entities.[2] This is a complicated compensation area that needs to be thoroughly vetted before entering into a revenue sharing agreement with a nonregistered entity. Care must also be taken when a broker-dealer determines what constitutes transactional-based compensation. In addition, the payment of a "marketing fee" might be deemed to be transactional-based depending on how the "marketing fee" is structured, paid, or computed.

Lift-outs and Other Hiring Decisions. Within any organization that is growing, hiring decisions are a common occurrence. A particular type of hiring transaction may occur when an organization executes an employee "lift-out." An employee lift-out may result when an organization hires a group of employees from another organization. An example of an employee lift-out would be a broker-dealer firm seeking to enter the institutional sales and trading space that hires away or enters into a transaction with another broker-dealer firm to hire a group of institutional salespeople and traders to establish that business and expertise on behalf of the hiring firm. As described later in this chapter, broker-dealers need to pay close attention to their FINRA membership agreement to ensure that the firm has the necessary authorization to engage in such activities. When hiring employees, particularly registered employees, a registered entity should perform a due diligence review to ensure that the employee or group of employees is qualified to perform the role(s) that the individuals are being hired to perform. Appropriate qualifications could involve having specific expertise, registrations, or regulatory backgrounds to perform the particular role. Likewise, a history of customer complaints or regulatory issues might be a telling sign of potential issues with a particular employee.

As part of the hiring process, organizations may also conduct criminal and/or financial background reviews to further evaluate the qualifications of the employee(s) being hired.

---

[2] *See* Section 15(a) of the Securities Exchange Act of 1934, as amended (the "Exchange Act"), which generally requires persons who seek to effect securities transactions to become registered as broker-dealers, unless an individual is an associated person of a broker-dealer. Any payments to nonregistered "finders" by broker-dealers may hinge on an analysis of the role of the "finder" and whether the finder made a particular representation or recommendation in relation to a particular security, negotiated the terms of a particular security, solicited the sale of the security, received transactional-based compensation, was previously an associated person at a registered broker-dealer, or engaged in other activities that are normally within the role of a registered broker-dealer. Some firms may enter into a form of a joint marketing or similar arrangement. However, caution must be exercised in structuring and reviewing such arrangements.

When a firm conducts criminal and financial background reviews, particular privacy-based laws come into play, some of which may relate to state and/or local provisions.[3] Conflicts may arise when managers seek to hire particular individuals with a demonstrated measure of success in generating revenues but with a prior history of regulatory issues. Poor hiring decisions can put organizations at risk for customer disputes and reputational concerns raised by both customers and regulatory organizations.

As part of any hiring decision that is not part of a corporate transaction, care must also be exercised with respect to the scope of the information that the new employee may be bringing from his or her prior firm. Many firms in the securities industry have their employees execute restrictive covenants that specify the employees' course of conduct while employed at a particular organization and thereafter. The employee may be restricted from:

- Sharing the organization's confidential and/or proprietary information with unaffiliated third parties;
- Disparaging the organization and its employees;
- Soliciting specified transactions, clients, or prospects of the organization;
- Soliciting employees of the organization; and/or
- Engaging in particular types of activities.

To the extent that the employee is seeking to transfer his or her existing "book of business," particularly with respect to retail clients, privacy concerns may arise if the underlying clients were unaware that their personal financial information was being shared with an unaffiliated organization. To address that situation, FINRA had sought to codify the process related to the removal of such information.[4]

Corporate Restructuring Transactions. A corporate restructuring transaction could result in an accretive transaction for an organization or, conversely, might be a necessary step to avoid bankruptcy or financial difficulty. From a positive perspective, the organization might have a particular division that has grown beyond expectations and may want to "spin off" or sell that division.[5] A spinoff or sale of a particular division may occur if there is a belief that the division might be worth more as a standalone entity or as part of a separate organization with a different culture, business plan, or compensation structure. Conversely, an organization that is contracting, as opposed to growing, might choose to cut expenses by closing a particular division, outsourcing

---

[3] Various federal and state laws need to be evaluated before a firm performs background reviews on prospective employees. Included within potentially applicable federal laws are the Fair Credit Reporting Act, the Employee Polygraph Protection Act, the Americans with Disabilities Act, and the Family Educational Rights and Privacy Act. Laws relating to criminal background checks must also be carefully evaluated prior to such reviews.

[4] FINRA Regulatory Notice 13-02 (January 2013), http://www.finra.org/web/groups/industry/@ip/@reg/@notice/documents/notices/p197599.pdf

[5] A spinoff transaction typically involves the transfer of a particular division of defined segment of a company into a newly created entity. Normally, the equity in the newly formed, entity is transferred to the parent company's existing shareholders. If the existing company is publicly traded, the newly formed entity will usually be publicly traded as well.

particular functions, or terminating groups of employees. A restructuring might also entail rebuilding an organization's existing capital structure, in which case the organization may seek to add new equity investors or lenders to address an existing capital need. Like the other corporate transactions described above, corporate restructurings often have collateral issues that may require compliance professionals' involvement.

The Anatomy of a Corporate Transaction

In most organizations, in-house counsel and/or outside counsel play a significant role in corporate and related transactions. There may be a level of confidentiality associated with a transaction, and access is necessarily limited to particular segments of the firm. Knowledge of the transaction itself might constitute "material nonpublic information" (discussed later in this chapter). In that regard, knowledge of a particular transaction might be limited to senior business leaders and in-house counsel.

The starting point for any corporate transaction is typically the execution of a nondisclosure or confidentiality agreement (NDA) between the parties to the transaction. A standard NDA is normally drafted such that one party, the disclosing entity, agrees to share confidential information with the receiving entity, often defined as the recipient. In transactions wherein both parties will disclose confidential information to one another, the NDA is drafted with both parties being mutually obligated to one another. The terms of an NDA normally include the following:

- A description of the confidential information and any exclusions therefrom;
- Limitations on the disclosure of the confidential information both internally and externally and provisions to follow if confidential information is required to be disclosed by the recipient in response to a regulatory or legal request;
- The ability of the disclosing entity to seek an injunction or other type of equitable relief, as opposed to monetary damages, in the event of a breach or threatened breach of the terms of the NDA;
- The period of time during which the confidential information must be held in confidence pursuant to the terms of the NDA;
- The specific state law that applies to the NDA and an agreement to pursue litigation in a particular venue or before a particular court; and
- Obligations to destroy or return confidential information.

Senior compliance professionals or the chief compliance officer (CCO) should be apprised of the existence of an NDA, particularly if a party to the NDA is a public company, to ensure that the company is added to the firm's restricted/watch list or related process to ensure that employees are not misusing material nonpublic information. Moreover, the Compliance Department should also be apprised of an NDA in the event of a regulatory request that touches upon the confidential information that an organization has received in connection with the execution of the NDA. Fundamentally, the execution of an NDA may be a good time for compliance professionals to be informed of a potential transaction so that the Compliance

Department can perform some preliminary due diligence on the counterparty, which might assist an organization in making an early determination of whether to proceed with a particular transaction.

Following the execution of an NDA, the process to complete a transaction typically involves (1) business negotiations to frame the terms of the transaction, (2) the drafting and negotiation of legal documentation to memorialize the transaction, and (3) due diligence to assess the representations and warranties of the parties and to ensure that each party is deriving the benefits of the transaction that it has entered into.

Normally, to avoid "deal fatigue" or a litany of other factors that might cause a party to back out of a corporate transaction, time is of the essence, and there is substantial time pressure to complete the necessary tasks accurately and expeditiously. Depending on the size of an organization, the firm may have a preestablished "deal team" that is quickly assembled to manage a particular transaction. Large firms with prior deal experience normally have dedicated personnel to lead and facilitate strategic deal opportunities or at least have personnel who can be quickly assembled and are familiar with the deal process. Smaller and entrepreneurial organizations with minimal prior deal experience may rely on one or more senior managers who typically tend to manage the process until they lack the requisite expertise or time to complete a transaction. Small firms that lack prior deal experience tend to focus on the closure of a transaction and may overlook particular details or the related consequences of a transaction consummated with minimal diligence or lack of attention to terms of the transaction. Similarly, the excitement surrounding a potential deal may outweigh a cautious approach of carefully proceeding though each stage of a transaction. Both in-house counsel and the Compliance Department should be the voice of reason and urge patience in making sure that all aspects of a transaction have been properly vetted and that issues collateral to a transaction have been identified and thought through.

In-house and/or outside counsel primarily focus on the memorialization of the transaction and conducting due diligence. When outside counsel is involved, at least with respect to corporate M&A transactions, the attorneys tend to be well versed in corporate finance transactions, contractual terms necessary to close a transaction, and related tax and accounting issues. However, an outside counsel is typically not well versed in securities regulatory issues and may not identify specific regulatory filing or disclosure obligations. Larger organizations routinely employ both deal attorneys and regulatory counsel. Smaller firms may not have the financial resources to afford regulatory counsel and may instead rely on their deal lawyers and/or in-house counsel.

In that regard, the expense associated with outside counsel is a factor to be considered in corporate transactions. Firms should be hesitant to pay outside counsel to educate itself in matters outside the expertise of counsel. Depending on the nature of the transaction, regulatory counsel may be engaged to address securities and related regulatory issues. However, the use of regulatory counsel comes with an added expense and regulatory counsel may not understand the firm's culture and personnel and may not understand or be familiar with the firm's policies and procedures and internal compliance processes. Similarly, although in-house counsel plays an important role in managing or fulfilling the legal aspects of the transaction, the regulatory expertise of in-house counsel may be limited, and the time pressures of completing a deal may cause in-house counsel to lose sight of or neglect to identify issues pertaining to compliance-related aspects of a transaction.

Cultural Impediments to the Compliance Department's Involvement in Corporate Transactions

What is the role of the Compliance Department? At many organizations, the answer to that question may be narrowly defined. Strictly speaking, the culture within each organization defines and dictates the role of the Compliance Department.

In a compliance-driven culture, the Compliance Department tends to be consulted on a broad spectrum of issues. Rank and file employees within an organization with a strong culture of compliance routinely involve compliance professionals as a matter of course without regard to the firm's policies and procedures. Compliance professionals are viewed as valued partners in generating new revenue for the firm and are involved in the performance of due diligence on new initiatives and business partners. FINRA touched on this role when it discussed the role of the Compliance Department with regard to vetting vendors.[6] The SEC also has commented on the importance of this role. However, the regulatory pronouncement on the Compliance Department's involvement with respect to the due diligence performed on third parties is narrowly focused on a small segment of corporate transactions and does not touch on the broader involvement of the Compliance Department in corporate and related transactions.

In a business-driven culture where the Compliance Department is perceived as a necessary function to "check the box" or perform a required regulatory or statutory responsibility, corporate and related transactions may follow an inefficient path from a cost, timing, or risk perspective. Firms exhibiting that type of culture typically take on greater risk, incur greater expense, and take longer to manage or close corporate and related transactions. Failing to involve the Compliance Department in a corporate transaction excludes a crucial knowledge base and skill set that could facilitate the smooth completion of a corporate transaction and/or avoid future problems or concerns. For example, absent the involvement of the Compliance Department, will an internal deal team be aware of FINRA's perspective on conflicts of interest or the SEC's guidance on information barriers and be able to analyze that perspective as it relates to a particular transaction?[7]

---

[6] *See*, e.g., NASD Notice to Members 05-48 (July 2005), http://www.finra.org/web/groups/industry/@ip/@reg/@notice/documents/notices/p014735.pdf

[7] *See* di Florio, *Conflicts of Interest and Risk Governance;* SEC Staff Summary Report on Examinations of Information Barriers: Broker-Dealer Practices Under Section 15(g) of the Securities Exchange Act of 1934 (Sept. 27, 2012).

Ensuring that the Compliance Department Has a "Seat at the Table"

The Compliance Department's participation in a corporate transaction tends to be a two-way street. Culturally, as discussed above, some firms are cognizant of the value that the Compliance Department brings to the table and routinely involve Compliance Department professionals in discussions of a wide array of issues. Conversely, other firms tend to view the Compliance Department as a potential impediment to taking advantage of business opportunities. Although that culture no longer pervades the securities industry, it may exist at some level in the securities industry, and firms may simply not recognize the value that the Compliance Department may offer with respect to a corporate transaction.

Although certain firms may still have outdated views of the role of the Compliance Department, the department needs to be a good partner in the process. There is an interesting divergence in the perspectives exhibited by lawyers and compliance professionals. Lawyers are trained to be advocates for their clients, and, in fact, take an ethical oath in that regard.[8] In certain respects, effective lawyers try to advocate for a solution based on their perception of the "gray" area when applying a set of facts to the applicable law, rule or regulation. Conversely, compliance professionals generally view issues in the frame of a black or white interpretation, at least with respect to addressing regulatory issues, as opposed to business issues. Firms that want a strong compliance program necessarily need their compliance professionals to undertake that black or white approach to resolving issues. The different approaches exhibited by lawyers and compliance professionals is part of a healthy discourse to ensure that firms pursue new business opportunities but do so in a thoughtful and measured approach. However, compliance professionals that are unable to distinguish between a business issue and a regulatory issue can be perceived as being heavy handed and overly rigid in resolving compliance-related issues. In such cases, the Compliance Department is not perceived to be a good "business partner."

Ensuring that the Compliance Department has a "seat at the table" is largely a function of delivery. Proper delivery by the Compliance Department entails a variety of factors. First, when approaching any issue, the Compliance Department professionals need to exhibit good listening skills. Being an effective listener is harder than it sounds in light of the volume of issues with which compliance professionals are confronted. There is a tendency for one's mind to wander, particularly when one has many tasks at hand Second, it is imperative that a compliance professional take the time to gather all the facts related to a particular issue. This starts with listening to the potential transaction to ensure that one has a grasp of nature of the transaction, at least as described by a businessperson. It is extremely easy to prejudge an issue based on some preconceived notion, being in a hurry or simply not taking the time to gather all the relevant information. Failing to capture all the relevant facts is the greatest cause of mistakes. In

---

[8] *See*, e.g., N.Y. Judiciary Law § 466; CA. Business and Professions Code § 6068; 705 Illinois Compiled Statutes 205/4; and Florida Board of Bar Examiners, Rules of the Supreme Court Relating to Admissions to the Bar, Rule 5-13.

that regard, part of capturing all relevant information is asking pertinent questions and making sure one has all relevant information related to the transaction. Third, properly applying the facts to the relevant policy, rule or statutory provision is important. This entails an understanding of the standard to which one is applying the relevant facts and then drawing the appropriate conclusion therefrom. Lastly, effective communication is absolutely critical. The Compliance Department is many times perceived as being too rigid by delivering its perspective without providing the underlying reasoning for that perspective. Being an effective communicator should never be underestimated and is a skill that can always be improved upon and refined. In fact, if one wants to grow professionally or if one is a compliance supervisor who wishes to enhance the skills of one's subordinates, taking a communication skills course or training seminar is crucial to becoming an effective and valued compliance professional.

III. LEGAL DEPARTMENT VERSUS COMPLIANCE DEPARTMENT

Functional Responsibilities of Each Department

At many organizations, the roles of the Legal Department and the Compliance Department are generally viewed as being one and the same. In fact, in organizations where I have worked, production employees may reach out to in-house counsel or compliance professionals without regard to their respective responsibilities or areas of expertise simply based on a prior existing relationship with the person or the ease of reaching a particular employee in the Legal Department or the Compliance Department. In reality, each department plays a distinct role with respect to an organization's risk management functions. Generally, in smaller organizations employees wear a variety of hats and in-house counsel or general counsel also serves as the organization's CCO. Yet, to the extent that these roles can be separated, the organization's risk management functions tend to be stronger based on the areas of expertise of the Legal Department and the Compliance Department. Given the increasing level of complexity within the securities industry and the increasing complexity of the scope of the business being conducted within particular firms, it is becoming more difficult to remain a generalist in legal matters and compliance matters within an organization.

What are the general functions of the Legal Department? As stated above, much like the Compliance Department, the primary role of the Legal Department is a risk management one. Although the Legal Department or a particular attorney in the department may focus on governance issues at either a publicly or privately held entity, the ultimate responsibility is to ensure that the organization is managing its risk particularly as it (1) manages its disputes with the individuals and entities with which the organization interacts and (2) enters into written agreements and contracts with employees, prospective employees, vendors, business partners, and prospective business partners. This responsibility takes on particular importance when the Legal Department is confronted with a corporate transaction. As discussed briefly above, lawyers undergo training in law school wherein they are taught to apply a set of facts to a particular body of law and draw a conclusion therefrom in accordance with the ethical obligations that such lawyers agree to in conjunction with the representation of their clients. Lawyers are taught to try to see the "forest through the trees" and anticipate various outcomes based on particular strategic alternatives. Good lawyers are very adept at quickly analyzing a particular situation and developing and espousing a viable position that benefits their clients or minimizes a potential negative result.

Conversely, what are the general functions of the Compliance Department? In October 2005 SIFMA published the *White Paper on the Role of the Compliance Department*.[9] It tracked the evolution of the Compliance Department and discussed its functions within a broker-dealer, although many of those functions similarly apply to role of compliance in other types of entities such as an investment adviser or entities exempt from registration such as a bank dealer. In March 2013, SIFMA published the *White Paper on the Evolving Role of Compliance Department*.[10] The 2013 paper acknowledges the fact that the role of the Compliance Department has evolved over time "in response to changes in market operations, business practices, and new regulatory mandates." Clearly, the role of the Compliance Department has become much more complicated given the changing regulatory landscape, which further illustrates the need for the department to play an involved role in connection with corporate transactions. For purposes of this chapter, I will only highlight the functions of the Compliance Department that come into play with respect to corporate transactions.

Although I will elaborate on the specific functions of the Compliance Department as they relate to corporate transactions later in this chapter, there are certain functions of the department that are integral to corporate transactions.

Policies and Procedures. One important function of the Compliance Department is the preparation of policies and procedures. Firms should consider whether policies and procedures related to corporate transactions are important to the firm (although existing policies and procedures may be drafted broad enough to encompass corporate transactions). A firm should never maintain a policy that it does not follow or create a policy for creation or appearance's sake. Policies and procedures outlining the involvement of compliance early in the genesis of a corporate transaction may be prudent so that the Compliance Department can participate in specifying the necessity of maintaining particular types of information in confidence, prohibiting trading in entities with which the firm may be negotiating a corporate transaction, establishing procedures for sharing confidential information with various departments within the firm, and highlighting the need to vet potential conflicts of interest or vet the backgrounds of registered employees that the firm might hire as a result of a corporate transaction.

---

[9] See SIFMA, *White Paper on the Role of Compliance* (October 2005), *available at* http://www.sifma.org/uploadedfiles/societies/sifma_compliance_and_legal_society/role_of_compliance_white_paper%20(2).pdf
[10] SIFMA, *White Paper on the Evolving Role of Compliance* (March 2013), http://www.sifma.org/issues/item.aspx?id=8589942363

Monitoring Employee Trading. Another important function of compliance concerns controls in place to monitor employee trading. If a registered entity is contemplating a transaction with a publicly held entity, it is important to monitor employee trading activity to ensure that employees are not misusing material information related to a corporate transaction. A vibrant restricted/watch list process coupled with preclearance requirements and monitoring of employee securities transactions are excellent controls to avoid the potential misuse of material nonpublic information. Similarly, if compliance professionals are advised in advance of a potential corporate transaction, they can evaluate the firm's existing physical boundaries or a lack thereof and advise management of any related issues. Additionally, the Compliance Department can fulfill an important control room function wherein it monitors the disclosure of confidential information internally amongst various departments or employees within the organization. That may allow particular employees with relevant expertise to be "brought over the wall" to assist in some aspect of a corporate transaction.

Licensing, Registration, and Regulatory Issues. Moreover, per their advisory capacity, the Compliance Department personnel are normally well versed in licensing and registration issues, regulatory approvals, particularly as they relate to the addition of new products and the scope of authority of the registered entity. Department personnel may opine on the strengths and/or weaknesses of a compliance program managed by a potential acquisition candidate.

Due Diligence and Contractual Agreements. Due diligence and contractual agreements related to corporate transactions are normally within the province of the Legal Department. The Legal Department is typically advised of a transaction, either upon being notified of an opportunity to participate in particular transaction (e.g., an investment banking firm is shopping a particular entity via a "book," which is an overview of the entity, including high-level financial and other data, to determine whether an organization is interested in participating) or once preliminary business terms have been generally agreed upon. Procedurally, as described above, most corporate transactions then begin with the execution of an NDA. Most organizations seek to limit the scope of the disclosure to those employees directly involved in the potential transaction, including senior management and affected supervisors within particular departments, in-house and outside counsel, outside financial advisors (e.g., investment bankers, accountants, etc.). From a best practices perspective, it is prudent to create a log in relation to each NDA, identifying the individuals that have been made aware of a particular transaction or confidential related information related. Similarly, it is always prudent to confirm the obligations of that employee to maintain the information in strict confidence, in writing to avoid any misunderstanding. Although this is normally handled by the Legal Department, the Compliance Department can also take on this role, which can be outlined in the Compliance Department's policies and procedures.

Privilege Considerations

In corporate transactions maintaining confidentiality or ensuring that advice is deemed to be "privileged" is often a reason that the Legal Department, as opposed to the

Compliance Department, plays a critical role in corporate transactions. However, in order for the Compliance Department to play a role in advising on corporate transactions, department professionals should understand the scope of the privileges that might attach to the involvement of counsel, which are primarily the work product privilege and the attorney-client privilege. Compliance professionals who understand the scope of legal privileges will make themselves better business partners if they have an appreciation for the best way to document their concerns with a particular corporate transaction. For example, a compliance professional who routinely highlights potential concerns in writing to other employees participating in the corporate transaction runs the risk of creating discoverable documents that may adversely affect the organization if litigation ensues with respect to the corporate transaction. Moreover, the compliance professional runs the risk of being viewed as a "chicken little," which serves no purpose other than to isolate the Compliance Department from participating in future corporate transactions. Understanding the relevant privileges may allow the compliance professional to raise bona fide concerns in a manner that is protected from disclosure in subsequent litigation.

The work product privilege generally protects documents that are prepared for litigation or in anticipation of litigation. Generally speaking, the work product privilege protects materials from being accessed by an opposing litigant. In order to be protected, the materials need to be prepared at the direction of counsel, which could include in-house or outside counsel. The work product privilege also includes materials prepared by consultants or experts retained by counsel. The scope of the materials could include a wide array of documents such as memoranda, notes, and chronologies, as well as other tangible items. Given the fact that the work product privilege is focused on litigation or anticipated litigation, this privilege is typically not relevant in corporate transactions, except, for example, in a corporate restructuring for which the transaction might result in litigation. Compliance professionals who opine on a particular corporate transaction and highlight in writing a mental impression as to the nature of the transaction should consult with counsel to determine whether a work product privilege might attach or whether their mental impression is better communicated orally.

The attorney-client privilege is more likely applicable in the context of corporate transactions. The attorney-client privilege was designed to facilitate the ability of an attorney to provide legal advice to his or her client. The elements of the attorney-client privilege are (1) an oral or written communication, (2) made between an attorney and his or her client, (3) in confidence and (4) for the purpose of seeking, obtaining or providing legal assistance to the client. There are a number of instances when the attorney-client privilege might not apply. The biggest misconception may be that the attorney-client privilege protects disclosure of the facts underlying the attorney's confidential legal advice. Compliance professionals should keep this in mind as they prepare written communications to counsel. Compliance professionals also need to keep in mind that disclosure of the privileged communication to an unaffiliated third party may result in the waiver of that privileged communication. Additionally, in *Upjohn v. United States*, the U.S. Supreme Court held that in a corporate setting the attorney-client privilege belongs to the corporation and not individual employees of the corporation.[11]

In a corporate transaction, there is a high likelihood that the attorney-client privilege will attach to particular communications surrounding the transaction. For example, a compliance professional may be asked by outside counsel representing the organization to provide information concerning the scope of the organization's compliance program. Compliance professionals should familiarize themselves with the scope of the various privileges and understand the parameters of the applicable privilege in order to avoid making comments that might later adversely impact the organization. I have worked in organizations in which employees, including nonattorney compliance professionals, send emails to in-house counsel and routinely note in the subject line that the communication is "privileged and confidential" or some other language to that effect. By including such language, the employee may feel comfortable sharing confidential information, but the email may not be privileged or confidential, and may be viewed by individuals outside of the organization. Education by in-house counsel or the Compliance Department is crucial to stem this type of conduct and avoid a potentially disastrous outcome. Regardless, compliance professionals need to be extraordinarily careful and circumspect when drafting documents or sending emails in relation to corporate transactions. If a compliance professional wants to memorialize a concern in writing, the best approach is to consult counsel in advance.

Areas of Expertise

The roles of the Legal Department and the Compliance Department are distinct and independent. Although it is not uncommon for the Compliance Department to report to the Legal Department in many organizations, the respective areas of expertise of the departments are entirely different. As the chief legal officer at two different firms, I observed this distinction on a daily basis. At its core, the Legal Department is responsible for providing legal advice and guidance to various constituencies within the organization and representing the organization in accordance with in-house counsel's ethical responsibilities.

From an ethical perspective, the conduct of in-house counsel is generally governed by the rules of professional conduct, although in-house counsel in publicly held corporations may have other ethical obligations, including those obligations under the Sarbanes-Oxley Act and those obligations promulgated by the SEC. Two of the ethical obligations of an in-house counsel, particularly a transactional attorney, are to maintain in confidence privileged communications concerning a transaction and to avoid conflicts of interest that might arise as a result of in-house counsel's prior employment. The in-house counsel who participates in corporate transactions also needs to carefully navigate the challenges associated with providing legal advice as opposed to business advice, whereby a privilege might not attach to a particular communication if in-house

---

[11] *Upjohn v. United States*, 449 U.S. 390 (1980).

counsel is wearing a "business hat" as opposed to its "legal hat." The ethical responsibility associated with maintaining the confidence of communications regarding a corporate transaction typically limits the in-house counsel's ability to interact with colleagues, potentially including those in the Compliance Department.

The Legal Department's legal advice or representation normally entails drafting memoranda, correspondence, pleadings in litigation, and/or transactional documentation. Besides taking a legal writing class in law school, law students may be taught by professors using the Socratic method of teaching, whereby law students are called on in a large class setting on a random basis and challenged by professors to address a variety of potential fact patterns. As a result of their law school training, graduating law students tend to be good writers who are capable of analyzing a complex set of facts and articulating a position as an advocate for their client. In that regard and based on this "expertise," the Legal Department routinely has responsibility for drafting documents associated with corporate transactions or managing members of outside counsel when they are drafting transactional documents. The Legal Department also has expertise in managing the closing process for corporate transactions, which entails all aspects of the closing process, including regulatory matters.

The "expertise" of the Compliance Department is different from that from the Legal Department. In my experience, successful compliance professionals are those individuals who can capture the relevant facts of a particular issue and be fully conversant regarding those facts, apply both firm policy and regulatory provisions to those facts, and draw a conclusion from a regulatory risk (as opposed to business risk) perspective and effectively communicate that decision to business personnel within the organization. Based on the Compliance Department's normal role in drafting policies and procedures and working within the confines of the body of regulatory law, the Compliance Department is much more effective than the Legal Department in identifying potential regulatory issues when a potential corporate transaction is evaluated. It is exceedingly important for legal professionals to know that they are not compliance professionals and for compliance professionals to know that they are not legal professionals, with the exception of individuals who serve in both capacities.

"Knowing what you do not know" is a simple concept but potentially difficult for particular individuals to follow. The old adage, "Why would you go to a lawyer if you need a doctor? " rings true in the context of a corporate transaction. In connection with a corporate transaction, why consult the Legal Department if you have a compliance question? Although that question is certainly an oversimplification of the capabilities of particular individuals employed in a dual legal and compliance capacity, there are specific areas of expertise possessed by legal and compliance professionals. Given the evolving complexity of the regulatory landscape, hopefully I have made the case that the Compliance Department should play an integral role in connection with corporate transactions. The following sections, describe the specific areas of expertise for which the Compliance Department's involvement can facilitate the corporate transaction or avoid future issues.

IV. THE ROLE OF THE COMPLIANCE DEPARTMENT IN CORPORATE TRANSACTIONS

Unless an organization routinely involves the Compliance Department at the onset of a corporate transaction, compliance professionals might not be consulted at the early stages of a corporate transaction. As discussed below, the nature of the corporate transaction might require regulatory approval with a lead time that may delay the closing date or even prevent the closing of a transaction altogether. Additionally, as previously discussed, one or both of the parties to an NDA might be publicly owned and have securities traded on an exchange. In that instance, the Legal Department may not be capable of implementing policies and procedures to ensure that (1) information is not being shared internally and (2) employees are not trading in the securities of one or both entities. Misuse of confidential information received via an NDA could have severe adverse consequences for an organization depending upon on the scope and nature of the corporate transaction and the materiality of the information being shared pursuant to the NDA. In either instance, the Compliance Department needs to be a strong advocate for its involvement in a corporate transaction at the earliest possible stage.

Once the business terms of a corporate transaction are generally agreed upon, the parties may enter into a nonbinding term sheet or letter of intent (NBLOI). The purpose of a NBLOI is permit the parties to begin the due diligence process in order to confirm the value of the proposed corporate transaction and to provide time for the parties to start the process of negotiating binding contractual deal documents. Drafting and/or reviewing the NBLOI is typically handled by in-house or outside counsel. An NBLOI is normally a relatively short agreement that:

- Identifies the parties to a proposed corporate transaction;
- Outlines the general business terms;
- Explains that the proposed transaction is nonbinding with respect to either party;
- Reiterates the need to maintain particular information about the proposed transaction in confidence; and
- Describes the process for terminating the transaction.

An NBLOI may also specify a timeframe during which the parties must proceed on an exclusive basis. During this stage of the corporate transaction, it makes sense for the parties to evaluate the inclusion of compliance matters in the due diligence process.

Engaging in robust due diligence is crucial to confirming that the organization is achieving the benefit of the corporate transaction it is negotiating. Normally, the due diligence process is managed by in-house or outside counsel. This makes sense given that the vast majority of the documents are related to the corporate structure or are financial or operational in nature. However, as described later in this chapter, it is important from a best practices perspective for the Compliance Department to participate in the due diligence process.

Concurrent with the due diligence process, outside counsel typically prepares definitive documentation to memorialize the corporate transaction. In an M&A transaction, there are a number of standard provisions included in the related purchase agreement (in the case of an asset acquisition, an asset purchase agreement, and in the case of a stock acquisition, a stock purchase agreement). These provisions typically:

- Specify the parties to the transaction;
- Describe the transaction in the recitals to the agreement;
- Confirm the nature of what the buyer is acquiring;
- Outline the consideration related to the transaction which may take the form of equity, assumption of debt, a cash payment or payments, earn-outs or a combination thereof, and the timing of such obligations;
- Include a series of representations and warranties given by each of the seller and the buyer;
- Contain particular restrictive covenants prohibiting one or both parties from engaging in certain conduct (e.g., competing with the buyer for a specified period of time);
- Describe the conditions to closing the transaction and the timing thereof;
- Outline the documents to be delivered at closing;
- Specify the indemnification obligations of one or both parties;
- Describe the information the parties can disclose publicly concerning the transaction; and
- Specify requirements regarding confidentiality, dispute resolution, choice of law, and notices.

In the "representations and warranties" section of the purchase agreement, the parties provide a number of statements that attest to the quality of the transaction and to ensure that the assets or business purchased by the buyer matches the representations of the seller regarding the same and that there are no impediments to proceeding with the transaction. The buyer may also obtain representations providing negative assurance that, for example, the seller has not violated the Foreign Corrupt Practices Act (FCPA), is in compliance with sanctions administered by the Office of Foreign Assets Control (OFAC), and is in compliance with all applicable antimoney laundering (AML) laws. There may be representations related to the facts that: the target entity was properly organized and is in good standing; the seller is authorized to engage in the transaction, that the financial information regarding the target entity or assets being sold has been accurately reported; the seller holds title to the securities of the target entity or assets being sold; and there are no impediments, liens, or encumbrances on the securities of the target entity or assets being sold, etc. In addition, many of these same representations and warranties will appear in underwriting agreements or purchase agreements for standalone offerings of securities (in which underwriters or initial purchasers purchase the securities from the issuer for resale to investors or other broker-dealers) and distribution agreements, program agreements, or selling agent agreements for programs for repeat issuances of securities.

The Compliance Department will perform due diligence to ensure that such representations and warranties are accurate, particularly those representations and warranties attesting to the nature of the assets or business being sold from a regulatory perspective. For example, representations and warranties may provide that the seller has implemented an AML program that has been managed in accordance with applicable law, the seller has made all required government filings, the seller has complied with all applicable regulatory requirements, the seller's employees are properly registered, the seller has not exceeded its regulatory authorization, the seller is not acting as a registered investment company, etc. Formulating and evaluating these types of representations and warranties might be accomplished by having the Compliance Department confirm that the relevant party has in fact taken the actions described in the representations and warranties and/or perform due diligence to independently confirm such matters.

As illustrated above, the participation of the Compliance Department in corporate transactions is an integral aspect of such transactions. The Compliance Department needs to ensure that it positions itself as a valued partner to ensure its participation in such transactions.

Advice and Guidance for Key Issues

Assuming that the Compliance Department is successful in getting a seat at the table with respect to a proposed corporate transaction, identifying issues and providing guidance and advice become invaluable in the process of closing a corporate transaction. From a best practices perspective, the following are some of the key issues that the Compliance Department needs to spot and address in a corporate transaction.

NASD Rule 1017. If the organization is registered as a broker-dealer or has an affiliated broker-dealer and is a FINRA member firm, it is crucial that the Compliance Department has a full understanding of the broker-dealer's FINRA membership agreement and understands the parameters of NASD Rule 1017.[12] Considerable time can be spent obtaining FINRA approval in relation to a change in the business of the broker-dealer. Failing to allocate sufficient time to obtain FINRA approval and to satisfy NASD Rule 1017 might delay the closing date of a proposed transaction or potentially result in the termination of a proposed transaction, particularly if time is of the essence. If the Compliance Department fails to identify and raise this issue and is blamed for the delay or lost opportunity, the Compliance Department will potentially lose substantial credibility within the organization.

NASD Rule 1017 governs the process for a change in ownership, control, or business operations. FINRA approval is required for a number of different types of changes in the organization's structure, including M&A, asset transfers, and material changes in the business of the broker-dealer.[13] Specifically, NASD Rule 1017 provides in relevant part that a FINRA member will file an application for approval for any of the following changes to its ownership, control, or business operations:

---

[12] NASD Rule 1017, Application for Approval of Change in Ownership, Control, or Business Operations.
[13] *See* FINRA Checklist for Changes in Firm Organization: Assistance with the Merger, Acquisition, and Succession Process (May 2011), http://www.finra.org/web/groups/industry/@ip/@comp/@regis/documents/industry/p014285.pdf

- A merger with another FINRA member;
- A direct or indirect acquisition by the FINRA member of another FINRA member;
- Direct or indirect acquisitions or transfers of 25 percent or more in the aggregate of the FINRA member's assets or any asset, business or line of operation that generates revenues composing 25 percent or more in the aggregate of the FINRA member's earnings measured on a rolling 36-month basis;
- A change in the equity ownership or partnership capital of the FINRA member that results in one person or entity directly or indirectly owning or controlling 25 percent or more of the equity or partnership capital; or
- A material change in business operations, which includes but is not limited to, removing or modifying a FINRA membership agreement restriction; market making, underwriting, or acting as a dealer for the first time; and adding business activities that require a higher minimum net capital under Exchange Act Rule 15c3-1.[14]

The application must be filed with FINRA's Department of Member Regulation and must include a FINRA continuing membership application, which includes a detailed description of the change in ownership, control or business operations. If the application requests the removal or modification of a FINRA membership agreement restriction, the application must also present facts showing that the circumstances that gave rise to the restriction have changed and state with specificity why the restriction should be modified or removed in light of the standards set forth in NASD Rule 1014[15] and the articulated rationale for the imposition of the restriction. FINRA members should file the application at least 30 days prior to such change. However, a FINRA member firm may effect a change in ownership or control prior to the conclusion of the proceeding, but FINRA's Department of Member Regulation may place new interim restrictions on the FINRA member based on the standards set forth in NASD Rule 1014, pending final approval. Alternatively, a FINRA member may file an application to remove or modify a FINRA membership agreement at any time. However, the existing restriction will remain in place during the pendency of the proceeding. Similarly, a FINRA member may also file an application for approval of a material change in business operations, other than the modification or removal of a restriction, at any time, but the FINRA member may not effect such change until the conclusion of the proceeding, unless FINRA's Department of Member Regulation and the FINRA member agree otherwise.[16] One should keep in mind that a corporate transaction that is covered by NASD Rule 1017 and involves an offshore entity may also require certain reporting and disclosure obligations with a foreign regulatory body.

The Compliance Department needs to be familiar with NASD Rule 1017. Normally, during the course of a transaction, neither in-house counsel nor outside counsel will be focused on the necessity of filing an application with FINRA to seek approval to close a transaction that affects the ownership of the organization. In-house and outside counsel will also likely not be focused on the timeframe associated with obtaining that

---

[14] If the counterparty or surviving entity is an NYSE company, an approval application may not need to be filed.
[15] NASD Rule 1014, Department Decision.
[16] See NASD Rule 1017(c).

approval. Consequently, the Compliance Department needs to take the lead on the regulatory approval process and coordinate all FINRA filing and disclosure requirements with in-house and outside counsel.

Regulation M. Regulation M under the Securities Act of 1933, as amended (the Securities Act), is intended to protect the trading markets by prohibiting activities by distribution participants that could manipulate the market for a security that is the subject of an offering. Regulation M impacts the activities that may be conducted by issuers' broker-dealers and other distribution participants around the time of a securities offering. Regulation M consists of the following six rules:

- Rule 100, Definitions;
- Rule 101, Activities of Distribution Participants;
- Rule 102, Activities of Issuers and Selling Security Holders;
- Rule 103, NASDAQ Passive Market Making;
- Rule 104, Stabilizing and Other Activities; and
- Rule 105, Short Selling.

Compliance professionals most frequently encounter Regulation M when they are determining whether a securities offering needs to be reported to FINRA and determining whether a "restricted period" applies to distribution participants in a particular offering. The rules under Regulation M are very technical, and Regulation M questions often turn on the specific facts of the offering in question. As a result, the Compliance Department needs to be informed of all of the facts at hand in order to properly advise the business professionals of FINRA reporting requirements (which may need to be timely made) and restrictions regarding distribution activity. Following is a summary of the main aspects of Regulation M.

Rule 101 prohibits distribution participants and their affiliated purchasers from bidding for, purchasing, or attempting to induce any person to bid for or purchase a covered security of a distribution during a restricted period. Rule 100 defines a *distribution* as a securities offering that is distinguished from ordinary trading transactions by the magnitude of the offering and the presence of special selling efforts and methods. The number of shares to be sold and the percentage of outstanding shares of the proposed distribution compared to the public float and the security's normal trading volume are factors to consider when firms determine the magnitude of an offering. Greater than "normal" compensation arrangements, delivery of sales documents such as a prospectus, and conducting road shows are generally indicative of special selling efforts and selling methods.[17] In the context of a shelf registration that contemplates various selling methods, each takedown needs to be individually assessed.[18] A "distribution" need not be a registered public offering; a private placement can also be a distribution under Regulation M.[19] A wide variety of private

---

[17] Exchange Act Release No. 34-33924 (April 26, 1994), at 6.
[18] *See* SEC Release Nos. 33-7375 and 34-38067 (April 1, 1997) (hereinafter the "Regulation M Adopting Release"), at 526.
[19] SEC Staff Legal Bulletin No. 9 (Oct. 27, 1999, revised Sept. 10, 2010) (hereinafter the "SEC Reg. M FAQ").

placement transactions can be considered distributions, depending on the circumstances, including Regulation D offerings and Rule 144 offerings.

Covered securities are securities that are the subject of a distribution or a *reference security*. A reference security is a security into which the covered security may be converted, exchanged, or exercised, or that may impact the value of the covered security. Derivative securities are not subject to Rule 101 and therefore, bids or purchases of options, warrants, rights, convertible securities, or equity-linked securities are not restricted by Rule 101.[20] However, during a distribution of derivative securities, Rule 101 does apply to the underlying security, the value of which affects the return of the derivative security.[21]

Distribution participants include any persons who have agreed to participate or are participating in a distribution, such as underwriters, prospective underwriters, brokers, and dealers. However, a broker-dealer who performs only ministerial duties and receives a fixed fee for its limited role is not considered a distribution participant.[22] A prospective underwriter is a person who has either (1) submitted a bid to the issuer or selling shareholder and who knows or is reasonably certain such bid will be accepted; or (2) has reached, or is reasonably certain to reach, an understanding that such person will become an underwriter regardless of whether the underwriting terms and conditions have been agreed upon. An *affiliated purchaser* includes a person acting in concert with or is controlled by or under common control with a distribution participant. The definition also includes any separate department or division that regularly purchases securities for its own account or the account of others or that recommends or exercises investment discretion with respect to the purchase or sale of securities.

Rule 101 applies only during a restricted period. The length of the restricted period will differ depending on the type of covered security. For securities with an average daily trading volume (ADTV) of $100,000 or more of an issuer whose common equity securities have a public float value of $25 million or more, the restricted period begins on the later of one business day prior to the pricing date or such time that a person becomes a distribution participant and ends on the completion of its participation in the distribution.[23] For all other securities, the restricted period begins on the later of five business days prior to the pricing date or such time that a person becomes a distribution participant, and ends on the completion of its participation in the distribution. In the case of convertible securities, the ADTV used to determine the restricted period is that of the convertible security itself and not the reference security.[24]

---

[20] Regulation M Adopting Release, at 524.
[21] *Id.*
[22] *See* SEC Reg. M FAQ.
[23] ADTV equals the worldwide average daily trading volume during the two full calendar months immediately preceding, or any 60 consecutive calendar days ending within the 10 calendar days preceding, the filing of a registration statement. If there is no registration statement or the sale is made on a delayed basis under Rule 415 under the Securities Act, it would be prior to the pricing date instead of the registration statement filing date.
[24] *See* SEC Reg. M FAQ.

In M&A transactions and exchange offers, the restricted period begins on the day proxy solicitation or offering materials are first distributed to security holders and ends upon the completion of the distribution. If the offering is in connection with an acquisition of a privately held company, the restricted period would commence one or five days (depending on the type of covered security as described above) prior to the day on which the target security holders are first asked to commit to the transaction.[25] If an underwriter joins the underwriting syndicate on the pricing date, its prior bids or purchases for the covered securities will not violate Rule 101. For such an underwriter, the restricted period begins when it joins the syndicate. Broker-dealers who become *prospective underwriters* often maintain restricted lists or watch lists in order to monitor bids for or purchases of covered securities, in order to avoid a violation of Regulation M.

The completion of participation in a distribution occurs when all the securities in the offering have been distributed and all stabilization arrangements and trading restrictions in connection with the distribution have terminated. For selling group members who are not part of an underwriting syndicate, the completion of the participation occurs when the selling group member has sold all of its allotment. The distribution period may also be modified for an offering with a "green shoe" option and for "sticky offerings."[26]

The following securities are exempt from Rule 101:

1. Actively traded securities with a worldwide ADTV of at least $1 million and issued by an issuer with common equity securities with a public float value of at least $150 million, unless those securities are issued by a distribution participant or its affiliate, in which case, only nonaffiliated participants are exempt;
2. Investment-grade nonconvertible securities and asset-backed securities;
3. "Exempt securities" as defined in Section 3(a)(12) of the Exchange Act, including but not limited to:
   a. Any security issued or guaranteed by the United States or issued by a religious or charitable organization or a Section 501(c) tax exempt nonprofit corporation;
   b. Any security issued by institutions which are supervised and examined by state and federal authorities; and
   c. Certain security futures product;
4. Face-amount certificates or securities issued by an open-end management investment company or unit investment trust (UIT).

---

[25] *Id.*
[26] In transactions in which an overallotment option is exercised, the exercise of the option does not affect the completion date, unless the underwriters exercise their over-allotment option for more shares than the net syndicate short position at the time that the option is exercised. In such cases, the completion date would be extended to the time at which all the excess shares have been sold. Furthermore, if there are any excess shares, any bids or purchases by the underwriters made before the exercise of the option could violate Rule 101 of Regulation M. In sticky offerings in which underwriters are unable to sell all of their allotted securities, the syndicate manager could keep the syndicate together and modify the selling concession or engage in unsolicited transactions or offers to sell or solicitations of offers to buy, both of which are exempted transactions under Rule 101. If the securities are taken in for the underwriter's own investment (an "unsold allotment"), the underwriter could resell the securities under a current prospectus or sell the securities after a significant holding period. The SEC usually presumes that an investment bank lacks the requisite investment intent to avail itself of exemptions from registration. As a consequence, most practitioners advise that an underwriter hold securities that form part of an unsold allotment for a substantial period of time.

Exemption (1) above for actively traded securities may apply to ordinary shares issued by foreign issuers. However, debt securities generally would not qualify for this exemption because of their lack of public trading history.[27]

In addition to the exempt securities, the following activities are exempt from Rule 101:

1. Publishing and disseminating research materials that are in compliance with Rules 138 and 139 under the Securities Act;
2. Engaging in transactions with respect to Securities Act Rule 144A eligible securities to "qualified institutional buyers" and non-U.S. persons;
3. Participating in unsolicited brokerage transactions or unsolicited purchases not effected from or through a broker or dealer, securities exchange or interdealer quotation system or electronic communications network;
4. Engaging in passive market making under Rule 103 or stabilizing transactions under Rule 104;
5. Purchasing a total of less than 2 percent of the ADTV of a security, if written procedures for Rule 101 compliance are in effect and enforced;
6. Exercising options, warrants, rights or conversion privileges;
7. Transactions in connection with a distribution not effected on a securities exchange or through an inter-dealer quotation system or electronic communications network;
8. Offers to sell or the solicitation of offers to buy securities;
9. Odd-lot transactions; and
10. Basket transactions.

In the case of exemption (3) above for unsolicited brokerage transactions and unsolicited purchases, participants must be careful: If a market transaction results from an original inquiry by a distribution participant, the original inquiry will be deemed "solicited" and will not fall under this exemption.[28]

Rule 103 allows broker-dealers who are registered NASDAQ market makers to engage in market making transactions in NASDAQ securities during the Rule 101 restricted period under certain conditions. However, Rule 103 market making is not allowed in at-the-market or "best efforts" offerings, or for a security for which a stabilizing bid subject to Rule 104 is in effect.

---

[27] *See* SEC Reg. M FAQ.
[28] In response to Regulation M violations in connection with the book-building activities for "hot" IPOs in 2005, the SEC published an interpretive release clarifying prohibited book-building activities under Regulation M. These prohibited activities include but are not limited to:
 - "Tie-in" arrangements where purchasers are induced to purchase securities in the form of tie-in agreements or solicitations of aftermarket bids or purchases prior to the completion of the distribution;
 - Solicitation of customers prior to the completion of the distribution regarding immediate aftermarket orders;
 - Accepting or soliciting interest from customers for purchases of shares in the aftermarket in an amount linked to the initial purchase; and
 - Soliciting aftermarket orders before the completion of the distribution or rewarding customers for aftermarket orders by allocating additional securities to those customers in the initial distribution. Exchange Act Release Nos. 33-8565 and 34-51500 (April 7, 2005).

Under Rule 104, stabilizing bid prices must be no higher than the lower of (i) the offering price and (ii) (a) the stabilizing bid for the security in the principal market if the principal market is open or (b) the stabilizing bid in the principal market at its previous close if the principal market is closed.

Under Rule 105, any person who has shorted an equity security that is subject to a public offering made on a firm commitment basis cannot purchase those securities from a distribution participant in the offering if the short sale was effected during a restricted period beginning either five business days before the pricing of the offering or the initial filing of the registration statement and ending with the pricing, whichever period is shorter. Such a practice can artificially decrease the price of the security, which would then reduce the issuer's net proceeds from the offering. Rule 105 does not apply to debt securities because they are less susceptible to manipulation, trade based on the yields and spreads of comparable securities, and are generally fungible with other similarly rated securities.[29]

FINRA members must notify FINRA when participating in a distribution of an exchange-listed security or an over-the-counter (OTC) equity security that meets the definition of distribution under Regulation M and is not subject to an exemption under Rule 101. FINRA Rule 5190[30] requires FINRA member firms to provide information related to the distribution, such as the determination of the restricted period, whether they are relying on the actively traded securities exemption and pricing information. Since June 2012, broker-dealers have been required to effect these notices electronically through the FINRA "Firm Gateway." The exchanges (e.g., the NYSE and NASDAQ) also require reporting transactions that qualify as "distributions" under Regulation M.

Advertising Rules. Undoubtedly, in a corporate transaction, there will be a desire to publicize the transaction in order to draw attention to the transaction or the resulting business changes as a result of the transaction. Accordingly, the Compliance Department needs to coordinate with the organization's Marketing Department or the relevant business unit that seeks to issue the press release or other form of communication. Various regulatory rules come into play when a firm intends to issue a marketing or advertising piece regarding a corporate transaction. Regardless of the applicable rules, caution must also be exercised when compliance (or marketing) professionals broadly disseminate marketing or advertising communications in relation to the corporate transaction. Any public communication that is broadly disseminated may be closely scrutinized from a potential litigation perspective.

Fundamentally, a determination should be made whether the marketing communication is intended for institutional or retail customers. An example of an institutional communication would be an announcement of a joint venture directed to the firm's institutional client base. An *institutional investor* generally refers to the account of:

---

[29] SEC Release No. 34-56206 (Aug. 6, 2007).
[30] FINRA Rule 5190, Notification Requirements for Offering Participants.

- A bank, savings and loan association, insurance company, or registered investment company;
- An investment adviser registered either with the SEC under Section 203 of the Investment Advisers Act or with a state securities commission (or any agency or office performing like functions); or
- Any other person (whether a natural person, corporation, partnership, trust, or otherwise) with total assets of at least $50 million.[31]

Institutional communications require principal approval, and the firm's policies and procedures must address employee education and training in relation to the issuance of institutional communications.[32] However, there is no requirement to file institutional communications with FINRA.[33] Nonetheless, many firms file institutional communications out of an abundance of caution or to avoid future regulatory scrutiny with respect to such communications. If the FINRA member firm has reason to believe that the communication will be forwarded to retail investors, the communication is then deemed to be a retail communication.[34]

Retail communications require principal approval and may need to be filed with FINRA.[35] An example of a retail communication would be an announcement of a merger between two broker-dealers and a description of the enhanced services and capabilities of the surviving broker-dealer. However, if that announcement is not recommending or promoting a particular security or is only disseminated or made available to media outlets, then the communication does not need to be filed with FINRA.[36] Assuming that the communication does not qualify for an exemption from filing, if the surviving broker-dealer is newly registered, then the communication must be filed at least ten business days prior to first use.[37] If the broker-dealer responsible for issuing the communication has been a FINRA member for at least one year, then the communication must be filed with FINRA within ten business days of first use. Irrespective of how long the broker-dealer has been registered with FINRA, if the retail communication is a *free writing prospectus* (FWP) that has been filed with the SEC pursuant to Securities Act Rule 433(d)(1)(ii),[38] then the broker-dealer may file such retail communication within ten business days of first use rather than at least ten business days prior to first use.[39]

In addition, FINRA has provided a filing exemption for the following types of communications:[40]

---

[31] FINRA Rules 2210(a)(4) and 4512(c).
[32] FINRA Rule 2210(b)(3).
[33] FINRA Rule 2210(c)(7)(K).
[34] FINRA Rule 2210(a)(4).
[35] FINRA Rule 2210(b)(1)(A).
[36] FINRA Rules 2210(c)(7)(3) and (8).
[37] FINRA Rule 2210(c)(1)(A).
[38] *Id.*
[39] *Id.*
[40] FINRA Rule 2210(c)(7).

- Retail communications that previously have been filed with FINRA and that are to be used without material change;
- Retail communications that are based on templates that were previously filed with FINRA the changes to which are limited to updates of more recent statistical or other nonnarrative information;
- Retail communications that do no more than identify a national securities exchange symbol of the FINRA member or identify a security for which the FINRA member is a registered market maker;
- Retail communications that do no more than identify the FINRA member or offer a specific security at a stated price;
- Prospectuses, preliminary prospectuses, fund profiles, offering circulars, and similar documents that have been filed with the SEC or any state, or that is exempt from such registration, and free writing prospectuses that are exempt from filing with the SEC, except that an investment company prospectus published pursuant to Securities Act Rule 482 and a free writing prospectus that is required to be filed with the SEC pursuant to Securities Act Rule 433(d)(1)(ii) will not be considered a prospectus for purposes of this exclusion;
- Retail communications prepared in accordance with Section 2(a)(10)(b) of the Securities Act, as amended, or any rule thereunder, such as Rule 134, and announcements as a matter of record that a member has participated in a private placement, unless the retail communications are related to publicly offered direct participation programs or securities issued by registered investment companies;
- Any reprint or excerpt of any article or report issued by a publisher, provided that:
  - The publisher is not an affiliate of the member using the reprint or any underwriter or issuer of a security mentioned in the reprint that the FINRA member is promoting;
  - Neither the FINRA member using the reprint nor any underwriter or issuer of a security mentioned in the reprint has commissioned the reprinted article or report; and
  - The FINRA member using the reprint has not materially altered its contents except as necessary to make the reprint consistent with applicable regulatory standards or to correct factual errors;
- Correspondence;
- Communications that refer to types of investments solely as part of a listing of products or services offered by the FINRA member;
- Retail communications that are posted on an online interactive electronic forum.
- Press releases issued by closed-end investment companies that are listed on the NYSE pursuant to Section 202.06 of the NYSE Listed Company Manual (or any successor provision); and
- Research reports as defined in NASD Rule 2711 that concern only securities that are listed on a national securities exchange, other than research reports required to be filed with the SEC pursuant to Section 24(b) of the Investment Company Act.

FWPs. FWPs are governed by Rule 405 under the Securities Act. An FWP is defined as any written communication that both:

- Is an offer to sell or a solicitation of an offer to buy SEC-registered securities that is used after the registration statement (www.practicallaw.com/4-382-3743) for an offering is filed (or, in the case of a "well-known seasoned issuer," whether or not a registration statement has been filed); and
- Is made by means other than:
  - A statutory prospectus (a final prospectus, a preliminary prospectus or certain other categories of prospectus that meet the requirements of Section 10(a) of the Securities Act (www.practicallaw.com/1-382-3805));
  - A written communication used in reliance on Rule 167 and Rule 426 under the Securities Act (special rules for issuers of asset-backed securities); or
  - A communication that is given together with or after delivery of a final prospectus (which therefore falls into the exception from the definition of prospectus in Section 2(a)(10)(a) of the Securities Act).

An example of an FWP would be a communication regarding the issuance and offer of a registered security. This could include an advertisement in a newspaper announcing the offer, a term sheet describing the terms of the security, or a banner ad on the broker-dealer's website announcing the offering.

Consequently, if the broker-dealer is participating in the offer and distribution of a registered security either as an underwriter or selling group member or as an affiliate of the issuer involved in the distribution, care must be taken to ensure that the FWP is permitted by the issuer and the communication has been filed with the SEC and FINRA. It is not unusual for issuers to prohibit underwriters and selling group members from creating and distributing an FWP. If the Compliance Department is asked to review a communication related to a newly issued registered security, the Compliance Department should coordinate with the Legal Department to determine whether the related underwriting, purchase, or distribution agreement with the issuer or a selected dealer agreement executed between the broker-dealer and the underwriter or another broker-dealer participating in the reoffer of a newly issued security prohibits such broker-dealer from creating a FWP. Normally, an issuer is reluctant to permit a broker-dealer to prepare an FWP absent the prior written approval of the issuer or the lead underwriter. In addition, failure to file an FWP under Rule 433 under the Securities Act could have adverse consequences for the issuer, including a possible right of rescission.[41] The Legal Department typically is not informed about the issuance of marketing communications and may be unaware of the nature and type of marketing communications being issued. Conversely, the Compliance Department works directly

---

[41] Failure to comply with the conditions of Rule 433 under the Securities Act will essentially result in a violation of Section 5(b)(1) of the Securities Act. Section 12(a)(1) of the Securities Act provides a rescission right to any investor who buys securities in a transaction violating Section 5 of the Securities Act. In other words, an investor can rescind the sale and recover the purchase price paid (plus interest, less any amount received on the securities) if the offering is conducted in violation of Section 5 of the Securities Act. An investor who no longer owns the securities can recover damages equal to the difference between the purchase and the sale price of the securities, again, plus interest, less any amount received on the securities. Beyond the statutory remedies available to purchasers, a rescission offer can be very costly to the issuer, making it very important to follow the Securities Act restrictions on communications and offers.

with the organization's Marketing Department and should be aware of the marketing communications being issued. As a result, the Compliance Department needs to identify this issue and coordinate with the Legal Department.

Regulation FD. In August 2000, the SEC adopted Regulation FD in an effort to eliminate the selective disclosure of "material nonpublic information."[42] The SEC was concerned in particular with issuers making selective disclosure, such as advanced warnings of earnings results, to securities analysts or selected institutional investors.[43] Regulation FD generally provides that whenever any issuer, or any person acting on its behalf, discloses any material nonpublic information regarding that issuer or its securities to certain "enumerated recipients," then the issuer must publicly disclose that information.[44] However, the definition of material nonpublic information remains elusive and the SEC has, to date, not offered a definitive definition or standard, except as articulated in a long line of SEC enforcement proceedings.[45]

Regulation FD applies to companies that have a class of securities registered under Section 12 of the Exchange Act or companies required to file periodic reports under Section 15(d) of the Exchange Act, as well as closed-end investment companies. However, Regulation FD does not apply to foreign private issuers, foreign government issuers or open-end investment companies. Regulation FD covers communications by an issuer and communications made by persons acting on behalf of the issuer, which could include senior executive officers, directors, investor relations or public relations officers, and employees or agents of the issuer who regularly communicate with the enumerated recipients or with shareholders of the issuer.

In recognition of the challenges that social media present both for issuers and the SEC, in April 2013 the SEC issued a report regarding its investigation of Netflix, Inc. and its chief executive officer (CEO).[46] Netflix's CEO had made a posting on his personal Facebook page that essentially touted the fact that monthly viewing of Netflix content exceeding one billion hours for the first time ever during a particular point in time. The SEC noted that the posting was not accompanied by a press release or a posting on the Netflix website, so the communication was not made in compliance with Regulation

---

[42] 17 C.F.R. 243.100–243.103.
[43] Securities Act Release No. 33-7881 (Aug. 15, 2000).
[44] *Enumerated recipients* include broker-dealers, investment advisers, institutional investment managers, investment companies, affiliates of these entities, and particular shareholders of the issuer if it is reasonably foreseeable that the shareholder would engage in a purchase or sale transaction in the issuer's securities based on such information.
[45] Information is material if "there is a substantial likelihood that a reasonable shareholder would consider it important" in making an investment decision. To fulfill the materiality requirement, there must be a substantial likelihood that a fact "would have been viewed by the reasonable investor as having significantly altered the 'total mix' of information made available." Information is nonpublic if it has not been disseminated in a manner making it available to investors generally (*TSC Industries, Inc. v. Northway, Inc.*, 426 U.S. 438, 449 (1976)); *see Basic v. Levinson*, 485 U.S. 224, 231 (1988) (materiality with respect to contingent or speculative events will depend on a balancing of both the indicated probability that the event will occur and the anticipated magnitude of the event in light of the totality of company activity); *see also* Securities Act Rule 405, 17 CFR 230.405; Exchange Act Rule 12b-2, 17 CFR 240.12b-2; Staff Accounting Bulletin No. 99 (Aug. 12, 1999) (64 FR 45150) (discussing materiality for purposes of financial statements).
[46] Exchange Act Release No. 69279 (Apr. 2, 2013).

FD. However, the SEC decided not to pursue enforcement action against Netflix and its CEO for violating Regulation FD. In its report, the SEC sought to clarify any confusion with respect to it guidance with respect to social media that dated back to 2008. In the report, the SEC essentially reiterated its 2008 guidance and suggested that communications through social media require a careful analysis under Regulation FD and the investing public should be notified of the distribution channels that a company will use to disseminate material nonpublic information. At the end of the day, compliance with Regulation FD remains a facts and circumstances test.

The Compliance Department should also be aware of the parameters of Regulation FD if the company or the parent is a public company. IPOs and mergers with public entities create scenarios whereby a Regulation FD analysis should be undertaken as the company or senior management desire to disclose material nonpublic information on through social media channels. Ensuring that the Compliance Department is notified in advance of such postings or disclosures is a key element in avoiding issues under Regulation FD. Training and education of the company's employees with respect to the parameters of Regulation FD is important as well.

Social Media. Social media presents a unique set of challenges that the Compliance Department cannot often control except through training and education. As described above, information disclosed on a social media site could, depending on the circumstances, be construed as an FWP or a violation of Regulation FD. Likewise, material nonpublic information could inadvertently be made public if the circumstances or details surrounding a corporate transaction involve a public company. As discussed below, the Compliance Department must play an integral role with respect to information barriers, but current technology permits individual employees to issue broad-based communications without prior review, approval, or oversight. How does the Compliance Department address the use of social media by employees as it relates to corporate transactions?

Well-communicated policies and procedures are the first line of defense for the Compliance Department that seeks to control the use of social media. Firms first need to decide the role of social media within the organization. Many organizations prohibit the use of social media and are able to block access through the firm's computer network. Although that may sound appealing from a risk management perspective, firms that fail to embrace the use of social media or limited segments thereof are likely limiting their upside potential and are restricting potential revenue opportunities. Once the scope of the firm's permitted use of social media is defined, the Compliance Department must draft or assist with the implementation of clear and concise related policies and procedures. These policies and procedures need to be specifically tailored to the business and customer mix of the firm, and the Compliance Department should never use or rely on canned policies and procedures. The use of canned policies and procedures may place the firm at risk for being named in a regulatory enforcement action if the firm fails to fails to abide by those policies and procedures.

Well-written policies and procedures on social media should accomplish a variety of goals. First, well-written policies and procedures on social media should be easily understood by employees. Second, well-written policies and procedures on social media should be drafted with an eye toward an applicable control. If employees are prohibited from maintaining a LinkedIn account, the Compliance Department can easily perform a search on LinkedIn to determine whether employees have violated such policy. Third, senior management needs to "buy in" to those policies and procedures on social media so that they can articulate them to employees at appropriate times and support disciplinary action if an employee violates a particular policy or procedure. Senior management buy-in is crucial in developing a culture of compliance within the firm. Additionally, supervisors need to fully understand their role and responsibilities. The Compliance Department should ask supervisors to recite the firm's policies with respect to social media, and if the supervisors are unable to do so, that may be a reflection of the Compliance Department's failure to educate and train not only supervisory personnel but also the rank and file. Training and education with respect to firm policies and procedures on social media are just as important as the actual policies and procedures regarding social media. Most firms typically spend more time training employees on issues pertaining to human relations then they do on compliance policies and procedures. Although there are important reasons for training employees on human relations issues, such as harassment in the workplace, firms should consider focusing training on an overview of the firm's policies and procedures on social media (in addition to policies and procedures on insider trading and material nonpublic information).

The second line of defense for the Compliance Department that seeks to control the use of social media is technology. This chapter is intended to provide an overview of the technology available to the Compliance Department to preclude or monitor particular types of activity or provide an endorsement of such tools, but there are many excellent tools available to support the policies and procedures governing the use of social media. Current technology can provide the Compliance Department with preapproval workflow, real-time alerts, supervision and approval trails, and infraction resolution, all from a central dashboard. It is also possible to capture, monitor, and archive social communications among employees and between employees and their clients from mobile devices, remote locations, and the corporate network. Specific functions may include preapproval of static content (including ads, tabs and profiles), capturing and archiving all social activity, receiving notifications about keyword infractions, real-time remediation of problematic posts and tweets, maintaining a history of supervisory and review actions in context, integrating with existing email supervision and archiving software, and quickly retrieving social data for internal spot-checks, external audits, or eDiscovery.

The third and perhaps most important line of defense for the Compliance Department that seeks to control the use of social media is a culture of compliance within the firm. Having senior management support the Compliance Department, particularly with respect to policies and procedures on social media, is crucial to avoiding risk in relation to the use of social media sites. The regulatory perspective on social media remains cautious because the technology available to many regulated entities from a cost perspective continues to lag behind the capabilities available to users of social media sites. Absent good controls and an ability to preview postings or comments on social media sites, ensuring that senior management will agree to some form of material retribution for employees who violate the organization's social media policy will go a long way toward avoiding problematic situations in relation to the disclosure of corporate transactions on social media sites.

Due Diligence

General Due Diligence Issues. As discussed above, the Compliance Department's involvement in the due diligence process is integral to a successful corporate transaction. The Compliance Department necessarily needs to evaluate a variety of regulatory matters concerning a potential corporate transaction, including one involving a targeted entity. For example, in the case of an M&A transaction, the due diligence review may include the following regulatory matters:

- The scope of the targeted entity's regulatory authorizations and consents;
- Prior regulatory issues;
- Operational capabilities;
- The creation and retention of required books and records;
- Compliance with the net capital rules;
- The scope of the targeted entity's compliance program (e.g., written policies and procedures, written supervisory procedures, code of conduct, etc.) and related controls;
- Any regulatory issues related to the associated personnel of the targeted entity;
- Findings in prior regulatory examinations and audits;
- The targeted entity's marketing and advertising materials and the scope of compliance review thereof;
- The targeted entity's AML program and any suspicious activity reports submitted by the targeted entity;
- The targeted entity's existing information barriers and any related issues; and
- Personal trading activity by associated personnel of the targeted entity.

Although each corporate transaction is unique from a due diligence perspective, many of the matters above also apply to other types of corporate transactions, such as offerings of existing or newly issued securities by a regulated issuer.

The lack of a robust due diligence process often leads to failed transactions or unwanted regulatory scrutiny, particularly when assets are purchased or liabilities are assumed and there is no clear determination of the scope of the liabilities or the nature of any deficiencies associated with the purchased assets. For example, if the assets of an investment adviser are purchased and it is later discovered that the investment adviser's investment performance was materially misstated, even if no liabilities related to such misstatement have been assumed, reputational value may be lost and/or regulatory requests might be made regarding the books and records that were acquired or the personnel that were hired. To the extent that business personnel seek to limit or minimize the scope of the due diligence review in order to facilitate an expedient closure of a particular transaction or to avoid an appearance of distrust by the acquiring entity, legal, and compliance professionals need to carefully evaluate such requests and potentially avoid the "easy path" to closing a transaction.

Normally, the due diligence process begins with both parties submitting written due diligence questions and due diligence request lists to one another. Conversely, the parties could meet in person to cover broad due diligence questions or set forth the framework for the due diligence process, including document requests. In a purchase transaction, the buyer should be focused on all aspects of the business which it is acquiring. In a typical M&A transaction, the buyer might be focused on the following fundamental issues:

- Confirmation that the target entity was legally established, is a bona fide corporate or partnership entity, and all requisite organizational documents and filings are up to date;
- Confirmation of the target entity's current ownership structure;
- Understanding any assumed or hired employees' prior criminal or regulatory issues, as well as any history of performance related issues including customer complaints or instances of insubordination;
- Understanding all material contracts that the target entity has entered into, particularly business terms, indemnification provisions, "evergreen provisions" (whereby the contract automatically renews without any independent action by the parties to the contract), and dispute resolution procedures;
- Understanding all employment agreements;
- Understanding all intellectual property owned by the target entity;
- Reviewing all pending and historic litigation and customer complaints;
- Reviewing all accounting statements and understanding the financial reporting systems, including any regulatory net capital computations and filings;
- Understanding the regulatory structure of the target entity (for example, when the target entity is a registered broker-dealer, the target entity's FINRA membership agreement, Form BD, Form ADV (Parts I and II), and all prior iterations of these documents for a specified period of time), as well as all FINRA or other regulatory examinations, audits, and CEO certifications;[47]
- Reviewing the target entity's compliance program in its entirety, including policies and procedures, exception reports, and internal and regulatory audit reports;
- Vetting the scope of the business and the nature of the target entity's clientele (e.g., seniors citizens, foreign residents, foreign governmental officials, and state and local officials,); and
- Performing such other due diligence reviews based on the nature of the corporate transaction to confirm the scope of the target entity's business.

Many of the matters above also apply to other types of corporate transactions, such as offerings of existing or newly issued securities by a regulated issuer. A number of the due

---

[47] FINRA Rule 3130.

diligence items pertaining to a corporate transaction with or involving a registered entity or registered employees necessarily involve the scope of the registered entity's compliance program and/or the regulatory history of registered employees involved in the corporate transaction. These areas of due diligence are clearly within the purview of the Compliance Department. Therefore, absent the involvement of the Compliance Department, the firm may not avail itself of expertise relevant to the corporate transaction and may not achieve the full benefits of the corporate transaction. In addition, the nature and structure of the registered entity's business model (e.g., foreign and domestic business units, business units in various states, holding company structure, etc.), will impact the scope of the due diligence review from the standpoint of the Compliance Department.

Specialized Due Diligence Considerations

FCPA/Anti-Bribery Provisions. The FCPA and foreign antibribery statutes, such as the UK Bribery Act 2010, seek to prohibit the payment of bribes to foreign governmental officials for the purposes of securing new business in a foreign jurisdiction or maintaining existing business in a foreign jurisdiction.[48] Registered entities that are currently doing business overseas should be knowledgeable with respect to the FCPA and the foreign laws that affect doing business in such countries, particularly the relationship of the registered entities with foreign governmental officials. Firms should also have policies and procedures and adequate controls to ensure that they are their employees do not run afoul of such provisions. However, recent case law highlights the risks related to successor liability when an acquiring firm becomes liable for the violative conduct of the target entity under the FCPA even if such conduct occurred prior to the acquisition or merger and was unknown to the acquiring entity.[49] This is important because violations of the FCPA entail both civil and criminal penalties.

The SEC has established a specialized unit within the Division of Enforcement to enhance its enforcement of the FCPA. In July 2010, General Electric agreed to pay a $1 million fine and disgorge $22.4 million to settle a complaint brought by the SEC for violations of the FCPA.[50] The case is noteworthy because the kickback scheme in question occurred at two foreign subsidiaries of General Electric and occurred before General Electric purchased the subsidiaries. According to the SEC, the corporate acquisitions did not provide General Electric with immunity from FCPA enforcement regarding the two subsidiaries.

---

[48] *See* Criminal Division of the U.S. Department of Justice and the Enforcement Division of the U.S. Securities and Exchange Commission, *A Resource Guide to the U.S. Foreign Corrupt Practices Act* (Nov. 14, 2012), http://www.justice.gov/criminal/fraud/fcpa/guide.pdf

[49] *See* Philip Urofksy, What You Don't Know Can Hurt You: Successor Liability Resulting From Inadequate FCPA Due Diligence in M&A Transactions, 1763 PLI/Corp. 631, 637 (2009) ("As a legal matter, when one corporation acquires another, it assumes any existing liabilities of that corporation, including liability for unlawful payments, regardless of whether it knows of them."). Whether successor liability applies to a particular corporate transaction depends on the facts involved and state, federal, and, potentially, foreign law.

[50] SEC Litigation Release No. 21602 (July 27, 2010); *Securities and Exchange Commission v. General Electric Company; Ionics, Inc.; and Amersham plc*, Civil Action No. 1:10-CV-01758 (D.D.C.)(RWR).

Performing thorough due diligence when an offshore entity or domestic entity that engages in offshore business is acquired, particularly with governmental entities, is crucial. For example, if a firm is acquiring a registered investment adviser that manages assets for sovereign wealth funds, due diligence should be performed to evaluate the relationship with those sovereign wealth funds. In performing such due diligence, it is imperative that the following areas be reviewed:

- The target entity's FCPA policies and procedures, as well as any controls related thereto;
- The target entity's books, records, and accounts;
- The target entity's contracts; and
- The target entity's offshore clients and contacts.

In addition, interviews should be conducted with the target entity's employees to understand the nature of any offshore transactions and unusual payments or patterns of payments. Furthermore, any red flags should be carefully evaluated to determine whether there is any problematic activity.[51]

Conflicts of Interest/Associated Persons Outside Business Activities. Practically every financial firm, including those regulated by FINRA, faces potential conflicts of interest in its business. In order to address those conflicts, a firm should be able to recognize conflict of interest situations and take measures to manage them appropriately. Firms should address conflicts of interest through proactive decision making involving the Compliance Department, rather than ad hoc responses to conflict-related events. The framework for this proactive decision making though is dependent on the nature and business model of the firm. Thus, it will look vastly different for a small introducing broker than for a large firm with multiple affiliates engaged in a broad range of businesses on a national or global scale. For example, large firms may address conflicts of interest through their enterprise risk management or operational risk frameworks, whereas the conflicts management framework at a small firm selling basic products might rely largely on the ethical tone set by the firm owner coupled with required supervisory controls, especially those related to suitability, and the firm's compensation structure.

Although conflict management frameworks may differ among firms, small and large firms alike often face some of the same basic conflicts of interest. For example, a firm or its registered representatives may have an incentive to recommend one product over another. Conflicts of interest may also exist between an associated person's activities as a broker and their "outside business" activities, which entail those activities outside of the firm and the individual's work responsibilities. Firms may be tempted to hire an associated person in spite of a poor regulatory history if they believe that the individual can boost firm profitability.

---

[51] *See* The Foreign Corrupt Practices Act and Global Anti-Corruption Law, FCPA & Anti-Corruption Task Force of Morrison & Foerster LLP (Dec. 2010), http://media.mofo.com/files/Uploads/Images/110118-FCPA-White-Paper.pdf

Establishing a "tone at the top" that stresses the importance of ethical decision making and fair treatment of customers is critical for managing conflicts of interest. This tone is set by a firm's executive managers in their day-to-day actions and decisions. It is important for the firm's executive managers to consistently communicate and demonstrate the values to which they expect their employees to adhere, and to monitor employees' behavior to ensure that it aligns with the firm's stated values.

Effectively managing conflicts of interest that arise in a firm's business also requires establishing carefully designed and articulated structures and policies and procedures. This includes clearly defining the roles and responsibilities of the individuals, committees, and other bodies that play key roles in that structure, including the Compliance Department. Managing conflicts of interest at the enterprise level is usually accomplished with either a distributed model or a centralized model. In a distributed model, responsibility for identification and oversight is spread within a firm with no single office or department having overall ownership. In this model, the business lines typically bear front-line responsibility for identifying and managing conflicts of interest. In a centralized model, a centralized conflicts office manages a firm's conflicts framework. Firms that use this model emphasize that although they operate a centralized office, responsibility for identifying conflicts rests first and foremost with the business lines.

FINRA Conflicts of Interest Report. On October 14, 2013, FINRA issued a report on conflicts of interest that summarizes FINRA's observations following an initiative, launched in July 2012, to review conflict management policies and procedures at a number of broker-dealer firms.[52] The report focuses on approaches to identifying and managing conflicts of interest in three broad areas: enterprise-level conflicts governance frameworks; new product conflicts reviews; and compensation practices. Although the report does not break new ground or create or alter legal or regulatory requirements, it offers insight into the approach that FINRA expects firms to take in implementing a robust conflict management framework. In particular, the report identifies effective practices that FINRA observed at various firms.

The report outlines the following key features of an effective and comprehensive conflict management framework:

- Tone at the top establishing a culture of ethics and compliance;
- Organizational structures that facilitate conflict management;
- Policies, procedures, and processes for conflict management;
- Appropriate incentive standards; and
- Adoption of "best interest of client" policies.

Other key features of an effective framework identified are articulated structures, policies and processes, which should include the following:

---

[52] *See* SEC Staff Summary Report on Examinations of Information Barriers (Sept. 27, 2012).

- Descriptions of conflicts of interest containing examples relevant to the firm;
- Delineation of employees' responsibilities in identifying and managing conflicts of interest;
- Defined escalation procedures;
- Ongoing and periodic systematic identification and categorization of conflicts of interest;
- Disclosures that go beyond the minimum legal and regulatory requirements to help achieve a customer's understanding of the product;
- Disclosure to customers of multiple roles that the firm plays;
- Obtaining customer consent and requiring investors to attest to their understanding of more complex products when appropriate; and
- Transparent reporting of material conflicts to the firm's management and the firm's board of directors.

FINRA noted that some firms have not adequately addressed conflicts of interest that arise in two related circumstances: conflicts present in the business or product and conflicts that may exist when a firm evaluates whether to engage in a new business line or offer a new product or service. FINRA indicated that these conflicts of interest may be particularly prominent in the case of complex financial products that are sold to less knowledgeable investors, including retail investors. FINRA noted two underlying themes in its examination of practices used by firms to mitigate potential conflicts of interest: firms must invest in and document proper processes and systems that identify and mitigate conflicts, and at the same time, these efforts must not lapse into pro forma procedures or be too narrowly defined in scope. FINRA indicated that it will continue to focus on the substance of such practices when evaluating firms, including the tone at the top, "thoughtful analysis," and a culture of "robust debate."

FINRA also examined potential conflicts of interest in compensation arrangements, focusing particularly on brokerage and other compensation for associated persons. The report highlights the following examples of effective practices used by firms to mitigate instances in which the compensation structure may potentially affect the behavior of registered representatives:

- Avoiding compensation thresholds in which a registered representative can increase his or her compensation disproportionately after reaching a certain threshold of sales;
- Using neutral compensation grids, which avoid favoring one product over another by having a flat payout percentage regardless of product type sold;
- Introducing fee caps to minimize the incentive to favor one mutual fund over another;
- Refraining from higher compensation or other rewards for the sale of proprietary products when there are comparable products;
- Implementing surveillance and monitoring to ensure that registered representatives are not being unduly motivated by thresholds that qualify the representative to receive a back-end bonus, qualify the representative to participate in a recognition club, or move the representative to a higher payout level in the firm's compensation grid;

- Monitoring the suitability of recommendations around key liquidity events in the investor's lifecycle where the recommendation is particularly significant; and
- Using red flag processes and clawbacks to penalize employees for not properly managing conflicts of interest.

FINRA suggested that firms establish compensation governance structures that mandate identifying and managing the conflicts of interest that compensation structures may create, in order to allow firms to adjust the compensation structure to eliminate or reduce conflicts of interest and establish oversight mechanisms appropriate to the scale of conflicts that may remain. FINRA further noted that firms should consider using clawbacks throughout their businesses and not just for senior executives. Finally, FINRA recommended that firms that are dually registered as a broker-dealer and an investment adviser consider whether a commission-based or fee-based account is more appropriate for a customer.

Compliance with Rule G-37/Lobbyist Provisions. In addition to conducting due diligence with respect to an entity's compliance with the FCPA in connection with a corporate transaction, the Compliance Department needs to be cognizant of specific rules pertaining to lobbying activities, which may even apply to the firm itself. The Rule G-37[53] of the Municipal Securities Rulemaking Board, which has been in effect since 1994, has provided substantial benefits to the securities industry and the investing public by greatly reducing the direct connection between political contributions given to issuer officials and the awarding of municipal securities business to dealers. Rule G-37 requires municipal securities broker-dealers to disclose (on Form G-37) certain contributions to issuer officials, contributions to bond ballot campaigns, and payments to political parties of states and political subdivisions made by covered parties. Rule G-37 prohibits municipal securities broker-dealers from engaging in municipal securities business within two years after proscribed contributions made by: the broker-dealer; any municipal finance professional associated with the broker-dealer; or any political action committee (PAC) controlled by the broker-dealer or any such associated municipal finance professional, to an official of the issuer, who can, directly or indirectly, influence the awarding of municipal securities business. The Rule G-37's prohibition on engaging in municipal securities business is not triggered by contributions that are made to bond ballot campaigns by covered parties.

Under Rule G-37, "municipal securities business" includes certain broker-dealer activities such as the purchase of a primary offering of municipal securities from the issuer on other than a competitive bid basis (i.e., acting as a managing underwriter or as a syndicate member in negotiated underwritings), and acting as a financial advisor, consultant, placement agent, or negotiated remarketing agent. Rule G-37 defines an *official of an issuer* as any incumbent, candidate (or successful candidate) for elective office of the issuer, which office is directly or indirectly responsible for, or can influence the outcome of, the hiring of a broker-dealer for municipal securities business.

---

[53] MSRO, Political Contributions and Prohibitions on Municipal Securities Business, 1994.

"Contributions" include any gift, subscription, loan, advance, or deposit of money or anything of value made:

- For the purpose of influencing any election of any official of a municipal securities issuer for federal, state, or local office;
- For payment or reduction of debt incurred in connection with any election; or
- For transition or inaugural expenses incurred by the successful candidate for state or local office.

Knowledge of Rule G-37 is particularly important for compliance professionals given the recent volatility and regulatory scrutiny of the municipal bond market and the increased competition among securities firms for business in this market. FINRA has also recently sanctioned several member firms for unfairly obtaining the reimbursement of fees paid to a state lobbying entity from the proceeds of municipal and state bond offerings.[54]

Information Barriers

Information barriers are a fundamental component of a compliance program for an organization in possession of material nonpublic information. Section 15(g) of the Exchange Act ("Section 15(g)") requires that broker-dealers in possession of material nonpublic information establish, maintain and enforce written policies and procedures reasonably designed to prevent the misuse of such material nonpublic information. Likewise, Section 204A of the Investment Advisers Act places similar requirements on registered investment advisers. It is critical in drafting policies and procedures on material nonpublic information that they align with the business operations of the firm. Policies and procedures on material nonpublic information taken from third parties or purchased from vendors that are unfamiliar with the organization create the potential for an enforcement action if such policies and procedures do not reflect the specific characteristics of the organization's business operations. Additionally, a firm that is registered as both a broker-dealer and an investment adviser also needs to ensure that the policies and procedures on material nonpublic information account for both aspects of the firm's operations.

Effective policies and procedures on material nonpublic information identify the types of material nonpublic information that the firm may possess. Typically, such information may be in the possession of the investment banking department if the firm is representing a publicly held organization in connection with an M&A or corporate finance transaction. Another type of material nonpublic information may be related to trading information shared by an institutional account. Clearly, large institutional securities orders may create an opportunity to "front run" an order in order to take advantage of a perceived price increase in the security or to avoid a potential loss in that security. Likewise, publicly disseminated research reports may also affect the prices of securities

---

[54] See FINRA News Release, FINRA Sanctions Five Firms $4.4 Million for Using Municipal and State Bond Funds to Pay Lobbyists (Dec. 27, 2102), http://www.finra.org/newsroom/newsreleases/2012/p197554

and advance knowledge of the information contained in a report might allow the recipient of such report to improperly profit from the information contained therein.

In September 2012, the SEC issued a report regarding information barriers and the types of material nonpublic information that the SEC identified in the course of performing examinations of broker-dealers and their information barrier programs.[55] In the report, the SEC noted the following specific concerns arising in the course of the examinations:

- A significant amount of interaction between groups that have material nonpublic information and internal and external groups that have sales and trading responsibilities occurred on an informal (undocumented) basis. Broker-dealers instructed groups with material nonpublic information to refrain from discussing material nonpublic information (and sometimes any specific issuer) and instructed groups with sales and trading responsibility to identify themselves as groups that should not be provided with material nonpublic information. However, the frequency of the discussions and the absence of documentation may make it difficult to trace any inadvertent (or even intentional) disclosures that may occur.
- At some broker-dealers, senior executives, referred to as "above-the-wall," received material nonpublic information with no related monitoring or restrictions. Many of these senior executives had managerial responsibilities for business units involved in sales and trading on behalf of the broker-dealer. The absence of any documentation that these executives were receiving material nonpublic information, in view of the natural motivation to have business units within one's areas of responsibility excel, as well as the apparent absence of related monitoring or other controls, raises serious concerns about the ability of broker-dealers to guard adequately against misuse of material nonpublic information in firm and customer trading.
- Formal and documented discussions may occur between two internal business groups of a broker-dealer, in which material nonpublic information is provided to sales, trading, or research personnel for business purposes. Broker-dealers must make judgment calls between the need for information against the restrictions required, such as on the trading of securities or issuance of research reports in companies to which the material nonpublic information related. In some cases, broker-dealers were not conducting any focused review of the trading that occurred after traders were provided with material nonpublic information.
- The SEC staff identified gaps in oversight coverage at most broker-dealers, although such gaps differed. Some broker-dealers did not review trading within accounts of institutional customers, asset management affiliates, or retail customers, or the broker-dealers did not conduct any review when material nonpublic information came through business activities outside of the investment banking department—such as participation in bankruptcy committees, employees serving on the boards of directors of public companies, changes in research ratings, or insiders of companies placing unusual trades.

---

[55] *See* SEC Staff Summary Report on Examinations of Information Barriers (Sept. 27, 2012).

The SEC indicated that these concerns by themselves may not necessarily suggest violations of Section 15(g), but broker-dealers may find it helpful to consider them in reviewing their policies and procedures. The SEC also indicated that the following practices were effective in its view:

- Broker-dealers were developing processes that differentiated between types of material nonpublic information based on the source (e.g., business unit) from which the information originated within the broker-dealer or the nature (e.g., transaction type) of the information. In some cases, broker-dealers were creating tailored exception reports that took into account the different characteristics of the information.
- Broker-dealers were expanding the scope of instruments that they reviewed for potential misuse of material nonpublic information by traders, including: credit default swaps, equity or total return swaps, loans, components of pooled securities such as UITs and exchange traded funds, warrants, and bond options.

However, the SEC noted that a practice that is effective in one context may be less effective in another and that any practices identified as effective are not necessarily exhaustive. The SEC further emphasized that in order to comply with Section 15(g), a broker-dealer must not only establish but also must maintain and enforce written policies and procedures reasonably designed to prevent the misuse of material nonpublic information. Ultimately, the Compliance Department must design policies and procedures that are appropriate for the broker-dealer's particular size and business model.

Reputational and Headline Risk Considerations

In the wake of the 2008 financial crisis, regulators now view the Compliance Department as an important resource for firmwide risk assessments. The Compliance Department often reviews risk controls and performs an independent, broad assessment of a firm's general regulatory risk and reputational risk, whereas other risk management functions focus on specific credit, finance and operational risks. When a firm conducts broad-based risk assessments, the Compliance Department should participate and provide advice on the assessment of regulatory risk for the firm.

Concern with reputational risk has grown in recent years with the increasing use and importance of social media. Firms are keenly interested in what customers and competitors are saying about them and may rank reputational interest ahead of threats to their business model and the impact of economic trends and competition. However, there are two main challenges to managing reputational risk. First, traditional risk management has historically been focused inward, on the workings of the firm itself, which are typically within the control of the firm. Reputational risk, though, is shaped outside the firm. Second, the tools and analyses used to measure and monitor reputational risk are different from measuring legal or regulatory risk, because reputational risk involves the media and what the firm's customers, employees, and other stakeholders are saying in the public domain.

In order to adequately manage reputational risk, the Compliance Department needs to be involved in the early stages of corporation transactions. For each corporate transaction, the firm must weigh the financial benefits of the corporate transaction against various risks, including reputational risk. However, this deliberation may be difficult to accomplish if assessments are only made after the corporate transaction has been completed. For example, in the case of bad publicity surrounding a failed corporate transaction, the firm may have compliance, legal, and marketing professionals meet to conduct an analysis in order to help avoid a similar event. This response, though, would essentially be crisis management, rather than true reputational risk management, and although crisis management is important, it may not be enough when dealing with reputational risk issues because it typically entails taking backward-looking, reactive measures.

Managing reputational risk should start with looking at the firm's strategy, what markets a company is entering, what products or services it is offering, and what the critical risks and value killers are that could sink the firm's brand. The next step is developing an early warning system to see and head off an adverse event before it can impact reputation. This forward-looking approach is fundamental to anticipating and managing the new risks that social media are presenting. However, in order to accomplish this, the Compliance Department needs to be able to provide input on some level with respect to the firm's activities, business strategy, and marketing practices. Again, having open lines of communication between the Compliance Department and other units within the firm (e.g., business, legal, and marketing) is critical.

Regulatory Considerations

Although the Compliance Department of a securities firm traditionally focuses on satisfying securities laws and regulations, regulators increasingly expect the Compliance Department to expand its traditional scope and cover a much broader range of compliance and control issues. For example, both regulators and Congress have created new obligations for firms to identify and mitigate broad conflicts of interest. Congressional and regulatory focus also has expanded regulation and the application of regulatory requirements to a wider spectrum of activities and personnel, including those employees who do not directly interact with customers, handle customer funds or securities, or otherwise engage in securities activities. In addition, new disclosure and recordkeeping rules, intended to promote market transparency and integrity, have created new duties for the Compliance Department and have increased its accountability for any inaccuracies.[56]

Similarly, the expectations of nonsecurities regulators have also begun to affect the Compliance Department's mandate in securities firms. In particular, the Federal Reserve Board's guidance on compliance programs is focused on implementing a firmwide, global approach to risk management and oversight increasingly influencing the securities

---

[56] See SIFMA *White Paper on the Evolving Role of Compliance* (March 2013).

industry even though many securities firms are not affiliated with bank holding companies. The guidance emphasizes the importance of a strong compliance function, which is broader than the traditional mandate. The guidance also states that a firm's board of directors should review and approve key elements of the firm's compliance risk management program and oversight framework. Finally, the guidance endorses the principles of the Basel Committee on Banking Supervision, which require firms to adhere to certain principles that guide the operation and function of the Compliance Department.[57]

Firms also encounter competing and, in some cases, conflicting regulatory demands, particularly if they operate in multiple markets or jurisdictions or employ employees that may wear a variety of hats. For example, depending on a firm's products and services, the CCO, who traditionally heads the firm's Compliance Department, may be subject to various overlapping requirements set out under, among others, the Securities Act, the Exchange Act, the Investment Company Act, the Investment Advisers Act, the Commodity Exchange Act, FINRA rules, and the rules of the various securities exchanges. If the firm conducts financial or securities-related business outside of the United States, the Compliance Department and the CCO also have to satisfy non-U.S. regulatory requirements.[58]

Regulators also routinely examine firms to ensure that they satisfy applicable laws, rules, and regulations, but for many firms, handling the increasing number of requests from multiple regulators has placed the Compliance Department, usually with limited resources, under tremendous strain. Regulatory requests for information are becoming more data-intensive and frequently require analytical components and conformity with detailed formatting requirements. The Compliance Department must effectively monitor and track all requests and respond with the requested materials or information in the regulator's allotted timeframe in order to avoid penalties, which may not necessarily be reasonable. However, timeliness and accuracy of a response to a regulator are critical, particularly to avoid any suggestion of a lack of cooperation. Furthermore, the involvement of multiple regulators has also created the risk that any penalty or wrongdoing identified by one regulator may quickly escalate into additional, parallel investigations by other regulators.[59] In an environment of increasing regulatory complexity and limited resources, it is critical for the Compliance Department to develop an effective organizational structure and clear policies and procedures for navigating the various regulatory regimes applicable to the firm.

V. CONCLUSION

Today's quickly shifting business and regulatory landscape requires that the Compliance Department adjust and evolve at an ever accelerated pace. As a result, it is essential that the function of the Compliance Department with respect to corporate transactions is

---

[57] *Id.*
[58] *Id.*
[59] *See id.*

clearly defined and that information is shared among the Compliance Department, the Legal Department, and the organization's business and marketing units so that the Compliance Department is adequately and timely informed of all corporate transactions and is in the best position to address the organization's regulatory requirements and effectively manage regulatory and reputational risk. Having a seat at the table will be most effective though if the organization has the right tone at the top and a culture of robust debate, which the Compliance Department can help foster by taking a practical approach to compliance issues with respect to corporate transactions and by engaging in open dialogue with the organization's business units and management.

It is also critical for the Compliance Department to have sufficient resources to be able to train compliance professionals effectively, to create effective policies and procedures, and to function independently from the other parts of the organization. The Compliance Department must view corporate transactions differently from the Legal Department and the organization's business units and cannot be unduly influenced to allow corporate transactions to proceed at the expense of the organization's reputation, legal liability, and satisfaction of applicable regulatory requirements. Furthermore, compliance professionals should also independently foster strong relationships and open lines of communication with business managers, irrespective of the organization's formal structure, so that issues are properly escalated and addressed in a timely manner.

ABOUT THE AUTHOR

A. Brad Busscher is general counsel of Incapital Holdings LLC, a financial services holding company with offices in Chicago, Boca Raton, and Toronto. Incapital underwrites and distributes a wide array of fixed income investments including corporate notes, agencies, structured securities, and certificates of deposit through a distribution network of over 800 broker-dealers and RIAs. Incapital is also a sponsor of unit investment trusts (UITs) and distributes a wide array of annuities. Prior to joining Incapital, Mr. Busscher spent several years as general counsel of Mesirow Financial and had previously served as an enforcement branch chief for the U.S. Securities and Exchange Commission.

He holds a bachelor of arts degree from Cornell University, a juris doctor degree from the University of Miami, and a master of business administration from the University of Chicago. He is a former board member of the National Society of Compliance Professionals.

The author wishes to thank the invaluable assistance provided by Anna Pinedo and Ze'ev Eiger of Morrison & Foerster.

CHAPTER 15

Affiliated Transactions Under the Advisers Act

By Joseph McDermott
  Keeley Asset Management Corp., Keeley Investment Corp., and the KEELEY Funds, Inc.

I. INTRODUCTION

Affiliated transactions[1] under the Investment Advisers Act of 1940, as amended ("Advisers Act") are one of the business practices where the proverbial "rubber meets the road." Although such transactions are permissible, they can present significant challenges to an investment adviser if not done properly. Affiliated transactions lie very close to the heart of the Advisers Act because of two issues: fiduciary duty and conflicts of interest. In fact, the Advisers Act was passed in large part due to questionable affiliated transactions taking place in the industry during the early 20th century. Some abusive practices that occurred at the time included:

- Excessively trading in clients' accounts to generate increased commission revenue for an affiliated broker;
- Transferring or selling worthless securities ("dumping") from one advised client/fund to another or from firm/affiliated accounts to clients; and
- Inflating or manipulating the value of securities through one or more cross trades between clients/funds;[2]

Additionally, the congressionally mandated study that preceded the passage of the Investment Company Act of 1940, as amended ("1940 Act"), also noted that some investment advisers used client accounts to purchase securities in which affiliated parties had a personal financial interest.[3] It was clear that there was a problem with these transactions and Congressional action was needed.

To address these abusive trading practices, Congress passed the Advisers Act to, among other things, codify the fiduciary duty owed to clients by investment advisers and

---

[1] Transactions in which the adviser or an affiliated person, either an individual or an entity, is engaged in a transaction with a client either on a principal or agency basis and has some financial interest in the trade.
[2] Jerry W. Markham, *The Financial History of the United States*, Volume II, M.E. Sharpe, Inc. (2002).
[3] SEC, *Investment Trusts and Investment Companies: Report of the Securities and Exchange Commission : Pursuant to Section 30 of the Public Utility Holding Company Act of 1935*, Washington, DC, U.S. Government Printing Office (19391942) (1939).

establish a framework required to be followed in order for such transactions to be permitted. Although many commentators at the time felt that an adviser could not do its job properly unless all such conflicts of interest were completely removed,[4] Congress did not issue an outright ban of these practices. Rather, the legislation and subsequent adopting rules required substantial disclosure of all conflicts of interest, including affiliated transactions. It was noted that the prohibitions were apparently removed from the final version of the Advisers Act at the urging of investment advisers concerned about the permanent damage that such a public indictment would have on their young and growing profession.[5]

Whether your firm conducts affiliated transactions or not, all compliance professionals should have an understanding of what these dealings are and their requirements. Before getting into those specifics, however, I will briefly touch on three reasons for their importance to compliance professionals. First, it is quite common for investment advisers to have affiliates that are also involved in the financial services industry. A recent study of the profession noted that each registered investment adviser has on average two financial industry affiliates.[6] Some of the more common types of affiliates, as disclosed on the Form ADV, are broker-dealers, investment companies, other investment advisers, future commission merchants, commodity pool operators/trading advisers, insurance companies, and general partners/managers of private funds.

A second and more serious reason why affiliated transactions are important is that violations of the antifraud provisions of the Advisers Act do not require scienter or intent on the part of the investment adviser for a violation to occur.[7] In its 1963 ruling, the U.S. Court of Appeals for the Second Circuit stated:

> Congress, in empowering the courts may enjoin any practice which operates "as a fraud or deceit" upon a client, did not intend to require proof of intent to injure and actual injury to the client; it intended the Act [Advisers Act] to be construed like other securities legislation "enacted for the purpose of avoiding frauds," not technically and restrictively, but rather flexibly to effectuate its remedial purposes.[8]

Because intent to defraud or scienter is not required, unlike many of the other securities laws, rules, and regulations, this theoretically lowers the threshold needed for regulatory authorities to bring an enforcement action for potential infractions. This means that an adviser firm and its officers/employees may be found in violation of the Advisers Act even if it and/or they engaged in certain affiliated transactions that were accidental

---

[4] SEC, *Investment Trusts and Investment Companies,* at 28.
[5] Financial Planners, Report of the Staff of the U.S. Securities and Exchange Commission to the House Committee on Energy and Commerce's Subcommittee on Telecommunications and Finance (Feb. 1988).
[6] The Investment Adviser Association and National Regulatory Services, *2014 Evolution Revolution: A Profile of the Investment Adviser Profession,* Washington, DC (2014).
[7] Thomas P. Lemke and Gerald T. Lins, *Securities Law Handbook Series: Regulation of Investment Advisers,* Thomson Reuters (Feb. 2014).
[8] *U.S. Securities and Exchange Commission v. Capital Gains Research Bureau,* 375 U.S. 18 (1963).

or unintended and even if there was no financial loss or harm to the client. As such, it is clear that investment advisers unaware of the potential pitfalls related to affiliated transactions can be significantly penalized if they are not careful and aware of the specific regulatory requirements. Unfortunately in the current regulatory environment, an enforcement action can be potentially fatal to an advisory firm.

Lastly, conducting affiliated transactions can increase a firm's risk profile in the eyes of the regulators, particularly the U.S. Securities and Exchange Commission (SEC), and lead to more frequent examinations. More examinations lead to more scrutiny of these transactions and potential problems if the transactions were not all done in compliance with the rules.

Years ago, the SEC followed a more simplistic examination approach whereby the commission attempted to examine advisory firms once every so many years based on the underlying activities of the advisory firm. Some of the bigger, more complex firms would be examined once every year or two, whereas, smaller, less complex advisers might only be examined on average once every seven years. With the increased number of registrants in recent years coupled with the resources available to SEC, a new approach to examinations was needed.

Nowadays, the SEC uses an internally generated risk score to determine the firms it will examine in any given year (the higher the risk score, the more frequent the examinations). The metrics used to generate this risk score have never been publically disclosed, but it appears they use a combination of sources including responses submitted in the Form ADV Parts 1 and 2A, a firm's regulatory history, and information received through tips, complaints, and referrals (TCRs). With Form ADV Part 2As now filed electronically, the SEC has never had more timely information about advisers in its possession than it has today, and there is no doubt that the data reported on the Part 2As is included in the commission's risk scoring process. Thus, any changes to a firm's business activities such as brokerage and trading practices noted in either the Part 1 or 2A of the ADV are likely to have an impact on the firm's risk profile and examination frequency.

II. IDENTIFYING AFFILIATES

To better understand affiliated transactions, we must first understand who are considered to be affiliates. In the Advisers Act statute, Congress referred to the 1940 Act for the definition of affiliated person. The 1940 Act defined *affiliated persons* as:

> (A) Any person directly or indirectly owning, controlling, or holding with power to vote, 5 per centum or more of the outstanding voting securities of such other person; (B) any person 5 per centum or more of whose outstanding voting securities are directly or indirectly owned, controlled, or held with power to vote, by such other person; (C) any person directly or indirectly controlling, controlled by, or under com-

mon control with, such other person; (D) any officer, director, partner, copartner, or employee of such other person; (E) if such other person is an investment company, any investment adviser thereof or any member of an advisory board thereof; and (F) if such other person is an unincorporated investment company not having a board of directors, the depositor thereof.

The Advisers Act defines "person" as a natural person or a company. Although this definition seems pretty straightforward, from a practical standpoint, it can be challenging to monitor (especially in situations where the ownership of an adviser is complex or there are many affiliates). As a best practice, advisers should create and maintain a listing of all entities and persons that meet this definition and update it as there are changes with the firm's ownership, personnel, or affiliations. The Compliance Department is not always the first to know about such changes, and in a lot of cases only learns of them annually during the update of the Form ADV Part 1. Senior management must understand the importance of keeping the Compliance Department appraised of such changes so it can effectively review for affiliated transactions. Receiving information about these changes only once a year during the update of the Form ADV can lead to potential violations and holes in a firm's compliance program.

III. LEGISLATION AND ADOPTING RULES

Under the Advisers Act, principal and cross transactions are governed by Section 206, and Rules 206(3)-1, 206(3)-2, and 206(3)-3T. Section 206 of the statute sets out the framework or guiding principles established by Congress and states that it is unlawful for any investment adviser, by use of the mails or any means or instrumentality of interstate commerce, directly or indirectly:

- To employ any device, scheme, or artifice to defraud any client or prospective client;
- To engage in any transaction, practice, or course of business that operates as a fraud or deceit upon any client or prospective client;
- To act as principal for his or her own account, knowingly to sell any security to or purchase any security from a client, or acting as broker for a person other than such client, knowingly to effect any sale or purchase of any security for the account of such client, without disclosing to such client in writing before the completion of such transaction the capacity in which he is acting and obtaining the consent of the client to such transaction; or
- To engage in any act, practice, or course of business that is fraudulent, deceptive, or manipulative.[9]

Advisers Act Rule 206(3)-1 provides an exemption from the disclosure and consent requirements of Section 206(3) for dual registrants who render objective investment advice exclusively through:

---

[9] *See* Advisers Act Section 206(4).

- Publication and dissemination of written materials (e.g., newsletters) to 35 or more paying customers[10];
- Materials or statements that do not claim to meet the investment objectives/needs of any individual(s);
- Issuance of statistical information that does not contain opinions on the merits of a particular investment/security; or
- Any combination of the three.[11]

In order for the exemption to apply, any such materials or statements made *must* disclose to the paying customer that, if he or she decides to use the firm's brokerage services to conduct a transaction in the security which was the subject of the communication, the firm may act as principal for its own account or as an agent for some other person (cross trade).

Advisers Act Rule 206(3)-2 specifically deals with agency cross trades and provides some relief from the trade-by-trade disclosure and consent requirements for dual registrants, and registered brokers that either control, are controlled by, or are under common control with an investment adviser. In order to obtain this relief, four provisions must be satisfied:

- After full disclosure of the nature of these transactions, the conflicts of interest involved, and the compensation to be received, the client provides prospective consent in writing;
- A written confirmation of each such trade must be sent to clients;[12]
- At least annually, the firm must send a statement to each affected client summarizing all such transactions that have occurred and the total commissions/revenue received since such transactions started occurring or since the last annual summary was provided; and
- All client statements and confirmations inform the clients that their previously provided consent and authorization to engage in agency cross transactions can be revoked at any time by providing written notice.[13]

This relief under Rule 206(3)-2 does not apply to situations when the investment adviser or any person controlling, controlled by, or under common control is recommending the transaction to both the buyer and seller.

In 2007, the SEC adopted Rule 206(3)-3T to provide dual registrants time to make necessary organizational and operational changes as the result of a court decision that eliminated the investment adviser registration exemption provided by Rule 202(a)

---

[10] This would also apply to oral comments and statements made to an audience of 35 or more paying customers.
[11] See Rule 206(3)-1 of the Advisers Act.
[12] Although Rule 206(3) -2 details specific information required to be on the confirmation, most confirmations delivered by brokers that comply with Rule 10b-10 of the Securities Exchange Act of 1934, as amended (the "Exchange Act") contain this information. It is advised that a review of the confirmations be conducted periodically to ensure that the required information is included.
[13] See Rule 206(3)-2 of the Advisers Act.

(11)-1 of the Advisers Act for firms that offered asset-based and fixed-fee accounts.[14] When initially adopted, Rule 206(3)-3T was to expire on December 31, 2014, but the expiration date has since been extended to December 31, 2016. It provides relief of the requirements of Section 206(3) for such firms engaging in principal trades provided that the following conditions are satisfied:

- The adviser does not exercise "investment discretion" over the client's account, except discretion may be granted by the client on a temporary or limited basis;
- Neither the adviser firm nor any of its affiliates is the issuer of, or at the time of the sale, an underwriter or sponsor (or performing similar functions) for the security involved;
- After full disclosure of the nature of these transactions, the conflicts of interest involved, and the manner in which the adviser addresses those conflicts, the client provides a prospective, revocable consent in writing;
- Prior to executing a principal trade, the adviser discloses either orally or in writing the firm's proposed capacity in the transaction and receives the client's consent either orally or in writing to act as principal in the transaction;
- A written confirmation of each such trade that complies with Rule 10b-10 of the Exchange Act must be sent to the client. The confirmation must also note that the adviser firm disclosed to the client prior to the execution of the trade that it may be acting in a principal capacity and that the client consented to the transaction;
- At least annually, the firm sends a statement to each affected client a summary of all such transactions that have occurred including dates and prices of such transactions since such transactions started occurring or since the last annual summary was provided; and
- All client statements and confirmations inform clients that their previously provided consents and authorizations to engage in these principal transactions can be revoked at any time without penalty by providing written notice.[15]

This relief under Rule 206(3)-3T only applies to dual registrants where the activities occur in brokerage accounts subject to Exchange Act and SRO rules and regulations. Additionally, relying on Rule 206(3)-3T does not relieve a firm of its obligations to seek the most favorable price and execution under the circumstances then prevailing (i.e., best execution) on behalf of its clients.

IV. PRINCIPAL AND CROSS TRADES

In their simplest form, principal trades and cross trades[16] are transactions that are arranged by the investment adviser and/or an affiliated broker whereby the adviser/affiliated broker has both an order to buy a certain security and an order to sell the same

---

[14] See Financial Planning Association v. Securities and Exchange Commission, 482 F.3d 481, 492 (D.C. Cir. 2007).
[15] See Rule 206(3)-3T of the Advisers Act.
[16] Although cross trades are not considered to be affiliated transactions, they are operationally conducted in essentially the same manner as principal trades and are therefore included in this discussion because of these similarities.

security from two or more different clients/customers. In such a situation, the orders can be placed into the open market for execution or the firm may decide to handle the transaction internally either through a principal trade or a cross trade. The adviser or broker may find it advantageous for many reasons to trade the orders opposite each other instead of going to the open market. For example, if the trading volume of the security is so low that executing the orders in the open market would lead to significant market impact risks for the clients, the firm may determine that trading them internally through such a transaction is the best interests of its clients.

These types of transactions are of particular interest to the SEC because of the potential for abuse: The trades are prearranged and there is significant potential for financial harm to the client accounts involved. The adviser and/or affiliated broker has complete and total control of all aspects of these trades. The adviser gets to determine the price at which the trade will be affected as well as the timing of the transaction. Thus, the adviser arranging the trade can have a significant impact on the economic outcome of the transaction. If not priced correctly, the transaction can be beneficial to one side and detrimental to the other. For example, if the trade was priced at the daily low, the buyer would benefit and the seller would be disadvantaged; the opposite would be true if the trade was priced at the daily high.

The operational mechanics of principal and cross trades are similar. The adviser and/or affiliate has orders on both sides of the market in the same security (orders to both buy and sell) and conducts an off-market transfer between the buyer's account and the seller's account at the price it establishes based on the market for the security. As noted earlier, the key differences between these transactions are the types of the accounts involved. If one of the accounts involved is beneficially owned by the adviser, principal, owner, officer, or employee, the transaction would be considered to be a principal trade. However, such trades that only have clients or one client and an unaffiliated brokerage customer involved would be considered a cross trade. It is important to note that the SEC considers any pooled investment vehicles that are substantially owned[17] by an adviser's employees and officers to be proprietary accounts. Thus, any trades in which such an account is involved would be considered to be principal transactions.

Under Section 206(3) of the Advisers Act, investment advisers must not engage in a principal trade with a client unless, prior to the completion of the trade, the advisers (i) provide the client adequate disclosure regarding its role in the transaction and (ii) obtain the client's consent to the transaction. Both must be done prior to the completion of the trade, which according to the SEC is considered the trade's settlement date. The disclosure must be in writing and must disclose to the client the exact capacity in which the adviser is acting in the transaction (agency for cross trades, or principal). Following the disclosure, an adviser must receive the client's consent to proceed with

---

[17] If an adviser, its controlling persons, or other related parties own, in aggregate, 25 percent or more of the investment vehicle, the SEC considers the account to be an account of the adviser and any such trades to be considered principal trades. *See* SEC No Action Letter, Gardner, Russo & Gardner. File No. 801-41357 Ref. No. 2005518927.

the transaction as disclosed. Although the statue does not specify that the consent be in writing, it would be considered best practice to get the client's consent in writing. If the consent is not maintained in writing, it may be difficult for an adviser to adequately demonstrate to the SEC that it satisfied both the disclosure and consent requirements *prior* to the completion of the transaction. This may sound simple enough—making a disclosure and getting client consent—but it can be a logistical nightmare given the tight timeframe within which the requirements must be satisfied. The current settlement cycle for trades done in the United States is three business days after trade date (commonly referred to as T + 3). This means an adviser must make the disclosure to a client and received their consent essentially within four business days of initiating a trade requiring such consent.

As noted earlier, advisers who are dual registrants can take advantage of the exemptions and/or relief provided by Rules 206(3)-1, 206(3)-2, and 206(3)-3T. Such firms should review these rules closely and determine whether their current activities could fulfill the requirements. If the requirements aren't being satisfied, firms should consider any necessary changes to meet them. A firm that can avail itself of either the exemptions or the relief would make it operationally more efficient to engage in principal and cross transactions.

Best Practices

Form ADV Part 2A requires investment advisers to disclose information to clients and prospective clients regarding their brokerage practices. Advisers should consider including some language in Form Part 2A about any principal or cross trades in which they are likely to engage. Although this does not alleviate the adviser from providing specific disclosure on a trade-by-trade basis as required under Section 206(3), it may be useful to include so it can be referenced when making future transaction disclosures. An adviser need not make such a disclosure in Part 2A if the adviser does not intend to engage in such transactions or considers the possibility of such trades unlikely. As noted in the instructions for Part 2A, the brochure should discuss only conflicts the adviser has or is reasonably likely to have, and practices in which it engages or is reasonably likely to engage.[18] If it is included in the Part 2A, the disclosure must not require clients to consent to all such transactions presented to them by the adviser in the future. Rather, the disclosure should note that from time to time such a transaction may occur in the future and that the client would be provided with specific disclosure from the adviser in the future regarding any such proposed trades for their account and would be asked to consent to proceed with the transaction(s).

Advisers have many more options today for making specific transaction disclosures than when the requirement was first enacted. Before the days of facsimile machines and electronic communications, an adviser's options for providing its disclosure was limited. Disclosures were done in hard copy and delivered either via courier or overnight

---

[18] *See* Form ADV, Uniform Requirements for the Investment Adviser Brochure and Brochure Supplements: General Instructions for Part 2 of Form ADV. OMB No. 3235-0049.

delivery, which provided the adviser with a little more breathing room in order to satisfy its obligations. When making these disclosures, firms should try to do them as soon as possible once it is known that the transaction will occur or has occurred. Valuable time is lost if the disclosure attempt doesn't begin until T + 1 or later. It's also wise to handle the disclosure through some form of electronic communication, such as email. In many cases, this approach will make the disclosure almost instantaneous[19] and is a quick and convenient method for the client to provide permission/consent or refusal of the transaction.

The disclosure should be clear, unambiguous, and concrete in terminology. For example, an adviser may say, "In this transaction, we will be acting as principal, and the shares you are purchasing will be sold from our inventory account (the account of affiliated broker-dealer or the personal account of the firm's sole proprietor)." Indicate to the client that the firm has a conflict of interest in the trade and the nature of the conflict (additional compensation, etc.). Then, request the client's consent to proceed with the transaction. You may also want to include a rationale about why, given the conflict, the adviser still considers the transaction to be suitable for the client and in the client's best interest. In the end, even if an adviser goes through all the hoops to meet the requirements, the transaction could still end up in violation if the disclosure isn't done properly. So make sure it counts.

It is also a good idea for advisers to put together a listing of their clients that they believe would be good candidates for such transactions. Although all clients would certainly be eligible to engage in such transactions,[20] there may be some whose personal or professional lives may make it logistically impossible to meet the rules' requirements. For example, an adviser to high net worth individuals may know of some clients who are frequently travelling and are unavailable, or clients who habitually don't respond promptly to calls or emails. Given the time requirements involved, it might make sense to screen clients based on their unique characteristics. Other potential factors to consider could be a client's level of sophistication and/or work experiences. Some clients may have a better understanding of the process or the conflicts involved in these transactions, thus making the disclosure process smoother, increasing the likelihood that the client understands the proposed transactions, and providing the clients' informed consent in a timelier manner.

Reviewing for potential principal and cross trades should be a part of every compliance program and will hinge greatly on the frequency and volume of transactions that occur at the firm. When advisers are in the market daily conducting transactions, it's best to have some way to monitor every day's trading activities, whether through an in-house developed system or an off-the-shelf, commercial application. When advisers don't trade as frequently, a less rigorous, manual review may be reasonable. Regardless of the

---

[19] This assumes the adviser has a compliant email system with archiving capabilities that can sufficiently demonstrate that the disclosure requirement was satisfied.
[20] Eligibility excludes clients who may be prohibited from participating in such transactions because of statues, such as ERISA, or due to contractual provisions.

frequency, it is important to review all client, firm, and employee trading activity at the same time. Once the data is laid out on a security-by-security basis, the reviewer should focus on looking for trades in the opposite direction, which occurred at or about the same time, and at the same execution prices. If any such trades are identified, they should be scrutinized further to determine the type of trade (principal or cross trade) and, if so, whether the disclosure and consent requirements were complied with properly and in a timely manner. Advisers should also understand that they cannot avoid the rules' requirements by simply sending both orders (a buy and sell) to an unaffiliated, third-party broker who in turn crosses them.[21] The SEC considers these types of transactions to be principal/cross trades that are subject to the same requirements.

Upon discovery of apparent principal/cross trades that did not satisfy all of the requirements of the rule, the adviser should determine which course of action it should follow to correct the error. If such trades are identified prior to settlement date (i.e., the trades haven't been "completed"), the adviser may still have time to satisfy the requirements or cancel the transactions and process them through an error account to prevent any financial harm to the client(s). If the erroneous transaction(s) is discovered post-settlement (i.e., the trade has been completed), the adviser must take a different approach. As with any error, the client should not suffer any financial harm as a result of the adviser's mistake. One way to make a client "whole" in such a situation would be to reimburse the client for any:

- Transaction costs associated with the trade (commissions, markups, markdowns, etc.);
- Loss of principal value on the investment[22]; and
- Opportunity cost or interest on the lost commissions/principal value since the time the trade occurred.

Once the reimbursement amount is known and the facts and circumstances have been reviewed, the client should be provided with notification of the matter, including the details of the trade(s), and asked how the firm should proceed with the reimbursement. Many clients appreciate open and honest dialogue about errors that occur. Keep in mind that the regulators understand that there will be errors but are more concerned with how errors are dealt with once discovered rather than the fact that they occurred.

Recent Disciplinary Actions

In November 2011, the SEC took action against Feltl & Company, Inc. (Feltl), for, among other things, violating Section 206(3) by engaging in hundreds of principal transactions with its advisory clients' accounts without making the proper disclosures and obtaining client consent over the course of several years.[23] It was noted that Feltl's

---

[21] See U.S Securities and Exchange Commission Administrative Action—January 27, 2014 (Investment Advisers Act of 1940 Rel. No. 3762; Investment Company Act of 1940 Rel. No. 30893).
[22] If the investment resulted in a gain to the client, the client should be entitled to keep the profits.
[23] See U.S Securities and Exchange Commission Administrative Action—November 28, 2011 (Securities Exchange Act of 1934 Rel. No. 65838; Investment Advisers Act of 1940 Rel. No. 3325; Investment Company Act of 1940 Release No. 29875).

violations were caused, at least in part, by its failure to invest the necessary resources in its advisory business as it changed and grew in relation to its brokerage business. Advisers cannot claim ignorance of the rules and regulations or blame their failures on lack of compliance resources. Firms must proactively monitor for changes in their business activities and make the necessary changes to their compliance programs in order to detect, correct and prevent violations related to these new or enhanced activities.

The SEC announced an administrative action against Western Asset Management Co. (Western) in January 2014 noting that, among other things, the firm violated Section 206(2) of the Advisers Act by arranging dealer-interposed cross trade transactions in which counterparty dealers purchased fixed-income securities from certain Western advisory client accounts, then resold the same securities to certain other Western advisory client accounts.[24] Because many of these cross trades involved one or more mutual fund clients, Western also aided, abetted, and caused certain of its advisory clients to unwittingly to violate Sections 17(a)(1) and (2) of the 1940 Act. The case also highlighted that Western provided favorable treatment to certain advisory clients over others by pricing the transactions in a manner that was advantageous to the buyers over the sellers, even though both were advisory clients of the firm and both owed the same fiduciary duty. The takeaway in this case is that firms can't do something indirectly that they can't do directly without complying with the requirements imposed by the Advisers Act and the 1940 Act.

V. AFFILIATED BROKERAGE

Affiliated brokerage is a practice whereby an investment adviser places client brokerage orders with a registered broker-dealer that is controlling, controlled by, or under common control with the investment adviser. For its services, the affiliated broker charges an agency commission on each trade. As a result of the relationship between the adviser and the broker-dealer, a number of questions and potential conflicts of interest arise, including but not limited to:

- Is the affiliate obtaining best execution?
- What is the rationale for sending orders to the affiliate?
- Is the use of the affiliate in the best interest of clients?
- Are the commission rates being charged in line with industry rates?
- Is the account trading more frequently than it would otherwise resulting in more commission revenue to the affiliate?

So, it's easy to see why affiliated brokerage is a concern for investors and regulators alike. However, even with the conflicts, there are legitimate reasons why an adviser might want to send orders to an affiliate rather than an unaffiliated firm. Some of these reasons include:

---

[24] *See* SEC. Administrative Action—January 27, 2014.

- The affiliated broker is more responsive and allows adviser more control when executing orders given sometimes rapidly changing market conditions;
- The adviser deals in low volume or illiquid names and needs more control over client orders in the marketplace so as to not adversely impact the market; and
- Execution quality by other brokerage firms is poor.

Also, let's not forget the negative perceptions that are sometimes out there in the market that the large firms are only out there to make money for themselves rather than service clients. This perception was clearly on full display a few years ago when an op-ed article was published in *The New York Times* regarding the reason why an industry executive was resigning from a larger Wall Street firm.[25] It should be clear, however, that this was just one person's opinion/perception and did not result directly in any meaningful disciplinary actions. However, the article did cause some embarrassment to the firm involved and the industry as a whole. On the flip-side, there also have been significant actions taken against other prominent Wall Street insiders that have also added to these negative perceptions. A former chairman of NASDAQ by the name of Bernard Madoff (some of you may have heard of him) was sanctioned in a highly publicized action, as well as a former president of NASDAQ, Alfred Berkeley, among others.[26]

Requirements

The Advisers Act[27] does not specifically prohibit firms from executing transactions themselves, in the case of a dual registrant, or from using the services of an affiliated broker. However under the antifraud provisions of the Advisers Act, advisers are required to provide clients and prospective clients with full, fair, and accurate disclosures about many of their business activities, including their brokerage practices. The SEC has mandated that such disclosures be included in a firm's Form ADV Part 2A. With that being said, it would most likely be considered fraudulent for an adviser to engage in affiliated brokerage transactions without providing adequate disclosure to clients. Without such disclosure, clients and prospective clients do not possess all of the information necessary to make an informed decision when choosing one particular investment adviser over another. Because such a situation would most likely end up in some form of enforcement action, it is important to ensure that any usage of an affiliated broker is fully disclosed as clearly and as accurately as possible in the Form ADV as well as any other similar materials provided to clients and prospects (requests for proposals (RFPs,) compliance questionnaires, etc.).

---

[25] Greg Smith, "Why I am Leaving Goldman Sachs," *The New York Times* (Mar. 14, 2012).
[26] *See* Securities and Exchange Commission v. Bernard L. Madoff and Bernard L. Madoff Investment Securities LLC (S.D.N.Y. Civ. 08 CV 10791 (LLS)) and U.S Securities and Exchange Commission Administrative Proceeding —October 24, 2011 (Securities Act of 1933 Rel. No. 9271; Exchange Act of 1934 Rel. No. 65609).
[27] This discussion only addresses affiliated brokerages in the context of the Advisers Act and does not specifically address the requirements of Section 17(e) of the 1940 Act or Rule 17e-1 promulgated thereunder. Advisers to mutual funds or other regulated investment companies that engage in affiliated brokerage should review these additional requirements.

Best Practices

As the old saying goes, "Disclosure is your best friend." This is no different for advisers with an affiliated broker-dealer who executes trades for the adviser's clients. The adviser should include information about these practices in the firm's Form ADV Part 2A. As with all disclosures, the adviser should be as specific and as direct as possible. If the adviser knows with certainty that trades will be sent to its affiliate for execution, that should be clearly spelled out. Refrain from using terms such as *may* or *could*. For example, the adviser should say, "…When placing client orders for execution, the adviser *will* place trades with its affiliate for execution on an agency basis, and it *will* charge clients a commission for these services that is separate from the advisory fees paid" rather than, "When placing client orders for execution, the adviser *may* place trades with its affiliate for execution on an agency basis and, in such cases, it *could* charge clients a commission for these brokerage services that is separate from the advisory fees paid." If it's going to happen, say it's going to happen. Also, when it comes to disclosure, it is recommended that the adviser firm have a separate schedule or addendum to its advisory contract in which the client acknowledges the use of the affiliate and provides a "global" consent[28] to the practice. These disclosures should done in a manner that provides adequate evidence that the firm provided the necessary disclosures to clients regarding the use of an affiliated broker and the conflicts of interest presented under such a scenario.

Commission and portfolio turnover rates should be closely monitored. At least annually, the adviser should review the commission rates charged by the affiliated broker and determine whether the rate(s) charged are in line with going market rates. This review can be done by collecting information from all of the brokers used by the adviser for executing client transactions[29] and analyzing the information. Alternatively, the adviser can obtain an analysis conducted by a nonaffiliated firm and comparing its affiliate's commission rates to those contained therein. If the commission rates aren't "in the ballpark" as compared to the analysis, it is clear that an adjustment is necessary. Turnover rates should be monitored and compared to historical turnover rates for the account or strategy to gauge the level of trading that is occurring. If the current turnover rate is significantly higher than the historical averages, additional analysis should be done to better understand the circumstances surrounding the level of portfolio trading and its appropriateness.

An adviser should be reviewing the executions received from an affiliated broker consistent with the disclosures made to clients (Form ADV Part 2A, RFPs, compliance questionnaires, etc.). If, for example, an adviser firm states that it reviews the affiliate's trades quarterly for best execution purposes, then it had better be conducting and documenting these reviews quarterly. The SEC has taken disciplinary action against advisers who have disclosed one thing to their clients and then, in practice, have either

---

[28] This type of consent is opposed to a trade-by-trade consent such as the one generally required to principal and cross trades.
[29] This assumes the adviser uses a large enough number of brokers to provide a meaningful analysis.

not done what they said or have done something completely different. It's critical to periodically review all disclosures to ensure that they are consistent, accurate, and reflective of current business practices. The SEC will review them for accuracy during the next examination and will take action if they are misleading or egregious.

Recent Disciplinary Actions

In July 2013, the SEC took action against Goelzer Investment Management, Inc., and its principal. Among other things, the action stated that Goelzer misrepresented in its Form ADV that it considered a list of factors and conducted comparative commission rate analysis before recommending itself as broker for its advisory clients, when in actuality the firm failed to perform any such analysis. It was determined that the firm also misrepresented in its Form ADV that clients who used the firm as their broker stood to benefit from lower commission costs as a result of trade aggregation, when no such benefit was provided.[30] This action clearly demonstrates the need to review disclosures to determine whether they are accurate and current and to make revisions when they are no longer correct. When it comes to disclosures, do what you say and say what you do.

The SEC took an administrative action against Manarin Investment Counsel, Ltd., Manarin Securities Corp., an affiliated broker, and its principal in October 2013 for, among other actions, charging an affiliated mutual fund commissions that exceeded the usual and customary broker's commission on transactions effected on a securities exchange.[31] Advisers need to periodically review and assess the commission structures charged to their clients to ensure that they are in line with current rates in the marketplace.

VI. OTHER CONSIDERATIONS

Investment advisers to registered mutual funds should also be aware of the 1940 Act rules regarding affiliated transactions. These rules include 10f-3, 17a-7, and 17e-1. As with the rules under the Advisers Act, these 1940 Act rules do not prohibit affiliated transactions but do require, among other things, certain disclosure and board reporting requirements. Compliance with the rules and regulations of the 1940 Act is handled by the SEC through periodic examinations.

Advisers to client accounts subject to the requirements of the Employee Retirement Income Security Act of 1974 (ERISA) should be aware of the Prohibited Transaction Exemption 86-128. Under ERISA PTE 86-128, advisers are prohibited from certain affiliated transactions but allowed to engage in others. PTE 86-128 also imposes certain reporting requirements on advisers engaging in such transactions. Compliance with

---

[30] *See* U.S Securities and Exchange Commission Administrative Action —July 31, 2013 (Securities Exchange Act of 1934 Rel. No. 70083; Investment Advisers Act of 1940 Rel. No. 3638).

[31] *See* U.S Securities and Exchange Commission Administrative Action—October 3, 2013 (Securities Act of 1933 Rel. No. 9462; Securities Exchange Act of 1934 Release No. 70595; Investment Advisers Act of 1940 Rel. No. 3686; Investment Company Act of 1940 Release No. 30740).

ERISA requirements is reviewed for by the U.S. Department of Labor (DOL) through periodic examination. Advisers to ERISA clients should pay close attention to these requirements because the DOL can and does levy fines against firms for noncompliance, and any actions could have a negative impact on a firm's advisory business.

ABOUT THE AUTHOR

Joseph McDermott, FRM, CSCP, is the chief compliance officer for Keeley Asset Management Corp., Keeley Investment Corp., and the KEELEY Funds, Inc. in Chicago. Prior to joining Keeley, he was a director with Alaric Compliance Services, LLC, in Chicago where he provided outsourced CCO and other compliance consulting services to investment advisers, regulated investment companies, and broker-dealers. Mr. McDermott has more than 20 years of compliance experience and has previously served as CCO or compliance director for Driehaus Capital Management, Artisan Partners L.P., and First Trust Portfolios L.P. From 1996 to 2000, he was a field supervisor in the Chicago office of the NASD (now known as FINRA), where he was responsible for conducting financial and operational audits of NASD registered broker-dealers. Prior to joining the NASD, Mr. McDermott was an investigator with the Chicago Board of Trade's Office of Investigations and Audits. Mr. McDermott received a master of business administration from De Paul University and an undergraduate degree from Loras College. In addition to holding the Series 3, 4, 7, 24, 27, 53, 55 and 66 licenses, Mr. McDermott also holds the Financial Risk Manager (FRM) certification from the Global Association of Risk Professionals and the Certified Securities Compliance Professional (CSCP) designation from the National Society of Compliance Professionals.

The opinions expressed herein are those of Mr. McDermott and not his current or any former employers, their owners, officers, or employees and are not to be considered as legal advice.

CHAPTER 16

Adviser Custody: What You Need to Know

By Elizabeth M. Knoblock
Matson Money, Inc.

I. INTRODUCTION

Custody is a fiduciary issue applicable to all federal and state investment advisers. Federally registered advisers are subject to the requirements of Rule 206(4)-2 under the Investment Advisers Act of 1940, also known as the Custody Rule. For state registrants, the North American Securities Administrators Association (NASAA) adopted a nearly identical Model Rule.[1] Although not every state has adopted the Model Rule in its entirety, virtually every state that regulates investment advisers has adopted some form of custody rule. In addition, federally registered advisers who work with state registered advisers, whether as solicitors or coadvisers, must require and supervise compliance with federal requirements to avoid being deemed to have violated the Custody Rule themselves.

Although most advisers would never intentionally violate the Custody Rule or misappropriate client assets, failure to understand the parameters of the Custody Rule have resulted in both inadvertent and intentional violations by advisers. This chapter addresses the regulatory issues surrounding adviser custody.

II. WHY IS CUSTODY SO IMPORTANT?

When the Office of Compliance Inspections and Examinations (OCIE) of the Securities and Exchange Commission (SEC) published its 2014 National Exam Program (NEP) priorities, the topic of custody and safekeeping of client assets was identified as the number one "core risk" facing SEC-registered investment advisers.[2] According to OCIE:

---

[1] *See* NASAA Model Rule 102(e)(1)-1, Custody of Client Funds or Securities by Investment Advisers, http://www.nasaa.org/wp-content/uploads/2011/07/IA-Model-Rule-Custody.pdf. *See also* NASAA, "Amendments to Model Custody and Recordkeeping Rules Under the Uniform Securities Acts of 1956 and 2002 to Clarify Requirements Relating to Inadvertent Custody of Client Funds," adopted April 15, 2013, http://www.nasaa.org/wp-content/uploads/2011/07/Redline-of-Revisions-to-Model-Custody-Effective-04152013.pdf

[2] *See* OCIE National Exam Program, "Examination Priorities for 2014" (Jan. 9, 2014),http://www.sec.gov/about/offices/ocie/national-examination-program-priorities-2014.pdf. As defined by OCIE, *core risks* are "those risk areas that are common to the business model utilized by a particular category of registrant and that have existed for a sustained period and are likely to continue for the foreseeable future," page 3.

> If the markets run on trust, then few things are more important than the safekeeping of clients' assets. Yet, the NEP continues to observe non-compliance with Rule 206(4)-2 under the Advisers Act ("Custody Rule")....Given the importance of this requirement for a fiduciary, the staff will continue to test compliance with the Custody Rule and confirm the existence of assets through a risk-based asset verification process. Examiners will pay particular attention to those instances where advisers fail to realize they have custody and therefore fail to comply with requirements of the Custody Rule.

Shortly before announcing its exam priorities, the NEP published a risk alert on the most commonly observed Custody Rule violations.[3] After reviewing all recent examinations containing significant deficiencies, the NEP found that approximately one-third of the exams, representing 140 advisers, had custody-related violations.

The NEP documented four categories of custody-related deficiencies:

- Failures to recognize the existence of "custody" as defined under the Custody Rule;
- Failures to comply with the rule's "surprise exam" requirement;
- Failures to comply with the "qualified custodian" requirements; and
- Failures to comply with the audit approach for pooled investment vehicles.

Although all such failures may result in enforcement actions,[4] this chapter focuses on the first category of deficiencies, because it is the one most likely to occur. NEP staff observed the following situations where an adviser failed to recognize that it had custody of client assets:[5]

- *Role of employees or related persons:* Adviser's personnel or a "related person" serves as trustee or have been granted power of attorney for client accounts;
- *Bill-paying services:* Adviser provides bill-paying services for clients and, therefore, is authorized to withdraw funds or securities from the client's account;
- *Online access to client accounts:* Adviser manages portfolios by directly accessing online accounts using clients' personal usernames and passwords without restrictions and, therefore, has the ability to withdraw funds and securities from the clients' accounts;
- *Adviser acts as a general partner:* Adviser serves as the general partner of a limited partnership or holds a comparable position for a different type of pooled investment vehicle;
- *Physical possession of assets:* Adviser has physical possession of client assets, such as securities certificates;
- *Check-writing authority:* Adviser or a related person has signatory and check-writing authority for client accounts; and

---

[3] *See* NEP Risk Alert, "Significant Deficiencies Involving Adviser Custody and Safety of Client Assets" (Mar. 4, 2013), http://www.sec.gov/about/offices/ocie/custody-risk-alert.pdf
[4] For example, in 2013 alone, the SEC brought the following custody-related enforcement actions: *In re GW & Wade, LLC* (Oct. 28, 2013), *In re Further Lane Asset Management, LLC* (Oct. 28, 2013); *In re Knelman Asset Management Group, LLC* (Oct. 28, 2013); and *SEC v. OM Investment Management LLC* (Sept. 27, 2013).
[5] NEP Risk Alert, n. 3, at 3–4.

- *Receipt of Checks Made to Clients:* Adviser receives checks made out to clients and fails to return them promptly to the clients.

III. WHAT DOES "CUSTODY" MEAN?

To avoid these violations, advisers must understand when they are deemed to have custody of client funds. As defined in the Custody Rule, custody occurs whenever an adviser holds "directly or indirectly, client funds or securities" or has "any authority to obtain possession of them" [206(4)-2(d)(2)]. Custody examples include any:

- *Arrangement*—especially a general power of attorney—under which an adviser or any supervised person or agent of the adviser is authorized or permitted to withdraw client funds or securities maintained with a custodian upon instruction to the custodian;
- *Capacity*—such as trustee of a trust or executor of an estate (unless the trustee or executor position arose out of a family or personal relationship with the beneficiary, decedent or grantor and not as a result of employment with the adviser), general partner of a limited partnership, or managing member of a limited liability company—that gives an adviser or any supervised person or affiliate legal ownership of or access to client funds or securities; or
- *Possession* of client funds or securities (but not of checks drawn by clients and made payable to third parties)—unless an adviser receives them inadvertently and returns them to the sender promptly but in any case within three business days of receiving them.[6]

In addition, advisers authorized to deduct fees from client accounts are deemed to have custody. However, if this is the only reason the adviser has custody, SEC registrants need not disclose custody on Form ADV.[7] State registrants may be required to disclose fee deduction authority as custody.

IV. WHAT DOES THE CUSTODY RULE REQUIRE?

An adviser with custody of client assets (with some exceptions) is required to:

- Maintain client assets with a "qualified custodian" (usually a bank or broker-dealer) in an account either under the client's name or under the adviser's name as agent or trustee for its clients;[8]

---

[6] An SEC Staff no-action letter modified the three-day return rule for any adviser that inadvertently receives: (1) settlement checks from class action lawsuits; (2) tax refund checks from the IRS, state, or other governmental taxing authorities; or (3) dividend payments or stock certificates, if the adviser has appropriate policies and procedures and forwards these assets to the client or a qualified custodian within five business days. See Investment Adviser Association (pub. avail. Sept. 20, 2007), http://sec.gov/divisions/investment/noaction/2007/iaa092007.pdf

[7] SEC, Uniform Application for Investment Adviser Registration and Report by Exempt Reporting Advisers.

[8] The term *qualified custodian* technically includes any regulated financial institution that customarily provides custodial services, including banks, savings associations, full-service (not introducing) broker-dealers, and in some cases, futures commission merchants. See 206(4)-2(d)(6).

- Have a reasonable belief, after due inquiry, that the qualified custodian sends account statements directly to clients; and
- Undergo an annual surprise examination by an independent public accountant.

An adviser with custody of client assets that opens a custodial account on behalf of a client must notify the client in writing of the qualified custodian's name, address, and the manner in which the funds or securities are maintained. If the adviser also sends account statements to such clients, the notification must include a *legend* urging the client to compare the account statements received from the adviser with account statements the client receives from the custodian. Similar disclosures are also required in an adviser's Form ADV Part 2A, Item 15. Because both federal and state-registered advisers use Form ADV, this disclosure applies to all advisers registered or required to be registered.

An adviser who maintains physical custody of client assets as a qualified custodian, or with an affiliate or related person who acts as a qualified custodian of client assets in connection with advisory services the adviser provides to clients, is required to have its surprise examination conducted by an independent accountant who is registered with, and subject to regular inspection by, the Public Company Accounting Oversight Board (PCAOB). In addition, the adviser must obtain an internal control report from an independent accountant registered with and subject to regular inspection by the PCAOB, attesting to the qualified custodian's controls related to safekeeping of client assets.

The two exceptions to the surprise examination requirement are:

- Advisers deemed to have custody over client assets solely because they have authority to deduct fees. These advisers are expected to have policies and procedures in place that address the risk that the adviser or its personnel could deduct fees to which the adviser is not entitled under the terms of the advisory contract; and
- Advisers deemed to have custody because their related person has custody of client assets are excepted from the exam requirement if they can demonstrate that they are "operationally independent" of their affiliate.

The Custody Rule also contains special requirements relating to custody of private pooled investment vehicles and privately offered securities. These aspects of the Custody Rule are beyond the scope of this discussion. However, if an adviser offers these investments to clients, the adviser will also need to understand these requirements.

V. PROCEDURES FOR COMPLYING WITH THE CUSTODY RULE

Advisers need to establish custody procedures covering at least the areas discussed here.

Determining Custody

Assess the arrangements of adviser and any related persons to determine whether adviser has custody:

- Do you have custody only because you can deduct fees from client accounts?
- If so, adopt safekeeping policies and procedures that
  - Address the risk that the adviser or its personnel could deduct fees to which the adviser is not entitled under the terms of the advisory contract;
  - Take into account how and when clients will be billed; and
  - Are reasonably designed to ensure that the assets under management (AUM) on which the fee is billed are accurate and have been reconciled with the AUM reflected on statements of the client's qualified custodian; and to ensure that clients are billed in accordance with the terms of their advisory contracts.
- Relevant procedures to consider include
  - Periodic testing of a sample of client account fee calculations to determine their accuracy,
  - Test overall reasonableness of fees deducted from all client accounts for a period of time based on the adviser's aggregate AUM, and
  - Segregate personnel duties, including
    - Personnel responsible for processing client billing invoices or fees provided to custodians to deduct fees from clients' accounts,
    - Personnel responsible for reviewing the invoices for accuracy, and
    - Personnel responsible for reconciling the invoices with deposits of advisory fees by the custodians into the adviser's proprietary bank account to confirm that accurate fee amounts were deducted.

Avoiding Custody

Advisers who do not want to be deemed to have custody of client assets (other than by deducting fees) should also establish procedures, such as:

- Requirement for advisory personnel to consult with compliance officer or firm's legal counsel before entering into any power of attorney, executor, or trustee arrangements with a client or agreeing to serve as general partner of a limited partnership, plus
  - Compliance Department and/or Legal Department must review all client documents that provide the adviser with any authority other than trading and fee deduction authority over the account, including any documents that provide the adviser with access to or authority to access, client funds or securities, and
  - Document in writing any preexisting personal relationship with a decedent or beneficiary to support service by advisory personnel as a personal fiduciary, such as serving as an executor or trustee for an estate or trust;
- All personnel must be trained to send all securities and checks (other than checks to third parties, settlement checks from class action lawsuits, tax refund checks, dividend payments, and stock certificates) back to the sender immediately or instruct all personnel to notify the compliance officer immediately when such funds or securities are received and follow further instructions from the compliance officer.

- For inadvertently received settlement checks, tax refund checks, and dividend payments, adopt procedures reasonably designed to ensure that adviser
  - Promptly identifies inadvertently received client assets;
  - Promptly identifies client (or former client) to whom such client assets are attributable;
  - Promptly forwards client assets to client (or former client) or qualified custodian, but in no event later than five business days following adviser's receipt of such assets;
  - Promptly returns to sender any inadvertently received client assets that adviser does not forward to client (or former client) or qualified custodian, but in no event later than five business days following adviser's receipt of such assets; and
  - Maintains and preserves appropriate records of all client assets inadvertently received, including a written explanation of whether (and, if so, when) client assets were forwarded to client (or former client) or qualified custodian, or returned to third party senders.

Qualified Custodian

When a client opens a new account, advisers should check whether the client's custodian is a qualified custodian. Advisers should also determine that all securities it manages on the client's behalf are held by the qualified custodian or are otherwise exempt under the Custody Rule.

Notice to Clients. If the adviser opens custodial accounts on behalf of clients, the adviser must provide the following information to the client:

- Custodian's name, address, and manner in which funds or securities are maintained;
- A revised notice when any custodial information changes; and
- If adviser also sends account statements to such clients, inclusion of a legend urging clients to compare account statements received from adviser with account statements received from custodian. Consider adding this legend to *all* account statements sent to clients, regardless of whether you open custodial accounts on clients' behalf.

Quarterly Account Statement. Establish a procedure for forming a reasonable basis after "due inquiry" for believing that the qualified custodian sends each of its clients (or the client's independent representative) account statements identifying the amount of funds and the amount of each security in the account at the end of the period and setting forth all transactions in the account during that period, on at least a quarterly basis. For example, advisers could form such a reasonable basis if:

- Adviser arranges for qualified custodian to mail or email copies of account statements to adviser at the same time statements are sent to clients;
- Custodian provides confirmation (in the form of an attestation or otherwise) to adviser that custodian is sending account statements to adviser's clients on a quarterly basis;
- Custodian sends CD, download, or other medium to adviser with copies of account statements sent to adviser's clients by custodian on a quarterly basis;

- Adviser has access to or can otherwise review account statements on custodian's website or
- Custodian either sends adviser notice that it has mailed or emailed clients' account statements or
- Custodian or client confirms that client obtained account statements via custodian's website;
- Adviser's affiliated custodian's SAS 70 service auditor's report includes an attestation or other statement that it sends account statements to clients on a quarterly basis or
- Adviser contacts clients on a periodic basis to confirm that they received account statements directly from custodian;
- Adviser could also perform periodic testing or regularly ask clients to contact adviser whether they are receiving account statements directly from custodian; and
- In the event that custodian delivers client account statements electronically, adviser may want to confirm that custodian is complying with SEC guidelines on delivering documents electronically; Consider requesting (from custodian or client) a copy of client's signed form consenting to electronic delivery of custodian account statements, coupled with sampling or testing of the custodian's electronic delivery (e.g., by confirming with a sampling of clients).

Account statements must *not* be routed through the adviser prior to delivery to clients. This measure is designed to ensure that advisory personnel have no opportunity to alter, divert, or falsify custodial statements.

Surprise Exam. If an adviser has custody of client assets for any reason other than the deduction of fees, the adviser must enter into a written agreement to retain an independent public accountant to conduct an annual surprise exam (unless it advises a pooled vehicle that is subject to an annual audit or it is operationally independent from its related person that has custody of client assets). The adviser should maintain a list of all accounts subject to the surprise exam requirement in order to be able to provide that information to the accountant conducting the surprise exam.

The accountant's written agreement must require accountant to:

- File a Form ADV–E certificate with the SEC within 120 days of the time chosen by accountant for the exam, stating that accountant has examined adviser's funds and securities and describing nature and extent of examination;
- Upon finding any material discrepancies during the course of the examination, notify the SEC within one business day of the finding, by fax or email, followed by first class mail, sent to the attention of the Director of OCIE;
- Upon resignation or dismissal from, or other termination of, the engagement, or upon removing itself or being removed from consideration for being reappointed, file within four business days Form ADV–E accompanied by a statement that includes:
  - The date of such resignation, dismissal, removal, or other termination,
  - The name, address, and contact information of the accountant, and
  - An explanation of any problems relating to examination scope or procedure that contributed to such resignation, dismissal, removal, or other termination;

- At the end of each calendar year, adviser should confirm that a surprise exam commenced during the past year. If exam was completed, review a copy of the report, confirm that accountant filed Form ADV-E, and address any material discrepancies identified by accountant on Form ADV-E;
- Advisers should seek confirmation annually that accountant is independent;
- For advisers that self-custody client assets or have a related person that serves as a qualified custodian of client assets, and cannot demonstrate "operationally independent" from related person, accountant must be registered with and subject to regular inspection by the PCAOB. These advisers should seek annual confirmation that accountant is registered with and subject to regular inspection by the PCAOB; and
- If adviser has custody of privately offered securities, adviser should confirm that those securities were subject to the surprise exam.

Internal Control Report. If an adviser serves as a qualified custodian or has an affiliate that serves as a qualified custodian in connection with advisory services the adviser provides to clients, the adviser:

- Must obtain a surprise exam from an accountant registered with and subject to regular inspection by the PCAOB, unless adviser demonstrates it is "operationally independent" of related person—
  - If the adviser can demonstrate it is "operationally independent" of related person, document adviser's relationship with related person, including an explanation of adviser's basis for determining that it has overcome presumption that it is not operationally independent of the related person and
  - As long as adviser relies on this exception, adviser needs procedure reasonably designed to ensure that it continues to overcome the presumption that it is not operationally independent;
- Adviser must annually obtain or receive from its related person a written internal control report prepared by an independent public accountant. Adviser should confirm that the internal control report—
  - Includes an opinion of an independent public accountant about whether
    - Controls were in operation as of a specific date, and
    - Controls are suitably designed and operating effectively to meet the control objectives relating to custodial services, including safeguarding of funds and securities held by adviser or related person on behalf of adviser's clients;
- Adviser should seek annual confirmation that accountant is independent and is registered with and subject to regular inspection by the PCAOB;
- Adviser should institute policies and procedures to
  - Segregate duties of advisory personnel from those of custodial personnel to make it difficult for any one person to misuse client assets without being detected, and
  - Separate personnel responsibilities so that personnel that authorize custodial transfers from client accounts are different from personnel that reconcile adviser's client account balances with custodian's records of client transactions and holdings.

Form ADV. Advisers must ensure that custody responses in Form ADV, Parts 1 and 2, are accurate:

- *Part 1, Item 9:* If federal adviser has custody only because it has authority to deduct advisory fees, it does not have to indicate that it has custody on Part 1, Item 9. State-registered advisers may be required to respond "yes." Also, a federal adviser that satisfies the "operationally independent" exception does not have to indicate the existence of custody even though a related person has custody of client assets. However, if adviser has custody for any other reason, Form ADV must disclose; and
- *Part 2, Item 15:* If adviser has custody of client funds or securities and a qualified custodian does not send account statements with respect to those assets directly to your clients, state that you have custody and explain the risks to clients. Alternatively, if adviser has custody of client funds or securities and a qualified custodian sends quarterly, or more frequent, account statements directly to clients, explain that clients will receive account statements from the qualified custodian and that clients should carefully review those statements.

Advisory Agreement and Third-Party Contracts. Advisory contract and third party agreements should appropriately describe custody arrangements. Contracts with service providers and other third parties should include descriptions regarding custody issues.

VI. CUSTODY REVIEW PROCESS

In addition to adopting policies and procedures to address custody rule compliance, an adviser should consider policies and procedures to safeguard client assets from conversion or inappropriate use by advisory personnel. Those policies and procedures may include:

- *Trading authority:* Limit personnel authorized to trade client accounts. Adviser could use special passwords for electronic trading software and systems, provide custodians with a list of personnel authorized to provide instructions, or otherwise limit the number of employees who are permitted to interact with custodians with regard to client assets. Large firms may rotate authorized employees on a periodic basis. Require authorization of more than one employee before assets can be moved, withdrawn, or transferred from a client's account or before allowing changes to client account ownership information, including address changes. In addition, compliance officer or designee should periodically review account trading patterns to monitor for signs of unauthorized trading.
- *Background checks:* Consider background and/or credit checks on employees who have, or could acquire, access to client assets to determine whether those employees should have such access.
- *Custodial statements:* Reconcile custodial statements to adviser's internal records and resolve differences.
- *Identity theft:* Protect client assets by maintaining confidentiality of client account information.
- *Escalation of compliance issues:* Requirement that "red flags," or problems, be brought to the immediate attention of firm management.

VII. MONITORING AND TESTING

As part of an overall compliance program, an adviser should monitor and test its custody and safeguarding procedures. Tests are summarized here.

Transactional Testing

The following actions are actions performed in transactional testing:

- Confirm that adviser has copies of or ready access to accurate and complete records of securities each custodian holds for each client;
- Reconcile custodial statements with adviser's records on a timely basis. Look for patterns among the reconciling items used over a period of time such as six months or a year to balance custodians' positions to those shown on advisers' books;
- In addition to regular internal reconciliations, compliance officer or independent third party may reconcile sample of custodial reports with a sample of adviser's account statements;
- Review any available internal and external audits that test securities held and transactions recorded by qualified custodians. Try to obtain copies of any SAS 70 report(s), internal or external audit papers, and/or reports from custodian supporting reliability of custodian's records; and
- Review contracts with custodians to ensure that proper controls are in place.

Forensic Testing

The following actions are actions performed in forensic testing:

- Ask custodian to supply list of addresses for each client account to which account statements are sent and compare those addresses to addresses maintained in advisers' records. Any differences should trigger further investigation to confirm that client assets are not being converted and that clients are receiving statements as required by Custody Rule;
- Look for anomalies in client addresses, such as frequent use of post office boxes, use of the same address by unrelated clients, or other inconsistencies or patterns that suggest possible manipulation of address information as a means for concealing misappropriation from these accounts by advisory personnel;
- For fund of fund advisers, request formal written confirmations of account balances from custodians and underlying fund managers;
- Reconcile custodial records with information received directly from clients. Periodically contact a sampling of clients and ask them to confirm the balances in their accounts. Use this information to reconcile the third-party custodial records to confirm that information is consistent;
- Request formal written confirmations of account balances from Depository Trust Company (DTC) (or other relevant securities depositories). Reconcile client account

balances, as reported on custodian's books, directly with DTC (or other relevant securities depositories);
- Increase the scrutiny of signatory authorities on client accounts;
- Consider hiring independent third party to request holdings reports directly from outside custodians and use them to reconcile a sample of adviser account statements to custodial statements, in order to provide an independent check on regular reconciliations performed by the firm;
- Periodically review account trading patterns to monitor for signs of unauthorized trading;
- Review any transfers or withdrawals from client accounts to make sure they are appropriate;
- Verify that custodian meets definition of "qualified custodian" under Custody Rule; and
- Perform on-site due diligence visits of custodians.

VIII. CONCLUSION

Other than an adviser's overarching fiduciary duty to put clients' interests ahead of their own, there is no more important obligation than an adviser's duty to safeguard client's assets against theft or misappropriation. This chapter demonstrates the considerable difficulties advisers face in meeting the requirements of the Custody Rule.

ABOUT THE AUTHOR

Elizabeth M. Knoblock, as of March 2015, is the general counsel of Matson Money, Inc. Prior to joining the Matson Money team, Elizabeth satisfied a long-held dream by establishing and, for the past two years, running her own private law practice, Elizabeth M. Knoblock, PLLC, based in Fort Lauderdale, Florida. Ms. Knoblock is a member of the state bars of New York, Florida, and the District of Columbia. Her educational degrees include a magna cum laude bachelor of arts from Stetson University in Deland, Florida; a juris doctor degree from Georgetown University Law Center in Washington, DC, and a master's in securities regulation, also from Georgetown, plus a master of business administration from NOVA University, in Fort Lauderdale, both of which were obtained while working full-time as a securities lawyer.

CHAPTER 17

Protecting the Privacy of Client Information

By David E. Rosedahl, *Briggs and Morgan, P.A.*
  Keith Loveland, *Loveland Consulting*
  Andrew C. Small, *Craig-Hallum Capital Group LLC*

I. INTRODUCTION

Personal information received by securities firms[1] must be used properly and protected from improper disclosure to unauthorized viewers. Initially, congressional concerns about client confidentiality arose out of how firms would share information with related and third parties for commercial reasons, e.g., selling client information to third-party marketers. The risk of inadvertent disclosures by firms has grown enormously since the Securities and Exchange Commission (SEC) Regulation S-P was adopted. Protecting the confidentiality of clients' personal information has become a far more challenging enterprise with the advent of very sophisticated technology. Although the ability to collect and store large amounts of financial information has grown enormously, so too have the threats of sophisticated thieves gaining access to and using that information to steal from clients and firms. Federal, state and self-regulators have been guided by laws requiring broker-dealers and investment advisers to manage the use and protection of client information. This chapter provides an overview of the laws affecting customer privacy and the regulations adopted to enforce those laws. Compliance officers are commonly responsible for establishing and overseeing procedures to assure client information is kept private and used in accordance with customer preferences.

II. GRAMM-LEACH BLILEY ACT

Enacted in 1999, the Gramm-Leach Bliley (GLB) Act granted broad new powers to financial holding companies enabling major changes in the financial services industry regulatory environment. Concerns arose about consumer privacy and the anticipated affiliation of service providers that could share data about customers, exposing those customers to a broad range of solicitations from multiple, but affiliated vendors. The ability for accelerated sharing of confidential information among many entities,

---

[1] Firms include broker-dealers, investment advisers and investment companies. Reg. S-P applies to SEC-registered firms. Most states have adopted Reg. S-P requirements that would apply to state-registered investment advisers.

together with the potential irresponsible use of that information, posed several threats to customers.

The GLB Act's privacy provisions require federal financial institution regulators, including the SEC, to implement specific rules to protect customers' *nonpublic personal information* (NPI). Financial institutions are required to:

- Disclose their policies for sharing NPI of current (and former) customers with affiliates and third parties;
- Notify customers of their intent to share NPI with nonaffiliated third parties;
- Allow customers in certain situations to *opt out* of the sharing of NPI; and
- Implement policies for protecting customers' NPI.

III. SEC REGULATION S-P: BROKER-DEALERS/INVESTMENT ADVISERS

The SEC adopted Regulation S-P (Reg S-P)[2] in response to the privacy provisions of the GLB Act. SEC Reg S-P governs the treatment of NPI about customers by broker-dealers (BDs), investment companies, and SEC-registered investment advisers (RIAs). The regulation requires firms to notify customers concerning the collection, use and sharing of their NPI, which is defined in more detail in Reg S-P than in the GLB. Reg S-P limits the disclosure of NPI to anyone not affiliated with the firm unless customers have been notified of the way their NPI will be shared and offered the opportunity to direct firms not to share it. Customers are entitled to opt out of a firm's plan to share their NPI with others not affiliated with the firm. However, Reg S-P contains an important exception to providing customers with opt-out rights.

In order to implement Reg S-P, firms must establish procedures for: (a) providing privacy notices to customers; (b) assuring that information is properly shared and, when applicable, used in accordance with customers' directions; and (c) safeguarding customer information. This chapter describes the basic elements of what is required for compliance with Reg S-P.

SEC Reg. S-P establishes four basic requirements for BDs and IAs. Firms must:

- Provide customers with *clear and conspicuous* initial and annual notices of their privacy policies;
- Provide consumers and customers with an opportunity to *opt out* of NPI disclosure to nonaffiliated third parties in certain situations;
- Adopt written policies and procedures reasonably designed to ensure the security, confidentiality, and integrity of customer records and information; and
- Properly dispose of customer information.

---

[2] 17 CFR § 248.1–248.100 (2014); 17 C.F.R. § 248 app. A, subpt. A Model Forms (2014).

Definition of Nonpublic Personal Information

Regulation S-P protects the NPI of consumers/customers of BDs and RIAs. NPI is defined as: (i) personally identifiable financial information; and (ii) any list, description, or other grouping of customers (and publicly available information pertaining to them) that is derived using any personally identifiable financial information that is not publicly available.

Personally identifiable financial information is defined as any information:

- A consumer provides to obtain a financial product or service;
- About a consumer resulting from any transaction involving a financial product or service; and
- Obtained in connection with providing a financial product/service to that consumer.[3]

Examples of personally identifiable financial information include:

- New account information provided to open a securities account or advisory account;[4]
- Account balance, position or activity information;
- The fact than an individual is or has been a customer or has obtained a financial product or service from a firm;
- Any list of names and addresses derived from a source that is not publicly available, e.g., list of names, addresses, and account numbers; and
- Any information collected, through an internet "cookie" (an information-collecting device from a web server).

NPI does not include publicly available information, e.g., any list, description or other grouping of consumers not derived from NPI. For example, NPI does not include any list of names and addresses that contains only publicly available information and that is not disclosed in a way indicating anyone on the list is a firm's customer.

Disclosure Requirements

Initial Privacy Notices. Firms must provide a clear and conspicuous notice that accurately reflects their privacy policies and practices to:

- Customers, when the relationship with the customers is established. A relationship with a customer is established when a firm and customer enter into a continuing relationship. Examples of the commencement of a continuing relationship include
  - A customer effects a securities transaction through the firm or opens a brokerage account with the firm,
  - Opening an account with an introducing broker/dealer that clears transactions with or for its customers on a fully-disclosed basis, and
  - Entering into an advisory contract with the customer;

---

[3] 17 CFR § 248.3(t)(1).
[4] *See* FINRA Rule 4512 for list of customer information that broker-dealers are expected to obtain and maintain.

- Consumers before passing any NPI to a nonaffiliated third party unless an exception applies. (A consumer is essentially a single transaction user of a firm's services. If there is no continuing relationship with a firm, the consumer does not become a customer.); and
- The law distinguishes between consumers and customers. Although the law and rules technically make this distinction, the interpretations and amendments to various applicable rules suggest that firms might well apply the same approach to all persons providing NPI to them. The distinction in how to address consumer NPI versus customer NPI has become fuzzy. For readers having a more intensive interest in this subject the author refers them to Reg S-P and some scholarly articles.[5]

Exceptions to Privacy Notice and Opt-Out Requirement. There are very limited circumstances in which a privacy notice may not be required, for example, if a firm does not disclose NPI to nonaffiliated third parties. Also, when customers purchase a new product or service, a new privacy notice may not be required. Here is a description of those situations:

- A firm does not have to provide an initial notice if
  - It does not disclose any NPI about the consumer to nonaffiliated third parties, except under an authorized exception, and
  - It does not have a customer relationship with the consumer.
- For existing customers who purchase a new product or service from the firm for personal, family, or household use, the firm satisfies the notice requirements if
  - The firm provides a revised privacy notice to the customers covering the new product or service, or
  - The initial, revised or annual privacy notices most recently provided to the customer are accurate with respect to the new product.
- The firm may postpone delivery of the initial notice to the customer for a reasonable time if
  - Establishing the customer relationship is not at the customer's choice. For example, where the customer's account is transferred to the firm by a securities investor protection corporation (SIPC) trustee,
  - Providing notice at the time the relationship is established would substantially delay the customer's transaction and the customer agrees to receive the notice later. An example would be a telephone transaction between the firm and the customer involving the prompt delivery of the financial service or product, or
  - A nonaffiliated broker/dealer establishes a customer relationship between the firm and the customer without the firm's prior knowledge.

The initial notice to the customer must be delivered so that each customer can reasonably be expected to receive actual notice in writing or, if the customer agrees, electronically.

---

[5] *See* Reg S-P, 17 C.F.R. § 248.3(g)(1); Stephanie Nicholas and Elena Schwieger, "Privacy of Client Information," in 1 *Practicing Law Institute Treatise Broker-Dealer Regulation*, 27-14–27-22; Securities and Exchange Commission, *Staff Responses to Questions About Regulation S-P* (Jan. 23, 2003), https://www.sec.gov/divisions/investment/guidance/regs2qa.htm

In limited circumstances, NPI may be disclosed to third parties to facilitate processing and servicing of transactions the consumer authorizes. Reg S-P provides an important exception to requirement of having to offer customers the right to opt out of sharing NPI with nonaffiliated third parties. The opt-out right does not apply when a firm provides NPI to a nonaffiliated third party to perform services for it or the third party functions on its behalf, so long as the firm provides the required privacy notice and enters into a contractual agreement with the third party that prohibits the third party from disclosing or using the information other than to carry out the purposes for which the information was disclosed.

In these circumstances a firm can employ a simplified notice that includes the following:

- Categories of NPI collected by firm;
- The firm's policies and practices to protect the confidentiality, security and integrity of NPI;
- A statement that the firm makes disclosures permitted by laws; and
- A statement that the firm neither discloses nor reserves the right to disclose NPI to affiliated or nonaffiliated third parties.

Annual Privacy Notices. A firm must provide a clear and conspicuous notice about its privacy policies to customers at least once every twelve consecutive months during which the relationship exists.

A firm is not required to provide annual notices to a former customer. Examples of former customers include ones who have closed their brokerage accounts, terminated their advisory contracts, or (if the firm is an investment company—mutual fund), the individual is no longer the record owner of the securities issued by the fund company.

The annual notice to the customer must be delivered so that each customer can reasonably be expected to receive actual notice in writing or, if the customer agrees, and the firm meets the regulatory requirements, electronically.

Content of Notices. A firm must include the following information:

- Categories of NPI collected. *Example*: information on the customer's transactions with the firm or its affiliates;
- Categories of NPI disclosed. The firm should provide examples to illustrate the types of categories of information to be disclosed;
- Types of affiliated and nonaffiliated third parties with whom the NPI will be shared. The firm should provide examples of affiliates and nonaffiliated third parties that are financial services providers, nonfinancial companies, and others;
- Categories of NPI about former customers and the categories of affiliated and nonaffiliated third party to whom the disclosures are made, except as allowed by the rule;
- For disclosures made to nonaffiliated third parties who are service providers or joint marketers, a statement describing the categories of information disclosed and the categories of third parties involved. The firm should state whether

- The service provider performs marketing services on the firm's behalf (and another financial institution, if applicable), or
- The third party is a financial institution with which the firm has a joint marketing agreement;
- An explanation of the right to opt out, including how the customer may exercise that right;
- An explanation of how to opt out of disclosures of information among affiliates if applicable; and
- The firm's policies and practices for protecting the confidentiality and security of NPI. The firm should describe in general terms who has access to the information and whether the firm has security practices in place to ensure the confidentiality of the information.

Form of Opt-Out Notice. If a firm wishes to disclose NPI about its customer, it must provide a clear and conspicuous notice that accurately explains the customer's right to opt out of the information sharing. The opt-out notice must also include:

- A statement that the firm will disclose or reserves the right to disclose NPI;
- A statement about the customer's right to opt out;
- A reasonable means to opt out;
- The categories of information to be disclosed and the categories of entities the information will be shared with; and
- The financial services or products subject to the customer's opt-out direction.

Opt-Out Methods. Reasonable opt-out methods include:

- Designating checkboxes in a prominent place on forms with the opt-out notice;
- Including a reply form with the opt-out notice;
- Providing an electronic means to opt out; and
- Providing a toll-free number.

Unreasonable opt-out methods include:

- The customer having to write a letter to exercise opt-out; and
- The only means to opt out as described in a subsequent notice to the initial notice is to use a checkbox supplied in the initial notice.

The firm may require a specific means for opting out. The opt-out notice may be included in the same form as the initial notice. When the opt-out notice is provided after the initial notice, a copy of the initial notice must accompany the opt-out notice. When two or more customers jointly obtain one product, the firm may provide one opt-out notice. However, individual opt-out notices may be required if the firm allows each individual to opt out.

Revised Privacy Notices. A revised privacy notice meeting the requirements of the initial notice must be issued when a firm wishes to:

- Disclose a new category of NPI to an unaffiliated third party;
- Disclose NPI to a new category of unaffiliated third party; or
- Disclose NPI about a former customer to a nonaffiliated third party if that former customer did not have the opportunity to opt out.

Delivery of Privacy and Opt-Out Notices. Firms must provide any privacy and opt-out notices so that all customers can reasonably be expected to receive the actual notice in writing or if they agree, electronically.

Examples of reasonable means of delivering the privacy and opt-out notices include:

- Hand delivery of printed notice;
- Mail delivery of a printed notice to the customer's last known address; and
- When the transaction is electronic, post the notice on the site and require the consumer to acknowledge the notice before completing the transaction.

Examples of unreasonable means of delivery include:

- Posting a sign in the branch office or publishing general advertisements of the privacy policy;
- Sending the notice via e-mail when the consumer does not obtain the financial product or service from the firm electronically; and
- Oral delivery of the notice by itself is never sufficient to meet the requirements of Reg S-P.

Delivery of annual notices is sufficient when:

- The customer uses a firm's website to access financial products and services, agrees to receive notices through the website, and the notice is posted in a conspicuous place on the website; or
- The customer has asked the firm not to send any information regarding the customer relationship, and the current privacy notice remains available to the customer upon request.

Firms must provide required notices in a manner that customers can retain them, obtain them later in writing or if the customer agrees, electronically.

Joint notices (with other financial institutions) may be used, provided the notice is accurate with respect to the firm and the other financial institutions.

Model Forms for Privacy Notices

The SEC has published model privacy and opt-out notice forms. Appendix I to this chapter provides copies of these templates. There are four versions of the model form, and the one employed depends upon what the firm shares with third parties and the methods offered for customers to opt out:

- Version 1: Model Form with No Opt Out;
- Version 2: Model Form with Opt Out by Telephone and/or Online;
- Version 3: Model Form with Mail-In Opt-Out Form; and
- Version 4: Optional Mail-In Form.

The model forms provide a legal safe harbor, although firms may continue to use other types of notices that vary from the model form so long as those notices comply with the privacy rule. For example, an institution could continue to use a simplified notice if it does not have affiliates and does not intend to share nonpublic personal information with nonaffiliated third parties outside of the exceptions provided.

The model form has two pages and may be printed on a single piece of paper. Together, pages one and two address the legal requirements of applicable federal financial privacy laws and are designed to increase comprehension.

Page one of the model form has five parts:

- Title;
- An introductory section called the "key frame" that provides context to help the consumer understand the required disclosures;
- A disclosure table that describes the types of sharing used by financial institutions consistent with federal law, which of those types of sharing the institution actually does, and whether the consumer can limit or opt out of any of the institution's sharing;
- Only if needed, a box titled "To limit our sharing" for opt-out information; and
- The institution's customer service contact information. When the firm provides a mail-in opt-out form, that form may appear at the bottom of page one.

The second page of the model form provides additional explanatory information that, together with page one, ensures that the notice includes all elements described in the GLB Act as implemented by Reg S-P. Supplemental information in the form of frequently asked questions (FAQs) appears at the top and definitions are below.

Need to Keep Policies Current

It is important that privacy policies are current and accurately reflect a firm's information-sharing practices. Enforcement cases have been brought against firms when firm information-sharing practices are not properly reflected in the firm's privacy statement. Those cases will be reviewed later in this chapter.

Caution Regarding Departing Registered Representatives. The privacy notices for your firm must accurately reflect how it manages obtaining, using, and protecting NPI. Consider for example the ability of registered representatives (RRs) to retain NPI about customers if they relocate with another firm. Are they permitted to take information with them? Consider your firm's privacy notice and the Protocol for Broker Recruiting, which is administered by Bressler, Amery & Ross P.C., and addresses what information transitioning RRs can take with them.

The protocol is an agreement voluntarily entered into by more than 400 brokerage firms, and is administered by the Securities Industry and Financial Markets Association (SIFMA). Firms that are signatories to the protocol agree not to sue one another if RRs moving from one protocol firm to another take with them client names, addresses, telephone numbers, email addresses, and account title information, but no other documents of information.[6]

Here is some language firms have used in privacy notices to describe the potential use of information by departing representatives:

Example 1. Nonprotocol Firm

Your registered representative having account access. If your representative's relationship with XYZ ends, he or she may want to transfer your account(s) to a new firm. To assist with this transfer, we allow your representative to maintain copies of your account records and provide your personal information to the new firm. If you do not wish for your representative to share your personal information with his or her new firm, you may choose to "opt out" of this arrangement by calling us at 888-666-1969, or by writing us at the address or email address below. Your election will apply to all of your accounts with XYZ unless you specify which account(s) to apply it to. If you have previously elected to opt out, no further action is required. Certain states require your written consent before your representative can share your personal information with a new firm. These states include Arizona, California, Georgia, Maine, Minnesota, Montana, New Jersey, New Mexico, North Carolina, North Dakota, Ohio, and Vermont. If you are a permanent resident of any of these states, then you must provide us with your written consent at the address or email address below before we will allow your representative to share your personal information with a new firm.

Example 2. Protocol Firm

If your primary address is in a state that requires your affirmative consent to share your personal information with the new firm (such as Alaska), then you must give your written consent before we will allow your financial advisor to take any of your personal information to that new firm.

Please be aware that [current firm name] entered into the Protocol for Broker Recruiting on September 4, 2008, with certain other brokerage firms, and if [current firm name] remains a signatory to the protocol as of the effective date of your advisor's termination from [current firm name], then [current firm name] will permit your financial adviser to

---

[6] See a description of NEXT Financial Groups SEC Admin. Law Judge decision later in the chapter ; *Dante J. DiFrancesco*, Exchange Act Rel. No. 66113, 2012 WL 32128, at 12–13 (Jan. 6, 2012).

take your name, address, phone number, email address, and the account title of the accounts services (or additional information as permitted if the Protocol is amended) while your financial advisor was associated with [current firm name] if your adviser joins one of these protocol brokerage firms. The retention of this limited information by your advisor under the protocol may occur even if you have exercised your rights to limit information sharing as described above.

Proposed Regulations

Potential Exception to Notice and Opt-Out Requirements—Limited Information Disclosure When Personnel Leave Their Firms. In 2008, the SEC proposed amending Reg S-P to provide a limited exception to address the movement of financial advisers from one firm to another.[7] The Safeguards Rule has long provided a challenge to covered firms addressing privacy issues when investment adviser representatives (IARs) and RRs change firms. The securities brokerage industry has had extensive experience with RRs moving between broker-dealers and encouraging their clients to follow them to a new broker-dealer. Although RRs believed the clients "belonged" to them, the broker-dealers they left generally believed otherwise. Broker-dealers and RRs have engaged in extensive litigation and arbitration disputes concerning, among other issues, the transfer of customers' personal information.

In 2004, major brokerage firms reached a truce on the issue of RRs moving between these firms. The firms signed on to the Protocol for Broker Recruiting permitting RRs to take certain customer-related information with them.[8] The proposed Reg S-P amendments would include a new exception to the privacy notice and opt-out requirements providing relief similar to the terms of the Broker Protocol.[9] Recognizing the close relationship of trust and confidence representatives have established with their clients, the exception would permit limited information sharing, within an orderly framework, facilitated by supervision of the transfer of such information.[10] The exception would work as follows.

A broker-dealer or investment adviser (Old Firm) could share information with a departing representative to join another broker-dealer or investment adviser (New Firm) provided:

---

[7] Regulation S-P: Privacy of Consumer Financial Information and Safeguarding Personal Information, Exchange Act Rel. No. 57,427 (Mar. 4, 2008) [hereinafter Proposed Rule Release], www.sec.gov/rules/proposed/2008/34-57427.pdf. All page references are to the PDF version available on the SEC website.

[8] For a discussion of the Protocol for Broker Recruiting, see Initial Decision *In Re NEXT Financial Group, Inc.* Exchange Act Rel. No. 349 (July 18, 2008), www.sec.gov/litigation/aljdec/2008/id349jtk.pdf [hereinafter NEXT Decision], at 30–31. The Initial Decision was made a Final Decision on July 18, 2008; *see also* Notice That Initial Decision Has Become Final, Exchange Act Rel. No. 58192 (July 18, 2008), www.sec.gov/litigation/aljdec/ 2008/34-58192.pdf; *see* Woodbury Financial Services, Exchange Act Rel. No. 59740 (Apr. 9, 2009).

[9] Proposed Rule Release, at 40–45, 93.

[10] *Id.*

- The information is limited to: customer name, a general description of the type of account and products held by the customer, and the customer's contact information (address, telephone number, and e-mail address);
- The customer information does not include: any customer account number, Social Security number, or securities positions;
- The departing representative provides the old firm, no later than the date of his or her separation from employment, with a written record of the information that will be disclosed; and
- The old firm maintains and retains these records.[11]

Effect of Stalled SEC Rulemaking on Transitioning Representatives. The SEC proposed the amendments in March of 2008.[12] During 2008, the SEC received more than 430 comments, both in written submissions and by persons meeting with SEC commissioners and staff members. A substantial number of commentators (at least three-fourths) addressed the issue of allowing

> [D]eparting financial advisers the unfettered right to utilize the client's name, address, telephone number, email information, and a general description of the client's account and products held to facilitate account portability and investor choice without interference from their prior broker-dealer. The proposed amendment falls short by making the exception available at the option of the prior broker-dealer firm.[13]

As of July 2015, the SEC has not acted on the proposed amendments. In 2013, the proposed amendments were dropped from the SEC's filings on the federal Unified Agenda of Federal Regulatory and Deregulatory Actions.[14] Thus several open issues posed by the SEC's NEXT decision[15] remain open. The NEXT matter is discussed later in this chapter. In summary, firms and individual advisers do not have clear guidance when advisers migrate between firms.

Safeguarding Customer Information

Reg S-P explicitly requires written safeguarding policies and procedures.[16] Currently, the Reg S-P Safeguards Rule provides little detail on how to safeguard customer records and information.[17] The rule restates the safeguarding provisions of the GLB.[18]

---

[11] Proposed Rule Release, at 42–44.
[12] *Id* at 105
[13] *See* www.sec.gov, comments on File No. S7-06-08; *see*, e.g., Comment from T. Robert Talbot (Apr. 9, 2008), https://www.sec.gov/comments/s7-06-08/s70608-6.htm
[14] *See*, generally, http://www.reginfo.gov/public/do/eAgendaMain
[15] *See* NEXT Decision, at 32–34 for a discussion of SEC enforcements action against NEXT Financial Group.
[16] The SEC amended Reg S-P in 2004 to require written procedures. *See Disposal of Consumer Report Information*, Exchange Act Rel. No. 50781 (Dec. 8, 2004), www.sec.gov/rules/final/34-50781.htm. At the same time, Reg S-P was also amended to incorporate a provision of the Fair and Accurate Credit Transactions Act of 2003, P.L. No. 108-159, 117 Stat. 1952 (2003) (FACTA), that set forth requirements for the disposal of credit reports and customer records. *See also* FINRA Regulatory Notice 08-69, http://www.finra.org/industry/notices/08-69 (discussing FACTA and the Red Flags Rule).
[17] 17 C.F.R. § 248.30.
[18] Stephen Lofchie, *Lofchie's Guide to Broker-Dealer Regulation* (2005), at 259–60.

Firms must adopt policies and procedures that contain administrative, technical, and physical safeguards to protect customers' NPI.[19]

The SEC's approach to safeguarding customer information permits firms to decide for themselves what policies and procedures are needed to comply with the Safeguards Rule. However, this principles-based approach presents the overworked compliance officer with the daunting task of deciding where to start the process.

In 2008, the SEC proposed modifying the Safeguards Rule with more specific requirements. Although the proposed amendments have not yet been adopted (and may never be), there are some important aspects of the proposal that firms should consider when designing/modifying their customer data protection processes.

Procedures for Safeguarding Customer Records (Safeguards Rule). Reg S-P requires firms to safeguard customer records and information. It also requires the proper disposal of customer information. Every firm must adopt written policies and procedures that address the administrative, technical, and physical safeguards for the protection of customer records and information. These policies and procedures must be reasonably designed to:

- Insure security and confidentiality of customer records and information;
- Protect against any anticipated threats or hazards to the security or integrity of customer records and information; and
- Protect against unauthorized access to or use of customer records and information that could result in substantial harm or inconvenience to the customer.

Disposal of Customer Information. Every firm that maintains or possesses customer information must properly dispose of the information by taking reasonable steps to protect against unauthorized access or use of the information in connection with its disposal.

The other details provided by the Safeguards Rule specify that policies and procedures must be reasonably designed to:

- Insure the security and confidentiality of customer records and information;
- Protect against any anticipated threats or hazards to the security or integrity of customer records and information; and
- Protect against unauthorized access to or use of customer records or information that could result in substantial harm or inconvenience to any customer.[20]

---

[19] The SEC Safeguards Rule does not apply to private investment companies (such as hedge, buyout, private equity, venture capital, and other private funds), and state registered or nonregistered investment advisers. The Federal Trade Commission's Privacy Rules apply to these types of firms. See 17 C.F.R. § 248.3(u) ("[p]ersonally identifiable financial information"). Nonpublic personal information includes identifying information such as name, address, phone number, Social Security number, financial information, and credit scores. It also includes a customer's portfolio information, including balances, positions, transaction history, and other information about a customer's account.

[20] 17 C.F.R. § 248.30(a).

As noted above, in 2008, the SEC proposed modifying the Safeguards Rule with more specific requirements. Citing concerns about the challenges posed by recent information security breaches, the SEC asserted that "perhaps most disturbing is the increase in incidents involving the takeover of online brokerage accounts, including the use of the accounts by foreign nationals as part of 'pump-and-dump' schemes."[21] The SEC described several areas of concern ranging from 'phishing attacks,' in which fraudsters set up phony internet sites mimicking legitimate sites, to the negligent disposal of client records by firms and their employees from which journalists have been able to remove sensitive securities-related data.[22]

Concluding that many firms do not regularly reevaluate and update their safeguarding programs to deal with increasingly sophisticated attacks and that some firms have improperly gained customer information from competitors, the SEC proposed expanding requirements involving the collection, use, and safeguarding of customer information.[23] The proposed revision is modeled upon the safeguards rules currently mandated by banking agencies and the Federal Trade Commission (FTC).[24]

Reg S-P would be changed in four principal ways:

- To require more specific standards under the Safeguards Rule, including safeguards that would apply to data security breach incidents;
- To amend the scope of the information covered by the safeguards and disposal rules and broaden the types of institutions covered by the rules;[25]
- To require firms to maintain written records of their policies and procedures and compliance with those policies and procedures; and
- To adopt a new exception from Reg S-P's notice and opt-out requirements to allow investors to more easily follow a financial adviser moving from one firm to another.[26]

Information Security Programs

The first proposed change under Reg S-P would require every SEC-registered investment adviser, investment company, registered broker-dealer, and transfer agent

---

[21] Proposed Rule Release, at 9.
[22] SEC Release, No. 34-57427, Regulation S-P, at 9–10.
[23] SEC Release, No. 34-57427, Regulation S-P, at 11.
[24] SEC Release, No. 34-57427, Regulation S-P, at 13.
[25] SEC Rel. No. 34-57427, Regulation S-P, at 100–01; 17 C.F.R. § 248.3(t). The proposed rule change has effectively broadened the scope of personal information covered by the rule. Firms should be cautious about allowing any information about a client to be disclosed to any third-party. The proposed rule change defines personal information as "any record containing consumer report information, or nonpublic personal information…that is identified with any consumer, or with any employee, investor, or security holder who is a natural person, whether in paper, electronic, or other form, that is handled or maintained by you or on your behalf." A "customer" is a "consumer" who has a continuing relationship with the securities firm. 17 C.F.R. § 248.3(j). A "consumer" is an individual (or an individual's legal representative) who obtains a financial product or service from the securities firm that is to be used primarily for personal, family, or household purposes. 17 C.F.R. § 248.3(g)(1).
[26] Proposed Rule Release, at 12.

(covered firms) to maintain a comprehensive Information Security Program (ISP).[27] The objectives of the ISP must be designed to:

- Ensure security and confidentiality of personal information;
- Protect against threats or hazards to the security of personal information; and
- Protect against any unauthorized access or use of personal information resulting in substantial harm or inconvenience to a consumer, employee, investor, or security holder who is a natural person.[28]

To achieve these ends, a covered firm would be required to have written policies and procedures to protect personal information and respond to unauthorized access or use of personal information, and have an appropriately-sized ISP for its business.[29] A designated employee would be required to coordinate the covered firm's ISP.[30]

The first step toward creating an ISP would entail performing a risk assessment to identify internal and external risks to personal information and related systems.[31] A risk assessment should include the following:

- Identifying reasonably foreseeable internal and external threats that could result in unauthorized disclosure, misuse, alteration, or destruction of customer information;
- Assessing the likelihood and potential damage of these threats, taking into consideration the sensitivity of customer information; and
- Assessing the sufficiency of policies, procedures, customer information systems, and other arrangements in place to control risks.[32]

Internal and External Risk Assessment. Once the risks to data security have been identified, the covered firm would be required to design, implement, and document the safeguards it proposes to address the identified risks. Reg S-P and its proposed amendments are silent as to what these safeguards should entail.

Developing Safeguarding Policies. The banking agencies and the FTC have actively provided resources, guidelines, and analytical frameworks for assisting companies in developing procedures and controls for protecting customer data. These resources are readily available on the Federal Financial Institution Examination Council (FFIEC)

---

[27] Proposed Rule Release, at 13–14. The scope of the rule would be expanded to include transfer agents.
[28] Proposed Rule Release, at 14.
[29] Proposed Rule Release, at 94.
[30] Id.
[31] In 2001, the Department of the Treasury, the Federal Reserve System, and the Federal Deposit Insurance Corporation (collectively, the banking agencies) issued joint regulations at about the same time the SEC adopted Reg S-P. See Interagency Guidelines Establishing Standards for Safeguarding Customer Information, 66 Fed. Reg. 8816 (Feb. 1, 2001) (to be codified at various parts of 12 C.F.R.) [hereinafter "Bank Guidelines"]. The Bank Guidelines go beyond policies and procedures and require banks, thrifts, and credit unions (referred to collectively as "banks") to develop and implement an ISP, Bank Guidelines at 8633. Like Reg S-P, the Bank Guidelines do not dictate specific bright line safeguarding rules. Rather, the Bank Guidelines specify the processes that banks should implement to safeguard customer information on an ongoing basis. Bank Guidelines at 8633-34. The FTC adopted similar safeguards rules in 2002. See Standards for Safeguarding Customer Information, 67 Fed. Reg. 36,484 (May 23, 2002).
[32] Proposed Rule Release, at 94–95.

and FTC websites.[33] The following is a high-level summary of key topics to address in developing safeguarding policies, procedures, and controls, regardless of whether the proposed changes to Reg S-P are finalized:[34]

- *Data Procedures.* Firms should maintain information security throughout the life cycle of customer information, from entry to data disposal, by knowing where and how confidential customer information is processed and stored. Data procedures should include ensuring that only authorized employees have access to customer information; storing records in a room or cabinet that is locked when unattended; ensuring that information stored on PCs, servers, and other computer storage devices or systems is accessible only with a "strong" password or stronger safeguards and is kept in a physically secure area. Data procedures should include procedures for creating backup records and keeping backup data secure by storing it offline and in a physically secure area;
- *Physical Access Restrictions.* Firms should restrict physical access to customer information to authorized individuals with specific provisions for building, area, and workplace locations;
- *Technical Access Controls.* It is important to implement appropriate access controls on customer information systems, including controls to authenticate and permit access only to authorized individuals and controls to prevent employees from providing customer information to unauthorized individuals who may seek to obtain this information through fraudulent means;
- *Traditional Information Security.* Firms should implement procedures and technologies to protect against loss, destruction, and alteration of customer data by using firewalls, backup procedures and facilities, intrusion prevent/detection systems, server-based technical safeguards, system modification protocols and change management, application development standards, system logging and monitoring, network security, and system security architecture;
- *Employee Procedures.* Firms must train staff to implement its ISP. This should also include conducting background checks of employees who have responsibilities for or access to customer information; training employees on safeguarding so that employees can avoid inadvertent or unauthorized disclosure of customer information (for example, using laptops, PDAs, cell phones and Wi-Fi; emailing; disposing of customer data properly; avoiding deception by pretext calls);[35] segregating job duties;
- and establishing job controls; and
  Testing Procedures. Periodic testing should be conducted to ensure the ongoing effectiveness of the ISP. The covered firm should document the effectiveness of key controls, including the effectiveness of access controls on personal information systems; controls to detect, prevent, and respond to unauthorized access to personal information; and employee training related to the ISP.

---

[33] *See* FFIEC home page, www.ffiec.gov; FTC home page, www.ftc.gov
[34] This summary is generally taken from a guide published by the FTC. *See* FTC, *Protecting Personal Information: A Guide for Business* (2011) [hereinafter FTC, *Protecting Personal Information*], https://www.ftc.gov/tips-advice/business-center/guidance/protecting-personal-information-guide-business
[35] Pretext calling is a method of impersonation that fraudsters use to obtain biographical and account-related information. *See* Office of the Comptroller of the Currency Advisory Letter, Identity Theft and Pretext Calling (Apr. 30, 2001), http://ithandbook.ffiec.gov/media/resources/3327/occ-al2001-04-identity_theft_pretext_call.pdf.

On a periodic but ongoing basis, firms should also evaluate whether adjustments to their ISP are necessary. The factors to take into consideration in evaluating an ISP include the result of testing and monitoring of key controls, changes in technology relevant to the ISP, material changes in operations or business, and any other circumstance that would have a significant impact on the ISP. Firms should also keep in mind the sensitivity of the customer information and any new internal or external threats to the information.[36]

Third-Party Service Providers. The Reg S-P amendments also would require covered firms to protect customer private information when that data is shared with third-party service providers.[37] The covered firm must retain written documentation of its efforts to select and retain service providers capable of maintaining safeguards over personal information. If the covered firm either uses a third-party service provider or is considering a third-party service provider with whom it would share customer nonpublic information, the covered firm would exercise appropriate due diligence in selecting these service providers; ensure its service providers agree in a contract to implement appropriate measures designed to meet safeguard-objectives; and monitor its service providers to confirm that they have satisfied their contractual obligations. As part of this monitoring, the covered firm should also review audits, summaries of test results, or other equivalent evaluations of its service providers.

Additional ISP Safeguards. There are other elements of an ISP that would not be required by Reg S-P but may be prudent additions whether or not the amendments become final. First, a high-level governance plan for safeguarding customer information should be encouraged.[38] In particular, it might be appropriate for the firm's board to receive an annual security report that describes the overall status of the ISP. The report would discuss material matters related to the ISP, addressing issues such as risk assessment, risk management and control decisions, wider arrangements, results of testing, security breaches or violations, management's responses, and recommendations for changes in the program.[39] Second, steps should be taken to educate the firm's customers about security concepts, and major threats and precautions against transmitting sensitive data (such as account numbers) via e-mail or in response to unsolicited e-mails or pop-up messages. Third, firms should take care to comply with the SEC and FTC's "Red Flag Rules," which require the adoption of written policies intended to identify and detect risks of identity theft and respond appropriately.[40]

Responding to Data Breaches. The proposed amendments to the Reg S-P Safeguards Rule would also require covered firms to have in place procedures for responding to unauthorized access or use of personal information.[41] At a minimum, each covered firm's ISP would be required to have procedures to:

---

[36] See Bank Guidelines, at 8634.
[37] Proposed Rule Release, at 26.
[38] See Bank Guidelines, at 8635.
[39] For broker-dealers, such a governance plan would be consistent with FINRA Rules 3012 and 3130. See also Rule 206(4)-7 of the Investment Advisers Act and Rule 38a-1 of the Investment Company Act.
[40] See SEC, *Identity Theft Red Flags Rules, A Small Entity Compliance Guide* (May 17, 2013) http://www.sec.gov/info/smallbus/secg/identity-theft-red-flag-secg.htm#_ftn1 [hereinafter "Identify Theft Red Flags Rules"].
[41] Proposed Rule Release, at 22–23.

- Assess the nature and scope of any incident of unauthorized access or use of personal information, and create a record of what information may have been compromised;
- Establish containment and control measures to avoid further unauthorized access or use of personal information, and document the mitigation steps taken;
- Promptly investigate any unauthorized access to determine whether personal information has been or will be misused, and create a written record of the covered firm's determination;
- Notify each affected individual if the covered firm's determination is that personal information is reasonably likely to be misused; and
- Notify the covered firm's self-regulatory organization (SRO) (if a broker-dealer) or the SEC (if an SEC-registered investment adviser, investment company, or transfer agent) on proposed Form SP-30 when:
  - There is significant risk that the person identified with the personal information might suffer substantial harm or inconvenience; or
  - The unauthorized access or misuse of personal information was intentional.[42]

Disposal of Personal Information. The proposed amendments to Reg S-P would require firms to properly dispose of personal information.[43] Any firms that maintain or process personal information must properly dispose of the information by taking reasonable measures to protect against unauthorized access or use.[44] Currently, Reg S-P only applies this requirement to firms that maintain consumer credit reports.[45] The SEC also seeks to expand the scope of the rule to apply to any natural person who is an associated or supervised person of the firm and employee records.[46] These obligations are expressly extended to firms' representatives while with the firm and when they leave.[47] Each firm would be required to adopt written policies and procedures that address the proper disposal of personal information.[48] Disposal includes discarding or abandoning personal information, or selling, donating, or transferring the storage medium such as computers, PDAs, computer disks, and tapes.[49]

Recordkeeping. Each covered firm would be required to maintain records documenting creation of records and the proper disposal of records as follows (the times listed below begin to run when the record is created or a written policy was last modified):

- Investment adviser—five years (first two years in easily accessible place);
- Broker-dealer—three years (first two years in easily accessible place);
- Transfer agent—two years (first year in easily accessible place); and
- Investment company—six years (first two years in easily accessible place).[50]

---

[42] Proposed Rule Release, at 23–24.
[43] Proposed Rule Release, at 98–99. The FTC has published a guide that includes a section on the proper disposal of personal information. See FTC, *Protecting Personal Information*.
[44] Proposed Rule Release, at 98–99. FACTA also requires proper disposal of "consumer report information." See FACTA Disposal Rule, R-411007, Disposal of Consumer Report Information and Records, 16 C.F.R. 682 (2014).
[45] 17 C.F.R. § 248.30.
[46] Proposed Rule Release, at 98.
[47] Id.
[48] Proposed Rule Release, at 99.
[49] Proposed Rule Release, at 100.
[50] Proposed Rule Release, at 99.

In February 2015, the SEC office of Compliance Inspections and Examinations published its OCIE's Cyber Security Examination Sweep Summary.[51] The OCIE summary indicated several positive aspects about security including efforts to protect customer and transaction information from intrusion by cyber hackers. The summary also indicates that an industry-wide standard for managing information security does not exist. It is reasonable to expect that the SEC and FINRA should revisit the rulemaking process to guide firms in establishing standards for confidential data management. The proposed rules could serve as the starting point for this process.[52]

IV. REGULATION S-AM: LIMITATIONS ON AFFILIATE MARKETING

The SEC adopted Regulation S-AM ("Reg S-AM") in 2010 in response to requirements in the Fair Credit Reporting Act (FCRA). The FCRA requires the SEC to adopt rules limiting a firm's use of certain information received from an affiliate to solicit a customer for marketing purposes unless the customer has had an opportunity to opt out of such solicitations. Reg S-AM complements the Reg S-P restrictions on sharing with nonaffiliated third parties with limitations on the extent to which firms can use customer information obtained from affiliates for marketing purposes.

SEC Reg S-AM permits a customer to block affiliates of firms[53] from soliciting him or her in certain circumstances. Firms cannot use "eligibility information" received from an affiliate to solicit a customer unless:

- The potential marketing use of that information has been clearly, conspicuously, and concisely disclosed to the customer;
- The customer has been provided a reasonable opportunity and simple method to opt out of receiving the marketing solicitations; and
- The customer has not opted out.

Eligibility information is defined broadly to include personally identifiable information obtained as a result of a relationship with a firm, e.g., information about a customer's account history, personal identifiers such as account numbers, names, addresses, telephone numbers, website passwords, screen names, user names, email addresses, and internet protocol addresses.

Notice and Opt-Out Opportunity Requirement

The notice and opt-out opportunity must go to the customer before an affiliate uses that customer's eligibility information to solicit the customer. The notice and opt-out opportunity must be provided to the customer either by:

- The firm having a customer relationship, or
- By joint notice of the firm and its affiliate(s).

---

[51] SEC OCIE, *National Exam Program Risk Alert*, Volume IV, Issue 4 (Feb. 3, 2015), https://www.sec.gov/about/offices/ocie/cybersecurity-examination-sweep-summary.pdf

[52] *See also* FINRA, Report on Cyber Security Protection (Feb. 15, 2015), http://www.finra.org/sites/default/files/p602363%20Report%20on%20Cybersecurity%20Practices_0.pdf

[53] Affiliates include broker-dealers, investment advisers, investment companies, and transfer agents.

Contents of Notice and Opt-Out Opportunity

The notice must be clear, conspicuous and concise, and identify the affiliate providing the notice. Two or more joint customers may receive a single opt-out notice. The notice and opt out may be coordinated with other privacy notices and opt-out opportunities.

See Appendix II for model privacy forms. Firms may use and amend the model forms. Remember, they must be clear, conspicuous, and concise. And up to date!

Opt-Out Notice Contents. A customer may choose from alternative elections to prohibit marketing solicitations, e.g., to prohibit:

- Solicitations from certain types of affiliates;
- Certain types of delivery methods; and
- All solicitations from all affiliates (mandatory).

Opt outs must be effective for at least five years. Customers can opt out at any time. A customer may choose an opt-out period that does not expire unless revoked by the customer.

Reasonable Opportunity to Opt Out. Customers must be given a reasonable opportunity to opt out. Examples of reasonable opportunities include:

- By mail;
- By electronic means: posting on website or through email (customer address provided to receive email disclosure);
- At time of an electronic transaction, e.g., transaction on website is necessary part of proceeding with the transaction;
- At time of in-person transaction, in writing, necessary to proceed with transaction; and
- Including Reg S-AM notice and opt-out opportunity as part of a Reg S-P privacy notice.

Reasonable/Simple Method to Opt Out. Examples of reasonable methods to opt out include:

- Prominent check-off box on opt-out form;
- Reply form and self-addressed envelope supplied with notice;
- Electronic means to opt-out form that can be emailed/processed on website;
- Toll-free telephone number customers can call to opt out; and
- Consolidated notice and form for customer to exercise all opt-out rights.

Delivery of Opt-Out Notice. Notices must be delivered so that each customer can reasonably be expected to receive actual notice. Examples of acceptable opt-out notice delivery include:

- Hand delivery of printed notice to customer;
- Mail delivery to customer's last known mailing address;
- Email delivery if customer has agreed to delivery; and
- Put notice on website where customer obtains product/service and customer must acknowledge receipt of notice.

Renewal of Opt-Out Elections. After an opt-out period has expired, a firm cannot solicit a customer who has previously opted out *unless* the customer has (i) received a renewal notice; (ii) been given a reasonable opportunity to renew the opt out; and (iii) not renewed the opt-out. Renewed opt outs must be effective for at least five years. The renewal opportunity notice must be provided by the affiliate that provided the previous opt-out notice (or its successor). A renewal notice may be provided jointly by the firm and affiliates. The renewal notice must:

- Identify firm(s) providing the renewal notice;
- Identify the affiliate and type of affiliate whose use of eligibility information is covered by the notice;
- Describe the types of information that may be used to solicit;
- Indicate that the customer has previously opted out;
- Indicate that the previous opt out has or is about to expire;
- Indicate that the customer may renew the previous opt-out;
- Indicate the time period the opt out would apply and that customer will be able to renew the opt out when that time expires; and
- Provide a reasonable and simple method for opting out.

Renewal notices may be sent to customers within a reasonable time before the current opt-out period has expired. Renewal notices may be included with annual Reg. S-P privacy notices. An opt-out period may not be shortened by sending a renewal notice before the expiration date, even if the customer does not renew the opt out.

V. IDENTITY THEFT PREVENTION PROGRAMS: THE RED FLAGS RULE

Another complement to the Reg S-P Safeguards Rule is the SEC Red Flags Rule that is intended to help consumers fight the growing crime of identity theft. Whereas the Safeguards Rule requires a program to safeguard customer records and information, the Red Flags Rule requires firms to have specific policies and procedures in place to help combat identity theft by responding to a laundry list of "red flags" that indicate a security breach may have occurred.

The Identity Theft Red Flags rules adopted by the SEC and the CFTC require establishing many of the same procedures proposed in the Reg S-P amendments. As a practical matter, developing written supervisory procedures that reflect the proposed amendments could be accomplished simultaneously. The compliance officer might consider implementing procedures consistent with the proposed amendments. These could be adjusted as necessary if the proposed Reg S-P amendments are eventually adopted.

The SEC adopted Regulation S-ID ("Reg S-ID") in 2013 in response to requirements of the Fair and Accurate Credit Transactions Act of 2003 (FACTA), which amended the Fair Credit Reporting Act to protect consumers from identity theft.[54]

---

[54] 15 U.S.C. § 1681 (2015).

Reg S-ID is known as the Red Flags Rule because it requires firms to develop programs to reduce and respond to potential identity theft risks and to update those programs at least annually. Although separate from Reg S-P, the Red Flags Rule requirements parallel proposed Reg S-P mandates. Accordingly, chief compliance officers (CCOs) should consider red flags requirements in designing their firm's information security program.

Reg S-ID requires broker-dealers and SEC registered investment advisers to develop, implement and maintain a written identity theft prevention program (ITPP).[55]

ITPPs must be designed to detect, prevent, and mitigate identity theft in connection with the opening and maintenance of "covered accounts."[56] Those programs must include four basic steps to be in compliance:[57]

- Identify relevant red flags for a firm's covered accounts and incorporate those red flags into its ITPP;
- Implement procedures to detect red flags;
- Assess whether a red flag indicates evidence of identity theft and respond appropriately according to the level of risk; and
- Update the ITPP periodically to reflect changes in risks to customers and to the safety and soundness of the financial institution or creditor from identity theft.

Reg S-ID contains guidelines must be considered when implementing and administering an ITPP. The guidelines outline methods to identify red flags by outlining risk factors and potential sources of red flags.[58]

The rule identified four main steps a firm must take to implement its program:[59]

- Obtain approval of the written ITPP from its Board of Directors or an appropriate committee thereof;
- Involve the Board of Directors or appoint an employee of at least senior status to oversee, develop, implement, and administer the ITPP;
- Train staff to implement the ITPP and detect red flags; and
- Exercise appropriate and effective oversight of service provider arrangements.

The Identity Theft Prevention Program

In designing its ITPP, a firm may incorporate, as appropriate, its existing policies, procedures, and other arrangements that control reasonably foreseeable risks to customers or to the safety and soundness of the firm from identity theft.

---

[55] Identity Theft Red Flags Rules, 78 Fed. Reg. 23,638 (Apr. 19, 2013); FINRA, Red Flags Rule, www.finrag.org/Industry/Issues/CustomerInformationProtection/p118480. FINRA includes a template for written supervisory procedures at this location. See also FINRA Information Notice, New FTC Red Flags Rule Template (July 1, 2009), https://www.finra.org/industry/information-notice-070109

[56] A covered account is any other account that a firm or creditor offers or maintains for which there is a reasonably foreseeable risk to customers or to the safety and soundness of the financial institution or creditor from identity theft, including financial, operational, compliance, reputation or litigation risks.

[57] "Financial institutions" including broker-dealers, investment advisers and investment companies. See SEC, *Identity Theft Red Flags Rules*.

[58] SEC, *Identity Theft Red Flags Rules*, at 34–40.

[59] SEC, *Identity Theft Red Flags Rules*, at 32–33.

Identifying Relevant Red Flags

Risk Factors. Firms should consider the following factors in identifying relevant red flags for covered accounts, as appropriate.

- The types of covered accounts it offers or maintains;
- The methods it provides to open its covered accounts;
- The methods it provides to access its covered accounts; and
- Its previous experiences with identity theft.

Sources of Red Flags. Firms should incorporate relevant red flags from such sources as:

- Incidents of identity theft that the firm has experienced;
- Methods of identity theft that the firm has identified that reflect changes in identity theft risks; and
- Applicable regulatory guidance.

Categories of Red Flags. The ITPP should include relevant red flags from the following categories, as appropriate.

- Alerts, notifications, or other warnings received from consumer reporting agencies or service provider, such as fraud detection services;
- The presentation of suspicious documents;
- The presentation of suspicious personal identifying information, such as a suspicious address change;
- The unusual use of, or other suspicious activity related to, a covered account; and
- Notice from customers, victims of identity theft, law enforcement authorities, or other persons regarding possible identity theft in connection with covered accounts held by the financial institution or creditor.

Detecting Red Flags

The ITPP policies and procedures should address the detection of red flags in connection with the opening of covered accounts and existing covered accounts, such as by:

- Obtaining identifying information about, and verifying the identity of, a person opening a covered account, for example, using the policies and procedures regarding identification and verification set forth in the firm's antimoney laundering customer identification program; [31 U.S.C. 5318(1) (31 CFR 1023.220 (broker-dealers) and 1024.220 (mutual funds))]; and
- Authenticating customers, monitoring transactions, and verifying the validity of change of address requests, in the case of existing covered accounts.

Preventing and Mitigating Identity Theft

The ITPP's policies and procedures should provide for appropriate responses to the red flags the firm has detected that are commensurate with the degree of risk posed. In determining an appropriate response, a firm should consider aggravating factors that may heighten the risk of identity theft, such as a data security incident that results in unauthorized access to a customer's account records held by the firm or third party, or notice that the customer has provided information to someone fraudulently claiming to represent the firm or to phishing or other type of fraudulent website. Appropriate responses may include the following:

- Monitoring the customer's account for evidence of identity theft;
- Contacting the customer;
- Changing any passwords, security codes, or other security devices that permit access to the account;
- Reopening the customer's account with a new account number;
- Not opening a new account;
- Closing an existing account;
- Not attempting to collect on an account or not selling an account to a debt collector;
- Notifying law enforcement; or
- Determining that no response is warranted under the particular circumstances.

Updating the Program

Firms should update their ITPPs (including the red flags determined to be relevant) periodically, to reflect changes in risks to customers or the safety and soundness of the firm from identity theft, based on factors such as:

- The firm's experiences with identity theft;
- Changes in methods of identity theft;
- Changes in methods to detect, prevent, and mitigate identity theft;
- Changes in the types of accounts that the firm offers or maintains; and
- Changes in the business arrangements of the firm, including mergers, acquisitions, alliances, joint ventures, and service provider arrangements.

Methods for Administering the Program

Oversight of the ITPP. Oversight by the board of directors, an appropriate committee of the board, or a designated employee at the level of senior management should include:

- Assigning specific responsibility for the ITPP's implementation;
- Reviewing reports described below prepared by staff regarding compliance by the firm with Reg S-ID; and
- Approving material changes to the ITPP as necessary to address changing identity theft risks.

Reports. In general, a compliance report must be provided to the governing committee or person the firm has designated as being the person or persons responsible for development, implementation, and administration of the ITPP at least annually.

Contents of Report. The report should address material matters related to the ITPP and evaluate issues such as: the effectiveness of the firm's policies and procedures in addressing the risk of identity theft in connection with the opening of customer accounts and with respect to existing customer accounts; service provider arrangements; significant incidents involving identity theft and management's response; and recommendations for material changes to the ITPP.

Oversight of Service Provider Arrangements. Whenever the firm engages a service provider to perform customer related activities, it should take steps to ensure that the activity of the service provider is conducted in accordance with reasonable policies and procedures designed to detect, prevent, and mitigate the risk of identity theft. For example, the firm could require the service provider by contract to have policies and procedures to detect relevant red flags that may arise in the performance of the service provider's activities, and to report the red flags to the firm.

Other Applicable Legal Requirements

Firms should be mindful of other related legal requirements that may be applicable, such as:

- Filing a FinCEN Suspicious Activity Report (SAR) in accordance with applicable law and regulation;
- Implementing any requirements under 15 U.S.C. 1681c-1(h) regarding the circumstances under which credit may be extended when the financial institution or creditor detects a fraud or active duty alert;
- Implementing any requirements for furnishers of information to consumer reporting agencies under 15 U.S.C. 1681s-2, for example, to correct or update inaccurate or incomplete information, and to not report information that the furnisher has reasonable cause to believe is inaccurate; and
- Complying with the prohibitions in 15 U.S.C. 1681m on the sale, transfer, and placement for collection of certain debts resulting from identity theft.

In addition to incorporating red flags from the sources recommended in the Guidelines each firm may consider incorporating into its program, whether singly or in combination, red flags from the following illustrative examples in connection with covered accounts:

Alerts, Notifications, or Warnings from a Consumer Reporting Agency

- A fraud or active duty alert is included with a consumer report;
- A consumer reporting agency provides a notice of credit freeze in response to a request for a consumer report;
- A consumer reporting agency provides a notice of address discrepancy, as referenced in Sec. 605(h) of the Fair Credit Reporting Act (15 U.S.C. 1681c(h));

- A consumer report indicates a pattern of activity that is inconsistent with the history and unusual pattern of activating of an applicant or customer, such as
  - A recent and significant increase in the volume of inquiries,
  - An unusual number of recently established credit relationships,
  - A material change in the use of credit, especially with respect to recently established credit relationships, or
  - An account that was closed for cause or identified for abuse of account privileges by a financial institution or creditor.

Suspicious Documents

- Documents provided for identification appear to have been altered or forged;
- The photograph or physical description on the identification is not consistent with the appearance of the applicant or customer presenting the identification;
- Other information on the identification is not consistent with readily accessible information that is on file with the financial institution or creditor, such as a signature card or recent check; and
- An application appears to have been altered or forged, or gives the appearance of having been destroyed and reassembled.

Suspicious Personal Identifying Information

- Personal identifying information provided is inconsistent when compared against external information sources used by the financial institution or creditor—
  - The address does not match any address in the consumer report, or
  - The Social Security number (SSN) has not been issued, or is listed on the Social Security Administration's Death Master File;
- Personal identifying information provided by the customer is not consistent with other personal identifying information provided by the customer. For example, there is a lack of correlation between the SSN and the date of birth;
- Personal identifying information provided is associated with known fraudulent activity as indicated by internal or third-party sources used by the financial institution or creditor—
  - The address on an application is the same as the address provided on a fraudulent application, or
  - The phone number on an application is the same as the number provided on a fraudulent application;
- Personal identifying information provided is of a type commonly associated with fraudulent activity as indicated by internal or third-party sources used by the financial institution or creditor—
  - The address on an application is fictitious, a mail drop, or a prison, or
  - The phone number is invalid or is associated with a pager or answering service;
- The SSN is provided is the same as that submitted by other persons opening an account or other customers;
- The address or telephone number provided is the same as or similar to the address or telephone number submitted by an unusually large number of other persons opening accounts or by other customers;

- The person opening the covered account or the customer fails to provide all required personal identifying information on an application or in response to notification that the application is incomplete;
- Personal identifying information provided is not consistent with personal identifying information that is on file with the financial institution or creditor; and
- For firms that use challenge questions, the person opening the covered account or the customer cannot provide authenticating information beyond that which generally would be available from a wallet or consumer report.

Unusual Use of, or Suspicious Activity Related to, the Covered Account

- Shortly following the notice of a change of address for a covered account, the firm receives a request for a new, additional, or replacement means of accessing the account or for the addition of an authorized user on the account;
- A covered account is used in a manner that is inconsistent with established patterns of activity on the account, such as
  - Nonpayment when there is no history of late or missed payments,
  - A material increase in the use of available credit,
  - A material change in purchasing or spending patterns, or
  - A material change in electronic fund transfer patterns in connection with a deposit account;
- A covered account that has been inactive for a reasonably lengthy period of time is used (taking into consideration the type of account, the expected pattern of usage and other relevant factors);
- Mail sent to the customer is returned repeatedly as undeliverable although transactions continue to be conducted in connection with the customer's covered account;
- The firm is notified that the customer is not receiving paper account statements; and
- The firm is notified of unauthorized charges or transactions in connection with a customer's covered account.

Notice from Customers, Victims of Identity Theft, Law Enforcement Authorities, or Other Persons Regarding Possible Identity Theft in Connection with Covered Accounts Held by the Firm

- The firm is notified by a customer, a victim of identity theft, a law enforcement authority, or any other person that it has opened a fraudulent account for a person engaged in identity theft.

VI. RECENT SEC AND FINRA INITIATIVES

This section summarizes recent SEC and FINRA initiatives, including exam priorities, guidance, enforcement actions relating to safeguarding customer information and preventing identity theft. This section also highlights some of the key questions that one should expect the SEC or other regulators to ask in examinations.

Comparable state laws and regulations are summarized. This section also provides tips firms should consider when developing and revising safeguarding policies and procedures.

The safeguarding of customer information is an important regulatory priority for the SEC. For 2015, the SEC staff identified "cybersecurity" as one of its exam priorities. In 2014, the SEC Office of Compliance Inspections and Examinations (OCIE) launched an initiative to examine broker-dealers' and investment advisors' cybersecurity compliance and controls. In early 2015, OCIE issued a risk alert that summarized its observations from examinations of certain broker-dealers and investment advisers as part of its April 2014 Cybersecurity Examination Initiative.

Similarly, in its 2013 Examination Priorities Letter, the Financial Industry Regulatory Authority (FINRA) also addressed the necessity of protecting customer data and preventing unauthorized access to account information.[60] The letter noted that "the frequency and intensity of threats, such as denial of service attacks and the number of data security breaches, raises concerns that the securities industry is vulnerable to disruption and unauthorized access to customer account information," and considered "the integrity of firms' policies, procedures, and controls to protect sensitive customer data" to be its primary concern.[61] Since 2000, SEC Reg S-P[62] has required firms[63] to safeguard customer information. FINRA has described the regulation as requiring firms to implement "policies and procedures that address administrative, technical, and physical safeguards for the protection of customer information and records," while ensuring that those WSPs are designed to reasonably protect against any anticipated threats or hazards to the security and integrity of customer records and information."[64]

As a result of technological advances, and instances of mishandling or lack of care by firms, the SEC has proposed amendments to Reg S-P (the "Proposed Rule").[65] When the amendments were proposed, SEC Chairman Christopher Cox noted:

> [A] lot has changed throughout the first decade of the 21st century. The securities industry uses a lot of information technology in new and different ways than it did before. And as a result of these developments, we and other federal regulators have increased our focus on protecting the privacy of investors and consumers.[66]

---

[60] FINRA 2013 Regulatory and Examination Priorities Letter 3 (Jan. 11, 2013), http://www. finra.org/industry/2013-exam-priorities-letter
[61] *Id.*
[62] SEC Regulation S-P: Privacy of Consumer Financial Information, 17 C.F.R. 248.
[63] SEC-registered investment advisers, investment companies, and broker-dealers must comply with Reg S-P.
[64] FINRA 2010 Regulatory and Examination Priorities Letter (Mar. 1, 2010), http://www. finra.org/industry/2010-exam-priorities-letter
[65] Proposed Rule Release.
[66] Press Release, SEC, SEC Proposes Amendments to Safeguard Customer Privacy (Mar. 4, 2008), www.sec.gov/news/press/2008/2008-31.htm (video and press release).

The SEC's concern was well founded. Reports at the time indicated that fraud and cybercrime incidents were dramatically increasing in the financial services industry.[67] According to the Identity Theft Resource Center's 2014 breach report, there were 783 reported breaches in 2014, exposing 85,611,528 records,[68] as more personal data is released through the internet and more sophisticated hacking tools are developed, it is likely that breaches will continue to be high. The Target, Home Depot, and SONY hacking incidents during 2014 highlighted the risks for all to see.

FINRA and the SEC have addressed the protection of customers' data both within rule-making, guidance and through examination and enforcement initiatives.

FINRA Guidance: Registered Representatives Changing Firms

In August 2007, FINRA published Regulatory Notice 07-36. The notice was intended to clarify guidance relating to Reg S-P under NASD Notice to Members 07-06, Special Considerations When Supervising Recommendations of Newly Associated Representatives to Replace Mutual Funds and Variable Products.[69]

NTM 07-06 recommended that firms should have procedures in place, including supervisory procedures, that are specifically designed to review and evaluate investment recommendations relating to mutual funds and variable products that are made by newly associated persons to their existing customers. Specifically, the NTM recommended procedures providing that when a firm conducts due diligence concerning a prospective new registered representative, the new firm should seek to learn the nature of the representative's business and the extent to which he or she offers investment products for which the new firm would need a dealer or servicing agreement in order for the representative to sell and provide service.

Some firms questioned the scope of due diligence described in the NTM and specifically asked whether any such due diligence procedures may conflict with a firm's obligations under Reg S-P. FINRA asserted that:

> The obligations set forth in NTM 07-06 do not conflict with a firm's obligations under SEC Regulation S-P. Indeed, in establishing due diligence procedures, NTM 07-06 does not recommend, nor does it suggest, that

---

[67] Ellen Messmer, "Banking's Big Dilemma: How to Stop Cyberheists Via Customer PCs," *Bloomberg Bus. Week* (June 17, 2010), www.businessweek.com/idg/2010-06-17/banking-s-big-dilemma-how-to-stop-cyberheists-via-customer-pcs.html (reporting that unauthorized use of account data, "along with a slew of other incidents in the past year, has many bank officials worried"). *The Wall Street Journal* also reported at the beginning of 2009 that cyberattacks on banks had doubled in the latter half of 2008. M.P. McQueen, "Cyber-Scams on the Uptick in Downturn," *The Wall Street Journal* (Jan. 29, 2009), at Dl. In early 2010, *The Wall Street Journal* reported cybercrime complaints increased in 2009 by 22.3 percent, according to. M.P. McQueen, "Cybercrime Complaints, Reported Losses Increase," *The Wall Street Journal* (Mar. 12, 2010), http:// www.wsj.com/articles/SB10001424052748704131404575117862249387610.

[68] Data Breach Reports, Identity Theft Resource Center (Jan. 12, 2015), http://www.idtheftcenter.org/ITRC-Surveys-Studies/2014databreaches.html. The Identity Theft Resource Center (ITRC) is a nonprofit organization that tracks many facets of personal information compromise and provides resources to those who have experienced identity theft. The ITRC also advises governmental agencies, legislators, law enforcement, and businesses about the evolving problem of personal information theft. *See* ITRC Home Page, www.idtheftcenter.org

[69] *See* Notice to Members 07-06, NASD (Feb. 2007), *available at* https://www.finra.org/industry/ notices/07-06

a firm obtain nonpublic personal information about any customers the prospective registered representative may seek to bring to the new firm. FINRA expects firms to keep in mind that the goal of such due diligence procedures is for the firm and its prospective new registered representative to understand the extent to which there exist mutual funds and variable products currently held in the representative's customer accounts that may not be serviced or sold by the new firm.

Therefore, in conducting reasonable due diligence of the prospective registered representative's customer base, the new firm needs to learn only the identity of the various mutual fund and variable products held by the registered representative's customer base. Detailed, nonpublic, personal information about individual customers and their particular investments is not necessary or relevant to meet the objectives of this review.

Information Encryption Requirements: FINRA Rule 8210

FINRA Rule 8210 mandates encryption for all information provided to it on a portable media device.[70] Recognizing that "data security issues regarding personal information have become increasingly important in recent years," FINRA amended Rule 8210 in 2010 regarding encryption requirements for providing documents or information via a portable media device. A *portable media device* is any "storage device for electronic information, including but not limited to a flash drive, CD-ROM, DVD, portable hard drive, laptop computer, disc, [or] diskette."

Verification of Emailed Instructions

Regulatory Notice 12-05 gives us the punch line right up front in its title: Verification of Emailed Instructions to Transmit or Withdraw Assets from Customer Accounts. FINRA has received an increasing number of reports of incidents of customer funds stolen as a result of instructions emailed to firms from customer email accounts that have been compromised. These incidents highlight some of the risks associated with accepting instructions to transmit or withdraw funds via email.

Customer funds have been stolen as a result of instructions emailed to firms from customer email accounts that have been compromised. Firms should review their policies and procedures to ensure they are adequate to protect customer funds from such risks. FINRA recommends that WSPs include a way to verify that the email was sent by the customer and be designed to identify and respond to red flags, including:

- Transfer requests that are out of the ordinary or just don't seem to be typical of the client;
- Requests that funds be transferred to an unfamiliar third-party account (i.e., a transmittal that would result in a change of beneficial ownership);

---

[70] FINRA Regulatory Notice 10-59, SEC Approves Amendments to FINRA Rule 8210 to Require Encryption of Information Provided Via Portable Media Device (Nov. 2010), https://www.finra.org/industry/notices/10-59

- Requests from customer accounts to outside entities (e.g., banks investment companies);
- Requests for transmittal of funds (e.g., wires or checks) from customer accounts to locations other than the customer's primary residence (e.g., post office box, "in care of" accounts, alternate address);
- Requests between customers and registered representative (including the hand delivery of checks); and
- Requests that indicate urgency or appear designed to deter verification of the transfer instructions.

FINRA recommended that firms reassess their WSPs to ensure they are adequate to protect customer assets from such risks. The Federal Bureau of Investigation (FBI), Financial Services Information Sharing and Analysis Center (FS-ISAC) and Internet Crime Complaint Center (I3C) recently released joint fraud alert describing a similar trend.

VII. SEC ENFORCEMENT ACTIONS

The SEC's attention to Reg S-P issues resulted in a number of significant enforcement actions beginning in 2008. Recently, FINRA has also stepped up its examination and enforcement program. FINRA and the SEC have targeted firms that have violated Reg S-P through improper recruiting practices, insecure disposal of client records, insufficient antivirus protection, fraudulent use of client information, and inadequate server and web portal security. These enforcement actions provide some practical guidance for firms to consider.

Improper Recruiting Practices

In 2008, an SEC administrative law judge (ALJ)[71] ordered NEXT Financial Group to cease and desist from any recruiting tactics that violated Reg S-P, and pay a $125,000 penalty.[72] The SEC's ALJ determined that NEXT violated Reg S-P's Safeguards Rule in a number of ways. The firm directly violated Reg S-P by disclosing nonpublic personal information about a consumer to nonaffiliated third parties without proper notice and a reasonable opportunity to opt out of the disclosure, and failing to have "reasonably designed" safeguarding policies and procedures. The firm indirectly violated Reg S-P by willfully aiding and abetting and causing other firms' violations of Reg S-P.

---

[71] Initial Decision, *In Re NEXT Financial Group, Inc.* The Initial Decision was made a Final Decision on July 18, 2008; *see also* Notice That Initial Decision Has Become Final, Exchange Act Rel. No. 58192 (July 18, 2008), www.sec.gov/litigation/aljdec/ 2008/34-58192.pdf; *see* Woodbury Financial Services, Exchange Act Rel. No. 59740 (Apr. 9, 2009).

[72] The ALJ found that NEXT's conduct violated the following Reg S-P rules:
- Rule 4, which requires a firm to provide customers with clear and conspicuous notice of the Firm's privacy policies and practices;
- Rule 6, which requires the privacy notices to include the types of NPI that will be disclosed, and the types of third parties to which such information may be disclosed;
- Rule 10, which mandates that customers be provided with a proper opt-out opportunity prior to the Firm's disclosure of nonpublic personal information to nonaffiliated third parties; and
- Rule 30, which requires all firms to adopt policies and procedures intended to safeguard customer information and records.

See In Re NEXT Financial Group, at 32–37.

The firm employed a "transition team" to actively obtain nonpublic information about customers of other independent broker-dealers/investment advisers from individuals it was recruiting. The transition team required new recruits to acquire and submit personal nonpublic information, including their Social Security numbers, passport numbers, driver's license numbers, annual income, occupations, and net worth.

The transition team members accessed recruits' current broker-dealer computer systems using the recruits' usernames and passwords in order to download NPI. Further, NPI on the recruits' customers was kept in the firm's system, even though many of them never became the firm's customers. These customers were unaware of this practice and were never given the opportunity to opt out. Additionally, when representatives left, they were permitted to take copies of all customer files, electronic information, and documents, including NPI. The firm's privacy policy did not adequately inform customers of this practice until its privacy notice was revised in June 2006. Further, the ALJ concluded that the firm acted negligently in its adoption of safeguarding policies and practices.[73]

Although the ALJ determined that the firm violated numerous Reg S-P provisions, he did not impose the $325,000 fine originally requested by the SEC. The ALJ acknowledged that there is general confusion within the securities industry about Reg S-P. But the firm did receive a scolding from the ALJ, who concluded that, even in the face of industry-wide uncertainty about how to comply with Reg S-P, the firm's "conduct was extremely reckless and that NEXT must have known that its conduct was highly improper."[74] The ALJ also concluded that unnamed broker-dealers acted negligently.[75]

As a case of first impression by any adjudicatory body, the ALJ's decision presents a thorough review of the legislative and regulatory history of Reg S-P. Interestingly, the ALJ rejected the argument that many of the practices alleged to be violations by the SEC Enforcement Division had been long-term industry practices known to the SEC's Market Regulation Division. Of interest, the ALJ also declared that unnamed firms had also violated Reg S-P because their "policy statements were deficient because they failed to inform customers that departing representatives were likely to disclose nonpublic personal information to successor brokerage firms and failed to afford customers a reasonable opportunity to opt out of such disclosure."[76] The firm was found to have aided, abetted, and caused those violations. The firm did not appeal the ALJ's decision.

---

[73] *See In Re NEXT Financial Group,* at 38 ("Viewing these circumstances in their entirety I conclude that NEXT acted at least negligently when implementing Regulation S-P drafting its early privacy notices and adopting safeguarding policies and practices.").

[74] *In Re NEXT Financial Group,* at 46.

[75] *See In Re NEXT Financial Group,* at 41–42(citations omitted), the ALJ concluded that:
[T]he nonparty brokerage firms acted negligently. By 2004-2005, Regulation S-P had existed for a sufficient length of time to charge the non-party brokerage firms with notice of their obligations under the law. In general, these independent brokerage firms knew that registered representatives who moved to other firms would disclose customer nonpublic personal information to the new firms before the registered representatives resigned from their current firms. Negligent conduct includes the failure to do an act which is necessary for the protection or assistance of another and which the actor is under a duty to do....On this basis, I conclude that the recruits' current brokerage firms negligently violated Rule 10 of Regulation S-P.
In Re NEXT FinancialGroup, at 41–42 (citations omitted).

[76] *In Re NEXT Financial Group,* at 41.

Improper Recruiting Practices

In another example of improper recruiting practices,[77] the SEC announced the settlement of an enforcement action against a broker-dealer with more than 1,800 independent contractor RRs nationwide in April 2009. The SEC asserted that the firm had violated Reg S-P while recruiting RRs from other broker-dealers. The firm allowed newly recruited RRs to send nonpublic client information such as Social Security numbers, account numbers, and account registrations to the firm before leaving their former broker-dealer.[78] This practice helped newly recruited RRs complete customer transfer forms more efficiently once they were registered with the new firm. The firm never determined whether the customers had consented to the release of this nonpublic personal information. The firm agreed to revise its practices to comply with Reg S-P and pay a $65,000 fine.[79]

Departing Registered Representative Downloaded Nonpublic Information. In 2014, the SEC affirmed FINRA's finding that an RR engaged in conduct inconsistent with just and equitable principles of trade when he downloaded NPI about more than 2,000 customers from his former firm's computer system onto a personal flash drive without the customers' consent and then shared that NPI with his new firm.

In October 2008, after attending a recruiting meeting, the RR decided to leave his firm and join a new firm. Before resigning, the RR downloaded onto his personal flash drive, which was not encrypted or password-protected, and personal laptop confidential customer NPI. The NPI included customers' names, addresses, account numbers and balances, quarterly account statements, Social Security numbers, and birth dates.

The RR left his old firm shortly before 6:00 p.m. on his last day of work and went to his new office. He met with an administrative assistant who had been assigned to help him prepare announcements of his move. He gave the assistant his personal flash drive but, because it was late in the day and had started to snow, they agreed to wait until the next day to work on the announcements. He allowed the assistant to keep the flash drive in her possession overnight without informing her that it contained confidential NPI and was not encrypted or password-protected.

A FINRA hearing panel found that the RR engaged in unethical conduct, in violation of NASD Conduct Rule 2110, by downloading confidential customer information protected as NPI under Regulation S-P, without authorization. The panel decided that disclosing that information to his new firm warranted imposition of a ten business-day suspension in all capacities and ordered the RR to pay costs.

As a result of the RR's appeal to FINRA's National Adjudicatory Council (NAC) his suspension was increased to 90 days in all capacities.

Citing the Restatement (Third) of Agency and SEC case law for the proposition that an agent has a duty not to use confidential information of the principal for his own, or

---

[77] *Woodbury Financial Services, Inc.*, Exchange Act Rel. No. 59740, 2009 WL 960760 (Apr. 9, 2009).
[78] *Woodbury Financial Services*, at 1.
[79] *Woodbury Financial Services*, at 2–3.

third-party's, interest, and is obligated to act in his customer's best interests, the SEC said the RR's conduct implicated the duty, "grounded in fundamental fiduciary principles," to maintain the confidentiality of customers' nonpublic information.

The SEC also found that the RR's actions were "self-interested and for his own purposes," i.e., he favored his own financial interest in building a book of business over his customers' interests in the privacy of their confidential NPI. Moreover, the absence of demonstrable harm to customers was not held to excuse his actions. Harm is not an element of a Rule 2100 violation.

Given these circumstances, the commission agreed with the NAC's determination to impose on the RR a ninety-day suspension in all capacities. They stated, "The ability to credibly assure a client that [confidential] information will be used solely to advance the client's own interests is central to any securities professional's ability to provide informed advice to clients."

The panel further stated, "Disclosure of such information jeopardizes the foundation of trust and confidence crucial to any professional advising relationship." The RR's misconduct showed a "careless" breach of his duty of client confidentiality.

Insufficient Antivirus Protection on RRs' Computers.[80] In 2009, the SEC settled an enforcement action against a broker-dealer and investment adviser with more than 1,600 RRs. The firm agreed to SEC findings that it had violated Reg S-P's Safeguards Rule by not requiring its RRs to maintain antivirus software on their computers.[81] As a result, customer information was vulnerable to cyberattack. A hacker obtained the login credentials of an RR by installing a virus on an RR's computer. The hacker gained access to 368 customer accounts and quickly placed more than $500,000 worth of unauthorized trades using those account numbers. The firm detected the unauthorized activity, canceled the unauthorized transactions, absorbed the cancellation penalties resulting from the transactions, and notified the SEC.[82] The firm agreed to cease and desist from committing or causing any future violations of Reg S-P's Safeguards Rule and paid a $100,000 fine.[83]

Nonsecured Disposal of Client Records

In an enforcement action against a broker-dealer with approximately 488 independent contractor RRs nationwide,[84] the SEC ALJ found the firm had violated Reg S-P's Safeguards Rule by failing to adopt written policies and procedures to protect customer records and information. The firm argued that its employee manual and customer privacy statement fulfilled Reg S-P's Safeguards Rule, but the SEC held that none of

---

[80] Commonwealth Equity Servs., LLP, Admin. Proc. No. 3-13631 (Sept. 29, 2009), https://www.sec.gov/litigation/admin/2009/34-60733.pdf
[81] Commonwealth Equity Services, at 1.
[82] Commonwealth Equity Services, at 2–3.
[83] Commonwealth Equity Services, at 64.
[84] J.P. Turner & Co., LLC, Admin. Proc. No. 3-13550, at 3 (May 19, 2010), https://www.sec.gov/litigation/aljdec/2010/id395rgm.pdf (a three-day public hearing on the matter).

these materials adequately explained a process for RRs to safeguard customer information.[85] Because of the firm's failure to adopt customer-protection procedures, RR left a box full of unsecured customer records at the curbside of his personal residence. The records were left unprotected for two weeks until they were retrieved by firm officials. The SEC discovered this situation when an SEC staff person saw a news story about it on the evening news. The SEC issued a cease and desist order, requiring the firm to adopt written policies to comply with Reg S-P[86] and to pay a $65,000 fine.[87]

Fraudulent Use of Client Information

Sale of Information.[88] In a civil injunctive action, the SEC charged an RR with aiding and abetting violations of Reg S-P, as well as violations of section 10(b) of the Exchange Act and Rule 10b5-2.[89] As part of a consent decree,[90] the RR consented to findings that he reaped illegal profits by selling the names and other confidential personal information of more than 500 of his customers—the majority of them elderly—to six different insurance agents. Information sold included contact information and, sometimes, the dollar figure that an investor had spent on the last annuity. This sale allowed the insurance brokers to sell the investors more annuity products, even though the majority of them had already purchased equity-indexed or fixed annuities. The insurance brokers reportedly paid the RR anywhere from $50 to $150 per lead. The RR also consented to findings that he received customer commissions from the investors that employed his services to sell securities so they could buy the new annuities.

The RR was permanently enjoined from violating Section 10(b) of the Exchange Act and Rule 10b-5 thereunder, and from aiding and abetting any violations of Rules 4(a), 5(a), and 10(a)(1) of Reg S-P. The RR was ordered to disgorge ill-gotten gains of $53,000 and pay a penalty of $45,000. The broker-dealer, UNCI, Inc., was dismissed by the court upon the SEC's motion.[91] In a separate related action, the SEC barred the RR from associating with any broker-dealer, with a right to reapply after five years.[92]

Fraudulent Use of Information.[93] A broker-dealer and its CEO and general counsel-chief compliance officer (GC/CCO) agreed to settle an SEC enforcement alleging that the firm failed to supervise its managing director of Client Services (MD), who had a history of FINRA violations and perpetrated two fraudulent schemes while employed at the firm. First, the MD gave customer account statements to a personal friend,

---

[85] In the Matter of J.P. Turner, at 17.
[86] In the Matter of J.P. Turner, at 18–19.
[87] In the Matter of J.P. Turner, at 19–20.
[88] *SEC v. Mondschein & UNCI, Inc.*, No. 07-6178 (N.D. Cal. Apr. 14, 2008) (Final Judgment).
[89] *Id.*
[90] *Final Judgment Entered Against Former San Francisco-Area Stockbroker Concerning Fraudulent Scheme That Violated the Privacy Rights of His Elderly Customers*, SEC Litigation Rel. No. 20,531 (Apr. 17, 2008), www.sec.gov/litigation/litreleases/2008/lr20531.htm
[91] *Id.*; *Mondschien*, Exchange Act Rel. No. 57680 (Apr. 17, 2008), www.sec.gov/litigation/admin/2008/34-57680.pdf
[92] *Final Judgment Entered Against Former San Francisco-Area Stockbroker.* SEC Litigation Release No. 20,531.
[93] *Merriman Curhan Ford & Co.*, Exchange Act Rel. No. 60976, 2009 WL 3757969 (Nov. 10, 2009).

allowing the friend to pledge those accounts as collateral in obtaining more than $45 million in personal loans.[94] Second, the MD used customer accounts to make unauthorized purchases of risky securities in order to receive the commissions generated by the trades.[95] The SEC initially brought a civil enforcement action against the MD and subsequently brought an enforcement action against the firm and its officers.

Both the CEO and the GC/CCO were aware that the MD had been fined by FINRA before joining their firm, and they placed him under a special supervision plan that was to be carried out by the GC/CCO.[96] The GC/CCO delegated his supervisory responsibilities to a Compliance Department subordinate who was also responsible for reviewing more than 100 other RRs. The SEC found the firm's Compliance Department to be "thinly staffed" and unable to properly review all of the MD emails.[97] The MD used the firm's e-mail system to send numerous customer account statements to his personal friend. The fraud was discovered when SEC staff members conducted an examination of the firm.[98]

The firm, CEO, and GC/CCO "unreasonably delegated their supervisory responsibilities" over the MD and "failed to act on red flags relating to [his] unauthorized trading."[99] The firm agreed to hire a private consultant to review its procedures for supervising RRs and pay a $100,000 fine.[100] The CEO and GC/CCO were suspended from acting as supervisors of RRs for one year and paid fines totaling $115,000.[101]

Inadequate Server and Web Portal Security

No Written Supervisory Procedures.[102] In 2008, the SEC settled an enforcement action against an independent BD firm financial corporation, LPL, finding violations of Reg S-P's Safeguards Rule. The enforcement action was based upon the firm's failure to adopt policies and procedures to safeguard customers' personal information, leaving at least 10,000 customers vulnerable to identity theft following a series of account intrusion incidents involving the firm's online version of its broker workstation. The firm was required to adopt written policies and procedures reasonably designed to safeguard customer information.[103] The SEC order included findings that the firm conducted an internal audit in mid-2006 that identified inadequate security controls to safeguard customer information at its branch offices. That audit specifically identified the risk that an intruder could hack into its web portal and cause financial loss to advisers and customers by accessing customer

---

[94] Merriman Curhan Ford, at 3.
[95] *Id.*
[96] Merriman Curhan Ford, at 4.
[97] *Id.*
[98] Merriman Curhan Ford, at 7.
[99] Merriman Curhan Ford, at 8-9.
[100] Merriman Curhan Ford, at 154.
[101] *Id.* At 15-16 (CEO paid $75,000 fine; GC/CCO paid $40,000 fine).
[102] *LPL Financial Corp.*, Exchange Act Rel. No. 58515 (Sept. 11, 2008). LPL is a broker-dealer and registered investment adviser that employs an "independent contractor" business model.
[103] 17 C.F.R. § 248.30(a).

nonpublic information and executing unauthorized trades. That firm failed to take timely corrective action because, by the time that hacking incidents began in July 2007, the firm had not implemented increased security measures in response to the identified weaknesses.

The firm experienced multiple hacking incidents between July 2007 and early 2008, and unauthorized persons gained access to several brokers' accounts on its web portal, which contained personal NPI and had order entry capability for all the accounts under the brokers' management. Once logged onto the firm's online tracking platform, perpetrators placed or attempted to place 209 unauthorized securities trades worth more than $700,000 combined in 68 customer accounts. The firm was required to hire an independent consultant to enhance its safeguarding policies, procedures, and controls and pay a $275,000 penalty, and the firm was subject to a cease and desist order.

Open Web Portal Access.[104] In 2010, FINRA settled an enforcement action against a broker-dealer for failing to secure customer data from hackers. The firm placed all of its customer data on a web server with a constantly open internet connection. The database was not encrypted and had no password. An international crime syndicate hacked into the system and accessed the nonpublic data of more than 190,000 of the firm's customers. The firm did not discover the breach until one of the criminals e-mailed it with a blackmail attempt. The firm promptly reported the incident and assisted the Secret Service in apprehending at least three of the criminals responsible for the breach. FINRA considered the firm's quick response and assistance of law enforcement authorities, but still enforced a $375,000 fine against the firm.

Weak Access Controls.[105] In February 2011, FINRA fined an independent model BD firm for failing "to require brokers working remotely to install security application software on their own personal computers used to conduct the firm's securities business." Employees, including ex-employees, were able to access customer accounts via any internet browser by using shared login credentials. More than 1 million customer accounts were accessed this way. FINRA concluded that the firm's lackadaisical policies regarding the shared login credentials resulted in "weaknesses in access controls to the firms' system, confidential customer records including names, addresses, Social Security numbers, account numbers, account balances, birth dates, email addresses, and transaction details." FINRA fined the firm $600,000 for its failure to properly monitor internet access to customer accounts available to employees and ex-employees.

---

[104] Press Release, FINRA, FINRA Fines D.A. Davidson & Co. $375,000 for Failure to Protect Confidential Customer Information (Apr. 12, 2010), www.finra.org/Newsroom/NewsReleases/2010/P121262

[105] Press Release, FINRA, FINRA Imposes Fines Totaling $600,000 Against Lincoln Financial Securities and Lincoln Financial Advisors for Failure to Protect Confidential Customer Information (Feb. 17, 2011), www.finra.org/Newsroom/NewsReleases/2011/P122940

Supervisors/Executives Accountable

In April 2011, the SEC charged three brokerage executives for failing to protect client information.[106] While winding down business operations for an independent model BD firm, the president and national sales manager failed to protect client information by improperly transmitting the information to another firm. More than 16,000 client records were transferred to the sales manager's new firm without allowing the clients an opportunity to opt out. The CCO was also charged because he failed to ensure that the firm's policies and procedures would adequately protect client information. The firm's policies and procedures were vague, and did little more than cite the Safeguards Rule. Without admitting or denying the allegations, the firm executives consented to an SEC order of censure and fines totaling $55,000. Notably, "This is the first time that the SEC has assessed financial penalties against individuals charged solely with violations of Regulation S-P."[107]

Transmitting Information to Nonaffiliates

A general securities principal and senior compliance analyst[108] "improperly transferred confidential and proprietary information outside of" his firm "for purposes other than [his firm's] business." The principal sent two internal compliance reports, one of which contained NPI regarding six of the firm's customers, to another firm. On another occasion, the analyst sent two of the firm's internal documents to his personal email address. That report contained NPI for seventy individuals derived from a request by the Financial Crimes Enforcement Network (FinCEN) of the U.S. Treasury Department. On a third occasion, he sent three documents that contained information of another customer to his personal email address. FINRA asserted that his actions caused his firm to violate both Regulation S-P and FinCEN's regulations. In April 2011, he consented to a fine of $5,000 and a fifteen-day suspension (for violating NASD Conduct Rule 2110 and FINRA Rule 2010).

Failure to Safeguard Hard Copy Records

When a branch[109] manager resigned from his firm, he failed to safeguard hard copy business records containing customer personal confidential information located in the branch. The former manager left the keys for filing cabinets containing customer information with the office's landlord. This failure to safeguard information made such information available to a nonaffiliated third party without providing appropriate notice to customers. For violating FINRA Rule 2010 and causing his firm to violate Rules 10 and 30 of Reg S-P, the branch manager consented to a twenty-day suspension and a fine of $10,000.

---

[106] SEC Press Rel. No. 2011-86, SEC Charges Brokerage Executives with Failing to Protect Confidential Customer Information (Apr. 7, 2011), https://www.sec.gov/news/press/2011/ 2011-86.htm

[107] Id.

[108] FINRA Letter of Acceptance, Waiver and Consent No. 20100235371-01 (Apr. 9, 2011), FINRA website's Disciplinary Actions: http://disciplinaryactions.finra.org/Search/ViewDocument/14681

[109] FINRA Letter of Acceptance, Waiver and Consent No. 2010022715603 (Oct. 1, 2011), FINRA website's Disciplinary Actions, http://disciplinaryactions.finra.org/Search/ViewDocument/26308

Failure to Update Written Supervisory Procedures

Patrick Walker, a firm's former president and CCO consented to a finding[110] that he failed to update written supervisory procedures covering a number of areas. Notwithstanding receipt of a letter of caution resulting from a previous FINRA examination, the president/CCO failed to update procedures identified as deficient. That letter of caution "indicated that the firm's written supervisory procedures were deficient with respect to Regulation S-P, in that these procedures failed to include policies in areas such as: the disposal of consumer report information, and safeguarding customer information." Walker consented to the findings that he had violated NASD Rules 3010 and 2110, a fine of $5,000, and a suspension in all supervisory and principal capacities for ten business days.

VIII. STATES' EFFORTS TO SAFEGUARD CUSTOMER INFORMATION

The vast majority of states have recently enacted privacy-related laws or amended existing privacy laws. The state laws share many common features. These laws typically fall into one of the following categories: breach notification, security freeze, social security number protection, disposal of personal information, or encryption. Each state's laws vary, however, and firms must identify the nuances for each state in which they do business in order to achieve compliance. The most comprehensive of these state laws is Massachusetts' security breach statute.[111] The statute and its regulations provide detailed duties and procedures for firms handling the personal information of Massachusetts clients.[112]

Breach Notice Statutes

Forty-seven states, the District of Columbia, Guam, Puerto Rico, and the Virgin Islands all have some form of security breach notice laws.[113] California was the first state to enact a security breach notice law, and the subsequent state laws find their genesis in California's model.[114] These laws generally require that when an entity reasonably believes a breach of its security system involving unencrypted computerized information has resulted in the information being acquired by an unauthorized person, the entity must promptly notify potentially affected customers.[115] Some

---

[110] FINRA Letter of Acceptance, Patrick Walker Waiver and Consent No. 2008011724302 (Aug. 19, 2011), FINRA website's Disciplinary Actions, http://disciplinaryactions.finra.org/Search/ViewDocument/21168
[111] Mass. Gen. Laws ch. 93H, §§ 1-6 (2014).
[112] *See Id.*; 201 Mass. Code Regs. 17.00 (2010).
[113] *See* Susan Lyon, "United States: An Overview of Significant U.S. Data Breach Cases and Enforcement Actions," *Cybercrime and Security,* § 13B:4, at 1 (July 2013); Patricia Covington and Meghan Musselman, "Privacy and Data Security Developments Affecting Consumer Finance in 2008," 64 *Bus. Law* 533, 534–35 (2009). Ms. Covington and Ms. Musselman have also authored Annual Surveys for 2007 and 2008. These articles provide excellent summaries of each area, together with recent developments in most states. It should be the starting point for any survey research concerning privacy and data security. *See also State Security Breach Notification Laws,* National Conference of State Legislatures (June 11, 2015), http://www.ncsl.org/issuesresearch/telecom/ security-breach-notification-laws.aspx
[114] Covington and Musselman, "Privacy and Data Security Developments," at 536.
[115] *See, e.g.,* Cal. Civ. Code § 1798.29 (West Supp. 2013).

states have varied the form of the notice required and some have added a "risk-of-harm" trigger.[116]

Security Freeze Laws

All fifty states and the District of Columbia have credit report freeze laws.[117] These laws allow a consumer who has been or believes he will be a victim of identity theft to request that a consumer reporting agency place a "freeze" on his credit report, thereby blocking any unauthorized access to it.[118]

Social Security Number Protection Laws

Forty-eight states have Social Security number protection laws of some sort.[119] These laws generally restrict the way Social Security numbers are used or displayed by restricting the following:

- The posting or display of the numbers;
- The printing of the numbers on identification cards; and
- The printing of the numbers on any document mailed to a customer's home unless otherwise required by law.[120]

The laws also usually prohibit requiring a consumer to transmit his or her Social Security number over the internet, unless it is through a secure connection or the number is encrypted.[121]

Disposal of Personal Information Laws

Thirty-six states now require the secure disposal of personal information.[122] These laws are relatively straightforward and generally require personal information held by a company to be completely destroyed before disposal.[123]

---

[116] Covington and Musselman, "Privacy and Data Security Developments," at 536.
[117] See National Conference of State Legislatures, Consumer Report Security Freeze State Laws, http://www.ncsl.org/research/financial-services-and-commerce/consumer-report-security-freeze-state-statutes.aspx
[118] *Id.*
[119] See Covington and Musselman, "Privacy and Data Security Developments," at 540 (listing thirty-three states with Social Security number protection laws); *see also* Social Security protection laws in Delaware (Del. Code Ann. tit. 6 §§ 12B–101 *et seq.*); District of Columbia (D.C. Code §§ 28–3851 *et seq.*); Florida (Fla. Stat. § 507.171), Georgia (Ga Code. Ann. § 10-1-393.8); Idaho (Idaho Code. Ann. §§ 28-51-104 *et seq.*); Iowa (Iowa Code § 715C.1), Mississippi (Miss. Code Ann. § 75-24-29); Montana (Mont. Code Ann. § 30-14-1701 *et seq.*); Nevada (Nev. Rev. Stat. §§ 603A.010 *et seq.*); New Hampshire (N.H. Rev. Stat. Ann. §§ 359-C:1 *et seq.*); North Dakota (N.D. Cent. Code §§ 51-30-01 *et seq.*); Oklahoma (Okla Stat. tit. 24, §§ 161 *et seq.*); Tennessee (Tenn. Code. Ann. § 47-18-2110); Washington (Wash. Rev. Code §§ 19.255.010 *et seq.*); West Virginia (W. Va. Code §§ 46A-2A-101 *et seq.*); and Wyoming (Wyo. Stat. Ann. §§ 40-12-501 *et seq.*).
[120] See Covington and Musselman, "Consumer Report Security Freeze Law."
[121] *Id.*
[122] See Covington and Musselman, "Consumer Report Security Freeze Law," at 541–42 (reporting that twenty-two states have enacted safe disposal laws); *see also* Raymond Nimmer and Holly Towle, "Disposal of Data," *Law of Elec. Com. Trans.* § 16.12 n. 30 (Apr. 2013) (reporting an additional thirteen states). Hawaii has also enacted a law requiring the secure disposal of personal information. Haw. Rev. Stat. § 487R-2 (2015).
[123] Covington and Musselman, "Consumer Report Security Freeze Law," at 542; Andrew B. Serwin, "Data Security and Destruction," *Information Security & Privacy: A Guide to Fed & State Law & Compliance* § 24:18 (May 2013).

Encryption Statutes

At present, only Nevada, Massachusetts, and Washington have encryption statutes on their books.[124] These statutes generally require protection of customer data by encrypting customer information on portable devices and any time the information is transmitted electronically.[125] Maryland has not required the encryption of personal information, but provides limited legal immunity for companies that suffer a data breach of encrypted data.[126] Regulations under the Massachusetts statute went into effect in March 2010, requiring employee training, regular security audits, and a Comprehensive Written Information Security Program (WISP) for all records containing personal information.[127] In December 2010, FINRA modified Rule 8210, which now mandates encryption for all information provided to it on a portable media device.[128]

IX. DEVELOPING CUSTOMER DATA SECURITY PROCESSES

Compliance officers need to work closely with their colleagues to develop safeguarding procedures. When it comes to certain compliance issues, the compliance officer is not always the subject matter expert. The trader, portfolio manager, specialist, or in this case, the information security analyst, typically has a greater understanding of the complexities and nuances of his or her specialty. Still, it is the role of the compliance officer to focus on the big picture to keep the safeguarding process on track. If an officer is not careful, the focus of safeguarding efforts may turn into an exercise in the implementation of security technologies instead of the realization of the firm's true goal.

The proposed Reg S-P amendments, banking guidelines, the FTC's recommendations, and the examples of real-life data breaches should give compliance officers the tools needed to develop customized safeguarding policies and procedures for their firms. Additional resources are available online. These resources include information security checklists, worksheets, risk assessment matrices, sample contract provisions and draft policies, and procedures for safeguarding customer information in a financial services environment.[129]

---

[124] *See* Ben Worthen, "New Data Privacy Laws Set for Firms," *The Wall Street Journal* (Oct. 16, 2008), http://www.wsj.com/articles/SB122411532152538495. Washington enacted its encryption law in 2010. Wash. Rev. Code § 19.255 (2013); *see also* Richard Fisher, "Other State Data Security Laws Relating to Personal Information," *The Law of Financial Privacy*, § 5.06[7], (Feb. 2013) (discussing encryption statutes in Nevada and Massachusetts as noteworthy).

[125] Worthen, "New Data Privacy Laws Set for Firms;" *see also* David Navetta, "Legally Mandated Encryption," InfoSECCompliance.com (Nov. 15, 2008), http://www.infolawgroup.com/2008/11/articles/encryption/ legally-mandated-encryption/

[126] *See* Michael Greenberger, "The Maryland Personal Information Protection Act: Strengthening Maryland's Security Breach Notification Law," 42 *U. Balt.* L.F. 129, 149–50 (2012) ("[T]o encourage encryption, [Md. Code Ann., Com. Law §§ 14-3501–3508] provides a safe harbor for data that has been encrypted...Any information that is specifically protected in this manner is exempt from the statute's definition of personal information.").

[127] *See* Keith Vance, "Keeping Pace with Data Encryption Laws," eSecurity-Planet.com (June 11, 2010), www.esecurityplanet.com/trends/article.php/3887111/Keeping-Pace-with-Data-Encryption-Laws.htm; 201 Mass. Code Regs. 17.00 (2010).

[128] FINRA, SEC Approves Amendments to FINRA Rule 8210

[129] *See* BankersOnline, Banker Tools, http://www.bankersonline.com/tools/tools.html# Informationsecurity

X. CUSTOMER SELF-PROTECTION OF DATA

Even the best safeguarding procedures cannot prevent all instances of identity theft and cybercrime because many vulnerabilities begin with the customer. Some identity thieves use keystroke-logging software to capture usernames and passwords, or "phish" for sensitive information via phony emails purporting to originate from a legitimate financial institution. Sixty-one percent of all client-side attacks observed in 2012 used malicious PDFs to attack Adobe Acrobat users.[130] Even "dumpster-diving" for discarded financial statements or old credit cards can pose a real security threat. To mitigate these risks, FINRA has published a simple checklist that describes a variety of simple actions customers can take to protect themselves against unauthorized account access and identity theft.[131] It may be useful for firms to advise their customers of simple self-protection techniques:

- ***Protect Login Information***. Passwords and PIN codes should never be disclosed to anyone, and passwords should be changed regularly. "Brute-force" crackers guess passwords by cycling through every possible permutation of letters, so it is generally recommended that passwords contain at least eight characters and be composed of both letters and symbols. However, the difficulty of remembering complicated passwords may lead to users writing them down, a serious security risk in itself. To compensate, customers may want to consider using a "pass phrase" instead. A five or six word pass phrase is as difficult to crack as a completely random nine-letter password,[132] but the former is much easier for most people to remember than the latter. Additionally, substituting symbols for letters further increases the effectiveness of a pass phrase (for instance, substituting 0 for O and $ for S would result in Microsoft becoming Micr0$0ft).
- ***Maintain Computer Security.*** Customers should invest in antivirus, antispam, and spyware detection software, and ensure that it is regularly updated and running. The user's operating system should be configured to automatically download and install updates. Firewalls should never be disabled unless absolutely necessary. Laptops and mobile phones should use encryption software that provides remote access and data wipe capabilities. Employees should never use public computers to access a brokerage account, as their security cannot be guaranteed. If using a nonsecure machine is necessary, employees should ensure that the "history," "cookies," and "temporary internet files" or "cache" are deleted after every session. The browser's help function can assist in instructing customers and employees how to delete that data.
- ***Maintain Internet Vigilance.*** Employees should never download or install suspicious looking files and ensure that websites handling sensitive data are transmitting over a secure connection, denoted by a URL beginning with https:// rather than the normal http://. Employees should log off completely after every session. Everyone

---

[130] Trustwave.com, *2013 Global Security Report Preview.*
[131] FINRA, Keeping Your Account Secure: Tips for Protecting Your Financial Information, http://www.finra.org/file/keeping-your-account-secure-tips-protecting-your-financial-information-pdf-english
[132] Jesper Johansson, *The Great Debates: Pass Phrases vs. Passwords. Part 3 of 3*, Microsoft.com (Dec. 1, 2004), http://technet.microsoft.com/library/cc512624

should ensure that browsers do not save passwords and not allow websites to "keep me logged in" or "save my login information." Also be wary of using public Wi-Fi "hotspots" that may not be secure.
- **Proactively Monitor Credit.** Customers should read account statements regularly to check for unusual activity. Americans can check their credit for free every 12 months by contacting the Annual Credit Report Request Service at www.AnnualCreditReport.com.

XI. SAFEGUARDING EXAMINATIONS

The following list offers possible requests for information and questions that firms may receive from the SEC or FINRA in the course of a Safeguards Rule exam:

- A copy of the firm's written policies and procedures on safeguarding customer information;
- A copy of all customer complaints dealing with safeguarding customer information or fraud;
- A copy of any risk assessment, audit, third-party tests, and other reviews dealing with safeguarding customer information or fraud;
- A copy of the firm's privacy policy and customer agreements, if they describe how the firm will safeguard customer information;
- A copy of informational materials (for example, emails, statement stuffers) that inform customers about the risks of certain practices, including online activity, online security practices, and internet fraud;
- A copy of each report that the firm uses to monitor for identity theft, wire fraud, or unauthorized account activity;
- A copy of the relevant provision from each contract that the firm has with third-party service providers to whom the firm has provided nonpublic customer information;
- A copy of the due diligence report for each of the third-party service providers to whom the firm has provided nonpublic customer information;
- A copy of all documentation that shows the last time the firm reviewed and, if necessary, updated its information security practices and procedures;
- A copy of employee training materials on safeguarding customer information and evidence that relevant employees have received training;
- A statement identifying all known instances of security breaches at the firm;
- A statement identifying the person who oversees the firm's Safeguards Rule compliance and third-party service provider arrangements to ensure compliance with the firm's policies;
- A statement that describes whether supervisors monitor phone calls for compliance with security and privacy laws and policies;
- A statement that describes the controls used to prevent employees from providing information to unauthorized individuals; and
- A statement that describes the access controls to the physical locations containing customer information and to the firm's customer website.

The above suggestions are by no means comprehensive. Like the other information provided, these ideas should be helpful in developing the necessary policies and procedures.

For more information, visit the following pages on FINRA's website:

- Customer Information Protection (www.finra.org/customer protection);
- Firm Identity Protection (www.finra.org/customerprotection/firmid); and
- Firm Checklist for Compromised Accounts (www.finra.org/industry/firm-checklist-compromised-accounts).

XII. "REPORT ON CYBERSECURITY PRACTICES"

In February 2015, FINRA published a "Report on Cybersecurity Practices." Although the report does not establish any new rules relating to cybersecurity, it does set forth FINRA's expectation that firms adopt a risk management-based approach to cybersecurity. FINRA emphasized that firms tailor their program to their particular circumstances and there is no on-size-fits-all approach to cybersecurity. The report is helpful in that it addresses the main cybersecurity issues faced by broker-dealers as well as recommendations for mitigating the risks/adverse effects of each.

An important component of the report is that it defines cybersecurity. Cybersecurity is "the protection of investor and firm information from compromise through the use—in whole or in part—of electronic digital media, (e.g. computers, mobile devices or Internet protocol-based telephony systems). 'Compromise' refers to a loss of data confidentiality, integrity, or availability." As such, cybersecurity is much broader in scope than firm obligations under the Safeguards Rule and red flags rule. Nevertheless, the Cybersecurity Report highlights principles and effective practices that firms can use in developing compliance programs for Reg S-P and Reg S-ID.

The FINRA report is divided into eight primary segments of concern:

- Governance and Risk Management for Cybersecurity;
- Cybersecurity Risk Assessment;
- Technical Controls;
- Incident Response Planning;
- Vendor Management;
- Staff Training;
- Cyber Intelligence and Information Sharing; and
- Cyber Insurance.

The report reviews each of these topics in detail and provides recommendations for mitigating the risks/adverse effects of such issue. The report also provides a number of real-life case study analyses in order to highlight the respective subject cybersecurity concerns. Moreover, the report includes the very useful appendices, including a summary of cybersecurity principles and effective practices, a thorough description of the

U.S. government National Institute of Standards and Technology (NIST) cybersecurity framework, and an examination of the use of encryption technology.

The "Report on Cybersecurity Practices" is an important resource for compliance officers developing the Safeguards Rule and the Reg S-ID compliance programs. FINRA cautioned that failure to address cybersecurity risks adequately "increases regulatory risks for firms, for example under Rule 30 of SEC Regulation S-P or SEC Regulation S-ID (the 'Red Flags Rule')."

XIII. CONCLUSION

Safeguarding customer information has become an increasingly important focus of the SEC and of the states as the SEC's proposed amendments to the Reg S-P Safeguards Rule, the SEC's enforcement actions in this area, and the rash of new state safeguarding laws show. This chapter should assist firms to learn about this burgeoning area of responsibility and help in the development of more effective compliance programs.

APPENDIX I. APPENDIX A TO 17 CFR 248 SUBPART A
Version 1: Model Form With No Opt-Out

Rev. [insert date]

FACTS	**WHAT DOES [NAME OF FINANCIAL INSTITUTION] DO WITH YOUR PERSONAL INFORMATION?**
Why?	Financial companies choose how they share your personal information. Federal law gives consumers the right to limit some but not all sharing. Federal law also requires us to tell you how we collect, share, and protect your personal information. Please read this notice carefully to understand what we do.
What?	The types of personal information we collect and share depend on the product or service you have with us. This information can include: ■ Social Security number and [income] ■ [account balances] and [payment history] ■ [credit history] and [credit scores] When you are *no longer* our customer, we continue to share your information as described in this notice.
How?	All financial companies need to share customers' personal information to run their everyday business. In the section below, we list the reasons financial companies can share their customers' personal information; the reasons [name of financial institution] chooses to share; and whether you can limit this sharing.

Reasons we can share your personal information	Does [name of financial institution] share?	Can you limit this sharing?
For our everyday business purposes— such as to process your transactions, maintain your account(s), respond to court orders and legal investigations, or report to credit bureaus		
For our marketing purposes— to offer our products and services to you		
For joint marketing with other financial companies		
For our affiliates' everyday business purposes— information about your transactions and experiences		
For our affiliates' everyday business purposes— information about your creditworthiness		
For our affiliates to market to you		
For nonaffiliates to market to you		

Questions?	Call [phone number] or go to [website]

APPENDIX I. APPENDIX A TO 17 CFR 248 SUBPART A
Version 1: Model Form With No Opt-Out— *Cont'd*

Page 2

Who we are	
Who is providing this notice?	[insert]

What we do	
How does [name of financial institution] protect my personal information?	To protect your personal information from unauthorized access and use, we use security measures that comply with federal law. These measures include computer safeguards and secured files and buildings. [insert]
How does [name of financial institution] collect my personal information?	We collect your personal information, for example, when you ■ [open an account] or [deposit money] ■ [pay your bills] or [apply for a loan] ■ [use your credit or debit card] [We also collect your personal information from other companies.] OR [We also collect your personal information from others, such as credit bureaus, affiliates, or other companies.]
Why can't I limit all sharing?	Federal law gives you the right to limit only ■ sharing for affiliates' everyday business purposes—information about your creditworthiness ■ affiliates from using your information to market to you ■ sharing for nonaffiliates to market to you State laws and individual companies may give you additional rights to limit sharing. [See below for more on your rights under state law.]

Definitions	
Affiliates	Companies related by common ownership or control. They can be financial and nonfinancial companies. ■ *[affiliate information]*
Nonaffiliates	Companies not related by common ownership or control. They can be financial and nonfinancial companies. ■ *[nonaffiliate information]*
Joint marketing	A formal agreement between nonaffiliated financial companies that together market financial products or services to you. ■ *[joint marketing information]*

Other important information
[insert other important information]

APPENDIX I. APPENDIX A TO 17 CFR 248 SUBPART A
Version 2: Model Form with Opt-Out by Telephone and/or Online

Rev. [insert date]

FACTS	WHAT DOES [NAME OF FINANCIAL INSTITUTION] DO WITH YOUR PERSONAL INFORMATION?
Why?	Financial companies choose how they share your personal information. Federal law gives consumers the right to limit some but not all sharing. Federal law also requires us to tell you how we collect, share, and protect your personal information. Please read this notice carefully to understand what we do.
What?	The types of personal information we collect and share depend on the product or service you have with us. This information can include: ■ Social Security number and [income] ■ [account balances] and [payment history] ■ [credit history] and [credit scores]
How?	All financial companies need to share customers' personal information to run their everyday business. In the section below, we list the reasons financial companies can share their customers' personal information; the reasons [name of financial institution] chooses to share; and whether you can limit this sharing.

Reasons we can share your personal information	Does [name of financial institution] share?	Can you limit this sharing?
For our everyday business purposes— such as to process your transactions, maintain your account(s), respond to court orders and legal investigations, or report to credit bureaus		
For our marketing purposes— to offer our products and services to you		
For joint marketing with other financial companies		
For our affiliates' everyday business purposes— information about your transactions and experiences		
For our affiliates' everyday business purposes— information about your creditworthiness		
For our affiliates to market to you		
For nonaffiliates to market to you		

To limit our sharing	■ Call [phone number]—our menu will prompt you through your choice(s) or ■ Visit us online: [website] **Please note:** If you are a *new* customer, we can begin sharing your information [30] days from the date we sent this notice. When you are *no longer* our customer, we continue to share your information as described in this notice. However, you can contact us at any time to limit our sharing.
Questions?	Call [phone number] or go to [website]

PAGE 1 OF 2

APPENDIX I. APPENDIX A TO 17 CFR 248 SUBPART A

Version 2: Model Form with Opt-Out by Telephone and/or Online— *Cont'd*

Page 2

Who we are	
Who is providing this notice?	[insert]

What we do	
How does [name of financial institution] protect my personal information?	To protect your personal information from unauthorized access and use, we use security measures that comply with federal law. These measures include computer safeguards and secured files and buildings. [insert]
How does [name of financial institution] collect my personal information?	We collect your personal information, for example, when you ■ [open an account] or [deposit money] ■ [pay your bills] or [apply for a loan] ■ [use your credit or debit card] [We also collect your personal information from other companies.] **OR** [We also collect your personal information from others, such as credit bureaus, affiliates, or other companies.]
Why can't I limit all sharing?	Federal law gives you the right to limit only ■ sharing for affiliates' everyday business purposes—information about your creditworthiness ■ affiliates from using your information to market to you ■ sharing for nonaffiliates to market to you State laws and individual companies may give you additional rights to limit sharing. [See below for more on your rights under state law.]
What happens when I limit sharing for an account I hold jointly with someone else?	[Your choices will apply to everyone on your account.] **OR** [Your choices will apply to everyone on your account—unless you tell us otherwise.]

Definitions	
Affiliates	Companies related by common ownership or control. They can be financial and nonfinancial companies. ■ *[affiliate information]*
Nonaffiliates	Companies not related by common ownership or control. They can be financial and nonfinancial companies. ■ *[nonaffiliate information]*
Joint marketing	A formal agreement between nonaffiliated financial companies that together market financial products or services to you. ■ *[joint marketing information]*

Other important information	
[insert other important information]	

APPENDIX I. APPENDIX A TO 17 CFR 248 SUBPART A
Version 3: Model Form with Mail-In Opt-Out Form

Rev. [insert date]

FACTS	**WHAT DOES [NAME OF FINANCIAL INSTITUTION] DO WITH YOUR PERSONAL INFORMATION?**
Why?	Financial companies choose how they share your personal information. Federal law gives consumers the right to limit some but not all sharing. Federal law also requires us to tell you how we collect, share, and protect your personal information. Please read this notice carefully to understand what we do.
What?	The types of personal information we collect and share depend on the product or service you have with us. This information can include: ■ Social Security number and [income] ■ [account balances] and [payment history] ■ [credit history] and [credit scores]
How?	All financial companies need to share customers' personal information to run their everyday business. In the section below, we list the reasons financial companies can share their customers' personal information; the reasons [name of financial institution] chooses to share; and whether you can limit this sharing.

Reasons we can share your personal information	Does [name of financial institution] share?	Can you limit this sharing?
For our everyday business purposes— such as to process your transactions, maintain your account(s), respond to court orders and legal investigations, or report to credit bureaus		
For our marketing purposes— to offer our products and services to you		
For joint marketing with other financial companies		
For our affiliates' everyday business purposes— information about your transactions and experiences		
For our affiliates' everyday business purposes— information about your creditworthiness		
For our affiliates to market to you		
For nonaffiliates to market to you		

To limit our sharing	■ Call [phone number]—our menu will prompt you through your choice(s) ■ Visit us online: [website] or ■ Mail the form below **Please note:** If you are a *new* customer, we can begin sharing your information [30] days from the date we sent this notice. When you are *no longer* our customer, we continue to share your information as described in this notice. However, you can contact us at any time to limit our sharing.
Questions?	Call [phone number] or go to [website]

✂--

Mail-in Form

Leave Blank OR [If you have a joint account, your choice(s) will apply to everyone on your account unless you mark below. ☐ Apply my choices only to me]	Mark any/all you want to limit: ☐ Do not share information about my creditworthiness with your affiliates for their everyday business purposes. ☐ Do not allow your affiliates to use my personal information to market to me. ☐ Do not share my personal information with nonaffiliates to market their products and services to me.	
	Name	**Mail to:**
	Address	[Name of Financial Institution] [Address1] [Address2] [City], [ST] [ZIP]
	City, State, Zip	
	[Account #]	

PAGE 1 OF 2

APPENDIX I. APPENDIX A TO 17 CFR 248 SUBPART A
Version 3: Model Form with Mail-In Opt-Out Form— *Cont'd*

Page 2

Who we are	
Who is providing this notice?	[insert]

What we do	
How does [name of financial institution] protect my personal information?	To protect your personal information from unauthorized access and use, we use security measures that comply with federal law. These measures include computer safeguards and secured files and buildings. [insert]
How does [name of financial institution] collect my personal information?	We collect your personal information, for example, when you ■ [open an account] or [deposit money] ■ [pay your bills] or [apply for a loan] ■ [use your credit or debit card] [We also collect your personal information from other companies.] OR [We also collect your personal information from others, such as credit bureaus, affiliates, or other companies.]
Why can't I limit all sharing?	Federal law gives you the right to limit only ■ sharing for affiliates' everyday business purposes—information about your creditworthiness ■ affiliates from using your information to market to you ■ sharing for nonaffiliates to market to you State laws and individual companies may give you additional rights to limit sharing. [See below for more on your rights under state law.]
What happens when I limit sharing for an account I hold jointly with someone else?	[Your choices will apply to everyone on your account.] OR [Your choices will apply to everyone on your account—unless you tell us otherwise.]

Definitions	
Affiliates	Companies related by common ownership or control. They can be financial and nonfinancial companies. ■ *[affiliate information]*
Nonaffiliates	Companies not related by common ownership or control. They can be financial and nonfinancial companies. ■ *[nonaffiliate information]*
Joint marketing	A formal agreement between nonaffiliated financial companies that together market financial products or services to you. ■ *[joint marketing information]*

Other important information	
[insert other important information]	

APPENDIX I. APPENDIX A TO 17 CFR 248 SUBPART A

Version 4. Optional Mail-in Form

Mail-in Form

Leave Blank OR [If you have a joint account, your choice(s) will apply to everyone on your account unless you mark below. ❑ Apply my choices only to me]	Mark any/all you want to limit: ❑ Do not share information about my creditworthiness with your affiliates for their everyday business purposes. ❑ Do not allow your affiliates to use my personal information to market to me. ❑ Do not share my personal information with nonaffiliates to market their products and services to me.
	Name
	Address
	City, State, Zip
	[Account #]

Mail To: [Name of Financial Institution], [Address1]
[Address2], [City], [ST] [ZIP]

PAGE 1 OF 1

NOTE: These forms can be downloaded from the Electronic Code of Federal Regulations (eCFR): http://www.ecfr.gov/cgi-bin/text-idx?SID=7f132c1a6b219f6f66356272f60b3067&mc=true&node=ap17.4.248_131_6248_1100.a&rgn=div9

APPENDIX II. APPENDIX TO 17 CFR 248 SUBPART B – MODEL FORMS
A-1 Model Form for Initial Opt Out Notice (Single-Affiliate Notice)

- [Name of Affiliate] is providing this notice.

- [Optional: Federal law gives you the right to limit some but not all marketing from our affiliates. Federal law also requires us to give you this notice to tell you about your choice to limit marketing from our affiliates.]

- You may limit our affiliates in the [ABC] group of companies, such as our [investment adviser, broker, transfer agent, and investment company] affiliates, from marketing their products or services to you based on your personal information that we collect and share with them. This information includes your [income], your [account history with us], and your [credit score].

- Your choice to limit marketing offers from our affiliates will apply [until you tell us to change your choice]/[for x years from when you tell us your choice]/[for at least 5 years from when you tell us your choice]. [Include if the opt out period expires.] Once that period expires, you will receive a renewal notice that will allow you to continue to limit marketing offers from our affiliates for [another x years]/[at least another 5 years].

- [Include, if applicable, in a subsequent notice, including an annual notice, for consumers who may have previously opted out.] If you have already made a choice to limit marketing offers from our affiliates, you do not need to act again until you receive the renewal notice.

To limit marketing offers, contact us [include all that apply]:

- **By telephone:** 1-877-###-####
- **On the Web:** www.—-.com
- **By mail:** check the box and complete the form below, and send the form to:

    [Company name]

    [Company address]

☐ Do not allow your affiliates to use my personal information to market to me.

APPENDIX II. APPENDIX TO 17 CFR 248 SUBPART B – MODEL FORMS — *Cont'd*

A-2 - Model Form for Initial Opt Out Notice (Joint Notice)—[Your Choice to Limit Marketing]/ [Marketing Opt Out]

- The [ABC group of companies] is providing this notice.

- [Optional: Federal law gives you the right to limit some but not all marketing from the [ABC] companies. Federal law also requires us to give you this notice to tell you about your choice to limit marketing from the [ABC] companies.]

- You may limit the [ABC] companies, such as the [ABC investment companies, investment advisers, transfer agents, and broker-dealers] affiliates, from marketing their products or services to you based on your personal information that they receive from other [ABC] companies. This information includes your [income], your [account history], and your [credit score].

- Your choice to limit marketing offers from the [ABC] companies will apply [until you tell us to change your choice]/[for x years from when you tell us your choice]/[for at least 5 years from when you tell us your choice]. [Include if the opt out period expires.] Once that period expires, you will receive a renewal notice that will allow you to continue to limit marketing offers from the [ABC] companies for [another x years]/[at least another 5 years].

- [Include, if applicable, in a subsequent notice, including an annual notice, for consumers who may have previously opted out.] If you have already made a choice to limit marketing offers from the [ABC] companies, you do not need to act again until you receive the renewal notice.

To limit marketing offers, contact us [include all that apply]:

- **By telephone:** 1-877-###-####
- **On the Web:** www.—-.com
- **By mail:** check the box and complete the form below, and send the form to:

    [Company name]

    [Company address]

    ☐ Do not allow any company [in the ABC group of companies to use my personal information to market to me.

© MODERN COMPLIANCE 2015

APPENDIX II. APPENDIX TO 17 CFR 248 SUBPART B – MODEL FORMS — *Cont'd*
A-3 - Model Form for Renewal Notice (Single-Affiliate Notice)— [Renewing Your Choice to Limit Marketing]/[Renewing Your Marketing Opt Out]

[Name of Affiliate] is providing this notice.

- [Optional: Federal law gives you the right to limit some but not all marketing from our affiliates. Federal law also requires us to give you this notice to tell you about your choice to limit marketing from our affiliates.]

- You previously chose to limit our affiliates in the [ABC] group of companies, such as our [investment adviser, investment company, transfer agent, and broker-dealer] affiliates, from marketing their products or services to you based on your personal information that we share with them. This information includes your [income], your [account history with us], and your [credit score].

- Your choice has expired or is about to expire.

To renew your choice to limit marketing for [x] more years, contact us [include all that apply]:

- **By telephone:** 1-877-###-####
- **On the Web:** www.—.com
- **By mail:** check the box and complete the form below, and send the form to:

    [Company name]

    [Company address]

☐ Renew my choice to limit marketing for [x] more years.

APPENDIX II. APPENDIX TO 17 CFR 248 SUBPART B – MODEL FORMS — Cont'd

A-2 - Model Form for Initial Opt Out Notice (Joint Notice)—[Your Choice to Limit Marketing]/[Marketing Opt Out]

- The [ABC group of companies] is providing this notice.

- [Optional: Federal law gives you the right to limit some but not all marketing from the [ABC] companies. Federal law also requires us to give you this notice to tell you about your choice to limit marketing from the [ABC] companies.]

- You previously chose to limit the [ABC] companies, such as the [ABC investment adviser, investment company, transfer agent, and broker-dealer] affiliates, from marketing their products or services to you based on your personal information that they receive from other ABC companies. This information includes your [income], your [account history], and your [credit score].

- Your choice has expired or is about to expire.

To renew your choice to limit marketing for [x] more years, contact us [include all that apply]:

- **By telephone:** 1-877-###-####
- **On the Web:** www.—-.com
- **By mail:** check the box and complete the form below, and send the form to:

    [Company name]

    [Company address]

    ☐ Renew my choice to limit marketing for [x] more years.

APPENDIX II. APPENDIX TO 17 CFR 248 SUBPART B – MODEL FORMS — *Cont'd*

A-5 - Model Form for Voluntary "No Marketing" Notice—Your Choice to Stop Marketing

- [Name of Affiliate] is providing this notice.

- You may choose to stop all marketing from us and our affiliates.

- [Your choice to stop marketing from us and our affiliates will apply until you tell us to change your choice.]

To stop all marketing, contact us [include all that apply]:

- **By telephone:** 1-877-###-####
- **On the Web:** www.—-.com
- **By mail:** check the box and complete the form below, and send the form to:

    [Company name]

    [Company address]

☐ Do not send me marketing material.

NOTE: These forms can be downloaded from the Electronic Code of Federal Regulations (eCFR): http://www.ecfr.gov/cgi-bin/text-idx?SID=7f132c1a6b219f6f66356272f60b3067&mc=true&node=ap17.4.248_131_6248_1100.a&rgn=div9

ABOUT THE AUTHORS

David E. Rosedahl is of counsel; Business Litigation Section, Financial Markets Group of the law firm of Briggs and Morgan in Minneapolis, Minnesota. Mr. Rosedahl has more than 30 years of experience in the financial markets industry, specifically in the securities regulatory area. His unique background as a former chief regulatory officer of the Pacific Exchange; managing director and general counsel for Piper Jaffray Companies; and associate general counsel and corporate secretary for the Securities Industry Association allows him to provide a balanced perspective when advising clients concerning investment and financial services issues, regulatory investigations, enforcement actions, remedial work and general inquiries.

In addition to his experience as a chief regulatory officer of a national securities exchange, Mr. Rosedahl maintains ongoing participation in securities industry activities today. He is active in the National Society of Compliance Professionals (NSCP) and has served on policy advisory committees for the New York Stock Exchange (NYSE), the National Association of Securities Dealers (NASD) (now FINRA) and the Minnesota Commerce Department. His experience also includes leadership positions with SROs, such as serving as chair of the International Intermarket Surveillance Group.

Keith Alden Loveland is a nationally recognized author, attorney, consultant, and teacher within the fields of investments, securities and securities offerings, ethical versus fraudulent practices regarding investments and securities, and fiduciary matters. He has been qualified as an expert regarding the above matters in state and federal courts, and in American Arbitration Association and NASD/FINRA arbitrations, and also has served as an arbitrator and qualified neutral mediator.

Mr. Loveland served as a subject matter expert to the New York Stock Exchange Qualification Committee from 1983 to 2001 as to all matters related to business entity formation and offerings of investments, among other matters. He currently serves as a subject matter expert to the North American Securities Administrators' Association as to the requirements necessary for offerors of investments and securities under state law, and fraudulent practices related thereto, among other matters. Mr. Loveland has been a teacher for many years. Among other engagements, he was adjunct professor, William Mitchell College of Law, from 1978 to 1987. He is currently adjunct faculty for The Center for Fiduciary Studies, teaching the Prudent Practices for Investment Stewards course. Mr. Loveland is a member of the American Bar Association, Business Law Section, Committee on Federal Regulation of Securities, and Committee on State Regulation of Securities. He has been a member of the Financial Planning Association since 1983, serving on its Board of Directors from 2011 to 2013. He was a recipient of their Heart of Financial Planning Award in 2010.

Andrew C. Small is general counsel for Craig-Hallum Capital Group. Previously, he served in a variety of legal, compliance and risk roles, including most recently as chief legal and risk officer, of Scottrade Financial Services, Inc., the parent of Scottrade, a leading online brokerage. Prior to joining Scottrade in August 2003, Mr. Small was vice president and compliance counsel at A.G. Edwards & Sons, Inc. where he was responsible for legal, regulatory, and compliance issues relating to e-commerce, technology, operations and antimoney laundering. He formerly served as an enforcement attorney with both FINRA and the Chicago Board Options Exchange. He is currently a member of the Board of Trustees of the Securities Industry Institute, the premier executive development program for financial industry professionals, hosted by SIFMA and The Wharton School. Mr. Small has previously served the securities industry in a variety of capacities, including as a member of the Securities Industry/Regulatory Council on Continuing Education, FINRA's e-Brokerage Committee, FINRA's District Committee for District 4 and as a board member for the National Society of Compliance Professionals. Mr. Small is a graduate of Michigan State University's James Madison School and received his law degree from DePaul University School of Law.

CHAPTER 18

Cybersecurity

By Krista Zipfel, *Advisor Solutions Group, Inc.*
Craig Watanabe, *Core Compliance & Legal Services, Inc.*

I. INTRODUCTION

This is a "how to" chapter on cybersecurity for compliance professionals. There is ample guidance on what to do but little on how to do it. Whenever possible this chapter will eschew technical jargon and translate cybersecurity into terms familiar to compliance professionals: policies and procedures. Moreover, at the end of this chapter are templates and a checklist to aid in implementing the procedures. Cybersecurity is a daunting subject, but this chapter provides a good start on the knowledge and tools needed to implement a robust cybersecurity program.

The centerpiece of this chapter is an annotated copy of the SEC's cybersecurity sweep exam letter that incorporates the National Institute of Standards and Technology (NIST) Cybersecurity Framework (identify, protect, detect, respond, recover) and applies it to the financial services industry. The sweep letter poses twenty-eight questions and this annotated letter includes twenty-eight answers so the reader has actionable guidance on how to create and implement a cybersecurity program.

Essential to designing a cybersecurity program is the prioritization of resources and risks. The top priority should be securing the data. To this end, the modules on data backup and data encryption are critical. Whether the data is in transit or at rest, backup and encryption are essential elements of a robust cybersecurity program. Even if perimeter defenses are breached, the data will still be secure if backed up and encrypted.

Cybersecurity touches upon human elements as well as technical elements, so user awareness training is essential. This chapter includes nine sample cybersecurity memos that can be tailored to a particular firm to aid in the training. Training topics include the safe use of email, websites, mobile devices, home computers, and public Wi-Fi, among others.

It is essential to understand and appreciate the vulnerability of information systems. This chapter includes a discussion on hiring outside consultants to perform vulnerability assessments and penetration testing. These are highly technical areas best left to IT security professionals, and the extremely high rate of success in penetration testing highlights the need for cyber insurance. This chapter discusses what these policies cover and considerations in purchasing cyber insurance.

> The best way to get something done is to begin!
> — Anonymous

If you are anxious to get started, you may skip the first four sections and get right to the annotated sweep letter. Determine with whom you may need to collaborate and start going through the items one-by-one until you have developed your cybersecurity program. The authors have provided their contact information in their biographies and welcome any comments or questions.

The fastest growing threats to the financial services industry are cyber espionage, cybercrime and cyber terrorism.[1] Thus, cybersecurity is a focus area for regulators and needs to be a priority for financial services firms. This chapter provides a practical guide for compliance officers to implement the NIST Cybersecurity Framework[2] (identify, protect, detect, respond, recover) with references to various resources, such as sample policies and procedures covering perimeter defenses, interior defenses and assessments as well as user awareness training.

II. THE GROWING CYBER THREAT

Cyberattacks in the financial services industry are on the rise, and broker-dealers, registered investment advisers, investment companies, and private funds need to be aware of the risks to their firms. The threat is spreading from large institutions to smaller firms as increasingly sophisticated cybercriminals seek softer targets. According to the Symantec 2014 Internet Security Report,[3] small businesses were the victim in 30 percent of targeted attacks in 2013. Symantec dubbed 2013 the year of the "Mega-breach," with eight breaches that exposed more than 10 million identities, including the headline breaches of Target and Neiman Marcus. However, cybersecurity officials in firms of all sizes need understand they are a potential target. Many small firms are in denial, believing "we are too small that hackers won't bother us." That assumption just isn't true. Cybercriminals are increasingly employing multipronged attacks against multiple targets, and small firms rarely have the robust defenses employed by large firms. Small and mid-size firms are the "low-hanging fruit" to cybercriminals.

In January 2014, BAE Systems, a cybersecurity contractor, reported to the press that one of its clients, a large hedge fund, was hacked in late 2013.[4] The hackers installed

---

[1] Michael Morell, Speech at the SIFMA Operations and Technology Conference (June 18, 2014).
[2] National Institute of Standards and Technology, "Framework for Improving Critical Infrastructure Cybersecurity," (Feb. 12, 2014), http://www.nist.gov/cyberframework/upload/cybersecurity-framework-021214-final.pdf
[3] Symantec, "Internet Security Threat Report," Volume 19 (Apr. 2014), http://www.symantec.com/content/en/us/enterprise/other_resources/b-istr_main_report_v19_21291018.en-us.pdf
[4] Eamon Javers, "Cybersecurity Firm Says Large Hedge Fund Attacked" (June 19, 2014), http://www.cnbc.com/id/101770396

malicious programs on the hedge fund's servers that crippled their high-frequency trading strategy and sent trade information to unknown offsite computers. It was reported that this incident cost the hedge fund "millions of dollars over just a few months' time." This incident was not an attempt to steal Social Security numbers or credit card information; and the target was not Goldman Sachs or Morgan Stanley. The attack was highly sophisticated and the perpetrators had the financial and market savvy to replicate intricate high-frequency trading strategies. This should be the proverbial wake-up call for anyone still in denial. Cybersecurity is a high priority for every financial services firm.

III. REGULATIONS, POLICIES, AND GUIDANCE

Since the 1990s the internet has transformed the world. New business models have emerged, and old business models have been automated to take advantage of the technology. However, the internet age has spawned a new form of criminal activity: cybercrime. This section explores the regulations, policies, and guidance underpinning cybersecurity in the financial services industry.

Federal Privacy Regulations

The Gramm-Leach-Bliley Act of 1999 (GLB): To comply with GLB the U. S. Securities and Exchange Commission (SEC) enacted Regulation S-P, Privacy of Consumer Financial Information[5] ("Reg S-P") in June 2000. Compliance professionals are reminded annually of their obligations under Reg S-P when their firms distribute their privacy notice to clients. However, Rule 30 of Reg S-P (the "Safeguard Rule") that implements the information security provisions of Title V, Subtitle A of GLB is far-reaching and stipulates:

> Every broker, dealer, and investment company, and every investment adviser registered with the commission must adopt written policies and procedures that address administrative, technical and physical safeguards for the protection of customer records and information. These written policies and procedures must be reasonably designed to:
>
> 1. Insure the security and confidentiality of customer records and information;
> 2. Protect against any anticipated threats or hazards to the security or integrity of customer records; and
> 3. Protect against any unauthorized access to or use of customer records or information that could result in substantial harm or inconvenience to any customer.

Although the word *cybersecurity* does not appear in Rule 30 of Reg S-P, this is clearly a cybersecurity mandate. Later in a discussion of case law we will highlight some cases brought under Rule 30 of Reg S-P for cybersecurity violations.

---

[5] SEC, Regulation S-P Privacy of Consumer Financial Information, 17 CFR Part 248, Rel. Nos. 34-42974, IC-24543, IA-1883 (June 22, 2000).

Federal Identity Theft Red Flags Regulations

Regulation S-ID,[6] Identity Theft Red Flags Rules ("Reg S-ID"), approved April 10, 2013, requires financial institutions that offer or maintain one or more covered accounts to develop and implement an ongoing written program to detect, prevent, and mitigate identity theft in connection with any covered accounts as defined in the rule. Identity theft is only one form of cybercrime, and Reg S-ID significantly overlaps with Reg S-P of Rule 30, No. 3: Protect against any unauthorized access to or use of customer records or information that could result in substantial harm or inconvenience to any customer.

Business Continuity and Disaster Recovery

Two critical aspects of cybersecurity are incident management and recovery. Cybersecurity, particularly responding to cyber terrorist attacks, has significant overlap with business continuity planning.

For SEC-Registered Investment Advisers. The SEC has not established specific requirements for firms to implement business continuity plans. However, in the releases adopting compliance rules for investment advisers (Rule 206(4)-7) and investment companies (Rule 38a-1)[7] the SEC stated its expectations that firms' policies and procedures, at a minimum, should include business continuity plans:

> An adviser's fiduciary obligation to its clients includes the obligation to take steps to protect the clients' interests from being placed at risk as a result of the adviser's inability to provide advisory services after, for example, a natural disaster or in the case of some smaller firms, the death of the owner or key personnel. The clients of an adviser that is engaged in the active management of their assets would ordinarily be placed at risk if the adviser ceased operations.

For Broker-Dealers. The Financial Industry Regulatory Authority (FINRA) broker-dealer self-regulatory organization has adopted Rule 4370—the emergency preparedness rule.[8] Rule 4370 requires broker-dealers to create and maintain business continuity plans appropriate to the scale and scope of their businesses, and to provide FINRA with emergency contact information.

State Data Security Breach Notification Laws. GLB preserves state authority to address privacy issues and allows states to enact legislation that is more stringent than GLB. As of the date of this writing, 47 states as well as the District of Columbia, Guam, Puerto Rico, and the U.S. Virgin Islands have adopted state data security/breach notification

---

[6] SEC, Adopting release of SEC Regulation S-ID (2003), http://www.sec.gov/rules/final/2013/34-69359.pdf
[7] Final Rule: *Compliance Programs of Investment Companies and Investment Advisers,* Rel. Nos. IA-2204; IC-26299; File No. S7-03-03.
[8] FINRA Rule 4370, Business Continuity Plans and Emergency Contact Information.

laws. The only states that have yet to do so are Alabama, New Mexico, and South Dakota.[9] Security breach laws typically stipulate:

- Who is subject to the law (e.g., businesses, data/ information brokers, government entities, etc.);
- Definitions of "personal information" (e.g., name combined with SSN; driver's license or state ID; account numbers; etc.);
- What constitutes a breach (e.g., unauthorized acquisition of data);
- Breach notification provisions (e.g., timing or method of notice, who must be notified); and
- Exemptions (e.g., for encrypted information).

Finally, Arkansas, California, Connecticut, Indiana, Maryland, Massachusetts, Nevada, Oregon, Rhode Island, and Utah have adopted data security laws that require companies to protect state residents' personal information from data breaches and identity theft.[10] Massachusetts state law in particular has some specific requirements including the use of 128-bit encryption to protect the personal information of the state's residents.[11] A detailed discussion of state law is beyond the scope of this chapter; however, compliance professionals need to be aware of the laws in the states where they conduct business.

SEC Policy and Guidance Regulation is shaped through speeches, guidance, and enforcement. These are important tools regulators use to establish guidance. The SEC conducted a Cybersecurity Roundtable[12] on March 26, 2014, to discuss cybersecurity issues and challenges it raises for market participants and public companies, and how they are addressing those concerns. Among Chair Mary Jo White's opening remarks was:[13]

Cyber threats are of extraordinary and long-term seriousness. They are first on the Division of Intelligence's list of global threats, even surpassing terrorism. And Jim Comey, director of the FBI, has testified that resources devoted to cyber-based threats are expected to eclipse resources devoted to terrorism. What emerges from this arresting view of the cybersecurity landscape is that the public and private sectors must be riveted, in lockstep, in addressing these threats. The president's 2013 Cybersecurity Executive Order and the Cybersecurity Framework issued in 2014 by the National Institute of Standards and Technology are reflective of the compelling need for stronger partnerships between the government and the private sector. The SEC's formal jurisdiction over cybersecurity is directly focused on the integrity of our market systems, customer data protection, and disclosure of material information. But it is incumbent on every government agency to be informed on the full range of cybersecurity risks and to actively engage to combat those risks in our respective spheres of responsibility."

---

[9] National Conference of State Legislatures, "State Security Breach Notification Laws" (Apr. 11, 2014), Security Breach Notification Laws.
[10] Id.
[11] Massachusetts Law, Part I, Title XV, Chapter 93H, General Laws: Chapter 93H, Section 1.
[12] SEC, Cybersecurity Roundtable webcast and additional information (Mar. 26, 2014).
[13] Mary Jo White, opening remarks at the Cybersecurity Roundtable (Mar. 26, 2014), http://www.sec.gov/News/PublicStmt/Detail/PublicStmt/1370541286468#.U77QtiLji70

On April 15, 2014, the SEC Office of Compliance Inspections and Examinations (OCIE) announced a Cybersecurity Initiative.[14] OCIE conducted a sweep exam of nearly fifty advisory firms of varying size and clients served to assess cybersecurity preparedness and obtain information about the industry's recent experiences with certain types of cyber threats. This will be covered in great detail later.

On February 3, 2015, OCIE released a summary of its examination sweep.[15] The risk alert merely provided a statistical summary of its observations of how broker-dealers and investment advisers address various legal, regulatory, and compliance issues related to cybersecurity but provided no practical guidance or suggestions for advisers. Of the firm's examined, 88 percent of the broker-dealers and 74 percent of the advisers reported having been subject to cyberattacks either directly or through one or more of their vendors; providing further evidence of the prevalence of the risk to firms. Advisers should take away from the sweep results that activities performed by a large percentage of the broker-dealers and advisers examined are likely best practices and may become the standard by which the SEC measures other examined firms. For example, 93 percent of the broker-dealers and 83 percent of the advisers examined had adopted written information security policies. Also, in most cases firms conducted inventories and catalogued or mapped their technology resources. More than 90 percent of both advisers and broker-dealers make use of encryption in some form. Broker-dealers and advisers showed a great disparity in conducting risk assessments of their vendors to identify cybersecurity threats. Thus, 84 percent of broker-dealers but only 53 percent of advisers required cybersecurity risk assessments of their vendors with access to their firm's networks. Advisers should do much more in the area of conducing due diligence of their vendors.

At nearly the same time that the SEC's issued its risk alert, FINRA issued its own findings based on examinations FINRA conducted in 2014.[16] Although FINRA regulates broker-dealers and not advisers, the cybersecurity risks and challenges are substantially the same for both types of firms such that the much more practical guidance provided in FINRA's report is beneficial to advisers, and they are encouraged to use this report as another tool in building their own cybersecurity program.

Finally, on April 28, 2015, the SEC's Division of Investment Management issued IM Guidance Update No. 2015-2 on cybersecurity.[17] The guidance suggests that advisers may wish to consider conducting various periodic assessments relating to cybersecurity; create a strategy that is designed to prevent, detect, and respond to cybersecurity threats; and implement that strategy through written policies and procedures and training. Once again, the SEC provided no practical suggestions on how advisers might go about performing any of the recommendations.

---

[14] SEC, OCIE Cybersecurity Initiative, National Exam Program Risk Alert, Volume IV, Issue 2 (Apr. 15, 2014), http://www.sec.gov/ocie/announcement/Cybersecurity+Risk+Alert++%2526+Appendix+-+4.15.14.pdf

[15] SEC, Cybersecurity Examination Sweep Summary, National Exam Program Risk Alert Volume IV, Issue 2, (Feb. 3, 2015), http://www.sec.gov/about/offices/ocie/cybersecurity-examination-sweep-summary.pdf

[16] The Financial Industry Regulatory Authority, Report on Cybersecurity Practices (Feb. 2015), http://www.finra.org/sites/default/files/p602363%20Report%20on%20Cybersecurity%20Practices_0.pdf

[17] SEC Division of Investment Management, IM Guidance Update No. 2015-2, Cybersecurity Guidance (Apr. 2015), http://www.sec.gov/investment/im-guidance-2015-02.pdf

IV. ENFORCEMENT CASES

CCO Liability: In the Matter of Marc A. Ellis

This is a case against Marc Ellis,[18] the former chief compliance officer (CCO) of GunnAllen Financial, Inc. for aiding, abetting and causing GunnAllen's violations of Regulation S-P, Rule 30. Notably, this was the first enforcement action in which an individual was charged solely with violating Reg S-P. CCO liability is also an issue in this case.

> Although GunnAllen maintained written supervisory procedures for safeguarding customer information, the y were inadequate and failed to instruct the firm's supervisors and registered representatives on how to comply with the Safeguard Rule. As CCO, Ellis was responsible for maintaining and reviewing the adequacy of GunnAllen's procedures for protecting customer information.

Theft of Laptop Computers and Passwords: Failure to Take Remedial Steps. Four separate incidents occurred between August 2006 and February 2008.

> The laptop computers belonging to three registered representatives and the computer password credentials belonging to a fourth were misappropriated from the firm. GunnAllen's senior managers, including Ellis and the firm's general counsel, learned of the thefts, but no single person or department directed or coordinated the firm's responses to the thefts. As a consequence, GunnAllen failed to assess what, if any, risks the thefts posed to its customers and failed to take follow-up and remedial steps recommended by its employees. A senior GunnAllen officer sent an email to the general counsel and Ellis stating that a letter should be sent to the affected customers, but no letter was ever sent.

The case was settled and Ellis agreed to pay a $15,000 penalty.

FINRA Letter of Acceptance, Waiver, and Consent: Lincoln Financial Advisors Corporation

Inadequate Controls for Accessing Web-Based Customer Information and Lack of Encryption Security on RR Laptops.[19] FINRA fined Lincoln Financial Securities, Inc. and Lincoln Financial Advisors Corporation a combined $600,000 for violating Rule 30 of Regulation S-P and NASD and FINRA rules.

Between 2002 and 2009, the firms allowed employees to access their web-based customer account system by using one of two shared user names and passwords. The firms had no

---

[18] SEC, *In the Matter of Marc A. Ellis,* Rel. No. 34-64220 (Apr. 11, 2011), https://www.sec.gov/litigation/admin/2011/34-64220.pdf

[19] FINRA, Letter of Acceptance, Waiver and Consent, No. 2009020074601, Lincoln Financial Advisors Corporation (Feb. 16, 2011), and FINRA Letter of Acceptance, Waiver and Consent, No. 200901872051, Lincoln Financial Securities (Feb. 16, 2011), http://www.finra.org/web/groups/industry/@ip/@enf/@ad/documents/industry/p122941.pdf

procedures to monitor the distribution of the common login credentials; were unable to determine which employees (current or former) had the login credentials; had no procedures to disable or change user names or passwords regularly or when associates left the firm; had not changed the shared credentials between 2002 and 2009; and had no means of determining who had accessed the web-based system or from where.

Additionally, the firms failed to require their registered representatives to use security software, such as antivirus, encryption, or firewall software, on their personal computers or to audit computers owned by their registered representatives and used in connection with firm business to determine whether they contained any kind of security application software.

Failure by the firms in both of these areas put customer information at risk of being obtained through any number of hacking or intrusion schemes. As a result, the firms were found to have violated Rule 30 of Regulation S-P, NASD Rules 3010 and 2110, and FINRA Rule 2010.

Failure to Require RRs/IARs to Maintain Antivirus Software on Computers

Failure to Audit RRs Computer Security Measures: *In the Matter of Commonwealth Equity Services, LLP d/b/a Commonwealth Financial Network.*[20] In a case that led to an actual breach of client information, Commonwealth Financial Network was found to have willfully violated Rule 30(a) of Regulation S-P in 2009. Commonwealth, both a broker-dealer and investment adviser, recommended, but did not require, that its registered representatives maintain antivirus software on their computers, which the registered representatives used to access customer account information on the firm's internal network and clearing firm's trading platform. Commonwealth also did not have procedures in place to adequately review its registered representatives' computer security measures. In particular, Commonwealth did not audit branch office computers to determine whether antivirus software was installed, nor did Commonwealth have procedures in place to follow up on potential computer security issues.

In November 2008, an unauthorized party obtained the login credentials of a Commonwealth registered representative through the use of a computer virus placed on the registered representative's computer, which at the time did not have antivirus software properly employed, and was thereby able to access Commonwealth's internal network. The intruder accessed a list of the representative's Commonwealth customer accounts and entered unauthorized purchase orders in several of those accounts before the activity was detected by Commonwealth's clearing broker-dealer and the intruders were blocked from further trading.

In addition to the approximately $8,000 in net trading losses Commonwealth had to absorb, the SEC censured Commonwealth and ordered the firm to pay a monetary penalty of $100,000.

---

[20] SEC, *In the Matter of Commonwealth Equity Services, LLP* d/b/a Commonwealth Financial Network, Administrative Rel. No. 34-60733 (Sept. 23, 2009), http://www.sec.gov/litigation/admin/2009/34-60733.pdf

FINRA Fines Centaurus Financial $175,000 for Failure to Protect Confidential Customer Information

Inadequate Firewall Controls. The Centaurus case provides a different important lesson.[21] FINRA found that between April 2006 and July 2007, Centaurus Financial, Inc., failed to safeguard customer information because it had failed to change the manufacturer default user name and password on the firm's firewall and had ineffective access controls to the firm's facsimile server. These failures resulted in unauthorized persons accessing stored images of faxes that contained confidential information, including Social Security numbers, account numbers, and dates of birth. Additionally, on July 15, 2007, Centaurus' fax server was used by an unauthorized third party to host a phishing scam.

FINRA found that Centaurus violated Regulation S-P by failing to protect confidential customer information. FINRA announced on April 28, 2009, that it fined Centaurus $175,000, required Centaurus to send notifications to affected customers and their brokers, and required the company to provide one year of credit monitoring at no cost to the affected customers.

FINRA Letter of Acceptance, Waiver, and Consent, D.A. Davidson & Co.

Failure to Encrypt or Password Protect Firm's Database. This case[22] illustrates, in particular, some of the various costs and serious implications to a firm and its clients for failing to have adequate policies and controls. D.A. Davidson, a broker-dealer, maintained a database server containing customer account numbers, Social Security numbers, names, addresses, dates of birth, and certain other confidential data. Davidson did not encrypt or password-protect the database. In December 2007, the database was compromised when an unidentified third party downloaded the confidential data of 192,000 customers through a sophisticated network intrusion. The firm learned of the breach through an email that the hacker sent to the firm in January 2008 in which the person demanded a ransom for the data.

FINRA found that the firm had failed to adopt and implement policies and procedures reasonably designed to safeguard customer records and information and to establish and maintain a system, including written supervisory procedures, reasonably designed to achieve compliance with Rule 30 of Regulation S-P, NASD Rule 2110, and NASD Rules 3010(a) and (b).

The FINRA letter of acceptance, waiver, and consent show the cost to the firm for this failure. Davidson took "prompt remedial steps after the hacker attacks, including issuing a press release to the public reporting the incident; preparing a detailed communication

---

[21] FINRA, FINRA Fines Centaurus Financial $175,000 for Failure to Protect Confidential Customer Information (Apr. 28, 2009), http://www.finra.org/Newsroom/NewsReleases/2009/P118550
[22] FINRA, FINRA Letter of Acceptance, Waiver, and Consent, No. 20080152998, D.A. Davidson & Co. (Apr. 9, 2010), http://www.finra.org/web/groups/industry/@ip/@enf/@ad/documents/industry/p121260.pdf

plan for employees, including establishing internal and external call centers to respond to customer inquiries; providing written notice to its affected customers; and voluntarily offering affected customers a subscription to a credit-monitoring service for a two year coverage period at a cost to the firm of $1.3 million." Davidson also resolved a class action suit with its affected customers, which included providing loss reimbursement for potential victims of the hacking of up to an aggregate of $1,000,000. Finally, Davidson also consented to being censured and fined $375,000.

V. THE NIST CYBERSECURITY FRAMEWORK

Framework Core

On February 12, 2014, NIST published "Framework for Improving Critical Infrastructure Cybersecurity,[23]" which provides a common language for understanding, managing and expressing cybersecurity risk. The framework can be used to help identify and prioritize actions for managing cybersecurity risk and is a useful tool for aligning policy.

The framework provides a set of activities to achieve specific cybersecurity outcomes and is built around five functions that organize cybersecurity activities at their highest level: identify, protect, detect, respond, and recover—organizational aids facilitating management of cybersecurity risks. The functions align with existing methodologies for incident management while demonstrating the impact of investments in cybersecurity.

Identify

The identify function instructs program leaders to develop the organizational knowledge to manage applicable cybersecurity risks to systems, assets, data, and capabilities. The activities in the identify function are foundational for effective use of the framework. Adequate knowledge and identification of the business context, the resources available to support critical functions, and the applicable risks enables an organization to focus and prioritize its efforts consistent with its risk management strategy and business needs.

Protect

The protect function instructs program leaders to develop and implement the necessary procedures to safeguard the consistent delivery of critical infrastructure services. The protect function supports the ability to limit or contain the impact of a potential cybersecurity event. Examples of outcome categories within this function include: access control; awareness and training; data security; information protection processes and procedures; maintenance; and protective technology.

---

[23] NIST, "Framework for Improving Critical Infrastructure: Cybersecurity," (Feb. 12, 2014), http://www.nist.gov/cyberframework/upload/cybersecurity-framework-021214-final.pdf

Detect

Using the detect function, program leaders develop and implement the necessary procedures to facilitate detection of a cybersecurity event. The detect function enables timely discovery of cybersecurity events. Examples of outcome categories within this function include: anomalies and events; continuous security monitoring; and detection processes.

Respond

Program leaders employ the respond function to develop and implement the necessary procedures to mitigate a cybersecurity event occurrence. The respond function supports the ability to contain the impact of a potential cybersecurity event. Examples of outcome categories within this function include: response planning, communications, analysis, mitigation, and improvements.

Recover

Using the recover function, program leaders develop and implement the necessary procedures to ensure effectiveness of plans and restoration of any impaired operational systems. The recover function supports timely recovery and reduces the impact of a cybersecurity event. Examples of outcome categories within this function include: recovery planning, improvements, and communications.

VI. SEC OFFICE OF COMPLIANCE INSPECTIONS AND EXAMINATIONS (OCIE) CYBERSECURITY INITIATIVE

National Exam Program Risk Alert: OCIE Cybersecurity Initiative

On April 15, 2014, OCIE published a National Exam Program Risk Alert outlining its cybersecurity initiative.[24] The SEC examined 57 broker-dealers and 49 investment advisers. In the last seven pages of the risk alert sweep exam letter, the Risk Alert provides excellent guidance on what issues should be addressed. However, many readers were left not knowing how to implement the guidance, and in many cases the Risk Alert raised more questions than it answered.

The Risk Alert incorporates the NIST cybersecurity framework tailored to financial services firms and will serve as the roadmap for implementation of the cybersecurity policies and procedures described in this chapter. Below is an annotated copy of the sweep letter referencing various cybersecurity issues and providing references and templates to address these issues. The Risk Alert did an excellent job of "telling you what you may be required to do." The annotations and supporting material given here will tell you how to do it and provide tools to aid in implementation.

---

[24] SEC, OCIE Cybersecurity Initiative, National Exam Program Risk Alert Volume IV, Issue 2 (Apr. 15, 2014), http://www.sec.gov/ocie/announcement/Cybersecurity+Risk+Alert++%2526+Appendix+-+4.15.14.pdf

In the annotations there are numerous references to sample policies. One free resource is the SANS Institute.[25] In addition to the free policy templates SANS offers a wealth of helpful guidance. Other additional free resources include the Federal Communications Commission (FCC) Small Biz Cyber Planner 2.0,[26] and Greater Houston Partnership cybersecurity resources, including a cybersecurity assessment tool.[27]

Annotated Cybersecurity Sweep Exam Letter[28]

UNITED STATES
SECURITIES AND EXCHANGE COMMISSION
OFFICE OF COMPLIANCE INSPECTIONS AND EXAMINATIONS
100 F STREET, NE
WASHINGTON, DC 20549

This document provides a sample list of requests for information that the U.S. Securities and Exchange Commission's Office of Compliance Inspections and Examinations (OCIE) may use in conducting examinations of registered entities regarding cybersecurity matters. Some of the questions track information outlined in the "Framework for Improving Critical Infrastructure Cybersecurity" released on February 12, 2014 by the National Institute of Standards and Technology. OCIE has published this document as a resource for registered entities. This document should not be considered all-inclusive of the information that OCIE may request. Accordingly, OCIE will alter its requests for information as it considers the specific circumstances presented by each firm's particular systems or information technology environment.

Identification of Risks/Cybersecurity Governance

1. For each of the following practices employed by the Firm for management of information security assets, please provide the month and year in which the noted action was last taken; the frequency with which such practices are conducted; the group with responsibility for conducting the practice; and, if not conducted firm wide, the areas that are included within the practice. Please also provide a copy of any relevant policies and procedure.

---

[25] SANS Institute, www.sans.org/security-resources/policies/
[26] FCC, Small Biz Cyber Planner 2.0, http://www.fcc.gov/cyberplanner
[27] Great Houston Partnership, http://www.houston.org/cybersecurity/
[28] The statements and annotations expressed in this sweep exam letter are not those of the SEC or staff of the OCIE. This letter is not a rule, regulation, or statement, nor does it serve as any endorsement of the SEC, OCIE staff or any governmental agency.

> This cybersecurity chapter references to policy templates that can be customized and implemented.

- Physical devices and systems within the Firm are inventoried.
- Software platforms and applications within the Firm are inventoried.

> The end of this cybersecurity chapter includes an inventory checklist.

- Maps of network resources, connections, and data flows (including locations where customer data is housed) are created or updated.

> Network schematics are not required, but like organizational charts, can be a useful visual aid to see the components of a network and how they are connected. For examples, do a Google search for <network map> and select <images>. Creating network maps can be done easily in MS Power Point, or graphics software such as Visio or SmartDraw.

- Connections to the Firm's network from external sources are catalogued.

> External connections are the doors and windows to your network. They need to be identified and subsequently addressed. Be diligent in cataloguing external connections. Often a hacker's first step is to probe a network for vulnerabilities so an external connection that is not catalogued may be akin to leaving a door or window unlocked.

- Resources (hardware, data, and software) are prioritized for protection based on their sensitivity and business value.

> Resource prioritization lays the foundation for risk assessment. For most firms your data, especially client data, should be your top priority. Also high on the list would be proprietary trade secrets such as databases or software programs. Most hardware and commercially available software is replaceable, although potentially at great cost and effort. There are many ways to prioritize resources. One is to use a simple "high, medium, low" ranking. Another method is a forced ranking where all assets are prioritized in a single list from most important to least important. Use the method that best suits you and your firm.

- Logging capabilities and practices are assessed for adequacy, appropriate retention, and secure maintenance.

> Logs are the heart of network monitoring and are critical to ensure the network is functioning properly and to identify problems and anomalies (potential problems). Unfortunately, generating and monitoring logs is very technical. Large firms with IT staff will have trained personnel to perform these functions. There are dedicated programs to analyze network logs, however, small firms typically do not review network logs.
>
> According to data breach statistics from the annual Verizon data breach report, the typical breach is discovered nine months after the initial penetration. Even large firms with sophisticated network monitoring systems and trained security personnel are often unable to immediately detect a breach. The reason is hackers are adept at avoiding detection. Network monitoring and reviewing logs is important but is far from being a strong safeguard.

2. Please provide a copy of the Firm's written information security policy.

> This cybersecurity chapter includes references to policy templates that can be customized and implemented.

3. Please indicate whether the Firm conducts periodic risk assessments to identify cybersecurity threats, vulnerabilities, and potential business consequences. If such assessments are conducted:

   a. Who (business group/title) conducts them, and in what month and year was the most recent assessment completed?
   b. Please describe any findings from the most recent risk assessment that were deemed to be potentially moderate or high risk and have not yet been fully remediated.

> If you follow through using this tool, and you complete the Inventory Checklist, you are conducting a cybersecurity risk assessment. It is advisable to at a minimum include some testing in your annual review.

4. Please indicate whether the Firm conducts periodic risk assessments to identify physical security threats and vulnerabilities that may bear on cybersecurity. If such assessments are conducted:

   a. Who (business group/title) conducts them, and in what month and year was the most recent assessment completed?

b. Please describe any findings from the most recent risk assessment that were deemed to be potentially moderate or high risk and have not yet been fully remediated.

> If you follow through using this tool, you are conducting a cybersecurity risk assessment. It is advisable to at a minimum include some testing in your annual review.

5. If cybersecurity roles and responsibilities for the Firm's workforce and managers have been explicitly assigned and communicated, please provide written documentation of these roles and responsibilities. If no written documentation exists, please provide a brief description.

> If you follow through using the policy templates, you will be assigning cybersecurity roles and responsibilities.

6. Please provide a copy of the Firm's written business continuity of operations plan that addresses mitigation of the effects of a cybersecurity incident and/or recovery from such an incident if one exists.

> Business continuity planning overlaps cybersecurity when we address risk mitigation and recovery. This is a good opportunity to review your BCP. A fundamental truth is some systems are more robust and secure than others. The process of creating a BCP starts with an assessment and hopefully actions to improve the security of the system. For example, if all records are on paper there is little hope of creating a robust BCP. A firm can create policies and memorialize the BCP but the paper system is inherently insecure. The firm should consider a robust electronic storage system which would actually improve the BCP. Creating a BCP goes beyond simply customizing a template and posting it on your website.

7. Does the Firm have a Chief Information Security Officer or equivalent position? If so, please identify the person and title. If not, where does principal responsibility for overseeing cybersecurity reside within the Firm?

8. Does the Firm maintain insurance that specifically covers losses and expenses attributable to cybersecurity incidents? If so, please briefly describe the nature of the coverage and indicate whether the Firm has filed any claims, as well as the nature of the resolution of those claims.

> This cybersecurity chapter addresses cyber insurance.

Protection of Firm Networks and Information

9. Please identify any published cybersecurity risk management process standards, such as those issued by the National Institute of Standards and Technology (NIST) or the International Organization for Standardization (ISO), the Firm has used to model its information security architecture and processes.

> If you follow through using the policy templates, you will have used the NIST framework.

10. Please indicate which of the following practices and controls regarding the protection of its networks and information are utilized by the Firm, and provide any relevant policies and procedures for each item.

   - The Firm provides written guidance and periodic training to employees concerning information security risks and responsibilities. If the Firm provides such guidance and/or training, please provide a copy of any related written materials (e.g., presentations) and identify the dates, topics, and which groups of employees participated in each training event conducted since January 1, 2013.

   > A library of sample user awareness training memos is included in this chapter.

   - The Firm maintains controls to prevent unauthorized escalation of user privileges and lateral movement among network resources. If so, please describe the controls, unless fully described within policies and procedures.

   > A fundamental principle of cybersecurity is minimalism. Users should not have any more permissions or access than is necessary. The minimalist philosophy is a more secure philosophy and has application beyond account management. Fewer targets are easier to defend so firms with less hardware and software onsite will be inherently more secure. Reference Server Security policies on the SANS website (http://www.sans.org/security-resources/policies/).

   - The Firm restricts users to those network resources necessary for their business functions. If so, please describe those controls, unless fully described within policies and procedures.

   > Reference Server Security policies.

   - The Firm maintains an environment for testing and development of software and applications that is separate from its business environment.

- The Firm maintains a baseline configuration of hardware and software, and users are prevented from altering that environment without authorization and an assessment of security implications.

> Reference Server Security policies. Industry trends are moving toward cloud computing for services and storage over the traditional client-server model. Although this brings with it its own set of security and auditing challenges, cloud based applications and storage may be a safer alternative for small firms that lack the resources to create and maintain a sufficiently secure computing environment.

- The Firm has a process to manage IT assets through removal, transfers, and disposition.

> Reference Server Security-Technology Equipment Disposal policies.

- The Firm has a process for ensuring regular system maintenance, including timely installation of software patches that address security vulnerabilities.

> Reference Server Security policies.

- The Firm's information security policy and training address removable and mobile media.

> Reference Removable Media and Remote Access policies.

- The Firm maintains controls to secure removable and portable media against malware and data leakage. If so, please briefly describe these controls.

> Reference Removable Media and Remote Access policies.

- The Firm maintains protection against Distributed Denial of Service (DDoS) attacks for critical internet-facing IP addresses. If so, please describe the internet functions protected and who provides this protection.

- The Firm maintains a written data destruction policy.

> This should be addressed in the books and records section of the firm's compliance manual.

- The Firm maintains a written cybersecurity incident response policy. If so, please provide a copy of the policy and indicate the year in which it was most recently updated. Please also indicate whether the Firm conducts tests or exercises to assess its incident response policy, and if so, when and by whom the last such test or assessment was conducted.

    > Reference Security Response Plan policies.

- The Firm periodically tests the functionality of its backup system. If so, please provide the month and year in which the backup system was most recently tested.

    > This should be covered in your BCP. Data backup is one of the most important considerations but overlaps BCP. Statistics have shown that most firms that lose their data go out of business within a year. Hardware and software is largely replaceable, albeit at potentially great cost and effort. However, your data is irreplaceable. Have multiple independent backups. At least two parties in the firm should be backing up data and neither should have access to the other's backup. This control can protect against a rogue person in the firm from intentionally destroying all of the firm's data. "No single person should have all of the keys to the kingdom."

11. Please indicate whether the Firm makes use of encryption. If so, what categories of data, communications, and devices are encrypted and under what circumstances?

    > Reference Acceptable Encryption policies. Along with data backup, data encryption is a top priority. The reality of cybersecurity is it is extremely difficult to prevent unauthorized access to your network. Firms can hire "white hat ethical hackers" to perform penetration tests of their system. A very high percentage of these tests are successful which highlights the vulnerability of perimeter defenses. However, firms can employ interior defenses such as data backup and data encryption that are more robust defenses.

12. Please indicate whether the Firm conducts periodic audits of compliance with its information security policies. If so, in what month and year was the most recent such audit completed, and by whom was it conducted?

    > At a minimum this should be incorporated into the firm's annual compliance review.

Risks Associated With Remote Customer Access and Funds Transfer Requests

13. Please indicate whether the Firm provides customers with on-line account access. If so, please provide the following information:

    a. The name of any third party or parties that manage the service.
    b. The functionality for customers on the platform (e.g., balance inquiries, address and contact information changes, beneficiary changes, transfers among the customer's accounts, withdrawals or other external transfers of funds).
    c. How customers are authenticated for on-line account access and transactions.
    d. Any software or other practice employed for detecting anomalous transaction requests that may be the result of compromised customer account access.
    e. A description of any security measures used to protect customer PINs stored on the sites.
    f. Any information given to customers about reducing cybersecurity risks in conducting transactions/business with the Firm.

14. Please provide a copy of the Firm's procedures for verifying the authenticity of email requests seeking to transfer customer funds. If no written procedures exist, please describe the process.

> Due to the high incidence of fraudulent requests from compromised email accounts, firms should authenticate email requests by speaking directly with the client. This is addressed in the user awareness training section of this chapter. This should also be addressed in the firm's Reg S-ID policies.

15. Please provide a copy of any Firm policies for addressing responsibility for losses associated with attacks or intrusions impacting customers.

    a. Does the Firm offer its customers a security guarantee to protect them against hacking of their accounts? If so, please provide a copy of the guarantee if one exists and a brief description.

Risks Associated with Vendors and Other Third Parties

16. If the Firm conducts or requires cybersecurity risk assessments of vendors and business partners with access to the Firm's networks, customer data, or other sensitive information, or due to the cybersecurity risk of the outsourced function, please describe who conducts this assessment, when it is required, and how it is conducted. If a questionnaire is used, please provide a copy. If assessments by independent entities are required, please describe any standards established for such assessments.

© MODERN COMPLIANCE 2015

> This should be covered in the firm's policies on due diligence of third-party vendors.

17. If the Firm regularly incorporates requirements relating to cybersecurity risk into its contracts with vendors and business partners, please describe these requirements and the circumstances in which they are incorporated. Please provide a sample copy.

> This should be covered in the firm's policies on due diligence of third-party vendors.

18. Please provide a copy of policies and procedures and any training materials related to information security procedures and responsibilities for trainings conducted since January 2013 for vendors and business partners authorized to access its network.

19. If the Firm assesses the segregation of sensitive network resources from resources accessible to third parties, who (business group/title) performs this assessment, and provide a copy of any relevant policies and procedures?

20. If vendors, business partners, or other third parties may conduct remote maintenance of the Firm's networks and devices, describe any approval process, logging process, or controls to prevent unauthorized access, and provide a copy of any relevant policies and procedures.

> This should be covered in the firm's policies on due diligence of third-party vendors.

Detection of Unauthorized Activity

21. For each of the following practices employed by the Firm to assist in detecting unauthorized activity on its networks and devices, please briefly explain how and by whom (title, department and job function) the practice is carried out.

    - Identifying and assigning specific responsibilities, by job function, for detecting and reporting suspected unauthorized activity.
    - Maintaining baseline information about expected events on the Firm's network.
    - Aggregating and correlating event data from multiple sources.
    - Establishing written incident alert thresholds.
    - Monitoring the Firm's network environment to detect potential cybersecurity events.

- Monitoring the Firm's physical environment to detect potential cybersecurity events.
- Using software to detect malicious code on Firm networks and mobile devices.
- Monitoring the activity of third party service providers with access to the Firm's networks.
- Monitoring for the presence of unauthorized users, devices, connections, and software on the Firm's networks.
- Evaluating remotely-initiated requests for transfers of customer assets to identify anomalous and potentially fraudulent requests.
- Using data loss prevention software.
- Conducting penetration tests and vulnerability scans. If so, please identify the month and year of the most recent penetration test and recent vulnerability scan, whether they were conducted by Firm employees or third parties, and describe any findings from the most recent risk test and/or assessment that were deemed to be potentially moderate or high risk but have not yet been addressed.
- Testing the reliability of event detection processes. If so, please identify the month and year of the most recent test.
- Using the analysis of events to improve the Firm's defensive measures and policies.

> Reference Information Logging Standard policies.

Other

22. Did the Firm update its written supervisory procedures to reflect the Identity Theft Red Flags Rules, which became effective in 2013 (17 CFR § 248—Subpart C—Regulation S-ID)?

    a. If not, why?

23. How does the Firm identify relevant best practices regarding cybersecurity for its business model?

24. **Since January 1, 2013**, has your Firm experienced any of the following types of events? If so, please provide a brief summary for each category listed below, identifying the number of such incidents (approximations are acceptable when precise numbers are not readily available) and describing their significance and any effects on the Firm, its customers, and its vendors or affiliates. If the response to any one item includes more than 10 incidents, the respondent may note the number of incidents and describe incidents that resulted in losses of more than $5,000, the unauthorized access to customer information, or the unavailability of a Firm service

for more than 10 minutes. The record or description should, at a minimum, include: the extent to which losses were incurred, customer information accessed, and Firm services impacted; the date of the incident; the date the incident was discovered and the remediation for such incident.

- Malware was detected on one or more Firm devices. Please identify or describe the malware.
- Access to a Firm web site or network resource was blocked or impaired by a denial of service attack. Please identify the service affected, and the nature and length of the impairment.
- The availability of a critical Firm web or network resource was impaired by a software or hardware malfunction. Please identify the service affected, the nature and length of the impairment, and the cause.
- The Firm's network was breached by an unauthorized user. Please describe the nature, duration, and consequences of the breach, how the Firm learned of it, and how it was remediated.
- The compromise of a customer's or vendor's computer used to remotely access the Firm's network resulted in fraudulent activity, such as efforts to fraudulently transfer funds from a customer account or the submission of fraudulent payment requests purportedly on behalf of a vendor.
- The Firm received fraudulent emails, purportedly from customers, seeking to direct transfers of customer funds or securities.
- The Firm was the subject of an extortion attempt by an individual or group threatening to impair access to or damage the Firm's data, devices, network, or web services.
- An employee or other authorized user of the Firm's network engaged in misconduct resulting in the misappropriation of funds, securities, sensitive customer or Firm information, or damage to the Firm's network or data.

25. **Since January 1, 2013**, if not otherwise reported above, did the Firm, either directly or as a result of an incident involving a vendor, experience the theft, loss, unauthorized exposure, or unauthorized use of or access to customer information? Please respond affirmatively even if such an incident resulted from an accident or negligence, rather than deliberate wrongdoing. If so, please provide a brief summary of each incident or a record describing each incident.

26. For each event identified in response to Questions 24 and 25 above, please indicate whether it was reported to the following:

    - Law enforcement (please identify the entity)
    - FinCEN (through the filing of a Suspicious Activity Report)
    - FINRA
    - A state or federal regulatory agency (please identity the agency and explain the manner of reporting)
    - An industry or public-private organization facilitating the exchange of information about cybersecurity incidents and risks

27. What does the Firm presently consider to be its three most serious cybersecurity risks, and why?

28. Please feel free to provide any other information you believe would be helpful to the Securities and Exchange Commission in evaluating the cybersecurity posture of the Firm or the securities industry.

VII. USER AWARENESS: NINE TRAINING MEMOS

To help comply with a firm's security training policy this chapter includes nine sample memos that can be customized and distributed to employees. There is a human element to cybersecurity, and training is the best way to address this area. The first memo is detailed and fairly comprehensive. The other nine are very brief and at times repetitive; however, "repetition is the mother of all learning."

Memo 1 Re: Employee's Home Computer and Personal Devices

Cybersecurity

The Threat

Home and Small Business Computers Are Easy Prey. Hackers may want to gain access to your financial accounts, or the target could be someone that you know that is a bigger target and the hacker is using you as a conduit. Another common reason home and small business systems are attacked is to gain control and use your computer (along with many others) in a coordinated cyberattack. Finally, there is malicious mischief when a hacker gains satisfaction from harming others, which could be you. According to the Symantec 2013 Internet Security Report, 31 percent of cyberattacks were aimed at home users and small businesses because they are soft targets. *You need to be aware of the threat and we will discuss specific steps you can take to protect yourself and your computers.*

Nomenclature and General Principles

Perimeter, Interior and User Defenses. We will break down this discussion into three sections: perimeter defenses, interior defenses, and user defenses. There is an overemphasis on perimeter defenses. The truth is, it is extremely difficult to keep a hacker out of your system even with the most hardened perimeter. However, what you can do is make it very difficult for the hacker to do harm once inside the system by hardening the interior. Think of an M&M candy, which is hard on the outside but soft on the inside. What we want to create is a peanut M&M which is hard on the outside and hard on the inside. This is analogous to protecting your privacy such as your Social Security number. If someone really wants to get your SSN, there is little you could do to stop him or her. However, by freezing your credit, you could make it very difficult for someone to abuse your information. There are technological and human elements to security. Cybersecurity is not wholly a technological issue. One of the biggest vulnerabilities is a compromised user. Hackers can trick and trap users into compromising information or enabling a vulnerability that can be exploited (such as a virus). Awareness is the best protection much like being aware when in an unfamiliar and potentially dangerous neighborhood.

Minimalist ("Less is more"). Fewer targets are easier to defend so a minimalist philosophy is a more secure philosophy. This theme will recur throughout this discussion.

Virtualization. Virtualization means using the internet ("the cloud") for services and data storage. Generally, reputable cloud delivered services and data storage will be more resilient and more secure than analogous applications on your own hardware. Your computers could be stolen, maybe damaged in a disaster, and are difficult to keep updated. Although cloud delivered applications are not perfect, they are probably better than the alternative on your own system. This will also be a recurring theme in this discussion.

Perimeter Security: "Close and Lock All of the Doors and Windows to Your System"

Inventory. The first step to securing your perimeter is to define your perimeter by taking an inventory of your devices and connections to your network (computers, mobile devices, remote access.) This inventory is a list of the entry points to your network and will be the focus of your perimeter defense. Remember one open window is all a hacker will need to easily breach your system so *every* entry point must be secured.

Physical Security. One of the most common breaches emanates from lost or stolen equipment. In particular, mobile devices and portable storage (flash drives) are highly susceptible, so be diligent and develop good habits including not leaving devices unattended for any length of time and not placing a phone on the table at a restaurant where it could be inadvertently left behind. If your home or office is vulnerable, consider upgrading the security which could be as simple as installing deadbolts on doors or an alarm system.

Firewall. A firewall is a hardware or software system that creates a secure environment for network computing. This can be accomplished through a number of devices. Windows has a built in firewall that can be activated here:

<Start><Control Panel><System & Security><Windows Firewall>

Most of the comprehensive software security packages (antivirus software) also include firewall protection (covered below). In the case of a wireless network, the wireless router will serve as a firewall (also covered below). Regardless of which system is acting as the firewall, the important point is to make sure you have one and are thus operating in a secure environment. Note: We use the term *secure environment*, but there are levels of security, with some definitely more secure than others. The levels of security are beyond the scope of this discussion; however, be aware that most secure networks can be penetrated so the firewall is just one component of your defenses.

Wireless Networks. Wireless networks are inherently vulnerable, but that must be weighed against the low cost and convenience. An open network is an open door, so make sure you secure the wireless network. Here are a few steps that should be taken:

- Change the administration password. The two most common wireless routers on the market are Linksys and Netgear and hackers know the default Admin passwords so make sure you change the password.
- Use WPA or preferably WPA2 encryption. If you are required to enter a password to allow a device to connect to your wireless then you have enabled encryption.
- Change the default service set identifier (SSID) (name your network). Again, if you have the factory default, a hacker will target your system on the assumption that if you did not name the network you probably did not take other steps such as encryption. To see the name of your network go to:

<Start><Control Panel><Network and Internet>

If it needs to be changed, consult the manual for your wireless router. If you have misplaced the manual, conduct an internet search on the name of your router and you should be able to find a manual online.

Antivirus Software. There are many good vendors and even free products. For example, centrally managed client-server solutions are offered by such companies as ESET, TrendMicro, Kaspersky, Norton Internet Security, and others. Each of these includes the options of antivirus, malware, and firewall protection. Antivirus software has become somewhat of a misnomer because many of these programs perform other critical functions. Having a robust security program is *absolutely* essential.

Antivirus Vendor Websites

- http://us.norton.com/internet-security/
- www.eset.com
- www.trendmicro.com
- usa.kaspersky.com

Operating System Patches. Make sure you turn on Windows Automatic Updates

<Start><All Programs><Windows Update>

On the second Tuesday of each month (dubbed "patch Tuesday") when you turn off your computer you should see "installing update 1 of __" and this is how you will know that you have automatic updates turned on. Windows is updated when vulnerabilities are identified and patched. Hackers exploit known vulnerabilities on systems that have not been updated, so make sure you turn on automatic updates. Incidentally, the second Wednesday of each month is called "hacker Wednesday" because hackers attempt to exploit vulnerabilities immediately and the highest number of breaches occurs on the second Wednesday of the month.

Mobile Devices. Smartphones and tablets are a window to your network, so make sure they are secured using these four steps:

- Password protect *and* encrypt your data. This may be done via <Settings> in either Apple or Android systems. Although inconvenient, you should be required to sign in when turning on the device. Without the password, the encrypted data on the device will be secure. If your Smartphone does not have an encryption option, you can purchase a third-party solution.
- Install antivirus software. Android is particularly vulnerable, and an example of a mobile antivirus application for mobile Android devices is Avast Mobile Security & Antivirus: http://www.avast.com/en-us/free-mobile-security
- If you are a typical iPhone user, you probably don't need antivirus software because apps via iTunes are screened by Apple for malware.
- Virtualize your data using iCloud (Apple devices) or Gmail (Android devices). Your data will be automatically backed up in the cloud. Avast has a backup utility with instructions to setup iCloud. http://www.apple.com/icloud/setup/
- Have the ability to remotely locate or wipe the device if it is lost or stolen. Avast Anti-theft and Google's Android Device Manager have these capabilities. For the iPhone the free app "Find My Phone" works well. With these apps you can use your computer to bring up a GPS map showing the location of your phone, and if necessary, you can wipe the data from the device.

Browser Security. Many viruses are transmitted via websites, so browser security is important. One browser does not preclude you from using another. You can install and use multiple browsers depending on the needs of the websites you are visiting. Consider using Chrome as your default browser. From Chrome, type in Chrome://extensions and <Get More Extensions>. Here are three security extensions to consider:

- HTTPS Everywhere. Many websites offer a secure connection. With HTTPS Everywhere installed Google Chrome will automatically create a secure connection to the supported website.
- Ad Block Plus. As the name implies this is an ad blocker, however this extension as well as the others mentioned here could cause some websites to malfunction. In this case you might need to switch to Firefox or Internet Explorer.
- Ghostery. Like Ad Block Plus, Ghostery is a privacy extension that blocks unwanted ads.

In Firefox go to <Tools><Options><Security> and check the boxes for "Warn me when sites try to install add-ons," "Block reported attack sites," "Block reported web forgeries."

In Internet Explorer go to <Tools><Internet Options><Security> and make sure the slider bar is set at least to <Medium-high>.

User Privileges. Consistent with the minimalist philosophy set up User Accounts without Administrator Privileges. This way if your user account is compromised, the hacker will be restricted in what they can do.

<Start><Control Panel><User Accounts>

Add User Account as a Standard User

Strong Passwords. Passwords are the keys to the locked doors and windows, and they must be protected. Don't share passwords! One of the most common sources of system breaches is a compromised password. The most critical element of password strength is the length of the password. Any eight-character password can be cracked with readily available internet tools in a matter of minutes. A twenty-character password would take weeks to hack. One technique to lengthen a password without compromising on convenience is called *padding,* when you add characters to the end of an easily remembered password such as $$$$$$$$ or 1234567890. Here is a website that explains the technique in more detail: GRC's | Password Haystacks: How Well Hidden is Your Needle?

Password managers are a highly recommend tool because they enable you to easily use different passwords on different sites by encrypting all your passwords in one application that requires you to only memorize one password to access that application. Using the same password for all sites is a poor safety practice. Moreover, Roboform and Lastpass, two examples of password managers, have features that are extremely convenient and actually make accessing password-protected websites easier by securely storing the web address, user ID, and password, and allowing you login with a single click. Finally, there are mobile versions, and all of the passwords can be virtualized and automatically synced with all devices. Thus, if you change a password using your phone, the password will be changed for all devices.

Roboform: Best Password Manager & Form Filler | RoboForm

Lastpass: https://lastpass.com

Finally, you should make use of multifactor authentication, which is readily available on commonly used websites such as Facebook, Yahoo Mail, and Gmail:

http://www.cnet.com/how-to/how-to-enable-two-factor-authentication-on-popular-sites/

When you enable multifactor authentication, you will be required to enter the password AND answer challenge questions or enter a token (six-digit code) sent to your phone via text message. Email accounts get hacked frequently; however, one with multifactor authentication is less likely to become compromised.

Interior Security

Data Backup. If you could do only one thing mentioned in this discussion, it would be to back up your data in the cloud. The services mentioned below are well worth the cost and operate seamlessly and effectively. Hardware and software can be replaced, but your data is critical so make sure you back it up. There are many services and most new computers come with a service preloaded. However, consider using Mozy and Carbonite:

> Mozy: https://mozy.com/#slide-5
> Carbonite: Carbonite Cloud Backup Services—Online Computer Data Backup

One big advantage of Mozy is you can access your data from all of your devices, including your work computer, netbook, and home computers. When you work on a file, it is saved online and there is no problem with accessing a prior version from a different device. This is consistent with the theme of virtualization and analogous to using iCloud or Gmail for your smartphone.

Finally, if there are multiple users of data such as in a small business, it is highly recommended to have at least two independent backups, so that the backups are done by different people and each does not have access to the other. This follows the principle that "no one should have all the keys to the kingdom." Many businesses have been wiped out by a disgruntled employee who is intent on harming the company and deleting all of its data. Having independent backups is a critical control if there are multiple users of the data.

Encryption. Encrypting your data is the second most important protection behind backing up your data. Note: the two most important safeguards are interior defenses because the perimeter is extremely difficult to guard. Encrypting the data on your smartphone and on your computer was discussed previously. There are built in encryption programs such as Bitlocker that will encrypt your entire hard drive. However, as "leaked" by Edward Snowden, Microsoft has cooperated with federal law enforcement and turned over the encryption key. Bitlocker is still extremely secure. There are alternatives, for example AxCrypt:

> Axantum Software AB | AxCrypt | File Encryption Software

This is a free open-source program and encrypts individual files and is a most convenient encryption program. Functionality is as simple as right-clicking on the file, and the passphrase can be stored and need only be entered once. Note: If you leave your computer (or it is generally acceptable for employees to leave their computers) alone, it is recommended not to enable this feature. In that case you would be required to enter the passphrase every time you open a protected file. Entire folders can be selected so it is easy to encrypt or decrypt multiple files at once.

Portable Storage. Flash drives (thumb drives) are handy (no pun intended) but vulnerable. Make sure all important content on flash drives is encrypted using AxCrypt or something similar. Also be aware of a hacker trick of leaving a flash drive to be found so that a curious person inserts the drive into his or her computer and unknowingly downloads a virus. Don't fall for this! If anyone gives you a flash drive, even someone known to you, get in the habit of holding down the left shift key while inserting the device. This will prevent any autoexecutable files on the flash drive from running. Another option is to disable autoplay on your computer.

Human Elements of Security: Awareness and Safe User Practices

Social Engineering. Social engineering are methods hackers use to trick users into revealing sensitive information such as passwords or to unknowingly download a harmful virus. Your best protection is awareness.

Phishing. Protect against phishing which is a technique used by online criminals to trick people into revealing information. Most are fairly easy to recognize as scams but some can emulate notifications from well-known vendors such as Bank of America, UPS, Federal Express, Amazon, or Ebay. Examine emails carefully, especially the sender's email address. If the email domain does not match the sender's company, it is likely fake. Also examine any links by hovering your mouse over the link to see the linked address. This is not 100 percent reliable, so the best policy is to not click on any links. Instead, open your browser and enter the address manually.

Spear phishing, also known as pretexting, is more insidious. Spear phishing attacks are targeted, and the criminal will often glean information from social media sites including names of family or friends to tailor the phishing attack. These can be much more difficult to detect so be careful.

Public Wi-Fi. Public Wi-Fi such as free wireless at airports, hotels, and internet cafes is inherently dangerous and should be avoided if possible. Learn how to use your phone as a mobile hotspot by contacting your cellular provider, for example:

> http://www.verizonwireless.com/insiders-guide/tech-smarts/how-to-use-your-smartphone-as-a-mobile-hotspot/

If you must use public Wi-Fi, set up a virtual private network (VPN). Here is a link to an example of an application, which also offers a more limited free version:

> http://www.hotspotshield.com/

Securely Empty the Recycle Bin. Most people don't know this but when you "empty" the recycle bin the file is still intact on your drive and could be easily retrieved. This is analogous to taking the trash out and having a dumpster diver pick out important information. To securely erase files from your system, you need to use an eraser (sometimes called a shredder). Here is an example of such an application:

> Eraser (free) http://download.cnet.com/Eraser/3000-2092_4-10231814.html

Malware. Malware includes viruses, spyware and other malicious programs that can be downloaded to aid a hacker or compromise your system. Unfortunately, many of these programs are not detected by antivirus software, so you need to be careful.

Two email tips:

- Do not open suspicious emails or attachments; and
- Do not click on links within an email.

Scareware. A common ploy is fake antivirus security warnings, also called scareware. Everyone on the [COMPANY] network has antivirus software but you should also know what type of antivirus software is protecting your other computers. If a warning pops up react calmly and with caution.

Ransomware. This is a virus payload that will encrypt your data which will be held for ransom to decrypt. If you backup your data online you can delete the encrypted files, remove the virus and restore your data from the backup.

Removing browser pop-ups and adware is both an annoyance and a security problem and it is very good to know if you are being bombarded with browser pop-ups (adware). Try:

> http://malwaretips.com/blogs/remove-adware-popup-ads/

Memo 2 Re: Strong Passwords

One of the greatest threats to our clients and our firm is the risk of an electronic breach (getting hacked.) We will talk about two very simple but effective measures to reduce this risk by strengthening passwords.

- Don't share passwords and make sure your passwords are strong. The best indicator of password strength is the length of the password. Any 8-character password can be cracked in less than 30 minutes with readily available hacker tools on the internet. However a 16-character password would take weeks to crack. An easy method of creating strong passwords is the technique of padding. For example MarengoPasadenaCA123123123 is a 26-character password that would be extremely difficult to crack. MarengoPasadenaCA was padded with 123123123. It could have been padded with any repetitive character such as 9 periods, dollar signs, pound signs or exclamation points. Padding is an easy way to lengthen your passwords and thus significantly increase their strength; and
- Password keepers are highly recommended. There are many free password keepers but here are two examples: RoboForm, www.roboform.com or Lastpass, https://lastpass.com/. Using a password keeper will allow you to not use the same password for multiple sites without sacrificing convenience. Roboform or Lastpass will not only securely maintain your passwords, it will make logging in a one-button function so you don't need to look up and enter the password. Roboform and Lastpass are simple, effective, and very convenient.

Memo 3 Re: Red Flag Rules

Identity Theft

Identity theft is a crime where the perpetrator wrongfully obtains and uses the victim's personal data in a way that involves fraud, typically for personal gain. Some law enforcement authorities have called identity theft the fastest growing crime across the country right now.

On May 30, 2013 the SEC passed Reg S-ID to combat identity theft and the attached procedures have been implemented to protect our clients.

Most of the red flags are common sense, but identity thieves are often fairly sophisticated and can prey upon the unsuspecting. Don't be complacent!

Compromised Email Accounts

Client email accounts are prime targets for identity thieves. We have all received numerous bogus emails from hacked email accounts, however, many are being used to fraudulently request money from an investment account. Here are some signs to be aware of.

Email addresses can be spoofed by changing the domain from .com to .net, adding a character to the address or domain, or substituting a character such as zero for the letter O. Be alert when you receive email message from clients and look at the email address and header.

Many firms will require written authentication of a request. The FBI reports that given access to the subject's email account, many thieves were able to cut and paste the client's signature to the written authentication.

The "Fraud Alert Involving E-mail Intrusions to Faciliate Wire Transfers Overseas" issued by the Internet Crime Compliant Center (January 20, 2012) cited that in a typical scenario:

> The identity thief will send an email to a financial institution, brokerage firm employee, or the victim's financial advisor pretending to be the victim and request the balance of the victim's account. When the request for balance information is successful, the identity thief then sends another email providing a reason why they can only communicate via email and asks that a wire transfer be initiated on their behalf. The excuse is typically based on an illness or death in the family which prevents the account holder from conducting business as usual.

Memo 4 Re: Mobile Computing

This memo will address security on mobile devices such as smartphones and tablets. The [COMPANY] policies and procedures address three safeguards with respect to mobile devices:

- **Password protect your device.** Think about the consequences if your device is lost. What information would the finder have access to? Your first line of defense is to password protect the device. This is mandatory: Don't leave your device unprotected.
- **Make sure any data stored on the device (such as passwords or client data) is encrypted.** It is best not to store sensitive data on the device and use a password keeper to store your passwords. There are many good password keepers and most are free. Two that are very popular are RoboForm and LastPass.
- **Have the ability to remotely wipe the device if it is lost.** There are apps such as Android Device Manager, Avast, or FindMyPhone that allow users to remotely wipe a device if it is lost. This is the final measure of protection mandated by our procedures.

Please let me know if you have any questions about these procedures or need any assistance implementing them. Protection of sensitive information is critical and mobile devices are a common source of security breaches.

Memo 5 Re: Email and Texting

Compliance Reminders and Best Practices When You Using Email

- Never use your personal email account for business. If a client happens to send a business related email to your personal address, forward it to your business email account and continue the string from your business account; and
- Business email should always be professional. Be aware that anything you write could be read by an auditor or regulator.

Text Messaging

Reminder: Because we don't have the ability to archive and review SMS text messages, our procedures prohibit the use of text messages to communicate with clients.

Reminders to Keep your Disclosures Current

- All personnel (registered and unregistered) must keep their disclosures current;
- Common disclosures are your home address. If you move you must not only notify the Human Resources Department but also the Compliance Department so your U-4 can be amended; and
- If you have any "yes" answers on the U-4, these require an amendment to the document. Common "yes" answers are financial (bankruptcies, liens, offers in compromise,

etc.), criminal (misdemeanors and felonies), regulatory (issues with any federal or state regulator such as insurance or real estate), and customer complaints. A complaint is defined very broadly as any written grievance. There may be times when a client is "complaining about poor performance" and this comes very close to meeting the definition of a complaint. When in doubt, contact a compliance officer.

Memo 6 Re: Hacking and Malware

Information Security

Information security is an important priority at [COMPANY]. In this month's memo we will address how to protect against hacking and malware.

Phishing

Protect against phishing, which is a technique used by online criminals to trick people into revealing information. Most are fairly easy to recognize as scams but some can emulate notifications from well-known vendors such as UPS, Federal Express, Amazon, or Ebay. Examine emails carefully, especially the sender's email address. If the email domain does not match the sender's company, it is likely fake. Also examine any links by hovering your mouse over the link to see the linked address. This is not 100 percent reliable, so the best policy is to not click on any links. Instead, open your browser and enter the address manually.

Spear phishing, which is also known as pretexting or social engineering, is more insidious. Spear phishing attacks are targeted and the criminal will often glean information from social media sites including names of family or friends to tailor the phishing attack. These can be much more difficult to detect, so be careful.

Scareware

A common ploy is fake antivirus security warnings also called scareware. Everyone on the [COMPANY] network has antivirus software, but you should also know what type of antivirus software is protecting your other computers. If a warning pops up, react calmly and with caution.

Malware

Malware is malicious software that can be loaded via the internet, downloads, attachments, email, social media, and other platforms. The most damaging variant of malware is keyloggers that log every keystroke enabling the hacker to obtain usernames and passwords typed on the computer. The best defense against malware is a combination of current antivirus software, up-to-date systems, proper browser security settings, and user awareness. Every browser should restrict cookies to some degree and block pop-ups. A security setting of "medium" or higher should be used.

Flash Drives

Many flash drives contain preinstalled viruses. Be aware of the source of a flash drive and do not use a drive from an unknown or untrustworthy source. When you use a new flash drive for the first time, hold down the left Shift key when inserting the drive to block viruses or malware from autoexecuting.

Prepare and Be Aware

The key to strong information security is to prepare and be aware. Be sure to report any incidents or suspicions. Please contact [BLANK] if you have any questions or concerns regarding information security.

Memo 7 Re: Emergency Contact Information

Emergency Contact Information

Communications are critical in an emergency. In this month's compliance memo I have very little to say but two favors to ask:

- **Print out the attached list of emergency contact information and take it home.** It has key contact information for all of our offices, <list custodians, clearing firms and other key contacts> as well as all employees' email addresses and cell phone numbers. In an emergency power could be down and travel may be impaired, so it will be good to have a hard copy so we can communicate. Please print out this list *now* and put it in your purse, briefcase or pocket. It will make its way home and you can file it; and
- **Store at least a handful of coworkers' cell phone numbers in your phone.** In an emergency you may not be home but you will likely have your cell phone with you. Our first priority will be to establish communications and you don't want to be scrambling for phone numbers when needed. Please use the attached list and store the numbers in your cell phone *now*.

Procrastination is the number one enemy of preparedness, so please print out the list and store the numbers right now. [Insert your call tree or similar procedure here.] [COMPANY] is small enough that we will be able to account for everyone and implement our business continuity plan.

Memo 8 Re: Fraudulent Emails and Two-Factor Authentication

Fraudulent Emails

A common and frequent fraud is being committed via hacked email accounts. If a client's email account has been hacked, the hacker may be able to see emails sent to and from [COMPANY]. Mimicking the style and knowing key personal information, the hacker could send a fraudulent email to us attempting to steal assets in the form of a third-party wire transfer. Our red flags identity theft procedures require us to call the client to verify the transaction. Moreover, our custodians require us to speak with the client prior to executing any third-party wire transfer. I am confident there is high awareness and that our procedures are being followed to protect the clients from this type of fraud, but this will serve as a reminder to maintain diligence.

Criminals are innovative and new threats emerge constantly. Here are some less common threats to be aware of. A client's email address has been hacked and instead of requesting a third-party wire, the hacker could request an address change, new bank ACH information, a buy transaction or request to transfer securities. *All* of these could be part of a fraudulent scheme, so be vigilant when you receive *any* email request from a client.

What if a [COMPANY] employee's email got hacked? A hacker could send one of us an email requesting a third-party wire transfer, and the email would state the adviser has spoken with the client to confirm. We would call a client to verify a client email, but what about an email from a one of our advisers? Even these emails should be verified with the adviser by a phone call.

Two-Factor Authentication (2FA)

A password is one factor to authenticate a user. In addition to the password, two-factor authentication (2FA) requires a second factor, such as a token sent via SMS text to your cell phone, a fingerprint, or an answer to a challenge question. Most free email providers, including Gmail and Hotmail, have the ability to activate two-factor authentication. It is highly recommend that you do so on your personal email accounts. It is a slight inconvenience but well worth the additional protection.

Memo 9 Re: Public Wi-Fi

Public Wi-Fi

Public Wi-Fi such as free wireless at airports, hotels, and internet cafes is inherently dangerous and should be avoided if possible. Learn how to use your phone as a mobile hotspot by contacting your cellular provider, for example:

> http://www.verizonwireless.com/insiders-guide/tech-smarts/how-to-use-your-smartphone-as-a-mobile-hotspot/

If you must use public Wi-Fi set up a virtual private network (VPN). Here is a link to an example of an application, which also offers a more limited free version: Hotspot Shield.

VIII. CYBER INSURANCE

The Need for Cyber Insurance

The October 20, 2014, headline in *USA Today* read "Officials Warn 500 Million Financial Records Hacked."[29] This is just in one year, and when one considers the entire population of the United States is 316 million, the number of hacks is an astounding and even frightening statistic. In the article Joseph Demarest, assistant director of the FBI's Cyber Division, stated bluntly, "You're going to be hacked. Have a plan." One critical aspect of planning is consideration of cyber insurance.

A common rationalization for those associated with small firms is, "We are too small and don't have the high-value targets that hackers covet." This myth can be discounted with a factual scenario. JP Morgan was in the news and announced the firm had 76 million individuals and 7 million businesses compromised in a cyberattack allegedly carried out by the Russian government in retaliation for U.S. sanctions related to the Ukraine conflict.[30] It was also disclosed that the breach occurred through an employee's personal computer.[31] Most firms have a client or investor who is an employee of a Fortune 500 company, or the friend/relative of an employee at a Fortune 500 company. Consider the possibility that the easiest way into that employee's computer may be through information gleaned through your firm. Even worse, if an attack were successful, the hackers often don't stop with what they wanted; they will post the hack for sale on the dark web. There someone who may want the identities of all of your clients/investors could purchase the information with very bad intentions for your firm. If you are not fearful of a cyberattack, you may be easy prey for hackers.

According to a 2014 Ponemon Institute study,[32] the cost of a data breach was up 15 percent from 2013 and cost $201 per record versus $188 in 2013. Moreover, Ponemon reported that the rate of customers terminating their relationship after a breach increased 15 percent from 2013. Multiply your number of clients / investors times $201 and you get a sense of how costly a breach could be, and this does not include lost business.

Risk Transfer

Insuring a risk is simply a way to transfer the risk to an insurance company in exchange for the premium payment. If a covered risk occurs the cost would be paid by the insurance company per the terms of the insurance policy. Risks can be insured

---

[29] Erin Kelly, "Officials Warn 500 Million Financial Records Hacked," *USA Today* (Oct. 20, 2014).
[30] "Data Breach Detected Involving KMART Credit Card Customers"(Oct. 11, 2014),http://www.inquisitr.com/1533464/data-breach-detected-involing-kmart-credit-card-customers-company-says-no-personal-data-was-stolen/
[31] Emily Glazer and Danny Yadron, "J.P. Morgan Says About 76 Million Households Affected by Cyber Breach," *The Wall Street Journal* (Oct. 2, 2014).
[32] Ponemon Institute, "2014 Cost of Data Breach: Global Analysis" (May 5, 2014).

(transferred), accepted, avoided, or mitigated. Two factors that weigh heavily in the decision of whether or not to insure are the frequency of the risk and the severity of the risk. Because cyberattacks are both frequent and costly, cyber insurance should be considered.

Cyber Insurance: Covered Risks

Cyber insurance can cover myriad risks including:

- *Crisis management coverage.* This would include expenses related to the investigation, remediation, notification, communication, credit monitoring for victims, legal and court costs, and regulatory fines. Although the term *cyber insurance* is used here, most policies define a breach to include physical theft; thus, the breach does not need to occur electronically to be covered.
- *Multimedia liability coverage.* This covers infringement of intellectual property rights, disruption of e-commerce, or defacement of the victim's web presence.
- *Cyber terrorism coverage.* This primarily covers losses due to extortion and the costs related to the event. One common manifestation of this risk is "ransomware," when the victim's data is encrypted and the perpetrator demands a ransom to unlock the data.
- *Network and data security coverage.* This covers denial of service attacks as well as data breaches from third-party vendors.

Considerations in Purchasing Cyber Insurance

First, inventory your information assets. Any databases, electronic files, and program data need to be identified. Next, attempt to assess the risks by quantifying the value of the data and anticipating potential threats. This risk assessment will provide the foundation for the type of coverage to consider as well as a cost-benefit analysis of the coverage. Finally, work with a knowledgeable insurance agent. A good agent will be invaluable, especially because cyber insurance policies tend to be nonstandard and have many different features and benefits.

IX. VULNERABILITY ASSESSMENTS AND PENETRATION TESTING

Vulnerability assessments and penetration testing enter the realm of information security (IS) professionals. It is important to note that IS is a subspecialty of information technology, and most "IT guys" are not trained in information security. There have been many articles and conference sessions on cybersecurity and one common takeaway is to "talk to your IT guy." For some, this may be helpful, but for most, not at all. Not only is IS a subspecialty but not all IS professionals are familiar with the financial services industry and specifically the SEC cybersecurity initiative. So, it is important to work with an IS professional who is familiar with our industry. The third question in the OCIE Cybersecurity Initiative sweep letter asks:

Please indicate whether the firm conducts periodic risk assessments to identify cybersecurity threats, vulnerabilities, and potential business consequences. If such assessments are conducted:

a. Who (business group/title) conducts them, and in what month and year was the most recent assessment completed?
b. Please describe any findings from the most recent risk assessment that were deemed to be potentially moderate or high risk and have not yet been fully remediated.

Of the twenty-eight questions posed in the sweep letter, this may be the most important one.

Vulnerability Assessments

Vulnerability assessments can be complex, and the scope can vary widely, depending on whether it includes "white hat" versus "black hat" external as well as internal testing, and testing of physical security. The IS professional can help define the scope, but cost will also be a consideration. The Federal Financial Institutions Examination Council (FFIEC) defined five information security processes as core components of an IS program:

- Risk identification and assessment;
- Develop a written plan and policies and procedures to address the risks;
- Implement the policies and procedures;
- Test the policies and procedures to assure they are performing as intended; and
- Monitor and update the policies and procedures, as necessary.

This methodology should be familiar to compliance professionals because it is the same methodology we apply in compliance, only in an IS context. A detailed dissertation of vulnerability testing is beyond the scope of this chapter; however, the SANS Institute has published a very helpful guide with more detail, "Security Assessment for Financial Institutions."[33]

Penetration Testing

Penetration testing (pen test) differs from a vulnerability assessment in objective. The objective of a pen test is to breach a system and deliver a report whereas a vulnerability assessment goes through the five steps outlined above and suggests remediation. A vulnerability assessment is much more practical for most firms. And for most small firms, a pen test is a waste of money. One of the most famous hackers in the world is Kevin Mitnick, who is now an ethical hacker. His company, Mitnick Security, performs pen tests. On his website, www.mitnicksecurity.com, they proudly advertise, "Our Team Has a 100 Percent Success Rate!" Unfortunately, this is very believable and probably not unique to Mitnick Security. So, why would a small firm pay for a pen test when

---

[33] Karen Nelson, "Security Assessment Guidelines for Financial Institutions," SANS Institute (Dec. 8, 2002).

the organization will almost certainly fail and have to go through a vulnerability assessment and remediation anyway? For a more detailed dissertation on penetration testing, we recommend the sister to the vulnerability testing article from the SANS Institute, "Penetration Testing in the Financial Services Industry."[34]

X. RISK ANALYSIS CHECKLIST

Technology	Product or Vendor	Risk of Failure	Risk of Breach	Risk Rating	Risk Mitigation
Internet Service Provider					
Servers/Software					
Web Server					
File Server or Vendor					
Firewall					
Intrusion Detection					
Antivirus					
Wireless					
Data Backup					
Email Server or Vendor					
Social Media Vendor					
CRM					
Custodial or Clearing Interface					
Performance Reporting					
Order Management					
Financial Planning					
Workstations					
Network Devices (Printers, Scanners, Copiers)					
Mobile Devices					
Telephone					

XI. CONCLUSION

Cybersecurity is an issue that affects nearly all financial services firms; for most, it should be a high priority. Compliance professionals need to take steps to make sure there is a reasonable cybersecurity program in place. After reading this chapter, hopefully you know what needs to be done and how to do it. It is time to execute.

---

[34] Christopher Olson, "Penetration Testing in the Financial Services Industry," SANS Institute (2010).

ABOUT THE AUTHORS

Krista S. Zipfel, CFA, has been president and chief executive officer (CEO) of Advisor Solutions Group, Inc., since June 2003, a firm that she wholly owns and operates. She founded ASG in 2003 after a decade of working for registered investment advisory firms ranging from $50 million to $5 billion in assets under management, serving both retail and institutional clients. She has worked in the areas of compliance, portfolio management, client service, marketing, research, portfolio administration, operations, trading, and accounting. She has provided valuable advice to CEOs, presidents, chief investment officers (CIOs), portfolio managers, analysts, and administrative and operational staff. Krista graduated summa cum laude with a bachelor of arts degree in Management and Business Administration from Pacific Christian College. She earned a master of business administration degree with a Finance emphasis from California State University, Fullerton. She holds the Chartered Financial Analyst designation from the CFA Institute.

Ms. Zipfel is a member of and serves on the board of directors for the National Society of Compliance Professionals (NSCP). She is a past president of the Southern California Compliance Group (SCCG). She has been a speaker on regulatory topics at NSCP, CFAOC, IAWatch, and other events. She is a member of the CFA Institute, and an active member and former president of the CFA Society of Orange County (CFAOC). She is the founder and former chair of the CFA Society of Orange County Foundation (CFAOCF).

Craig R. Watanabe, CFP®, AIF®, CSCP® has been a compliance consultant with Core Compliance & Legal Services, Inc. since May 2015. Mr. Watanabe entered the securities industry in 1983 and has been a successful financial planner, branch manager, operations manager, chief compliance officer, and chief operating officer. Mr. Watanabe has broker-dealer and investment adviser compliance experience covering retail brokerage, market making, research, investment banking, insurance, commodities, retail investment advisory and ERISA plans.

Mr. Watanabe served on the FINRA District 2 Committee from 2008-11 and was chairman of the committee in 2011. He also served six years on the NSCP Board of Directors and was chairman of the Board in 2013. Mr. Watanabe is a frequent speaker at compliance conferences and has authored numerous articles and training modules for compliance professionals. Mr. Watanabe's experience in senior management as well as a producing financial adviser brings an extremely valuable perspective to compliance consulting.

CHAPTER 19

Forensic Testing

By Jeffrey Hiller
Principal Global Investors, LLC

I. INTRODUCTION

Rule 206(4)-7 under the Investment Advisers Act of 1940 ("Advisers Act") mandates that investment advisers review, no less frequently than annually, the adequacy of the policies and procedures established and the effectiveness of their implementation.[1] In order to meet this requirement, investment advisers should incorporate forensic testing as a critical component of their compliance program.

Forensic tests are broad tests of policies and procedures, including tests of the existing daily and periodic monitoring by the adviser that may assist in determining whether firms' activities are consistent with their compliance policies and procedures.[2] For example, although investment advisers may conduct daily tests for fair allocation of securities to client accounts, an effective forensic test will accumulate data over time to determine whether there are exceptions, trends, or enhancements needed to the firms' policies and procedures?

This chapter will address the types of forensic tests that may be used in order to prevent and detect violations of the federal securities laws. In addition, the chapter will discuss the implementation of such tests, recognizing that tests must be adapted to the unique characteristics of each firm.

II. FORENSIC TESTING DEFINED

The SEC has mandated that advisers must implement policies and procedures in a manner designed to detect violations of the securities laws.[3] The SEC does not specifically mandate forensic testing, nor has it specifically defined *forensic testing*. However, the SEC stated in its Adopting Release to Rule 206(4)-7 as follows:

---

[1] SEC, Final Rule, *Compliance Programs of Investment Companies and Investment Advisers*, IA Rel. No. 2204 (Dec. 13, 2003).
[2] *See* CCOutreach National Seminar, Forensic Measures for Funds and Advisers (Nov. 14, 2007), www.sec.gov/info/cco/forensictesting.pdf
[3] SEC, Final Rule, *Compliance Programs of Investment Companies and Investment Advisers*.

> Where appropriate, advisers' policies and procedures should employ, among other methods of detection, compliance tests that analyze information over time in order to identify unusual patterns, including, for example, an analysis of the quality of brokerage executions (for the purpose of evaluating the adviser's fulfillment of its duty of best execution), or an analysis of the portfolio turnover rate (to determine whether portfolio managers are overtrading securities), or an analysis of the comparative performance of similarly managed accounts (to detect favoritism, misallocation of investment opportunities, or other breaches of fiduciary responsibilities).[4]

Accordingly, forensic tests analyze information over time to identify patterns and trends to determine whether advisers' activities are consistent with its compliance policies and procedures.[5] Forensic tests are designed to find matters that may not be detected through your daily transactional and other compliance testing. As Lori Richards, former director of the SEC's Office of Compliance Inspections and Examinations (OCIE) expressed it, "A good forensic test has three characteristics. First, it provides a real test. Second, it helps you answer the question: what am I missing? Third, it adds current value."[6]

Forensic tests should be distinguished from the daily tests, such as guideline monitoring, approved broker monitoring, and the like, that are embedded in your routine monitoring and testing program. In addition, forensic tests should be distinguished from periodic tests, such as review of approved brokers and the like, that may be conducted quarterly or on a less frequent basis but are designed to identify current exceptions, not trends and patterns of inappropriate conduct. Forensic tests are designed to identify trends and patterns in determining whether the daily and periodic tests are effective in preventing and detecting violations of the securities laws.

> **Compliance Example:** As an example, your daily allocation test may find that the allocations to client accounts were fair and reasonable for the specific allocation tested. Some accounts may have been omitted from the allocation in accordance with your policies and procedures. A forensic test of allocation will look at all of the allocations over a period of time to identify whether there are trends or patterns that may identify issues not previously noted in the daily and periodic tests. In the case of an allocation, an account may have been omitted because it is determined an account did not have sufficient cash to participate and thus was appropriate for exclusion. However, the forensic test may identify that that particular account was omitted from 25 percent of all allocations over the tested period, even though the allocations passed the daily or routine tests. This finding would raise a red flag and trigger an inquiry into why this account was omitted so frequently.

---

[4] SEC, Final Rule, *Compliance Programs of Investment Companies and Investment Advisers*, fn. 15.
[5] *See* CCOutreach National Seminar, Forensic Measures for Funds and Advisers.
[6] *See* Lori Richards, Remarks before the National Society of Compliance Professional National Membership Meeting (Oct. 25, 2005), www.sec.gov/news/speech/spch102605lr.htm

Finding Compliance Exceptions

In each forensic test an adviser should ask, "What is the objective of the test?" Forensic tests are designed to find exceptions to the adviser's policies, procedures, practices, and applicable rules and regulations that you may not find in daily and periodic transaction testing. You should expect to find issues or matters that raise red flags of which you should follow up for further examination. Moreover, in addition to reviewing documents and records the adviser should, as appropriate, supplement what it learns through forensic testing with discussions with people within the firm to get a full picture of how the policies and procedures work in practice.

Maintain Documentation of Testing

Advisers are required to maintain any records documenting the investment adviser's annual review of those policies and procedures conducted pursuant to Rule 206(4)-7.[7] As a practical matter, the SEC will likely request the backup material to your reports of forensic testing to understand and examine the methodology employed in your testing and to verify that the adviser completed the tests claimed.

When to Conduct Testing

Rule 206(4)-7 requires advisers to review, no less frequently than annually, the adequacy of their policies and procedures and the effectiveness of their implementation.[8] As a practical matter, compliance officers should consider conducting forensic tests throughout the year and incorporating their findings into their annual review and report. This will help the Compliance Department avoid a year-end rush and allow for time to plan for exams in a manner that can be thorough. This approach also facilitates time for matters that arise in the normal course of business that may warrant more robust forensic tests.

What to Test

Advisers should conduct risk assessments of compliance with the federal securities laws to identify the risks associated with their specific business model and nature of their operations.[9] This review should cover all conflicts and potential conflicts of interest. The risk assessment may be used to identify the appropriate subjects of forensic testing and to determine the frequency of such tests.[10]

> **Compliance Tip:** It is critical that an adviser follow the specific firm's own internal compliance policies, even if they are not required by regulation. These internal rules should be included in the forensic testing program. During an examination the SEC may find certain internal

---

[7] See IA Rule 204(2)(a)(17).
[8] Rule 206(4)-7(b) under the Advisers Act.
[9] See CCOutreach National Seminar, Common Examination Areas (Nov. 14, 2006).
[10] See Gene Gohlke, Examination of "Annual" Reviews Conducted by Advisers and Funds, SEC Press Release (Apr. 7, 2006); CCOutreach Regional Seminars, Investment Adviser Case Study Discussion Guide (2006).

practices inadequate that may arguably not be proscribed by the federal securities laws, but the examiner will nonetheless comment on their deficiency. As a hypothetical example, an adviser has a policy that portfolio managers may not accept any honorarium from public or private companies because it considers it a conflict of interest. This policy is not required by any federal regulation but because the adviser established the policy itself, the firm must have a process in place to monitor this policy, either through certifications, periodic internet searches, or other means. If the SEC found the adviser did not implement its own policy, the SEC would likely cite this in a deficiency letter.

In addition, advisers should consider SEC priorities and recent issues and enforcement actions. The SEC's OCIE periodically announces its examination priorities.[11] The SEC also issues National Exam Program Risk Alerts.[12] These alerts announce issues that the SEC staff perceives to have heightened risk. Accordingly, when advisers develop and prioritize their forensic testing program they should incorporate the SEC's current priorities.[13]

As a general practice, you should look at any point in the firm's operation where there may be an opportunity to disadvantage the client to the benefit of the firm or other clients, such as custody, allocation, soft dollars and other brokerage and personal trading by investment personnel, among others.

III. TESTS AND ANALYSIS

In all cases an adviser should compare its written policies and procedures to its actual practice in implementing them to ensure the adviser is following its own policies and procedures. As a practical matter, the SEC takes a harsh view when it determines an adviser's firm cannot even follow its own policies. Such a determination erodes confidence and results in closer scrutiny by the SEC.

It is important to note that firms are varied in their organization and operations and Compliance officers should tailor their tests to the particular nature of their firms operations.[14]

Prior Compliance Exceptions, Changes in Business Arrangements, and Regulatory Developments

The SEC has mandated that advisers should review any compliance matters that arose during the previous year, any changes in the business activities of the adviser or its af-

---

[11] OCIE, NEP, Examination Priorities for 2014 (Jan. 9, 2014); *see also* CCOutreach National Seminar, Forensic Measures for Funds and Advisers; CCOutreach National Seminar, Top Deficiencies Identified in Examinations (2008); CCOutreach Regional Seminars, The Evolving Compliance Environment: Examination Focus Areas (Apr. 2009), www.sec.gov/info/iaiccco/iaiccco-focusareas.pdf
[12] *See*, e.g., *National Exam Program Risk Alert*, Vol. II, Issue 3 (Aug. 27 2013); Gohlke, Examination of "Annual" Reviews.
[13] *Id.*.
[14] *See* Adopting Release 206(4)-7.

filiates, and any changes to applicable regulations that might suggest a need to revise the adviser's policies and procedures.[15]

Prior Compliance Exceptions

As a matter of course, the adviser's Compliance Department should detect compliance exceptions throughout the year and during its annual review of its compliance program. The SEC expects advisers to find violations and is skeptical when they do not.[16]

Prior compliance exceptions or violations should be logged to track for trends and patterns. When reviewing the results of your forensic tests, you should ask whether there are common issues, personnel, locations, clients, and times of year, among other questions depending on the nature of the exception. Moreover, the prior compliance exceptions should be rereviewed periodically (at least annually and more frequently depending on the severity of the violation) to ensure that they do not recur, that the corrective actions have been fully implemented, and that it is not indicative of a larger, systemic problem.

> **Compliance Example:** In the previous year's review of marketing and advertising material, the Compliance Department found that the performance numbers in several advertising pieces were inaccurate and used stale numbers. Once identified, this exception should be regularly reviewed until it is determined that the corrective actions were effective on an ongoing basis. In the event of material exception, even after corrective action has been implemented and tested for effectiveness, it is advisable to review, at least semiannually, the prior exception to ensure that the corrective action is effective on an ongoing basis.

The SEC Division of Enforcement's Asset Management Unit has instituted a Compliance Program Initiative that focuses on advisers that have previously received letters from the SEC finding compliance deficiencies but failed to correct them.[17] The SEC takes a dim view of repeat violations and imposes stiff penalties in such cases.[18] When SEC examiners identify deficiencies in a firm's compliance program, those deficiencies need to be corrected before they lead to other securities law violations that could harm investors. Investment advisers that essentially ignore SEC examination warnings risk being the subject of SEC enforcement actions.[19]

---

[15] Adopting Release 206(4)-7.
[16] *See* CCOutreach Regional Seminars, The Evolving Compliance Environment; Gohlke, Examination of "Annual" Reviews; SEC, Questions Advisers Should Ask While Establishing or Reviewing Their Compliance Program, SEC Press Release (May 2006).
[17] *See* SEC Penalizes Investment Advisers for Compliance Failures, SEC Press Release 2011-248 (Nov. 28, 2011).
[18] *See e.g., In the Matter of Asset Advisers, LLC,* Investment Advisers Act of 1940 Rel. No. 29874 (Nov. 28, 2011); *In the Matter of FELTL & Company, Inc.,* Investment Advisers Act of 1940 Rel. No. 3325 (Nov. 28, 2011); *In the Matter of OMNI Investment Advisers Inc. and Gary R. Beynon,* Investment Advisers Act of 1940 Rel. No. 3323 (Nov. 28, 2011).
[19] *See* SEC Penalizes Investment Advisers for Compliance Failures.

> **Compliance Tip:** Advisers that have been examined by the SEC should keep a list of all deficiencies identified. Advisers should catalog all deficiencies noted by examiners and not just those from the most recent exam. The past deficiencies should be reviewed at least annually, or more often depending on the nature, severity, and complexity of the compliance deficiency, to ensure that the matters have been corrected and that there has been no recurrence.

Changes in Business Arrangements

Changes to an adviser firm's business or that of its affiliates can have a substantial impact on its compliance program. Changes in business activities of the adviser that would warrant additional review or heightened scrutiny include, but are not limited to, mergers and acquisitions, expansion of the adviser's activities to new jurisdictions, internal reorganizations and newly created offices or divisions, turnover of key personnel, new product development, changes in fee arrangements, and systems and technology changes. Changes in business activities may also give rise to the need for new or revised policies and procedures, coordination among advisers and their affiliates, and training of appropriate personnel, to ensure that compliance requirements are understood and implemented effectively.

> **Compliance Example:** An adviser that is acquired by a broker-dealer or by the corporate parent of a broker-dealer should assess whether its policies and procedures are adequate to guard against the conflicts that arise when the adviser uses that broker-dealer to execute client transactions, or invests client assets in funds or other securities distributed or underwritten by the broker-dealer.[20]

Regulatory Changes

Advisers must have a process in place to identify in a timely manner any changes in the Investment Advisers Act of 1940 or other applicable regulations that might suggest a need to revise the policies and procedures.[21] Advisers should identify all such changes and test their compliance policies, procedures, and practices against these revisions in order to demonstrate their compliance with the regulatory changes and SEC priorities. While the adviser's firm should implement the changes in a timely manner as proscribed by the regulator, it should test annually that the new requirements are being met.

> **Compliance Tip:** Advisers should scrutinize SEC enforcement actions to get a good understanding of the areas of SEC focus and test their compliance program against the violations announced in applicable enforcement actions. You may find that you have not been testing a particular subject

---

[20] Adopting Release 206(4)-7.
[21] *Id.*

because it did not seem to present a risk or just fell through the cracks. Scrutinizing SEC actions is a good way to identify risks. In addition, advisers may decide that they do not need a policy if they do not engage in a certain practice. For example, an adviser may prohibit all internal cross trades and thus see no need for a cross trade policy beyond its prohibition and no need for testing. Notwithstanding its policy, the adviser should regularly test to ensure there were no cross trade transactions and should have a procedure to address how the adviser will manage an inadvertent cross trade.

Compliance Example: The SEC announced with *In the Matter of Western Asset Management Company*[22] (WAM) that it imposed sanctions against the adviser for concealing investor losses that resulted from a coding error and engaging in cross trading that favored some clients over others.[23] According to the SEC order instituting settled administrative proceedings, WAM served as an investment manager primarily to institutional clients, many of which were ERISA plans. Western Asset breached its fiduciary duty by failing to disclose and promptly correct a coding error that caused the improper allocation of a restricted private investment to the accounts of ERISA clients. The private investment that was off-limits to ERISA plans had plummeted in value by the time the coding error was discovered, and Western Asset had an obligation to reimburse clients for such losses under the terms of its error correction policy. Instead, WAM did not notify its ERISA clients until nearly two years later.[24] Once this action was announced by the SEC, a diligent Compliance Department would take the following actions: ensure that it policies and procedures required timely correction of all errors, test its systems for similar coding errors, and verify that it had not engaged in the improper allocation of a restricted private investments to the accounts of ERISA clients. This review should be documented and incorporated into the advisers annual compliance review pursuant to Rule 206(4)-7.

Investment Adviser Code of Ethics

The SEC's Final Rule 204A-1implementing the Investment Advisers Code of Ethics mandates registered investment advisers to adopt a code of ethics designed to promote compliance with fiduciary standards by advisers and their personnel.[25] The rule requires advisers to review periodically the personal securities transactions and holdings of its access persons[26] and to review all violations.[27]

---

[22] *See In the Matter of Western Asset Management Company,* Investment Advisers Act Rel. No. 3763 (January 27, 2014).
[23] *Id.*
[24] *Id.*
[25] Rule 204A-1, 17 CFR 275.204A-1.
[26] Rule 204A-1(a)(3).
[27] Rule 204A-1(a)(4).

In practice, most mid- to large-sized adviser firms have automated personal securities trading systems tied to their firm's trading desks that monitor personal trading and address preclearance. Smaller firms may do this manually. The process usually requires access persons to preclear their personal securities transactions in the system, and the system either grants or denies permission to trade in the requested security based on current data. Even after approval, violations can occur as a result of failure to preclear a transaction, purchasing/selling the wrong security or more shares than approved, violations of the 7-day rule prohibiting trading 7days before and after a client transaction, failure to submit required reports, and other matters depending on the requirements contained in the adviser's code of ethics.

The SEC has suggested that advisers should conduct forensic tests regarding the personal trading of access persons as follows:[28] First, assess whether the access person is trading for his or her own account in the same securities he is trading for clients, and if so, whether clients are receiving terms as favorable as the access person takes.[29] If the access person is trading the same securities for his or her personal account as the person uses for clients, you should compare the prices of the security and transaction costs received by the access person and client to ensure the access person is not giving him- or herself favorable treatment. Further, it is advisable to examine the time of the placement of trades for the access person and the client. You want to determine whether the access person buys before placing the client's purchase or sells before he or she places the client's sell order to identify whether the access person is taking advantage of the clients' larger trades that may impact the market price. In the event you determine that the access person does get more favorable price and or terms, you should follow up to determine whether there is anything inappropriate occurring.

Second, periodically analyze the access person's trading for patterns that may indicate abuse.[30] In this instance, you should look to see whether the access person is trading frequently in and out of the same fund managed by the adviser that may indicate impermissible market timing. Also, the adviser should examine trading in a security on the restricted list or trading in a security shortly before it is placed on the restricted list that may indicate possible misuse of material nonpublic information.

Third, you should investigate any substantial disparities between the quality of performance the access person achieves for his or her own account and that the person achieves for clients.[31] In the event the access person is getting better performance than his or her client, you must understand why this is occurring. Is the access person trading in securities that he or she could purchase for the client but took for him- or herself? Is the access person purchasing before the client purchase to get a better price or selling before the client sale in the same security that may drive down the price?

---

[28] Rule 204A-1.
[29] Final Rule, Investment Adviser Code of Ethics, IA Rel. No. 2256 (July 2, 2004).
[30] *Id.*
[31] *See* Final Rule, Investment Adviser Code of Ethics; *see also* OCIE, NEP, Examination Priorities for 2014 (Jan. 9, 2014); *see also* CCOutreach National Seminar, Forensic Measures for Funds and Advisers; CCOutreach National Seminar, Top Deficiencies Identified in Examinations (2008); and CCOutreach Regional Seminars, The Evolving Compliance Environment.

Fourth, investigate any substantial disparities between the percentage of trades that are profitable when the access person trades for his or her own account and the percentage that are profitable when he or she places trades for clients.[32] You would ask the same questions posed above to determine whether the access person might have traded inappropriately.

Additionally, the SEC staff has specifically suggested the following tests when reviewing personal trading at an adviser:

- Review of access persons' trades—
  - Consider including proprietary and other related trades in the adviser's electronic trading system, allowing for electronic tracking of access persons' trades,
  - Systematically compare personal trading to any restricted lists,
  - Periodically analyze access persons' trading for patterns that may indicate abuse, such as consistently trading ahead of client accounts, and
  - Review client files of affiliated persons for any unreported brokerage accounts;
- Performance disparities among clients and accounts of insiders—
  - Calculate one- and three-year average annual total returns for every proprietary account of the adviser and every account of an access person. Compare the returns on these accounts to those earned by clients and further analyze any wide discrepancies, and
  - Compare performance among client and proprietary accounts managed under similar investment styles over a one or two year period. Identify accounts whose performance is significantly higher than the average of all accounts in a style. Review trading in such accounts to determine whether a reason for the unusual performance may be due to the unfair or fraudulent allocation of trades. For example, check whether a trade intended for one client was diverted to a proprietary account or the account of an insider by changing the allocation or settlement instructions given to the executing broker;
- Percentage of profitable trades in an access person's accounts—
  - Calculate the number of profitable trades in each proprietary and access person's account over the previous 12 months and the average number of such trades for these accounts. Compare the number of profitable trades in these propriety/access persons accounts to those in clients' accounts and if there are significant discrepancies, determine the reason.[33]

  > **Compliance Tip:** You may elect to review a percentage of the access people each quarter until you complete all of the access employees. In the event you find unusual trading by an access person, you should continue to monitor that person on an ongoing basis, even if you find no wrongdoing until you determine that the pattern is no longer a red flag.

---

[32] Final Rule, Investment Adviser Code of Ethics; see also OCIE, NEP, Examination Priorities for 2014 (Jan. 9, 2014); see also CCOutreach National Seminar, Forensic Measures for Funds and Advisers; CCOutreach National Seminar, Top Deficiencies Identified in Examinations (2008); CCOutreach Regional Seminars, The Evolving Compliance Environment.
[33] CCOutreach National Seminar, Forensic Measures for Funds and Advisers.

Code of ethics violations should be reviewed year-over-year and a trend analysis should be conducted to identify any patterns. If possible, you should compare data over a three- to four-year period. The objective of this trend analysis is to identify a pattern in specific violations to see whether there are broader concerns; to identify areas where you can take action to enhance your compliance policies, procedures, and practices including training programs to make them more effective; and to determine whether prior changes to policies, procedures, and practices were effective in their implementation.

Compliance Tip: Examine trends of violations of the code of ethics to identify whether a particular type of violation, such as failure to preclear a trade or failure to report an outside business interest is increasing or decreasing. You will then have substantive reasons to direct your training on this type of violation or identify other enhancements to your compliance program that can be made to reduce these violations. You should examine the following:

- Compare the number of violations year-over-year: Are they increasing or decreasing? Note that when reviewing this it is more effective to compare the number of violations on a percentage basis because the number of employees at the adviser may change year-to-year;
- Whether specific types of violations such as failure to pre-clear a security or report an outside business activity are increasing or decreasing;
- Whether there are specific jobs, such as trader or portfolio manager, in which more violations are committed than others;
- Whether there are specific systems where more violations occur;
- Whether certain employees are committing more violations than others and whether they are repeat offenders; and
- Whether certain violations occur at a specific time each year, such as summer vacation, holidays or the end of the reporting period.

Compliance Example: Table 1 shows a sample, abbreviated report that can be done either manually at small advisers or automated at large advisers.

TABLE 1.			
SEC Divisions	2011	2012	2013
Number of Employees	30	45	50
Preclearance violations	2 (6.6%)	7 (15.5%)	7 (14%)
Failure to report outside business interests	1 (3%)	1 (2.2%)	1 (2%)
Total Violations	3 (10%)	8 (17.7%)	16 (18%)

When looking at this data you should ask the following questions, among others:

- Why has the total number of violations increased? Did you cut back on training? Are there a lot of new rules or policies that need to be explained? Are there new employees or people in new job functions that are causing the errors? Is the preclearance system accurate and system appropriately tied to the trading desks? Are there appropriate backup personnel when the primary person responsible is on holiday? Is the number of violations high or low in relation to other advisers in the industry? You want to ask questions to determine why there was an increase in violations and what can be done to reduce them;
- Preclearance violations increased dramatically in 2012 from 2011 and remained high in 2013. Why did employees fail to preclear trades? Was it forgetfulness, inability to access system, human error or other reasons? Do you need to conduct more training? Are these occurring at particular times of the year? Are there actions you can take to reduce the violations?
- Failure to report outside business interests remained essentially constant over the three-year period; and
- Are there factors, such as increased training and awareness or past compliance initiatives that account for this remaining steady and relatively low? Are there actions that the Compliance Department can take to reduce the violations?

Valuation

Valuation has an impact on performance and the fees advisers charge to clients, so it is critical to test the fairness and accuracy of the firm's valuation of securities. A firm should test the adequacy and effectiveness of its valuation policies and procedures to detect situations where market values materially deviate from values used to price client portfolios.[34]

The adviser should maintain a list of all securities that have been fair valued or priced by the adviser and compare them to the selling price to determine the accuracy of the fair value price.[35] In addition, it should maintain a list of securities where the adviser overrode the price provided by the pricing service.[36] This data is critical in determining whether the procedures used are fair and reasonable over time. The SEC has suggested the following tests applicable to advisers when examining valuation:

- Pricing of securities—
  - Review the pricing of securities prior to the sale date. Compare selling prices to the price used the previous day or to prices used over the previous several days,
  - Review portfolios for static prices (i.e., positions that have had the same value for a significant period;

---

[34] CCOutreach Regional Seminars, The Evolving Compliance Environment: Examination Focus Areas (April 2009).
[35] Id.
[36] See SEC Penalizes Investment Advisers for Compliance Failures.

- Differences between selling prices and fair values—
  - Compare fair values with selling prices to evaluate the accuracy of fair value pricing procedures,
  - Compare prices realized upon the sale of securities with the valuation applied to those securities at their most recent valuation dates. Aggregate the results of these individual tests across longer periods and use market factors to test the efficacy of fair value pricing processes, and
  - Evaluate results to determine if fair value pricing processes produce systemic overvaluations;[37]
- Other facts and circumstances reviewed during its tests of valuation—
  - Examine the dates of the valuations for several quarters to ensure that valuations are not inflated at quarter end to show better results,
  - Review minutes of Brokerage Committee or Fair Value Committee (if the firm has such committees), to ensure processes were followed and to understand how the valuation was determined,
  - Identify the participants in the process and the portfolios impacted by the valuation to determine whether certain individuals may be inflating prices or whether certain portfolios are seeking higher values to show better performance in their fund,
  - Review all backup documentation to ensure you are not only meeting books and records requirements but to understand why the action occurred, and
  - Review all fair-valued and illiquid securities held by clients and compare the fair value to the price of any securities sold to determine the accuracy and effectiveness of the fair value process and procedures and whether any changes to the valuation policy and practices needs enhancements.

Compliance Tip: Many firms use third-party pricing services and quotation services to value their securities. It is important to conduct service provider due diligence on the pricing services to ensure that their processes are consistent, appropriate and that their methodology is reasonable. See the later discussion of third-party services providers.

Trade Aggregation, Block Trades, or "Bunching"

Trade aggregation occurs when the adviser combines client accounts to buy or sell the same security and trades them in a block. The adviser purchases securities and then allocates them back to clients based on the existing allocation policy of the adviser.

The objective of testing trade allocation is to determine whether there was any favoritism for certain accounts, whether all policies and procedures were followed, and whether all required books and records were maintained. When testing to determine the appropriateness of aggregated trades, the adviser should do the following:

- Compare the advisers' policies and procedures to the actual aggregated trade to ensure the policy is being followed;

---

[37] CCOutreach National Seminar, Forensic Measures for Funds and Advisers.

- Examine accounts that were excluded from the aggregated trade to determine whether their exclusion was appropriate and consistent with the policy; and
- Review the excluded accounts to determine whether there is any pattern of exclusion of some accounts over time (quarterly or semiannually) that may give rise to a pattern of favoring some accounts over others. Is there a pattern of omitting certain accounts on a regular or on a more frequent basis than other accounts? Why were they left out of the aggregation? Did they trade anyway? Did they get a better price?[38]

Trade Allocation

Trade allocation tests review whether over time one account is treated more favorably than another when an adviser is purchasing the same security for several clients.[39] This situation generally arises when there are a limited number of securities available and the adviser is not able to get all of the securities sought for clients. In that case, the adviser must allocate the securities among clients based on the firm's policies and procedures to ensure fairness to all clients.

Generally, advisers have daily trade allocation reports that are reviewed for consistency with the advisers' policy. The forensic test of allocations will review the allocated trades over a period of time (quarterly or semiannually) to see whether there are patterns or trends not identified in the daily tests. The advisers should ask the following questions and take the following steps[40]:

- Was the allocation made before the trade was placed with the broker or after the broker filled the order (if the allocation was made after the order was filled then it should be closely scrutinized to make sure no accounts were excluded in order to favor others and consistent with disclosures)?
- Are allocations of limited investment opportunities such as hot initial public offerings (IPOs) dispersed among clients in ways that fairly reflect clients' investment objectives and restrictions, disclosures made to clients, and your fiduciary relationship with the clients?
- Are allocations of positions among clients acquired in block or bunched trades consistent with disclosures and the adviser's fiduciary relationship with clients?[41]
- Are proprietary accounts' and access person participation in investment opportunities, including blocked or bunched trades, consistent with the adviser firm' code of ethics and disclosures made to clients? Also, is any SEC staff issued interpretive guidance, such as no-action letters, applicable?[42]

---

[38] *See* SEC, Questions Advisers Should Ask While Establishing or Reviewing their Compliance Programs; Gohlke, Examination of "Annual" Reviews; CCOutreach National Seminar, Forensic Measures for Funds and Advisers; Office of Compliance Inspections and Examinations, Core Initial Request for Information (Nov. 2008), www.sec.gov/info/requestlistcore.com

[39] *See* Generally Final Rule, Compliance Programs of Investment Companies and Investment Advisers, IA Rel. No. 2204, fn. 15 (Dec. 13, 2003).

[40] *See* SEC, Questions Advisers Should Ask While Establishing or Reviewing their Compliance Programs; Gohlke, Examination of "Annual" Reviews; CCOutreach National Seminar, Forensic Measures for Funds and Advisers; OCIE, Core Initial Request for Information.

[41] *Id.*

[42] *Id.*

- When changes are made to the initial decisions regarding the allocation of trades among client, proprietary, and/or access persons' accounts, are these changes supported by fully documented and approved audit trails?[43]

Side-by-Side Management of Client Accounts

It is not unusual for advisers to manage registered investment companies and hedge funds side-by-side on the same trading desk. Generally, advisers have the potential to earn higher compensation if the hedge fund performs well, thus presenting a conflict that must be managed. The Compliance Department must monitor these arrangements to determine that the adviser is not favoring higher-paying clients over lower-paying ones.

Compliance officers should routinely (monthly or quarterly) segregate and review such accounts to ensure that all allocations among hedge funds and other, lower-paying clients are fair and equitable over time. Compliance officers should review accounts excluded from the allocation to make sure they were not excluded to make additional shares available to other accounts.

Additionally, compliance professionals should test the firm's policies to ensure that they do not facilitate unequal treatment. For example, a policy may exclude accounts from an allocation or IPO unless the account purchases a certain number or dollar amount of the securities. Although such exclusion may seem *de minimis* for any single transaction, if looked at over a longer period of time—say six months to a year—it may cause a significant difference in performance. If so, compliance officers should look for other methods of fair and reasonable allocation.

Another review should look at large transactions in other accounts managed by the adviser that may inflate the price of the same security held in the hedge fund. This review can be accomplished by examining the ten largest trades or all trades that moved the market at a set threshold to determine the impact on other portfolios.

Finally, for accounts that are managed in a similar style, are in the same composite, and are appropriate for comparison, a performance dispersion test will identify differences in accounts. You should question disparate performance to ensure that there were legitimate reasons for the discrepancy and not favoritism of one account or group of accounts over others.

Brokerage Arrangements and Best Execution

Brokerage arrangements and best execution are nearly always part of a routine SEC examination of registered investment advisers.[44] This is because there has been a history of misuse of such requirements to benefit the adviser at the expense of clients.

---

[43] *Id.*

[44] *See* OCIE, NEP, Examination Priorities for 2014 (January 9, 2014); *See also* CCOutreach National Seminar, Forensic Measures for Funds and Advisers; CCOutreach National Seminar, Top Deficiencies Identified in Examinations (2008); CCOutreach Regional Seminars, The Evolving Compliance Environment.

The objective in testing brokerage arrangements and best execution is to ensure that the firm is meeting its fiduciary duty to clients in the trade and execution of client assets and to ensure no accounts are favored over others. With regard to brokerage arrangements and execution, the SEC staff has suggested the following forensic tests[45]:

- Average commission rates paid to broker-dealers;[46] and
- Compute the average commission rates paid to broker-dealers used during a period to identify brokers with whom the adviser may have undisclosed conflicts of interest.

By identifying commission rates outside the norm, the adviser can examine the reasons for the rates, including favoritism to such broker.

Most firms have implemented an approved broker or counterparty list that has been vetted by the firm for appropriate use by its traders. Generally, traders may only trade with counterparties on the approved list. Advisers should identify any trades executed by brokers not on the approved counterparty list and examine the reasons the broker was used and any potential violations of policies and procedures.

Average Commission Rates Paid by Advisory Clients.[47] Calculate the average commission rates paid by various advisory clients and compare the individual client averages to the average commission rate paid by all clients. Identify significant disparities among clients and identify clients that have been referred or have directed brokerage arrangements, which may result in these clients paying different (often higher) commission rates than other clients of the adviser or getting less effective executions.

Total Commission Paid to Broker-Dealers.[48] Calculate the total commissions paid to each broker-dealer used during a period to identify brokers with whom the adviser has a significant relationship. This forensic measure may show the relative importance of each broker-dealer with whom an adviser maintains an arrangement and may reveal undisclosed conflicts of interest.

Because best execution is a constant focus of SEC examinations of investment advisers,[49] adviser firms should have robust policy and procedures describing how they will attempt to achieve best execution. It is advisable to test the application of the procedures quarterly to ensure that the requirements are being met.

Most policies mandate that an adviser firm establish a Brokerage Committee to review whether the adviser is achieving best execution and have incorporated approved counterparty lists, third-party trade cost analysis, and other measures to evaluate best

---

[45] *See* SEC, Questions Advisers Should Ask While Establishing or Reviewing their Compliance Programs; Gohlke, Examination of "Annual" Reviews; CCOutreach National Seminar, Forensic Measures for Funds and Advisers; OCIE, Core Initial Request for Information.
[46] *Id.*
[47] *Id.*
[48] *Id.*
[49] *See* OCIE, NEP, Examination Priorities for 2014 (Jan. 9, 2014).

execution. When testing for whether the adviser is achieving best execution, you should ask the following questions:

- Is the best execution policy consistent with the advisers' disclosure documents?
- If the firm has a Brokerage Committee, does it meet as scheduled and is there documentation of the actions and conclusions of the committee?
- Do you periodically evaluate arrangements with broker-dealers to determine that those broker-dealers continue to provide best execution of client orders? Are clients' orders consistently placed with broker-dealers that are likely to provide best execution?[50]
- Based on post-trade analysis of client order execution, are the full costs incurred by clients (market impact, opportunity, spreads, and commissions) consistent with your duty to seek best execution, disclosures regarding your practices in placing orders, and your status as a fiduciary?[51]
- Periodically compare brokerage commissions paid to executing broker-dealers with the value of products and services (i.e., research) you and clients have obtained from these brokers? Are the outcomes consistent with your disclosures?[52]

Soft Dollars

The SEC has defined *soft dollar practices* as arrangements under which products or services other than execution of securities transactions are obtained by an adviser from or through a broker-dealer in exchange for the direction by the adviser of client brokerage transactions to the broker-dealer.[53] Money managers who obtain brokerage and research services with client commissions do not have to purchase those services with their own funds, which creates a conflict of interest for the money managers. Section 28(e) of the Securities Exchange Act of 1934 addresses these conflicts by permitting money managers to pay higher commissions on behalf of a client than otherwise are available to obtain brokerage and research services, if managers make their good faith determination regarding the reasonableness of commissions paid.[54] The objective of testing soft dollars is to manage the inherent conflicts of interest by identifying all soft dollar arrangements and any instances that fall outside the Section 28(e) safe harbor. To that end, advisers should ask the following questions:

- Have all soft dollar arrangements been approved as required by the firm's policies and procedures?
- Are only client commissions on agency transactions and fees on certain riskless principal transactions designated by the SEC used to generate soft dollars?
- Do the soft dollar services meet the definition of "research" or "brokerage" as defined by Section 28(e)?

---

[50] SEC, Questions Advisers Should Ask While Establishing or Reviewing Their Compliance Programs.
[51] Id.
[52] Id.
[53] See Inspection Report on the Soft Dollar Practices of Broker-Dealers, Investment Advisers and Mutual Funds (Sept. 22, 1998), www.sec.gov/news/studies/softdolr.htm
[54] See Commission Guidance Regarding Client Commission Practices Under Section 28(e) of the Securities Exchange Act of 1934, Rel. No. 34-54165; File No. S7-13-06, www.sec.gov/rules/interp/2006/34-54165.pdf

- Do the services actually provide lawful and appropriate assistance in the performance of investment decision-making responsibilities?
- Is the amount of client commissions paid reasonable in light of the value of products or services provided by the broker-dealer? Compare brokerage commissions paid to executing broker dealers with the value of products and services obtained. Are the outcomes consistent with the adviser's disclosures and status as a fiduciary?[55]
- If soft dollar services are used for both eligible and ineligible ("mixed-use") purposes under Section 28(e), has a good faith allocation of the actual use been made and documented? Can you verify that hard dollars were actually paid for the "ineligible" portion of a mixed-use service? In practice, is this good faith allocation conducted and documented at least annually to ensure that circumstances have not changed that would cause the allocation of actual use to be unreasonable or inaccurate?
- Are all books and records regarding soft dollar arrangements, determinations, and reviews maintained so that the adviser can demonstrate compliance with the requirements, Section 28(e) and its analysis of soft dollars?

Portfolio Pumping and Window Dressing

The objective of a test for portfolio pumping (as the SEC defines it) is to identify whether the adviser is buying shares of stocks the fund or client already owns on the last day of the reporting period or shortly before, in order to drive up the price of the stocks and inflate the fund's performance results.[56]

In a test for window dressing (as the SEC defines it), the objective is to identify whether the adviser is buying or selling portfolio securities shortly before the date as of which a fund's holdings are publicly disclosed, in order to convey an impression that the manager has been investing in companies that have had exceptional performance during the reporting period.[57]

The SEC staff has suggested the following test for advisers to review portfolio pumping and window dressing:

> Compare portfolio turnover at the end of several reporting periods in comparison to portfolio turnover during longer periods to identify patterns of activity that could demonstrate the intent to pump the portfolio (i.e., manipulate trading to boost performance at the end of a period) or to window dress (i.e., improve the appearance of the portfolio or its performance before it is reported to clients or fund shareholders). Compute portfolio turnover rates for the five or ten days before and after quarter ends for a two or three-year period and compare these short-period turnover rates, both individually and on average, to the portfolio turnover for the account or fund for one year periods.[58]

---

[55] See SEC, Questions Advisers Should Ask While Establishing or Reviewing Their Compliance Programs.
[56] See, e.g., *Shareholder Reports and Quarterly Portfolio Disclosure of Registered Management Investment Companies*, SEC Rel. No. 33-8164 (Feb. 14, 2003).
[57] *Id.*
[58] CCOutreach National Seminar, Forensic Measures for Funds and Advisers.

To review portfolio pumping the adviser should review purchases and sales within seven to ten days of the reporting period and a few days to a week thereafter to identify any trends or patterns that might give rise to a concern the manager is engaging in portfolio pumping. When reviewing this record, you should compare daily trading patterns during the period to trading patterns at the end of the reporting period and ask:

- Did the fund increase buying at the end of the period?
- Have concentrations in a well-known or high performing stock or stocks increased at quarter end?
- Was there a big purchase that may have moved the market?
- Did you see any trends that would give rise to red flags?
- Did the adviser liquidate or sell stocks shortly after the end of the reporting period that were purchased shortly before the reporting period ended?
- If you find a pattern, does it repeat each reporting period end or is it an anomaly?

To test window dressing review trading for a week or two before the holdings are publicly disclosed and review the securities in and out of the portfolio and ask the following questions:

- Did the adviser increase buys and sells at quarter end?
- What securities were purchased? Did the adviser sell lower-quality stocks and buy higher-quality stocks?
- Are the period end purchases and sells consistent with the trading patterns during the rest of the period?

> **Compliance Tip:** Window dressing tests are normally conducted at the same time as portfolio pumping because you are using the same portfolio securities holding reports and transaction reports to identify trends and patterns in trading that occur usually at quarter end.

Trade Errors

Trade errors occur at all firms. Compliance should take steps to minimize them through identification of their cause and implementation of actions to address identified trends of exceptions.

The SEC has suggested the following forensic test for trade errors:

- Select accounts in which trade errors have occurred for a sample period and review the entries to make sure errors have been corrected promptly; and
- Identify any concentration of errors by a single broker-dealer. Follow up on any efforts to get the broker to reduce its error rate and to ensure that there were no undisclosed conflicts of interest.[59]

---

[59] CCOutreach National Seminar, Forensic Measures for Funds and Advisers.

> **Compliance Tip:** Advisers should test and analyze all trade errors and not just those that resulted in a loss to the client or firm. Generally, the cost of the error is immaterial for testing and analytical purposes and unrelated to the cause of the error itself. Depending on the number of errors, advisers should conduct this test quarterly and accumulate data for longer periods of comparison to identify significant trends and patterns.

Look for trends regarding errors at particular brokers, specific traders who may have caused errors, particular clients that had a concentration of errors, systems issues that may not meet expectations to prevent errors, overrides that may have caused the error, and timing regarding when errors occur. Select accounts in which trade errors have occurred for a sample period and review the entries to make sure errors have been corrected promptly. Identify any concentrations of errors by a single broker-dealer. Follow up on any efforts to get the broker to reduce the error rate and to ensure that there are no undisclosed conflicts of interest.

> **Compliance Example**: In one instance an adviser identified that errors more frequently occurred during the summer months when some traders and operations personnel were on holiday and the backup personnel were not as familiar with the processes. In another case, the adviser learned that new employees at the trading desk made an average of five errors their first month due to lack of appropriate training and oversight. Thereafter, such errors trailed off. Once these patterns were identified through forensic testing, corrective actions were taken to reduce the number of errors, including more supervision of new traders, additional training, and assignment of trained backup personnel during holidays.

Advertising Review

Advisers' dissemination of advertising and marketing materials is subject to the antifraud provisions of the Investment Advisers Act of 1940 and the rules thereunder as well as other rules and regulations regarding the form and content of such advertising and marketing materials.[60] Advisers must have a process in place to timely review all such material on an ongoing or daily basis.

The process for approval and the substantive review of the advertising and marketing material should be tested periodically (quarterly, semiannually, or annually as circumstances dictate) depending on the size of the firm, volume of material generated, and number of issues identified in prior reviews. The objective is to identify any exceptions to the rules and regulations as well as the advisers' written policies and procedures and to identify patterns of violations in the production of advertising materials.

---

[60] *See* Investment Advisers Act of 1940, Section 206; Rule 206(4)-1.

The SEC staff has recommended the following tests for an adviser to conduct when reviewing performance composites for marketing material compliance:

- Periodically review client account holdings for an account's appropriateness to be included in a composite, including sector and security concentrations;
- Compare client account asset levels to composite asset minimums;
- Review accounts that are excluded from composites to ensure that reasons for the exclusion are adequate and documented;
- Periodically review composite disclosures to ensure the information reported is accurate; and
- Review the appropriateness of the timing of accounts being added or removed from composites to ensure compliance with applicable policies and procedures.

Recordkeeping Related to Marketing and Performance Advertisements. Periodically test recordkeeping practices to ensure that all documents necessary to substantiate advertised performance are being appropriately created and retained.

Claims of Compliance with Global Investment Performance Standards (GIPS) or Other Ethical Standards.

- Review claims of compliance with GIPS standards for accuracy. An inaccurate claim of compliance in advertisements and other correspondence could constitute a false and misleading statement under Rule 206(4)-1(a)(5);
- Responses to requests for proposals and consultant questionnaires; and
- Periodically review responses to ensure the information reported is truthful and not misleading.[61]

When conducting the review, the reviewer should take, depending on the volume, a random sample of advertising pieces that were reviewed and compare them to the mandates of the rules and regulations, as well as the adviser's policy to ensure that all requirements were met. As an alternative, if several people review advertising material you could review each individual's work periodically to identify issues with a specific reviewer. In the event you identify a reviewer that makes more issues than others, you should review his/her work more often.

For each sampled advertising piece reviewed, the adviser should identify who reviewed the piece and ask questions such as the following:

- Are all performance numbers accurate?
- Are all disclosures contained on the piece in the form and substance required?
- Are all statements of fact accurate and not misleading?
- Are claims for of compliance with GIPS standards accurate?
- Are the books and records being maintained as required?

---

[61] CCOutreach National Seminar, Forensic Measures for Funds and Advisers.

- Is the advertisement being used only in permissible jurisdictions where the adviser is appropriately licensed?
- If errors are found are they concentrated in a particular area, such as incorrect or inaccurate numbers, missing disclosers, or other similarity? Are frequent errors made by a particular person or at a particular time of year?

In the event you find exceptions to the rules, regulations, and policies you should look at other pieces by the reviewer to ensure it is not a systemic problem.

> **Compliance Tip:** The adviser should review requests for proposals and consultant questionnaires to be sure the responses reported are truthful and not misleading. In some cases, advisers use a database of preapproved responses to questions that change frequently. In those cases make sure that responses are up to date with changes that may have occurred at the advisers firm and reflect compliance with regulatory changes.

Solicitors Agreements

The SEC mandates that advisers may not pay compensation to solicitors unless certain conditions are met. The conditions include, among others, prohibitions on compensating solicitors that have engaged in prohibited conduct defined by the SEC and that the cash payment must be made pursuant to a written agreement to which the adviser is a party.[62] Moreover, the solicitor must provide the client with a current copy of the investment adviser's required written disclosure statement (brochure) and a separate solicitor's written disclosure document. The adviser must receive from the client a signed, dated acknowledgment of receipt of both the adviser's and the solicitors written disclosure statements.

The objective of this test is to identify exceptions to the Solicitors Rule (Rule 206(4)-3) so that the adviser can be sure that the client has received all disclosures and that the adviser and solicitor are acting in accordance with the rule.

The adviser should gather all solicitors' agreements, client acknowledgments and payment records to solicitors and ask the following questions:

- Are there signed agreements in place and maintained between the adviser and solicitor consistent with the requirements of Rule 206(4)-3?
- Has the adviser conducted appropriate checks on the solicitor to ensure that he or she has not engaged in disqualifying conduct as defined by the SEC? The adviser should conduct a review of the solicitor to ensure that the solicitor has not engaged in any of the prohibited conduct set forth in the rule since the last time that the adviser examined the conduct. As a general rule, this review should be done at least annually and should be current at the time any cash payment is made to the solicitor.
- Does that solicitor maintain current licenses and registrations if they are necessary for the solicitation?

---

[62] *See* Restriction on Payment of Referral Fees, IA Rule 206(4)-3.

- Were all client acknowledgments received? Advisers may elect to contact some clients to ensure that the solicitor met the obligations expected by the adviser and that client received all required disclosures.

Portfolio Restriction and Guideline Monitoring

Generally, advisers monitor their clients' investment guidelines and regulatory restrictions through the use of an automated system. Account trades and holdings are monitored against the guidelines and usually pass through a daily pretrade check and nightly post-trade check to ensure that all guidelines and restrictions are met. The success of these daily checks is dependent on the guidelines and restrictions being coded or entered into the system accurately and that alerts or warnings generated by the system are approved or denied consistent with the clients' directions.

The objective of the test is to identify any transactions that fall outside the client's objectives and mandated guidelines and restrictions that were not identified by the daily pre- and post-trade checks. Advisers should:

- Compare a sample of clients' guidelines and restrictions to transactions on behalf of the clients and the clients' holdings. Are any disparities identified?
- Sample guidelines and restrictions in the system. Are they are coded correctly?
- If there were guideline or restriction errors, was the client notified of the error and the corrective action in a timely manner?
- Review the process for overriding system alerts and warnings, and identify individuals authorized to approve and deny alerts and warnings in the system. Are the approvers the correct persons to be assigned this task?
- Are clients' holdings consistent with the client's objectives even if all of the holdings passed the automated check?

> **Compliance Tip:** Some guidelines and restrictions can only be monitored manually even when the adviser has an automated system. Advisers should create a log of all manually monitored guidelines and restrictions and test them quarterly to identify any trends or patterns of exceptions and the effectiveness of the manually monitored restrictions and guidelines.

Safety of Client Assets: Custody

If an investment adviser holds, directly or indirectly, client funds or securities or has any authority to obtain possession of them the adviser is deemed to have custody and must comply with the Custody Rule.[63] The adviser must have policies and procedures in place to prevent and detect any misuse of client funds of which the adviser maintains custody.[64]

---

[63] See Investment Advisers Act Rule 206(4)-2, Custody of Funds or Securities of Client Accounts; see also Rule 206(4)-2 Adopting Release 206(4)-7.
[64] See IA Rule 206(4)-2.

The objective of this forensic test is two-fold: first, to determine whether the adviser has custody under the SEC's definition; and second, if the adviser does have custody, to ensure that it is meeting all of the custody rule requirements.

Even if the firm does not believe it has custody, it is prudent to do a review to make sure this continues to be the case. The SEC has provided three examples to help identify whether an adviser firm has custody under Rule 206(4)-2:

> The first example clarifies that an adviser has custody when it has possession of client funds or securities, even briefly. An adviser that holds clients' stock certificates or cash, even temporarily, puts those assets at risk of misuse or loss. The [rule], however, expressly exclude inadvertent receipt by the adviser of client funds or securities, so long as the adviser returns them to the sender within three business days of receiving them. The rule does not permit advisers to forward clients' funds and securities without having "custody," although advisers may certainly assist clients in such matters. In addition, the amendments clarify that an adviser's possession of a check drawn by the client and made payable to a third party is not possession of client funds for purposes of the custody definition.

> The second example clarifies that an adviser has custody if it has the authority to withdraw funds or securities from a client's account. An adviser with power of attorney to sign checks on a client's behalf, to withdraw funds or securities from a client's account, or to dispose of client funds or securities for any purpose other than authorized trading has access to the client's assets. Similarly, an adviser authorized to deduct advisory fees or other expenses directly from a client's account has access to, and therefore has custody of, the client funds and securities in that account. These advisers might not have possession of client assets, but they have the authority to obtain possession.

> The last example clarifies that an adviser has custody if it acts in any capacity that gives the adviser legal ownership of, or access to, the client funds or securities. One common instance is a firm that acts as both general partner and investment adviser to a limited partnership. By virtue of its position as general partner, the adviser generally has authority to dispose of funds and securities in the limited partnership's account, and thus has custody of client assets.[65]

If you have determined that you do not have custody, the SEC staff has suggested the following steps to address third-party custodian statements and book reconciliations:

---

[65] *See* Adopting Release Rule 206(4)-2.

- Review periodic reconciliation of client account statements to look for patterns among the reconciling items used over a period of time such as six months or a year to balance the positions shown by custodians to those shown on the adviser's books;[66] and
- Identify any reconciling items that consistently appear from one reconciliation to the next. These items may indicate a misuse or misappropriation of client assets. Alternatively, they may indicate sloppy recordkeeping that could result in misuse or misappropriation of client assets.[67]

If the adviser determines that it does not meet any of the exemptions and has custody, then it must review the facts and circumstances to ensure that it meets the requirements of the rule. The adviser should ask the following questions and verify that the following are in place:[68]

- Are client assets held in accounts maintained by qualified custodians as required by Rule 206(4)-2?
- If you inadvertently obtain possession of clients' assets (e.g., if a client sends you stock certificates), are required actions taken to dispose of those assets within the time periods specified in Rule 206(4)-2?
- Does the custodian of each client's account independently monitor corporate actions (e.g., stock splits and dividends) affecting the account?
- Does the custodian of each client's account independently determine the value of each position on a date near the date of each statement sent to the client and communicate such valuations and the total value of the account in its statements sent to clients?
- Are securities lending practices that involve loans of clients' securities consistent with clients' contracts and disclosures made to clients?
- Do you periodically verify the postal/email addresses to which clients' account statements are sent)?
- Do you regularly reconcile account balances and transaction detail shown on your records with information reported by clients' custodians? Is there follow-up to resolve all reconciling items?
- Are pooled vehicles over whose assets you have custody annually audited by an independent auditor in accordance with generally accepted accounting principles?
- Does the auditor performing the financial statement audit of each pooled vehicle confirm the activity in and balances of their account and appropriately follow-up with all participants in the pool on any discrepancies identified (not a specific requirement)?
- Does the auditor send a copy of the pooled vehicles' audited financial statements directly to each participant in the pooled vehicle or to a representative of the participant (this is not a specific requirement)?

---

[66] CCOutreach National Seminar, Forensic Measures for Funds and Advisers.
[67] Id.
[68] The following were derived from the SEC, Questions Advisers Should Ask While Establishing or Reviewing their Compliance Programs.

Cybersecurity

The SEC's OCIE announced that its national examination priorities for 2014 included a focus on technology and cybersecurity.[69] OCIE has conducted, and will continue to conduct, cybersecurity examinations focusing on the following topics: the entity's cybersecurity governance, identification and assessment of cybersecurity risks, protection of networks and information, risks associated with remote customer access and funds transfer requests, risks associated with vendors and other third parties, detection of unauthorized activity, and experiences with certain cybersecurity threats.[70] OCIE is using these exams to assess preparedness of advisers and identify areas where the SEC can work with advisers to protect investors and the markets from cybersecurity treats.[71] Although the 2014 OCIE initiative appears directed at information gathering, at some point the OCIE's focus will likely turn to issuing deficiency letters and, ultimately, enforcement actions.

Generally, the adviser's Compliance Department will work with operations, technology, and others to develop this policy. Compliance professionals will monitor and oversee that the policies and procedures are adequate and effective in their implementation to prevent and detect violations or breaches of its information technology environment. OCIE's Risk Alert of April 15, 2014 was accompanied by a sample request for information and documents used in its initiative.[72] The OCIE examinations will address the following areas:

- Identity of risks/cybersecurity governance;
- Protection of firm networks and information;
- Risks associated with remote customer access and funds transfer requests;
- Risks associated with vendors and other third parties;
- Detection of unauthorized activity; and
- Other matters including whether the adviser's policies and procedures include identity theft red flag rules and how the firm incorporates best practices to it specific business model, among other inquiries.[73]

In addition, the SEC will request the adviser's risk assessment, policies and procedures, information security architecture and processes,[74] practices and controls regarding the protection of its networks and information, mitigation of risks with use of vendor and service providers, and processes to detect unauthorized activity.[75]

---

[69] SEC Office of Compliance Inspections and Examinations, National Exam Program, Examination Priorities for 2014 (Jan. 9, 2014), http://www.sec.gov/about/offices/ocie/national-examination-program-priorities-2014.pdf
[70] Risk Alert, National Exam Program, SEC's Office of Compliance, Inspections and Examinations, OCIE Cyber Security Initiative (Apr. 15, 2014), http://www.sec.gov/ocie/announcement/Cybersecurity-Risk-Alert--Appendix---4.15.14.pdf.
[71] Id.
[72] Id.
[73] Id.
[74] See National Institute of Standards and Technology, Framework for Improving Critical Infrastructure Cybersecurity (Feb. 12, 2014).
[75] OCIE Cyber Security Initiative.

The objective of testing the adviser's cybersecurity policy is to determine the adequacy of the adviser's policies and procedures designed to prevent and detect violations or breaches of its information technology environment. The adviser must prepare for cybersecurity threats coming both internally and externally. The advisers should gather relevant documents and information, then speak with the personnel responsible for implementation of the policy and procedures and ask the following questions:[76]

- Does the adviser have a written information security policy and procedures?
- Can the firm establish that it has physical devices, systems, software platforms, and applications within the adviser are inventoried; maps of network resources, connections, and data flows (including locations where customer data is housed) are created or updated; connections to the adviser's network from external sources are catalogued; resources (hardware, data, and software) are prioritized for protection based on their sensitivity and business value and logging capabilities; and practices are assessed for adequacy, appropriate retention, and secure maintenance?
- Does the adviser conduct periodic risk assessments to identify cybersecurity threats, vulnerabilities, and potential business consequences? If such assessments are conducted, who conducts them, when are they conducted, and has the risk assessment identified matters that may be potentially moderate or high risk and have not yet been addressed with compensating controls?
- Does the adviser conduct periodic risk assessments to identify physical security threats and vulnerabilities that may bear on cybersecurity? Have these been addressed?
- Does the adviser have a written business continuity of operations plan that addresses mitigation of the effects of a cybersecurity incident and/or recovery from such an incident if one exists?
- Does the adviser provide written guidance and periodic training to employees concerning information security risks and responsibilities?
- Has the adviser maintained controls to prevent unauthorized escalation of user privileges, lateral movement among network resources, restricted users to those network resources necessary for their business functions, an environment for testing and development of software and applications that is separate from its business environment, a baseline configuration of hardware and software, and users are prevented from altering that environment without authorization and an assessment of security implications, a process to manage IT assets through removal, transfers, and disposition and a process for ensuring regular system maintenance, including timely installation of software patches that address security vulnerabilities?
- Does the adviser maintain a written data destruction policy?
- Does the adviser maintain a written cybersecurity incident response policy?
- Does the adviser periodically test the functionality of its backup system?
- Does the adviser conduct periodic audits of compliance with its information security policies?

---

[76] *Id.*

- If the adviser provides customers with online account access, how are customers authenticated for online account access and transactions to prevent breaches of their information security? Does the firm have procedures for verifying the authenticity of email requests seeking to transfer customer funds?
- Does the adviser conduct or require cybersecurity risk assessments of vendors and business partners with access to the adviser's networks, customer data, or other sensitive information, or due to the cybersecurity risk of the outsourced function? If so, are the third parties' procedures and practices reasonably designed to prevent and detect violations of the adviser's information technology environment?
- Does the adviser have procedures and practices to detect unauthorized activity on its networks and devices?[77]

Cybersecurity is a relatively new and complex area for advisers and their compliance departments. Depending on the size and complexity of the adviser, the review and testing of cybersecurity will likely necessitate cooperation and coordination with other functional areas including operations, technology, risk, and others with appropriate expertise, such as internal audit.

Business Continuity and Disaster Recovery Plans

The SEC expects that the adviser's policies and procedures will address business continuity plans.[78] The SEC stated that

> ...An adviser's fiduciary duty to its clients includes the obligation to take steps to protect the clients' interests from being placed at risk as a result of the adviser's inability to provide advisory services after, for example, a natural disaster or, in the case of some smaller firms, the death of the owner or key personnel. The clients of an adviser that is engaged in the active management of their assets would ordinarily be placed at risk if the adviser ceased operations.[79]

As noted earlier, compliance programs must be tailored to the unique characteristics of each adviser, depending on its size, organization, and complexity of the adviser's business, among other factors. The business continuity and disaster recovery plans of small advisers will differ substantially from those of large advisers with a global presence. An adviser should review its "business continuity plan to ensure that it covers risks to all important resources, including facilities, utilities, personnel, communications, and market access. In good practice, the business continuity plan's primary focus should be clients' prompt access to funds, securities, and account information in the event of an emergency."[80]

The objective of testing business continuity and disaster recovery plans (BCP) is to ensure that in the event the adviser's business is disrupted through a natural disaster

---

[77] *See* OCIE Cyber Security Initiative, Appendix.
[78] Adopting Release IA 206(4)-7.
[79] Adopting Release 206(4)-7, at note 22.
[80] 2008 CCOutreach Regional Seminars, Top Deficiencies Identified in Examinations.

or other event the adviser can continue to conduct business and meet the needs of its clients. When testing its BCP plans, an adviser should determine whether the following objectives are being met:

- Rapid recovery and timely resumption of critical operations following a wide-scale disruption;
- Rapid recovery and timely resumption of critical operations following the loss or inaccessibility of staff in at least one major operating location; and
- A high level of confidence, through ongoing use or robust testing, that critical internal and external continuity arrangements are effective and compatible.[81]

At a minimum, advisers should determine whether their BCP plan addresses the widespread disruption considerations, alternative locations considerations, vendor relationships, telecommunications services and technology considerations, communication plans, and regulatory and compliance considerations.[82] In addition, they should consider adopting contingencies in the event key personnel are unavailable, among other factors. In reviewing policies the adviser should consider the following disaster recovery provisions that the SEC has found effective:

- A prearranged remote location for short-term and possible long-term use;
- Alternate communication protocols to contact staff and clients, such as cell phones, text messaging, web-based email accounts, or an internet website;
- Remote access to business records and client data through appropriately secured means that ensure ongoing compliance with Regulation S-P[83] and other confidentiality requirements;
- Temporary lodging for key staff where necessary as a result of a relocation of the firm;
- Maintaining accurate and up-to-date contact information for all third-party service providers, including custodians, broker-dealers, transfer agents, pricing services, and research firms;
- Familiarity with the BCP plans of such third-party service providers;
- Contingency arrangements for loss of key personnel, such as the president or primary portfolio manager, either temporarily or permanently;
- Effective training of staff on how to fulfill essential duties in the event of a disaster, including compliance matters;
- Periodic testing, evaluation, and revision of disaster preparedness plan; and
- Maintaining sufficient insurance and financial liquidity to prevent any interruption to the performance of compliant advisory services.[84]

---

[81] Interagency Paper on Sound Practices to Strengthen the Resilience of the U.S. Financial System, SEC rel. No. 34-47638 (Apr. 7, 2003); Joint Review of Business Continuity and Disaster Recovery of Firms by the Commission's National Examination Program, the Commodity Futures Trading Commission's Division of Swap Dealers and Intermediary Oversight and the Financial Industry Regulatory Authority (Aug. 16, 2013).
[82] Risk Alert, National Exam Program, *SEC Examinations of Business Continuity Plans of Certain Advisers Following Operational Disruption Caused by Weather-Related Events Last Year*, Volume II, Issue 3 (Aug. 27, 2013).
[83] 17 CFR 248, Regulation S-P.
[84] SEC Compliance Alert (June 2007), www.sec.gov/about/offices/ocie/complialert.htm

When testing their BCP plans, advisers should consider the following actions, taking into account the nature and complexity of their business:

- Conducting full BCP tests and participating in industry testing, at least annually, but more frequently if changes are made. Firms should consider full staff BCP tests to evaluate whether all day-to-day functions, including trade processing, can be performed regardless of staff location. In addition, firms are encouraged to keep their BCPs up to date and to amend their BCPs to incorporate testing results;
- Conducting annual or more frequent training on their BCPs to familiarize all personnel with the plan and their critical pre-established roles; and
- Incorporating stress tests into their BCPs. For example, firms could perform a stress test on their liquidity position and review the level of excess customer reserves. Based on this analysis, firms may be better prepared to adjust liquidity or excess reserves (e.g., term repos versus overnight, ability to liquidate money market funds, ability to meet margin calls in a potentially volatile market, and adding excess segregation reserves) prior to an event.[85]

Form ADV Disclosure

Registered investment advisers are required to complete Form ADV. The ADV is a disclosure document that provides clients with information about the adviser. ADV Part 2, commonly called the "brochure," sets forth the minimum required disclosures that the adviser's brochure must contain:

> Under federal and state law, an adviser is a fiduciary and must make full disclosure to its clients of all material facts relating to the advisory relationship. As a fiduciary, it also must seek to avoid conflicts of interest with its clients, and, at a minimum, make full disclosure of all material conflicts of interest between the adviser and its clients that could affect the advisory relationship. This obligation requires that advisers provide the client with sufficiently specific facts so that the client is able to understand the conflicts of interest you have and the business practices in which you engage, and can give informed consent to such conflicts or practices or reject them. To satisfy this obligation, advisers therefore may have to disclose to clients information not specifically required by Part 2 of Form ADV or in more detail than the brochure items might otherwise require. You may disclose this additional information to clients in the brochure or by some other means.[86]

The SEC will examine the advisers' disclosures contained in Form ADV and test them for accuracy and to determine whether the adviser follows the practices that it discloses to its clients. As a general rule, the adviser should have a process in place to

---

[85] Joint Review of Business Continuity and Disaster Recovery of Firms by the Commission's National Examination Program, the Commodity Futures Trading Commission's Division of Swap Dealers and Intermediary Oversight and the Financial Industry Regulatory Authority (Aug. 16, 2013).
[86] Form ADV, General Instructions for Part 2 of Form ADV, www.sec.gov/about/forms/formadv-part2.pdf

ensure that all items in the form are accurate and current. The objective of testing is to ensure the accuracy of the disclosures in the form and to verify that the adviser is following its disclosed policies. The adviser should periodically test the accuracy of its statements in Form ADV, ensuring that the firm timely files its annual update and any required amendments.

In Form ADV Part 2 the firm is required to disclose among many other matters, its policies regarding code of ethics; participation or interest in client transactions and personal trading; brokerage practices including soft dollars; review of client accounts; client referrals and other compensation; custody; investment discretion; and voting client securities.

> **Compliance Example:** As an example of a Form ADV Part 2 test to assess the accuracy of the adviser's ADV, the following is an excerpt from an ADV Part 2, item 12—Brokerage Practices disclosed by an adviser (all references to names and other identifying data have been excerpted):
>
> **Selection of Brokers and Dealers**
> The [Adviser] seeks to obtain the best overall execution when selecting a broker or dealer for Client portfolio transactions. *In selecting brokers and dealers, [Adviser] considers a variety of factors including, but not limited to*:
>
> - Their financial strength and stability;
> - Best price for the trade;
> - Reasonableness of their commission, spreads, or markups;
> - Their ability to execute and clear the trade in a prompt, orderly, and satisfactory manner;
> - Quality of their executions in the past and existing relationship to date;
> - The confidentiality they provide as to the trades placed through them by the Adviser;
> - Their execution capabilities and any related risks in trading a particular block of securities;
> - Their broad market coverage resulting in a continuous flow of information concerning bids and offerings;
> - The consistent quality of their services, including the quality of any investment-related services provided (e.g. a first call on the release of influential securities reports);
> - Their record keeping practices (e.g. timely and accurate confirmations); and
> - Their cooperation in resolving differences.
>
> The [Adviser] may also use the above factors to establish generally the proportion of the overall commissions to be allocated to each broker or dealer used in effecting equity trades on behalf of its clients. There is a semiannual broker voting process that includes research analysts, portfolio managers and traders. The broker vote is designed to rank brokers based on the quality of research and trading services provided. Recommendations

are made for commission allocation based on the results of the vote. These factors and the results of the broker vote are used as general guidelines by the equity trading desk in deciding which broker-dealer to use for specific securities transactions. Because of the variety of factors used to select brokers or dealers, the determining factor in seeking best execution is not the lowest possible commission, but whether the transaction represents the best overall execution for the client. In some instances, [Adviser] will pay a broker commissions that are higher than the commissions another broker might have charged for the same transaction. Further, in the case where a firm bundles research services with its execution services, [Adviser] may consider the receipt of research services provided (including soft dollar services) if it does not compromise the selection of best overall execution. Please see the section on Soft Dollar Practices below for additional information about brokerage and research services received by the Adviser.

The [Adviser] maintains an approved list of brokers and dealers. New counterparty arrangements must be reviewed and approved by the Counterparty Team of the Adviser before trading can begin through the new counterparty. Alternative trading systems that meet the guidelines are also eligible for consideration. The traders at [Adviser] are required to direct trades only through approved counterparties. Counterparties are regularly monitored by the Counterparty Team for signs of deterioration in business operations, creditworthiness and rating changes. [Adviser] does not use affiliated broker-dealers to place client trades.

In its review, the adviser should compare what it states in its ADV to its actual practice and maintain documentation of its response to the following questions:

- Does the adviser, in fact, consider the listed factors when selecting a broker for execution of client transactions? Does the adviser have documentation to establish this?
- Does the adviser have documentary evidence of its semiannual broker voting process and are its practices consistent with the results of the vote?
- Is the approved list of brokers readily available and current? Have all counterparties on the list been approved as claimed?
- Have all trades been directed only to approved brokers? If there are exceptions, have you identified any patterns or trends, and have they been addressed in a manner that will prevent violations in the future?
- Is there documentary evidence that the counterparty team has monitored all brokers on the approved counterparty list for signs of deterioration in business operations, creditworthiness, and rating changes? Are they regularly monitored as claimed?
- If the adviser has an affiliated broker-dealer but discloses that it does not use the affiliated broker-dealer to place client trades, has the adviser reviewed transaction sheets and other reports to establish this claim is accurate?

The adviser should also verify that it has reflected appropriate changes to its policies and procedures in its Form ADV as well as other timey requirements.

Third-Party Service Providers

In many cases an adviser will use the services of a third-party service provider, such as a subadviser, pricing service, broker-dealer, transfer agent, or others that are unaffiliated with the adviser. There is an obligation to conduct due diligence on such service providers.[87] The SEC takes a broad view of the definition of *service provider* and it includes, but is not limited to, pricing services, transfer agents, auditors, custodians, and other entities employed by the adviser.[88] Because the adviser often selects these service providers to conduct activities on behalf of clients, the adviser must determine that they adequately carry out their responsibilities. With regard to service provider oversight, the SEC has been fairly specific:

> The Commission understands that, in some cases, the fund may employ the services of a service provider that is not an affiliated person of the fund, such as a transfer agent or administrator, and that provides similar services to a large number of funds. In such cases, it may be impractical for the fund or its compliance officer to directly review all of the service provider's policies and procedures. In such cases, we will consider a fund's policies and procedures to have satisfied the requirements of this rule if the fund uses a third-party report on the service provider's procedures instead of the procedures themselves when the board is evaluating whether to approve the service provider's compliance program. The third-party report must describe the service provider's compliance program as it relates to the types of services provided to the fund, discuss the types of compliance risks material to the fund, and assess the adequacy of the service provider's compliance controls....
>
> The chief compliance officer, in exercising her responsibilities under the rule, will oversee the fund's service providers, which will have their own compliance officials. A chief compliance officer should diligently administer this oversight responsibility by taking steps to assure herself that each service provider has implemented effective compliance policies and procedures administered by competent personnel. The chief compliance officer should be familiar with each service provider's operations and understand those aspects of their operations that expose the fund to compliance risks. She should maintain an active working relationship with each service provider's compliance personnel. Arrangements with the service provider should provide the fund's chief compliance officer with direct access to these personnel, and should provide the compliance officer with periodic reports and special reports in the event of compliance problems. In addition, the fund's contracts with its service providers might also require service providers to certify periodically that they are in compliance with

---

[87] *See* Adopting Release IA 206(4)-7.
[88] *See* Adopting Release of Rule 206(4)-7, fn.28.

applicable federal securities laws, or could provide for third-party audits arranged by the fund to evaluate the effectiveness of the service provider's compliance controls. The chief compliance officer could conduct (or hire third parties to conduct) statistical analyses of a service provider's performance of its duties to detect potential compliance failures.[89]

Thus, when reviewing service providers, the adviser should:

- Review the service provider's compliance policies and procedure to determine whether they are adequate and effective;
- Determine that the service provider's compliance personnel are qualified;
- Understand the service provider's operations and identify and review risks that may be present to the adviser's business; and
- Develop and request that the service provider complete certifications and periodic reports (generally submitted quarterly) and special reports in the event of compliance problems.

It is a good practice for advisers to require service providers to complete and submit a quarterly questionnaire and periodic certifications of compliance. In addition, it is advisable to periodically visit the operations of the service provider to identify ant compliance issues that may arise and to meet and develop relationships with the service provider's compliance personnel in order to facilitate resolution of any possible compliance concerns.

Books and Records

The Advisers Act and Rule 204-2, promulgated thereunder, mandate that an investment adviser must make and keep true, accurate, and current certain required books and records. The rule enumerates the specific types of records that must be maintained as well as the duration of their maintenance and place where they must be kept.[90] Other sections of the Advisers Act similarly require books and records maintenance of certain documents.[91]

Generally, an adviser's records are created and maintained by different people in the firm, such as the portfolio manager, trader, operations personnel, finance personnel, and others. As a practical matter, the adviser should establish a matrix of all required books and records set forth in the Advisers Act and include the required holding period, location of each record, and personnel required to maintain the documents. The adviser may store records electronically but must comply with the SEC rules on electronic storage.[92] Your matrix should include the following fields:

- Description of required record;
- Date record created;

---

[89] Final Rule, *Compliance Programs of Investment Companies and Investment Advisers,* IA Rel. No. 2204 (Dec. 13, 2003).
[90] Rule 204-2(e)(1) and Rule 204-2(e)(3).
[91] *See* IA Act Rule 204A-1.
[92] *See* IAA Rule 204-2(g).

- Location of record;
- Person responsible for creating and maintaining record;
- Date of review;
- Issues or comments.

At least annually, the adviser should use the books and records matrix to test whether the firm is in compliance with the requirements. Depending on the size of the firm, you may elect to sample records to see that they are adequately maintained.

In addition, the adviser should test to see that the documents are maintained in a manner that secures them from unauthorized alteration and protects them from untimely destruction.

Email Review

Registered investment advisers are not required by statue or other rules and regulations to review email.[93] However, as a best practice, firms should consider incorporating review of email into their annual review program because it is an effective way to identify issues and prevent and detect securities law violations. Moreover, SEC examiners are routinely requesting email documents when they conduct their exams.

As a best practice, an adviser may select certain employees each quarter, such as portfolio managers, traders, and sales personnel to ensure that their correspondence is true, accurate, and not misleading. Also, advisers can review their employees' emails to brokers, clients, and others to ensure that there are no issues that may arise. In addition, in the event you identify any red flags regarding the conduct of an employee it is advisable to review their email to assist in determining the appropriateness of their conduct.

When testing email, advisers should identify key words relevant to their inquiry and review emails that are produced. For example, an adviser could use key word searches for items such as "sure thing," "hot IPO," "guarantee," or "promise" to monitor the practices of its sales team.

Contradictory Positions

An adviser may manage both long only and long/short portfolios for its clients. At times, this may result in holding contradictory securities positions in different funds or client accounts.[94] For example, an adviser may hold a long position in a security in one account and a short position in the same security in another account that he or she manages.

The adviser should monitor such holdings to prevent and detect violations of the federal securities laws and manage any potential conflicts or the appearance of such conflicts that may arise. The adviser should check that its trading practices are appropriately disclosed and examine the reasons for holding contradictory positions in its client

---

[93] If an adviser is associated with a related or affiliated broker-dealer and has representatives registered with FINRA, there may be some email review requirements imposed by FINRA rules.
[94] See 2009 CCOutreach Regional Seminars, The Evolving Compliance Environment.

accounts. In many cases the adviser has established a procedure requiring the manager who seeks to take a contradictory position to complete and submit an approval form explaining why the manager seeks to take that position and that the manager's supervisor approves of the action. Acceptable reasons likely differ depending on the policies and procedures of the adviser but could include, for example, a nonvolitional trade consistent with an index or purchase or sale of an overweight or underweight position due to market factors, among other reasons.

IV. CONCLUSION

Forensic testing is one of the most important tasks of an effective Compliance Department. Each firm must tailor its policies and procedures to the particulars of its business, consistent with the securities laws, and ensure that they are effective in their implementation. To that end, forensic tests, properly documented, will assist you in preventing, detecting and correcting securities laws violations on a timely basis. Your testing should evolve with changes in your business, new products and developments in the industry, and regulatory changes.

ABOUT THE AUTHOR

Jeffrey Hiller J.D. serves as the chief compliance officer and head of global compliance at Principal Global, Investors, LLC. Mr. Hiller joined Principal Global Investors in 2007 in his present role. Prior to joining Principal, Mr. Hiller served as managing director, first vice president and chief compliance officer for Merrill Lynch Investment Managers/Blackrock) as well as managing director and chief compliance officer (global) for major asset management companies headquartered in New York City. Additionally, he served as the senior counsel in the Securities and Exchange Commission Division of Enforcement in Washington, DC, from 1990 to 1995. Mr. Hiller is the coauthor of "*The Salomon Case* and the Supervisory Responsibilities of Lawyers and Compliance Personnel," *INSIGHTS*, Vol. 7, No. 5 (May 1993) and *Legal Agreements in Plain English* (Contemporary Books, Chicago, 1982).

Born in Trenton, New Jersey, and raised in Bucks County, Pennsylvania, Mr. Hiller earned his bachelor of arts degree in Political Science from Pennsylvania State University, his juris doctor degree from American University, Washington College of Law, and studied graduate law in tax at the Georgetown University Law Center. He is a member of the Washington, DC, and Maryland Bar Associations and serves as an advisory director to the Rock Ethics Institute of the Pennsylvania State University.

CHAPTER 20

Regulatory Examinations and Audits

By Michelle Jacko, Esq., CSCP
    Jacko Law Group, PC | Core Compliance & Legal Services, Inc.

I. THE PURPOSE OF SEC EXAMINATIONS

Overview of the National Exam Program

All investment advisers who are registered with the Securities and Exchange Commission (SEC) are obligated to comply with the Investment Advisers Act of 1940 (the "Advisers Act"). The Office of Compliance Inspections and Examinations (OCIE) is responsible for overseeing the activities of investment advisers to ensure they comply with the rules set forth in the Adviser Act. For such oversight, OCIE conducts examinations through the National Examination Program (NEP).

Mission of the Office of Compliance Inspections and Examinations

The OCIE's mission is to protect investors; maintain fair, orderly, and efficient markets; and facilitate capital formation by conducting examinations.[1] Examination teams are based in eleven regional offices located in Atlanta, Boston, Chicago, Denver, Fort Worth, Los Angeles, Miami, New York, Philadelphia, Salt Lake City, and San Francisco. Washington, DC, serves as the headquarters for OCIE.

The NEP is responsible for examining investment advisers, investment companies, broker-dealers, municipal securities dealers, transfer agents, clearing agencies, self-regulatory organizations, and municipal advisors. Its objectives are threefold:

- To protect investors;
- To maintain market integrity; and
- To gather information for rulemaking.

---

[1] *See* https://www.sec.gov/about/offices/ocie/ocieoverview.pdf

Administration of Examinations

Whether your firm is a target to be examined depends upon your business model. The SEC's examination priorities change year after year. But one thing that remains a constant is the collaboration of the SEC's divisions and offices to perform assessments based on a variety of risk-based factors. They include:

- Gathering information about registrants through filings, examinations conducted by the NEP, records maintained in third-party databases, and media publications;
- Communications with other regulatory agencies and tips from investors; and
- Interactions with various industry groups and service providers.

Each year the OCIE's NEP issues a report of its examination priorities. In recent years, examinations have focused on:

- New investment advisers to private-equity and hedge funds;[2]
- Never-before-examined registered investment advisers;[3]
- Municipal advisors;[4]
- Fraud and prevention;[5]
- Technology (including internal controls, market access, operational capabilities, cybersecurity, and preparedness for system outages and malfunctions);[6]
- Dual registrants, and in particular, supervisory structures and whether a customer is placed in a brokerage or investment advisory account;[7] and
- Advisers who switch from SEC to state registration to unveil potential deficiencies in areas such as suitability and books and records maintenance.[8]

In addition, if a tip, referral, or complaint against a firm is received by a regulator, that firm is more likely to be examined and classified as a "higher risk" adviser. Moreover, if a firm made an investment in a Ponzi scheme, even if that firm is far removed, it is likely that the adviser will be examined as part of the staff's investigation of the underlying issuer.

The SEC's annual request for budgetary resources also impacts the examination process. With additional resources the commission is able to hire additional examiners, expand technology, and advance current regulatory initiatives. Consequently, this has enabled the

---

[2] See http://www.sec.gov/about/offices/ocie/national-examination-program-priorities-2013.pdf
[3] See http://www.sec.gov/about/offices/ocie/nbe-final-letter-022014.pdf
[4] See http://www.sec.gov/about/offices/ocie/national-examination-program-priorities-2015.pdf
[5] See http://www.sec.gov/about/offices/ocie/national-examination-program-priorities-2014.pdf
[6] See http://www.sec.gov/about/offices/ocie/national-examination-program-priorities-2014.pdf, and Risk Alert on SEC Examinations of Business Continuity Plans of Certain Advisers Following Operational Disruptions Caused by Weather-Related Events Last Year (Aug. 27, 2013), http://www.sec.gov/about/offices/ocie/business-continuity-plans-risk-alert.pdf, and CCLS Risk Management Update on Cybersecurity: Important Considerations for Investment Advisers and Broker-Dealers (May 2014), http://www.corecls.com/cybersecurity-important-considerations-for-ias-and-bds/
[7] See http://www.sec.gov/about/offices/ocie/national-examination-program-priorities-2014.pdf
[8] See "State Exams Target Former SEC Registered Advisers," *Institutional Investor Compliance Intelligence* (Aug. 22, 2013).

staff to increase the proportion of advisers examined each year and to concentrate on what is deemed to be "higher risk" focus areas, such as custody and performance advertising.

II. THE EXAMINATION PROCESS

Types of Examinations

The SEC generally has four types of examinations. This includes risk-based routine examinations, limited-focus examinations, "sweep" examinations, and for cause examinations as a result of a tip, referral or complaint, whistleblower, rule violation, or emerging risk.

Risk-Based Routine Examinations. Historically, the SEC conducted routine examinations based upon an examination cycle over a set period of time. Today, the NEP conducts its routine examinations based on risk matrices. Consequently, compared to FINRA examinations that typically occur on a two- to three-year cycle, investment advisers may not be aware of the exact timing of their examination. Generally, the longer the period during which an adviser has not been examined, the more likely it is that the firm will be placed in a "higher" risk category.

Limited-Focus Examinations. A limited focus exam is just that: It is an examination that focuses on a particular area such as the compliance program of new advisers to hedge funds and documents such as the Form ADV and compliance manual.

For the risk-based routine and limited-focus examinations discussed above, there are several factors which trigger these types of examinations. Risk analytics are used to help prioritize which firms should be examined first and for how long. Here, the SEC reviews regulatory reports on Form ADV, Form PF, Forms 13F, 13G, and 13H, and other industry databases to determine which advisers pose the highest degree of risk. The staff also considers the date that the adviser was last examined as well as prior deficiencies. Based on performing these quantitative analytics, advisers are strategically selected for examination.

The SEC also will take into consideration its examination priorities and program initiatives. This includes evaluating an adviser's core risks such as fraud prevention and investor protections; corporate governance and the firm's control environment; use of technology and operational capabilities; conflicts of interest, including compensation arrangements, allocation of investment opportunities, and investment strategies for retirees; marketing and performance claims; compliance program advocacy; and complex business structures, including dual registrant models and wrap-fee programs. In addition, SEC staff takes into account new laws and regulations, product risks, and examination priorities. For example, a focused examination may concentrate on an area such as cybersecurity so that the SEC can assess the adviser's security and potential threats, including malware, network breaches, compromises with client accounts, and safeguards for those that have client log-ins.

"Sweep" Examinations. A third type of examination is a sweep examination. During a sweep examination, the SEC conducts an investigation of a particular set of business practices across numerous advisers or funds. Generally, such exams are spurred due to particular business concerns, such as use of social media, disaster recovery efforts, and sale of structured products.

For Cause Examinations. Finally, "for cause" examinations typically are triggered by some event, such as receipt of a customer complaint or receipt of a "tip" from a particular employee or former employee. It also may be triggered based on examination findings that the staff believes warrants further investigation for potential federal security law violations. When a for cause examination commences, the commission may provide the adviser's custodian of records with a letter notifying the firm of the SEC's commencement of an investigation accompanied by either a request list or a subpoena to provide documents and give sworn testimony described in an accompanied attachment. Commonly requested areas include all books and records related to the subject area of the investigation, banks and other financial records, formal testimonies by employees, and interviews with clients. The purpose of this type of examination is to determine whether some type of egregious behavior, such as lying, cheating, or stealing may have occurred, and if it did, whether the adviser was or should have been aware of it. In more formal investigations, the SEC will evaluate scienter and potential violation of the antifraud prohibitions found in Rule 206 of the Advisers Act.

Stages of an Examination

One of the most frequently asked questions posed by advisers is whether they will receive notification prior to the staff coming onsite. The answer: not necessarily. For most examinations, typically the SEC will send an initial document request list to the representative agent listed on the organization's Form ADV. Generally, the adviser will have a certain period of time to respond to the SEC's requests, which may range from a couple of days to two weeks, depending upon the volume of the specific requests. Should the SEC not provide notice prior to entering an organization, the adviser will be given a reasonable period of time, typically between 24 to 48 hours, to readily produce all requested information.

During this initial inquiry and identification stage, the examiner will review the firm's risk factors and assess the adequacy of the firm's policies and procedures for addressing those risks. The examiner will focus on whether firm policies are clearly defined, whether the procedures are followed by personnel, and whether the organization's procedural controls clearly articulate duties for personnel to perform. Concurrently, the examiner will evaluate the effectiveness of supervisory controls, including the type and frequency of supervisory reviews, the records created by the adviser to track and report forensic and transactional test outcomes, and the existence of escalation procedures for exception or outlier results. In assessing organizational risks, the examiner will review past SEC deficiency letters, assess past and current compliance discrepancies, and consider current priorities in the SEC's examination process. In addition, the examiner will inquire about changes in the firm's business, including new lines of products and services offered, and consider what, if any, potential conflicts of interest might exist as a result. If conflicts are identified, the examiner will explore what checks and balances might be needed to address those conflicts. Finally, the examiner will consider changes that occurred in applicable regulations that might necessitate having the firm revise its policies and procedures.

During the onsite portion of the examination, the commission will continue its evaluation of the firm's compliance program. Similar to an adviser's own annual review process, the examiner will conduct forensic testing using, among other things, its national examination analytics tool (NEAT) to determine whether there is a suspicion of subversion of the compliance system through some means that may be difficult to detect through some other form of testing. For example, the staff will look for aberrational performance and for trends to detect whether there was any insider training at the advisory firm. In other circumstances, the examiner may review broker delegation processes and then listen to telephone calls between the trade test and the broker dealer to help ensure that there are no "arrangements" that would influence brokerage allocation. The ultimate goal during this stage is to help determine and identify whether trends and patterns exist that could evidence misconduct by advisory personnel.

While onsite, the examiners will request to speak with certain personnel at the organization, which typically include C-level executives (i.e., the chief executive officer (CEO), the chief investment officer (CIO), the chief financial officer (CFO), the chief compliance officer (CCO), the chief information officer, etc.). In order to evaluate internal controls, the examination team also may request demonstrations, which typically involve mid-level employees showing the day-to-day processes and protocols they use for surveillance and supervision efforts. Consequently, it is imperative that employees are well prepared in advance prior to speaking to examination staff; (a process described in detail later).

As a result of the interview process and internal demonstrations, the staff may have additional follow-up requests. They may include, among other things, additional interviews, documents, and written explanations describing the firm's compliance control efforts.

Prior to the examiner's departure, the adviser should request an exit interview. During this phase, the adviser will become aware of areas of potential concern that the staff may have found deficiencies on during the course of its onsite review. This will enable the adviser to both clarify any misunderstandings that the examiners may have related to the firm's compliance program as well as to proactively respond to any concerns. If there are areas identified that require action by the adviser, it is best to act immediately and, if possible, provide documentation subsequent to the examination demonstrating what actions were taken or will be taken by the firm.

After the staff has concluded its review, the examiners will determine what type of action(s) should be taken as a result of the findings. The outcomes of an examination generally are memorialized in the form of a response letter from the SEC. Response letters generally take one of five forms:

- No findings of deficiencies and no further action by the staff;
- A deficiency letter;
- A deficiency letter and request for special meeting;
- Referral of the matter to the SEC Division of Enforcement for a formal investigation; and for reoccurring or recidivist deficiencies; or
- A deficiency letter and referral to another office or division in the SEC, such as the Division of Investment Management.

In some instances, the adviser may not receive any formal letter from the SEC (although this is rare). Most commonly, when a deficiency letter is received, the adviser is requested to respond in writing to the staff about what steps the firm will take to correct any noted deficiencies. It is critical for the CCO to share the deficiency letter with members of the senior management team for collaboration on how the firm will address each of the noted areas.

What Advisers Can Do to Prepare for an SEC Exam

Understanding how an SEC examination is performed is critical to an advisory firm. The keys to a successful examination occur in the preparatory stages, well before the regulators arrive. As part of the overall compliance review, it is important to evaluate the risks within the organization. There are several ways to accomplish this evaluation:

- *Conduct a conflict inventory.* Detecting conflicts and mitigation thereof is one of the most important steps to unveiling potential areas that the regulators will focus on during an examination. Outside business activities, compensation arrangements, side by side management, and most favored nation clauses are some of the most common conflicts that exist for investment advisers. Consider developing a conflicts inventory worksheet, which should be evaluated no less than annually in your organization. Exhibit A at the end of this chapter is a sample Conflict Inventory Worksheet;
- *Review the prior examination's regulatory deficiency letter.* Deficiencies that were noted in the prior examination typically require attention. Ensure that if action steps were noted on the firm's response letter to the SEC, they actually occurred. If changes in business model resulted in the firm not taking such actions, ensure that the firm can document and demonstrate why those actions were not taken. For example, if the adviser noted during the examination that the firm would cease placing performance marketing materials on its website and three years later, the adviser elected to place performance numbers on the website, the firm must be able to demonstrate what internal controls the organization developed to allow it to take actions contrary to representations provided in the response letter (e.g., performance numbers audited and reviewed by auditing firm);
- *Review the latest SEC examination focus areas and any new risk alerts.* Such materials are available at www.sec.gov. These updates will include important information on current examination focus areas. Based on this information, compliance officers should work with senior management to identify potential risk areas;

- *Consider new regulations that were recently promulgated.* Determine whether the firm needs to develop new policies and procedures or enhance existing processes. To conduct this task, compliance officers may wish to consider using an annual compliance policies and procedures worksheet. A sample of this is provided in Exhibit B;
- *Make notes of customer complaints and allegations of wrongdoing.* Timely investigate the legitimacy of such allegations to ensure that internal controls are addressed accordingly.
- *Conduct a risk assessment.* Consider whether the organization should engage an independent third party to conduct a risk assessment of the firm not only to ensure whether books and records are in order, but moreover to identify areas that may require additional attention or enhancement. Should the compliance officer conduct the risk assessment internally, when possible, use independent managers for reviewing the subject areas. A sample of a compliance risk focus matrix may be found in Exhibit C;
- *Gather evidence that the compliance program is "dynamic."* The SEC is evaluating the competency of compliance officers. Therefore, it is important that the CCO be able to demonstrate his or her ongoing continuing education through participation in industry conferences, industry work groups, certification programs, and training. Consider whether to develop a report on all of the different actions that compliance has taken during the course of the year to enhance its competency and increase the dynamics of the firm's overall compliance efforts. Exhibit D provides a sample report;
- *Consider performing a mock SEC regulatory examination.* The NEP initial document request list is readily available on the internet and should be reviewed frequently by the firm's compliance officers to determine whether the firm has such books and records and their preparedness for gathering such information on a timely basis. A sample of a document request list is provided in Exhibit E; and
- *Review SEC "compliance alerts."* This letter addressed to CCOs summarizes select areas that SEC examiners have recently reviewed during examinations and the compliance practices they observed. One recent compliance alert[9] provided various suggestions on notable practices that can help address top examination deficiencies:
  - Test whether the firm's code of ethics is incomplete, not followed, and/or monitoring not performed;
  - Check whether procedures are in place to ensure that trading does not occur in client accounts, employee personal accounts, or the adviser's proprietary accounts while the adviser or its employees are in possession of material, nonpublic information pertaining to that security;
  - Compare performance of client accounts with the performance of personal and firm proprietary accounts employing similar investment strategies to see whether there is any indication of preferential treatment;
  - Ensure that trade allocations are determined prior to or soon after the trades were executed and documented to ensure allocations are consistent with firm policies;
  - Determine how the adviser is managing conflicts of interest in proxy voting and document the process accordingly;
  - Be able to express how the firm is conducting its review of conflicts of interest;

---

9   *See* https://www.sec.gov/about/offices/ocie/complialert0708.htm. In addition, advisers should consider staff Letters, Risk Alerts and Special Studies and Reports that can be found at https://www.sec.gov/about/offices/ocie/ocie_guidance.shtml

- Ensure that the firm is providing adequate disclosures of increased risk with respect to liquidity and valuation, as required for riskier investment strategies and products;
- Be sure that the firm is conducting a best execution analysis (including soft dollar usage) and that it is documented;
- Analyze whether high-risk areas are sufficiently staffed, and/or are staffed with individuals that have adequate experience to supervise those areas (examples could include trading, portfolio management, valuation, and performance advertising reviews); and
- Review the advertising and sales literature, including responses to requests for proposal, to ensure that they contain neither false nor misleading information.

Prior to even receiving an examination notice from the commission, the CCO should prepare for the firm's next SEC examination. This can be accomplished by testing whether key personnel within the organization are able to gather the items listed on the NEP document request list on a timely basis. Organization and strong communications are essential to orchestrating an effective system of document retrieval. Protocols on the maintenance of these records should be reviewed by the CCO on a periodic basis, and no less than annually.

Advanced Preparations by the Staff

In preparation for examining an investment adviser, the staff takes very deliberate steps to learn about the registrant, its structural risks, compliance systems, and conflicts of interest that affect its customers and investors. Typically, OCIE begins by reviewing the registrant's Form ADV, website, and marketing collateral to learn how the adviser is representing the firm, its products, and services to its clients, including material disclosures related to its business. From this, OCIE customizes an initial document request list that is delivered to the adviser for production of certain books and records. Among other considerations, OCIE assesses the ability of the adviser to readily produce such documents and evaluates whether they are being maintained in accordance with the Adviser's Act recordkeeping requirements. Data analytics is commonly used by the staff to identify potentially fraudulent, suspect, or illegal activity, to spot adviser representatives who may be circumventing firm policies or federal regulatory requirements, and to evaluate the compliance controls employed by the investment adviser, such as for best execution analysis and insider trading detection.

Depending upon the type of examination, the staff often focuses on how the registrant responds to certain requests for information on current SEC priority areas in which OCIE has found higher levels of deficiencies on previous examinations. Recent examples include business continuity plans, compliance program documents of never-before-examined advisers, and cybersecurity controls.

Areas where potential deficiencies are noted will become a focal point of the staff's onsite portion of the exam.

III. CUSTOMARY REGULATORY REQUESTS

Books and Records Document Requests

Prior to coming onsite to conduct an examination, the SEC staff will review various documents as prepared by the adviser. Most commonly this will include the firm's disclosure documents, marketing efforts and materials (including the firm's website, social media channels, and promotional materials), communications with clients, internal communications, and trade blotter. With this information, the staff will prepare for the onsite examination, focusing on particular areas to gain additional insights and information. Specifically, the examiner will analyze how the firm is proactively addressing higher risk areas through internal controls, considering:

- Does the adviser manage risk effectively at the product and asset class level?
- Are key risk management, control, and compliance functions structured and resourced to be effectively embedded in the business process, while having the necessary independence, standing, and authority to be effective in helping the organization identify, manage and mitigate risk?
- Does senior management exercise effective oversight and is risk management embedded in key business processes, including strategic planning, performance management, and compensation incentives?
- How are internal reviews used to help verify and provide assurance regarding the operating effectiveness of risk management, compliance, and control functions?
- Is the governance of the organization staffed and structured to effectively set risk parameters, foster an effective risk management culture, oversee risk-based compensation systems, and effectively oversee the risk profile of the firm?

Notably, the SEC recognizes that small advisers (defined as five or fewer employees) and/or newly registered advisers face distinct compliance issues. The staff will concentrate on how a small adviser is addressing enterprise risks, particularly because in many instances the small adviser has professionals holding multiple roles. Based on this, the commission will evaluate how conflicts are being managed and what risk management strategies are employed, which will differ for each particular firm and business model.

Finally, the staff will review the adviser's risk management techniques and will reference the adviser's policies and procedures and annual review report for essential elements. During examination, the SEC then will assess not only whether such policies and procedures are effectively implemented but also whether management is setting a "tone at the top" of the organization for fiduciary and regulatory obligations to be taken very seriously. Among other things, the staff will assess the system for oversight of both compliance and risk management generally.

To assist in its assessment of the organization's risk, expect document requests to cover a one- to two-year period to include the following:

- Recent policies and procedures, including any changes made and the date of those changes;
- Client disclosure documents, such as Forms ADV Part 2 and offering materials;
- Investment advisory agreements;
- Solicitor and revenue sharing agreements;
- Code of ethics and corresponding personal trading records;
- Trade blotter, including identification of the firm's ten most and least profitable trades;
- List of terminated client accounts;
- Examples of any violations of firm policies and procedures;
- Soft dollar budget or similar document that describes the products and services obtained using clients' brokerage commissions;
- Description of all positions held in side-pockets or special situation accounts together with their valuation on the date of the related calculation of net asset values;
- Minutes of investment and/or portfolio management committee meetings;
- A list of the firm's investment strategies (e.g., global equity, high-yield, aggressive growth, and long-short), the corresponding performance composite in which the strategies are included, if any, and the identity of the portfolio managers;
- The CCO's written annual review report;
- Risk assessments and internal audit reports;
- Cybersecurity controls;
- Conflict of interest assessments;
- Financial records;
- Organization charts;
- Proprietary performance reports;
- Customer complaints;
- Business continuity plans;
- Corporate records;
- Electronic emails of C-level executives;
- Materials used to promote the firm, including prospective client marketing pieces; and
- Due diligence reports.

The aforementioned documents should be readily available to produce to the staff upon request.

Management and Employee Interviews

The SEC's examination program focuses strongly on the firm's culture of compliance, including tone at the top and effectiveness of the compliance program. To evaluate these areas, the staff frequently reviews such items as firm e-mail communications (particularly to and from senior management team members), the compliance program's annual review report, and prior examination findings, and thereafter, conducts employee interviews.

It is critical for senior management and key employees to be prepared for and understand the examination interview process. Prior to the examination, compliance should meet with such individuals to provide insight into what to expect.

Typically, the staff will ask to speak to specific employees responsible for business risk areas such as trading, portfolio management, operations, finance, and legal/compliance. Employees will be asked about their role(s) and responsibilities within the organization, including firm policies, procedures, reports and forensic tests that they oversee, administer, and become accountable.

Sometimes an employee may be asked about an internal control that he or she may not be completely familiar with. In those circumstances, the employee should be up front and let the examiner know that another individual may be more knowledgeable about that area. It is imperative to always be honest and forthcoming. If the employee does not know the answer to a question, he or she should simply respond "I don't know." The compliance officer also can let the examiner know that he or she will research the answer to the inquiry and get back to the staff as soon as possible.

Many times when conducting an interview, the staff will ask a question, listen to the answer, and then wait a moment to see whether the interviewee has anything to add. Employees should not feel compelled to fill that moment of silence. As a good rule of thumb, examination interviews should be treated and viewed with the same protocols as a deposition; i.e., the interviewee should listen carefully to the question and respond only to the question that is asked. If the staff poses a yes/no question, the employee should simply respond yes or no. Once the question is answered, the employee should stop talking and wait for the next question. Although it is important to be open, the interviewee should not volunteer any information unnecessarily. Moreover, if the employee does not understand the question being asked, he or she should not hesitate to let the examiner know.

As a general rule, the CCO should always be present during the interview process. The CCO is in the best position to help clarify responses relating to the firm's internal controls, clarify the question posed by the staff to the respondent, and help ensure that the most knowledgeable employees are responding to a particular set of inquiries. If the firm determines that the CCO's presence is required during employee interviews, consider documenting this requirement within the firm's compliance policies and procedures manual so that both employees and the staff is aware.

Spend sufficient time training employees on how to prepare for an SEC examination interview. In addition to the above guidance, the following is a list of considerations to address during training:

- Do not interrupt the examiner; let the staff finish asking the question before responding;
- Pause to think before responding to the examiner's question;
- Do not speculate; it is better to reply "I will get back to you";
- Provide concise, clarifying answers;
- Respond only to the question asked;
- Always have the CCO, or a competent delegate, present during employee interviews to take notes, document subsequent books and record requests from the staff, and clarify responses;
- Be professional and respectful; do not provide sarcastic remarks;

- Review key documents, such as the Form ADV, firm policies and procedures manual and investor documents prior to the interview;
- Be able to clearly articulate their role(s) and responsibilities, and particularly how the firm supervises a particular area; and
- If a question is too broad, ask for the examiner to clarify its scope.

It is important for supervisors to be aware of any "gaps" within their area and how to best respond to inquiries when asked. It is important to prepare with outside counsel, as necessary, who can provide guidance on how to address sensitive areas.

Review of Firm Operations and Systems

During the onsite portion of the exam, it is customary for the staff to ask for demonstrations of the firm's operational systems, including those used to survey portfolio management, trading, emails, advertisements, personal trading, and any other area where technology is used to supervise an activity. While firm members should cooperate, it is important to manage this process.

The management should establish a contact person for demonstrating the firm's operational systems. Do not give the examiners free reign to view and access any and all technologies or computer files. Rather, identify what specifically the staff would like to see and have the contact person sit behind the keyboard and demonstrate how the firm performs certain internal control functions.

The contact person should note each area that was demonstrated to the staff. Keep a running list of any specific records requested. This way, the CCO will be able to identify what area(s) the examination team is focusing on and provide supplemental information, as necessary, to further clarify internal controls that the firm has established. If any of the records contain sensitive information, work with outside counsel to determine whether confidential treatment should be requested.

IV. PREPARING FOR A REGULATORY AUDIT

In the continuing aftermath of the Bernard Madoff scandal and the passage and implementation of the Wall Street Reform and Consumer Protection Act of 2010[10] ("Dodd-Frank") there is enhanced focus by federal, self-regulatory, and state regulators to continuously monitor and audit investment advisers and other financial industry participants to foster compliance with the various statutory and regulatory requirements. For advisers and their personnel tasked with designing and implementing the firm's compliance program, this enhanced scrutiny can heighten anxiousness felt in the face of an impending SEC examination. However, with careful and deliberate preparation, anxieties will hopefully lessen while the firm derives several important potential outcomes. They include:

- *A stronger, more effective, compliance program.* The process of preparing for a regulatory examination necessarily entails an internal examination of a firm's compliance

---

[10] P.L. 111–203, H.R. 4173.

program focused on its design, implementation, and effectiveness. As gaps or deficiencies are identified and addressed, the overall compliance system will become more robust and effective;

- *Increased firm value through reduced risk and enhanced efficiencies.* Compliance programs are designed to enable a firm to fulfill the various statutory and regulatory requirements under which they operate. These requirements are designed to protect investors from bad, unfair, or malicious business practices. The failure of a firm to adhere to these requirements can create a range of liabilities, including fines and other penalties imposed by regulators in enforcement proceedings; costs, including legal fees and human capital expended by the firm to defend a lawsuit or customer complaint; and associated reputational harm and damages that may result. In addition, the more time, money, and attention a firm must devote to putting out "compliance fires" means the less time, money, and attention that firm can devote to its core business. Firms can mitigate compliance risks and address areas of potential concern by conducting periodic internal risk assessments, testing the effectiveness of policies and procedures, ensuring all required records are maintained, and conducting a mock SEC examination to identify and address potential internal control deficiencies. Taking these steps will help to identify areas of the business that could negatively impact investors and expose the firm to liability. At the same time, such steps also will help to identify where protocols need to be enhanced, which will help to create a more efficient and effective compliance program—invaluable to the firm enterprise; and
- *Better responsiveness to examiner requests.* Firms that proactively prepare for a regulatory examination are better prepared to more readily produce requested documents and provide targeted, responsive answers to staff inquiries. One way to accomplish this is to obtain a copy of a recent OCIE examination document request list. This will provide guidance as to specific areas of focus the SEC will concentrate on during the examination and help the firm to organize books and records in advance.

To position the firm for a successful examination, it is essential to plan ahead and establish a solid compliance program. Consider taking the following steps to identify areas that may require attention prior to the staff's arrival:

- Assess the strengths and weaknesses of the firm's compliance program by reviewing policies and procedures, thinking about what risks the compliance program is designed to address. Consider the firm's annual review and assess how effective it is in identifying and ameliorating risks and improving controls so that clients and the firm are better protected;
- Consider changes to the firm's business and whether to modify the compliance program to address such changes. Changes may include new product and service offerings, implementing new investment strategies, expanding into new markets, using new distribution channels, entering into new contractual arrangements, making staff changes, and undertaking strategic outsourcing;
- Evaluate the firm's compliance training program. Make sure all employees are educated about the firm's compliance program, how it works, what responsibilities they

have in connection with the program, and the importance of faithfully administering the program. Senior management should be visibly engaged and supportive of the training program with an eye toward fostering a "culture of compliance";
- Review prior regulatory examination results and ensure that any identified deficiencies have been addressed. To the extent that the firm made a representation that something was done and is no longer applicable, be sure to make a note to the compliance file about what occurred;
- Inventory the firm's books and records to ensure required records are being maintained;
- Consider how compliance officers are documenting compliance and supervisory reviews. Generally, oral reviews do not sufficiently demonstrate to examiners that a review actually took place. Consider the mantra, "if it's not in writing, it's as if the review did not occur";
- Timely review audited financial statements and auditor internal control reports to assess the impact they may have on the firm's compliance program; and
- Be aware of current SEC initiatives and recent enforcement actions. These may be found in a variety of sources—the SEC's website,[11] industry compliance seminars, compliance publications, law firm newsletters, and compliance consultants. Consider how these areas affect your compliance program in light of your business model and how you would respond to an examiner's inquiries on the subject.

Building a dynamic and effective compliance program will position the firm for a successful regulatory examination. The program will help to demonstrate a strong culture of compliance and help to demonstrate the seriousness with which the firm approaches its compliance obligations. This in turn may help boost the examiner's confidence in a compliance professional's explanations if a compliance program deficiency is discovered. On the flip side, failure to demonstrate a positive culture of compliance will likely result in the examiner having an enhanced degree of skepticism toward the firm, its personnel, and its compliance program.

Getting Organized

Strong communication and organization are keys to a successful examination. Senior management should announce to employees that the firm is about to undergo a regulatory exam. To the extent it is known, share information related to when the examination is scheduled to start, the expected duration of the exam, where the staff will be located, and general office protocols. Remind employees that they should:

- Adhere to a "clean desk" policy, whereby all confidential and sensitive information (such as client identifiers) is secured at night;
- Lock file cabinets and secure office doors at night;
- Shred unwanted documents containing confidential client information;
- Guide persons they do not recognize to their destination; and
- Be mindful of conversations within earshot of the examiners.

---

[11] OCIE publishes National Examination Risk Alerts, available on the SEC's website, to draw attention to areas of SEC focus.

To initiate document production, identify a central person to collect and organize all submissions to the staff. Make sure that all files are clearly labeled and in the order requested by the examiners. Remember that the goal of document production is to demonstrate the effectiveness of the firm's compliance processes. Therefore, documentation should reflect how the organization's daily processes and workflows help to achieve compliance with the firm's policies and industry regulations. Consider whether a brief memo or narrative may be needed to describe the purpose and flow of the firm's internal controls.

In addition, determine whether the firm will provide copies to the staff of those documents they wish to duplicate. To control the process, consider providing the examiners with Post-it Notes and ask them to tag which documents they wish to have. Then, duplicate copies of all documents produced to the SEC examiners for the firm and consider a third set for the firm's outside counsel. That way should an issue arise, the compliance officer will know the sources from which the staff is obtaining its information. For production of sensitive information, contact outside counsel to discuss whether to have documents Bates stamped and obtain Freedom of Information Act treatment. This will help to more easily reference such documents, which should also be kept on the firm's privilege logs.

Establish a Primary Contact with the SEC Staff

During the initial interview, establish who the firm's primary contact is to the staff (which typically is the CCO). This will help to streamline the examination process and avoid unnecessary confusion.

The role of the primary contact is multifaceted and includes educator, gatherer, provider, and advocate.

Educator. The primary contact generally is present for most, if not all interviews, and educates the staff about the firm, its products and services, and how they have changed since the last examination. The primary contact also answers or finds the answers to questions that the firm's employees may not readily know.

Gatherer. During the course of the examination, the staff may ask for new or supplemental documents to review. The primary contact is responsible for ultimately gathering, organizing and presenting these documents for production. But beware: Sometimes examiner requests may involve documents from nonregulated members in the firm's group of companies that the firm may not be obligated to produce, such as an affiliated trust company or CPA firm. In these instances, the firm should carefully review each document request prior to production and question the staff about its relevance or applicability if it appears the request goes outside the scope of the examination. As a practice tip, carefully review the disclosure documents that the SEC provides at the inception of the exam. These disclosures will help the firm to understand the SEC's lawful reach and to recognize when it is exceeded.

Provider. The primary contact often liaises between the examiners and firm's senior management team. This includes, among other duties, establishing what days and times interviews will be conducted, who from the staff will explain the purpose and scope of the interview, which employee of the firm is to be interviewed, persons to be present during the interviews (e.g., CCO or legal counsel), the inventory of documents requested by the staff, expected duration of the staff's in-house examination, and the timing of the exit interview.

Advocate. The primary contact also may serve as an advocate for your firm—and the compliance program it has developed. For example, if the staff is concerned about a violation that the firm does not believe has been interpreted correctly, the primary contact may become an advocate, explaining why the questioned practices are legal or inadvertent.

Prepare Employees for the Examination

Throughout the exam, it is critical for firm members to demonstrate competency and knowledge of not only the latest rules, but of the firm's compliance program, particularly for their personal areas of responsibility. Can firm supervisors clearly articulate their risk controls, oversight, and supervision of critical practice areas? Do managers understand their roles, responsibilities, and escalation processes within the organization? Can employees express the firm's email etiquette—what to say and what not to say? Do personnel know how the firm communicates newly adopted firm policies—through departmental meetings, trainings, e-news bulletins, or teleconferences?

In her 2004 speech, "The New Compliance Rule: An Opportunity for Change," Lori Richards, director of the SEC's OCIE, provided the following guidance.

> Compliance staff should continually be asking: Are we detecting problematic conduct with this policy? Based on what we've detected, should we alter our policy? Is there a better way to detect problematic conduct?... Were the actions we took, once problematic conduct was detected, adequate to deter problematic conduct by this individual or others?[12]

Being able to answer these questions articulately and competently is essential to success in today's examination process.

Be Aware of SEC Examination Priorities and Focus Areas

Understanding the SEC's current examination priorities is critical to help prepare the firm for a regulatory exam. As previously mentioned, each year the SEC releases an examination priority document that identifies those areas OCIE believes represents heightened risk to the financial industry and to investors.

---

[12] Lori Richards, The New Compliance Rule: An Opportunity for Change (June 28, 2004).

Recent OCIE priorities include assessing issues related to market-wide risks, retail investors and retirement investors, cybersecurity controls, investment recommendations and related marketing, suitability and fee structures, proxy services, never-before-examined advisers and investment companies, and newly registered municipal advisors.[13]

Information about the SEC's priorities and focus areas is available from a wide array of sources. Visit the SEC's website,[14] which features the NEP's issuance of annual examination priorities, risk alerts, staff letters, and commissioner speeches which often focus on current examination objectives. Also, consider third-party sources, such as law firms, consultants, custodians, and other vendors, who often regularly hold seminars and publish articles that report on current developments in SEC examination and enforcement activities and provide general compliance program guidance.

V. MANAGING A REGULATORY EXAMINATION

Making Good First Impressions

First impressions say a lot about the firm and its culture of compliance. The opening interview often sets the tone for the examination. Consider preparing a presentation that covers, among other matters, an overview of the organization, the firm's affiliates, the products and services offered, the firm's internal control environment, and its compliance culture. This may further support information requested by the staff in its initial document production letter.

In addition, during the examination process the staff will evaluate how the firm embeds risk management into key business processes and decision making. At the onset of the exam, make an effort to outlining for the staff how the firm addresses risks to help set the tone for the firm's culture of compliance.

Finally, be sure to proactively establish the firm's internal control and risk management environment at the onset. This is accomplished by:

- Demonstrating how the firm has updated its policies and procedures to prevent, detect, and correct violations of the federal securities laws;
- Evidencing where the compliance program enhanced its tests that were done previously; and
- Explaining the type of testing performed on various policies and procedures (transactional, periodic, and forensic) to help identify circumvention and ensure efficacy.

Setting Ground Rules and Controlling the Process

During the initial interview, set the ground rules for the examination. Establish what time the examination will commence each day, who will serve as the firm's primary

---

[13] This list is not all-inclusive. For additional information, see http://www.sec.gov/about/offices/ocie/national-examination-program-priorities-2015.pdf
[14] See http://www.sec.gov/about/offices/ocie.shtml

contact for the staff, what days and times interviews will be conducted, and the expected duration of the staff's in-house examination.

The examination can be further managed and controlled by having key firm personnel proactively take the following steps:

1. Identify the securities regulations that govern the firm's practice areas;
2. Review policies and procedures for clarity and effectiveness, noting any potential areas of concern; and
3. Gather compliance program documentation in advance, such as risk assessments, annual review reports, exception reports, training program documents, and books and records substantiating the strength of the organization's internal and supervisory controls.

These advanced preparations will help the firm's management team to refresh their knowledge in key areas and be organized for both interviews and subsequent document production.

Demonstrating the Dynamics of the Compliance Program

The SEC is increasingly interested in evaluating whether a firm's compliance program is *dynamic*. To prove that the compliance program is robust, it is important to demonstrate the adequacy of resources dedicated to compliance and the effectiveness of compliance controls (e.g., supervision, compliance training initiatives, and technology management). Show examples of the firm's proactiveness in detecting and preventing potential compliance concerns, and illustrate support for compliance by senior management (the tone at the top). Consider formulating a one-page report highlighting those efforts.

For example, begin by gathering supporting documentation of the compliance efforts. If the risk management or compliance officer has a formal process for reviewing and identifying risk in the organization, have it available for review by the staff. Be prepared to discuss how the analysis was prepared (often termed risk mapping) and what procedures are in place to evaluate enterprise risk.

To help demonstrate the compliance process, consider maintaining a log and supporting documentation of when policies and procedures change or new ones are implemented. This may help the staff to better understand which policies and procedures were in place when the activity or transaction they are examining occurred.

In addition, gather documents evidencing the firm's investment in compliance. If the firm has purchased new compliance software, hired new compliance personnel, or encouraged compliance staff to participate in industry conference or compliance membership organizations, document this. List third-party sources, such as outside counsel, consultants, and others used to provide compliance training.

Perhaps most importantly, demonstrate that compliance personnel are competent. Discuss how the CCO keeps abreast of new laws, regulations, and interpretations, such as by attending educational meetings and reading industry periodicals. List how the CCO has taken this information and applied it to the compliance program, such as through enhancements made to review processes, exception reports, and the forensic testing performed on the organization's procedures. Maintain copies of conference and reference materials to help further support the initiatives.

Advocating the Organization's Position

A prime goal once the examination begins is to be an advocate for the firm—and the compliance program it has developed. If the staff is concerned about a violation that the firm member does not believe has been interpreted correctly, advocate the case to the staff. Be able to explain why the questioned practices are legal or why they are inadvertent. In doing so, be careful to avoid confrontations with the SEC. If the liaison believes something is awry, he or she should request a meeting with the senior inspection staff to further advocate the firm's position.

When to Create Custom Reports

Many advisers struggle as to how proactive they should be during an SEC exam. Although the liaison does want to provide the staff with meaningful information responsive to the regulator's inquiries, he or she also does not necessarily want to provide custom reports that could confuse or mislead the commission. The following are some dos and don'ts to consider:

- Do ask the regulator staff whether to create a customized report created to assist in the review;
- Do not imply or infer that a "new" report was part of your compliance program (unless it really was);
- Do create a custom report if it will be helpful to explain the firm's controls;
- Do not create a custom report if the report itself is complex or would raise additional questions;
- Do negotiate cumbersome requests; and
- Do not fail to provide the staff with reports and documents requested during the investigation which are responsive to their requests.

The Advisers Act sets forth various books and records requirements that may or may not include these customized reports. However, even if not required, should certain reports and records be maintained and presented in the examination process, that practice may go a long way in making the examination run as smoothly and as efficiently as possible. For example, if the firm has a formal process for reviewing and identifying risk, have it available for review by the staff. Be prepared to discuss how the risk manager or CCO went about preparing the analysis (risk mapping) and what procedures keep the document organic and representative of the organization's business, regulatory, operations, and reputation risk. Although examiners are focused on the firm's compliance with the Advisers Act, other applicable regulations, and written policies and procedures, there is a certain amount of comfort that comes with examining a well-run, thoughtful business organization that evaluates risk at all levels. In addition, it is likely that the staff may ask to see documentation of how the organization's policies and procedures address and mitigate the risks that have been identified.

Reports that demonstrate compliance processes and trends are important. Consider maintaining a log and supporting documentation of changes or implementation of new policies and procedures. This may help the staff to better understand which policies and procedures were in place when the activity or transaction they are examining occurred.

Reports also can help demonstrate your review plan for the organization's compliance program, including projects completed and/or scheduled and timelines for performance. Be sure to include supporting documentation: the review process, exception reports, and forensic testing performed on the organization's procedures. Remember to maintain copies of all work papers.

Finally, "gap reports," which capture weaknesses identified within the compliance program, are helpful to demonstrate that a gap was identified and timely corrected. Consider maintaining records that evidence the timeline of detection, corrective steps taken, and preventative plans for the future. If a resolution has not been reached, include a proposed action plan and keep track of its implementation.

VI. FINAL STAGES OF THE EXAMINATION PROCESS

Generally, the SEC will advise a firm when it is nearing the completion of its onsite portion of the exam. Often, this is accompanied by final document requests and perhaps an exit interview with the senior management team, as further described below. However, typically, the examination process will not end here. The staff often returns to their offices and continue the examination by reviewing and analyzing additional documents, consulting with other departments, finalizing their conclusions, and preparing finding. Consequently, the final portion of the onsite exam presents a critical opportunity for the firm's employees and leaders to make a lasting impression.

The Exit Interview

Depending upon the type of exam and initial findings, the staff may communicate potential problems they detected so the liaison gains a sense of the examiners' concerns. If not, he or she should attempt to engage them to ascertain this vital information. This can be accomplished during one of two stages: the preliminary exit interview or the exit interview.

The preliminary exit interview is an informal meeting that takes place prior to the examiners' conclusion of the onsite portion of the exam. Initial findings, follow-up inquiries, and areas of potential concern may be discussed. The exit interview generally consists of a meeting with the staff and advisory personnel to discuss preliminary exam results. Although the exit interview may be done at the conclusion of the onsite exam, typically it occurs telephonically. If the examiner does not schedule an exit interview, the liaison should request one.

The exit interview provides several important opportunities, including the opportunity to gain a greater understanding of the examiner's preliminary concerns and conclusions. By discussing these concerns, the liaison may have the opportunity to provide additional information, context, or insight that could soften or ameliorate the staff's concerns. Keep in mind that part of the examination process involves the staff learning the firm's business. The regulatory staff may not have received or understood all of the information that may be relevant to a concern. By understanding the factors that led to the examination's conclusions, the liaison may be able to provide additional insights and information about the business or compliance program that can clear up a potential gap prior to a deficiency letter being issued or other action taken. By gaining an understanding of the examiners' concerns, the liaison may also be able to take corrective action that will cause that finding to come off of a deficiency letter. An exit interview is also a good opportunity to reinforce to the examiners the firm's commitment to compliance at a time when the examiners are determining whether a matter of concern rises to the level of a deficiency or warrants a referral to enforcement. Remember, examiners are people, and reinforcing the organization's eagerness to maintain an effective compliance program at a critical time in the staff's decision making could make a difference during the final stage of analysis.

Post-Fieldwork

After the onsite portion of examination is completed, the staff will continue to work to refine the preliminary analyses into final conclusions. During this period, the examiners may request supplemental information either through interviews or document requests. The staff also may consult other staff members or divisions within the SEC for input for the analysis. In addition, opinions of SEC legal and accounting staff may be sought to ensure consistency, and the staff may compare preliminary findings with those of similar firms.

It is during this post-fieldwork time that the examiners finalize their conclusions as to the results of the examination. If a long period of time has passed and the organization has not heard from the staff, consult with counsel about whether to contact the staff to learn the findings.

Examination Outcomes

Depending on the scope and complexity of the examination, the length of the examination may be as short as a few days or weeks or it could take months to complete. In general, the SEC will seek to complete the examination within 120 days after it commences. However, if the staff is unable to complete its work within that timeframe, the SEC will notify the firm and provide an estimate about when the examination's estimated completion is. Once the staff finalizes the examination results and determines what actions should be taken as a result of its findings, the firm will be notified in writing.

Several results can occur from an examination, each representing a different level of seriousness and severity.

The most desirable finding is a closing letter with no comments or recommendations at this time. If the firm fortunate enough to receive this notice, keep in mind that the staff is simply stating that it did not uncover any deficiencies during the examination and not that there were no deficiencies that could be found. Continue to actively refine and implement the compliance program so it remains as robust as practicable.

The most common result, however, is for some deficiencies to be discovered during the course of the examination. In these cases, the advisory firm will receive a deficiency letter, generally within 90-days of the exam's conclusion that describes the issues discovered by the staff during the examination. The letter typically cites regulations supporting the staff's findings and could also describe remedial steps the adviser should take to address the deficiencies. The deficiency letter requires the recipient to submit a written response to each deficiency, including the steps the firm plans to take to address any noted gaps. The response to the deficiency letter generally is due within 30 days from receipt.

When serious deficiencies are discovered, and particularly those that harm investors by putting client funds or securities at risk, the staff may refer the deficiencies to the SEC's Enforcement Program or another regulator (such as the state, and SRO or other federal agency). Based on this referral, the Division of Enforcement or other regulator will make a determination whether and to what extent it will investigate those areas. Should a formal investigation ensue, the adviser will receive a formal order, which typically is accompanied by a subpoena for certain books and records. As further described below, at the conclusion of the investigation, the Division of Enforcement or other regulator will either conclude the matter with no findings or recommend an enforcement proceeding against the firm.

Considerations for Responding to a Deficiency Letter

The firm's response to a deficiency letter is of critical importance. Deficiency letters should be addressed as soon as practical, with high priority placed by the firm on how areas of concern will be addressed.

In the event the firm is unable to address a deficiency in the time frame set forth in the deficiency letter, request more time and explain why additional time is necessary. The staff generally will grant a request for extension if the rationale provided for the delay is reasonable.

If the firm had an exit interview, the liaison likely has a good idea of the issues that will be identified in the deficiency letter well in advance. Accordingly, consider the feedback already received from the staff on areas of potential concern. Take steps where necessary to remediate those deficiencies so that the firm's proactiveness can be highlighted in the response letter.

Be deliberate and exacting when describing the firm's corrective actions in the response. The SEC will be looking for the firm to memorialize and demonstrate its understanding and awareness of risk identification and mitigation by carefully managed protocols to both correct infractions and prevent future violations from occurring.

Responses to a particular deficiency often acknowledge the issue and describe the remedial steps that the firm intends to, or has already, implemented. Some firms may wish to communicate with the examiners, particularly on more serious infractions, because the remedial action plan is formulated to ascertain whether the proposed steps address the staff's concerns. Although the staff will not provide guidance on the adequacy of the control measures, they may provide feedback as to whether the control appears reasonable.

In other instances, the firm may disagree with the staff's conclusion. In those instances, carefully work with outside counsel to formulate a well-thought out written response to articulate the organization's position. There may be additional information that the staff was not aware of that could impact their findings and alter their conclusions.

The response letters to a deficiency letter are carefully analyzed by the staff. To the extent that the staff is satisfied with the proposed remedial steps set forth by the firm, the examination is closed. However, if the examiners find the response unacceptable—either because the firm has not taken the examination findings seriously or the proposed remedial actions are inadequate (among other things)—the examiners may request additional information or schedule an additional onsite visit to the firm to further investigate or they may simply refer the deficiencies to the Enforcement Division.

Formal Inquiries

When the staff discovers matters of serious concern, the Division of Enforcement will launch a formal inquiry to investigate the facts and circumstances to help ascertain whether any illegal activity has occurred and if enforcement proceedings or other actions are warranted.

Formal inquiries are launched by the director of the Enforcement Division or his or her designees issuing a formal order for investigation. If a copy of the formal order is not given to the subject of the investigation, it should be requested. The formal order may give valuable insight into aspects of the investigations such as the scope of the investigation and the securities law violations that are suspected to have taken place. In addition, the formal order can inform the firm which individuals and entities are "targets" of the investigation, the activities being investigated, and key documents and other evidence that may be pertinent to the investigation.

Unless related to a perceived industry-wide problem, formal inquiries are typically private matters. Although initially this may help to shield the firm and its principals from potential negative fallout in the form or reputational risk and/or loss of goodwill from being the subject of a formal inquiry, the recipient will nevertheless need to determine if and when disclosure of the investigation is necessary. For example, a hedge or private equity fund that is actively raising capital will need to determine whether and when the formal investigation becomes a material risk based on the nature of the investigation and the surrounding facts and circumstances. If the general partners of the fund believe that the investigation has a strong likelihood of leading to an administrative proceeding that would materially and negatively impact the financial condition of the fund, then they should weigh whether disclosure of the investigation to investors is appropriate so as to not be fraudulent and misleading. Actively continuing to raise funds while the investigation is undisclosed could lead to rescission rights of the investors and potential lawsuits.

Anyone who is the subject of a formal inquiry should engage legal counsel to advise and represent them throughout the process. Counsel can help the firm launch its own internal investigation into the area(s) of concern. This may help to ascertain whether there is indeed a problem, and if so, allow the firm to determine the best course of action to take (which could include self-reporting, preparing employees for on-the-record interviews, responding to subpoena requests for information, and, if applicable, designing and implementing a remedial action plan to address identified issues). Keep in mind, however, that the firm should not interfere with the SEC's investigation or take steps to cover anything up if something negative is discovered. If the firm does embark on its own internal review, consider whether these efforts should be directed through counsel. In most circumstances, this will help to ensure that the results of the investigation are protected by attorney-client privilege.

Enforcement Proceedings

When a serious problem is found during the course of an examination, the staff will refer the matter to the SEC's Division of Enforcement. In making this referral, the staff will consider, among other things, whether investors are harmed; whether there are indications of fraud; whether misconduct is ongoing or severe; whether the perpetrator profited from illicit activity; whether the firm's supervisory procedures are appropriate and adequate; whether there is intentional misconduct; the statutes or rules potentially violated and whether the alleged misconduct touches upon an area of emphasis for the SEC.

Each year, a significant portion of the SEC's enforcement cases come against regulated entities referred by the staff through the examination process. The Division of Enforcement reviews all referred matters by the staff and then decides whether to conduct a formal investigation. To proceed, the staff must obtain authorization from the commission through the issuance of a formal order of investigation ("formal order") (as further described above). Once a formal order of investigation is issued, the staff embarks on broad fact finding and investigation that could involve administration of oaths, subpoena of witnesses, compelling document production and taking testimony.[15]

---

[15] 15 U.S. Code §80b-9.

Following the investigation, the SEC staff will determine whether to take no action or to present the findings to the commission for its review and consideration of bringing enforcement proceedings.[16] Based on its findings, the SEC will determine whether to pursue prosecution through a civil suit either in the federal courts or an administrative proceeding.

In civil actions, it is common for the commission to seek an injunction to prohibit future violations, request monetary penalties, seek the disgorgement of ill-gotten gains and even bar or suspend individuals from acting in certain capacities within the securities industry.[17]

Administrative proceedings result in similar orders from the commission. However, in addition, for regulated persons and entities, the commission may revoke or suspend a license or registration and impose bars and sanctions.

For individuals and entities that do cooperate with the commission's investigation, certain benefits may accrue. These can range from reduced charges and sanctions to taking no enforcement action at all.[18]

In the event that the staff will be recommending an enforcement proceeding, Securities Act Release 5310 permits persons involved in an investigation to present a statement to the staff setting forth their position.[19] This is known as a "Wells Notice." The purpose of the Wells Notice is to inform the firm or individual of the nature of the charges the staff is considering and permit the proposed defendant a unique opportunity to respond to allegations prior to the commencement of enforcement proceedings. Although a Wells Notice is not required to be delivered to potential targets of an enforcement action, it is the general practice of the SEC to issue the notice.[20]

The potential defendant is provided with an opportunity to submit a brief, referred to as a "Wells Submission." The purpose of this response is to communicate to the staff the factual, legal and/or policy reasons why the commission should not bring an enforcement action under the circumstances. Although a Wells Submission is usually driven by the submitter's sincere hope that the response will influence the staff not to recommend the firm to enforcement, it is more likely that the Wells Submission will be used for purposes of settlement discussions and mitigating potential penalties for alleged infractions.

Wells Submissions are not required, and the question of whether to make one can be extremely difficult. This is because the Wells Submission is not privileged. In fact, a

---

[16] See http://www.sec.gov/News/Article/Detail/Article/1356125787012#.VR3S52cU-Uk
[17] For more information, see http://www.sec.gov/divisions/enforce/about.htm
[18] See http://www.sec.gov/spotlight/enfcoopinitiative.shtml
[19] See Sec. Act Rel. No. 5,310, 1972 WL 18218 (SEC) (Sept. 27, 1972).
[20] In 1972, SEC Chairman William J. Casey appointed a committee (chaired by John Wells and commonly referred to as the Wells Committee) to make recommendations as to the SEC's enforcement actions. As part of this, the Wells Committee recommended an opportunity for the prospective defendant to submit a response to the staff, which would be forwarded to the commission along with the staff's memorandum recommending an enforcement proceeding.

Wells response can provide a blueprint of the defense strategy and be used against the potential defendant at hearing. Furthermore, the staff may share the Wells Submission with other governmental bodies, which may pursue additional actions. For private litigation matters, a Wells Submission is discoverable, which can be detrimental on numerous fronts.

On the other hand, a Wells Submission can accomplish various important objectives. It can be used to articulate deficiencies in the staff's record, which could help in negotiating less onerous charges and citing less egregious violations. The Wells response also provides an opportunity to highlight the firm's or individual's remedial actions and to persuade the staff not to go forward with an enforcement proceeding.

Accordingly, a Wells Notice recipient should work closely with experienced counsel to consider all of these relevant factors in order to determine whether to make a Wells Submission and, if so, what arguments and information to include within it.

Finally, a Wells Notice allows the potential defendant an opportunity to pursue settlement discussions. Factors to consider in determining whether to pursue settlement discussions include: the strength of the firm's case; the magnitude of the negative impact on the firm's business; the organization's ability to fund litigation; and the potential magnitude of sanctions from an adverse result.

Pursuant to the Dodd-Frank Act, the SEC is required to notify a potential defendant no later than 180 days from issuance of the Wells Notice of the commission's intention to proceed with an enforcement proceeding or its decision not to recommend the potential defendant to enforcement. For cases that the director of the Division of Enforcement or his or her designees determine are sufficiently complex, the deadline can be extended for up to two additional 180-day periods.

If the staff does proceed with recommending a matter to enforcement, then the five-member commission must vote to authorize the case. The commission will receive from the staff its recommendation in an action memo, which details the facts and legal basis for the claims, outlines any policy issues or litigation risks, and lists the proposed remedies, which may include cease and desist orders, fines and penalties, disgorgement, engagement of an independent consultant or monitor, permanent bars from the industry, and admissions of guilt, among others.

The SEC's *Enforcement Manual*[21] provides invaluable information relating to the enforcement process, including the initiation of an investigation, the Wells process, enforcement recommendations, what to expect at enforcement proceedings, and other procedural considerations.[22] The commission will review the recommendations of the SEC staff in the action memo and will decide whether to proceed with enforcement. Once the matter is heard, at the conclusion of the proceeding, the court or judge will

---

[21] SEC, http://www.sec.gov/divisions/enforce/enforcementmanual.pdf
[22] Additional guidance, e.g., on the assessment of money penalties, may be found at 15 U.S. Code §78u-2.

render a decision. If a decision is rendered against the defendant, then that entity and/or individual is either directed or ordered to comply with the judgment. Once the defendant complies with the terms of any orders and decisions that have been entered, then the enforcement process concludes.

VII. CONCLUSION

The key to a successful SEC examination is preparation. Having a robust, well thought out compliance program that is supported by senior management will go a long way to demonstrate to the staff the firm's culture of compliance. Do take time to truly test the effectiveness of policies, procedures, and internal controls during the annual review. Engage an independent third party to conduct a mock SEC examination. Review conflicts of interest frequently and ensure that they are disclosed to your clients and investors. Be proactive to promote compliance education. Ensure that supervisors are competent and understand their roles and responsibilities. Taking these steps will not only prepare the firm for a regulatory examination, but will help foster the firm's reputation and instill confidence with investors.

EXHIBIT A. SAMPLE CONFLICTS INVENTORY WORKSHEET

	Business Area	Conflict	Type of Conflict	Control	Potential Impact	Material[1]	Does this Need to be Disclosed?	If Not, Why Not?
1	Brokerage/Trading	Trading Execution Including Commissions	Client/Firm	☐ Avoid by Elimination ☐ Firm Approach ☐ Mitigate & Disclose ☐ Manage & Disclose	☐ Low ☐ Medium ☐ High	☐ Yes	☐ Yes ☐ No	
2	Brokerage/Trading	Principal Transactions	Client/Firm	☐ Avoid by Elimination ☐ Firm Approach ☐ Mitigate & Disclose ☐ Manage & Disclose	☐ Low ☐ Medium ☐ High	☐ Yes	☐ Yes ☐ No	
3	Brokerage/Trading	Affiliated Underwriting Activities	Client/Affiliate	☐ Avoid by Elimination ☐ Firm Approach ☐ Mitigate & Disclose ☐ Manage & Disclose	☐ Low ☐ Medium ☐ High	☐ Yes	☐ Yes ☐ No	
4	Brokerage/Trading	Cross Transactions	Client/Client	☐ Avoid by Elimination ☐ Firm Approach ☐ Mitigate & Disclose ☐ Manage & Disclose	☐ Low ☐ Medium ☐ High	☐ Yes	☐ Yes ☐ No	
5	Brokerage/Trading	Soft Dollar Arrangements	Client/Firm	☐ Avoid by Elimination ☐ Firm Approach ☐ Mitigate & Disclose ☐ Manage & Disclose	☐ Low ☐ Medium ☐ High	☐ Yes	☐ Yes ☐ No	
6	Brokerage/Trading	Step-Out Trades	Client/3rd Party/Firm	☐ Avoid by Elimination ☐ Firm Approach ☐ Mitigate & Disclose ☐ Manage & Disclose	☐ Low ☐ Medium ☐ High	☐ Yes	☐ Yes ☐ No	
7	Brokerage/Trading	Client Directed Trading	Client/Firm	☐ Avoid by Elimination ☐ Firm Approach ☐ Mitigate & Disclose ☐ Manage & Disclose	☐ Low ☐ Medium ☐ High	☐ Yes	☐ Yes ☐ No	
8	Brokerage/Trading	Directed Brokerage Arrangements (Clients instruct an adviser to send transactions to a specific broker-dealer for execution.)	Client/3rd Party/Firm	☐ Avoid by Elimination ☐ Firm Approach ☐ Mitigate & Disclose ☐ Manage & Disclose	☐ Low ☐ Medium ☐ High	☐ Yes	☐ Yes ☐ No	
9	Brokerage/Trading	Trade Aggregation and Block Trading	Client/Firm	☐ Avoid by Elimination ☐ Firm Approach ☐ Mitigate & Disclose ☐ Manage & Disclose	☐ Low ☐ Medium ☐ High	☐ Yes	☐ Yes ☐ No	
10	Brokerage/Trading	Allocation of Investment Opportunities	Client/Firm	☐ Avoid by Elimination ☐ Firm Approach ☐ Mitigate & Disclose ☐ Manage & Disclose	☐ Low ☐ Medium ☐ High	☐ Yes	☐ Yes ☐ No	
11	Brokerage/Trading	Sequential Transactions (Engaging in securities transactions in one account that closely precede transactions in related securities in a different account.)	Client/Client	☐ Avoid by Elimination ☐ Firm Approach ☐ Mitigate & Disclose ☐ Manage & Disclose	☐ Low ☐ Medium ☐ High	☐ Yes	☐ Yes ☐ No	

CHAPTER 20 | Regulatory Examinations and Audits

12	Brokerage/Trading	Trading with Affiliated Broker-Dealers	Firm/Affiliate/Clients	☐ Avoid by Elimination ☐ Firm Approach ☐ Mitigate & Disclose ☐ Manage & Disclose	☐ Low ☐ Medium ☐ High	☐Yes	☐Yes ☐No
13	Brokerage/Trading	Investments in issuers of securities that are also Firm clients	Client/3rd Party/Firm	☐ Avoid by Elimination ☐ Firm Approach ☐ Mitigate & Disclose ☐ Manage & Disclose	☐ Low ☐ Medium ☐ High	☐Yes	☐Yes ☐No
14	Brokerage/Trading	Solicitation Arrangements/Payment for Client Referrals	Firm/3rd Party	☐ Avoid by Elimination ☐ Firm Approach ☐ Mitigate & Disclose ☐ Manage & Disclose	☐ Low ☐ Medium ☐ High	☐Yes	☐Yes ☐No
15	Brokerage/Trading	Trade Errors	Client/Firm	☐ Avoid by Elimination ☐ Firm Approach ☐ Mitigate & Disclose ☐ Manage & Disclose	☐ Low ☐ Medium ☐ High	☐Yes	☐Yes ☐No
16	Brokerage/Trading	Proprietary Investing	Employee/Firm	☐ Avoid by Elimination ☐ Firm Approach ☐ Mitigate & Disclose ☐ Manage & Disclose	☐ Low ☐ Medium ☐ High	☐Yes	☐Yes ☐No
17	Portfolio Management	Consistency with Investment Style	Client/Firm	☐ Avoid by Elimination ☐ Firm Approach ☐ Mitigate & Disclose ☐ Manage & Disclose	☐ Low ☐ Medium ☐ High	☐Yes	☐Yes ☐No
18	Portfolio Management	Side-by-Side Portfolio Management (Commingled Products vs. Separate Accounts) Trade Allocation	Client/Firm	☐ Avoid by Elimination ☐ Firm Approach ☐ Mitigate & Disclose ☐ Manage & Disclose	☐ Low ☐ Medium ☐ High	☐Yes	☐Yes ☐No
19	Portfolio Management	Side-by-Side Portfolio Management (Long/Short vs. all Long Accounts) Trade Allocation	Client/Firm	☐ Avoid by Elimination ☐ Firm Approach ☐ Mitigate & Disclose ☐ Manage & Disclose	☐ Low ☐ Medium ☐ High	☐Yes	☐Yes ☐No
20	Portfolio Management	Serving as Subadviser to Registered Mutual Funds	Client/Firm	☐ Avoid by Elimination ☐ Firm Approach ☐ Mitigate & Disclose ☐ Manage & Disclose	☐ Low ☐ Medium ☐ High	☐Yes	☐Yes ☐No
21	Portfolio Management	Performance Fees (i.e. side-by-side management of accounts that pay performance fees and those that do not.)	Client/Firm	☐ Avoid by Elimination ☐ Firm Approach ☐ Mitigate & Disclose ☐ Manage & Disclose	☐ Low ☐ Medium ☐ High	☐Yes	☐Yes ☐No
22	Portfolio Management	Allocation of IPOs	Client/Firm	☐ Avoid by Elimination ☐ Firm Approach ☐ Mitigate & Disclose ☐ Manage & Disclose	☐ Low ☐ Medium ☐ High	☐Yes	☐Yes ☐No
23	Portfolio Management	Fair Valuation	Client/Firm	☐ Avoid by Elimination ☐ Firm Approach ☐ Mitigate & Disclose ☐ Manage & Disclose	☐ Low ☐ Medium ☐ High	☐Yes	☐Yes ☐No
24	Portfolio Management	Portfolio Pumping	Client/Firm	☐ Avoid by Elimination ☐ Firm Approach ☐ Mitigate & Disclose ☐ Manage & Disclose	☐ Low ☐ Medium ☐ High	☐Yes	☐Yes ☐No

© MODERN COMPLIANCE 2015

EXHIBIT A. SAMPLE CONFLICTS INVENTORY WORKSHEET Cont'd

	Business Area	Conflict	Type of Conflict	Control	Potential Impact	Material[1]	Does this Need to be Disclosed?	If Not, Why Not?
26	Portfolio Management	Dumping/Cherry Picking	Client/Firm	☐ Avoid by Elimination ☐ Firm Approach ☐ Mitigate & Disclose ☐ Manage & Disclose	☐ Low ☐ Medium ☐ High	☐ Yes	☐ Yes ☐ No	
27	Portfolio Management	Selective Disclosure of Portfolio Holdings	Client/3rd Party	☐ Avoid by Elimination ☐ Firm Approach ☐ Mitigate & Disclose ☐ Manage & Disclose	☐ Low ☐ Medium ☐ High	☐ Yes	☐ Yes ☐ No	
28	Portfolio Management	Proxy Voting	Client/Firm	☐ Avoid by Elimination ☐ Firm Approach ☐ Mitigate & Disclose ☐ Manage & Disclose	☐ Low ☐ Medium ☐ High	☐ Yes	☐ Yes ☐ No	
29	Portfolio Management	Brokers Affiliated with Consultants	Firm/3rd Party	☐ Avoid by Elimination ☐ Firm Approach ☐ Mitigate & Disclose ☐ Manage & Disclose	☐ Low ☐ Medium ☐ High	☐ Yes	☐ Yes ☐ No	
30	Code of Ethics	Possession of Material, Nonpublic Information	Client/Firm/3rd Party	☐ Avoid by Elimination ☐ Firm Approach ☐ Mitigate & Disclose ☐ Manage & Disclose	☐ Low ☐ Medium ☐ High	☐ Yes	☐ Yes ☐ No	
31	Code of Ethics	Personal Trading Activities	Client/Firm	☐ Avoid by Elimination ☐ Firm Approach ☐ Mitigate & Disclose ☐ Manage & Disclose	☐ Low ☐ Medium ☐ High	☐ Yes	☐ Yes ☐ No	
32	Code of Ethics	Charitable Contributions	Client/Firm/3rd Party/Employee	☐ Avoid by Elimination ☐ Firm Approach ☐ Mitigate & Disclose ☐ Manage & Disclose	☐ Low ☐ Medium ☐ High	☐ Yes	☐ Yes ☐ No	
33	Code of Ethics	Political Contributions	Client/Firm/3rd Party/Employee	☐ Avoid by Elimination ☐ Firm Approach ☐ Mitigate & Disclose ☐ Manage & Disclose	☐ Low ☐ Medium ☐ High	☐ Yes	☐ Yes ☐ No	
34	Code of Ethics	Gifts and Entertainment	Client/Firm/3rd Party/Employee	☐ Avoid by Elimination ☐ Firm Approach ☐ Mitigate & Disclose ☐ Manage & Disclose	☐ Low ☐ Medium ☐ High	☐ Yes	☐ Yes ☐ No	
35	Code of Ethics	Outside Employment	Employee/Firm	☐ Avoid by Elimination ☐ Firm Approach ☐ Mitigate & Disclose ☐ Manage & Disclose	☐ Low ☐ Medium ☐ High	☐ Yes	☐ Yes ☐ No	
36	Code of Ethics	Outside Employment, Directorships and Other Business Activities	Client/Firm/Employee	☐ Avoid by Elimination ☐ Firm Approach ☐ Mitigate & Disclose ☐ Manage & Disclose	☐ Low ☐ Medium ☐ High	☐ Yes	☐ Yes ☐ No	
37	Code of Ethics	Participation of Interest in Client Transactions	Client/Firm	☐ Avoid by Elimination ☐ Firm Approach ☐ Mitigate & Disclose ☐ Manage & Disclose	☐ Low ☐ Medium ☐ High	☐ Yes	☐ Yes ☐ No	

#	Category	Description	Parties	Approach	Risk		Disclosed	Material[1]
38	Code of Ethics	Affiliate Stock Transactions	Client/Firm/Employee	☐ Avoid by Elimination ☐ Firm Approach ☐ Mitigate & Disclose ☐ Manage & Disclose	☐ Low ☐ Medium ☐ High		☐ Yes	☐ Yes ☐ No
39	Code of Ethics	Possession and Use of Sensitive or Confidential Information	Employee/Firm	☐ Avoid by Elimination ☐ Firm Approach ☐ Mitigate & Disclose ☐ Manage & Disclose	☐ Low ☐ Medium ☐ High		☐ Yes	☐ Yes ☐ No
40	Compensation	Fee Differentials (Proprietary vs. Non-Proprietary)	Client/Firm	☐ Avoid by Elimination ☐ Firm Approach ☐ Mitigate & Disclose ☐ Manage & Disclose	☐ Low ☐ Medium ☐ High		☐ Yes	☐ Yes ☐ No
41	Compensation	Employee Compensation	Employee/Firm	☐ Avoid by Elimination ☐ Firm Approach ☐ Mitigate & Disclose ☐ Manage & Disclose	☐ Low ☐ Medium ☐ High		☐ Yes	☐ Yes ☐ No
42	Compensation	Employee Compensation - Commissions	Employee/Firm	☐ Avoid by Elimination ☐ Firm Approach ☐ Mitigate & Disclose ☐ Manage & Disclose	☐ Low ☐ Medium ☐ High		☐ Yes	☐ Yes ☐ No
43	Compensation	Separate Side Arrangements	Client/Client	☐ Avoid by Elimination ☐ Firm Approach ☐ Mitigate & Disclose ☐ Manage & Disclose	☐ Low ☐ Medium ☐ High		☐ Yes	☐ Yes ☐ No
44	Miscellaneous	Purchasing Goods/Services From Clients	Client/Firm	☐ Avoid by Elimination ☐ Firm Approach ☐ Mitigate & Disclose ☐ Manage & Disclose	☐ Low ☐ Medium ☐ High		☐ Yes	☐ Yes ☐ No
45	Miscellaneous	Affiliate serves as general partner or managing member of a pooled investment vehicle subadvised by Firm.	Client/Affiliate/Firm	☐ Avoid by Elimination ☐ Firm Approach ☐ Mitigate & Disclose ☐ Manage & Disclose	☐ Low ☐ Medium ☐ High		☐ Yes	☐ Yes ☐ No
46	Miscellaneous	Employees attending or participating in Conferences/Workshops sponsored by an entity or individual that has a business relationship with Firm or its clients.	Client/Firm/3rd Party/Employee	☐ Avoid by Elimination ☐ Firm Approach ☐ Mitigate & Disclose ☐ Manage & Disclose	☐ Low ☐ Medium ☐ High		☐ Yes	☐ Yes ☐ No
47	Miscellaneous	Revenue Sharing or "Shelf Space" Payments	Client/Firm/3rd Party/Employee	☐ Avoid by Elimination ☐ Firm Approach ☐ Mitigate & Disclose ☐ Manage & Disclose	☐ Low ☐ Medium ☐ High		☐ Yes	☐ Yes ☐ No
48	Miscellaneous	Purchasing Products & Services From Consultants Who Recommend Clients/Prospects to Firm	Client/Firm/3rd Party	☐ Avoid by Elimination ☐ Firm Approach ☐ Mitigate & Disclose ☐ Manage & Disclose	☐ Low ☐ Medium ☐ High		☐ Yes	☐ Yes ☐ No
49	Miscellaneous	Other Business Activities	Client/Firm/3rd Party/Affiliate	☐ Avoid by Elimination ☐ Firm Approach ☐ Mitigate & Disclose ☐ Manage & Disclose	☐ Low ☐ Medium ☐ High		☐ Yes	☐ Yes ☐ No
50	Custody	Custody Arrangements	Client/Firm	☐ Avoid by Elimination ☐ Firm Approach ☐ Mitigate & Disclose ☐ Manage & Disclose	☐ Low ☐ Medium ☐ High		☐ Yes	☐ Yes ☐ No

[1] The standard of materiality under the Advisers Act is whether there is a substantial likelihood that a reasonable investor/client would have considered the information important.

EXHIBIT B. ANNUAL COMPLIANCE POLICIES AND PROCEDURES REVIEW WORKSHEET

FOR YEAR 20??

		Responsible Party	Method of Review	Findings	Summary and Conclusions	Recommended Change/Update	Reviewer & Date of Review
A.	**Regulatory Filings**						
A. 1.	Form ADV – Annual Amendments The firm has amended its Form ADV at least annually and made the annual amendments w/in 90 days of the fiscal year end	Compliance					
A. 2.	Form ADV – Interim "Prompt" Amendments The firm has amended its Form ADV promptly whenever certain changes occurred to information provided by the adviser, as described in the instructions to Form ADV	Compliance					
A. 3.	State Notice Filings; Licensing of IA Representatives. The Firm has made all required state notice filings and ensured that its "investment adviser representatives" are properly licensed with the states, if applicable.	Compliance					
A. 4.	Schedules 13D and 13G. If the Firm has "beneficial ownership" of more than five percent of a class of an issuer's registered equity securities, it has filed an appropriate Schedule 13D or 13G as follows: (a) Schedule 13D. A Schedule 13D within 10 days of exceeding the 5% threshold (b) Schedule 13G. Alternatively, if the Firm meets the Schedule 13G eligibility requirements, an abbreviated Schedule 13G within 45 days of the end of the calendar year after exceeding the 5% threshold (c) Subsequent Filings. The Firm has made all subsequent filings as required	Compliance					
A. 5.	Form 13F. If the Firm exercises investment discretion with respect to accounts holding at least $100 million in "Section 13(f) securities", it has filed initial and periodic Forms 13F	Compliance					
B.	**Marketing**						
B. 1.	Advertising – General and Specific Prohibitions. The Firm has identified all materials that may constitute an advertisement, including materials posted on its website, to ensure that the materials do not result in any fraudulent, deceptive, or manipulative advertising practices and that the materials do not contain any specifically prohibited forms of advertising under Rule 206(4)-1, which relate to (a) The use of testimonials; (b) The use of past specific recommendations (c) References to graphs, charts, formulas, and similar devices; (d) The use of the term "free of charge"	Marketing					
B. 2.	Performance Advertising – Calculation. The Firm has calculated composite performance in accordance with procedures.	Marketing					
B. 3.	Performance Advertising – General Use. The Firm's presentation of performance information contained in any of its advertisements has conformed to procedures	Marketing					

B. 4.	Performance Advertising - Net of Fees Requirement. The Firm has presented performance information in advertisements net-of-fees unless the presentation is a one on one presentation or presented in equal prominence to gross-of-fees information	Marketing						
B. 5.	Performance Advertising - Supporting Records. The Firm maintains books and records necessary to demonstrate the calculation of the performance of accounts used in connection with performance advertising	Marketing						
B. 6.	Performance Advertising - Use of Performance Generated at Prior Firms. The Firm has not used advertisements that contain performance information generated by an employee while working at a prior firm unless it satisfies certain requirements	Marketing						
B. 7.	GIPS Compliance. The Firm has not falsely stated, suggested or implied in advertisements that any of its performance information is GIPS compliant.	Marketing						
B. 8.	Use of Solicitors. The Firm has not paid a cash fee, directly or indirectly, to any person in return for client referrals unless the Firm has complied with the requirements of Rule 206-(4)-3 including - Solicitor not disqualified, written agreement in place, client disclosure, record of agreements and client disclosure, and supervision of solicitors	Marketing						
C. The Client Relationship								
C. 1.	Initial Form ADV Delivery. The Firm has delivered to each client and prospective client an initial copy of its Form ADV Part II at least 48 hours prior to accepting a new client or when the account started and allowed the right to terminate w/o penalty w/in 5 business days	Marketing						
C. 2.	Annual Form ADV Part II Delivery Offer. The Firm has annually and without charge delivered, or offered in writing to deliver upon request, to each client a copy of the ADV Part II. Any request for the ADV has been filled w/in 7 days of receipt. The Firm has maintained a record of each annual delivery or offer, as well as any client correspondence related to any request for a copy of the brochure.	Accounting						
C. 3.	Acceptance of New Clients. The Firm has reviewed all documentation required of new clients, prior to accepting a new clients	Marketing						
C. 4.	Financial and Disciplinary Disclosures. The Firm has disclosed to existing and prospective clients, if applicable, (i) all materials facts with respect to the Firm's financial condition that are reasonably likely to impair the Firm's ability to meet its contractual commitments to clients and (ii) material legal and disciplinary events involving the Firm or its management.	Compliance						
C. 5.	Advisory Contracts - The firm has not entered into any contracts that (i) does not contain a clause stating that the Firm cannot assign the contract without the consent of the client (ii) contains an impermissible hedge clause that may mislead a client into believing that the client has waived any right of action (iii) does not specify the amount of the Firm's fees and the method of calculation.	Marketing/ Compliance						
C. 6.	Advisory Contracts - Performance based Fees. The firm has received sufficient information to ensure that the client may be charged a performance based fee. The Firm's Form ADV reflects the fact that it charges performance-based fees.	Marketing/ Compliance						

© MODERN COMPLIANCE 2015

EXHIBIT B. ANNUAL COMPLIANCE POLICIES AND PROCEDURES REVIEW WORKSHEET *Cont'd*

FOR YEAR 20??

		Responsible Party	Method of Review	Findings	Summary and Conclusions	Recommended Change/Update	Reviewer & Date of Review
C. 7.	Custody of Client Assets. To the extent that the Firm is deemed to have custody of client assets, it has complied with the requirements of Rule 206(4)-2, including the following: (1) Qualified Custodians hold client assets (2) Account Statement Delivery - has a reasonable basis to believe that the custodian has sent at least quarterly statements to clients or has arranged for an annual audit or the clients' assets deemed to be in the custody of the Firm.	Accounting					
C. 8.	Proxy Voting. The Firm has (i) adopted and implemented written policies and procedures designed to ensure that it votes client proxies in the best interest of the clients; (ii) provided clients with a written description of the Firm's policy and procedures, and how they can obtain a copy of the policies and procedures; and (iii) provided clients with instructions about how they may obtain information about how the Firm voted with respect to their securities	Accounting					
C. 9.	Privacy. The Firm has (i) adopted and maintained written policies and procedures designed to safeguard the privacy of personal financial information and (ii) delivered a statement of its privacy policies and procedures to new clients and annually thereafter.	All					
C. 10.	Settlement. The firm has reviewed settlement procedures to ensure accurate trade data is provided to custodians and clients.	Accounting					
C. 11.	Accuracy of Information sent to clients. Settlement and Reconciliation Procedures to ensure information provided to clients about their accounts is accurate.	Marketing/ Accounting					
C. 12.	Management Fee Calculation. The Firm has accurately calculated the fees charged to clients.	Accounting					
C. 13.	AML Review - no clients that have been accepted are on the OFAC list.	Marketing					
D. Managing Client Accounts							
D. 1.	Suitability. The Firm has made only suitable investment recommendations.	Portfolio Management					
D. 2.	Investment Recommendations. The Firm has conducted reasonable due diligence with respect to any security that it acquires for clients.	Portfolio Management					
D. 3.	Adherence to Investment Objectives. The Firm has periodically reviewed each client portfolio holdings to ensure that the securities held by each client are consistent with the respective client's stated investment objectives.	Portfolio Management					

D. 4.	Allocation of Investment Opportunities. The Firm has allocated investment opportunities fairly between the disciplines managed.	Trading					
D. 5.	Best Execution. The Firm has sought best execution when effecting client transactions.	Trading					
D. 6.	Directed Brokerage. The Firm has received direction from the client and disclosures about the practice have been made.	Trading					
D. 7.	Soft Dollar Arrangements. The Firm has (i) disclosed its use of soft dollars and (ii) complied with the safe harbor provisions of Section 28(e). The Firm has documented and reviewed all third party research services utilized.	Compliance					
D. 8.	Allocation and Aggregation of Client Trades. The Firm has (i) allocated investment opportunities among the clients promptly and on a documented, equitable basis and (ii) disclosed its allocation and aggregation policies and procedures to clients in its Form ADV.	Trading					
D. 9.	Principal Transactions. The Firm has (i) provided written disclosure to clients about the Firm's role and the material terms of each principal transaction and (ii) obtained prior client consent.	Trading					
D. 10.	Internal Cross Transactions.						
D. 11.	Agency Cross Transactions. Rule 206(3)-2 is followed for any such transactions where the adviser acts as broker and adviser	Trading					
D. 12.	Affiliated Brokerage	Trading					
D. 13.	Trade Errors. The Firm has corrected any trade errors in a manner consistent with its stated policies and procedures and has not (i) used soft dollar credits with brokers to cover any costs or (ii) used other client accounts to correct errors.	Trading/ Compliance					
D. 14.	Valuation. The Firm has valued the securities held by clients according to procedures.	Accounting					
F. 1.	Supervisory Functions. The Firm has (i) established procedures, and a system for applying the procedures, which would reasonably be expected to prevent and detect, insofar as practicable, any such violation by a person subject to the Firm's supervision, and (ii) reasonably discharged the duties and obligations incumbent upon the Firm by reason of the Firm's supervisory procedures and system without reasonable cause to believe that such procedures and systems were not being complied with.	Compliance					
F. 2.	Insider Trading. The Firm has established, maintained, and enforced written policies and procedures reasonably designed to prevent the misuse of material, nonpublic information by the Firm and any person associated with the Firm.	Compliance					

EXHIBIT B. ANNUAL COMPLIANCE POLICIES AND PROCEDURES REVIEW WORKSHEET *Cont'd*

FOR YEAR 20??

		Responsible Party	Method of Review	Findings	Summary and Conclusions	Recommended Change/Update	Reviewer & Date of Review
F. 3.	Code of Ethics. The Firm has established, maintained, and enforced a written code of ethics that meets the requirements of Rule 204A-1, and pursuant to the code has at least (i) obtained initial and annual holdings reports from its "access persons"; and (ii) obtained quarterly transaction reports from its "access persons"; and (iii) precleared acquisitions of IPOs and private placements by its "access persons". The Firm has reviewed personal securities transactions against client transactions for conflicts of interest with clients. The Firm has included in its Form ADV a description of its codes of ethics and a statement that, upon request, the Firm will furnish clients with a copy of the code of ethics.	Compliance					
F. 4.	Compliance Manual and Related Training. The Compliance Officer has (i) met with each new Employee shortly after the start of employment to discuss provisions of the Manual applicable to the Employee and (ii) held an annual compliance meeting to review any changes to the policies and procedures contained in the manual, as well as to review the Firm's Code of Ethics and Insider Trading Policies and Procedures.	Compliance and supervisors					
F. 5.	Initial and Annual Employee Acknowledgements. The Firm has obtained from each Employee a signed acknowledgement stating that the employee has received a copy of the Manual, a copy of the Firm's insider Trading policies and procedures and the Firm's Code of Ethics, and including that the employee has read and understands the materials contained in the materials after the start of employment and annually thereafter except for Code of Ethics and insider shortly trading procedures which require acknowledgements of any changes.	HR and Compliance					
F. 6.	Role of Compliance Officer. The Firm has designated a Chief Compliance Officer who has responsibility for administering the Firm's written compliance policies and procedures.	Firm Partners					
F. 7.	Accuracy of Disclosures. The Firm has taken steps to ensure the accuracy of its regulatory filings, including its Form ADV, and any communications sent to clients and potential clients	Supervisors / Compliance					
F. 8.	Maintenance of Required Books and Records. The Firm has made and kept the specified books and records described in Rule 204-2 for the length of time specified in the Rule.	Corporate accounting/ reconciliation/ client service					
F. 9.	Business Continuity Procedures. The Firm has developed a written Business Continuity Plan to protect employees and client assets in the case of a natural disaster or other event that may cause a prolonged business outage.	Technology					

EXHIBIT C. COMPLIANCE RISK ASSESSMENT MATRIX			
YES	NO	FOCUS AREA	NOTES
		IARD— ■ Is the Firm required to file on the IARD System? Is the Firm's ADV Part I on the IARD System current? ■ Has the annual filling been filled in a timely manner? ■ Ensure that firm's contact information is current with regard to who should receive information from the SEC.	
		Filings & Reports— ■ Were all required Forms 13-F, Schedule 13-D and Schedule 13-G filings made with the SEC?	
		Form ADV/Brochure Disclosure and Delivery— ■ Is the Firm's Form ADV Part II current and accurate? ■ If Firm has custody of client securities and/or funds or collects management fees of more than $500 from each client more than 6 months in advance has a Schedule G been completed? ■ Is the Firm in compliance with Rule 204-3, does the adviser provide prospective clients with: Form ADV Part II or an Alternative Brochure? If an alternative brochure is furnished, does it contain at least the information required to be maintained in Form ADV, Part II? ■ Was the registrant's Form ADV, Part II, or its brochure delivered or offered for delivery in writing annually to clients? (Rule 204-3(c)(1))4-3) ■ Does the adviser give a copy of Form ADV, Part II, or its brochure to new clients in a timely manner? ■ Is Forms ADV, Part II, or alternative brochures sent to clients that request the document? ■ Does the Firm maintain a record of clients and prospective clients to whom copies of the document were furnished initially and offered annually in fulfillment of the brochure rule requirement? (Rule 204-2(a)(14))	
		Investment Advisory Agreements— ■ Does the Firm use written contracts? *(Note: While recommended, there is no statutory requirement that advisers enter into a <u>written</u> agreement with their clients.) (Sec. 205)* **Note: It is very important for the firm to know who its client is and their financial status?** ■ Are copies of all written contracts maintained? (Rule 204-2(a)(10)	
		■ Does the Firm's Investment Advisory Agreements contain a non-assignment clause as required by Section 205(a)(2)? ■ If the Firm is organized as a partnership, does the agreement with clients provide for notification to clients of any change in the membership of such partnership within a reasonable time after such change? (Section 205(a)(3)	
		Custody— ■ Does the Firm disclose in its Form ADV Part I that it has custody of client funds or securities? ■ *Does a* qualified custodian maintain those funds and securities -- (i) In a separate account for each client under that client's name; or (ii) In accounts that contain only your clients' funds and securities, under the Firm's name as agent or trustee for its clients. *Notice to clients.* If the Firm opens an account with a qualified custodian on the client's behalf, either under the client's name or under the Firm's name as agent, the Firm must notify the client in writing of the qualified custodian's name, address, and the manner in which the funds or securities are maintained, promptly when the account is opened and following any changes to this information.	

© MODERN COMPLIANCE 2015

EXHIBIT C. COMPLIANCE RISK ASSESSMENT MATRIX *Cont'd*			
YES	NO	FOCUS AREA	NOTES
		Custody—*cont'd* *Account statements to clients. (i) By qualified custodian.* The Firm has a reasonable basis for believing that the qualified custodian sends an account statement, at least quarterly, to each of its clients for which it maintains funds or securities, identifying the amount of funds and of each security in the account at the end of the period and setting forth all transactions in the account during that period; or ▪ Does the Firm send a quarterly account statement to each of its clients for who it has custody of funds or securities, identifying the amount of funds and of each security of which you have custody at the end of the period and setting forth all transactions during that period; ▪ Does an independent public accountant verify all of those funds and securities by actual examination at least once during each calendar year at a time that is chosen by the accountant without prior notice or announcement to you and that is irregular from year to year, and files a certificate on Form ADV-E [17 CFR 279.8] with the SEC within 30 days after the completion of the examination, stating that it has examined the funds and securities and describing the nature and extent of the examination; and The independent public accountant, upon finding any material discrepancies during the course of the examination, notifies the Commission within one business day of the finding, by means of a facsimile transmission or electronic mail, followed by first class mail, directed to the attention of the Director of the Office of Compliance Inspections and Examinations; and	
		Books & Records— ▪ Does the Firm maintain a backup of its system in case of system failure or corruption of files? If yes, how often is the system backed-up? (*Daily backups with weekly backups maintained until the next weekly backup would indicate a good internal control.*) If the Firm does maintain a system backup, is this backup maintained off-site? (*Off-site backups are preferable.*) ▪ Does the system of accounting and recordkeeping appear adequate in relation to the Firm's business and is the staff responsible for these accounting and recordkeeping activities adequate, given the nature and size of registrant's business? ▪ Does the Firm retain source documents supporting transaction journals and all other required books and records required under the Books and Records Rule? Where and by whom are the Firm's principal books and records maintained? *Records Retention - Paragraph 204-2(e)* ▪ Does it appear that the Firm retains its books and records for the required five years, the first two years located at the Firm's offices? ▪ Are articles of incorporation, by-laws, charter, minute books etc maintained at the Firm's principal office?	
		Financial Condition of the Firm— ▪ Did a review of the Firm's financial records indicate that it is capitalized with client funds through either loans or equity? If yes, have adequate disclosures been made to clients about the risks and conflicts of interest involved with this transaction? ▪ Does the Firm's current financial condition raise concerns as to its solvency or its ability to otherwise continue to provide advisory services? (*Note: Although the SEC does not have any specific standards for an adviser's financial condition, an adviser who contracts to provide extensive services while insolvent may violate the anti-fraud provisions of Section 206. If yes, is the Firm complying with the disclosure requirements of Rule 206(4)-4?*	

EXHIBIT C. COMPLIANCE RISK ASSESSMENT MATRIX *Cont'd*

YES	NO	FOCUS AREA	NOTES
		Internal Controls— ▪ If the Firm has internal control procedures in place, does it appear that such control procedures are being consistently and correctly applied and being adhered to? ▪ Review the Firm's internal control procedures; did the review reveal any specific areas of concern? ▪ Who monitors the Firm's internal control procedures? Does the Firm have an independent compliance department to monitor/test its internal controls? ▪ Did the Firm have an internal audit conducted, or any other examination by an outside agency or its parent if applicable, for which a comment letter or report was provided? If so, ensure that any issues found have been documented and corrected.	
		Suitability— The Firm should provide its services in a manner consistent with the way in which its services have been described in disclosure documents, marketing documents, electronic media and oral representations. ▪ Does the Firm collect the necessary information from clients, initially and on a continuing basis, to make suitability determinations and ensure advice provided is consistent with the clients' needs and objectives? ▪ Does the Firm or a representative of the Firm, contact each client at least annually to review the client's current investment objectives and financial condition to assure that future purchases of securities for the client's account are suitable investments? ▪ Do purchases and sales generally conform to clients' investment objectives? ▪ Does the firm offer individualized account management? Do clients maintain all indicia of ownership of their securities, including right to pledge them as collateral and right to vote proxies? ▪ Are clients' individual financial needs and objectives assessed initially and updated periodically? ▪ Do securities recommended appear to be suitable in light of clients' financial circumstances, risk tolerance and sophistication? ▪ Do clients have direct access to portfolio managers or other representatives of the adviser at least annually? ▪ Do the Firm's custodians track ownership of securities on a client by client basis? ▪ Do clients have the ability to place limitations and restrictions on securities purchased for or sold from their accounts? ▪ Review terminated accounts; did the review of clients who terminated their investment advisory contracts reveal any significant problems? ▪ Did a review of client complaint files indicate any problems or concerns?	
		Portfolio Management— ▪ Does the Firm manage accounts in a manner consistent with the clients' investment objectives, subject to any client investment restrictions or other special instructions? ▪ Are client accounts maintained on an automated system? If the Firm uses an automated order management system, does this system produce exception reports (*i.e.*, restrictions report, turnover reports, portfolio diversification reports, maturity schedules, ex-dividend reports, call-date reports, schedules of available cash, percentage of security held, etc?) ▪ Are available cash balances identified and invested for the benefit of clients on a timely basis?	

© MODERN COMPLIANCE 2015

EXHIBIT C. COMPLIANCE RISK ASSESSMENT MATRIX *Cont'd*			
YES	NO	FOCUS AREA	NOTES
		Portfolio Management—*cont'd* ▪ Are account rebalances executed on a timely basis? (account maintenance due to client account deposits & withdraws) ▪ Is the investment adviser adhering to individual client investment restrictions? ▪ Does transaction volume (portfolio turnover) appear excessive considering each client's stated investment policies and their individual circumstances? ▪ Does the adviser have a basis for investment decisions? (*i.e.,* research, on-site visits, interviews)	
		Prohibited Transactions – Principal & Agency Transactions **Rule 206(3)-2** ▪ Is the Firm engaging in any prohibited transactions without first obtaining prior client approval? Is the approval in writing? *The rule refers to the firm and any other person relying on the rule.* ▪ Has the advisory client executed a written consent prospectively authorizing the Firm to effect agency cross transactions for the advisory client, provided that the written consent is obtained after full written disclosure that with respect to agency cross transactions the investment adviser or other person will act as broker for, receive commissions from, and have a potentially conflicting division of loyalties and responsibilities regarding, both parties to the transactions; ▪ Does the Firm send to each client a written confirmation at or before the completion of each transaction, which confirmation includes (i) a statement of the nature of the transaction, (ii) the date the transaction took place, (iii) an offer to furnish upon request, the time when the transaction took place, and (iv) the source and amount of any other remuneration received or to be received by the investment adviser in connection with the transaction. *Please be aware that there are caveats about participating in a distribution or tender offer.* ▪ Does the Firm send to each client, at least annually, and with or as part of any written statement or summary of the account from the investment adviser or other person, a written disclosure statement identifying the total number of transactions during the period since the date of the last statement or summary, and the total amount of all commissions or other remuneration received or to be received by the investment adviser in connection with transactions during the period; ▪ Each written disclosure statement and confirmation required by this rule includes a conspicuous statement that the written consent referred to in paragraph (a)(1) of this section may be revoked at any time by written notice to the investment adviser; and ▪ No such transaction is effected in which the same investment adviser or an investment adviser and any person controlling, controlled by or under common control with such investment adviser recommended the transaction to both any seller and any purchaser. ▪ For purposes of this rule the term *agency cross transaction for an advisory client* shall mean a transaction in which a person acts as an investment adviser in relation to a transaction in which such investment adviser, or any person controlling, controlled by, or under common control with such investment adviser, acts as broker for both such advisory client and for another person on the other side of the transaction. This rule shall not be construed as relieving in any way the investment adviser from acting in the best interests of the advisory client, including fulfilling the duty with respect to the best price and execution for the particular transaction for the advisory client; nor shall it relieve such person or persons from any disclosure obligation which may be imposed by subparagraphs (1) or (2) of section 206 of the Act or by other applicable provisions of the federal securities laws.	

EXHIBIT C. COMPLIANCE RISK ASSESSMENT MATRIX *Cont'd*			
YES	NO	FOCUS AREA	NOTES
		Prohibited Transactions—Principal & Agency Transactions Rule 206(3)-2—*cont'd* - Does a review of the trading blotter or other documents containing similar information reveal that the Firm or an affiliate has effected transactions in a principal capacity for registered investment company or ERISA clients? *If yes, these transactions may be prohibited. Obtain full explanations for these transactions and documentary record of the details of each transaction. (Section 17(a) of the Investment Company Act generally prohibits such transactions).* - Does a review of a sample of trades indicate that the Firm or affiliate obtained the client's written consent? - If applicable, have investment company clients purchased new issues in which the adviser or affiliate was a principal underwriter? *If yes, determine if these purchases were effected under Rule 10f-3 of the Investment Company Act.* - Perform a review of the trading blotters, order tickets, or other documents to determine if the adviser or an affiliate has effected transactions in an agency capacity for both sides of the trade in which the advisory clients took part ("agency cross transactions"). Did the adviser, or the affiliated broker, receive any compensation for effecting any agency-cross transactions? *If no, then the transaction would not be considered to be an agency-cross.*	
		Conflicts of Interest— Review the adviser's business practices, products and services offered to determine if any conflicts of interest exist. Did the adviser provide clients with proper disclosures to address the adviser's conflicts of interest or did the adviser's conflicts of interest require corrective action so that the conflict would not harm its clients? - Does the adviser have a "code of ethics" and/or "code of conduct"? If so, does the adviser's code require employees to pre-clear all personal trades? - Are employee personal transactions reviewed after they are executed for potential conflicts of interest? Does the adviser have an automated system to match the employees' personal securities transactions with those of advisory clients, especially those on behalf of investment companies, if applicable? If no, how does the adviser control such transactions so as to prevent unauthorized and/or inappropriate securities transactions by employees? Does someone independent from the person who regularly collects and monitors/reviews employee transactions review the securities transactions of the person who performs the regular reviews of employee transactions? - Does the Firm and any persons falling within Rule 204-2(a) (12) the definition of an "advisory representative" file quarterly statements of their personal securities transactions, regardless of activity during the period? Are the records properly maintained and are the records reviewed by an officer of the Firm or some one independent from the Firm and if so, note by whom? - Does the adviser's code require all advisory representatives to provide the adviser with a copy of all confirmations of trades they effect in their personal accounts? Review employee personal transactions. Did the review of these transactions in conjunction with the trading activity of the firm for clients indicate any instance where the adviser or an advisory representative may have engaged in improper trading activities (*i.e.*, "front-running")? - Does the adviser maintain written policies and procedures "reasonably designed to prevent the misuse of material non-public information?" (Sec. 204A) If the adviser has adopted these policies & procedures, review and evaluate these policies and procedures in light of the firm's organization, affiliations and activities. Do these policies and procedures appear to be comprehensive and designed to reasonably prevent the misuse of material non-public information? - Does the adviser actively enforce these policies and procedures? If yes, describe generally the procedures used to prevent the deliberate or inadvertent dissemination of non-public information.	

© MODERN COMPLIANCE 2015

EXHIBIT C. COMPLIANCE RISK ASSESSMENT MATRIX *Cont'd*

YES	NO	FOCUS AREA	NOTES
		Conflicts of Interest—*cont'd* - Perform a review of the firm's investment files to determine if there are any instances in which non-public information may have been received or given. - Perform a review of the trading records and or the trading blotter, including particularly any consolidated holdings reports (if available), to determine if anyone may have received or acted on non-public information? - Upon completion of the review of the trading records and or the trading blotter was any evidence found that would suggest that transactions occurred just prior to the release of public information?	
		Brokerage/Trade Execution— - Does any one in the firm or an affiliate act in any of the following capacities in which he or she or a related party receives a commission for the placement of transactions: Registered Representative, Broker-Dealer, Registered Principal or a Purchaser Representative? - Do the adviser's disclosure documents and marketing material disclose the receipt of the commissions? Do the disclosures provide adequate information to the firm's clients about the activities of the firm and/or its affiliates? - Do the firm's controls appear adequate to prevent them from disadvantaging any of its clients? - Are commission reports (Brokerage Allocation Report) utilized to monitor to whom commissions are paid and the amount? - Does the firm monitor & review trade errors and failed trades? Does there appear to be an excessive number of trade errors and failed trades in light of the nature of the trades executed? If yes, review the trades to identify if there are valid reasons for the error/fails or whether the problem appears to be systemic. - Upon completion of your review does it appear that clients are ever disadvantaged as a result of trading errors? If yes, review each incident and make sure you determine and verify that the client was made whole with the cost being borne by the firm if the error or fail was caused by the firm. *The firm has a fiduciary duty to its clients to take responsibility for any losses which result from it making an error and placing an unauthorized trade in a client's account, unless the adviser was acting in good faith at the time of such execution.* - Does the firm participate in any soft-dollar arrangements with broker-dealers, review all products and services. If you determine that the firm is receiving products and services that are not used entirely for research, classify them as mixed-use arrangements: mixed research and non-research items. Does the firm make a good faith allocation of the non-research costs? Ensure that the firm pays for these products and services with hard dollars only. - Does the firm participate in any soft-dollar arrangements with broker-dealers, review all products and services. If you determine that the firm is receiving products and services that are not used entirely for research, classify them as mixed-use arrangements: mixed research and non-research items. Does the firm make a good faith allocation of the non-research costs? Ensure that the firm pays for these products and services with hard dollars only. - Perform a review of the firm's commission rates paid to broker-dealers. How do the rates paid to brokers with whom the firm has soft-dollar arrangements compare to the rates paid to broker-dealers with whom there are no soft-dollar arrangements? *If you uncover significant differences in these commission rates, determine if the differences are justified based on the services received or if there are other undisclosed reasons for such differences.* - Does the firm make adequate disclosures to clients regarding its soft-dollar arrangements? - Does the firm produce any soft-dollar reports? If yes, make sure you review the reports to ensure that policies & procedures are being adhered to and that the reports do not illustrate any patterns.	

EXHIBIT C. COMPLIANCE RISK ASSESSMENT MATRIX *Cont'd*

YES	NO	FOCUS AREA	NOTES
		Brokerage/Trade Execution—*cont'd* Best Execution – Review the firm's policies & procedures with regard to best execution and review any reports produced. Make sure you review the reports to ensure that policies & procedures are being adhered to and that the reports do not illustrate any patterns. **Note:** *During your review of the firm's records, do you see any signs that indicate excessive commissions, churning, trading errors, "as of" trades, or other unusual or abusive items regarding price, commissions, mark-ups/downs, execution, timing, broker or dealer used or market in which executed?* ▪ Test the accuracy of the trading blotter provided by testing a sample of transactions back to source documentation such as order tickets and broker-dealer confirms. Review the executed transactions and commissions assessed clients on a cents/share basis. ▪ Does the commission rates paid appear to be in the range of what institutions normally pay (industry standard), uniformly imposed, and appropriate in light of the transactions made? Is there a reason(s) for the higher commission rates? Are they justifiable? Are there any specific clients or group of clients that are consistently paying higher commission rates than other clients in general? Why? ▪ Did the review of the trading blotter indicate that the firm is executing cross transactions between clients such as buys and sells of the same security on the same day by different clients? Why? Were these trades executed as principal transactions? Are disclosures about this practice made to clients? ▪ Did the review of the trading blotter reveal evidence that only one or merely a few broker-dealers are used to execute trades for any given client? Is the trade placement made pursuant to direction by the client, *Directed Brokerage Arrangements?* Are disclosures about *Directed Brokerage* (Mark Bailey) made to clients? Did the client request such arrangement and has it been documented in writing by the client? Review the commission rates for these trades. Are they excessive? **Note:** *All Investment Advisers have a fiduciary duty at minimum to make its clients aware of the Directed Brokerage commission rates they are paying and that they appear excessive even if the client still wishes to remain party to the arrangement.* ▪ Did the review of the trading blotter reveal evidence of any material, aggressive short-term trading in any security, particularly contrary to the firm's normal practices or policies & procedures? ▪ **If applicable:** Did the review of the trading blotter or other records reveal that the adviser or an affiliate has effected transactions in an agency capacity for its investment company clients? Are the commission rates paid on these transactions at the most favorable rates that the adviser or affiliate can obtain and/or offer? Are the commission rates paid on such transactions competitive with those of non-affiliated broker-dealers for similar trades? **Note:** *The practice above may constitute a violation of Section 17(e) and Rule 17e-1 of the Investment Company Act of 1940 if the client is an investment company or Section 206(1) or (2) for other clients.* ▪ Did the review of the trading blotter reveal evidence that only one or merely a few broker-dealers are used to execute trades for any given client? Is the trade placement made pursuant to direction by the client, *Directed Brokerage Arrangements?* Are disclosures about *Directed Brokerage* (Mark Bailey) made to clients? Did the client request such arrangement and has it been documented in writing by the client? Review the commission rates for these trades. Are they excessive? **Note:** *All Investment Advisers have a fiduciary duty at minimum to make its clients aware of the Directed Brokerage commission rates they are paying and that they appear excessive even if the client still wishes to remain party to the arrangement.*	

EXHIBIT C. COMPLIANCE RISK ASSESSMENT MATRIX Cont'd

YES	NO	FOCUS AREA	NOTES
		Brokerage/Trade Execution—*cont'd* ■ Did the review of the trading blotter reveal evidence of any material, aggressive short-term trading in any security, particularly contrary to the firm's normal practices or policies & procedures? ■ **If applicable:** Did the review of the trading blotter or other records reveal that the adviser or an affiliate has effected transactions in an agency capacity for its investment company clients? Are the commission rates paid on these transactions at the most favorable rates that the adviser or affiliate can obtain and/or offer? Are the commission rates paid on such transactions competitive with those of non-affiliated broker-dealers for similar trades? **Note:** *The practice above may constitute a violation of Section 17(e) and Rule 17e-1 of the Investment Company Act of 1940 if the client is an investment company or Section 206(1) or (2) for other clients.* ■ Review trades to determine whether or not broker-dealers used by the adviser are paid for order flow. Why are they making these payments? Are an unusually large number of trades going to broker-dealers that reportedly pay for order flow? ■ Does the firm regularly include all client accounts in bunched trades for which a particular instrument is appropriate and who have available resources in their accounts (if it is a purchase)? If not, what are the apparent reasons certain accounts do not participate? If securities acquired through bunched trades are purchased at different prices, was each client participating in the bunched trade allocated the security at the average price, including any commissions paid? ■ If the securities in a bunched trade are purchased at different prices during the day and the adviser does not use average pricing, is the methodology used by the adviser fair and reasonable to participating accounts? ■ Do order tickets/confirms identify accounts participating and the extent of each account's participation in each bunched trade? Review the commission rates to determine if they are competitive and in line with regular institutional rates? ■ Are proprietary accounts, either those of individuals of the firm, the firm or pension or profit sharing plans included in bunched trades with clients? If proprietary accounts are bunched with client accounts, review the trades that occurred for a period of time (1-2 years) to determine if the proprietary account(s) was in any way advantaged to the detriment of the firm's clients. **Note:** *Is the performance of the proprietary accounts whose trades are regularly bunched with those of clients substantially different than the performance of client accounts that are managed in the same investment style? If yes, why?* ■ Is the firm's disclosure to its clients about its bunching practices sufficiently clear and understandable? If no, what information is missing? ■ Does the firm participate in any Wrap Fee Programs? Wrap Fee Programs raise a number of concerns. Among the major issues are the amount and clarity of disclosure that wrap fee clients receive regarding the wrap arrangements and the amount of fees the client pays, suitability, best execution, and conflicts of interest. Review and test for the areas mentioned.	
		Marketing Material & Performance Calculations – Rule 206(4)-1 contains a general prohibition against the use of any advertisement that is false or misleading as well as a number of additional specific prohibitions. The Advisers Act defines the term "advertisement" broadly to include most communications that are addressed to more than one prospective client. ■ Does the firm use marketing material and advertisements to attract clients? If so, review presentation content and materials provided to potential clients for objectionable items or missing disclosures.	

EXHIBIT C. COMPLIANCE RISK ASSESSMENT MATRIX *Cont'd*			
YES	NO	FOCUS AREA	NOTES
		■ Does the firm claim to be GIPS compliant? Does the firm prepare and present its marketing material in compliance with the GIPS standards for marketing material? ■ Does the firm maintain a file of all advertisements utilized? (Rule 204-2(a)(11)) ■ Does the firm conduct seminars to attract clients? If so, review presentation content and materials provided attendees for objectionable items or missing disclosures. ■ Does the firm use performance figures in attracting prospective clients or in reports to current clients? If yes, does the firm maintain the necessary records that support the performance calculations and source documents? (Rule 204-2(a) (16)) Do these records and documents support the firm's performance computations? Did the performance history include inappropriate periods? Do the performance figures represent: model results? or performance of actual accounts? **Note:** *If the performance figures represent model results, were the results calculated using actual investment decisions and market activity subsequent to completion of development of the model? "Back-tested" results are generally not allowable. Can the adviser prove the timing of the model trades or if a timed account, the dates of timing switches?* ■ What method is used to calculate performance, e.g. Internal Rate of Return (IRR) or Time Weighted Rate of Return (TWRR) or a hybrid (linked short period IRR's)? ■ Does the firm utilize a portfolio management software system? If yes pick some samples and perform some testing.	
		Compensation / Client Fees— ■ Are all clients being charged the correct fees as specified in each client's contract? ■ Are client bills verified for accuracy and compliance with each client's contract by a person other than the preparer prior to sending them to the client? ■ Do the investment advisory fees, in general, appear excessive considering the nature of the services provided? (Sec. 206(1), (2), & (4)) ■ Perform an independent computation of a sample of accounts to confirm the accuracy of the firm's application of its advisory fee schedule? (Form ADV, Contract) Does the firm charge clients different fees for essentially the same service? ■ Does the firm offset part of its advisory fee with commissions which it or an affiliate receives? If yes, explain the conditions associated with the payments. Is this procedure disclosed to its clients? ■ Does the firm have a pro-rata refund policy if fees are received in advance? ■ Do any client investment advisory contracts contain a performance based fee provision? If yes, did registrant satisfy the conditions of Rule 205-3? *Please keep in mind certain factors such as the identity of the client, including whether or not they are "qualified clients," look through provisions and the transition rules.* Are these fee arrangements disclosed in Form ADV?	
		Client Referrals – ■ Does the firm participate in any client referrals? Do all referred clients receive adequate disclosure of all material facts related to such arrangements and receive adviser's Form ADV, Part II or alternative brochure? If no, describe all weaknesses found. ■ How does the firm assure that solicitor provides all prospective clients with the adviser's Form ADV or brochure and the disclosure document required by Rule 206(4)-3?	

EXHIBIT C. COMPLIANCE RISK ASSESSMENT MATRIX *Cont'd*			
YES	NO	FOCUS AREA	NOTES
		Client Referrals – *cont'd* ■ Does the firm compensate anyone other than an officer or employee of the firm for referring clients? ■ Does the firm direct or appear to direct client brokerage to any broker-dealers in exchange for client referrals? ■ Is the solicitor a related party? If yes, has the firm disclosed this affiliation to its clients? ■ If arrangements are with an unaffiliated solicitor for personal advisory services, does the agreement between the investment adviser and the solicitor comply with Rule 206(4)-3(a) (2) (iii) (A)? ■ **Specifically, does it:** (1) contain a description of the solicitation activities and the compensation arrangements; and (2) contain an undertaking by the solicitor to perform his duties under the agreement consistent with the investment adviser's instructions and provisions of the Advisers Act and rules? ■ Does the firm require the solicitor to provide the client, at the time of the solicitation, the investment adviser's disclosure brochure and separate solicitor's disclosure document? ■ Is there a separate solicitor's disclosure document which contains information required by Rule 206(4)-3? Does the solicitor's disclosure document contain the information required by paragraph (b) of Rule 206(4)-3? ■ Has the adviser made a bonafide effort to ascertain whether the solicitor has complied with the agreement?	
		Proxy Voting – ■ Does the firm vote proxies on behalf of its clients? ■ If the firm votes proxies on behalf of clients, do any conflicts exist? Are policies & procedures in place to address the conflicts and/or eliminate them? ■ Are proxy vote ballots reconciled? Does the firm reconcile proxy ballets received vs. the proxies actually voted? ■ If the firm has Taft-Hartley Union accounts and votes in accordance with the AFL-CIO Letter for these accounts, does the firm vote the same way for its non Taft-Hartley Union accounts? **Note:** *This could be a conflict and/or problem.* ■ If the firm utilizes a service provider to handle proxies for the firm, does the firm perform due diligence on the service provider? ■ How often? Has the firm incorporated the service provider's policies & procedures into their Proxy policies and procedures? - - Has the firm made appropriate disclosure about its proxy voting process in its Form ADV Part II? Is it current and accurate? ■ Does the firm vote proxies for mutual funds that it advises? ■ Does the firm have policies & procedures in place to vote such proxies? ■ Do any conflicts exist? Are policies & procedures in place to address the conflicts and/or eliminate them? ■ Does the adviser perform continued due diligence/oversight of the third party proxy voting service provider? ■ Regulation S-P (Privacy Policy & Procedures)—Does the Adviser periodically provide clients with privacy policy notices, as required? ■ Does the Adviser effectively safeguard information it is required to maintain from unauthorized access, alteration, loss, or destruction? ■ Does the adviser have security measures to properly safeguard personal and financial information of clients, including consumer credit report information, from unauthorized access, disclosure or use? Does it ensure that the security measures of its service providers also safeguard this information?	

EXHIBIT C. COMPLIANCE RISK ASSESSMENT MATRIX *Cont'd*

YES	NO	FOCUS AREA	NOTES
		Proxy Voting – *cont'd* • Does the adviser's electronic information systems, both internal and those supplied by third parties, effectively detect and prevent malicious intrusions from internal and external sources? Does it have effective oversight measures to protect its electronic infrastructure, operating systems, files and databases? • Does the Adviser have procedures in place for the disposal of consumer information?	
		Antimoney Laundering— • Does the adviser ensure that its staff has sufficient knowledge and skills to effectively carry out their AML responsibilities? • Does the adviser's AML program appear to be effective in identifying suspicious cash/ currency activity and reporting such activities to appropriate authorities? • With respect to its AML program, is documentation or other output generated to substantiate that you obtained all related information in a timely, accurate, and complete manner? Does the adviser ensure that this information is preserved for the required period of time and protected from unplanned destruction, loss, alteration, compromise, or use? • Does it comply with the U.S. Treasury Office of Foreign Asset Control's (OFAC) requirements by restricting its business transactions with certain individuals, entities, and/or countries on lists compiled by OFAC? • Does the adviser maintain evidence of initial checking of OFAC lists for each new client, and periodic re-checking of OFAC lists for existing clients?	
		Disaster Recovery— • Does the adviser comply with SEC guidance regarding disaster recovery plans? • Does the adviser have procedures in place to be prepared for and test operations during human or natural emergencies? • Does the adviser have procedures in place provide for the availability of critical personnel and systems in the event of a disaster? • Do the adviser's procedures contain verification of business continuity plans of its third-party service providers? • Do the adviser's policies and procedures contain contingencies that have been sufficiently contemplated? For example, determine whether the policy, among other things, i) discusses what will happen in the event of the death or incapacitation of key personnel, ii) includes information regarding how to reach employees and service providers, iii) provides for back-up facilities in the event of dislocation due to a natural disaster or otherwise. • Does the adviser's plan detail how customers can reach the firm in the event of an emergency? • Does the plan address procedures for how employees can communicate with each other, and with key service providers, • And does the plan provide for back-up facilities in the event of dislocation? • Does the adviser maintain documentation of regular reviews and adjustments of the plan as a result of such reviews and testing, to account for changes in the adviser, its business, and needs, such as ensuring alternative worksites are adequate, evidence of actual testing of the plan to determine if it will be successful, and whether changes should be made to the plan?	

EXHIBIT D. SAMPLE REPORT TO DEMONSTRATE THAT YOUR COMPLIANCE PROGRAM IS DYNAMIC

Step 1: Gather the following:

1. Supporting documentation of compliance efforts (conflict reviews, testing results, etc.)
2. Documents evidencing the firm's investment in compliance
3. List of third-party sources (including outside counsel, consultants, attorneys, etc.) used to access training – conferences, webinars, and publications

Step 2: Author the Annual Review summary for management, including the following structure and sample language:

The Compliance Program. The following report has been prepared by the Chief Compliance Officer (CCO) of XYZ Co. based on the CCO's annual review and assessment of the firm's compliance policies and procedures.

Compliance Support. XYZ management and the XYZ Co., an SEC registered investment adviser (the *"Adviser"*), fully support the firm's compliance program and the XYZ CCO in performing her duties with respect to the investment adviser. To this end, XYZ management provided the following support to the CCO in 2009:

1. The following attorneys and compliance consulting resources were made available to the CCO during the period: Legal and Compliance Department resources of the Administrator, Outside Counsel, XYZ's compliance consultant and other sources that the Adviser consults with on issues.
2. In the capacity as the CCO to an investment adviser, the CCO kept abreast of new laws, regulations and interpretations of rules by attending educational meetings and reading industry periodicals.

    In addition, the CCO attended the following continuing education meetings in 2010:

    - NSCP Conference in Boston, MA in March
    - NRS Conference in Orlando, FL in April
    - SEC's CCOutreach Program in Philadelphia, PA in June
    - Stradley Ronan Mutual Fund and Investment Adviser Seminar in Philadelphia in June
    - ACA Compliance Roundtable Meeting in Philadelphia in September
    - NSCP National Meeting in Philadelphia in October
    - Philadelphia Compliance Roundtable in December

The CCO reviews numerous industry periodicals including: Investment Company Institute memorandums, IA Week, Core Compliance & Legal Services, Inc. Monthly Risk Management Updates, regulatory newsletters and summaries from a number of law and accounting firms.

EXHIBIT E. SAMPLE 2015 SEC DOCUMENT REQUEST LETTER (00088737XD690E)

**UNITED STATES
SECURITIES AND EXCHANGE COMMISSION
CHICAGO REGIONAL OFFICE
SUITE 900
175 WEST JACKSON BLVD.
CHICAGO, IL 60604**

 2015

DELIVERY VIA E-MAIL

Mr. ▇
Chief Compliance Officer
▇

Re: Examination of ▇ (the "Adviser") and ▇ (the "Funds")

Dear ▇:

The staff of the U.S. Securities and Exchange Commission is conducting an examination of the Adviser and the Funds pursuant to Section 204 of the Investment Advisers Act of 1940 (the "Advisers Act") and Section 31(b) of the Investment Company Act of 1940 (the "Investment Company Act"), respectively. The purpose of the examination is to assess the Adviser's compliance with provisions of the Advisers Act and the rules thereunder as well as the Funds' compliance with the provisions of the Investment Company Act and rules thereunder.

Additional information about compliance examinations and the examination process is included in the enclosed "*Examination Information*" brochure (SEC Form 2389). Also enclosed is information regarding the Commission's authority to obtain the information requested and additional information: "*Supplemental Information for Entities Directed to Supply Information to the Commission Other Than Pursuant to a Commission Subpoena*" (SEC Form 1661) and *Supplemental Information for Persons Requested to Supply Information Voluntarily to the Commission's Examination Staff* (SEC Form 2866).

Information is Requested

Please provide all of the information specified in the enclosed information request list. The staff requests that responses be provided in an electronic format to the extent possible by the dates indicated in the document request list. Additional information about the desired electronic format is included in the document request list.

EXHIBIT E. SAMPLE 2015 SEC DOCUMENT REQUEST LETTER (00088737XD690E)

If the Adviser becomes aware of the need for delay in the production of any requested information, the Adviser should immediately contact the undersigned at the telephone number indicated. During the examination, the staff may also request additional or follow-up information, and will discuss timeframes for the Adviser to produce this information.

The On-Site Phase of Examination

The on-site phase of the examination will begin on ▊▊▊▊ 2015. The staff appreciates the Adviser's cooperation in facilitating the examination process.

We request that you make adequate office facilities available to the staff during the on-site examination, to ensure the confidentiality and efficiency of the examination.

Background Regarding the Information Requested

Each investment adviser and investment company that is registered with the Commission is required to adopt and implement written policies and procedures reasonably designed to prevent violations of the federal securities laws, and to review those policies and procedures annually for their continued adequacy and the effectiveness of their implementation. In addition, registered advisers and funds are required to designate a chief compliance officer responsible for administering the policies and procedures. Each adviser should adopt policies and procedures that take into consideration the nature of that firm's operations. The policies and procedures should be designed to prevent violations from occurring, detect violations that have occurred, and correct promptly any violations that have occurred.

The initial phase of an examination generally includes a review of the firm's business and investment activities and its corresponding compliance policies and procedures. The examination staff will request information and documents and speak with the firm's employees to ensure an understanding of the firm's business and investment activities and the operation of its compliance program. Using the information obtained, the staff will assess whether the firm's policies and procedures appear to effectively address the firm's compliance risks. The initial phase of an examination also includes testing of the firm's compliance program in particular areas. The information requested and the purpose for requesting the information is described below.

- Certain general information is requested, such as the firm's organizational charts, demographic and other data for advisory clients, including privately offered funds, and a record of all trades placed for its clients/funds (trade blotter) -- to provide an understanding of the firm's business and its investment activities.

- Information about the firm's compliance risks is requested, and the written policies and procedures that the firm has established and implemented to address those risks -- to provide an understanding of the firm's compliance risks and its corresponding controls. This information would include, for example, any inventory performed of the firm's compliance risks and its compliance manual or policies and procedures.

EXHIBIT E. SAMPLE 2015 SEC DOCUMENT REQUEST LETTER (00088737XD690E)

- Documents relating to the firm's compliance testing is requested -- to provide an understanding of how effectively a firm has implemented its compliance policies and procedures. This information would include, for example, the results of any compliance reviews, quality control analyses, surveillance, and/or forensic or transactional tests performed by the firm.

- Information regarding actions taken as a result of compliance testing is requested -- to provide an understanding of steps taken by the firm to address the results of any compliance reviews, quality control analyses, surveillance, and/or forensic or transactional tests performed by the firm. This information would include, for example, any warnings to or disciplinary action of employees, changes in policies or procedures, redress to affected clients, or other measures.

- Other information is requested -- to allow the staff to perform testing for compliance in various areas.

As part of the pre-examination planning process, the staff actively coordinates examination oversight to ensure that regulatory efforts are not duplicative. If you have any concerns in this regard, please contact the undersigned.

Your cooperation is greatly appreciated in the examination process. If you have any questions, please contact me, at (312)

Sincerely,

Staff Accountant

Enclosures:
   Information Request List
   Exhibit 1: Layout for Securities Trading Blotter/Purchase and Sales Journal
   Examination Information Brochure (Form 2389)
   Supplemental Information (Forms 1661 & 2866)

EXHIBIT E. SAMPLE 2015 SEC DOCUMENT REQUEST LETTER (00088737XD690E)

Examination Information Request List

Examination Period

Information is requested for the period **January 1, 2013** through **December 31, 2014** (the "Examination Period") unless otherwise noted.

Organizing the Information to be Provided

Please label the information so that it corresponds to the item number in the request list. This list is divided between Part I and Part II. Items should be provided on or before the date stated at the top of Part I and Part II. If information provided is responsive to more than one request item, you may provide it only once and refer to it when responding to the other request item numbers. If any request item does not apply to your business, please indicate "N/A" (not applicable).

Please provide the information requested below and hereafter during the examination in electronic format, and please ensure that all electronic information provided is "read-only."

PART I: Information to be Provided by ▬▬▬▬ 2015

General Information

1. Adviser's organization chart with ownership percentages showing the adviser, control persons, and all affiliates.

2. List of current employees, partners, officers and/or directors and their respective titles, office location, and hire date.

3. List of any of the Adviser's employees, partners, officers and/or directors who resigned or were terminated during the Examination Period and information regarding the reason for their departure.

4. A list of any employees of the Adviser who resigned or were terminated and who filed or stated complaints against the firm or its employees, alleging potential violations of securities laws as the cause for the resignation or termination.

5. Any threatened, pending and settled litigation or arbitration involving the Adviser or any "supervised person" (if the matter relates to the supervised person's association with the Adviser or a securities-related matter) including a description of the allegations, the status, and a brief description of any "out of court" or informal settlement. Note that "supervised person" is any partner, officer, director (or other person occupying a similar status or performing similar functions), or employee of an investment adviser, or other person who provides investment advice on behalf of the investment adviser and is subject to the supervision and control of the investment adviser (defined in Section 202(a)(25) of the Advisers Act). If none, please provide a written statement to that effect.

EXHIBIT E. SAMPLE 2015 SEC DOCUMENT REQUEST LETTER (00088737XD690E)

6. Current standard client advisory contracts or agreements.

7. List of any sub-advisers.

8. Part 2B of Form ADV ("Brochure Supplement") furnished to clients during the Examination Period.

9. A list of all committees including a description of each committee's responsibilities, meeting frequency, and a list of the members of each committee. State whether the committees keep written minutes.

10. Names of any joint ventures or any other businesses in which the Adviser or any officer, director, portfolio manager, or trader participates or has any interest (other than their employment with the Adviser), including a description of each relationship.

11. The names and location of all affiliated and unaffiliated key service providers and the services they perform.

12. Compliance and operational policies and procedures in effect during the Examination Period for the Adviser and its affiliates. Please be sure to also include any Code of Ethics, insider trading, fair valuation, remote office monitoring, contractor oversight, and GIPS policies and procedures that are created and maintained.

Portfolio Management and Trading

13. A trade blotter (*i.e.*, purchases and sales journal) that lists transactions (including all trade errors, cancellations, re-bills, and reallocations) in securities and other financial instruments (including privately offered funds) for: current and former clients; proprietary and/or trading accounts and access persons. The preferred format for this information is to provide it in Excel as indicated in Exhibit 1.

14. Provide the information below for all advisory clients, including privately offered funds and wrap clients. The preferred format for this information is in Excel.

    A. Current advisory clients including:

        a. the account number;
        b. the account name;
        c. account balance as of **December 31, 2014**;
        d. whether the client is a related person, affiliated person, or a proprietary account;
        e. the type of account (*e.g.*, individual, defined benefit retirement plan, registered fund, or unregistered fund);
        f. the account custodian and location;
        g. whether the custodian sends periodic account statements directly to the client; whether the delivery is electronic, if so, a copy of the authorization; and the form of electronic delivery (*e.g.*, email or website login);

EXHIBIT E. SAMPLE 2015 SEC DOCUMENT REQUEST LETTER (00088737XD690E)

    h. whether the Adviser has discretionary authority;
    i. whether the Adviser, an officer, an employee, or an affiliate acts as trustee, co-trustee, or successor trustee or has full power of attorney for the account;
    j. whether the Adviser or related persons are deemed to have custody of, possession of or access to the client's assets, and if so, the location of the assets;
    k. the investment strategy (*e.g.*, global equity, high-yield, aggressive growth, long-short, or statistical arbitrage) and the performance composite in which it is included, if any;
    l. the account portfolio manager(s);
    m. whether the client has a directed brokerage arrangement, including commission recapture;
    n. the value of each client's account that was used for purposes of calculating its advisory fee for the most recent billing period;
    o. whether the client pays a performance fee and the most recent performance fee amount;
    p. whether advisory fees are paid directly from the client's custodial account;
    q. account inception date; and
    r. name(s) of consultant(s) related to obtaining the client, if any.

B. Names of advisory clients lost, including the reason, method that the termination was communicated, termination date, and asset value at termination.

C. Names of any financial planning, pension consulting or other advisory clients not named in response to section A above.

Financial Records

15. Adviser's balance sheet, trial balance, income statement, and cash flow statement as of the end of its most recent fiscal year and the most current year to date.

16. List the terms of any loans from clients to the Adviser, including promissory notes, or sales of the Adviser's or any affiliate's stock to clients.

17. List all fee splitting or revenue sharing arrangements.

Custody

18. Provide the account number and contact information (e.g., name, mailing address, phone number and e-mail address) for the entities that maintained custody of the cash and securities of each client's account during the Examination Period. For private fund clients, please be sure to include all bank and brokerage accounts. For any securities that were not maintained with a qualified custodian, please include a description of the security, security name, location of the security, and the name of the clients who held such securities. For purposes of this request, you may exclude any assets held pursuant to a derivative or swap contract. Such information, if applicable, may be requested later.

EXHIBIT E. SAMPLE 2015 SEC DOCUMENT REQUEST LETTER (00088737XD690E)

Advisers Sponsoring or Managing Privately Offered Funds

19. Preferably in Excel format, information regarding each private and/or unregistered investment fund (and any co-investment or other parallel vehicles) sponsored and/or managed by the Adviser, including:

    a. name as shown in organizational documents (as amended);
    b. domicile (country);
    c. investment strategy (e.g., buyout, venture, mezzanine, fund-of-funds, etc.);
    d. name of the sub-adviser, if applicable;
    e. if funds are part of a master/feeder fund structure, full name and domicile of each fund;
    f. number of investors and total assets as of **December 31, 2014**;
    g. amount, if any, of Adviser's equity interest in each fund as of **December 31, 2014**;
    h. amount, if any, of Adviser's affiliated persons' interest as of **December 31, 2014**;
    i. date the fund began accepting unaffiliated investors;
    j. offering size;
    k. whether the fund is currently closed to new investors and when it closed;
    l. lock up periods for both initial and subsequent investments;
    m. specific exemption(s) from registration under the Securities Act of 1933 and/or the Investment Company Act of 1940 upon which the fund relies;
    n. the current stage of the fund's lifecycle, if applicable. Also indicate if the fund has been extended beyond its expected lifespan;
    o. services the Adviser or an affiliate (e.g., general partner, adviser, managing member) is providing;
    p. amount of leverage, both explicit (on-balance sheet) and off-balance sheet (futures and certain other derivatives), used by the fund as of **December 31, 2014**;
    q. whether the fund was created to offer investors participation in subsequent private funds offered by the Adviser;
    r. the value of each fund's account that was used for purposes of calculating its advisory fee for the last billing period;
    s. the advisory fee charged for the last billing period;
    t. whether the fund pays carried interest and whether the fund is currently in-the-money or out-of-the-money for earning carried interest; and
    u. whether the fund is currently in a clawback position and the amount of the clawback.

20. For each of the funds, the most recent audited financial statements. In addition, please provide documentation indicating when audit reports were delivered to investors.

Advisers to Registered Investment Companies ("RIC")

RIC: General Information

21. A chart listing all Funds with the following information as of **December 31, 2014**:

    a. fund/portfolio name;

EXHIBIT E. SAMPLE 2015 SEC DOCUMENT REQUEST LETTER (00088737XD690E)

      b. share class;
      c. registration number;
      d. net asset value;
      e. total shares outstanding;
      f. number of shareholder accounts;
      g. maximum sales load;
      h. investment objective;
      i. portfolio turnover rate for last 2 years;
      j. commencement date of operations; and
      k. whether the Fund was classified as aggressive capital appreciation, balanced, capital appreciation, growth and income, foreign issuer, growth, income, long term debt (taxable), long term debt (tax-free), money market (taxable), money market (tax-free), precious metals, index, or other.

22. A list of threatened, pending and settled litigation or arbitration to which the Fund was a party during the Examination Period. Provide a description of the allegations forming the basis for each issue, the status of each pending issue, and a brief description of any "out of court" or informal settlement. If none, please provide a written statement to that effect.

23. The Fund's policies and procedures adopted pursuant to the Compliance Rule. Please be sure to also include Code of Ethics, insider trading, gift giving/receiving, 2a-7, securities lending, and valuation policies and procedures.

Advisers That Are Money Managers in Wrap Fee Programs

24. Names of wrap fee programs in which one or more clients participate, including for each program:

      a. name of custodian/sponsor/broker-dealer;
      b. program name and the acronym;
      c. whether the program is a single or a dual contract program;
      d. total fee percentage charged by the sponsor;
      e. terms of Adviser's compensation;
      f. total value of client assets in each program as of the most recent billing date; and
      g. state whether the program permits "trading away" or "stepping out" from the wrap broker-dealer; and
      h. if applicable, state whether the adviser traded away during the Examination Period.

PART II: Information to be Provided by ▇▇▇▇▇ 2015

Information Regarding the Adviser's Compliance Program, Risk Management and Internal Controls

25. Any written interim or annual compliance reviews, internal control analyses, and forensic or transactional tests performed. Include any significant findings, both positive and negative, and any information about corrective or remedial actions taken regarding these findings.

EXHIBIT E. SAMPLE 2015 SEC DOCUMENT REQUEST LETTER (00088737XD690E)

26. A current inventory of the Adviser's compliance risks that forms the basis for its policies and procedures. Note any changes made to the inventory during the Examination Period and the dates of the changes.

27. Written guidance the Adviser provided to its employees regarding the compliance program and documents evidencing employee compliance training during the Examination Period.

28. Internal audit review schedules and completed audits for a three year period, including the subject and the date of the report.

29. A list of all client or investor complaints and information about the process used for monitoring client/investor correspondence and/or complaints.

30. A record of any non-compliance with the Adviser's compliance policies and procedures and of any action taken as a result of such non-compliance.

Portfolio Management and Trading

31. Names of securities held in all client portfolios (aggregate position totals for all instruments) for each quarter-end of the Examination Period including:

    a. security name;
    b. CUSIP (or other identifier);
    c. client name;
    d. client account number;
    e. quantity or principal/notional amount owned by each client;
    f. cost basis;
    g. whether the position was fair valued; and
    h. market value of the position.

    The preferred format for this information is in Excel.

32. Any restricted, watch, or grey lists that were in effect for the Examination Period.

33. A list of employees of the Adviser or its affiliates that performed a role for a publicly traded company or served on a creditor's committee. Include the name of the company or committee and the dates of the employee's service.

34. Please provide a list of all securities for which the Adviser or its related persons made 13F, 13D and/or 13G filings for the relevant reporting dates, including corresponding ownership percentages.

35. List of all PIPE investments that the Adviser participated in during the Examination Period.

EXHIBIT E. SAMPLE 2015 SEC DOCUMENT REQUEST LETTER (00088737XD690E)

36. A list of all initial public offerings and secondary offerings in which clients, proprietary accounts or access persons participated and, if not stated in policies and procedures or if the allocation did not follow standard policies and procedures, information regarding how allocation decisions were made. Include the trade date, security, symbol, total number of shares, and participating accounts. For initial public offerings, indicate whether shares traded at a premium when secondary market trading began. The preferred format for this information is in Excel.

Advisers to Registered Investment Companies

RIC: General Information

37. Any correspondence with the staff of the Commission or other regulatory agencies and any no-action letters or exemptive orders relied upon by the Fund, including those relied upon for engaging in securities lending.

RIC: Compliance Policies and Procedures

38. The annual reports submitted to the Board by the CCO during the Examination Period. Please include any attachments to the report.

39. A current inventory of compliance risks. If changes were made to this inventory of risks during the Examination Period, please indicate what these changes were and the corresponding date of the change. Please provide this information, if possible, in Word, Excel or the equivalent format.

RIC: Fund Corporate Governance

40. Identify any relationships that the Fund or any affiliate may have with any service provider, (e.g., custodian, transfer agent, administrator, pricing service, accountant, marketing firm), and provide documents indicating that these relationships were disclosed to the Fund's Board in connection with its review of the contract with the service provider or otherwise. This would include, for example, whether a broker-dealer affiliate has an investment banking relationship with a service provider; whether the Fund's adviser manages the corporate pension plan of a service provider; whether the Fund or its adviser has investments in the service provider; whether the service provider also provides services to the Fund's adviser or an affiliate, etc.

41. Information regarding any compensation, whether direct or indirect, received by the Fund's adviser from any of the Fund's service providers. Please include information provided to the Board regarding this compensation.

EXHIBIT E. SAMPLE 2015 SEC DOCUMENT REQUEST LETTER (00088737XD690E)

EXHIBIT 1

Layout for Securities Trading Blotter/Purchase and Sales Journal

In conjunction with the scheduled examination, the staff requests records for all purchases and sales of securities for portfolios of advisory clients and proprietary accounts being advised. Please provide this record in Excel. This record should include the fields of information listed below in a similar format.

Please provide separate worksheets for: *(i)* equities (Note: ETF trades should be included with equities); *(ii)* cash or cash equivalents, maturities, calls, pay-downs, expirations, or reinvestments of mutual fund dividends or capital gains distributions; *(iii)* fixed income; *(iv)* mutual funds; and *(v)* options, futures, swaps and other derivatives.

Examples:

I. Sample Trading Blotter for Equity Securities

Client Name/#	Trade Date	Settle Date	Buy/Sell	CUSIP	Security Symbol	Security Description	Quantity	Unit Price	Principal/Proceeds/Notional Value	Total Commission	Fees	Net Amount	Broker
155	1/1/00	1/3/00	B	1234567	MSFT	Microsoft Corp	100	$100.00	$10,000	$10.00		$10,010.00	ABC
123	1/2/00	1/5/00	S	89101112	IBM	IBM Corp.	500	$100.00	$50,000	$50.00	$1.67	$49,948.33	DEF

II. Sample Trading Blotter for Fixed-Income Securities

Client Name/#	Trade Date	Settle Date	Buy/Sell	CUSIP	Security Description 1 (Issuer)	Security Description 2 (Coupon Maturity, etc)	Quantity	Unit Price	Accrued Interest	Principal Value/Proceeds	Total Commission	Net Amount	Broker
155	4/2/98	4/6/98	B	802586AG2	SANTA ROSA CA PKG FACS DIST	4.60% 07-02-2004	50,000	100	$95.83	$50,000	$0	$50,095.83	GHI

© MODERN COMPLIANCE 2015

EXHIBIT E. SAMPLE 2015 SEC DOCUMENT REQUEST LETTER (00088737XD690E)

III. Sample Trading Blotter for Derivative Securities

Client Name/#	Trade Date	Settle Date	Buy/Sell	CUSIP	Security Description 1 (Issuer)	Security Description 2 (Coupon Maturity, etc)	Quantity	Unit Price	Payments	Principal Value/Proceeds	Total Commission	Net Proceeds	Broker	Security Type	Economic Position "Long or Short" Position
178	4/1/05	4/3/05	B	DR80258RG	Deutsche Bank AG, Microsoft Corp., Credit Default Swap	6 Months 10-01-2005	100,000	100	$95.83	$100,000	$0	$100,095.83	DB	Credit Default Swap	Buying Protection
182	2/1/07	2/3/07	S	MOSMS149	Morgan Stanley; PD: If credit spreads as represented by the Barclays Capital U.S. CMBS AAA 8.5+ index widen, pays the spread change minus 50 basis points*; RD: If credit spreads as represented by the Barclays Capital U.S. CMBS AAA 8.5+ index narrow, receives the spread change*. (TWSP)	9 Months 11-01-2007	150,000	100	$0	$150,000	$0	$150,000	MOR	Total Return Swap	Economic Long

2

EXHIBIT E. SAMPLE 2015 SEC DOCUMENT REQUEST LETTER (00088737XD690E)

EXAMINATION INFORMATION FOR ENTITIES SUBJECT TO EXAMINATION OR INSPECTION BY THE COMMISSION

> The examination staff of the Office of Compliance Inspections and Examinations (OCIE) of the Securities and Exchange Commission (Commission) has prepared this brochure to provide information about examinations it conducts, including information about the examination process and the methods the examination staff employs for resolving issues identified during examinations. This information, provided to entities undergoing examination or inspection, should help entities to understand better the examination staff's objectives in this area.

I. PURPOSE OF EXAMINATIONS

Commission representatives have statutory authority to conduct, at any time or from time to time, reasonable periodic, special and other examinations of the records of specified Commission-regulated entities. OCIE carries out these examination responsibilities through the National Examination Program (NEP) comprised of examination staff in 11 regional offices and the home office in Washington, D.C. OCIE's mission is to protect investors, ensure market integrity and support responsible capital formation through risk-focused strategies that: (1) improve compliance; (2) prevent fraud; (3) monitor risk; and (4) inform policy.

During examinations, the examination staff will seek to determine whether the entity being examined is: conducting its activities in accordance with the federal securities laws and rules adopted under these laws (as well as, where applicable, the rules of self-regulatory organizations subject to the Commission's oversight); adhering to the disclosures it has made to its clients, customers, the general public and/or the Commission; and implementing supervisory systems and/or compliance policies and procedures that are reasonably designed to ensure that the entity's operations are in compliance with the applicable legal requirements. The examination staff appreciates each entity's cooperation with the examination process as it will greatly facilitate the examination staff's ability to complete the examination in a timely manner. Therefore, entities should work to ensure that the examination staff is provided promptly with complete information and knowledgeable employees are made available to help the examination staff better understand the entity and its operations.

II. THE EXAMINATION PROCESS

The Commission's examination program is a risk-based program. An entity may be selected for examination for any number of reasons including, but not limited to, a statutory mandate that requires the Commission to examine the entity; the entity's risk profile; a tip, complaint or referral; or a review of a particular compliance risk area. To help evaluate the effectiveness of our risk-based selection process, the NEP may also randomly select some firms for examination. The reason an entity has been selected for examination is non-public information, and typically will not be shared with the entity under examination. As part of their pre-examination planning

SEC 2389 (6/14)

EXHIBIT E. SAMPLE 2015 SEC DOCUMENT REQUEST LETTER (00088737XD690E)

process, the examination staff actively works to allocate efficiently examination resources and to determine whether an examination's scope might overlap with the scope of any recent or ongoing examinations or investigations by other regulators or staff in other Commission offices or divisions. Sometimes an examination may overlap with ongoing examinations or investigations by other regulators or Commission staff because of legal requirements or otherwise. If an entity has any concerns with respect to overlapping examinations or investigations, as described above, the entity should contact the examination team(s) involved.

In addition, throughout the examination process, the examination staff may consult and/or coordinate with other Commission staff, including supervisory examination staff and staff in other Commission offices and divisions, regarding any issues identified as well as interpretation and application of the securities laws and rules adopted under these laws, and, to the extent applicable, self-regulatory organization rules. As a result, examination staff may share information and documents received from the entity during the examination with other Commission staff to the extent the examination staff deems necessary or appropriate. This and other possible uses of information and documents provided to the examination staff are described in the Commission's Form 1661, which may be accessed at www.sec.gov/about/forms/sec1661.pdf.

Examinations may be conducted on an announced or unannounced basis. When the examination is announced, the examination staff may send the entity a letter notifying it of the examination and containing a request list that identifies certain information or documents that the examination staff will review as part of the examination. In most instances, the examination staff will request that certain of the information and documents be provided in electronic format, if available. The letter may ask that the information and documents: (1) be delivered to the Commission's offices by a specified date; and/or (2) be made available for review at the entity's offices on a specified date. When the examination is unannounced, the examination staff may provide the entity with an information or document request list upon arrival and may conduct an initial interview.

In addition to the letter and/or request list identified above, the examination staff will provide the entity with the Commission's Form 1661, and, upon request, the examination staff will also provide the name and telephone number of their supervisor.

In many examinations, the examination staff will visit the physical premises of the entity to conduct examination work. Upon arrival, the examination staff will identify themselves and present their Commission credentials. The examination staff may conduct an initial interview. During this initial interview, the examination staff will ask questions about the entity and the activities to be examined. This information assists the examination staff in understanding the entity and its operations. The examination staff may also ask for a tour of the entity's offices to gain an overall understanding of the entity's organization, flow of work, and control environment. The initial interview and tour can be critical because they may determine the tone and focus of the examination. Some examinations may be completed without an on-site visit through a review of records in the Commission's offices along with interviews conducted by telephone, as needed. A cooperative approach by the entity being examined will help facilitate the examination.

Following this initial phase of the examination, the examination staff will review the information and documents the entity has provided. During this review, the examination staff may make

SEC 2389 (6/14)

EXHIBIT E. SAMPLE 2015 SEC DOCUMENT REQUEST LETTER (00088737XD690E)

supplemental requests for additional information and documents. Throughout the examination, the entity should communicate promptly to the examination staff any questions or concerns regarding the documents and information that have been requested. In all cases, producing requested information and documents in a timely manner will facilitate the efficient completion of the examination. The examination staff may also request meetings (in person or by telephone) with entity employees to discuss the entity's operations and the information and documents provided. The entity should make knowledgeable employees or other knowledgeable persons available to participate in the meetings. These meetings help the examination staff gain a better understanding of the entity's activities and compliance processes. The examination staff may also request relevant information and documents held by third party service providers or agents (including custodians) that, for example, perform work for, or in conjunction with, the entity or whose activities may have a material impact on the entity. Examination staff may send such requests to the entity or directly to the third party service provider or agent. In addition, the examination staff routinely contacts the entity's clients, customers, or other knowledgeable persons, as necessary, to gather and/or verify relevant information.

Typically, on the last day of the on-site visit, the examination staff may conduct a preliminary "exit interview" during which they will discuss the status of the examination and any outstanding information and document requests and, if appropriate, raise any issues identified during the examination to that point. During the preliminary exit interview, the entity will be given an opportunity to discuss any of the issues that the examination staff raises and provide additional relevant information, including any actions the entity has taken or plans to take to address those issues. Entities are also encouraged to keep the staff informed of any relevant changes that occur after the on-site portion of the examination has been completed.

Following the on-site visit, the examination staff, in many cases, will perform additional analyses of the information or data obtained during the on-site examination. This may include contacting the entity to ask clarifying questions or to request additional information or documents. If the analysis performed subsequent to completion of the on-site portion of the examination reveals issues in addition to those discussed during the preliminary exit interview, the examination staff, under most circumstances, will contact the entity, usually by telephone, to discuss these additional issues as part of a "final exit interview." During the final exit interview, the entity will typically be given an opportunity to discuss any of the issues that the examination staff has raised with the entity during the course of the examination and provide additional relevant information, including any actions that the entity has taken or plans to take to address the issues raised. In limited situations, the examination staff may not conduct preliminary or final exit interviews. In connection with either a "preliminary exit interview" and/or "final exit interview," staff may speak with the entity's senior management and/or its board of directors.

III. COMPLETING AN EXAMINATION

Section 4E of the Securities Exchange Act of 1934 requires the examination staff to complete compliance examinations within 180 days from the latter occurrence of one of two specified events. Specifically, Section 4E (b)(1) provides that:

> Not later than 180 days after the date on which Commission staff completes the on-site portion of its compliance examination or inspection **or** receives all records requested from the entity being examined or inspected, **whichever is later**, Commission staff shall

SEC 2389 (6/14)

EXHIBIT E. SAMPLE 2015 SEC DOCUMENT REQUEST LETTER (00088737XD690E)

provide the entity being examined or inspected with written notification indicating either that the examination or inspection has concluded, has concluded without findings, or that the staff requests the entity undertake corrective action. (Emphasis added)

For certain complex examinations, the examination deadline may be extended for an additional 180-day period. Generally, the examination staff will provide an entity with written notification of an examination's completion by sending a deficiency letter. If the examination staff identifies serious issues during an examination, in addition to sending the entity a deficiency letter, the examination staff may refer the issues to the Commission's Division of Enforcement, a self-regulatory organization, state regulatory agency, or others, including criminal authorities, for possible action. On occasion and usually in the context of exigent circumstances, the examination staff may make a referral to the Division of Enforcement without conducting an exit interview.

The examined entity will be asked to respond in writing to any issues identified in a deficiency letter, including any steps that it has taken or will take to address the issues and to prevent their reoccurrence. The entity's response will generally be due within 30 days of the date of the deficiency letter.

An entity's submission of a timely and complete response to a deficiency letter will facilitate the examination staff's ability to complete the examination in a timely manner. In particular, an entity should make sure to address all of the issues identified in the deficiency letter. If the examination staff has comments on an entity's response, the examination staff generally will either provide them to the entity within 60 days of receipt of the entity's response, or contact the entity within the 60-day period to discuss when the examination staff will be able to provide comments. If the examination staff has no further comments after receiving an entity's response to a deficiency letter, the examination staff will send no further communication and the examination will be closed. The NEP conducts a limited number of Corrective Action Reviews in order to verify whether entities, including investment advisers, investment companies, and transfer agents, take the corrective actions discussed in their response to a deficiency letter. FINRA reviews corrective action taken in response to NEP deficiency letters during certain FINRA examinations of member broker-dealers; the NEP may also, on a limited basis, review broker-dealers for corrective action taken.

* * *

If you have any questions, comments, complaints, or concerns during an examination or after it is completed, please raise them with the examination staff or with their supervisors in the respective regional office or the home office. Most questions and issues can be resolved by discussing them with the examination staff. You may also communicate comments, complaints, or concerns through the *Examination Hotline*, (202) 551-EXAM. The *Examination Hotline* offers callers a choice to speak with either an attorney in the Office of Compliance Inspections and Examinations in Washington, DC, *or* staff in the Commission's Office of Inspector General. The Office of Inspector General is an independent office within the Commission that conducts audits of Commission programs and investigates allegations of employee misconduct. Persons speaking with staff on the *Examination Hotline* may identify themselves or request anonymity.

SEC 2389 (6/14)

EXHIBIT E. SAMPLE 2015 SEC DOCUMENT REQUEST LETTER (00088737XD690E)

IV. **INFORMATION REGARDING THE COMMISSION'S OFFICE OF THE WHISTLEBLOWER**

The Commission is authorized by Congress to provide monetary awards to eligible individuals who voluntarily come forward with high-quality, original information that leads to a Commission enforcement action in which over $1,000,000 in sanctions is ordered. The range for awards is between 10% and 30% of the money collected. An "eligible whistleblower" is an individual who voluntarily provides original information about a possible violation of the federal securities laws that has occurred, is ongoing, or is about to occur. Information is provided "voluntarily" if it is provided to the Commission or another regulatory or law enforcement authority before (i) the Commission requests it from an individual or his/her lawyer; or (ii) Congress, another regulatory or enforcement agency, or self-regulatory organization (such as FINRA) asks the individual to provide the information in connection with an investigation or certain examinations or inspections. One or more people are allowed to act as a whistleblower, but companies or organizations cannot qualify as whistleblowers. A person is not required to be an employee of an entity to submit information about that entity.

The Commission's Office of the Whistleblower administers the whistleblower program. Additional information about the program, including how to submit a tip under the program, is available at www.sec.gov/whistleblower. The Office of the Whistleblower may be reached at (202) 551-4790.

SEC 2389 (6/14)

EXHIBIT E. SAMPLE 2015 SEC DOCUMENT REQUEST LETTER (00088737XD690E)

SECURITIES AND EXCHANGE COMMISSION
Washington, D.C. 20549

Supplemental Information for Entities Directed to Supply Information to the Commission Other Than Pursuant to Commission Subpoena

A. Freedom of Information Act

The Freedom of Information Act, 5 U.S.C. 552 (the "FOIA"), generally provides for disclosure of information to the public. Rule 83 of the Commission's Rules on Information and Requests, 17 CFR 200.83, provides a procedure by which a person can make a written request that information submitted to the Commission not be disclosed under the FOIA. That rule states that no determination as to the validity of such a request will be made until a request for disclosure of the information under the FOIA is received. Accordingly, no response to a request that information not be disclosed under the FOIA is necessary or will be given until a request for disclosure under the FOIA is received. If you desire an acknowledgement of receipt of your written request that information not be disclosed under the FOIA, please provide a duplicate request, together with a stamped, self-addressed envelope.

B. Authority for Solicitation of the Information

1. Mandatory Information.

    (a) All records of persons identified in Section 17(a) of the Securities Exchange Act of 1934 and investment advisers, including but not limited to required records, must be made available for examination by representatives of the Commission.[1] See Sections 17(a) and (b) of the Securities Exchange Act of 1934 and rules thereunder, and Section 204 of the Investment Advisers Act of 1940 and rules thereunder. Records required to be maintained and preserved pursuant to Section 31(a) of the Investment Company Act of 1940 and rules thereunder must be made available for examination by representatives of the Commission. See Section 31(b) of the Investment Company Act of 1940. Other persons subject to examination by representatives of the Commission pursuant to the Federal securities laws and rules must make certain records, as described by statute or rule, available for examination by representatives of the Commission.[2] See Sections 13(n)(2), 13A(c)(2), and 15F(f)(1)(C) of the Securities Exchange Act of 1934 and Section 32(c) of the Investment Company Act of 1940.

    (b) Security-based swap execution facilities registered with the Commission are required to provide certain information to the Commission pursuant to Section 3D(d)(5) of the Securities Exchange Act of 1934.

    (c) Persons subject to Section 106 of the Sarbanes-Oxley Act of 2002, as amended by the Dodd-Frank Wall Street Reform and Consumer Protection Act, shall make any production required by that section.

    (d) The Commodity Exchange Act requires certain persons who are required to maintain books and records prescribed by the United States Commodity Futures Trading Commission to keep certain books and records open to inspection and examination by the Commission or representatives of the Commission.

2. Other Information. The production of information other than the records and documents described in paragraph B.1 above is voluntary.

C. Effect of Not Supplying Information

1. Mandatory Information.

    (a) A willful failure to permit inspection by authorized Commission personnel of the records and documents described in paragraph B.1 may result in legal proceedings the penalty for which, upon conviction, is a fine of not more than $5,000,000 or imprisonment for not more than 20 years, or both. When the person failing to permit inspection is a person other than a natural person, a fine not exceeding $25,000,000 may be imposed.

    (b) Failure to produce the records and documents described in paragraph B.1 for inspection, and/or aiding or abetting someone in such failure may have the following consequences: (i) regulated persons may be censured or their registration and/or exchange or association status may be suspended, revoked, or subject to

---

[1] Section 204(a) of the Investment Advisers Act of 1940 provides that all records of investment advisers, other than investment advisers specifically exempt from registration pursuant to Section 203(b) of the Act, are subject to examination by representatives of the Commission.

[2] Any person that is subject to regulation and examination by a Federal financial institution regulatory agency (as defined under 18 U.S.C. 212(c)(2)) may satisfy an examination request, information request, or document request described under Section 204(d)(1) of the Investment Advisers Act or Section 31(b)(4)(A) of the Investment Company Act of 1940, by providing the Commission with a detailed listing, in writing, of the securities, deposits or credits of the client or registered investment company within the custody or use of such person. See Section 204(d)(2) of the Investment Advisers Act of 1940 and Section 31(b)(4)(B) of the Investment Company Act of 1940.

SEC 1661 (09-14)

EXHIBIT E. SAMPLE 2015 SEC DOCUMENT REQUEST LETTER (00088737XD690E)

various other sanctions; (ii) members of national securities exchanges may be censured, suspended or expelled from membership; and (iii) members of a registered securities association may be censured, suspended or expelled from membership in a registered association, or subject to various other sanctions. Employees of and persons associated with the foregoing may be suspended or barred from association with regulated entities and/or they may be censured or subject to various other sanctions.

(c) If there is a failure to permit inspection of the records and documents described in paragraph B.1, the Commission may seek an injunction against, among other things, continuing to fail to permit an inspection. The continuance of such failure thereafter may result in civil and/or criminal sanctions for contempt of court.

(d) A willful refusal to comply with a request, in whole or in part, under Section 106 of the Sarbanes-Oxley Act of 2002 may result in civil or administrative remedies or sanctions.

2. Other Information. There are no direct sanctions and thus no direct effects for failure to provide all or any part of the information requested to be supplied on a voluntary basis.

D. False Statements and Documents

Section 1001 of Title 18 of the United States Code provides as follows:

[W]hoever, in any matter within the jurisdiction of the executive, legislative, or judicial branch of the Government of the United States, knowingly and willfully—
(1) falsifies, conceals, or covers up by any trick, scheme, or device a material fact;
(2) makes any materially false, fictitious, or fraudulent statement or representation; or
(3) makes or uses any false writing or document knowing the same to contain any materially false, fictitious, or fraudulent statement or entry;
shall be fined under this title, imprisoned not more than 5 years . . . or both.

E. Submissions and Settlements

Rule 5(c) of the Commission's Rules on Informal and Other Procedures, 17 CFR 202.5(c), states:

Persons who become involved in . . . investigations may, on their own initiative, submit a written statement to the Commission setting forth their interests and position in regard to the subject matter of the investigation. Upon request, the staff, in its discretion, may advise such persons of the general nature of the investigation, including the indicated violations as they pertain to them, and the amount of time that may be available for preparing and submitting a statement prior to the presentation of a staff recommendation to the Commission for the commencement of an administrative or injunction proceeding. Submissions by interested persons should be forwarded to the appropriate Division Director or Regional Director with a copy to the staff members conducting the investigation and should be clearly referenced to the specific investigation to which they relate. In the event a recommendation for the commencement of an enforcement proceeding is presented by the staff, any submissions by interested persons will be forwarded to the Commission in conjunction with the staff memorandum.

The staff of the Commission routinely seeks to introduce submissions made pursuant to Rule 5(c) as evidence in Commission enforcement proceedings, when the staff deems appropriate.

Rule 5(f) of the Commission's Rules on Informal and Other Procedures, 17 CFR 202.5(f), states:

In the course of the Commission's investigations, civil lawsuits, and administrative proceedings, the staff, with appropriate authorization, may discuss with persons involved the disposition of such matters by consent, by settlement, or in some other manner. It is the policy of the Commission, however, that the disposition of any such matter may not, expressly or impliedly, extend to any criminal charges that have been, or may be, brought against any such person or any recommendation with respect thereto. Accordingly, any person involved in an enforcement matter before the Commission who consents, or agrees to consent, to any judgment or order does so solely for the purpose of resolving the claims against him in that investigative, civil, or administrative matter and not for the purpose of resolving any criminal charges that have been, or might be, brought against him. This policy reflects the fact that neither the Commission nor its staff has the authority or responsibility for instituting, conducting, settling, or otherwise disposing of criminal proceedings. That authority and responsibility are vested in the Attorney General and representatives of the Department of Justice.

F. Principal Uses of Information

The Commission's principal purpose in soliciting the information is to gather facts in order to determine whether any person has violated, is violating, or is about to violate any provision of the federal securities laws or rules for which the Commission has enforcement authority, such as rules of securities exchanges and the rules of the Municipal Securities Rulemaking Board. Facts developed may, however, constitute violations of other laws or rules. Information provided may be used in Commission and other agency enforcement proceedings. Unless the Commission or its staff explicitly agrees to the contrary

EXHIBIT E. SAMPLE 2015 SEC DOCUMENT REQUEST LETTER (00088737XD690E)

in writing, you should not assume that the Commission or its staff acquiesces in, accedes to, or concurs or agrees with, any position, condition, request, reservation of right, understanding, or any other statement that purports, or may be deemed, to be or to reflect a limitation upon the Commission's receipt, use, disposition, transfer, or retention, in accordance with applicable law, of information provided.

G. Routine Uses of Information

The Commission often makes its files available to other governmental agencies, particularly United States Attorneys and state prosecutors. There is a likelihood that information supplied by you will be made available to such agencies where appropriate. Whether or not the Commission makes its files available to other governmental agencies is, in general, a confidential matter between the Commission and such other governmental agencies.

Set forth below is a list of the routine uses which may be made of the information furnished.

1. To appropriate agencies, entities, and persons when (a) it is suspected or confirmed that the security or confidentiality of information in the system of records has been compromised; (b) the SEC has determined that, as a result of the suspected or confirmed compromise, there is a risk of harm to economic or property interests, identity theft or fraud, or harm to the security or integrity of this system or other systems or programs (whether maintained by the SEC or another agency or entity) that rely upon the compromised information; and (c) the disclosure made to such agencies, entities, and persons is reasonably necessary to assist in connection with the SEC's efforts to respond to the suspected or confirmed compromise and prevent, minimize, or remedy such harm.

2. To other federal, state, local, or foreign law enforcement agencies; securities self-regulatory organizations; and foreign financial regulatory authorities to assist in or coordinate regulatory or law enforcement activities with the SEC.

3. To national securities exchanges and national securities associations that are registered with the SEC, the Municipal Securities Rulemaking Board; the Securities Investor Protection Corporation; the Public Company Accounting Oversight Board; the federal banking authorities, including, but not limited to, the Board of Governors of the Federal Reserve System, the Comptroller of the Currency, and the Federal Deposit Insurance Corporation; state securities regulatory agencies or organizations; or regulatory authorities of a foreign government in connection with their regulatory or enforcement responsibilities.

4. By SEC personnel for purposes of investigating possible violations of, or to conduct investigations authorized by, the federal securities laws.

5. In any proceeding where the federal securities laws are in issue or in which the Commission, or past or present members of its staff, is a party or otherwise involved in an official capacity.

6. In connection with proceedings by the Commission pursuant to Rule 102(e) of its Rules of Practice, 17 CFR 201.102(e).

7. To a bar association, state accountancy board, or other federal, state, local, or foreign licensing or oversight authority; or professional association or self-regulatory authority to the extent that it performs similar functions (including the Public Company Accounting Oversight Board) for investigations or possible disciplinary action.

8. To a federal, state, local, tribal, foreign, or international agency, if necessary to obtain information relevant to the SEC's decision concerning the hiring or retention of an employee; the issuance of a security clearance; the letting of a contract; or the issuance of a license, grant, or other benefit.

9. To a federal, state, local, tribal, foreign, or international agency in response to its request for information concerning the hiring or retention of an employee; the issuance of a security clearance; the reporting of an investigation of an employee; the letting of a contract; or the issuance of a license, grant, or other benefit by the requesting agency, to the extent that the information is relevant and necessary to the requesting agency's decision on the matter.

10. To produce summary descriptive statistics and analytical studies, as a data source for management information, in support of the function for which the records are collected and maintained or for related personnel management functions or manpower studies; may also be used to respond to general requests for statistical information (without personal identification of individuals) under the Freedom of Information Act.

11. To any trustee, receiver, master, special counsel, or other individual or entity that is appointed by a court of competent jurisdiction, or as a result of an agreement between the parties in connection with litigation or administrative proceedings involving allegations of violations of the federal securities laws (as defined in section 3(a)(47) of the Securities Exchange Act of 1934, 15 U.S.C. 78c(a)(47)) or pursuant to the Commission's Rules of Practice, 17 CFR 201.100 – 900 or the Commission's Rules of Fair Fund and Disgorgement Plans, 17 CFR 201.1100-1106, or otherwise, where such trustee, receiver, master, special counsel, or other individual or entity is specifically designated to perform particular functions with respect to, or as a result of, the pending action or proceeding or in connection with the administration and enforcement by the Commission of the federal securities laws or the Commission's Rules of Practice or the Rules of Fair Fund and Disgorgement Plans.

EXHIBIT E. SAMPLE 2015 SEC DOCUMENT REQUEST LETTER (00088737XD690E)

12. To any persons during the course of any inquiry, examination, or investigation conducted by the SEC's staff, or in connection with civil litigation, if the staff has reason to believe that the person to whom the record is disclosed may have further information about the matters related therein, and those matters appeared to be relevant at the time to the subject matter of the inquiry.

13. To interns, grantees, experts, contractors, and others who have been engaged by the Commission to assist in the performance of a service related to this system of records and who need access to the records for the purpose of assisting the Commission in the efficient administration of its programs, including by performing clerical, stenographic, or data analysis functions, or by reproduction of records by electronic or other means. Recipients of these records shall be required to comply with the requirements of the Privacy Act of 1974, as amended, 5 U.S.C. 552a.

14. In reports published by the Commission pursuant to authority granted in the federal securities laws (as such term is defined in section 3(a)(47) of the Securities Exchange Act of 1934, 15 U.S.C. 78c(a)(47)), which authority shall include, but not be limited to, section 21(a) of the Securities Exchange Act of 1934, 15 U.S.C. 78u(a)).

15. To members of advisory committees that are created by the Commission or by Congress to render advice and recommendations to the Commission or to Congress, to be used solely in connection with their official designated functions.

16. To any person who is or has agreed to be subject to the Commission's Rules of Conduct, 17 CFR 200.735-1 to 200.735-18, and who assists in the investigation by the Commission of possible violations of the federal securities laws (as such term is defined in section 3(a)(47) of the Securities Exchange Act of 1934, 15 U.S.C. 78c(a)(47)), in the preparation or conduct of enforcement actions brought by the Commission for such violations, or otherwise in connection with the Commission's enforcement or regulatory functions under the federal securities laws.

17. To a Congressional office from the record of an individual in response to an inquiry from the Congressional office made at the request of that individual.

18. To members of Congress, the press, and the public in response to inquiries relating to particular Registrants and their activities, and other matters under the Commission's jurisdiction.

19. To prepare and publish information relating to violations of the federal securities laws as provided in 15 U.S.C. 78c(a)(47)), as amended.

20. To respond to subpoenas in any litigation or other proceeding.

21. To a trustee in bankruptcy.

22. To any governmental agency, governmental or private collection agent, consumer reporting agency or commercial reporting agency, governmental or private employer of a debtor, or any other person, for collection, including collection by administrative offset, federal salary offset, tax refund offset, or administrative wage garnishment, of amounts owed as a result of Commission civil or administrative proceedings.

* * * * *

Small Business Owners: The SEC always welcomes comments on how it can better assist small businesses. If you would like more information, or have questions or comments about federal securities regulations as they affect small businesses, please contact the Office of Small Business Policy, in the SEC's Division of Corporation Finance, at 202-551-3460. If you would prefer to comment to someone outside of the SEC, you can contact the Small Business Regulatory Enforcement Ombudsman at http://www.sba.gov/ombudsman or toll free at 888-REG-FAIR. The Ombudsman's office receives comments from small businesses and annually evaluates federal agency enforcement activities for their responsiveness to the special needs of small business.

EXHIBIT E. SAMPLE 2015 SEC DOCUMENT REQUEST LETTER (00088737XD690E)

SECURITIES AND EXCHANGE COMMISSION
Washington, D.C. 20549

Supplemental Information for Persons Requested to Supply Information Voluntarily to the Commission's Examination Staff

A. Introduction

This document is being provided to you because the Commission's examination staff has requested that you voluntarily provide information. For your reference, this document describes the principal purposes that the information may be used for, the Commission's statutory authority for soliciting the information, the effects of not supplying information or of supplying false information, the routine uses of information provided, and how to request confidential treatment for the information provided.

The examination program's mission is to protect investors, ensure market integrity and support responsible capital formation through risk-focused strategies that: (1) improve compliance; (2) prevent fraud; (3) monitor risk; and (4) inform policy. Please visit the following website for more information about the examination program http://www.sec.gov/about/offices/ocie.shtml.

B. Principal Uses of Information

The Commission's principal purposes in soliciting the information are:

1. Asset Verification: To obtain independent confirmations of account balances or positions from various persons over whom the Commission does not have examination authority, including clients or shareholders;

2. Risk Assessment: To monitor risk and gather information about areas of interest or concern to the Commission; and

3. Assist with Examinations and Other Inquiries: To gather facts in order to determine whether an entity or person is complying with applicable federal securities laws and rules, and to determine whether any entity or person has violated, is violating, or is about to violate any provision of the federal securities laws or rules for which the Commission has enforcement authority, such as rules of securities exchanges and the rules of the Municipal Securities Rulemaking Board. Facts developed may, however, constitute violations of other laws or rules. Information provided may be used in Commission and other agency enforcement proceedings.

Unless the Commission or its staff explicitly agrees to the contrary in writing, you should not assume that the Commission or its staff acquiesces in, accedes to, or concurs or agrees with, any position, condition, request, reservation of right, understanding, or any other statement that purports, or may be deemed, to be or to reflect a limitation upon the Commission's receipt, use, disposition, transfer, or retention, in accordance with applicable law, of information provided.

C. Authority for Solicitation of the Information

One or more of the following provisions authorizes the Commission to solicit the information requested: Section 20 of the Securities Act of 1933; Section 21 of the Securities Exchange Act of 1934; Section 321 of the Trust Indenture Act of 1939; Section 42 of the Investment Company Act of 1940; Section 209 of the Investment Advisers Act of 1940, and 17 CFR 202.5. Disclosure of the requested information to the Commission is voluntary on your part.

D. Effect of Not Supplying Information

There are no direct sanctions and thus no direct effects for failure to provide all or any part of the information requested to be supplied on a voluntary basis.

E. False Statements and Documents

Section 1001 of Title 18 of the United States Code provides as follows:

> whoever, in any matter within the jurisdiction of the executive, legislative, or judicial branch of the Government of the United States knowingly and willfully (1) falsifies, conceals, or covers up by any trick, scheme, or device a material fact; (2) makes any materially false, fictitious or fraudulent statement or representation; or (3) makes or uses any false writing or document knowing the same

SEC 2866 (9/14)

EXHIBIT E. SAMPLE 2015 SEC DOCUMENT REQUEST LETTER (00088737XD690E)

to contain any materially false, fictitious or fraudulent statement or entry, shall be fined under this title, imprisoned not more than five years, ..., or both.

F. Routine Uses of Information

The Commission often makes its files available to other governmental agencies, particularly United States Attorneys and state prosecutors. There is a likelihood that information supplied by you will be made available to such agencies where appropriate. Whether or not the Commission makes its files available to other governmental agencies is, in general, a confidential matter between the Commission and such other governmental agencies.

Set forth below is a list of the routine uses which may be made of the information furnished.

1. To appropriate agencies, entities, and persons when (a) it is suspected or confirmed that the security or confidentiality of information in the system of records has been compromised; (b) the SEC has determined that, as a result of the suspected or confirmed compromise, there is a risk of harm to economic or property interests, identity theft or fraud, or harm to the security or integrity of this system or other systems or programs (whether maintained by the SEC or another agency or entity) that rely upon the compromised information; and (c) the disclosure made to such agencies, entities, and persons is reasonably necessary to assist in connection with the SEC's efforts to respond to the suspected or confirmed compromise and prevent, minimize, or remedy such harm.

2. To other federal, state, local, or foreign law enforcement agencies; securities self-regulatory organizations; and foreign financial regulatory authorities to assist in or coordinate regulatory or law enforcement activities with the SEC.

3. To national securities exchanges and national securities associations that are registered with the SEC; the Municipal Securities Rulemaking Board; the Securities Investor Protection Corporation; the Public Company Accounting Oversight Board; the federal banking authorities, including, but not limited to, the Board of Governors of the Federal Reserve System, the Comptroller of the Currency, and the Federal Deposit Insurance Corporation; state securities regulatory agencies or organizations; or regulatory authorities of a foreign government in connection with their regulatory or enforcement responsibilities.

4. By SEC personnel for purposes of investigating possible violations of, or to conduct investigations authorized by, the federal securities laws.

5. In any proceeding where the federal securities laws are in issue or in which the Commission, or past or present members of its staff, is a party or otherwise involved in an official capacity.

6. In connection with proceedings by the Commission pursuant to Rule 102(e) of its Rules of Practice, 17 CFR 201.102(e).

7. To a bar association, state accountancy board, or other federal, state, local, or foreign licensing or oversight authority; or professional association or self-regulatory authority to the extent that it performs similar functions (including the Public Company Accounting Oversight Board) for investigations or possible disciplinary action.

8. To a federal, state, local, tribal, foreign, or international agency, if necessary to obtain information relevant to the SEC's decision concerning the hiring or retention of an employee; the issuance of a security clearance; the letting of a contract; or the issuance of a license, grant, or other benefit.

9. To a federal, state, local, tribal, foreign, or international agency in response to its request for information concerning the hiring or retention of an employee; the issuance of a security clearance; the reporting of an investigation of an employee; the letting of a contract; or the issuance of a license, grant, or other benefit by the requesting agency, to the extent that the information is relevant and necessary to the requesting agency's decision on the matter.

10. To produce summary descriptive statistics and analytical studies, as a data source for management information, in support of the function for which the records are collected and maintained or for related personnel management functions or manpower studies; may also be used to respond to general requests for statistical information (without personal identification of individuals) under the Freedom of Information Act.

11. To any trustee, receiver, master, special counsel, or other individual or entity that is appointed by a court of competent jurisdiction, or as a result of an agreement between the parties in connection with litigation or administrative proceedings involving allegations of violations of the federal securities laws (as defined in section 3(a)(47) of the Securities Exchange Act of 1934, 15 U.S.C. 78c(a)(47)) or pursuant to the Commission's Rules of Practice, 17 CFR 201.100 – 900 or the Commission's Rules of Fair Fund and Disgorgement Plans, 17 CFR 201.1100-1106, or otherwise, where such trustee, receiver, master, special counsel, or other individual or entity is

SEC 2866 (9/14)

EXHIBIT E. SAMPLE 2015 SEC DOCUMENT REQUEST LETTER (00088737XD690E)

specifically designated to perform particular functions with respect to, or as a result of, the pending action or proceeding or in connection with the administration and enforcement by the Commission of the federal securities laws or the Commission's Rules of Practice or the Rules of Fair Fund and Disgorgement Plans.

12. To any persons during the course of any inquiry, examination, or investigation conducted by the SEC's staff, or in connection with civil litigation, if the staff has reason to believe that the person to whom the record is disclosed may have further information about the matters related therein, and those matters appeared to be relevant at the time to the subject matter of the inquiry.

13. To interns, grantees, experts, contractors, and others who have been engaged by the Commission to assist in the performance of a service related to this system of records and who need access to the records for the purpose of assisting the Commission in the efficient administration of its programs, including by performing clerical, stenographic, or data analysis functions, or by reproduction of records by electronic or other means. Recipients of these records shall be required to comply with the requirements of the Privacy Act of 1974, as amended, 5 U.S.C. 552a.

14. In reports published by the Commission pursuant to authority granted in the federal securities laws (as such term is defined in section 3(a)(47) of the Securities Exchange Act of 1934, 15 U.S.C. 78c(a)(47)), which authority shall include, but not be limited to, section 21(a) of the Securities Exchange Act of 1934, 15 U.S.C. 78u(a).

15. To members of advisory committees that are created by the Commission or by Congress to render advice and recommendations to the Commission or to Congress, to be used solely in connection with their official designated functions.

16. To any person who is or has agreed to be subject to the Commission's Rules of Conduct, 17 CFR 200.735-1 to 200.735-18, and who assists in the investigation by the Commission of possible violations of the federal securities laws (as such term is defined in section 3(a)(47) of the Securities Exchange Act of 1934, 15 U.S.C. 78c(a)(47)), in the preparation or conduct of enforcement actions brought by the Commission for such violations, or otherwise in connection with the Commission's enforcement or regulatory functions under the federal securities laws.

17. To a Congressional office from the record of an individual in response to an inquiry from the Congressional office made at the request of that individual.

18. To members of Congress, the press, and the public in response to inquiries relating to particular Registrants and their activities, and other matters under the Commission's jurisdiction.

19. To prepare and publish information relating to violations of the federal securities laws as provided in 15 U.S.C. 78c(a)(47), as amended.

20. To respond to subpoenas in any litigation or other proceeding.

21. To a trustee in bankruptcy.

22. To any governmental agency, governmental or private collection agent, consumer reporting agency or commercial reporting agency, governmental or private employer of a debtor, or any other person, for collection, including collection by administrative offset, federal salary offset, tax refund offset, or administrative wage garnishment, of amounts owed as a result of Commission civil or administrative proceedings.

G. Freedom of Information Act

The Freedom of Information Act, 5 U.S.C. 552 (the "FOIA"), generally provides for disclosure of information to the public. Rule 83 of the Commission's Rules on Information and Requests, 17 CFR 200.83, provides a procedure by which a person can make a written request that information submitted to the Commission not be disclosed under the FOIA. That rule states that no determination as to the validity of such a request will be made until a request for disclosure of the information under the FOIA is received. Accordingly, no response to a request that information not be disclosed under the FOIA is necessary or will be given until a request for disclosure under the FOIA is received. If you desire an acknowledgement of receipt of your written request that information not be disclosed under the FOIA, please provide a duplicate request, together with a stamped, self addressed envelope.

* * * * *

Small Business Owners: The SEC always welcomes comments on how it can better assist small businesses. If you have comments about a voluntary request for information you received from staff in the SEC's examination program, please contact the Office of Small Business Policy, in the SEC's Division of Corporation Finance, at 202-551-3460. If you would prefer to comment to someone outside of the SEC, you can contact the Small Business Regulatory

EXHIBIT E. SAMPLE 2015 SEC DOCUMENT REQUEST LETTER (00088737XD690E)

Enforcement Ombudsman at http://www.sba.gov/ombudsman or toll free at 888-REG-FAIR. The Ombudsman's office receives comments from small businesses and annually evaluates federal agency enforcement activities for their responsiveness to the special needs of small business.

SEC 2866 (9/14)

ABOUT THE AUTHOR

Michelle L. Jacko, Esq., is the managing partner and CEO of Jacko Law Group, PC, a securities law firm which offers securities and corporate legal services to broker-dealers, investment advisers, hedge/private funds, and financial professionals. In addition, Ms. Jacko is the Founder and CEO of Core Compliance & Legal Services, Inc., a compliance consultation firm. She specializes in investment advisory and broker-dealer firm formation, hedge and private fund development, mergers and acquisitions, transition risks, and investment counsel on regulatory compliance and securities law. Her practice is focused on the areas of corporate and compliance risk management, contracts, policies and procedures, testing of compliance programs (including evaluation of internal controls and supervision), performance advertising, soft dollar arrangements, best execution, separation agreements, and more.

Previously, Ms. Jacko served as Of counsel at Shustak & Partners, PC. Prior to that, she was vice president of compliance and branch manager of the Home Office Supervision team at LPL Financial Services, Corporation (Linsco/Private Ledger). Ms. Jacko has also served as legal counsel of investments and chief compliance officer at First American Trust, FSB and held the position of compliance manager at Nicholas-Applegate Capital Management. In addition, Ms. Jacko was with PIM Financial Services, Inc., and Speiser, Krause, Madole & Mendelsohn, Jackson. She regularly presents at conferences throughout the nation and is a frequent contributor to various industry journals. In 2013, Ms. Jacko was appointed to the Editorial Advisory Board for the Wolters Kluwer publication *Practical Compliance and Risk Management for the Securities Industry*. She is speakers bureau chair and co-founder of the Southern California Compliance Group and is involved in the American Bar Association (Business Law Section), State Bar of California (Corporations Committee), and San Diego County Bar Association, where she served as co-chair of the Business & Corporate Law Section from 2012 to 2014. She also is a FINRA arbitrator. Ms. Jacko has been named as a *Top 20 Rising Star for "Who's Who" in Upcoming Compliance Professionals* by Compliance Reporter magazine. In 2014, Ms. Jacko was named as a finalist for *San Diego Magazine's* 2014 Woman of the Year Award. She was also recognized as a finalist for *San Diego Business Journal's* 2014 Women Who Mean Business Awards. Ms. Jacko received her juris doctor degree from St. Mary's University School of Law and a bachelor of arts degree in International Relations from the University of San Diego. She is admitted to the State Bar of California and United States District Court, Southern District of California. Michelle is a past two-term board member for the National Society of Compliance Professionals (NSCP) and holds the Certified Securities Compliance Professional (CSCP) designation sponsored by NSCP.

CHAPTER 21

Your Relationship with FINRA

By David Sobel
   Abel/Noser Corp.

I. INTRODUCTION

The securities industry is one of the most regulated industries in this country. We all understand that and live with it on a daily basis. Feeling under the gun at all times makes most of the participants in this industry shy away from interaction with the regulators. The only interaction they have is when there is an examination. Those examinations take a number of forms: FinOp (financial operations), cycle (every year or two or three), sales practice, sweeps, etc. It is often during these examinations that Financial Industry Regulatory Authority (FINRA), the Securities and Exchange Commission (SEC), or the state finds a problem (or two or three). At this point, your relationship with the regulator becomes paramount.

If the problems they find are minor, then they should be corrected as soon as possible—preferably before the examiner leaves your shop. However, this does not mean that you have to agree with the examiner on every issue. Cooperation with the examiners does not necessarily mean that you have to submit to their whims. If you feel that you are right, you can and should challenge their decision. If you believe that their requests are too demanding, overreaching, or misguided, you should make your case. Making your case, however, becomes more effective if you have a history of being cooperating and have a good relationship with the regulator.

Flying under the regulator's radar might make you feel safer and more secure that they don't know you exist, but that is a Pollyanna view of regulation. You should be in contact with your liaison from whatever regulator you are working with. Most of you will be dealing on a regular basis with FINRA if you are a broker-dealer, or the state and SEC if you are a registered investment adviser. For purposes of this chapter, I will be focusing on interactions with FINRA.

I have found that being in regular contact with my liaison from FINRA has stood me in good stead for many years. When the regulators hear from you for whatever reason, they come to know you and trust you. That trust is probably one of the most important parts of your relationship with regulators. That relationship is the focus of this chapter and will color your interactions with them whether it's an exam, an enforcement action, or just a simple query.

II. DEVELOPING A RAPPORT

How do you start to cultivate that rapport? A simple phone call to your contact could be the beginning. Maybe it's a question about a new rule; maybe it's a request for clarification of a new regulatory alert; or something you intend to do such as adding a new silo of business. Perhaps you need to prepare a 1017 request; perhaps a new rule may apply to your specific business line; or perhaps you simply want to introduce yourself to your new compliance officer. Talking to regulators when there is no potential for recriminations or enforcement action develops the rapport you need for when there is a real problem. During that first phone call, invite the liaison to your shop. Let him or her know that you are not afraid of the regulator's presence in your office. Introduce your liaison to your C-suite officers (all of those having *chief* in their titles) so that the regulator can see that your firm's leadership is on board with your compliance efforts.

Take this opportunity to discuss your specific business. The more the regulator knows about your business model the less "shotgun scattering" the requests will be when it is time for an examination. For instance, if you only have an institutional business, then all the regulator's normal requests for retail information can be eliminated. If you only service mergers and acquisitions, then all the requests for blotters are eliminated. The examination can be shorter and more focused, and be far less frustrating than explaining to the examiner that you don't do "retail" so you don't have those issues.

Most of you will spend many hours and many dollars making sure that your relationship with your clients is on solid ground. Obviously, that's where the revenue stream comes from. However, your relationship with your regulator(s) is just as important. It's the regulator who can make your life miserable. Regulators can drag out an investigation, fine your firm (or you), suspend you, or, finally, bar you from the industry. The larger your firm, the more visibility it has. With that visibility has to come a more comprehensive relationship with regulators. That does not mean, however, that a small firm can sneak by. To say it succinctly, your regulatory agency is there at your company's birth and it will most likely be there after you are long gone. The regulator must approve your license, your business, and your leadership. Therefore, it behooves any broker-dealer that intends to be around a while to be in contact with and develop a relationship with your regulators.

III. GETTING INVOLVED

I know that it will sound like I have been drinking the FINRA Kool-Aid, but I can tell you from experience that getting involved with FINRA has been incredibly beneficial for me personally and for my firm in general. What do I mean by getting involved? I believe that participating in conferences and committees is a great first step. Meeting your peers and discussing issues as well as hearing from experienced practitioners in the field makes you a part of the industry and gives you a better understanding of the industry in general, not just your problems.

Conferences

At most conferences, and especially at the FINRA annual conference, the regulators appear as panelists. They could be from the SEC or FINRA or North American Securities Administrators Association (NASAA, the state regulator organization), but they all come to the conference to tell you what is happening, what is new, and what they are looking for. They are telling you how to be compliant. Listen to them! This also gives you the opportunity to meet and talk to regulators that are pretty high up in the food chain—people that you would not normally have the opportunity to meet. After a panel discussion, go up and introduce yourself to the speakers. Prepare a question or comment to present to them. If they can't answer right then, they will ask for your information and get back to you—they will! Maintain that relationship.

Committees

Once you have established yourself at these conferences, and met a number of, let's say FINRA, executives; it is time to move ahead. Your firm is in one of (at the time of this writing) 11 FINRA districts. Each district has a committee with industry representatives that are elected from your district. These committees usually meet about twice a year. At these meetings, FINRA executives are in attendance to discuss new initiatives, rules, and general issues that the industry committee members raise. This gives you the opportunity to make personal inroads with the executives (district head of regulation, head of enforcement, head of exams, etc.). You bring these relationships and the knowledge gained at these meetings back to your firm.

Issues raised at these meetings are usually six months ahead of the curve. These new rules are still in the formative stage, and the meeting gives you a chance to have input into shaping the new rule. It also gives you a chance to prepare long in advance for some new compliance issue that is coming down the pike and that will affect your firm. If you don't think that having an additional six months to prepare will stand you in good stead with your superiors at your firm, then you are not the executive material you think you are.

Wouldn't it have been useful to know about the incoming supervision rules well in advance? Wouldn't it have been informative to understand the regulator's thinking about those supervision rules—what they are expecting, how they think it could be complied with? Your firm would have lots of time to have those never-ending committee meetings on how your firm could comply and what money and resources it would need to put in place. And, you would be cementing your importance with your firm by bringing these insights to them so far in advance.

Up the Ladder

Now that you have established yourself on a district committee, it is time for you to move up the ladder at FINRA. There a number of roads available to you that would move you into the next realm. If you are part of a small firm, then maybe the next step for you is the

Small Firm Advisory Board (SFAB). If enforcement is more your bent, there is the National Adjudicatory Council (NAC), and many more very specific committees (examples involve trading and finance). Why bother to spend your time doing this? The first reason is what I discussed previously: knowledge and connections. The SFAB meets five times a year. And it gives you the opportunity to establish a personal relationship with many of the executives of FINRA. That personal relationship leads to the trust mentioned earlier.

The second reason may be a bit altruistic, but valid nonetheless. This industry has provided most of us with a fairly decent living (granted some more decent than others). This is a chance for you to give something back to that industry. If you are on the SFAB, you are representing all firms that have fewer than 150 representatives. You are there because you know the problems facing those small firms and to give FINRA the low-down on how any new rule or requirement would affect small firms both financially and in compliance. By protecting small firms, you are giving back to the industry.

A third reason is a little more selfish. The others on the SFAB are very bright people. You can learn so much from them, because in most cases we are locked into the knowledge of what our firms do. This gives you the opportunity to expand your horizons.

The NAC is another way of influencing the industry. The NAC is the appeal board for FINRA enforcement actions. It also makes decisions on membership issues. But if you want to know more about these elected and/or appointed positions, go to the FINRA website.[1] Service on either the SFAB or NAC involves three-year terms.

My personal path was through the district committee and onto a four-year stint on the SFAB (the last year as chair). I found it rewarding, helpful, informative and impressive to both the executives and employees of my firm.

The final stage that you can aspire to is election to the FINRA Board of Governors.

I don't want to give you the impression that by being on these committees or boards you will change the course of regulation in our time. There are many, many rules that were enacted during my time on the SFAB that we argued vehemently against but lost. The SFAB is an advisory board; members don't have veto power. Then again there were many times that if we didn't kill a rule, we were at least able to modify it so that it would be less onerous on small firms. There were times that the board had to agree to disagree with FINRA.

IV. EXAMINATIONS

Many of you will never meet a regulator until he or she comes into your office for your cycle examination. This examination may be every year, every other year, or every three years. The decision on how often your firm is examined depends on its regulatory record and how risky FINRA believes your firm is—because of the type of business you

---

[1] FINRA's website is www.FINRA.org

do or the products you sell or the Central Registration Depository (CRD) records of your personnel. If this is your only contact with regulators, you are doing something wrong. If, as discussed earlier, you have established a relationship with your liaison and maybe even your district director, your examination will be shorter and more focused. FINRA will understand your business and will know of your leadership. That overused phrase of a "culture of compliance" is very important to FINRA, and if the authority realizes that your firm has that culture, the regulator will trust that you are doing the right thing. And, if something is amiss, the regulator will understand that it was unintentional and that once pointed out, you will fix it.

Additionally, the newest format for examinations is for FINRA to send a document request well in advance of the on-site visit. Those documents are uploaded onto the FINRA website and reviewed in the FINRA office so as not to intrude too much on the daily workings of your firm. However, if a document request is off-base or overly burdensome, or you feel that another document would better show what the regulator is looking for, it is time to call the examination director or your liaison. If you have already established a relationship with the authority, then your conversation will be much less onerous. You should have already established that trust relationship. If so, the conversation will be received by your FINRA examiner in a much more receptive way. Plus, you will not be afraid to disagree with him or her. I believe that not being afraid to question or disagree with the examination team is a key to being an effective compliance officer.

V. ENFORCEMENT

I don't want to get too involved in the enforcement of regulations because enforcement is explored elsewhere in this book. However, there is an overlap between examinations and enforcement.

There are a number of ways that you may interact with the FINRA. The most common way is that the FINRA examination team makes a referral to enforcement personnel after having found a serious violation during your examination. This sort of referral will begin a long and arduous process of investigation, with possible depositions and piles of document requests.

The key to making enforcement go smoothly is to maintain constant contact with the team that is investigating your firm. If the team sends a document request, it is up to you to make sure that the documents are produced in a timely and organized manner. If for some reason you do not understand the request or cannot meet the deadline in the request, you must call the enforcement attorney and discuss the options. The investigator will work with you if he or she believes that you are seriously cooperating. This is the minimum type of cooperation that FINRA expects, but it will not get you the kind of credit that FINRA described in Regulatory Notice 08-70.[2] It will, however, make the process a bit less stressful and make it more palatable.

---

[2] Regulatory Notice 08-70, FINRA Investigations: FINRA Provides Guidance Regarding Credit for Extraordinary Cooperation (Nov. 2008).

Then there is self-reporting, a topic of great debate. Should you report a violation that you have discovered to FINRA if you believe that FINRA would never find the problem on its own? Or should you take the chance that your corrections will suffice for FINRA to not discipline you? I can't give you the answer to that. However, if FINRA discovers the issue and finds that you knew about the violation and didn't report it, then you have violated a second rule; the requirement to self-report. Your relationship with FINRA comes into play at this point. If it is a good relationship, then the process could be less onerous.

VI. CONCLUSION

I hope that I didn't sound like a FINRA toady in this chapter, but I really believe that involvement in FINRA will advance your career and help you protect your firm. This does not mean that you will never get an inquiry letter, or be issued a letter of acceptance, waiver and consent (AWC). However, the resolution of those problems may be a lot easier if you have been involved on the level where you can make a call to a department head or another individual who can help you; and the respondent will answer the phone!

Know your rules, regulations, latest news, and best practices; make sure that your firm is compliant; and, get involved with the regulator. This can be a formula for your success.

ABOUT THE AUTHOR

David M. Sobel is executive vice president, general counsel and chief compliance officer for Abel/Noser Corp. He is past chair of the National Association of Independent Broker/Dealers, past chair of the SFAB, and a past director on the Board of the National Society of Compliance Professionals.

From 1982 to 1991, Mr. Sobel was a floor member of the New York Stock Exchange, and from 1991 to1996 he was an OTC market maker. He is admitted to practice in New York and Connecticut.

CHAPTER 22

Compliance Professionals' Relationships with Endangered Populations

By Theodore J. Sawicki, *Alston & Bird LLP*
   Melissa J. Gworek, *Alston & Bird LLP*

I. INTRODUCTION

A disposition toward paternalism is permeating the laws and regulations governing the relationships between financial services firms and their customers. This trend can be seen in the increasingly complex prescriptive rules and regulations being promulgated by government agencies and self-regulatory organizations and the insidious expansion of the types of customer relationships governed by the fiduciary standard.

By way of example, the relationships between firms and senior investors have become the current focus of this policy of paternalism. And by virtue of the confluence of certain transcendent socioeconomic and political factors with this regulatory approach, investors who are seniors now constitute the single most valuable and vulnerable group of current and prospective consumers of financial services.

Given the huge impact that seniors will have on the industry in the coming years in terms of both profit and risk, securities compliance professionals have no choice but to embrace seniors as one of the key constituencies compliance serves and to make a special effort to proactively address the unique risks and challenges that attend this particularly vulnerable group of current and prospective customers. In the same vein, compliance professionals should be prepared to develop and implement effective policies and procedures to protect other "special classes" of customers and address the risks and vulnerabilities that may be specific to them.

This chapter discusses the most significant and prevalent senior investor issues that now face, or are on the horizon for, securities compliance professionals. It will then provide practical guidance and identify suggested "best practices" to enable compliance professionals to effectively protect their firms, as well as senior investors and other "special classes" of customers, from illicit schemes and inappropriate and unlawful sales practices, and to meet the expectations of the relevant regulatory authorities.

II. DUTIES OWED TO SENIOR INVESTORS

With myriad overlapping and increasingly protective regimes designed to prevent the financial abuse of the elderly, an understanding of the legal framework governing financial advisors who work with senior investors is imperative to the development of a functional compliance program. In the last decade alone, industry and regulatory guidance has proliferated as compliance professionals and regulators turn their attention to the ongoing retirement boom. Laying the groundwork for this expansion is a scheme of general common law rules, state statutes, and regulatory guidance that are ripe for new applications to protect the aging financial consumer. This section surveys the legal backdrop against which financial advisors operate, starting with the common law duties enunciated by courts and then turning to the state statutes and regulatory schemes that supplement these duties.

Broker-Dealers

A broker owes basic duties to all clients, which may be heightened depending on the type of account at issue, the sophistication of the client, and the relationship between the client and the registered representative. As an initial matter, a broker owes duties of diligence and competence in executing a client's trade orders and should give honest and complete information when recommending the purchase or sale of securities.[1] Courts have held that a broker's basic duties include:

- A duty to refrain from self-dealing;
- A duty to recommend an investment after studying it sufficiently to become informed as to its nature, price, and financial prognosis;
- A duty to transact business only after receiving customer authorization;
- A duty not to misrepresent material facts, including facts about the securities recommended, the risks involved, or the ability of the customer or the broker to limit these risks, the broker's commissions, and the broker's claimed possession of inside information;
- A duty to observe all industry rules, regulations, customs, and practices, including internal policies and procedures intended to protect the customer; and
- A duty to carry out the customer's orders promptly, in a manner best suited to serve the customer's interests, and at the best reasonably available price.[2]

The breadth and duration of these basic duties often turns on whether an account is nondiscretionary or discretionary. A nondiscretionary account involves the customer, rather than the broker, determining purchases and sales based on the recommendation and information provided by the broker.[3] With a nondiscretionary account, a broker's

---

[1] *De Kwiatkowski v. Bear Stearns & Co.*, 306 F.3d 1293, 1302 (2d Cir. 2002).
[2] *See, e.g., Leib v. Merrill Lynch, Pierce, Fenner & Smith, Inc.*, 461 F. Supp. 951, 952-53 (E.D. Mich. 1978); *Newton v. Merrill Lynch, Pierce, Fenner & Smith, Inc.*, 135 F.3d 266, 270 (2d Cir. 1998); Jeanne Crandall, *Establishing a Reasonable Standard of Responsibility for Broker-Customer Relationships in Securities Arbitration 2006: Taking Responsibility*, 323, 328–330 (2006).
[3] *See Leib*, at 461 F. Supp., at 953.

duties are triggered by individual transactions.[4] In other words, the broker owes the customer the duties outlined above with respect to each transaction only. This means that the broker generally has no continuing duty to monitor the account or to tell the customer of new developments that might affect the customer's investments.[5] For instance, the courts have held that a customer has no legal claim to the broker's ongoing attention.[6] Moreover, the giving of advice generally triggers no duty to do so going forward.[7]

As such, in the context of nondiscretionary accounts, a broker should carefully observe the duties above with respect to each transaction, particularly with respect to his or her obligation to provide honest and complete information. This obligation is of particular importance when the broker works with inexperienced or unsophisticated investors who require the broker's assistance to make informed investment decisions.[8] In such situations, a broker should define the potential risks of a particular transaction carefully and cautiously.[9] On the other hand, a broker's explanation of such risks may be perfunctory if the customer purports to understand the stock market or is personally familiar with the security.[10]

The suitability rules of the Financial Industry Regulatory Authority (FINRA), discussed further below, provide an important layer to this backdrop. FINRA is an independent organization that oversees securities firms and brokers. FINRA writes rules governing investment services providers, examines firms, and produces educational materials for investment. In 2014, FINRA brought 1,397 disciplinary actions against registered brokers and firms, levied $134 million in fines, and referred more than 700 fraud and insider trading cases to the SEC. Essentially, FINRA is the private-sector watchdog of the industry with significant oversight authority.[11]

Under FINRA Rule 2111, recommended investment strategies must be suitable to a customer's investment objectives, based on a variety of factors to be considered by a broker.[12] FINRA's regulatory notices make clear that the rule is triggered regardless of whether the recommendation results in a transaction, and that an explicit recommendation to hold a security constitutes a recommended strategy.[13] The rule applies on a recommendation-by-recommendation basis and does not impose ongoing monitoring obligations.[14]

---

[4] *Leib*, 461 F. Supp., at 952.
[5] *Leib*, at 953.
[6] *See*, e.g., *De Kwiatkowski*, 306 F.3d, at 1302.
[7] *Id.*
[8] *See Leib*, at 461 F. Supp. at 953; *De Kwiatkowski*, 306 F.3d, at 1308–09.
[9] *Id.*
[10] *Id.*
[11] FINRA, http://www.finra.org/about (last accessed May 11, 2015).
[12] FINRA Rule 2111, Suitability, http://finra.complinet.com/en/display/display_main.html?rbid=2403&element_id=9859&print=1; *see also* Regulatory Notice 11-02, FINRA (Jan. 2011); Regulatory Notice 11-25, FINRA (May 2011); Regulatory Notice 12-25, FINRA (May 2012); Regulatory Notice 12-55, FINRA (Dec. 2012).
[13] *Id.*
[14] *Id.*

As might be suspected, when more discretion and control are vested in a broker, the greater his or her duties to the customer. When a broker either has the authority to make (e.g., power of attorney or a written grant of discretion), or in fact makes purchase and sale decisions without specific prior authorization from the customer, courts have held that the broker becomes a fiduciary of the customer in the broadest sense.[15] The implication is that the broker has duties that extend beyond each transaction, including duties to:

- Manage the account in a manner directly comporting with the needs and objectives of the customer as stated in the authorization papers or as apparent from the customer's investment history;
- Keep informed regarding changes in the market that affect the customer's interest and act responsively to protect those interests;
- Keep his or her customer informed as to each completed transaction; and
- Explain forthrightly the practical impact and potential risks of the course of dealing in which the broker is engaged.[16]

Indeed, courts have observed that brokers who handle discretionary accounts tend to concentrate on conservative investments and brokers who act otherwise must explain the possible consequences of their actions to the customer.[17] Importantly, these duties are in addition to the duties discussed above for nondiscretionary accounts. Finally, FINRA's suitability rule requires a quantitative suitability assessment for discretionary accounts. The quantitative suitability assessment looks to whether a series of recommended transactions is excessive when taken together in light of the customer's investment profile.[18]

The label assigned to an account does not always determine whether it is discretionary. Courts, perhaps cognizant of the potential for abuse, have held that brokers assumed actual control over nondiscretionary accounts in certain circumstances.[19] In these cases, the broker is designated the customer's fiduciary from the moment the broker assumes control of the account.[20] The determination that a broker has assumed control of a customer's account is based on several factors, including an evaluation of the customer's age, intelligence, education, and investment acumen. If the customer is particularly young, old, or naïve with regard to financial matters, the courts may find that the broker assumed *de facto* control over the account.[21] For instance, one court found that a broker sufficiently controlled the nondiscretionary account of a 77-year-old widow because she was relatively naïve and unsophisticated and invariably relied on the broker's recommendations.[22] Indeed, FINRA's suitability rule recognizes that a broker may have

---

[15] *Leib*, 461 F. Supp., at 953–54.
[16] *Id.*
[17] *Id.*
[18] FINRA Rule 2111; *see also* Regulatory Notice 11-02, FINRA (Jan. 2011); Regulatory Notice 11-25, FINRA (May 2011); Regulatory Notice 12-25, FINRA (May 2012); Regulatory Notice 12-55, FINRA (Dec. 2012).
[19] *Id.*
[20] *Leib*, 461 F. Supp., at 953–54.
[21] *Id.*
[22] *Hecht v. Harris, Upham & Co.*, 283 F. Supp. 417, 433 (N.D. Cal. 1968).

actual or *de facto* control over a customer account and requires a quantitative suitability analysis in either situation.[23]

Broker-dealers may also be subject to the Investment Advisers Act of 1940 (the "Advisers Act"). Although the Advisers Act nominally applies to investment advisers, in practice, a broker must also be sensitive to whether he or she falls within the Advisers Act's definition of an *investment adviser*. An individual is considered an investment adviser if he or she engages in the business of advising others as to the value of securities or as to the advisability of investing in, purchasing, or selling securities.[24] Notably, a person will be considered an investment adviser if he or she provides such information directly or indirectly through writing or publications.[25] Persons who issue or promulgate analyses or reports concerning securities also fall within the Advisers Act's coverage. Some brokers offering certain types of accounts may be subject to regulation as investment advisers.[26] For example, a broker-dealer that provides advice and offers fee-based accounts (i.e., accounts that charge an asset-based or fixed fee rather than a commission, mark-up, or mark-down) must treat those accounts as advisory because an asset-based fee is considered "special compensation."[27] Excluded from the Advisers Act are brokers whose performance of advisory services is solely incidental to the conduct of their business and who receive no special compensation for such advice.[28]

Courts have routinely held that investment advisers owe a heightened fiduciary duty to their customers, one that is arguably greater than the duties owed by brokers managing nondiscretionary accounts.[29] For instance, advisers must fully and fairly disclose all material facts to their clients.[30] Indeed, investment advisers invite litigation when they promise, but fail to provide, investment advice, research, and monitoring services, or fail to disclose when such services prove unproductive.[31] Financial firms should also be on notice that liability is not always confined to the individual broker who violates these duties. Liability has been extended to reach employers based on their registered representatives' conduct via the provisions of the Securities Exchange Act.[32] For instance, an appellate court upheld a failure-to-supervise penalty of $310,000 that was imposed by the SEC on an employer.[33] In that case, the court noted that the employer failed to investigate its employee's conduct with respect to marketing variable annuities to elderly customers, even after the broker lost his Florida license for such practices.[34]

---

[23] FINRA Rule 2111; *see also* Regulatory Notice 11-02, FINRA (Jan. 2011); Regulatory Notice 11-25, FINRA (May 2011); Regulatory Notice 12-25, FINRA (May 2012); Regulatory Notice 12-55, FINRA (Dec. 2012).
[24] Investment Advisers Act of 1940 § 202(a)(11), 15 U.S.C. § 80b-2.
[25] *Id.*
[26] SEC, Comm'n, *Guide to Broker-Dealer Registration*, http://www.sec.gov/divisions/marketreg/bdguide.htm
[27] *Id.*
[28] *Id.*
[29] *Norman v. Salomon Smith Barney, Inc.*, 350 F. Supp. 2d 382, 392 (S.D.N.Y. 2004).
[30] *Id.*
[31] *Id.*
[32] *See, e.g., Hecht*, 283 F. Supp. 417, 438–39.
[33] *Collins v. SEC*, 736 F.3d 521, 527 (D.C. Cir. 2013).
[34] *Id.*

Finally, although FINRA does not have regulatory authority over professionals registered solely as investment advisers, it is often the forerunner in addressing nascent regulatory issues and impacts the overall dialogue in the regulatory community. FINRA rules, SEC rules and guidance, and the law tend to develop in tandem with each other. Accordingly, investment advisers may experience downstream effects of FINRA's rules and interpretations thereof.

Courts have used a variety of phrases to describe the duties that a broker owes to clients (e.g., fiduciary, loyalty, reasonable care, full disclosure, and good faith). Importantly, the SEC has undertaken a study of proposed rulemaking that would unify the duties owed by investment advisors and broker-dealers by imposing clear fiduciary responsibilities on broker-dealers.[35] The SEC is responding to perceived investor confusion on the difference between a broker and an advisor, but the discussion is ongoing and the SEC has declined to state a deadline for any formal decision.[36] For the time being, the specific facts determine the scope and duration of the duty owed by broker-dealers: the type of account, the broker's control over the account, the relationship between the broker and the customer, and the customer's sophistication. In other words, a fact-specific assessment of each situation determines the level of duty owed to a client, with age one of the many variables to be considered.

Elder Abuse Statutes

Because individuals age 50 and above control at least seventy-five percent of the nation's household wealth and nearly half of all elder abuse involves some form of financial exploitation, nearly every state has a statute directly or indirectly addressing the financial exploitation of the elderly.[37] These statutes can be separated into three basic categories: (1) general application statutes; (2) statutes specifically making unlawful the financial abuse of the elderly and vulnerable; and (3) statutes enhancing penalties for crimes against elderly and vulnerable victims.[38] Importantly, some of these statutes specifically address the financial abuse of the elderly and may provide a basis for actions against broker-dealers and investment advisers.

Statutes of General Application. Many states use their general theft statutes to address the financial abuse of the elderly, rather than relying on targeted legislation.[39] Carolyn L. Dessin has noted, "Since financial abuse involves a wrongful deprivation of the assets of another, much financial abuse could be classified as a form of theft."[40] As a result, general application statutes can at least theoretically be used to prohibit financial abuse and to

---

[35] See "Mary Jo White: The 2014 IA 25 Extended Profile," *ThinkAdvisor* (Apr. 28, 2014); Mark Schoeff Jr., "SEC Keeps Fiduciary Promises Vague for 2015," *Investment News* (Nov. 18, 2014).
[36] *Id.*
[37] John B. Breaux and Orrin G. Hatch, "Confronting Elder Abuse, Neglect, and Exploitation: The Need for Elder Justice Legislation," 11 *ELDER L.J.*, 207, 221–222 (2003).
[38] Carolyn L. Dessin, "Financial Abuse of the Elderly: Is the Solution a Problem?" 34 *McGeorge L. Rev.*, 267, 289 (2003).
[39] Dessin, "Financial Abuse of the Elderly," at 289.
[40] Dessin, "Financial Abuse of the Elderly," at 288.

punish the abuse if it occurs. Notably, this approach mirrors certain regulatory efforts to target financial abuse through the application of general regulations, as discussed below.

General statutes pose certain limitations as applied to broker-dealers and investment advisers. Although general theft statutes may be applied to instances of financial exploitation, one wrinkle that may arise is the issue of consent. In the average theft prosecution, there is rarely a question about whether the victim consented to the asset transfer.[41] In contrast, allegations of exploitation often, if not always, will raise the issue of whether the victim intended to consent to the transaction at issue. "[T]he question of whether the alleged victim consented should always be considered if the victim's autonomy rights with respect to the disposition of his property are to be adequately taken into account."[42] Indeed, there is a corresponding interest in protecting the right of the elderly to manage and dispose of their assets. As such, states using general application statutes will likely encounter difficulty distinguishing between exploitation and the conduct traditionally considered theft.[43]

Statutes Specifically Addressed to Financial Abuse of the Elderly and Vulnerable. Statutes specifically addressing the financial abuse of the elderly and vulnerable can be further separated into three subcategories: those that make unlawful financial abuse of both the elderly and the "vulnerable;" those that make unlawful the exploitation of the elderly; and those that make unlawful the financial exploitation of the "vulnerable."[44] Regardless of the statutory scheme, recent trends indicate an expansion of the statutory protections and some state courts are receptive to claims brought based on alleged violations of the statutes.

In Florida, with its large population of seniors, the Adult Protective Services Act creates a private cause of action for so-called "vulnerable" persons.[45] The statute provides that "a vulnerable adult who has been abused, neglected, or exploited as specified in this chapter has a cause of action against any perpetrator and may recover actual and punitive damage for such abuse, neglect or exploitation."[46] With such an expansive definition of exploitation and limited case law construing the statutory scheme, plaintiffs in Florida may successfully argue that the statute applies to broker-dealer or investment adviser abuses.[47] In addition to this broad statute, Florida's criminal law makes the exploitation of an elderly or disabled person illegal.[48] Notably, legislation proposed in both 2013 and 2014 would further expand the protections of the criminal statute.

Similarly, Georgia has a statute designed to protect the vulnerable and elderly. The Georgia statute's purpose is to "provide protective services for abused, neglected,

---

[41] *Id.*
[42] Dessin, "Financial Abuse of the Elderly," at 288.
[43] *Id.*
[44] *Id.* at 289.
[45] *See* Fla. Stat. § 415.101-415.113.
[46] Fla. Stat. § 415.1111.
[47] Geralyn M. Passaro, "Claims of Exploitation of the Elderly in the Sale of Financial Products," 80 *Fla. B.J.* 81 (2006).
[48] *See* Fla. Stat. § 825.103.

or exploited disabled adults and elder persons."[49] Interestingly, the Georgia statute also acknowledges that its provision may impinge upon the rights and preferences of elderly individuals, and directs that it is expressly not seeking "to place restrictions upon the personal liberty of disabled adults or elder persons...."[50] The statute was amended in 2013 to expand certain protections and expressly defined "exploitation" as "the illegal or improper use of a disabled adult or elder person or that person's resources through undue influence, coercion, harassment, duress, deception, false representation, false pretense, or other similar means for one's own or another's profit or advantage."

California's statute, the Elder Abuse and Dependent Adult Civil Protection Act, likewise protects both elders and dependent adults from financial abuse.[51] The statute defines financial abuse to include actions of a person who does any of the following:

- Takes, secretes, appropriates, obtains, or retains real or personal property of an elder or dependent adult for a wrongful use or with intent to defraud, or both;
- Assists in taking, secreting, appropriating, obtaining, or retaining real or personal property of an elder or dependent adult for a wrongful use or with intent to defraud, or both; or
- Takes, secretes, appropriates, obtains, or retains, or assists in taking, secreting, appropriating, obtaining, or retaining, real or personal property of an elder or dependent adult by undue influence, as defined [elsewhere in the statute].[52]

The statute provides civil remedies, including potential attorneys' fees and damages, to any protected person who sustains fiduciary abuse.[53] California courts are increasingly allowing claims of elder abuse premised on this statute, as well as claims for breach of fiduciary duty, to proceed against persons acting as investment advisers who use deceptive sales materials to procure investments.[54]

Statutes Enhancing Penalties for Crimes Against the Elderly and Vulnerable. In contrast to the above categories, some states enhance criminal penalties for those convicted under general application statutes when the victim is elderly.[55] For instance, Arizona's statute treats the victim's status as a senior citizen (a person older than age 65) or a disabled person as an aggravating circumstance that enhances potential punishment for the underlying crime.[56] Nevada provides additional penalties for crimes committed against individuals who are 65 or older.[57] If the exploitation of a senior citizen was for an amount over $5,000, the perpetrator can be subject to a fine up to

---

[49] O.C.G.A. § 30-5-2.
[50] Id.
[51] Cal. Welf. & Inst. Code § 15656.
[52] Cal. Welf. & Inst. Code § 15610.30.
[53] Cal. Welf. & Inst. Code § 15657; see also Dessin, "Financial Abuse of the Elderly," at 386; Passaro, "Claims of Exploitation of the Elderly, at 81.
[54] See, e.g., Negrete v. Fidelity and Guar. Life Ins. Co., 444 F. Supp. 2d 998 (C.D. Cal. 2006).
[55] See Dessin, "Financial Abuse of the Elderly," at 289.
[56] Ariz. Rev. Stat. Ann. § 13-701(D)(13).
[57] See Nev. Rev. Stat. § 200.5099.

$25,000 or a prison term of two to ten years.[58] In keeping with trends elsewhere, the potential fine was just recently increased to $25,000. In determining the appropriate punishments, the statute recommends combining the "monetary value of all of the money, assets, and property of the older person or vulnerable person which have been obtained or used."[59]

Elder abuse has garnered federal attention as well. In 2010, Congress passed the Elder Justice Act, which is the first comprehensive federal legislation to address elder abuse. [60] The Elder Justice Act directs for federal resources to be used to "prevent, detect, treat, understand, intervene in and, where appropriate, prosecute elder abuse, neglect, and exploitation," and imposes various requirements on the Department of Health and Human Services and the Department of Justice with the goal of protecting elders from abuse, including financial abuse. [61] The Elder Justice Act also provides for grants to state and community agencies to promote awareness of financial fraud and abuse.[62] Although the act is expansive in scope, Congress has yet to appropriate any of the funds authorized by the Elder Justice Act.

Financial professionals can further run into complications when they detect, and attempt to take action on, suspicions of financial abuse. Absent appropriate permissions, a firm may violate privacy laws or industry regulations if a member reports questionable account activity to relatives or friends.[63] Although FINRA is expected to issue guidance on this topic, regulators cannot prevent private lawsuits by clients for such actions. One potential safeguard, if implemented by Washington, could be laws that permit brokerages to place holds on clients" accounts if there is a concern about diminished capacity.[64]

Regulatory Oversight

Regulatory efforts to curtail abusive practices with regard to senior investors have dramatically increased throughout the last decade. Recognizing the potential threat to the growing retiree market, FINRA and the Securities and Exchange Commission (SEC) have prioritized protecting this investor market from unscrupulous practices. The agencies have been actively guiding investment professionals on working with senior investors.

Indeed, in 2006, the SEC and the North American Securities Administrators Association (NASAA) announced a coordinated national initiative to protect seniors from investment fraud.[65] The initiative also enlists FINRA in a collective effort toward active investor

---

[58] *Id.*
[59] Nev. Rev. Stat. § 200.5099(3).
[60] The Elder Justice Act is a part of the Patient Protection and Affordable Care Act. Public Act. 42 U.S.C. § 1305, et seq.
[61] *Id.*
[62] *Id.*
[63] *See* Suzanne Barlyn, "Client Dementia Vexes Financial Brokerages, Regulators," Reuters (May 29, 2010).
[64] *Id.*
[65] *See* Office of Compliance Inspections and Examinations Securities and Exchange Commission, *Protecting Senior Investors: Report of Examinations of Securities Firms Providing "Free Lunch" Sales Seminars* (Sept. 2007), available at http://www.sec.gov/spotlight/seniors/freelunchreport.pdf

education and outreach, targeted examinations to detect abusive sale tactics aimed at seniors, and aggressive enforcement of securities laws in cases of fraud against seniors.[66]

Most notably, agencies have pushed investment professionals to be cognizant of the suitability and "know your customer" rules when working with seniors.[67] FINRA's suitability rule requires that in making a recommendation, "[a] member or an associated person must have a reasonable basis to believe that a recommended transaction or investment strategy involving a security or securities is suitable for the customer, based on the information obtained through the reasonable diligence of the member."[68] The factors to be considered in determining whether an investment is suitable include the customer's age, investment time horizon, and liquidity needs, each of which is particularly applicable in the case of senior investors.[69] The rule works in tandem with FINRA Rule 2090, which requires firms to use "reasonable diligence" to ascertain "essential facts" concerning each customer. Prior to the implementation of FINRA's suitability Rule 2111, which specifically includes age as a factor in the suitability analysis, FINRA released a regulatory notice focused on senior investors that advised that a customer's age and life stage "are important factors to consider in performing a suitability analysis."[70]

Courts also take note of these rules. For instance, one court cited the former suitability rules and FINRA's supervisory guidance on senior investors as relevant to assessing industry standards in an action brought by senior investors for professional malpractice and breach of fiduciary duty.[71] Plaintiffs in that case alleged that an investment advisory firm failed to consider their ages and investment strategies in investing their portfolios. In finding the former suitability rules and FINRA's guidance relevant, the court ignored the fact that the firm was not even a FINRA member. The adoption of the FINRA rule specifically referencing investors' ages will likely strengthen the attention placed on this factor by courts and regulators.

FINRA has also turned its attention to sales practices targeting military personnel and their dependents. In February 2015, the authority announced that it was developing

---

[66] *Id.*
[67] Formerly governed by NASD 2310, the suitability rule is now embodied in FINRA Rule 2111.
[68] FINRA Rule 2111. FINRA has explained that there are three main suitability obligations: reasonable basis suitability, customer-specific suitability, and quantitative suitability. Reasonable basis suitability requires a broker to have a reasonable basis to believe, based on reasonable diligence, that the recommendation is suitable for at least some investors. Customer-specific suitability requires that a broker have a reasonable basis to believe that the recommendation is suitable for a particular customer based on that customer's investment profile. Quantitative suitability requires a broker who has actual or *de facto* control over a customer account to have a reasonable basis for believing that a series of recommended transactions, even if suitable when viewed in isolation, are not excessive and unsuitable for the customer when taken together in light of the customer's investment profile. Regulatory Notice 11-02, FINRA (Jan. 2011); *see also* Regulatory Notice 11-25, FINRA (May 2011); Regulatory Notice 12-25, FINRA (May 2012); Regulatory Notice 12-55, FINRA (Dec. 2012).
[69] FINRA Rule 2111; *see also* Regulatory Notice 11-02, FINRA (Jan. 2011); Regulatory Notice 11-25, FINRA (May 2011); Regulatory Notice 12-25, FINRA (May 2012); Regulatory Notice 12-55, FINRA (Dec. 2012).
[70] Regulatory Notice 07-43, FINRA (Sept. 2007). The former suitability rules did not specifically mention age as a component of the analysis.
[71] *Rioseco v. Gamco Asset Management, Inc.*, No. 15862/10, 2011 WL 4552544 (2011).

potential rules to govern sales practices targeting this group, which follows up on reports from the early 2000s that certain firms deceptively sold armed services members expensive or unnecessary investment products.[72] As this action demonstrates, regulatory supervision over practices targeting potentially vulnerable investors extends beyond the limited demographic of seniors.

In the absence of statutes and regulations specifically targeting seniors, the agencies look to apply their general regulations to senior investments and have issued guidance to ensure broker-dealers and investment advisers comply. For instance, the 2007 FINRA notice also reminded investment professionals that the rules governing false and misleading statements apply to communications with senior investors.[73] Specifically, FINRA Rule 2210[74] and New York Stock Exchange (NYSE) Rule 472 prohibit firms and registered representatives from making false, exaggerated, unwarranted, or misleading statements or claims in communications with the public. Thus, it is clear that regulators are closely examining sales materials and communications targeting seniors.

The agencies have also focused on the use of senior certifications or designations by professionals. Following an investigatory sweep by FINRA in 2005, the NASAA issued a model rule for such designations in 2008, which has been adopted by several states.[75] Likewise, in 2011, FINRA issued a regulatory notice on senior designations, reiterating the rules regarding false and misleading communications with the public and noting that under NASD Rule 3010 firms are required to establish and maintain a supervisory system that is reasonably designed to achieve compliance with applicable securities laws and regulations and FINRA rules.[76]

These regulatory efforts have been impactful. The SEC has pursued numerous administrative actions against individuals for targeting senior citizens with fraudulent investment schemes.[77] FINRA has barred brokers found to have defrauded elderly customers.[78] As discussed above, the SEC has pursued penalties against firms for failing to supervise members' transactions with senior customers. In short, both individuals and firms targeting this investment market must be cognizant of the growing legal and regulatory landscape in which they operate.

---

[72] *See* Ed Beeson, "FINRA Eyes New Rules on Fired Brokers, Military Sales," *Law*360 (Feb. 4, 2015), http://www.law360.com/securities/articles/618466?utm_source=shared-articles&utm_medium=email&utm_campaign=shared-articles

[73] Regulatory Notice 07-43, FINRA (Sept. 2007).

[74] Formerly NASD 2210.

[75] SEC, NASAA Model Rule on the Use of Senior-Specific Certifications and Professional Designations; *Protecting Senior Investors: Compliance, Supervisory and Other Practices Used by Financial Services Firms in Serving Senior Investors*, 2010 Addendum.

[76] Regulatory Notice 11-52, FINRA (Nov. 2011).

[77] *See* Luis A. Aguilar, Protecting the Financial Future of Seniors and Retirees (Feb. 4, 2014), http://www.sec.gov/News/Speech/Detail/Speech/1370540744550

[78] *See* Everdeen Mason, "FINRA Bars Two Former Chase Brokers for Allegedly Stealing $300,000 from Elderly Widow," *The Wall Street Journal* (Dec. 3, 2013).

III. REGULATORY CONCERNS ABOUT SALES PRACTICES AND INVESTMENT PRODUCTS

As exemplified by a 2014 speech by SEC Commissioner Luis Aguilar, regulatory agencies are focused on safeguarding retirement assets and are strengthening examination programs with a keen eye trained on sales practices targeting senior investors:

> [T]he importance of regulatory oversight cannot be understated. As one survey shows, most seniors do not have all the information they need to pick a financial adviser to help protect their retirement assets. And about three in five experts said that seniors are not able to determine the "legitimacy, value, and authenticity of credentials held by their financial advisers and planners." For this and other reasons, the SEC and other regulators must continue to play an important role in securing the financial future of American retirees....[79]

This section discusses the product and sales practice issues that frequently arise in the context of senior investors and touches on pertinent regulatory directives.

Product Offerings

It should come as no surprise that regulators have fixated on certain product offerings that potentially pose a risk to senior investors who fail to truly comprehend the features, limitations, risks, and costs of those products. Three investments have drawn particular attention: variable annuities, life settlements, and equity-indexed annuities.

In general, the product concerns relate to the horizon of the investment or the investment's status as being outside the scope of traditional securities regulation.[80]

Variable Annuities. For years, regulators have focused on the sale and exchange of deferred variable annuities.[81] Variable annuities offer several desirable benefits to certain investors, such as death benefits and tax savings. But the product is also viewed as a long-term investment better suited to long-range goals because of the product's built-in accumulation period and diminishing surrender charges (among other features and reasons).[82] Problems arise when the long-term nature of the product conflicts with investor goals. For instance, many variable annuities impose surrender charges if the product is held for less than seven years, meaning the product may be unsuitable for

---

[79] See Aguilar, Protecting the Financial Future of Seniors and Retirees.
[80] Other issues of concern may include lack of liquidity, volatility, and inflation risk.
[81] A variable annuity is a contract between an investor and an insurance company, under which the insurer agrees to make periodic payments to the investor either immediately or at some future date. A typical variable annuity offers a range of investment options, such as mutual funds that invest in stocks, bonds, money market instruments, or some combination of the same. See SEC, Variable Annuities: What You Should Know, http://www.sec.gov/investor/pubs/varannty.htm (last accessed Oct. 14, 2014).
[82] Id.

investors with short-term investment horizons.[83] In fact, many of the legitimate benefits offered by variable annuities may not be appropriate or desirable for many senior investors. Indeed, regulators have observed that even variable annuities that offer riders specifically designed for seniors, such as guaranteed life benefits, may not be suitable for some senior investors.[84]

Regulators' concerns are fueled by the reported cases of unscrupulous sales tactics related to variable annuities. It seems certain that the regulatory scheme as it now exists was driven in part by a Seniors Summit hosted by the SEC in 2006, which suggested that seniors submitted roughly 44 percent of all investor complaints about variable annuities.[85] Similarly, a 2007 investigation showed that, at one firm, most of the customers who purchased annuities had time horizons that were incompatible with the surrender charges contained in the product.[86]

Over the next several years, FINRA Rule 2330 was developed specifically to govern the sale of deferred variable annuities.[87] In its current form, FINRA Rule 2330 applies to recommended transactions and contains four general directives.

First, the rule outlines specific suitability requirements intended to supplement, not supplant, the general suitability Rules. At the outset, a representative must take reasonable steps to ascertain customer-specific information when recommending a customer purchase a variable annuity, including the customer's age, investment horizon, and investment objectives. Although not explicitly stated in the rule, the related regulatory notice observes that the product is generally considered to have a long-term horizon and therefore is not suitable for investors with short-term investment horizons (i.e. senior investors).[88] From there, the representative must have a reasonable basis to believe that the customer would benefit from certain features of the deferred variable annuity, such as the tax savings or death benefit, and that the customer has been informed of the material features of the product. Finally, the representative must assess whether the particular product-offering is suitable as a whole.

Second, a registered principal must review a customer's application for a deferred variable annuity before it is submitted to the insurance company for processing. The principal reviewer must assess information about both the customer and the product(s), and determine whether the transaction is suitable. If the transaction is unsuitable, the principal must reject the transaction unless the customer is informed of the reason why the principal found it to be unsuitable and confirms that he or she wants to proceed.[89]

---

[83] See SEC, *Protecting Senior Investors: Report of Examinations of Securities Firms Providing "Free Lunch Sales Seminars*(Sept. 2007), at 22.
[84] See Regulatory Notice 07-43 (Sept. 2007).
[85] U.S. Securities and Exchange Commission, Seniors Summit (July 17, 2006).
[86] See *Protecting Senior Investors*, at 22.
[87] Formally NASD Rule 2821.
[88] See Regulatory Notice 07-53 (Nov. 2007).
[89] For further detail on the period governing in the principal review, see Regulatory Notice 07-53; Regulatory Notice 09-32 (June 2009).

Third, a firm must establish and maintain written supervisory procedures designed to achieve compliance with the rule. As a part of its procedures, the firm must implement surveillance procedures to determine whether any associated persons' rates of effecting exchanges evidences conduct inconsistent with the rule or other applicable rules and laws. Likewise, a firm must have policies and procedures designed to implement corrective measures to address inappropriate exchanges.

Fourth, firms must include training programs on the material aspects of the products for representatives and principals who work with it.

FINRA's unprecedented adoption of Rule 2330—a supplemental suitability rule targeting a specific product—exemplifies the heightened concern regarding the sale of variable annuity products to seniors. Rule 2330 details exacting requirements for specific transactions and for the general oversight of such transactions. Not only are individual transactions alone subject to scrutiny but firms must also be cognizant of the policies and procedures in place to educate their sales forces and to deter and detect unscrupulous sales practices.

Life Settlements. A *life settlement,* sometimes called a *viatical settlement,* is a transaction wherein an insured person sells his or her life insurance policy to an investor. The seller of the policy receives an immediate cash payment of a portion of the policy that will be due upon his or her death and is no longer obligated to make payments on the policy. The investor assumes the payment of the policy premiums and collects the benefits when the insured person dies. Generally, the insured person has a shortened life expectancy, making senior investors ripe targets of these transactions.[90]

Life settlements can be beneficial to investors and sellers alike. Research suggests that seniors receive four times more from settlement investors than they would receive selling the policies back to the insurance company.[91] On the other side of the transaction, the average expected return to investors ranged from 11 percent to 18 percent from 2001 to 2011.[92] Investors accept the risk, however, that the insured will outlive the anticipated life expectancy and thereby erode the return on the policy. Although demand for life settlements dropped during the financial crisis, investors seeking higher yields have returned, and the demand for life settlements increased by 20 percent in 2013.[93]

Life settlements present certain industry challenges. First, many companies and brokers selling life settlements are not licensed, and the commissions paid to brokers can be exorbitant—up to 30 percent or more of the purchase price.[94] Naturally, exorbitant commissions can lead to deceptive practices by brokers seeking to capitalize. Indeed, the SEC

---

[90] *See S.E.C. v. Tyler,* No. 3:02-cv-282-P, 2003 WL 21281646, at *1 (N.D. Tex. May 28, 2003).
[91] *See* Allison Schrager, "Investing in Other People's Life Insurance Makes a Comeback," *Bloomberg Businessweek* (July 30, 2014); Afonso V. Januário and Narayan Y. Naik, *Empirical Investigation of Life Settlements: The Secondary Market for Life Insurance Policies,* London Business School Working Paper (June 10, 2013), http://www.coventry.com/assets/Marketing_Tools_Pdfs/LifeSettlementsStudy_LBS.pdf
[92] *Id.*
[93] *Id.*
[94] *See* Regulatory Notice, 06-38 (Aug. 2006).

has succeeded in a number of actions alleging fraud in connection with life settlement securities.[95] Second, demand for life settlements may drive some investment professionals to canvass their book of business for seniors who may be interested in selling their policies, even if they had not previously considered doing so.[96] Finally, life settlements often raise privacy concerns because the policy's seller usually authorizes disclosure of certain medical and personal information to the buyer. Depending on the agreement, the information may be shared with other parties such as third-party investors or lenders.

In 1993, the National Association of Insurance Commissioners (NAIC) adopted the Viatical Settlements Model Act to address concerns about life settlements.[97] The Model Act, or similar legislation, has been adopted in most states and only five states have failed to adopt any relevant laws. The Model Act requires all viatical settlement providers or brokers to obtain a license from the state insurance commissioner and to provide annual reports to the commission.

The Model Act attempts to addresses privacy concerns. For instance, a broker cannot disclose the insured's identity or medical information to any other person, except in limited circumstances. Further, several disclosure obligations are detailed in the Model Act, including that a broker must:

- Identify possible alternatives to the viatical settlement contract;
- Explain that the broker represents the viator and owes a fiduciary duty to the viator, including a duty to act according to the viator's instructions and in the best interest of the viator;
- Identify the amount and method of calculating the broker's compensation on the transaction; and
- Describe certain tax and benefit consequences that might occur as a result of receiving proceeds from the viatical settlement.

In addition to state laws regulating the sale of life settlements, FINRA has clarified that life settlements involving variable insurance policies are securities transactions subject to applicable FINRA rules, including the suitability rule.[98] Likewise, a SEC Task Force examining life settlements observed that variable life settlements are subject to the federal securities laws and found that the commission should recommend that Congress amend the definition of *security* to include all life settlements, in order to resolve a conflict among courts regarding this issue.[99]

Although FINRA has not issued specific rules governing life settlements, regulatory guidance describes considerations that may apply in the context of these transactions. For instance, a FINRA regulatory notice instructs that an appropriate suitability

---

[95] *See* SEC Life Settlements Task Force, *Staff Report to the United States Securities and Exchange Commission* (July 22, 2010), at 30–33.
[96] *Id.*
[97] The Model Act has been amended throughout the years, with the most recent amendments adopted in 2007. *See* generally Viatical Settlements Model Act, available at http://www.naic.org/store/free/MDL-697.pdf
[98] *See* Regulatory Note 06-38 (Aug. 2006); Regulatory Notice 09-42 (July 2009).
[99] SEC Life Settlements Task Force, *Staff Report.*

analysis in the context of a life settlement must account for the customer's continued need for insurance coverage, tax and welfare implications, and whether comparable or adequate coverage will be available if the customer plans to replace the existing policy.[100] Moreover, FINRA's due diligence rules require that a firm understand the confidentiality policies that apply to the transactions and explain to their customers any ongoing obligations, such as continued reporting of medical developments. Finally, practitioners are reminded that any commissions received from life settlements must be supportable under the FINRA rules.[101]

Equity-Indexed Annuities. An equity-indexed annuity is a type of hybrid product that combines the guaranteed interest rate of a fixed annuity with the market-indexed returns of a variable annuity. By combining the features of fixed and variable annuities, equity indexed annuities offer an intermediate level of risk and return compared to their counterparts.[102] Equity-indexed annuities are considered long-term investments and early surrenders often come with tax penalties and significant surrender charges.

Although it is settled that variable annuities are securities regulated by the SEC and fixed annuities are not, regulators have struggled with the appropriate supervision for equity-indexed annuities. Historically, equity-indexed annuities were not registered securities, limiting regulatory oversight of their marketing and sales. Not surprisingly, the product is sold widely to elderly and unsophisticated customers.[103]

After failed attempts by the SEC to regulate the product, the Wall Street Reform and Consumer Protection Act of 2010 (Dodd-Frank Act) left regulation of equity-indexed annuities to the individual states. Many states subsequently promulgated laws and/or regulations imposing compliance or suitability requirements for equity-indexed annuities.[104] For example, some states impose specific disclosure requirements at the time of purchase and may require a seller to take additional training on the products or to include information on how value will be calculated.[105]

A 2005 FINRA[106] notice also recognized the potential dangers of improperly marketed equity-indexed annuities. In the notice, members were warned of potentially misleading marketing claims and were encouraged to adopt enhanced supervisory procedures for the sale of these products.[107] As with other products targeting senior investors, FINRA

---

[100] See Regulatory Note 06-38; Regulatory Notice 09-42.
[101] Regulatory Notice 09-42 (July 2009).
[102] See FINRA, Investor Alert, *Equity-Indexed Annuities: A Complex Choice* (2012), https://www.finra.org/web/groups/investors/@inv/@protect/@ia/documents/investors/p125847.pdf
[103] See Jane Quinn, "Congress Sells Out Seniors: No SEC Regulation for Indexed Annuities," *CBS Money Watch*, (July 2, 2010), http://www.cbsnews.com/news/congress-sells-out-seniors-no-sec-regulation-for-indexed-annuities/
[104] See Zeke Faux and Margaret Collins, "Indexed Annuities Cap Gains, Obscure Fees as Sellers Earn Trip to Disney," Bloomberg (Jan. 20, 2011), http://www.bloomberg.com/news/2011-01-20/indexed-annuities-obscure-fees-as-sellers-earn-trip-to-disney.html
[105] *Id.*
[106] Formerly, the NASD.
[107] See Regulatory Note 05-50 (Aug. 2005).

noted the difficulty of assessing the suitability of the product for senior investors in light of the product's investment time horizon.

Recent evidence shows that senior investors will demand even more from their investment professionals in the coming years. For instance, one study shows that 67 percent of baby boomers expect their investment advisers to play a role in their consideration of health care costs, such as long-term care insurance.[108] As the market steps in to fill these demands, the regulators will almost certainly be scrutinizing all new product offerings and advice that target senior investors.

As demonstrated by the discussion of these three relatively novel and complex investment products that appeal to or are designed to target senior investors, a savvy compliance professional should be aware of each particular product's characteristics, features, and restrictions that are prone to scrutiny by regulators, in order to adapt existing policies and procedures, and/or develop new ones so his or her firm is prepared to deal with such scrutiny.

Advertising and Marketing

In addition to suitability issues and sales practices targeting a particular group, regulators are focusing on the advertising and marketing practices of investment firms, particularly practices targeting persons with diminished capacity. Under FINRA Rule 2210, "[N]o member may publish, circulate, or distribute any communication that the member knows or has reason to know contains any untrue statement of a material fact or is otherwise false or misleading." Certain marketing techniques raise particular concern in the context of senior investors. As a result, compliance professionals must strike a fine balance of ensuring compliance with the applicable laws and regulations without stifling legitimate marketing activities.

Senior Certifications and Sales Materials. For several years, FINRA has focused on the use of senior-oriented certifications and designations, with a particular focus on professionals using "empty" designations that are not supported by any specialized training or experience. In the 2000s, regulators found that senior designations abounded, including titles such as "senior specialist," "certified senior adviser," and "retirement specialist."[109] When the agencies dug into the designations, however, there was a noticeable disparity in the qualifications required to use the designations. Although some designations required formal certification, others could be obtained by paying membership dues. Further, a 2011 FINRA survey found that although 68 percent of the surveyed firms allowed

---

[108] "Advisors: What Boomers Want from You," *Financial Planning* (Oct. 27, 2014), http://www.financial-planning.com/news/retirement_planning/advisors-baby-boomers-want-help-on-retirement-health-care-costs-2690798-1.html (reporting 67 percent of baby boomers expect an advisor to play at least some role in discussions about health care costs in retirement); see also Steven Podnos, "Dealing with Client Incapacity," *Wealth Management* (June 2, 2014), http://www.wealthcarellc.com/sitebuildercontent/sitebuilderfiles/2014-6-2incapacitywmanagement.pdf (recommending that advisors review long-term care insurance policies with families of senior investors).

[109] See Regulatory Notice, 07-43 (Sept. 2007).

registered persons to use senior designations, but only two firms required professionals to obtain senior designations before marketing products to senior investors.[110]

Senior designations may be inaccurate or misleading when they suggest expertise that does not exist. Such misrepresentations can run afoul of FINRA rules, state laws, and potentially the federal securities laws. For instance, FINRA has advised that "[f]irms that allow the use of any title or designation that conveys an expertise in senior investments or retirement planning where such expertise does not exist may violate FINRA Rule 2010, [FINRA] Rule 2210, NYSE Rule 472, and possibly the antifraud provisions of the federal securities laws...."[111] Likewise, the NASAA issued a model rule on senior certifications in 2008, which prohibits the use of misleading certifications, and certain states have restricted the use of senior designations.[112]

Similarly, general sales materials can violate FINRA rules and federal laws, such as giving the impression of specialized expertise, promising exaggerated returns, or employing manipulative marketing schemes. For instance, third-party publishing companies may provide agents with prewritten books, articles, and newsletters for prospective clients that carry imprimaturs of authority where none exists.[113] Notably, some senior investors may be more easily persuaded by these materials than younger investors who are more prone to validate the information through alternative sources, such as internet research.

Free Lunch Seminars. Although free lunch seminars have historically been a legitimate marketing tool, many seminars targeting senior citizens have raised concerns because of high-pressure sales tactics used to persuade seniors to purchase unsuitable or overly risky financial products. For instance, seminars like "Senior Financial Survival Seminar" and "Senior Financial Safety Workshop," among others, advertise a suite of products and services for seniors, including investment advice, estate planning, retirement planning, and inheritance advice.[114] The proliferation of these marketing efforts is notable. One SEC study showed the 78 percent of seniors received a free lunch seminar invitation in the past three years.[115]

A regulatory sweep of free lunch seminars confirmed that in many instances the so-called free lunches came with a catch.[116] Contrary to representations that the sessions were educational or simply workshops, the overwhelming finding was that

---

[110] See SEC, *Protecting Senior Investors: Compliance, Supervisory and Other Practices Used by Financial Services Firms in Serving Senior Investors* (Sept. 22, 2008).
[111] Regulatory Notice, 11-52 (Nov. 2011).
[112] See SEC, *Protecting Senior Investors*; *State Securities Regulators Announce New Model Rule on the Use of Senior Certifications and Professional Designations*, NASAA (Apr. 1, 2008), http://www.nasaa.org/5685/state-securities-regulators-announce-new-model-rule-on-the-use-of-senior-certifications-and-professional-designations/
[113] See Testimony of William Francis Galvin, Secretary of State, Commonwealth of Massachusetts, Before the Special Committee on Aging, United States Senate (Sept. 5, 2007).
[114] SEC, Seniors Summit, at 56 (July 17, 2006).
[115] SEC, " 'Free Lunch' Investment Seminar Examinations Uncover Widespread Problems, Perils for Older Investors" (Sept. 10, 2007), http://www.sec.gov/news/press/2007/2007-179.htm
[116] See SEC, *Protecting Senior Investors*.

the seminars were designed to sell investment products, including equity-indexed annuities and speculative securities. Particularly troublesome was the finding that in more than half of the seminars examined, the firms used misleading, exaggerated, or unwarranted claims. The most common types of misleading statements were claims about the safety, liquidity, or anticipated rates of return on investment products, and in many instances, broker-dealers had not submitted their sales materials to FINRA for review.[117]

In the course of the examinations, regulators also concluded that unsuitable products were offered to participants and reported some indications of possible fraudulent practices.[118] In contrast, attendees may not have even been aware that the seminars were sponsored by investment firms, making them particularly susceptible to dubious sales practices.[119] Of note for compliance professionals, the study found weak supervisory practices in more than half of the examinations.[120]

Marketing investments to seniors serves legitimate goals, but such activities also present opportunities for unscrupulous practices. Compliance professionals must be vigilant in establishing and monitoring systems to detect abusive marketing practices.

Selling Away and Fraudulent Schemes

As is well known in the industry, "selling away" is "so named because the registered representative sells a product that is not approved by the firm."[121] Unapproved products are more susceptible to fraudulent or aggressive marketing schemes because (among other reasons) the firm does not engage in any due diligence of the product.

FINRA Rule 3040 prohibits a representative from selling away without his or her firm's approval of the proposed transaction. If approved, a firm assumes supervisory obligations over the transaction. FINRA has consistently imposed sanctions on representatives who violate the selling away mandate.[122] In so doing, the organization admonishes that representatives are not to sell unapproved products, even if they are the type of product that the representative ordinarily sells.[123]

Unlike selling away, which can be a legitimate and excellent practice in certain circumstances, Ponzi and pyramid schemes are inherently fraudulent in nature. In general, a Ponzi scheme promises investors exorbitant returns and uses money from "new" investors to pay "old" investors.[124] Ponzi schemes exhibit the following characteristics:

---

[117] *Id.*
[118] SEC, *Protecting Senior Investors*, at 5.
[119] *Id.*
[120] *Id.*
[121] Susan Antilla, "Hey Wall Street, Tell Why You Booted That Broker," *Bloomberg News*, Nov. 21, 2005, http://www.bloomberg.com/apps/news?pid=newsarchive&sid=awfQdEqf5fJk
[122] *See* NASD Investor Alert, Promissory Notes Can Be Less Than Promised (Jan. 11, 2001), http://www.finra.org/InvestorInformation/InvestorAlerts/PromissoryNotes/PromissoryNotesCanBeLessThanPromised/P006050; Dep't of Enforcement v. Nugent, NASD, Complaint No. C01040010, 2006 WL 462014 (Feb. 23, 2006).
[123] *See Dep't of Enforcement v. Ryerson*, NASD, Complaint No. C9B040033, 2006 WL 2335513 (Aug. 3, 2006).
[124] 'Lectric Law Library, How to Avoid Ponzi and Pyramid Schemes, http://www.lectlaw.com/files/inv01.htm

- Reliance on funds from new investors to provide returns, commissions, or bonuses to old investors;
- The need for an inexhaustible supply of new investors; and
- The absence of profitable products or efforts to make profits through productive work.[125]

Ponzi schemes abound on the internet. For instance, high yield investment programs are a common scheme offered online with eye-catching pitches like "How to Make Money from Your Home Computer!" These programs offer unregistered investments created and sold by unregistered individuals and often use social media to lure investors by fabricating "buzz" about the product.[126] The programs have proliferated with the growth of the internet. Both FINRA and the SEC have issued alerts to help investors protect themselves.[127] According to the SEC:

> High-yield investments tend to involve extremely high risk. [Investors should]:
>
> - Never invest in an opportunity that promises "guaranteed" or "risk-free" returns;
> - Watch out for claims of astronomical yields in a short period of time;
> - Be skeptical of "off-shore" or foreign investments; and
> - Beware of exotic or unusual sounding investments, especially those involving so-called "prime bank" securities.[128]

This section covered only the most recent prominent and pervasive examples of regulatory and compliance challenges regarding products and sales practices that targeted seniors and other vulnerable investors within the last several years. We have done so in order to orient the reader to the current regulatory landscape and the types of products, sales practices, and circumstances that have been prone to abuse and regulatory concern. As financial services continue to evolve to meet growing and changing customer demand from seniors and other types of vulnerable investors, compliance professionals must be cognizant of and facile with the tools, techniques, and processes that can help them manage this important and growing segment of the financial services market. The next section of this chapter discusses many of those tools, techniques, and processes.

IV. SUGGESTED BEST PRACTICES

A close look at the studies, reports, and rules applicable to senior investors sheds light on important steps that compliance professionals can take to improve policies and procedures associated with endangered investor populations. Based on the information and concepts outlined above, we now turn to a series of practical ideas and suggested

---

[125] *Id.*
[126] FINRA Investor Alert, HYIPs—High Yield Investment Programs Are Hazardous to Your Investment Portfolio (July 15, 2010), http://www.finra.org/Investors/ProtectYourself/InvestorAlerts/FraudsAndScams/P121728
[127] *Id.*
[128] SEC, *Avoiding Internet Investment Scams: Tips for Investors*, http://www.sec.gov/investor/pubs/scams.htm. (last accessed Nov. 9, 2014).

"best practices" for compliance professionals to consider. Each firm should assess the nature of the risks it faces to determine whether and the extent to which some or all of these suggestions can bolster its compliance program.

Training/Client Communication

Firms are well-served by mandatory training for registered representatives and advisers to put them on notice of diminished capacity issues, including how diminished capacity affects a person's ability to understand and retain information that is exchanged in the normal course of a brokerage or advisory relationship. Training programs can set the tone and expectations about the firm's commitment to senior customers and should be mandatory for both new and existing financial professionals.

The training should include instructions on indicators of possible changes in comprehension, signs of dementia, and the like. Although every diminished capacity situation will be different, firms should aim to provide hands-on training that incorporates relevant examples, in addition to providing the applicable rules and policies. Relevant topics include:

- Education on red flags of diminished capacity;
- Training on how to advise clients on planning for dementia;
- Education on sales practices and products scrutinized by regulators, including examples of abusive practices;
- Information on common scams and fraudulent conduct by con artists targeting senior investors, such as fraudulent lotteries /sweepstakes and sweetheart scams;
- Special considerations posed by senior clients and shifting investment goals;
- Potential alternatives, such as powers of attorney, and signs of their abuse; and
- The potential application of privacy regulations, such as the Exchange Act's privacy regulation, Regulation S-P.

One of the most important training components is education on client communications. Financial professionals should be prepared to obtain information relevant to assessing diminished capacity issues and should be knowledgeable of listening and communication skills that can be used when working with persons who may have diminished capacity. Finally, a firm should develop policies and procedures on when and how a financial professional can collaborate with family and other professionals in working with a person with diminished capacity.

The first step is to maintain current client information. For both new and existing customers, professionals should be trained to obtain and document investment goals and stage of life information, such as age, employment, and retirement status. Investment advisers can also obtain emergency contact information at the client intake stage and inquire whether the client has executed a power of attorney directing who can act in his or her stead. This information can be included on standardized intake forms, but should be updated periodically for accuracy. Because of the significance of customer information in the context of senior and other vulnerable investors, a firm should consider specialized procedures for documentation, including:

- Requiring in-person meetings to finalize new account information, and requiring more than one person from the firm to attend such a meeting;
- Requiring independent documentation of total net worth for all customers over a certain age;
- Requiring special supervisory review of all new account forms that include an investment objective that is more aggressive than "income" for customers over a certain age;
- Regularized procedures for the detailed review of clients' financial status, needs, and investment objectives as they near retirement age or enter retirement; and
- Regularized procedures for seeking to update information regarding financial status, personal circumstances (including ability to make decisions for themselves), and investment objectives.

As a final check, firms may wish to conduct quality assurance calls with a random sample of clients to provide a check on adviser compliance.

The next step is to provide advisers and representatives with education on strong communication skills. Financial professionals should be cognizant of client health conditions and should note clients who are more comfortable with in-person communications or letters, rather than electronic updates.

If there are potential cognition issues, professionals should be trained to set meetings at a slower pace, document the conversations, and ask clients to repeat information to ensure that they understand. Effective and active listening is key: Face the speaker, maintain eye contact, minimize distractions, respond to show you understand, and use visual aids.

Further, training should emphasize the importance of detecting and responding to client health conditions. For instance, if a client appears to have hearing problems, training should guide the adviser to close the door to block outside noises and speak slowly and distinctly. If a client has poor vision, training should guide the adviser to increase lighting, use larger fonts in communications, and position the client with his or her back to the window. In the event dementia or diminished capacity is suspected, training should guide the adviser to suggest a visit to the doctor to assess the concern.

The final step is to develop policies and procedures designed to encourage advisers and representatives to seek appropriate ways to involve children, beneficiaries, other professional advisers and/or third parties (e.g., guardians, concerned relatives, or even Adult Protective Services) in the financial planning process. Problems frequently arise when relatives and loved ones in the next generation review how the client's finances have been managed. To the extent feasible, the bridging of the generations through involvement of children in the planning process once the client reaches a certain age will in many cases protect the client, the family, and the firm. Family members can also provide feedback if diminished capacity is suspected. Working with a client's accountants, estate attorney, and other professional advisers can also lead to a better understanding of how to invest for the client over his or her lifetime and create the opportunity to collaborate as to the best course of action to meet the client's needs and goals.

Written policies and procedures, and training on their consistent application, can make it easier for financial professionals to broach this sensitive issue. Such policies and procedures could include:

- Procedures for seeking written permission, if and when appropriate and feasible, to contact and consult children, beneficiaries, and other professionals;
- Policies and procedures formalizing referral arrangements between registered representatives, advisers, and other professionals; and
- Implementation of an approval process for any such collaborative arrangements.

Of course, privacy considerations are of paramount importance in developing procedures for collaboration with others. Compliance professionals should be mindful to guard against the firm's violation of privacy laws and industry regulations when discussing personal financial information of a customer with others, particularly in the absence of documented consent by the customer. The strictures of Regulation S-P should be taken into account, including disclosure of the conditions under which contact with family and other professionals would be made and how a client's information can be used in such circumstances. Further, financial professionals must understand and communicate the client's right to withdraw consent to collaborative arrangements and/or information-sharing at any time.

Helpfully, in October 2013, the Federal Reserve, CFTC, FDIC, SEC, and other regulatory agencies issued guidance clarifying that reporting *suspected financial abuse* of older adults to appropriate *local, state, or federal agencies* does not generally violate the privacy provisions of the Gramm-Leach-Bliley Act or its implementing regulations.[129] Unfortunately, the guidance does not address diminished capacity issues in the absence of suspected abuse or the privacy implications of reporting suspected conduct to private parties. Although states and regulatory agencies may further clarify the scope of a firm's authority to respond to diminished capacity suspicions in the future, for the time being, firms must be sensitive to general privacy laws that may inhibit their ability to act and proactively address this subject.

Internal Controls

Internal controls should be used to monitor the compliance of financial professionals with relevant policies and procedures and to flag potential problem areas. Best practices for internal controls can be grouped into three categories: oversight, reporting, and escalation; communication networks; and policies and procedures.

---

[129] *See* Interagency Guidance on Privacy Laws and Reporting Financial Abuse of Older Adults, https://www.fdic.gov/news/news/press/2013/Interagency-Guidance-on-Privacy-Laws-and-Reporting-Financial-Abuse-of-Older-Adults.pdf?source=govdelivery

Oversight, Reporting, and Escalation. As an initial matter, firms should consider designating an individual or department to supervise practices and policies related to endangered population investors, including seniors, vulnerable persons, and persons with diminished capacity. The designated individual could be tasked with establishing firm protocols and processes specific to these issues, implementing internal audits or trend reports to identify red flags in senior transactions, and escalating reports of suspected abuse. Oversight could include enhanced surveillance tools and exception reports that capture transactions and changes in senior customer accounts that increase the firm's potential exposure to regulatory action or civil litigation. For instance, exception reports could be generated based on (among other things):

- Losses in customer accounts in relation to account/portfolio value;
- Losses in customer accounts in relation to customer reported net worth;
- Percentage of customer reported net worth in alternative or illiquid investments;
- Asset allocation mix limits for customer portfolio (or reported net worth);
- Changes in reported investment objectives; and
- Failure to change investment objectives or income at certain ages.

Finally, this individual could be tasked with establishing processes for monitoring fee-based account and investment advisory arrangements to ensure continuing suitability for accounts that are not active.

Although some firms may lack the resources to dedicate a full position to policing these issues, every firm should consider implementing some system of reports and accountability tools to flag potential abuse. For instance, firms should work to identify professionals that consistently target senior investors to ensure proper supervision. Firms should also consider using client demographics to help identify clients with diminished capacity issues and to provide a back-end check on the training provided to advisers and representatives. Red flags should be raised when seniors ask for unsuitable products. Most importantly, reports must be escalated when a potential problem is identified, and prompt remedial action should be taken as appropriate. Documentation policies regarding monitoring, escalation, and action are of course essential to the efficacy of such enhanced policies and procedures.

Communication Networks. One simple tool firms can employ is to create internal communication networks to provide information and feedback on endangered population investor issues. This can be as simple as designating an e-mail address or telephone hotline that is accessible to persons with questions about a particular situation or these issues generally.

Similarly, firms should connect with and/or monitor other organizations and agencies serving seniors and other vulnerable populations to remain informed and up-to-date on the concerns and issues affecting those populations and how those concerns and issues are being addressed. For example, the American Association of Retired Persons and the Alzheimer's Association provide a wealth of information about emerging issues and concerns affecting seniors. For some firms, it may be worthwhile to appoint a person or committee as the designee for monitoring such groups and staying current on the issues and trends specific to seniors and other vulnerable populations.

Policies and Procedures. The principal/supervisory relationship is an important area for policy making with respect to endangered population investors, including seniors, vulnerable persons, and persons with diminished capacity, because it provides the essential means for oversight of representatives' individual client relationships. In light of the additional risks associated with these investor relationships, firms must assure more direct and substantive involvement of line supervisors—and documentation thereof—concerning the opening and handling of such customers' accounts and investments, including:

- Mandatory client contact at specific periods, including at the commencement of each customer relationship, once the client reaches retirement age, once the client retires, and an annual contact to verify objectives and knowledge of their account performance;
- Mandatory periodic supervisory interview of the registered representative or adviser regarding the portfolios of their endangered population investors;
- Mandatory prior approval of all, or certain types, of higher risk products or alternative investments;
- Detailed procedures requiring the client to affirm in writing the receipt of risk disclosure documents for higher risk products (e.g., variable annuities and equity-indexed annuities); and
- Formalized procedures for review and approval of direct investments made by seniors or otherwise vulnerable customers.

In addition to the proposed changes and policies outlined above, a few additional changes to the firm's written supervisory and compliance procedures may be warranted. For instance, firms should consider limitations on product offerings with respect to endangered population investors. Limitations could take the form of outright prohibitions, size, volume, or dollar amount caps, required prior written customer consent, required participation of a supervisor in the product pitch, and/or required post-transaction review and approval.

Further, firms should review the regulatory guidance when designing policies for specific product offerings and then determine the appropriate actions that the firm should take in light of its client and product mix, history of complaints, size, and resources. Potential actions include:

- Providing guidance on how to identify, and what to do, if a registered person suspects that his or her customer is experiencing diminished capacity or is being abused, financially or otherwise, by a family member, caregiver, or other person;
- Banning the use of any designation that includes the word *senior* or *retirement* or maintaining a list of designations approved by a committee, including supervisory,

legal, and/or compliance personnel, based on curriculum, examinations, and continuing education requirements;
- Imposing prohibitions or limitations regarding the sale or exchange of certain types of products to customers older than a certain age;
- Placing additional and more specific restrictions on the list of approved products for endangered population investors;
- Placing more specific restrictions and requirements for prior written approval for any recommendation or sales to senior customers that deviate from the list of approved products or other established parameters concerning investment objections, asset allocation mix, net worth, or personal circumstances;
- Requiring two persons from the firm to attend any in-person consultations, seminars, dinners, or other sales presentations or similar events targeted at customers over a certain age;
- Prohibiting or strictly limiting sales calls on customers in nursing homes, assisted living facilities, or similar special care or elder living settings;
- Developing more specific and detailed requirements regarding the disclosures (and documentation thereof) of the features, risks, and fees of certain products for endangered population investors;
- Mandating secondary, centralized supervisory review of transactions of a certain size involving endangered population investors;
- Requiring enhanced and more specific compliance certifications addressed to diminished capacity issues; and
- Developing specialized policies for communications with senior customers and additional recordkeeping requirements documenting the same, including confirmatory writings of all meetings and phone calls.

Marketing Tactics and Product Evaluation

The final area we focus on for best practice development is the firm's marketing and product materials. Because advertising is closely scrutinized by regulators, member firms and compliance professionals should be cognizant of the content and design of written materials so as to not mislead investors or omit necessary information. For guidance on this, we turn to some items that have been noted by the regulators as "helpful to consider" in reviewing and updating a firm's written procedures addressing sales seminars and advertising:[130]

- Centralizing the process for reviewing and approving proposed seminars and advertising and other materials for the seminars, and including a dedicated compliance person with knowledge of the securities laws and rules with respect to advertising materials. The firm's policies and procedures should clearly set forth the process for proposing seminars and advertising materials, and be made known to all firm employees. Supervisory reviews of advertising and sales materials should generally

---

[130] *See* FINRA, *Protective Senior Investors: Report of Examinations of Securities Firms Providing "Free Lunch" Sales Seminars* (Sept. 2007), http://www.sec.gov/spotlight/seniors/freelunchreport.pdf, Appendix B.

identify disclosure mistakes and potential problem areas to be corrected prior to the time the advertising materials are to be used;
- Policies and procedures for submitting proposals for sales seminars should include specific timeframes for supervisory review and approval. For example, the approval and review process for seminar and advertising material may require submission of all materials three to four weeks prior to the seminar date. This would allow adequate time for supervisors and compliance personnel to review and correct disclosure issues and any other issues identified prior to the seminar;
- All advertising material should be forwarded to the home office for review and approval prior to use, as well as information on seminar guest speakers;
- Creating two levels of supervisory approval for seminars and all sales materials and advertisements to be used at those seminars, including a first level review and approval by a branch manager, followed by a second level review and approval process at the firm's main office;
- Providing written guidance to all individuals who may be involved in sales seminars, including the registered representatives who conduct sales seminars, the branch office manager and other supervisors who review and approve the seminars and sales materials, and also any compliance staff who may review the sales seminars and materials prior to use. The guidance should provide clear explanations of what is permissible and impermissible, both in terms of compliance with the securities laws, and compliance with the firm's own policies;
- Using written checklists to aid firm employees in reviewing and approving sales seminar advertisements and sales literature to ensure that the materials comply with regulatory requirements and the firm's policies;
- Requiring supervisors and/or compliance staff to make written edits to proposed sales seminar materials or advertising, and requiring that such marked-up drafts be provided along with a final copy of the materials (showing that the changes had been made) to the reviewing official for the permanent file;
- Developing and using only standardized, preapproved materials and advertisements for sales seminars, such as requiring that all marketing materials be created at a central level and prohibiting individual registered representatives from creating their own seminar materials or advertisements;
- Maintaining materials for sales seminars in a centralized location, including a copy of the request to host the seminar with indications of approval by the branch office manager and any other authorized approving official. Such a centralized file should include the title of the seminar, date, location, speaker, any guest speakers, the company(ies) they represent, the date the approval was given, and the list of people invited to attend the seminar. The file should also contain a list of attendees, whether they are clients or prospects, a photocopy of the actual seminar ad that ran in the newspaper, the approved marketing pieces that were distributed at the seminar, approved copies of the slide presentation, and any other information given to attendees;
- Expecting branch managers to attend a percentage of the sales seminars presented by the sales people they supervise;

- Using "mystery shoppers" (who are firm employees) on a random basis to attend sales seminars and identify potential disclosure and compliance weaknesses, and report any issues back to the direct supervisors of the seminar hosts; and
- Requiring all registered representatives to certify to their branch manager each month that they provided all advertisements, sales literature, and correspondence items used during the month.

V. CONCLUSION

The retirement boom presents an unprecedented and momentous opportunity for the financial services industry. The needs of seniors and endangered population investors for sound investment advice and appropriate investment vehicles will continue to be critically important to their lives and well-being. These needs provide substantial opportunity for broker-dealers and investment advisers to expand their businesses. Yes, as is often the case, such opportunity comes with risks of potential investor abuse and potential exposure to liability for wrongful conduct.

The risks are magnified because of the nature and vulnerability of senior and other diminished capacity customers. Moreover, the regulators' recent focus on these issues and the documented incidents of actual abuse suggest that each firm must proactively address these issues.

The efforts to refine, tailor, and upgrade a firm's compliance efforts to address the specialized and heightened needs and risks of endangered population investors will involve significant additional costs, time, and complexity. Nevertheless, the added effort is an inevitable consequence of the regulators' focus on senior and vulnerable investor issues. The effort will also enable firms to serve the investment needs of the burgeoning senior population and to avoid the all-too-real and expensive risks of litigation and regulatory sanctions.

At the bottom line, given the huge impact that seniors and other vulnerable investors will have on the financial services industry, it seems that each firm and its investment, supervisory, and compliance professionals have no choice but to proactively address these issues in their business models, compliance efforts, and supervisory policies and procedures.

ABOUT THE AUTHORS

Theodore J. Sawicki is a partner in the Alston & Bird's Securities Litigation Group with more than 28 years of experience in broker-dealer and investment advisory litigation, arbitration, regulatory counseling and representation. He has acted as lead counsel in court cases and arbitrations in 26 states and the Territory of Puerto Rico.

In June 2004, Mr. Sawicki traveled to Dubai, U.A.E., to present a four-day program on securities enforcement and market oversight along with representatives of the SEC and the Dubai Financial Services Authority. In September 1997, he spent two weeks in Croatia as part of a Financial Services Volunteer Corps' independent expert assessment team evaluating shareholder rights following that country's privatization effort and then provided commentary and proposed revisions to the Varazdin, Croatia, OTC Market Surveillance and Enforcement Rules in March 1999. Mr. Sawicki regularly speaks and writes on the topics of arbitration, securities litigation, and SEC regulatory issues and trends and is listed in the 21st edition of *The Best Lawyers in America* for securities litigation.

Melissa J. Gworek is an associate at Alston & Bird LLP and is a member of the firm's Securities Litigation Group. Her practice focuses primarily on securities fraud actions, shareholder derivative suits, corporate investigations, and other complex commercial litigation.

Ms. Gworek received her juris doctor degree in 2012 from the University of Chicago School of Law. While in law school, she served as a comment editor for *The Chicago Journal of International Law* and as a member of the Gendered Violence and the Law Clinic. She completed her undergraduate studies in 2008 at the University of Texas at Austin, majoring in public relations and government, with a minor in business.

CHAPTER 23

Seeking to Avoid Chief Compliance Officer Liability

By J. Christopher Jackson
Calamos Investments

I. INTRODUCTION

It is clear to me that the vast majority of CCOs are working hard and getting good results. But many of you are nonetheless concerned about possible enforcement actions against CCOs....If you read the facts in the cases we bring, you will see that they are not cases against CCOs that were promoting compliance. Instead, they are cases against CCOs that were assisting fraud, ignoring red flags, not asking the tough questions, and not demanding answers.[1]

Chief compliance officers (CCOs) serving in that role in financial services firms are subject to liability. That is a fact. It is reality. It is unlikely to change. That does not mean, however, that the CCO is powerless, that such liability is inevitable, or that there are not a number of "best practices" that can help ensure that your exposure to such liability can be greatly reduced. This is not rocket science, and as we continue to evolve from what I believe to be the "real start" of CCO liability—the passage and enactment of the Final Compliance Rule in the Code of Federal Regulations in December 2003[2]—we continue to gain insight into the types of activities that are likely to lead to the Securities and Exchange Commission (SEC) Division of Enforcement's scope to be trained on the CCO as a defendant.

I submit that in looking at the concept of CCO liability, it is too limiting and myopic to look just at SEC rules or case law. At least two other areas bear examination, but they are in some respects less tangible and more subjective in nature. The first is you, the CCO, and what types of traits, background, and experience it is important that you possess. If you lack certain traits and abilities, you may fall more easily prey to attracting an enforcement action. The second is your firm. What is the "tone at the

---

[1] SEC Commissioner Kara M. Stein, Keynote Address at Compliance Week 2014, Washington, DC, May 19, 2014.
[2] Final Rule: Compliance Programs of Investment Companies and Investment Advisers, 17 CFR Parts 270 and 275; Release Nos. IA-2204 and IC-26299, adopted Dec. 17, 2003; hereinafter, the "Final Compliance Rule."

top"? What is the firm's true belief and commitment to compliance? What resources does your firm devote to compliance, including personnel, training, and technology? Although "one size does not fit all" in the compliance world, certain basic understandings and commitments on behalf of the firm's senior executives, board of directors, and employees need to exist. This is an area where the old adage "actions speak louder than words" is applicable.

This chapter will be laid out sequentially, examining the role of compliance and the CCO, certain of the enforcement actions against CCOs, and finally some key steps CCOs can take to seek to avoid liability.

II. THE ROLE OF COMPLIANCE AND THE CCO

Compliance as a Profession

John H. Walsh, the then-chief counsel of the SEC's Office of Compliance Inspections and Examinations, delivered what has become a seminal speech for the compliance profession in 2002.[3] In his speech entitled "What Makes Compliance a Profession?" Walsh borrowed the characteristics of what makes an occupation a profession from a 1914 book authored by Louis M. Brandeis entitled *Business—A Profession*. Brandeis put forth that in order to be deemed a profession such as law, medicine, and theology, the three characteristics the occupation requires to be present are:

- The necessary training is intellectual, involving knowledge and learning as distinguished from skill;
- Pursuit of the occupation largely for others; and
- The amount of financial return is not the accepted measure of success.[4]

Walsh methodically walked his audience through the case for compliance as a profession, taking each of the Brandeis-identified elements and demonstrating emphatically how the practice of compliance met each one.[5] But importantly, and I would submit, somewhat omnisciently, Walsh argued for yet an additional characteristic of an occupation deemed to be a profession:

> To be truly professional, compliance's special status must be recognized by its practitioners, by those who employ them, and by the members of the public who deal with them. All should respect the public interest that fills this work. Earning compliance that recognition and respect is part of our mission.[6]

---

[3] John H. Walsh, "What Makes Compliance a Profession?" NRS Symposium on the Compliance Profession, Miami Beach, Florida, April 11, 2002.
[4] Id.
[5] Walsh stated: "I think compliance satisfies Brandeis's definition of a profession. Moreover, in these characteristics, we can see some of the professional standards that it should meet. The practice of compliance is an intellectual challenge that should be met through the exercise of expert judgment. Compliance should make sure the customer's interests, and the customer's perspective, are not forgotten. Finally, the successful practice of compliance should be measured by discrete and distinctive standards: does it prevent problems, does [it] establish understandable ethics?"
[6] Walsh, "What Makes Compliance a Profession?"

Final Compliance Rule

In February 2003 the SEC proposed what would become known as the Final Compliance Rule.[7] The SEC proposed that each fund and adviser designate an individual responsible for administering the compliance policies and procedures. To accomplish same, Rule 206(4)-7 and Rule 38a-1 under the Investment Advisers Act of 1940, as amended (Advisers Act) and Investment Company Act of 1940, as amended (1940 Act), respectively, were proposed. Each rule as proposed required certain policies and procedures be adopted by advisory and fund firms and that these policies and procedures be reviewed on an annual basis.[8] The SEC anticipated some concerns regarding potential liability arising from such designation. In footnote 38 of the Proposed Compliance Rule, the SEC noted as follows:

> Designation of a person by an adviser as its chief compliance officer would not, in and of itself, impose upon the person a duty to supervise another person. Thus, a chief compliance officer appointed in compliance with the Proposed Rules would not necessarily be subject to a sanction by us for failure to supervise. A compliance officer that does have supervisory responsibilities will have available the defense discussed above. *See supra* note 13.[9]

It should be noted that the above language was carried over for the most part to the Final Compliance Rule and can be found in footnote 73.[10]

Among the approximately 48 comments received to the Proposed Compliance Rule, the Investment Company Institute picked up on the issue of liability and argued for any final rule to include a safe harbor from liability for persons who reasonably discharge their responsibilities under the rule.[11]

---

[7] Proposed Rule, "Compliance Programs of Investment Companies and Investment Advisers," 17 CFR Parts 270 and 275, Release Nos. IC - 25925 and IA - 2107 (Feb. 5, 2003); hereinafter, the "Proposed Compliance Rule."
[8] *Id.*
[9] *Id.* The Commission's reference to footnote 13 in the Proposed Rule goes to the defense permissible under Section 203 (e)(6) of the Advisers Act. As pointed out in footnote 13, "Section 203(e)(6) of the Advisers Act [15 U.S.C. 80b-3(e)(6)] provides that a person shall not be deemed to have failed to supervise any person if: (i) the adviser had adopted procedures reasonably designed to prevent and detect violations of the federal securities laws; (ii) the adviser had a system in place for applying the procedures; and (iii) the person had reasonably discharged his supervisory responsibilities in accordance with the procedures and had no reason to believe the supervised person was not complying with the procedures."
[10] Final Compliance Rule.
[11] Craig S. Tyle, General Counsel, Investment Company Institute Letter dated April 17, 2003 to Mr. Jonathan G. Katz, available at www.sec.gov/rules/proposed/s70303/s70303-15.pdf. Mr. Tyle noted: "We are concerned that the absence of a safe harbor provision in the rule may result in any violation of law by a fund or its service providers being deemed either a *de facto* violation of the compliance rule or a failure to supervise. To avoid this result, we recommend that Rule 38a-1 expressly provide that no person would be liable under the rule solely because a violation of the securities laws occurs if he or she (1) had a reasonable basis to believe that the compliance policies and procedures adopted pursuant to the rule were not deficient and (2) reasonably discharged his or her obligations under the rule....Moreover, including such a provision in the rule would recognize that persons should not be held liable for violating the rule merely because a compliance failure occurs if they have no reasonable basis to question the established compliance procedures and they have reasonably discharged the duties imposed on them pursuant to the rule."

The Final Compliance Rule noted the need to foster improved compliance by clarifying firms' compliance obligations and to strengthen the hand of compliance personnel in deal with them.[12] In imposing the requirement for a CCO to be designated by advisers, the SEC noted that: "An adviser's chief compliance officer should be competent and knowledgeable regarding the Advisers Act and should be empowered with full responsibility and authority to develop and enforce appropriate policies and procedures for the firm."[13] Likewise, in requiring a CCO for funds, the SEC stated such person should be competent and knowledgeable regarding the federal securities laws and be empowered to develop and to enforce appropriate compliance policies and procedures.

In the Final Compliance Rule, the commission was straightforward in addressing the role of the CCO for a fund, acknowledging that a CCO who is an employee of the fund's investment adviser might be conflicted in his or her duties, and that the nature of the adviser's business may be such so as to "discourage the adviser from making forthright disclosure to fund directors of its compliance failures."[14] The commission noted:

> Thus, a chief compliance officer who fails to fully inform the board of a material compliance failure, or who fails to aggressively pursue noncompliance within the service provider, would risk her position. She would also risk her career, because it would be unlikely for another board of directors to approve such person as a chief compliance officer.[15]

FINRA and the Role of the Chief Compliance Officer

The Financial Industry Regulatory Authority (FINRA), as part of its FINRA Manual, adopted Rule 3130, Annual Certification of Compliance and Supervisory Processes. Rule 3130(a) specifically requires each member firm to designate and specifically identify to FINRA on Schedule A of Form BD one or more principals to serve as a CCO. Unlike the Final Compliance Rule, multiple CCOs are permitted; however, several conditions must be met in such an instance.[16] The CCO for a member firm plays a vital role in the annual certification process undertaken by the member firm's chief executive officer. The chief executive officer (CEO) must have conducted one or more meetings with the CCO(s) in the preceding 12 months, the subject of which satisfies the obligations set forth in FINRA Rule 3130.[17]

The role of the CCO to member firms is of paramount importance. As noted in Supplementary Note .05 to Rule 3130, FINRA points out that a CCO is a primary advisor to

---

[12] Final Compliance Rule.
[13] *Id.*
[14] *Id.*
[15] *Id.* The commission pointed out further that should the CCO go to another fund, the staff would enhance its scrutiny of the fund accordingly. (See footnote 90 of the Final Compliance Rule.)
[16] FINRA Rule 3130 Supplemental Note .02 For example, each designated CCO must be a principal and the member firm shall have precisely defined and documented the areas of primary responsibility assigned to each designated CCO and makes specific provisions for which of the designated CCOs has primary compliance responsibility in areas that can reasonably be expected to overlap.
[17] FINRA Rule 3130(c)2.

the member on its overall compliance scheme and the particular rules, policies and the particularized rules, policies and procedures that the member adopts.[18] This is because the CCO should have expertise in the process of:

- Gaining an understanding of the products, services, or line functions that need to be the subject of written compliance policies and written supervisory procedures;
- Identifying the relevant rules, regulations, laws, and standards of conduct pertaining to such products, services, or line functions based on experience and/or consultation with those persons who have a technical expertise in such areas of the member's business;
- Developing, or advising other business persons charged with the obligation to develop, policies and procedures that are reasonably designed to achieve compliance with those relevant rules, regulations, laws and standards of conduct;
- Evidencing the supervision by the line managers who are responsible for the execution of compliance policies; and
- Developing programs to test compliance with the member's policies and procedures.[19]

Participation in Firm Oversight: Back to Fundamentals

One of a CCO's primary responsibilities concerns firm oversight. This should be systematic and comprehensive in nature. In a speech given in early 2004 to a best practices summit, Lori Richards outlined a seven-step approach that is as sound today as it was when she articulated it in 2004.[20] In summary fashion, those seven steps consist of the following:

1. Conduct an inventory of your firm's compliance obligations under both the federal securities laws and pursuant to your firm's disclosures to investors. This should be done and revisited no less frequently than annually.
2. Identify areas of conflicts of interest. Again, this list will change frequently, as for example where new products or investment strategies are added to the firm. Think about how clients could be harmed. Take into account what types of abusive conduct have been identified in SEC enforcement actions. "Your goal here is to identify conflicts of interest that, if unmitigated, could lead to violations of any type."[21]
3. Match existing compliance practices to your inventory of obligations and conflicts of interest and find any gaps. Word of caution here: Never assume. Never assume when you come into the role of CCO that your firm has all necessary and required policies and procedures in place. Never assume that individuals and departments assigned responsibility under a particular policy and procedure do not need to be reviewed and revisited as it is carried out.
4. Assess the effectiveness of your firm's current compliance functions. "In this stage, determine whether a particular compliance function makes violations less likely and results in the prompt identification of violations."[22] This is particularly

---

[18] FINRA Rule 3130, Supplemental Note .05, "Role of Chief Compliance Officer."
[19] Id.
[20] Lori Richards, "Put the Compliance Rule to Work"; IA Compliance Best Practices Summit; Washington, DC; March 15, 2004.
[21] Id.
[22] Id.

challenging because this step will require the constant assessment of compliance resources in terms of personnel as well as technology that will aid you and your firm in its compliance oversight and obligations. In turn, this assessment will impact at a minimum compliance as well as information technology budgets.

5. Identify additional compliance procedures that are warranted for your firm. This step seems basic and straightforward, but needs to be constantly "top-of-mind" with CCOs. The more obvious triggers for additional compliance policies and procedures are new rules and regulations promulgated by regulatory agencies that impact and oversee your firm, new products or strategies employed by your firm, as well as any new businesses added. A particular note of caution and warning here: More and more frequently the SEC's Division of Enforcement is bring actions and relying on the failure of firms to have in place policies reasonably designed to prevent violations of the Investment Advisers Act or the federal securities laws. Again, this step is basic, but the consequences for missing can be severe.

6. Implement your firm's policies and procedures, in writing, in clear, plain English, setting forth the goal of the compliance procedure, the regularity with which it will be performed and who will perform it. Ensure those responsible understand they are responsible and their role and are adequately trained.

7. Test the compliance procedures. Ms. Richards was correct when she admonished: "You can only ensure your compliance program is working if you test all the various components—and improve any weaknesses found. You should be tweaking your program over time—not simply until the annual review."[23]

There is no question when it comes to firm oversight from a compliance point of view that the CCO is the key driver of the initiative to seek to ensure the firm remains compliant. This can only be done with buy-in from the top, a strong tone-at-the-top, a strong "culture of compliance," the time and resources to systematically assess the firm's business and products and determine the adequacy and need of policies and procedures, the continued surveillance and testing of the compliance system, the identification and timely correction of compliance issues and the reporting out to required constituencies to members of senior management, including any fund and corporate boards, the results of violations and issues found. Such a process is required if a CCO hopes to avoid or insulate him- or herself from the specter of an enforcement action.

III. THE QUESTION OF SUPERVISION

I hope to use my current role to further promote a strong, empowered legal and compliance presence at firms, in part by encouraging legal and compliance personnel to engage and become involved when they see an issue that raises a concern. You should not hesitate to provide advice and help remediate when problems arise. And I do not want you to be concerned that by engaging, you will somehow be exposed to liability. As recent SEC staff guidance makes clear, compliance personnel do not

---

[23] *Id.*

become supervisors solely because they provide advice to, or consult with, business line personnel and the staff does not view compliance or legal personnel generally as supervising business personnel (footnote omitted).[24]

Notwithstanding the words of the SEC's director of the Division of Enforcement, Andrew Ceresney, CCOs, compliance, and legal personnel face a real issue in terms of whether and under what circumstances their conduct and/or role within their organization may be deemed to be "supervisory" in nature. Although a comprehensive discussion of what constitutes supervision is beyond the scope of this chapter, the question of "supervision" is important to the determination of and defenses to possible liability by CCOs. It influences decisions by compliance—as well as by legal personnel of a firm—about whether and to what extent to participate in various aspects of their organization's business, e.g., whether or not to participate as "members" or "voting members" of various committees established at their firms to address various compliance-driven matters such as brokerage practices, soft dollars, valuation and pricing, proxy voting, conflicts of interest, and enterprise risk.

Framework

In considering whether a CCO or compliance officer has taken on supervisory responsibility, there are some key precedents that need to be considered, among which are the Section 21(a) Report in *In the Matter of John H. Gutfreund*,[25] the Ted Urban decision,[26] speeches by SEC Commissioner Daniel M. Gallagher, and frequently asked questions (FAQs) issued by the SEC's Division of Trading and Markets in 2013.[27]

A key precedent in the area of supervisory responsibility involves the Section 21(a) proceeding brought by the SEC against John H. Gutfreund, Thomas W. Strauss, and John W. Meriwether, each of whom were officers of Salomon Brothers, Inc. Donald M. Feuerstein, although not a named respondent in the Section 21(a) proceeding, was a key player in the facts concerning the proceeding and one on whom our focus turns. During the relevant time period covered by the proceeding, Mr. Feuerstein served as the chief legal officer of Salomon and the head of its Legal Department. The head of the Compliance Department reported directly to Mr. Feuerstein. The proceeding turned on certain false bids submitted by Salomon in connection with U.S. Treasury securities auctions that occurred in early 1991. Information was brought to the attention of senior management—Gutfreund, Strauss, and Meriwether—by the head of Salomon's Government Trading Desk, Paul Mozer. Mr. Feuerstein advised senior management that submission of the false bid appeared to be a criminal act and although not legally

---

[24] Andrew Ceresney, director of Division of Enforcement, SEC, Keynote Address at Compliance Week 2014, Washington, DC, May 20, 2014.
[25] *In re John H. Gutfreund*, Exchange Act Release No. 31554, Dec. 3, 1992.
[26] *In the Matter of Theodore W. Urban*, Admin. Proc. File No. 3-13655, Initial Decision Rel. No. 402, Sept. 8, 2010.
[27] Frequently Asked Questions about Liability of Compliance and Legal Personnel at Broker-Dealers Under Sections 15(b)(4) and 15(b)(6) of the Exchange Act(Sept. 30, 2013), http://www.sec.gov/decisions/marketreg/faq-cco-supervision-093013.htm

required to be, ought to be reported to the government. Senior managers indicated they would do so as well as undertake an investigation. For a period of months senior management neither investigated the matter nor disciplined or imposed limitations on the head of the Government Trading Desk: Mozer. Further, senior management did not report the initial false bid to the government for a period of months. Meanwhile, during this period of nonaction, Mr. Mozer committed additional violations of the federal securities laws with respect to two subsequent U.S. Treasury auctions. In its proceeding, the SEC did not charge Gutfreund, Strauss, or Meriwether with participation in the underlying violations but with a failure to supervise. The SEC, in reliance on Section 15(b)(4)(E) of the Securities Exchange Act of 1934, cited these individuals with a failure to supervise, noting:

> The supervisory obligations imposed by the federal securities laws require a vigorous response even to indications of wrongdoing. Many of the Commission's cases involving a failure to supervise arise from situations where supervisors were aware only of 'red flags' or 'suggestions' of irregularity, rather than situations where, as here, supervisors were explicitly informed of an illegal act (footnote omitted).

With respect to Mr. Feuerstein, our primary focus here, the SEC noted that although he pointed out the activity might rise to criminal activity and should be reported to the government, he did not direct that an inquiry be undertaken and he did not recommend appropriate procedures be implemented, which procedures should have been reasonably designed to prevent and detect future misconduct and he did not advise his firm's Compliance Department of the false bid. The SEC made the decision that the facts presented in this proceeding provided "an appropriate opportunity to amplify our views on the supervisory responsibilities of legal and compliance officers in Feuerstein's position, we have not named him as a respondent in this proceeding."[28] The commission went on to point out:

> Employees of brokerage firms who have legal or compliance responsibilities do not become 'supervisors' for purposes of Sections 15(b)(4)(E) and 15(b)(6) solely because they occupy those positions. Rather, determining if a particular person is a "supervisor" depends on whether, under the facts and circumstances of a particular case, that person has a requisite degree of responsibility, ability or authority to affect the conduct of the employee whose behavior is at issue. (footnote omitted) Thus, persons occupying positions in the legal or compliance departments of broker-dealers have been found by the Commission to be "supervisors" for purposes of Sections 15(b)(4)(E) and 15(b)(6) under certain circumstances. (footnote omitted).[29]

---

[28] *In re John H. Gutfreund.*
[29] *Id.*

Under the facts and circumstances—given Feuerstein's position—the commission stated that such a person "shares in the responsibilities to take appropriate action to respond to the misconduct."[30] The SEC went further noting that once someone in Feuerstein's position becomes involved in formulating management's response to a problem, "he or she is obligated to take affirmative steps to ensure appropriate action is taken to address the misconduct."[31]

What if a person in Feuerstein's position takes "appropriate steps," but management fails to act? The commission stated that in that situation, one would have to consider "additional steps" appropriate to address the matter. "These steps may include disclosure of the matter to the entity's board of directors, resignation from the firm, or disclosure to regulatory authorities."[32]

As we will see, *In re John H. Gutfreund* is oft cited when considering whether as a CCO one is taking on supervisory responsibility. As noted by the commission in *Gutfreund*, based upon the facts and circumstances, a CCO may be considered to have picked up "supervisory responsibility."[33] Our analysis, however, must not stop here.

In an action that captivated the entire compliance industry, *In the Matter of Theodore W. Urban,* an administrative proceeding brought by the SEC against Ted Urban,[34] the commission charged Mr. Urban with a failure to supervise. Although the case against Mr. Urban is "a sobering one"[35] in that Mr. Urban, the firm's general counsel, was held to be a supervisor under the *Gutfreund* standard, the case was dismissed[36] because the administrative law judge held that Mr. Urban did not fail in his duties as a supervisor. A thorough understanding of the facts leading up to the administrative proceeding is important for any CCO to understand. Some key facts in the *Urban* case were that Mr. Urban's legal and compliance opinions were viewed as "authoritative"; Urban's recommendations were generally followed by people in the business units; and Urban

---

[30] *Id.*
[31] *Id.*
[32] *Id.*
[33] Commissioner Daniel M. Gallagher, in his speech at "The SEC Speaks in 2012" (Feb. 24, 2012), in addressing the very issue of the failure to supervise by chief compliance officers and in-house legal counsel, noted the following: "Although *Gutfreund* was a report issued in connection with a settlement, and therefore, its precedential value is not the same as a formal commission adjudication, for those struggling for resolution on the question of supervisory authority, *Gutfreund* remains a key authority."
[34] *In the Matter of Theodore W. Urban* (Initial Decision Rel. No. 402, Admin Pro File No. 3-13655, Sept. 8, 2010).
[35] *See* Commissioner Daniel M. Gallagher, Keynote Address: Investment Adviser Association Investment Adviser Compliance Conference/2012 (March 8, 2012), http://www.sec.gov/News/Speech/Detail/Speech/1365171490028
[36] *In the Matter of Theodore Urban* (Sept. 8, 2010, Admin. Proc. File No. 3-13655). This administrative proceeding followed an order instituting proceedings (OIP) issued by the SEC (Oct. 19, 2009) pursuant to Section 15(b) of the Securities Exchange Act of 1934 and Section 203(f) of the Investment Advisers Act of 1940. The OIP alleges that Theodore Urban of Ferris, Baker Watts, Inc.'s general counsel, executive vice president, and voting member of the FBW Board of Directors, the Executive Committee of the Board of Directors, and the Credit Committee failed reasonably to supervise Stephen Glantz, a broker, with a view to detecting and preventing Glantz's violation of Section 17(a) of the Securities Act of 1933. The SEC concluded that "in view of the allegations made by the Division of Enforcement, the commission deems it necessary and appropriate in the public interest that public administrative proceedings be instituted [to make certain enumerated findings]."

served as a member of the firm's Credit and Risk Committees that reviewed compliance concerns. In the Urban administrative proceeding, Chief Administrative Law Judge Brenda Murray reviewed the testimony, of among others, an expert witness for the SEC's Division of Enforcement, David E. Paulukaitis, who was qualified as an expert on the operations and supervision of broker-dealers. Based upon the facts presented, Mr. Paulukatis saw a "direct parallel" between Urban and the chief legal officer, Donald M. Feuerstein in *Gutfreund*.[37]

The *Urban* case will continue to be a pivotal case when it comes to the whole area of CCO liability, albeit, we will see that the SEC clarifies that the *Urban* case "shall be of no effect."[38]

After the decision in *Urban,* SEC Commissioner Daniel M. Gallagher, in a series of speeches given in 2012 and 2013, took up the entire area of failure to supervise by compliance and legal officers, noting, among other things a dearth of guidance for determining whether a given member of a firm's legal or compliance staff is a "supervisor" for purposes of Exchange Act liability.[39] Commissioner Gallagher, who is one of the smartest and most articulate spokesmen for issues facing the legal and compliance professions in the financial services industry, frames the issue in the following way:

> Broker-dealers and investment advisers employ legal and compliance personnel to provide advice and guidance to firms and their employees regarding the application of laws and regulations to their businesses. Almost by definition, legal and compliance personnel work outside the direct chain of supervision for business activities, and few, if any, would think of themselves as "supervising" day-to-day activity. A key question, therefore, is at what point can legal and compliance personnel be reasonably deemed "supervisors" as they carry out their responsibility to prevent and, if necessary, address violations of laws or regulations by firm employees and to provide advice and guidance to management?[40]

Commissioner Gallagher reviewed the decisions in both the *Gutfreund* and *Urban* matters, noting that once a person becomes involved in formulating management's response to a problem, he or she is obligated to take affirmative steps to ensure appropriate action is taken.[41] Gallaher points out the critical role played by compliance and legal personnel within regulated firms, noting the "dilemma" that may arise when seeking to carry out their roles and becoming very engaged in issues facing their firms and the inevitable question of whether they have somehow crossed the line into being deemed a "supervisor." "Thus, the commission's position on supervisory liability for

---

[37] *In the Matter of Theodore Urban* at page 40. As noted, "Paulukaitis contended that Urban failed reasonably to supervise Glantz with a view to preventing violations of the Exchange Act because he did not reasonably and decisively respond to 'red flags' concerning Glantz's conduct and deficiencies in Glantz's supervision."
[38] *In the Matter of Theodore Urban* at FAQ No. 7.
[39] Gallagher, Remarks at "The SEC Speaks in 2012," Washington, DC (Feb. 24, 2012).
[40] Gallagher, Remarks at "The SEC Speaks in 2012" at page 3.
[41] Gallagher, Remarks at "The SEC Speaks in 2012," at page 5.

legal and compliance personnel may have had the perverse effect of increasing the risk of supervisory liability in direct proportion to the intensity of their engagement in legal and compliance activities."[42] Commissioner Gallagher sounded the call for the SEC to provide a "framework" that would allow compliance and legal officers of a company "to jump into crisis" when required without having to worry that they may have picked up the role of a supervisor.

Committee Involvement

Commissioner Gallagher, in his speech above, after sounding the need for further guidance in the area of supervision, concluded his presentation by admonishing legal and compliance officers of the types of activities that might place them squarely within the sight of being deemed a supervisor.[43] Commissioner Gallagher pointed to participation by legal and compliance officers on boards and committees within their firm. In my view, participation by legal and compliance personnel in the various committees established by their firms is a key role that such personnel play and need to play within their firms. But, it is how and in what way they participate that create a key question. To foreshadow my view and strong admonition, legal and compliance personnel should only function in a nonmember, nonvoting, advisory capacity only. In other words, legal and compliance personnel's presence at committee meetings (depending upon the type of committee) is critical, but the role they play is equally important to the question of taking on supervisory responsibility.

Commissioner Gallagher continued to sound the call for increased guidance in the area of legal and compliance personnel and the issue of supervision in a speech he gave shortly after his SEC Speaks remarks noted above.[44] He echoed the themes of his recent speech and emphasized again: "The business of regulated entities inherently involves regulatory issues at every turn, and, accordingly, the commission should want legal and compliance departments involved in the discussion of most issues. We must strive to ensure that failure-to-supervise liability never deters legal and compliance personnel from diving into the firm's real-world legal and compliance problems."[45]

Commissioner Gallagher, perhaps under the theory that "three times is a charm," again raised the issue of failure-to-supervise in his 2013 speech delivered to the National Compliance Outreach Program for Broker-Dealers.[46] Sounding his familiar themes and concerns, Commissioner Gallagher noted:

---

[42] Gallagher, Remarks at "The SEC Speaks in 2012," at page 6.
[43] Commissioner Gallagher put it this way: "At the same time, however, it is critically important for in-house lawyers and compliance officers to be mindful of the types of activities that might indicate the type of supervisory control the commission discussed in *Gutfreund*."
[44] Keynote Address: Investment Adviser Association Investment Adviser Compliance Conference/2012, Arlington, Va.(March 8, 2012), http://www.sec.gov/News/Speech/Detail/Speech/1365171490028
[45] Keynote Address at page 10.
[46] Remarks at The 2013 National Compliance Outreach Program for Broker-Dealers, Washington, DC (Apr. 9, 2013), http://www.sec.gov/News/Speech/Detail/Speech/1365171515226

I worry, however, that the commission's current position on supervisory liability skews in the opposite direction, reducing the risks of liability only for those who intentionally chose inaction over action. As we pursue clarity on this issue, we must avoid establishing a rigid set of expectations based on bright-line rules that further discourage compliance officers from acting out of fear that any "wrong" decision they make might subject them to heightened regulatory scrutiny. Rather, an optimal compliance regime requires a flexible regulatory framework that incentivizes compliance officers to fully engage in the many difficult regulatory and business decisions that firms face every day.

In late 2013, the SEC's Division of Trading and Markets issued its Frequently Asked Questions About Liability of Compliance and Legal Personnel at Broker-Dealers under Sections 15(b)(4) and 15(b)(6) of the Exchange Act.[47] In its preamble to its FAQs, the Division of Trading and Markets noted:

> Liability for failure to supervise is a facts and circumstances determination. The purpose of these FAQs is to provide staff guidance to consider in assessing whether particular facts and circumstances result in potential supervisory liability for broker-dealers' compliance and legal personnel. The Exchange Act does not presume that a broker-dealer's compliance or legal personnel are supervisors solely by virtue of their compliance or legal functions. Rather, the question is whether compliance or legal personnel have supervisory authority over business units or other personnel outside the compliance and legal departments as could be the case, for example, if a chief executive or operating officer also is the firm's chief compliance officer. Supervisory authority also can be implicitly delegated to, or assumed by, compliance or legal personnel" (footnotes omitted).[48]

There are a number of key points to take from the Division of Trading and Markets' FAQs, which are set forth below and some of which will be addressed when we address key steps and considerations CCOs can take to seek to delimit the specter of attracting liability because of their compliance role. Key points include the following:

- As specifically pointed out by the Division of Trading and Markets, the FAQs represent the views of the Division of Trading and Markets and not the views of the SEC;
- These are the FAQs of the Division of Trading and Markets going to the liability compliance and legal personnel at broker-dealers. There are not currently FAQs issued by the SEC's Division of Investment Management regarding the liability of compliance and legal personnel at investment advisory firms (some take the view that the FAQs apply equally to CCOs of investment advisory firms);

---

[47] Frequently Asked Questions About Liability of Compliance and Legal Personnel at Broker-Dealers under Sections 15(b)(4) and 15(b)(6) of the Exchange Act, http://www.sec.gov/divisions/marketreg/faq-cco-supervision-093013.htm
[48] *Id.*

- Liability for failure to supervise is a facts and circumstances determination. The FAQs look at certain facts and circumstances;
- SEC notes most enforcement actions against individuals for failure to supervise have involved business line personnel. Cases involving compliance and legal personnel are brought when they have been delegated or have assumed "supervisory responsibility" for particular activities or situations;
- "Supervisory responsibility" equals the requisite degree of responsibility, ability or authority to affect the conduct of the employee whose behavior is at issue;
- Compliance and legal personnel are not "supervisors" of business line personnel for Exchange Act purposes solely because they occupy compliance or legal positions[49];
- A person's actual responsibilities and authority, rather than, for example, his or her "line" or "nonline" status, determine whether he or she is a supervisor[50];
- Compliance and legal personnel do not become "supervisors" solely because they have provided advice or counsel concerning compliance or legal issues to business line personnel, or assisted in the remediation of an issue[51];
- Compliance and legal personnel can establish and implement a robust compliance program without being considered "supervisors"[52];
- Compliance and legal personnel do not become supervisors solely because they participate in, provide advice to, or consult with a management or other committee[53] (serving on company committees is a key concern of CCOs and in-house legal personnel and is worth considered thought)[54]; and
- Compliance and legal personnel do not become supervisors solely because they provide advice to, or consult with, senior management.[55]

IV. ENFORCEMENT ACTIONS AGAINST CCOs

CCOs are not immune from enforcement actions. Although this statement is nothing new, it would appear that cases against those in compliance have been on the increase and as well, the concern among compliance officers that the "target on their back" has increased in both size and hue. I believe there are at least two main factors behind this trend: the Final Compliance Rule (discussed above) and Bernie Madoff, the crime by whom, as we have seen, has caused a move toward increased commission action in the area of enforcement.[56] Under the leadership of the SEC's Division of Enforcement's Robert Khuzami—he himself a former federal prosecutor with the U.S. Attorney's

---

[49] Frequently Asked Questions FAQ 1.
[50] Frequently Asked Questions FAQ 2. The Division of Trading and Markets sets forth in its Answer to FAQ 2 six key questions to consider in this regard.
[51] Frequently Asked Questions FAQ 3.
[52] Frequently Asked Questions FAQ 4.
[53] Frequently Asked Questions FAQ 5.
[54] Indeed, and as discussed later in this chapter, the Division of Trading and Markets points out in footnote 10 of the FAQs as follows: "Firms should evaluate what role legal or compliance personnel perform on management or other committees. In this regard, broker-dealers could consider whether legal or compliance should serve ex officio, as nonvoting members, serving in an active but advisory role to the committee." Service on committees will be discussed.
[55] Frequently Asked Questions FAQ 6.
[56] See SEC Press Release 2008-293, "SEC Charges Bernard L. Madoff for Multi-Billion Dollar Ponzi Scheme."

Office for the Southern District of New York—the Division of Enforcement established specialized units to focus on specific areas, including, asset management.[57] Mr. Khuzami, in the SEC press release announcing his appointment as the new director of the SEC's Division of Enforcement, had this to say: "As head of the SEC's Division of Enforcement, the staff and I will relentlessly pursue and bring to justice those whose misconduct infects our markets, corrodes investor confidence, and has caused so much financial suffering."[58] The work and efforts commenced by Mr. Khuzami are alive and working today. One has to look no further than current Chairman Mary Jo White's "broken windows" speech as evidence of this fact.[59] Indeed, in its 2014 Agency Financial Report, it was noted that the Enforcement Division continued to bring new and innovative approaches to widen its enforcement footprint and deter wrongdoers.[60] The SEC noted in that report: "The successful results over the past year sent a strong message to the financial markets that violations would be uncovered and punished, *regardless of the size of the entity, position of the individual or magnitude of the wrongdoing*" (emphasis added.)[61]

Any chapter on CCO liability would naturally review a number of enforcement actions brought against CCOs. Such enforcement actions are covered elsewhere in this book.

V. KEY STEPS TO TAKE TO SEEK TO AVOID LIABILITY

Recommended Actions to Prevent the Specter of an Enforcement Action Against Compliance Officers

There are a number of steps you can take as a compliance or legal officer to seek to avoid the specter of an enforcement action against you during your compliance/legal

---

[57] *See* SEC Press Release 2010-5, "SEC Names New Specialized Unit Chiefs and Head of New Office of Market Intelligence" (Jan. 13, 2010). Mr. Khuzami noted: "Two great challenges face every enforcement authority policing our securities markets: the complexity and high-velocity pace of innovation in financial products, transactions, and markets, and the willingness of violators to use every trick to cover their tracks.... These specialized units address both challenges through improved understanding of complex products and markets, earlier and better capability to detect emerging fraud and misconduct, greater capacity to file cases with strike-force speed, and an increase in expertise throughout the division. And by making connections between similar tips from different outside sources, our new Office of Market Intelligence will enable the division to better focus resources on those tips and referrals with the greatest potential for uncovering wrongdoing."

[58] *See* SEC Press Release 2009-31 (Feb. 19, 2009).

[59] Mary Jo White, "Remarks at the Securities Enforcement Forum," Washington, DC (Oct. 9, 2013). The theory is that no infraction is too small to be uncovered and punished. As explained by Ms. White, "The underpinning for this strategy was outlined in an article, which many of you will have read or heard of, titled, 'Broken Windows' (citation omitted). The theory is that when a window is broken and someone fixes it, it is a sign that disorder will not be tolerated. But, when a broken window is not fixed, it 'is a signal that no one cares, and so breaking more windows costs nothing' (citation omitted). The same theory can be applied to our securities markets: Minor violations that are overlooked or ignored can feed bigger ones, and, perhaps more importantly, can foster a culture where laws are increasingly treated as toothless guidelines. And so, I believe it is important to pursue even the smallest infractions. Retail investors, in particular, need to be protected from unscrupulous advisers and brokers, whatever their size of the violation that victimizes the investor."

[60] SEC, Agency Financial Report, Fiscal Year 2014.

[61] SEC, Agency Financial Report, page 13.

career. Many of the suggestions covered here are themselves covered in part or in whole by other chapters in this book. None of the suggested actions, in and of itself, will "insulate" you from liability, but taken collectively will provide a powerful deterrent to possible enforcement actions. None of these suggestions is "cosmic" or requires the proverbial "rocket scientist" to deduce or figure out. In fact, none of the suggestions is intended to be so characterized. I submit that if you adhere to each suggestion in your firm, your chances of drawing an enforcement action will be diminished. The suggestions are derived in part from existing case law, regulatory guidance and based on experienced. There is no order of priority.

Step 1: Help to Set the Tone at the Top. For years the SEC has admonished firms on the need for a clear and definitive tone at the top: the true "buy-in" by members of senior management to compliance. The tone at the top cannot be fabricated or faked. It either exists or it does not exist. The careful compliance officer will take steps to help ensure its existence by his or her frequent meetings with top executives, documented agenda items covered in those meetings, firmwide communications by senior executives on the importance of compliance, as well as communications on distinct compliance issues under certain circumstances. For example, if a new regulation has come into effect that affects the firm, a brief and concise directive from the firm's CEO to all associates highlighting the change and stressing the need to be aware and comply is beneficial. As another example, the Compliance Department picks up on a number of violations in the same area or involving a particular policy or procedure, so a well drafted reminder to all associates by the CEO may be in order.

A warning must be made here because it can sometimes determine or dictate the fate of a CCO or legal personnel in dealing with their firms. If the CCO believes—or there is any doubt—that the firm for which he or she works has a very strong tone at the top, then he or she needs to strongly consider whether to remain at the firm.

Step 2: Design Policies and Procedures. For compliance officers, a comprehensive set of compliance policies and procedures is vitally important. As is often noted, "canned" versions or "off-the-shelf" versions of policies and procedures need to be avoided and instead a comprehensive set of policies and procedures designed for the specific firm need to be adopted and followed.[62] All policies and procedures must be reviewed at least annually, and these reviews need to be documented.[63]

---

[62] *See, e.g., In the Matter of Du Pasquier & Co., Inc.* (IAA Rel. No. 4004; Jan. 21, 2015). The SEC noted, among other things, that the firm failed to adopt a comprehensive set of policies and procedures and those that it did adopt came from a template that was not in all cases customized to the firm. The SEC stated: "From at least 2009 forward, du Pasquier relied on an off-the-shelf investment advisory compliance manual template. Du Pasquier tailored a number of sections of the template appropriately but failed to edit certain others, leaving the firm without a customized set of established procedures. For example, on the issue of safeguarding client information, the template provided a number of different possible procedures and advised that certain security measures 'should' be taken by the firm. Du Pasquier retained that language from the template unedited, without clarifying which of the measures it would use."

[63] Rule 38a-1 of the Investment Company Act of 1940 contains specific provisions relating to fund policies and procedures, among which are that such policies and procedures of the fund and each investment adviser, principal underwriter, administrator, and transfer agent be reviewed annually.

Step 3: "Mind the Gap." –Borrowing a phrase from London's subway system, the Tube, it is important that compliance personnel undertake systematically a gap analysis of the firm's existing policies and procedures. New laws, regulations, and new products introduced by the firm must be taken into consideration when the CCO performs a gap analysis. The SEC's Division of Enforcement has been quick to bring actions alleging violations of the Investment Advisers Act of 1940, as amended Rule 206(4)-7, as well as the Investment Company Act of 1940, as amended Rule 38a-1.[64] Before leaving this key step, in a recent action against a firm and its CCO, the SEC found there to be a willful violation of Rule 206(4)-7, in that the firm failed to adopt and implement policies and procedures to assess and monitor the outside business activities of its employees and disclose conflicts of interest to the funds' boards and to advisory clients.[65]

Step 4: Map the Policies and Procedures. For each policy and procedure, a mapping should be performed that clearly lays out for each policy and each procedure what is being addressed and by whom specifically. What role does compliance/legal play? What is the construct? Do your policies and procedures, or other documents, identify persons other than compliance/legal personnel as responsible for supervising, or for overseeing, one or more business persons or activities?[66]

Step 5: Undertake Awareness and Training. Ensure that those specifically responsible for a specific policy and procedure are aware they are responsible and are properly trained to help ensure full adherence to the particular policy or procedure. Firmwide training

---

[64] 17 CFR 270.38a-1, Compliance Procedures and Practices of Certain Investment Companies. Rule 38a-1(a) provides as follows: (a) Each registered investment company and business development company ("fund") must: (1) *Policies and procedures*. Adopt and implement written policies and procedures reasonably designed to prevent violation of the federal securities laws by the fund, including policies and procedures that provide for the oversight of compliance by each investment adviser, principal underwriter, administrator, and transfer agent of the fund; (2) *Board approval*. Obtain the approval of the fund's Board of Directors, including a majority of directors who are not interested persons of the fund, of the fund's policies and procedures and those of each investment adviser, principal underwriter, administrator, and transfer agent of the fund, which approval must be based on a finding by the board that the policies and procedures are reasonably designed to prevent violation of the federal securities laws by the fund, and by each investment adviser, principal underwriter, administrator, and transfer agent of the fund; (3) *Annual review*. Review, no less frequently than annually, the adequacy of the policies and procedures of the fund and of each investment adviser, principal underwriter, administrator, and transfer agent and the effectiveness of their implementation[.]

[65] *In the Matter of Blackrock Advisors, LLC and Bartholomew A. Battista,* Inv. Adv. Rel. 4065/April 20, 2015. As noted by SEC in its Order: "As a result of the conduct described above, BlackRock willfully violated Section 206(4) of the Advisers Act and Rule 206(4)-7 thereunder by failing to adopt and implement written policies and procedures reasonably designed to prevent violations of the Advisers Act and its rules. BlackRock failed to adopt and implement written policies and procedures to assess and monitor the outside activities of its employees and to disclose conflicts of interest to the funds' boards and to advisory clients. Battista caused BlackRock's compliance-related violations. "36. As a result of the conduct described above, BlackRock and Battista caused certain BlackRock funds' violations of Rule 38a-1(a) under the Investment Company Act. Rule 38a-1(a)(4)(iii)(B) requires registered investment companies, through their chief compliance officer, to provide a written report at least annually to the fund's board of directors that addresses each material compliance matter that occurred since the date of the last report. Rule 38a-1, in pertinent part, defines a "material compliance matter" as any compliance matter about which the fund's board of directors would reasonably need to know to oversee fund compliance, and that involves, without limitation, a violation of the policies and procedures of its investment adviser. BlackRock and Battista caused the failures by certain BlackRock funds to report all material compliance matters —namely Rice's violations of BlackRock's private investment policy—to their Boards of Directors."

[66] Frequently Asked Questions at page 2.

is a necessity and should be undertaken with respect to new regulations, as part of an annual or more frequent refresher, or when specific compliance issues have surfaced.

Step 6: Decide About Committees—To Serve or Not to Serve? It is, will, and should be expected and anticipated that compliance and legal personnel will serve in some capacity in a number of committees within their firms; e.g., enterprise's Risk Committee, Conflicts of Interest Committee, Brokerage Practices (soft dollars/best execution) Committee, Proxy Voting Committee, Valuation Committee, etc. Should compliance professionals be actual "members" of these committees? Should they be a "voting members" of the committees? These are questions that several years ago would not necessarily have been asked. That is no longer the case. Compliance and legal personnel serve a vital role and function on committees. That said, compliance and legal personnel should position themselves as "advisors" to committees upon which they sit, but not as members or voting members.

Consider the SEC's Division of Trading Markets' carefully worded answer to Question 5 set forth in its Frequently Asked Questions about Liability of Compliance and Legal Personnel at Broker-Dealers under Sections 15 (b)(4) and 15(b)(6) of the Exchange Act, wherein the commission states:

> Compliance and legal personnel do not become 'supervisors' solely because they *participate in, provide advice to, or consult with a management or other committee.* As explained above, the determination whether a particular person is a supervisor depends on whether, under the facts and circumstances of a particular case, that person has the requisite degree of responsibility, ability or authority to affect the conduct of the employee whose behavior is at issue (citation omitted) (emphasis added).

The division FAQ goes on, however, in endnote 10 to state: "Firms should evaluate what role legal or compliance personnel perform on management or other committees. In this regard, broker-dealers could consider whether legal or compliance personnel should serve ex officio, as nonvoting members, serving in an active but advisory role to the committee."

Each committee established by your firm should operate pursuant to a well thought out and written charter. Among the items covered in the committee charter will be those firm members who participate as members—voting and nonvoting—on the committee. I advise that legal and compliance personnel be neither, but rather, as noted above, serve in an advisory capacity. This role serves at least two key purposes: With respect to compliance personnel, this role helps with the argument that compliance personnel are not taking on a supervisory function; second, with respect to legal personnel, an advisory role can aid in seeking to protect the attorney-client privilege that may arise in the providing of legal advice and judgments to the committee.

Lastly, to emphasize a previous point with respect to the FAQs issued by the Division of Trading and Markets, the FAQs are addressed to broker-dealers and are not specifically aimed at investment advisers. Notwithstanding, this guidance can (and should) serve investment advisory firms as well.

Step 7: Ensure Competency and Stay Current. It should go without saying that in order to serve in the role of a CCO one must be competent to do so. There are many different paths into the role of compliance as well as a number of different innovative strategies to launch an individual in a compliance career described in this book. It is vitally important for anyone in the field of compliance to ensure he or she has developed the required skills to deal in this important area. Constant learning must be undertaken, and staying abreast of key developments is a must.[67]

Step 8: Perform Testing and Surveillance. The importance of testing—periodic, transactional, and forensic—should not be underestimated when it comes to compliance programs and helping to avoid major compliance issues,. Some of these issues could lead to sanctions against compliance personnel. Compliance testing is a key function undertaken by the Compliance Department. Testing and surveillance, properly done, can help to identify and deal with red flags before they become much bigger and widespread issues.

Step 9: – Hire Resources (Personnel). Having and maintaining an adequately staffed Compliance Department will help to ensure that compliance functions cover the operations and business of the firm. Overextended CCOs or CCOs wearing multiple hats can be key contributors to compliance issues, problems, and enforcement actions. For example, insufficient time and attention paid to the firm's policies and procedures may result in gaps, leading the firm and its CCO to being exposed to violations of Rule 206(4)-7 of the Investment Advisers Act of 1940, as amended.

Step 10: Provide Resources (Technology). As a corollary to the previous step, firms engaged in the asset management business must ensure they have adequate technology in place to aid in the overall compliance function, whether that be effective trade and order management systems, investment guideline and restriction monitoring systems (allowing for pro forma and post-trade testing), systems that allow for implementation of codes of ethics (including the preclearance of trades by access persons and investment personnel), contract monitoring systems, or other. Technology is constantly evolving—witness the cloud—and it is key in order to run a comprehensive and efficient compliance system that the firm allocates sufficient resources to technology and to technological advances.[68]

Step 11: Achieve Board and Firm-Wide Buy-In. As a corollary to Step 1, the value of a well-educated and well-advised board, both at the corporate level and the fund

---

[67] *See,* e.g., Rita Drew, founder and president, National Compliance Services White Paper, Liability Exposure of Chief Compliance Officers," National Compliance Services, page 6, www.ncsonline.com. Ms. Drew submits the following: "CCOs can avoid sanctions and harsh words from the SEC by documenting their efforts to increase their knowledge of their compliance obligations." Ms. Drew suggests participating in the SEC's annual Compliance Outreach Program, attending compliance seminars, and documenting their attendance and by providing training to advisory personnel.

[68] At most major compliance conferences, several software vendors will attend and not only encourage conference attendees to review various vendors and their products, but to engage in live demonstrations as well. This presents one way for CCOs and compliance personnel to stay current on the tools available to help them and their firms implement various aspects of their compliance program and/or monitor various parts of the firm's activities.

level, is indispensable to the overall compliance effort of any firm and its registered investment companies. For the CCO the board can be used as both a "sword" and a "shield." In the first instance, the governing body of your firm—whether set up as a limited liability company, a corporation, or a general or limited partnership—helps to set the overall compliance tone of the organization along with members of senior management. This can be done in several ways (1) allowing for direct reporting of the CCO to the board or head of an Audit Committee, (2) requiring routine in-person reporting to the corporate board, (3) using executive sessions with the CCO attended by only independent board members and their counsel, (4) the budgeting process (seeking to determine whether adequate resources are devoted to the firm given its size, nature of its products and services and complexity), (5) following up on red flags or compliance issues identified by the firm's CCO and (6) ensuring a direct pipeline at all times in the event the CCO believes something needs to be brought to the board's attention during a time when no board meeting is scheduled to occur.

Fund boards can serve the same purpose as a firm's corporate board in addition to the matters that are already incumbent upon the board by various federal securities laws, the primary one among which is the 1940 Act. Although a discussion of a registered investment company's corporate governance and the responsibilities of fund boards is beyond the scope of this chapter, it is important to note the board's role in fund and service provider policies and procedures. As noted in Steps 2 and 3, having comprehensive policies and procedures, having them reviewed and approved by the fund board as required, is absolutely essential to having a sound compliance program and will protect a firm's CCO.[69]

The key relationship played by a fund board and relationship with the CCO is examined in the Report of the Mutual Fund Directors Forum: The Board/CCO Relationship.[70] The report addresses the board's role in fostering a strong culture of compliance. It states, in part:

> While the board is not physically present at the adviser's place of business every day, the board nonetheless plays an important role in establishing the compliance tone at the organization. The board itself can set a tone during board meetings that compliance is a priority by addressing compliance and related breeches with an appropriate level of seriousness and weight. The board can work to establish and promote an environment at the adviser that supports the CCO, in part by making clear to the adviser that the CCO acts as the representative of the board.[71]

Step 12: Respond to Red Flags/Documentation. CCOs need to respond affirmatively to issues giving rise to potential compliance problems, whether the issue be conflicts of interest, code of ethics violations, investment guidelines and restriction monitoring

---

[69] Rule 38a-1 of the Investment Company Act of 1940.
[70] Available at: http://www.mfdf.org/images/uploads/newsroom/Board-CCO_Relationship._4.2015.pdf
[71] Report of the Mutual Fund Directors Forum at page 6.

and violations, trade errors, policy and procedure violations, or some other among the other seeming ubiquitous issues that can arise during the course of overseeing a firm's compliance program. Red flags need to be identified and systematically dealt with, and resolutions should be documented in a form that can demonstrate the process followed and the result obtained. CCOs can and will be held liable when they either fail to act or their actions failed to properly address a compliance matter.

Step 13: Undertake the Annual Review. The Advisers Act and the 1940 Act require that an annual review be undertaken.[72] Unlike Rule 38a-1 of the 1940 Act, Rule 206(4)-7 of the Advisers Act does not require the annual review to be in writing. In my view the annual review should always be written and its contents include, but not by way of limitation, an executive summary, an adequate review the CCO's and firm's activities, policies and procedures, testing, material compliance matters (as defined in Rule 38a-1),[73] any enhancements to the compliance program and personnel, and new products and strategies introduced—all within the year covered by the review.[74]

Step 14: Use Outside Experts. A comprehensive compliance program should include a budget for use of outside compliance and legal experts on an annual basis. Too often, problems arising at investment advisory and investment companies present various issues of first impression, complexity, or scope that often require the need to consult with industry, legal and/or compliance experts in the field. Often a quick call to one's expert outside counsel can provide just the right guidance and judgment to guide the course of a response to a thorny, complicated compliance question. Finding the right expert is key. Consulting with outside experts can provide added support when CCOs are presenting to members of senior management, their boards, and their regulators on various compliance issues and how to address them.

---

[72] Rule 38a-1a4(iii) states with respect to the requirement that each fund appoint a CCO and that the CCO "must, no less frequently than annually, provide a written report to the board that, at a minimum, addresses: (A) The operation of the policies and procedures of the fund and each investment adviser, principal underwriter, administrator, and transfer agent of the fund, any material changes made to those policies and procedures since the date of the last report, and any material changes to the policies and procedures recommended as a result of the annual review conducted pursuant to paragraph (a)(3) of this section; and (B) Each Material Compliance Matter that occurred since the date of the last report..."
See Investment Advisers Act of 1940 § 275.206(4)-7 Compliance procedures and practices. Rule 206(4)-7(b) states as follows: "(b) Annual review. Review, no less frequently than annually, the adequacy of the policies and procedures established pursuant to this section and the effectiveness of their implementation..."

[73] See 1940 Act Rule 38a-1(e)(2): (2) A Material Compliance Matter means any compliance matter about which the fund's board of directors would reasonably need to know to oversee fund compliance, and that involves, without limitation: (i) A violation of the federal securities laws by the fund, its investment adviser, principal underwriter, administrator or transfer agent (or officers, directors, employees or agents thereof), (ii) A violation of the policies and procedures of the fund, its investment adviser, principal underwriter, administrator or transfer agent, or (iii) A weakness in the design or implementation of the policies and procedures of the fund, its investment adviser, principal underwriter, administrator or transfer agent.

[74] For a more comprehensive view of the annual review from the SEC's perspective, see Gene A. Gohlke, Examiner Oversight of "Annual" Reviews Conducted by Advisers and Funds (Apr. 7, 2006), https://www.sec.gov/info/cco/ann_review_oversight.htm. See also the SEC's "Questions Advisers Should Ask While Establishing or Reviewing Their Compliance Programs" (May 2006), https://www.sec.gov/info/cco/adviser_compliance_questions.htm

Step 15: Mock Audits—To Engage or Not to Engage. The use of mock audits serves a good and viable purpose for the CCO, the firm, and its compliance program. Some argue that mock audits have in essence been replaced by the need to have an annual review under the Advisers Act and 1940 Act.[75] Notwithstanding that an annual review is required by regulation and, if done correctly, provides an annual review of the compliance program, a mock audit can provide an outside "test" of how well your compliance program or various components of your compliance stack up. Mock audits can be conducted at key inflection points; such as (a) for new firms, (b) in the event your firm has yet to be subject to an SEC exam, (c) when the firm has not been examined for a number of years (with the belief that your firm's "number is up") (d) to review a particular process (such as the annual Section 15 (c) process required under the 1940 Act) or (e) due to a key regulatory initiative (such as business continuity, antimoney laundering, or cybersecurity). Conducting a mock audit through a law firm expert in undertaking them can provide the benefit of the attorney-client privilege. Mock audits, particularly ones that are comprehensive in scope and performed by a law firm, are not cheap. That said, the specter of an enforcement action against the firm (and possibly its CCO) is not to be taken lightly and will have a more severe impact to the firm, its reputation, and its overall business, than seeking to help ensure such an action is not brought in the first place by adding a mock audit to the firm's overall compliance effort.

Step 16: Decide to Become a Whistleblower. On August 29, 2014,[76] and April 22, 2015,[77] the SEC announced whistleblower awards for compliance officers. In its August 29, 2014 press release, the SEC's head of the Office of the Whistleblower stated the following:

> "Individuals who perform internal audit, compliance, and legal functions for companies are on the front lines in the battle against fraud and corruption. They often are privy to the very kinds of specific, timely, and credible information that can prevent an imminent fraud or stop an ongoing one," said Sean McKessy, chief of the SEC's Office of the Whistleblower. "These individuals may be eligible for an SEC whistleblower award if their companies fail to take appropriate, timely action on information they first reported internally."[78]

---

[75] Rule 38a-1 of the Investment Company Act of 1940.
[76] Available at: http://www.sec.gov/News/PressRelease/Detail/PressRelease/1370542799812. Under Rule 21F-4(b)(4)(iii)(B), unless an exception applies, "[t]he Commission will not consider information to be derived from[a whistleblower's] independent knowledge or independent analysis" if the whistleblower "obtained the information because" the whistleblower was "[a]n employee whose principal duties involve[d] compliance or internal audit responsibilities[.]"17 C.F.R. § 240.21F-4(b)(4)(iii)(B).
[77] Director of SE Division of Enforcement Andrew Ceresney stated of a compliance officer: "When investors or the market could suffer substantial financial harm, our rules permit compliance officers to receive an award for reporting misconduct to the SEC," http://www.sec.gov/news/pressrelease/2015-73.html. This compliance officer reported misconduct after responsible management at the entity became aware of potentially impending harm to investors and failed to take steps to prevent it."
[78] Rule 38a-1 of the Investment Company Act of 1940.

Generally, members of the Compliance Department are prohibited from pursuing a whistleblower action unless an exception can be found.[79] Ropes & Gray issued a concise analysis of the Whistleblower Award announced on April 22, 2015.[80] This key analysis examines the impact of Dodd-Frank for a compliance officer but raises concern in terms of how the exceptions set forth in the whistleblower rules are being interpreted by the SEC. They point out the following:

> Because yesterday's SEC press release does not provide factual details about the company involved, the misconduct at issue, or the potential injury to which the misconduct exposed investors, it is unclear how broadly the SEC is prepared to interpret the Rule 21F-4(b)(v)(A) exception. If this lack of clarity lingers, it may have negative consequences that the SEC does not intend. For example, it may increase the risk that compliance employees will too often choose to eschew their companies' internal compliance processes in favor of an immediate report to the SEC, a result that would both impair companies' critical ability to self-remediate and unduly burden the SEC. *This possibility is especially salient given recent speeches by SEC and DOJ officials suggesting that compliance officers could face personal liability if they fail to effectively prevent and remediate company misconduct; compliance employees could view an immediate whistleblower report to the SEC as an expedient way to immunize themselves from potential personal liability* (emphasis supplied).[81]

Although the submission of a whistleblower claim to the SEC is a possibility in the right set of circumstances meeting the required exceptions to the prohibition on the submission of such claims by compliance personnel, in an extreme situation, this may be a possible avenue that should be considered.

---

[79] *Id.* As set forth on the Office of the Whistleblowers' website: "The SEC's whistleblower program went into effect on July 21, 2010, when the president signed into law the Dodd-Frank Wall Street Reform and Consumer Protection Act. The same law also established a whistleblower incentive program at the Commodity Futures Trading Commission that rewards individuals who submit tips related to violations of the Commodity Exchange Act." The exceptions to a compliance person filing a whistleblower complaint are set forth in Rule 21F-4(b)(v) and are as follows: (v) Exceptions. Paragraph (b)(4)(iii) of this section shall not apply if: (A) You have a reasonable basis to believe that disclosure of the information to the commission is necessary to prevent the relevant entity from engaging in conduct that is likely to cause substantial injury to the financial interest or property of the entity or investors; (B) You have a reasonable basis to believe that the relevant entity is engaging in conduct that will impede an investigation of the misconduct; or (C) At least 120 days have elapsed since you provided the information to the relevant entity's audit committee, chief legal officer, chief compliance officer (or their equivalents), or your supervisor, or since you received the information, if you received it under circumstances indicating that the entity's audit committee, chief legal officer, chief compliance officer (or their equivalents), or your supervisor was already aware of the information. (vi) If you obtained the information from a person who is subject to this section, unless the information is not excluded from that person's use pursuant to this section, or you are providing the commission with information about possible violations involving that person.

[80] Ropes &Gray Alert, available at: https://www.ropesgray.com/news-and-insights/Insights/2015/April/SEC-Announces-Dodd-Frank-Whistleblower-Award-for-Compliance-Professional.aspx

[81] Ropes & Gray Alert at page 2.

Step 17: Decide to Resign. Do I need to resign? My sincere desire for all of my compliance brethren is that this question never arise during your career in compliance. That said, the possibility of having to resign remains real and ever present. The type of situation that might merit resignation could involve misconduct by the CCO's firm that was egregious, was known, and was not addressed—prevented or rectified—despite a CCO's best efforts. If a CCO or compliance professional works in a firm where there is a lax tone at the top or worse yet, one that is the antithesis of a sound and compliant compliance system, then a CCO is well advised to consider resigning and seeking employment elsewhere. These decisions are not undertaken lightly and for most, the pressures that are present when the full ramifications of what it means to resign are taken into account (e.g., family hardship, creditors, ability to be employed in the future, etc.), resignation is made that much more difficult. However, the decision to become a compliance professional should not be undertaken lightly and should not be undertaken without the distinct possibility that one may, under the right set of circumstances, have to resign.[82]

VI. CONCLUSION

A chapter devoted to seeking to avoid liability as a CCO is unfortunate because, as we have seen, compliance is a "profession" and, done correctly, serves a real benefit and need for firms, investors, and regulators alike. As is often said, "Good compliance is good for business." Seeking to avoid liability as a CCO is really the other side of the coin of how to establish, implement, and maintain a sound compliance program. As we have seen from the steps set forth in this chapter, with few exceptions, each step goes to making a good Compliance Department. Without each step being undertaken, the CCO risks more than just an enforcement action against his or her firm; he or she risks an action directly against him- or herself for failing as a CCO.

---

[82] As noted above, and in coming full circle, the SEC's admonition in *In the Matter of Gutfreund* bear repeating here; namely, "If such a person takes appropriate steps but management fails to act and that person knows or has reason to know of that failure, he or she should consider what additional steps are appropriate to address the matter. These steps may include disclosure of the matter to the board of directors, resignation from the firm, or disclosure to regulatory authorities."

ABOUT THE AUTHOR

J. Christopher Jackson is senior vice president and general counsel of Calamos Investments in Chicago. Prior to this, Mr. Jackson was director and head of U.S. Retail Legal at Deutsche Asset Management. Mr. Jackson has been chairman of the National Society of Compliance Professionals, is a nationally recognized contributor to numerous professional periodicals, and is a frequent speaker on compliance issues.

CHAPTER 24

Avoiding Supervisory Liability

By Ted Urban
    Former General Counsel, Ferris, Baker Watts, Inc.

I. INTRODUCTION

One of the ongoing challenges confronting compliance professionals is ensuring that their exercise of compliance responsibilities remains "compliance" and does not inadvertently cross over an ill-defined line into the exercise of supervisory responsibility. Compliance professionals generally acknowledge that in circumstances when they have been assigned or otherwise knowingly accepted specifically defined supervisory responsibilities, they can become liable as supervisors if they fail to perform those responsibilities in a reasonable manner. Recent enforcement actions, however, have raised concerns in the compliance community that the Securities and Exchange Commission (SEC) had expanded the circumstances where compliance personnel may be viewed as "supervisors." Regulatory actions charging compliance personnel for "failure to supervise" violations have included situations in which compliance personnel *have not* knowingly accepted or assumed supervisory responsibility in the normal exercise of their compliance responsibilities. And, in the recent SEC enforcement action in which I was the target, finding of the administrative law judge (ALJ) that I was a supervisor was based largely upon others' *perception* that I had the ability to "affect the conduct" of an individual who engaged in unlawful conduct, regardless of the accuracy of that perception. Standards that place compliance officers at risk of liability for supervisory responsibilities that they are unaware they exercise, or for others' subjective perceptions of their supervisory authority clearly threaten the effectiveness of the compliance community.

When I was asked to provide a chapter on the subject of avoiding Supervisory Responsibility," my initial reaction was: "Why me?" Although I prevailed against charges of "failure to supervise" in the administrative action brought by the SEC's Division of Enforcement against me, and the commission dismissed the division's subsequent appeal,[1] I had failed to convince the Enforcement Division that I was not a supervisor and thus could not be prosecuted on this charge. Although the ultimate result was satisfying, the division's

---

[1] In her Initial Decision, the ALJ found that I was a supervisor, but dismissed the charges, finding that I had exercised my alleged supervisory responsibilities in a reasonable manner. *In re Urban*, SEC Admin. Proc. File No. 3-13655 (Dec. 7, 2010). On appeal, the commission was evenly divided as to whether the Division of Enforcement's charges had been established, and summarily dismissed the entire proceeding. *In re Urban*, SEC Admin. Proc. File No. 3-13655 (Jan. 26, 2012).

widely publicized investigation and issuance of charges, the administrative proceeding, and subsequent appeal to the commission cumulatively extended over six years and were professionally disruptive, personally traumatic, and neither rewarding nor pleasurable.

Given my failure to avoid this disruption and pain, in this chapter I share insights from my experience that may assist compliance officers to avoid a "failure to supervise" charge when performing their responsibilities *as* compliance officers. In this chapter I will review the legal bases for supervisory liability; analyze the evolution of the Commission's legal standards for this liability, including *Gutfreund*; examine the *Urban* case in the context of the Commission's evolving standards; explain the legal landscape post-*Urban*; and offer practical advice for compliance officers seeking to avoid supervisory liability in this landscape.

II. LEGAL BASES FOR SUPERVISORY LIABILITY

Prior to 1964, the federal securities laws did not establish liability for supervisors who had failed to supervise the persons under their supervision who had committed securities law violations. By contrast, broker-dealers were held liable on various grounds for the conduct of their employees resulting in violations. Broker-dealer liability was often predicated on the agency and tort law doctrine of *respondent superior,* under which a firm could be held vicariously liable for its employees' violations of the law if conducted in the course of a firm's business.[2] Moreover, the commission considered a firm that had failed adequately to supervise an employee to have participated in, and thus to be liable for, an employee's wrongful conduct.[3]

The Securities Exchange Act of 1934 (SEA) was amended in 1964 to include a provision that became section 15(b)(4)(E). Section 15(b)(4)(E) authorizes the commission to sanction a broker-dealer, if the sanction "is in the public interest" and the broker dealer or associated person "has failed reasonably to supervise, with a view to preventing violations of [federal securities laws and regulations], another person who commits such a violation, if such other person is subject to his supervision." By a cross-reference to Section 15(b)(4)(E), Section 15(b)(6) authorizes an action against "any person associated" with a broker-dealer on similar grounds.[4]

---

[2] Securities Industry Association Compliance and Legal Division, *White Paper on the Role of Compliance* (Oct. 2005), at 11, note 55 (summarizing the early development of supervisory liability). Cited herein as the "2005 SIA White Paper."

[3] This theory is articulated in *In re Reynolds & Co.*, Exchange Act Release No. 6273, 39 S.E.C. 902 (May 25, 1960).

[4] This chapter mainly looks at supervisory liability under the SEA and the potential liability of broker dealer compliance officers for failure to supervise. Other federal securities laws and financial regulations have comparable provisions for supervisory liability. *See*, e.g.,. the Investment Advisers Act of 1940 ("Advisers Act"), which includes at Sections 203(e)(6) and 203(f) provisions comparable to SEA Sections 15(b)(4) and (6). The Advisers' Act authorizes the commission to sanction investment advisers and persons associated with investment advisers for failing to supervise, within the procedures established by the adviser, with a view to preventing violations of the federal securities laws and the Commodity Exchange Act and rules under those statutes, as well as the rules of the Municipal Securities Rulemaking Board. Depending on the substantive and geographic scope of a firm's securities-related business, compliance and related supervisory obligations may arise from guidance of the Federal Reserve Board or other domestic banking regulatory authorities or, in some instances, non-U.S. regulatory requirements.

Section 15(b)(4)(E) includes the following fact-based defenses to a charge of failure to supervise:

> [N]o person shall be deemed to have failed reasonably to supervise any other person, if—
>
> i. there have been established procedures, and a system for applying such procedures, which would reasonably be expected to prevent and detect, insofar as practicable, any such violation by such other person, and
> ii. such person has reasonably discharged the duties and obligations incumbent upon him by reason of such procedures and system without reasonable cause to believe that such procedures and system were not being complied with.

It would appear that, if compliance officers were charged with a failure to supervise, a defense would be available to them if they had dispatched their duties in a reasonable manner. Although the "established procedures" refer to supervisory procedures that typically do not apply to a firm's compliance officers (who after all generally do not have supervisory responsibilities), they nonetheless might be used to refute charges that a compliance officer had failed reasonably to perform the "duties and obligations incumbent upon him."

In addition to supervisory obligations under the SEA, the Financial Industry Regulatory Authority (FINRA), as a self-regulatory organization, requires its member firms to "establish and maintain a system to supervise the activities of each associated person that is reasonably designed to achieve compliance with applicable securities laws and regulations, and with applicable FINRA Rules."[5] As a key element of such supervisory systems, FINRA requires each member to "establish, maintain, and enforce written procedures to supervise the types of business in which it engages and the activities of its associated persons that are reasonably designed to achieve compliance with applicable securities laws and regulations, and with applicable FINRA Rules."[6] Although FINRA's supervisory rules differ from Section 15(b)(4)(E) in that they enumerate what should be the elements of a supervisory system, in effect they provide FINRA with even broader authority than the commission to seek sanctions against its members and their associated persons for failure to supervise.[7]

---

[5] See FINRA Rule 3110(a).
[6] See FINRA Rule 3110(b). See also FINRA, Consolidated Supervision Rules, Regulatory Notice 14-10 (Mar. 2014) at www.finra.org/notices/14-10.
[7] In an appeal to the commission of an National Association of Securities Dealers (NASD) disciplinary proceeding, Conrad Lysiak, a part-time compliance officer and previously the firm's outside general counsel, challenged NASD's finding that he had failed to supervise a branch office of his member firm (*In the Matter of Conrad C. Lysiak*, 15 SEC 841, SEA Release No. 33245 (Nov. 24, 1993)). The commission affirmed that he was a supervisor under the standards the Commission would apply under the SEA at that time (post-*Gutfreund*) and, notably, that "[t]he instant action against Lysiak is based on Section 27 of the NASD's Rules [now FINRA Rule 3110], which has an even broader scope than Section 15(b)." *Lysiak* at 4, and note 13. Lysiak appealed the commission's decision to the U.S. Court of Appeals, which affirmed the Commission (*Lysiak v. SEC*, No. 94-70021; 47 F. 3d 1175, 1995 WL 57177 (C.A.9)).

Given how commission standards applicable to supervisory liability have evolved, this chapter primarily focuses on issues raised by the requirement in Section 15(b)(4)(E) that the person who committed the violation be "subject to the supervision" of the person charged with failure to supervise. Specifically, the chapter addresses this fundamental question for compliance personnel: Under what circumstances might a violator of the securities laws who is not directly managed by a compliance officer nonetheless be found to have been "subject to the supervision" of that compliance officer?

III. THE EVOLUTION OF COMMISSION STANDARDS FOR SUPERVISORY LIABILITY

Actions Under Section 15(b)(4)(E): Pre-*Gutfreund*

With the adoption in 1964 of explicit statutory authority for the SEC to sanction broker dealers and associated persons for supervisory failures, enforcement actions and administrative proceedings pursuant to the new statutory authority began to define the commission's expectations for the exercise of supervisory responsibilities under the new statutory authority, the protections that the adoption and discharge of established supervisory procedures might provide against such charges, and the circumstances that would cause a compliance officer (among others) to be charged with failure to supervise.

One of the first actions against a compliance officer for failure to supervise was *In re Alfred Bryant Tallman*.[8] In *Tallman*, the SEC found that a compliance director failed reasonably to supervise a registered representative and his branch manager because he did not make sufficient inquiry upon learning of their activity in speculative stocks. Without explaining what facts showed that the branch manager and the registered representative were subject to the compliance officer's supervision, the commission determined that "the public interest did not require a sanction, due to the compliance officer's lack of experience and young age, and the fact that it was the first case involving charges against a compliance employee."[9] Thus, notwithstanding the commission's unexplained determination that the persons committing the violations were subject to Tallman's supervision and Tallman had failed to exercise his supervisory authority reasonably, the commission relied on its sympathy for the compliance officer involved to conclude that the public interest did not justify any sanction.

By contrast, *In re Michael E. Tennenbaum*[10] more directly addressed under what circumstances a violator of the securities laws might be found to have been "subject to the supervision" of a firm principal who is also performing functions that might otherwise be performed by a compliance officer. Tennenbaum, the head of a broker

---

[8] *In re Alfred Bryant Tallman*, 44 SEC 230 (1970). In a brief filed by the Division of Enforcement in the *Huff* matter, the division noted *Tallman* as precedent for its authority to bring a failure to supervise action against a nonline supervisor. *Reply Brief of the Division of Enforcement* (May 10, 1988), reprinted in Ferrara, Rivkin & Crespi, *Stockbroker Supervision*, Butterworth Legal Publishers (1989); App. L., at 355–366.
[9] 44 SEC, at 233.
[10] *Michael E. Tennenbaum*, Exchange Act Release No. 18429, 47 SEC 703, 24 SEC Docket 676, 1982 WL 31984 (Jan. 19, 1982).

dealer's arbitrage department, was asked "to set up an options department." He was appointed senior registered options principal (SROP) and "was responsible for establishing compliance procedures for option transactions." Management approved his proposed options compliance program, which included direct supervision of associated persons authorized to transact options business by supervisory sales personnel who "were to become [registered options principals] ROPs and assume responsibility for the options transactions in their branches," as well as oversight of the options program by resident partners of the firm. As SROP, Tennenbaum retained sole authority to approve the exercise of discretion in option accounts. Compliance officers were to monitor options sales practices and trading and bring matters of concern "to the attention of appropriate supervisory personnel, who would deal with the problem."[11]

After an associated person in a branch office engaged in the abusive exercise of discretionary options trading authority and settled charges that his conduct constituted securities law violations, the SEC Enforcement Division charged Tennenbaum with failure to supervise. Tennenbaum's defense was to analogize his status to that of a compliance officer: He alleged that he had devised the firm's options compliance system and played a role in monitoring its operation but had had no supervisory responsibility over the violator. He contended that branch management and others in the firm's management hierarchy were responsible for supervision, and his function, like that of a compliance officer, was to bring problems to management's attention.

The commission disagreed with this characterization, stating that "[o]f critical importance is the fact that Tennenbaum had sole authority to permit a salesman to handle discretionary option accounts." It noted that "[o]nce Tennenbaum had given…his approval, he assumed responsibility for ensuring that this grant of authority, over which he continued to exercise control, was not being abused."[12] The SEC also noted that Tennenbaum's reliance on other supervisors was predicated on the "presence of a qualified supervisor at the local level" and that in this instance he was aware both that options trading problems existed at the branch in question, and that it lacked an ROP (or any other person) upon whom he could rely for local supervision of options trading. Significantly, the commission did not base Tennenbaum's supervisory liability upon the exercise of his compliance functions (the design and monitoring of an options program), but rather upon the specific approval authority he exercised and his failure to assure that the abuse of options trading discretion he had approved was being addressed in any manner by any other supervisor.

In *In re Louis R. Trujillo*,[13] the commission applied a similar analysis to that in *Tennenbaum* but reached a different result. Trujillo was an assistant branch manager whose duties "included administrative matters and several compliance functions." When confronted with sales abuses by a registered representative within the branch, Trujillo

---

[11] *Michael E. Tennenbaum*, Exchange Act Release No. 18429, at *3.
[12] *Id.*
[13] *In re Louis R. Trujillo*, SEA Release No. 26635 (Mar. 16, 1989).

performed his duties in "a less than exemplary" manner.[14] Because the commission assumed that Trujillo's title and stated job responsibilities placed him in the role of a supervisor, its analysis focused on whether he acted reasonably within the scope of those responsibilities. The commission stated that:

> Critical to our decision in this case is the limited scope of Trujillo's authority. Trujillo's functions were largely advisory. His primary job was to apprise [the branch manager] of situations that needed his attention, and it was up to [the manager] to decide what action, if any, should be taken. It was the [manager] who had the power to discharge, restrict, or otherwise take effective action against [the representative].[15]

The SEC concluded that Trujillo exercised his limited authority in a reasonable, even if imperfect, manner and dismissed the charges against him. Although it is unclear to what degree the violator ultimately was subject to Trujillo's control, the determinative factor in absolving him of supervisory liability appears to be that Trujillo acted reasonably in relying upon the branch manager to take such actions as the branch manager believed were necessary to address the noncompliant conduct. In contrast, Tennenbaum's defense failed because he was aware that violations were occurring, had the authority to control the violator, and knew that no other supervisor was in a position to address the situation.

Several years after *Tennenbaum*, in *In the Matter of Arthur J. Huff*,[16] the Commission again emphasized the importance of the authority to exercise control in determining whether one person was subject to the supervision of another. Huff was a vice president and SROP in a major firm's Compliance Department. A registered representative of the firm pled guilty to criminal charges for improperly using customer funds to trade in options. The Order Instituting Proceedings (OIP) charged the branch manager with failure to supervise the representative, and charged a regional manager and Huff with failure to supervise both the branch manager and the representative. Both the branch and regional managers consented to the commission's entry of an order imposing sanctions based on its findings of supervisory failure.[17] When Huff challenged the charges and proceeded to a hearing on the record, the ALJ found that he was a supervisor and, as such, had failed to exercise his supervisory responsibilities reasonably. The commission granted Huff's petition for review.

At the time, the *Huff* proceeding attracted significant attention in the compliance community because it raised fundamental questions about whether compliance officers could be deemed supervisors if they did not have the authority to exercise control over the person they were charged with failing to supervise. The Securities Industry Association's (SIA) Compliance and Legal Division submitted a statement of views

---

[14] *In re Louis R. Trujillo,* at 1.
[15] *In re Louis R. Trujillo,* at 4.
[16] *In the Matter of Arthur J. Huff,* 48 SEC Docket 767, 191 WL 296561 (Mar. 28, 1991).
[17] SEA Release No. 23542, August 18, 1986.

in the adjudicative proceeding and then a letter to the commission during the SEC's review.[18] The C&L Letter asserted that the question of supervision over an individual engaging in misconduct was in each case a question of fact, and that "[o]ne who lacks authority and power to comply with the [SEA's] implicit injunction to 'supervise' the transgressing employee cannot be liable under this statute."[19]

Based on differing analyses, the commissioners reached the same outcome and dismissed the charges against Huff. Chairman Breeden and Commissioner Roberts concluded that the Division of Enforcement had not met its burden of showing Huff had failed to reasonably supervise the guilty representative, and thus it was not necessary to determine whether he had been subject to Huff's supervision.[20] In a concurring opinion, Commissioners Lochner and Schapiro concluded that the representative was not subject to Huff's supervision, thus rendering the reasonableness analysis unnecessary. The concurrence stated that a supervisory relationship "can only be found in those circumstances when, among other things, it should have been clear to the individual in question that he was responsible for the actions of another and that he could take effective action to fulfill that responsibility."[21] In the view of the concurrence, "The most probative factor that would indicate whether a person is responsible for the actions of another is whether that person has the power to control the other's conduct.... Control...is the essence of supervision and it is unlikely that anyone would consider his or her self another's employment 'supervisor' if he or she did not have authority to control the other's actions."[22] In explaining why so few actions for failure to supervise are brought against legal and compliance personnel (in contrast to line supervisors), the concurrence attributed the disparity to the fact that line supervisors "have clear and direct authority and responsibility to control the conduct of salespersons, including the power to hire or fire, and to reward and punish."[23]

Gutfreund

Less than two years after the *Huff* concurrence's emphasis on "control" as the key element in determining the existence of a supervisory relationship, the SEC took a decidedly new tack and identified additional circumstances in which a person could be liable for supervisory failures, even if the person possessed none of the traditional supervisory attributes of control or authority addressed in *Huff* and other predecessor cases. In a Section 21(a) Report of Investigation, the commission set out its view that one's possession of the "responsibility, ability, or authority to affect the conduct of the employee whose conduct is at issue" was sufficient to make that person a supervisor.

---

[18] SIA Letter to the SEC Regarding *In the Matter of Arthur James Huff* (Administrative Proceeding File No. 3-6700) (Mar. 31, 1988). Published in Ferrara, Rivkin, and Crespi, *Stockbroker Supervision*, Butterworth Legal Publishers (1989) at App. K; pp. 329–352.
[19] SIA Letter to the SEC, at 337.
[20] *In the Matter of Arthur J. Huff*, 48 SEC Docket at 767-771; at 769. SEA Rel. No. 34-29017 (Mar. 28, 1991). Opinion of the Commission (Chairman Breeden and Commissioner Roberts); in which Commissioners Lochner and Schapiro concurred in part and filed a separate opinion.
[21] *Huff* (Commissioners Lochner and Schapiro, concurring), at 772.
[22] *Id.*
[23] *Id.*

This language marked a new, more expansive standard for identifying the existence of a supervisory relationship and threatened to sweep in as "supervisors" a larger number of compliance officers called upon by their firms to provide expertise in responding to problem situations. Nonetheless, *Gutfreund* remains today the prevailing test of whether one may be viewed as subject to supervisory liability.

In the *Gutfreund* administrative proceeding, three senior management executives of Salomon Brothers, Inc. (the chairman and chief executive officer (CEO), president, and vice chairman)) were charged with failing to supervise the head of the firm's Government Trading Desk staff, who had submitted false bids in auctions of U.S. Treasury securities. [24] All three settled the charges and accepted sanctions for their failure reasonably to supervise the trader. The firm's chief legal officer, Donald Feuerstein, consented to the issuance and findings of the Section 21(a) Report of Investigation, which the commission used as "an appropriate opportunity to amplify [its] views on the supervisory responsibilities of legal and compliance officers in [his] position."[25]

Feuerstein was not a direct supervisor, but he provided advice to the other executives and participated in their consideration of the trader's actions. The management executives and Feuerstein participated collectively in numerous discussions concerning various aspects of the submission of the false bid and its consequences, and Feuerstein advised the management group that the submission was a criminal act and should be reported to the government. He urged them on several occasions to proceed with this disclosure when he learned that the report had not been made. Until other events intervened, however, there was no internal investigation of the trader's conduct, the involvement of others, or the consequences of the false bid, nor discussion of possible discipline or other restrictions upon the trader's activities. In the investigative report, the commission stated:

> Employees of brokerage firms who have legal or compliance responsibilities do not become "supervisors" for purposes of Sections 15(b)(4)(E) and 15(b)(6) solely because they occupy those positions. Rather, determining whether a particular person is a "supervisor" depends on whether, under the facts and circumstances of a particular case, that person has a requisite degree of responsibility, ability, or authority to affect the conduct of the employee whose conduct is at issue.[26]

---

[24] In re *John H. Gutfreund, et al.*: Order Instituting Proceedings and Report of Investigation pursuant to Section 21(a), 52 SEC Docket 2849, 1992 WL 362753 (Dec. 3, 1992).

[25] Section 21(a) Report of Investigation, 1992 SEC Lexis 2939; 51 S.E.C. 93, at 13.The report imposed no sanctions upon Feuerstein, but it noted he had "represented that he does not intend to be employed in the securities industry in the future."

[26] Section 21(a) Report of Investigation, at 13, note 24. The report also noted that the concurring opinion in *Huff* was "consistent with this principle" in that the *Huff* concurrence cites to "a person's actual responsibilities and authority rather than…his or her 'line' or 'non-line' status" as the determinant of whether he or she is a supervisor.

Applying this principle to Feuerstein, the commission stated:

> In this case, serious misconduct...was brought to the attention of the firm's chief legal officer...by other members of senior management in order to obtain his advice and guidance, and to involve him as part of management's collective response to the problem. Moreover, in other instances of misconduct, that individual had directed the firm's response and had made recommendations concerning disciplinary action, and management had relied upon him to perform those tasks.
>
> Given the role and influence within the firm of a person in a position such as Feuerstein's and the factual circumstances of this case, such a person shares in the responsibility to take appropriate action to respond to the misconduct. Under those circumstances, we believe that such a person becomes a "supervisor"...[and] is responsible, along with other supervisors, for taking responsible and appropriate action. It is not sufficient for one in such a position to be a mere bystander to the events that occurred.

The *Gutfreund* report left the compliance community with a critical dilemma. An effective Compliance Department typically is recognized, through its advice and others' receptivity to such advice, as having the "ability to affect the conduct" of other personnel within a firm. *Gutfreund* diminished the assurance in the *Huff* concurrence that "[c]ontrol...is the essence of supervision" and threatened to expose an effective compliance officer to supervisory liability simply for providing advice and guidance, even if the officer did not have the concomitant ability to exercise the elements of control present in a traditional supervisory relationship.[27]

In a speech to the SIA Compliance and Legal Seminar shortly after the release of the *Gutfreund* order and 21(a) report, Commissioner Schapiro expressed her concern that *Gutfreund* and prior cases on supervision were "being misinterpreted," and she reasserted her belief that they "display a consistent emphasis on authority, responsibility and control as the hallmarks of a 'supervisor.' "[28] She noted that "these attributes are present in the direct supervisory chain of command, and they must also be the defining characteristics of a non-line supervisor."[29] Yet, in particular, she noted that if the ability to "hire, fire, reward, or punish" were the only markers of supervisory status (as she asserted some were reading her concurrence in *Huff* to suggest), such a reading would

---

[27] Section 21(a) Report of Investigation, at 13. The Commission appeared to anticipate this dilemma, but did not resolve it in any meaningful manner. It added in its Report that a person who becomes involved in management's collective response to a problem has an affirmative obligation to "ensure that appropriate action is taken to address the misconduct" and if that person "knows or has reason to know" that management has failed to act, "he or she should consider what additional steps are appropriate" including "disclosure of the matter to the entity's Board of Directors, resignation from the firm, or disclosure to regulatory authorities."

[28] Mary L. Schapiro, *Broker-Dealer Failure to Supervise: Determining Who Is a 'Supervisor,'* Remarks at SIA Legal and Compliance Seminar (Mar. 24, 1993).

[29] Schapiro, *Broker-Dealer Failure to Supervise*, at 16.

allow "persons who are on notice of the occurrence of violative behavior, *and* are in a position to influence the outcome, to merely stand by and let it happen."[30]

Commissioner Schapiro was not alone in addressing perceived inconsistencies between *Huff* and *Gutfreund*. In an address to the NSCP, Commissioner Roberts observed that "there has been a great deal of concern, bordering on hysteria, among legal and compliance personnel...over the language in the Report."[31] Taking a somewhat contradictory and less conciliatory position than Commissioner Schapiro, he too cited the "affect the conduct" phrasing of the Section 21(a) Report of Investigation as definitive, but added his view that "the guideline for determining a 'supervisor'...is considerably broader than the definition of 'supervisor' contained in the concurring opinion of *Huff* and is somewhat broader than the definition of 'supervisor' that appeared in most of the prior case law in this area."[32]

Supervisory Cases After *Gutfreund*

Following *Gutfreund*, enforcement actions against compliance personnel for failure to supervise generally looked first to whether the compliance officer had the power to control the person alleged to be subject to his or her supervision. Guided by the language of *Gutfreund*, these proceedings frequently characterized the supervisor as having the ability to "affect the conduct" of the violator, although in many instances the supervisor's ability to affect the conduct was based on the authority to control at least some aspects of the violator's conduct.

For example, in *In the Matter of Marion Bass Securities Corp. and Gerald Chandik*, a compliance officer accepted findings that he failed reasonably to supervise firm employees who charged excessive markups and markdowns.[33] The commission noted that Chandik was given, and at times exercised, the authority to cancel trades and have them reexecuted at different prices and to discipline firm employees for charging excessive markups. Citing *Gutfreund*, the commission concluded that Chandik had the responsibility, ability, and authority to affect the conduct of employees who charged excessive markups and thus was a supervisor. Presumably, the commission could have applied the more rigorous *Huff* "control" standard to Chandik and reached the same result.

In the Matter of George J. Kolar, the SEC considered an appeal of an ALJ decision finding that Kolar, a regional manager of a major firm, had failed reasonably to supervise a broker who had unlawfully engaged in selling away from the firm.[34] Kolar argued that, because his involvement in investigating the conduct of the offending broker occurred prior to the issuance of *Gutfreund*, he did not have fair notice that the *Gutfreund*

---

[30] Schapiro, *Broker-Dealer Failure to Supervise*, at 17 (emphasis in original).
[31] Richard Y. Roberts, "Failure to Supervise Revisited," Remarks at National Society of Compliance Professionals 1993 National Membership Meeting (Oct. 7, 1993).
[32] Roberts, "Failure to Supervise Revisited," at 3.
[33] *In the Matter of Marion Bass Securities Corp. and Gerald Chandik*, 73 SEC Docket 2916, 2000 WL 1862850 (Dec. 20, 2000).
[34] *In the Matter of George J. Kolar*, 77 SEC Docket 2944, 2002 WL 1393652 June 26, 2002).

Section 21(a) Report of Investigation had expanded the grounds for potential liability as a supervisor beyond that set forth in *Trujillo* and *Huff*. The commission rejected Kolar's arguments that he lacked the elements of control that the concurring opinion in *Huff* cited as the "essence of supervision." The SEC also noted that the views expressed in the *Huff* concurrence had never been adopted by the commission and affirmed the standards set forth in the Section 21(a) Report of Investigation as authoritative.

In *Bellows*, a compliance officer of a broker-dealer, who was also a vice president and member of the Executive Committee, was charged with failure to supervise when a representative of the firm engaged in fraudulent activity, misappropriating customer funds by circumventing the compliance and operational policies of the firm and its clearing firm.[35] Relying on the securities industry's common understanding of the responsibilities of line managers and the SEC's opinion and concurrence in *Huff,* the ALJ found that Bellows was not a supervisor and reaffirmed that individuals who serve as compliance officers, and those who assume limited executive or committee positions, do not automatically become supervisors. In finding in the alternative that the compliance officer acted reasonably in the exercise of whatever supervisory responsibilities she may have assumed, the ALJ also found that individuals "who may have overarching supervisory responsibilities for thousands of employees must be able to delegate supervisory responsibility to subordinate qualified individuals."

The ALJ's pinion did not cite (or even mention) the commission's Section 21(a) Report of Investigation for *Gutfreund* or the standard set forth in that report. Enforcement sought review of the initial decision, seeking clarification that executive officers and members of a firm's Executive Committee did not assume absolute liability as supervisors, as the Enforcement Division contended the ALJ had characterized its position. In rejecting the Enforcement Division's petition and affirming the ALJ's decision, the commission noted that the ALJ's determination that Bellows was not a supervisor did not mean that compliance personnel can never be found liable for failing to supervise. To the contrary, the commission stated that "[s]uch a holding would embody an erroneous legal conclusion" and itself cited (among other authorities) the standard set forth in the *Gutfreund* Section 21(a) Report of Investigation as authority for finding that compliance personnel could be found liable for failing to supervise in appropriate circumstances, thereby reaffirming *Gutfreund* as the standard for determining supervisory liability, while nonetheless absolving Bellows of such liability.[36]

In a proceeding in which the ALJ elaborated upon the defenses available to a compliance officer against a finding of supervisory liability, the Division of Enforcement charged a registered representative (RR) with improper mutual fund switches and Kirk Montgomery, the firm's chief compliance officer (CCO), with failure reasonably to supervise the RR to prevent the alleged violations.[37] The ALJ found that the RR did not commit

---

[35] *In the Matter of Patricia Ann Bellows*, 67 SEC Docket 1426, 1998 WL 409445 (July 23, 1998).
[36] *In the Matter of Patricia Ann Bellows*, at 3.
[37] *In the Matter of Richard Hoffman and Kirk Montgomery*, Initial Decision Release No. 158 ; 71 SEC Docket 1247, 2000 SEC LEXIS 105 (Jan. 27, 2000).

the violations charged, thus eliminating any possible finding of a failure to supervise, but nonetheless examined the bases upon which a failure to supervise charge otherwise also would have failed. As CCO, Montgomery was not the RR's direct line supervisor and the ALJ found that "Montgomery lacked the responsibility, ability, or authority to affect the conduct of [the RR]; or to discipline [the RR] or any other RR or OSJ," citing the standard in *Gutfreund* and its recognition in *Bellows*.[38] She noted that Montgomery could "bring problems or potential problems to the attention of senior management, but, at times, his recommendations to discipline, fire, or not to hire were ignored." The CCO had also attempted to improve supervisory practices within the firm, including those relevant to mutual fund switches, but the ALJ noted that he could only make recommendations to management, which would at times reject them. In this regard, *Montgomery* supports the proposition that a compliance officer's good faith, reasonable efforts to remedy a problem situation—even if unsuccessful—may provide a defense to charges that the officer had failed reasonably to supervise.

SIA *White Paper on the Role of Compliance*

As the preceding cases illustrate, enforcement actions alleging supervisory failures following *Gutfreund* did not differ materially from those preceding the 21(a) report, notwithstanding concerns that the "affect the conduct" standard could encourage more aggressive enforcement and expose compliance officers to greater uncertainty as to when their role might be viewed as supervision. In the aftermath of the "tech bubble" and intense scrutiny of improper business conduct and conflicts of interest in the corporate world and financial services industry at that time, considerable attention was directed to the role of compliance programs in both the corporate world at large as well as the securities industry. Concerned that the role of compliance in preventing and addressing abuses within the securities industry was not well understood, in 2005 the Securities Industry Association's (SIA's) *White Paper on the Role of Compliance* specifically addressed the distinctions between the responsibilities of compliance departments and those of business line supervisors and senior management, and the need to differentiate the advisory role of compliance officers from business management.

In that context, the SIA 2005 White Paper discussed the potential liability of compliance officers for failure to supervise. It observed that the SEC and self-regulatory organizations (SROs) had brought cases "only in limited circumstances" when compliance personnel had been "specifically delegated, or ha[d] assumed, supervisory authority for particular business activities or situations" and thus met the *Gutfreund* standard of having the "requisite degree of responsibility, ability, or authority to affect the conduct of the employee whose behavior is at issue."[39] The SIA 2005 White Paper noted that "*Gutfreund* and other deficient supervision cases...give few specifics as to the responsibilities that would expose compliance officials to supervisory responsibility" and that a "broad application of these general considerations would be inconsistent with the traditional role

---

[38] In the Matter of Richard Hoffman and Kirk Montgomery, at 24.
[39] Securities Industry Association, *White Paper on the Role of Compliance* (" SIA 2005 White Paper") (Oct. 2005), at 11–12.

of the compliance function."[40] The SIA 2005 White Paper optimistically concluded that the commission's prior enforcement actions "suggest that the commission will find that Compliance Department officials have supervisory authority only in those rare circumstances when officials have authority and responsibility over the conduct at issue," citing to the concurring opinion in *Huff* for support of this expectation.[41] Unfortunately, the paper's optimism that the commission or its prosecutors would base their determinations of supervisory liability on the *Huff* standards of actionable authority and responsibility over the conduct at issue, as opposed to on the expansive "affect the conduct" language of *Gutfreund*, proved to be unfounded, and the seeds of a new and troubling look at supervisory liability by the commission had already been sown.

IV. THE *URBAN* MATTER

Background: FBW Supervisory Structure

During the period of 2003 through 2005, I served as general counsel of Ferris, Baker Watts, Inc. (FBW), an employee-owned broker-dealer and investment advisor. I supervised three FBW departments, Legal and Compliance, Human Resources, and Internal Audit, and reported directly to the CEO. Neither I nor any person reporting to me had any supervisory responsibility over personnel in any other department. My role as general counsel was to provide legal advice to management and other employees throughout the firm, and to manage the three departments reporting to me. I was a member of FBW's Board of Directors, and the board's Executive Committee and Credit Committee, the latter of which included the CEO, chief financial officer (CFO), and director of operations, all of whom also were members of the board.

FBW had a traditional organizational structure, with the directors of both business line and administrative/operations control departments responsible for overseeing their organizational units and reporting to the CEO. The firm's written supervisory procedures (WSPs) were drafted by compliance officers in collaboration with, and approved by, the managers within each business line and control department in order to reflect its specific business practices, control functions, and regulatory requirements. "Retail Sales" generated the most significant portion of the firm's revenues and was headed by Louis Akers, with his deputy, Patrick Vaughan, responsible for the Retail Sales branch network. Both were members of the board.

Glantz: Supervision, Issues, and Interaction with Compliance

In January 2003 Stephen Glantz joined FBW from another regional firm as a broker, and brought to FBW a mix of both institutional and individual retail accounts. He divided his time between a retail sales branch and the Institutional Sales Department and, accordingly, was supervised by both a branch manager and the head of the

---
[40] SIA 2005 White Paper, at 12–13.
[41] SIA 2005 White Paper at 13, note 60.

Institutional Sales Department, who also oversaw the institutional trading desk. The arrangement was unusual for FBW, but was approved by the directors of both Retail Sales and Institutional Sales, as well as by the CEO.[42]

Shortly after Glantz joined FBW, compliance and operations personnel expressed concerns about the trading activity that they observed in one of Glantz's institutional accounts, the IPOF Fund (IPOF). IPOF and a number of Glantz's retail accounts held large positions, and were accumulating additional shares, in Innotrac Corporation (INOC), a NASDAQ-listed security. Many of Glantz's clients, including IPOF, had transferred large margin balances into FBW. Compliance officers expressed concerns about these positions and the margin balances, and also about possible manipulative trading in INOC and the adequacy of Glantz's supervision. I encouraged them to consolidate all information available at that time into a written report and directed them to send it to the Credit Committee, as well as to Akers and Vaughan.

Compliance officers and I provided ongoing advice and made numerous recommendations to guide the firm's efforts to supervise Glantz, and to ensure that he and his clients complied with applicable regulatory and reporting requirements. Those actions, among others, included the following:

- In early 2003, I ensured that the Credit Committee discussed the above compliance report and, as a member of the Credit Committee, I caused IPOF to make required, antimanipulative disclosures to the SEC on Forms 13G and Form 4 in response to issues raised in that report.[43] Throughout the year, I and compliance officers repeatedly urged the head of Retail Sales and other business managers to increase their vigilance in supervising Glantz;
- In February 2004 I alerted the Credit Committee to the continued growth of IPOF's margin position in INOC and expressed ongoing concerns about whether Glantz was being properly supervised. As a result, the committee prohibited all additional purchases by IPOF of INOC stock through FBW and adopted additional restrictive measures applicable to IPOF's account. The head of Retail Sales reassigned Glantz to the Baltimore headquarters retail branch, where he was supervised by a senior branch manager widely recognized within the firm as effective;
- In November 2004 I instructed compliance personnel to perform additional diligence on Glantz's activities, which examination disclosed suspicious transactions in INOC in certain of Glantz's client accounts, including trading on discretion without written authorization. I reported these findings to CEO, Akers and Vaughan, and advocated strongly to Akers and Vaughan that they terminate Glantz's employment with FBW; and

---

[42] Initial Decision, *In re Urban,* Initial Dec. Rel. No. 402, 99 SEC Docket 32157 (Sept. 8, 2010), at 5.

[43] These public filings by IPOF necessarily disclosed that they were not timely and the continued accumulation of shares by IPOF in small transactions during 2003. INOC corporate management and independent legal counsel also confirmed to FBW that neither IPOF nor its general partner/manager was a control person of INOC.

- When Akers refused to terminate Glantz, I advocated for (and obtained Akers' agreement to) strict terms of special supervision over Glantz. I reported Akers' resolution of the Glantz situation to the CEO, who expressed no disagreement with Akers' course of action, and I instructed compliance officers to file a New York Stock Exchange (NYSE) Form RE-3 report regarding Glantz's failure to obtain written customer authorization to exercise discretion in their accounts.

Throughout this period, the Credit Committee, supported by compliance officers, focused considerable attention on the trading in, and margin status of, Glantz's accounts, imposing increasingly restrictive controls upon IPOF's trading through FBW, while all the time struggling to get the branch managers, Akers and Vaughn, and Institutional Sales management to fulfill their responsibilities to supervise Glantz effectively. Although I played an ongoing role in advising the Credit Committee and communicating many of its directives to both direct and executive level managers, I was never assigned by that committee, the CEO, or the board to be, nor did I ever view myself as, personally responsible for Glantz's supervision. I clearly did not have the authority to terminate his employment or otherwise take disciplinary actions against him.

Enforcement Investigation; Order Instituting Proceedings

In November 2005 investors in IPOF initiated legal proceedings against IPOF and its general partner for securities fraud and against FBW and other firms to protect IPOF's assets. Ultimately, Glantz pled guilty to criminal charges of manipulating the price of INOC and making false statements to law enforcement officials, and in related SEC actions was barred from association with any broker-dealer or investment advisor.[44] In 2009, FBW, Akers, and Vaughan settled SEC administrative actions, accepting the findings of their failure to supervise Glantz and the sanctions against them.[45]

Unfortunately, the Enforcement Division's perception of my role, as well as its understanding of who at FBW had the ability, authority, and responsibility to exercise control over Glantz, differed distinctly from mine. Almost four years after the division's investigation began, the commission issued an order instituting proceedings (OIP) charging solely that I had "failed reasonably to supervise Glantz with a view to detecting and preventing Glantz's violations" of the securities laws.[46] My answer to the OIP denied that Glantz was ever subject to my supervision, and asserted that, under the circumstances, my advice and actions in response to the "red flags" cited by the Enforcement Division were reasonable.

Administrative Proceeding: Initial Decision

Once the OIP was issued, the matter proceeded through a briefing schedule; a 13-day hearing, during which the testimony of 20 fact and 3 expert witnesses was heard; and

---

[44] *Stephen J. Glantz*, Exchange Act Rel. No. 59373 (Feb. 10, 2009).
[45] *Ferris, Baker Watts, Inc.*, Exchange Act Rel. No. 59372, (Feb. 10, 2009); *Louis J. Akers*, Exchange Act Rel. No. 60628 (Sep. 4, 2009); and *Patrick J. Vaughan*, Exchange Act Rel. No. 59375 (Feb. 10, 2009).
[46] Securities Exchange Act Rel. No. 60837 (Oct. 19, 2009), 96 SEC Docket 21500.

the submission of post-hearing briefs. On September 8, 2010, Commission Chief ALJ Murray issued her initial decision.[47] Following a lengthy summary of the evidence presented and the legal arguments of the parties, she reached four conclusions:

- First, based on his guilty plea to securities fraud charges, she found that Glantz had violated the securities laws;
- Second, relying primarily upon *Gutfreund*, she concluded that "the case law dictates that Urban be found to be Glantz's supervisor";[48]
- Third, she found that I performed the responsibilities for which she believed I was accountable as a supervisor "in a cautious, objective, thorough, and reasonable manner" and thereby "did not fail to supervise Glantz";[49] and
- Fourth, she found that Enforcement "had failed to prove the allegations in the OIP and that it is not in the public interest to impose the recommended sanctions."[50]

Accordingly, she concluded that no remedial action was appropriate under the SEA or the Advisers Act, and dismissed the proceeding.

Although I was relieved to be exonerated of the charges brought against me, Chief ALJ Murray's determination that I was a supervisor of Glantz was troubling and raised serious concerns within the legal and compliance community. She recognized that, although I had the authority to advise and make recommendations, I "did not have any of the traditional powers associated with a person supervising brokers," and "did not direct FBW's response to dealing with Glantz."[51] She added that "there are significant factual differences that distinguish" *Gutfreund* from my situation, noting with approval that "Urban was not a bystander, he took actions, and he shared information."[52] As she explained, I had shared that information with the Compliance Department, which actively monitored Glantz; the Credit Committee, with which compliance officers also provided their own report; and with the managers (Akers and Vaughn) who had direct supervisory responsibility over Glantz. Chief ALJ Murray observed that "[p]erhaps the most significant difference between the posture of Urban and Feuerstein…is that almost all of the business leaders at FBW either lied to Urban or kept information from him, and people with clear supervisory responsibility over Glantz did not carry out their supervisory responsibilities."[53]

With these clear differences between my situation and Feuerstein's, on what basis did she conclude that I was a supervisor? Citing *Gutfreund*, she found that my status as general counsel and participation on FBW's Credit Committee gave me the "requisite degree of responsibility, ability, or authority to affect the conduct" of Glantz. Although

---

[47] Initial Decision, *In re Urban*.
[48] Initial Decision, *In re Urban*, at 52.
[49] Initial Decision, *In re Urban*, at 56.
[50] Initial Decision, *In re Urban*, at 57.
[51] Initial Decision, *In re Urban*, at 52. In reviewing the evidence, she had previously noted that "Urban was not responsible and had no authority for hiring, assessing performance, assigning activities, promoting, or terminating employment of anyone, outside of the people in the departments he directly supervised," at 35.
[52] Initial Decision, *In re Urban*, at 49–50.
[53] *Id.*

she acknowledged that I lacked the traditional powers associated with a supervisor, she articulated two reasons for her conclusion that "case law dictates" a finding that I was Glantz's supervisor.[54] First, my "*opinions* on legal and compliance issues *were viewed* as authoritative" and my "*recommendations* were generally followed by people in FBW's business units" (although, critically, "not by [those in] Retail Sales," the department within which Glantz was subject to direct supervision).[55] Second, she found that "Urban did not direct FBW's response to dealing with Glantz; however, he was a member of the Credit Committee and dealt with Glantz on behalf of the committee."[56]

Chief ALJ Murray effectively disavowed control as a necessary element of the ability to "affect the conduct" of a violator with her adoption of an entirely subjective measure of this criterion. In her analysis, the question of whether Glantz was subject to my supervision was dependent not upon my *actual* authority to control or ability to affect his conduct, but instead upon others' perception of my authority. A subjective standard is problematic, however, because a firm and its management convey supervisory authority through WSPs written specifically to define supervisors and their responsibilities, and do not include those who are simply "perceived" to have the ability to affect the conduct of another. General perceptions as to one's authority are not reliable evidence of actual authority or one's ability to "affect the conduct" of another in a specific situation; it is the objective accuracy of the perception applied to the specific situation which must be assessed. In this instance the ALJ herself acknowledged that such perception was inaccurate when it came to my authority over Retail Sales and Akers.

A subjective measure based upon perceptions also poses the risk of being circular and places the measure of supervisory status in the eyes of the beholder, not within management's expectations or intent. *Gutfreund* states emphatically that a person is not a supervisor solely because he or she carries the title of compliance officer. Yet a primary reason that compliance officers' opinions are generally viewed as authoritative and their recommendations are typically followed is the understanding—or, if you will, the perception—that the officers' qualifications and experience in compliance provide a sound basis for relying upon their opinions and recommendations. In effect, a compliance title may impart an appearance of authority that was not intended by management in establishing the firm's supervisory structure. This creates an unmanageable standard whereby nonline employees involved in advisory functions cannot discern when they will be regarded as supervisors or who might thereby become subject to their supervision. Moreover, a conclusion that a person becomes a supervisor because he or she is thought to give sound advice, or because he or she took the initiative and became involved in attempting to resolve a problem situation, is both counterintuitive and

---

[54] Initial Decision, *In re Urban,* at 49–50, 52.
[55] Initial Decision, *In re Urban,* at 52 (emphases added).
[56] *Id.* This finding raises a collateral question of why the Enforcement Division chose not to charge other committee members with failure to supervise. The committee was headed by FBW's CEO, to whom Akers reported, and with whom "Glantz was in good standing," notwithstanding the information provided to the committee by compliance and operations, and at least one branch manager, at 50. The other two members of the committee were FBW's CFO and chief operations officer (COO), both of whom also made recommendations to the committee.

counterproductive; it sweeps in the astute and the diligent, and protects ineffectual personnel who seek to avoid involvement in controversy.

Finally, Chief ALJ Murray acknowledged, in agreement with both parties' expert witnesses, that "the language in *Gutfreund*, taken literally, would result in Glantz having many supervisors because many people at FBW acted to affect Glantz's conduct in a variety of different ways."[57] Thus, many, if not all, legal, compliance, financial, and operational personnel who interacted with Glantz might be viewed as his supervisors. As expressed in the expert reports of both Marc I. Steinberg, on my behalf, and David Paulaukitis, on behalf of the Enforcement Division, "The consequence of conducting an investigation by itself (even if the broker is not ultimately subject to discipline) likely will affect the future conduct of the broker."[58] The difficulty with this conclusion by Chief ALJ Murray is that if all (or many) are supervisors, how do those individuals, or regulators, identify which of them bears primary responsibility for the conduct at issue? If line supervisors with undisputed authority to control a situation fail to act when urged to do so, what regulatory objective is achieved by charging those who urged action with supervisory failures when others of the potential multiple supervisors failed to heed their advice?

Based on all of the above, Chief ALJ Murray concluded her analysis by finding that any sanction for my "failing to supervise" was not in the public interest. She stated that "[t]he division's thorough presentation and its regulatory zeal are admirable, but as I noted, I disagree with its judgment and conclusions, and I disagree further with what it believes is in the public interest in this situation. Urban was the only person in FBW management who tried to deal with Glantz, a problem he did not create and I find his actions, in these facts and circumstances, reasonable." I greatly appreciated her concluding statement, although it further illustrates the peril to which her decision exposes legal and compliance personnel. If the *Gutfreund* standard is understood to make a supervisor of every compliance officer who is involved in dealing with a potential violator, then the only defense against a zealous prosecutor lacking judgment is contending with a prolonged investigation and a hindsight analysis of the facts and circumstances of the violations and your purported "supervision," and then prevailing in a determination that your actions and/or omissions nonetheless were reasonable.

Appeals to the Commission and Dismissal

Shortly after Chief ALJ Murray issued her initial decision, the Enforcement Division filed a petition for review, asserting that her finding that I had acted reasonably as a supervisor was "incorrect." In response, counsel on my behalf filed a conditional cross petition for review challenging her determination that Glantz was subject to my supervision. The SEC granted both parties' petitions for review, leading the industry to anticipate resolution of the tension between the *Huff* concurrence and *Gutfreund*, and in general more definitive guidance from the commission on what standards it would

---

[57] Initial Decision, *In re Urban*, at 52.
[58] Expert Witness Report of Marc I. Steinberg, at 5; Expert Witness Report of David E. Paulukaitis, at 7–8.

apply to determine whether a compliance officer, without direct line supervisory authority, might otherwise be a supervisor. The potential significance of the commission's consideration of the matter was recognized throughout the securities industry, and within the corporate legal community. Amicus briefs were submitted by the National Society of Compliance Professionals and jointly by Securities Industry and Financial Markets Association (SIFMA), including its Compliance and Legal Society, with the Association of Corporate Counsel, a professional bar association of corporate legal counsel. The commission also agreed to hear oral argument by the parties.

On January 26, 2012, following the submission of briefs by the parties and *amicae*, and the scheduling of oral arguments, the commission (with Chairman Schapiro and Commissioners Walter and Gallagher not participating) abruptly announced (without hearing the scheduled arguments) that it was "evenly divided as to whether the allegations in the OIP have been established" and ordered the proceeding dismissed.[59] Under the SEC's Rules of Practice (Rule 411(f)), the legal impact of the dismissal was that the initial decision "shall be of no effect." Accordingly, neither Chief ALJ Murray's determination that I was a supervisor nor her finding that I had exercised that supervision in a reasonable manner is of any precedential value.

Since the commission's nondecision effectively wipes the legal impact and history of this matter clean, *Gutfreund* remains the commission's uncontroverted legal standard for determining whether a person without specifically assigned supervisory responsibilities may be deemed a supervisor. However, although any legal impact of Chief ALJ Murray's decision is now moot, her analysis and application of *Gutfreund* to conclude that I was a supervisor will continue to pose a threat to compliance personnel. If the commission's chief ALJ (and at least one of the two nonrecused commissioners) could analyze the facts and circumstances of my situation and conclude that I was a supervisor, what assurance exists that the Enforcement Division, faced with similar facts and circumstances, would not bring the same case again, or that a future ALJ or commission would not find that, under "the case law" a legal or compliance officer in a similar situation also was a supervisor? More importantly, to what definitive standard can compliance personnel look for guidance to avoid inadvertently becoming a supervisor?

V. DEVELOPMENTS AFTER *URBAN*: SEEKING CLARITY IN MURKY WATERS

Remarks of Commissioner Gallagher

With the recusal of three commissioners and a divided decision between the remaining two, the SEC lost a rare opportunity to revisit, in the context of a fully contested, litigated matter, what legal authorities, facts, and circumstances it would look to in determining whether a legal or compliance professional in the securities industry might become a supervisor. As Commissioner Gallagher observed shortly after the dismissal,

---

[59] SEA Rel. No. 34-66359, 2012 WL 1024025 (ALJ January 26, 2012).

"For those struggling for resolution on the question of supervisory authority, *Gutfreund* remains a key authority." He also observed that although the "commission's failure-to-supervise cases, including [*Urban*], have provided some modicum of clarity on the responsibilities of a person deemed to be a supervisor...[t]he question of what makes a legal or compliance officer a supervisor, however, remains disturbingly murky."[60]

In this same speech, Commissioner Gallagher emphasized the importance of the legal and compliance role, and the ability of compliance personnel to carry out their responsibilities. He expressed concern that under the existing case law "robust engagement on the part of legal and compliance personnel raises the specter that such personnel could be deemed to be 'supervisors,'" creating a "dangerous dilemma" in which "the commission's position on supervisory liability for legal and compliance personnel may have had the perverse effect of increasing the risk of supervisory liability in direct proportion to the intensity of their engagement."[61] He stressed the critical importance of such engagement in resolving "thorny regulatory issues" and other matters calling for "the benefit of sage regulatory counseling," and concluded by stating that the commission should "strive to ensure...that the fear of failure-to-supervise liability never deters legal and compliance personnel from carrying out their own critical responsibilities."[62]

In subsequent remarks, Commissioner Gallagher emphasized the need for "failure-to-supervise" to mean what it says, and for regulators to focus on "business line supervisors, not the compliance official who steps in and takes action in good faith, even if the results of his or her actions are less than ideal."[63] He stated that the commission must "avoid establishing a rigid set of expectations based on bright line rules that further discourage compliance officers from acting" and that "an optimal compliance regime requires a flexible regulatory framework that incentivizes compliance officers to fully engage in the many difficult regulatory and business decisions." Although noting that the "vast majority of failure-to-supervise cases will not be close calls," he also expressed his belief that "the commission has an obligation to provide regulated entities with clarity on supervisory liability in those close cases that do arise."[64]

The Failure of the *Gutfreund* Standard

John Walsh, former associate director chief counsel of the commission's Office of Compliance Inspections and Examinations (OCIE), provides a convincing analysis that the *Gutfreund* standard for evaluating whether a compliance officer was a supervisor has failed, as demonstrated by the confusion arising from Chief ALJ Murray's decision in the *Urban* matter.[65] He argues that all cases involving individual failures to supervise

---

[60] Daniel M. Gallagher, Remarks at The SEC Speaks in 2012 (Feb. 24, 2012), at 3, http://www.sec.gov/News/Speech/Detail/Speech/1365171489872
[61] Gallagher, The SEC Speaks, at 4.
[62] Gallagher, The SEC Speaks, at 5–6.
[63] Daniel M. Gallagher, Remarks at the 2013 National Compliance Outreach Program for Broker Dealers, April 9, 2013, http://www.sec.gov/news/speech/2013/spch040913dmg.htm
[64] Gallagher, Remarks at the 2013 National Compliance Outreach Program, at 3.
[65] John H. Walsh, "The Time has Come to Reconsider the *Gutfreund* Standard," *The Review of Securities and Commodities Regulation*, Vol. 45, No. 15 (Sept. 12, 2012).

likely could be determined with the same outcome through application of the "control" standard as articulated in the *Huff* concurrence: Did the person charged with a supervisory failure have the power to control the violator's conduct?

He reasons that *Gutfreund* should be read as it initially applied to Feuerstein, that is, to the exercise of collective responsibility. Once Feuerstein became involved in formulating management's response to a problem, he was obligated to ensure through affirmative steps that appropriate action was taken to address the misconduct. Knowing that no participant in the collective response had initiated a further investigation, disciplined the trader, or reported the matter as agreed upon, Feuerstein (along with each of the other participants in the management group) became responsible for ensuring that effective action was taken; he could not remain a bystander even if he had no direct supervisory authority over the government bond trading desk. His supervisory authority in these circumstances arose from his participation in the collective response of the management group. Thus, it was not his advice to the group that made him a supervisor, but his participation in the group's response to the violations and his failure, once involved, to ensure that action was taken to "affect the conduct" of the traders violating the securities laws. As to more straightforward questions of supervision, i.e., where one is not part of a collective response to a violation, the *Huff* standard of "control" would be the determinative test. Under it, no person would be deemed to be a supervisor of a person whose conduct the person is not authorized or does not have the power, to control.

SIFMA *White Paper: The Evolving Role of Compliance*

In 2013, SIFMA revisited the role of compliance in the aftermath of changes following the 2008 financial crisis. The SIFMA *White Paper: The Evolving Role of Compliance*[66] reaffirmed SIFMA's continued belief in the traditional line of demarcation between, on the one hand, compliance's advisory role and responsibility for maintaining the firm's compliance program and, on the other, management's authority and responsibility to implement and enforce supervisory and compliance obligations. It criticized, however, an apparent change in the views of enforcement authorities who, unsupported by legislative mandate or administrative rulemaking, had adopted "differing and more expansive views of compliance responsibilities relative to management's supervisory responsibilities."[67] The 2013 White Paper cited three theories (from the administrative actions discussed above) that in its view exposed compliance officers to the risks of being deemed supervisors:

- Control (as recognized as the critical element of supervision in the *Huff* concurrence);
- Ability to affect conduct (as set forth in *Gutfreund*); and
- A new "blended theory," which it recognized as emerging from Chief ALJ Murray's analysis in *Urban*.

---

[66] SIFMA, *White Paper: The Evolving Role of Compliance* (Mar. 2013) ("2013 White Paper"), http://www.sifma.org/issues/item.aspx?id=8589942363
[67] 2013 White Paper, at 9–10.

The 2013 White Paper characterized the blended theory as "deeply problematic," in that it elevated the appearance of authority from one's position as a trusted advisor to the equivalent of actual control, noting that "compliance should be influential and affect the decision-making of supervisors, but influence does not equate with control."[68] The 2013 White Paper additionally concluded that because the *Urban* decision was dismissed, "The precise point at which the performance of compliance activities would cause a Compliance professional to be deemed a supervisor remains unclear."[69]

The 2013 White Paper expressed these concerns within the context of its focus on the dramatic changes in the role of compliance since the 2005 White Paper and its continuing evolution. The 2013 document discussed the proliferation of new and complex financial products, each with its own attendant regulatory requirements; legislative initiatives—particularly pursuant to Dodd-Frank—that have increased the subject matter areas which firms and their compliance departments must address; the significant growth and changes in technology available to firms and compliance; the increasing demands upon compliance for involvement in risk assessment and management; and the increased focus on internal reviews and testing of supervisory systems. The growth in all of these areas and responsibilities has increased the need for compliance's interaction with both business and product line management, as well as with other control groups, and likely will foster greater reliance upon compliance advice, and an expanded role for compliance as an intermediary among business lines and between business lines and their respective control groups. As compliance's role as advisor and intermediary increases, there inevitably will be an increased perception that compliance has the ability to affect the conduct of the business lines or control groups which it is advising. To the extent compliance proves effective in that role, it will presumably garner greater respect and appreciation for its efforts, which may further enhance the perceived importance of its role, even if not its actual authority.

To avoid the dangers that the increased compliance responsibilities and potential perception of its intermediary roles could lead to increased supervisory liability, the 2013 White Paper recommended that senior management "clearly define and memorialize the role and responsibilities of compliance in a way that allows compliance to exist and operate independently and without undue pressure from any business unit or other control function" and that regulators "be aware of, and focus on, the role agreed to and ordinarily undertaken by compliance professionals…" recognizing that "[a]ctive

---

[68] 2013 White Paper, at 10.

[69] *Id*. As noted above, SIFMA had filed a brief in support of my cross-appeal of the Initial Decision in the *Urban* matter, challenging ALJ Murray's conclusion that I was a supervisor and criticizing the vagueness of the *Gutfreund* standard. SIFMA argued strongly that the "commission should explicitly recognize that neither the ability of legal and compliance professionals to provide advice and recommendations, nor their participation in firm credit or similar committees, constitutes sufficient authority to make them 'supervisors.' " Brief of *Amici Curiae* SIFMA and The Association of Corporate Counsel, at 27; Administrative Proceeding File No. 3-13655 (Nov. 22, 2010), http://www.sifma.org/issues/item.aspx?id=22405

involvement in advising business personnel should not transform compliance professionals into business personnel or line supervisors."[70]

Supervision in Another Context

A consistent refrain in critiques of the commission's *Gutfreund* "affect the conduct" standard (and Chief ALJ Murray's interpretation of that standard to include the "appearance of authority") is the vagueness of the standard and the resulting uncertainty when compliance professionals seek to make a reasonable determination whether, in given circumstances, they are supervisors. In *Vance v. Ball State University*,[71] the U.S. Supreme Court recently addressed similar concerns about vagueness in defining supervision. Under Title VII of the Civil Rights Act of 1964, employer liability for harassment depends on the status of the harasser. In cases when the harasser is a "supervisor," and the harassment results in a significant change in employment status of the victim, the employer is strictly liable for the injury caused by the harassment.[72] If the harasser is the victim's coworker, the employer is liable only if it was negligent in controlling working conditions. Thus, a determination of whether a coworker who engages in harassment is a supervisor may be critical under Title VII to the liability of the employer.

In *Vance,* the court held that an employee is a "supervisor" for purposes of vicarious liability under Title VII only if he or she is empowered by the employer to take "tangible employment actions" against the victim. The court noted that prior cases had established "tangible employment actions" to mean "the power to hire, fire, demote, promote, transfer, or discipline" the person supervised. In adopting this standard, the court reasoned that this definition of a supervisor is one that is capable of being discerned, and thus can readily be applied, before litigation commences, and contrasted its clarity with the vagueness of the existing Equal Employment Opportunity Commission (EEOC) standard for identifying a supervisor.

The Supreme Court's ruling on Title VII in *Vance* is, admittedly, not directly relevant to the interpretation of supervisory liability under the SEA and the Advisers Act. However, the need for clarity about who is a supervisor is the same in the securities law context: Compliance officers should have sufficient guidance to determine reliably when they may be exposed to liability for failing to supervise, in the same manner that employers under Title VII are entitled to know which of their employees might cause them to be subject to strict liability for harassment offenses. The absence of a clearly defined standard for identifying a supervisor under the SEA or Advisors Act could invite similar challenges to the SEC's prosecution of supervisory failure. Indeed, the lack of guidance on the question of who is a supervisor under Section 15(b)(4)(E) of

---

[70] 2013 White Paper, at 29–30.
[71] 133 S. Ct 2434 (2013).
[72] See *Burlington Industries, Inc. v. Ellerth* (524 U. S. 742, 761).

the SEA was one of the additional bases included in my petition for review challenging Chief ALJ Murray's finding that I was a supervisor.

Division of Trading and Markets Frequently Asked Questions

In September, 2013, the SEC's Division of Trading and Markets (T&M) sought to alleviate at least some of the murkiness following the commission's dismissal of the *Urban* matter, by issuing "Frequently Asked Questions about Liability of Compliance and Legal Personnel at Broker-Dealers Under Sections 15(b)(4) and 15(b)(6) of the Exchange Act" (FAQs).[73] Although the responses provided by T&M to the FAQs are a useful summary of many issues raised by the *Huff, Gutfreund,* and *Urban* matters, they are solely the views of T&M and are not rules, regulations, or statements of the commission. Moreover, they are offered by T&M solely with respect to compliance personnel of broker-dealers, although it is likely that the same or similar principles would apply to investment advisers under the Advisers Act.

In general, the FAQs offer some encouragement that T&M is aware of the compliance community's desire for more definitive guidance in this area. They also recognize (FAQ No.6) the critical role of compliance personnel in developing and maintaining effective compliance systems, and encourage active engagement by affirming that compliance officers do not become supervisors solely because they provide advice to, or consult with, senior management. As a whole, the FAQs offer a synopsis of the prevailing commission standards for analyzing potential supervisory liability of compliance officers. The FAQs do so, however, primarily by restating standards from *Gutfreund* and are thus disappointing in that they do not offer any new guidance on the facts and circumstances that may arise within the gaps of those standards.

For example, FAQ No. 2 addresses the application of the *Gutfreund* "affect the conduct" standard and lists six factors, set forth as "questions to consider," as relevant to such determination. At least three of the six factors listed, however, raise additional issues that undermine the usefulness of the questions to be considered. One question, for example, asks whether a person "clearly has been given, or otherwise assumed, supervisory authority or responsibility for particular business activities or situations." How are compliance officers to know that they have "otherwise assumed supervisory authority" if it has not been clearly given? How are they to know that a "situation" exists and that they are responsible for supervising it if not explicitly assigned and accepted?

Another question to consider asks, "did the person otherwise have authority such that he or she could have prevented the violation from continuing" absent the person's possession of traditional indicia of control? A third asks whether the person should "nonetheless reasonably have known in light of all the facts and circumstances that he or she had the authority or responsibility within the administrative structure to exercise control to prevent the underlying violation." These questions presume a lack of

---

[73] The FAQs and any subsequent updates are found at http://www.sec.gov/divisions/marketreg/faq-cco-supervision-093013.htm

notice of assigned authority to "prevent" a continuing violation and the possibility that such authority can exist outside the defined administrative structure or, as Chief ALJ Murray found, that it may exist subjectively because others believed you possessed it.

The difficulty in assessing the facts and circumstances relevant to answering each of the questions to consider in FAQ No. 2 is that the full range of facts and circumstances known to investigators after a situation has "gone bad" rarely are as readily apparent when the situation is developing; and the degree to which a situation has gone bad may subsequently influence interested persons' recollections of their knowledge or involvement in the situation as it was developing. If the FAQs are to assist compliance officers in evaluating their potential supervisory liability as or before events unfold, the commission or Division of T&M should make clear that the factors would be evaluated from the perspective of the compliance officer at the time they were involved. Thus, the evaluation would focus on indicia that compliance officers to be charged for failing to perform supervisory duties not expressly assigned had unequivocal notice they were expected to be involved in investigating the problem situation, were conferred some meaningful authority to address the situation, and were clearly aware that management expected them to report on the resolution or with a recommendation as to how management should resolve the situation.

T&M also takes note of the Supreme Court's *Vance* decision and points out that it is distinguishable from the situation of compliance officers. T & M asserted that *Vance's* definition of supervisory authority as the empowerment of a person by his employer to take tangible employment actions "does not reflect all of the factors that are relevant to establishing such responsibility under the Exchange Act."[74] Yet the FAQs do not meaningfully define what other "factors" the T&M staff might look to in determining whether one individual has the ability to affect the conduct of another under *Gutfreund*. In fact, the commission has never attempted to address broader concerns as to the vagueness of the phrase "subject to the supervision" under the SEA. The proposal and adoption of rules in this area would provide clarity to both industry personnel and regulatory staff in the interpretation of this phrase, and would better protect commission actions under the SEA from justifiable challenge on grounds of vagueness similar to those asserted in *Vance*.

VI. PRACTICAL CONSIDERATIONS

Given the imperfect statutory authority, lack of definitional clarity, anomalies of administrative and case law precedent, and the resultant uncertainties of compliance officers' exposure to potential supervisory liability, how can these officers best ensure that they will not become the target of a failure to supervise charge? This section will attempt to identify specific circumstances that might expose one to supervisory liability, and identify firm, Compliance Department, and personal practices to minimize or avoid those risks.

---

[74] Frequently Asked Questions, at 6–7, fn 8.

Have I Been Assigned or Otherwise Assumed Supervisory Responsibilities?

A firm's WSPs should specifically identify who is responsible for, and has the authority to, supervise each business line and operating unit of a firm, and the measures that the supervisor is expected to employ in exercising that authority. If the role of compliance at your firm is solely advisory, no compliance officer should be listed as responsible for, or authorized to control, any business line supervisory procedure. In practice, however, even well-drafted WSPs are not immune from practical issues:

- SIFMA's 2013 White Paper notes the growing interactions among compliance officers, business units, and control groups within a firm, and "the possibility for misunderstanding, both inside and outside the firm, of [compliance's] advisory role."[75] When a compliance officer serves as a coordinator among business units, and particularly if the officer becomes the person who communicates the joint work of the units, it creates a risk that the compliance official will be perceived (within the firm, and possibly even within the units involved) as exercising supervisory authority over the coordinating units and their personnel. A compliance officer serving as a coordinator should take precautions to ensure that the management mandate of the coordinating units is well defined and explicitly recognizes the advisory role of compliance, and that the results of the coordinated work are communicated by the business unit(s) or control group(s) that has(ve) supervisory responsibility for the work product;
- T&M FAQ No. 2 asks whether the firm's policies or procedures "or other documents" identify a person as responsible for supervising another. What other documents might exist that speak to supervisory authority? Can memoranda or emails among firm personnel create a perception that a compliance officer (or other nondesignated person) has been given, or otherwise assumed, supervisory responsibility? The firm's WSPs should establish that they are the definitive documentation for the assignment of supervisory responsibilities, and they should state firm policy that supervisory responsibilities may not be assigned or accepted without inclusion in the WSPs and written acknowledgment of acceptance by the designated supervisor (typically by signoff upon the WSPs that define his or her responsibilities);
- Who is the responsible supervisor when the designated supervisory position is vacant or a gap in responsibility arises? Although the WSPs should identify individuals within a unit with temporary or backup authority, it should be clear in the WSPs that it is the default responsibility of the next level supervisor to fill the vacancy or assume responsibility for the supervisory tasks performed during the subordinate's absence. If a manager looks to compliance officers to fill a vacancy or a gap in supervision, the terms of the assignment should be documented and the exercise of the temporary responsibilities routinely reviewed with the next level business line supervisor, and any material issues that may arise resolved subject to his or her approval. Your objective as a compliance officer is to ensure that business line personnel are reasonably performing their assigned supervisory responsibilities, not to substitute your performance for theirs; and

---

[75] 2013 White Paper, at 6.

- A more critical situation may arise when a lack of resources or personnel causes a suspension or gap in performance of a business unit's supervisory procedures, or monitoring of the procedure by compliance. Senior management personnel who are aware of, and fail to remedy, a suspension of supervisory procedures caused by a lack of resources (or other factors) and compliance personnel who are aware of the suspension and fail to take appropriate steps to cause the procedures to be performed also may be held liable for failure to supervise.[76]

Routine Compliance Administrative Actions

A number of the administrative proceedings discussed earlier in this chapter based their findings of a supervisory relationship and failure to supervise on the authority of the person charged to take routine administrative or disciplinary action (e.g., closing an account, rebilling a trade to adjust commissions or execution price, and nominal fines) during the course of performing routine supervision, or as part of compliance oversight of such supervision. These actions remain a part of many firms' supervisory systems for taking what they view as corrective actions for routine errors or mistakes. Compliance personnel risk exposure for broader supervisory responsibility when such actions identify a potentially suspicious pattern of trading or other unlawful activity, but the actions do not prompt an appropriate investigation or response beyond the routine administrative action. Although compliance systems may identify the possible need for such routine administrative actions, the decision to impose fines or other actions should be made by a business line supervisor, after appropriate inquiry into the circumstances of the error or need for the corrective action.

Situations and a Collective Response

Another area of concern is dealing with particular "situations" (see, e.g., T&M FAQ No. 2). Frequently, when a problem situation arises, it may call for multiple parties from different disciplines to collaborate in the investigation, review, and resolution of that problem without there being established a predefined chain of authority among the parties. In *Gutfreund*, three business executives and the general counsel of the firm were participants in a "collective response" to a serious Treasury bond trading violation. Their collective inaction permitted serious violations to continue and the SEC found that all had failed to supervise, including the general counsel, who, as a participant in the collective response, had the authority and ability to take the remedial actions agreed upon by the group.

If you are called to be part of the firm's collective response to a situation, you should seek a clear definition of the situation the group is called on to address, the scope of your individual and collective authority and responsibility to investigate and respond to the situation, and to whom you and the group will be accountable. Documentation of the collective group's work—including scope, findings, response, and responsibility

---

[76] See *Dennis S. Kaminski*, SEA Rel. No. 65347 (Sept. 16, 2011).

for any necessary further action or follow-up—is critical. If the situation that you believe you addressed later becomes the subject of further scrutiny, you will want to be able to demonstrate that your efforts were taken in good faith and, given the facts and circumstances, reasonably designed at the time to prevent further violations, even if your or the group's efforts did not prove fully successful.

Board and Committee Participation

The potential benefits and perils of board or committee participation by legal and compliance personnel remains one of the most debated questions of potential exposure to supervisory liability. Although almost all in this industry agree that participation by compliance officers on the board or a board committee benefits a firm's compliance culture, many express concern that it provides a compliance officer with authority to affect the conduct of firm personnel in particular situations or at a minimum enhances the perception that one has such authority.

In the Initial Decision of *In re Urban*, my participation as a member of the board's Credit Committee was one of the factors cited by Chief ALJ Murray in determining that I was a supervisor, although she did not explain how my dealings with Glantz "on behalf of the committee" contributed to my ability to affect his conduct. Commissioner Gallagher cited the benefits of legal or compliance participation on a board and committees, but cautioned, in light of *Gutfreund*, that "one must carefully weigh the consequences of full voting membership in light of the substantial benefits of being a valued but nonvoting advisor to the board or committee."[77] SIFMA's 2013 White Paper also examined the role of compliance officers on committees and recognized its considerable value to firms. It also stated that "compliance professional participation on committees should not be viewed as indicative of the exercise of managerial or supervisory activity. This should be the case even where a committee requires or allows compliance officers to record votes on matters. A determination by compliance to approve, or to not object to, a particular activity or decision is not an exercise of supervisory control."[78]

Finally, T&M FAQ No. 5 acknowledges that compliance officers and legal personnel do not become supervisors solely by participating in or providing advice to committees, but the FAQ again provides little prospective guidance on the facts and circumstances which would provide a committee participant with the responsibility, ability or authority to affect the conduct of a person whose actions may be at issue.

Compliance and legal participation on boards or committees clearly brings value to a firm, and enables compliance officers to be heard at levels of management that might not otherwise routinely be available. The question of board and committee participation, however, must be evaluated in the context of the size, history, and management structure of the firm, and the expectations of management and ownership. There is no

---

[77] *See* Gallagher, The SEC Speaks, at 5, note 70.
[78] 2013 White Paper, at 7.

uniform answer for all firms or compliance personnel, and if the decision is to participate on a board or committee, the participation must be tailored to meet the needs of the firm and protection of the advisory role of compliance officers.

Indemnification and Insurance

Responding to a regulatory investigation and effectively defending against criminal, civil, or administrative charges in a legal proceeding can be a prohibitively demanding and expensive proposition. In reality, the primary reason that there are so few contested actions for failure to supervise is the time commitment and costs involved in the underlying investigation and legal proceedings. In my case, the investigation took almost four years; the subsequent administrative proceeding and appeal took an additional two and a half years. I was the beneficiary of our corporation's effective indemnification policies and a commitment from the firm with its adequate financial resources for my defense. Many compliance personnel may not have these benefits or firm commitment, or the officers may not be in a situation where they can devote the time and attention necessary to defending themselves effectively while continuing to pursue or advance their professional careers. In short, they may often find it wiser to devote a much more limited time to achieving the most advantageous settlement terms possible. I hope that you will never confront these issues. Nonetheless, I would suggest that the time to examine your firm's indemnification provisions and to understand the availability and effectiveness of individual or firm professional liability insurance, is before you are charged with a supervisory failure.

VII. CONCLUSIONS

The legislative authority of the SEC under the SEA and Advisers Act to sanction for failure to supervise is relatively straightforward for associated persons who have line management authority over others. The application of that authority to compliance and legal personnel who are serving in the traditional role of advisors to management and business line supervisors is considerably less clear. Recent cases, in particular *Urban*, have raised more questions than they have answered, providing little guidance to legal and compliance personnel on how best to advise and guide management without assuming supervisory liability. These cases seemingly expanded the circumstances by which the prevailing *Gutfreund* standard may be applied to legal and compliance personnel to charge that they are supervisors under the SEA and Advisers Act.

The securities industry continues to grow and become increasingly complex, and the reliance of the public investor, the industry, and regulatory authorities upon effective regulation becomes ever greater. Within that growth and increasing complexity, compliance's role continues to evolve, necessarily increasing the interaction of compliance with business and other control groups, and potentially making it even more difficult to distinguish the advisory role of compliance from the supervisory responsibilities of those who manage the firm's lines of business.

Although the commission staff and individual commissioners have sought to assure compliance personnel that their role within the securities industry and in support of the commission's mission and regulatory objectives is critical and valued, the commission has not proposed or adopted regulations that would provide the necessary guidance so that compliance personnel serving as advisors are not unduly exposed to liability as supervisors. *Urban* highlighted the need for such regulatory guidance, and the attention that it attracted and the resulting commentary should encourage the commission to provide definitive guidance in this area.

ABOUT THE AUTHOR

Ted Urban served as general counsel of Ferris, Baker Watts, Inc. (FBW), a regional broker dealer and investment advisor. He was named in a recent widely followed SEC action regarding the supervisory duties of compliance officers. The commission's chief ALJ determined he had no liability and, following the Enforcement Division's appeal, the commission dismissed all charges against him.

Mr. Urban currently provides independent consulting and expert witness services to a wide range of investors and other participants in the securities industry. He serves as vice chair of the Board of Investment Trustees for the Montgomery County, Maryland, Public Schools' Employee Pension and Retirement System, and as a board member of TCA TrustCorp America. He has been engaged in USAID-sponsored assignments to promote the development of capital markets and reform of the pension system in Ukraine. At FBW, he served for 23 years as executive vice president and general counsel, where he was a member of the board and the Executive Committee, a trustee of the firm's employee pension and benefit plans, and chair of the affiliate trust company. Mr. Urban has served on numerous FINRA and NYSE self-regulatory committees, and he was elected to the NASD's National Adjudicatory Counsel. Prior to joining the private sector, for nine years he held both staff attorney and management positions at the SEC and CFTC. He graduated with a bachelor of science degree from Cornell University, and a juris doctorate from the Columbus School of Law at Catholic University.

CHAPTER 25

Enforcement Actions Against Chief Compliance Officers

By Brian L. Rubin, *Sutherland Asbill & Brennan LLP*
   Irene A. Firippis, *Sutherland Asbill & Brennan LLP*

I. INTRODUCTION

If you're a chief compliance officer (CCO), you've got a target on your back. (Go ahead. Take a look. You may need to get a couple of mirrors. And don't be afraid to squint—reading all of those compliance manuals, policies, and procedures really has made your eyesight worse.) Whenever something bad (or arguably not-so-good) happens at a broker-dealer (BD) or investment adviser (IA), the regulators want to review the relevant policies and procedures, learn who was in charge of supervision, and examine how the firm was monitoring compliance, among other things. This fact-finding mission often leads directly to the CCO or his or her designees, who sometimes find themselves on the receiving end of an enforcement action brought by the Securities and Exchange Commission (SEC), the Financial Industry Regulatory Authority (FINRA), or the states. Therefore, if you are a CCO or a compliance officer, you may want to learn about what conduct has gotten other compliance officers in trouble and how you might avoid a similar fate.

How common are these actions? That's a good question, but as we'll see in a minute, that statistic doesn't tell the whole story. From January 1, 2013, to December 31, 2014, FINRA brought 44 cases involving compliance officers.[1] Although it is sometimes difficult to determine the role in which someone is acting and whether someone is being charged purely for compliance-related conduct, it appears that in 41 of those cases, a compliance officer was charged for compliance-related conduct and, in some of those 41 cases, for noncompliance-related conduct as well. In three of those cases, CCOs were charged for conduct related to another function, such as being a supervisor of a registered representative. During that same period, the SEC brought 54 SEC administrative actions involving CCOs, 46 of which concerned investment advisory conduct and nine of which involved broker-dealer conduct (two of the cases involved both IA and BD conduct). Of the 46 IA cases, it appears that in 25 of those cases, a compliance officer was charged for compliance-related conduct and, in certain instances,

---

[1] FINRA Disciplinary Actions Online, www.finra.org/Industry/Enforcement/DisciplinaryActions/FDAS/

other conduct as well. In 21 IA cases, compliance officers were charged for conduct related only to a noncompliance function. Of the nine BD cases, it appears that five cases involved a compliance officer who was charged for compliance-related conduct and sometimes other conduct as well. In four BD cases, it appears that compliance officers were charged for noncompliance related functions.

These statistics are interesting but possibly of questionable significance for CCOs. For each case in which an action was filed, there were other matters for which the regulators considered bringing charges by providing a Wells notification to the CCO but ultimately did not bring an action.[2] And for each of those matters, there were others in which CCOs were investigated but did not receive a Wells notification. There were also countless others in which CCOs had to provide investigative on-the-record testimony even though, at the time of the testimony, they technically may not have been the subject of the investigation. Thus, given the regulatory climate, CCOs should be concerned. Indeed, recent enforcement actions seem to indicate that CCOs may face increasing exposure to disciplinary liability related to business and supervisory activities as new regulations and constraints in firm resources force CCOs to take on more responsibilities and become more actively involved in business activities.[3]

II. THE RELEVANT RULES AND THE ROLE OF THE CCO

Traditionally, the role of the CCO has been to provide advice and guidance to business units and senior management on the overall compliance program of the BD and IA without assuming supervisory authority over business functions.[4] FINRA Rule 3130 requires BDs to designate at least one principal to serve as the CCO and further requires the BD's chief executive officer (CEO) or equivalent to certify annually that the firm "has in place processes to establish, maintain, review, test, and modify written compliance policies and written supervisory procedures reasonably designed to achieve compliance with applicable FINRA rules, MSRB rules and federal securities laws and regulations."[5]

The CEO also must certify that he or she has met annually with the CCO to discuss the firm's compliance efforts. This meeting requirement illustrates the "unique and integral role" of the CCO in the firm's compliance program.[6] The Supplemental Material for the rule provides that the CCO is "a primary advisor to the member on its

---

[2] If the staff of the SEC or FINRA has preliminarily determined that securities laws or regulations were violated, they will usually initiate the "Wells process," informing the potential respondent or defendant of the staff's proposed violations. See Securities and Exchange Commission Division of Enforcement, § 2.4 (Oct. 9, 2013), www.sec.gov/divisions/enforce/enforcementmanual.pdf; "Investigations and Formal Disciplinary Actions: FINRA Provides Guidance on Its Enforcement Process," FINRA Reg. Notice 09-17, at 3-4 (Mar. 2009), www.finra.org/web/groups/industry/@ip/@reg/ @notice/documents/notices/p118171.pdf. Potential respondents or defendants often convince the staff that the SEC or FINRA should not bring an action.
[3] White Paper: *The Evolving Role of Compliance, Securities Industry and Financial Markets Association*, at 4–5 (Mar. 2013), http://www.sifma.org/issues/item.aspx?id=8589942363
[4] See White Paper, *The Evolving Role of Compliance*, at 4.
[5] FINRA Conduct Rule 3130.
[6] FINRA Conduct Rule 3130, Supplemental Material .05.

overall compliance scheme and the particularized rules, policies, and procedures that the member adopts" and should therefore have expertise in the following: understanding the firm's lines of business; identifying the relevant rules, regulations, laws, and standards of conduct pertaining to those lines of business; developing policies and procedures reasonably designed to achieve compliance with those rules, regulations, laws, and standards of conduct; evidencing supervision by line managers responsible for executing those policies and procedures; and testing compliance with the firm's policies and procedures.[7]

Under FINRA Rule 3110, BDs are required "to establish and maintain a system to supervise the activities of each associated person that is reasonably designed to achieve compliance with applicable securities laws and regulations, and with applicable FINRA rules."[8] As a part of that supervisory system, a firm must "establish, maintain, and enforce written procedures to supervise the types of business in which it engages and the activities of its associated persons that are reasonably designed to achieve compliance with applicable securities laws and regulations, and with applicable FINRA rules." Firms often delegate to the CCO overall responsibility for the supervisory systems and written procedures, called written supervisory procedures (WSPs).

Rule 206(4)-7 under the Investment Advisers Act of 1940 (Advisers Act) requires IAs to adopt and implement written policies and procedures reasonably designed to prevent violations of the Advisers Act and rules promulgating thereunder. Investment advisers are also required to designate a CCO who is responsible for administering these policies and procedures.[9] When the SEC adopted Rule 206(4)-7, it explained that an IA's CCO "should be empowered with the full responsibility and authority to develop and enforce appropriate policies and procedures for the firm" and therefore "should have a position of sufficient seniority and authority within the organization to compel others to adhere to the compliance policies and procedures."[10]

III. THEORIES OF LIABILITY

CCOs may find themselves the subject of enforcement actions under a variety of theories. First, CCOs may be found liable if they directly violate the federal securities laws, either acting in their role as CCO or acting in another capacity. Second, they may be found to have aided and abetted or caused a securities law violation. For example, if a BD or an IA is found to have violated a specific rule, depending on the facts, the CCO may be found liable for aiding and abetting or causing that violation. Third, CCOs may be found liable for failing to supervise another person who committed a violation. Sometimes, that other person may be a direct report, or in other situations, because of the CCO's position at the firm, the other person may not be a direct report.

---

[7] *Id.*
[8] FINRA Rule 3110 is effective on December 1, 2014. Prior to its effective date, FINRA Rule 3010 sets forth substantially similar requirements for supervisory systems and written procedures.
[9] Advisers Act Rule 206(4)-7.
[10] *Final Rule: Compliance Programs of Investment Companies and Investment Advisers, Investment Advisers Act* Rel. No. 2204, Investment Company Act No. 26299, File No. S7-03-03 (Dec. 17, 2003).

IV. DIRECT VIOLATIONS

BD CCOs may be disciplined as direct violators of SEC and FINRA rules, and IA CCOs as direct violators of SEC rules. Sometimes CCOs are charged for direct violations related to their function as CCO, and sometimes they are charged for conduct they engaged in while wearing other "hats," such as being the firm's president.

Conduct Related to the Role of the CCO

As discussed above, CCOs of BDs serve as a primary adviser to the firm on its overall compliance scheme and the rules, policies, and procedures that the firm adopts. CCOs of IAs administer their firms' IA compliance policies and procedures. Therefore, CCOs may be found liable for failing to establish, maintain, or enforce adequate supervisory systems and/or WSPs. In addition, CCOs also may have other responsibilities delegated to them by their firms and may be found liable for failing to adequately carry out those responsibilities.

Supervisory Systems and WSPs

Inadequately Tailored WSPs. CCOs have been found liable when their firms' WSPs failed to adequately address part of the firms' business. In an April 2013 FINRA settlement, a CCO was disciplined in connection with his firm's sale of nonexempt unregistered securities.[11] Three customers had opened accounts at the firm, deposited shares of unregistered securities into their accounts, and then sold the unregistered shares to others. FINRA determined that the firm failed to have adequate WSPs in place designed to prevent the sale of nonexempt unregistered securities. According to FINRA, adequate procedures "would have communicated each step in the review and approval process, including background inquiry, information gathering, and required documentation." In the absence of such WSPs, FINRA concluded that the CCO, who was responsible for his firm's WSPs, violated NASD Rule 3010[12] (FINRA's prior rule on supervisory systems, including WSPs) and FINRA Rule 2010. The CCO was suspended in any principal capacity for six months but was not fined due to a demonstrated inability to pay.

A July 2013 decision by FINRA's National Adjudicatory Council (NAC) also illustrates the perils of WSPs that are not adequately tailored to a firm's business.[13] In that case, the NAC found that a CCO was responsible for his firm's failure to have an adequate supervisory system to monitor markups and markdowns. The CCO was designated as the individual responsible for establishing the firm's overall supervisory system and was the principal responsible for supervising the corporate fixed income transactions of a particular registered representative engaged in that business. From January 2004 to

---

[11] *Michael A. Zurita*, FINRA AWC No. 2009019534203 (Apr. 4, 2013).
[12] NASD Rule 3010, Supervision, http://finra.complinet.com/en/display/display.html?rbid=2403&element_id=3717
[13] *Department of Market Regulation v. Robert N. Drake*, NAC Decision, Complaint No. 20060053785-02 (July 25, 2013).

December 2004, the firm failed to report 34 corporate bond transactions that should have been reported during that time period. Beginning in October 2004, the firm executed a reporting agreement with its clearing firm, whereby the clearing firm would perform TRACE reporting on behalf of the firm. However, the firm's WSPs—which were the responsibility of the CCO—did not contain any procedures for supervisory review of the clearing firm's reporting. The NAC decision characterized the TRACE reporting WSPs as "boilerplate." For these and other supervisory failures, the NAC affirmed the hearing panel's imposition of a bar in principal and supervisory capacities and fined the CCO $5,000.

> *Takeaway:* CCOs may be sanctioned for their firms' failure to have and maintain procedures relating to, and appropriately tailored to, the business in which their firms are engaged.

Failure to Follow WSPs. CCOs may be liable where firms do not act in accordance with their procedures. In an August 2013 settlement order, FINRA disciplined a CCO for failing to adopt and implement adequate WSPs regarding outside business activities (OBAs) and private securities transactions (PSTs).[14] From 2004 to 2008, the CCO was directly responsible for reviewing and supervising OBAs and PSTs. For much of that time period, two registered representatives at the firm were selling investments away from the firm. In total, the two registered representatives solicited approximately 30 investors, many of whom were firm customers, to invest more than $4 million in investments held away from the firm with nonbroker-dealer custodians. The investors lost all of their money. The CCO had approved the registered representatives' participation in the outside company as an OBA, but did not require the registered representatives to submit written notice detailing their managerial activities with the outside company or written notice of their solicitation of firm customers for investments in the outside company. These notices were required by the firm's compliance manual. The order accepting the offer of settlement stated that the CCO "failed to make appropriate and reasonable inquiries prior to approving the brokers' involvement" in the OBA.

When the CCO later required all registered representatives to submit new written requests for approval for existing OBAs, the registered representatives failed to comply, and the CCO never followed up. Finally, the firm failed to review the registered representatives' sale of the outside investments (which were private securities transactions) and failed to receive copies of statements or confirmations because the investments were not held with the firm's clearing firm. In addition to failing to have adequate procedures in place to supervise OBAs and PSTs, the firm failed to have adequate procedures in place to prevent registered representatives from using outside custodians for selling away. Because the CCO was responsible for drafting and implementing supervisory practices and procedures at the firm, he was sanctioned for violating NASD Rules 3010 and 2110. The CCO was suspended for three months in a principal capacity and fined $10,000.

---

[14] *Department of Enforcement v. David Walton Matthews, Jr.*, Disciplinary Proceeding No. 2009017195204 (Aug. 19, 2013).

In a 2011 settlement, the SEC found that a CCO aided and abetted his firm's failure to have written policies and procedures reasonably designed to ensure compliance with the Advisers Act and caused his firm's violations relating to principal trades with advisory clients.[15] Over the course of approximately two and a half years, the firm effected thousands of securities transactions without disclosing to its advisory clients that the firm was acting as principal for its own account, violating the disclosure and consent requirements of Section 206(3) of the Advisers Act. During this time, the CCO was responsible for monitoring the firm's overall compliance with the Advisers Act, including the disclosure and consent requirements. The firm, at the CCO's suggestion, had hired an outside consultant to review the firm's advisory business and the outside consultant had brought the rules regarding principal transactions to the CCO's attention. Nevertheless, the CCO failed to determine whether the firm had adequate written policies and procedures regarding principal transactions and failed to adopt and implement such procedures on behalf of the firm. Through this conduct, the CCO caused his firm's violations related to principal trades. The firm was dually registered, and the SEC found that, although the firm had policies and procedures in effect with respect to its broker-dealer business, it had only an "off-the-shelf" investment adviser compliance manual. The CCO was responsible for revising and implementing the investment adviser manual to address the firm's business practices. By the time of the outside consultant's review, several months after the firm's SEC registration, the CCO had not completed the revisions. The outside consultant's report specifically recommended that the firm adopt a compliance manual tailored to its advisory business and further pointed out the need for a written code of ethics. Neither the CCO nor the firm's president took any action. Consequently, the CCO was censured and assessed a civil penalty of $50,000.

Takeaway: CCOs (and others) may be sanctioned if they fail to follow firm procedures.

Reporting Violations

Firms are subject to various reporting obligations, including FINRA Rule 4530, which governs the reporting of customer complaints, litigation, and non-FINRA arbitrations, as well as obligations under FINRA's bylaws to amend Forms U4, U5, and BD to reflect events such as arbitration settlements. These responsibilities are often delegated to CCOs and, therefore, CCOs may be held liable where there are failures to timely or accurately disclose reportable items. For example, in an October 2011 settlement, FINRA found that a CCO, along with his firm, violated reporting obligations when he failed to report an arbitration settlement within the 10-day period required by FINRA Rule 3070 (the predecessor to FINRA Rule 4530).[16] FINRA also found that the CCO and the firm violated FINRA's bylaws and Rule 2010 for failing to disclose the settlement on the appropriate Form U4. FINRA noted that the CCO "was responsible for ensuring [the firm] filed all necessary Forms U4, Forms U5, and Rule 3070 reports."

---

[15] Wunderlich Securities, Inc., et al., Exch. Act. Rel. No. 3-14403, 2011 SEC LEXIS 1859 (May 27, 2011).
[16] *Internet Securities and Michael W. Beardsley*, FINRA AWC No. 20090209303-02 (Oct. 3, 2011).

For these and other violations, he was suspended in any principal capacity for one year. Due to his inability to pay, no fine was imposed.

Takeaway: CCOs may be sanctioned for their firms' reporting failures.

Inadequate Responses to FINRA Rule 8210 Requests

FINRA Rule 8210 empowers FINRA to compel member firms and associated persons to produce documents and information and to require individuals to appear for testimony. CCOs are regularly involved in responding to document and information requests, or are required to appear for testimony. Failure to respond adequately could subject a firm or an individual to liability. For example, in an August 2013 FINRA settlement, a CCO (who was also a CEO and a chief operating officer) was disciplined for failing to respond to Rule 8210 requests and failing to appear for testimony.[17] First, in the context of a cycle examination, the CCO failed to respond completely to a Rule 8210 request and failed to provide the balance of the information requested until after a notice of suspension was issued. Second, in the context of an investigation of the firm's distribution of investors' funds from an investment group for which the CCO was the manager, the CCO failed to appear for testimony and failed to provide requested documents and information. For this conduct, the CCO was barred from associating with any FINRA member firm in any capacity.

In a December 2013 NAC appeal, a CCO was disciplined for failing to respond to Rule 8210 requests in a timely manner.[18] The CCO, who was also the firm's chief financial officer, responded to two Rule 8210 requests that FINRA staff initially sent. More than seven months later, the CCO responded to a third request for correspondence and account documents and then produced responsive documents only after the staff issued a notice of suspension to the CCO and to another principal of the firm. For this and other conduct, the CCO was suspended in all capacities for two years and fined $25,000.

Takeaway: CCOs may be sanctioned if they fail to respond to Rule 8210 requests adequately.

Misleading the Public or the Regulators

False Compliance Reviews. In one of the Bernard Madoff-related cases, Peter Madoff, Bernie's brother who was CCO of Bernard L. Madoff Investment Securities, LLC (BMIS), settled with the SEC in July 2012 for allegedly making "false and misleading entries in numerous documents at BMIS that were designed to make it appear that Respondent performed various compliance reviews of BMIS's IA operations and that BMIS maintained an effective compliance program."[19] The SEC's settlement order stated that Peter Madoff's "false and misleading statements made it appear to regulators and

---

[17] *William Edward Hogan,* AWC No. 2013036782802 (Aug. 21, 2013).
[18] *Robert Marcus Lane and Jeffrey Griffin Lane,* NAC Decision, Disciplinary Proceeding No. 20070082049 (Dec. 26, 2013).
[19] *Peter Madoff,* Admin. Proc. File No. 3-14963, 2012 SEC LEXIS 2367 (July 26, 2012).

the firm's advisory clients that [the firm] actually had a CCO who performed required compliance functions, when in reality Respondent did nothing of the sort." For this conduct, Peter Madoff was found to have violated Section 15(b) of the Securities and Exchange Act of 1934 (Exchange Act) (which deals with the registration of BDs) and Section 203(f) of the Advisers Act (which deals with the registration of IAs). Peter Madoff was barred from associating with any investment adviser or broker-dealer.

> *Takeaway:* CCOs may be sanctioned if they make false statements to regulators or clients, including statements related to compliance functions (or if they assisted their brother, Bernie Madoff).

False Form ADV. In the *Peter Madoff* case, he was also sanctioned for allegedly submitting false and misleading Forms ADV. Similarly, in an October 2012 case, another CCO was barred, with the right to reapply after one year, for filing a false Form ADV with the SEC staff.[20]

> *Takeaway:* CCOs may be sanctioned if the firm's Form ADV is false.

False Books and Records. BDs and IAs are required to maintain certain books and records under Securities Exchange Act Rules 17a-3 and 17a-4, Advisers Act Rules 204-2, and related FINRA Rules, including NASD Rule 3110. CCOs may face liability if they fall short in maintaining truthful books and records, or tamper with them in some fashion.

In a May 2014 settlement, FINRA disciplined a CCO for submitting to FINRA backdated documents related to customer complaints.[21] During the course of a routine examination, the CCO's firm produced to FINRA Excel spreadsheets showing customer complaints received during a defined time period. The spreadsheets included a notation showing a false date on which the firm's compliance department had supposedly reviewed the complaints, with the CCO's initials near the notation. The Letter of Acceptance, Waiver and Consent (AWC) alleged that "[a]ccording to [the CCO], the date approximated the date on which he had reviewed the spreadsheets." FINRA noted that the CCO "knew the spreadsheets he marked would be provided to FINRA staff." FINRA found that the CCO violated NASD Rule 3110(a), which provides that firms have to keep books and records in accordance with applicable laws, rules, regulations, and statements of policy as prescribed in SEC Rule 17a-3 and FINRA Rule 2010. The CCO was suspended in any principal capacity for 20 business days and fined $7,500.

> *Takeaway:* CCOs may be sanctioned for falsifying books and records and providing them to regulators.

Inadequate Antimoney Laundering Program

FINRA Rule 3310 requires BDs to implement an effective Anti-Money Laundering (AML) program designed to achieve compliance with the Bank Secrecy Act, 31 U.S.C.

---

[20] *Rick Cho,* Admin. Proc. File No. 3-15067, 2012 SEC LEXIS 3258 (Oct. 15, 2012).
[21] *Robert Henry Decker,* FINRA AWC No. 2011025434002 (May 22, 2014).

§ 5311 et seq. An AML compliance officer (AMLCO) is responsible for creating policies and procedures to detect and deter money laundering. In addition, Rule 17a-8 of the Exchange Act also requires BDs to comply with reporting obligations under the Bank Secrecy Act.

In a May 2014 settlement, FINRA disciplined an AMLCO, who was also the firm's president and CCO, in connection with the firm's AML supervisory system.[22] FINRA found that the firm, "through" the AMLCO, "demonstrated an ongoing pattern of noncompliance with the antimoney laundering rules" and that the firm and the AMLCO "failed to establish and implement an adequate AML supervisory system, reasonably designed to ensure compliance with the Bank Secrecy Act." The settlement order enumerated a number of examples in which the firm and the AMLCO failed to follow their AML procedures. For example, even though the firm had a procedure in place to detect red flags that should have prompted an investigation, the AMLCO failed to investigate the red flags. The red flags included a high volume of trading of low-priced securities, accounts domiciled or maintained offshore, and wire activity associated with liquidation of low-priced securities transactions. Additionally, the firm did not use exception reports to monitor unusual trading activity, but instead relied on inadequate daily reviews of customer trades.

The settlement order also noted that the firm failed to implement other components of a reasonably designed AML system, including "failing to properly respond to requests under Section 314(a) of the USA PATRIOT Act of 2001, which authorizes law enforcement to communicate with broker-dealers to request information regarding persons or entities of interest to an investigation so that any accounts or transactions involving these individuals or entities can be promptly located." FINRA found that the AMLCO was "responsible for the creation and failed implementation of the policies that led to the AML violations by the firm." Accordingly, by failing to "adequately identify, investigate, or report suspicious activity," the AMLCO was found to have violated NASD Rules 3011(a) and 2110 and FINRA Rules 3310(a) and 2010. He was fined $25,000, jointly and severally with the firm, and suspended for three months in a principal capacity.

> *Takeaway:* AMLCOs may be sanctioned if they do not adequately monitor and respond to red flags, even if their firms maintain AML policies and procedures.

Other Conduct

In addition to liability related to their CCO responsibilities, CCOs who act in other capacities may be found to have directly violated certain statutes or rules. For example, in January 2013, through a settlement, FINRA disciplined a CCO in connection with his firm's allegedly inadequate due diligence of private placement investments.[23] Under

---

[22] *Department of Enforcement v. Capital Path Securities, Inc. and William John Davis*, Order Accepting Offer of Settlement, Disciplinary Proceeding No. 2011025869201 (May 8, 2014).
[23] *Enforcement v. Marc Holzberg*, Order Accepting Offer of Settlement, Disciplinary Proceeding No. 2009018956001 (Jan. 24, 2013).

the firm's WSPs, the CCO was responsible for "the due diligence investigation of private placements, including the acquisition and review of relevant documents, discussions with product sponsors, review of third party due diligence reports, monitoring of the affairs of the issues during the period that a private placement was being offered for sale by the firm's representatives and, where applicable, establishing conditions upon the offer and sale of private placement securities." FINRA determined that the CCO failed to respond reasonably to red flags indicating risks associated with a particular private placement offering. For example, in August 2008, the CCO approved a private placement offering despite knowing that (1) the issuer of that private placement had missed payments of distributions to customers on a prior offering and eventually suspended sales in that offering, and (2) the Private Placement Memorandum (PPM) for the offering falsely claimed that the issuer had never missed any interest payments on its offerings. Additionally, after approving the private placement, the CCO created a disclosure form to accompany the private placement, which failed to inform investors that the issuer was delinquent in payments to investors on at least one previous offering. Finally, after at least one prior offering was declared in default, the CCO instructed the firm's representatives to disclose the delinquent payments but did not establish any procedures to monitor compliance with this condition on the sale of the offering. Based on this conduct, FINRA concluded that the CCO violated NASD Rule 3010 and FINRA Rule 2010. Under the terms of the settlement, the CCO was suspended from participating in any principal capacity for six months. No monetary sanction was imposed because the CCO had filed for bankruptcy.

As another example, in May 2012 an administrative law judge (ALJ) found that a CCO willfully violated Exchange Act Rule 10b-5 and Sections 206(1) and 206(2) of the Advisers Act (each of which prohibits fraudulent conduct) by engaging in a "mark-the-close" scheme whereby the CCO instructed a trader to execute trades to inflate the prices of certain thinly traded securities held by the firm's advisory clients by placing buy orders at prices higher than the most recent previous trades just before the markets closed.[24] For this conduct and other related violations, the ALJ assessed a civil penalty of $75,000, jointly and severally against the CCO and his firm, and barred the CCO.

> *Takeaway:* CCOs may be sanctioned if they fail to comply with their noncompliance responsibilities (or if they commit fraud).

V. AIDING AND ABETTING AND/OR CAUSING A VIOLATION

Another way that CCOs may face liability is through aiding, abetting, and/or causing a violation by another party. Liability for aiding and abetting requires an underlying violation, substantial assistance in connection with the primary violation and scienter,

---

[24] *Donald L. Koch and Koch Asset Management, LLC,* Admin. Proc. File No. 3-14355, 2012 SEC LEXIS 1645 (May 24, 2012).

which is satisfied by recklessness.²⁵ Similarly, liability for "causing" a violation requires a primary violation and an act or omission by the person or entity that causes the violation. Causing liability, however, requires only negligence in some cases.²⁶

Policies and Procedures

In a November 2011 SEC settlement, a CCO, who was also the CEO and sole owner of the firm, was found to have aided, abetted and caused his firm's violations. The SEC had found that the IA "failed to adopt and implement written compliance policies and procedures as required by Section 206(4) of the Advisers Act."²⁷ The CCO/CEO/owner "was living in Brazil on a religious mission" when he assumed his responsibilities and therefore "failed to perform virtually any compliance responsibilities." As a result, the firm was found to have violated Section 206(4) of the Advisers Act, and the CCO/CEO/owner was found to have aided, abetted, and caused the violations. He was barred from the industry and assessed a civil penalty of $50,000.

In May 2011 a CCO was sanctioned for causing his firm's violations related to inadequate policies and procedures.²⁸ This firm, Wunderlich Securities, Inc., was dually registered, and the SEC found that, although the firm had policies and procedures in effect with respect to its BD business, it had only an "off-the-shelf" IA compliance manual. The CCO was responsible for revising and implementing the IA manual to address the firm's business practices. The firm hired an outside consultant to review its policies and procedures. By the time of the outside consultant's review, which was several months after the firm's SEC registration, the CCO had not completed the revisions to the IA compliance manual. The outside consultant's report specifically recommended that the firm adopt a compliance manual tailored to its advisory business and further pointed out the need for a written code of ethics. The CCO failed to take action in response to these recommendations, and he was found to have aided and abetted and caused the firm's violations related to its inadequate policies and procedures and failure to maintain and enforce a written code of ethics. The CCO was censured and assessed a civil penalty of $50,000.

Principal Trades

In the *Wunderlich Securities* case discussed above, the CCO was also found to have aided and abetted and caused his firm's violations relating to principal trades with advisory clients.²⁹ Over the course of approximately two and one-half years, the firm effected

---

[25] Section 15 of the Securities Act of 1933 (Securities Act), Section 20(e) of the Exchange Act, and Section 209(f) of the Investment Advisers Act of 1940 provide for aiding and abetting liability for reckless, as well as knowing, conduct. *See In the Matter of MidSouth Capital, Inc. and Mark D. Hill*, Admin. Prof. File No. 3-14852, 2012 SEC LEXIS 1254 (Apr. 18, 2012) (finding aiding and abetting liability premised on recklessness).

[26] *Mark T. Schwetschenau*, Admin. Proc. File No. 3-13995, 2010 SEC LEXIS 2534 *9 (Aug. 5, 2010) ("Negligence is sufficient to establish liability for causing a primary violation that does not require scienter").

[27] *OMNI Investment Advisors, Inc., and Gary R. Beynon*, Admin. Proc. File No. 3-14643, 2011 SEC LEXIS 4176 (Nov. 28, 2011).

[28] *Wunderlich Securities, Inc., et al.*, Admin. Proc. File No. 3-14403, 2011 SEC LEXIS 1859 (May 27, 2011).

[29] *Id.*

thousands of securities transactions without disclosing to its advisory clients that the firm was acting as principal for its own account. This conduct violated the disclosure and consent requirements of Section 206(3) of the Advisers Act. During this time, the CCO was responsible for monitoring the firm's overall compliance with the Advisers Act, including the disclosure and consent requirements.

Books and Records

In the *Gary R. Beynon* case (in which the CCO worked remotely from Brazil), the firm also failed to maintain certain books and records, as required by Section 204A of the Advisers Act. The CCO was found to have aided and abetted the firm's violation.[30]

Through a May 2011 SEC settlement decision, a CCO was sanctioned in connection with his responsibility for receiving and maintaining employee written acknowledgments of the firm's code of ethics.[31] For a two-year period, the firm did not keep any records of these acknowledgments. Consequently, the CCO was found to have willfully aided and abetted the firm's violations of Rule 204-2(a)(12) under the Advisers Act, which requires firms to maintain a record of such acknowledgment pages. For this and other violations, the CCO was censured and assessed a civil penalty of $100,000.

In July 2010, the SEC upheld an ALJ's decision that a CCO willfully aided and abetted his firm's recordkeeping and document production violations of Section 17(a) of the Securities Exchange Act of 1934.[32] The CCO was responsible for preserving records at the firm, including email and instant messages. In July 2003, the CCO approved a revised written policy requiring registered representatives either to disable their computers' instant messaging programs or to preserve paper copies of their instant messages. Contrary to this policy, at the end of 2003, the CCO approved a registered representative's practice of storing instant messages electronically. At this time, the CCO also became aware that the same registered representative was using a personal email address for business purposes, contrary to the registered representative's written affirmation to the contrary during a branch audit. In connection with branch audits during the following two years, the CCO failed to alert the firm's auditors about the personal email account, and the CCO continued to approve electronic storage of instant messages. The CCO repeatedly threatened to take disciplinary action against the representative for using a personal email account, but the CCO never took any action.

The SEC Enforcement staff contacted the CCO in July 2005 requesting firm documents, including electronic materials, relating to the representative's trading of a particular stock. In response to this request, the CCO assigned to the representative the responsibility for producing records of correspondence and then relayed to the SEC the representative's false assertion that he had no responsive

---

[30] *OMNI Investment Advisors, Inc., and Gary R. Beynon*, Admin. Proc. File No. 3-14643, 2011 SEC LEXIS 4176 (Nov. 28, 2011).
[31] *Aletheia Research and Mgmt., Inc., et al.*, Admin. Proc. File No. 3-14374, 2011 SEC LEXIS 1637 (May 9, 2011).
[32] *In the Matter of vFinance Investments, Inc. and Richard Campanella*, Exchange Act Release No. 62448, 2010 SEC LEXIS 2216 (July 2, 2010).

correspondence to produce. During the next several months, the SEC sent at least five request letters to the CCO, spoke with him by telephone, and contacted the registered representative through his counsel. Although the firm produced limited emails, without attachments, and the representative's phone records, the CCO never visited the representative's office to search for responsive documents. The representative made multiple incomplete email productions and declined to produce his computer's hard drive.

In January 2006, the CCO threatened to terminate the representative if he did not comply with the SEC's request. Weeks later, the representative finally provided his hard drive, but by that time he had "electronically shredded" approximately 1,000 messages. Finally, in response to a July 2006 SEC subpoena directed at the firm, the firm produced emails from the registered representative's firm email account. Not until March 2007 did the CCO visit the representative's branch office to collect additional responsive documents. At that time, he found two boxes of responsive documents.

Based on the firm's underlying failure to preserve records and to produce business records in a timely fashion, and the CCO's "substantial assistance" to those failures, which the SEC characterized as "variously knowing and extremely reckless," the SEC concluded that the CCO had willfully aided and abetted the firm's violations. The SEC affirmed the ALJ's decision to assess a $30,000 penalty against the CCO, but added to his sanction by imposing a two-year bar, with the right to reapply. Finally, the SEC also upheld a $100,000 penalty against the firm.

Fraudulently Responding to Requests for Proposal

In a May 2011 settlement, the SEC found that an IA CCO had aided and abetted a number of his firm's underlying violations related to responding to requests for proposal (RFPs).[33] In response to a number of RFPs from prospective clients, the firm either misrepresented or omitted information related to prior SEC examinations and, in one instance, provided a copy of an SEC deficiency letter for the firm's BD, rather than for the IA that was the subject of the RFP. The SEC found that the CCO, who reviewed the firm's RFP responses, knew or should have known about the firm's examination deficiencies and, at a minimum, should have verified that the correct deficiency letter was provided. Because of this conduct, the SEC found that the CCO willfully aided and abetted the firm's violation of Section 206(2) of the Advisers Act, which prohibits fraudulent conduct. For these and other violations, the CCO was censured and assessed a civil penalty of $100,000.

> *Takeaway:* CCOs may be sanctioned not only for their own violations, but also for contributing to another's violation.

---

[33] *Id.*

VI. FAILURE TO SUPERVISE

Section 15(b)(6) of the Securities Exchange Act of 1934 authorizes the SEC to institute proceedings against an individual where a person under that individual's supervision violates the securities laws or rules. Similarly, FINRA Rule 3110 provides liability for failure to supervise an individual (although, unlike Section 15, it does not require that the supervised individual actually commit an underlying violation). Section 203(e)(6) of the Advisers Act contains similar language as Section 15(b)(6). Typically, CCOs are not part of the direct supervisory line and, therefore, would not be subject to such liability. There are instances, however, where CCOs are designated as supervisors or act as direct-line supervisors, and they may be subject to liability for failure to supervise individuals. For example, CCOs traditionally have supervisory responsibility for Compliance Department employees.[34] In other instances, even where the CCOs are not in the direct supervisory chain, they may nonetheless be found to be supervisors by virtue of their conduct and, therefore, be subject to liability for failure to supervise.

Direct-Line Supervision

Sometimes CCOs supervise employees directly in their supervisory chain in the Compliance Department. A CCO also may directly supervise employees outside of the Compliance Department when the CCO and the employee have noncompliance functions. For example, in a March 2013 settlement, FINRA disciplined a CCO for failing to supervise his firm's owner (and producing manager) who excessively traded in at least five customer accounts.[35] FINRA noted that the CCO had no experience in a supervisory or compliance role prior to becoming CCO and the producing manager's supervisor. It further noted that the firm's WSPs required the CCO to review the producing manager's trading activity but that the CCO failed to identify and follow up on red flags indicating excessive trading. For violations of NASD Rule 3010 and FINRA Rule 2010, the CCO was suspended for 30 business days in a principal capacity, but was not fined due to a demonstrated inability to pay.

In a July 2012 settlement, the SEC disciplined a CCO for allegedly failing to supervise an investment adviser representative (IAR) who misappropriated $7 million from 15 clients.[36] The IAR accomplished the misappropriations by forging client signatures on wire requests and causing funds to be transferred to entities linked to him. On some occasions, the IAR liquidated securities in clients' accounts to fund the transfers. According to the SEC, the CCO "had supervisory responsibility over" the IAR but "failed reasonably to investigate or otherwise respond to the numerous red flags indicating possible violations." The SEC concluded that the CCO failed to supervise the IAR reasonably in accordance with Section 203(e) of the Advisers Act. Accordingly, the SEC barred the CCO from associating in a supervisory capacity and imposed a civil penalty of $25,000 (based on the CCO's sworn statement regarding her financial condition).

---

[34] *See, e.g., Trillium Brokerage Services, LLC, Letter of Acceptance, Waiver, and Consent*, No. 20070076782-01 (July 7, 2010) (FINRA sanctioned a CCO for failing to supervise two compliance employees).
[35] *Brady Castille*, FINRA AWC No. 2011025843302 (Mar. 15, 2013).
[36] *Charles L. Rizzo and Gina M. Hornbogen*, Admin. Proc. File No. 3-14641, 2012 SEC LEXIS 2299 (July 20, 2012).

In a July 2013 settlement, the SEC disciplined a CCO for allegedly failing to supervise a representative who misappropriated $16 million of client funds.[37] The CCO was the direct supervisor for all of the registered personnel at the firm for a period of time. Over an eight year period, the representative transferred mutual fund shares and cash from client accounts at a custodial broker dealer to a nominee account under his control. The representative misappropriated the funds by using falsified transfer authorization forms and abusing the standing authority his clients had given him over their advisory accounts. The SEC alleged that as the representative's direct supervisor, the CCO failed to reasonably supervise him and prevent the violations. For example, the CCO was aware that client assets were transferred to the nominee account but took no action to ensure, consistent with the IA's policies, that the representative did not directly or indirectly hold client assets or have access to them through the nominee account. Accordingly, the SEC found that the CCO violated Section 203(e)(6) of the Advisers Act. The SEC barred the CCO from associating with any broker, dealer, IA, or municipal securities dealer for twelve months. The SEC did not impose a civil penalty, due to the CCO's sworn testimony asserting his inability to pay.

Urban: Indirect Line Supervision

As discussed above, CCOs traditionally have supervisory responsibility for Compliance Department employees, but generally have not been viewed as supervisors of business activities.[38] Nonetheless, CCOs may face liability for failing to supervise individuals not directly in their chain of command. When CCOs have sufficient "responsibility, ability, or authority to affect the conduct of the employee whose behavior is at issue," even if those employees do not report directly to the CCO, the CCO may be deemed a supervisor and become subject to liability for supervisory failures.[39] Some observers have suggested that in recent years regulators have taken a more expansive view of the potential supervisory liability of compliance officers.[40] Indeed, a recent SEC case involving Theodore Urban, a former general counsel of Ferris, Baker Watts, arguably indicates an expansion of the contours of the test for supervisory liability.

In October 2009, the SEC's Division of Enforcement filed an administrative action against Mr. Urban, general counsel and executive vice president of a BD and IA, who oversaw the Compliance Department. Enforcement alleged that Mr. Urban failed reasonably to supervise a broker who was involved in a $50 million Ponzi scheme. In September 2010, after a 13-day hearing, the SEC ALJ ruled that Mr. Urban was, indeed, a supervisor, but found that he acted reasonably.[41] In that decision, the ALJ analyzed

---

[37] *Ronald Rollins*, Admin. Proc. File No. 3-15392, 2013 SEC LEXIS 2204 (July 29, 2013).
[38] *See* White Paper, *The Evolving Role of Compliance*, at 10 ("The management function in a securities firm, not the Compliance Department function, has the responsibility to supervise business units and to direct firm and employee activities to achieve compliance with applicable laws."), http://www.sifma.org/uploadedfiles/societies/sifma_compliance_and_legal_society/role_of_compliance_white_paper%20(2).pdf
[39] *George J. Kolar*, 55 S.E.C. 1009, 2002 SEC LEXIS 1647, *13 (June 26, 2002) (quoting *John H. Gutfreund*, 51 S.E.C. 93, 113, 1992 SEC LEXIS 2939, *47 (Dec. 3, 1992)).
[40] *See* White Paper, *The Evolving Role of Compliance*, at 4–5.
[41] *Theodore W. Urban*, Admin. Proc. File No. 3-13655, 2010 SEC LEXIS 2941 (Sept. 8, 2010).

the meaning of "responsibility, ability, and authority," and suggested a broader scope of supervisory liability than had been previously understood for nonline supervisors, like in-house counsel and CCOs. In concluding that Mr. Urban was a supervisor, the ALJ noted that, while Mr. Urban did not have any of the traditional powers associated with a person supervising brokers, his legal and compliance opinions were viewed as "authoritative" and his "recommendations were generally followed by people in [the firm's] business units." The ALJ also noted that, although Mr. Urban did not direct the firm's response to concerns about the broker, he was a member of the firm's Credit and Risk Committee that reviewed compliance employees' concerns about the broker, and the general counsel dealt directly with the broker on behalf of the committee.

The ALJ ultimately found that Mr. Urban had fulfilled his supervisory obligations because he had "performed his responsibilities in a cautious, objective, thorough, and reasonable manner." Mr. Urban believed those he supervised were carrying out their responsibilities and "repeatedly prodded them to do so." The ALJ's decision was then appealed by both sides to the full commission. In January 2012, the SEC summarily dismissed the case on appeal based on a one-to-one vote (with then-Chairman Mary L. Schapiro and Commissioner Elisse B. Walter recusing themselves).[42]

The significance of the *Urban* case is unclear and has proven to be unsettling for those in the securities industry. Enforcement's position, along with the ALJ's determination that Mr. Urban was a supervisor, seems to create a standard that legal and compliance professionals could face supervisory liability simply for doing their jobs. *Urban* reduces the standard for supervisory liability to include someone whose recommendations are respected and who participates in problem solving. Arguably, this analysis could create an incentive for legal and compliance personnel not to involve themselves in potential legal and compliance issues at all, for fear of subjecting themselves to supervisory liability.

Certain SEC commissioners have acknowledged concerns regarding this type of liability. For example, in a speech at the Practising Law Institute's SEC Speaks in February 2012, SEC Commissioner Daniel M. Gallagher characterized the question of what makes a legal or compliance officer a supervisor as "disturbingly murky," but he emphasized that the SEC must ensure that "the fear of failure-to-supervise liability never deters legal and compliance personnel from carrying out their own critical responsibilities."[43] Moreover, he suggested that the consequences of the ALJ decision in *Urban* would not be an expansion of liability for legal and compliance personnel, saying, "If a firm employee in a traditionally nonsupervisory role has expertise relevant to a compliance matter, that employee shouldn't fear that sharing the expertise could result in a commission action for failure to supervise."[44] Similarly, SEC Commissioner Luis Aguilar stated that CCOs and general counsel who do their jobs "rationally, reasonably and

---

[42] SEC, Order Dismissing Proceeding, *In the Matter of Theodore W. Urban*, http://www.sec.gov/litigation/admin/2012/34-66259.pdf

[43] Daniel M. Gallagher, Remarks at "The SEC Speaks in 2012" (Feb. 24, 2012), http://www.sec.gov/news/speech/2012/spch022412dmg.htm

[44] *Id.*

professionally" have nothing to fear.[45] Commissioner Gallagher has also indicated that specific guidance from the SEC on this issue may not be forthcoming, saying, "It's hard to give particular guidance because the facts can be so nuanced—they're infinite in the number of permutations they can take."[46]

In an attempt to provide some guidance on supervisor liability, the SEC issued "frequently asked questions" regarding the liability of compliance and legal personnel in September 2013.[47] It assured CCOs and others that they are not subject to supervisory liability simply by virtue of their compliance positions and stated that the SEC "has brought failure to supervise actions against broker-dealer legal or compliance personnel only in limited circumstances in which these individuals have been delegated, or have assumed, supervisory responsibility for particular activities or situations, and therefore have 'the requisite degree of responsibility, ability, or authority to affect the conduct of the employee whose behavior is at issue.'" Current SEC Chair Mary Jo White sought to reassure compliance personnel by stating that "compliance officers who perform their responsibilities diligently, in good faith, and in compliance with the law are our partners and need not fear enforcement action."[48] Of course, whether people are performing their responsibilities adequately is in the eye of the regulator rather than the beholder (or compliance officer, if you prefer).

Guidance Regarding Indirect Line Supervision

In the absence of more concrete guidance from the SEC, CCOs may want to ensure that their roles remain advisory in nature, and that their firms document that compliance officers are not supervisors and do not have sufficient responsibility, ability, or authority to affect the conduct of employees. Specifically, to minimize exposure to findings of supervisory responsibility in the future, firms and CCOs may want to consider implementing the following steps:

- Adopt written supervisory policies and procedures that
  - Identify the direct supervisors of all employees; and
  - Specifically state that
    - Limit compliance officers' responsibilities to offering advice and recommendations, and
    - Do not assign compliance officers the responsibility, ability, or authority to affect the conduct of employees outside of their departments;
- When the firm is addressing misconduct of employees or representatives, the firm could document which business line supervisor is handling the issue and how;

---

[45] Julie Goodman, "Aguilar Queries Value of CCO Liability Guidance," *Compliance Intelligence* (Aug. 9, 2012), http://www.complianceintel.com/Article/3073517/Search/Aguilar-Queries-Value-Of-CCO-Liability-Guidance.html
[46] *Id.*
[47] SEC, *Frequently Asked Questions About Liability of Compliance and Legal Personnel at Broker-Dealers under Sections 15(b)(4) and 15(b)(6) of the Exchange Act, Division of Trading and Markets* (Sept. 30, 2013) http://www.sec.gov/divisions/marketreg/faq-cco-supervision-093013.htm
[48] Mary Jo White, *Remarks at National Society of Compliance Professionals National Membership Meeting* (Oct. 22, 2013), http://www.sec.gov/News/Speech/Detail/Speech/1370539960588

- When compliance officers serve on firm committees, the firm could document that their role is only advisory in nature; and
- When a compliance officer does have serious concerns about potential violations of the law, he or she may want to consider escalating the matter to senior management.

VII. CONCLUSION

Although being a compliance officer can be a rewarding career, like all careers, it can have some downsides. One of them is that every decision you make could be scrutinized by the regulators. And if regulators disagree with your decision (applying after-the-fact, 20/20 hindsight analysis), you may find yourself at the receiving end of a Wells notification or ultimately a disciplinary action. Regulators often don't understand that all of us—well, most of us anyway—make mistakes. And there's nothing wrong with that. As Albert Einstein (who, rumor has it, always wanted to be a CCO when he was a child) said, "A person who never made a mistake never tried anything new."[49] So, compliance officers should continue to do the best job they can by trying new things, and keeping up with changes in rules, regulations, and enforcement priorities by attending conferences and reading articles and books (like this one). And don't forget to use those mirrors to check out that target on your back. (And to see if anyone is following you.) It may help to motivate you.

---

[49] Brainy Quote, http://www.brainyquote.com/quotes/quotes/a/alberteins148788.html (last visited Dec. 31, 2014).

ABOUT THE AUTHORS

Brian L. Rubin is the Washington office leader of Sutherland Asbill & Brennan's Litigation group and the administrative partner in charge of the Securities Enforcement and Litigation Team. With more than 20 years of experience in federal securities law, first prosecuting and now defending, Brian represents clients being examined, investigated, and prosecuted by the U.S. Securities and Exchange Commission (SEC), the Financial Industry Regulatory Authority (FINRA), other self-regulatory organizations, and states. As former NASD (now FINRA) deputy chief counsel of Enforcement and Senior Enforcement Counsel at the SEC, he brings an insider's perspective to defending broker-dealers, investment advisers, investment companies, public companies and individuals in examinations, investigations, enforcement proceedings, litigation, arbitrations and in counseling.

Recently, Mr. Rubin represented firms and individuals on matters involving REITs, variable annuities, variable life insurance, mutual funds, advertising, email retention and surveillance, advisory accounts, insider trading, trade reporting, markups/markdowns, registration, privacy and supervision. He regularly litigates against regulators and claimants, counsels clients on regulatory and compliance matters, and conducts internal investigations. He has been named to The Best Lawyers in America in the areas of securities law, securities litigation and securities regulation and he has been selected for inclusion in Washington, DC, Super Lawyers® in the area of securities litigation. He received his juris doctor degree and his master of arts in Economics from Duke University and his bachelor of science degree, *cum laude*, from the Wharton School of Business of the University of Pennsylvania.

Irene A. Firippis is a member of Sutherland Asbill & Brennan's Litigation Practice Group. She focuses on an array of business and commercial litigation matters, including unclaimed property audits and securities litigation and enforcement. Her work also includes conducting internal investigations.

Prior to law school and her career at Sutherland, Ms. Firippis worked for the United States Department of Justice in Washington, DC, in its Aviation and Admiralty Section. She is admitted to the Maryland State Bar. Her work is supervised by District of Columbia Bar members. Ms. Firippis received her bachelor of arts degree from Pennsylvania State University and her juris doctor degree, *summa cum laude*, from American University Washington College of Law.

CHAPTER 26

Preparing to Become a Compliance Officer, and the Academy

By James A. Fanto
Brooklyn Law School

I. INTRODUCTION

This chapter is a reflection on the different kinds of backgrounds and academic preparations that are most useful for someone who would like to enter the compliance field. It is an understandable kind of review for a professor in a professional school, like me, who, aside from research interests, spends much time preparing students for future careers, generally in legal practice. This subject particularly interests me not only because I closely follow compliance in broker-dealers and investment advisers but also because in recent years many of my students are taking entry-level jobs as compliance officers and my former students are established in the compliance field. As a result, I have had to think about how to alter my teaching and courses to put students in the best position to find compliance jobs and to do well in them. Moreover, because I have taught for several years compliance-related subjects at the Financial Industry Regulatory Authority (FINRA) Institute at Wharton, which has a Certified Regulatory and Compliance Professional (CRCP) program, I have had the opportunity to meet many experienced compliance officers and to learn the various career paths that they took to achieve their current positions.

The first section of this chapter discusses the traditional backgrounds of compliance officers, which have been in the law, business, and accounting, and the strengths associated with these backgrounds. The next section examines why there has been a recent focus upon legal training in compliance and what law schools can do to prepare their students for this field. This section also considers how compliance officers can become involved in teaching compliance at local colleges, universities, and professional schools. The next section offers observations about the kinds of skills that are important in compliance and about how schools may contribute to developing those skills in future compliance officers.

II. TRADITIONAL BACKGROUNDS OF COMPLIANCE OFFICERS

A few words about the history of the compliance function are in order here, without entering much into the subject, which is examined elsewhere in this volume in depth. Compliance became a necessary firm function in broker-dealers when, in the Securities Act Amendments of 1964, Congress imposed supervisory liability explicitly upon broker-dealers and their supervisors for violations by those under their supervision.[1] Although supervisory liability for the firm was not new at that time, for the SEC had used other liability theories to reach broker-dealers for their supervisory violations,[2] it was a new risk for supervisors. While imposing liability, the statute also gave the firm and the supervisors statutory defenses, which essentially required a firm to have a supervisory system with written procedures and to implement it adequately.[3] This meant that, for the defenses to work, brokers and other firm employees had to be appropriately supervised to ensure their compliance with the law, regulations, and professional standards.

As a result of this supervisory liability, in all but the smallest firms, there had to be a separate department or group of specialized employees who would help create and implement the compliance and supervisory system, which entailed, among other assignments, drafting compliance procedures for the brokers and supervisory procedures for the supervisors, conducting training on these procedures, monitoring the firm's operations and employees for compliance with the procedures, and following up and investigating any indication that the procedures were not being followed, which might indicate a legal or professional violation.[4] Historically, the responsibility for compliance fell to a subdivision within a broker-dealer's legal department.[5] Because the ultimate purpose of compliance was to prevent legal violations, it made sense that legal expertise was useful for the design and implementation of supervisory and compliance systems and that, accordingly, some compliance officers were lawyers.

But many compliance officers then, as today, were and are not legally trained. Some, in fact, had the same origin as supervisors and supervisory assistants. They came from a

---

[1] P.L. 88-467, 78 Stat. 565, 571-72 (1964) (adding, for firms, 15 U.S.C. § 78o(b)(5)(E) (1964) (now codified at 15 U.S.C. § 78o(b)(4)(E)) and, for associated persons, 15 U.S.C. §§ 78o(b)(7)) (now codified at 15 U.S.C. § 78o(b)(6)). I use the origin of compliance in broker-dealers just as an example here because it was established as a firm obligation well before compliance became required in investment advisers. For the latter, see Compliance Programs of Investment Companies and Investment Advisers, Advisers Act Release No. 2204, 68 Fed. Reg. 74,714 (Dec. 24, 2003) (imposing compliance obligations upon investment companies and investment advisers).

[2] Task Force on Broker-Dealer Supervision and Compliance of the Committee on Federal Regulation of Securities, "Broker-Dealer Supervision of Registered Representatives and Branch Office Operations," 44 *Business Lawyer* 44 (1989): 1361, 1363–64 (discussing early theories of supervisory liability used by the SEC).

[3] 78 Stat. at 572 (15 U.S.C. § 78o (b)(5)(E)(i) & (ii)) (now codified at 15 U.S.C. § 78o(b)(4)(E)(i) & (ii)).

[4] John H. Walsh, "Right the First Time: Regulation, Quality, and Preventive Compliance in the Securities Industry," *Columbia Business Law Review* (1997): 165, 189–91 (describing compliance procedures and activities).

[5] O. Ray Vass, "The Compliance Officer in Today's Regulatory Environment," in *Broker-Dealer Institute* (New York: PLI Corp. Law & Practice, Course Handbook Ser. No. 579, 1987) 49 (discussing early configuration of compliance in firms).

background in the securities business: They had been brokers or traders, or worked in the operations part of the firm. They thus knew well the business, or a part of the business, and learned the basic legal and professional obligations associated with it, at the very least to be able to pass the qualification examinations that test knowledge of this subject matter. From one perspective, having securities business experience is an ideal, or at least necessary, background for a compliance officer who must guide employees in, and remind them of, their legal and professional obligations because, having been "in the trenches," these employees understand the business, as well as the typical forms of misconduct possible in it.

Another traditional background for compliance was (and is) in another control function, such as internal auditing. This, too, makes perfect sense because a major task of internal auditing is to ensure that a firm's controls, including its compliance controls, have been followed. It is true that the main focus of internal auditing is on the reliability of the financial statements and of the supporting documents for them. But to do this task well demands a knowledge of the securities business, its controls, and the detailed ways in which funds and securities move through the broker-dealer. An internal auditor with this background would be well prepared for the monitoring and investigative aspects of compliance.

Today, we think of compliance officers in broker-dealers or investment advisers as having one or more of these three general backgrounds, which all have their respective benefits.[6] They may be legally trained, with a specialty in financial regulation, which gives them familiarity with the applicable law and regulations and with the skills of statutory and regulatory interpretation, all of which are useful in a highly regulated financial industry (more on this below). Compliance officers may also come from a securities business or other financial services position, which background provides them with a knowledge of that business and its finance and economic foundations, as well as the "nuts and bolts" of operations. Finally, compliance officers may have been trained in, and practiced, accounting and auditing, whether in the public or private sector, with its useful "control" discipline. It may well be that, when a prospective compliance officer is hired, a CCO looks for a combination of these backgrounds: e.g., a recent law school graduate who worked before law school in the financial industry or as an accountant,[7] a recent university graduate with a major in accounting or finance with summer internships in financial firms, or an accountant or examiner with the Securities and Exchange Commission (SEC) or FINRA.[8]

---

[6] A good example of the diversity of backgrounds is reflected in an article in which the authors interview chief compliance officers (CCOs) precisely about their views on key skills and career paths for compliance officers. Ann Oglanian and David Thetford, "CCO Insights: Key Skills and Career Paths," 6 *Practical Compliance & Risk Management for the Securities Industry* 6, Issue No. 1 (Jan.–Feb. 2013): 5. The interviewees of this article have educational backgrounds in accounting, business, and economics (but, interestingly, not the law), and business backgrounds in back office operations, internal accounting, and securities trading, respectively.

[7] My students who become compliance officers often have this combination of background and skills.

[8] Even if they do not have these skills when they start their job, compliance officers are expected to develop them as soon as possible. Todd L. Spillane, "So You Are a Compliance Officer. Now What?" 3, *Practical Compliance & Risk Management for the Securities Industry* 3, Issue No. 6 (Nov.–Dec. 2010) (online): 1 (discussing skills expected of a new compliance officer, including business, operations and regulatory knowledge).

Schools of course have a significant role in providing future compliance officers with the educational foundations for law, business, and accounting. For example, universities and colleges train their students about the subjects (finance and financial markets) and skills (understanding financial statements and conducting valuations) that will be useful in compliance, and law schools provide a student with the knowledge of financial law and regulation and an introduction to the skills of legal reasoning and statutory interpretation. Here schools are just doing for the compliance field what they have done for other professions: providing prospective employees with the knowledge that is necessary, but not sufficient, for practice. But this issue of the role of educational institutions in preparing people for a compliance career naturally leads to a discussion of the recent focus on legal training for the compliance officer position.

III. INCREASED FOCUS ON LEGAL TRAINING FOR COMPLIANCE OFFICERS

Why Legal Training?

As noted above, in its origins with broker-dealers compliance generally fell under the authority of the Legal Department and the general counsel, given that its main focus was to ensure that a firm and its employees complied with the applicable law and regulations. Recently, there are anecdotal reports that Compliance Departments are looking for legally trained individuals and that there is a resulting influx of lawyers into the field. To give an admittedly unscientific example of this trend, in recent graduating classes at my law school, nearly one-fifth of the students have entered into entry-level compliance positions with financial firms, or with firms consulting on compliance and regulatory matters. Moreover, even compliance officers who are not legally trained may see the need to increase their knowledge of the laws and regulations governing their firms' activities, such as by returning to an academic program to be "certified" in legal compliance, as in FINRA's CRCP program mentioned above.[9]

There are many reasons for this trend, if it in fact exists. Having an advanced degree, such as a juris doctor, may increase the likelihood that a compliance officer will rise in the compliance managerial ranks, particularly in a law-oriented field like compliance.[10] My own experience confirms this motivation: Our law school has a part-time program with courses given at night, and I have had students who are compliance officers by day and who go to school at night to obtain their juris doctor degree for career advancement. Obtaining a master of business administration or other kind of relevant degree or certification might serve the same purpose.[11]

---

[9] For example, in Ann Oglanian's and David Thetford's interview with CCOs, one of them, Adam Reback, observed that, though not a lawyer, he was referred to by his colleagues as "the best legal counsel 'without a JD.'" Oglanian and Thetford, "CCO Insights," 10. Mr. Reback was emphasizing how necessary legal knowledge is for the compliance position.

[10] Todd Spillane emphasizes the importance of regulatory knowledge for the compliance officer position. Spillane, "So You Are a Compliance Officer," 2–3.

[11] Roy V. Washington, "Knowledge, Skills and Abilities CCOs Need to Be Effective and Successful—A Way of Traveling," *Practical Compliance & Risk Management for the Securities Industry* 4, Issue No. 1 (Jan.–Feb. 2011) (online): 13–14 (emphasizing the importance of continuing education and certification for CCOs).

The increased focus on legal training and background also reflects the growing number of legal obligations that are being imposed upon broker-dealers, investment advisers, and other financial firms and that must inevitably fall under the responsibility of compliance officers. The number and different kinds of laws that are applicable to financial firms make one's head spin. Compliance officers have a familiarity with the federal securities laws and regulations (and, if employed by a broker-dealer, FINRA rules) applicable to the kind of financial institution where they work, whether it be a broker-dealer, an investment adviser, or an investment fund—and these are numerous, including matters involving registration, books and records, conflicts of interest, custody, employee practices, fiduciary duties, marketing materials, use of solicitors, regulatory reporting, and trading practices, to name just a few. But compliance officers must also be familiar with other legal domains that affect their firm's business, such as those dealing with antimoney laundering and antiterrorism, escheat laws, foreign corrupt practices, margin and other lending, and privacy, whether under federal or state law. There is always a new law or regulation that a compliance officer must know. In addition, depending upon the kind of firm that employs the compliance officer and the firm's products, he or she will need an understanding of and familiarity with multiple laws and regulations in non-U.S. jurisdictions.

The legislative, regulatory, and enforcement reaction to the financial crisis, as exemplified by the Dodd-Frank Wall Street Reform and Consumer Protection Act of 2010,[12] may have been the final step in the legalization of compliance. Dodd-Frank led to new regulations and swept financial firms, such as investment advisers advising private funds, into potential SEC registration and regulation. The new laws and regulations increased the demand for compliance officers at all levels, particularly as some investment advisers were required for the first time to have a CCO, and as that CCO needed compliance officers to accomplish the compliance mandate. The renewed enforcement activity of the SEC, FINRA, and state attorneys general enhanced the importance of compliance within firms, either to guard against the increased risk of enforcement or as a required part of a settlement. An example that comes to mind is J.P. Morgan's employment of thousands of compliance officers after the London whale episode and other regulatory missteps.[13]

Regulators appear to be of two minds about the influx of lawyers into compliance. On the one hand, I have heard anecdotally that the regulators sometimes prefer not to have lawyers in compliance positions because legal training teaches compliance officers to be adept at finding narrow ways to satisfy the law or to be able to evoke attorney-client privilege on certain matters.[14] On the other hand, because the SEC and FINRA staff sometimes think of compliance officers as an extension of themselves, their "eyes and

---

[12] P.L. No. 111-203, 124 Stat. 1376 (July 21, 2010).
[13] Monica Langley and Dan Fitzpatrick, "J.P. Morgan Bulks Up Oversight," *Wall Street Journal* (Sept. 12, 2013), accessed September 13, 2013, online.wsj.com/article/SB10001424127887324755104579071304170686532.html#printMode (discussing bank's plans to hire up to 5,000 compliance and other control officers).
[14] On the problems associated with a lawyer in a compliance position evoking attorney-client privilege when providing legal advice, see Edward T. Dartley, "The Combined Role of General Counsel and the Chief Compliance Officer—Opportunities and Challenges," *Practical Compliance & Risk Management in the Securities Industry* 7, Issue No. 3 (May–June 2014): 21.

ears," in the firm, they may prefer to have compliance officers who are, like many of them, legally trained. They might even prefer compliance officers to be former regulators.[15]

It is unclear whether all the legal hiring and emphasis on legal training in compliance are ultimately beneficial for the field, which may change as a result. Certainly, one would not want compliance to end up like the SEC staff of a few years ago: having too many lawyers and inadequate representation from those with expertise in securities trading and risk analysis. Although, as discussed above, legal knowledge and training will always be required of all compliance officers, a well-functioning Compliance Department will benefit from having compliance officers from the diverse financial, internal control, legal, and operational backgrounds discussed above.

The Role of Law Schools in Compliance Officer Preparation: One Example and Its Implications

Whatever the reasons for the increased hiring of lawyers in Compliance Departments, law schools like my own would be well advised to take notice of the trend and respond to it. This is especially the case because, as has been well publicized, recent law graduates continue to face a tough job market. If, therefore, we find an area of growing employment, such as compliance, we do everything in our power to prepare our students for employment in it.

I would like to discuss here what we have done to train students for the compliance field, not just to highlight our school's program (although that is an incidental benefit). Rather, the program is described because it could also serve as one model for compliance officer involvement in education: It gives compliance officers the opportunity to publicize their field and to form their future employees. Our school's Center for the Study of Business Law & Regulation, which I codirect, has a compliance program.[16] Because Brooklyn Law School is an educational institution, one of the purposes of this program is to reflect upon, and to study, the growth and structure of compliance, particularly in financial firms such as broker-dealers and investment advisers. For example, we held an all-day conference on "The Growth and Importance of Compliance in Financial Firms: Meaning and Implications" on February 8, 2013, which both focused legal scholars on the development of compliance and which brought practicing compliance officers and compliance advisors to the school to discuss their practice and, frankly, to bring a "reality check" to the professors.[17] We had no trouble getting compliance officers to participate in the conference because we have graduates who are established CCOs and are eager to talk about their profession to an educational audience.

---

[15] This does not necessarily mean that they will be "easy" on former SEC or FINRA staff members in compliance officer positions, however. *In re Theodore W. Urban*, SEC Initial Decision Release No. 402 (Sept. 8, 2010). Moreover, compliance officers with a regulatory background are not always lawyers. Oglanian and Thetford, "CCO Insights," 6 (recounting that CCO Patricia Flynn, who was with the SEC as an assistant regional director, has an accounting background).

[16] The program is described at http://www.brooklaw.edu/intellectuallife/centerforbusinesslawregulation/ComplianceProgram.aspx

[17] *See* James A. Fanto, "Advising Compliance in Financial Firms: A New Mission for the Legal Academy," *Brooklyn Journal of Corporate, Financial and Commercial Law* 8 (2013): 1 (providing an introduction to the symposium).

On the classroom front, we feel that we must offer the students "transition to practice" courses in compliance, because traditional law school courses cover only subject matter areas like banking, securities regulation, and securities market regulation. So I devised an evening course (to enable part-time working students to attend) entitled "An Introduction to Compliance and Risk Management," for which I enlisted six practitioners, i.e., CCOs, risk managers, legal counsel, and compliance advisers, to "team teach" with me. In this class I offered a few background sessions on compliance and risk management, and each practitioner was responsible for two sessions on particular compliance areas (sometimes, two practitioners would assume responsibility for several classes).[18] Students would have background reading on the particular compliance topic for the session, and the practitioners would discuss it from a real-life perspective, offering students problems and hypotheticals. The class design was to promote as much interaction between the practitioners and the students as possible and not to burden the practitioners with the time-consuming duties that go along with teaching, such as grading. Part of the interaction of each class involved the practitioners offering their own views on how best to prepare for a job in compliance and, frankly, provided networking opportunities for the students. In fact, some of my students obtained a job indirectly as a result of the class, during which a practitioner would counsel them about applying for positions or refer them to a firm (including the practitioner's) that was hiring entry-level compliance officers.

This class was only one part of the student preparation for compliance. Our school encourages students to do outside externships.[19] They receive course credit for this work, which must be approved by our clinical faculty. Students in the "compliance track" generally spend a semester in the New York offices of FINRA or the SEC, or in a Compliance Department of a financial firm. There they become familiar with regulatory practice and the issues of interest to the examination and enforcement staff, or with the practices of a compliance department. Some students, in fact, elect to do two externships, ideally one with a regulator and the other with a private firm. As part of their first externship, they enroll in a weekly seminar taught by a compliance officer with a major securities firm, in which they reflect on their outside work and are further introduced to issues of interest to the compliance community (again, generally through guest speakers). These externships enable the students to gather knowledge about compliance practice and to build resumés that make them credible as entry-level compliance officers, i.e., people with basic experience in the field and familiarity with regulators and regulatory approaches.

Finally, we make the networking between compliance officers and students more regular with the help of our Career Services Office. That office and our compliance program cosponsor evening compliance program sessions where compliance officers (generally, but not exclusively, alumni of the school) conduct a short program on a compliance topic. A recent one, for example, dealt with compliance issues in the offering and trading of municipal securities. Following the program, the featured compliance officers,

---

[18] Topics included, with respect to broker-dealers or investment advisers, registration and qualification, privacy and antimoney laundering, supervision, sales practices, fiduciary duties, information barriers, and conflicts of interest, internal investigations and risk management.

[19] An externship helps satisfy a "skills" requirement for graduation at our school.

as well as others invited to come to the event, engage in an informal career networking discussion with the students. Members of the Advisory Board of our center who work in the compliance field advise us on topics for the programs, and our alumni office helps us identify possible program participants.

Our law school is one of the few in having this kind of compliance program, and we take advantage of our location in the greater New York City area with its heavy concentration of financial firms. Yet other law schools are beginning to develop their own programs and are reaching out to compliance officers who are their alumni or who work near them. In my view—and this is the main point of the account of our program—compliance officers in any part of the country should be receptive to outreach from law schools, business schools or universities, or colleges in their areas and might even consider contacting the schools to have compliance professionals volunteer their services.[20] They will likely find deans and professors who will be receptive to them and to the possibility of establishing programs similar to the one described above. Compliance officers will benefit from talking about and reflecting upon their occupation in a setting removed from the demands of business, and may be introduced to ideas and perspectives that they can use in their job. They also receive the satisfaction of knowing that their profession is now one receiving considerable interest in higher education. Again, from a purely instrumental perspective, they can identify interested students to put on the career path of compliance, who may well be future employees, and have a hand in their formation.

IV. SKILLS TRAINING FOR COMPLIANCE OFFICERS IN THE ACADEMY

As noted above, whether in law schools, business schools, or local colleges and universities, compliance officers could have a hand in alerting students about, and preparing them for, a career in compliance. But what other skills, in additional to substantive knowledge about accounting, finance, laws, regulations, and the operations of securities firms should the officers value in future employees, and can the academy have a role in imparting this knowledge? I shall answer this question from the perspective of the law school, but I shall refer to other educational settings as well.[21]

Compliance today demands highly educated employees and probably no longer allows for what was possible in a former time, i.e., having a noncollege-educated person enter the back office of a securities firm and climb the compliance ranks. The sheer financial complexity of the securities business, the large number of applicable laws and regulations governing it, and the increased exposure of compliance professionals to potential liability demand the kind of knowledge and skills that should be imparted by an advanced education—the ability to conduct both numerical and verbal analysis, which itself demands a high level

---

[20] Since it became known that our center has a compliance program, our alumni in the field regularly contact me to offer their services, and I do my best to get them involved in the program.

[21] I have some experience in these other settings because I have a doctorate degree and, before attending law school, taught undergraduates in several universities.

of mathematical and verbal skills. Certainly, universities and colleges pride themselves on producing graduates who have these skills, which could come from a number of majors. In their interaction with these institutions, compliance officers could echo the need for these skills and underscore that an ideal compliance officer would not be "one-sided," i.e., inclined to shy away from, or to be disdainful of, either numerical or verbal reasoning.

As a result of the field's complexity, it is absolutely essential for the compliance officer to have the ability to write and to speak well and clearly. Almost all compliance officers' tasks today demand writing, whether in drafting compliance and supervisory procedures and providing continuous and updated training to employees regarding those procedures, providing explanations of regulatory developments or the regulatory consequences of new products, conducting educational sessions, or reporting to senior executives or to regulators.[22] Although legal writing has its own characteristics, generally relating to the manner of legal arguments and to the support that is credible for the law, we place great emphasis in law schools on the ability to explain in writing complex factual scenarios and to convey clearly complex analysis and reasoning. The new generations of students, who will be future compliance officers, have to understand that their social media skills with their abbreviated, cryptic language will be no substitute for the traditional skill of written exposition. Similarly, students have to be able to explain simply and clearly complex regulatory issues to a specialist and nonspecialist audience. This message about verbal skills has to go to universities and colleges from the compliance officers who are participating in the educational development of the students interested in the field. The CCOs in my class echoed that message. We also emphasized the message by giving students a writing project in which they had to explain a compliance development to senior executives in a firm, which task demanded both a full analysis of a compliance issue as well as the ability to write a clear executive summary for the busy executives.

Future compliance officers should also have the ability to analyze a situation to identify problems—legal or otherwise—in it and to be creative in arriving at solutions to them.[23] Universities and colleges pride themselves on producing critical thinkers, the traditional hallmark of a liberal education. However, it is not at all clear that they have adequately emphasized the problem-solving focus in all of their disciplines, except perhaps in engineering. This is the one consistent criticism that I hear from compliance officers or practitioners who provide compliance advice (and that is echoed at sessions at National Society of Compliance Professionals meetings): New compliance employees do not always realize that they are supposed to be, rather than "naysayers,"

---

[22] Robert Schlangen and Jennifer M. Selliers, "The Foundation of a Compliance Professional's Role," *Practical Compliance & Risk Management for the Securities Industry* 6, Issue No. 1 (Jan.–Feb., 2013): 23, 27. Here the authors emphasize that nearly every task in a typical compliance department demands "exceptional verbal and written skills." Ms. Selliers emphasizes different writing approaches in compliance tasks in Jennifer M. Selliers, "No "Right" Way to Write?!?," *Practical Compliance & Risk Management for the Securities Industry* 7, Issue No. 7 (July–Aug. 2014): 13.

[23] Jiliane Bauer suggests this point about creativity by affirming that compliance officers must be focusing on the future "unknowns" and be curious about everything that touches their job. Jiliane Hummel Bauer, "The Compliance Officer's Survival Guide: Six Practices That Are Vital to Your Success," *Practical Compliance & Risk Management for the Securities Industry* 4, Issue No. 5 (Sept.–Oct., 2011) (online): 1–2.

problem solvers, which is a large part of their value added to the business.[24] It seems to me that the problem-solving orientation, if not the actual practice of compliance problem solving, can be taught through creative classroom exercises. As an aside, the ideal law school examination question in a business law subject would test a student's ability to come up with a solution to a factual scenario, given the client's goals and the law's constraints. Being a *creative* problem solver is no doubt a special talent. To identify it, CCOs and compliance managers have to be open to considering prospective employees of diverse subject matter backgrounds (but with the skills already discussed) and then must train and test the employees in their early years as a way to develop in them the problem-solving skills and to see how talented the employees are at those skills. [25]

Whether those of us who are, say, more advanced in age like it or not, compliance officers increasingly have to have computer and technology skills. Admittedly, law school is not going to be at the forefront of the institutions imparting them. As compliance officers today know, much of what they do demands the use (and thus a knowledge) of automated systems, such as those that make possible surveillance of communications and trading or those that allow for automation of other compliance tasks.[26] Moreover, the steady refrain from the SEC and FINRA is that they are employing automation and the tools of "big data" in their own surveillance of and interaction with financial firms.[27] It is not necessary that compliance officers be computer programmers conversant in coding, although I have met those who have this background. In light of global technological developments, however, compliance officers cannot simply rely upon their Information Technology Department, especially since they are ultimately responsible for the automated systems that they use and depend upon. Compliance officers have to have a basic computer literacy so that they can discuss technology critically and creatively with that department, and explain their technology needs to firm management.[28] Moreover, because they conduct educational programs inside the firm and, if they follow the encouragement of this chapter, outside it as well,

---

[24] Spillane, "Spillane, "So You Are a Compliance Officer ," 3, states the point well:
Another danger is to simply say "NO." While this is certainly an option, the risk is developing the perception of compliance becoming "profit prevention" or "antibusiness." Additionally, by simply saying "no" when an activity may have been permissible, we may raise the question whether we as compliance really did act in the best interest of the clients and the best interest of your firm. This is why I earlier said that the role of compliance in any company is to assist our business partners in navigating the regulatory framework to help them meet their business objectives.

[25] Schlangen and Selliers, "The Foundation," 26–27 (discussing ways for compliance managers to identify talents in their compliance officers).

[26] David Tilkin, "The Landscape of Broker-Dealer Compliance and Exception Reporting Systems," *PIABA Bar Journal* 17, No. 1 (2010): 65 (discussing the prevalence of compliance software systems in most firms).

[27] To take a few examples, *see* Mary Jo White, Testimony on "Examining the SEC's Agenda, Operations and FY 2016 Budget Request" (House Committee on Financial Services, Washington, DC (Mar. 24, 2015) (discussing SEC's plans to modernize its technology systems, including with respect to data analytics tools used to analyze data for indications of fraud, EDGAR modernization to enhance automation of company filings, examination improvements through regulatory surveillance, and an enterprise data warehouse where the SEC would organize all of its collected data); Rick Ketchum, FINRA Chairman/CEO, "Restoring Investor Trust in the Markets" (Speech at FINRA Annual Conference, Washington, DC, May 19, 2014) (explaining how FINRA must be "data informed," "technology empowered," so as to respond more quickly to trends and to discipline bad actors, and how the Comprehensive Automated Risk Data System ("CARDS") initiative fits into this); http://www.finra.org/industry/issues/cat/ (discussing the Consolidated Audit Trail).

[28] *See* Schlangen and Selliers, "The Foundation," at 26–27 (noting that part of compliance is determining the proper allocation between manual and automated processes and that some tasks demand "exceptional data entry skills").

they need to be conversant with all the presentation techniques that are used in live and remote education.[29] Certainly, universities and colleges have the programs to help future compliance officers, and even current officers, obtain these necessary technology skills.

Finally, there are all of the important "people" skills that are so critical to success as a compliance officer and, in fact, for so many other jobs. These include the ability to listen to other people to understand their needs and motivation,[30] to assume responsibility and leadership for, and to work cooperatively in, a team project,[31] and to be able to stand one's ground when necessary.[32] Perhaps business schools alone try to impart some of these skills because they encourage team projects and devote time to leadership. However, in recruiting people for compliance positions, CCOs have to look beyond educational training and background for other indications of these skills, such as recommendations, participation in extracurricular activities and their own interviews with candidates. For the difficulty is trying to identify a socially astute and ethical individual. What educational institutions can do with respect to these "people" skills, other than weeding out bad actors (which they do not always do successfully or at all),[33] is to impart in students a knowledge of psychology and social processes. The advances in knowledge of our cognitive, emotional, and social makeup have literally exploded in recent years, such as with respect to common cognitive and emotional limitations of people and problems in group dynamics.[34] It would be invaluable for a compliance officer to possess knowledge of these developments, which are critical for understanding, for instance, how people make errors in decision-making and what techniques they can use to promote compliant conduct.

V. CONCLUSION

This chapter reflected on the different kinds of backgrounds and academic preparations that are useful to prospective compliance officers. It first discussed the traditional three backgrounds of law, securities business and finance and accounting, the strengths associated with each of these backgrounds and the contributions of educational institutions to imparting them to students. The chapter then considered why, in recent years, there

---

[29] Wendy Snyder, "Maintaining an Effective Firm Element Training Program," *Practical Compliance & Risk Management for the Securities Industry* 7, Issue No. 6 (Nov.–Dec., 2014): 5, 10–11 (among other topics, discussing the electronic ways to deliver education and suggested approaches to this delivery).

[30] Spillane, "Compliance Officer," 3 ("The most important skill that I can encourage any young compliance officer to develop is the basic skill of listening closely, not only to what is being said but also how it is said.").

[31] Washington, "A Way of Traveling," 12 (discussing, among other things, team building skills of CCOs).

[32] Oglanian and Thetford, "CCO Insights," 9 (in their article, interviewees discuss the importance of "courage" in compliance).

[33] Robert Giacalone and Mark Promislo, "Broken When Entering: The Stigmatization of Goodness and Business Ethics Education," *Academy of Management Learning & Education* 12 (2013): 86 (explaining how many business students have been taught to belittle ethics and to espouse materialistic values, before they enter business schools); Dennis A. Gioia, "Business Education's Role in the Crisis of Corporate Confidence," *Academy of Management Executive* 16 (2002): 142, 143(discussing how business schools promote unethical conduct in their graduates).

[34] The works here are too numerous to list. But several of particular interest to compliance officers would be Daniel Kahneman, *Thinking, Fast and Slow* (New York: Farrar, Straus and Giroux, 2011) (discussing our automatic and rational selves in general) and Max H. Bazerman and Ann E. Tenbrunsel, *Blind Spots: Why We Fail to Do What's Right and What to Do About It* (Princeton: Princeton University Press, 2011) (discussing, among other things, how and why "ethical" fading occurs, which is a process whereby ethical dimensions of a decision "fade" at the time of decision making).

appears to be an increased focus upon legal training in compliance and the hiring of more lawyers into entry-level compliance officer positions. This consideration led to a discussion about how law schools might prepare students for these positions, with my school's compliance program used as an example. The program highlighted a broader point that could be applied to other educational settings, such as business schools, universities, and colleges—the useful involvement of compliance officers in assisting educational institutions to prepare future compliance officers. The chapter then identified the kinds of skills that are essential for compliance officers, such as mathematical and verbal reasoning, excellent writing and verbal skills, critical thinking, problem solving, and computer literacy, and discussed how educational institutions provide expertise in some of them, as well as how compliance officers might encourage schools to focus on these skills. Finally, this discussion pointed to the important "people" skills that compliance officers should possess, but that are difficult to identify and to teach.

The above reflection about preparing future compliance officers matters because compliance has become so important in financial services—a fact to which this book attests. That is, since compliance is well established, as evidenced by its professional societies, journals, and programs of continuing education, it makes sense to discuss and to debate the issue of the proper educational background and training for prospective compliance officers. As this chapter's discussion shows, there are still diverse paths to a career in compliance, with law school being the one that has received recent attention. The message of this chapter is that, whatever form this training takes in colleges, universities, and professional schools, compliance officers should be encouraged to take part in it, and their involvement will make the educational preparation more effective and will frankly be rewarding to the officers themselves.

ABOUT THE AUTHOR

James A. Fanto is the Gerald Baylin Professor of Law and codirector of the Center for the Study of Business Law & Regulation at Brooklyn Law School. Professor Fanto teaches courses on banking, broker-dealer law, regulation and compliance, corporate and securities law, and corporate finance. He coauthors a treatise on broker-dealer law with Norman Poser, *Broker-Dealer Law and Regulation* (New York: Wolters Kluwer, 2007, updated annually) and is co-editor in chief of the Wolters Kluwer journal, *Practical Compliance & Risk Management for the Securities Industry.* Before entering academia, Professor Fanto practiced banking, corporate, and securities law with the firm of Davis Polk & Wardwell.

CHAPTER 27

Is It Time to Go?

By Kathleen Edmond
Robins Kaplan LLP

I. INTRODUCTION

> Should I stay or should I go now?
> If I go, there will be trouble.
> And if I stay it will be double.
>
> — The Clash

The Executive Committee leaves you off a newly formed antifraud taskforce. The board asks you to assume the responsibilities of the departing general counsel because the compliance work is "on auto-pilot." Despite your counsel to the contrary, senior leadership increasingly tolerates bad behavior by certain key employees because of their perceived value to the organization. Your organizational value becomes more difficult to articulate and defend. The company that so recently spent months recruiting you now compromises your ability to do your job.

The sad truth remains that the average tenure of a compliance officer can be short-lived, either by choice or circumstance. Headlines abound of fallen and departing senior compliance officers, amid questionable circumstances. Some depart involuntarily; others leave "to spend more time with family." Too often, the compliance officer becomes the sacrificial lamb when organizational adversity strikes. Compliance leaders caught in the line of fire face grave consequences, including job loss, reputational harm, and, more recently, financial and legal liability.

What do you do when the bull's eye appears on your back? What is your responsibility when the ethics culture erodes from the top and an entitled leadership team rewards cutting corners? What is your duty to the organization's stakeholders to take a stand and object to questionable business conduct? Can you stay in your role or should you head for the hills? If you do depart, how do you protect your reputation, career, and dignity? Although every journey into the compliance crossroads looks different, threshold questions and practical protections help you recognize and navigate your responsibilities and limitations on this perilous trip.

II. READ THE TEA LEAVES

To control your professional destiny and preserve your dignity during organizational strife, you must anticipate and recognize when your ability to competently perform your role starts to deteriorate through no fault of your own. Whether management deliberately sabotages your efforts or a decaying corporate culture prevents you from effectively fulfilling your responsibilities, recognizing your predicament and planning proactively help mitigate your personal toll.

Are You Being Groomed to Go?

Your concerns may arise from a series of subtle actions or overt snubs. You continually find yourself in situations that give you pause. The company conducts an investigation of a senior executive without your involvement. The board completely ignores your risk mitigation recommendations. The leadership team attributes your successes to someone else while attaching unpopular outcomes to you. The bottom line is that your position no longer feels secure, and you question your ability to make an impact and manage effectively.

Your primary role as a compliance executive is to protect the organization. At times, this may mean conducting sensitive investigations, delivering harsh messages, and uncovering corporate failures. Not surprisingly, your reward for a job well done may be a target on your back. All too easily, organizations may blame the messenger for the revealed shortcomings. As a result, you may find yourself isolated from peers, stripped of responsibilities, deprived of professional growth opportunities, and, potentially, pushed out the door. Although unlimited and varied, other signals that your organization may have alternative plans for you may be telegraphed when senior leadership or the board:

- Disinvites you to board meetings;
- Leaves you off an Audit Committee but incorporates your report into someone else's work;
- Questions your investigative approach when the result is unpopular;
- Strips you of crucial decision-making authority, but leaves you the accountability; and
- Changes your reporting structure in ways that diminish your authority and visibility within the organization.

As these small and large affronts occur, you must evaluate your strategic role and relevancy to determine whether you have been rendered ineffective. The greater your disempowerment, the more likely your career, reputation, and attitude will suffer if you stay in your position. When you can no longer adequately carry out your compliance duties, you face significant risk of misdirected accountability. In addition, you must critically assess your ability to fulfill the responsibilities expected of the compliance officer role. By anticipating and preempting the company's actions, and being brutally honest about your own contribution to the disintegrating relationship, you retain greater control over your future and dignity.

Is It Too Risky to Stay?

Sometimes your professional woes might not be the result of deliberate efforts to remove you but rather organizational mismanagement. The Executive Committee asks you to investigate an allegedly corrupt supply chain but refuses to provide you necessary additional resources. The board alters your reporting structure, effectively depriving you of the necessary visibility to competently perform your job.

You must pay careful attention when a company's actions or failures compromise your ability to manage the controls you hold the responsibility—and, possibly, the legal and financial liability—for enforcing. Other organizational mistakes that may put you in jeopardy include when senior management or the board:

- Unreasonably increases your job responsibilities, making it impossible for you to manage effectively;
- Declines to take your admonitions or recommendations seriously;
- Pressures you not to investigate a controversial matter; and
- Requires the organization to incur unreasonably high business risk.

When a deteriorating environment interferes with your responsibilities, know that the company may blame you if regulators or others take notice of resulting compliance breaches. To avoid unearned accountability, you must evaluate whether you can rescue the situation or whether extracting yourself is your best option. Avoid the temptation to play hero when objectively you lack the ability or resources to redeem the organization. You often have a brief window when you can responsibly end the deteriorating professional situation before others inextricably and indefinitely link you to the organization's failures. Neglecting to take advantage of this opportunity may unjustly and irreparably damage your reputation, career, and dignity.

Avoid Blind Spots

Sometimes circumstances cloud your ability to recognize when it is time to leave your position, either as a result of the company's pressure or because you simply are no longer the right person for the job. When seen in hindsight, the red flags are impossible to ignore. In reality, they are often more subtle and lost in the noise of day-to-day activities. Heightening your sensitivity, through frequent and honest reflection and evaluation, can help you remain objective and better determine when your situation renders you stagnate and ineffective.

When you read stories of epic corporate failures leading to departing executives or, worse, criminal indictments, you likely shake your head and say, "What were they thinking?" and "Where was the compliance or ethics officer?" These cases do not always result from bad actors' malicious intents but often a pattern of line blurring or crossing. Repeated overstepping desensitizes organizations to once firmly held boundaries. Persistent institutional overreaching can result in a loss of your objectivity as a compliance leader, blinding you to the very principles the organization hired you to protect.

© MODERN COMPLIANCE 2015

Recall the values and boundaries you had when you came in the door. Is your company asking you to tread on them? Be wary of an organizational culture that regularly pressures you and other employees to take advantage of loopholes, acquiesce to aggressive business goals, or incur unacceptable risks. Obviously, survival depends on meeting metrics. But singular focus on these quantitative markers without equal regard to ethical compliance can lead to disastrous results. Also, be concerned if senior management continually makes it impossible for you to implement your objectives. Repeatedly justifying an organization's bad behavior is equally perilous. To avoid your own slippery slope, reflect honestly and objectively on your organization's questionable acts.

Test Your Theories

Corporate pressures and dynamics can undermine job confidence. If this occurs frequently, you should investigate whether these forces constitute business as usual or something potentially more sinister. Examine whether your heightened sensitivity to internal politics or the personal toll the job inflicts on you is causing you to be unjustifiably insecure. Question whether you are overreacting. Look at the issues that generate concern, both in isolation and in context to improve your ability to investigate their legitimacy. Focus on objective fact rather than unsubstantiated rumor. Have the company activities changed since you arrived? What are the root causes of the change? Have personnel changes altered the compliance perspective of the firm?

Although the issues that worry you may be steeped in confidentiality, you may still safely seek the guidance and counsel of others by omitting identifiable information when you ask for their thoughts on your situation. Relying on the judgment of trusted colleagues, within or external to the organization, can help you maintain your objectivity and validate your concerns. Other compliance professionals, or your personal independent compliance counsel with whom you can confide confidentially, likely are the most relevant sounding boards.

Listen to Your Gut

Although significant decisions should not stem from your feelings alone, your initial emotional response to a situation often proves to be accurate. Listen carefully when your gut alerts you, while always substantiating your suspicions and testing your hypotheses. If no facts support your emotional response, put the matter aside and consider whether something else going on in your life triggered your reaction.

III. DO YOU REALLY *HAVE* TO GO?

Once you acknowledge that your role is in jeopardy and that you can no longer protect the organization or its stakeholders, your next steps are crucial. Your reputation, career, and dignity, as well as potential liability, depend on careful consideration of how you proceed. You can gain or lose the trust of your professional constituents depending on how you wind up handling the remediation or termination of your position. As previously stated, when your organization significantly compromises your ability to competently perform your job, self-preservation usually dictates leaving the organization.

Occasionally, circumstances may not be so toxic that you must leave immediately, but instead, you may safely, but cautiously, continue in your role in an attempt to "right the ship." Before you make the decision to stay with your organization, carefully examine the potential consequences. Carefully and honestly consider these questions:

- What is your "true north" or touchstone for evaluating your situation?
- Can you realistically restore your authority if it has been undermined?
- Do you have adequate allies within the organization to achieve results?
- Do you still have respect for the organization? Will you be respected and valued if you remain?
- Can you do your job without compromising your own compliance program and core values?
- Will you be incurring substantial risk, including potential legal and financial liability?
- Do you have a duty to report the misconduct to the board or outside authority?
- Are you trying to figure this out by yourself? Or are you accessing trusted and necessary sounding boards?

Staying in your current compliance role may provide short-term security and decreased stress. The potential long-term consequences may produce the opposite effects. Although your personal tendencies to be competitive, stubborn, or irrationally persistent may drive you to stay and restore your authority or "fix" a troubled environment, many compliance professionals in this position regret not leaving sooner. Too often, compliance officers admit regretting staying too long with their organizations after recognizing a precarious environment.

IV. PROTECT YOURSELF WHEN YOU DEPART

If you decide you must leave your job or your organization decides that outcome for you, available safeguards can help protect your dignity, reputation, professionalism, and career.

Leave a Trail

Obviously, as a matter of course, you document your relevant findings, decision making, and actions in a timely and comprehensive manner. When your corporate environment begins to destabilize, you should document the company's acts and omissions that impede you from carrying out your compliance responsibilities. If the organization comes under regulatory scrutiny after you leave, a careful record of events, including obstacles that prevented you from doing your job, can help insulate you. This record also may protect others potentially harmed by the company's misdeeds.

Repair Bridges

Prior to departing, do what you can internally to mend any frayed relationships. Do not let ego, hurt feelings, or other emotions prevent you from maximizing your available network. Chances are that you own some part of the broken relationship. Learn what you can, discard what does not apply, and consistently act with grace.

Negotiate Safeguards

To prevent defamation after your departure, require a nondisparagement clause in any separation agreement the company provides you. Limit the firm's ability to discuss your departure to a select few within the organization. Carefully tailor what this select few may lawfully say about your separation from the company.

If your company might issue a press release or any other statement about your departure, make sure that you negotiate into any separation agreement a clause specifying the precise wording of any communications.

V. CONSIDER OTHER PRECAUTIONS

Create Ongoing Safety Nets

Maintain a Financial Cushion. If possible, structure your personal finances so that you maintain a financial cushion at all times. Keeping these reserves available affords you freedom to separate from a precarious position quickly with your soul, sanity, and reputation intact.

Continue to Network. No one wants to start a new position thinking about the next one. Yet, given the truncated nature of the compliance role, you should always think strategically about your next move and foster your relationships and personal brand. This foresight benefits you in your current role, as well as in future positions.

Stay current in your field, keeping up with increasingly complex technologies and regulatory environments, as well as rapidly changing issues facing business operations. Always keep an eye on the marketplace in the event you may need alternative employment.

Do not let gainful employment curb your networking. Continue outside activities and cultivate your relationships within professional organizations. Having a solid, entrenched reputation among your industry peers outside of your current organization will keep you engaged and energized in your current role, and prove vital if your job crumbles.

If the (un)expected happens, such strategic planning, as well as quality contacts and an established reputation within the industry, could likely be invaluable in establishing your next position.

Plan Strategically for Your Next Job

First, Get Over It. Before engaging your next move, shake off the disappointment and frustration of your past situation. Badmouthing your previous employer or airing the negatives of the job left behind only makes you look bad. And, that's a reputation you don't want.

Clarify the Scope of the Job and Available Resources. When you are ready—but before stepping into your next job—make certain you comprehend the specific scope of your future responsibilities, which the prospective employer should reasonably and clearly proscribe. Seek clarification and be wary in the event you receive overly broad, narrow, or vague information concerning the potential span of your position.

Additionally, ask a prospective employer what resources would be available to you in your compliance role. Ask questions about the sufficiency of these resources, as well as the availability and likelihood of obtaining additional resources should you deem them necessary.

Ask About Ongoing Investigations. During the interview process with a future employer, ask about the existence of ongoing significant internal or external compliance-related investigations. Although you seek information that is likely confidential, request general, nonidentifying facts so you understand your potential involvement and exposure. Clarify your prospective role in these matters, making sure you grasp how you avoid accountability for prior acts and omissions of others.

Determine D&O Coverage. Given the inherent sensitivity and risks associated with the compliance officer role, ask upfront whether the company would cover you under its directors' and officers' (D&O) insurance policy.

Learn About Your Predecessor. Although specifics of your predecessor's departure may be confidential, use formal and informal channels to learn whatever you can. This historic information may inform your decision whether to accept a position. Do not rely on cursory or unsubstantiated anecdotes. Rather, attempt to obtain as full an account as possible to avoid stepping into a situation that will set you up for failure.

Seek an Employment Agreement. Consider asking your next employer for an employment agreement including a severance package. Although this may not be the company's standard practice, you can argue that the unique and independent nature of the compliance officer's role necessitates this protection.

© MODERN COMPLIANCE 2015

VI. CONCLUSION

You likely know good compliance professionals who left their jobs under unfortunate circumstances. By anticipating the transitory nature of your role, asking threshold questions, and implementing available safeguards, you can protect yourself if and when you find yourself on this slippery slope. Proactively responding to organizational pressures and failings enables you to control the forces that shape your compliance program as well as your reputation, career, and dignity, while you grow personally and professionally in the process.

ABOUT THE AUTHOR

Kathleen Edmond has spent the majority of her legal career in corporate ethics and compliance. As chief ethics officer for a Fortune 100 company from 2004 to 2014, she built and subsequently led the company's Ethics Office. She is currently a partner at Robins Kaplan LLP, a national law firm based in Minneapolis, and leads the firm's corporate compliance and ethics practice. Ms. Edmond is probably best known for her leading-edge communications initiatives in creating a connected, ethical culture within the organization that supported business strategy, vendor integrity, and customer engagement. She has won national awards for her innovative and exemplary leadership in her field, and her original use of social media in furthering a transparent, ethical business operation is groundbreaking.

Prior to practicing law, Ms. Edmond earned a master of business administration with a concentration in Business Ethics, from the University of St. Thomas, and a master's in social work from the University of Minnesota. Over the course of her career she has worked with a wide range of clients representing industries ranging from retail, healthcare, professional sports, and insurance, to nonprofit, public institutions.

CHAPTER 28
Compliance as a Profession

By John H. Walsh
    Sutherland Asbill & Brennan

I. INTRODUCTION

Is compliance a profession? If one were to judge by how it is described, compliance already qualifies. Practitioners are routinely called "compliance professionals." Trainers offer "professional education programs" concluding in professional certifications. Professional associations have issued professional codes of ethics. If self-designation were enough, compliance would have arrived. Unfortunately, however, professional status requires much more. Most importantly, the professionalism of any group of practitioners must be recognized by society at large. In a recent decision, discussed below, the highest court in the State of New York held that compliance was not a profession and thus was not entitled to the recognition given to more established professions, such as the law. This decision is a reminder that despite its increasing professionalism, compliance has not yet achieved full professional status.

I have been a proponent of compliance as a profession for many years, beginning with my April 2002 speech to the NRS Symposium on the compliance profession, *What Makes Compliance a Profession?* This chapter reviews the current status of compliance as a profession and concludes that although there have been setbacks, significant progress toward professionalism continues. Importantly, there are steps every compliance practitioner can take to help the profession's progress. Finally, the chapter concludes by proposing an objective methodology for testing and validating the future progress of compliance toward professionalism.

II. IS COMPLIANCE A PROFESSION?

Joseph Sullivan was the chief compliance officer (CCO) of an asset management partnership.[1] He held several other positions at the firm, including chief operating officer (COO). He claimed he was terminated after he objected to certain stock sales by the partnership's majority owner and chief executive officer (CEO). According to Sullivan, the sales amounted to frontrunning, that is, an abusive practice in which an adviser sells in anticipation of transactions by the firm's clients. Sullivan also alleged that the sales enabled the CEO and

---

[1] *Sullivan v. Harnisch, et al.*, 19 N.Y. 3d 259, 969 N.E. 758 (Court of Appeals of New York, 2012).

his family to take advantage of an opportunity from which the clients were excluded. Sullivan confronted the CEO, raised objections, and insisted that the trades be reversed or that other appropriate action to address the conflicts to be taken. The CEO refused and yelled at Sullivan for raising the topic. A few days later, Sullivan was terminated.

Sullivan sued for wrongful discharge, and the CEO moved for summary judgment, that is, to dismiss the claim as insufficient as a matter of law. The trial court held that Sullivan's claim was legally sufficient and could go forward. However, on appeal the first appellate level court disagreed and dismissed the claim. Sullivan then appealed the case to the highest court in the State of New York: its Court of Appeals, which consists of a chief judge and six associate judges who decide cases by voting amongst themselves.

In its analysis the Court of Appeals applied the legal doctrine known as "employment at will." The doctrine would not detain us here, except that it has an exception based on the professionalism of the employment. Under New York law, as a general matter, an employer has the right to terminate an employee at will at any time. Under this rule Sullivan would have no cause of action for wrongful discharge because he was an employee "at will." However, the New York Court of Appeals has recognized an exception to this rule when adherence to the ethical standards of a profession could be implied to be a fundamental and essential understanding of the employment in question. For example, when a law firm employs an attorney, the ethical and professional obligations of attorneys and the obligations of the employment relationship are "so closely linked as to be incapable of separation." If, therefore, the firm terminated the attorney in retaliation for the exercise of applicable professional ethics, the terminated employee could bring an action against the firm for his or her dismissal. Thus, in Sullivan's case before the Court of Appeals the question was clear: Is compliance a profession? On this question the judges disagreed.

A majority of the court answered: no. In an opinion written by Judge Smith, the court held that compliance was not a profession. Sullivan, it said, was not associated with other compliance officers in a firm where all were subject to self-regulation as members of a common profession. Indeed, the majority noted, Sullivan was not even a full-time compliance officer because he held other titles at the firm. "It is simply not true that regulatory compliance," the majority concluded, "was at the very core and, indeed, the only purpose of Sullivan's employment."[2]

Chief Judge Lippman disagreed. In his dissenting opinion, he said that Sullivan's:

> [S]ole function as compliance officer was to ensure compliance with the applicable internal and external ethical and legal requirements, his employer was bound by the same obligations, and his job as a compliance officer entailed fundamental self-regulatory functions.... In other words, it was Sullivan's responsibility to make certain that [the firm] engaged in the lawful and ethical provision of investment adviser services.[3]

---

[2] *Sullivan v. Harnisch*, at 264 (internal quotations omitted).
[3] *Sullivan v. Harnisch*, at 268.

From this the chief judge concluded that Sullivan was in a professional position comparable to that of an attorney. The chief judge rejected the argument that Sullivan was not a professional because he did not work in a firm of fellow compliance officers. Instead, the chief judge reasoned: "Sullivan was an employee of a business that was subject to certain legal and ethical obligations to its clients and his reason for being, as a compliance officer, was to ensure that in providing services to those clients, those rules were followed at all times."[4]

The spirited debate between Judge Smith and Chief Judge Lippman highlights the uncertain professional status of compliance. Of course, this was a decision by a New York court, whose jurisdiction is limited to that state. Nonetheless, as a decision by the highest court of law in a major commercial and financial jurisdiction, this case could have considerable influence even outside New York.

Three observations can be made about this case. First, as much as compliance practitioners may believe themselves to be professionals, compliance is not yet fully recognized as a profession. In *Sullivan v. Harnisch*, Judge Smith commanded a majority of the Court of Appeals and his opinion became law. His standards for a profession appear fairly simplistic: Professionals do nothing else and always work together in professional firms. Despite this limited definition of a profession, his opinion is controlling law in New York, at least for the moment and with respect to the narrow issue relating to an exception to the employment at will doctrine.

Second, compliance practitioners are not alone in believing themselves to be professionals. In his dissent Chief Judge Lippman recognized compliance's ethical and self-regulatory functions, even if he did not command a majority of the court. Moreover, his opinion should be taken seriously. In the American legal tradition, dissents often highlight developing trends that may require more time to reach majority status and to become the law. There are famous judges—U.S. Supreme Court Justice Oliver Wendell Holmes comes to mind—whose reputations were largely built on their thoughtful dissents. Outside of the narrow area in which Judge Smith's decision is dispositive law—the employment at will doctrine in New York State—Chief Judge Lippman's dissent could well be viewed as equally, or even more persuasive.

Third, the debate in the Court of Appeals was framed as a matter of employment law, but it touched on issues of critical importance to the professionalism of compliance. Chief Judge Lippman criticized the majority decision because it "undermines the exception to the at-will employment doctrine…by excluding arbitrarily hedge fund compliance officers from the protections extended to lawyers working in law firms." The result, he said, would be to give managers "carte blanche" to terminate the employees who are charged with the critical role "of ensuring adherence to ethical and legal obligations." These protections, the chief judge continued, "must exist not only to decrease the likelihood that such employees will succumb to pressures to ignore or violate their

---

[4] *Sullivan v. Harnisch*, at 269.

obligations for fear of terminations, but also to protect the public." This is a powerful statement on the role and importance of compliance as a profession.

Nevertheless, Chief Judge Lippman's eloquence cannot disguise the reality of the majority decision of the Court of Appeals. It was a setback for the professionalism of compliance.[5] Compliance was compared to the professional practice of law, and the majority concluded that it fell short. As a matter of law, the decision of the Court of Appeals was primarily focused on employment issues, specifically employment at will, and it may be read solely in that narrow doctrinal context. Nonetheless, when given an opportunity to recognize the professionalism of compliance, the court declined. With this in mind, let us review the current progress of compliance towards professionalism.

III. PROGRESS TOWARD PROFESSIONALISM

There is no standard definition for a profession. Scholars have used various descriptions and definitions, often based on their own ideological predilections.[6] Despite this lack of an official and binding definition, certain characteristics frequently recur in the literature and in everyday observation. Professionals enjoy a measure of autonomy in the workplace from those outside the profession; they apply a specialized body of knowledge; they practice according to an ethical code; and they have some degree of professional organization. Because our purpose is to assess compliance's progress as a social phenomenon—whether it has made progress in the characteristics generally associated with a profession—these recurring expectations should provide a working structure for our inquiry. Therefore, we will examine compliance's progress in these four categories: (1) control over the workplace, (2) expertise, (3) ethics, (4) and organization.

Control over the Workplace

Control over the workplace is a critical indicator of professionalism. Mature professions, such as medicine and law, insist on professional autonomy. Viewed as a measure of professionalism, only a physician should offer a dispositive medical opinion, and only a lawyer should offer one on a question of law. These concepts have been so widely accepted that they seem truisms. In many jurisdictions they have reached a sufficient level of social acceptance that they have been codified in law. For example, in some jurisdictions anyone other than a physician who purports to practice medicine may be subject to criminal liability. Stated as a matter of control over the workplace, this thinking often focuses on the need for autonomy: The professional must have ultimate control over his or her own professional judgment.

---

[5] The author wishes to note that in this discussion of the opinions of the Court of Appeals he states no view on the merits of the underlying claims, if they had gone to trial.
[6] *See* Elliott A. Krause, *Death of the Guilds: Professions, States and the Advance of Capitalism, 1930 to the Present* (Yale University Press, 1996), at 14–20 (surveying theories and definitions).

Compliance, of course, is not a mature profession. Rather, it must be considered among the many occupations that aspire to this status. The term *semiprofession* is often applied to these groups. They feel themselves to be professional but have not received the same level of social recognition as the more established professions. In a certain sense, labeling compliance one or the other—profession or semiprofession—would seem to be no more than an exercise in semantics. However, as shown by the majority decision of the New York Court of Appeals, the difference between the two statuses can have real consequences. We should also note that this exercise in classification is not free from invidious assumptions or subjectivity. Many observers have noted that the dividing line between professions and semiprofessions seems to follow gender. Men generally occupied the traditional professions—medicine, law, and academia—and women occupied the traditional semiprofessions—nursing, teaching, and librarianship. Hence, one must take care to avoid assumptions about the nature of an occupation that could conceal unstated or even unrecognized bias. As recently as the 1970s, it was news when a woman worked in compliance.[7] More recently, compliance has been a field in which women have played a significant role and have had success. When one assesses the professionalism of an occupation, control over the workplace provides an important objective measure, relatively free of subjective bias. The question is twofold: why should a particular occupation have control over its own workplace, and then, how should that control be achieved?

Among semiprofessions, nursing has enjoyed perhaps the longest debate over its status. As a result, many of the issues that are just taking shape among compliance practitioners have been thoroughly discussed among nurses. Control over the workplace has played an important role. For example, in an incisive, peer-reviewed piece, one scholar of the field said nurses need more "power" to accomplish their function.[8] Most importantly, she said, "powerless nurses are ineffective nurses." She continued:

> Of all decision makers in the hospital environment, only the bedside nurse, who is in closest proximity to the patient, can fully appreciate subtle patient cues and trends as they arise and act on them to properly care for that patient. To identify the appropriate course of action and effectively function, professionals must have understanding and control over the entire spectrum of activities associated with the job at hand [citations omitted].[9]

This analysis precisely illustrates the question. What is it about the particular practice that warrants giving it greater control—or power—over its own work?

More particularly, what is it about compliance that warrants giving it greater control over its own work? In recent years several groups have taken on this question as a matter

---

[7] "Miss Allen One of Few Women to Become Compliance Officer," *Baltimore Afro-American* (Apr. 15, 1972), page 13.
[8] Milisa Manojlovich, "Power and Empowerment in Nursing: Looking Backward to Inform the Future," *The On-Line Journal of Issues in Nursing, A Scholarly Journal of the American Nurses Association* 12 (Jan. 31, 2007).
[9] Id.

of public policy and private best practice. Generally, they have expressed the concept of control as "independence" and the social value to be achieved as "objectivity." For example, in a supervisory letter the U.S. Board of Governors of the Federal Reserve System stated, "Compliance independence facilitates objectivity and avoids inherent conflicts of interest that may hinder the effective implementation of a compliance program."[10] In other words, to perform its function compliance should be objective, and to be objective it should be independent. The Basel Committee on Banking Supervision described this quest for objectivity in more detail in a white paper issued in 2005.[11] The purpose of independence, it said, was to "help ensure the effectiveness of the compliance function." Moreover, that effectiveness could be threatened if the head of compliance and other compliance staff are "placed in a position where there is a real or potential conflict between their compliance responsibilities and their other responsibilities."

These concepts of independence and objectivity are standard fare among professionals, when a social function is deemed of sufficient importance that it warrants professional attention, free from conflicts of interest. Mature professions generally have extensive controls in this area. Lawyers, for example, have elaborate standards (among lawyers we would expect no less) governing potential conflicts of interest. Much like the bedside nurse who requires power to care for the patient, compliance requires objectivity to administer the compliance program, and professional control over the workplace helps deliver that capability.

This leads to the second question: How should greater control be achieved? The Basel Committee has taken a strong view. In a statement reminiscent of the majority opinion written by Judge Smith of the New York Court of Appeals, the Basel Committee said, "It is the preference of the committee that compliance function staff perform only compliance responsibilities."[12] It admitted that this type of specialization might not be practicable in smaller institutions. When compliance performs non-compliance functions, the Basel Committee notes, potential conflicts of interest must be avoided. Other sources of guidance have highlighted that compliance should not be subject to instructions or adverse influence in their compliance activities;[13] that compliance should enjoy ultimate authority regarding compliance matters;[14] that its advice should not be subject to the approval of senior management, its personnel should be solely responsible for performing compliance functions; and that it should have sufficient tools and expertise to fulfill its responsibilities.[15] All of these share the common theme that compliance must enjoy sufficient organizational independence to remain objective in its work.

---

[10] Board of Governors of the Federal Reserve System, *Compliance Risk Management Programs and Oversight at Large Banking Organizations with Complex Compliance Profiles*, SR 08-8 (Oct. 16, 2008).
[11] Basel Committee on Banking Supervision, *Compliance and the Compliance Function in Banks*, Bank for International Settlements (Apr. 2005).
[12] *Compliance and the Compliance Function in Banks*, at 12.
[13] European Securities and Markets Authority, *Final Report, Guidelines on Certain Aspects of the MiFID Compliance Function Requirements*, ESMA 2012/388 (July 6, 2012).
[14] Board of Governors of the Federal Reserve System, *Compliance Risk Management Programs*.
[15] Securities Industry and Financial Markets Association, *White Paper: The Evolving Role of Compliance* (Mar. 2013).

Granting the importance of independence and objectivity in the work of compliance, what does this importance mean in practice? Could compliance ever be fully independent? Many who have reflected on the compliance function have recognized that the challenge for compliance is to preserve its independence while working closely, and in a collaborative fashion, with the organization's line operations. Admittedly, greater objectivity is possible with independent compliance firms, such as those that provide third-party compliance services and audits. The rise of third-party providers has been a notable development of compliance over the last few years. Even Judge Smith of the New York Court of Appeals would likely recognize the professionalism of these third-party providers. Nonetheless, third-party providers must also work effectively with their clients. In any event, whether one considers in-house or third-party compliance, compliance officers should recognize that independence remains an elusive goal and that the same is true among established professions. Physicians in the United States worry about the growing ability of insurance companies to limit their professional judgment. Legal scholars recognize that the ideal of lawyer independence continues to raise many difficult questions.[16] In sum, no one should consider independence an easily attainable panacea. Professional independence will always be a pragmatic and qualified tool for achieving identified social benefits.

The attention given to the need for greater independence and objectivity among compliance practitioners suggests greater potential support for the idea of compliance as a profession. The efforts to give compliance greater control over its own work imply that society is at last recognizing compliance as among those occupations—still few in number—in which the social benefits of an autonomous practice warrant professional status. In this sense, compliance is making progress toward professionalization.

Expertise

Expertise is another indicator of professionalism because it has played a critical role in the development of the established professions. During the 19th and 20th centuries the development of dynamic capitalism was accompanied by the development of expertise-based professionalism. Historians recognize that professions flourished during this period because "both the state and the universities were persuaded of the virtues of tested and regulated expertise in a wide range of occupations and, therefore, made it relatively easy for occupations to claim professional status by adopting the forms of professionalism."[17] Steven Brint has noted that capitalism and professionalism "are quite closely connected."[18] As he put it:

> New organizational forms and new technological achievements produced by capitalist enterprise called forth new professions – in engineering and other applied sciences, in accounting, in corporation law. The problems of

---

[16] *See*, e.g., the thoughtful discussion in: Kevin M. Michels, "Lawyer Independence: From Ideal to Viable Standard," 61 *Case Western Reserve Law Review* 85 (2010).
[17] Steven Brint, *In an Age of Experts: The Changing Role of Professionals in Politics and Public Life* (Princeton University Press, 1994), page 31.
[18] *Id.*

poverty created, in large part, by a highly dynamic, but weakly regulated capitalism, also called forth new aspiring professions – in city planning, social work, public health, and again, teaching. And finally, new wealth, also the by-product of capitalist expansion, called forth the growth or development of new cultural or consumer service professions: university teachers, journalists, curators, librarians, psychologists, and other therapists.

The result, he concluded, was a new "occupational professionalism" fostered by aspiring white-collar occupations and governments "convinced of the civic virtues" of trained expertise and professional ethics.[19]

Other scholars have noted that the demand for specialized knowledge and skill is likely to rise, not shrink, in the economy of the future. As Eliot Freidson expressed it, "Virtually all prophets—or, as they are now called, futurologists—seem agreed that the future will see ever-increasing reliance on specialized knowledge and skill, and on applying that knowledge to the solution of practical problems by specially trained men."[20] However, he continues, knowledge "is not disembodied spirit." Rather, the questions are: Where does it come from, how is it recognized, and how is it organized, evaluated, and controlled? When we answer these questions for compliance, we can see that it has made progress toward being a profession.

One of the most important developments for compliance over the last decade has been the growing recognition that its practice requires special expertise. Practitioners have long understood this, and others have slowly come to recognize it as well. This recognition has taken various forms. The Federal Reserve Board, for example, has recognized that compliance risk is unique, not susceptible to the same kinds of controls as other, more quantitative, risks and therefore, that firmwide compliance programs and strong cultures of compliance are necessary.[21] Unique risks, one can easily infer, must be addressed with unique skills. Similarly, when the European Securities and Markets Authority (ESMA) issued guidelines on the compliance function for investment firms, it emphasized the necessary expertise of compliance practitioners. ESMA said, "The compliance officer should have sufficiently broad knowledge and experience and a sufficiently high level of expertise so as to be able to assume responsibility for the compliance function as a whole and ensure that it is effective."[22]

ESMA then identified three elements of this expertise:

- All compliance staff must have knowledge of applicable laws and regulations, receive regular training to maintain their knowledge, and the senior compliance officer, known in the European regime as the "designated compliance officer," shall have a "higher level of expertise";

---

[19] *Id.*
[20] Eliot Freidson, *Professionalism Reborn: Theory, Prophecy, and Policy* (The University of Chicago Press, 1994), pages 66–67.
[21] Federal Reserve, *Compliance Risk Management Programs*.
[22] ESMA, *Final Report*.

- The "compliance officer shall demonstrate sufficient professional experience as is necessary to be able to assess the compliance risks and conflicts of interest inherent in the investment firm's business activities"; and
- The compliance officer shall have specific knowledge of the different business activities provided by the investment firm.[23]

This triad suggests the unique combination of skills necessary for the field: knowledge of applicable legal and regulatory standards, professional expertise in assessing the compliance risks of a particular firm, and knowledge of the firm's business so as to be able to apply appropriately the legal knowledge and the professional risk-assessment expertise.

In addition, recognition of the special expertise required to be an effective compliance practitioner can be seen in the growing importance of specialized training programs. Several organizations have developed programs to train compliance professionals and award them some form of professional recognition upon completion of the program. The Compliance Certification Board (CCB) offers a variety of certifications.[24] The CCB was established by the Society of Corporate Compliance and Ethics and the Health Care Compliance Association in 1999. Its designations include Certified Compliance & Ethics Professional (CCEP), Certified Compliance & Ethics Professional-International (CCEP-I), Certified in Healthcare Compliance (CHC), as well as specialized compliance designations for health care privacy and healthcare research. Certifications require work experience, continuing education units, and an examination. The CCB states that more than 7,800 people actively hold at least one of these designations. Another certification is available for practitioners who work with asset managers. National Regulatory Services created the program in 2005, and the Investment Adviser Association has been a cosponsor since 2007. Completion of the program requires 18 months of course work and an examination, and results in designation as an Investment Adviser Certified Compliance Professional (IACCP).[25] The program states that more than 360 individuals have earned the designation. A third designation is available for compliance practitioners who work with broker-dealers. Sponsored by the Financial Industry Regulatory Authority (FINRA) and the Wharton School of Business of the University of Pennsylvania, the program requires two weeks of residential courses, an examination, and results in designation as a Certified Regulatory and Compliance Professional (CRCP).[26] Finally, the National Society of Compliance Professionals offers an examination-based certification for compliance professionals who work with both asset managers and broker-dealers. Successful completion of the examination results in designation as a Certified Securities Compliance Professional (CSCP).[27]

---

[23] ESMA, *Final Report*, Supporting Guidelines 5-50–5-52.
[24] Descriptions of the certifications may be found on the CCB's website.
[25] A description of the program may be found on the IACCP's website. The author wishes to note that he has served as a faculty member for the IACCP program.
[26] A description of the program may be found on the CRCP's website. The author wishes to note that he has also served as a faculty member for the CRCP program.
[27] A description of the program may be found on the CSCP's website. The author wishes to note that he serves on the Board of Directors of the National Society of Compliance Professionals.

The collaboration between FINRA and the Wharton School is suggestive of another trend in this area: the increasing interest of universities. For example, the University of Albany and the Albany Law School have developed the Institute for Financial Market Regulation (IFMR) to foster scholarship and research on regulation, including compliance. Similarly, New York University Law School has established a Program on Corporate Compliance and Enforcement (PCCE) to encourage a dialogue among academic and legal experts on compliance, among other topics. Other universities and law schools have developed specific classes for their curricula. As this trend continues it will be interesting to see how compliance develops as a scholarly field.

As public authorities recognize the special expertise required for the compliance function, and educational organizations offer to provide professional training and certifications, we can see compliance developing into what scholars would call an occupational profession. The growing interest of institutions of higher learning adds even more weight to this trend. Special expertise is a growing requirement for the practice of modern compliance. As recognition of this reality spreads beyond practitioners, compliance makes progress toward full professionalism.

Ethics

Ethics has always been an indicator of professionalism. Some observers have identified professionalism's high ethical tone as the characteristic that distinguishes it from business and the trades. Louis M. Brandeis, a great progressive of the early 20th century and justice of the U.S. Supreme Court, reflected this perspective when he defined *professionalism:* A profession is an occupation for which the necessary training is intellectual and involves knowledge and learning as opposed to technical skill, it is pursued largely for others, and the amount of financial return is not the accepted measure of success.[28] Brandeis' description of a profession reminds us that professional ethics require more than mere adherence to accepted social norms—although many professions expect this from their members. Rather, professional ethics are based upon the nature of the work, the intended beneficiary, and the quality (not solely the profit) of the work provided.

Steven Brint, a well-known scholar of professionalism, argues that the ideology of professionalism has both a technical and a moral aspect.[29] Technically, it promises skilled work based on broad and complex knowledge. In the previous section we discussed this as "occupational professionalism." Morally, it promises to be guided by an appreciation for the important social ends it serves. Brint labels this perspective "social trustee professionalism."[30] Beyond doing competent work, Brint says, the professional is focused on achieving the larger public purpose of his or her work. Many advocates for professionalism, he notes, have understood the professions as activities "that embodied and expressed the idea of larger social purposes." In this sense, we can see Brandeis' view that the professional is a trustee for the delivery of a socially valuable service to

---

[28] Louis M. Brandeis, *Business—A Profession* (1914).
[29] Brint, *In an Age of Experts,* page 7.
[30] Brint, *In an Age of Experts,* page 36.

others, and the mark of success is not solely monetary compensation—although many professions are highly lucrative[31]—but also the quality of the service provided.

These principles are reflected in the codes of ethics of many established professions.

Medicine, for example, has been governed by a code of ethics for thousands of years. The Hippocratic Oath was drafted in the 5th century B.C. As a more contemporary statement, the American Medical Association (AMA) adopted Principles of Medical Ethics that reflect the goals of professionalism.[32] It is worth quoting the Preamble to the Principles in its entirety:

> The medical profession has long subscribed to a body of ethical statements developed primarily for the benefit of the patient. As a member of this profession, a physician must recognize responsibility to patients first and foremost, as well as to society, to other health professionals, and to self. The following Principles adopted by the American Medical Association are not laws, but standards of conduct, which define the essentials of honorable behavior for the physician.

In its focus on the patient, society, the respect of other professionals, and the responsibility of the practitioner as such, the statement reflects Brandeis' understanding of a profession.

The AMA's Principles of Medical Ethics reflect another aspect of professionalism that has had a powerful role, that is, the deeply conservative nature of the professional mindset.[33] The AMA's Principles describe the conduct that the association's members seek as "honorable." Honor, discretion, judgment, and character are all terms one often hears when discussing professionals. Some scholars of professionalism have attributed this emphasis on honor to professionals' possession of "guilty knowledge." To do their work professionals must learn about the "diseases, impecunities, illegalities, and moral sins" of their clients.[34] This places a premium on the honor with which they will handle such knowledge. But beyond this functional approach (we must have confidence in the honor of those to whom we reveal our weaknesses) ethical professionalism reflects a social ideal that has remained alive from an earlier age in our history. As Steven Brint explains, professionalism shows a "remarkable resonance with older cultural and political priorities in the Anglo-American world: the idea of work in a calling, a rationalist frame of mind, collective self-governance, and high levels of self-direction in day-to-day work activities."[35]

---

[31] So lucrative, in fact, that critics on both the ideological left and right wing, Marxists and Libertarians alike, have criticized the professions' ability to produce rewarding incomes.
[32] American Medical Association, *Principles of Medical Ethics, Preamble.*
[33] The author wishes to note that the term *conservative* has taken on a political and even partisan meaning. He uses it here in a sense Edmund Burke would have appreciated, not as it would be understood in a contemporary partisan setting.
[34] Brint, *In an Age of Experts*, page 27 (citing to Everett Hughes).
[35] Brint, *In an Age of Experts*, page 7.

What, then, is the public purpose that ethical compliance practitioners hold in trust? Chief Judge Lippman of the New York Court of Appeals suggested an answer in the dissent discussed above.[36] He said:

> In the wake of the devastation caused by fraudulent financial schemes—such as the Madoff Ponzi operation, infamous for many reasons including the length of time during which it continued undetected—the courts can ill afford to turn a blind eye to the potential for abuses that may be committed by unscrupulous financial services companies in violation of the public trust and law. In the absence of conscientious efforts by those insiders entrusted to report and prevent such abuses of investors, such behavior can run rampant until a third party outside the company discovers it and takes action.[37]

The Chief Judge also asserted that the compliance official's sole function as a compliance official was to ensure compliance with applicable internal and external ethical and legal requirements. Therefore, he wrote in dissent, the compliance officer exercised an internal self-regulatory function over the ethical and legal duties of the employer asset manager. Ultimately, in the chief judge's words, compliance should be treated as a profession "to protect the public."

Although Chief Judge Lippman did not use the term *social trustee professionalism*, we can hear the concept expressed in his dissent. Compliance is a function imbued with a public purpose: protecting the public from organizational malfeasance. Failure to accomplish this public purpose can and does result in social devastation, as his reference to the Madoff fraud shows. Moreover, compliance should be recognized as a profession because a lack of this recognition prevents it from fulfilling its public purpose. Finally, the conscientious efforts of compliance practitioners themselves, not the intervention of outsiders, fulfill this public purpose.

Indeed, the relationship between compliance practitioners and outsiders, or "third parties," in the chief judge's terms, warrants attention. Chief Judge Lippman suggests that the intervention of outside third parties, such as regulators, demonstrates not the ultimate purpose of compliance, but its failure. This reflects an important understanding about the nature of compliance. As a provider of a professional service, compliance stands on its own. At each stage of the discussion in this chapter, compliance's autonomy has played an important role: It must be independent to provide an objective perspective on a unique type of risk; it requires special expertise and training; and here, its ethics embody an important public purpose. This concept of functional autonomy is at the heart of compliance as a profession, as it is for every profession. Yet, it is not the only vision for the role of compliance. For example, in his majority opinion, Judge Smith suggested that compliance practitioners could earn legal recognition by reporting adverse

---

[36] See Sullivan v. Harnisch, § 31.02.
[37] Sullivan v. Harnisch, at 265.

information to regulators and then claiming the legal protections accorded whistleblowers.[38] Judge Smith appeared to find fault in the plaintiff compliance official's failure to tell "the SEC or anyone else" outside the asset manager about the CEOs misconduct. Instead, he says, Sullivan only "confronted" the CEO himself. This poses a vision of compliance that is diametrically opposed to its professionalism and turns the idea of professional honor and discretion on its head. Instead of taking the guilty knowledge to the client and working for its correction, Judge Smith would have the compliance professional take the information to the government and demand whistleblower status. In Judge Smith's view compliance achieves its public purpose by informing on its clients. Chief Judge Lippman brushed aside the majority's analysis on this point, stating simply that compliance officials should be protected from the inception of an investigation, even before they have made any report to the government. Nonetheless, as long as Judge Smith's view prevails—that compliance practitioners will be recognized not by preventing problems but rather by being informers for the government—professionalism for compliance is certainly a distant dream.

One can see a growing recognition for compliance's public purpose in how society has responded to instances of organizational malfeasance. With remarkable regularity, over the last several decades, a new understanding of the role and value of compliance has followed each new round of scandal and crisis. As long ago as the early 1990s, when compliance was still in an early stage of development, contemporaries recognized this role. Following scandals at major securities firms, such as Drexel, Burnham Lambert and Salomon Brothers, the press reported about compliance practitioners: "Firms are learning that their reputations, perhaps their very survival, might rest on these professional worrywarts."[39] As a result of recent developments, the press reported, practitioners were being given higher status, higher salaries, larger staffs, and more access to the highest levels of the organization. In particular, firms caught in the scandals gained new recognition for compliance's value. At the heart of the scandals of the early 1990s, Salomon Brothers implemented various enhancements to its compliance program and issued a statement that the new compliance measures "should go a long way toward advancing the firm's efforts to restore the trust and confidence of our clients, shareholders, and of government regulators."[40] Decades later, there was even more widespread appreciation for compliance after the devastation of the financial crisis of 2008. In fact, as one reporter put it, after the crisis compliance finally got "a corner office."[41] In following years the appreciation of compliance also spread around the world, with the press reporting new attention to compliance and growing numbers of professionals in countries like China and Brazil.[42] Certainly, recognizing that compliance provides a response to these crises shows an appreciation for the public purpose it serves.

---

[38] *Id.*
[39] Alison Leigh Cowan, "Compliance Officers' Day in the Sun: Investment Houses Have Elevated the Status of Their In-House Cops," *The New York Times* (Oct. 20, 1991), page F10.
[40] Michael Siconolfi, "Salomon Beefs Up Compliance Rules in Wake of Scandal," *Wall Street Journal* (Aug. 30, 1991), page C13 (quoting a statement by Salomon Brothers).
[41] Carol E. Curtis, "Compliance Gets a Corner Office…," *Securities Industry News* (Nov. 30, 2009), page 16.
[42] *See e.g.,* Gregory J. Millman and Ben DiPetro, "For Compliance Chiefs, Who's the Boss?" *Wall Street Journal* (Jan. 16, 2014), page B7.

How then do compliance practitioners put this public purpose to work in their day-to-day work? At least two professional groups have issued codes of ethics for compliance professionals: the National Society for Compliance Professionals (NSCP)[43] and the Society of Corporate Compliance and Ethics (SCCE).[44] The two codes show many similarities. Professionals should avoid conflicts of interest, preserve client confidences (unless disclosure is authorized or compelled), and serve their clients with appropriate knowledge or expertise. In some areas the two codes differ somewhat, but a similar meaning can be understood. For example, the NSCP says compliance professionals should have sufficient "independence," whereas SCCE says they should not "agree to unreasonable limits that would interfere with their professional ethical and legal responsibilities." Both organizations also agree on the basic steps professionals should take when they discover misconduct and the client fails to respond, including reporting the matter to the highest levels of the organization and considering resignation if those efforts are unsuccessful. There are a few interesting nuances between the codes. For example, in commentary the SCCE says professionals should consider resignation as a last resort, because they may be the only remaining barrier to misconduct. Moreover, whereas the NSCP states that professionals should consider reporting unresolved misconduct to regulatory authorities, the SCCE says a professional should only do so "when required by law." Even so, both codes suggest fundamentally similar approaches to fulfilling compliance's public purpose. As SCCE states in commentary to its code, "The duty of a compliance and ethics professional goes beyond a duty to the employing organization, inasmuch as his/her duty to the public and to the profession includes prevention of organizational misconduct."

Compliance has made great progress in obtaining recognition for its social purpose and in articulating ethical standards that should guide compliance practitioners as they work to achieve that purpose. Chief Judge Lippman's dissent was a ringing endorsement of the public purpose compliance holds and serves. In the codes of ethics adopted by professional groups, such as NSCP and SCCE, we can see statements of the specific ethical requirements for achieving those goals. In this regard, as in the others discussed above, compliance continues to make progress toward professionalism.

Organization

Organization of the occupation is widely recognized as an indication of professionalism. Indeed, in the scholarship of professions, there have been efforts to describe a standard life or development cycle for professions. According to these theories, the process begins when an occupation or trade like any other begins to imagine it is more than simply another job. One scholar described a five-step process[45]:

- First, a group of people begins doing full time "the thing that needs doing";
- Second, they form an association for "socializing, study, and the discussion of common problems";

---

[43] National Society for Compliance Professionals, Code of Ethics: Standards of Professional Conduct and Guidance for Compliance Professionals. NSCP's code is available on its website.
[44] Society of Corporate and Compliance Ethics, Code of Professional Ethics for Compliance and Ethics Professionals. SCCE's code is available on is website.
[45] Brint, *In an Age of Experts*, page 32 (citing to Harold Wilensky).

- Third, the group seeks a course of professional training, either in the universities or outside;
- Fourth, the state is approached to "protect the public interest by licensing as competent only those who have the proper qualifications"; and
- Fifth, the group establishes a code of ethics to protect the public from unscrupulous practitioners and to reinforce professional status by providing evidence of a sense of public responsibility.

This cycle has been followed, the scholar notes, by many professions in both the United States and the United Kingdom. Two critical steps in the process are organizational. The aspiring profession forms an association and seeks the protection of the government. In this area, compliance has had mixed results.

At least two associations have been formed for compliance professionals. NSCP was founded in 1986 and claims a membership of several thousand. NSCP focuses on compliance professionals in financial services and offers a variety of professional activities, including professional education, conferences, certification, standards, and networking. SCCE is newer, having been established in 2004. It claims a membership of more than 4,500. SCCE is distinguishable from NSCP in that it covers a wide range of industries including academics; aerospace; banking; construction; entertainment; government; financial services; food and manufacturing; insurance; and oil, gas, and chemicals. It also provides training, certification, and networking. Both of these organizations are active, as can be seen by the crowded schedule of events, programs, and publications they offer.

The second development, protection of the government, has been much less developed. Compliance professionals in certain positions in certain sectors must achieve designated qualifications. For example, CCOs for broker-dealers in the United States must qualify as a General Securities Principal.[46] This requirement has been in place since 2001[47] and usually requires CCOs to pass a test known as the Series 24. However, this is not a specialized test for compliance professionals, but a test generally applicable to senior broker-dealer officials. More generally, however, the government does not license compliance professionals in the same sense as physicians and lawyers. Indeed, as shown by the majority opinion of the New York Court of Appeals, discussed above, in some cases compliance is not even recognized as a profession, let alone one deserving public protection. In a recent development that holds out a great deal of future promise, the American Law Institute (ALI) has announced a new project on corporate compliance.[48] According to the ALI the target audience for this project:

> [I]ncludes outside counsel specializing in the areas of compliance and risk management; in-house attorneys, compliance officers, and other personnel who carry out internal control responsibilities; government regulators and prosecutors; and commentators, scholars, and people involved in law reform initiatives.

---

[46] FINRA Rule 1022(a), General Securities Principal.
[47] National Association of Securities Dealers, *Notice to Members 01-51* (Aug. 2001).
[48] American Law Institute, The American Law Institute Announces Four New Projects, Press Release by the American Law Institute (Nov. 14, 2014).

Nonetheless, although the ALI project holds out great promise for the future, as of this writing compliance has not yet fulfilled all of the steps in a typical professional life cycle.

Although compliance enjoys the benefits of thriving professional associations, it has not yet made significant progress in obtaining governmental recognition, let alone protection. Of all the characteristics of a profession, protection remains the most underdeveloped. In this regard, compliance's progress towards professionalism is mixed.

IV. GETTING TO THE NEXT LEVEL

Compliance continues to make progress toward professionalism. Its independence has been recognized in several settings, public and private. Its special expertise has been recognized, both as a requirement for success in the field, and also through increasing attention to professional training and certification. Its public purpose and the professional ethics supporting that purpose have also been noted and codified in codes of ethics. Finally, professional organizations have been created and are active in the field, even if progress toward governmental recognition has been mixed. In light of all of these developments, one could view compliance as already highly professionalized.

This reality leads to a difficult question. Why can compliance be so professional and yet, when a moment arrives for recognition, most recently before the New York Court of Appeals, it could all appear for naught? This question is particularly significant because we should recognize that professionalism is not simply a form of status. It is a tool that would help compliance achieve its mission. Professionalism serves the underlying purpose that has been entrusted to compliance practitioners: achieving their firms' compliance with applicable laws, regulations, and ethical standards. Professionalism will help practitioners overcome the diverse and ever present challenges that they face, which fall into three broad categories: knowing when to say "no;" the potential for retaliation; and pressures from outside the firm.

One challenge is universal to the practice. To do their job well, from time to time compliance officers have to define the limits of permissible conduct: they have to be able to say "no." Whenever people hear that word, or any verbal formulation that has the same effect, you can expect them to be unhappy and offer opposition. This is inherent in the compliance field. For example, collegiate sports are a relatively new entrant into the world of modern compliance. Yet the dynamic long experienced in financial and other forms of compliance has already manifested itself there. As William Rhoden, a sports columnist, has put it:

> In a highly scrutinized world of big-time intercollegiate athletics, where one violation of the rules can embarrass a university and cause head coaches to lose their jobs and players their eligibility, compliance officers have become an athletics department's most important employee. Also the most resented. Theirs is a cordial but often contentious relationship.[49]

---

[49] William C. Rhoden, "Compliance Officers: Good Cop, Bad Cop," Sports of the Times, *The New York Times* (Apr. 11, 2009), page D2.

The columnist concluded that despite all the talk of coaches and compliance "being on the same team," the compliance director's works primarily for the university's best interest. Seasons may end, he said, but the "internecine game of cops and robbers never will." In this environment, a compliance practitioner will always face a certain degree of opposition from those he or she advises and monitors. The stature and credibility provided by professionalism should help overcome this opposition.

Another challenge is less common, but practitioners must always be sensitive to the risk that opposition to compliance will escalate into retaliation against the practitioner. After the collapse of MF Global, a financial firm made famous by the founder's prior service as a U.S. senator, the firm's former risk officer suggested that he had been dismissed as retaliation for the concerns he had expressed about its aggressive risk practices.[50] In regards to compliance and risk officers, one reporter covering the story said, "Potential retaliation goes with the territory."[51] Retaliation could be explicit or subtle. But the more that compliance is vulnerable to retaliation within a single organization, the more likely retaliation becomes. Professionalism should give compliance a frame of reference and perspective beyond the individual employer. This is not a full defense to retaliation, for which there is probably no silver bullet defense. Nonetheless, professional status may provide compliance officers with some insulation and protection from retaliation because business line executives might be reluctant to be seen, particularly by regulators, as dismissing professionals who oppose their plans.

A final challenge is even less common, luckily. Beyond the reality of opposition and the risk of retaliation, compliance crises are always a danger. In a compliance crisis there will always be outside pressures that can threaten a compliance practitioner. This threat means that, when a crisis occurs, a firm's executives, the media, or regulators often look someone to blame, create a narrative of missed opportunities, or simply assume that everyone who was near the scene of an incident must share in the guilt, whatever role each individual played or attempted to play. If good faith compliance cannot survive these pressures and this blame, the entire practice, and the social purpose it serves will be at risk. No one is immune from allegations and litigation. Nonetheless, professionalism, with social recognition of professional standards of care, as discussed below, should help good faith practitioners navigate through crises.

Given the potential benefits of professionalism, what can an individual practitioner do to foster its progress? Sitting back and waiting for outside recognition serves no one. Indeed, as long as compliance practitioners wait for someone else to award them recognition, one can question whether they are ready for professionalism. Instead, practitioners must push forward, especially with the developments that are under their own control. Each practitioner should ask what he or she could do to further the progress

---

[50] Emmanuel Olaoye, "Evidence, Access Aid Job Security When Compliance Staff Raise a Red Flag," Complinet, Thomson Reuters Accelus (Feb. 8, 2012). In describing public reportage on this incident, the author states no view on the merits of the risk officer's allegations. Rather, whether true or not in this instance, the allegations articulated a risk potentially faced by compliance professionals.

[51] Id.

of compliance toward professionalism. Potential helpful actions are almost unlimited. They range from speaking with pride, in social settings, about the important role of compliance in modern society, to playing an active role in public policy to help shape the laws and regulations governing compliance and to volunteering time and energy to professional associations. Every contribution helps build upon the others and advances the cause. Three additional suggestions are offered below.

Make Professionalism Personal

Every practitioner can further the progress of compliance by making professionalism personal. Compliance is not alone in this regard. Other professions have paid attention to the role of the individual in enhancing professionalism. Richard Bowman is a senior professor of education who has written on the role of the individual in professionalism. He has said:

> Being a professional is not merely an intellectual exercise but, rather, involves a commitment to being something compelling and transformative in the workplace. Self-images have transformational power: they define who we think we are. Viewing oneself as a professional elicits one's best work, essentially because it involves living up to a set of ideals.…In that sense, professionalism is less a matter of what professionals actually do and more a matter of who they are as human beings. [52]

Professionals, Bowman continued, view themselves as such "because they choose to, regardless of the quality of the culture around them." Indeed, he said, the "most powerful form of human influence is inspiration," and in "a morally interdependent world, professionals inspire principled conduct by enlisting others in a common cause."

The sense that professionalism emerges from within, as a personal experience rather than an external standard, has also been discussed in the context of nursing. Milisa Manojlovich, a professor of nursing who was quoted earlier in regards to a professional's power over the workplace, suggests that empowerment is both a structural and a psychological experience.[53] In the latter dimension, known as "psychological empowerment," doing what is necessary to get the job done is a motivational construct with several attributes:

- Practitioners derive meaning from the congruence between their personal beliefs and their job requirements;
- They have feelings of competence or self-efficacy when they have confidence in their ability to perform the job;
- They have a sense of self-determination and autonomy when they have feelings of control over their work; and
- They feel they have an impact when they have a sense they can influence important organizational outcomes.

---

[52] Richard Bowman, *Understanding What It Means to Be a Professional,* 86 The Clearing House (2013), pages 17–20 (citations and internal quotations deleted).
[53] Manojlovich, *Power and Empowerment in Nursing* (summarizing the work of several other scholars).

This kind of empowerment gives practitioners an active orientation toward their work, contributes to professional practice behaviors, and appears to have a positive effect on job satisfaction and avoiding burnout.

The lesson for compliance professionals is that professionalism should be a personal experience. One can call the experience either inspiration or psychological empowerment. In either case, the result is the same. Practitioners achieve professionalism and have an impact through their own internal experience of their work. In other words, progress towards professionalism comes from within.

Emphasize Professional Judgment

Every practitioner can further the progress of compliance by emphasizing professional judgment. This is an area in which compliance continues to lag the mature professions. Judgment adds subjective depth and quality to a profession. When a profession is recognized as capable of judgment beyond mere expertise, it is given special respect.

Respect for professional judgment seems to be particularly applicable to the practices, such as law and medicine, where society pays a particularly terrible price if the profession's social purpose is not served. One can see this judgment in the law, when a lawyer counsels a client not to assert a legal right, because, in his or her professional judgment, the harmful consequences to the client's overall interests would outweigh the benefits. One can also see it in medicine, when a treating physician uses a prescription drug for a purpose other than its designated use, because, again in his or her professional judgment, it will be efficacious in treating the patient's condition. In both instances judgment supersedes mere technical expertise. Importantly, as with these mature professions, society pays an especially high price when compliance's social purpose is not served. Accordingly, compliance officers must be allowed and encouraged to use their professional judgment.

Respect for this type of judgment also carries with it an important corollary: social recognition that professional judgment is just that—judgment. Such judgment does not guarantee a specified outcome, as would the operation of a machine producing specified outputs. Medicine has given us the most famous statement of this point: "The operation was a success, but the patient died." A physician, performing brilliantly, against the odds, delivers an extraordinary professional service, but nonetheless, the patient dies. To achieve this kind of respect—recognition for the professionalism of the service, even when the outcome is ultimately unsuccessful—compliance must give greater attention to how its capability for judgment and advice transcends its technical expertise.

In this regard, compliance remains something of a prisoner of its past. When compliance first appeared, its practitioners were generally operational staff who operated broker-dealers' supervisory controls. The first major statement on modern compliance, the *Guide to Broker-Dealer Compliance* issued by an advisory committee of the Securities and Exchange Commission in 1972,[54] simply compiled control processes that broker-dealers could operate. As compliance developed and spread to other sectors, such as banks, asset managers, and health care providers, it again appeared as a set of operational control practices targeting the individual compliance requirements of each new field. As each round of crisis brought new attention to the value of compliance, as discussed above, the importance and value of compliance grew. Now, as time has gone by, the challenges involved in delivering compliance have become more apparent, compliance practitioners have become more sophisticated with more expertise, and judgment has come to play an important role at the highest levels of the profession. Nonetheless, many observers continue to view compliance in terms of its origins, many years ago, and its current line operations, down on the shop floor, where practitioners do nothing more than operate the control machinery. This lingering image of compliance as solely an operational function must be brought up to date.

Compliance also remains a prisoner of its regulators. At least one regulator has discouraged compliance practitioners from exercising judgment and giving advice, by suggesting that if compliance officers give advice, and it is usually taken, they could be liable even when it is not.[55] This strange and counterintuitive suggestion has given rise to discussions of whether compliance practitioners should serve on firm committees, and to guidance from the same regulator about what sorts of advice they may safely give.[56] In this environment one could understand a reluctance to emphasize one's judgment. However, if compliance practitioners wish to be fully recognized as professionals, they cannot retreat into their operational past.

The lesson for compliance practitioners is that if they are afraid to exercise their judgment and offer advice, they cannot expect the recognition given to the mature professions. Of course, it would be better if those who support compliance's social purpose were to avoid undermining its judgment, but compliance practitioners cannot stand by and wait. In other words: Progress toward professionalism requires courage.

View Compliance as One Practice and One Profession

Every compliance practitioner can further the professionalization of the field by viewing compliance as one practice and one profession wherever it appears. Compliance first emerged in the 1960s as a method for controlling the sales practices of securities salespeople.[57] Over the following years it has reached into multiple business sectors, organizations, and the public sector. In this environment, so different from compliance's

---

[54] *Guide to Broker-Dealer Compliance, Report of the Broker-Dealer Model Compliance Program Advisory Committee to the Securities and Exchange Commission*, Securities Exchange Act Release No. 11,098, 5 SEC Docket 472 (Nov. 13, 1974). A copy of the full report is available in the SEC Library.
[55] *See, e.g., In the Matter of Theodore W. Urban*, Initial Decision, Initial Decision Release No. 402 (Sept. 8, 2010). The SEC later vacated this decision without issuing any decision or opinion: *In the Matter of Theodore W. Urban*, Order Dismissing Proceeding, Release No. 34-66259 & IA-3366 (Jan. 26, 2012).
[56] *See* SEC Division of Trading and Markets, *Frequently Asked Questions About Liability of Compliance and Legal Personnel at Broker-Dealers under Sections 15(b)(4) and 15(b)(6) of the Exchange Act* (Sept. 30, 2013).
[57] Modern compliance is detailed by other contributors to this text.

origins fifty years ago, one need no longer suggest that the learning developed in financial compliance could have a wider application. It has already happened. Compliance is being practiced across American society and around the world.

Within this global environment we should recognize that in the past, many practitioners viewed their work solely in terms of their narrow area of specialized expertise. They did not recognize themselves as practicing compliance. Instead they believed they practiced broker-dealer compliance, or asset management compliance, or bank compliance, or health care compliance, and so on. More generally, though less explicitly, they also defined themselves by the local regulatory regime in which they worked, be it the United States, the United Kingdom, China, or any of the myriad other local regulatory regimes in which compliance has appeared. In other words, by defining their practice by the specific problems they faced and the specific tools with which they worked, compliance practitioners defined themselves as craftspeople. As time went by they became increasingly sophisticated, but craftspeople nonetheless. Compliance practitioners who continue to define themselves as craftspeople should expect society to agree with their assessment. To be professionals they should raise their horizon and their self-image to compliance's new world stage.

The new global ISO Standard for Compliance Management, issued in December 2014,[58] is an important step away from the lingering image of compliance as a craft. As an ISO standard, it is global in its reach. Participants from Australia, Austria, Canada, China, France, Germany, Malaysia, Netherlands, Portugal, Singapore, Spain, and Switzerland drafted the standard. Several others, including Japan and the United Kingdom, had observer status. Moreover, the standard explicitly applies to all types of organizations. In other words, the standard is all encompassing. It applies to any organization, anywhere in the world. Moreover, the compliance management tools it sets out are already familiar to experienced practitioners: identifying and analyzing compliance risks; compliance leadership; planning and achieving compliance objectives; resources, training, awareness, communication, and documented information; operation of controls and procedures; monitoring and audits; escalating and correcting nonconformance; and continual improvement. The new ISO Standard 19600 can be used whether one is the CCO for a broker-dealer, an asset manager, a bank, a medical practice, a manufacturer, a software developer, a chain of retail stores, a university, a charity, or any other organization. ISO recognition makes the underlying continuities in the practice of compliance explicit and measurable against a global benchmark.

The lesson for compliance practitioners is that they should recognize that they share a profession with all other compliance practitioners, wherever they practice and in whatever organization they practice. Indeed, the lessons in this book are largely based on the long-term experience of financial compliance, but they should prove helpful as compliance practitioners in other sectors around the world take up the challenge. This continuity among practices, highlighted by ISO Standard 19600 should make

---

[58] ISO, *Compliance Management Systems: Guidelines*, ISO 19600, First ed. (Dec. 15, 2014).

learning developed in any sector useful to all sectors. Envisioning and aiming for these broad horizons will be the next step in compliance's development as a profession. In other words: Progress toward professionalism will open the world.

V. UNFINISHED BUSINESS

Compliance is making progress toward professionalism. Today, more than ever, we can see its professionalism taking shape, with enhanced control over its workplace, expertise, professional ethics, and thriving professional associations. However, much work remains to be done. Until their professionalism is recognized, compliance practitioners will remain handicapped as they seek to achieve the important public purpose entrusted to them. Nonetheless, as we have seen, practitioners can help advance the cause of professionalism. They can look to the professionalism within themselves, emphasize their professional judgment, and recognize the profession's global stature. Every practitioner can foster compliance's progress. Through all of these means, compliance can continue to develop as a profession.

Of course, if we can't test and validate this progress toward professionalism, are we really talking about compliance? Any compliance practitioner would say, "Don't expect me to believe we are making progress, unless we can test and validate those assertions." To this end: How can we measure progress towards professionalism? For many years compliance practitioners have focused on the government, and the recognition it could potentially bestow. After years of frustration, perhaps the time has come to choose a new path. Let us propose a measure for testing compliance's progress in society at large. To be effective, the measure should be precise, with measurable indicators, as well as meaningful. That is, the measure should capture how compliance is viewed at a macro and impactful level in society. Some recent work associated with the University of Houston will be helpful in this regard.

In June 2014 the University of Houston Law Center held a symposium on compliance and ethics.[59] The symposium focused on Fortune 500 corporations—the largest and most significant corporations in the United States—including speakers from Walmart and Google. Following the symposium, Ryan McConnell and Erin Mitchell, both of whom are associated with the Law Center, published some interesting statistics. They reported that of the Fortune 500 Corporations, only 9 had directors with a background in compliance.[60] By way of comparison: 473 corporations had directors with backgrounds in finance, 225 had directors with backgrounds in law; and 165 had directors with backgrounds in accounting. In other words, in only a small number of major corporations have compliance professionals reached the highest organizational level, the senior governing body.

---

[59] University of Houston Law Center, University of Houston Law Center Hosts Ethics & Compliance Symposium, Professionals from a Broad Range of Industries Will Share Expertise at June 13 Conference (May 20, 2014).
[60] Ryan McConnell and Erin Mitchell, "Where's the Compliance Experience on Corporate Boards?" *Corporate Counsel* (July 9, 2014).

This could serve as a test to validate the future progress of compliance toward professionalism. As compliance is recognized as a profession, as practitioners are respected for their professional judgment, and as corporations understand and value the social purpose they serve, practitioners should be increasingly welcomed onto boards, and the number of corporations with directors whose backgrounds are in compliance should climb. Law, as a mature profession that is represented on 45 percent of Fortune 500 boards, establishes an interesting benchmark. Starting at less than 2 percent of the boards, compliance has lots of room to grow. It will be interesting to see how that growth unfolds. In the future, when we wonder whether compliance is continuing to make progress toward professionalism, let us see what membership on boards tells us.

Index

A

Accountability
Is it Time to Go? ... 766, 767, 771

Adequacy
Core Requirements of a Compliance Program ... 100, 105, 108, 110, 111, 114, 117, 121, 122, 123, 124, 125, 126
Cybersecurity ... 499, 506
Forensic Testing ... 533, 535, 543, 558, 564
Regulatory Examinations and Audits ... 572, 586, 591

Administrator Privileges
Cybersecurity ... 519

Adopting release
A History of Compliance ... 36, 40

Adult Protective Services Act
Compliance Professionals' Relationships with Endangered Populations ... 655

Advanced training
Compliance Training ... 234, 238

Advertising Regulation Department
Navigating Marketing and Distribution ... 312, 321, 323

Advertising Review
Forensic Testing ... 551

Advertising Rules
Corporate Transactions
The Role of the Compliance Department ... 386

Advisers Act fiduciary duty
Fiduciary Duty ... 81, 82, 86, 87, 89, 91

Affiliated brokerage
Affiliated Transactions Under the Advisers Act ... 417, 418

Affiliated person
Affiliated Transactions Under the Advisers Act ... 407, 409

Affiliated purchaser
Corporate Transactions
The Role of the Compliance Department ... 383

After Use Filing
Navigating Marketing and Distribution ... 323

Agency cross trades
Affiliated Transactions Under the Advisers Act ... 411
Enforcement Actions Against Chief Compliance Officers ... 735, 738, 742, 743, 744, 745

American Law Institute (ALI)
Compliance as a Profession ... 787, 788

American Stock Exchange
A History of Compliance ... 10, 11, 13, 14

Annual assessment
Compliance Training ... 236

Annual Certification of Compliance and Supervisory Processes
Seeking to Avoid Chief Compliance Officer Liability ... 682

Annual compliance report
Core Requirements of a Compliance Program ... 107, 116, 111, 115, 116, 117, 118, 121, 122, 123, 124, 125, 126, 127, 128, 133
Regulatory Examinations and Audits ... 577, 578

Annual Privacy Notices
Protecting the Privacy of Client Information ... 439

Annual review
Forensic Testing ... 535, 537, 566
Overview of the Regulatory Framework for SEC-Registered Investment Advisers ... 147
Regulatory Examinations and Audits ... 573, 577, 578, 581, 586, 595
Seeking to Avoid Chief Compliance Officer Liability ... 684, 698, 699

Annual review requirement
Core Requirements of a Compliance Program ... 110

Annual security report
Protecting the Privacy of Client Information ... 450

Antifraud provisions
Affiliated Transactions Under the Advisers Act ... 408, 418
Navigating Marketing and Distribution ... 283

Anti-Money Laundering (AML)
Enforcement Actions Against Chief Compliance Officers ... 740, 741
Corporate Transactions
The Role of the Compliance Department ... 379, 380, 393

Anti-Referral Payments Law
A History of Compliance ... 29, 30

Antivirus software
Cybersecurity ... 500, 516, 517, 518, 522, 525

Article Reprints
Navigating Marketing and Distribution ... 288, 293

Attorney-client privilege
Core Requirements of a Compliance Program ... 133
Corporate Transactions

The Role of the Compliance Department ... 375, 376
Regulatory Examinations and Audits ... 592

Average commission rates
Forensic Testing ... 547

Average daily trading volume (ADTV)
Corporate Transactions
The Role of the Compliance Department ... 383, 384, 385

B

Back-tested performance
Navigating Marketing and Distribution ... 300, 301, 320, 321, 331, 355

Baker, R. Gerald
A History of Compliance ... 52, 56

Bank Secrecy Act
Enforcement Actions Against Chief Compliance Officers ... 740, 741

Bankers Code Committee
A History of Compliance ... 10

Barkley, Alben
A History of Compliance ... 10

Barnier, Michel
A History of Compliance ... 54

Basel Committee on Banking Supervision
A History of Compliance ... 46
Compliance as a Profession ... 778

Basic training
Compliance Training ... 232, 238

Benchmark
Navigating Marketing and Distribution ... 301, 318, 328, 334, 338, 340, 342, 343

Best execution
Fiduciary Duty ... 83, 87
Forensic Testing ... 534, 546, 547, 548, 563
Regulatory Examinations and Audits ... 576, 642

Beynon, Gary R.
Enforcement Actions Against Chief Compliance Officers ... 743, 744

Bharara, Preet
What is Compliance? ... 65

Blackout periods
Fiduciary Duty ... 85

Blue sky laws
Overview of the Regulatory Framework for SEC-Registered Investment Advisers ... 143

Books and records
Forensic Testing ... 544, 549, 552, 565, 566
Overview of the Regulatory Framework for SEC-Registered Investment Advisers ... 146, 150, 151, 161
Regulatory Examinations and Audits ... 570, 572, 575, 576, 581, 582, 586, 587, 590

Breach notice law
Protecting the Privacy of Client Information ... 472

Brokerage arrangements
Forensic Testing ... 547

Browser Security
Cybersecurity ... 518

Business continuity plan (BCP)
Cybersecurity ... 496, 507, 526
Forensic Testing ... 559, 560, 561
Regulatory Examinations and Audits ... 576

C

Cambiar Investors, Inc.,
Navigating Marketing and Distribution ... 285

CAMELS
Overview of the Regulatory Framework for SEC-Registered Investment Advisers ... 166

Caremark International, Inc. (Caremark)
A History of Compliance ... 29, 30, 31, 38

Carve-outs
Navigating Marketing and Distribution ... 332, 343

Cash flow
Navigating Marketing and Distribution ... 325, 329, 330, 343, 344

Catchall provision
Navigating Marketing and Distribution ... 280, 286, 296, 297

Centaurus Financial
Cybersecurity ... 501

Central Registration Depository (CRD)
Your Relationship with FINRA ... 647

Certified Compliance & Ethics Professional
Compliance as a Profession ... 781

Certified in Healthcare Compliance
Compliance as a Profession ... 781

Certified Regulatory and Compliance Professional (CRCP)
Compliance as a Profession ... 781
Preparing to Become a Compliance Officer, and the Academy ... 753, 756

Certified Securities Compliance Professional (CSCP)
Compliance as a Profession ... 781
Ethics Standards Governing Compliance Professionals ... 193

Cherry picking
Navigating Marketing and Distribution ... 291, 295, 333, 356

Chief risk officer (CRO)
Compliance and Risk Management ... 259, 272, 274

Closing letter
Regulatory Examinations and Audits ... 590

Clover Capital
Navigating Marketing and Distribution ... 279, 297, 298, 300, 302, 303, 306, 329, 331, 341

Code of conduct
How Compliance Can Teach Ethics ... 185, 186, 190

Code of ethics
A History of Compliance ... 5, 6, 8, 9, 10, 35, 41, 42, 43

Enforcement Actions Against Chief Compliance
  Officers ... 738, 743, 744
Ethics Standards Governing Compliance
  Professionals ... 193, 199
Fiduciary Duty ... 85, 88
Forensic Testing ... 539, 540, 542, 545, 562
Game Plan for the New CCO ... 171
How Compliance Can Teach Ethics ... 179, 185
Overview of the Regulatory Framework for SEC-
  Registered Investment Advisers ... 147, 148
Regulatory Examinations and Audits ... 575

Cohen, Milton
A History of Compliance ... 11

Committee of Sponsoring Organizations of the Treadway Commission (COSO)
A History of Compliance ... 33, 34
Compliance and Risk Management ... 259, 260, 275

Commodities Futures Trading Commission Act of 1974 (CFTCA)
Overview of the Regulatory Framework for
  SEC-Registered Investment Advisers ... 158, 159

Commodity Exchange Act
Navigating Marketing and Distribution ... 345
Overview of the Regulatory Framework for
  SEC-Registered Investment Advisers ... 158, 159, 160

Commodity Exchange Authority
Overview of the Regulatory Framework for SEC-
  Registered Investment Advisers ... 158

Commodity Exchange Commission
Overview of the Regulatory Framework for
  SEC-Registered Investment Advisers ... 158

Commodity Futures Trading Commission (CFTC)
Navigating Marketing and Distribution ... 342, 345, 346, 347, 348, 349, 350, 352, 353, 354, 355, 356, 357, 358
Overview of the Regulatory Framework for
  SEC-Registered Investment Advisers ... 142, 157, 158, 159, 160, 161, 162
What is Compliance? ... 70

Commodity pool operators (CPOs)
Navigating Marketing and Distribution ... 345, 346, 347, 348, 349, 351, 354, 357

Commodity trading advisor (CTA)
Overview of the Regulatory Framework for SEC-
  Registered Investment Advisers ... 160, 161, 162
Navigating Marketing and Distribution ... 345, 346, 347, 348, 349, 351, 354, 357

Communication skills
Soft Skills
  Presenting Compliance ... 212, 213

Compliance and Ethics Leadership Council
How Compliance Can Teach Ethics ... 182, 187, 188

Compliance Certification Board
Compliance as a Profession ... 781

Compliance Committee
Core Requirements of a Compliance Program ... 110, 125, 127, 135

Compliance culture
What is Compliance? ... 65, 66

Compliance goals
Core Requirements of a Compliance Program ... 99

Compliance Official
A History of Compliance ... 15

Compliance procedures
Core Requirements of a Compliance Program ... 101, 103, 109, 112

Compliance Program Initiative
Forensic Testing ... 537

Compliance Program Rule
Fiduciary Duty ... 84, 85
Overview of the Regulatory Framework for
  SEC-Registered Investment Advisers ... 146, 147, 149, 150, 156, 167

Compliance rules
A History of Compliance ... 36, 37, 38, 40, 43
Core Requirements of a Compliance Program ... 93, 94, 95, 99, 100, 101, 102, 103, 104, 107, 108, 109, 111, 113, 114, 115, 116, 117, 123, 126, 128, 129, 130, 137
Cybersecurity ... 496

Composites
Navigating Marketing and Distribution ... 304, 326, 330, 341

Concept release
A History of Compliance ... 36

Conflict management
Soft Skills
  Presenting Compliance ... 218

Conflicts inventory
Regulatory Examinations and Audits ... 574

Conflicts of interest
Compliance as a Profession ... 778, 781, 786
Core Requirements of a Compliance Program ... 94, 97, 100, 103, 105, 108, 118, 140
Corporate Transactions
  The Role of the Compliance Department ... 370, 373, 376, 396, 397, 398, 399, 403
Ethics Standards Governing Compliance
  Professionals ... 195, 200, 201, 203
Fiduciary Duty ... 87
Regulatory Examinations and Audits ... 571, 573, 575, 576, 578, 595

Consolidated Supervision Rules
Overview of the Regulatory Framework for
  SEC-Registered Investment Advisers ... 156, 157

Contradictory securities positions
Forensic Testing ... 566

Control structures
Core Requirements of a Compliance Program ... 93, 96, 115, 116

Cook, Bradford
A History of Compliance ... 13

Corporate Executive Board
How Compliance Can Teach Ethics ... 182

Corporate restructuring transaction
Corporate Transactions
  The Role of the Compliance Department ... 367

Cox, Christopher
A History of Compliance ... 48

Credit report freeze law
Protecting the Privacy of Client Information ... 473

Crisis management coverage
Cybersecurity ... 529

Cross trades
Affiliated Transactions Under the Advisers Act ... 407, 412, 413, 414, 415, 416, 417, 419

Culture of compliance
A History of Compliance ... 22, 23, 46, 59
Core Requirements of a Compliance Program ... 95, 96, 97, 99, 112, 128, 135
Corporate Transactions
The Role of the Compliance Department ... 370, 392
Regulatory Examinations and Audits ... 578, 582, 585, 595
Seeking to Avoid Chief Compliance Officer Liability ... 684, 697
What is Compliance? ... 64, 65, 66, 69, 78

Custody procedures
Adviser Custody
What You Need to Know ... 426

Custody Rule
Adviser Custody
What You Need to Know ... 423, 424, 425, 426, 428, 432, 433
Forensic Testing ... 554

Customer privacy
Protecting the Privacy of Client Information ... 435, 467

Customized reports
Regulatory Examinations and Audits ... 587

Cyber insurance
Cybersecurity ... 494, 528, 529

Cyber Security Examination Sweep Summary
Protecting the Privacy of Client Information ... 452

Cyber terrorism coverage
Cybersecurity ... 529

Cybersecurity
Forensic Testing ... 557, 558, 559
Protecting the Privacy of Client Information ... 461, 477, 478

Cybersecurity Examination Initiative
Protecting the Privacy of Client Information ... 461

Cybersecurity Framework
Cybersecurity ... 493, 494, 497, 502

Cybersecurity Initiative
Cybersecurity ... 498, 503, 529

D

D.A. Davidson & Co
Cybersecurity ... 501

DALBAR, Inc.,
Navigating Marketing and Distribution ... 284, 287

Data Backup
Cybersecurity ... 520, 531

Data destruction
Cybersecurity ... 509

Data security
Game Plan for the New CCO ... 175

Deficiency letter
Enforcement Actions Against Chief Compliance Officers ... 745
Regulatory Examinations and Audits ... 572, 574, 589, 590, 591

Denver Investment Advisors, Inc.,
Navigating Marketing and Distribution ... 284, 285

Desktop procedures
Core Requirements of a Compliance Program ... 103

Directive on Markets in Financial Instruments (MiFid)
A History of Compliance ... 54, 55

Disaster recovery
Forensic Testing ... 559, 560

Disclosures
Navigating Marketing and Distribution ... 341

Discretion
Navigating Marketing and Distribution ... 324, 325, 341

Distribution participants
Corporate Transactions
The Role of the Compliance Department ... 383

Division of Enforcement
Avoiding Supervisory Liability ... 703, 706, 709, 713
Corporate Transactions
The Role of the Compliance Department ... 395
Enforcement Actions Against Chief Compliance Officers ... 734, 747
Forensic Testing ... 537, 567
Overview of the Regulatory Framework for SEC-Registered Investment Advisers ... 145, 159
Regulatory Examinations and Audits ... 574, 590, 591, 592, 594

Division of Investment Management (IM)
Compliance and Risk Management ... 265, 266, 268, 278
Navigating Marketing and Distribution ... 279, 289, 320
Overview of the Regulatory Framework for SEC-Registered Investment Advisers ... 145

Division of Trading and Markets (T&M)
Avoiding Supervisory Liability ... 726, 727, 728, 729, 730
Seeking to Avoid Chief Compliance Officer Liability ... 685, 690, 691, 695
What is Compliance? ... 68, 70, 74

Document request list
Game Plan for the New CCO ... 174, 177

Dodd, Christopher
A History of Compliance ... 50

Dodd-Frank Wall Street Reform and Consumer Protection Act of 2010
A History of Compliance ... 50, 51
Avoiding Supervisory Liability ... 724
Compliance and Risk Management ... 266, 269, 271, 272

Compliance Professionals' Relationships with
  Endangered Populations ... 664
Overview of the Regulatory Framework for
  SEC-Registered Investment Advisers ... 143, 144,
  150, 159, 163, 164
Preparing to Become a Compliance Officer, and the
  Academy ... 757
Regulatory Examinations and Audits ... 580, 594
Seeking to Avoid Chief Compliance Officer
  Liability ... 700

Donaldson, William
A History of Compliance ·42, 44

Dow Theory Forecasts, Incorporated
Navigating Marketing and Distribution ... 293

Due diligence ... 578
Corporate Transactions
  The Role of the Compliance Department ... 364,
  366, 369, 370, 374, 378, 379, 380, 393, 394,
  395, 396, 399
Protecting the Privacy of Client Information ... 450,
  462, 463, 476

Due diligence process
Core Requirements of a Compliance
  Program ... 117, 119

E

Effectiveness
Core Requirements of a Compliance Program ...
  100, 101, 108, 110, 111, 114, 117, 121, 123, 124,
  125, 126, 129, 132, 135
Forensic Testing ... 533, 535, 537, 543, 544,
  554, 565
Regulatory Examinations and Audits ... 572, 577,
  578, 581, 583, 586, 595

Elder abuse
Compliance Professionals' Relationships with
  Endangered Populations ... 657

Elder Abuse and Dependent Adult Civil
  Protection Act
Compliance Professionals' Relationships with
  Endangered Populations ... 656

Elder Abuse Statutes
Compliance Professionals' Relationships with
  Endangered Populations ... 654

Elder Justice Act
Compliance Professionals' Relationships with
  Endangered Populations ... 657

Electronic data processing (EDP)
A History of Compliance ... 12, 14

Email Review
Forensic Testing ... 566

Employee lift-out
Corporate Transactions
  The Role of the Compliance Department ... 366

Employee Retirement and Income Security
  Act of 1974 (ERISA)
Fiduciary Duty ... 89, 91

Employee surveys
How Compliance Can Teach Ethics ... 189

Employee trading
Corporate Transactions
  The Role of the Compliance Department ... 374

Employment at will
Compliance as a Profession ... 774, 775, 776

Encryption
Cybersecurity ... 493, 497, 498, 500, 510, 517,
  518, 520

Encryption Statutes
Protecting the Privacy of Client Information ... 474

Enforcement actions
Seeking to Avoid Chief Compliance Officer Liability
  ... 679, 680, 683, 691, 692, 693, 696

Enforcement Division
Overview of the Regulatory Framework for
  SEC-Registered Investment Advisers ... 145

Enforcement Manual
Regulatory Examinations and Audits ... 594

Enterprise risk
Compliance and Risk Management ... 259, 260,
  264, 275, 277

Equal Employment Opportunity Commission (EEOC)
Avoiding Supervisory Liability ... 725

Equity-indexed annuity
Compliance Professionals' Relationships with
  Endangered Populations ... 664

Ethics Resource Center (ERC)
How Compliance Can Teach Ethics ... 181, 189

Ethisphere Institute
How Compliance Can Teach Ethics ... 183

European Securities and Markets Authority (ESMA)
A History of Compliance ... 54, 55, 56, 59
Compliance as a Profession ... 778, 780, 781

Examination interviews
Regulatory Examinations and Audits ... 579

Examination notice
Regulatory Examinations and Audits ... 576

Examination priorities
Forensic Testing ... 536, 557
Regulatory Examinations and Audits ... 570, 571,
  584, 585

Exit interview
Regulatory Examinations and Audits ... 573, 584,
  588, 589, 590

Extracted performance
Navigating Marketing and Distribution ... 349, 350

F

Failure to supervise
Avoiding Supervisory Liability ... 703, 704, 705,
  706, 707, 708, 709, 712, 713, 714, 717, 719, 722,
  727, 729, 731
Core Requirements of a Compliance Program ... 102,
  112

Enforcement Actions Against Chief Compliance
    Officers ... 746, 748, 749
Ethics Standards Governing Compliance
    Professionals ... 197
Overview of the Regulatory Framework for
    SEC-Registered Investment Advisers ... 151
Seeking to Avoid Chief Compliance Officer Liability
    ... 681, 686, 687, 688, 690, 691

Fair and Accurate Credit Transactions Act of 2003 (FACTA)
Protecting the Privacy of Client Information ... 445, 451, 454

Fair Credit Reporting Act (FCRA)
Protecting the Privacy of Client Information ... 452, 454, 458

Federal Deposit Insurance Corporation (FDIC)
A History of Compliance ... 28
Overview of the Regulatory Framework for
    SEC-Registered Investment Advisers ... 163, 164, 165

Federal Financial Institution Examination Council
Protecting the Privacy of Client Information ... 448

Federal Financial Institutions Examination Council (FFIEC)
Cybersecurity ... 530
Protecting the Privacy of Client Information ... 448, 449

Federal Reserve
A History of Compliance ... 28, 45, 46, 47, 53, 55, 56, 59

Federal Reserve Act of 1913
Overview of the Regulatory Framework for
    SEC-Registered Investment Advisers ... 162

Federal Reserve System
Overview of the Regulatory Framework for
    SEC-Registered Investment Advisers ... 162, 164

Federal Sentencing Commission
How Compliance Can Teach Ethics ... 184, 185

Federal Sentencing Guidelines
Compliance Training ... 227
Core Requirements of a Compliance Program ... 93
Ethics Standards Governing Compliance
    Professionals ... 196
How Compliance Can Teach Ethics ... 185

Feltl & Company, Inc
Affiliated Transactions Under the Advisers Act ... 416

Feuerstein, Donald M.
Seeking to Avoid Chief Compliance Officer
    Liability ... 685, 688

Fiduciary duty
Affiliated Transactions Under the Advisers
    Act ... 407, 417
Fiduciary Duty ... 81
Overview of the Regulatory Framework for
    SEC-Registered Investment Advisers ... 150

Fiduciary principles
Fiduciary Duty ... 81, 82, 84

Final Compliance Rule
Seeking to Avoid Chief Compliance Officer
    Liability ... 679, 681, 682, 691

Financial Action Task Force (FATF)
A History of Compliance ... 19, 20, 21, 22, 23, 40

Financial Industry Regulatory Authority (FINRA)
A History of Compliance ... 10
Fiduciary Duty ... 90
Overview of the Regulatory Framework for
    SEC-Registered Investment Advisers ... 154
What is Compliance? ... 64, 68, 69, 70, 72, 75, 78

Financial Market Regulation
Compliance as a Profession ... 782

Financial Stability Board (FSB)
Compliance and Risk Management ... 272, 273, 274

Financial Stability Forum (FSF)
Compliance and Risk Management ... 272

Financial Stability Oversight Council (FSOC)
Compliance and Risk Management ... 264, 266, 269, 270
Overview of the Regulatory Framework for
    SEC-Registered Investment Advisers ... 164

FINRA Board of Governors
Your Relationship with FINRA ... 646

FINRA districts
Your Relationship with FINRA ... 645

FINRA Notice 14-10
Overview of the Regulatory Framework for
    SEC-Registered Investment Advisers ... 156

Firewall protection
Cybersecurity ... 516, 517

Firm element
Compliance Training ... 227, 235

Firm oversight
Seeking to Avoid Chief Compliance Officer
    Liability ... 683, 684

Flannery, Anne
A History of Compliance ... 26, 53

Flash drives
Cybersecurity ... 516, 520, 526

Fleischman, Edward
A History of Compliance ... 16

Following the money
Core Requirements of a Compliance Program ... 106

For cause examinations
Regulatory Examinations and Audits ... 571, 572

Foreign Corrupt Practices Act (FCPA)
Corporate Transactions
    The Role of the Compliance Department ... 379, 395, 396, 399

Forensic testing
Adviser Custody
    What You Need to Know ... 432
Core Requirements of a Compliance Program ... 107, 108
Forensic Testing ... 533, 535, 536, 551
Regulatory Examinations and Audits ... 573, 587, 588

Form ADV Disclosure
Forensic Testing ... 561

Form ADV Part 2A
  Fiduciary Duty ... 88
Form ADV Part 2B
  Fiduciary Duty ... 88
Form ADV-E
  Adviser Custody
    What You Need to Know ... 430
Framework for Improving Critical Infrastructure Cybersecurity
  Cybersecurity ... 494, 502, 504
Frank, Barney
  A History of Compliance ... 50
Franklin Management, Inc.
  Navigating Marketing and Distribution ... 285, 291, 294, 295, 297
Fraud Alert Involving E-mail Intrusions to Faciliate Wire Transfers Overseas
  Cybersecurity ... 523
Fraudulent Emails
  Cybersecurity ... 526
Free lunch seminars
  Compliance Professionals' Relationships with Endangered Populations ... 666
Free writing prospectus (FWP)
  Corporate Transactions
    The Role of the Compliance Department ... 387, 388, 389, 391
Freedom of Information Act
  Regulatory Examinations and Audits ... 583
Frontrunning
  Core Requirements of a Compliance Program ... 96, 103
Fund rankings
  Navigating Marketing and Distribution ... 315, 316
Future Trading Act (FTA)
  Overview of the Regulatory Framework for SEC-Registered Investment Advisers ... 158

G

Gallagher, Daniel M.
  Seeking to Avoid Chief Compliance Officer Liability ... 685, 687, 688
Gap analysis
  Seeking to Avoid Chief Compliance Officer Liability ... 694
General Securities Principal
  Compliance as a Profession ... 787
General theft statutes
  Compliance Professionals' Relationships with Endangered Populations ... 654, 655
Gibbs Brown, June
  A History of Compliance ... 31, 32
Gifts
  Ethics Standards Governing Compliance Professionals ... 202

Glantz, Stephen
  Avoiding Supervisory Liability ... 715
Glass-Steagall Act of 1933
  Overview of the Regulatory Framework for SEC-Registered Investment Advisers ... 162, 163
Glauber, Robert R.
  A History of Compliance ... 41
Global Investment Performance Standards (GIPS)
  Forensic Testing ... 552
  Navigating Marketing and Distribution ... 298, 306, 310, 323, 324, 325, 326, 327, 328, 329, 330, 331, 332, 333, 334, 335, 336, 337, 338, 339, 340, 341, 342, 343, 344, 345, 352, 353, 355, 356, 357, 360
Goelzer Investment Management, Inc.
  Affiliated Transactions Under the Advisers Act ... 420
Goldstein v. SEC
  Overview of the Regulatory Framework for SEC-Registered Investment Advisers ... 150
Gohlke, Gene
  A History of Compliance ... 39
Grain Futures Act (GFA)
  Overview of the Regulatory Framework for SEC-Registered Investment Advisers ... 158
Grain Futures Commission
  Overview of the Regulatory Framework for SEC-Registered Investment Advisers ... 158
Gramm-Leach-Bliley Act of 1999 (GLB)
  Cybersecurity ... 495, 496
  Compliance Professionals' Relationships with Endangered Populations ... 671
  Overview of the Regulatory Framework for SEC-Registered Investment Advisers ... 163
  Protecting the Privacy of Client Information ... 435, 436, 442, 445
Graphs and charts
  Navigating Marketing and Distribution ... 315
Gross-of-fee performance
  Navigating Marketing and Distribution ... 302, 303, 304, 342
Group of Seven (G-7)
  A History of Compliance ... 19, 58
Guide to Broker-Dealer Compliance
  A History of Compliance ... 13, 14, 15
  Compliance as a Profession ... 791, 792
Guideline Monitoring
  Forensic Testing ... 554
Gutfreund, John H.
  Avoiding Supervisory Liability ... 704, 705, 706, 709, 710, 711, 712, 713, 714, 715, 718, 719, 720, 721, 722, 723, 724, 725, 726, 727, 729, 730, 731
  Ethics Standards Governing Compliance Professionals ... 197, 198
  Overview of the Regulatory Framework for SEC-Registered Investment Advisers ... 151
  Seeking to Avoid Chief Compliance Officer Liability ... 685, 686, 687, 688, 689, 701

H

Holdings charts
Navigating Marketing and Distribution ... 292

House Committee on Energy and Commerce
A History of Compliance ... 18

Huff, Arthur James
A History of Compliance ... 23, 24, 51

Hypothetical performance
Navigating Marketing and Distribution ... 300, 312, 320, 331, 349, 350, 358, 359

I

ICI II no-action letter
Navigating Marketing and Distribution ... 302, 303

Identity theft prevention program (ITPP)
Protecting the Privacy of Client Information ... 455, 456, 457, 458

Identity Theft Red Flags
Protecting the Privacy of Client Information ... 450, 454, 455

Identity Theft Red Flags Rules
Cybersecurity ... 496, 513

Identity Theft Resource Center
Protecting the Privacy of Client Information ... 462

IM Guidance Update No. 2015-2
Cybersecurity ... 498

In re Alfred Bryant Tallman
Avoiding Supervisory Liability ... 706

In re LBS Capital Management, Inc.
Navigating Marketing and Distribution ... 297, 301, 302

In re Louis R. Trujillo
Avoiding Supervisory Liability ... 707, 708

In re Michael E. Tennenbaum
Avoiding Supervisory Liability ... 706

In re Spear & Staff, Incorporated
Navigating Marketing and Distribution ... 297

In re Urban
Avoiding Supervisory Liability ... 703, 716, 718, 719, 720, 730

In the Matter of Arthur J. Huff
Avoiding Supervisory Liability ... 708, 709

In the Matter of Commonwealth Equity Services, LLP d/b/a Commonwealth Financial Network
Cybersecurity ... 500

In the Matter of George J. Kolar
Avoiding Supervisory Liability ... 712

In the Matter of John H. Gutfreund
Seeking to Avoid Chief Compliance Officer Liability ... 685

In the Matter of John H. Gutfreund et al
Overview of the Regulatory Framework for SEC-Registered Investment Advisers ... 151
Seeking to Avoid Chief Compliance Officer Liability ... 685, 686, 687

In the Matter of Marc A. Ellis
Cybersecurity ... 499

In the Matter of Marion Bass Securities Corp. And Gerald Chandik
Avoiding Supervisory Liability ... 712

In the Matter of Theodore W. Urban (Urban matter)
Avoiding Supervisory Liability ... 722, 724, 726
Seeking to Avoid Chief Compliance Officer Liability ... 685, 687

In the Matter of Western Asset Management Company
Forensic Testing ... 539

Indirect Training
Compliance Training ... 246

Information barriers
Corporate Transactions
  The Role of the Compliance Department ... 400

Information security
Cybersecurity ... 495, 498, 504, 506, 508, 509, 510, 512, 526, 529, 530
Forensic Testing ... 557, 558, 559

Information Security Program (ISP)
Protecting the Privacy of Client Information ... 448, 449, 450, 474

Inherent risk
Compliance and Risk Management ... 259, 261, 276

Initial document request list
Regulatory Examinations and Audits ... 572, 575, 576

Initial Privacy Notices
Protecting the Privacy of Client Information ... 437

Initial public offering (IPO)
Corporate Transactions
  The Role of the Compliance Department ... 362, 363, 364

Insider trading
A History of Compliance ... 17, 18, 19
Regulatory Examinations and Audits ... 576

Insider Trading and Securities Fraud Enforcement Act of 1988 (ITSFEA)
A History of Compliance ... 18, 19

Institute for Financial Market Regulation (IFMR)
Compliance as a Profession ... 782

Institutional investor
Corporate Transactions
  The Role of the Compliance Department ... 386

Internal control report
Adviser Custody
  What You Need to Know ... 426, 430

Internal controls
Regulatory Examinations and Audits ... 570, 573, 574, 575, 577, 579, 580, 583, 595, 642

International Organization of Securities Commissions (IOSCO)
A History of Compliance ... 49, 50

International Standards Organization (ISO)
A History of Compliance ... 58, 59, 60, 61

Internet Crime Compliant Center
  Cybersecurity ... 523

Investment Adviser Certified Compliance Professional (IACCP)
  Compliance as a Profession ... 781

Investment Adviser Codes of Ethics rule
  Fiduciary Duty ... 85

Investment Adviser Registration Depository (IARD)
  Overview of the Regulatory Framework for SEC-Registered Investment Advisers ... 154

Investment Advisers Act of 1940
  Adviser Custody
    What You Need to Know ... 423
  Affiliated Transactions Under the Advisers Act ... 407, 408, 409, 410, 411, 412, 413, 416, 417, 418, 420
  Avoiding Supervisory Liability ... 704, 718, 725, 726, 731
  Compliance and Risk Management ... 263, 264
  Compliance Professionals' Relationships with Endangered Populations ... 653
  Corporate Transactions
    The Role of the Compliance Department ... 365, 387, 400, 404
  Enforcement Actions Against Chief Compliance Officers ... 735, 738, 740, 742, 743, 744, 745, 746, 747
  Forensic Testing ... 533, 535, 537, 538, 539, 551, 554, 565
  How Compliance Can Teach Ethics ... 185
  Navigating marketing and distribution ... 279, 280, 281, 282, 283, 284, 288, 289, 295, 296, 299, 300, 301, 302, 306, 307, 308, 309, 310, 314, 315, 317, 318, 330, 331, 332, 337, 344, 347, 348, 352, 353, 354, 355, 356, 357
  Overview of the Regulatory Framework for SEC-Registered Investment Advisers ... 143, 144, 147, 148, 150, 151, 160, 167
  Regulatory Examinations and Audits ... 569, 572, 587

Investment Advisers Association
  Navigating Marketing and Distribution ... 287

Investment Advisers Supervision Coordination Act
  Overview of the Regulatory Framework for SEC-Registered Investment Advisers ... 143

Investment Bankers Code Committee
  A History of Compliance ... 9

Investment Company Act of 1940 (Investment Company Act)
  Affiliated Transactions Under the Advisers Act ... 407, 416, 420
  Compliance and Risk Management ... 263, 268
  How Compliance Can Teach Ethics ... 185
  Overview of the Regulatory Framework for SEC-Registered Investment Advisers ... 143, 144, 150

Investment risk management
  Compliance and Risk Management ... 270

ISO Standard 19600
  Compliance as a Profession ... 793

ISO Standard for Compliance Management
  Compliance as a Profession ... 793

J

Joint venture
  Corporate Transactions
    The Role of the Compliance Department ... 362, 364, 365, 366, 386

K

Khuzami, Robert
  Seeking to Avoid Chief Compliance Officer Liability ... 691

L

Learning model
  Compliance Training ... 231, 232, 234, 235, 236, 238, 242, 243, 247, 248

Learning styles
  Compliance Training ... 228, 230, 242, 249, 252, 253

Lehman Brothers
  A History of Compliance ... 45

Letter of Acceptance, Waiver and Consent
  Enforcement Actions Against Chief Compliance Officers ... 740

Life settlement
  Compliance Professionals' Relationships with Endangered Populations ... 662, 663, 664

Limited-focus examinations
  Regulatory Examinations and Audits ... 571

Lincoln Financial Advisors Corporation
  Cybersecurity ... 499

Live training
  Compliance Training ... 243

M

Maloney Act
  Overview of the Regulatory Framework for SEC-Registered Investment Advisers ... 153

Malware
  Cybersecurity ... 514, 522, 525

Manarin Investment Counsel, Ltd
  Affiliated Transactions Under the Advisers Act ... 420

Material compliance matter
  Core Requirements of a Compliance Program ... 115, 124, 139

Material nonpublic information
  Corporate Transactions
    The Role of the Compliance Department ... 368, 374, 390, 391, 392, 400, 401, 402
  Regulatory Examinations and Audits ... 575

Materiality
  Navigating Marketing and Distribution ... 330

Measurement Period
  Navigating Marketing and Distribution ... 292, 293

Mergers and acquisitions (M&A)
  Corporate Transactions
    The Role of the Compliance Department ... 362, 369, 379, 380, 384, 393, 394, 395, 400

Meriwether, John W.
  Seeking to Avoid Chief Compliance Officer Liability ... 685

Midwest Stock Exchange
  A History of Compliance ... 14

Minimum asset levels
  Navigating Marketing and Distribution ... 335

Mobile devices
  Cybersecurity ... 493, 513, 516, 524

Mobile Devices
  Cybersecurity ... 518, 531

Mock audit
  Seeking to Avoid Chief Compliance Officer Liability ... 699

Mock SEC regulatory examination
  Regulatory Examinations and Audits ... 575

Model Act
  Compliance Professionals' Relationships with Endangered Populations ... 663

Model fee
  Navigating Marketing and Distribution ... 304, 340

Model Guide
  A History of Compliance ... 5, 13, 14, 15, 16, 21, 25, 56, 57, 61

Model performance
  Navigating Marketing and Distribution ... 299, 300, 320

Model Rule
  Adviser Custody
    What You Need to Know ... 423

Mozer, Paul
  Seeking to Avoid Chief Compliance Officer Liability ... 685

Multimedia liability coverage
  Cybersecurity ... 529

Municipal Securities Rulemaking Board (MSRB)
  Compliance Training ... 227
  Overview of the Regulatory Framework for SEC-Registered Investment Advisers ... 155, 165
  Corporate Transactions
    The Role of the Compliance Department ... 399

N

NASD Notice to Members 07-06
  Protecting the Privacy of Client Information ... 462

NASD Rule 1014
  Corporate Transactions
    The Role of the Compliance Department ... 381

NASD Rule 1017
  Corporate Transactions
    The Role of the Compliance Department ... 380, 381

National Adjudicatory Council (NAC)
  Enforcement Actions Against Chief Compliance Officers ... 736, 737, 739
  Protecting the Privacy of Client Information ... 466, 467
  Your Relationship with FINRA ... 646

National Association of Insurance Commissioners (NAIC)
  Compliance Professionals' Relationships with Endangered Populations ... 663

National Association of Securities Dealers (NASD)
  A History of Compliance ... 10, 14, 27, 36, 38, 41, 44
  Overview of the Regulatory Framework for SEC-Registered Investment Advisers ... 153, 154, 156, 157
  What is Compliance? ... 69

National Business Ethics Survey (NBES)
  How Compliance Can Teach Ethics ... 181, 182

National Currency Act
  Overview of the Regulatory Framework for SEC-Registered Investment Advisers ... 162

National Exam Program Risk Alert
  Compliance and Risk Management ... 264, 265
  Cybersecurity ... 498, 503

National Exam Program Risk Alerts
  Forensic Testing ... 536

National examination analytics tool (NEAT)
  Regulatory Examinations and Audits ... 573

National Examination Program (NEP)
  Regulatory Examinations and Audits ... 569, 570, 571, 575, 576, 585

National Futures Association (NFA)
  Navigating Marketing and Distribution ... 323, 345, 346, 347, 348, 349, 350, 351, 352, 353, 354, 355, 356, 357, 358
  Overview of the Regulatory Framework for SEC-Registered Investment Advisers ... 154, 161, 162

National Industrial Recovery Act of 1933
  A History of Compliance ... 9

National Institute of Standards and Technology (NIST)
  Cybersecurity ... 493, 494, 497, 502, 503, 504, 508

National Recovery Administration (NRA)
  A History of Compliance ... 9

National Securities Markets Improvement Act (NSMIA)
  Overview of the Regulatory Framework for SEC-Registered Investment Advisers ... 143

National Society of Compliance Professionals (NSCP)
  A History of Compliance ... 52, 53
  Avoiding Supervisory Liability ... 712, 721
  Compliance as a Profession · 781, 786, 787
  Corporate Transactions
    The Role of the Compliance Department ... 361

Networking
  Soft Skills
    Presenting Compliance ... 212

Never-before-examined
Regulatory Examinations and Audits ... 576, 585

New York Investors Group, Inc.
Navigating Marketing and Distribution ... 284, 288, 293, 347

New York Stock Exchange
A History of Compliance ... 8
History of Compliance ... 8, 9, 12, 14

NFA Compliance Rule 2-29
Navigating Marketing and Distribution ... 345, 346, 347, 348, 350

No-action letters
Navigating Marketing and Distribution ... 280, 281, 284, 298, 305, 353

Nonbinding letter of intent (NBLOI)
Corporate Transactions
The Role of the Compliance Department ... 378

Nondisclosure agreement (NDA)
Corporate Transactions
The Role of the Compliance Department ... 368, 369, 374, 378

Nondiscretionary
Navigating Marketing and Distribution ... 325, 326, 340, 341

Nonpublic personal information (NPI)
Protecting the Privacy of Client Information ... 436, 437, 438, 439, 440, 441, 442, 446, 447, 463, 464, 465, 466, 467, 470, 471

Nonqualified eligible persons (QEPs)
Navigating Marketing and Distribution ... 349, 350, 358

North American Securities Administrators Association (NASAA)
Adviser Custody
What You Need to Know ... 423
Compliance Professionals' Relationships with Endangered Populations ... 657, 659, 666

NSCP Code of Ethics
Ethics Standards Governing Compliance Professionals ... 193, 194, 195, 196, 198, 199, 201, 202, 203, 204

NTM 07-06
Protecting the Privacy of Client Information ... 462

O

Office of Compliance Inspections and Examinations (OCIE)
Compliance and Risk Management ... 264, 265, 266, 267, 268
Overview of the Regulatory Framework for SEC-Registered Investment Advisers ... 145, 146, 151
What is Compliance? ... 64, 70

Office of Foreign Assets Control (OFAC)
Corporate Transactions
The Role of the Compliance Department ... 379

Office of the Comptroller of the Currency (OCC)
Overview of the Regulatory Framework for SEC-Registered Investment Advisers ... 142, 162, 163, 164, 165, 166

Office of the Whistleblower
Seeking to Avoid Chief Compliance Officer Liability ... 699

Office of the Whistleblower Protection
Overview of the Regulatory Framework for SEC-Registered Investment Advisers ... 155

Office of Thrift Supervision (OTS)
A History of Compliance ... 28
Overview of the Regulatory Framework for SEC-Registered Investment Advisers ... 163

Onion Futures Act of 1958
Overview of the Regulatory Framework for SEC-Registered Investment Advisers ... 158

Operational risk
Compliance and Risk Management ... 269

Opt-Out Methods
Protecting the Privacy of Client Information ... 440

Opt-Out Notice
Protecting the Privacy of Client Information ... 436, 439, 440, 441, 442, 443, 452, 453, 465, 471
Order Instituting Proceedings (OIP)
Avoiding Supervisory Liability ... 708, 717, 718, 721

Original 1971 manual
A History of Compliance ... 13

Outside business activities
Enforcement Actions Against Chief Compliance Officers ... 737

Oversight responsibilities
Compliance and Risk Management ... 261

Oxley, Michael
A History of Compliance ... 33

P

Partial client lists
Navigating Marketing and Distribution ... 284, 286, 356

Partial List of Recommendations
Navigating Marketing and Distribution ... 292

Password manager
Cybersecurity ... 519

Past specific recommendations
Navigating Marketing and Distribution ... 280, 282, 288, 291, 292, 293, 294, 295, 317, 356

Patient Protection and Affordable Care Act
A History of Compliance ... 50

Pay-to-Play
Overview of the Regulatory Framework for SEC-Registered Investment Advisers ... 149

Penetration testing
Cybersecurity ... 493, 494, 529, 531

Periodic review
Core Requirements of a Compliance Program ... 107

Personal securities trading
Game Plan for the New CCO ... 172
How Compliance Can Teach Ethics ... 179, 185
Overview of the Regulatory Framework for SEC-Registered Investment Advisers ... 147, 148

Personal securities transactions
Forensic Testing ... 539, 540

Personal trading
Ethics Standards Governing Compliance Professionals ... 201, 202
Fiduciary Duty ... 85, 88

Personally identifiable financial information
Protecting the Privacy of Client Information ... 437

Peters, Aulana
A History of Compliance ... 16

Phishing
Cybersecurity ... 521, 525

Pitt, Harvey
A History of Compliance ... 37, 38, 40

Plaze, Robert
A History of Compliance ... 37, 38, 39, 40, 41, 42, 43, 44

Policies and procedures
Compliance Professionals' Relationships with Endangered Populations ... 649, 650, 662, 665, 668, 669, 670, 671, 672, 674, 676
Corporate Transactions
    The Role of the Compliance Department ... 361, 370, 373, 374, 377, 378, 387, 391, 392, 393, 394, 395, 396, 397, 400, 402, 404, 405
Cybersecurity ... 493, 494, 495, 496, 498, 501, 503, 508, 512, 524, 530
Enforcement Actions Against Chief Compliance Officers ... 733, 735, 736, 738, 741, 743, 749
Forensic Testing ... 533, 534, 535, 536, 537, 538, 539, 543, 544, 545, 547, 548, 551, 552, 554, 557, 558, 559, 563, 564, 567
Navigating Marketing and Distribution ... 283, 309, 310, 336, 337, 338
Regulatory Examinations and Audits ... 572, 573, 575, 577, 578, 579, 580, 581, 585, 586, 587, 588, 642
Seeking to Avoid Chief Compliance Officer Liability ... 681, 682, 683, 684, 693, 694, 695, 696, 697, 698

Political action committee (PAC)
Corporate Transactions
    The Role of the Compliance Department ... 399

Pooled Vehicle Antifraud
Overview of the Regulatory Framework for SEC-Registered Investment Advisers ... 150

Portability
Navigating Marketing and Distribution ... 298, 305, 306, 330, 331, 332, 355

Portability standards
Navigating Marketing and Distribution ... 331, 355

Portable media
Cybersecurity ... 509

Portable Storage
Cybersecurity ... 520

Portfolio pumping
Forensic Testing ... 549, 550

Portfolio Restriction
Forensic Testing ... 554

Post-effective period
Corporate Transactions
    The Role of the Compliance Department ... 363

Preeffective period
Corporate Transactions
    The Role of the Compliance Department ... 363

Prefiling period
Corporate Transactions
    The Role of the Compliance Department ... 363

Press releases
Navigating Marketing and Distribution ... 295

Principal trades
Affiliated Transactions Under the Advisers Act ... 412, 413

Principles of Medical Ethics
Compliance as a Profession ... 783

Privacy policy
Protecting the Privacy of Client Information ... 441, 465, 476

Private equity transactions
Corporate Transactions
    The Role of the Compliance Department ... 362, 364

Private funds
Navigating Marketing and Distribution ... 294, 312, 313, 327, 354

Private Placement Memorandum (PPM)
Enforcement Actions Against Chief Compliance Officers ... 742

Private placement offering
Enforcement Actions Against Chief Compliance Officers ... 742

Private securities transactions
Enforcement Actions Against Chief Compliance Officers ... 737

Professionalism
Compliance as a Profession ... 773, 774, 775, 776, 777, 779, 780, 782, 783, 784, 785, 786, 788, 789, 790, 791, 792, 794, 795

Program on Corporate Compliance and Enforcement (PCCE)
Compliance as a Profession ... 782

Prohibited testimonials
Navigating Marketing and Distribution ... 290

Prohibited Transaction Exemption 86-128
Affiliated Transactions Under the Advisers Act ... 420

Proprietary risks
Compliance and Risk Management ... 263

Prospective clients
Navigating Marketing and Distribution ... 281, 283, 285, 291, 292, 294, 303, 306, 310, 324, 326, 327, 328, 345, 352

Protecting the Privacy of Client Information - 15 U.S.C. 1681c-1(h)
Protecting the Privacy of Client Information ... 458

Protecting the Privacy of Client Information - 15 U.S.C. 1681m
Protecting the Privacy of Client Information ... 458

Protecting the Privacy of Client Information - 15 U.S.C. 1681s-2
Protecting the Privacy of Client Information ... 458

Protocol for Broker Recruiting
Protecting the Privacy of Client Information ... 442, 443, 444

Proxy voting
Overview of the Regulatory Framework for SEC-Registered Investment Advisers ... 146, 149

Proxy voting rule
Fiduciary Duty ... 85

Public Wi-Fi
Cybersecurity ... 521, 527

Q

Qualified custodian
Adviser Custody
What You Need to Know ... 424, 425, 426, 427, 428, 430, 431, 433

Qualified institutional buyers (QIB)
Navigating Marketing and Distribution ... 319

R

Ransomware
Cybersecurity ... 522

Re, Re and Sagarese
A History of Compliance ... 10

Reasonably designed
Core Requirements of a Compliance Program ... 94, 100, 101, 102, 104, 105, 107, 110, 112, 113, 122, 123, 132, 140

Recommendation 20
A History of Compliance ... 19, 20, 21, 40

Recordkeeping
Forensic Testing ... 552, 556
Navigating Marketing and Distribution ... 307, 309, 310, 324, 330, 332

Red Flag Rules
Protecting the Privacy of Client Information ... 445, 450, 454, 455, 478

Red flags
Forensic Testing ... 535, 550, 566
Is it Time to Go? ... 767
Protecting the Privacy of Client Information ... 454, 455, 456, 457, 458, 463, 469, 477
Seeking to Avoid Chief Compliance Officer Liability ... 698

Reference security
Corporate Transactions
The Role of the Compliance Department ... 383

Reg M, Rule 100
Corporate Transactions
The Role of the Compliance Department ... 382

Reg M, Rule 101
Corporate Transactions
The Role of the Compliance Department ... 382, 383, 384, 385, 386

Reg M, Rule 102
Corporate Transactions
The Role of the Compliance Department ... 382

Reg M, Rule 103
Corporate Transactions
The Role of the Compliance Department ... 382, 385

Reg M, Rule 104
Corporate Transactions
The Role of the Compliance Department ... 382, 385, 386

Reg M, Rule 105
Corporate Transactions
The Role of the Compliance Department ... 382, 386

Registered investment adviser
Navigating Marketing and Distribution ... 289, 291, 307, 337

Regulation 4.25(a)(7)
Navigating Marketing and Distribution ... 348

Regulation 4.35(a)(6)
Navigating Marketing and Distribution ... 348

Regulation 4.41
Navigating Marketing and Distribution ... 345, 346, 347, 350

Regulation D
Corporate Transactions
The Role of the Compliance Department ... 383

Regulation FD
Corporate Transactions
The Role of the Compliance Department ... 390, 391

Regulation M
Corporate Transactions
The Role of the Compliance Department ... 382, 383, 384, 385, 386

Regulation S-AM (Reg S-AM)
Protecting the Privacy of Client Information ... 452, 453

Regulation S-ID (Reg S-ID)
Cybersecurity ... 496, 513, 523
Protecting the Privacy of Client Information ... 454, 455, 457, 477, 478

Regulation S-P (Reg S-P)
Compliance Professionals' Relationships with Endangered Populations ... 669, 671
Cybersecurity ... 495, 496, 499, 500, 501
Protecting the Privacy of Client Information ... 435, 436, 437, 438, 439, 441, 442, 444, 445, 446, 447, 448, 449, 450, 451, 452, 453, 454, 455, 461, 462, 464, 465, 466, 467, 468, 469, 471, 472, 474, 477, 478

Regulatory Notice 07-36
Protecting the Privacy of Client Information ... 462

Regulatory Notice 08-70
Your Relationship with FINRA ... 647

Regulatory Notice 12-05
　Protecting the Privacy of Client Information ... 463

Regulatory Notice 14-10
　Overview of the Regulatory Framework for SEC-Registered Investment Advisers ... 156

Reputational risk
　Corporate Transactions
　　The Role of the Compliance Department ... 402, 403, 405

Requests for proposal (RFPs)
　Enforcement Actions Against Chief Compliance Officers ... 745

Reserve Primary Fund
　A History of Compliance ... 45

Reservoir Capital Management, Inc.
　Navigating Marketing and Distribution ... 285

Residual risk
　Compliance and Risk Management ... 259, 261, 276

Response letters
　Regulatory Examinations and Audits ... 574

Revenue sharing agreements
　Corporate Transactions
　　The Role of the Compliance Department ... 362, 364, 365

Richards, Lori A.
　A History of Compliance ... 47, 48
　Regulatory Examinations and Audits ... 584

Risk Alert
　Navigating Marketing and Distribution ... 290, 291, 309

Risk Appetite Framework (RAF)
　Compliance and Risk Management ... 273

Risk appetite statement (RAS)
　Compliance and Risk Management ... 273

Risk assessment
　Compliance and Risk Management ... 263, 271, 275, 276
　Cybersecurity ... 498, 506, 511, 530
　Forensic Testing ... 535, 557, 558
　Game Plan for the New CCO ... 172, 174, 177
　Protecting the Privacy of Client Information ... 448, 450, 474, 476
　Regulatory Examinations and Audits ... 575

Risk inventory
　Core Requirements of a Compliance Program ... 104, 105, 108, 110, 123

Risk management
　Core Requirements of a Compliance Program ... 111
　Corporate Transactions
　　The Role of the Compliance Department ... 361, 372, 391, 396, 402, 403, 404
　Preparing to Become a Compliance Officer, and the Academy ... 759
　Regulatory Examinations and Audits ... 577, 585, 586, 642

Risk management framework
　Compliance and Risk Management ... 261, 267, 270, 271, 272, 274

Risk oversight
　Compliance and Risk Management ... 262, 267

Risk-based routine examinations
　Regulatory Examinations and Audits ... 571

Roberts, Richard Y.
　A History of Compliance ... 26, 27

Roosevelt, Franklin D.
　A History of Compliance ... 8, 9, 10

Rule 10b-5
　Enforcement Actions Against Chief Compliance Officers ... 742

Rule 10b5-2
　Protecting the Privacy of Client Information ... 468

Rule 1120
　What is Compliance? ... 69

Rule 1250
　Compliance Training ... 227, 235
　What is Compliance? ... 69

Rule 134
　Corporate Transactions
　　The Role of the Compliance Department ... 388

Rule 144
　Corporate Transactions
　　The Role of the Compliance Department ... 383

Rule 167
　Corporate Transactions
　　The Role of the Compliance Department ... 389

Rule 17a-3
　Enforcement Actions Against Chief Compliance Officers ... 740

Rule 17a-4
　Enforcement Actions Against Chief Compliance Officers ... 740

Rule 17a-8
　Enforcement Actions Against Chief Compliance Officers ... 741

Rule 2010
　Enforcement Actions Against Chief Compliance Officers ... 736, 738, 740, 742, 746
　Protecting the Privacy of Client Information ... 471

Rule 204-2
　Enforcement Actions Against Chief Compliance Officers ... 740, 744
　Forensic Testing ... 565
　Navigating Marketing and Distribution ... 306, 307, 308, 309, 332
　Overview of the Regulatory Framework for SEC-Registered Investment Advisers ... 146, 150

Rule 204-2(a)(16)
　Navigating Marketing and Distribution ... 306, 307, 308

Rule 204-3
　Navigating Marketing and Distribution ... 281

Rule 204A-1
　Compliance Training ... 227
　Core Requirements of a Compliance Program ... 104
　Forensic Testing ... 539, 540

Overview of the Regulatory Framework for
    SEC-Registered Investment Advisers ... 147, 148
Rule 206
    Regulatory Examinations and Audits ... 572
Rule 206(3)-1
    Affiliated Transactions Under the Advisers Act ... 410, 411
Rule 206(3)-2
    Affiliated Transactions Under the Advisers Act ... 411
Rule 206(3)-3T
    Affiliated Transactions Under the Advisers Act ... 411, 412
Rule 206(4)
    Overview of the Regulatory Framework for SEC-Registered Investment Advisers ... 146, 149, 150, 156, 166
Rule 206(4)-1
    Navigating Marketing and Distribution ... 279, 280, 281, 282, 283, 284, 285, 286, 287, 288, 291, 292, 293, 294, 295, 296, 297, 298, 299, 300, 301, 302, 305, 306, 310, 317, 318, 331, 344, 347, 352
Rule 206(4)-1(a)(5)
    Forensic Testing ... 552
Rule 206(4)-2
    Adviser Custody
        What You Need to Know ... 423, 424
Rule 206(4)-3
    Corporate Transactions
        The Role of the Compliance Department ... 365
    Forensic Testing ... 553
Rule 206(4)-7
    A History of Compliance ... 37, 39
    Compliance and Risk Management ... 265
    Core Requirements of a Compliance Program ... 93, 94, 100, 104, 107, 108, 115, 126, 127, 128, 130, 134
    Cybersecurity ... 496
    Enforcement Actions Against Chief Compliance Officers ... 735
    Forensic Testing ... 533, 535, 539, 564
    Overview of the Regulatory Framework for SEC-Registered Investment Advisers ... 146, 150, 156, 166
    Seeking to Avoid Chief Compliance Officer Liability ... 681, 694, 696, 698
Rule 2090
    Compliance Professionals' Relationships with Endangered Populations ... 658
Rule 2100
    Protecting the Privacy of Client Information ... 467
Rule 2111
    Compliance Professionals' Relationships with Endangered Populations ... 651, 652, 653, 658
    Fiduciary Duty ... 90
Rule 2210
    Compliance Professionals' Relationships with Endangered Populations ... 659, 665, 666
    Navigating Marketing and Distribution ... 311, 312, 313, 314, 315, 317, 318, 320, 321, 322, 323, 354

Rule 2214
    Navigating Marketing and Distribution ... 312
Rule 2330
    Compliance Professionals' Relationships with Endangered Populations ... 661, 662
Rule 2711(a)(9)(A)
    Navigating Marketing and Distribution ... 321
Rule 28a-1
    Core Requirements of a Compliance Program ... 116
Rule 30 of Reg S-P
    Cybersecurity ... 495
Rule 3010
    Compliance Professionals' Relationships with Endangered Populations ... 659
    Enforcement Actions Against Chief Compliance Officers ... 735, 736, 742, 746
Rule 3010(b)
    A History of Compliance ... 38
Rule 3010(d)
    Navigating Marketing and Distribution ... 322
Rule 3013
    Overview of the Regulatory Framework for SEC-Registered Investment Advisers ... 156
Rule 3040
    Compliance Professionals' Relationships with Endangered Populations ... 667
Rule 3070
    Enforcement Actions Against Chief Compliance Officers ... 738
Rule 3100
    Overview of the Regulatory Framework for SEC-Registered Investment Advisers ... 156
Rule 3110
    Enforcement Actions Against Chief Compliance Officers ... 735, 740, 746
Rule 3130
    Core Requirements of a Compliance Program ... 94, 100, 116, 128
    Enforcement Actions Against Chief Compliance Officers ... 734
    Overview of the Regulatory Framework for SEC-Registered Investment Advisers ... 156
    Seeking to Avoid Chief Compliance Officer Liability ... 682, 683
Rule 3220
    Ethics Standards Governing Compliance Professionals ... 203
Rule 3310
    Enforcement Actions Against Chief Compliance Officers ... 740
Rule 38a-1
    A History of Compliance ... 37, 39, 41, 42
    Core Requirements of a Compliance Program ... 94, 100, 101, 104, 107, 108, 115, 116, 117, 124, 126, 127, 128, 129, 130, 131, 134, 135, 138
    Cybersecurity ... 496
    Ethics Standards Governing Compliance Professionals ... 199, 200

Overview of the Regulatory Framework for SEC-Registered Investment Advisers ... 146
Seeking to Avoid Chief Compliance Officer Liability ... 681, 693, 694, 697, 698, 699

Rule 4.14(a)(8)
Overview of the Regulatory Framework for SEC-Registered Investment Advisers ... 161

Rule 405
Corporate Transactions
The Role of the Compliance Department ... 388, 390

Rule 411(f)
Avoiding Supervisory Liability ... 721

Rule 426
Corporate Transactions
The Role of the Compliance Department ... 389

Rule 433(d)(1)(ii)
Corporate Transactions
The Role of the Compliance Department ... 387, 388

Rule 4370
Cybersecurity ... 496

Rule 4530
Enforcement Actions Against Chief Compliance Officers ... 738

Rule 472
Compliance Professionals' Relationships with Endangered Populations ... 659, 666

Rule 482
Corporate Transactions
The Role of the Compliance Department ... 388

Rule 8210
Enforcement Actions Against Chief Compliance Officers ... 739
Protecting the Privacy of Client Information ... 463, 474

Rule G-3
Compliance Training ... 227

Rule G-37
Corporate Transactions
The Role of the Compliance Department ... 399, 400

Rules of Practice
Avoiding Supervisory Liability ... 721

S

S&L Crisis
A History of Compliance ... 28

Safeguarding customer information
Cybersecurity ... 499

Safeguards Rule
Protecting the Privacy of Client Information ... 444, 445, 446, 447, 450, 454, 464, 467, 469, 471, 476, 477, 478

Safety of Client Assets
Forensic Testing ... 554

Salomon Brothers, Inc
Seeking to Avoid Chief Compliance Officer Liability ... 685

SANS Institute
Cybersecurity ... 504, 530, 531

Sarbanes, Paul
A History of Compliance ... 33

Sarbanes-Oxley Act of 2002 (SOX)
A History of Compliance ... 33, 34, 35, 36, 38, 41, 42
Corporate Transactions
The Role of the Compliance Department ... 376
Overview of the Regulatory Framework for SEC-Registered Investment Advisers ... 143

Saul, Ralph S.
A History of Compliance ... 13

Scareware
Cybersecurity ... 522, 525

Seat at the table
Corporate Transactions
The Role of the Compliance Department ... 371, 380, 405

Section 12 of the Exchange Act
Corporate Transactions
The Role of the Compliance Department ... 390

Section 15(b)
Enforcement Actions Against Chief Compliance Officers ... 740, 746

Section 15(b)(4)(E)
Avoiding Supervisory Liability ... 704, 705, 706, 725

Section 15(b)(6)
Avoiding Supervisory Liability ... 704

Section 15(d) of the Exchange Act
Corporate Transactions
The Role of the Compliance Department ... 390

Section 15(f)
A History of Compliance ... 18

Section 15(g)
A History of Compliance ... 18
Corporate Transactions
The Role of the Compliance Department ... 370, 400, 402

Section 17(a)
Enforcement Actions Against Chief Compliance Officers ... 744

Section 2(a)(10)(a)
Corporate Transactions
The Role of the Compliance Department ... 389

Section 2(a)(10)(b)
Corporate Transactions
The Role of the Compliance Department ... 388

Section 203(e)
Enforcement Actions Against Chief Compliance Officers ... 746, 747

Section 203(e)(6)
Core Requirements of a Compliance Program ... 113
Enforcement Actions Against Chief Compliance Officers ... 746, 747

Section 203(f)
Enforcement Actions Against Chief Compliance Officers ... 740

Section 204A
Corporate Transactions
The Role of the Compliance Department ... 400

Section 204A of the Investment Advisers Act
A History of Compliance ... 18

Section 206
Overview of the Regulatory Framework for SEC-Registered Investment Advisers ... 148, 149, 150

Section 206(3)
Enforcement Actions Against Chief Compliance Officers ... 738, 744

Section 206(4)
Navigating Marketing and Distribution ... 279, 280, 283, 285, 296, 305

Section 208(b)
Navigating Marketing and Distribution ... 289

Section 21(a)
Seeking to Avoid Chief Compliance Officer Liability ... 685

Section 21(a) Report of Investigation
Avoiding Supervisory Liability ... 709, 710, 711, 712, 713

Section 28(e)
Forensic Testing ... 548, 549

Section 3(a)(26)
Overview of the Regulatory Framework for SEC-Registered Investment Advisers ... 153

Section 3(c)(7)
Navigating Marketing and Distribution ... 319, 327

Section 314(a) of the USA PATRIOT Act of 2001
Enforcement Actions Against Chief Compliance Officers ... 741

Securities Act Amendments of 1964
Preparing to Become a Compliance Officer, and the Academy ... 754

Securities Act Amendments of 1975
Overview of the Regulatory Framework for SEC-Registered Investment Advisers ... 153

Securities Act of 1933 (Securities Act)
Overview of the Regulatory Framework or SEC-Registered Investment Advisers ... 142, 143, 152, 153
Navigating Marketing and Distribution ... 312, 323

Securities Act Release 5310
Regulatory Examinations and Audits ... 593

Securities and Exchange Commission (SEC)
A History of Compliance ... 5
History of Compliance ... 11, 14
What is Compliance? ... 64, 65, 69, 74

Securities Exchange Act of 1934 (SEA, Securities Exchange Act, Exchange Act)
Avoiding Supervisory Liability ... 704, 705, 707, 708, 709, 718, 721, 725, 726, 727, 729, 731
A History of Compliance ... 9, 10, 11, 14, 18
Compliance Professionals' Relationships with Endangered Populations ... 653
Enforcement Actions Against Chief Compliance Officers ... 740, 741, 742, 743, 744, 746, 749

Overview of the Regulatory Framework for SEC-Registered Investment Advisers ... 142, 143, 151, 152, 153, 158, 159, 160

Securities Industry and Financial Markets Association (SIFMA)
A History of Compliance ... 52, 53, 56
Avoiding Supervisory Liability ... 721, 723, 724, 728, 730
Corporate Transactions
The Role of the Compliance Department ... 361, 373, 403
Protecting the Privacy of Client Information ... 443, 491
What is Compliance? ... 63, 72, 78, 79

Securities Industry Association (SIA)
A History of Compliance ... 13, 17, 25, 26, 27, 52, 53, 56
Avoiding Supervisory Liability ... 704, 708, 709, 711, 714, 715

Selective disclosure
Corporate Transactions
The Role of the Compliance Department ... 390

Self-directed
Compliance Training ... 247

Self-evaluation
Soft Skills
Presenting Compliance ... 208, 209

Self-regulatory organization (SRO)
Avoiding Supervisory Liability ... 714
Compliance Professionals' Relationships with Endangered Populations ... 649
Overview of the Regulatory Framework for SEC-Registered Investment Advisers ... 152, 153, 154, 158, 162
What is Compliance? ... 64

Selling away
Compliance Professionals' Relationships with Endangered Populations ... 667

Semiprofession
Compliance as a Profession ... 777

Senator, Charles
A History of Compliance ... 52

Senior designations
Compliance Professionals' Relationships with Endangered Populations ... 666

Senior investors
Compliance Professionals' Relationships with Endangered Populations ... 649, 650, 657, 658, 659, 660, 661, 662, 664, 665, 666, 668, 669, 672

Senior registered options principal (SROP)
Avoiding Supervisory Liability ... 707, 708

Separation of duties
Core Requirements of a Compliance Program ... 106, 128, 129, 135

Service providers
Core Requirements of a Compliance Program ... 94, 116, 117, 121, 129, 131, 132

Service set identifier (SSID)
Cybersecurity ... 517

Shad, John
A History of Compliance ... 17

Schapiro, Mary L.
A History of Compliance ... 27, 60
Ethics Standards Governing Compliance Professionals ... 197

Side-by-Side Management
Forensic Testing ... 546

Small Firm Advisory Board (SFAB)
Your Relationship with FINRA ... 646, 648

Social engineering
Cybersecurity ... 521

Social media
Corporate Transactions
The Role of the Compliance Department ... 390, 391, 392, 393, 402, 403
Navigating Marketing and Distribution ... 289, 290, 291, 309, 310, 322

Society of Corporate Compliance and Ethics (SCCE)
Compliance as a Profession ... 781, 786, 787

Soft dollar arrangements
Fiduciary Duty ... 87
Forensic Testing ... 536, 548, 549, 562

Solicitors Rule
Forensic Testing ... 553

Special Study of the Securities Markets (Special Study)
A History of Compliance ... 10, 11, 12, 13, 14, 16, 23, 26

Specific training
Compliance Training ... 232, 233

SR 08-8
A History of Compliance ... 45, 46, 47, 56

Standards for Safety and Soundness
A History of Compliance ... 28, 29

Standards of Practice of the Investment Adviser Association
Fiduciary Duty ... 83, 84

Strategic plan
Core Requirements of a Compliance Program ... 125, 126, 127, 138

Strauss, Thomas W.
Seeking to Avoid Chief Compliance Officer Liability ... 685

Suitability
Compliance Professionals' Relationships with Endangered Populations ... 651, 652, 653, 658, 661, 662, 663, 664, 665, 672

Sullivan v. Harnisch
Compliance as a Profession ... 773, 774, 775, 784

Summit of the Arch
A History of Compliance ... 19

Supervision
Seeking to Avoid Chief Compliance Officer Liability ... 683, 685, 688, 689, 690, 696

Supervisory
Seeking to Avoid Chief Compliance Officer Liability ... 681, 683, 685, 686, 687, 689, 690, 691, 695

Supervisory controls
Regulatory Examinations and Audits ... 572, 586

Supervisory Letter SR 08-8
A History of Compliance ... 45

Supervisory liability
Avoiding Supervisory Liability ... 704, 706, 707, 708, 710, 711, 713, 715, 722, 724, 725, 726, 727, 730, 731
Core Requirements of a Compliance Program ... 113
Preparing to Become a Compliance Officer, and the Academy ... 754
Seeking to Avoid Chief Compliance Officer Liability ... 688, 689, 690

Supervisory procedures
Avoiding Supervisory Liability ... 705, 706, 715, 729
Compliance Professionals' Relationships with Endangered Populations ... 662, 664
Cybersecurity ... 499, 501, 513

Supervisory responsibility
A History of Compliance ... 15
Seeking to Avoid Chief Compliance Officer Liability ... 685, 687, 689, 691

Supervisory structure
Core Requirements of a Compliance Program ... 96, 111, 112, 113, 135

Surprise examination
Adviser Custody
What You Need to Know ·424, 426, 429, 430

Suspicious Activity Report (SAR)
Protecting the Privacy of Client Information ... 458

Sweep examination
Regulatory Examinations and Audits ... 572

Symantec 2013 Internet Security Report
Cybersecurity ... 515

Symantec 2014 Internet Security Report
Cybersecurity ... 494

Systemically important financial institutions (SIFIs)
Overview of the Regulatory Framework for SEC-Registered Investment Advisers ... 164

T

Talent management
Soft Skills
Presenting Compliance ... 210, 216

Testimonial
Navigating Marketing and Distribution ... 280, 283, 284, 285, 286, 287, 288, 289, 290, 291, 310, 314, 335, 346, 347, 356

The Cash Solicitation Rule
Overview of the Regulatory Framework for SEC-Registered Investment Advisers ... 149

The Custody Rule
  Overview of the Regulatory Framework for SEC-Registered Investment Advisers ... 149
The Evolving Role of Compliance
  What is Compliance? ... 72, 78
The TCW Group, Inc.
  Navigating Marketing and Distribution ... 291, 292, 293
Third-party rating
  Navigating Marketing and Distribution ... 286, 287, 349
Third-party service provider
  Forensic Testing ... 564
  Protecting the Privacy of Client Information ... 450, 476
Third-party social media
  Navigating Marketing and Distribution ... 289, 290
Title V, Subtitle A of GLB
  Cybersecurity ... 495
Title VII of the Civil Rights Act of 1964
  Avoiding Supervisory Liability ... 725
Tolar, Martin
  A History of Compliance ... 58
Tone at the top
  Compliance Training ... 230
  Core Requirements of a Compliance Program ... 97, 98, 99, 106, 127
  Corporate Transactions
    The Role of the Compliance Department ... 397, 398, 405
  Fiduciary Duty ... 86, 91
  Regulatory Examinations and Audits ... 577, 578, 586
  Seeking to Avoid Chief Compliance Officer Liability ... 680, 684, 693, 701
  What is Compliance? ... 65, 69
Trade aggregation
  Forensic Testing ... 544
Trade allocation
  Forensic Testing ... 545
Trade errors
  Forensic Testing ... 550, 551
  Game Plan for the New CCO ... 172
Training material
  Compliance Training ... 230, 240, 243, 250, 253
Training methods
  Compliance Training ... 242
Transactional testing
  Adviser Custody
    What You Need to Know ... 432
  Core Requirements of a Compliance Program ... 107
Trend analysis
  Forensic Testing ... 542
Triage
  Game Plan for the New CCO ... 173, 177
Trust Indenture Act of 1939
  Overview of the Regulatory Framework for SEC-Registered Investment Advisers ... 143

Two-factor authentication
  Cybersecurity ... 527

U

U.S. Commodity Futures Trading Commission
  Overview of the Regulatory Framework for SEC-Registered Investment Advisers ... 158, 159
U.S. Department of Health and Human Services (HHS)
  A History of Compliance ... 29, 31, 32, 38, 50
U.S. Sentencing Commission
  Compliance Training ... 227
UK Bribery Act 2010
  Corporate Transactions
    The Role of the Compliance Department ... 395
Unit investment trust (UIT)
  Corporate Transactions
    The Role of the Compliance Department ... 384
United States of America v. S.A.C. Capital Advisors, L.P., S.A.C. Capital Advisors, LLC, CR Intrinsic Investors, LLC, and Sigma Capital Management, LLC
  What is Compliance? ... 65
United States Sentencing Guidelines Manual (USSG)
USSG Manual
  A History of Compliance ... 21, 22, 23, 30
United States v. S.A.C. Capital Advisors LP
  What is Compliance? ... 65
Upjohn v. United States
  Corporate Transactions
    The Role of the Compliance Department ... 375, 376
Urban, Theodore W.
  A History of Compliance ... 51, 52, 53, 54, 59
  Enforcement Actions Against Chief Compliance Officers ... 747
  Ethics Standards Governing Compliance Professionals ... 197
  Seeking to Avoid Chief Compliance Officer Liability ... 685, 687

V

Valuation of securities
  Forensic Testing ... 543
Valuation Principles
  Navigating Marketing and Distribution ... 336, 337, 343
Vance v. Ball State University
  Avoiding Supervisory Liability ... 725
Variable annuities
  Compliance Professionals' Relationships with Endangered Populations ... 653, 660, 661, 664, 673
Viatical Settlements Model Act
  Compliance Professionals' Relationships with Endangered Populations ... 663

Voting member
Seeking to Avoid Chief Compliance Officer Liability ... 685, 695

Vulnerability assessments
Cybersecurity ... 529, 530

W

Wall Street Reform and Consumer Protection Act of 2010
Compliance Professionals' Relationships with Endangered Populations ... 664
Regulatory Examinations and Audits ... 580

Wells Notice
Enforcement Actions Against Chief Compliance Officers ... 734, 750
Regulatory Examinations and Audits ... 593, 594

Wells Submission
Regulatory Examinations and Audits ... 593, 594

Western Asset Management Co.
Affiliated Transactions Under the Advisers Act ... 417

Whistleblower
Compliance as a Profession ... 785
Core Requirements of a Compliance Program ... 105, 109
Ethics Standards Governing Compliance Professionals ... 205
Seeking to Avoid Chief Compliance Officer Liability ... 699, 700

White, Mary Jo
Compliance and Risk Management ... 264, 266, 268

White Paper on the Evolving Role of Compliance Department
Corporate Transactions
The Role of the Compliance Department ... 373

White Paper on the Role of Compliance
Avoiding Supervisory Liability ... 704, 714

White Paper on the Role of the Compliance Department
Corporate Transactions
The Role of the Compliance Department ... 373

White Paper: The Evolving Role of Compliance
A History of Compliance ... 56, 57
Avoiding Supervisory Liability ... 723

Whitney, Richard
A History of Compliance ... 8, 9, 10

Wilkins, William W. Jr
A History of Compliance ... 23

Window dressing
Forensic Testing ... 549, 550

Wireless Networks
Cybersecurity ... 517

Work product privilege
Corporate Transactions
The Role of the Compliance Department ... 375

Wrap accounts
Navigating Marketing and Distribution ... 304

Written code of conduct

Written Information Security Program (WISP)
Protecting the Privacy of Client Information ... 474
How Compliance Can Teach Ethics ... 185, 186

Written policies and procedures (WPPs)
A History of Compliance ... 18, 32
Core Requirements of a Compliance Program ... 100
Protecting the Privacy of Client Information ... 436, 446, 448, 451, 467, 469, 476
What is Compliance? ... 72, 73

Written supervisory procedures (WSPs)

Wsps
Avoiding Supervisory Liability ... 715, 719, 728
Enforcement Actions Against Chief Compliance Officers ... 734, 735, 736, 737, 742, 746
Game Plan for the New CCO ... 173
Protecting the Privacy of Client Information ... 461, 463, 464

Wunderlich Securities
Enforcement Actions Against Chief Compliance Officers ... 738, 743